ALPHA MATHE

David Barton

LONGMAN

CONTENTS

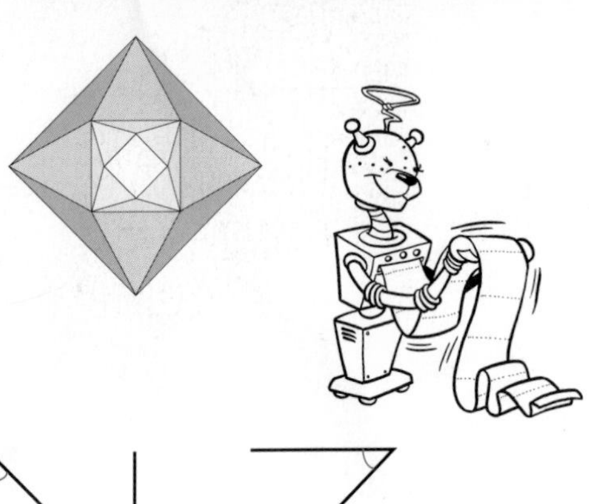

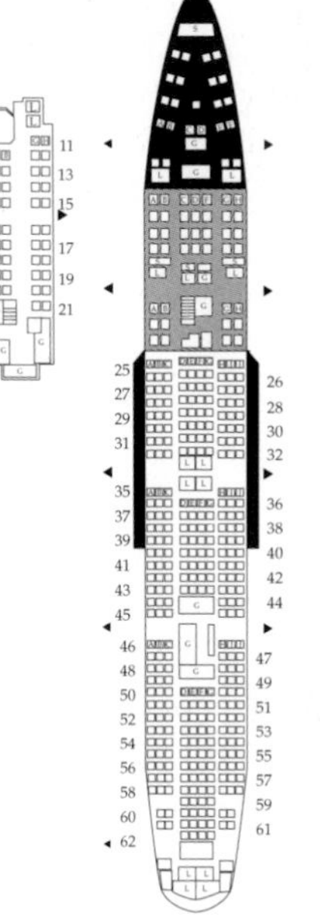

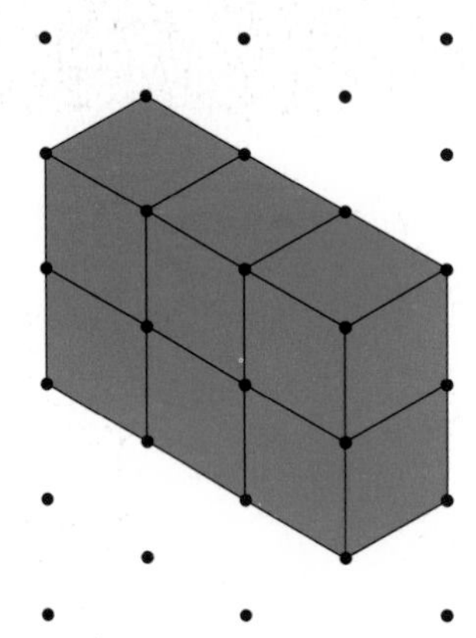

SPREADSHEET INVESTIGATIONS

PREFACE

To students

Welcome to your first year of studying Mathematics at secondary school. This will mark the beginning of a fascinating and challenging journey that you should pursue for as long as possible. Learning Maths is a wonderful process – you can relate it to many of your own experiences outside school, and a good understanding of the subject will mean you are well equipped for the future. I hope you'll also enjoy learning Maths for its own sake – it is an interesting and logical subject of pattern and symmetry.

Your teacher and this book will show you plenty of activities and investigations that introduce you to the ideas, and then there are exercises that help build and check your understanding. Maths is a subject that you learn by *doing*; and the harder you work, the better your results will be. Use the answers in the back of the book to check your understanding – do this frequently, and ask your teacher or refer to the explanations in the book if you are having difficulty. Have a go at the puzzles in *Alpha Mathematics* – they are not always as hard as they look, and some have unexpected results.

If your school has computers, or if you have one at home, then tackle some of the spreadsheet exercises in *Alpha Mathematics*. Using spreadsheets helps you understand mathematical ideas, and can save time on routine calculations. A calculator will help with some of the exercises, but it is also important to be able to explain what you are doing, and to have a good idea, in advance, of the kind of answer you might expect.

Year 9 is a very important one in Mathematics. You encounter many ideas for the first time – and it's the first year most of you will have a specialist Maths teacher and have lessons that are devoted only to this subject! I hope you have a worthwhile journey of learning and discovery in Mathematics this year.

David Barton

As you go through the book, watch out for Alpha's helpful hints:

Let's start

Here's a tip

The Professor speaks

Time for a calculator

Use a spreadsheet

Here's a puzzle

Extension work

1 Spreadsheets

What is a spreadsheet?

- A **spreadsheet** is a kind of large electronic table with rows and columns. You can type data in—both text and numbers. You can also do lots of different mathematical things.
- Spreadsheets are a type of computer software. The software used in this book is Microsoft Excel. Other spreadsheet software is very similar, as long as you use a computer with a mouse.

Looking for the mouse?

Starting up

You need to know how to run a software program, and how to exit. If you don't, ask your teacher.

Now, start Excel. After a few seconds, you will see a blank worksheet. It looks like this:

	A	B	C	D	E
1					
2					
3					
4					
5					
6					
7					
8					
9					
10					
11					
12					
13					
14					

- the **rows** are numbered 1, 2, 3, 4, 5, ... down the table
- the **columns** are labelled A, B, C, D, E .... across the table.

When you open a spreadsheet, all you see is the top left part. The actual spreadsheet is much bigger. It goes a long way in both directions—down, and across to the right.

Each **cell** in a worksheet has a name. This name tells you which column and row the cell is in.

The highlighted cell in this worksheet is C2. It is in column C and row 2.

	A	B	C	D	E
1					
2					
3					
4					
5					
6					
7					
8					
9					
10					
11					
12					
13					
14					

Moving around a worksheet

To move from one cell to another cell in a worksheet you can either:

- move the mouse and click
- use the arrow keys to move one cell at a time.

To move up or down quickly, these keys are useful:

- PgDn — moves one screen-sized page down
- PgUp — moves one screen-sized page up
- Control+Home — takes you to cell A1 (the first cell in the worksheet)
- Control+End — takes you to the last non-empty cell in the worksheet (i.e. the last place you typed something in)

If a + symbol is written between two keys, it means you press the two keys at the same time. For example, Control+Home means hold down Control and press Home as well. This is a key combination.

EXERCISE 1.1

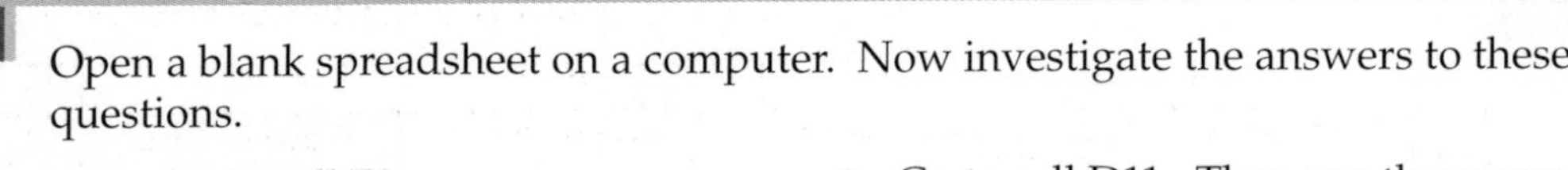

Open a blank spreadsheet on a computer. Now investigate the answers to these questions.

1 Go to cell E8.
   (a) What cell is just above cell E8?
   (b) What cell is just below cell E8?
   (c) What cell is on the left of cell E8?
   (d) What cell is on the right of cell E8?

2 Go to cell D11. Then use these arrow keys to move about. Press each key once only. Write down the cell you go to from D11 each time.
   (a) ←   (c) →
   (b) ↓   (d) ↑

3 Go to cell H13. Now press Control+Home (together). Explain what happens. Does this work from anywhere in the spreadsheet?

4 This is a 'scroll bar' below the worksheet, near the bottom of the screen. Use it to move right.

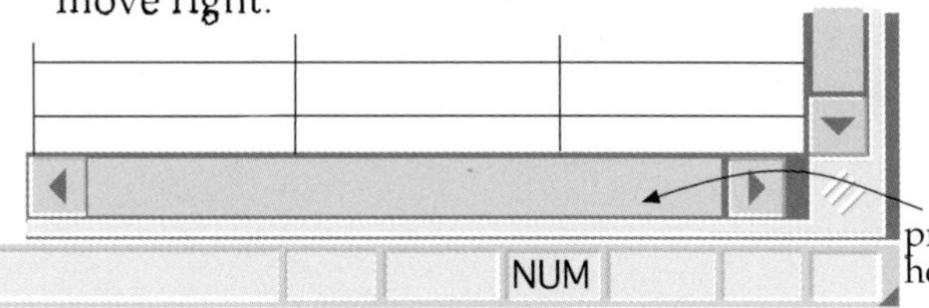

(a) What is the name of the next column after column Z?

(b) What would you call the next column after column DZ? Investigate.

(c) Keep moving right as far as you can. What is the name of the last column, at the right-hand edge of the worksheet?

5 Go back to cell A1. Then press Control+→ Explain what this key combination does.

6 Use the mouse and/or arrow keys to move to cell R100.

- Type your name in there.
- Go back to cell A1
- Press Control+End

Explain what the key combination Control+End does.

7 Open a new spreadsheet. One way of doing this is to click on File, then click on New. Type one word (e.g. red, or blue, or green) in each of these three cells:

B11, D9, E4

When you have done this, press Control+End. What cell do you go to?

8 Investigate what these two key combinations do:

(a) Control+↓ (b) Control+↑

9 What is the name of the bottom row in your worksheet?

10 What is the name of the cell at the bottom right-hand corner of your worksheet?

11 Try to work out the total number of cells in your worksheet.

In Excel version 7.0, it is 4 194 304. In Excel 97, it is 16 777 216.

Write down the calculation that gives the total number.

12 Click on File, then Exit. You don't want to save your work, so click on 'No'.

Entering data in a spreadsheet

STARTER

A class of students has been asked to type some information about themselves into a spreadsheet. The columns already have the headings in.

Here are the first few rows of this spreadsheet.

	A	B	C	D	E	F
1	**First name**	**Age**	**Eye colour**	**Phone number**	**Place of birth**	
2						
3	David	13	blue	6668472	Wellington	
4	Melanie	12	blue-green	3444575	Tawa	
5	Nga	13	brown	5038989	Wellington	
6	Chris	12	blue	4839449	Hutt	
7	Wei-Li	12	brown	6358200	Taiwan	
8						

- The spreadsheet is displaying numbers in a different way from text. How?
- The headings look different from the text and numbers below them. There are two differences. What are these?

There are many different ways to change the appearance of data in a spreadsheet. We can:

- decide how we want to align data in a cell (left, right or centred)
- adjust the width of columns
- make the contents of the cell look larger and/or **bolder**, etc.

The look of the cell contents is called the **format**.

Alignment

Spreadsheets handle text in a different way from numbers:

- text is left-aligned
- numbers are right-aligned.

If you want to change the alignment, follow these steps:

1. use the mouse to select the cells
2. click on Format, Cells, Alignment
3. choose the look you want—left, right, or centred.

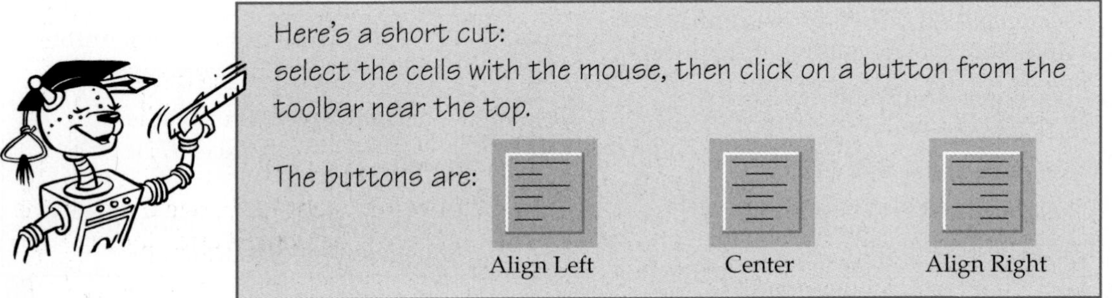

Here's a short cut:
select the cells with the mouse, then click on a button from the toolbar near the top.
The buttons are:
Align Left
Center
Align Right

Column width

In a new spreadsheet (worksheet), all the columns are set at the same width. Sometimes you will want to change the width of a column.

Here's an example of a worksheet with columns of *different* widths:

	A	B	C	D	E
1					
2					
3					
4					
5					

To change the width of a column:

- move the mouse pointer to the top row, the one with the column headings A B C D etc.
- move along this row, and watch the pointer. Most of the time the pointer looks like a cross. On the boundary line between columns it looks different, like this:
- when the pointer changes to this shape, hold the mouse key down. Then drag it left or right until you have the column width you want.

Appearance of text

Spreadsheets have a huge number of ways to make the data in cells look different. You can make text *and* numbers look different.

One way is to make text **bold**.

Example To make text in a cell bold:

- first click on the cell with the mouse
- then click on Format, Cells, Format, Bold.

Here's a shortcut: click on or select the cell(s), then click on the B key on the toolbar.

Type the data (text and numbers) into the spreadsheet first. Then fix up the formatting. It's much easier to do the formatting *after* all the data has been entered.

Fixing typos

No one is perfect. We all make typing/spelling mistakes—called typos. These need to be fixed. In a spreadsheet, it's easy to change what you have typed in a cell.

1 Deleting data in cells

- You can just delete the contents of the cell, and try again. To do this, click on the cell. Then press either the Delete or the ← (Backspace) key.
- You can click on the 'Undo' key on the toolbar.
  This takes the program back one step.
- You can just type something new. This then replaces the original text.

2 Changing data in a cell

Sometimes you want to change the contents of a cell *without* deleting it and starting again.

- Double-click on the cell you want to edit.
- Make your changes. You can use the mouse or arrow keys to move along *inside* the cell.
- Press ENTER when you have finished.

You can also use the special cell-editing box, above the worksheet and below the toolbar. Click in here, and make your changes. When you've finished, click on the green ✓ key to the left (or press ENTER).

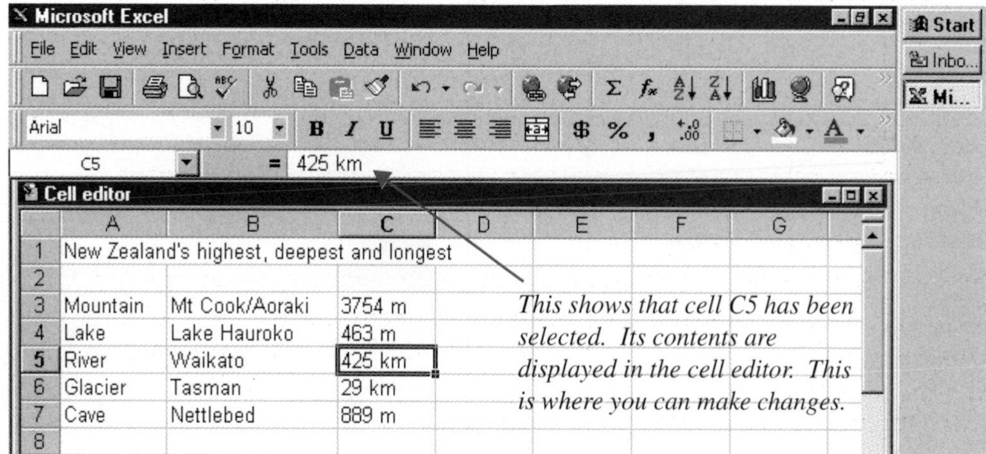

This shows that cell C5 has been selected. Its contents are displayed in the cell editor. This is where you can make changes.

EXERCISE 1.2

1 Run your spreadsheet software and start with a blank worksheet.

Produce this spreadsheet:

- Type in the data first
- Format it so that:
  —the columns are wide enough
  —the headings are bold
  —the numbers in column B are centred.
- Save your spreadsheet.

Do this by clicking on File, Save As and typing in Months of Year.xls as the name. You will be using it later on.

Exit the spreadsheet (File, Exit).

	A	B	C
1	**Month of Year**	**Number of Days**	
2			
3	January	31	
4	February	28	
5	March	31	
6	April	30	
7	May	31	
8	June	30	
9	July	31	
10	August	31	
11	September	30	
12	October	31	
13	November	30	
14	December	31	
15			

2 Open the spreadsheet you have just saved.

Do this by clicking on File, Open and then clicking on the name of the spreadsheet.

- Use the cell editor to change the months to their 3-letter abbreviations. For example, change January to Jan, etc.
- Remove the bold from the headings.
- Centre the names of the months.
- Right-align the number of days.

Exit the spreadsheet *without* saving it.

3 Display the information in this table in a spreadsheet.

Lake	Maximum depth (m)	Area (sq. km)
North Island		
Taupo	163	606
Rotorua	45	80
Wairarapa	3	80
Waikaremoana	248	54
South Island		
Te Anau	417	344
Wakatipu	380	293
Wanaka	311	193
Ellesmere	2	181
Pukaki	70	169
Manapouri	444	142
Hawea	384	141
Tekapo	120	88
Benmore (artificial)	120	75
Hauroko	462	71

Lake Wakatipu

The top five rows of the spreadsheet should look like this:

	A	B	C	D	E
1	**New Zealand's Principal Lakes**				
2					
3	**Lake**	**Island**	**Maximum depth (m)**	**Area (sq. km)**	
4					
5	Taupo	North	163	606	
6					
7					

When you have finished, save your spreadsheet with a name like NZ Lakes.xls

Doing simple calculations in a spreadsheet

You should know what the four main arithmetic operations mean:

Operation	Meaning	Symbol	Example
Adding	plus	+	8 + 2 = 10
Subtracting	minus	–	8 – 2 = 6
Multiplying	times	×	8 × 2 = 16
Dividing	divided by	÷	8 ÷ 2 = 4

We need to tell the spreadsheet **in advance** that we want it to carry out a calculation. Otherwise, it will just treat what is typed as data.
We do this by putting an equals sign (=) in front of what we want the spreadsheet to calculate.

Computer keyboards are not quite the same as the buttons on a calculator.
For example, you won't see the ÷ symbol anywhere on a computer keyboard.
Here are the keys we use for spreadsheet work:

On a calculator	In a spreadsheet
+	+
–	-
×	*
÷	/

Example What you type:

	A	B	C
1			
2			
3		=8+2	
4		=8-2	
5		=8*2	
6		=8/2	
7			
8			

What you get:

	A	B	C
1			
2			
3		10	
4		6	
5		16	
6		4	
7			
8			

If your calculation has brackets, use the round bracket keys on the keyboard. Remember to hold down the SHIFT key to type brackets.

Example To calculate (3.4 – 1.8) × 5, type = (3.4–1.8)*5 in a cell

EXERCISE 1.3

Open a blank worksheet in your spreadsheet program. Use spreadsheet operations to do these simple calculations.

1 $120 + 40$

2 $120 - 40$

3 120×40

4 $120 \div 40$

5 3.6×4.1

6 $40 + 12 \times 2$

7 $(40 + 12) \times 2$

8 $25 - 18 - 6$

9 $25 - (18 - 6)$

10 $23 + 56 + 18$

11 $4500 \div 150$

12 $180 - 180$

13 $(45 + 18) \div 9$

14 $(345 - 123) \times 21$

15 $580 - 247 - 192$

16 $180 \times 247 \times 0$

17 $36 \times (458 - 190)$

18 $30 - 29 + 1$

19 $44.6 - (51.3 \times 0.04)$

20 In Mathematics, dividing by 0 is *undefined*. (This means you don't get a result.)

(a) Use a calculator to divide a number by 0. What appears on the screen?

(b) Type =5/0 in a spreadsheet cell. Write down the error message that appears.

Formulas or formulae

A **formula** in a spreadsheet is a special sort of calculation. It uses values that have been entered in *other* cells.

A formula can be typed in *any* cell of a spreadsheet.

Here are some formulas:

=4*B7	this formula multiplies whatever is in cell B7 by 4
=A1+A2	this formula adds the numbers in cells A1 and A2
=C5*D5	this formula multiplies the numbers in cells C5 and D5

A formula always needs an = sign in front.

Formulas are very useful because:

- you can *copy* the formula to other cells to save repeating typing
- you can change values in cells, and instantly see the result updated.

How to copy a formula

Step	What you do in Excel
1 Choose what you want to copy.	Select a cell by clicking on it. Then click on Edit, Copy
2 Decide where you want to copy it to (the destination).	The mouse pointer changes to a cross shape. Move this pointer to the cell you want to copy to, and click. You can drag the pointer to copy into other cells too, if you want. Then click on Edit, Paste (or just press ENTER).

SPREADSHEET INVESTIGATION

A SPREADSHEET GAME

Choose a partner to work with on a computer. Call yourselves Alpha and Beta.

Open a blank spreadsheet. Enter these formulas into column C (as shown). Also enter what the formulas do (in the cells in column D).

	A	B	C	D	E
1			=A25+B25	Adding	
2			=A25-B25	Subtracting	
3			=A25*B25	Multiplying	
4			=A25/B25	Dividing	
5					
6					

Alpha now thinks of two numbers between 1 and 12. Alpha types these numbers in cells A25 and B25—while Beta looks away.

Alpha presses Control+Home to return to the top of the worksheet. Both of you can now look at the results in cells C1 to C4.

Beta has to work out what the numbers in cells A25 and B25 are.

Now swap over. Beta will enter numbers in cells A25 and B25, while Alpha looks away.

Take turns to do this three times. Do you both get a perfect record?

What happens when you copy

When formulas are copied downwards, the row numbers change too.

Let's look at an example.
We will copy a formula that does subtraction for us.

Example

This spreadsheet will calculate the difference between the maximum and minimum temperatures in a number of cities in New Zealand. The answers will appear in column D, Temp range.

	A	B	C	D
1	City	Max temp	Min temp	Temp range
2				
3	Whangarei			=B3-C3
4	Auckland			=B4-C4
5	Hamilton			=B5-C5
6	New Plymouth			=B6-C6
7	Napier			=B7-C7
8	Palmerston North			=B8-C8
9	Wellington			=B9-C9
10	Nelson			=B10-C10
11	Christchurch			=B11-C11
12	Dunedin			=B12-C12
13	Invercargill			=B13-C13

We only have to enter the formula *once* – in cell D3. When we copy this formula downwards, the row numbers change in exactly the way we would want them to.

Here is the result when temperature data is entered into columns B and C.

	A	B	C	D	E
1	City	Max temp	Min temp	Temp range	
2					
3	Whangarei	14.9	11.4	3.5	
4	Auckland	14.8	11.4	3.4	
5	Hamilton	13.8	6.8	7.0	
6	New Plymouth	11.7	7.9	3.8	
7	Napier	9.9	7.0	2.9	
8	Palmerston North	10.2	6.1	4.1	
9	Wellington	9.7	5.0	4.7	
10	Nelson	11.5	6.3	5.2	
11	Christchurch	9.8	2.3	7.5	
12	Dunedin	10.2	1.1	9.1	
13	Invercargill	8.7	1.8	6.9	
14					

EXERCISE 1.4

Open a blank worksheet in your spreadsheet program.

1 Produce this spreadsheet. In cell C3, enter a formula that adds the numbers in cells A3 and B3. Then copy this formula downwards. When completed, your spreadsheet should show numbers where the question marks are.

	A	B	C
1	First number	Second number	Sum
2			
3	4	10	?
4	11	39	?
5	780	519	?
6	8.9	17.1	?
7	19.83	0	?
8	0.4	0.7	?
9	519000	63700	?
10	0.49	9.51	?
11			
12			

2 Produce this spreadsheet. It will show the results of multiplying and dividing two numbers.

	A	B	C	D	E
1	First number	Second number	Multiplying	Dividing	
2					
3	8	4	=A3*B3	=A3/B3	
4	12	6	?	?	
5	99	100	?	?	
6	6.45	3.18	?	?	
7	256	512	?	?	
8	6.0001	5.9999	?	?	
9	100	0.01	?	?	
10	0.003	0.0006	?	?	
11					
12					

3 This spreadsheet is for showing how much money is paid in entrance fees at a zoo one day.

	A	B	C	D	E
1	Type of visitor	Number	Entrance fee	Amount received	
2					
3	Adult	74	$15	=B3*C3	
4	Senior citizen	14	$10	?	
5	Zoo member	63	$9	?	
6	Child (2-14)	150	$5	?	
7	Infant (0-2)	6	$0	?	
8				=D3+D4+D5+D6+D7	
9					
10					

(a) How much does it cost each adult to enter the zoo?

(b) How many children visited the zoo this day?

(c) What will the formula in cell D8 calculate?

Produce this spreadsheet yourself, and enter the data.

(d) What was the total amount of entrance fees received this day?

(e) Next day, the number of adults visiting was 85 rather than 74, and children were admitted free. Calculate the new total amount of entrance fees received.

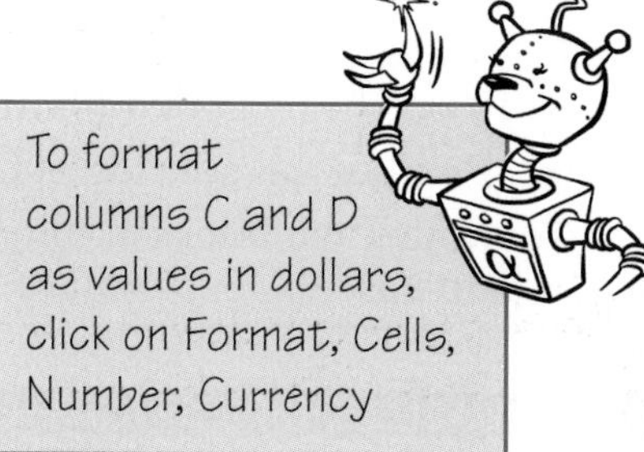

To format columns C and D as values in dollars, click on Format, Cells, Number, Currency

4 Here is some information about wages paid to staff at a restaurant one week.

The hourly wage rate for servers is $12.50, for kitchenhands is $9.50, and for assistant chefs is $14.90. The head chef is paid $19.20 an hour.

Name	Job description	Hours worked
Paolo Stella	Head chef	45
Nga Taumanu	Assistant chef	40
Darren Hinch	Server	18
Vanessa Smith	Server	23
Wiremu Ngatai	Server	22
John Jones	Kitchenhand	16
Ki Lim Liu	Kitchenhand	19

Produce a spreadsheet. It should show:

- how much was paid to each worker
- the total amount paid out in wages.

Here are the headings you will need:

	A	B	C	D	E
1	Name	Hourly Rate	Hours worked	Amount paid	
2					

5 This spreadsheet gives the population in several countries, and the number of doctors there.

	A	B	C	D	E
1	Country	Population	Number of doctors	Doctors per 1000 pop'n	
2					
3	New Zealand	3800000	8000	2.11	
4	Australia	18300000	40000		
5	Japan	125800000	214000		
6	Korea	45500000	45500		
7	Norway	4400000	12000		
8	UK	58800000	88000		
9	USA	266600000	586500		
10					
11					

The number of doctors per 1000 population is calculated using a formula in column D. This is done by dividing the number of doctors by the population, and then multiplying by 1000. The *result* of this formula is shown for New Zealand.

(a) Produce this spreadsheet.

(b) Round the values in column D to 2 decimal places. Use Format, Cells, Number to do this.

SPREADSHEET INVESTIGATION

MAGIC SQUARE

In a magic square, the numbers in each row, column and diagonal have the same total.

We can use a spreadsheet to keep track of these totals for a 3 by 3 square.

Produce a spreadsheet for a magic square.

- Format the 9 cells in colour and with borders.
- Enter formulas:
  —at the bottom of each column
  —at the end of each row
  —at the end of each diagonal.
  These formulas will add the numbers in the square.

This extract from a spreadsheet will show you how to start:

	A	B	C	D	E	F
1						
2					=B2+C2+D2	
3						
4						
5	=B4+C3+D2	=B2+B3+B4	=C2+C3+C4			

- Now try entering the numbers 1, 2, 3, 4, 5, 6, 7, 8, 9 in the nine cells so that each formula gives the same sum.

Sequences

Another use of formulas in spreadsheets is to produce sequences of numbers.

Here is one sequence: 1, 2, 3, 4, 5, 6, ...

It would take a long time to type every number from 1 to 1000 into cells in a spreadsheet. Luckily, these numbers are linked by a formula. The formula involves adding 1 to each number to get the next number in the sequence.

This shows where the formulas would be placed to give the numbers 1, 2, 3, 4, etc. going downwards:

	A	B	C
1	1		
2	=A1+1		
3	=A2+1		
4	=A3+1		
5	=A4+1		
6	=A5+1		
7	=A6+1		
8	=A7+1		
9	=A8+1		
10	=A9+1		
11	=A10+1		
12			
13			

	A	B	C
1	1		
2	2		
3	3		
4	4		
5	5		
6	6		
7	7		
8	8		
9	9		
10	10		
11	11		
12			
13			

We only have to type in the first number, and a formula that gives the second number. All the other formulas can be *copied* into the cells below. We can copy cell A2 down a long way, and the spreadsheet will calculate the values very quickly.

Formulas can also be copied sideways. To get 1, 2, 3, etc. to go across the page we would enter 1 in cell A1. We would then enter the formula =A1+1 in cell B1, and copy it to the right.

	A	B	C	D	E	F
1	1	=A1+1	=B1+1	=C1+1	=D1+1	
2						
3						

EXERCISE 1.5

Open a blank worksheet in your spreadsheet program.

1

	A	B	C
1	2		
2	=A1+2		
3			
4			
5			

Enter the value 2 into cell A1, and the formula given in cell A2.

Copy cell A2 downwards for several rows.

(a) Write down the sequence of numbers this gives.

(b) What do we call this sequence?

(c) Now change the value in cell A1 to 1. Explain what happens.

2 One way of producing a '9 times table' is to use a spreadsheet.

(a) Use a formula to place the numbers 1 to 12 in cells A1 to A12.

(b) In cell B1, type the formula =A1*9

(c) Copy cell B1 downwards.

3 Use the method in question 2 to produce an '11 times table'.

4 Follow these steps. You will produce a table of numbers from 1 to 100.

- Type 1 in cell A1
- In cell B1, enter the formula =A1+1
- Copy B1 to the *right* eight times
- In cell A2, enter the formula =A1+10
- Copy cell A2 *downwards* eight times
- Highlight the *block* of cells from A2 to A10 and copy it to the right nine times.

	A	B	C	D	E	F	G	H	I	J	K
1	1	2	3	4	5	6	7	8	9	10	
2	11	12	13	14	15	16	17	18	19	20	
3	21	22	23	24	25	26	27	28	29	30	
4	31	32	33	34	35	36	37	38	39	40	
5	41	42	43	44	45	46	47	48	49	50	
6	51	52	53	54	55	56	57	58	59	60	
7	61	62	63	64	65	66	67	68	69	70	
8	71	72	73	74	75	76	77	78	79	80	
9	81	82	83	84	85	86	87	88	89	90	
10	91	92	93	94	95	96	97	98	99	100	
11											
12											

If you can, print out this spreadsheet. You will find it useful in Chapter 4 when you are looking at prime numbers.

5 Produce this February calendar. Use a similar method to question 4.

	A	B	C	D	E	F	G
1	**February 2009**						
2							
3	Sunday	Monday	Tuesday	Wednesday	Thursday	Friday	Saturday
4	1	2	3	4	5	6	7
5	8	9	10	11	12	13	14
6	15	16	17	18	19	20	21
7	22	23	24	25	26	27	28

Sorting

Spreadsheets can sort data from smallest to largest (and from largest to smallest). This can be done in alphabetical order, or in numerical order.

In Excel:

- Select the block of cells to be sorted (click and drag with the mouse)
- Then click on Data, Sort
- Decide which column you want to sort with. If this is *not* Column A, use the dialogue box to select another column
- If you want to sort from smallest at the top to largest at the bottom, you want the 'Ascending' option.
  If you want to sort the other way, choose 'Descending'.
- Click on OK

Example Here are three views of a spreadsheet with the names and lengths (in km) of some New Zealand rivers. It is shown:

- entered in North to South order
- sorted alphabetically by river name
- sorted by the lengths of the rivers.

North to South

	A	B
1	New Zealand Rivers	
2		
3	**River**	**Length in km**
4		
5	Waikato	425
6	Mokau	158
7	Wanganui	290
8	Rangitikei	241
9	Manawatu	182
10	Wairau	169
11	Buller	177
12	Clarence	209
13	Waitaki	209
14	Clutha	322
15	Waiau	169

Alphabetical

	A	B
1	New Zealand Rivers	
2		
3	**River**	**Length in km**
4		
5	Buller	177
6	Clarence	209
7	Clutha	322
8	Manawatu	182
9	Mokau	158
10	Rangitikei	241
11	Waiau	169
12	Waikato	425
13	Wairau	169
14	Waitaki	209
15	Wanganui	290

Longest to shortest

	A	B
1	New Zealand Rivers	
2		
3	**River**	**Length in km**
4		
5	Waikato	425
6	Clutha	322
7	Wanganui	290
8	Rangitikei	241
9	Clarence	209
10	Waitaki	209
11	Manawatu	182
12	Buller	177
13	Waiau	169
14	Wairau	169
15	Mokau	158

EXERCISE 1.6

Open a blank worksheet in your spreadsheet program.

1 These are the six numbers and the bonus number for Lotto last Saturday night. They appear in the order in which they were drawn.
(a) Enter the numbers into a spreadsheet column.
(b) Sort the numbers from smallest to largest.
(c) Sort the numbers from largest to smallest.

	A	B
1	Lotto numbers	
2		
3	34	
4	5	
5	31	
6	18	
7	1	
8	29	
9	11	
10		
11		

2 Here is a list of decimal numbers. Enter them into cells of a spreadsheet, and then sort them from smallest to largest.
0.70001, 0.701, 0.711, 0.71, 0.7, 0.7107, 0.70017, 0.77, 0.71701

3 Here are the maximum temperatures one day in winter in several New Zealand cities.

City	Maximum temperature (°C)
Whangarei	15
Auckland	15
Tauranga	17
Hastings	10
Palmerston North	10
Wellington	10
Nelson	12
Christchurch	10
Timaru	7
Dunedin	8
Invercargill	9

(a) Enter this information into a spreadsheet.
(b) Sort the cities into alphabetical order. Print out the spreadsheet if possible.
(c) Sort the cities from highest temperature to lowest. Print out the spreadsheet if possible.

4 Find out the following information for at least six people you know. Enter it into a spreadsheet.
- First name
- Last name
- Phone number
- Address

Sort the information in these three different ways. Print each one out if possible.
(a) By first name
(b) By last name
(c) By telephone number.

Graphs

Spreadsheets can produce many different graphs.

The spreadsheet program can do much of the work automatically. In Excel you use the Chart-wizard button on the toolbar.

All you need to do is tell the Chart-wizard:

- what part of the spreadsheet to get the data from (use the mouse to select a block)
- what kind of graph you want
- where to place the graph.

Here are two of the most useful graphs, and how to get them in Excel 97.

Pie graph

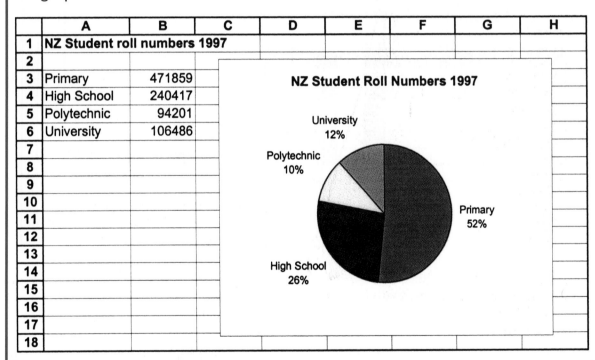

	A	B	C	D	E	F	G	H
1	**NZ Student roll numbers 1997**							
2								
3	Primary	471859						
4	High School	240417						
5	Polytechnic	94201						
6	University	106486						
7								
8								
9								
10								
11								
12								
13								
14								
15								
16								
17								
18								

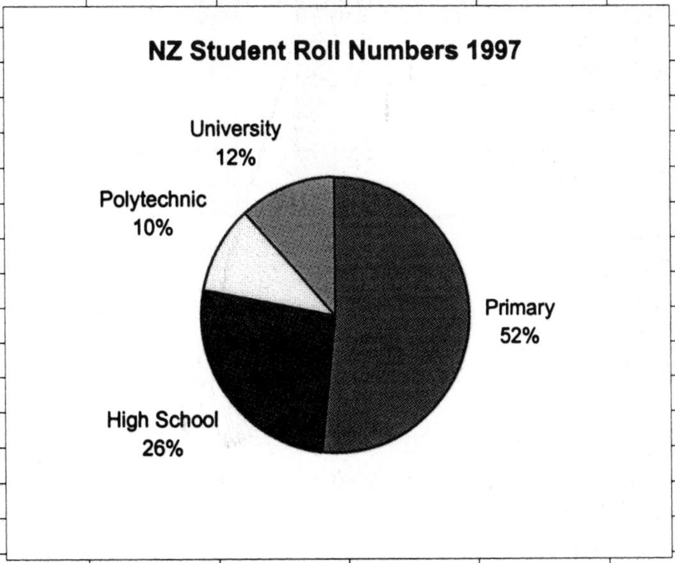

- Use the mouse (click and drag) to select from A3 down to A6 and across to B6
- Click on the Chart-wizard button
- Step 1 of 4 (Chart Type): choose Pie chart type (click on Next to confirm)
- Step 2 of 4 (Chart Source Data): click on Next to confirm the graph is what you want
- Step 3 of 4 (Chart Options): enter title in box (click on Finish)
- Step 4 of 4: if you want to move the graph, click inside it and drag to a suitable position.

Column graph

	A	B	C	D	E	F	G
1	**Continent**	**Size in square kilometres**					
2							
3	Asia	44391162					
4	Africa	30244049					
5	North America	24247038					
6	South America	17821028					
7	Antarctica	13338500					
8	Europe	10354636					
9	Australia	7682300					
10							
11							
12							
13							
14							
15							
16							
17							
18							
19							
20							
21							
22							
23							
24							
25							
26							
27							
28							
29							

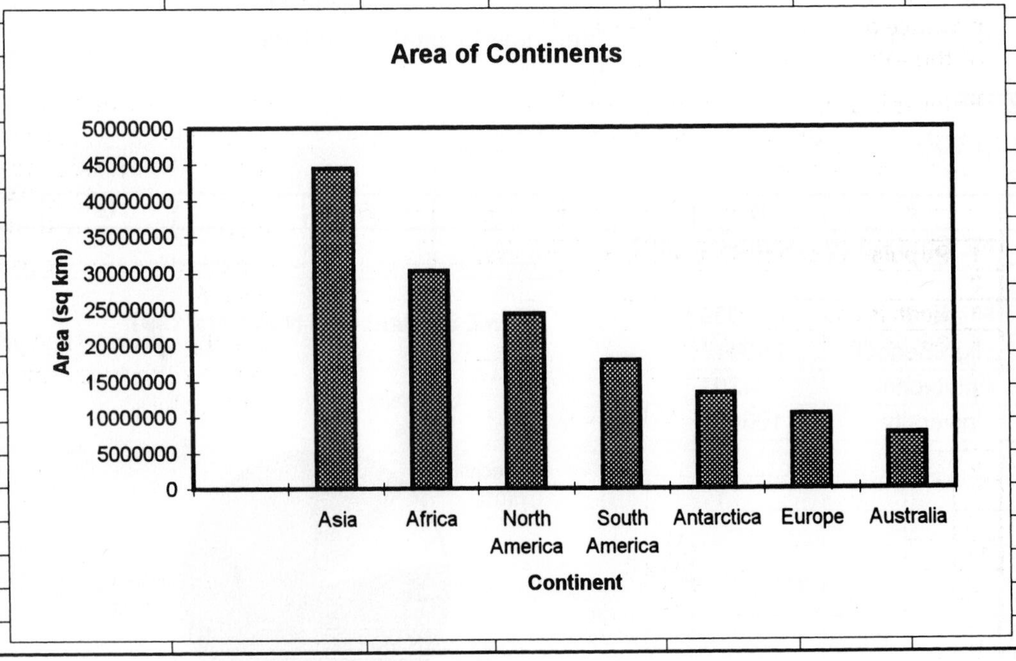

- Use the mouse (click and drag) to select from A3 down to A9 and across to B9
- Click on the Chart-wizard button
- Step 1 of 4 (Chart Type): choose Column chart type (click on Next to confirm)
- Step 2 of 4 (Chart Source Data): click on Next to confirm the graph is what you want
- Step 3 of 4 (Chart Options): enter titles in boxes (click on Finish)
- Step 4 of 4: if you want to move the graph, click inside it and drag to a suitable position.

EXERCISE 1.7

Open a blank worksheet in your spreadsheet program.

1 Here is data about the three longest rivers of the world, and the Waikato (New Zealand's longest river). Enter the data into a spreadsheet.

River	Length in km
Nile	6695
Amazon	6570
Mississippi	6020
Waikato	425

Use the spreadsheet graphing tools to produce a column graph of the lengths of the four rivers.

2 Enter this data into a spreadsheet. Use the graphing tools to produce a pie graph like this one:

	A	B	C	D	E
1	**Population of New Zealand at 30 June 1997**				
2					
3	North Island	2837000			
4	South Island	923700			
5					
6					
7					
8					
9					
10					
11					
12					
13					
14					
15					
16					

NZ Population 1997

South Island 25%

North Island 75%

3 Open the spreadsheet about New Zealand lakes you saved earlier. You were advised to save it as NZ Lakes.xls. If you didn't save it, the information you need is on page 6.

(a) Delete Columns B and D. Now you only have the name of the lake and its maximum depth.

(b) Use the spreadsheet graphing tools to produce a column graph showing the depths of the lakes.

4 Open the spreadsheet you saved earlier about months of the year. You were advised to save it as Months of Year.xls. If you didn't save it, the information you need is on page 6.

Use the spreadsheet graphing tools to produce a pie graph for the data.

5 Imagine you start with $1 and then double your money every day.

Day 1: $1

Day 2: $2

Day 3: $4

Day 4: $8

Use a spreadsheet to work out which day you will have one million dollars. Produce a graph to show how your money increases.

SPREADSHEET INVESTIGATION

DOMINOS

A domino is a tile with two squares on it.
In a double-six set of dominos, there are 28 tiles. Each tile is different.
The squares on the tiles have dots on them to represent numbers from 1 to 6.

Here are three tiles from a **double-six** set: 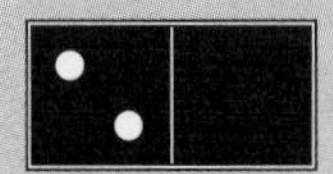 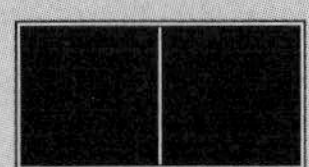 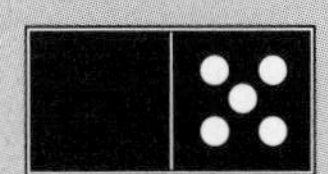

In a **double-two** set there are only 6 tiles. We could represent these by writing these pairs of numbers.

(0-0) (0-1) (1-1) (0-2) (1-2) (2-2)

There is a pattern you can use to work out the number of dominos in a set.

1 Copy this table, and complete it.

Highest number on domino	Number of dominos in set
0	
1	
2	6
3	
4	
5	
6	28
7	
8	

2 Produce a spreadsheet that shows the same information as the table above.

It should rely on formulas (using the pattern you have discovered).

3 Copy cells downwards a number of times. Now use your spreadsheet to predict the number of dominos in a double-twenty set.

2 Decimals

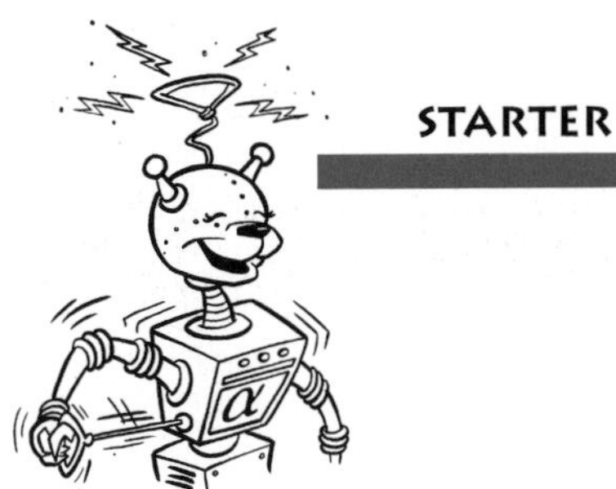

STARTER

- How many units of electricity have been used?
- How does this meter show tenths of units?
- Which dials would move most often?
- What would the meter have read when it was first installed?

Our **decimal** number system is based on the number 10.
Each place value is ten times larger than the place value on its right.

We can use place value to expand numbers.

Example 294 = 2 hundreds plus 9 tens plus 4 ones

$= 2 \times 100 + 9 \times 10 + 4 \times 1$

Here is how the place values work:

thousands	hundreds	tens	ones	•	tenths	hundredths	thousandths

We use a **decimal point** to show where the 'whole number' part ends and the 'fraction' part begins.

The decimal point acts as a separator.

A decimal point = I'm a dot in place.
This *anagram* shows the meaning of a decimal point quite nicely!
To make an anagram from a word or sentence, you move all the letters around to make new words.

Example 4.83 = 4 ones plus 8 tenths plus 3 hundredths

$$= 4 \times 1 \quad + \quad 8 \times \frac{1}{10} \quad + \quad 3 \times \frac{1}{100}$$

> Using 0 shows there is none of a particular unit. For example, 503.08 means 5 hundreds, no tens, 3 ones, no tenths and 8 hundredths.

EXERCISE 2.1

1 Write out these decimals in expanded form. The first one has been done for you.

(a) $14.67 = 1 \times 10 \quad + \quad 4 \times 1 \quad + \quad 6 \times \frac{1}{10} \quad + \quad 7 \times \frac{1}{100}$

(b) 29.83

(c) 5.917

(d) 30.05

(e) 0.028

2 These numbers are expressed in words. Write them as decimals:

(a) four tenths

(b) 8 tenths

(c) five and three tenths

(d) 17 and 4 tenths

(e) one and three tenths, two hundredths

(f) 5 and 6 tenths, 8 hundredths

(g) sixteen and no tenths, 7 hundredths

(h) 4 hundredths

3 How many *tenths* are there in each of these numbers?

(a) 0.9 (c) 809.167

(b) 1.38 (d) 41.05

4 How many *hundredths* are there in each of these numbers?

(a) 0.51 (c) 0.082

(b) 122.036 (d) 10.9084

5 How many *thousandths* are there in each of these numbers?

(a) 1.348 (c) 12.44832

(b) 0.0021 (d) 0.01975

6 Look at these diagrams. The columns represent tenths. The small squares represent hundredths. What is the value of the shaded part in each diagram? Write the answers as decimals.

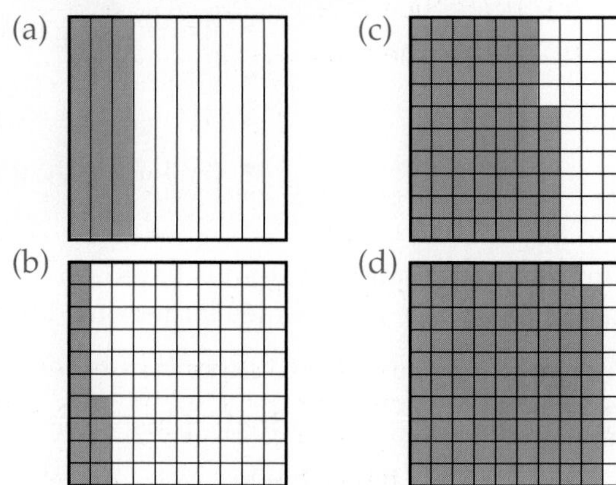

7 In each of these numbers, one digit has been underlined. Write down the place value of that digit. The first one has been done for you.

(a) $5.7\underline{2}1$ two hundredths

(b) $11.\underline{8}19$

(c) $\underline{4}1.06$

(d) $314.5\underline{6}$

(e) $0.06\underline{5}$

(f) $0.00\underline{1}8$

(g) $5000.\underline{1}$

(h) $4\underline{7}820$

8 Write these fractions as decimals. The first one has been done for you.

(a) $\frac{4}{10} = 0.4$ (e) $\frac{5}{1000}$

(b) $\frac{9}{10}$ (f) $\frac{63}{1000}$

(c) $\frac{7}{100}$ (g) $\frac{331}{1000}$

(d) $\frac{44}{100}$ (h) $\frac{87}{1000}$

9 Write these as decimals:

(a) twelve thousandths

(b) forty-five hundredths

(c) three hundred and fifty thousandths

10 Write *true* or *false* for each of these:

(a) 0.05 is the same as $\frac{5}{10}$

(b) $\frac{29}{100}$ is the same as 0.29

(c) 0.9 is the same as 0.90

(d) 0.70 is the same as 0.07

11 The World Record for the 100 m sprint is 9.89 seconds.

(a) Is this measurement given in tenths, hundredths or thousandths of seconds?

(b) One day, someone might run this distance 3 hundredths of a second faster. What would be the new World Record for the 100 m?

12 This is a reading from a trip recorder in a car. The first digit (white on black) represents hundreds of kilometres.

6 5 8 2

(a) What does the last digit (black on white) represent?

(b) Write the distance shown using decimals.

(c) What is the distance of the longest journey that this trip recorder can show?

(d) How much further will the car have to travel before the trip recorder shows

0 0 0 0 ?

Place value cross-number

Make a copy of this cross-number grid. Now look at the table. Each number in the table can be placed in the grid once only. There is only one possible way of doing this.

84 has been placed for you.

8	4								

6-digit numbers	5-digit numbers	4-digit numbers	3-digit numbers	2-digit numbers
498 336 698 336 869 336	47 536 47 935 49 336 49 833	4735 5935 7036	368 842	23 26 30 37 47 52 82 84 98

INVESTIGATION

BAR-CODES

Look at the back cover of this book. There is a bar-code there, with a number underneath.

This is a project that can be done in your own time. It involves collecting bar-codes, and investigating some of their features.

Here are some ideas:

- Why are there numbers underneath the bar-code? When would they need to be used?
- Can you match the different-sized lines on a bar-code to the digits 0–9?
- Find several bar-codes for products from the same country. Examples could include pasta and breakfast cereals from Australia, or wine and cheese from Germany.

  Do the products from a single country have any part of their bar-code the same? What about New Zealand bar-codes?
- Find several different products from the same manufacturer. You could try different books from one publisher, for example. What do the bar-codes have in common?

Further investigation

- Find out about the ISBN code for books.
- New Zealand has a four-digit postal code. What is your one? What is the postal code for an area near you? Do other countries use a similar system?
- Find out about codes used for telephone numbers. Are there special prefixes for certain kinds of numbers? Explain.
- What digits would a caller overseas have to dial to get:

  —New Zealand?

  —your town or city?

  —your suburb?

Decimal number lines

Look at these number lines. The top line is the whole-number line.

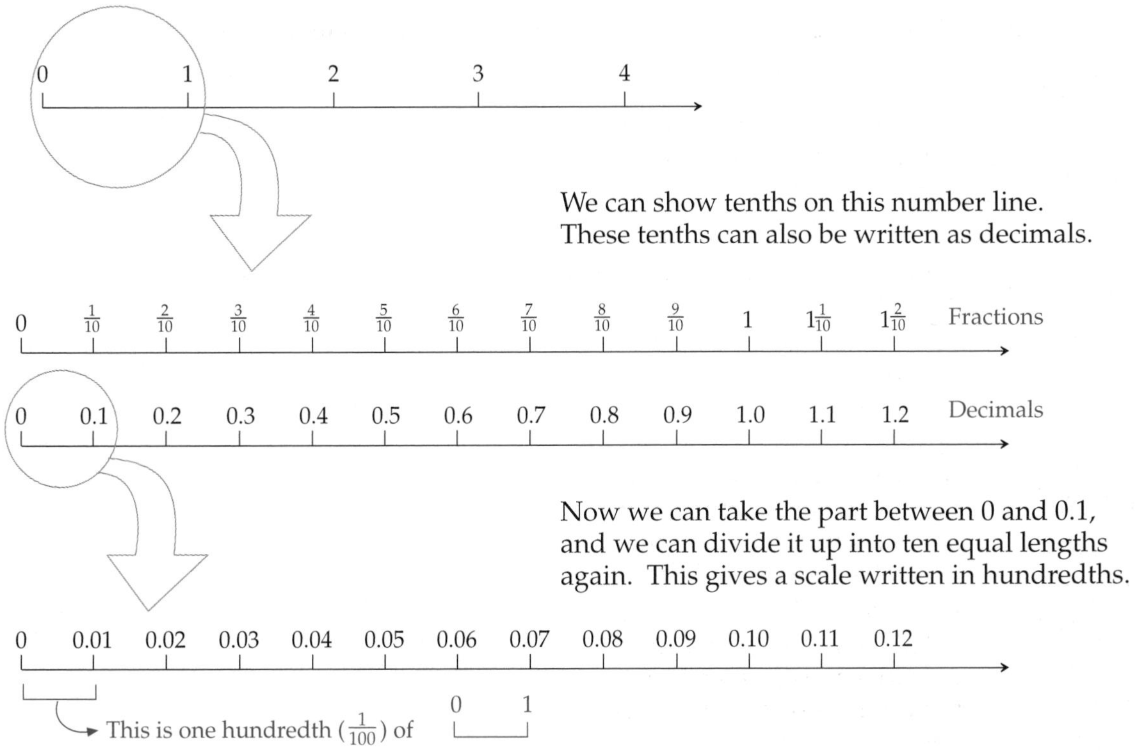

We can show tenths on this number line. These tenths can also be written as decimals.

Now we can take the part between 0 and 0.1, and we can divide it up into ten equal lengths again. This gives a scale written in hundredths.

A decimal number line shows how to **compare** decimals. This means saying whether one number is *greater than* or *less than* another number.

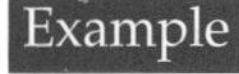

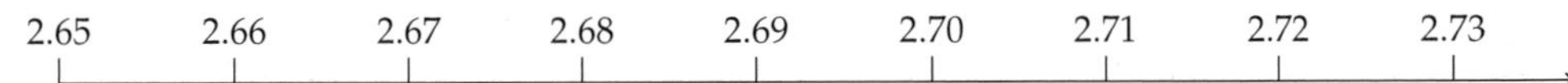

2.68 is less than 2.7. This is because 2.68 is to the left of 2.7. (Note that 2.7 is the same as 2.70).
2.73 is greater than 2.66. This is because 2.73 is to the right of 2.66.

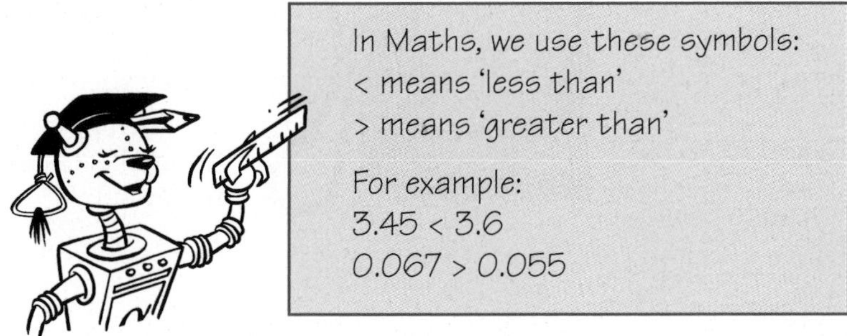

EXERCISE 2.2

1 Copy these number lines. Then complete the decimal scale.

(a)

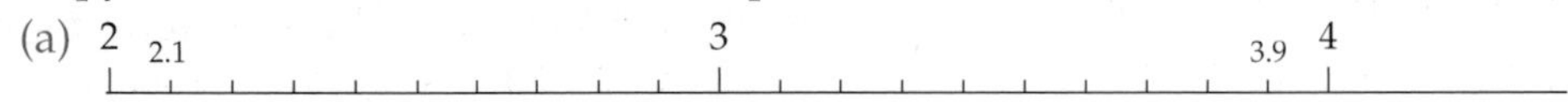

(b) 6.4 7

2 Look at these pairs of numbers. Write down which is the *greater* number.

(a) 4.82, 4.93 (b) 4.86, 4.84 (c) 4.8, 4.79 (d) 4.82, 4.9 (e) 4.84, 4.8

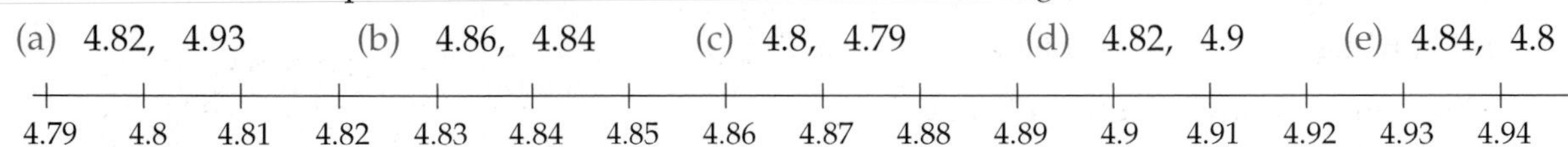

3 Look at these pairs of numbers. Then write down the *greater* number.

(a) 13, 12.85
(b) 14.05, 1.406
(c) 0.37, 0.6
(d) 0.941, 1.02

4 The symbol < means 'less than'. The symbol > means 'greater than'.

Write down *true* or *false* for each of these statements:

(a) 12.26 < 12.28
(b) 12.15 > 12.17
(c) 12.2 < 12.18
(d) 12.35 > 12.3
(e) 12.09 > 12.1

5 Here are the results for three events at the school sports day. For each event, write down the names in winning order (1st, 2nd, etc).

(a) Girl's high jump

Rachel	1.6 m
Nga	1.625 m
Christine	1.55 m
Sally	1.61 m
Amanda	1.63 m
Wei-Li	1.575 m

(b) Boy's shot-put

Steven	13.538 m
Bruce	15.319 m
Temoana	15.2 m
Wiremu	15.41 m
Mark	14.793 m
Ioane	15.082 m

(c) Boy's 100 m sprint

Bruce	12.1 s
Ralph	11.79 s
Wiremu	12.83 s
Derek	11.9 s
Ioane	12 s
Tuwhare	12.08 s

6 Here are displays from pumps at three different petrol stations:

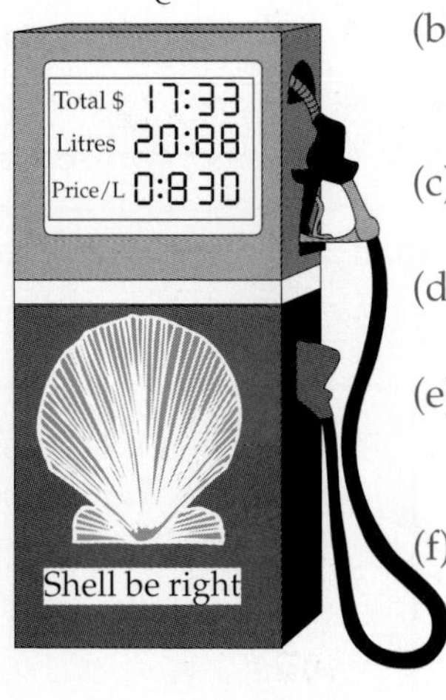

(a) Which pump (A, B or C) pumped the most petrol?

(b) Which pump (A, B or C) pumped the least petrol?

(c) Which station had the cheapest petrol?

(d) Which station had the most expensive petrol?

(e) At which pump was the largest amount of money spent?

(f) At which pump was the smallest amount of money spent?

7 Write these sets of numbers in order from smallest to largest.

(a) { 14, 13.18, 11.993, 12.5, 12.06 }

(b) { 0.71, 0.072, 0.705, 0.17, 0.057 }

8 (Multichoice) Here are the weights written on four different packets of gravy beef. Which packet is the heaviest?

A 1.593 kg C 1.608 kg

B 1.62 kg D 1.6 kg

9 This number line is divided into equal intervals.

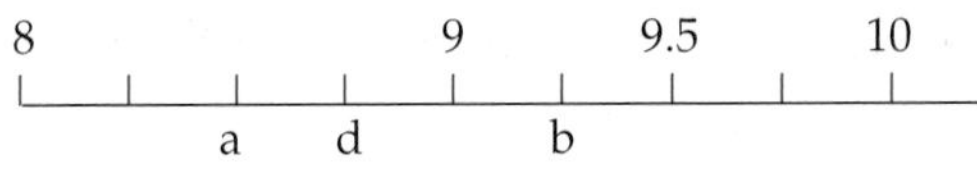

Write down the numbers represented by a, b, c and d.

10 Write down 12 different numbers between 6.11 and 6.18.

11 Alpha has forgotten the PIN (Personal Identification Number) on a credit card. There are four digits in the PIN. Here are the various PIN numbers Alpha tries. Each time two of the numbers are correct, and two are wrong:

6204
6108
8208
8198

Can you work out the four digits of the PIN, in their correct order?

Adding decimals

Decimals are added in the same way as whole numbers are.

Examples 40 + 30 = 70

4 + 3 = 7

0.4 + 0.3 = 0.7

Sometimes it helps to compare a decimal sum to a similar whole-number sum.

Example

Whole-number	Decimal
36 + 47 83	3.6 + 4.7 8.3

When writing down a decimal sum, make sure the decimal points line up vertically.

EXERCISE **2.3**

1–5 *Do the whole-number sum on the left. Then write down the answer to the decimal sum on the right.*

1 107 + 429 = ____   10.7 + 42.9 = ____ . ____

2 57 + 328 = ____   0.57 + 3.28 = ____ . ____

3	1673 + 2996 ______	1.673 + 2.996 ___.___
4	426 + 1537 ______	0.426 + 1.537 ___.___
5	29 + 86 ______	0.29 + 0.86 ___.___

6–15 *Work out the answers to these decimal sums.*

6 5.6 + 3.2

7 22.3 + 8.5

8 0.4 + 0.8

9 9.3 + 12.2

10 15.3 + 39.1

11 8.47 + 1.29

12 19.38 + 50.18

13 7.36 + 9.68

14 11.04 + 0.53

15 0.09 + 19.92

Sometimes we need to add extra 0s to decimals to show how they line up vertically.

Example Show how to add 15.8 + 6.29

Answer 15.8 is the same as 15.80. Here is the sum:

```
  15.80
 + 6.29
  22.09
```

EXERCISE 2.4

1–12 *Work out the answer to each of these addition problems.*

1 0.8 + 0.2

2 1.9 + 2.31

3 4.82 + 1.3

4 26.52 + 9.4

5 179.5 + 44.68

6 16.1 + 9.42

7 27.275 + 3.55

8 29 + 2.386

9 0.05 + 0.4

10 11.68 + 239.4

11 0.63 + 0.984

12 0.08 + 1.2 + 13.87

13 This is a reading from an odometer in a car. It shows the distance travelled, to the nearest tenth of a kilometre.

5	7	7	6	9	4

What will the odometer read after the car travels a further:

(a) 3 tenths of a kilometre?

(b) 12.6 km?

(c) 392.2 km?

(d) 32 288.7 km?

Subtracting decimals

Subtracting decimals works in the same way as subtracting whole numbers.

Sometimes it helps to compare a decimal subtraction to a similar whole-number subtraction.

Example

Whole-number	Decimal
85 − 27 58	8.5 − 2.7 5.8

Keep the decimal points lined up!

EXERCISE 2.5

1–5 *Do the whole-number subtraction on the left. Then write down the answer to the decimal subtraction on the right.*

1
```
  36       3.6
– 19     – 1.9
____     ___.__
```

2
```
  27      0.27
– 22    – 0.22
____     ___.__
```

3
```
 673      6.73
– 261   – 2.61
____     ___.__
```

4
```
  44      0.44
– 37    – 0.37
____     ___.__
```

5
```
 566      5.66
– 198   – 1.98
____     ___.__
```

6–15 *Work out the answers to these decimal subtractions.*

6 0.8 – 0.2

7 6.8 – 3.1

8 4.9 – 3.7

9 9.3 – 6.8

10 15.2 – 11.8

11 0.49 – 0.31

12 10.61 – 7.43

13 42.23 – 5.36

14 11.386 – 10.965

15 1.092 – 0.638

Decimal subtractions are easier to do when both numbers have the same number of digits after the decimal point. Add 0s if needed to the end of one of the numbers.

Example Work out 8.3 – 2.47

Answer Write 8.3 as 8.30. Then:

```
  8.30
– 2.47
  5.83
```

EXERCISE 2.6

1–12 *Work out the answer to each of these subtraction problems.*

1 6 – 3.4

2 11 – 10.9

3 5 – 2.31

4 14.5 – 9.82

5 21 – 19.86

6 43.24 – 29.4

7 18 – 0.02

8 531 – 6.86

9 0.4 – 0.15

10 0.05 – 0.025

11 7 – 0.018

12 31.86 – 2.047

13 In a 100 m freestyle swimming race, the winning time was 63.78 seconds. The swimmer who came second swam the distance in 65.11 seconds.

(a) Calculate the time difference between the winner and the swimmer who came second.

(b) The winner broke the previous race record by 0.46 seconds. Calculate the previous race record.

14 Before a journey, this was the reading on a car odometer. It showed the distance the car had travelled, to the nearest tenth of a kilometre.

4	3	0	9	5	8

At the end of the journey, the reading was:

4	7	8	0	6	2

(a) Work out the length of the journey. Give your answer to the nearest tenth of a kilometre.

(b) How much further would the car need to travel until the odometer read:

0	0	0	0	0	0

Write down the decimal subtraction you did to calculate this answer.

15 Copy this decimal addition table. Now complete it!

+		0.02		
0.7				0.9
2.18			4.33	
				3.2
	5.49		6.5	

16

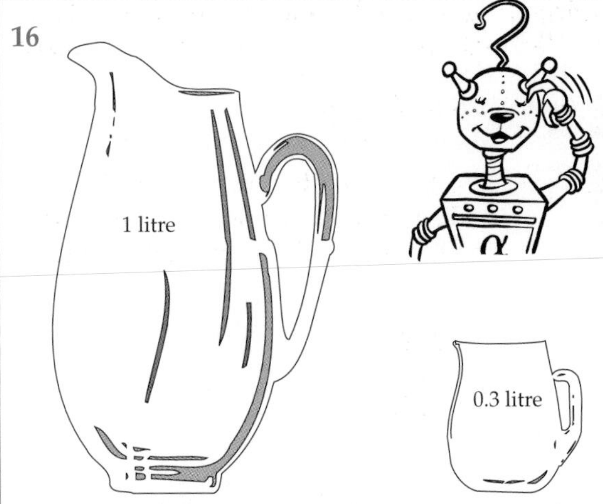

Explain how you could use these two jugs to measure exactly 0.4 litres of water. One jug holds 1 litre. The other jug holds 0.3 litres.

Multiplying decimals

STARTER

Each row in this square represents $\frac{1}{10}$ or 0.1 of the whole square.

Each column in this square represents $\frac{1}{10}$ or 0.1 of the whole square.

- What decimal fraction of the whole square does each *small square* represent?

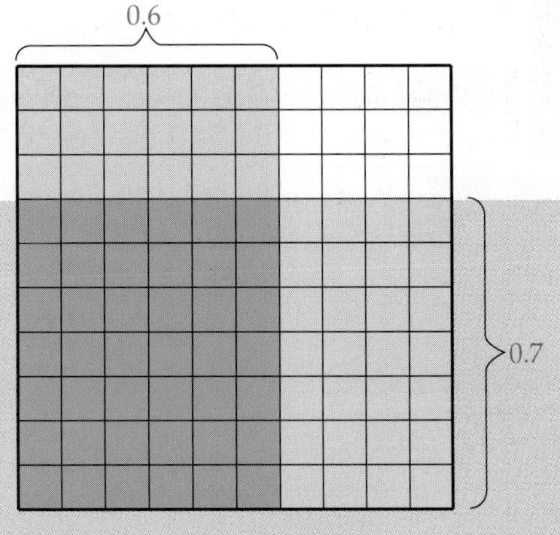

The diagram shows that:

0.6 (six-tenths) of the columns

0.7 (seven-tenths) of the rows are shaded

- How many *small* squares out of 100 have both kinds of shading?
- Write down a decimal that represents the squares with *both* kinds of shading.
- What is the answer to 6×7? What do you think 0.6×0.7 should be?

Multiplying decimals follows the same rules as multiplying whole numbers.
The decimal point in the answer must be placed so that the answer is the correct size.

Example Multiply 4.1×2.9

Answer 4.1×2.9 is close to $4 \times 3 = 12$.
Therefore, our answer should be near 12.
Doing the whole-number multiplication gives:

$$\begin{array}{r} 41 \\ \underline{\times 29} \\ 369 \\ \underline{820} \\ \underline{1189} \end{array}$$

It is a good idea to *estimate* the answer first. This will help to get the decimal point in the right place.

From our estimate: 0.1189 or 1.189 would be too small (not near 12).
118.9 or 1189 would be too large (not near 12).

There is only one possible place for the decimal point to go:

$$\begin{array}{r} 4.1 \\ \underline{\times 2.9} \\ = \underline{11.89} \end{array}$$

EXERCISE 2.7

These numbers have been multiplied on a calculator. But there's a problem—the decimal point is not showing up.
Write the number in the display column as it should appear, with a decimal point in the correct position.

	First number		Second number		Display
1	2.1	×	1.3	=	273
2	1.28	×	1.1	=	1408
3	0.9	×	2.1	=	189
4	10.8	×	2	=	216
5	5.3	×	6.8	=	3604
6	2.9	×	4.17	=	12093
7	20	×	0.8	=	16
8	0.99	×	0.98	=	09702
9	14	×	0.51	=	714
10	0.12	×	12	=	144
11	30.7	×	0.81	=	24867
12	0.75	×	38	=	285

Here's the first answer: 2.73! This is because the answer should be near 2 x 1 = 2. 27.3 would be too large, and 0.273 would be too small.

EXERCISE 2.8

Work out the answer to each of these multiplication problems.

1	1.2×0.9	6	37×0.4	11	32.6×0.4
2	4.8×2	7	0.5×63	12	0.7×1.9
3	2.1×0.8	8	16.1×0.2	13	13.1×1.5
4	1.1×1.1	9	1.6×8.2	14	802×0.7
5	2×0.3	10	2.9×7.9	15	4.3×62.8

When you multiply two numbers, there is a rule for where the decimal point goes in the answer.

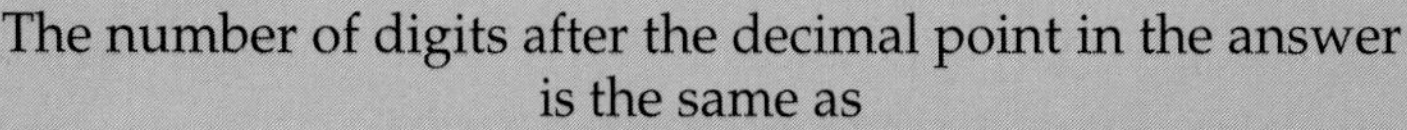

The number of digits after the decimal point in the answer is the same as the sum of the number of digits after the decimal point in the numbers being multiplied.

Example Work out 0.4×0.11

Numbers being multiplied	Number of digits after decimal point
0.4	1
0.11	2
Total	3

This means the answer must have 3 digits after the decimal point.

We know $4 \times 11 = 44$

Therefore, $0.4 \times 0.11 = 0.044$ (3 digits after the decimal point)

You can see how we have added an extra 0 to get the decimal places right.

EXERCISE 2.9

These numbers have been multiplied on a broken calculator. The decimal point and the zeros at the front are not showing up.

Write the number in the display column as it should appear.

	First number		Second number		Display
1	0.8	×	0.7	=	56
2	0.02	×	0.4	=	8
3	1.89	×	0.02	=	378
4	0.51	×	0.7	=	357
5	0.006	×	0.18	=	108

(continues)

6	0.3	×	0.001	=	3
7	37	×	0.0045	=	1665
8	1.963	×	0.9	=	17667
9	0.002	×	0.0007	=	14
10	0.87	×	10.056	=	874872
11	8000	×	0.0005	=	4
12	0.1	×	0.545	=	545

EXERCISE **2.10**

Work out the answer to each of these multiplication problems.

1 0.5×0.3
2 0.1×0.6
3 0.8×0.7
4 0.18×0.2
5 1.5×0.3
6 8×0.4
7 0.06×5
8 7×0.7
9 0.9×0.1
10 0.008×2
11 0.007×0.3
12 0.01×0.08
13 0.03×0.09
14 30×0.04
15 500×0.002
16 5.1×0.8
17 0.32×0.6
18 0.15×0.012
19 3.2×0.75
20 8.1×0.021

Multiplying by 10, 100, and 1000

Here's one reason the decimal number system is so useful. It makes multiplying by 10, 100, 1000, etc. very easy.

> The number of places the decimal point moves to the right
> is the same as
> the number of zeros in 10, 100, 1000, etc.

Examples

3.42×10	10 has 1 zero—so move decimal point 1 place:	$3.42 \times 10 = 34.2$
28.215×100	100 has 2 zeros—so move decimal point 2 places:	$28.215 \times 100 = 2821.5$
0.79×1000	1000 has 3 zeros—so move decimal point 3 places:	$0.79 \times 1000 = 790$

EXERCISE **2.11**

1 Work out each of these multiplications by 10.

(a) 0.6×10
(b) 1.2×10
(c) 0.78×10
(d) 10×0.4
(e) 312.4×10
(f) 31.18×10
(g) 0.004×10
(h) 0.0507×10

2 Work out each of these multiplications by 100.

(a) 0.55×100
(b) 0.6×100
(c) 1.34×100
(d) 12.6×100
(e) 0.007×100
(f) 65.182×100
(g) 0.00031×100
(h) 0.7312×100

3 Work out each of these multiplications by 1000.

(a) 0.625×1000
(b) 0.9×1000
(c) 0.0004×1000
(d) 1.11×1000
(e) 31.7×1000
(f) 4.5×1000
(g) 11.1255×1000
(h) $0.0080\ 66 \times 1000$

4 Copy this table. Then complete it to show multiplying by 10, 100, 1000 and 10 000.

	Number	× 10	× 100	× 1000	× 10 000
(a)	0.6				
(b)	53.1				
(c)	6.45				
(d)	0.026				
(e)	0.0008				
(f)	8.9				
(g)	0.16125				
(h)	93.182				

Decimals and money

In New Zealand we measure prices in dollars ($) and cents (c). There are 100 cents in $1.

Examples 635 c = $6.35
$0.75 = 75 cents

Example The price of petrol is 87 cents a litre. Calculate the cost of 12 litres.

Answer 87 cents × 12 = 1044 cents = $10.44
OR $0.87 \times 12 = 10.44$ (i.e. $10.44)

EXERCISE 2.12

1 Write these amounts in dollars ($).

(a) 335 c
(b) 690 c
(c) 4920 c
(d) 10550 c
(e) 75 c

2 Change these amounts to cents (c).

(a) $5.65
(b) $14.90
(c) $100.50
(d) $0.60
(e) $0.05

3–6 *For the next questions you will need this price list.*

3 Calculate the cost of these purchases:

(a) 2 tea towels
(b) 3 Bic Flik lighters
(c) 6 coffee mugs
(d) 1 triple pack of Bluebird chips and 1 packet of salted blanched peanuts
(e) 2 cans of Raid fly spray and 3 light bulbs
(f) 4 containers of detergent and 3 Jiffy firelighters

Snack Foods, Chips, Peanuts	
Krunchi Krisps (200 g)	1.80
Bluebird Chips (triple pack)	3.49
Peanuts Blanched Salted (250 g)	2.38
Peanuts Spanish Eta (250 g)	2.19
Detergent & Laundry Aids	
Lemon Detergent 900 mL	3.65
Miscellaneous	
Lighter Bic Flik	2.29
Air Freshener Ozore	3.80
Gloves Rubber Ambi ss	4.35
Coffee Mugs	3.88
Raid Fly Spray	3.95
Firelighters Jiffy	1.96
Phillips Light Bulbs 40, 60, 75 W	0.89
Teatowels	0.89
No Frills Disposable Razors 10s	3.69
BIC Disposable Razors 4s	1.75

4 How much change should you get when you pay for 1 Ozore air freshener with a $5 note?

5 How much change should you get when you pay for a packet of rubber gloves with a $20 note?

6 A catering firm wants to buy 130 packets of blanched salted peanuts for a wedding reception. Would $300 be enough money to pay for this? Show your working, and explain what you are calculating at each step.

7 Copy this table. Then complete it by working out the values marked a–h.

Item	Unit price	Price per 10	Price per 100
Bread	$2.33/loaf	a	b
Flour	$3.49/kg	c	d
Chicken (Size 9)	e	f	$899
Cola (1 litre bottles)	g	$12.40	h

At banks, exchange rates are expressed using decimals.

Here, the 'BUY NOTE' exchange rate shows how much foreign currency you will receive for 1 New Zealand dollar in cash.

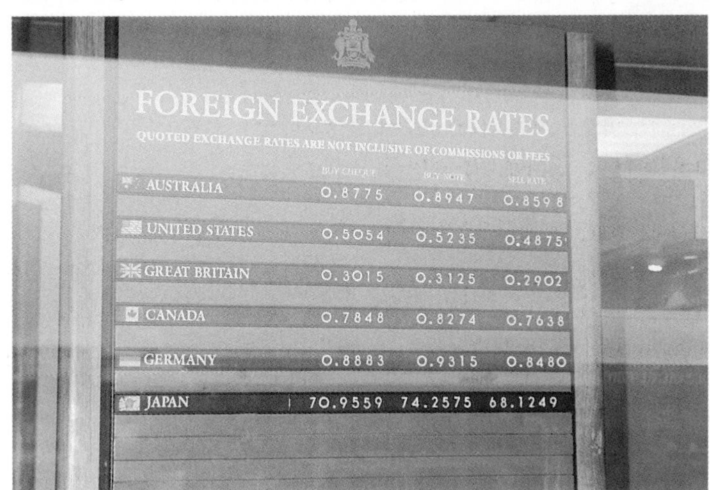

FOREIGN EXCHANGE RATES
QUOTED EXCHANGE RATES ARE NOT INCLUSIVE OF COMMISSIONS OR FEES
AUSTRALIA 0.8775 0.8947 0.8598
UNITED STATES 0.5054 0.5235 0.4875
GREAT BRITAIN 0.3015 0.3125 0.2902
CANADA 0.7848 0.8274 0.7638
GERMANY 0.8883 0.9315 0.8480
JAPAN 70.9559 74.2575 68.1249

Example Exchange rate for $US = 0.5235

This means $1 NZ will buy about 50 cents US.

To change $240 NZ to $US, do this calculation:

$NZ 240 × 0.5235 = $US 125.64

8 You are changing NZ cash into foreign currency. Calculate how much foreign currency you will receive when you change:

(a) $6 to US dollars
(b) $800 to US dollars
(c) $50 to Australian dollars
(d) $1042 to Australian dollars
(e) $66.50 to pounds sterling
(f) $812.78 to German marks
(g) $24 000 to Japanese yen
(h) $1388.66 to US dollars

Dividing decimals by whole numbers

There are several ways of writing a division.

'86 divided by 2' means the same as 'How many times does 2 go into 86?'

Using symbols, we could write this as either $86 \div 2$ or $2\overline{)86}$.

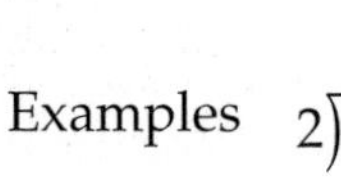

Examples $\begin{array}{r} 43 \\ 2\overline{)86} \end{array}$ $\begin{array}{r} 4.3 \\ 2\overline{)8.6} \end{array}$ $\begin{array}{r} 0.43 \\ 2\overline{)0.86} \end{array}$ $\begin{array}{r} 0.043 \\ 2\overline{)0.086} \end{array}$

↑ decimal points in line

- Write the decimal point in the answer so that it lines up with the decimal point in the number being divided.
- See how leading zeros are added in front if needed.

EXERCISE 2.13

1–6 *In each question, work out the answer to the first division problem. Then use it to help complete the second problem.*

1 (a) $6\overline{)42}$ (b) $6\overline{)4.2}$

2 (a) $5\overline{)210}$ (b) $5\overline{)2.10}$

3 (a) $8\overline{)1000}$ (b) $8\overline{)10.00}$

4 (a) $3\overline{)348}$ (b) $3\overline{)3.48}$

5 (a) $2\overline{)52}$ (b) $2\overline{)0.52}$

6 (a) $4\overline{)784}$ (b) $4\overline{)7.84}$

7–12 *Work out the answer to each of these division problems.*

7 $2\overline{)1.04}$

8 $5\overline{)38.75}$

9 $8\overline{)0.0544}$

10 $4.585 \div 7$

11 $0.284 \div 4$

12 $0.058\ 11 \div 3$

Sometimes you need to write some extra zeros at the end of the number being divided. This makes it easier to do the dividing steps.

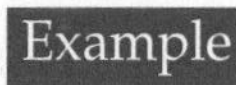

Example Show how to set out the division $1.7 \div 5$

Answer $5\overline{)1.7}$ is the same as $5\overline{)1.70}$

$$\begin{array}{r} 0\,.\,3\;\;4 \\ 5\overline{)\,1\,.\,{}^{1}7\;{}^{2}0} \end{array}$$

EXERCISE 2.14

Work out the answer to each of these division problems.

1 $5\overline{)2.8}$

2 $6\overline{)0.63}$

3 $4\overline{)30}$

4 $8\overline{)1}$

5 $0.01 \div 2$

6 $0.17 \div 4$

7 $81.9 \div 5$

8 $0.0078 \div 4$

Dividing by decimals

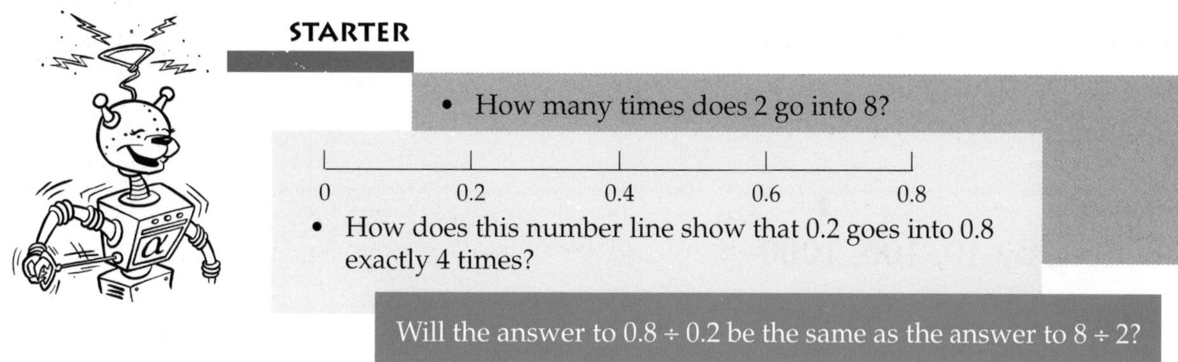

STARTER
• How many times does 2 go into 8?
0
0.2
0.4
0.6
0.8
• How does this number line show that 0.2 goes into 0.8 exactly 4 times?
Will the answer to 0.8 ÷ 0.2 be the same as the answer to 8 ÷ 2?

When we divide by a decimal, we can often make it easier to do. We change the problem so that we are dividing by a *whole number* instead. We do this by moving the decimal point in *both* numbers by the *same* number of places.

Examples To work out 20.3 ÷ 0.5 we work out 203 ÷ 5 instead (decimal point moves 1 place in each number)

To work out 18.295 ÷ 0.04 we work out 1829.5 ÷ 4 instead (decimal point moves 2 places in each number)

Example Work out 3.68 ÷ 0.2

Answer This has the same answer as 36.8 ÷ 2

$$2\overline{)36.8}\quad = 18.4$$

EXERCISE 2.15

1 In this table, each division in the right-hand column has the same answer as the division next to it in the left-hand column. Copy the table. Then complete the right-hand column.

	Division by a decimal	Division by a whole number that has the same answer
(a)	29 ÷ 0.2	290 ÷ ____
(b)	5.3 ÷ 0.5	53 ÷ ____
(c)	6 ÷ 0.03	____ ÷ 3
(d)	298 ÷ 0.4	____ ÷ 4
(e)	0.05 ÷ 0.12	____ ÷ 12
(f)	31.7 ÷ 0.06	3170 ÷ ____
(g)	0.3 ÷ 0.002	____ ÷ 2
(h)	50.2 ÷ 1.1	____ ÷ 11

2 Each of these decimal divisions has a whole-number division which gives the same answer. Write down the whole-number division.

(a) 6.7 ÷ 0.5
(b) 80 ÷ 0.2
(c) 15.73 ÷ 0.4
(d) 3 ÷ 0.05
(e) 602 ÷ 0.01
(f) 59.31 ÷ 0.8
(g) 0.52 ÷ 0.2
(h) 0.001 ÷ 0.5

3–12 *Work out the answer to each of these division problems.*

3 1.2 ÷ 0.4
4 82.5 ÷ 0.3
5 5 ÷ 0.2
6 7.39 ÷ 0.2
7 6.342 ÷ 0.02
8 1 ÷ 0.05
9 44.1 ÷ 0.5
10 0.204 ÷ 0.2
11 31.8 ÷ 0.04
12 0.584 ÷ 0.008

Dividing by 10, 100, 1000

Another good reason for using the decimal number system is that it makes division by 10, 100, 1000, etc. very easy.

Sometimes you will need extra leading zeros at the front.

> Just move the decimal point to the *left* by the same number of places as the number of zeros in 10, 100, 1000, etc.

Examples

3.42 ÷ 10	10 has 1 zero—so move decimal point 1 place:	3.42 ÷ 10 = 0.342
28.215 ÷ 100	100 has 2 zeros—so move decimal point 2 places:	28.215 ÷ 100 = 0.282 15
0.79 ÷ 1000	1000 has 3 zeros—so move decimal point 3 places:	0.79 ÷ 1000 = 0.000 79

Exercise 2.16

1 Work out each of these divisions by 10.
(a) 90.6 ÷ 10
(b) 1.2 ÷ 10
(c) 0.78 ÷ 10
(d) 4 ÷ 10
(e) 312.4 ÷ 10
(f) 31.18 ÷ 10
(g) 0.004 ÷ 10
(h) 0.0507 ÷ 10

2 Work out each of these divisions by 100.
(a) 445.5 ÷ 100
(b) 80.6 ÷ 100
(c) 1.34 ÷ 100
(d) 12.6 ÷ 100
(e) 0.007 ÷ 100
(f) 65.12 ÷ 100
(g) 0.031 ÷ 100
(h) 0.00731 ÷ 100

3 Work out each of these divisions by 1000.
(a) 2202.5 ÷ 1000
(b) 6000.9 ÷ 1000
(c) 80 000 ÷ 1000
(d) 1.11 ÷ 1000
(e) 31.7 ÷ 1000
(f) 4.5 ÷ 1000
(g) 11.1255 ÷ 1000
(h) 0.0086 ÷ 1000

4 Copy this table. Then complete it to show dividing by 10, 100, 1000 and 10 000.

	Number	÷ 10	÷ 100	÷ 1000	÷ 10 000
(a)	33				
(b)	788				
(c)	6.45				
(d)	733.5				
(e)	0.8				
(f)	12.97				
(g)	55 667				
(h)	1088.21				

Using a calculator for decimals

EXERCISE 2.17

1–10 *Use a calculator to work these out.*

1 6.189 + 13.04
2 59.035 – 8.981
3 1.121 × 6.78
4 846 ÷ 0.2
5 6.89 + 4.56 + 13.12
6 0.00635 ÷ 0.25
7 600.5 × 0.8
8 1.1 × 1.1 × 1.1
9 (7.445 – 0.92) × 0.18
10 (78.15 + 0.0035) ÷ 0.05

11 Here's a decimal hunt. Copy this multiplication table. Now use multiplication and division on your calculator to fill in the gaps.

×	**4**		**6.8**	
1.3		0.65		
	148.8			
		0.04		
	3			0.015

EXERCISE 2.18

1–12 *In each question, write down the answer* ***together with*** *the decimal calculation you used to work it out. The first one has been done for you.*

1 The record height for the high jump at school is 1.585 m. Chris breaks the record by 0.02 m. What is the new record?

Calculation: 1.585 + 0.02

Answer: 1.605 m

2 A cake recipe says: 'Add 0.65 kg of sugar to 1.125 kg of flour and mix'. What would you expect this mixture to weigh?

3 A swimmer breaks a race record by 1.27 seconds. The old record was 94.08 seconds. What is the new record?

4 A pencil measures 12.4 cm. It is then sharpened. Afterwards, it only measures 10.8 cm. What length has been removed?

5 A jar of marmalade weighs 0.454 kg. What would you expect 12 jars to weigh?

6 An empty glass jar weighs 0.268 kg. It is then filled with 0.957 kg of peanuts. The lid of the jar weighs 0.037 kg. What does the jar weigh when it is full and the lid is on?

7 A length of wood measures 3.48 m. It is then split into four equal pieces. What is the length of each piece?

8 A stake 1.8 m long is hammered into the ground. Afterwards, the length of stake above ground is 1.32 m. What length is below ground level?

9 Bottles of spring water sell for $2.29. Calculate the cost of 24 bottles.

10 How many 45 cent stamps can you buy for $30.60?

11 Debbie buys 8 bags of crisps for $9.20. What does one bag cost?

12 19 litres of petrol cost $17.48. How much does 1 litre of petrol cost?

13 6 stakes are placed in a line in a garden. The distance from each stake to the next stake is 0.84 m.

(a) Draw a diagram to show how the stakes are placed.

(b) Calculate the distance from the first stake to the last stake.

14 If 5 rabbits eat 12.5 lettuces in 5 days, how many lettuces will 10 rabbits eat in 10 days? The answer is NOT 25!

Recurring decimals

STARTER

- Use a calculator to work out 2 ÷ 9. Explain what happens.
- Now try working out 1 ÷ 7 on a calculator. Is there a pattern?
- Can you predict what the next decimal digit (not showing on the display) would be?
- Can you write out the answer to 1 ÷ 7 to twenty places of decimals?

Recurring decimals go on forever in a particular pattern. Here's a simple example. The decimal for the fraction one-third $\left(\frac{1}{3}\right)$ can be worked out by dividing: 1 ÷ 3

A calculator display will give 0.333333333 for this.

In short form, we write 0.333333333.... as $0.\dot{3}$

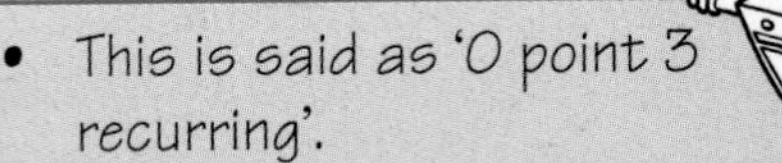

- This is said as '0 point 3 recurring'.
- The dot above the 3 shows where the repeating pattern begins.

Sometimes, a group of several digits repeats. To show this, we write dots over the *first* and *last* of the group. This shows that the whole group repeats.

Examples

Long form	Short form
0.28282828....	$0.\dot{2}\dot{8}$
0.714871487148....	$0.\dot{7}14\dot{8}$
0.58333333....	$0.58\dot{3}$

EXERCISE 2.19

1 Write these recurring decimals in long form.

(a) $0.\dot{6}$ (b) $15.\dot{2}$ (c) $18.\dot{2}\dot{7}$ (d) $4.1\dot{6}$ (e) $0.00\dot{3}$ (f) $0.\dot{3}0\dot{7}$ (g) $23.1\dot{8}1\dot{2}$ (h) $646.\dot{6}4\dot{6}$

2 Write these recurring decimals in short form.

(a) 0.8888.... (b) 10.5555.... (c) 1.633 33.... (d) 0.181 818 18.... (e) 0.562 626 262.... (f) 0.218 218 218.... (g) 0.113 131 313.... (h) 6.827 727 727....

3 The correct way of writing 0.6666.... as a recurring decimal is $0.\dot{6}$ rather than $0.\dot{6}\dot{6}$. Explain why.

4 Use a calculator to do these division problems. Write any recurring decimals in short form.

(a) 4.1 ÷ 3 (b) 49 ÷ 60 (c) 80 ÷ 11 (d) 31.6 ÷ 0.3 (e) 1.58 ÷ 0.9 (f) 355 ÷ 0.11 (g) 6.718 ÷ 0.15 (h) 55 ÷ 0.7

Rounding decimals

Sometimes a calculator will give a really accurate answer to a problem.

Example Calculate 150 ÷ 7 as a decimal.

Answer 150 ÷ 7 = 21.428 571....

Too much accuracy can be unhelpful. This is often true in measuring.
This division (150 ÷ 7) might be the answer to a practical problem:

Example A 150 cm plank of wood is divided into 7 equal pieces. How long is each piece?

Answer 21.428 571 cm (or 214.285 71 mm)

This length is roughly 21 cm, or 21.4 cm, or 214 mm.

Any value more accurate than this would be impossible to measure.

We could say that the answer to 150 ÷ 7 is 21.4. This is accurate to 1 decimal place.

Finding an approximate answer is called **rounding.**
We decide what approximate number is closest.

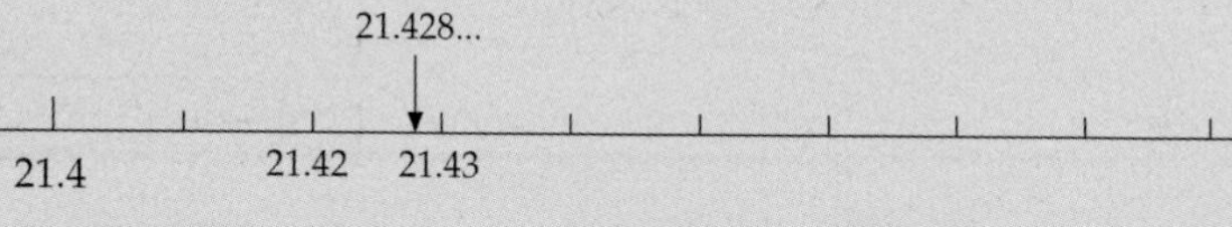

21.428 571 is closer to 21.4 than to 21.5.

We write this *rounded* answer as 21.4 (1 dp.)

The (1 dp) shows the number has been *rounded* to 1 decimal place.

Here are the rules for rounding numbers to any particular number of decimal places.

1. Decide which place you will round to. This will be the last digit in your answer. It will either be **rounded up** or be left unchanged (called **rounding down**).
2. Look at the digit just to the right of that place.
3. If the digit in step 2 is 5, 6, 7, 8 or 9 **round up**.
   If the digit is 0, 1, 2, 3, or 4, leave the last digit unchanged (**round down**).

Example Round 5.08 713 (a) to 2 dp (b) to 4 dp

Answer

(a) Look at the digit to right of the second decimal place: 5.08 713.
It is a 7, so round up.

5.08 713 = 5.09 (2 dp)

(b) Look at the digit to right of the fourth decimal place: 5.08 713.
It is a 3, so leave the digit in the fourth decimal place unchanged.

5.08 713 = 5.0871 (4 dp)

EXERCISE 2.20

1 Round these numbers to 1 decimal place.
(a) 3.125 (b) 4.863 (c) 0.428 37 (d) 0.068

2 Round these numbers to 2 decimal places:
(a) 1.3895 (b) 0.4418 (c) 0.0552 (d) 10.0209

3 Round these numbers to 3 decimal places:
(a) 0.4467 (b) 2.695 38 (c) 12.063 11 (d) 0.004 531

4 Copy this table. Then complete it to show rounding to 1, 2, 3 and 4 decimal places.

		to 1 dp	to 2 dp	to 3 dp	to 4 dp
(a)	7.091 83		7.09		
(b)	0.117 78				
(c)	16.995 46				

5 Use a calculator to work out these decimal problems. Write each answer rounded to 2 dp.
(a) $15 \div 7$ (b) 1.38×2.92 (c) $15.61 \div 8.692$ (d) 23.8×0.051 (e) $16.29 \div 23.6$ (f) $401.8 \div 79.6$

6 Work out these decimal problems. Write each answer rounded to 4 dp.
(a) $3 \div 7$ (b) $29 \div 87$ (c) 402.618×0.0106 (d) $37 \div 13$ (e) 15.162×89.61 (f) $73.61 \div 5.55$

7 Write down six different numbers that round to 6.41 (2 dp).
How would you describe *all* the numbers that round to 6.41?

Using a spreadsheet to do rounding

Produce a spreadsheet that shows this list of numbers rounded to 0, 1, 2 and 3 decimal places.

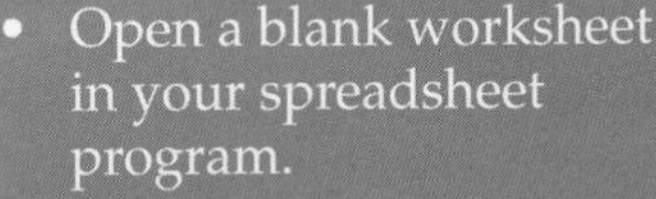

- Open a blank worksheet in your spreadsheet program.
- Type headings in row 1.
- Enter the numbers in column A.
- Copy the numbers into columns B, C, D and E.

	A	B	C	D	E
1	Number	to 0 dp.	to 1 dp.	to 2 dp.	to 3 dp.
2					
3	7.09183				
4	0.11778				
5	16.99546				
6	0.999888				
7	0.004639				

To round numbers in *Excel*, follow these steps:
1 select the cell(s) the numbers are in
2 click on Format, Cells, Number
3 make sure the 'Number' category is chosen
4 a dialog box will appear. Here you can choose the number of decimal places you want displayed.

In Mathematics, we can often get an answer which is more accurate than we need! Then, we need to consider how to round the answer sensibly.

Money calculations are one example. Here, we round to the nearest cent. In dollars, we round to 2 dp.

EXERCISE 2.21

1–5 *In each question,* ***round your answer sensibly****.*

1 A 63 cm strip of licorice is cut into 8 equal pieces. How long is each piece?

2 The price ticket on a packet of meat gives the weight (1.455 kg), and the price per kg ($7.99). What is the price of the meat?

3 Calculate the cost of buying 1.14 kg of capsicums at $5.39 a kg.

4 A bench in a grandstand is to be used for seating. The bench is 5.08 m long. 11 seats will be marked out on the bench. What is the width of each seat?

5 The Hopkins family pay annual rates of $1102.37. They pay in 6 equal instalments.

(a) How much is each instalment?

(b) If they pay the amount in (a) by 6 equal cheques, will they have overpaid or underpaid their rates? By how much?

6 An exchange rate table can be used to change foreign money into New Zealand currency.

This is done by *dividing* the amount of overseas money by the *selling* rate.

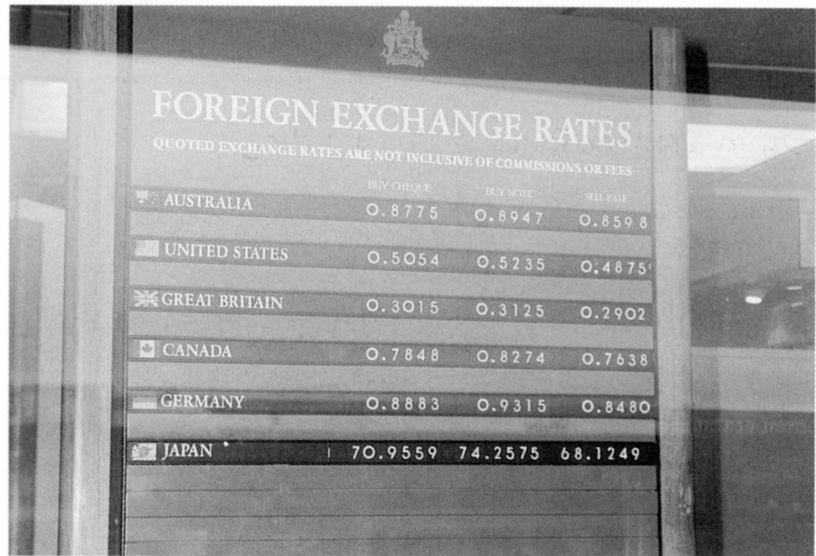

FOREIGN EXCHANGE RATES
QUOTED EXCHANGE RATES ARE NOT INCLUSIVE OF COMMISSIONS OR FEES
AUSTRALIA 0.8775 0.8947 0.8598
UNITED STATES 0.5054 0.5235 0.4875
GREAT BRITAIN 0.3015 0.3125 0.2902
CANADA 0.7848 0.8274 0.7638
GERMANY 0.8883 0.9315 0.8480
JAPAN 70.9559 74.2575 68.1249

Example Change $230 US in notes to New Zealand currency.

Answer The exchange rate for selling is 0.4875.

$230 ÷ 0.4875 = $471.79 (to the nearest cent)

To the nearest 5 cents, $471.80 would be paid for the US money.

Change these amounts of money into New Zealand currency.

(a) 80 US dollars

(b) 46 000 Japanese yen

(c) 2000 pounds sterling

(d) 89.41 German marks

(e) 308.45 Australian dollars

(f) 55 000 US dollars

INVESTIGATION

AEROBIC FITNESS TESTING

This investigation is about measuring your fitness level. It involves calculations using decimals.

Here is what you do:

- First practise taking your pulse. Place the tips of the fingers of one hand firmly onto the other wrist, just below the thumb. Get someone to time 30 seconds for you. Count the beats over this 30 seconds.
- Find a step that is about 16–20 cm high. Get someone to call out a rhythm, 1, 2, 3, 4. To this rhythm, step up and down:
  - — left foot up
  - — right foot up
  - — right foot down
  - — left foot down
- Step up and down for no more than 5 minutes. Take a note of how long you exercised, in seconds.
- Wait 1 minute. Then take your pulse for 30 seconds.

Here is how you work out your aerobic fitness index.

- Multiply your pulse count by 5.5
- Divide this result into the time you exercised (in seconds)

Show your working, and explain what you are calculating at each step.

Decide how your fitness rates using this scale:

Index	Description
above 1.4	athlete!
between 1.2 and 1.4	excellent
between 1 and 1.2	very good
between 0.8 and 1	good
between 0.5 and 0.8	fair
below 0.5	poor

3 Integers

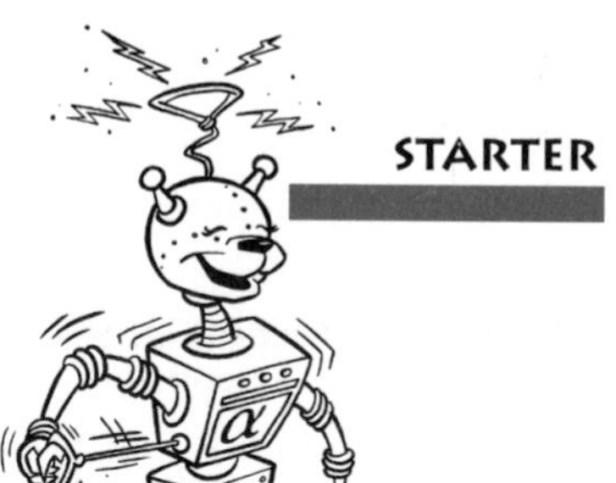

STARTER

The shore of the Dead Sea, between Israel and Jordan, is the lowest part of the Earth's land surface.

We could write the level of the Dead Sea using a *negative* number. This would be $^{-}394$ m.

- What would 0 represent?
- If the level of the Dead Sea rose by 2 m, how far below sea level would it be?
- If the level of the Dead Sea fell by 3 m, how far below sea level would it be?

What are integers?

We need to use negative numbers often in real life.

- A temperature of 12 degrees is not the same as a temperature of 12 degrees below zero.
- A bank balance of $100 is not the same as an overdraft of $100.

Counting numbers are positive numbers. They are not enough to answer some subtraction questions, such as 3 – 5. Instead, we use **integers**.

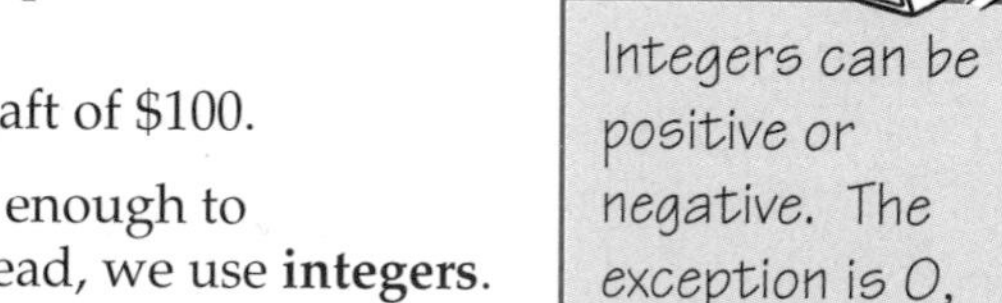

Integers can be positive or negative. The exception is 0, which is neither!

Here's how we represent integers.

1 We start with the whole-number line:

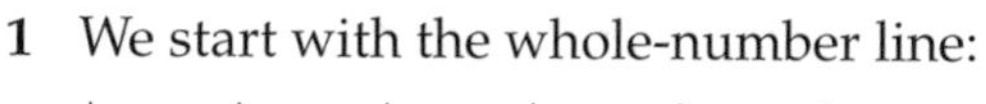

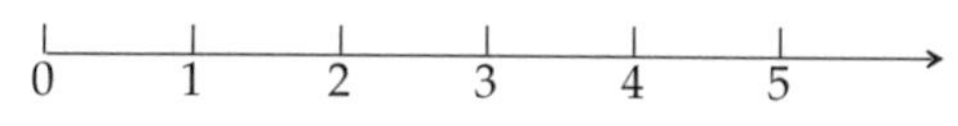

2 Turn it over to get a new line:

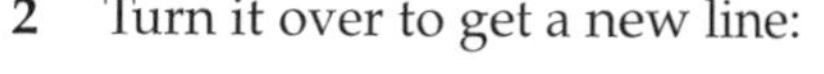

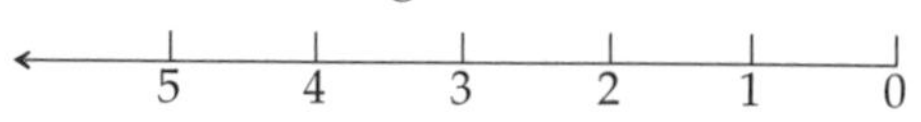

3 Join the two number lines together at 0:

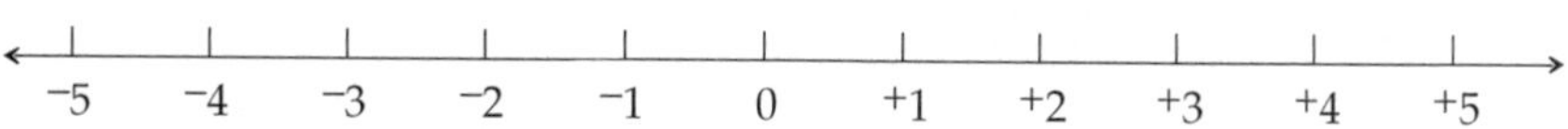

We write the left-hand numbers with a small – They are called **negative integers**	We can write the right-hand numbers with a small + They are called **positive integers**

EXERCISE 3.1

1 Write down the missing words or numbers.

(a) Deposit of $60 is $^{+}60$
Withdrawal of $40 is ____

(b) 70 m above sea–level is $^{+}70$
70 m _____ sea level is $^{-}70$

(c) 3 strokes over par in golf is $^{+}3$
3 strokes under par in golf is ____

(d) 20 seconds _____ take–off is $^{-}20$
40 seconds after take–off is $^{+}40$

(e) 4 floors _____ ground level is $^{+}4$
3 floors below ground level is $^{-}3$

(f) 9 °C above zero is $^{+}9$
4 °C ______ zero is $^{-}4$

2 Use integers to represent each of these:

(a) a deposit of $12 in the bank, a withdrawal of $100 from the bank

(b) two floors up, eight floors down

(c) 12 °C below zero, 19 °C above zero

(d) a score of 8 over par in golf, a score of 2 under par

(e) a fall of 40 points on the sharemarket, a rise of 65 points on the sharemarket

(f) 4 goals ahead, 15 runs behind

(g) 2 people absent, 5 people over

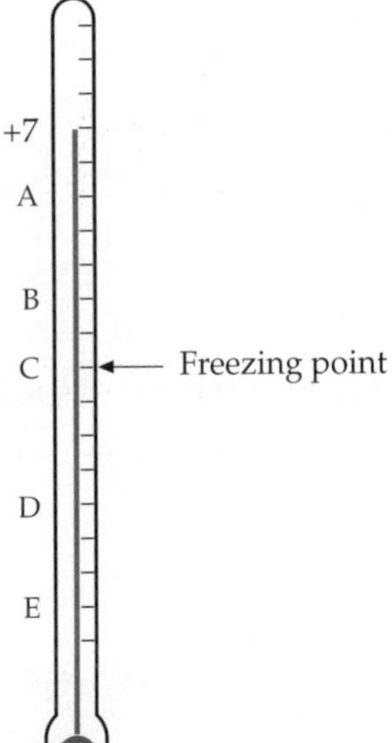

3 This thermometer shows a temperature of 7 °C.

(a) Look at the points on the scale marked A, B, C, D, and E. Write down the numbers that should appear.

(b) The temperature is 7 °C. What will the new temperature be if:
(i) it falls by 4 °C?
(ii) it falls by 9 °C?

(c) The temperature is $^{-}5$ °C. What will the new temperature be if:
(i) it falls by 4 °C?
(ii) it rises by 8 °C?
(iii) it rises by 2 °C?
(iv) it rises by 5 °C?

4 A company is allowed to have an *overdraft*. They can write cheques for amounts that are more than they have in their account. They have $1000 in the bank. They then write a cheque to pay one of their suppliers.

(a) How much money will they have if the cheque is for $400?

(b) How much money will they have if the cheque is for $1700?

5 This table shows the minimum and maximum temperatures in Calgary, Canada over three days in January.

	Jan 8	Jan 9	Jan 10
Min (°C)	$^{-}16$	$^{-}11$	$^{-}13$
Max (°C)	$^{-}7$	0	2

(a) What was the coldest temperature in Calgary over this period?

(b) What was the warmest temperature in Calgary over this period?

(c) Which day had the greatest *range* in temperature? (The range is the difference between the maximum and the minimum temperatures.)

Comparing integers

We can compare numbers by saying one number is **greater than** or **less than** another number. Here are the symbols we use:

Symbol	Meaning	Example
$<$	is less than	$6 < 13$
$>$	is greater than	$43 > 41$

How do we decide if a number is less than or greater than another number? We look at a number line. The further to the *right* a number is, the larger that number is.

One integer is **less than** another ($<$) if it is to the **left** on the integer number line.
One integer is **greater than** another ($>$) if it is to the **right** on the integer number line.

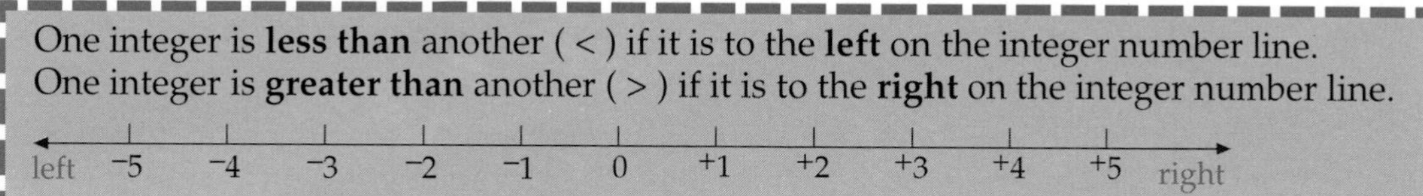

This number line shows $^{+}2$ is greater than $^{-}3$

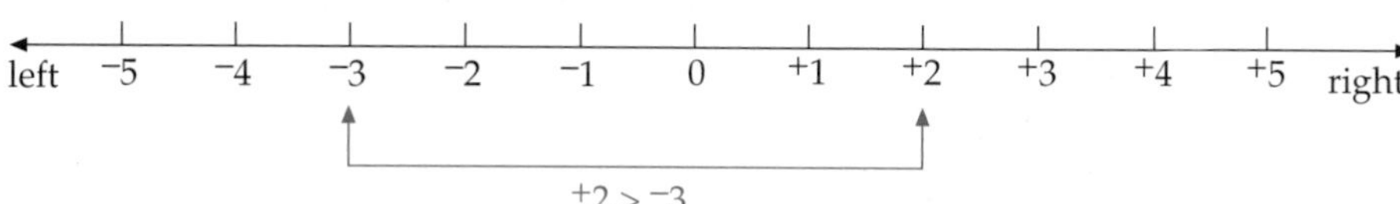

This number line shows $^{-}4$ is less than $^{-}1$

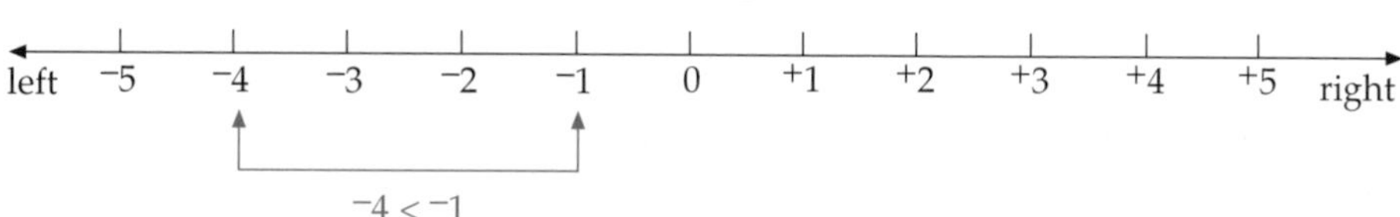

We can write the comparison between two numbers in two ways.
$^{+}2 > {}^{-}3$ means exactly the same as writing $^{-}3 < {}^{+}2$.
It's just a different way of writing down the same idea.

1 Here are some sets of numbers. Write them in order from smallest to largest.
   (a) { 1, 5, 0, 3, 6 }
   (b) { 1, 4, 7, 2, 5, 3 }
   (c) { 49, 17, 38, 52, 29 }
   (d) { 38, 192, 27, 93, 42, 138, 49 }

2 Copy each pair of numbers. Replace each box with a $<$ or $>$ symbol.
   (a) 3 ☐ 1
   (b) 5 ☐ 0
   (c) 1 ☐ 3
   (d) 0 ☐ 4
   (e) 1 ☐ 0

3 Use this drawing of a thermometer to help you answer these questions.

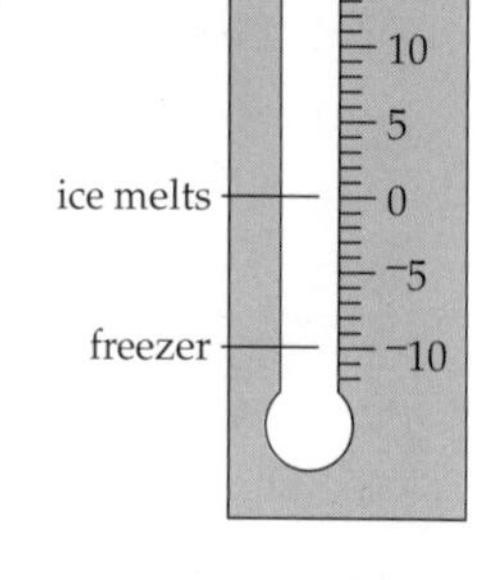

   (a) Which temperature is warmer: 2 °C or $^{-}8$ °C?
   (b) Which temperature is colder: $^{-}3$ °C or $^{-}7$ °C?
   (c) Which of these is the highest temperature? $^{-}5$ °C, 0 °C, or $^{-}2$ °C?

(continues)

(d) Which of these is the lowest temperature? $^{-}4$ °C, 0 °C, or 3 °C?

(e) Write down *two* temperatures that are higher than $^{-}10$ °C.

(f) Write down *two* temperatures that are lower than $^{-}10$ °C.

4–15 *Copy each pair of numbers. Replace each box with a < or > symbol.*

4 $^{+}7$ □ $^{+}2$

5 $^{-}3$ □ $^{+}4$

6 $^{-}2$ □ $^{-}5$

7 $^{-}8$ □ $^{-}3$

8 $^{+}5$ □ $^{-}2$

9 $^{+}3$ □ $^{-}8$

10 $^{-}10$ □ $^{-}1$

11 $^{+}16$ □ $^{-}11$

12 $^{+}57$ □ $^{+}73$

13 $^{-}25$ □ $^{-}84$

14 $^{-}93$ □ $^{+}12$

15 $^{+}3$ □ $^{-}467$

16–21 *Write each set of numbers in order from the smallest to the largest.*

16 { 0, $^{-}4$, $^{+}2$ }

17 { $^{+}5$, $^{-}5$, $^{+}2$, $^{-}3$, $^{+}7$ }

18 { $^{-}3$, $^{-}5$, $^{-}2$, $^{-}6$, $^{-}1$ }

19 { $^{-}5$, 0, $^{-}3$, $^{-}2$, $^{-}7$ }

20 { $^{+}98$, $^{-}78$, $^{-}80$, $^{-}31$ }

21 { $^{-}392$, $^{+}428$, $^{-}821$, $^{-}3$, $^{-}5$ }

22 Write down whether these statements are *true* or *false*.

(a) $^{-}6 > {}^{-}4$

(b) 0 is a positive integer

(c) $^{-}6$ is a negative integer

(d) $+7 > {}^{-}10$

(e) $0 < {}^{-}8$

(f) 0 is a negative integer

(g) $^{-}8.32$ is an integer

(h) All whole numbers are positive

23 Here are the results from a golf tournament. The winner is the player with the lowest score.

Player	Score (over or under par)
Jason Ng	$^{-}3$
Wiremu Rata	0
Alar Treial	$^{+}3$
Rex Hopkins	$^{-}5$
John Sutton	$^{+}2$
Tracey Meech	$^{-}4$

List the players in finishing order, starting from the winner.

24 The lowest points on six continents are given in this table. The elevation gives the height of each point compared with sea-level.

Continent	Lowest point	Elevation (m)
Africa	Lake Assai, Djibouti	$^{-}156$
Asia	Dead Sea (Jordan/Israel)	$^{-}394$
Australia	Lake Eyre	$^{-}16$
Europe	Caspian Sea, Russia	$^{-}28$
North America	Death Valley, USA	$^{-}86$
South America	Valdes Peninsula, Argentina	$^{-}40$

List the lowest points in order from highest to lowest.

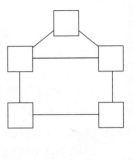

25 Copy this diagram. Place the integers $^{-}10$, $^{-}9$, $^{-}8$, $^{-}7$ and $^{-}6$ in different boxes. Make sure that consecutive integers are not directly connected. For example, $^{-}7$ must not be connected to $^{-}8$ or $^{-}6$.

Adding integers

STARTER

In golf, a very good golfer is expected to take a certain number of strokes to complete the course. This number is called a 'par' score. A winner takes fewer strokes than anyone else, and will probably have an 'under' par score. Players who do badly (take a lot more strokes) will have a score that is likely to be 'over' par.

We can represent an under par score with a negative number:

$^-2$ means two strokes under par

An over par score is represented by a positive number:

$^+6$ means 6 strokes over par

In the World Cup of Golf, two players make a team. The team's score is the combined score of the two players.

- Discuss how you would complete this table to show each team's score.

Team	Player A	Player B	Combined score	Integer sum
New Zealand	3 under	5 under	8 under	$^-3 + ^-5 = ^-8$
Fiji	1 under	6 over		
Australia	2 over	4 under		
Japan	1 over	1 over		
Scotland	par	1 under		

- Which team had the best score?

We can show how to add integers on an integer number line.

Adding integers

Always start from where the first integer is. Then:

- step **right** to add a **positive** integer
- step **left** to add a **negative** integer

Examples

(a) $^-2 + ^+3$ Start at $^-2$. Move 3 steps to the right.

$^-2 + ^+3 = ^+1$

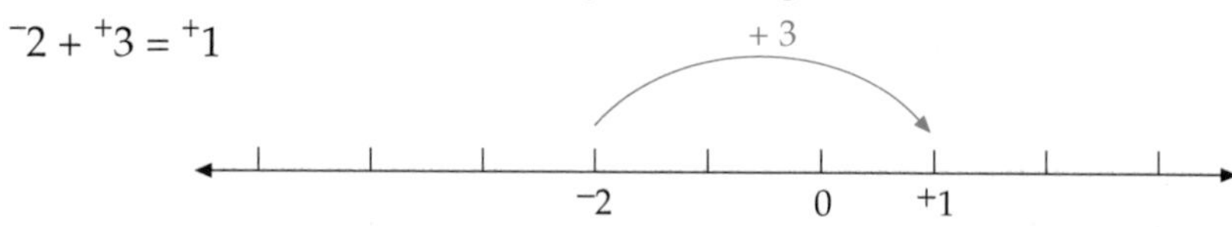

(b) ${}^{-}2 + {}^{-}4$ Start at ${}^{-}2$. Move 4 steps to the left. ${}^{-}2 + {}^{-}4 = {}^{-}6$

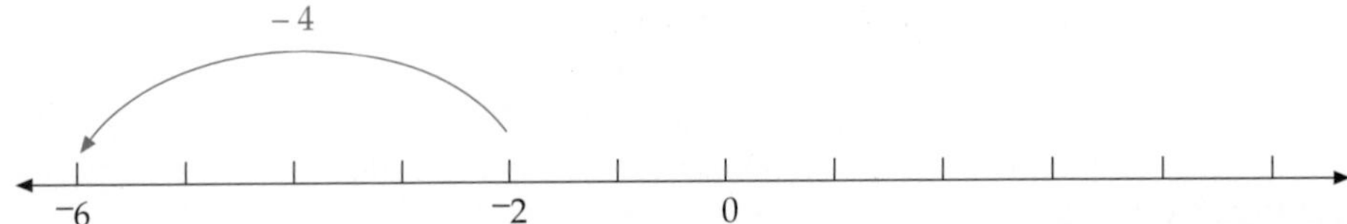

(c) ${}^{-}5 + {}^{+}3$ Start at ${}^{-}5$. Move 3 steps to the right.
${}^{-}5 + {}^{+}3 = {}^{-}2$

+ 3

${}^{-}5$ ${}^{-}2$ 0

EXERCISE 3.3

1–30 *Use this number line to help you work out the sums.*

${}^{-}13$ ${}^{-}12$ ${}^{-}11$ ${}^{-}10$ ${}^{-}9$ ${}^{-}8$ ${}^{-}7$ ${}^{-}6$ ${}^{-}5$ ${}^{-}4$ ${}^{-}3$ ${}^{-}2$ ${}^{-}1$ 0 ${}^{+}1$ ${}^{+}2$ ${}^{+}3$ ${}^{+}4$ ${}^{+}5$ ${}^{+}6$ ${}^{+}7$ ${}^{+}8$ ${}^{+}9$ ${}^{+}10$ ${}^{+}11$ ${}^{+}12$ ${}^{+}13$

1 ${}^{-}2 + {}^{+}4$
2 ${}^{-}2 + {}^{-}4$
3 ${}^{-}1 + {}^{+}5$
4 ${}^{+}4 + {}^{-}3$
5 ${}^{-}1 + {}^{+}1$
6 ${}^{-}1 + {}^{-}1$
7 ${}^{-}3 + {}^{-}5$
8 ${}^{-}4 + {}^{+}4$
9 ${}^{-}3 + {}^{+}5$
10 ${}^{+}7 + {}^{-}3$

11 ${}^{-}13 + {}^{+}4$
12 ${}^{+}5 + {}^{-}9$
13 ${}^{+}7 + {}^{-}8$
14 ${}^{-}11 + {}^{+}13$
15 ${}^{+}7 + {}^{+}3$
16 ${}^{-}5 + {}^{-}4$
17 ${}^{+}3 + {}^{+}9$
18 ${}^{-}12 + {}^{-}1$
19 ${}^{-}3 + {}^{+}3$
20 ${}^{-}7 + {}^{-}6$

21 ${}^{+}5 + {}^{-}11$
22 ${}^{-}7 + {}^{+}7$
23 ${}^{+}9 + {}^{-}12$
24 ${}^{-}8 + {}^{-}5$
25 ${}^{+}5 + {}^{+}3$
26 ${}^{-}2 + {}^{-}3 + {}^{-}5$
27 ${}^{+}3 + {}^{-}5 + {}^{-}3$
28 ${}^{+}12 + {}^{-}13 + {}^{+}1$
29 ${}^{-}6 + {}^{-}1 + {}^{-}2$
30 ${}^{+}4 + {}^{-}5 + {}^{-}2 + {}^{+}10$

31 You would need a very long number line for some sums! See if you can 'imagine' a line to work out these:
(a) ${}^{+}27 + {}^{+}7$
(b) ${}^{+}93 + {}^{-}3$
(c) ${}^{-}36 + {}^{-}2$
(d) ${}^{-}43 + {}^{+}5$
(e) ${}^{-}139 + {}^{-}7$
(f) ${}^{+}256 + {}^{-}9$
(g) ${}^{-}568 + {}^{-}32$
(h) ${}^{+}238 + {}^{-}27$

EXERCISE 3.4

1–4 *For each of these problems, write down the sum of two integers. Then add them to work out the answer.*

1 The temperature fell 1 °C, then fell a further 7 °C. How much did it fall altogether?

2 The reading on a barometer fell by 4 points, then rose by 9 points. By how much had the reading changed over this time?

3 The water level at a lake fell 10 cm, then rose 7 cm. How much did it fall altogether?

4 The value of some shares rose by 3 cents on Monday, then fell by 5 cents on Tuesday. What happened to their value overall?

5 Daniel played four rounds of golf. His scores were: 3 over, 5 under, 1 over, 2 under. What was his final combined score for the four rounds?

6 Sara made these transactions at her bank:

Deposit	\$120
Withdrawal	\$85
Withdrawal	\$70
Deposit	\$10

What single transaction would be the same as making these four?

Adding and subtracting integers on a spreadsheet

Let's see how a spreadsheet does adding of integers.
This spreadsheet will show the results of adding ⁻8, ⁻2 and +7 to each of the integers from ⁻6 to +6.

Enter this:

	A	B	C	D
1		adding -8	adding -2	adding 7
2				
3	-6	=A3+-8	=A3+-2	=A3+7
4	-5			
5	-4			
6	-3			
7	-2			
8	-1			
9	0			
10	1			
11	2			
12	3			
13	4			
14	5			
15	6			

Result:

	A	B	C	D
1		adding -8	adding -2	adding 7
2				
3	-6	-14	-8	1
4	-5			
5	-4			
6	-3			
7	-2			
8	-1			
9	0			
10	1			
11	2			
12	3			
13	4			
14	5			
15	6			

In column A, we have all the integers from ⁻6 to 6.

1 Produce a finished version of this spreadsheet by:
- entering formulas in cells B3, C3 and D3
- copying the formulas down.

2 Produce another spreadsheet showing how to *subtract* ⁻8, ⁻2 and 7 from each of the integers from ⁻6 to 6.

Adding integers on a calculator

Scientific calculators have a special key for entering *negative* numbers.

The key has both + (plus) and – (minus) symbols on it. It looks like [±], and is often called the 'sign change' key.

It is pressed after the number itself is entered.

Here is what you would enter, in order, to work out ⁻37 + ⁻14:

[37] [±] [+] [14] [±] [=]

The [=] key at the end is needed to complete the calculation.
The answer should be ⁻51. Check this on *your* calculator!

EXERCISE 3.5

Make two copies of this table.

+	$^{-}11$	89	$^{-}32$	41
$^{-}8$				
$^{-}35$				
$^{-}66$				
37				

- In the first copy, write down + or – signs only in the cells, to show whether the answers will be positive or negative.
- Complete the second copy by adding the integers on a calculator.

Subtracting integers

You will have noticed that:

$^{-}5 + {}^{+}5 = 0$ $\quad$ $^{+}3 + {}^{-}3 = 0$ $\quad$ $^{-}17 + {}^{+}17 = 0$ etc.

$^{+}5$ is called the *opposite* of $^{-}5$. $^{-}5$ is called the opposite of $^{+}5$; and so on.

If two integers add to 0, they are **opposites**.

EXERCISE 3.6

Write down the opposites of these integers.

1 $^{-}3$
2 $^{+}4$
3 $^{-}2$
4 $^{+}1$
5 0
6 $^{+}6$
7 $^{+}3$
8 $^{-}37$
9 $^{+}98$
10 $^{-}41$

We already know how to subtract whole numbers.

Example $6 - 5 = 1$

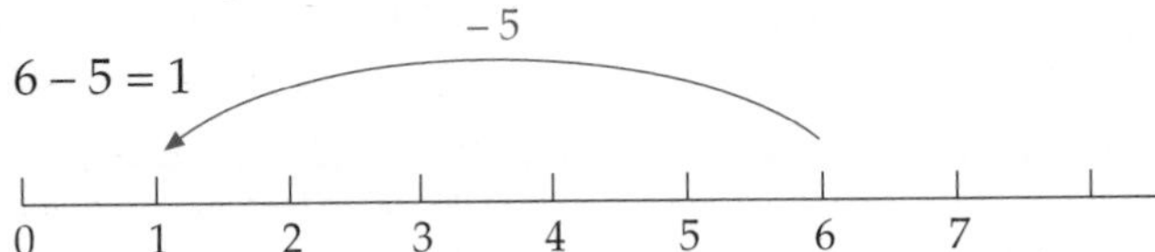

This is the same as adding $^{+}6 + {}^{-}5$

$^{+}6 + {}^{-}5 = +1$

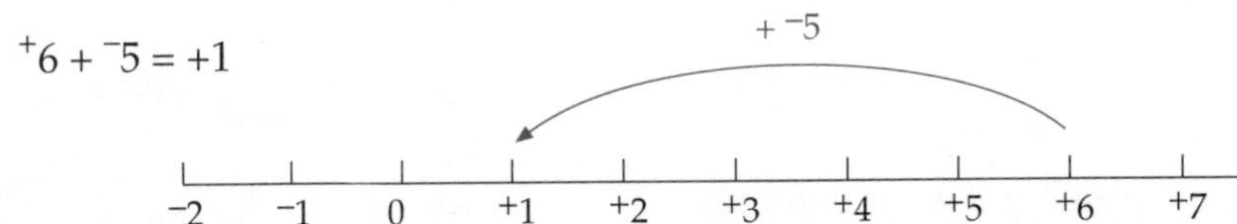

Subtracting 5 from 6 is the same as adding $^{-}5$ to 6.
This shows we can change a subtracting problem into an adding problem with the same answer.

Rule for subtracting integers

To subtract integers, we add the *opposite* of the second integer to the first integer.

Examples

Subtraction	Change to add the opposite	Answer
$^{+}7 - {}^{+}4$	$^{+}7 + {}^{-}4$	$^{+}3$
$^{-}3 - {}^{-}5$	$^{-}3 + {}^{+}5$	$^{+}2$
$^{-}10 - {}^{+}7$	$^{-}10 + {}^{-}7$	$^{-}17$
$^{+}4 - {}^{-}6$	$^{+}4 + {}^{+}6$	$^{+}10$

EXERCISE 3.7

Work out the answers to these subtractions.

1 $^{+}4 - {}^{+}7$
2 $^{-}6 - {}^{+}5$
3 $^{+}7 - {}^{-}4$
4 $^{+}6 - {}^{-}3$
5 $^{-}3 - {}^{-}5$
6 $^{+}1 - {}^{-}8$
7 $^{-}3 - {}^{+}9$
8 $^{+}5 - {}^{+}8$
9 $^{+}2 - {}^{+}7$
10 $^{+}1 - {}^{-}4$
11 $^{-}4 - {}^{+}3$
12 $^{-}7 - {}^{-}2$
13 $^{-}11 - {}^{+}5$
14 $^{-}6 - {}^{+}6$
15 $^{-}5 - {}^{+}2$
16 $^{+}3 - {}^{-}4$
17 $^{-}7 - {}^{+}9$
18 $^{-}1 - {}^{-}2$
19 $^{-}4 - {}^{+}4$
20 $^{-}29 - {}^{-}29$
21 $^{-}45 - {}^{+}52$
22 $^{-}81 - {}^{+}94$
23 $^{+}142 - {}^{+}64$
24 $^{+}294 - {}^{-}6$

EXERCISE 3.8

1 The temperature inside a house is 18 °C. Outside, it is 23 °C colder. What is the temperature outside?

2 A business has $1300 in their cheque account. They write a cheque for $1500. How much money do they now have in their cheque account?

3–4 *For each of these problems show your working. Write down a subtraction of two integers, and then write down the answer.*

3 The minimum temperatures in four South Island towns on July 17 were:

Alexandra	$^{-}9$ °C
Nelson	$^{-}1$ °C
Greymouth	3 °C
Queenstown	$^{-}5$ °C

(a) What is the difference in minimum temperatures between Alexandra and Nelson?

(b) How much warmer than Queenstown is Greymouth?

(c) By how much is Alexandra colder than Queenstown?

4 Here are four kitchen temperatures:

Oven	120 °C
Bench	19 °C
Refrigerator	4 °C
Freezer	$^{-}6$ °C

(a) A piece of pizza is taken out of the oven and left on the bench. By how much will it cool down?

(b) Some frozen scones are taken from the freezer and placed in the oven. By how much will they warm up?

(c) What is the difference in temperature between the refrigerator and the freezer?

(d) A carton of blackcurrants is washed, left to dry on the bench, and then put in the freezer. By how much will they cool down?

5 A dolphin is swimming at the bottom of a 5 m deep pool. It then leaps straight upwards to grab a fish from its trainer's hand, 2 m above the pool surface. What distance has the dolphin leapt? Write down an expression using integers to explain.

We don't normally use the + sign to show that an integer is positive. Usually, if a number has **no sign** in front of it, it is **positive**.

Examples $^{+}5 = 5$ $^{+}10 = 10$ $21 = {}^{+}21$ etc.

The rules for adding and subtracting don't change.

Examples

$^{-}5 + 2 = {}^{-}3$		$^{-}5 + {}^{+}2 = {}^{-}3$
$1 - 10 = {}^{-}9$	is the same as	$^{+}1 - {}^{+}10 = {}^{-}9$
$2 - {}^{-}8 = 10$		$^{+}2 - {}^{-}8 = {}^{+}10$

We always need the – to show a number is **negative**.

EXERCISE 3.9

Work out the answers to these addition and subtraction problems.

1 $4 + 5$	7 $^{-}2 + 3$	13 $5 + {}^{-}2$	19 $9 + {}^{-}11$
2 $^{-}3 + 1$	8 $1 - 4$	14 $^{-}6 + {}^{-}18$	20 $^{-}11 + 9$
3 $4 - 1$	9 $^{-}3 + {}^{-}6$	15 $4 - 17$	21 $69 - 73$
4 $3 - 5$	10 $^{-}11 - 4$	16 $11 - {}^{-}4$	22 $^{-}2 - 83$
5 $1 - {}^{-}2$	11 $^{-}14 - {}^{-}19$	17 $^{-}21 - 20$	23 $^{-}1 + 41$
6 $^{-}1 - {}^{-}4$	12 $^{-}11 + 2$	18 $^{-}18 - 13$	24 $^{-}43 + 17$

Several additions/subtractions in one problem!

To add more than two numbers, group the numbers in pairs. Work from left to right.

Example Work out $3 + {}^{-}7 + 2$

Answer

$$\begin{aligned} 3 + {}^{-}7 + 2 &= (3 + {}^{-}7) + 2 \\ &= {}^{-}4 + 2 \\ &= {}^{-}2 \end{aligned}$$

EXERCISE 3.10

Work out the answers to these addition problems.

1 $^{-}4 + 2 + {}^{-}3$	6 $^{-}9 + 4 + 7$
2 $7 + {}^{-}9 + {}^{-}3$	7 $^{-}3 + 2 + {}^{-}7$
3 $^{-}9 + {}^{-}2 + {}^{-}3$	8 $^{-}9 + {}^{-}3 + {}^{-}4$
4 $5 + {}^{-}8 + {}^{-}4$	9 $5 + 2 + {}^{-}10$
5 $^{-}3 + {}^{-}7 + 8$	10 $^{-}11 + 15 + {}^{-}12$

With subtractions, first change *all* the subtractions so that you are adding *opposites*. Then work from left to right.

Example Work out $5 - {}^{-}3 - 9$

Answer

$$\begin{aligned} 5 - {}^{-}3 - 9 &= 5 + 3 + {}^{-}9 \\ &= (5 + 3) + {}^{-}9 \\ &= 8 + {}^{-}9 \\ &= {}^{-}1 \end{aligned}$$

EXERCISE 3.11

Work out the answers to these subtraction problems.

1 $7 - {}^-2 - 5$
2 $12 - {}^-5 - 6$
3 ${}^-4 - 8 - {}^-9$
4 $8 - 2 - {}^-4$
5 $3 - 5 - {}^-9$
6 ${}^-15 - {}^-11 - 12$
7 ${}^-12 - 6 - {}^-2$
8 ${}^-1 - {}^-7 - {}^-7$
9 ${}^-42 - 36 - 90$
10 $80 - {}^-12 - 37$

Sometimes, there is addition and subtraction in the same problem. Change the subtractions to adding opposites. Then, work left to right.

Example Work out ${}^-2 + {}^-8 - {}^-5$

Answer

$$
\begin{aligned}
{}^-2 + {}^-8 - {}^-5 &= {}^-2 + {}^-8 + 5 \\
&= ({}^-2 + {}^-8) + 5 \\
&= {}^-10 + 5 \\
&= {}^-5
\end{aligned}
$$

EXERCISE 3.12

Work out these.

1 $4 + {}^-3 - {}^-8$
2 ${}^-8 + 2 - {}^-5$
3 $11 + {}^-4 - {}^-7$
4 ${}^-6 - {}^-2 + {}^-9$
5 $4 - {}^-3 + 2$
6 ${}^-12 - 8 + 18$
7 ${}^-15 - 8 + 14$
8 ${}^-24 - 7 + {}^-3 - {}^-2$
9 ${}^-18 + 4 - 2 - {}^-4$
10 ${}^-12 - 4 - {}^-3 - 12$
11 $7 + {}^-3 - 4 - {}^-8$
12 ${}^-2 + 5 - {}^-3 - 5$

EXERCISE 3.13

1 A class started the year with 29 students. During the year 6 students left, and 4 new students joined the class. How many students were in the class at the end of the year?

2 A golfer uses positive and negative numbers to record her score for each hole. These numbers show if her score was:

- under par (negative)
- even with par (0)
- over par (positive).

For example, she got 0, ${}^-1$, 2, ${}^-1$, 1, ${}^-2$, 0, 0, ${}^-1$ on nine holes. This gave an overall score of ${}^-2$ (2 under par).

What is the overall result for each of these rounds?

A (nine holes)	${}^-1$, 2, ${}^-1$, 0 , 0, 1, 3, ${}^-1$, 0
B (18 holes)	0, 0, 0, ${}^-1$, 1, ${}^-2$, 0, 0, 0, 2, 0, ${}^-1$, 0, 1, 0, ${}^-1$, 1, 1
C (18 holes)	${}^-1$, 0, 0, 0, ${}^-1$, 1, 0, 1, 0, 1, 0, 2, 3, 1, 0, ${}^-1$, 0, 2

3 A bank uses positive numbers to represent deposits, and negative numbers to represent withdrawals. Calculate the final balance for these transactions:

(a) Initial balance \$60, then ${}^-$\$45, ${}^-$\$30, \$55
(b) Initial balance \$80, then \$12, ${}^-$\$25, ${}^-$\$37, \$5
(c) Initial balance ${}^-$\$30, then ${}^-$\$48, \$70, ${}^-$\$36, \$10

4 This diagram shows the lift controls in a hotel. There are 6 floors of rooms, reception on the ground floor, and a 3-level parking garage below ground level. Each level is also linked by a flight of stairs.

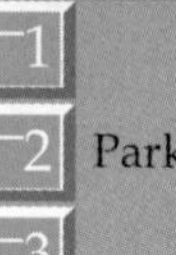

(a) How many flights of stairs are there between Floor 5 and Level 2 of the parking garage?

(continues)

(b) Lee rides the lift for several journeys in a row. It starts at level 1 of the parking garage. The lift then goes up 7 floors, down 3, down 2, up 4, down 8. Then Lee gets out of the lift. Where is he?

5 In a magic square, the sum of the numbers in any row, in any column, or in any main diagonal is the same.

Copy this 4-by-4 magic square. Complete the missing numbers.

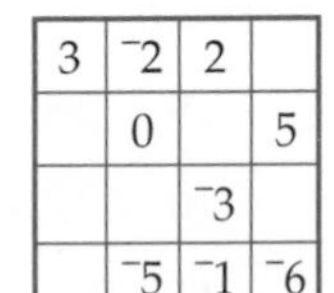

3	$^{-}2$	2	
	0		5
		$^{-}3$	
	$^{-}5$	$^{-}1$	$^{-}6$

6 Copy this diagram. Place each integer from the set { $^{-}5, ^{-}4, ^{-}3, ^{-}2, ^{-}1, 0, 1, 2, 3$ } in a circle. Make sure that the numbers on each line add to 0.

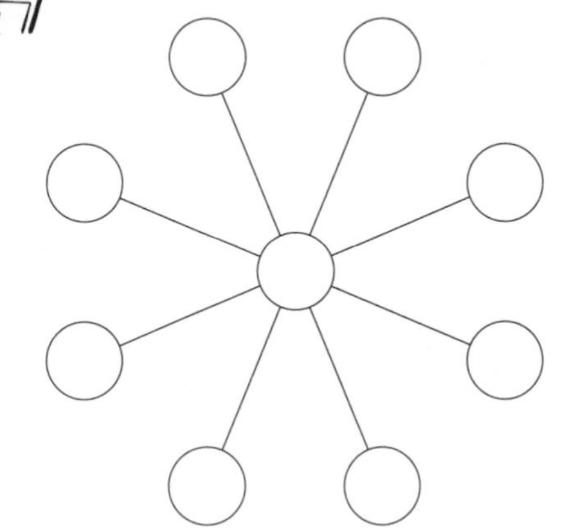

Multiplying integers

STARTER

- What is unusual about this sentence?

  'I do not know where family doctors acquired illegibly perplexing handwriting.'

- From a *mathematical* point of view, which of these words should be added to the end of the sentence?

  diversification

  distinctions

  ability

- Write down a set of numbers to explain the pattern shown in this sentence.

Sequences

A sequence is a set of numbers in a particular order. A sequence often has a pattern to it.

Examples $\{1, 3, 5, 7, 9, \ldots\}$ Each term is 2 more than the one before.

$\{6, 3, 0, {}^-3, {}^-6, {}^-9, {}^-12, \ldots\}$ Each term is 3 less than the one before.

Sequences can explain what happens to the plus and minus signs when we multiply integers. The next exercise shows how.

EXERCISE 3.14

Copy these columns of multiplication problems. Then fill in the answers. The answers are ***in sequence***.

1 $3 \times 5 = 15$
$3 \times 4 = 12$
$3 \times 3 = 9$
$3 \times 2 =$
$3 \times 1 =$
$3 \times 0 =$
$3 \times {}^-1 =$
$3 \times {}^-2 =$
$3 \times {}^-3 =$
$3 \times {}^-4 =$
$3 \times {}^-5 =$
$3 \times {}^-6 =$

Notice the sequence going down ↓

2 $6 \times 5 =$
$6 \times 4 =$
$6 \times 3 =$
$6 \times 2 =$
$6 \times 1 =$
$6 \times 0 =$
$6 \times {}^-1 =$
$6 \times {}^-2 =$
$6 \times {}^-3 =$
$6 \times {}^-4 =$
$6 \times {}^-5 =$
$6 \times {}^-6 =$

3 ${}^-2 \times 5 = {}^-10$
${}^-2 \times 4 = {}^-8$
${}^-2 \times 3 =$
${}^-2 \times 2 =$
${}^-2 \times 1 =$
${}^-2 \times 0 =$
${}^-2 \times {}^-1 =$
${}^-2 \times {}^-2 =$
${}^-2 \times {}^-3 =$
${}^-2 \times {}^-4 =$
${}^-2 \times {}^-5 =$

Notice the sequence going up ↑

4 ${}^-5 \times 4 = {}^-20$
${}^-5 \times 3 =$
${}^-5 \times 2 =$
${}^-5 \times 1 =$
${}^-5 \times 0 =$
${}^-5 \times {}^-1 =$
${}^-5 \times {}^-2 =$
${}^-5 \times {}^-3 =$
${}^-5 \times {}^-4 =$
${}^-5 \times {}^-5 =$
${}^-5 \times {}^-6 =$

5 ${}^-7 \times 4 = {}^-28$
${}^-7 \times 3 =$
${}^-7 \times 2 =$
${}^-7 \times 1 =$
${}^-7 \times 0 =$
${}^-7 \times {}^-1 =$
${}^-7 \times {}^-2 =$
${}^-7 \times {}^-3 =$
${}^-7 \times {}^-4 =$
${}^-7 \times {}^-5 =$
${}^-7 \times {}^-6 =$

Here are the rules for multiplying pairs of integers:

Rule	Example
1 multiplying two **positive** integers gives a **positive** answer positive × positive = positive	$^{+}7 \times {}^{+}2 = {}^{+}14$
2 multiplying two **negative** integers gives a **positive** answer negative × negative = positive	$^{-}3 \times {}^{-}4 = {}^{+}12$
3 multiplying a **positive** integer by a **negative** integer, in either order, gives a **negative** answer. positive × negative = negative negative × positive = negative	$^{-}7 \times 5 = {}^{-}35$ $3 \times {}^{-}8 = {}^{-}24$

EXERCISE 3.15

1–20 *Work out the following multiplication problems.*

1 $^{+}6 \times {}^{+}4$
2 $^{-}5 \times {}^{-}3$
3 $^{-}6 \times {}^{+}2$
4 $^{-}3 \times {}^{-}3$
5 $^{+}10 \times {}^{+}10$
6 $^{+}8 \times {}^{-}2$
7 $^{-}3 \times {}^{-}7$
8 $^{-}4 \times {}^{-}4$
9 $3 \times {}^{-}8$
10 $8 \times {}^{-}5$
11 $^{-}1 \times 8$
12 $1 \times {}^{-}4$
13 $^{-}7 \times {}^{-}6$
14 $^{-}3 \times 0$
15 $^{-}10 \times 2$
16 $^{-}1 \times {}^{-}5$
17 $^{-}9 \times 2$
18 $^{-}20 \times 6$
19 $24 \times {}^{-}3$
20 $7 \times {}^{-}10$

21 Copy this table. Then complete it to show the rules for multiplying integers. In each of the 4 spaces, you should have a + or a – sign.

×	+	–
+		
–		

22–40 *Calculate the answers to each of these multiplications. Hint: do them from left to right, so multiply the first pair first. The first one is done for you.*

22 $2 \times {}^{-}4 \times {}^{-}5 = {}^{-}8 \times {}^{-}5 = 40$
23 $^{-}1 \times {}^{-}3 \times 2$
24 $4 \times 8 \times {}^{-}1$
25 $^{-}6 \times {}^{-}1 \times 3$
26 $^{-}2 \times {}^{-}2 \times {}^{-}2$
27 $3 \times {}^{-}2 \times {}^{-}5$
28 $^{-}3 \times {}^{-}2 \times 5$
29 $^{-}5 \times {}^{-}1 \times 1$
30 $^{-}4 \times 3 \times 2$
31 $^{-}1 \times 0 \times 1$
32 $5 \times {}^{-}2 \times 10$
33 $^{-}4 \times {}^{-}4 \times 4$
34 $18 \times {}^{-}1 \times {}^{-}2$
35 $5 \times {}^{-}7 \times {}^{-}3$
36 $^{-}3 \times {}^{-}2 \times {}^{-}1 \times {}^{-}6$
37 $^{-}2 \times 8 \times {}^{-}2 \times 2$
38 $^{-}1 \times 3 \times {}^{-}5 \times 8$
39 $^{-}1 \times 0 \times {}^{-}7 \times 6$
40 $2 \times {}^{-}5 \times {}^{-}4 \times {}^{-}5$

Dividing integers

SPREADSHEET INVESTIGATION

Let's see how a spreadsheet handles dividing integers.
We'll use numbers like 60 and 120—small integers go into these exactly.
The spreadsheet will show the results when integers from $^{-}6$ to 6 are divided into $^{-}60$ and 120.

Enter this:

	A	B	C
1		-60	120
2			
3	-6	=-60/A3	=120/A3
4	-5		
5	-4		
6	-3		
7	-2		
8	-1		
9	0		
10	1		
11	2		
12	3		
13	4		
14	5		
15	6		

Result:

	A	B	C
1		-60	120
2			
3	-6	10	-20
4	-5	12	-24
5	-4	15	-30
6	-3	20	-40
7	-2	30	-60
8	-1	60	-120
9	0	#DIV/0!	#DIV/0!
10	1	-60	120
11	2	-30	60
12	3	-20	40
13	4	-15	30
14	5	-12	24
15	6	-10	20

In column A, we have integers from $^{-}6$ to 6.
Column B is headed $^{-}60$.
Column C is headed 120.

The calculations in columns B and C are completed by copying cells B3 and C3 downwards.

- The spreadsheet shows several patterns. What happens when:
  —two positive numbers are divided?
  —two negative numbers are divided?
  —a positive number divides a negative number, in either order?
- How does the spreadsheet show that it is not possible to divide by 0?

Produce a similar spreadsheet yourself. This should show the results when integers from $^{-}10$ to 10 are divided into 420 and $^{-}1260$.

The rules for dividing integers are the same as for multiplying:

Rule	Example
positive ÷ positive = positive	$60 \div 12 = 5$
negative ÷ negative = positive	${}^{-}35 \div {}^{-}5 = 7$
positive ÷ negative = negative	$24 \div {}^{-}6 = {}^{-}4$
negative ÷ positive = negative	${}^{-}18 \div 3 = {}^{-}6$

EXERCISE 3.16

1–16 *Work out these division problems.*

1. $12 \div {}^{-}4$
2. $18 \div {}^{-}6$
3. ${}^{-}16 \div 2$
4. $21 \div {}^{-}3$
5. ${}^{-}42 \div {}^{-}7$
6. ${}^{-}24 \div {}^{-}12$
7. ${}^{-}36 \div 2$
8. $60 \div {}^{-}12$
9. $30 \div {}^{-}2$
10. ${}^{-}38 \div {}^{-}19$
11. ${}^{-}1 \div {}^{-}1$
12. $1 \div {}^{-}1$
13. ${}^{-}41 \div 41$
14. $75 \div {}^{-}25$
15. ${}^{-}100 \div 20$
16. $0 \div {}^{-}2$
17. Copy and complete this table to show the rules for the division of integers. In each of the 4 spaces you should have a + or – sign.

÷	+	–
+		
–		

We finish the chapter with a practice exercise and a puzzle to revise all four operations with integers.

EXERCISE 3.17

Work out the value of each integer expression.

1. $8 - {}^{-}3$
2. ${}^{-}16 \div {}^{-}4$
3. $6 \times {}^{-}5$
4. ${}^{-}6 + 3$
5. ${}^{-}50 + {}^{-}20$
6. ${}^{-}6 \div {}^{-}3$
7. ${}^{-}3 \times {}^{-}8$
8. $4 + {}^{-}5$
9. ${}^{-}19 - 8$
10. ${}^{-}2 + 15$
11. ${}^{-}31 \div 31$
12. ${}^{-}12 - {}^{-}4$
13. ${}^{-}1 \times {}^{-}5$
14. $4 - 10$
15. $28 \div {}^{-}4$
16. ${}^{-}1 - {}^{-}15$
17. ${}^{-}40 \times {}^{-}2$
18. ${}^{-}200 \div {}^{-}50$
19. ${}^{-}20 + 4$
20. $300 \div {}^{-}3$

Use the clues here to work out the caption for this cartoon.

Clues:

A	${}^{-}12 \div 6$	N	${}^{-}1 - 5$
C	$1 - {}^{-}2$	O	${}^{-}1 \times {}^{-}7$
D	${}^{-}2 + {}^{-}3$	R	${}^{-}8 + 5$
E	${}^{-}2 \times {}^{-}2$	S	${}^{-}4 + 4$
F	${}^{-}1 - {}^{-}6$	T	$60 \div {}^{-}15$
G	${}^{-}40 \div {}^{-}5$	W	${}^{-}4 \times 2$
I	$17 - 18$	Y	${}^{-}14 - {}^{-}16$
L	$3 \times {}^{-}3$		

Caption: | $5\ 7\ {}^{-}3$ | $5\ {}^{-}2\ 0\ {}^{-}4$ | ${}^{-}2\ 3\ {}^{-}4\ {}^{-}1\ {}^{-}6\ 8$ |

| ${}^{-}3\ 4\ {}^{-}9\ {}^{-}1\ 4\ 5$ | ${}^{-}4\ {}^{-}3\ 2$ |

| $0\ {}^{-}9\ 7\ {}^{-}8\ {}^{-}1\ {}^{-}6\ 8$ | ${}^{-}5\ 7\ {}^{-}8\ {}^{-}6$ |

4 Multiples, factors and primes

Multiples

The **counting numbers** can be written as { 1, 2, 3, 4, 5, ... }

↑ The dots show that the pattern continues forever.

Sometimes we call these numbers the **natural numbers.**

STARTER

The cartoon shows some houses on one side of a street.

- What would be the number of the house to the left of number 18?
- What would be the number of the house to the right of number 22?
- What would be the number of the first house (on the left) on this side of the street?

- Explain whether number 39 would be on the same side of the street as these houses.
- What name do we give to numbers such as { .... 18, 20, 22, ... }?
- Explain how these house numbers are related to the counting numbers.

When we multiply each of the counting numbers by a particular number, we get **multiples** of that number.

Example Counting numbers: { 1, 2, 3, 4, 5, ...}

×8 ↓ ↓ ↓ ↓ ↓

Multiples of 8: { 8, 16, 24, 32, 40, ...}

EXERCISE 4.1

***1–5** List the first six numbers of:*

1 multiples of 4

2 multiples of 7

3 multiples of 10

4 multiples of 12

5 multiples of 200

6 List all the multiples of 5 that are between 32 and 56.

7 List all the multiples of 25 that are less than 140.

8 There are 24 hours in a day.

(a) Write down the first seven multiples of 24.

(b) What information does the last number in this list give?

9 *True* or *false*?

(a) 8 is a multiple of 2

(b) 51 is a multiple of 17

(c) 37 is a multiple of 3

(d) 25 is a multiple of 30

10 Write a sentence in English to describe these sets of numbers:

(a) { 6, 12, 18, 24, 30, 36, ... }

(b) { 13, 26, 39, 52, 65, 78, ... }

(c) { 44, 48, 52, 56, 60 }

11 This diagram is a floor plan for level 7 of a tall hotel. Each floor with guest rooms has the same layout.

N E S W

West	East
702	701
704	703
706	705
708	707
710	709
712	711
Lifts	Lifts
714	713
716	715
718	717
720	719
722	Stairs
724	

(a) How would you describe the room numbers on the west side of the hotel?

(b) You have been given room 413 in this hotel. Would you expect the view to be facing east or west?

(c) What is the number of the room one floor above room 706?

(d) What room(s) would share a common wall with room 1216?

(e) A guest wants to go from room 722 to 619. Which way would involve less walking—the lift or the stairs?

(f) The rooms in this hotel are numbered from 201 to 1324. How many rooms are there altogether?

12 (a) Explain in your own words what an *even* number is.

(b) Explain in your own words what an *odd* number is.

13 Even and odd numbers follow certain rules. For example, two even numbers *always* add to another even number. This is shown in table (a) below.
Copy the tables. Then write the words 'even' or 'odd' in the cells to show what happens with adding, subtracting and multiplying.

(a) Adding

+	Even	Odd
Even	Even	
Odd		

(b) Subtracting

−	Even	Odd
Even		
Odd		

(c) Multiplying

×	Even	Odd
Even		
Odd		

14 Here is a die with six numbers on it. Three are showing. The six numbers are *consecutive* multiples of 3. The two numbers on each pair of opposite faces add to the same amount.

What is the largest number on the die?

INVESTIGATION

ODDITIES

- Write down the odd numbers from 1 to 31.

Then:

- Calculate the sum of the first 2 odd numbers.
- Calculate the sum of the first 3 odd numbers.
- Calculate the sum of the first 4 odd numbers.

- What is the sum of the first 10 odd numbers?
- Explain how you could work out the sum of the first 20 odd numbers, without adding them all together.
- Explain in your own words what the pattern is.

Common multiples

Numbers can share multiples. For example, 24 is a multiple of 3. It is also a multiple of 4. Sometimes we have two lists of multiples, and some numbers are in *both* lists. These are called **common multiples**.

Example Write down the common multiples of 2 and 5.

Answer Multiples of 2 = { 2, 4, 6, 8, 10, 12, 14, 16, 18, 20, 22, 24, 26, 28, 30, 32, ... }

Multiples of 5 = { 5, 10, 15, 20, 25, 30, 35, ... }

The numbers in *both* lists are printed in green.

These are the common multiples of 2 and 5.

That is, { 10, 20, 30, ... }

The **lowest common multiple** is the first number that is in both lists.
Sometimes the lowest common multiple is written as LCM.
LCM of 2 and 5 is 10.

EXERCISE 4.2

1–4 Write down the first three numbers in each of these:

1 common multiples of 2 and 3

2 common multiples of 5 and 3

3 common multiples of 6 and 8

4 common multiples of 10 and 15

5–8 Work out each of these lowest common multiples:

5 LCM of 6 and 9

6 LCM of 14 and 21

7 LCM of 6 and 18

8 LCM of 30 and 45

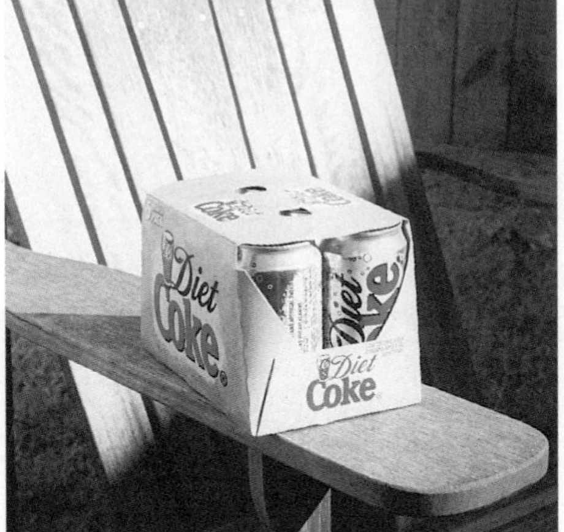

9 Cans of soft drink come in two different-sized packs: 4 and 6. For some numbers of cans, packs of either size would give you the same number of cans. What is the smallest number of cans you could buy this way?

10 A bank sells $US travellers cheques in two different denominations: $20 and $50. What is the smallest amount in dollars where either kind of travellers cheque would give you the amount you wanted?

11 A hairdresser works from home. She has two prices: $15 for adults and $9 for children. This table shows the money she makes one week. One of the figures is wrong.

Day	Takings ($)
Monday	$20
Tuesday	$18
Wednesday	$24
Thursday	$45
Friday	$30

(a) Which day has the wrong figure?

(b) Explain what kind of haircuts she must have done on Tuesday and Friday.

(c) The lowest common multiple of 15 and 9 is 45. Explain what information that gives you about the haircuts on Thursday.

12 One lighthouse flashes every 6 seconds. Another lighthouse flashes every 14 seconds. They have both just flashed at the same time. How many seconds will it take for them to both flash again *at the same time*?

13 Allie, Brian, Catina and Douglas each own a dog. All of them are exercising their dogs today.

- Allie exercises her dog every day
- Brian exercises his dog every second day
- Catina exercises her dog every third day
- Douglas exercises his dog every fourth day

In how many days' time will they all be exercising their dogs on the same day again?

Factors

STARTER

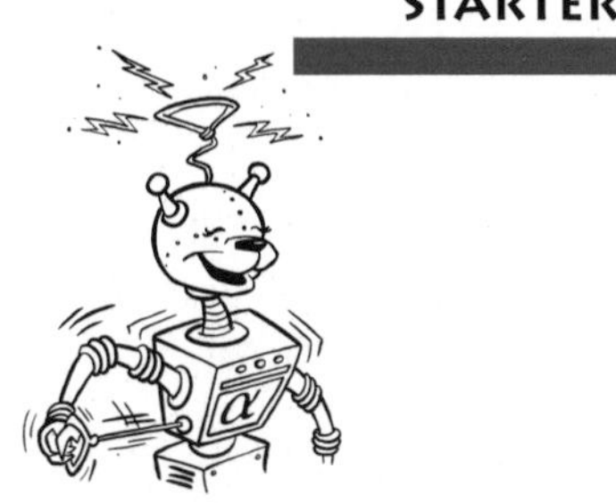

Here are all the different ways we can make up rectangles with 12 squares:

This shows we can multiply two numbers to make 12 in *three* different ways.

$3 \times 4 = 12$ or $2 \times 6 = 12$ or $1 \times 12 = 12$

- What property do all of the numbers { 1, 2, 3, 4, 6 and 12 } have?

The **factors** of a number are all the counting numbers that divide into it exactly.

Example The factors of 15 are { 1, 3, 5 and 15 }

1 is a factor of every counting number.
A number is always a factor of itself.

A calculator can be used to check for factors.
Here is an example to show how.

Example Write down the factors of 78.

Answer

1 divides 78 exactly $78 \div 1 = 78$ 1 and 78 are both factors
2 divides 78 exactly $78 \div 2 = 39$ 2 and 39 are both factors
3, 4, 5 do not divide into 78 exactly
6 divides 78 exactly $78 \div 6 = 13$ 6 and 13 are both factors
7, 8, 9 do not divide into 78 exactly
The factors of 78 are: { 1, 2, 6, 13, 39 and 78 }

Note $78 \div 10 = 7.8$.
When the result of dividing (7.8) is smaller than what you are dividing by (10), you can stop!

EXERCISE 4.3

1–7 *Write down these lists of factors:*

1 factors of 4
2 factors of 7
3 factors of 18
4 factors of 13
5 factors of 40

6 factors of 100
7 factors of 80
8 Use a calculator to help find all the factors of these numbers:
(a) 63 (c) 39
(b) 102 (d) 91

9 Write down whether each of these statements is *true* or *false*.
(a) 1 is a factor of every counting number
(b) 7 is a factor of 143
(c) 11 is a factor of 143
(d) Every counting number has itself as a factor
(e) 13 only has two factors
(f) 50 is a factor of 25
(g) All the factors of 16 are even numbers
(h) Odd numbers never have even-number factors

10 Write these numbers as *products* of two numbers in as many ways as you can. (A product is one number × another number.)
(a) 96 (b) 144

Rules of divisibility

You don't always need a calculator to check factors of large numbers. Here are some easy rules. They work for the factors 2, 3, 4, 5, 6, 8, 9, 10 and 12.

A number is divisible by:	Rule
2	if it is even (ends in 0, 2, 4, 6 or 8)
3	if the sum of the digits is divisible by 3
4	if the number formed by the last two digits is divisible by 4
5	if it ends in 0 or 5
6	if it is divisible by 2 *and* 3
8	if the number formed by the last three digits is divisible by 8
9	if the sum of the digits is divisible by 9
10	if it ends in 0
12	if it is divisible by 3 *and* 4

Example Check whether 58 576 is divisible by: (a) 8 (b) 9

Answer (a) Last three digits are 576. The division below shows that 8 divides into 576 exactly.

$$8\overline{)57\,{}^{1}6}\quad = 72$$

58 576 is divisible by 8

(b) The sum of the digits is 5 + 8 + 5 + 7 + 6 = 31. 31 is not divisible by 9. 58 576 is not divisible by 9.

EXERCISE 4.4

1–8 *Use the rules of divisibility to check these.*

1 Is 88 976 divisible by 2?
2 Is 358 divisible by 5?
3 Is 469 divisible by 9?
4 Is 4302 divisible by 3?
5 Is 4912 divisible by 6?
6 Is 66 814 divisible by 4?
7 Is 73 656 divisible by 8?
8 Is 4958 divisible by 12?

9 Here is the rule for deciding whether a year is a leap year:

> All years that are divisible by 4 are leap years,
> except for years that are divisible by 100,
> which are leap years only if they are divisible by 400

Here is a list of years. For each one, write down whether or not it is a leap year.

(a) 1964 (b) 2010 (c) 1700 (d) 2000

Common factors

Numbers can share factors – for example 6 is a factor of 18, and it is also a factor of 60. Sometimes we look at two lists of factors and decide which numbers are in *both* lists – these are called **common factors**.

Example Write down the common factors of 18 and 60.

Answer Factors of 18 = { 1, 2, 3, 6, 9, 18 }
Factors of 60 = { 1, 2, 3, 4, 5, 6, 10, 12, 15, 20, 30, 60 }

The numbers in *both* lists are printed in green.
These are the common factors of 18 and 60.
That is, { 1, 2, 3, 6 }

The **highest common factor** is the last number that is in both lists.
Sometimes the highest common factor is written as HCF.
HCF of 18 and 60 is 6.

EXERCISE 4.5

1–4 *Write down all the common factors of:*

1 15 and 20 2 16 and 24 3 15 and 16 4 18, 24 and 30

5–7 *Copy these tables. Then complete them. Write the highest common factor underneath.*

5

Number	Factors
4	
6	

HCF = ____

6

Number	Factors
30	
75	

HCF = ____

7

Number	Factors
36	
48	

HCF = ____

8–13 *Work out each of these highest common factors:*

8 HCF of 6 and 8

9 HCF of 7 and 5

10 HCF of 10 and 15

11 HCF of 1 and 13

12 HCF of 75 and 50

13 HCF of 16, 24 and 32

14 A piece of material has the shape of a rectangle. It measures 96 cm by 64 cm.
It is to be cut into *square* pieces. All of these are to be *equal* in size.
What is the largest possible size for these square pieces?

96 cm

64 cm

Three factor and multiple puzzles

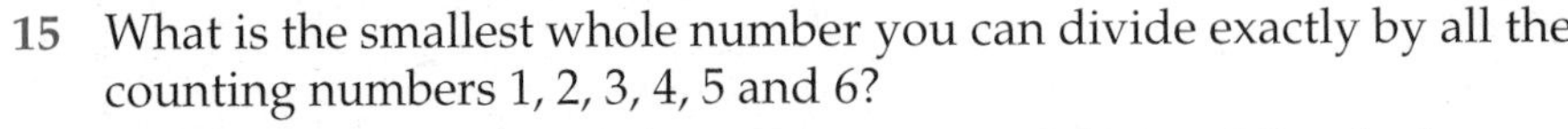

15 What is the smallest whole number you can divide exactly by all the counting numbers 1, 2, 3, 4, 5 and 6?

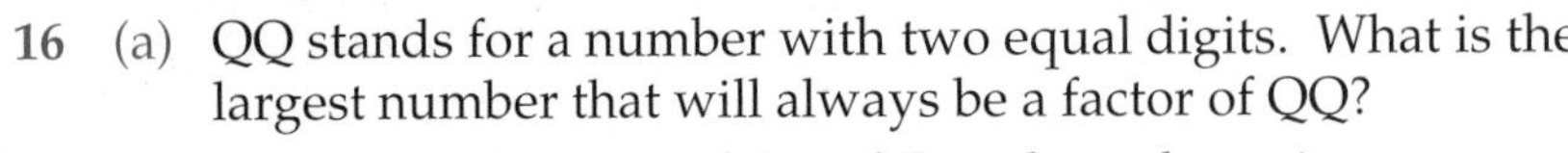

16 (a) QQ stands for a number with two equal digits. What is the largest number that will always be a factor of QQ?

(b) Work out the values of Q and R in this subtraction:

$$\begin{array}{r} QQ \\ -7 \\ \hline 4R \end{array}$$

17 What is the smallest number that has a remainder of 1 when you divide it by each of 2, 3, 4, 5, 6, 8, and 10, but has no remainder when you divide it by 11?

Primes

INVESTIGATION

RUPERT AND THE PASTA STRETCHING MACHINES

Rupert works as an apprentice to a pasta maker. The kitchen has 50 different machines—these produce ribbons of pasta in any length from 1 cm to 50 cm. The main machine makes 1 cm ribbons. These are then inserted into one of the other 49 machines and stretched out to some other length. For example, if a 1 cm ribbon is put into machine no. 24, it comes out 24 cm long.

This diagram shows how the forty-nine stretching machines are laid out in the kitchen:

	2	3	4	5	6	7	8	9	10
11	12	13	14	15	16	17	18	19	20
21	22	23	24	25	26	27	28	29	30
31	32	33	34	35	36	37	38	39	40
41	42	43	44	45	46	47	48	49	50

One day, the pasta maker was making 14 cm ribbons when machine number 14 broke down! Rupert thought about this for a while, and solved the problem.

'What about feeding ribbons into machine number 7 to make 7 cm ribbons, and then feeding these 7 cm ribbons through machine number 2? Their lengths will be doubled to make 14 cm ribbons!'

The pasta maker thought about this, tried it, and it worked! Result—machine number 14 didn't need fixing because it wasn't really needed. Machines 2 and 7 could be used instead.

- What would happen if machine number 6 broke down? Suggest what other machines could be used instead.
- Explain how we could do without machine number 39.
- Which of the machines are essential and can't be replaced? Investigate. Copy the grid of the numbers from 2 to 50, and cross out the machines that *can* be replaced.
- Make a list of the numbers of all the essential stretching machines.

Counting numbers that have exactly *two* factors are called **prime numbers**.

There are an infinite number of prime numbers. Here are the first ten:

{ 2, 3, 5, 7, 11, 13, 17, 19, 23, 29 , ... }

The two factors of any prime number are: the number itself, and 1. 1 is *not* a prime number, because it only has one factor.

Numbers that have *more than two* factors are called **composite numbers.**
Here are the first ten composite numbers:

{ 4, 6, 8, 9, 10, 12, 14, 15, 16, 18, ... }

EXERCISE 4.6

1 Each of these numbers is a prime number or a composite number. Write down which is which.

(a) 23 (e) 43
(b) 39 (f) 63
(c) 2 (g) 51
(d) 38 (h) 97

2 Write down all the prime numbers between 20 and 30.

3 What is the next prime number after 47?

4 Is 1 a prime number, a composite number, or neither?

5 What is the only *even* prime number?

6 The Sieve of Eratosthenes (275–195 BC)

Here is a method of discovering all the prime numbers up to a particular point—say 100. You will need a table that shows all the numbers from 1 to 100.

1	2	3	4	5	6	7	8	9	10
11	12	13	14	15	16	17	18	19	20
21	22	23	24	25	26	27	28	29	30
31	32	33	34	35	36	37	38	39	40
41	42	43	44	45	46	47	48	49	50
51	52	53	54	55	56	57	58	59	60
61	62	63	64	65	66	67	68	69	70
71	72	73	74	75	76	77	78	79	80
81	82	83	84	85	86	87	88	89	90
91	92	93	94	95	96	97	98	99	100

(If you saved the spreadsheet print-out from Exercise 1.5, Question 4 you could use that instead!)

- Cross out 1 (it isn't a prime number!).
- Cross out all the multiples of 2, except for 2 itself—that is, cross out 4, 6, 8, 10, 12 ....
- Cross out all the multiples of 3, except for 3 itself—that is, cross out 6, 9, 12, 15, ... (Some may already have been crossed out.)
- Cross out all the multiples of 5, except for 5 itself—that is, cross out 10, 15, 20, 25, 30, ...
- Cross out all the multiples of 7, except for 7 itself—that is, cross out 14, 21, 28, 35, 49, ...
- The numbers you are left with will be the prime numbers less than 100. Write them down.

Prime factors

Any composite number can be written by multiplying only prime numbers.

Example $28 = 2 \times 2 \times 7$

Here is a method for 'breaking down' a number into its prime number factors. We make a factor tree. We keep dividing by prime numbers, until we can't go any further.

Example Write 40 as a product of prime factors.

Answer

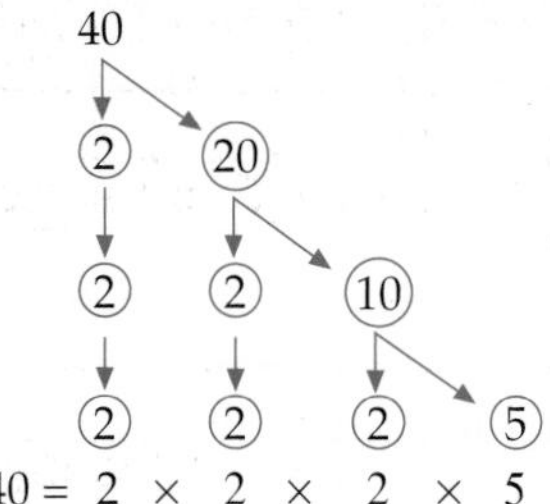

EXERCISE 4.7

1–4 *Copy these factor trees. Complete them, and write the result underneath.*

1

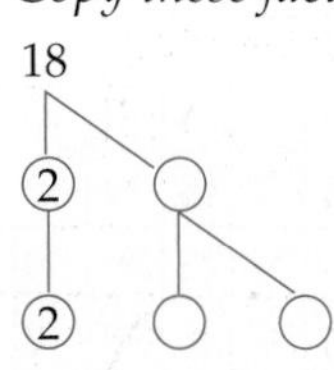

2

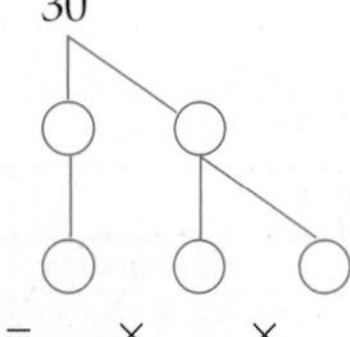

3

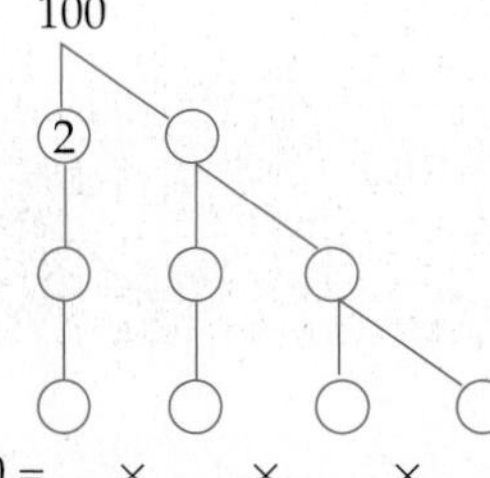

4

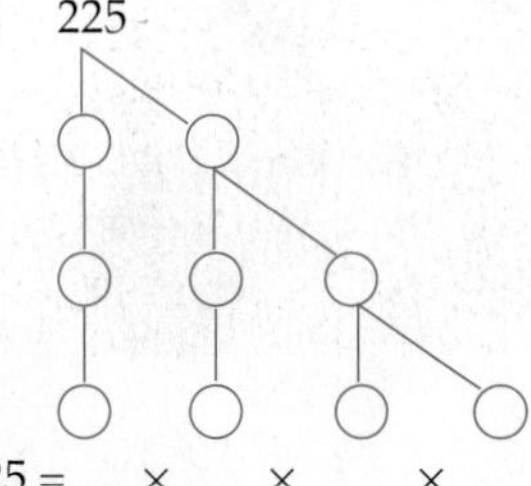

5–12 *Write each of these numbers as a product of prime factors.*

5 56	**6** 48	**7** 72	**8** 80
9 250	**10** 15	**11** 91	**12** 900

SPREADSHEET INVESTIGATION

TERMINATING DECIMALS

Have you noticed this—when you divide by some counting numbers, there are two kinds of result:

- the decimal may go on forever

Examples 7 ÷ 3 = 2.333 333 333 333 .... 6 ÷ 11 = 0.545 454 545 ....

OR

- the decimal may *terminate* (stop) after a certain point

Examples 7 ÷ 5 = 1.4 9 ÷ 20 = 0.45

We can use spreadsheet software to investigate this.

Here is the question to answer: What kind of numbers give terminating decimals when you divide by them?

- Open a blank worksheet in your spreadsheet program.
- In column A, produce a list of counting numbers from 1 to 200. These are the numbers we will *divide by*. In column B we will show the result of dividing 1 by these numbers.

What you type:

	A	B	C
1	Dividing by	Decimal result	
2			
3	1	=1/A3	
4	=A3+1		
5			
6			

What you get (first 12 rows)

	A	B	C
1	Dividing by	Decimal result	
2			
3	1	1	
4	2	0.5	
5	3	0.333333333	
6	4	0.25	
7	5	0.2	
8	6	0.166666667	
9	7	0.142857143	
10	8	0.125	
11	9	0.111111111	
12	10	0.1	

- Now use the results in column B to make a list of all the numbers, starting from 2, that give *terminating* decimals. The first five are 2, 4, 5, 8 and 10.

- Investigate to see what is special about these numbers. *Hint*—try writing each one as a product of prime factors. What do you notice about the kind of numbers that give terminating decimals?

5 Powers and roots

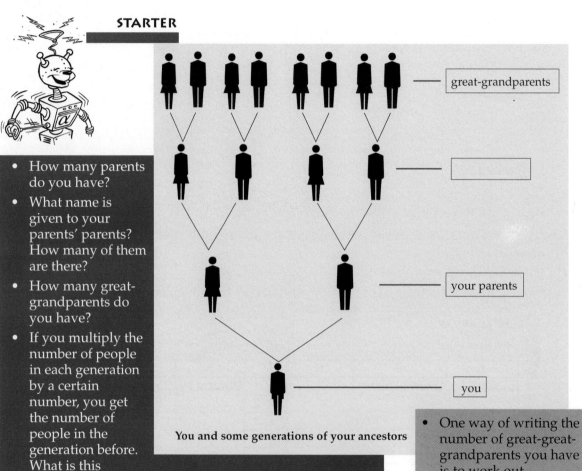

STARTER

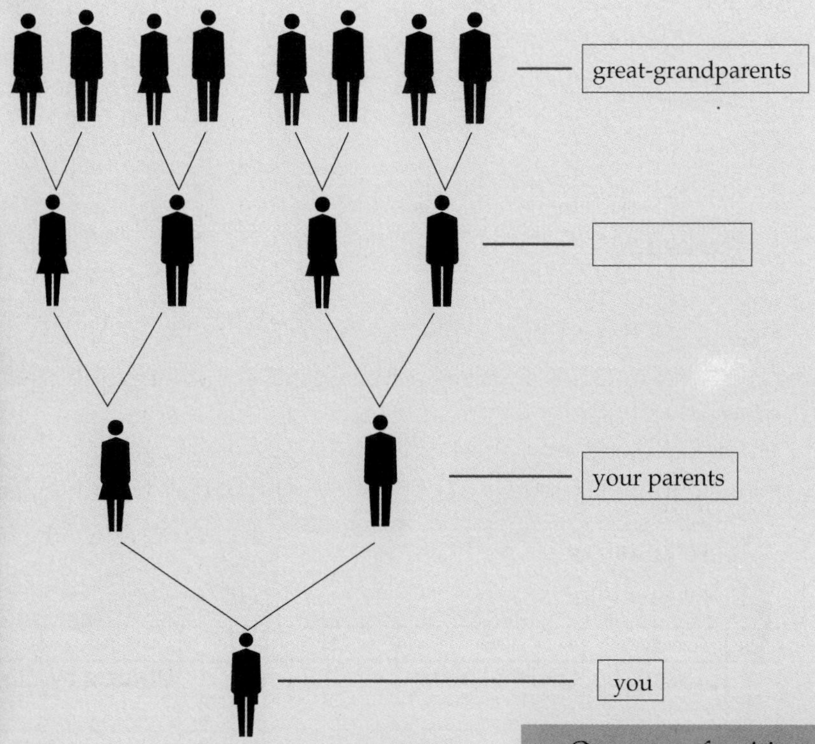

- How many parents do you have?
- What name is given to your parents' parents? How many of them are there?
- How many great-grandparents do you have?
- If you multiply the number of people in each generation by a certain number, you get the number of people in the generation before. What is this number?

great-grandparents

your parents

you

You and some generations of your ancestors

- One way of writing the number of great-great-grandparents you have is to work out $2 \times 2 \times 2 \times 2$.
- Discuss whether there is a short way of writing $2 \times 2 \times 2 \times 2$.
- What is the value of $2 \times 2 \times 2 \times 2$?

We use **powers** to show repeated multiplying.

Example $2 \times 2 \times 2 \times 2 \times 2 \times 2$ can be written as 2^6

5^3 can be written in full as $5 \times 5 \times 5$

We say 'to the power of' to describe this way of writing repeated multiplication.
For example, 2^6 is said as '2 to the power of 6'.
Two cases happen very often. For these, we use special wording:

- A power of 2 is said as 'squared' e.g. 7^2 is said as '7 squared'
- A power of 3 is said as 'cubed' e.g. 12^3 is said as '12 cubed'

EXERCISE 5.1

1–8 Write these expressions in power form.

1 $4 \times 4 \times 4$

2 $8 \times 8 \times 8 \times 8 \times 8 \times 8$

3 $2 \times 2 \times 2 \times 2 \times 2$

4 $3 \times 3 \times 3$

5 6×6

6 $7 \times 7 \times 7 \times 7 \times 7 \times 7 \times 7 \times 7$

7 $20 \times 20 \times 20$

8 $15 \times 15 \times 15 \times 15$

9–12 Write these in full, with multiplication signs.

9 2^3

10 10^4

11 7^2

12 3^6

13–18 Write each of these in power form.

13 '6 to the power of 4'

14 '4 to the power of 6'

15 '5 squared'

16 '8 cubed'

17 '10 squared'

18 '2 cubed'

In power form:

- the power is sometimes called the **index**
- the number that is being multiplied is called the **base.**

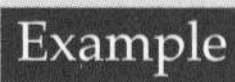
Example 4^9 ← index is 9
↑
base is 4

19 Write down the *base* for each of these expressions:

(a) 3^4 (b) 8^5 (c) 5^1 (d) 7^2

20 Write down the *index* for each of these expressions:

(a) 4^2 (b) 6^1 (c) 10^5 (d) 8

Working out powers

To work out the value of a power expression, write it out in full first. Then use repeated multiplication.

Example Work out the value of 2^5.

Answer

$$\begin{aligned} 2^5 &= 2 \times 2 \times 2 \times 2 \times 2 \\ &= 4 \times 2 \times 2 \times 2 \\ &= 8 \times 2 \times 2 \\ &= 16 \times 2 \\ &= 32 \end{aligned}$$

EXERCISE 5.2

Work out the values of these power expressions.

1 3^2

2 2^3

3 10^2

4 4^3

5 3^4

6 5^3

7 2^6

8 4^5

9 10^3

10 12^2

Calculators have a special key for working out powers.

On most calculators it will look like x^y It might look like y^x. This key is called the **power** key.

To work out the value of a power:

- enter the base number
- press the power key
- enter the index (power)
- press the = key to complete the calculation.

Here is the sequence of keys to press to work out 6^5 on a calculator:

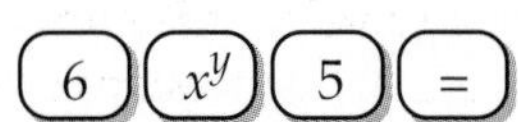

The result is 7776. Check that you get this answer on your own calculator.

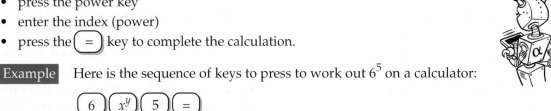

EXERCISE **5.3**

1–14 *Work out these powers on a calculator:*

1	4^7	8	16^3
2	3^5	9	3^{12}
3	11^3	10	45^2
4	17^3	11	103^3
5	12^4	12	29^5
6	2^{12}	13	83^2
7	18^4	14	421^3

15–20 *Use a calculator to work out these powers of decimal numbers:*

15 $(1.5)^3$

16 $(1.1)^4$

17 $(0.3)^4$

18 $(8.3)^3$

19 $(17.45)^2$

20 $(6.41)^3$

With powers of decimals, we use brackets around the decimal number. This shows that *all* of it is raised to the power.
The brackets don't need to be entered on a calculator.

Powers of negative numbers

Negative numbers can also be used in repeated multiplication.

Remember the rules for multiplying integers:

- negative × negative = positive
- positive × negative = negative

When the base number is negative, we write it in brackets.

Example Evaluate $(^-2)^3$

Answer $(^-2)^3 = {^-2} \times {^-2} \times {^-2}$

$= 4 \times {^-2}$

$= {^-8}$

EXERCISE 5.4

1–6 *Evaluate these powers.*

1 $(^-1)^4$

2 $(^-2)^6$

3 $(^-5)^3$

4 $(^-2)^7$

5 $(^-3)^6$

6 $(^-1)^9$

7 Copy this table. Complete it by evaluating the powers.

Column A	Column B
$(^-3)^7 =$	$(^-6)^4 =$
$(^-18)^3 =$	$(^-1)^{10} =$
$(^-54)^3 =$	$(^-11)^4 =$
$(^-8)^3 =$	$(^-7)^6 =$
$(^-29)^5 =$	$(^-5)^8 =$

8 (You'll need to do question 7 first.)

Copy these two sentences. Fill in the gaps using words from the list {odd, even, positive, negative }.

(a) In Column A, the index numbers are all ______ and the answers are ________

(b) In Column B, the index numbers are all ______ and the answers are ________

9 In your own words, write down a rule for what happens when negative numbers are raised to:

- even-number powers
- odd-number powers.

Squaring

Raising a number 'to the power of 2' is called squaring. That is, 6^2 can be said '6 squared'.

Calculators have a special key just for squaring. This looks like 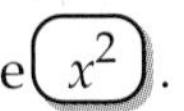.

Example To work out $(^-4)^2$, press these keys:

This will give an answer of 16.

EXERCISE 5.5

1–14 *Work out the squares of these numbers:*

1 3

2 15

3 $^-6$

4 $^-71$

5 1.4

6 23.6

7 $^-18.1$

8 $^-0.6$

9 11.9

10 320

11 $^-43$

12 $^-1$

13 0.87

14 $^-17.6$

15 Produce a spreadsheet that shows the squares of the counting numbers from 1 to 20.

This extract shows what the beginning should look like. *Hint*: the formula for squaring uses the keys ^2. For example, we write =A3^2 to square the number that is in cell A3.

	A	B	C
1	Number	Square	
2			
3	1	1	
4	2	4	
5	3		
6	4		

INVESTIGATION

LARGER AND SMALLER SQUARES

Are squares of numbers always larger than the number itself?

- Copy and complete this table:

Number	Square	The square is ______ than the number
39	1521	larger
2		
0.3		
0.767		
15		
1.2		
0.98		
5.001		

1 Some numbers in the table have a square which is *larger* than the number itself. Write them down.

2 Some numbers in the table have a square which is smaller than the *number* itself. Write these down.

3 Is there a number with a square which is the same as the number itself? Explain. (The number is not necessarily in this table.)

4 Describe these two groups of numbers:

(a) numbers whose square is larger than the number itself

(b) numbers whose square is smaller than the number itself

Applications—area and volume

One of the main uses of powers is to work out:

- the area of a square
- the volume of a cube (or amount of space in it).

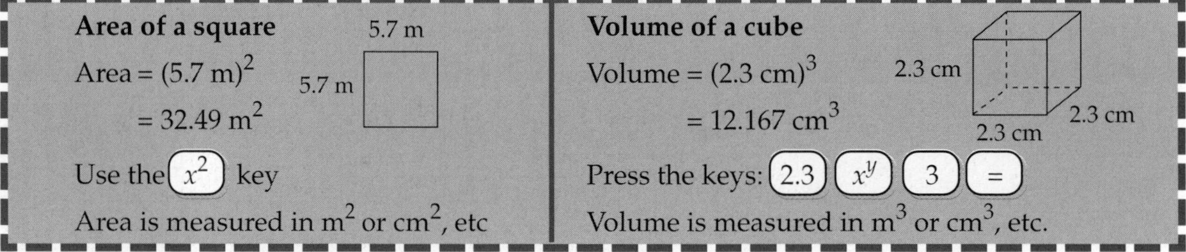

Area of a square

Area = $(5.7 \text{ m})^2$

= 32.49 m^2

Use the x^2 key

Area is measured in m^2 or cm^2, etc

Volume of a cube

Volume = $(2.3 \text{ cm})^3$

= 12.167 cm^3

Press the keys: 2.3 x^y 3 =

Volume is measured in m^3 or cm^3, etc.

EXERCISE 5.6

1–4 Calculate the area of each square.

1 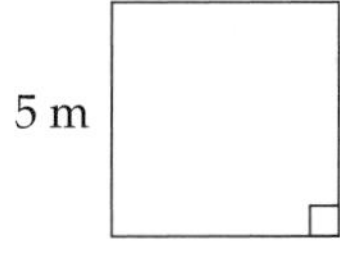

2 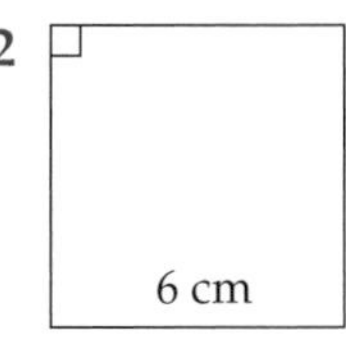

3 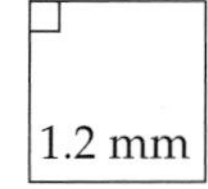

4 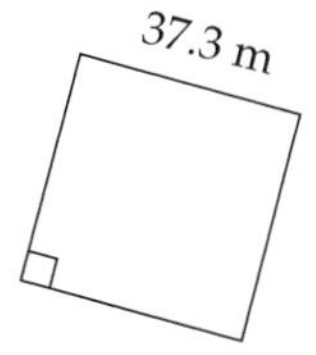

5 These are the side lengths of some squares. Work out their area.

(a) 73 m (b) 4.5 m (c) 31.2 cm (d) 49 mm

6–9 Calculate the volume of each cube.

6 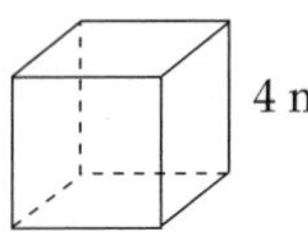

7 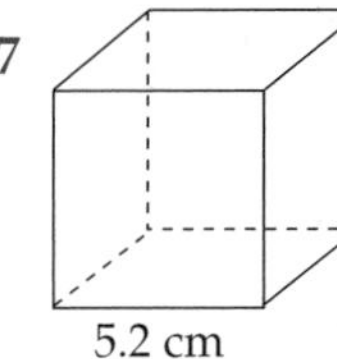

8 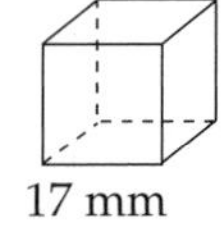

9 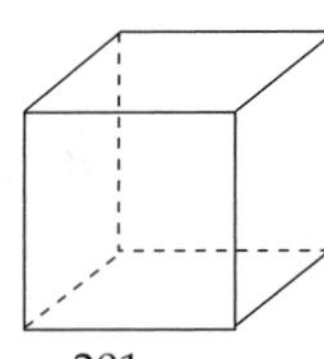

10 Work out the volume of a cube with each of these edge lengths:

(a) 5 m (b) 8 cm (c) 23 mm (d) 1.7 m

11 Next year Wiki's age will be a cube number. Last year her age was a square number. How old is she now?

INVESTIGATION

MERSENNE PRIMES

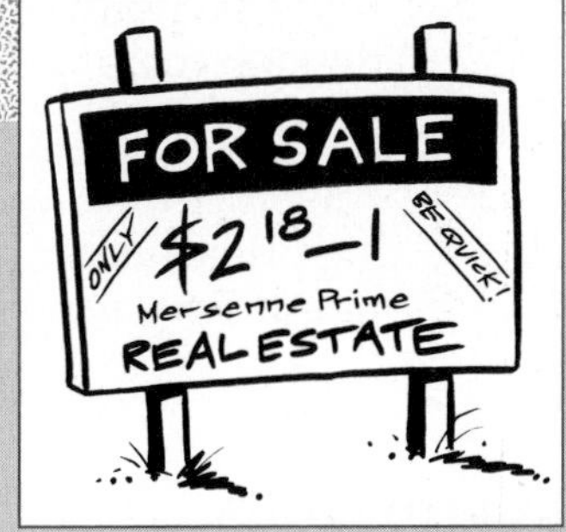

Mersenne numbers are named after Marin Mersenne (1588–1648). He was a Franciscan monk who lived in Paris.

They are numbers that are 1 less than a counting-number power of 2.
In algebra, we could write them as $2^n - 1$, where n stands for any counting number.

The first three Mersenne numbers are 1, 3 and 7

$n = 1$: $2^1 - 1 = 2 - 1 = 1$

$n = 2$: $2^2 - 1 = 4 - 1 = 3$

$n = 3$: $2^3 - 1 = 8 - 1 = 7$

1 What is the next Mersenne number?

2 Must Mersenne numbers always be odd?

Some Mersenne numbers are also prime numbers. These are called **Mersenne primes**.

3 What are the first four Mersenne primes?

So far, only 37 Mersenne primes have been discovered. The 37th of these is the largest known prime number. It can be written as $2^{3021377} - 1$. Altogether, it has 909 526 digits.

4 I want to print this 37th Mersenne prime. Estimate how many pages of a book like this it would take. Explain your method and show your calculations.

Why are these large numbers useful?
They form part of the testing of high-powered computers, and are also used in encryption programs. In these programs, data is transmitted in code to keep it private.

This information about the largest prime number may be out of date when you read it. The number was discovered on 27 January 1998 by Roland Clarkson. He was one of 4000 volunteers taking part in GIMPS (the Great Internet Mersenne Prime Search). Roland used a 200 mHz Pentium computer for 46 days to prove that this number was prime!

In GIMPS, thousands of volunteers all over the world run a special program on their desktop computers. A server in San Jose, California, distributes work to them and collects the results. It works just like operating as a single, massively-parallel supercomputer. In a typical day, the server processes more than an entire year of desktop computing power, and this rate grows daily.

A cash prize of $1000 has been offered for the next Mersenne prime to be discovered. Anyone with a reasonably powerful personal computer can join GIMPS and become a big prime hunter. It could be you! All the necessary software can be downloaded for free at www.mersenne.org/prime.htm

Square roots

STARTER

What number, multiplied by itself, gives 36?

We call this number the square root of 36.

If you multiply a number by itself, you get a second number. The first number is the **square root** of the second number.

Example The square root of 49 is 7. This is because $7 \times 7 = 49$, or $7^2 = 49$.

We use the symbol $\sqrt{\ }$ to show square roots.

Example $\sqrt{144} = 12$

EXERCISE 5.7

Write down the value of these square roots:

1 $\sqrt{36}$ 6 $\sqrt{64}$

2 $\sqrt{9}$ 7 $\sqrt{4}$

3 $\sqrt{100}$ 8 $\sqrt{16}$

4 $\sqrt{81}$ 9 $\sqrt{1}$

5 $\sqrt{25}$ 10 $\sqrt{0}$

STARTER

We can use multiplication to estimate the square root of a number.

$\sqrt{25} = 5$ (because $5 \times 5 = 25$)

$\sqrt{36} = 6$

$\sqrt{49} = 7$

$\sqrt{64} = 8$

- Which pair of numbers would you expect the square root of 61 to be between?

  5 and 6 OR 6 and 7 OR 7 and 8
- Explain why.

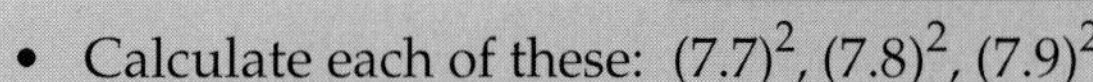

- Calculate each of these: $(7.7)^2$, $(7.8)^2$, $(7.9)^2$
- Use your calculations to estimate $\sqrt{61}$ (rounded to 1 decimal place).

The numbers in Exercise 5.7 were carefully chosen so that the square roots worked out exactly. Most numbers don't have an exact square root. However, we can work them out fairly accurately using a calculator.

The square root key on a calculator looks like $\boxed{\sqrt{x}}$

Example Use a calculator to work out $\sqrt{19}$

Answer The keys to press are: $\boxed{19}$ $\boxed{\sqrt{x}}$

A ten-digit display would show an answer of 4.358898944

This answer is too accurate for most purposes, so we **round** it.

To 2 dp, $\sqrt{19} = 4.36$

Note: the digit in the 3rd decimal place is 8. So, we increase the digit before it by 1.

One practical use of square roots is to work out the side length of a square when we know the area.

Example A gardener wants to make a square flower-bed and fill it with topsoil. There is enough topsoil for an area of 8 m^2. Calculate the length of each side of the flower-bed.

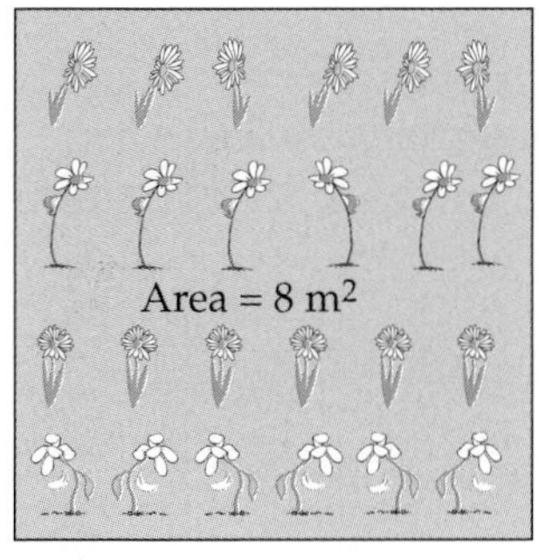

Answer Side length $= \sqrt{8}$

$= 2.828427125$ (calculator display)

$= 2.8$ m (1 dp) (rounded sensibly)

EXERCISE 5.8

1 Look at these pairs of numbers. Which pair would you expect the square root of 7 to be between—A, B, or C?

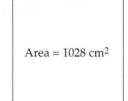

A 2 and 3

B 3 and 4

C 7 and 8

2 (a) Calculate each of these squares:

(i) 4^2 (iii) $(4.2)^2$

(ii) $(4.1)^2$ (iv) $(4.3)^2$

(b) Now estimate $\sqrt{17}$, accurate to 1 dp.

3 (a) Calculate each of these squares:

(i) $(7.5)^2$ (iii) $(7.7)^2$

(ii) $(7.6)^2$ (iv) $(7.8)^2$

(b) Now estimate $\sqrt{59}$, accurate to 1 dp.

4 Explain why $\sqrt{85}$ is between 9 and 10.

5–14 *Work out these square roots on a calculator. If they don't work out exactly, round to 2 dp.*

5 $\sqrt{3}$

6 $\sqrt{510}$

7 $\sqrt{5041}$

8 $\sqrt{169}$

9 $\sqrt{49.23}$

10 $\sqrt{200}$

11 $\sqrt{0.89}$

12 $\sqrt{38.44}$

13 $\sqrt{0.0049}$

14 $\sqrt{0.37}$

15–18 *Work out the side length of these squares. If they don't work out exactly, round to 2 dp.*

15 Area = 25 m²

16 Area = 47.2 m²

17 Area = 1028 cm²

18

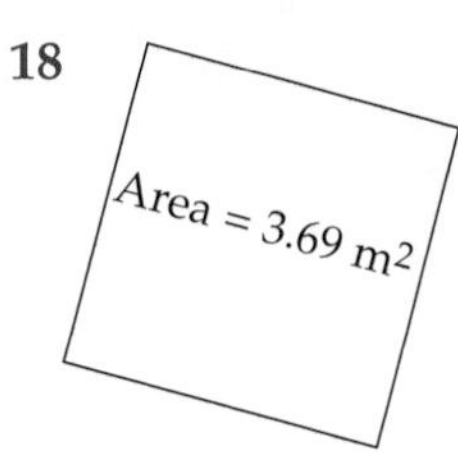

19 A square has an area of 196 cm². Calculate:

(a) the length of a side

(b) the perimeter (total length of the sides).

20 A square patchwork quilt was made by sewing 64 small squares of material together.

(a) How many squares of material are there along each side?

(b) How many squares of material are on the inside of the quilt?

(c) How many squares of material are on the outside of the quilt?

21 Is it possible to make a square patchwork quilt from exactly 200 small squares of material, with no overlapping? Explain.

22 The floor of a warehouse has an area of 1000 m². The floor is square. What is the length of each side?

23 A joiner wants to make a square tabletop with an area of 2 m².

(a) Explain how the joiner would work out the length of each side.

The joiner won't be able to work out the length exactly. Instead, it will need to be estimated.

(b) Copy this table. Complete it to show these different estimates of the length.

Accuracy	Estimate of length
to nearest m	
to 1 dp	1.4 m
to 2 dp	
to 3 dp	
to 4 dp	

(c) Explain which estimate in the table would be the most suitable.

6 Brackets and order of operations

STARTER

- Can you match these English instructions with the mathematical expressions?

English instruction	Mathematical expression
Subtract the result of 4 times 3 from 15	$(15 - 4) \times 3$
Subtract 4 from 15 and multiply the result by 3	$15 - (4 \times 3)$

- Explain what the job of the brackets is in each expression.

Brackets, written (and), are used in some mathematical expressions. They show that the part inside should be worked out first.

Example Evaluate $8 + (2 \times 5)$

Answer $8 + (2 \times 5) = 8 + 10$
$= 18$

EXERCISE 6.1

1–10 *Work out the value of these expressions:*

1 $6 + (3 - 1)$

2 $(8 + 4) \times 2$

3 $10 - (9 - 3)$

4 $8 - (3 + 1)$

5 $30 \div (6 - 4)$

6 $(20 + 1) \div 7$

7 $5 \times (2 + 1)$

8 $(5 \times 2) + 1$

9 $(36 \div 6) \div 3$

10 $36 \div (6 \div 3)$

11–15 *Each of these expressions can work out to 20 with brackets in the right places. Write the expressions with brackets.*

11 $2 \times 6 + 4$

12 $40 \div 8 \times 4$

13 $10 - 7 + 17$

14 $24 - 2 + 2$

15 $3 + 7 \times 5 - 3$

16–20 *Write these statements with brackets. Then work out their value.*

Example The sum of 3 and 15 is divided by 2

Answer $(3 + 15) \div 2 = 9$

16 The result of 4 times 2 is added to 3

17 The difference of 5 and 3 is multiplied by 8

18 5 is added to the difference of 6 and 2

19 The sum of 10 and 3 is multiplied by 2

20 The product of 7 and 2 is added to 4

Expressions with integers can also use brackets.

Example Work out the value of each of these:

(a) $(^{-}6 - 2) + {}^{-}3$

(b) $^{-}6 - (2 + {}^{-}3)$

Answer (a) $(^{-}6 - 2) + {}^{-}3 = {}^{-}8 + {}^{-}3$
$= {}^{-}11$

(b) $^{-}6 - (2 + {}^{-}3) = {}^{-}6 - {}^{-}1$
$= {}^{-}6 + 1$
$= {}^{-}5$

See how the position of the brackets makes a difference to the answer.

EXERCISE 6.2

Work out the value of each of these expressions:

1 $(3 - {}^{-}7) + 5$
2 $3 - (^{-}7 + 5)$
3 $^{-}2 + (^{-}3 - 4)$
4 $(^{-}2 + {}^{-}3) - 4$
5 $6 + (^{-}8 \times {}^{-}1)$
6 $(6 + {}^{-}8) \times {}^{-}1$
7 $5 - (^{-}2 \times 4)$
8 $(5 - {}^{-}2) \times 4$
9 $1 - (^{-}3 - {}^{-}10)$
10 $(1 - {}^{-}3) - {}^{-}10$
11 $(^{-}2 \times {}^{-}1) + {}^{-}4$
12 $^{-}2 \times (^{-}1 + {}^{-}4)$
13 $(16 \div {}^{-}4) \div {}^{-}2$
14 $16 \div (^{-}4 \div {}^{-}2)$
15 $^{-}1 - (2 + {}^{-}4)$
16 $(^{-}1 - 2) + {}^{-}4$
17 $(10 \times 2) - {}^{-}4$
18 $10 \times (2 - {}^{-}4)$
19 $5 \times (6 \div {}^{-}3)$
20 $(5 \times 6) \div {}^{-}3$

Order of operations (when there are no brackets)

SPREADSHEET INVESTIGATION

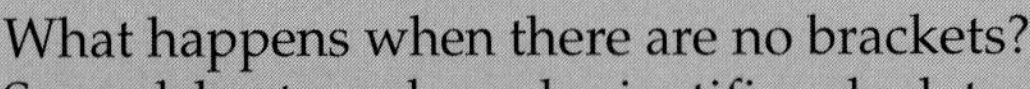

What happens when there are no brackets?
Spreadsheets and good scientific calculators follow rules to decide how to work out expressions. Some operations (e.g. × and ÷) have **priority** over others (e.g. + and –).

Look at this spreadsheet. Rows 3, 4 and 5 show three calculations and their answers:

$6 + 2 \times 3 = 12$

$10 + 1 \times 4 = 14$

$3 + 5 \times 8 = 43$

	A	B	C	D
1	First number (A)	Second number (B)	Third number (C)	=A1+B1*C1
2				
3	6	2	3	12
4	10	1	4	14
5	3	5	8	43
6				
7				
8	First number	Second number	Third number	=A8*B8-C8
9				
10	2	3	1	5
11	9	9	5	76
12	6	7	4	38

- Does the spreadsheet work out multiplication (×) or addition (+) first?
- If the numbers in columns A, B and C were 4, 5 and 10, would the answer in column D be 90 or 54?

Rows 10, 11 and 12 show three more calculations and their answers:

$2 \times 3 - 1 = 5$

$9 \times 9 - 5 = 76$

$6 \times 7 - 4 = 38$

- Does the spreadsheet work out multiplication (×) or subtraction (–) first?
- If the numbers in columns A, B and C were 8, 5 and 2, would the answer in column D be 38 or 24?

Here's how mathematicians treat the order of operations.

When we have no brackets in an expression, we follow this rule every time:

Multiplication and division are done before addition and subtraction

This means:

1 You work from **left to right** doing the multiplications and divisions first.

2 Then you work from **left to right** again, this time doing the additions and subtractions.

- If you only have additions (+) and/or subtractions (–), work **in order** from left to right.
- If you only have multiplications (×) and/or divisions (÷), work **in order** from left to right.

Here are some examples:

Expression	Comment
$12 - 3 + 4 = 9 + 4 = 13$	only has + and –, so work out from left to right
$15 + 9 \div 3 = 15 + 3 = 18$	do division (÷) before addition (+)
$2 \times 4 - 1 = 8 - 1 = 7$	do multiplication (×) before subtraction (–)
$5 + 1 \times 3 = 5 + 3 = 8$	do multiplication (×) before addition (+)

Scientific calculators follow these rules. But be careful—some other calculators don't. Check your one works correctly. Press the keys:

The correct result is 4. If your calculator gives an answer of 14, it won't be much use in Maths!

EXERCISE **6.3**

1–10 *Calculate the value of these. Work from left to right.*

1 $8 - 5 + 2$
2 $16 - 9 - 3$
3 $40 \div 2 \times 5$
4 $12 - 8 + 1$
5 $100 \div 10 \div 2$
6 $18 - 10 - 6 + 3$
7 $8 + 5 - 3 + 4$
8 $15 - 3 + 6 - 4$
9 $80 \div 4 \div 2 \div 2$
10 $20 \div 5 \times 4 \div 2$

11–30 *Use the rules for priority of operations to evaluate these:*

11 $3 \times 4 + 5$
12 $13 - 2 \times 3$
13 $24 \div 4 \div 2$
14 $18 - 7 \times 2$
15 $36 \div 6 \div 2$
16 $24 \div 6 \times 2$
17 $4 + 2 \times 5$
18 $15 - 5 - 2$
19 $18 \div 2 \times 9$
20 $10 + 8 \div 2$
21 $16 - 3 + 1$
22 $22 \div 11 \times 2$
23 $3 + 11 \times 3$
24 $20 + 30 \div 5$
25 $6 \times 5 + 9$
26 $24 \div 2 \times 6$
27 $30 - 4 + 6$
28 $100 + 4 \div 2$
29 $64 - 2 \times 3$
30 $20 \times 2 + 3$

31–40 *Evaluate these expressions:*

31 $2 + 1 \times 3 + 2$
32 $4 \times 3 + 1 \times 2$
33 $4 - 2 + 3 \times 9$
34 $2 + 14 \div 2 + 5$
35 $100 - 80 - 12 - 1$
36 $32 \div 4 \div 2 \div 2$
37 $2 \times 4 + 4 \div 2$
38 $25 - 2 \times 3 \times 4$
39 $17 - 5 + 2 \times 3$
40 $4 \times 4 - 3 \times 3 + 2 \times 2$

The NUT puzzle

Copy this diagram. Write the numbers 0, 1, 2, 3, 4, 5 and 6 in the circles so that:

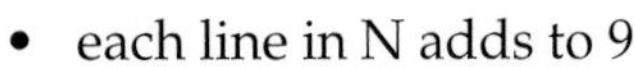

- each line in N adds to 9
- each line in U adds to 10
- each line in T adds to 11

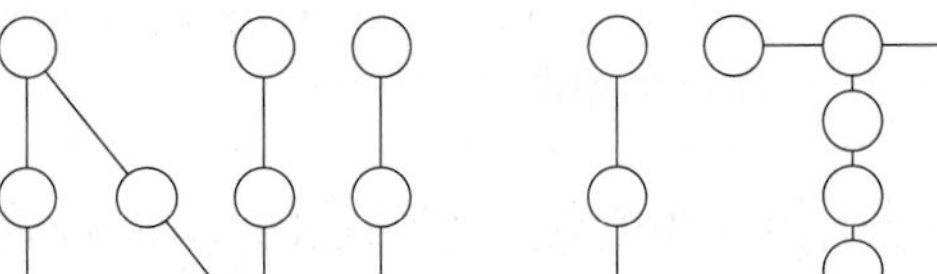

BODMAS

The rules for priority of operations can be summarised by BODMAS. This is a **mnemonic.**
A mnemonic is a 'word' where the order of the letters help us remember something.

B deal with **brackets** first
O work in **order** from left to right
D, M } do **division** and **multiplication**
A, S } before **addition** and **subtraction**

Example Evaluate $10 - (4 + 5) \div 3$

Answer

$10 - (4 + 5) \div 3 = 10 - 9 \div 3$ (deal with the brackets first)
$= 10 - 3$ (do division before subtraction)
$= 7$

EXERCISE **6.4**

1–15 *Use the 'order of operations' rules to work out each of these:*

1 $(3 + 2) \times 8$

2 $15 - (8 - 1)$

3 $40 - 6 + 5$

4 $40 - (6 + 5)$

5 $7 + 4 \times 2$

6 $(7 + 4) \times 2$

7 $30 + (6 - 5) \times 4$

8 $14 - (8 \div 2) \times 3$

9 $40 - 6 \div (12 \div 4)$

10 $21 - (10 - 3) - 5$

11 $(3 + 4) \times (8 - 6)$

12 $(27 - 3) - (14 - 2)$

13 $(4 + 4 \times 4) \div 4$

14 $3 \times (2 + 3 \times 6)$

15 $(13 - 8 - 1) \div 2$

16 Small squares are shown here instead of operations.

(7 □ 2) □ (10 □ 3).

Use each of the symbols ×, +, – once only to make the result as large as possible.

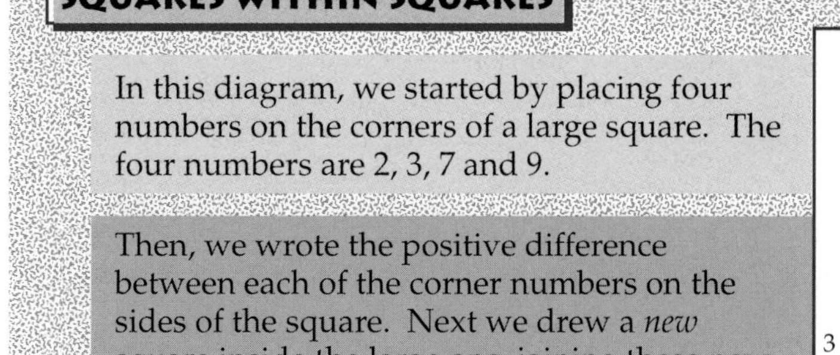

The 3333 puzzle

All the whole numbers between 0 and 9 can be made up using four threes:

$0 = 3 + 3 - 3 - 3$	$3 = ?$	$6 = ?$	$8 = ?$
$1 = 3 \div 3 + 3 - 3$	$4 = ?$	$7 = ?$	$9 = ?$
$2 = ?$	$5 = ?$		

(a) Try to write down each number from 2 to 9 using four threes. You may use the four main operations of +, –, × and ÷. You may also use brackets.

(b) What is the connection between the face on this badge and the numbers 0 to 9?

INVESTIGATION

SQUARES WITHIN SQUARES

In this diagram, we started by placing four numbers on the corners of a large square. The four numbers are 2, 3, 7 and 9.

Then, we wrote the positive difference between each of the corner numbers on the sides of the square. Next we drew a *new* square inside the large one, joining these new values.

This process is repeated until we get a square with 0 on each corner.

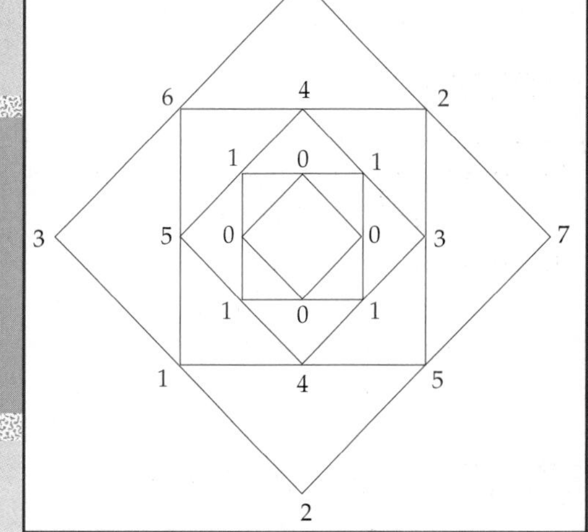

- Choose any four numbers of your own. Show that your numbers also end up giving a square with 0 on the four corners.
- Investigate whether this result occurs if you choose *three* numbers, and draw triangles within triangles.

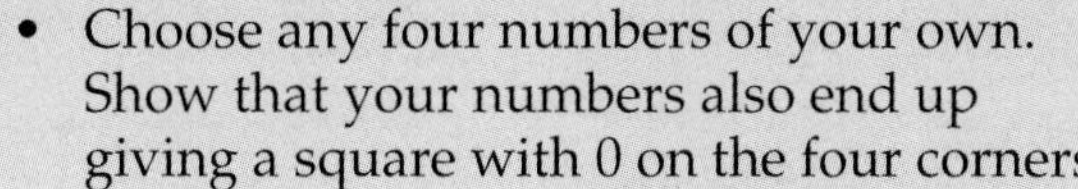

7 Fractions

STARTER

Here are several different ways of cutting an apple into equal pieces.

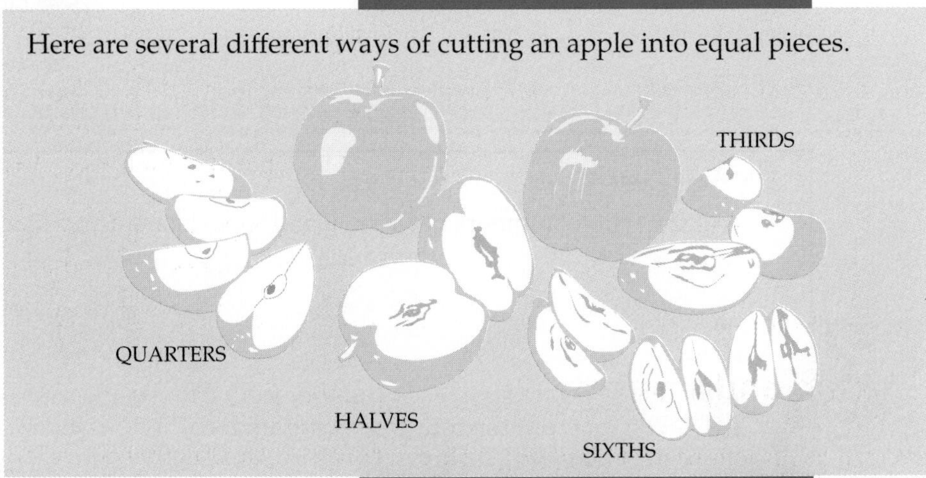

- Write down all the different fractions you can see here.

A **fraction** shows how *part* of an object is compared to the *whole* of the object.

This diagram shows the fraction two-fifths.
Two parts out of five altogether are shaded.
We write this fraction as $\frac{2}{5}$

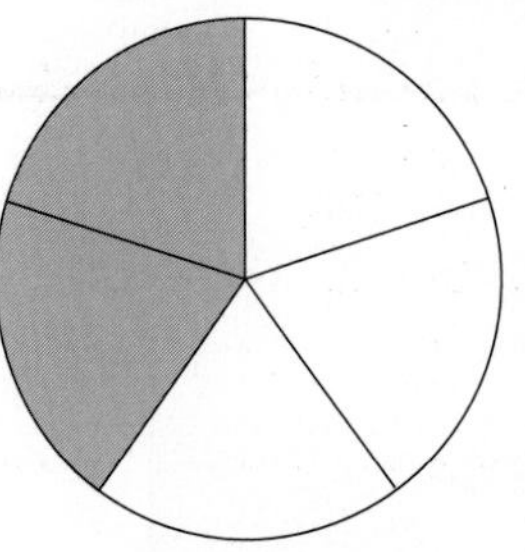

Any fraction can be written as $\frac{\text{part}}{\text{whole}}$. Sometimes we describe this as $\frac{\text{numerator}}{\text{denominator}}$

EXERCISE 7.1

1–9 *Each of these diagrams shows a fraction. Write down the fraction.*

1 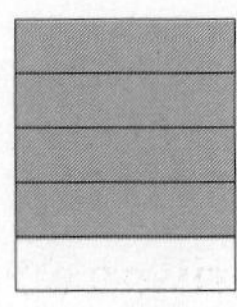

2 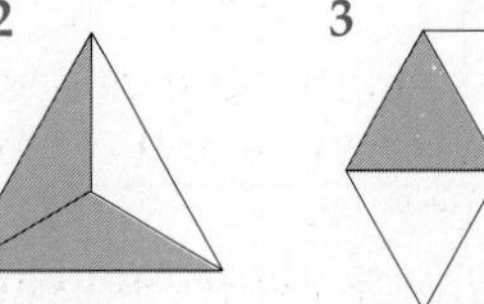

3 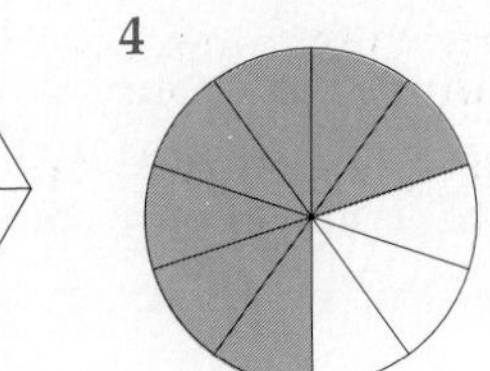

4

5 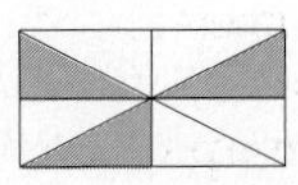

6 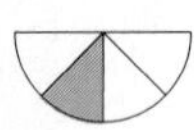

7 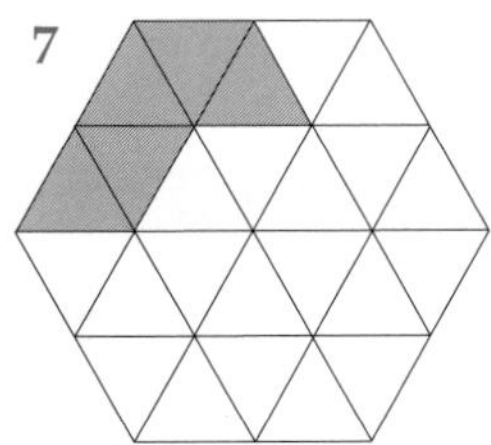

8 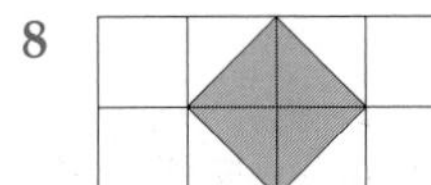

9 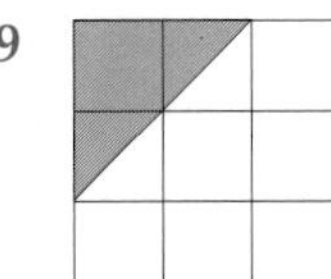

10–12 *Make three copies of the square. Then shade it to show these fractions:*

10 $\frac{1}{2}$ 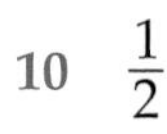

11 $\frac{3}{4}$ 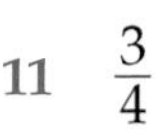

12 $\frac{9}{16}$ 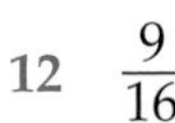

13 Make a copy of this diagram.

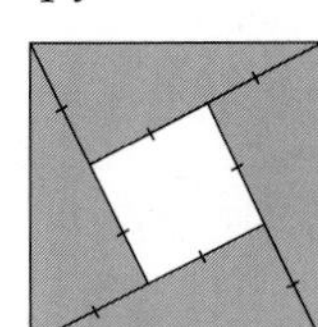

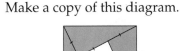

The eight marked line segments are the same length.

Divide the shape into smaller equal shapes to work out what fraction is shaded.

Sharing and fractions

We can use fractions for comparing. We can compare measurements, and numbers of objects.

Example What fraction of these apples are green?

Answer 5 out of the 6 apples altogether are green. The fraction that is green is $\frac{5}{6}$

Example A round post is placed in the ground. 1 m is below the ground and 2 m is above the ground. What fraction is above ground level?

Answer The length of the post is 3 m. 2 m is above ground level.

Fraction above ground level = $\frac{2}{3}$

EXERCISE 7.2

1 A bag holds 20 potatoes. 7 of the potatoes are rotten. What fraction is rotten?

2 Three biscuits in a packet of 28 are cracked. What fraction is cracked?

3 A survey shows that in every hour (60 minutes) of television, 13 minutes are taken up by advertising. What fraction is this?

4 In June (30 days) in Auckland last year, it rained on 17 days. What fraction of days in June is this?

5 4 pies are cooked for 7 people. The pies are shared equally. What fraction of pie will each person receive?

6 A police officer checks the licences of 15 car drivers. 4 of the drivers do not have a licence.

(a) What fraction of the drivers do not have a licence?

(b) What fraction of the drivers do have a licence?

7 Aroha buys 6 eggs. 2 of the eggs have white shells, and 4 have brown shells. One of the eggs is cracked.

(a) What fraction of the eggs is white?

(b) What fraction of the eggs is brown?

(c) What fraction of the eggs is cracked?

8 The weekly timetable for class 9Bn has 25 periods of equal length. The class have Music for 1 period a week, Phys Ed for two periods a week, and Maths for four periods a week. What fraction of the timetable is:

(a) Phys Ed?

(b) Music?

(c) Maths?

9 Over a period of one week, Tom kept simple records of the weather at midday each day.

	Sun	Mon	Tue	Wed	Thu	Fri	Sat
Sky	Cloudy	Wet	Fine	Fine	Cloudy	Wet	Wet
Wind	Windy	Calm	Windy	Calm	Calm	Calm	Windy
Maximum temperature (°C)	18	15	13	14	19	21	19

For what fraction of the days in this week was:

(a) the weather fine?

(b) the weather wet?

(c) the weather calm?

(d) the temperature over 20 °C?

10 Ngaire recorded a one-hour programme at the beginning of a new four-hour video-tape. What fraction of the video-tape is available for recording other programmes?

11 Jerry makes some orange drink by adding 1 litre of water to 4 litres of pure orange juice.

(a) How many litres of orange drink does this give?

(b) What fraction of the orange drink is pure orange juice?

Fractions on number lines

STARTER

You can see fractions when a line is marked into sections of equal lengths. This scale on a ruler shows centimetres (cm) and millimetres (mm).

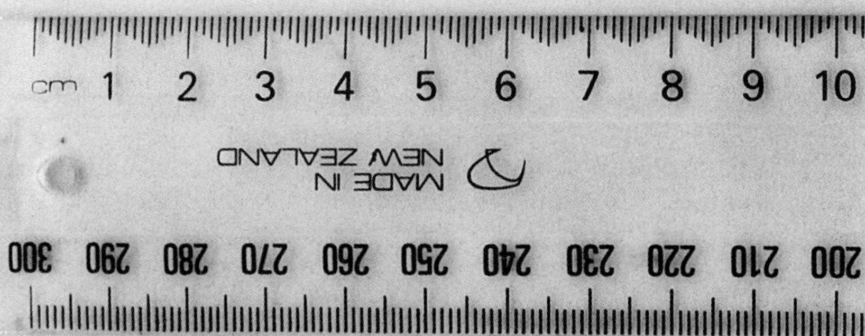

- What fraction of a cm is a mm?

The scale on this ruler starts at 0, and 1, 2, 3, etc. are marked in.

- Where on the scale would you mark $\frac{7}{10}$?

Any number line can be split into equal lengths to show fractions.

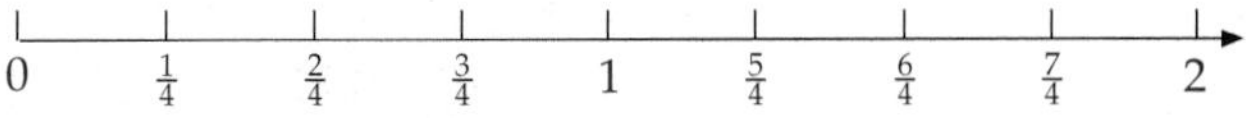

Each space on this number line represents one-quarter $\left(\frac{1}{4}\right)$.

Notice how the number line shows fractions **bigger** than 1.
For example, the fraction $\frac{5}{4}$ could represent five-quarters of an apple!

EXERCISE 7.3

1 This number line is marked in tenths.

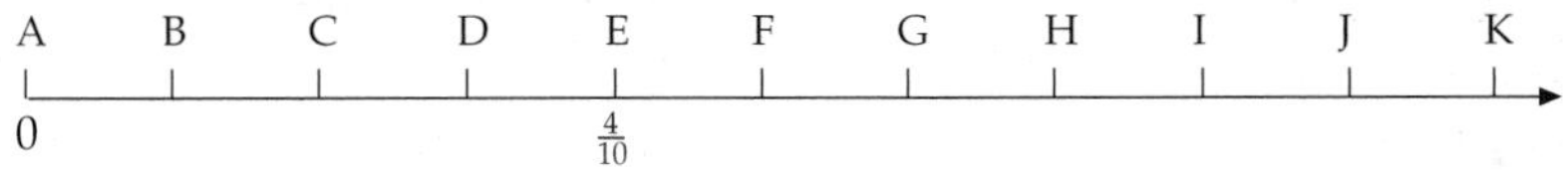

(a) Write down the fraction for each of these points on the line:
(i) B (ii) D (iii) G (iv) K

(b) Which letter on the number line would represent each of these fractions?
(i) $\frac{2}{10}$ (ii) $\frac{9}{10}$ (iii) $\frac{10}{10}$ (iv) $\frac{0}{10}$

2

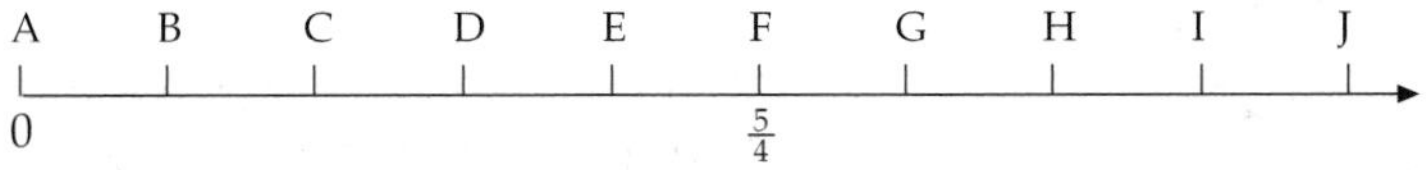

(a) Write down the fraction for each of these points on the line:
(i) D (ii) E (iii) J (iv) A

(b) Which letter on the number line would represent each of these fractions?
(i) $\frac{7}{4}$ (ii) $\frac{4}{4}$ or 1 (iii) $\frac{8}{4}$ (iv) 2

3 Draw a number line. Mark off equal lengths. Then label the line to show these fractions:
$\frac{1}{6}, \frac{3}{6}, \frac{5}{6}, \frac{6}{6}, \frac{9}{6}, \frac{12}{6}, \frac{13}{6}$

THE DEMOGRAPHIC CENTRE OF NEW ZEALAND

Half of New Zealand's population lives north of a line drawn through Taupo.
Half lives east of a line drawn through Auckland.

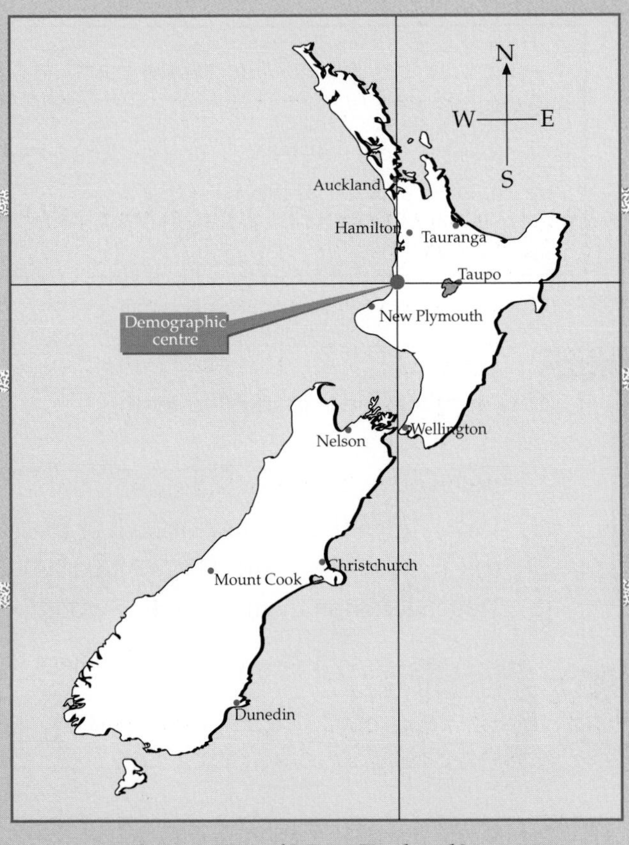

The two lines intersect at a small settlement called Mokau. (This is on the road from Hamilton to New Plymouth.)

- What fraction live to the west of Wellington?
- Is it possible to say what fraction live to the south and east of Mokau? Discuss in your class.

We could also show the *geographic* centre of New Zealand on a map. This point would have:
—half the land area to the north of it, and
—half the land area to the east of it.

- What city on this map is closest to the geographic centre of New Zealand?

Equivalent fractions

STARTER

Draw two equal circles.

Split the first circle into halves
Split the second circle into quarters

Shade the first circle to show one-half
Shade the second circle to show two-quarters

- What does this show about the two fractions $\frac{1}{2}$ and $\frac{2}{4}$?

Sometimes two fractions can be represented by the same point on a number line. Then, these two fractions are called **equivalent**.

Example This number line shows that $\frac{8}{10}$ is equivalent to $\frac{4}{5}$

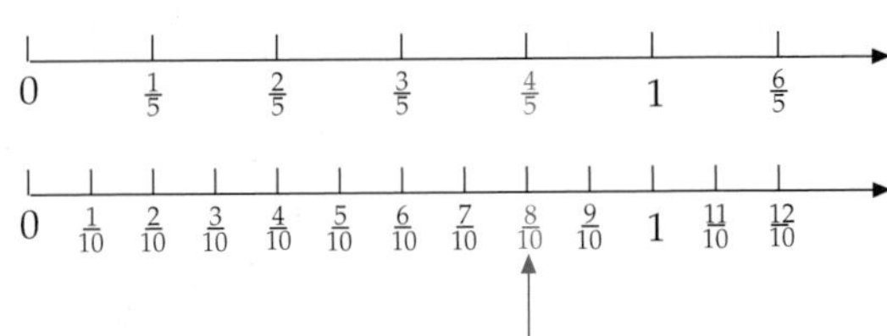

We can get equivalent fractions by **multiplying**. We multiply the top and bottom numbers in one fraction by the *same* number.

Example Write down a fraction equivalent to $\frac{4}{7}$

Answer Let's multiply both top and bottom numbers in the fraction by 2:

$$\frac{4 \times 2}{7 \times 2} = \frac{8}{14}$$

Some other fractions that are also equivalent to $\frac{4}{7}$ are $\left\{\frac{12}{21}, \frac{16}{28}, \frac{20}{35}, \ldots\right\}$

multiplied by 3 — multiplied by 4 — multiplied by 5

EXERCISE 7.4

1–6 *Write down at least two other fractions that are equivalent to these:*

1 $\frac{4}{5}$

2 $\frac{1}{3}$

3 $\frac{2}{4}$

4 $\frac{5}{6}$

5 $\frac{7}{10}$

6 $\frac{24}{36}$

7 Which two diagrams here show equivalent fractions?

A 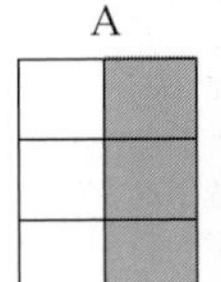 B 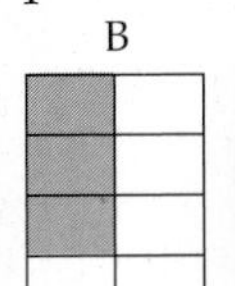 C 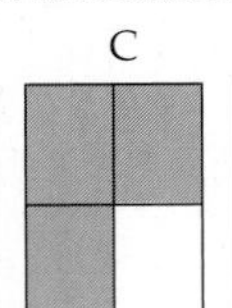 D 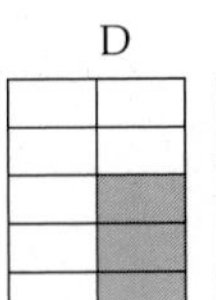 E 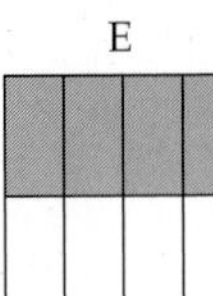

8 Which fraction in each list is *not* equivalent to the first (green) fraction in the list?

(a) $\left\{\frac{1}{5}: \frac{2}{10}, \frac{3}{15}, \frac{4}{20}, \frac{5}{30}, \frac{10}{50}\right\}$

(b) $\left\{\frac{3}{4}: \frac{6}{8}, \frac{15}{20}, \frac{18}{32}, \frac{30}{40}, \frac{36}{48}\right\}$

9 This diagram is a plan for a brick wall. The shaded part has been built already.

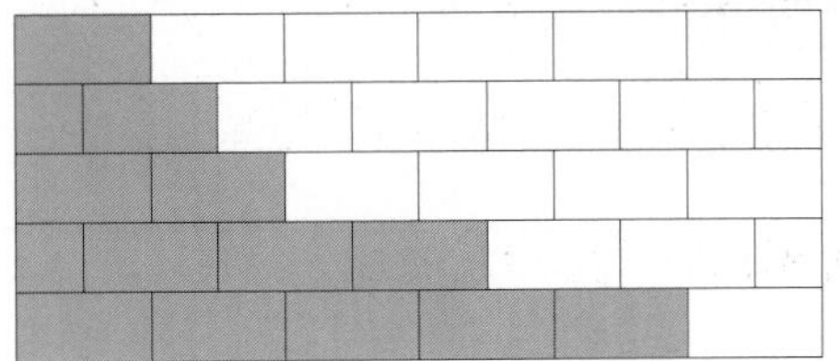

(a) Explain whether half the wall has been built.

(b) What fraction still has to be built?

Is $\frac{1}{2}$ empty equivalent to $\frac{1}{2}$ full?

'A bottle half empty equals a bottle half full. If two items are equal, then double each item must equal double the other item. Therefore, a full bottle equals an empty one.'

Simplifying fractions

In Mathematics, we want to write answers as simply as possible. So, we often need to change a fraction to a simpler, *equivalent* one.

Example The fraction $\frac{6}{9}$ can be simplified to $\frac{2}{3}$.

Look at the two diagrams below. The *same* proportion of the square is shaded, but 'two-thirds' is the *simplest* way of expressing (saying) this.

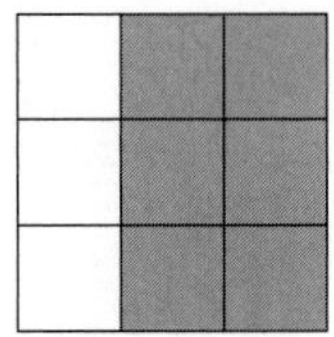
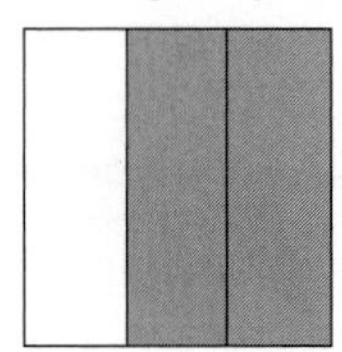

$$\frac{6}{9} = \frac{2}{3}$$

Here is how we simplify a fraction. We write it as an **equivalent** fraction using **smaller numbers** than in the original fraction.

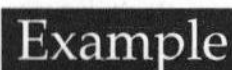

Example Simplify the fraction $\frac{20}{35}$

Answer We ask the question: 'What number divides exactly into both 20 and 35?'

5 does:

5 goes into 20 exactly 4 times

5 goes into 35 exactly 7 times

So, $\frac{20}{35}$ simplifies to $\frac{4}{7}$

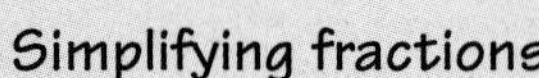

Simplifying fractions

Try dividing the top and bottom numbers by prime numbers like 2, 3, 5, 7, etc. Sometimes you'll need to do this more than once.

Example Simplify $\frac{48}{16}$

Answer $\frac{48}{16} = \frac{24}{8} = \frac{12}{4} = \frac{6}{2} = \frac{3}{1} = 3$

EXERCISE  7.5

1–3 *This diagram shows one-whole, and several different fractions. For example, the strip labelled* E *represents* 1. *The small pieces marked* D *each represent* $\frac{1}{3}$.

1 Write down the fractions represented by one piece of:

(a) A (c) C (e) G

(b) B (d) F (f) H

2 Use the C and D strips to simplify:

(a) $\frac{2}{6}$ (b) $\frac{4}{6}$

3 Use the diagram to simplify these fractions. Each time, explain which two strips you used.

(a) $\frac{6}{9}$ (c) $\frac{2}{4}$ (e) $\frac{9}{12}$

(b) $\frac{8}{12}$ (d) $\frac{6}{8}$

4–15 Write these fractions in their simplest form:

4 $\frac{8}{10}$ 8 $\frac{12}{20}$ 12 $\frac{60}{80}$

5 $\frac{9}{18}$ 9 $\frac{7}{14}$ 13 $\frac{12}{12}$

6 $\frac{10}{15}$ 10 $\frac{10}{30}$ 14 $\frac{2}{58}$

7 $\frac{12}{8}$ 11 $\frac{8}{4}$ 15 $\frac{26}{39}$

Multiplying fractions

STARTER

Jill has bought a pizza from a café. The pizza has already been cut into two equal pieces. Jill wants to share it with her friends Rana and Mike.

- Will one of the friends miss out?
- How could you solve this problem so that each friend gets the same amount of pizza?

In the starter above, each half of the pizza should be cut into three equal pieces.

We can write this as a calculation: $\frac{1}{3} \times \frac{1}{2}$. The answer to this calculation is $\frac{1}{6}$.

The working for the multiplication is: $\frac{1}{3} \times \frac{1}{2} = \frac{1 \times 1}{3 \times 2} = \frac{1}{6}$

Rule for multiplying two fractions
- Multiply the two numerators (top numbers)
- Multiply the two denominators (bottom numbers)
- Simplify the resulting fraction if possible

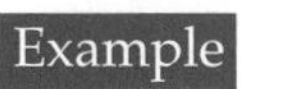

Work out $\frac{3}{4} \times \frac{2}{5}$

Answer $\frac{3}{4} \times \frac{2}{5} = \frac{6}{20}$

$= \frac{3}{10}$ (simplifying)

Sometimes you need to multiply a fraction and a whole number.
Write the whole number as a fraction with a denominator of 1.

Example Work out $\frac{1}{10} \times 4$

Answer $\frac{1}{10} \times 4 = \frac{1}{10} \times \frac{4}{1}$

$= \frac{4}{10}$

$= \frac{2}{5}$

Exercise 7.6

Multiply these fractions. Simplify your answer if possible.

1 $\frac{2}{3} \times \frac{4}{5}$

2 $\frac{3}{10} \times \frac{1}{2}$

3 $\frac{1}{4} \times \frac{5}{6}$

4 $\frac{1}{2} \times \frac{1}{3}$

5 $\frac{3}{4} \times \frac{3}{5}$

6 $\frac{3}{10} \times \frac{7}{10}$

7 $\frac{3}{4} \times \frac{3}{4}$

8 $\frac{1}{10} \times \frac{3}{5}$

9 $\frac{7}{8} \times \frac{3}{5}$

10 $\frac{2}{3} \times \frac{2}{5}$

11 $\frac{5}{4} \times \frac{1}{2}$

12 $\frac{3}{2} \times \frac{4}{3}$

13 $\frac{5}{8} \times \frac{3}{10}$

14 $\frac{2}{3} \times \frac{6}{1}$

15 $\frac{4}{5} \times \frac{10}{1}$

16 $\frac{2}{3} \times 9$

17 $\frac{3}{4} \times 2$

18 $5 \times \frac{4}{5}$

19 $3 \times \frac{1}{4}$

20 $0 \times \frac{1}{2}$

21 $\frac{2}{3} \times 15$

22 $10 \times \frac{1}{10}$

23 $\frac{2}{3} \times \frac{4}{5} \times \frac{1}{3}$

24 $\frac{2}{5} \times \frac{1}{2} \times \frac{3}{4}$

Exercise 7.7

1 A recipe for cooking rice requires two-thirds of a cup of milk. Mel is only cooking one-half of the quantity in the recipe. What fraction of a cup of milk will he need?

2 Two-fifths of a rugby squad of 30 players are injured. How many is this?

3 Paula works as a salesperson in a car yard. She keeps one-fifth of the sale price of a car as her commission. She has to pay one-third of her commission in tax. What fraction of the sale price does Paula pay in tax?

4 John plans to save two-thirds of his pocket money altogether. He wants to use a quarter of his savings on his model airplane collection. What fraction of his pocket money is he planning to save for his model airplanes?

5 At a school social, the band expects to play for two-thirds of the time. The social lasts for 4 hours (240 minutes). How long will the band be playing for?

6 In a sale, prices were calculated by working out four-fifths of the original price. Calculate the sale price for:

(a) an iron originally priced at \$30

(b) a toaster originally priced at \$55

7 Vinikolo watched a 72-minute programme on TV. He thought that about one-quarter of the programme was advertisements. How many minutes was this?

8 Three-quarters of the bicycles in the school bike sheds belong to boys. There are 32 bicycles there altogether.

(a) How many bicycles belong to boys?

(b) How many belong to girls?

9 6 chocolate bars can be shared equally between 8 people. Explain how.

10 In the last council elections, only three-fifths of the people on the electoral roll actually voted. Of the people who voted, one-third voted for the current mayor. What fraction of all the people on the electoral roll voted for the current mayor?

11 It takes Melanie a quarter of an hour to deliver newspapers to the houses in Hillary Street. Rana thinks she can do the same job in four-fifths of the time Melanie takes.

(a) What fraction of an hour does Rana think the job will take?

(b) How long will this be in minutes? Write down a fraction calculation that shows this.

Reciprocals of fractions

To get the **reciprocal** of a fraction, just turn it *upside-down*.

Examples The reciprocal of $\frac{3}{4}$ is $\frac{4}{3}$

The reciprocal of $\frac{1}{10}$ is $\frac{10}{1}$, or 10

The reciprocal of 8 is $\frac{1}{8}$

When you multiply a fraction and its reciprocal, you get 1. For example, the reciprocal of $\frac{2}{5}$ is $\frac{5}{2}$.

$\frac{2}{5} \times \frac{5}{2} = \frac{10}{10} = 1$

EXERCISE 7.8

1–11 Write down the reciprocal:

1 $\frac{2}{3}$

2 $\frac{4}{3}$

3 $\frac{3}{2}$

4 $\frac{5}{6}$

5 $\frac{7}{10}$

6 $\frac{7}{2}$

7 $\frac{1}{4}$

8 $\frac{7}{1}$

9 $\frac{1}{2}$

10 3

11 100

12–18 Are each of these pairs of numbers or fractions reciprocals? *Answer 'yes' or 'no'.*

12 $\frac{9}{10}$, $\frac{10}{9}$

13 $\frac{11}{12}$, $\frac{21}{11}$

14 $\frac{1}{5}$, 5

15 2, $\frac{1}{2}$

16 $\frac{16}{3}$, $\frac{13}{6}$

17 1, 1

18 $\frac{8}{6}$, $\frac{3}{4}$

Remember: turn a whole number into a fraction by putting it over 1; e.g. $3 = \frac{3}{1}$

Dividing by fractions

STARTER

- How many quarter pieces of apple could you cut from five apples?

- Does this mean the same as 'How many times does a quarter go into 5?
- Can this calculation by represented by writing $\frac{5}{1} \div \frac{1}{4}$?

With fractions, dividing is actually done by **multiplying**.
The first fraction stays unchanged. The second fraction gets changed to its reciprocal. We then multiply these together.

Example Work out $\frac{3}{5} \div \frac{2}{3}$

Answer $\frac{3}{5} \div \frac{2}{3} = \frac{3}{5} \times \frac{3}{2}$

$= \frac{9}{10}$

> To **divide** a number by a fraction, we **multiply** by its **reciprocal**.

EXERCISE 7.9

1–4 *Copy the working for these fraction divisions. Put numbers in place of the boxes, and then complete the working.*

1 $\frac{2}{3} \div \frac{1}{4} = \frac{2}{3} \times \frac{\square}{1} =$

2 $\frac{1}{5} \div \frac{2}{5} = \frac{1}{5} \times \frac{\square}{\square} =$

3 $\frac{3}{4} \div \frac{1}{3} = \frac{\square}{\square} \times \frac{3}{1} =$

4 $\frac{1}{2} \div \frac{7}{10} = \frac{\square}{\square} \times \frac{\square}{\square} =$

5–20 *Work out each of the following. Write each answer as simply as possible.*

5 $\frac{3}{10} \div \frac{1}{3}$

6 $\frac{1}{3} \div \frac{7}{10}$

7 $\frac{1}{2} \div \frac{3}{4}$

8 $\frac{1}{2} \div \frac{4}{5}$

9 $\frac{2}{5} \div \frac{3}{2}$

10 $\frac{1}{4} \div \frac{1}{3}$

11 $\frac{1}{8} \div \frac{1}{2}$

12 $\frac{3}{5} \div \frac{1}{5}$

13 $\frac{2}{3} \div \frac{4}{3}$

14 $\frac{3}{10} \div \frac{3}{5}$

15 $\frac{1}{4} \div \frac{1}{2}$

16 $8 \div \frac{1}{4}$

17 $6 \div \frac{3}{10}$

18 $\frac{1}{3} \div 2$

19 $\frac{4}{5} \div 8$

20 $1 \div \frac{2}{3}$

YOUNG MAN, YOU'VE LOST A SHOE!

Work out the fraction problems in the clues. Then swap the letters into the hippie's reply to find out what he said.

Here is the hippie's reply—in code:

6 $\frac{1}{2}$	$\frac{1}{10}$ 6	$\frac{2}{3}$ $\frac{1}{4}$ $\frac{6}{5}$
24 6 $\frac{3}{10}$ $\frac{1}{10}$ $\frac{1}{15}$	6 $\frac{1}{10}$ $\frac{6}{5}$	

Clues

$H = \frac{2}{3} \times \frac{3}{4}$	$O = \frac{3}{4} \div \frac{1}{8}$
$A = \frac{1}{7} \div \frac{2}{3}$	$I = \frac{1}{3} \times 2$
$U = \frac{3}{5} \times \frac{5}{10}$	$N = \frac{1}{5} \div 2$
$E = \frac{4}{5} \div \frac{2}{3}$	$D = \frac{1}{9} \times \frac{3}{5}$
$V = \frac{1}{2} \times \frac{1}{2}$	$F = 9 \div \frac{3}{8}$

Adding and subtracting fractions

STARTER

The diagram shows a chocolate bar that has been cut into 16 equal pieces.

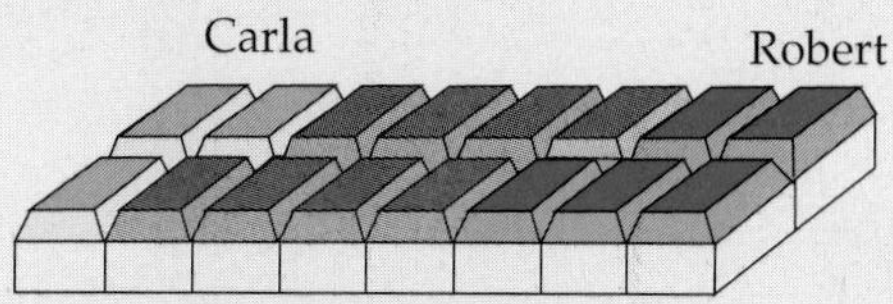

Robert wants to eat 5 pieces, and Carla wants to eat 3 pieces.

- What fraction of the whole bar does Robert want?
- What fraction of the whole bar does Carla want?
- What fraction do they want to eat altogether?
- What is the simplest possible answer to $\frac{5}{16} + \frac{3}{16}$?

Same denominator

To add two fractions with the same denominator:
add the two numerators and leave the denominator unchanged.

Example Add $\frac{1}{12} + \frac{7}{12}$

Answer

$$\frac{1}{12} + \frac{7}{12} = \frac{1+7}{12} = \frac{8}{12} = \frac{2}{3}$$

Always simplify your answer, if possible.

Subtracting fractions with the same denominator works in the same way.

To subtract two fractions with the same denominator:
subtract the two numerators and leave the denominator unchanged.

Example $\frac{4}{5} - \frac{1}{5} = \frac{3}{5}$

EXERCISE 7.10

1–10 *Add these fractions. Write each answer as simply as possible.*

1 $\frac{2}{5}+\frac{2}{5}$

2 $\frac{3}{7}+\frac{2}{7}$

3 $\frac{1}{8}+\frac{5}{8}$

4 $\frac{2}{9}+\frac{4}{9}$

5 $\frac{5}{12}+\frac{5}{12}$

6 $\frac{3}{10}+\frac{5}{10}$

7 $\frac{1}{11}+\frac{10}{11}$

8 $\frac{2}{15}+\frac{8}{15}$

9 $\frac{1}{5}+\frac{2}{5}+\frac{1}{5}$

10 $\frac{3}{20}+\frac{11}{20}+\frac{1}{20}$

11–20 *Subtract these fractions. Write each answer as simply as possible.*

11 $\frac{4}{5}-\frac{3}{5}$

12 $\frac{6}{11}-\frac{4}{11}$

13 $\frac{7}{10}-\frac{3}{10}$

14 $\frac{5}{8}-\frac{3}{8}$

15 $\frac{3}{4}-\frac{1}{4}$

16 $\frac{9}{10}-\frac{3}{10}$

17 $\frac{5}{6}-\frac{1}{6}$

18 $\frac{11}{12}-\frac{5}{12}$

19 $\frac{1}{2}-\frac{1}{2}$

20 $\frac{17}{20}-\frac{3}{20}$

Different denominators

STARTER

Mike has lots of pairs of socks. One-half of the socks are green, and two-fifths are grey.

These fractions are shown in the diagram:

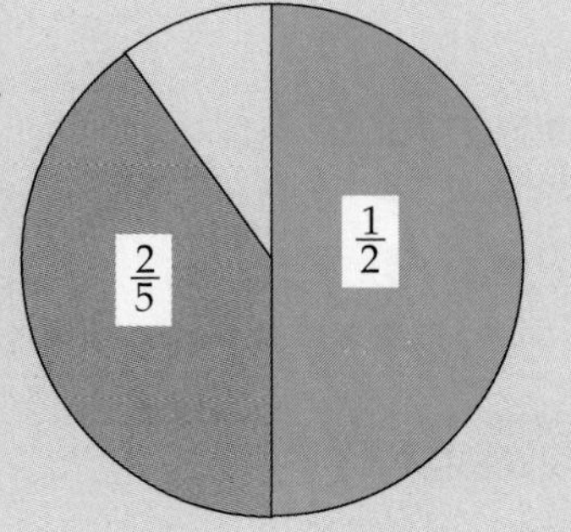

He wants to work out the fraction that are green or grey. In the diagram, this is shown by both shaded parts together.

Look at this list of fractions.

$$\left\{\frac{2}{10}, \frac{3}{10}, \frac{4}{10}, \frac{5}{10}, \frac{6}{10}, \frac{7}{10}\right\}$$

- Which fraction (in tenths) is equivalent to $\frac{2}{5}$?
  Explain how you chose your answer.
- Which fraction in the list is equivalent to $\frac{1}{2}$?

- Copy this working. Fill in the boxes to show the answer to Mike's question.

$$\frac{2}{5}+\frac{1}{2} = \frac{\square}{10}+\frac{\square}{10}$$
$$= \frac{\square}{10}$$

- Can you explain why we changed to equivalent fractions using tenths?

To add fractions with different denominators:

- change the fractions to equivalent fractions with the same denominator
- add these equivalent fractions
- simplify if possible

There are two ways of finding a denominator that will fit two fractions.

1 You can multiply the two denominators.

Example $\frac{1}{3}$ and $\frac{1}{5}$ will have a common denominator of 15 (because $3 \times 5 = 15$)

$$\frac{1}{3} + \frac{1}{5} = \frac{5}{15} + \frac{3}{15}$$
$$= \frac{8}{15}$$

2 You can look for the lowest common multiple of both denominators.

Example $\frac{1}{6}$ and $\frac{3}{4}$ will have a common denominator of 12:

multiples of 6 = { 6, **12**, 18, 24, 30, ... }
multiples of 4 = { 4, 8, **12**, 16, 20, 24, ... }
12 is the smallest number in *both* lists.

$$\frac{1}{6} + \frac{3}{4} = \frac{2}{12} + \frac{9}{12}$$
$$= \frac{11}{12}$$

We **subtract** fractions that have different denominators in the same way.

To subtract fractions with different denominators:

- change the fractions to equivalent fractions with the same denominator
- subtract these equivalent fractions
- simplify if possible

Example Work out $\frac{5}{6} - \frac{7}{10}$

Answer $\frac{5}{6} - \frac{7}{10} = \frac{\square}{60} - \frac{\square}{60}$ (both fractions can be written with a denominator of 60)

$$= \frac{50}{60} - \frac{42}{60}$$
$$= \frac{8}{60}$$
$$= \frac{2}{15}$$

EXERCISE 7.11

1–4 *Copy the working for these 'adding fraction' problems. Complete them by filling in the squares.*

1 $\frac{2}{3}+\frac{1}{5}=\frac{\square}{15}+\frac{\square}{15}$
$=\frac{\square}{15}$

2 $\frac{3}{10}+\frac{2}{5}=\frac{\square}{10}+\frac{\square}{10}$
$=\frac{\square}{10}$

3 $\frac{4}{5}+\frac{1}{7}=\frac{\square}{35}+\frac{\square}{35}$
$=\frac{\square}{35}$

4 $\frac{1}{4}+\frac{5}{6}=\frac{\square}{12}+\frac{\square}{12}$
$=\frac{\square}{12}$

5–16 *Add these fractions. Express your answer as simply as possible.*

5 $\frac{1}{3}+\frac{1}{2}$

6 $\frac{2}{5}+\frac{1}{3}$

7 $\frac{4}{9}+\frac{2}{3}$

8 $\frac{2}{3}+\frac{1}{4}$

9 $\frac{1}{6}+\frac{1}{2}$

10 $\frac{3}{5}+\frac{1}{10}$

11 $\frac{3}{4}+\frac{5}{6}$

12 $\frac{3}{10}+\frac{7}{15}$

13 $\frac{1}{7}+\frac{1}{9}$

14 $\frac{8}{15}+\frac{9}{20}$

15 $\frac{3}{20}+\frac{2}{5}$

16 $\frac{1}{2}+\frac{1}{4}+\frac{1}{8}$

EXERCISE 7.12

1–4 *Copy the working for these 'subtracting fraction' problems. Complete them by filling in the boxes.*

1 $\frac{2}{3}-\frac{1}{4}=\frac{\square}{12}-\frac{\square}{12}$
$=\frac{\square}{12}$

2 $\frac{9}{10}-\frac{1}{5}=\frac{\square}{10}-\frac{\square}{10}$
$=\frac{\square}{10}$

3 $\frac{2}{5}-\frac{1}{7}=\frac{\square}{35}-\frac{\square}{35}$
$=\frac{\square}{35}$

4 $\frac{5}{6}-\frac{1}{9}=\frac{\square}{18}-\frac{\square}{18}$
$=\frac{\square}{18}$

5–10 *Subtract these fractions. Express your answer as simply as possible.*

5 $\frac{3}{4}-\frac{2}{3}$

6 $\frac{7}{8}-\frac{1}{2}$

7 $\frac{5}{9}-\frac{2}{7}$

8 $\frac{5}{6}-\frac{3}{4}$

9 $\frac{3}{10}-\frac{1}{5}$

10 $\frac{11}{12}-\frac{2}{3}$

A prisoner has been given hard labour as a punishment. By making a statement, he can choose what he does—if the statement is true, he will break rocks; if the statement is false, he will dig ditches.

What should the prisoner say?

The prisoner should say:

$\frac{9}{10}$	$\frac{1}{3}$ $\frac{7}{12}$ $\frac{3}{4}$ $\frac{3}{10}$ $\frac{3}{10}$	$\frac{5}{8}$ $\frac{9}{10}$ $\frac{2}{3}$	$\frac{5}{8}$ $\frac{9}{10}$ $\frac{34}{35}$ $\frac{1}{2}$ $\frac{7}{12}$ $\frac{23}{35}$ $\frac{1}{3}$

Solve the fraction problems in the clues. Then swap the letters into the prisoner's reply to find out what he should say.

Clues

$S = \frac{2}{9} + \frac{1}{9}$	$C = \frac{5}{12} + \frac{1}{12}$	$T = \frac{4}{7} + \frac{2}{5}$	$I = \frac{1}{5} + \frac{7}{10}$	$D = \frac{3}{8} + \frac{1}{4}$
$A = \frac{7}{8} - \frac{1}{8}$	$L = \frac{4}{5} - \frac{1}{2}$	$E = \frac{6}{7} - \frac{1}{5}$	$G = \frac{11}{12} - \frac{1}{4}$	$H = \frac{3}{4} - \frac{1}{6}$

EXERCISE 7.13

1 In a class:

- $\frac{1}{5}$ of the students were absent on a sports visit
- $\frac{1}{4}$ were away sick.

What fraction of the class was not there?

2 Before a journey, the petrol gauge showed my car's tank was half full. When I returned home it was one-third full. What fraction of a tank of petrol had I used?

3 My brother, my sister and I are paying for a gift for our parents. My brother pays one-quarter of the total cost, and my sister pays one-third.

(a) What fraction of the total cost did they pay altogether?

(b) What fraction will I have to pay?

4 A bottle of tomato sauce is three-quarters full. A recipe requires one-third of a bottle of tomato sauce. What fraction will be left in the bottle after the recipe is made?

5 Peter and Wendy are planning their wedding. Wendy's parents have offered to pay $\frac{2}{3}$ of the cost. Peter's parents have agreed to pay $\frac{1}{4}$ of the cost.

(a) What fraction of the total cost will be paid for by the parents?

(b) What fraction of the total cost will Peter and Wendy have to pay themselves?

6 Rana and Vicki are each donating a litre of blood. So far Rana has donated $\frac{3}{4}$ of a litre, and Vicki has donated $\frac{5}{8}$ of a litre. How much more has Rana given so far?

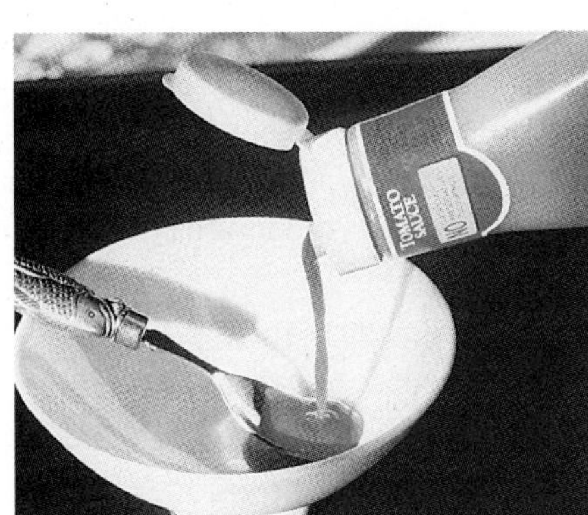

Mixed numbers

A **mixed number** is a combination of a counting number and a fraction smaller than 1 whole. This number line shows where the mixed numbers $4\frac{3}{4}$ and $5\frac{1}{2}$ would go:

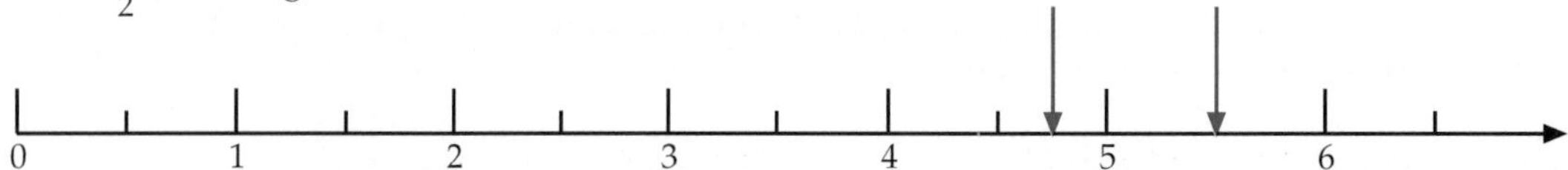

A mixed number like $2\frac{1}{4}$ really means $2 + \frac{1}{4}$. Some fraction calculations give a 'top-heavy' fraction (numerator larger than denominator) as the answer.
Sometimes we choose to write these as mixed numbers.

Example $\frac{3}{2} \times \frac{3}{2} = \frac{9}{4}$

$\frac{9}{4}$ is the same as $\frac{8}{4} + \frac{1}{4}$ or $2 + \frac{1}{4}$. So we can write $\frac{9}{4}$ as $2\frac{1}{4}$

Changing fractions to mixed numbers

- Divide the denominator into the numerator.
- The remainder (what is left over) gives the fraction part of the mixed number.

Example Change $\frac{11}{5}$ to a mixed number.

Answer When 11 is divided by 5 it goes in 2 times, with 1 left over: $5\overline{)11}$ gives 2, $11 - 10 = 1$. So, $\frac{11}{5} = 2\frac{1}{5}$

EXERCISE 7.14

1–10 *Change these fractions to mixed numbers.*

1 $\frac{7}{3}$ 2 $\frac{3}{2}$ 3 $\frac{11}{6}$ 4 $\frac{11}{4}$ 5 $\frac{29}{5}$ 6 $\frac{65}{6}$ 7 $\frac{17}{10}$ 8 $\frac{28}{7}$ 9 $\frac{19}{17}$ 10 $\frac{29}{12}$

11 A twist-tie is 11 cm long. It is to be cut into 3 equal pieces. Express the length of each piece as a mixed number.

12 A cake decorator has 29 bells to place on 4 cakes. Each cake has to have the same number of bells.

(a) Write $\frac{29}{4}$ as a mixed number.

(b) How many bells does each cake have?

(c) How many bells will be left over?

13 A small school has 32 students who want to play netball. A netball team has 7 players.

(a) Write $\frac{32}{7}$ as a mixed number.

(b) Will the school be able to have 5 netball teams? Explain.

(c) How would you organise the teams if you were in charge? Explain.

14 A rugby team has 15 players. Each player has a quarter of an orange at half-time. How many oranges are needed?

Changing mixed numbers to fractions

- Write the mixed number as a whole number plus a fraction.
- Change the whole number into a fraction with the same denominator as the fraction.
- Add.

Example Change $3\frac{2}{5}$ to a fraction.

Answer

$$3\frac{2}{5} = 3 + \frac{2}{5} = \frac{15}{5} + \frac{2}{5} = \frac{17}{5}$$

EXERCISE 7.15

1–10 *Change these mixed numbers to fractions:*

1 $2\frac{1}{4}$

2 $3\frac{1}{2}$

3 $1\frac{2}{5}$

4 $1\frac{3}{10}$

5 $6\frac{3}{5}$

6 $1\frac{1}{2}$

7 $2\frac{3}{8}$

8 $20\frac{1}{2}$

9 $2\frac{1}{20}$

10 $4\frac{13}{100}$

11 Some muffins were divided up among four people. Each person got $2\frac{1}{4}$ muffins.

(a) Change $2\frac{1}{4}$ to a fraction.

(b) How many muffins were there altogether?

In problems involving mixed numbers, we first change any mixed numbers to fractions.
Then we multiply, divide, add or subtract as usual.
Finally, we express the answer as a mixed number.

Multiplication

$1\frac{1}{2} \times 2\frac{2}{3} = \frac{3}{2} \times \frac{8}{3}$ (changing to fractions)

$= \frac{24}{6}$ (multiplying)

$= 4$ (simplifying)

Division

$3\frac{1}{3} \div \frac{2}{5} = \frac{10}{3} \div \frac{2}{5}$ (changing to fractions)

$= \frac{10}{3} \times \frac{5}{2}$ (changing from $\div$ to $\times$)

$= \frac{50}{6}$ (multiplying)

$= \frac{25}{3}$ (simplifying)

$= 8\frac{1}{3}$ (changing back to mixed number)

Addition

$$2\frac{1}{2} + 3\frac{3}{5} = \frac{5}{2} + \frac{18}{5} \quad \text{(changing to fractions)}$$
$$= \frac{25}{10} + \frac{36}{10} \quad \text{(writing with common denominator)}$$
$$= \frac{61}{10} \quad \text{(adding)}$$
$$= 6\frac{1}{10} \quad \text{(changing back to mixed number)}$$

Subtraction

$$3\frac{1}{5} - 1\frac{4}{5} = \frac{16}{5} - \frac{9}{5} \quad \text{(changing to mixed numbers)}$$
$$= \frac{7}{5} \quad \text{(subtracting)}$$
$$= 1\frac{2}{5} \quad \text{(changing back to mixed number)}$$

EXERCISE 7.16

Work out these multiplication and division problems. Write each answer as a mixed number.

1. $1\frac{1}{4} \times 2\frac{1}{2}$
2. $\frac{1}{2} \times 2\frac{1}{2}$
3. $2\frac{2}{3} \times \frac{3}{4}$
4. $2\frac{3}{7} \times 2\frac{1}{3}$
5. $2\frac{1}{2} \div 1\frac{1}{4}$
6. $3\frac{3}{5} \div 1\frac{1}{2}$

EXERCISE 7.17

Add or subtract these pairs of mixed numbers. Write each answer as a mixed number.

1. $1\frac{1}{2} + 2\frac{1}{2}$
2. $3\frac{1}{4} + 4\frac{3}{4}$
3. $4\frac{1}{5} + 2\frac{3}{5}$
4. $2\frac{1}{4} - 1\frac{1}{4}$
5. $6\frac{5}{6} - 4\frac{1}{6}$
6. $3\frac{1}{3} - 1\frac{2}{3}$
7. $8\frac{5}{8} + 1\frac{7}{8}$
8. $6\frac{4}{5} + \frac{3}{5}$
9. $1\frac{1}{2} + 2\frac{2}{3}$
10. $3\frac{3}{4} + 1\frac{4}{5}$
11. $3\frac{5}{8} - 2\frac{2}{3}$
12. $4\frac{1}{2} - \frac{3}{5}$

EXERCISE 7.18

1 A car radiator holds exactly 8 litres. A motorist checks the level of water, and needs to top it up with $1\frac{3}{4}$ litres of water. How much water was in the radiator before it was topped up?

2 A fruit punch is made up by adding $3\frac{1}{2}$ litres of water to $1\frac{1}{4}$ litres of orange concentrate. How many litres of punch will there be?

3 A nail $5\frac{1}{2}$ cm long is used to fix a piece of wood $2\frac{3}{4}$ cm thick to a wall.
(a) Show this by drawing a diagram.
(b) How far into the wall does the nail go?

4 One of the instructions in a chef's recipe says: 'Whisk $1\frac{1}{2}$ cups of cream'. The chef is cooking for $3\frac{1}{2}$ times as many people as usual. How many cups of cream will be needed?

5 There are $7\frac{1}{2}$ meat pies left in a fridge. They are to be shared equally between three people. Calculate the number of pies each person gets. Give your answer as a mixed number.

6 A fitness test involves running as many lengths of a gym as possible in 1 minute. The test is then repeated after a short break. Wanda runs $5\frac{1}{2}$ lengths the first time, and then $4\frac{4}{5}$ lengths the second time.
(a) How many lengths did she run altogether?
(b) How much further did she run the first time compared with the second?

7 Water is poured from a bottle and fills $3\frac{2}{3}$ glasses. How many glasses would be filled if only half the water in the bottle was poured out?

8 Two-thirds of a pizza has to be shared between five people. What fraction will each person get?

9 A book-binder can repair $12\frac{1}{2}$ books in $1\frac{2}{3}$ hours. How many books can the book-binder repair per hour? Divide one of these mixed numbers by the other to work this out.

10 Wiremu wants to share $3\frac{3}{4}$ Easter eggs equally among 5 people. Write down a mathematical calculation to explain how this could be done. Work out the answer.

INVESTIGATION

WHAT DAY OF THE WEEK WERE YOU BORN?

Caution: this method only works if you were born last century!

Here are instructions for working out which day of the week you were born on.

- Write down the last two digits of the year in which you were born e.g. 91. Call this number A. e.g. A = 91
- Divide this two-digit number by 4. Write the result as a mixed number. e.g. $\frac{91}{4} = 22\frac{3}{4}$
- Write down the whole-number part of the mixed number. Call this number B. e.g. B = 22
- Look up the month you were born in from this table. Call this number C.

Month	C =	Month	C =
January	1	June	5
January in a leap year	0	July	0
February	4	August	3
February in a leap year	3	September	6
March	4	October	1
April	0	November	4
May	2	December	6

- Take the date of the month. Call this number D.
- Add A + B + C + D
- Divide the sum by 7. Write your answer as a mixed number.
- Write down the remainder.
- This table then gives the day you were born:

Remainder	Day of week
1	Sunday
2	Monday
3	Tuesday
4	Wednesday
5	Thursday
6	Friday
0	Saturday

Here's an example for one of the most significant dates last century.
Neil Armstrong and Buzz Aldrin were the first people from our planet to land on the moon. The date was 21 July 1969.

- Last two digits of year = 69. A = 69
- Divide by 4 and write down whole-number part: $\frac{69}{4} = 17\frac{1}{4}$ B = 17
- Month is July. C = 0
- Date of month is 21. D = 21
- The sum A + B + C + D = 69 + 17 + 0 + 21 = 107
- Divide by 7: $\frac{107}{7} = 15\frac{2}{7}$
- The remainder is 2. The table tells us this date was a Monday.

- Work out the day of the week on which you were born. Show your working, and explain what you are calculating at each step.

Tenths, hundredths and thousandths

We know already the decimal system uses special fractions: like tenths, hundredths, thousandths, and so on.

Here are the three main decimal fractions:

	Fraction	Decimal
One tenth	$\frac{1}{10}$	0.1
One hundredth	$\frac{1}{100}$	0.01
One thousandth	$\frac{1}{1000}$	0.001

The number of 0s underneath the fraction line is the same as the number of places after the decimal point.

Fractions are more useful for showing how items are shared.
Decimals are more useful with measurement problems and money.

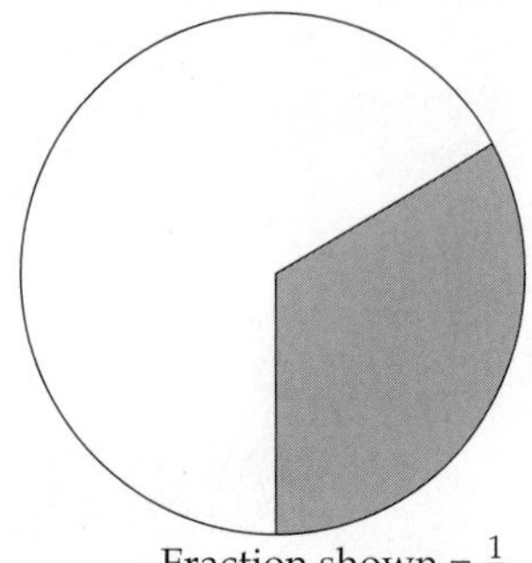

Fraction shown = $\frac{1}{3}$

Length of nail = 4.3 cm

Example A fraction of two-tenths can be written as:

(a) a fraction $\frac{2}{10}$ (b) a decimal 0.2

EXERCISE 7.19

1–4 *Here are some fractions, given in words. Write them as (a) ordinary fractions and (b) decimals.*

1 seven-tenths

2 nine-hundredths

3 forty-one hundredths

4 five-thousandths

5–8 *Write these fractions as decimals.*

5 $\frac{3}{10}$ 7 $\frac{22}{100}$

6 $\frac{5}{100}$ 8 $\frac{376}{1000}$

9–12 *Write these decimals as fractions.*

9 0.9 11 0.61

10 0.07 12 0.003

13–16 *Write these mixed numbers as decimals.*

13 $3\frac{5}{10}$ 15 $22\frac{3}{100}$

14 $6\frac{75}{100}$ 16 $1\frac{41}{1000}$

17–20 *Write these decimals as mixed numbers.*

17 1.9 19 31.3

18 5.07 20 7.023

Changing decimals to fractions

When we change a decimal to a fraction, we have to decide what to write under the fraction line (10, 100 or 1000, etc.). The number of places after the decimal point tells us what to write.

Example Write 0.48 as a fraction in its simplest form.

Answer 0.48 has two places after the decimal point. Therefore, it represents 48 *hundredths*.

$0.48 = \frac{48}{100}$

Writing as a simpler, equivalent fraction:

$\frac{48}{100} = \frac{12}{25}$

EXERCISE 7.20

Change these decimals into fractions. Write each fraction as simply as possible.

1	0.7	5	0.83	9	0.75	13	0.125
2	0.3	6	0.99	10	0.4	14	0.84
3	0.1	7	0.513	11	0.2	15	0.006
4	0.17	8	0.25	12	0.36		

To change a fraction to a decimal, *divide* the numerator (top) by the denominator (bottom).

Example Write $\frac{3}{8}$ as a decimal.

Answer

$$8\overline{)3.0\,{}^{6}0\,{}^{4}0}$$ = 0.3 7 5

You could also use your calculator.
Press these keys:

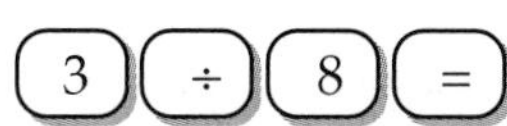

Done either way, the answer is 0.375.

Sometimes a fraction does not change exactly to a decimal. Then you have to round the decimal.

Example $\frac{2}{11} = 0.181\ 818\ 181\ ...$

$= 0.\dot{1}\dot{8}$

$= 0.182$ (3 dp)

EXERCISE 7.21

1–6 *Change these fractions to decimals:*

1 $\frac{2}{5}$

2 $\frac{1}{2}$

3 $\frac{11}{20}$

4 $\frac{7}{8}$

5 $\frac{3}{40}$

6 $\frac{37}{80}$

7–10 *Change these mixed numbers to decimals:*

7 $2\frac{3}{4}$

8 $7\frac{1}{2}$

9 $9\frac{3}{5}$

10 $17\frac{3}{16}$

11–16 *Change these fractions to decimals. Round your answers to 4 dp.*

11 $\frac{1}{3}$

12 $\frac{2}{7}$

13 $\frac{8}{9}$

14 $\frac{3}{13}$

15 $\frac{5}{11}$

16 $\frac{81}{110}$

Comparing fractions

It is useful to change fractions to decimals when **comparing**.

Example Sarah and Taewa are collecting for charity. In Sarah's street, people at 7 out of 16 houses give money. In Taewa's street, people at 9 houses out of 20 give money. Which street has the larger fraction of givers?

Answer This question is asking which of these fractions is larger: $\frac{7}{16}$ or $\frac{9}{20}$?

Change each fraction to a decimal:

Sarah's street: $\frac{7}{16} = 0.4375$

Taewa's street: $\frac{9}{20} = 0.45$

0.45 is the larger of these two decimals. Taewa's street has the larger fraction of givers.

EXERCISE 7.22

1–6 *Change these fractions to decimals. Then, write down the larger fraction in each pair.*

1 $\frac{1}{2}$ or $\frac{4}{9}$

2 $\frac{2}{3}$ or $\frac{4}{5}$

3 $\frac{4}{10}$ or $\frac{7}{20}$

4 $\frac{5}{16}$ or $\frac{4}{11}$

5 $\frac{3}{4}$ or $\frac{16}{25}$

6 $\frac{81}{100}$ or $\frac{71}{83}$

7–10 *Write* true *or* false *for each of these statements.*

7 $\frac{1}{4} > \frac{1}{5}$

8 $\frac{2}{3} < \frac{7}{10}$

9 $\frac{9}{20} > \frac{7}{8}$

10 $\frac{5}{18} < \frac{3}{11}$

11 Write this list of fractions in order from *smallest* to *largest*.

$\left\{\frac{1}{2}, \frac{2}{5}, \frac{3}{4}, \frac{5}{8}\right\}$

12 Write this list of fractions in order from *largest* to *smallest*.

$\left\{\frac{7}{9}, \frac{4}{5}, \frac{2}{3}, \frac{18}{25}, \frac{13}{20}\right\}$

13 Ngaire and Peter are each working separately on the same homework assignment.

Peter: 'I'm two-thirds of the way through.'

Ngaire: 'Oh, I think I've done three-fifths of mine!'

Who has done more?

14 Which contract, A or B, pays the salesperson more?

Contract A: for every \$8 of goods sold, the salesperson is paid \$1

Contract B: for every \$14 of goods sold, the salesperson is paid \$2

15 Three people changed money at different banks in the High Street:

Mr Atkinson changed \$106 US and got \$55 NZ

Mr Bean changed \$77 US and got \$40 NZ

Mr Rowan changed \$45 US and got \$23 NZ.

(a) The exchange rate at Mr Atkinson's bank was 0.5189. Write down the fraction that shows how this could be calculated.

(b) Who got the best (highest) exchange rate? Explain, showing your working.

16 Some crocodiles at two different crocodile farms in Queensland, Australia had an algal infection:

Name of crocodile farm	Total number of crocodiles	Number of crocodiles infected
Daintree	25	17
Trinity Bay	16	11

Which crocodile farm has the higher rate of infection? Explain so that someone else can follow your reasoning.

INVESTIGATION

FRACTION APPROXIMATIONS TO π

π is the number of times the diameter of a circle divides into the circumference.

It is impossible to calculate π exactly.

To ten decimal places, it is 3.141 592 653 5

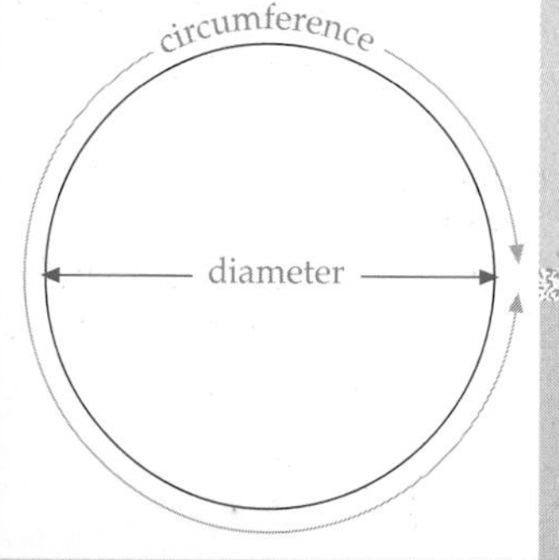

Mathematicians have tried for centuries to work out π more exactly.

Here are some fractions that have been used to approximate π over the years:

Mathematicians	Date	Fraction
NZ secondary school students	1980 AD	$\frac{22}{7}$
Johann Lambert (Switzerland)	1777 AD	$\frac{103\,993}{33\,102}$
Tsu Ch'ung-Chi (China)	501 AD	$\frac{355}{113}$

Mathematicians	Date	Fraction
Archimedes (Greece)	212 BC	$\frac{223}{71}$
Ahmes (Egypt)	1650 BC	$\left(\frac{16}{9}\right)^2$
Babylonians	2000 BC	$\frac{25}{8}$

1 Calculate each of the six approximate fractions as a decimal.

2 Copy this diagram.

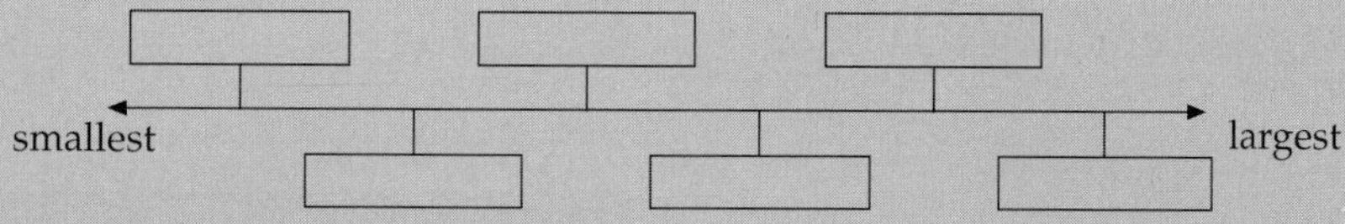

Add the six mathematicians from the table to the six boxes. Do this so that their approximations are in order from smallest to largest. Then add an arrow to show where you think π should be.

3 Which mathematician(s) in the table used the most accurate approximation? Explain.

8 Percentages

STARTER

Water crisis

The Auckland region suffered from a severe drought in 1993–1994. The main result for most residents was a shortage of water.

Local councils issued warnings. Mild restrictions—like a ban on watering gardens—were introduced.

By April, the problem had developed into a full-blown crisis. Cars went dirty as car-washes closed down. The water supply in public urinals was turned off. Residents were encouraged to place bricks in toilet cisterns, and wash clothing less frequently. The council considered measures such as emptying swimming pools. They also drew up plans for rationing residents to one hour of water supply per day.

Fortunately, the rains eventually came at the end of winter 1994, and the immediate crisis was over.

At the height of the crisis, the level of water in the Auckland reservoirs was down to about 25%. To avoid this happening again, regional planners want to arrange an alternative supply, from the Waikato River.

Five years later (in 1998), after a very wet winter, the storage lakes were 99.7% full.

- Explain in words what the two numbers 25 and 99.7 mean in this article.
- What does the symbol % mean?
- What number and symbol would be used to represent 'absolutely full'?
- What number and symbol would be used to represent 'half full'. Explain.

Per cent means 'out of 100'. A **percentage** is a 'part out of every hundred'.

The symbol for per cent is %.

Example 50% means 50 out of 100, or $\frac{50}{100}$

We know that $\frac{50}{100}$ simplifies to $\frac{1}{2}$.

So, we can use the terms 50% and one-half for the same thing.

> Many words use *cent* as a way of expressing one hundred.
> For example, there are 100 cents in a dollar. A century means 100 years.
> Can you think of any others?

EXERCISE 8.1

1 Look at these diagrams. What percentage of the whole square is shaded?

(a) 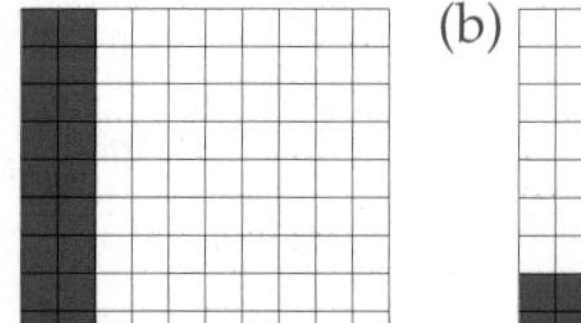 (b) 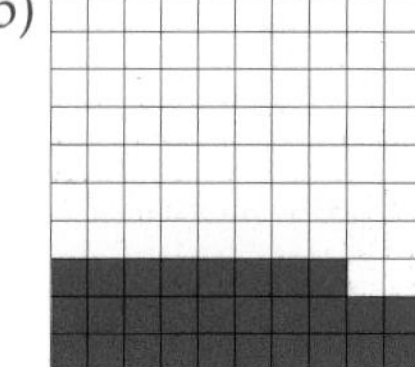

2 Draw two 10-by-10 grids of small squares. Shade them to show these percentages:

(a) 75% (b) 6%

3 Match each of these diagrams with the most likely percentage from the box:

(a) (d) 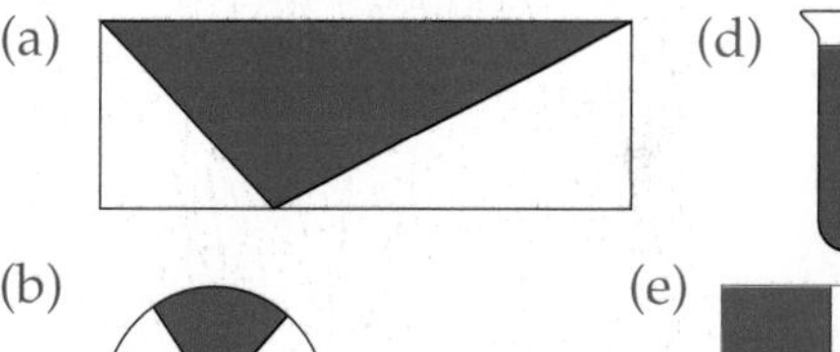

(b) (e) 

(c)

10%	25%	40%	50%	85%

Changing percentages to fractions

Percentages can be thought of as special fractions with a denominator of 100.
We use this idea to change percentages to fractions. If we can, we then simplify the fraction.

Example Change 45% to a fraction. Simplify if possible.

Answer $45\% = \frac{45}{100}$

$\frac{45}{100} = \frac{9}{20}$ (to simplify: 5 goes into both 45 and 100)

EXERCISE 8.2

Write these percentages as fractions. Simplify if possible.

1 17%	5 75%	9 6%	13 70%
2 30%	6 25%	10 60%	14 44%
3 99%	7 1%	11 50%	15 96%
4 49%	8 5%	12 40%	

Changing fractions to percentages

To change a fraction to a percentage, multiply it by 100 $\left(\text{or } \frac{100}{1}\right)$

Example Change $\frac{3}{4}$ to a percentage.

Answer $\frac{3}{4} \times \frac{100}{1} = \frac{300}{4}$

$= 75\%$

In some problems, fractions don't change *exactly* to whole-number percentages. It is useful to use a calculator here.

Example Change $\frac{2}{7}$ to a percentage. Round the answer to 2 dp.

Answer The working is: $\frac{2}{7} \times \frac{100}{1} = \frac{200}{7}$

On a calculator, the keys to use are:

[2] [÷] [7] [×] [100] [=]

This gives 28.57142857

$\frac{2}{7} = 28.57\%$ (2 dp)

EXERCISE 8.3

1–8 *Change these fractions to percentages:*

1 $\frac{2}{5}$

2 $\frac{3}{10}$

3 $\frac{49}{100}$

4 $\frac{3}{25}$

5 $\frac{1}{2}$

6 $\frac{1}{4}$

7 $\frac{7}{20}$

8 $\frac{19}{50}$

9–15 *Change these fractions to percentages. Round each answer to 2 dp.*

9 $\frac{1}{3}$

10 $\frac{2}{3}$

11 $\frac{4}{9}$

12 $\frac{31}{51}$

13 $\frac{3}{7}$

14 $\frac{6}{13}$

15 $\frac{5}{6}$

16 This table shows Ailsa's results in four Maths tests this year:

Topic	Mark out of total	Percentage
Integers	$\frac{11}{20}$	
Angles	$\frac{24}{30}$	
Area	$\frac{27}{50}$	
Fractions	$\frac{12}{25}$	

(a) Copy the table. Then complete it to show each mark as a percentage.

(b) Which topic got the lowest mark (as a percentage)?

(c) Which topic do you think Ailsa understood best?

(d) What do you need to assume to answer question (c)? Explain.

Linking decimals and percentages

To change a decimal to a percentage multiply by 100.

Example Change 0.43 to a percentage.

Answer $0.43 \times 100 = 43\%$

To change a percentage to a decimal write it out of 100, and do the division

Example Change 86% to a decimal.

Answer $\frac{86}{100} = 86 \div 100 = 0.86$

Remember:
- when **multiplying** a decimal by 100, the decimal point will move 2 places to the **right**
- when **dividing** a number by 100, the decimal point will move 2 places to the **left**.

EXERCISE 8.4

1–5 *Change these decimals to percentages:*

1 0.53
2 0.3
3 0.01
4 0.7
5 0.649

6–10 *Change these percentages to decimals:*

6 50%
7 29%
8 4%
9 125%
10 69.2%

11 Copy this table (except for the diagrams). Complete it by writing the shaded part of each diagram as a percentage, a decimal and a fraction (simplified as much as possible) of the whole square.

	Percentage (words)	Percentage (symbol)	Decimal	Fraction (symbol)	Fraction (words)
(a)					
(b)					
(c)					
(d)					

Percentages of quantities

STARTER

When people buy very expensive things they often pay a **deposit**—part of the cost—first. This deposit can be expressed as a percentage.

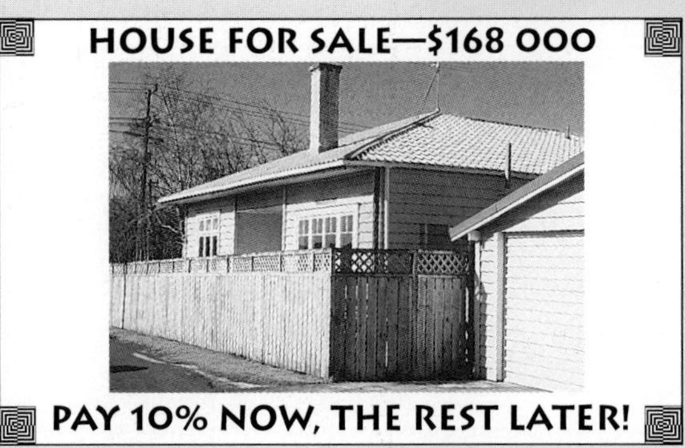

HOUSE FOR SALE—$168 000
PAY 10% NOW, THE REST LATER!

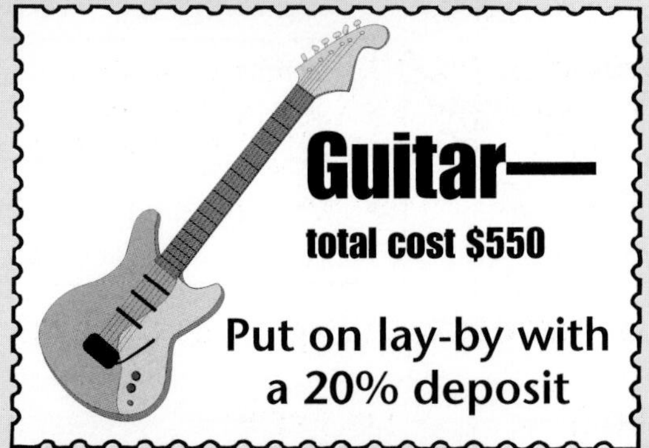

Guitar—
total cost $550
Put on lay-by with a 20% deposit

- How would you work out the amount of the deposit in each case?

To work out a percentage of a quantity we **multiply** the percentage by the quantity.

Example Calculate 30% of $120

Answer $30\% \times 120 = \frac{30}{100} \times \frac{120}{1}$

$= \frac{3600}{100}$ (this working uses fractions)

$= \$36$

With fractions and percentages, the word 'of' means we multiply.

Alternatively, we can use a calculator:

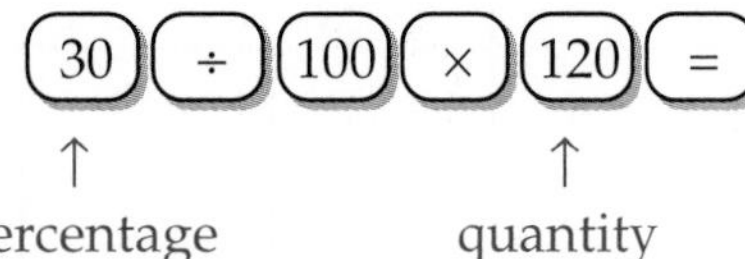

EXERCISE 8.5

1–7 Work out the following:

1 70% of 50
2 32% of 600
3 24% of 300
4 5% of 200
5 42% of $12
6 60% of $18
7 7% of 33 m

8 A soccer player scores with 40% of his shots at goal. He shoots for goal 30 times altogether. How many times would you expect him to score?

9 A church asks its members to pay a 'tithe' of 10% of their income. How much would a member with an income of $35 000 pay?

10 A serious drought affected kiwifruit production this year. The total weight of fruit at one orchard was only 70% of last year's figure, 6500 kg. Calculate the total weight produced this year.

11 These are instructions for mixing concrete:

the amount of cement added to the mixture should be 30% of the weight of gravel.

How much cement should be added to 150 kg of gravel?

12 Membership fees for senior citizens at a social club are 80% of the fee charged to ordinary members. The fee for ordinary members is $90. How much do senior citizens pay?

13 The government pays some retired people a pension of 60% of the average wage after tax. The average wage after tax is $26 500. Calculate the amount of the pension.

14 The owners of a hall hire it out for social events. They charge 15% of the total entrance fees taken. The hall has been hired out for a dance, and the total entrance fees were $1200. Calculate how much the owners should receive.

One amount as a percentage of another amount

STARTER

Your parents probably had to borrow money to pay for your home. To do this, they have to pay *interest* on a mortgage.

The interest rate is expressed as a percentage. Percentages are used because they give a standard way of comparing how expensive it is to borrow money.

Instead of saying that $60 000 has been borrowed and $4800 interest will be paid per year, the interest rate is given as 8%.

- Explain how you work out 8% from these two numbers ($60 000 and $4800).

Here's how to write one quantity as a percentage of another.
Write it as a fraction first. Then change it into a percentage.

Example In a Maths test, Lee got 42 questions correct out of 70. The teacher wrote $\frac{42}{70}$ on the front page. Write this mark as a percentage.

Answer $\frac{42}{70} \times \frac{100}{1} = 60\%$

EXERCISE 8.6

1 Paul got 28 out of 50 in a test. Express this as a percentage.

2 Jane got 72 out of 80 in an exam. What is this as a percentage?

3 A retailer sold a washing machine for \$800, and received a commission of \$40. What percentage commission is this?

4 In a referendum, 34 people out of 50 voted 'no'. What percentage voted 'no'?

5 Wayne was cycling the 75 km distance from Gore to Balclutha. He got blisters after 45 km and had to stop. What percentage of the distance had he completed?

6 Monica tests a coin to see if it is 'fair'. She tosses it 80 times. If it is 'fair', it should land heads up about half the time.
   (a) The coin lands with heads up 32 times. What is this percentage?
   (b) For a fair coin, what should this percentage be, approximately?

7 A speed camera takes photos of 16 cars out of 200 passing by. Calculate the percentage of cars that are photographed.

8 What percentage of \$90 is \$21.60?

9 What percentage of 14 km is 5.88 km?

10 Leanne borrowed \$750 for a year. She was charged interest of \$45. Calculate the interest as a percentage of the amount she borrowed.

11 The Rhodes family are driving from Picton to Invercargill.

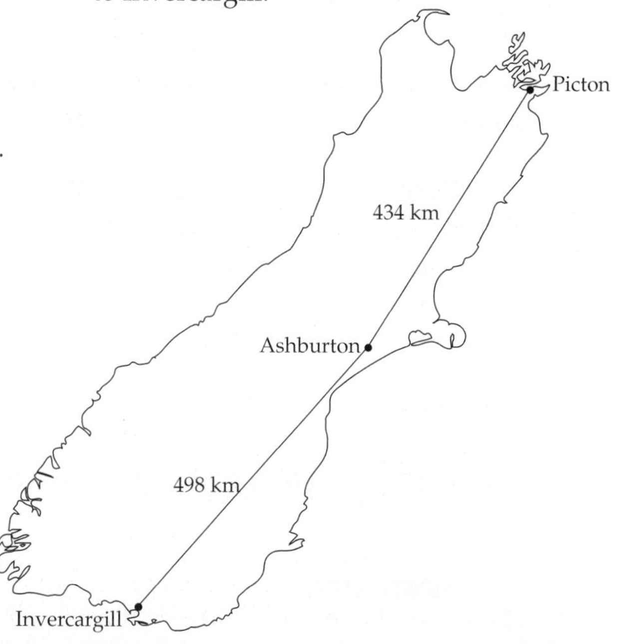

   (a) What is the total distance?
   (b) They stop overnight at Ashburton. What percentage of the journey have they covered so far? Give your answer to the nearest whole number.
   (c) From Ashburton, how many more km do they have to drive to be at the half-way point for the journey?

12 In the 1st term Science test, Kaitoa's mark was 24 out of 40. In the 2nd term Science test it was 17 out of 25. Has his result improved? Explain using percentages.

13 Mr and Mrs Taylor have eight children altogether: two girls and six boys.
   (a) What percentage of the children are boys?
   (b) What percentage of the children are girls?
   (c) What percentage of the *family* are males?
   (d) What percentage of the *family* are females?

INVESTIGATION

ADULT AND CHILD PRICING

We have a mixture of rules for deciding when people 'come of age' and are treated as adults.

Here are some:

Driving licence	15
Leaving school	16
Voting	18
Drinking alcohol	18

You may notice this when you pay for some services. At your age, you probably still qualify for some discounts as a 'child'.

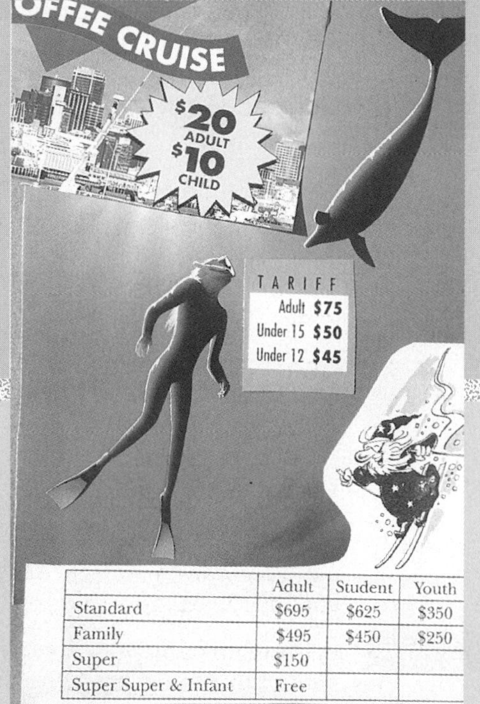

	Adult	Student	Youth
Standard	$695	$625	$350
Family	$495	$450	$250
Super	$150		
Super Super & Infant	Free		

- Choose at least three activities/services which have a 'child' price and an 'adult' price.

  Here are some suggestions:

Entrance fees:	e.g. the zoo
Membership fees	e.g. the SPCA
Entertainment	e.g. movie tickets
Bus fares	
Airline fares	

- Now do some research and make a presentation. Here are some of the details you will need to include:
  - child price
  - adult price
  - qualifying age for children.

- Produce a table like this one:

Activity/service	Qualifying age	Child price	Adult price	Child price as a percentage of the adult price

Percentage increases and decreases

You can also use percentages to look at increases and decreases. For example:

- profits and losses
- increases in population
- discounts.

We describe the change using percentages. The percentage always compares the change to the old, or **original**, quantity.

Example Gerald had a pay increase recently. His wage increased from \$8 per hour to \$10 per hour.

(a) How much was the increase?

(b) Calculate his *percentage* wage increase.

Answer (a) Increase = New wage rate – Old wage rate
= \$10 – \$8
= \$2

(b) As a percentage: compare the increase with the old wage rate.

$$\text{Percentage increase} = \frac{\text{Increase}}{\text{Original quantity}} \times \frac{100}{1}$$

$$= \frac{2}{8} \times \frac{100}{1}$$

$$= 25\%$$

Example A car dealership aims to make a 30% profit selling cars imported from Japan. One of these cars costs the dealership \$9000.

(a) Calculate the profit on this car.

(b) Calculate the price that the car will sell for.

Answer (a) The profit will be 30% of \$9000

$$\frac{30}{100} \times 9000 = \$2700$$

(b) The profit is added on to the cost price:

Selling price = Cost price + Profit
= \$9000 + \$2700
= \$11 700

A **profit** is the difference between:

- the money you get for selling an item

and

- the money you paid to buy the item.

This can be written as:
Profit = Money received – Expenses

Decreases work in the same way.

Example Last year 300 students took part in the athletic sports. This year there were only 240.

(a) How much have the numbers decreased by?

(b) Calculate the percentage decrease.

Answer (a) Decrease = 300 – 240 = 60

(b) $\text{Percentage decrease} = \frac{\text{Decrease}}{\text{Original quantity}} \times \frac{100}{1}$

$$= \frac{60}{300} \times \frac{100}{1} = 20\%$$

Example A music shop holds a sale. All prices are discounted (reduced in price) by 15%. A jazz CD usually sells for $26. Calculate:

(a) the discount (price reduction)

(b) the sale price of the CD.

Answer (a) The discount will be 15% of $26.

$\frac{15}{100} \times 26 = \$3.90$

(b) The discount is subtracted from the usual price:

Sale price = Usual – Discount

= $26.00 – $3.90

= $22.10

If a shop sells an item for *less* than it paid for it, we say the shop has made a **loss**.

EXERCISE 8.7

1 A rare stamp worth $8000 increases in value by 40%.

(a) Calculate the increase in value.

(b) What is the stamp now worth?

2 A fence 1.5 m high is raised to a new height of 1.8 m.

(a) Calculate the increase in height.

(b) What is the *percentage* increase in height?

3 A watch worth $70 is discounted (reduced in price) to $42. Calculate:

(a) the discount

(b) the discount as a percentage.

4 The roll at Te Kanawa High School has increased from 1200 students to 1500 students. Calculate the percentage increase.

5 A computer decreases in value by 20% over a year. When new, it was worth $4200. What is the computer worth at the end of the year?

6 One of these refrigerators will be cheaper than the other after the discount is taken off. Calculate which one. Show your calculations. Explain what you are working out at each stage.

7 The price of petrol has increased from 89.7 cents a litre to 92.9 cents a litre. Calculate:

(a) the amount of the increase

(b) the *percentage* increase.

8 Jan's typing speed increased from 40 words a minute in Year 9 to 70 words a minute in Year 10. Calculate the percentage increase in typing speed.

9 **Good day on sharemarket:**
Telco shares increase by 4%

At the beginning of the day, each Telco share was worth $6.34. Calculate how much each Telco share was worth at the end of the day.

10 Calculate the *percentage* price reduction on this TV set.

SPREADSHEET INVESTIGATION

COMPOUND INTEREST

If you keep money in a savings account at the bank, the bank pays you interest. This interest is added to the original amount in the account. If you leave the money there, you will earn interest on the new total.

The amount on which you earn money is the **principal.**

Example Deposit in the bank: $600
Interest rate: 5%

Year 1: Principal = original deposit = $600

At the end of 1 year: Interest = 5% of $600 = $\frac{5}{100} \times 600 = \$30$

The interest is then *added* to the original principal: 600 + 30 = $630

Year 2: Principal = $630

At the end of 2 years: Interest = 5% of $630 = $\frac{5}{100} \times 630 = \$31.50$

The interest is then *added* to the deposit: 630 + 31.50 = $661.50

Year 3: Principal = $661.50

At the end of 3 years: Interest = 5% of $661.50 = $\frac{5}{100} \times 661.50 = \$33.08$

The interest is then *added* to the deposit: 661.50 + 33.08 = $694.58

And so on!

We can use a spreadsheet to do these calculations.

Here are the headings and formulas you would type:

	A	B	C
1	Principal	Interest calculation	New principal
2			
3	600	=5/100*A3	=A3+B3
4	=C3	=5/100*A4	=A4+B4

Here are the first four rows of the spreadsheet:

	A	B	C
1	Principal	Interest calculation	New principal
2			
3	$600.00	$30.00	$630.00
4	$630.00	$31.50	$661.50

To get the $ signs in the cells, format the cells as currency! In Excel, do this by highlighting the block of cells, then click on Format, Cells, Currency.

Copy the bottom row (Row 4) downwards several times.

1 What will be the total amount in the bank after 8 years?

2 Produce spreadsheets for these savings:

(a) $4000 deposited in the bank at 12% interest for 10 years.

(b) $800 deposited in the bank at 25% interest for 10 years.

3 Would you rather have a large initial deposit or a high interest rate over a 10-year period? Use your spreadsheet results to explain.

9 Everyday measurements

Time

What time is it now?

- Write down at least five devices that tell you the time.
- Explain how they display or announce the time.

One of the most accurate time devices is the atomic clock. It works off the frequency at which the caesium-133 atom vibrates. The International System of Units defines a second as 'the duration of 9 192 631 770 periods of vibration of the caesium atom'. Sometimes scientists decide we need to change the time by adding an extra second. The reason: the Earth is gradually slowing down, and takes longer and longer to rotate.

Computers can download the correct time from the Internet. The address is http://www.timeanddate.com/worldclock/

Here's a printout from that address:

Current **UTC** (or GMT)-time used: **Tuesday August 11, 1998 at 09:12:36**
UTC is Coordinated Universal Time, GMT is Greenwich Mean Time

Some radio stations broadcast special pips (beeps) just before each hour. The sixth (and last) pip gives the exact hour. It's easy to use this to get the time on *your* watch exact.

The most common devices for measuring time are:

- the clock
- the watch.

These give time in hours, minutes, and sometimes seconds.

There are two kinds of display:

analogue

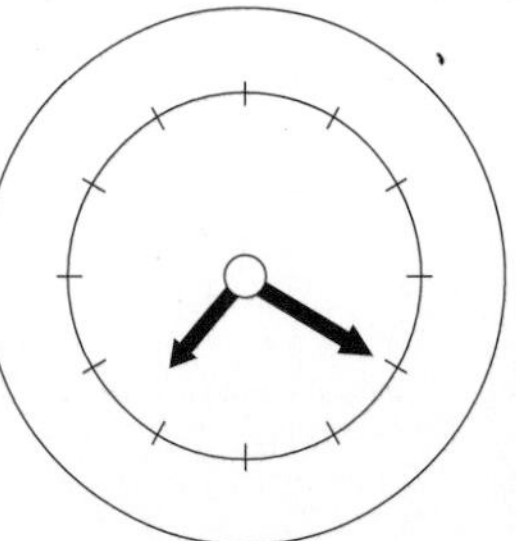

digital

In words, we would say this time is 'twenty past seven' or 'seven-twenty'.

Times in the morning and times in the afternoon/evening are marked by the letters am and pm.

Examples 6.30 am means half past six in the morning
2.45 pm means quarter to three in the afternoon.

We can do calculations with times.

> Remember there are 60 minutes in an hour. This is important when adding or subtracting time.

Example A concert started at 7.55 pm. It lasted for $2\frac{1}{2}$ hours. When did the concert finish?

Answer We add 2 hours 30 minutes to 7.55 pm
Adding 2 hours to the start time gives 9.55 pm
Adding 30 minutes takes us to 10.25 pm (5 minutes needed to get to 10 pm, then the remaining 25 minutes is after 10 pm)

The concert finished at 10.25 pm.

Example Lee left work at 4.50 pm, and arrived home at 5.15 pm. How long did the journey take?

Answer Look at this time line:

|← 25 min →| (from 4.50 to 5.15)

4.30 4.35 4.40 4.45 4.50 4.55 5.00 5.05 5.10 5.15 5.20

Each space represents 5 minutes.
The journey took 25 minutes.

> Why does half an hour in Mathematics go faster than half an hour in Science? I just don't understand time sometimes!

EXERCISE 9.1

1 What times are shown by these clocks?

(a)

(b)

(c)

(d)

2 Write these times using words only. (For example, 5.30 pm means half past five in the afternoon.)

(a) 10.30 am
(b) 9.15 am
(c) 8.45 am
(d) 7.30 pm
(e) 1.10 pm
(f) 12.45 pm
(g) 11.50 am
(h) 2.40 pm

3 Write these times using digits plus am or pm.

(a) half past four in the afternoon
(b) three o'clock in the morning
(c) quarter past one in the afternoon
(d) quarter to eight in the morning
(e) five past three in the afternoon
(f) ten to eleven in the morning

4 Sketch two circles. Draw these times on the circle, like a clock with an hour hand and a minute hand.

(a) 7.25
(b) quarter past ten

5 How many minutes are there in:

(a) an hour?
(b) quarter of an hour?
(c) half an hour?
(d) three-quarters of an hour?
(e) three hours?

6 A video cassette has the symbol 'E180' stamped on it. What you think this code means about the playing time?

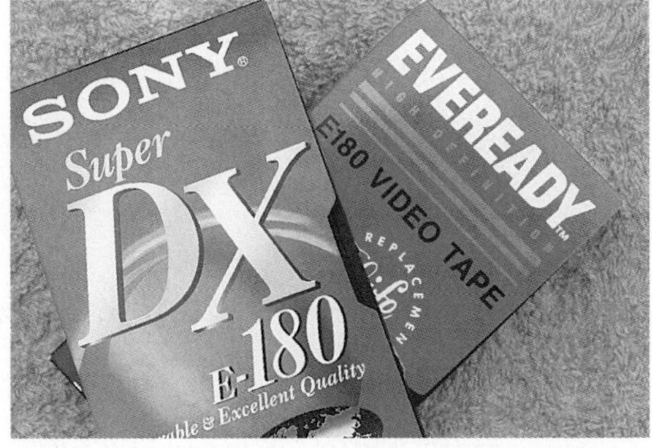

7 Sharon wants to watch the two movies *Dick Tracy* and *Star Trek: First Contact* on Sky TV. She will be out that night, so decides to record the two movies on video.

Here is the programme:

6.30 pm *Dick Tracy*
8.15 pm *Total Recall*
10.25 pm *Star Trek: First Contact*
12.30 am *The Prophecy*

She sets the video and inserts a tape marked E240. Will the tape be long enough? Make some calculations and use them to explain.

8 What is the time:

(a) 20 minutes after 10.40 am?
(b) 30 minutes before 8.40 am?
(c) 10 minutes before 6.05 pm?
(d) $1\frac{1}{2}$ hours after 11.45 am?

9 Work out the time interval between these times:

(a) 4.30 pm and 4.45 pm
(b) 9.20 am and 10.10 am
(c) 10.30 am and 2.15 pm

10 A rugby game started at 2.45 pm, and finished at 4.10 pm. For how long did the game last?

11 A school social will begin at 7.30 pm, and last for 3 hours and 45 minutes. When is it due to finish?

12 There are two main types of public transport in the Wellington region: train and bus. The next page shows the timetables for Sundays.

(a) How long does it take to travel from Trentham to Petone by train?
(b) How long does it take to travel from Wellington Hospital to Seatoun by bus?
(c) You catch the train from Upper Hutt at 1 pm. When is the earliest you can reach Seatoun?

(continues)

Hutt Valley to Wellington Train timetable

SUNDAY

Upper Hutt	Trentham	Silverstream	Taita	Naenae	Hutt Central	Petone	Ngauranga	Wellington
6.00	6.04	6.08	**6.18**	6.22	**6.27**	**6.35**	6.40	**6.50**
7.00	7.04	7.08	**7.18**	7.22	**7.27**	**7.35**	7.40	**7.50**
8.00	8.04	8.08	**8.18**	8.22	**8.27**	**8.35**	8.40	**8.50**
9.00	9.04	9.08	**9.18**	9.22	**9.27**	**9.35**	9.40	**9.50**
10.00	10.04	10.08	**10.18**	10.22	**10.27**	**10.35**	10.40	**10.50**
11.00	11.04	11.08	**11.18**	11.22	**11.27**	**11.35**	11.40	**11.50**
12.00	12.04	12.08	**12.18**	12.22	**12.27**	**12.35**	12.40	**12.50**
1.00	1.04	1.08	**1.08**	1.22	**1.27**	**1.35**	1.40	**1.50**
2.00	2.04	2.08	**2.08**	2.22	**2.27**	**2.35**	2.40	**2.50**
3.00	3.04	3.08	**3.08**	3.22	**3.27**	**3.35**	3.40	**3.50**
4.00	4.04	4.08	**4.08**	4.22	**4.27**	**4.35**	4.40	**4.50**
5.00	5.04	5.08	**5.08**	5.22	**5.27**	**5.35**	5.40	**5.50**
6.00	6.04	6.08	**6.18**	6.22	**6.27**	**6.35**	6.40	**6.50**
7.00	7.04	7.08	**7.18**	7.22	**7.27**	**7.35**	7.40	**7.50**
8.00	8.04	8.08	**8.18**	8.22	**8.27**	**8.35**	8.40	**8.50**
9.00	9.04	9.08	**9.18**	9.22	**9.27**	**9.35**	9.40	**9.50**
10.00	10.04	10.08	**10.18**	10.22	**10.27**	**10.35**	10.40	**10.50**

Bus timetable for Wellington Railway Station to Seatoun

SUNDAY						
Route No.	Railway Station	Polytechnic	Wellington Hospital	Kilbirnie Shops	Seatoun Park	
	Bus dep	Bus dep	Bus dep	Bus dep	Bus arr	
11	**8.05**	8.14	8.18	8.23	8.37	AM
11	**9.05**	9.14	9.18	9.23	9.37	
11	**10.05**	10.14	10.18	10.23	10.37	
11	**11.05**	11.14	11.18	11.23	11.37	
11	**11.35**	11.44	11.48	11.53	12.07	PM
11	**12.05**	12.14	12.18	12.23	11.37	
11	**12.35**	12.44	12.48	12.53	1.07	
11	**1.05**	1.14	1.18	1.23	1.37	
11	**1.35**	1.44	1.48	1.53	2.07	
11	**2.05**	2.14	2.18	2.23	2.37	
11	**2.35**	2.44	2.48	2.53	3.07	
11	**3.05**	3.14	3.18	3.23	3.37	
11	**3.35**	3.44	3.48	3.53	4.07	
11	**4.05**	4.14	4.18	4.23	4.37	
11	**4.35**	4.44	4.48	4.53	5.07	
11	**5.05**	5.14	5.18	5.23	5.37	
11	**5.35**	5.44	5.48	5.53	6.07	
11	**6.05**	6.14	6.18	6.23	6.37	
11	**7.05**	7.14	7.18	7.23	7.37	
11	**8.05**	8.14	8.18	8.23	8.37	
11	**9.05**	9.14	9.18	9.23	9.37	
11	**10.05**	10.14	10.18	10.23	10.37	

(d) The Heretaunga College waterpolo team have a game on Sunday night. This will be at the Aquatic Centre (next to the Kilbirnie shops) at 7 pm. When should the team leave from Trentham station?

13 Here are the cooking times for a vegetarian meal:

A Roast potatoes, parsnip and onions sprinkled with herbs (1 hour)

B Steam broccoli and asparagus (5 minutes)

C Roast capsicum (20 minutes)

D Boil pasta (10 minutes)

E Roast yams (40 minutes)

The cook wants to serve all the food at the same time. Dinner is planned for 8.15 pm.

(a) When should the potatoes, parsnip and onions go in the oven?

(b) When should the capsicum go in the oven?

(c) Draw a time-line to show when the cook should put each item on to cook. Use 5-minute intervals, and start at 7.15 pm.

7.15 7.20 7.25 etc.

Do this by placing the labels A, B, C, D and E on your time-line.

14 This diagram shows how long it takes to walk around a large zoo and see some of the animals.

(a) Your family wants to visit the kiosk and see each animal once only. Write down a route they could take. What is the total time for this route?

(b) Is it possible to see all these animals and visit the kiosk in under an hour? Explain.

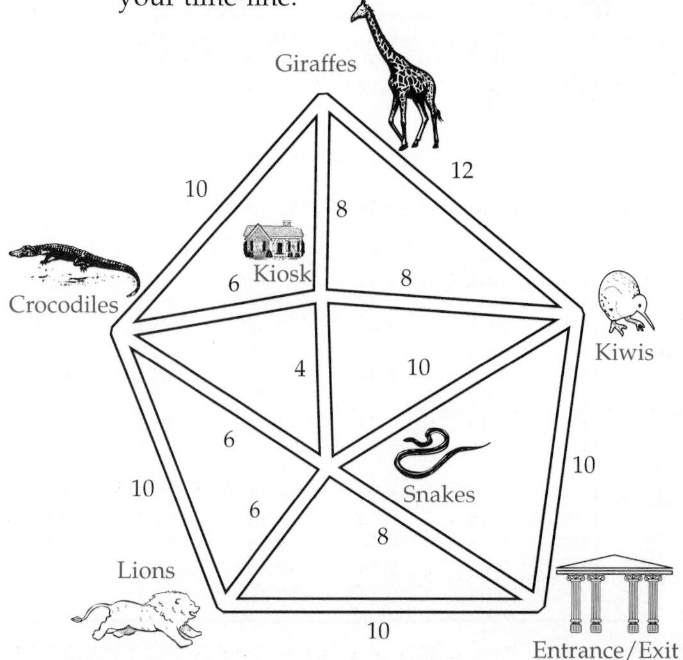

24-hour clock

STARTER

Rupert wants to record a movie that starts at 8.10 pm. He programmes his video by entering 4 digits. This diagram shows part of the display.

Start				
Stop	2	2	3	5

- What four digits should be entered in the start boxes?
- When is the movie due to finish?
- How long is the movie?
- What do the first two digits on the video display represent?
- What do the last two digits represent?

Times are written in the 24-hour clock to avoid confusion between am and pm times.
They are often used in airline timetables, alarm clocks, computers, video recorders, etc.

The 24-hour clock uses four digits to show time.

- The first two digits represent the number of hours that have passed since midnight.
- The last two digits represent the number of minutes after the hour.

Morning times: 0001–1159

Example 1130 in the 24-hour clock means 11.30 am, or half past eleven in the morning.
6.45 am (or quarter to seven in the morning) is written as 0645 in the 24-hour clock.

Afternoon/evening times: 1201–2359

Example 1715 in the 24-hour clock means 5.15 pm, or quarter past five in the afternoon
10 pm (or ten o'clock at night) is written as 2200 in the 24-hour clock.

Where the last two digits are zero, the times are exactly on the hour. These are said using the word 'hundred'.

Example 1600 is said 'sixteen hundred hours', and means exactly 4 pm.
Midday is 1200 (said 'twelve hundred hours')
Midnight is 0000 or 2400 (said 'zero hours' or 'twenty-four hundred hours')

Changing to 24-hour time:	**Examples**
Morning times (am): Write a zero in front if needed, so that the time has *four* digits	11.15 am = 1115 9.30 am = 0930
Afternoon time (pm): Add 12 to the hours	4.15 pm = 1615
Changing from 24-hour time	**Examples**
Morning times: The first two digits give the hours. If there is a 0 there, drop it	1020 = 10.20 am 0845 = 8.45 am
Afternoon/evening times: Subtract 12 from the first two digits	1950 = 7.50 pm

EXERCISE 9.2

1 Make a copy of this time-line.

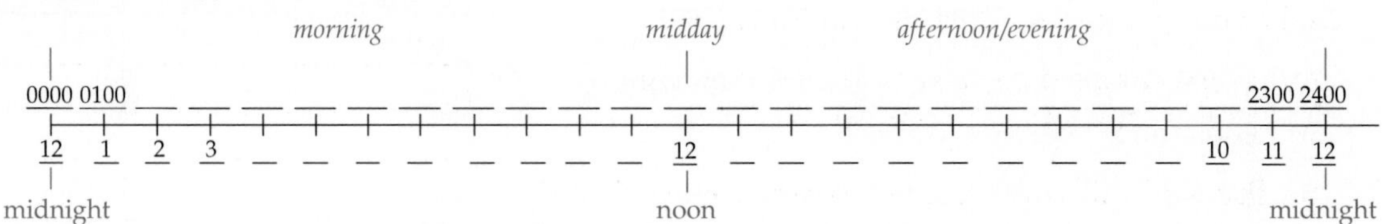

Complete the scale above and below the line, to show 24-hour time and am/pm time.

2 Change these 24-hour clock times to am/pm time:

(a) 0945 (e) 2020
(b) 1500 (f) 0815
(c) 0430 (g) 2330
(d) 1650 (h) 1215

3 Write these times using the 24-hour clock:

(a) 10.15 am (f) 11.10 pm
(b) 4.30 pm (g) 5.28 pm
(c) 11 pm (h) 8.40 am
(d) 6 am (i) midday
(e) 4.45 am (j) midnight

4 Write these times using the 24-hour clock:

(a) half past seven in the morning
(b) quarter past eight at night
(c) quarter to four in the morning
(d) twenty to nine at night
(e) half past two in the afternoon
(f) five to four in the afternoon

5 Copy these sentences. Complete them by adding the word *midday* or *midnight:*

(a) 1145 is 15 minutes before ....
(b) 0020 is 20 minutes after ....
(c) 1230 is half an hour after ....
(d) 2300 is one hour before ....

6 This table gives a programme schedule for the SKY Movie channel.

(a) Make a list of these times using the 24-hour clock.

(b) Which programme runs for the shortest time? For how long does it run?

(c) Which programme runs for the longest time? For how long does it run?

Midnight	Husbands and Lovers (R18) Drama
1.25 am	In the Bleak Midwinter (M) Comedy
3.00 am	Priest (R16) Drama
4.45 am	The Nurse (R16) Thriller
6.15 am	The Making of Daylight
6.45 am	Country Gold (PG) Drama
8.30 am	Empire of the Sun (PG) Drama
11.00 am	Silverado (PG) Western
1.15 pm	Cherokee Kid (PG)
2.45 pm	Perry Mason: Case of the Jealous Jokester (PG) Thriller
4.30 pm	Muppet Treasure Island (G) Family
6.15 pm	Sabrina (G) Comedy
8.30 pm	The Rich Man's Wife (R16) Thriller
10.05 pm	Stealing Beauty (M) Drama (115 minutes)

7 Write down when school finishes today in four different ways:

(a) as a pm time
(b) in words
(c) using the 24-hour clock
(d) on a drawn circle, with lines for the hour and minute hands.

8 Write your school timetable for today, using the 24-hour clock. Set it out in a table like the one here. Make sure you show intervals and lunchtime.

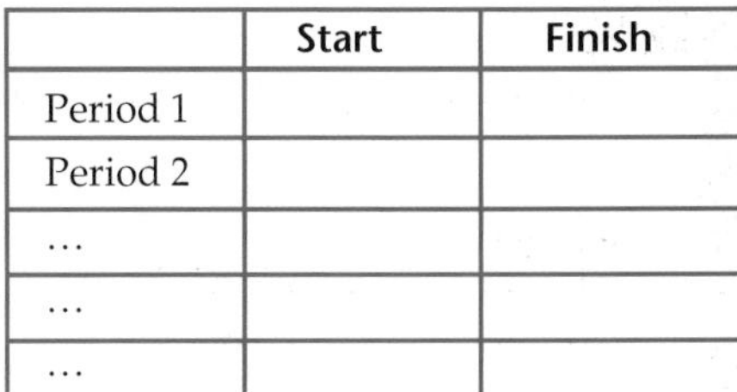

	Start	Finish
Period 1		
Period 2		
...		
...		
...		

9 How many hours and minutes are there between 2230 on Monday and 0415 on Tuesday?

10 The *Overlander* daytime train runs between Auckland and Wellington every day. Here is its timetable.

Station	Southbound	Northbound
Auckland	dep. 8.30 am	arr. 7.35 pm
Papakura	arr. 9.14 am	arr. 7.00 pm
Hamilton	arr. 10.43 am	arr. 5.32 pm
Taumarunui	arr. 1.01 pm	arr. 3.11 pm
National Park	arr. 1.53 pm	arr. 2.18 pm
Ohakune	arr. 2.25 pm	arr. 1.47 pm
Marton	arr. 4.27 pm	arr. 11.13 am
Palmerston North	arr. 5.12 pm	arr. 10.57 am
Levin	arr. 5.49 pm	arr. 10.17 am
Porirua	arr. 7.09 pm	arr. 9.05 am
Wellington	arr. 7.27 pm	dep. 8.45 am

arr. = arrival time; dep. = departure time.

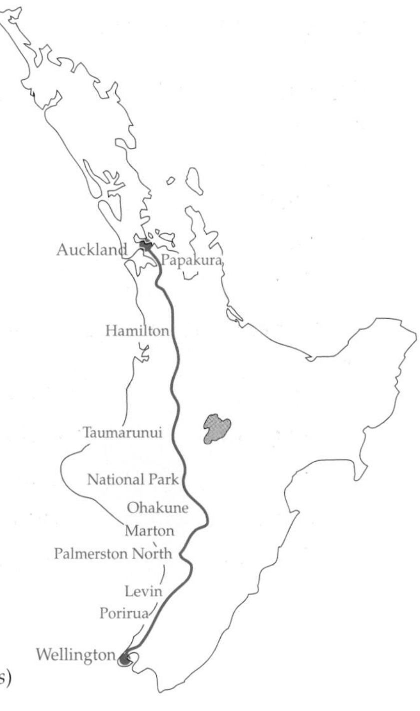

(a) When does the northbound train leave Wellington each day?

(b) Copy the station names for the southbound journey. Then change the departure/arrival times to the 24-hour clock.

(*continues*)

(c) The northbound train passes through Paraparaumu (not shown) at 0940. Which two stations listed here is Paraparaumu between?

(d) The northbound train passes through Middlemore (not shown) at 1916. Which two stations listed here is Middlemore between?

(e) The two trains pass each other during their journey. Between which two stations listed here will they pass?

(f) Which train trip takes more time—northbound from Wellington to Auckland, or southbound from Auckland to Wellington?

Write down your calculations. Explain each step so that someone who doesn't have this timetable can follow your working.

Different places, different seasons, different times

STARTER

There are times of the year when you have to change the time on all the clocks in your house.

- Do you change the minutes or the hours?
- How much of a change is made?
- Why is the change made?

Is the time in places overseas the same as in New Zealand?

- Where in the world would it be night time now?
- You turn on your television and watch a live rugby game that starts in Sydney at 8 pm. What would be the time where you are?

This band on the earth's surface is called the **terminator**. It marks the division between day and night.

Daylight saving

Daylight saving involves changing the time by exactly one hour. This is done in spring each year.
The main reason is to make us wake up earlier for school and work, so we are not asleep when it is light outside in the morning. This gives us longer evenings to relax, garden, have barbeques, or play sport outside.

We change to New Zealand **daylight time** on the first Sunday in October. We put clocks and watches *forward* by 1 hour.

Example 6.35 pm becomes 7.35 pm with daylight saving.

In autumn (the first Sunday on or after 15 March), we move back to standard time by going *back* 1 hour.

Example 6.40 pm becomes 5.40 pm when daylight saving is stopped and we go back to standard time.

Here's how to remember what happens with daylight saving: 'spring forward, fall back'.

EXERCISE 9.3

1 What time would these become when changed to daylight saving time?
   (a) 4 pm (c) quarter to seven at night
   (b) 1445 (d) midday

2 What time would these become when changed from daylight saving time to standard time?
   (a) 11 am (c) half past seven in the morning
   (b) 0910 (d) midnight

3 Here is an extract from the calendar for the year 2000. Only the months of March and October are shown.

March						
S	M	T	W	T	F	S
			1	2	3	4
5	6	7	8	9	10	11
12	13	14	15	16	17	18
19	20	21	22	23	24	25
26	27	28	29	30	31	

October						
S	M	T	W	T	F	S
1	2	3	4	5	6	7
8	9	10	11	12	13	14
15	16	17	18	19	20	21
22	23	24	25	26	27	28
29	30	31				

   (a) On what day in this year did daylight saving begin?
   (b) On what day in this year did daylight saving end?

Different time zones

Time is different in different places because of the rotation of the Earth. At midday in Wellington, the Sun is at its highest in the sky. It can't be midday in Perth, Western Australia, at the same time. There is a four-hour time difference between New Zealand and Western Australia.

To make times easier, we have a system of 24 different time zones. These give a clear idea of time anywhere in the world. The zones usually follow national boundaries on land; over the oceans, they are shown with straight lines.

The time zones are shown on the map on the next page.

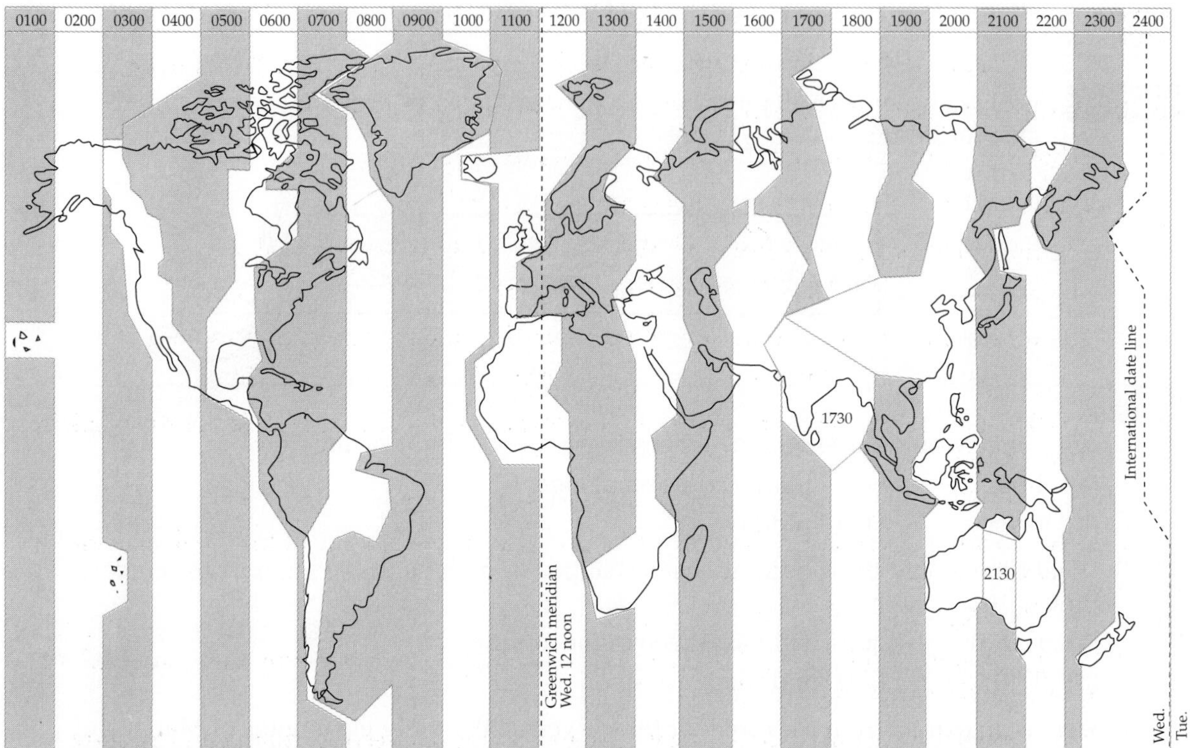

The International Date Line runs through the Pacific Ocean to the east of New Zealand. Our time zone is 23 hours (almost 1 day) ahead of countries like Samoa on the other side of the Date Line.

This map shows time zones in New Zealand's part of the world.

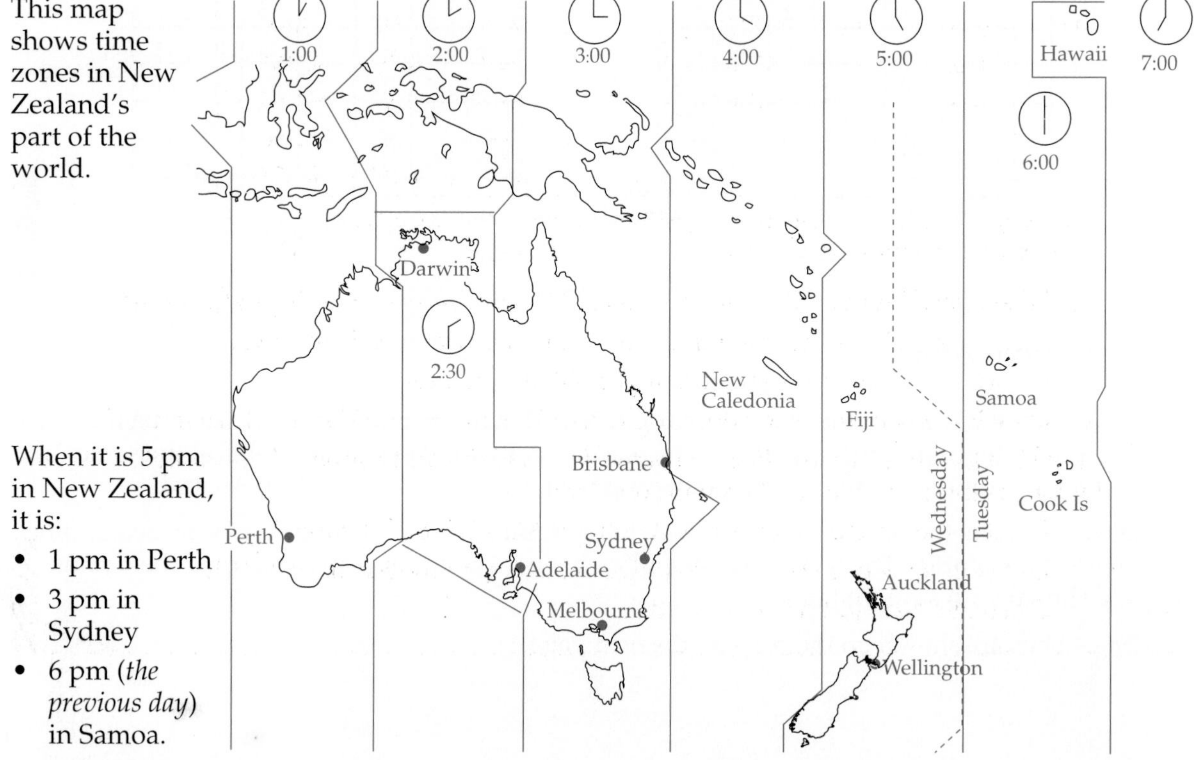

When it is 5 pm in New Zealand, it is:

- 1 pm in Perth
- 3 pm in Sydney
- 6 pm (*the previous day*) in Samoa.

EXERCISE 9.4

1–7 Use the Australia/Pacific time zone map on the previous page to answer these questions.

1 Which Pacific island(s) are in the same time zone as New Zealand?

2 What is the time difference between Perth and Melbourne?

3 Which other Australian city has the same time as Darwin?

4 The time in New Zealand is 10 am. Write down the time in these places:
(a) Samoa (b) New Caledonia (c) Hawaii (d) Adelaide

5 The time in Melbourne is midday. Write down the time in these places:
(a) Brisbane (b) Auckland (c) Perth (d) Darwin

6 It is 8.30 pm on Thursday in New Zealand. Write down the time and day of the week in these places:
(a) Sydney (b) Hawaii (c) Samoa

7 It is 6.15 am on Monday in Samoa. Write down the time and day of the week in these places:
(a) Wellington (b) Hawaii (c) Perth

8 The Chatham Islands are east of New Zealand. Can you explain why they expected a lot of worldwide interest on 1st January 2000?

9 This shows the timetable for Air New Zealand flights between Auckland and Sydney:

From Auckland to Sydney				From Sydney to Auckland			
Day	**Departs**	**Arrives**	**Flight No.**	**Day**	**Departs**	**Arrives**	**Flight No.**
D	0700	0830	NZ101	DX17	0700	1155	NZ100
D	0900	1030	NZ103	1	0800	1255	NZ100
D	1400	1530	NZ105	D	1000	1455	NZ102
DX6	1800	1930	NZ107	D	1200	1655	NZ104
				D	1800	2255	NZ106
				7	2035	0130*	NZ108

D = daily; 1 = Monday; 6 = Saturday; 7 = Sunday; X = except; * = following day.
All departure and arrival times are *local.*

(a) When does flight NZ105 leave Auckland? Write your answer in am/pm time.
(b) How many flights are there from Auckland to Sydney on Saturdays?
(c) On what days of the week does flight NZ100 operate?
(d) On what day of the week does flight NZ108 arrive in Auckland? At what time?

There is a two-hour time difference between Auckland and Sydney. For example, 8 am in Sydney is the same time as 10 am in Auckland.

(e) What is the time in Auckland when flight NZ 104 leaves Sydney?
(f) Use your answer to part (e) to calculate the flight time for flight NZ104.
(g) Calculate the flight time for NZ105.

The calendar

The only natural measurements of time are:

- day
- month
- year.

These are based on movements in the solar system.

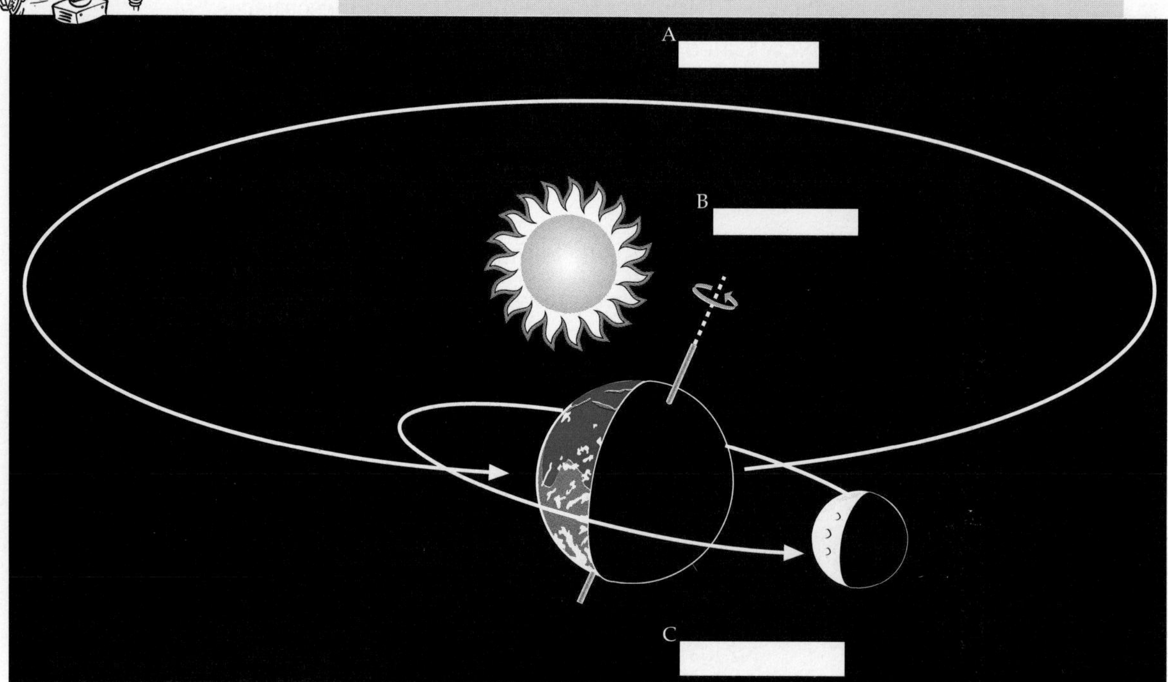

- Decide which word should go in each gap below. Choose from { year, month, day }.

  The Earth orbits the Sun. This takes 1 ....

  The Moon orbits the Earth. This takes about 1 ....

  The Earth rotates about its axis. This takes 1 ....
- Which word should go in each of the boxes marked A, B, C in the diagram?

Here are the main time units, from shortest to longest:

1 second 1 minute = 60 seconds 1 hour = 60 minutes 1 day = 24 hours	1 week = 7 days 1 month 1 year	1 decade = 10 years 1 century = 100 years 1 millennium = 1000 years

Many centuries ago, astronomers discovered there was no **exact** relationship between days, months and years.
This is why the months in our calendar have different numbers of days. It is also why there are leap years, with an extra day.

Thirty days has September,
April, June, and wild November.
All the rest have 31
excepting February alone,
which has 28 days clear
but 29 in each leap year.

We need leap years because actually it takes about $365\frac{1}{4}$ days for the Earth to orbit (move round) the Sun.

Most years are 365 days long. Every four years we have a leap year with 366 days to allow for the extra time. This extra day occurs on 29 February.

The numbers used to name leap years are normally divisible by 4. This is not true for years that are divisible by 100. These years are only leap years if they are divisible by 400.

Examples 2015 is not a leap year (it isn't divisible by 4).

2016 is a leap year, because 4 divides exactly into 2016. $\frac{2016}{4} = 504$

2100 is not a leap year, because it isn't divisible by 400.

HEARTBEAT

Work with another student.
Take each other's pulse. This is the number of times your heart beats in one minute.

The best method (unless you have a stethoscope!) is to place your finger firmly on your partner's wrist, just below their thumb.

Calculate how many times your heart will beat:

- in one hour
- in one day
- in one year.

EXERCISE 9.5

1 (a) How many minutes are there in 3 hours?
(b) How many hours are there in 2 days?
(c) How many minutes are there in half an hour?
(d) How many months are there in 4 years?

2 Marie has to make a time calculation. She multiplies 24 by 7 on a calculator, and gets 168.
Copy this sentence:

There are 168 .... in a ....

Choose two words from this list to fill the gaps: { minutes, hours, day, days, week, month }

3 There are just over 52 weeks in a year. This can be worked out using the numbers 365 (365 days in most years) and 7 (7 days in a week). Explain how.

4 To the nearest whole number, how many weeks are there in a month?

5 A fortnight is two weeks. How many days are there in a fortnight?

6 'Today will be yesterday tomorrow'.

(a) It will be Saturday tomorrow. What was it yesterday?
(b) It was Monday yesterday. What will it be tomorrow?
(c) The day before yesterday was Tuesday. What will it be the day after tomorrow?

7 How many days are there in each of these months:

(a) July
(b) September
(c) December
(d) November
(e) February 2007
(f) February 2008

8 This shows the calendar for the month of June. This calendar works for the years 1984, 1990, 2001, 2007, 2012, 2018, etc.

June						
Sunday	Monday	Tuesday	Wednesday	Thursday	Friday	Saturday
					1	2
3	4	5	6	7	8	9
10	11	12	13	14	15	16
17	18	19	20	21	22	23
24	25	26	27	28	29	30

(a) What day of the week is July 3 in this year?
(b) What day of the week was May 25 in this year?
(c) What will be the date three weeks after June 18?
(d) The 'Rally of New Zealand' runs from 14 June to 19 June inclusive. How many days is this?

9 The year is divided into four seasons. These are roughly the same length. The months of winter are { June, July, August }. Write down the months of:

(a) summer (b) autumn (c) spring

10 Which of these are leap years? (*Hint*: dividing by 4 on your calculator will help you.)

(a) 2004
(b) 1967
(c) 1942
(d) 2046
(e) 1900
(f) 2100
(g) 2000
(h) 3000

11 How many decades are there in a century?

12 It is Freya's birthday today. Using her calculator, she works out she has been alive for about 410 248 800 seconds.

Here are the keys she presses:

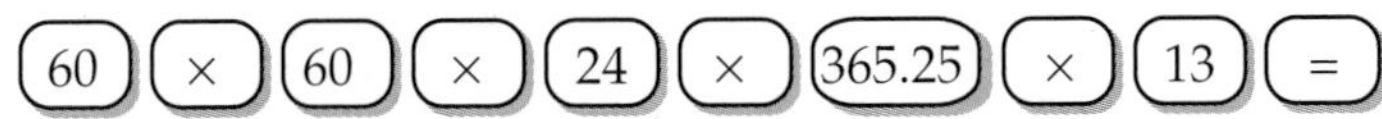

(a) Which birthday is Freya celebrating today?

(b) Use a calculator to work out about how many *minutes* Freya has been alive.

(c) Freya's life expectancy is 79 years. How many days is this (to the nearest 100)?

13 Dates are often written using only digits. For example, the date 18 June 2007 could be written as 18/6/07. This means the 18th day of the 6th month in the 7th year of this century.

Write these dates in full. (Assume they are in this century.)

(a) 12/10/04 (b) 1/3/00 (c) 29/2/12

14 We say that years like 2003, 2015 and 2078 are in the 21st century. In which century were these years?

(a) 1642 Abel Tasman visits New Zealand

(b) 1840 Treaty of Waitangi signed

(c) 1995 New Zealand wins America's Cup for the first time

Money

STARTER

New Zealand uses dollars and cents for its money.

- There are 6 different New Zealand coins. If you paid for an item using one of each of them, what would it cost?
- How much change would you get from a $5 note?

- How many other forms of money can you name?
- Is it possible to have amounts of money as small as 1 or 2 cents? Discuss.
- What happens in the supermarket when you buy some sliced ham that is marked $2.87?

Calculators can be used for working out money problems.

- We take dollars as the amount *before* the decimal point.
- Cents are the two digits *after* the decimal point.

Example Calculate the cost of buying 8 stamps worth 40 c each.

Answer $8 \times 0.40 = 3.2$

The 8 stamps cost $3.20

Example Anna pays $11.40 for 12 identical handibags. What did each handibag cost?

$11.40 ÷ 12 = 0.95

Each handibag cost 95 cents.

Rounding money

When paying in cash, amounts of money sometimes need to be *rounded*. The rounding depends on the last cent digit. We round 'to the nearest 5 or 10 cents'.

This table shows how amounts between 70 c and 80 c are rounded.

Amount in cents	Rounded for paying in cash
70	70 cents (no rounding needed)
71	70 cents
72	70 cents
73	75 cents
74	75 cents
75	75 cents (no rounding needed)
76	75 cents
77	75 cents
78	80 cents
79	80 cents
80	80 cents (no rounding needed)

Each amount is *rounded* to the closest possible amount that is a multiple of 5 or 10 cents.

Example Pita buys some prawns. They are priced at $5.42. If Pita pays cash, how much will he pay?

Answer The closest multiple of 5 or 10 cents to 42 cents is 40 cents. Pita will pay $5.40.

EXERCISE 9.6

You will find a calculator helpful for this exercise.

1 Calculate the cost of 6 movie tickets at $8.50 each.

2 (a) Calculate the cost of 4 ice-creams at $1.85 each.

(b) How much change would you get if you paid for the ice-creams with a $10 note?

3 (a) Calculate the total cost of:

- a pencil sharpener at 45 cents
- a rubber at 65 cents
- an A4 pad at $1.95.

(b) Work out the change for these items from a $20 note.

4 Quinta is paid $8.50 per hour for part-time babysitting. How much will she be paid for:

(a) 2 hours? (b) 5 hours? (c) $3\frac{1}{2}$ hours?

5 A computer game was reduced from $49.30 to the sale price of $28.75. How much was it reduced?

6 Deanna buys 2 boxes of tissues for \$4.20. How much does each box cost?

7 The stationery shop sells ballpoint pens for 85 c each. How many can you buy for \$5.10?

8 A motorist buys 22.4 litres of petrol. The price of petrol is 89 cents a litre.
   (a) Calculate the cost (to the nearest 5 or 10 cents).
   (b) What will be the change if the motorist pays with a \$50 note?

9 Ian has a part-time lawn-mowing job. He is paid \$9.50 per hour. One day he was paid \$23.75. How long did he work for?

10 Round these amounts of money to the nearest 5 or 10 cents:
   (a) 73 cents (b) \$1.62 (c) \$10.86 (d) \$15.39

11–12 *Use this advertisement for both questions 11 and 12.*
In question 11, people are paying by Eftpos and are charged the exact amount of money.
In question 12, people are paying with cash—their purchase is rounded to the nearest 5 or 10 cents.

Cutting food costs is our business

11 Calculate the cost of these purchases.
   (a) 1 French stick
       1 bottle of wine
   (b) 3 kg of rump steak
   (c) 2 heads of broccoli
       1 dozen scallops
       2 towels
   (d) 2.5 kg of corned silverside
       2 bottles of wine
       3 heads of broccoli

12 Calculate the cost of these purchases. Round the total to the nearest 5 or 10 cents.
   (a) 2 French sticks
   (b) 24 scallops
       1 head of broccoli
       1 towel
   (c) 4 kg of corned silverside
       3 heads of broccoli
   (d) 1.83 kg of rump steak
       2 towels
       4 bottles of wine
       6 scallops

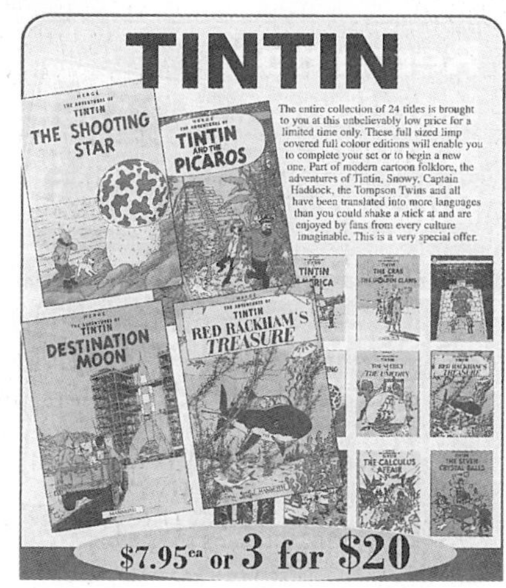

13 (a) What would it cost to buy all 24 Tintin books?
   (b) How much money do you save by buying 3 Tintin books as a set instead of buying them individually?

14 The bus fare (one way) from our place to town is $2.40. In town we want to go to a movie that costs $9.50. How much would it cost altogether for my two brothers and me to travel in to town, see the movie, and return home?

15 A golf club is running a special sale.

(a) How many golf balls can you buy for $50?

(b) How much change is there from $100 if you buy 3 caps and 4 golfballs?

16 A parking meter takes any kind of coin. 5 cents buys 3 minutes of parking. How much parking time would you get for $1?

Reading prices from tables

EXERCISE 9.7

1 Here are some of Telecom New Zealand's new national rates:

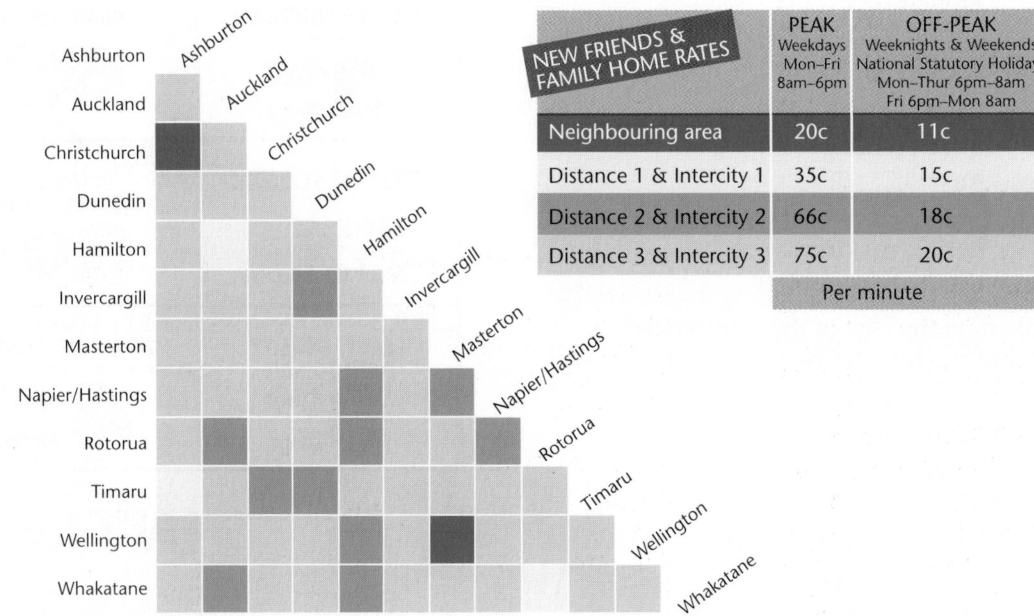

NEW FRIENDS & FAMILY HOME RATES	PEAK Weekdays Mon–Fri 8am–6pm	OFF-PEAK Weeknights & Weekends National Statutory Holidays Mon–Thur 6pm–8am Fri 6pm–Mon 8am
Neighbouring area	20c	11c
Distance 1 & Intercity 1	35c	15c
Distance 2 & Intercity 2	66c	18c
Distance 3 & Intercity 3	75c	20c
	Per minute	

(a) What is the peak rate per minute for calls between Timaru and Ashburton?

(b) What is the off-peak rate per minute for calls between Hamilton and Wellington?

(c) Sally, who lives in Invercargill, phones her friend in Whakatane on Sunday afternoon. They talk for 5 minutes. How much will the call cost?

(d) Bruce sends a fax from Wellington to Masterton on Tuesday morning at 8.30 am. The fax takes 2 minutes to send. How much will it cost?

2 Here is part of the price list from a burger bar:

Item	Price	
Chicken sandwich	\$3.85	
Burger	\$3.50	
Cheeseburger	\$3.95	
Fries	Small \$1.25	Large \$1.75
Cola	Small \$1.00	Large \$1.30

(a) What is the cost of these orders:
   (i) 2 chicken sandwiches
   (ii) 2 burgers and 3 small colas
   (iii) 1 cheeseburger, 2 large fries and 3 large colas

(b) How much change should you get if you bought 2 cheeseburgers with a \$20 note?

(c) Two customers write these calculations on paper napkins before they order. Explain what each customer is working out.
   (i) $2 \times 1.75 + 3.85$
   (ii) $20 - (3.95 + 1.75)$

(d) Kerry paid exactly \$5.20 for a burger and fries. What kind of burger and what size of fries did Kerry get?

3 **Swimming pool fees**

PRICES (inclusive of GST)

SWIM (includes Sauna, Steam, Spa)

ADULT

CASUAL	\$4.00	OR	**Monthly payment option**	
1 month	\$36.00		Joining fee	\$50.00
3 months	\$100.00		Monthly Automatic payments from your bank account (minimum 12 months)	\$27.50
6 months	\$190.00			
12 months	\$300.00			

CHILD (under 15 yrs) & **SENIOR** (over 60 years)

CASUAL	\$2.00
1 month	\$18.00
3 months	\$50.00
6 months	\$95.00
12 months	\$180.00

STUDENT (ID required)

CASUAL	\$3.00
1 month	\$27.00
3 months	\$65.00
6 months	\$120.00
12 months	\$220.00

(a) How much does it cost an adult and a child to go for a single swim?

(b) You can save money by paying monthly rather than per swim, if you go often enough. How many times would you need to go to the swimming pool *each month* to save money?

(c) An adult knows they will be away for two months next year, and won't be able to use the swimming pool. Would it be cheaper to pay for ten months' membership or to join for twelve months? Explain.

(continues)

(d) Hinemoa turns 15 in six months' time. She is a student at high school. Should she pay for:

- six months child membership and then six months student membership, or
- twelve months student membership?

Explain.

(e) Troy is an adult. He can only afford to pay for membership on a monthly basis. He plans to use the pool for 14 months until he goes overseas. He decides to pay by automatic bank payments instead of cash each month. How much money would he save altogether?

4 This table shows prices per minute for toll calls from New Zealand to some countries.

	WORLDWIDE PLAN RATES		
	Weekdays 8am–6pm	Weekdays 6pm–10pm	Weekdays 10pm–8am Weekends & National Statutory Holidays
Australia	$0.99	$0.75	$0.55
Canada	$1.69	$1.39	$1.09
Fiji	$1.52	$1.13	$0.89
Hong Kong	$1.83	$1.39	$1.09
Japan	$1.83	$1.39	$1.09
Samoa	$1.52	$1.13	$0.89
South Africa	$2.42	$1.85	$1.19
Taiwan	$2.25	$1.71	$1.19
UK	$1.69	$1.39	$1.09
USA	$1.69	$1.39	$1.09

Calculate the cost of these calls:

(a) a 10-minute call to Canada on Saturday morning

(b) a 2-minute call to South Africa at 9 am on Wednesday

(c) an 8-minute call to the UK at 7 pm on Friday

(d) a half-hour call to Taiwan at 7 am on Monday.

INVESTIGATION

PLAN A SCHOOL TRIP TO CHRISTCHURCH OR WELLINGTON

You have been placed in charge of:

- making the arrangements and
- finding the cost

of a school trip to either Christchurch or Wellington.

The other students in your class need to know well in advance how much the trip will cost them. They will pay the school for the travel and accommodation. Other costs, such as entry fees, food, etc., will be paid for by the students individually.

Your class will need 3 nights' accommodation.

Here is some of the information you will need to find out:

— Number of students in the class (this will be needed to split the cost equally between students).

— Cost of return travel for a group. (Check bus/train/air fares. Find out if discounts apply for a school party.)

— Price of accommodation, e.g. motel, motor-camp, etc. (Check in an AA travel guide.) Explain how you would decide on the number of units/cabins needed.

- Present your findings as a project.
- Make a recommendation about how much each student will need to pay.

Temperature

STARTER

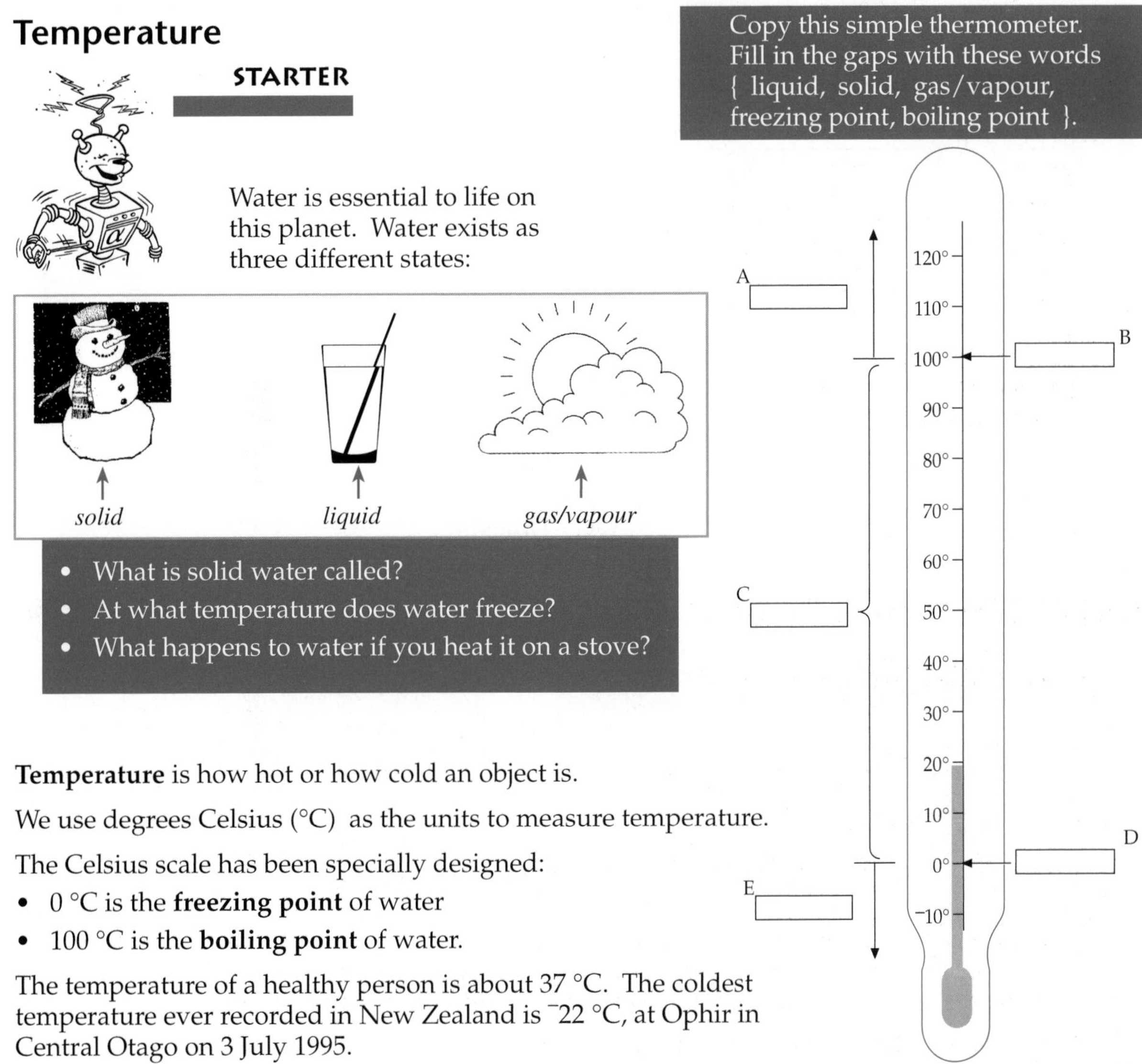

Water is essential to life on this planet. Water exists as three different states:

- What is solid water called?
- At what temperature does water freeze?
- What happens to water if you heat it on a stove?

Copy this simple thermometer. Fill in the gaps with these words { liquid, solid, gas/vapour, freezing point, boiling point }.

Temperature is how hot or how cold an object is.

We use degrees Celsius (°C) as the units to measure temperature.

The Celsius scale has been specially designed:

- 0 °C is the **freezing point** of water
- 100 °C is the **boiling point** of water.

The temperature of a healthy person is about 37 °C. The coldest temperature ever recorded in New Zealand is ⁻22 °C, at Ophir in Central Otago on 3 July 1995.

The Kelvin scale

The coldest temperature possible is 273 °C below zero. That is, ⁻273 °C.
This is called **absolute zero**.

Scientists use a basic unit called the **Kelvin** for measuring temperature.

The Kelvin scale starts at absolute zero:
0 K = ⁻273 °C

- To change a temperature on the Kelvin scale to °C, subtract 273.
- To change a temperature in °C to the Kelvin scale, add 273.

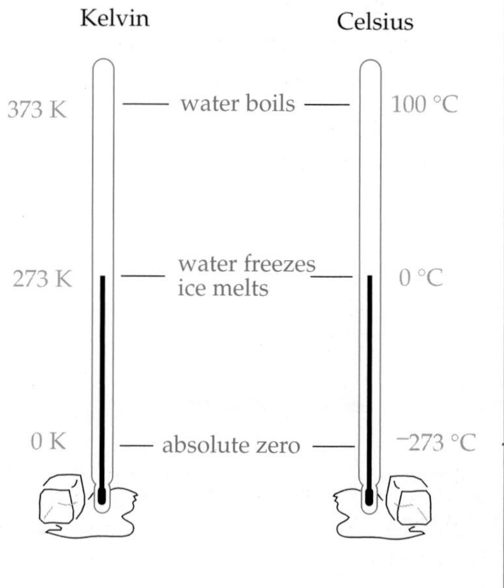

We use negative numbers to show temperatures below 0 °C.

EXERCISE 9.8

1 These daytime temperatures were recorded at 3 pm on March 22. Arrange the temperatures in order from hottest to coldest.

Auckland	18 °C	Christchurch	26 °C
Tauranga	21 °C	Dunedin	9 °C
Napier	25 °C	Invercargill	11 °C
Wellington	16 °C		

2 Match each of these examples with its most likely temperature:

	Example	Temperature
(a)	Hot shower	85 °C
(b)	Surface of the moon	800 °C
(c)	Glass of water from the tap	45 °C
(d)	A blast furnace in a steelworks	–4 °C
(e)	Cup of instant coffee just poured	–120 °C
(f)	Inside freezer compartment of fridge	350 °C
(g)	Inside a pizza oven	12 °C

3 Make a copy of this line. Add a scale to it, with °C marked in equal spaces of 10 °C.

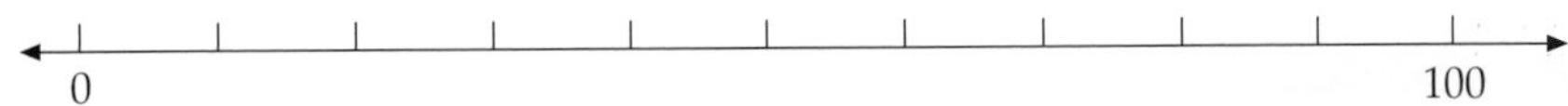

Draw arrows pointing to a likely temperature for each of these:

(a) your body
(b) a cube of ice
(c) water from an outside tap
(d) a warm summer's day
(e) a hot bath
(f) a jug of boiling water.

Hot and cold

4 This table shows the maximum and minimum temperatures recorded in several New Zealand towns for one day in August. It also shows the range of temperatures (the difference between the maximum and the minimum temperature).

All three figures are given for Whangarei and Alexandra. The other towns each have one missing measurement. Write down each of the missing measurements (a)–(f).

Town	Maximum temp.	Minimum temp.	Temperature range
Whangarei	21 °C	13 °C	8 °C
Tauranga	19 °C	7 °C	(a)
Wanganui	(b)	5 °C	11 °C
Lower Hutt	14 °C	(c)	6 °C
Alexandra	11 °C	$^{-}5$ °C	16 °C
Queenstown	10 °C	$^{-}2$ °C	(d)
Dunedin	(e)	$^{-}1$ °C	10 °C
Invercargill	8 °C	(f)	8 °C

5 Change these temperatures on the Kelvin scale to °C:

(a) 1140 K (blast furnace at steel mill)
(b) 186 K (estimated temperature on polar surface of Mars)
(c) 77 K (liquid nitrogen)
(d) 330 K (hottest temperature ever recorded on Earth—at Death Valley)

6 Change these Celsius readings to the Kelvin scale:

(a) 1064 °C (melting point of gold)
(b) $^{-}259$ °C (liquid hydrogen)
(c) 430 °C (estimated temperature on hot side of Mercury)
(d) $^{-}88$ °C (coldest temperature ever recorded on Earth—at Vostok base, Antarctica)

Reading scales

STARTER

This bathroom scale measures a person's weight in kg. The scale has three types of marking:

- long lines (e.g. showing 50, 60, 70, etc)
- medium length lines
- short lines.

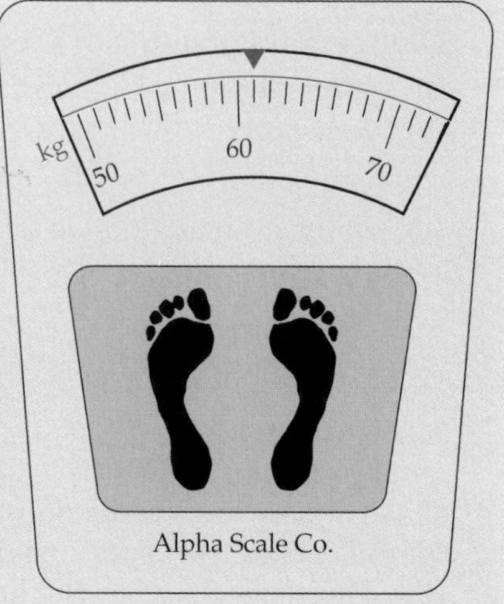

- What do the medium length lines represent?
- What do the short lines represent?
- Suggest a reason why long and medium length lines are used as well as short ones. (*Hint*: think about what the scale would look like if there were short markings only.)
- Estimate the weight shown on these scales.

EXERCISE 9.9

1 On this scale, each small unit or division stands for 0.2.

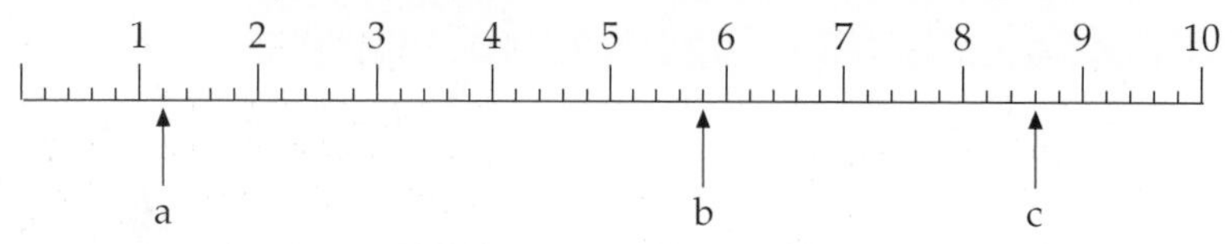

What are the readings shown by the arrows marked a, b and c?

2 (a) What do each of the *small* markings on this scale stand for?

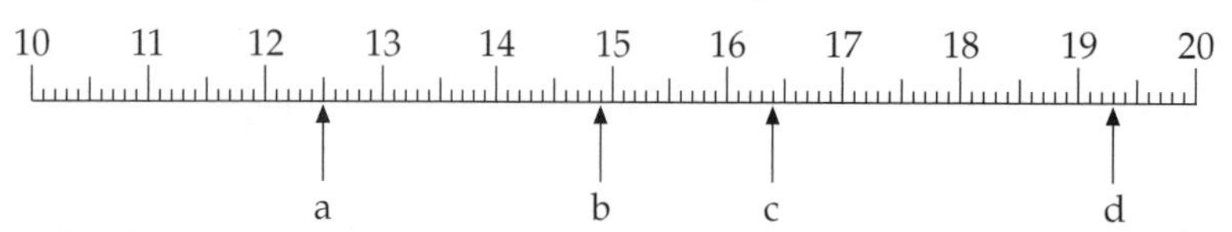

(b) What are the readings shown by the arrows marked a, b, c and d?

3 The large units on this scale are the same as most rulers: they are centimetres.

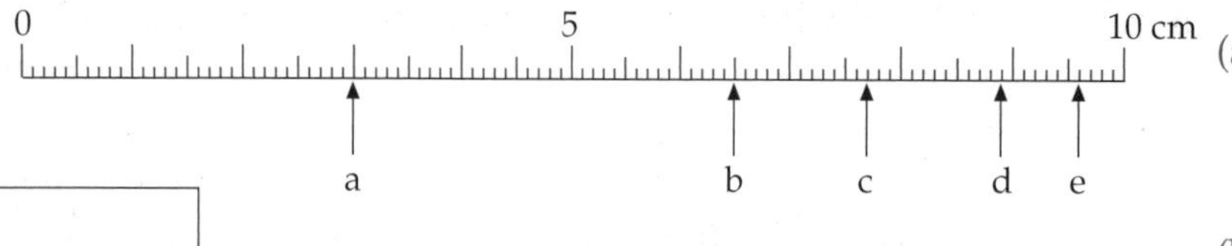

(a) What units are shown by the *small* divisions on this scale?

(b) What are the readings shown by the arrows marked a, b, c, d and e?

cm 1 2 3 4 5 6 7

300 290 280 270 260 250 240 230

MADE IN NEW ZEALAND

Addison Wesley Longman

Private Bag 102908
North Shore Mail Centre
Auckland 10
New Zealand

Telephone (09) 444 4968
Facsimile (09) 444 4957

4 This business card has been placed against a ruler. What is the height of the business card?

5 This diagram shows a car speedometer.

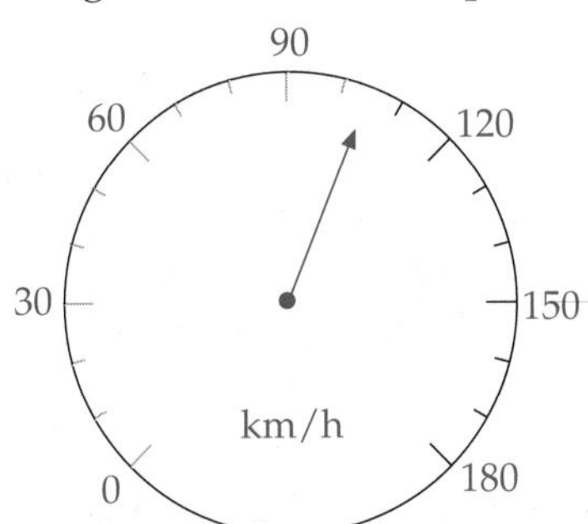

(a) What does each division of the scale represent?
(b) What reading is shown by the arrow?

6 What temperature (in °C) is shown on this thermometer?

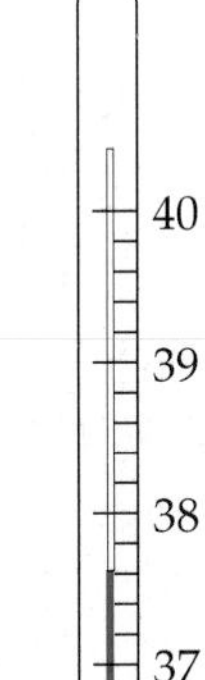

7 These are displays from weighing scales. Each scale is in kilograms (kg). What is the reading shown on each one?

(a) (b)

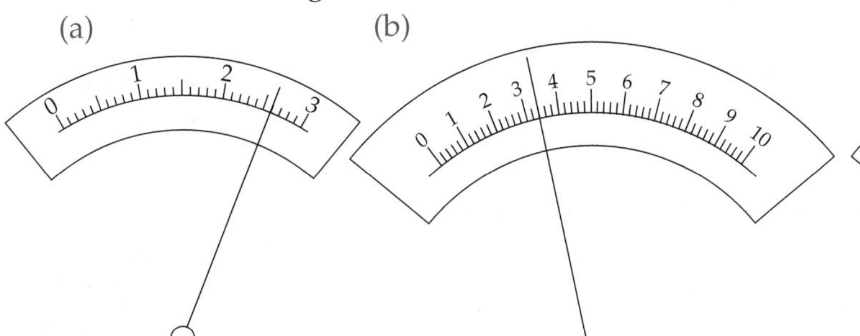

(c)

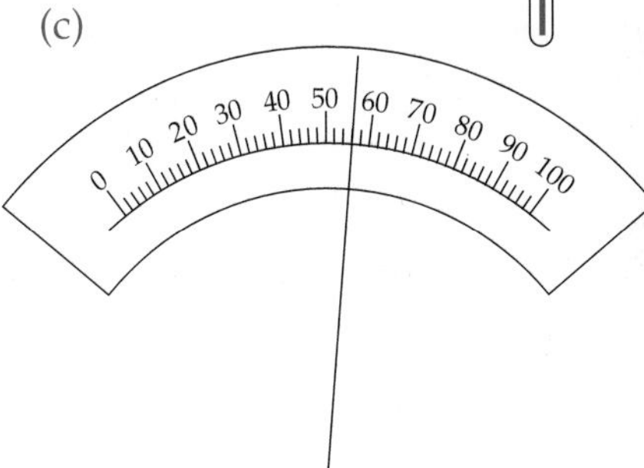

8 The scale on these measuring jugs is in millilitres (mL). Estimate the amount of liquid in each jug.

(a)

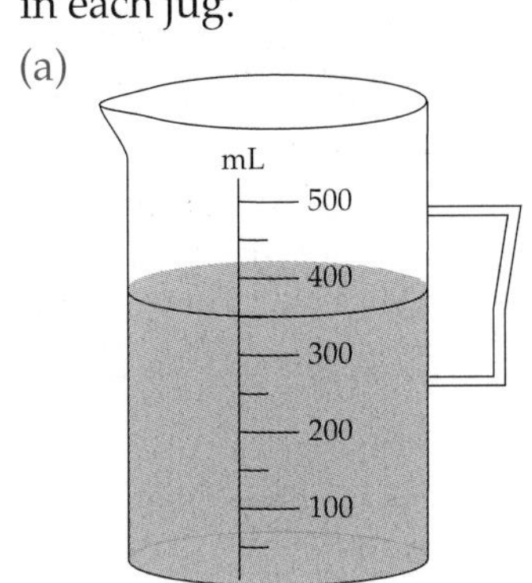

(b)

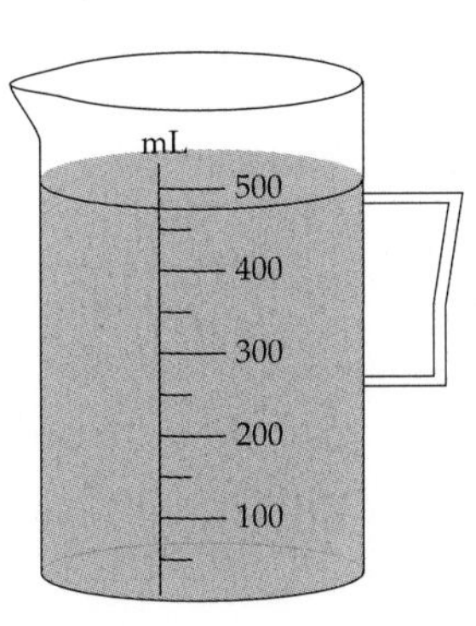

(c)

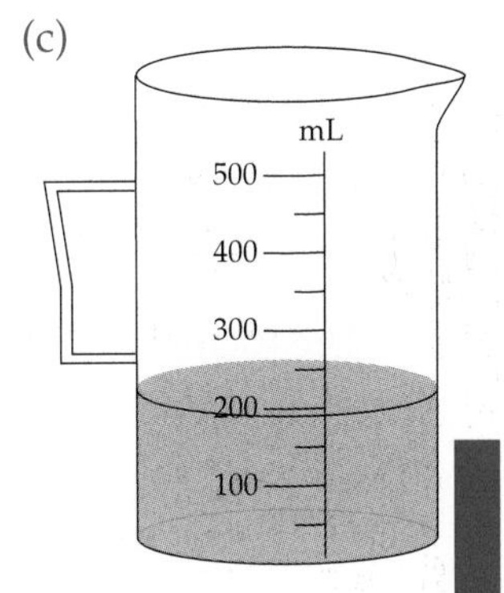

Non-uniform scales

On some scales each division is not the same length. These scales are **non-uniform**.

An example is the dial on an AM radio.

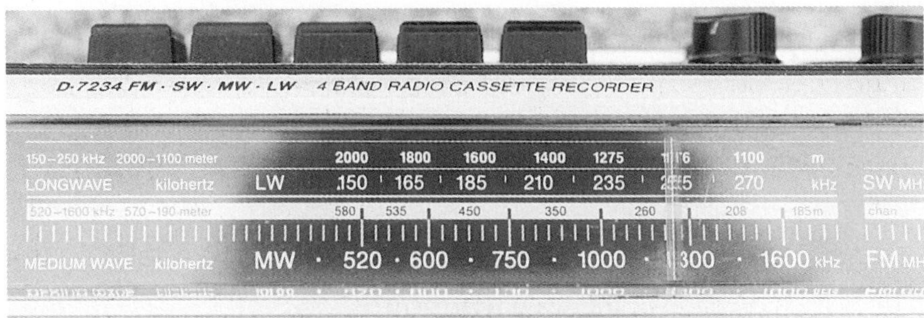

This radio is tuned to 1250 kHz.

Notice how the frequencies between 1400 and 1600 kHz are squeezed together, compared with the frequencies at the other end of the dial.

On a non-uniform scale, divisions represent equal quantities, even though they are not the same length.

Example

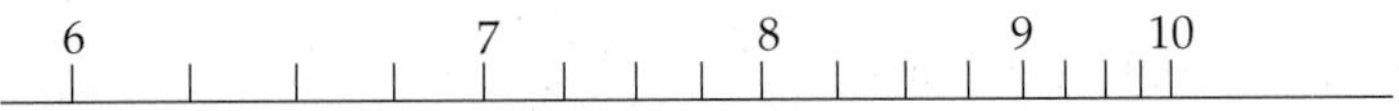

Each small division represents 0.25 units.

EXERCISE 9.10

1 This diagram shows a scale for an AM radio. Four different radio stations—A, B, C and D—are shown.

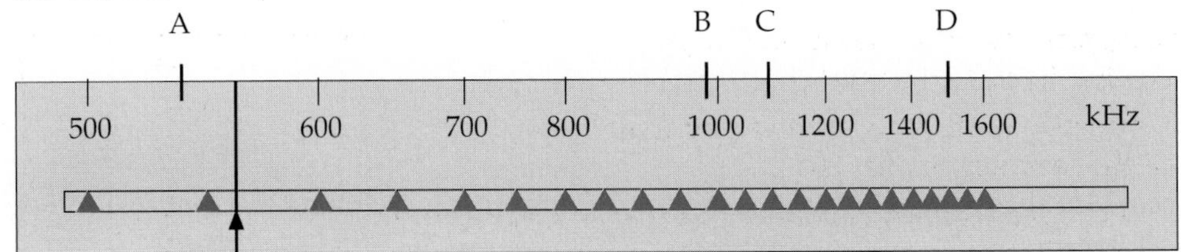

Match each letter A, B, C and D with one of these radio stations:

Radio Hauraki 1492 kHz
National Radio Wellington 530 kHz
Newstalk ZB Auckland 1080 kHz
Sports Station 981 kHz

2 The Richter scale is used to measure the strength of earthquakes. This scale is similar to the Richter scale.

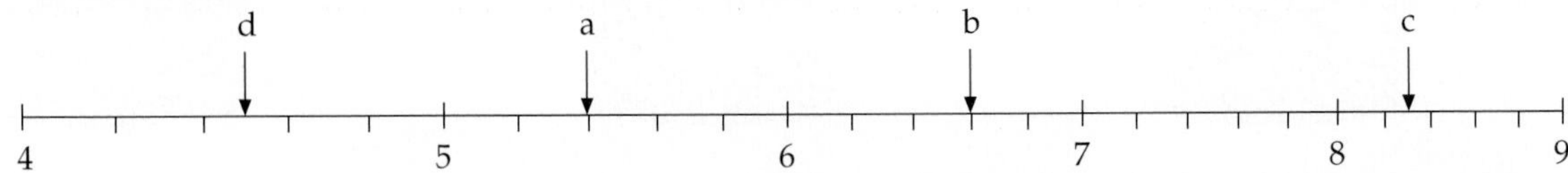

(a) How many units does each of the small divisions represent?

(b) Write down the readings at each of the points marked a, b, c and d.

3 This scale is from an FM radio.

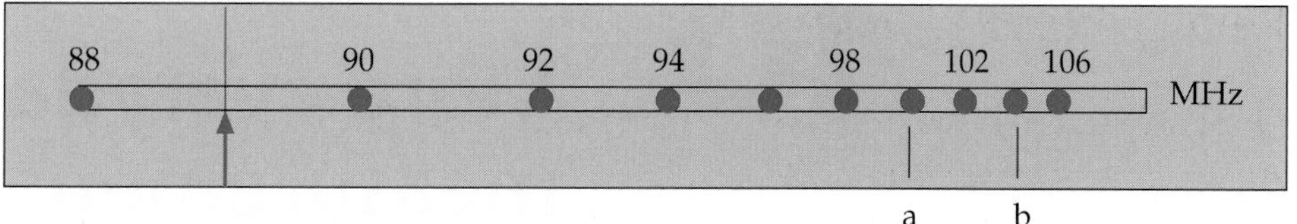

(a) What are the frequencies at the points marked a and b?

(b) The radio seems to be tuned to a point exactly half-way between 88 Mhz and 90 Mhz. Is this point more likely to be 88.8 Mhz, or 89.2 Mhz?

4 This scale is in decibels. Decibels are units used to measure the loudness of certain sounds.

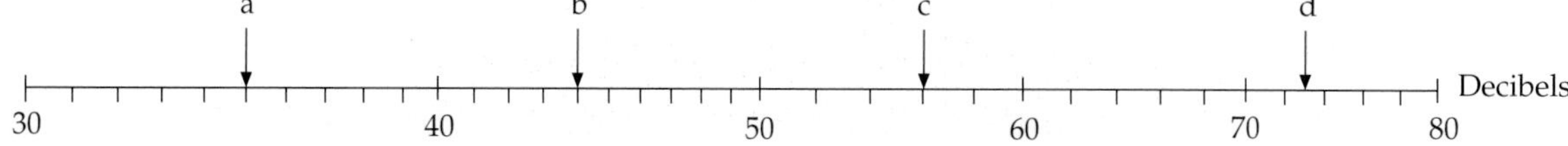

(a) Do the small units on this scale all represent the same units? Explain.

(b) Write down the readings at each of the points marked a, b, c and d.

5 An ammeter measures electrical current. The scale on this ammeter is non-uniform. The units are amps.

Write down the readings at each of the points marked a, b, c, d, e and f.

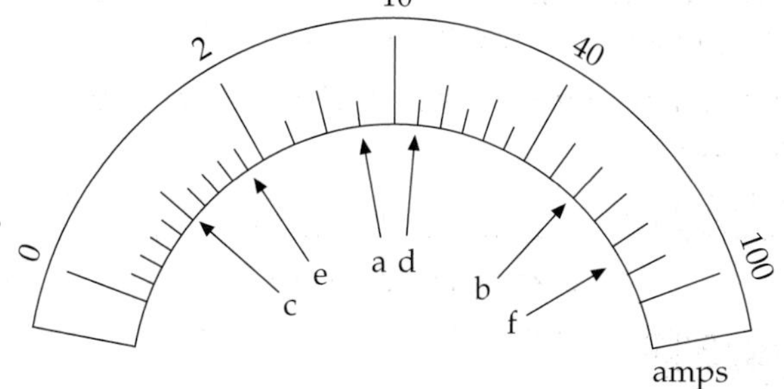

6 This diagram shows a measuring jug. The scale is in millilitres (mL).

(a) Write down the amount of liquid in the jug at each of the levels a, b, c and d.

(b) Use the scale (or otherwise) to write down the number of millilitres in 1 litre.

(c) Explain why this kind of jug gives a scale that is not uniform.

(d) What shape would the jug have to be for the scale to be uniform?

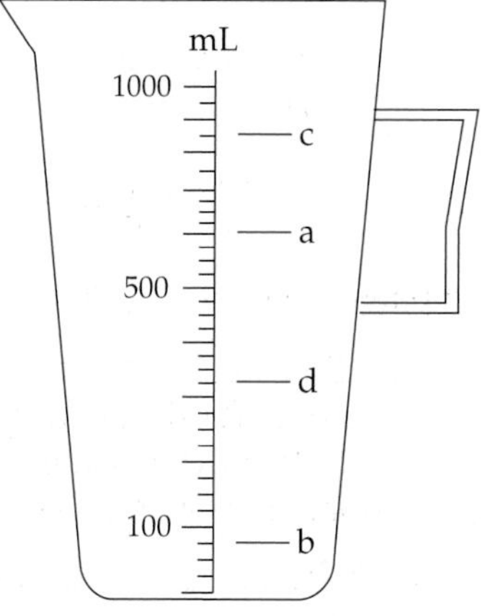

10 More everyday measurements

Length

CLASS INVESTIGATION

MEASURING LENGTHS

1 'A tall person can jump further than a short person.'
2 'Your height is the same as the distance between your finger-tips with your arms outstretched.'

Discuss how you could check these statements.

- What measuring instruments could you use?
- What units of measurement would you use?

Here's a way of checking the first statement.
You will need two measurements for each person.

- Measure their height by standing them against a scale on a wall.
- We will take the jump as being a 'standing' jump—the person stands on a line, and then jumps as far as they can. Measure the length of the jump using a tape measure.

Height

Distance jumped from a stand

- Write down the measurements (height and distance jumped) for each person.

Is there a pattern? One way of checking is to mark a cross for each person on a grid using squared paper:

The cross shows that a person who was 150 cm tall was able to jump 115 cm.

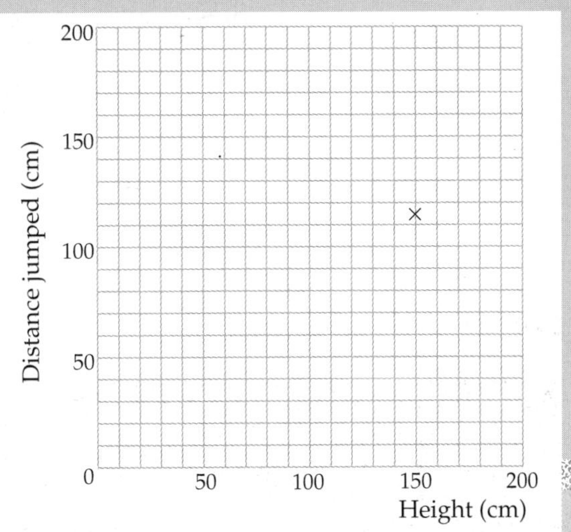

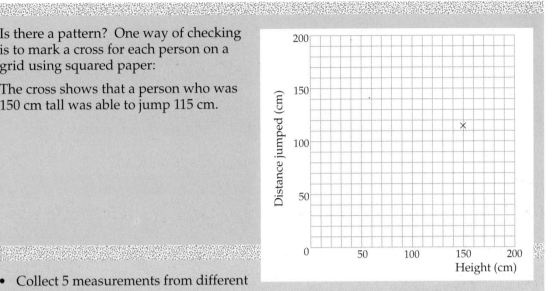

- Collect 5 measurements from different people in the class.
  Plot them on squared paper.
- What does your diagram show about the relationship between height and the distance jumped? Do your measurements agree with statement 1?
- Now try to check statement 2.

An **estimate** in Mathematics is an educated guess!

You should be able to do both of these:
- measure lengths accurately
- estimate lengths.

Example

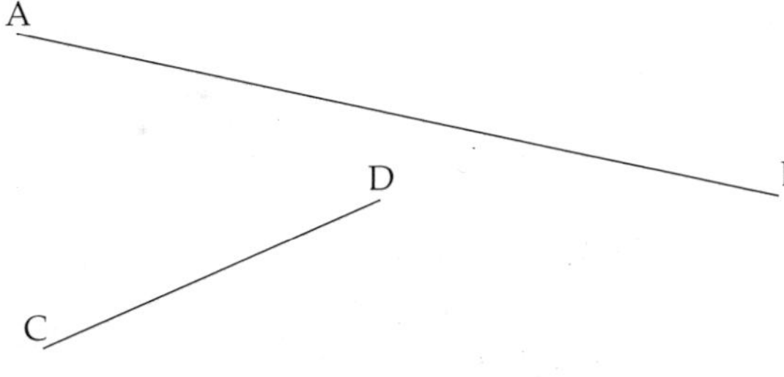

(a) Measure (in mm) the length of the line segment labelled AB.

(b) Estimate the length (in mm) of the line segment labelled CD.

Answer (a) The length is 72 mm.

(b) CD looks like it is about *half* the length of AB. A good guess would 35 mm (to take exactly half of 72 and say 36 mm would be too accurate.) In fact, it measures 34 mm.

EXERCISE 10.1

1 Use a ruler to measure the length of this key in mm.

2 Use a ruler to measure the length of this safety pin in cm.

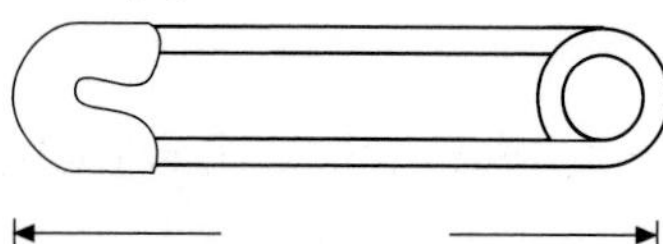

3 Estimate these lengths in mm.
Do not use a ruler. A line segment exactly 20 mm long has been shown as a guide.

20 mm

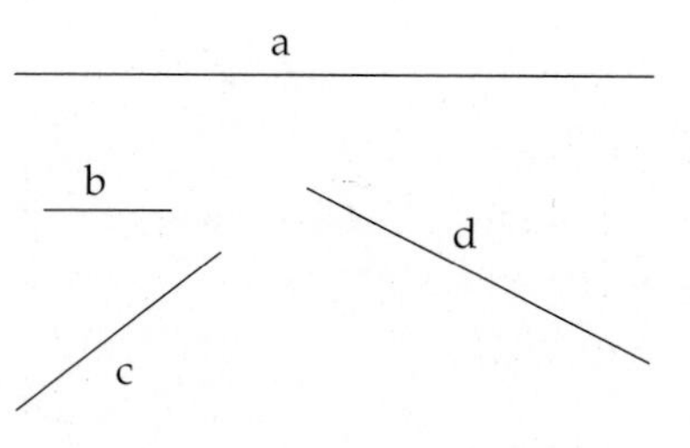

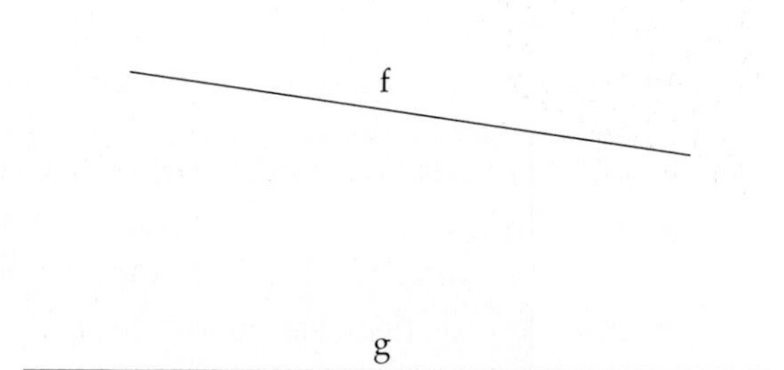

4 Here are six different line segments.

Make a copy of this table.

	Estimate of length (cm)	Actual measured length (cm)
a		
b		
c		
d		
e		
f		

1 cm

5 cm

a b c d e f

Follow these steps to complete the table:

- First write your estimate of the length (in cm) of each line segment.
- Then use a ruler to measure the length of each line segment.

5 Estimate the length of each of these objects. Choose your answers from this list of lengths: { 10 cm, 20 cm, 40 cm, 80 cm }
(a) the width of your foot (at its widest point)
(b) the length of a computer keyboard
(c) the width of a door
(d) the length of a telephone handpiece
(e) the length of your arm
(f) the height of a coffee mug
(g) the length of your hand span (distance from end of thumb to end of little finger when hand outstretched)

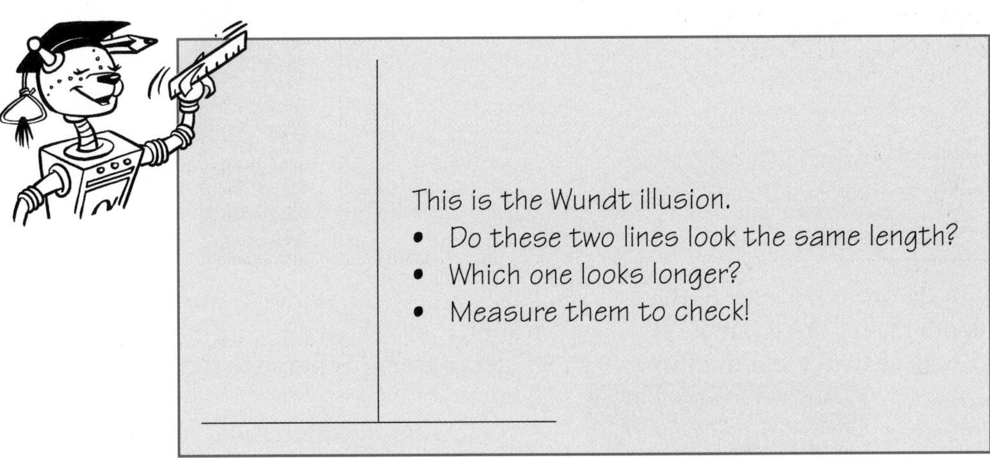

This is the Wundt illusion.
• Do these two lines look the same length?
• Which one looks longer?
• Measure them to check!

We measure length using **metric** units. Here are some:

Unit	Shortened to	Used for	Example
millimetres	mm	very accurate measurements	the diameter of a CD is 118 mm
centimetres	cm	approximate measurement of small objects, people, etc.	my height is 182 cm
metres	m	buildings, sport, etc.	the height of the Sky Tower is 328 m
kilometres	km	distances	it is 364 km from Dunedin to Christchurch

EXERCISE **10.2**

1 Which unit would you use to measure or estimate these lengths? Choose from this list: { millimetres, centimetres, metres, kilometres }.
(a) the width of a TV screen
(b) the distance from New Plymouth to Palmerston North
(c) the width of your little finger
(d) the distance from your Maths classroom to your English classroom
(e) the length of a cricket pitch
(f) the length of an ant

2 Choose the best measurement for each of these.

(a) length of a thumb nail: A 14 mm B 14 cm

(b) height at which a rescue helicopter flies: A 300 m B 300 km

(c) length of a ballpoint pen: A 15 mm B 15 cm

(d) height of a flagpole: A 7 cm B 7 m

3 The left-hand box contains distances to measure. The right-hand box contains measurements with units. Match each distance with the most likely measurement and unit.

(a) thickness of a credit card
(b) height of a door in a house
(c) the length of a hockey field
(d) the width of a ballpoint pen
(e) the length of a netball court
(f) the height of a student's desk
(g) the length of one of your shoes
(h) the thickness of a wooden door
(i) the distance a car can travel on a motorway in 4 minutes
(j) the length of a ballpoint pen

35 m
7 km
14 cm
1 mm
24 cm
2 m
100 m
70 cm
9 mm
4 cm

4 This road sign stands at the start of the main road south from Christchurch. It shows the distances to five main centres.

Ashburton	87
Timaru	164
Oamaru	248
Dunedin	364
Invercargill	585

(a) What units should be used in this sign?

(b) Use the information in the sign to work out these distances:

(i) Timaru to Oamaru

(ii) Ashburton to Invercargill

(c) Use the information in the sign to design another road sign showing the distances *north* from Oamaru.

5 The hair on your head grows at the rate of about 4 cm every 3 months.

(a) How many cm will it grow in six months?

(b) How many cm will it grow in one year?

(c) How many years would it take to grow from the top of your head to your waist?
(This is about 1 metre = 100 cm.)

6 Paul cycles from home to surf-lifesaving training and back, three times a week. The distance from his home to the surf-club is 6 km.

(a) How many km does he cycle each training day?

(b) How many km does he cycle in a week?

7 Jacqui cycled to school and back every day (Monday–Friday) for two weeks. Her bicycle odometer read 457 km at the beginning of the two weeks, and 511 km at the end. How far does Jacqui live from school?

8 The trip-meter on a rental car has four digits. The first three digits show kilometres. The last digit shows tenths of kilometres. Here is the distance travelled since the car was rented:

5 4 8 2/3

(a) How far has the car travelled (to the nearest km)?

(b) The car is driven another 832 km (exactly) before it is returned.

(i) What will be the distance for the whole trip?

(ii) What will be the reading on the trip-meter?

9 Here is the information on the back of a sewing pattern. It gives the length of material you need to make a T-shirt.

- There are three kinds of T-shirt: sleeveless, short-sleeved and long-sleeved
- Material comes in two widths: 115 cm and 150 cm
- Lengths are given for sizes 8 to 16

(a) Jill's measurements are: Bust 89, Waist 66, Hip 90. What size should she use?

(b) What length of material should each of these people buy?

(i) Delia is size 10 and wants to make a short-sleeved T-shirt. She has seen some material 115 cm wide that she wants.

4182 MISSES' T-SHIRTS
Close-fitting T-shirts have U-necklines and topstitch trim; raglan sleeves are very short, above-elbow or full-length with turned back cuffs. Purchased belts.
Pattern Sized For Moderate Stretch Knit Fabrics Only

6 Pattern Pieces
T - SHIRTS A, B, C
1. Front
2. Back
3. Sleeve A
4. Front Facing
5. Back Facing
6. Sleeve B, C

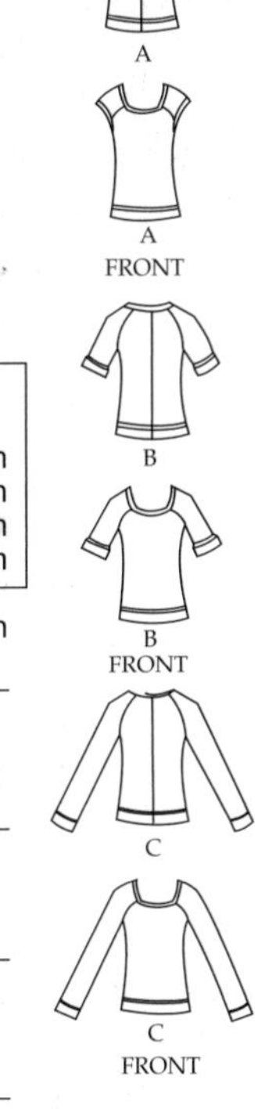

BODY MEASUREMENTS						
Size	8	10	12	14	16	
Bust	80	83	87	92	97	cm
Waist	61	64	67	71	76	cm
Hip	85	88	92	97	102	cm
Back Waist length	40	40.5	41.5	42	42.5	cm
BUST	80	83	87	92	97	cm
SIZES	**8**	**10**	**12**	**14**	**16**	
T -SHIRT A						
115 cm	0.90	1.00	1.10	1.10	1.10	m
150 cm	0.80	0.80	0.80	0.80	0.90	m
T-SHIRT B						
115 cm	1.30	1.30	1.30	1.40	1.40	m
150 cm	0.90	0.90	1.00	1.10	1.20	m
T-SHIRT C						
115 cm	1.50	1.60	1.60	1.60	1.60	m
150 cm	1.20	1.20	1.30	1.30	1.30	m
Width at lower edge						
T-Shirt A, B, C	87.5	90	94	99	104	cm
Finished back length from base of neck						
T-Shirt A, B, C	58.5	59	59.5	60.5	61	cm

(ii) Maree is size 16, and wants to make a sleeveless T-shirt. The only material she can buy is 150 cm wide.

(iii) Zara's measurements are Bust 90, Waist 70, Hip 95. She wants material that is 115 cm wide for a short-sleeved T-shirt.

(c) Rhonda has bought 0.90 m of material (115 cm wide) for a sleeveless T-shirt. What size is she?

Metric length conversions

STARTER

This shows part of a ruler with a scale in centimetres (cm).

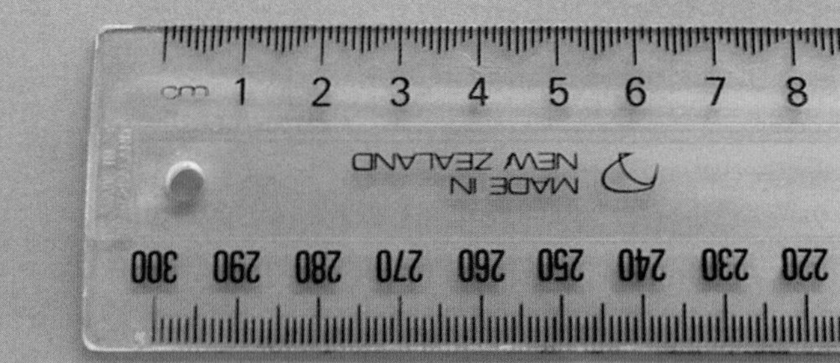

- The scale also shows millimetres (mm). How are the mm represented on this ruler?
- How many mm are there in 1 cm?

The length units mm, cm, m and km are all metric units.

The base unit is the metre (m). The other three are linked to this by multiplying/dividing by 10, 100, 1000, etc.

Example 1 m = 1000 mm

A millimetre is $\frac{1}{1000}$th of a metre

1 m = 100 cm

A centimetre is $\frac{1}{100}$th of a metre

1 km = 1000 m

You should choose a suitable unit depending on what you are measuring.

The width of this calculator could be written as 76 mm, or 7.6 cm, or 0.076 m.

It isn't appropriate to measure this in m!

76 mm
7.6 cm
0.076 m

This diagram shows the relationship between mm, cm, m and km. You can use it to convert (change) from one unit to another.

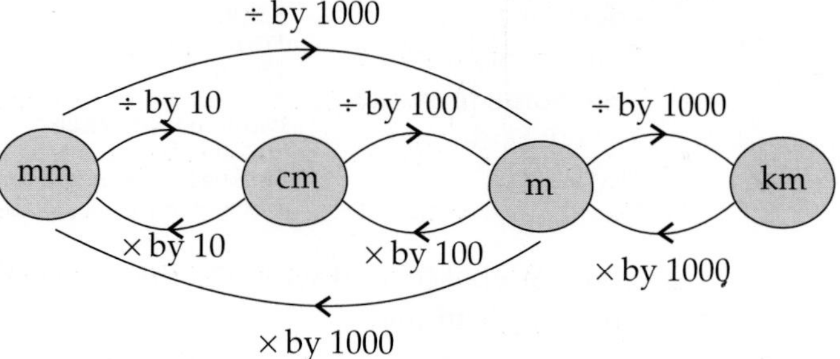

Examples Here are some conversions.

(a) **mm ⟷ cm**

Change 45 mm to cm	Divide by 10:	45 mm = 4.5 cm
Change 8 cm to mm	Multiply by 10:	8 cm = 80 mm

(b) **mm ⟷ m**

Change 850 mm to m	Divide by 1000:	850 mm = 0.85 m
Change 4.3 m to mm	Multiply by 1000:	4.3 m = 4300 mm

(c) **cm ⟷ m**

Change 120 cm to m	Divide by 100:	120 cm = 1.2 m
Change 1.82 m to cm	Multiply by 100:	1.82 m = 182 cm

(d) **km ⟷ m**

Change 3.8 km to m	Multiply by 1000:	3.8 km = 3800 m
Change 1600 m to km	Divide by 1000:	1600 m = 1.6 km

The metric system has been designed around multiples of 10. This is to make it easy to change from one unit to the other.

10.3

1

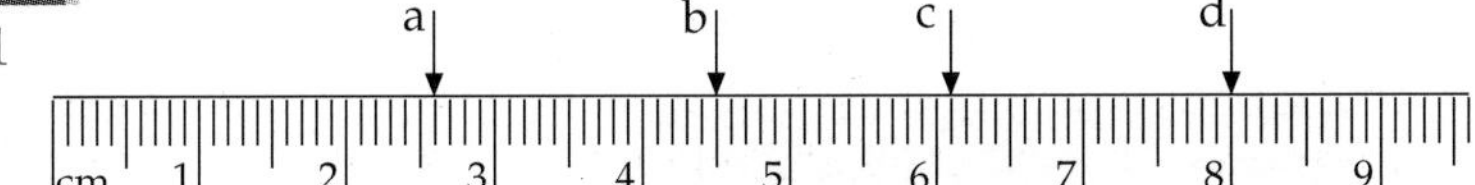

Write down each measurement a, b, c, and d in mm.

2 Write down each of the measurements in Question 1 in cm.

3 Change these lengths (given in mm) to cm.
(a) 80 mm (b) 35 mm (c) 120 mm (d) 94 mm

4 Change these lengths (given in cm) to mm.
(a) 6 cm (b) 4.2 cm (c) 13 cm (d) 8.3 cm

5 Change these lengths (given in mm) to m.
(a) 2000 mm (b) 1300 mm (c) 850 mm (d) 1479 mm

6 Change these lengths (given in m) to mm.
(a) 3 m (b) 4.6 m (c) 0.13 m (d) 0.018 m

7 Change these lengths (given in cm) to m.
(a) 400 cm (b) 530 cm (c) 80 cm (d) 73 cm

8 Change these lengths (given in m) to cm.
(a) 2 m (b) 1.7 m (c) 0.58 m (d) 0.08 m

9 Change these lengths (given in km) to m.
(a) 3 km (b) 4.2 km (c) 0.83 km (d) 0.075 km

10 Change these lengths (given in m) to km.
(a) 5000 m (b) 1350 m (c) 14 800 m (d) 500 m

11 Copy these conversions. Complete them so that the lengths are changed correctly.
(a) 4 m = ____ cm
(b) 60 cm = ___ mm
(c) 10 000 m = ____ km
(d) 2 km = ____ m
(e) 0.8 m = ____ mm
(f) 44 mm = ___ cm
(g) 830 mm = ___ m
(h) 900 cm = ___ m

12 Are the measurements in each of these pairs equal? Write *yes* or *no*.
(a) 80 m, 800 cm
(b) 9000 mm, 9 m
(c) 50 cm, 5 mm
(d) 1000 cm, 10 m

10.4

1 Paula swims 80 lengths of a swimming pool. The pool is 50 m long. How many km does she swim?

2 Tuariki entered for three races at the athletics sports: the 800 m, the 1500 m, and the 5000 m. What is the total length of these races? Give your answer in km.

3 A piece of wood 3.6 m long is cut into 4 equal lengths. What is the length of each piece, in mm?

4 A cook chops a stick of celery into 40 small pieces, of equal length. The celery originally measured 16 cm. How long is each piece in mm?

5 Here are two motorway signs:

A

Next exits:
Tristram Ave 1.2
Onewa Road 4.5

B

Clearance next bridge
4.72

(a) What units are being used in sign A?
(b) What units are being used in sign B?
(c) Change the units in sign A to m.
(d) Change the units in sign B to cm.
(e) Work out the distance between the two exits, to the nearest km.

INVESTIGATION

TOILET ROLLS

- How long is a roll of toilet paper? Investigate.
- Is the length given on the packaging? How would you check?
- Is it possible to work out the length of the whole roll by measuring individual pieces? Explain.

Set out your work as a project.

- Explain how you estimated or measured the length.
- Write down any calculations you made. Include any changing of units (mm, cm or m) you needed to do.

Further investigation

- Find out the price of singles, twin-packs, 4-packs and 6-packs of the same brand of toilet paper.
- Which pack represents the best value for money? Explain by writing down some calculations.

Estimating lengths from scale drawings and photos

Builders, architects and other designers often use scale drawings. A **scale drawing** represents a real-life situation. It shows all lengths in proportion, but is usually reduced to fit on paper or a computer screen. Scale drawings are often used as guides or plans.

Example

This is a scale-drawing of a basketball court. The scale is 1 : 500. This means that the lengths in the basketball court are actually 500 times as long as drawn here. So, 1 cm on the drawing represents 500 cm (or 5 m) on the court.

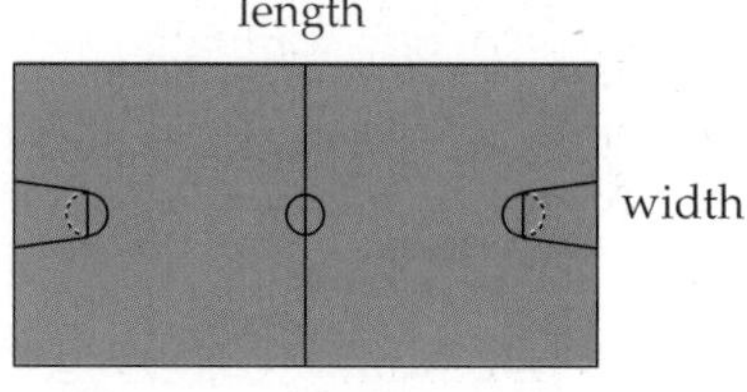

Scale: 1 : 500

(a) What are the measurements of length and width in the scale drawing?
(b) What are the measurements of length and width in the real basketball court?

Answer

(a) The length in the scale drawing is 4 cm.
The width in the scale drawing is 2 cm.

(b) Multiply these by 500 to work out the actual measurements:
Real length = 500 × 4 cm = 2000 cm. Changing this to m gives 2000 ÷ 100 = 20 m.
Real width = 500 × 2 cm = 1000 cm. Changing this to m gives 1000 ÷ 100 = 10 m.

EXERCISE 10.5

1 This is a scale drawing of a calculator. The scale is 1 : 3. This means the actual measurements are 3 times the length shown here.
(a) Measure the width and height in the drawing.
(b) Work out the actual width and height of the calculator.

2 This is a scale drawing of a rugby field.
The scale is 1 : 2000.

(a) Measure the length and width in the drawing.
(b) Work out the actual length and width of the rugby field. Give your answer in m.
(c) How far is it from one corner of the field to the opposite corner? Use the scale drawing to estimate.

3 This map of downtown Auckland has been drawn using a scale of 1 : 10 000. This means that 1 mm on the map = 10 000 mm (or 10 m) on the ground.

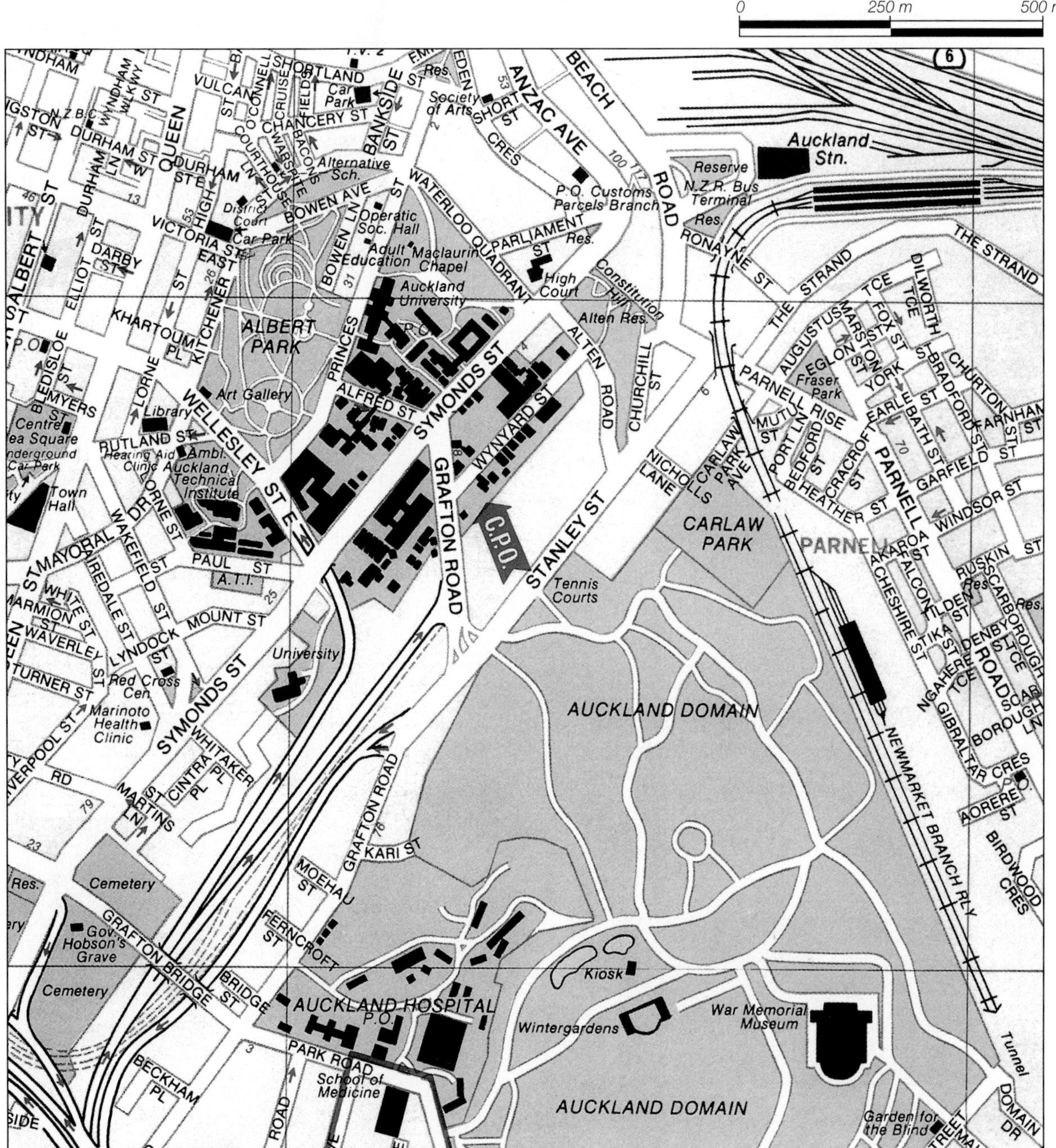

Make measurements and use the scale to estimate:

(a) the distance across Albert Park from Kitchener Street to Princes Street

(b) the distance along Symonds Street from the High Court to the Marinoto Health Clinic

(c) the length of Grafton Bridge (it starts at Symonds Street and ends at Grafton Road)

(d) the distance of railway track from the Auckland Station to the tunnel (allow for the bend in the track).

4 A scale of 1 : 200 has been used for this house plan.

(a) Work out the length of the hall in m.

(b) What is the width of the hall? Give your answer in cm.

(c) What are the dimensions (length and width) of the lounge?

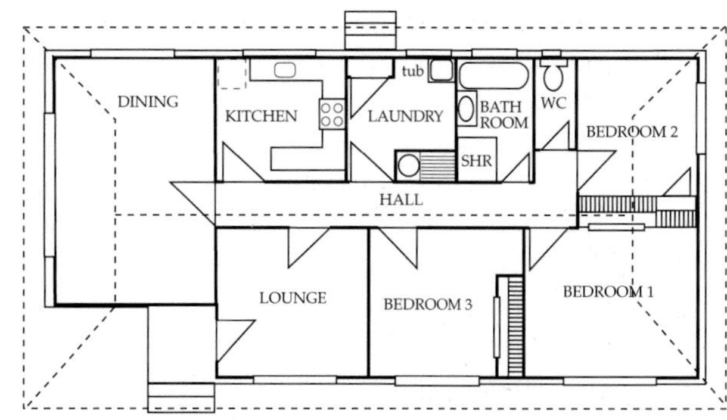

5 This is a plan of a small paddock. It has been drawn using a scale of 1 : 500. Give all your answers in metres.

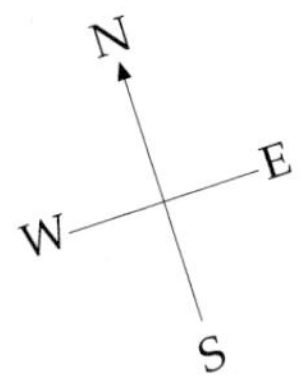

(a) How long is the fence along the western boundary?

(b) How long is the row of trees along the northern boundary?

(c) What is the distance from the gate to the avocado tree?

6 The diagram below shows a pup tent. It is *not* drawn to scale. The length of the base is 4 metres. The height of the tent is 3 metres.

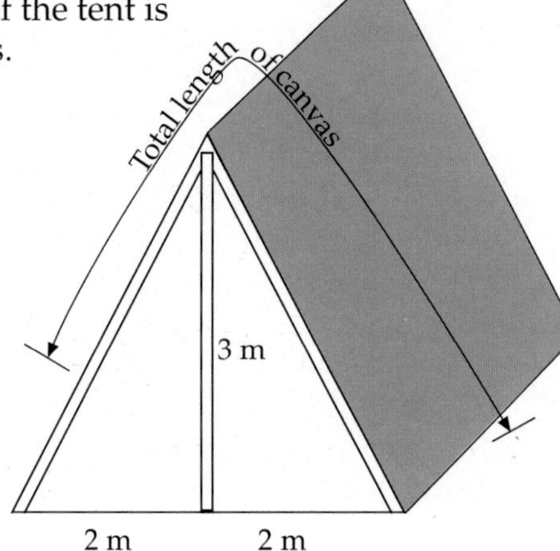

Make a scale drawing of the front of the tent (a triangle with a base of 4 cm and a height of 3 cm). Use this to estimate the total length of canvas needed to cover the tent. (This is the distance from ground level on one side, to ground level on the other side).

7 This is a blown-up diagram of an adult flea. The scale is 20 : 1, meaning 20 mm in the drawing is 1 mm in real life. Measure the length, and use the scale to estimate the actual length of an adult flea.

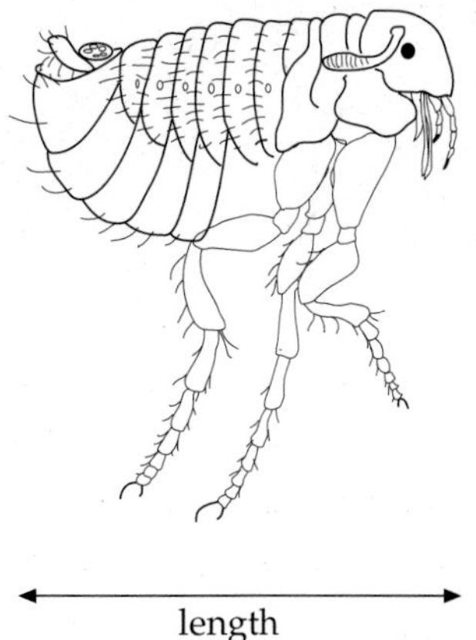

8 Included in this photo are a very large tree, some cars and two people underneath the tree.

(a) A tall person is about 2 m in height (to the nearest m). Use this approximation to estimate the height of the tree.

(b) One of these gives the best estimate of the length of a car (to the nearest m). Which one?

A 2 m B 4 m C 10 m

(c) Use your answer to part (b) to estimate the width of the tree at its widest part.

9

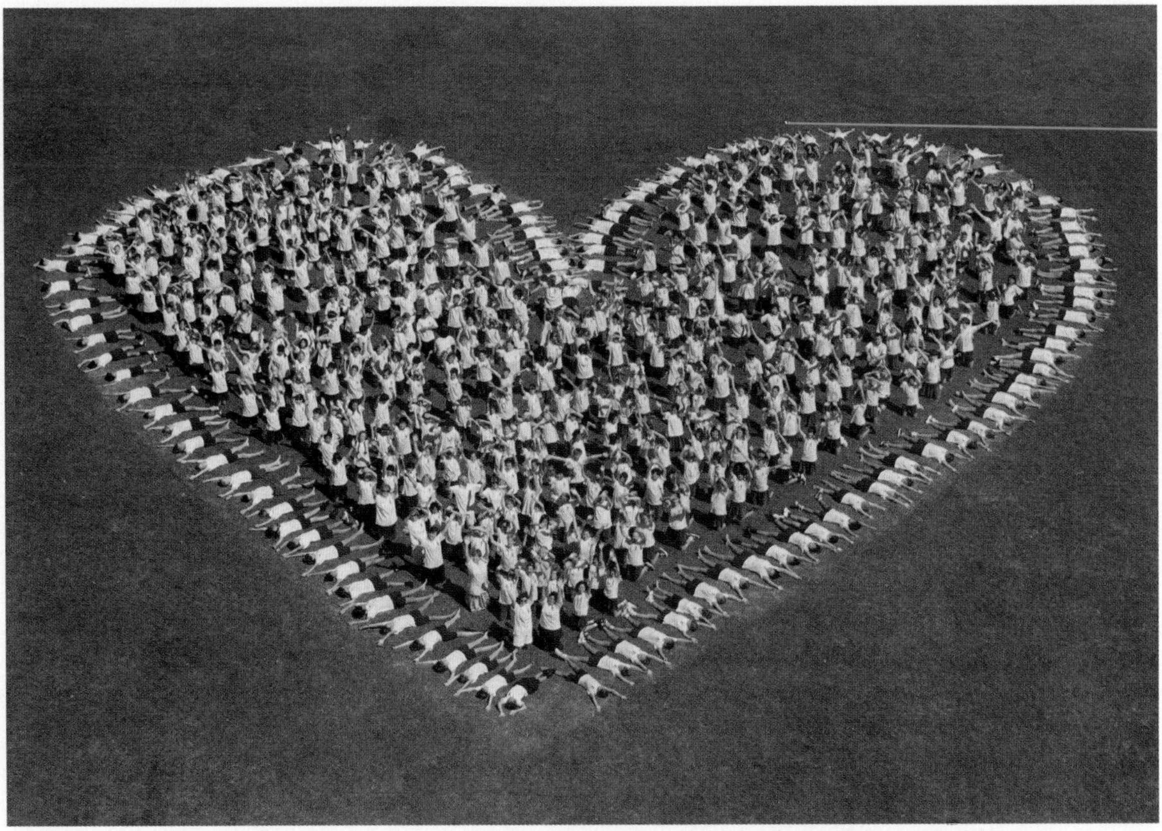

Here's a photo of one of the largest human hearts you are ever likely to see. It shows about 560 pupils from Takapuna Normal Intermediate School, positioned on the ground.

Estimate the width of the heart. Explain how you made your estimate.

Speed

STARTER

Two cars are being tested for fuel economy. They are driven steadily around a race-track.

Car A travelled 400 km in 5 hours

Car B travelled 600 km in 8 hours

- Which car travelled at the faster speed?
- Explain what calculations you make to work out speed.

The **speed** (or **velocity**) of an object measures how fast it is travelling.

In real life, the speed of an object tends to change. So, here we will only consider *average* speed.

We use km/h as our units for speed.

To calculate speed, we divide the *distance travelled* by the *time taken to cover that distance.*

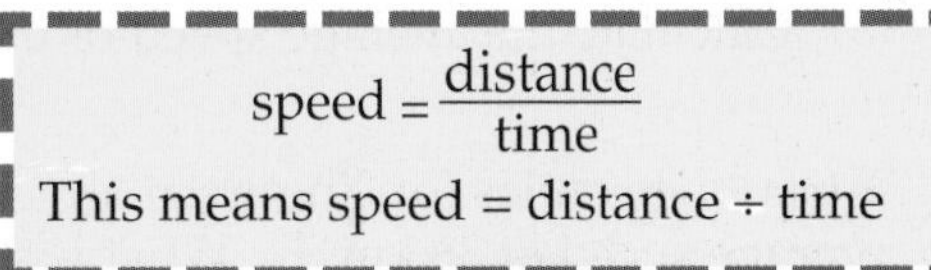

$$\text{speed} = \frac{\text{distance}}{\text{time}}$$

This means speed = distance ÷ time

Example A bus travels a distance of 300 km in 4 hours. Calculate the average speed of the bus.

Answer

$$\text{speed} = \frac{\text{distance}}{\text{time}} = \frac{300 \text{ km}}{4 \text{ h}} = 75 \text{ km/h}$$

With speed, distance and time, you only need two measurements to be able to work out the third one.

distance = speed × time

Example Jenny walks for 2 hours at an average speed of 4 km/h. How far did she walk?

Answer

$$\begin{aligned} \text{distance} &= \text{speed} \times \text{time} \\ &= 4 \times 2 \\ &= 8 \text{ km} \end{aligned}$$

$$\text{time} = \frac{\text{distance}}{\text{speed}}$$

or time = distance ÷ speed

Example Paul cycles 80 km at an average speed of 32 km/h. Work out how long it took him.

Answer

$$\text{time} = \frac{\text{distance}}{\text{speed}} = \frac{80}{32} = 2.5 \text{ hours}$$

EXERCISE 10.6

1 A train takes 10 hours to travel 800 km. What is its average speed?

2 A ship travels 360 km in a day (24 hours). What is the average speed of the ship?

3 A powerboat takes half an hour to travel 16 km.
   (a) How far would the powerboat travel in 1 hour if it kept the same speed?
   (b) Work out the speed at which the powerboat is travelling.

4 An airplane travels for 6 hours at an average speed of 850 km/h. What distance does it travel?

5 A racing car does 200 laps of a circuit 1.5 km long. This takes 2 hours.
   (a) What is the total distance that the car travels?
   (b) Calculate the average speed of the car.

6 A triathlete cycles for 2 hours at an average speed of 36 km/h. What is the total distance travelled?

7 A bus is travelling at an average speed of 75 km/h. How long would it take to complete a 300 km journey?

8 Calculate the average speed of these journeys:
   (a) 68 km in 4 hours
   (b) 1280 km in 2 hours
   (c) 50 km in half an hour (i.e. 0.5 h)

9 Calculate the distance travelled in these journeys:
   (a) 6 hours at an average speed of 30 km/h
   (b) 2 days (48 h) at an average speed of 15 km/h
   (c) 15 minutes (0.25 h) at an average speed of 100 km/h

10 Calculate the time taken for these journeys:
   (a) 100 km at an average speed of 50 km/h
   (b) 900 km at an average speed of 20 km/h
   (c) 1500 m (1.5 km) at an average speed of 3 km/h

11 Hemi ran for half an hour at an average speed of 16 km/h. He then walked for 2 hours at 5 km/h. What was the total distance he travelled?

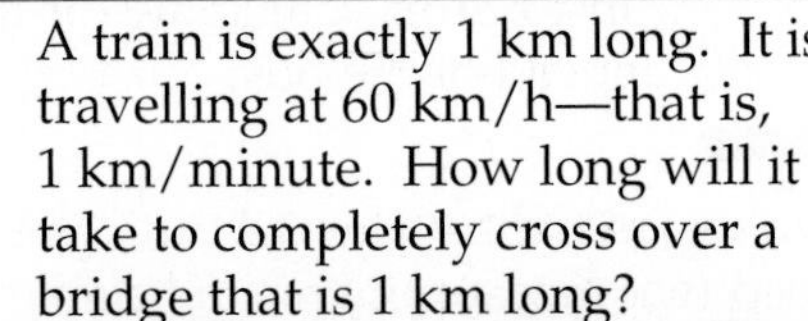

12 A train is exactly 1 km long. It is travelling at 60 km/h—that is, 1 km/minute. How long will it take to completely cross over a bridge that is 1 km long?

Weight or mass

There is a difference between **mass** and **weight.**

- Mass is the amount of matter in an object. This is the same everywhere.
- Weight depends on the pull of gravity. For example, astronauts on the Moon's surface feel 'lighter' than back on Earth. Their weight has changed, but they still have the same mass.

Because we are all on the Earth rather than the Moon, we can use the terms 'mass' and 'weight' for the same thing this year.

We measure mass and weight using metric units. Here are some examples:

Unit	Shortened to	Used for	Example
milligrams	mg	very accurate scientific measurement	a cup of instant coffee has 50 mg of caffeine
grams	g	accurate measuring	a recipe takes 10 grams of sugar
kilograms	kg	people, objects that can be carried	my weight is 52 kg
tonnes	t	heavy objects	a shipping container weighs 14 tonnes

EXERCISE 10.7

1–8 *Which unit of mass would be the most suitable unit for these?*

1 your own weight

2 an eyelash

3 a railway engine

4 a tea bag

5 a sack of potatoes

6 a Boeing 747 aircraft

7 a bag of cement

8 a box of matches

9 Choose the best measurement for each of these:

(a) mass of a cricket ball:
A 250 g B 250 kg

(b) weight of a raisin
A 2 kg B 2 g

(c) mass of a blue whale
A 70 kg B 70 tonnes

10 Match the objects in the left-hand box with the most likely mass in the right-hand box.

(a) a taxi	2 t
(b) this book	100 kg
(c) a full bucket of water	30 g
(d) a Boeing 747	10 kg
(e) a pencil	500 g
(f) a newborn baby	3 kg
(g) a drawing pin	2 g
(h) a refrigerator	45 kg
(i) a packet of butter	1 kg
(j) an average Year 9 student	380 t

Metric weight or mass conversions

The units mg, g, kg and tonnes are all metric units.

The base unit is the gram (g). The other three are linked to this by multiplying/dividing by 1000.

Examples

1 g = 1000 mg   A milligram is $\frac{1}{1000}$th of a gram

1 kg = 1000 g   A gram is $\frac{1}{1000}$th of a kilogram

1 tonne = 1000 kg   A kilogram is $\frac{1}{1000}$th of a tonne.

This diagram shows the relationship between mg, g, kg and tonnes. You can use it to convert (change) from one unit to another.

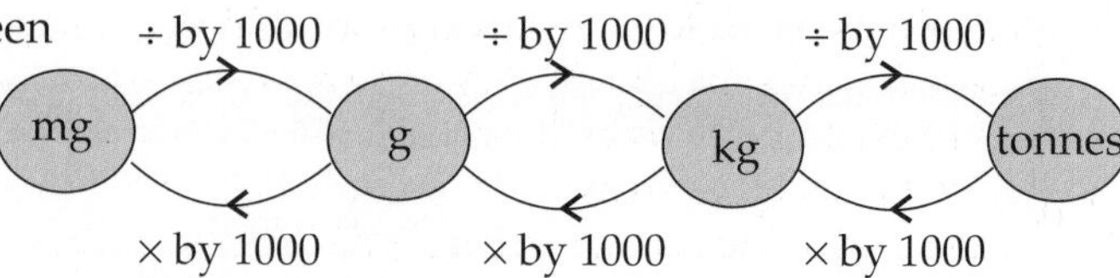

Examples Here are some conversions:

1 mg ⟷ g

Change 6000 mg to g	Divide by 1000:	6000 mg = 6 g
Change 8.5 g to mg	Multiply by 1000:	8.5 g = 8500 mg

2 g ⟷ kg

Change 3500 g to kg	Divide by 1000:	3500 g = 3.5 kg
Change 4 kg to g	Multiply by 1000:	4 kg = 4000 g

3 kg ⟷ tonnes

Change 1200 kg to t	Divide by 1000:	1200 kg = 1.2 t
Change 9.6 t to kg	Multiply by 1000:	9.6 t = 9600 kg

EXERCISE 10.8

1 Change these masses (given in mg) to g.
(a) 8000 mg (b) 3590 mg (c) 180 mg

2 Change these masses (given in g) to mg.
(a) 6 g (b) 12.9 g (c) 130 g

3 Change these masses (given in g) to kg.
(a) 2000 g (b) 4300 g (c) 850 g

4 Change these masses (given in kg) to g.
(a) 3 kg (b) 8.3 kg (c) 0.125 kg

5 Change these masses (given in kg) to tonnes.
(a) 4000 kg (b) 6530 kg (c) 850 kg

6 Change these masses (given in tonnes) to kg.
(a) 3 t (b) 5.9 t (c) 0.58 t

7 A cake recipe requires 750 g of flour, 300 g of butter and 400 g of sultanas. What is the total weight of this mixture, in kg?

8 A bookshop posts a parcel of 5 books, each weighing 850 g. What is the total weight in kg?

9 Three friends buy a tray of cherries weighing 1.2 kg. They share the cherries equally. What weight, in grams, should each friend get?

10 A carton contains 96 packets of cheese. Each packet weighs 400 g. What is the total weight (in kg) of the cheese?

11 A cake recipe requires half a 1.5 kg bag of flour. How much is this in grams?

12 A supermarket sells meat which is priced at $9.50 per kg. Work out the cost of:
(a) 2 kg (b) 3.6 kg (c) 500 g

13 Cashew nuts sell for $22 per kilogram at a bulk-bin shop. Calculate the cost of:
(a) 3 kg (b) 100 g (c) 250 g

14 At a wool auction, Merino fleece sells for $1200 per tonne. Calculate the cost of:
(a) 1 kg (b) 400 kg (c) 68 kg

15 This table gives average amounts of caffeine in some drinks and foods. Caffeine acts as a stimulant. In high doses it can cause insomnia (sleeplessness), jitteriness, and tension. Caffeine becomes toxic (poisonous) at about 5 grams—this would all need to be consumed in one hour.

Where does caffeine come from?	Amount
Instant coffee (200 mL cup)	50 mg
Espresso (200 mL cup)	190 mg
Cola drink (330 mL can)	40 mg
Cocoa (200 mL cup)	5 mg
Milk chocolate (100 g)	20 mg
Dark chocolate (100 g)	80 mg
Cold/flu tablets	25 mg
Nodoz tablet	100 mg
Jolt (soft drink) 330 mL	50 mg

Source: Consumer, *issue 352, Sept 1996.*

(a) Which kind of food or drink on the list has the least caffeine?

(b) Which kind has the most?

(c) How many cups of instant coffee would give you 1 g of caffeine?

(d) How much caffeine is there in a 400 g block of milk chocolate?

(e) To be poisoned by caffeine, you would need to consume 5 g in an hour. This is the equivalent of drinking 125 cans of cola (about 2 cans a minute!). Explain how this figure (i.e. 125 cans) is worked out using the information in the table. Write down your calculations, and any conversions from g to mg you need to make.

INVESTIGATION

UNIT PRICES IN SUPERMARKETS

Many large supermarkets have 'unit price' labels on the shelves. These allow you to compare prices quickly.

Example

Coffee sugar 500 g
$4.39
Unit price per 100 g: 87.8 cents
Coffee sugar 250 g
$2.29
Unit price per 100 g: 91.6 cents

- Which size of coffee sugar is the best value?
- Explain how the unit price for the 250 g packet is worked out from the information in the top two rows of the label. Write down the calculation that gives 91.6 cents.

- Choose **three** different supermarket products which are sold in different-sized packaging. Here are some suggestions:
  —cola drinks
  —jam
  —flour
  —tomato sauce
- In each case, work out the unit prices for the different sizes.
- Write two or three sentences about:
  —whether there is a significant saving in price
  —some of the advantages of buying in bulk
  —some of the disadvantages of buying in bulk.

- Present your findings in the form of a project.
- Write simple explanations so that a person who doesn't know about unit pricing could follow your reasoning.

Liquids

Liquids (such as water) are measured as volumes.
Units of volume are, for example, litres (L) and millilitres (mL).
There are 1000 mL in a litre.

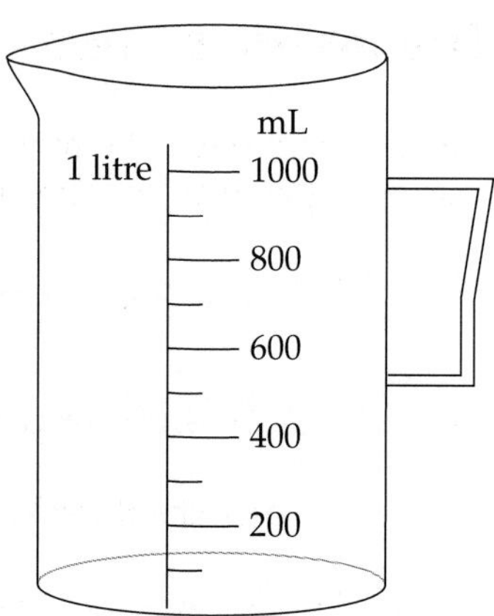

- Litres are used for units of volume because 1 litre of water weighs exactly 1 kg. Therefore, 1 mL weighs exactly 1 g.
- Sometimes the volume of liquids is called **capacity**.

This diagram shows the relationship between mL and litres.
Use it to convert (change) from one unit to the other.

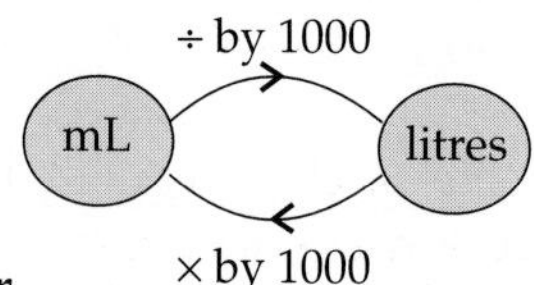

Example 200 mL of milk is poured from a 1 litre container. How much milk is left in the container?

Answer 1 litre = 1000 mL
Amount left = 1000 – 200 = 800 mL

EXERCISE 10.9

1 Write these liquid volumes in litres:
(a) 4000 mL
(b) 2250 mL
(c) 800 mL

2 Write these liquid volumes in millilitres (mL):
(a) 5 L
(b) 1.8 L
(c) 0.5 L

3 A family drinks 3 cartons of milk a day. Each carton holds 600 mL. How much milk do they drink:
(a) in mL?
(b) in litres?

4 A recipe uses 50 mL of milk. This is poured from a full 1 litre bottle. How much is left?

5 The instructions for making cordial say: 'add 400 mL of concentrate to 2 litres of water'. How much cordial will this produce?

6 Soft drinks are sold in cans that hold 333 mL. They are also sold in 2 litre plastic bottles. How many cans would hold about the same amount of soft drink as a 2 litre bottle?

7 Sue uses a old plastic milk-container (holding 600 mL) to carry water to her car radiator. She estimates that she poured in eight and a half containers-full. Estimate the amount of water poured in, to the nearest litre.

8 An ice-cream scoop holds about 80 mL. How many scoops of ice-cream could be taken from a 2 litre container of ice-cream?

9 A full coffee urn holds 2 litres. Mike uses it to fill up coffee mugs until the coffee runs out. Each mug holds 150 mL.
(a) How many coffee mugs will be needed?
(b) How much coffee will there be in the last mug?

The metric system—prefixes

One reason we use the metric system is because it has a good system of prefixes. The same prefixes are all used for length, weight and liquid volume.

Examples m is short for milli $\left(\frac{1}{1000}\right)$ e.g.: mm, mg, mL

c is short for centi $\left(\frac{1}{100}\right)$ e.g.: cm

k is short for kilo (1000 ×) e.g.: km, kg

The prefix tells you the *size* of the unit. The second letter tells you the base unit. This tells you what you are measuring.

EXERCISE 10.10

1 Which unit is used to measure these? (Choose from metre or kilometre, gram or kilogram, millilitre or litre.)
- (a) the amount of paint in a bucket
- (b) the height of your classroom
- (c) water in a hot-water cylinder
- (d) the amount of sliced ham bought at a supermarket
- (e) the distance travelled from Wellington to Picton across Cook Strait
- (f) soft drink in a plastic bottle
- (g) the length of Auckland's Harbour Bridge
- (h) the amount of potatoes in a sack

2 Copy these sentences. Then insert the correct numbers in the gaps. Choose from { 10, 100, 1000 }.
- (a) 1 km = ____ m
- (b) 1 m = ____ cm
- (c) 1 m = ____ mm
- (d) 1 cm = ____ mm
- (e) 1 kg = ___ g
- (f) 1 litre = ____ mL
- (g) 1 g = ____ mg
- (h) 1 tonne = ____ kg

3 Copy these sentences. Then insert the correct metric units.
- (a) 5000 m = 5 ____
- (b) 100 ____ = 1 m
- (c) 4 kg = 4000 ____
- (d) 600 ____ = 0.6 litres
- (e) 2 tonnes = 2000 ____

4 Change these units:
- (a) 3 km to m
- (b) 9300 g to kg
- (c) 630 cm to m
- (d) 4 m to cm
- (e) 3.2 kg to g
- (f) 5000 kg to tonnes
- (g) 80 mm to cm
- (h) 2.1 litres to mL
- (i) 13 000 m to km
- (j) 500 mL to litres
- (k) 40 cm to mm

INVESTIGATION

THE SPECTACULAR SKY TOWER

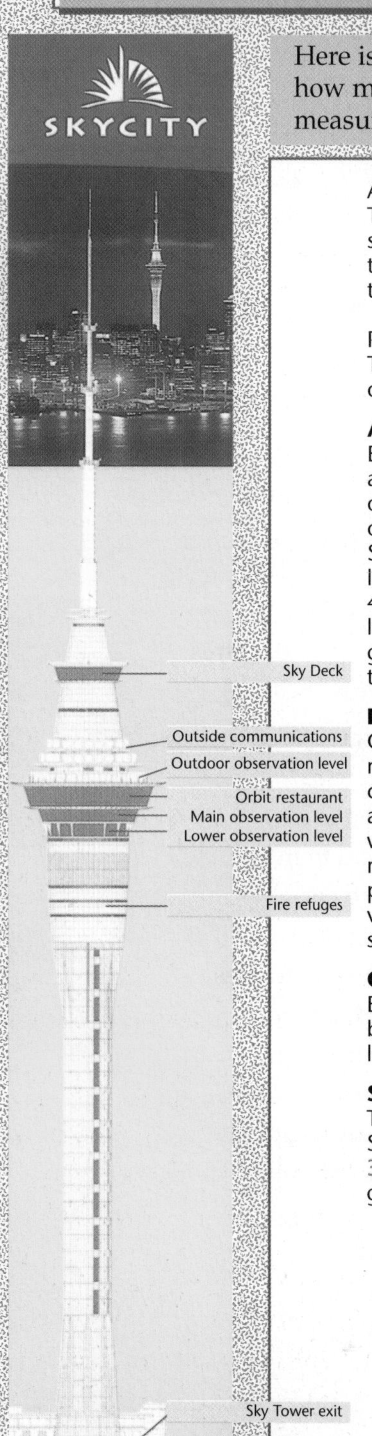

Here is an article about Auckland's Sky Tower. Read it, and notice how many metric measurements are given. 13 different measurements are mentioned—these have been highlighted.

At 328 metres (over 1000 feet), Sky Tower is New Zealand's tallest structure and most spectacular tourist, broadcasting and telecommunications facility.

Taller than the Eiffel Tower in Paris and Sydney's AMP Tower, Sky Tower is expected to attract almost one million visitors each year.

Access

Entry to Sky Tower's lifts is through an underground gallery at the base of the tower. Access to the observation and restaurant levels of Sky Tower is via three glass-fronted lifts capable of transporting 450 people every 30 minutes. The lift ride from the underground gallery to the main observation level takes a speedy 40 seconds.

Restaurant

Orbit, Sky Tower's revolving restaurant, offers innovative, contemporary New Zealand cuisine and a showcase of New Zealand wine. The restaurant makes a full revolution every 60 minutes, and provides guests with a stunning view of the cityscape and surrounding areas.

Outdoor observation level

Equipped with high-powered binoculars, the outdoor observation level is open to the elements.

Sky Deck

The highest public viewing area in Sky Tower, Sky Deck features 360 degree views through seamless glass.

Construction facts

The main structure of Sky Tower is a reinforced concrete shaft, measuring 12 metres in diameter. It is supported by eight reinforced concrete 'legs' at the base, connected to the shaft by a concrete collar and designed to spread force load. Sky Tower's foundations go down more than 15 metres into the earth.

The upper floors of Sky Tower have been constructed using composite materials, structural steel, pre-cast concrete and reinforced concrete.

Telecommunication facilities, above and below the centre pod, are housed on silver-aluminium clad communications floors.

Emergency stairs and service utilities are located within the centre of the shaft.

Some construction statistics

Sky Tower has used:

- 2000 tonnes of reinforcing steel
- 660 tonnes of structural steel, including 170 tonnes in the mast.

Safety

Sky Tower has been designed to provide a high level of performance in the event of earthquake, severe wind storms or fire.

Wind

The Sky Tower structure has been designed to remain essentially undamaged during storms with winds (at the restaurant level) gusting to 200 km/h. Such winds are assessed to have an average return period in the order of 1000 years, and are expected to result in sway at the top of the concrete shaft of approximately one metre.

Find each of these numbers in the article. Write the numbers down with their units. Next, write down what is being measured for each one. Choose from { time, length, weight, speed, angles }. 328 has been done for you.

1	
12	
15	
30	
40	
60	
170	
200	
328	328 m, length
360	
660	
1000	
2000	

11 Area

STARTER

- Draw a rectangle in your book. Make it 10 squares high and 20 squares wide.

Take out a 5 cent coin. Use it to draw circles inside the rectangle. The circles should be as close together as possible. Keep drawing circles until no more can fit inside.

- How many circles have you drawn?
- Copy and complete this sentence: 'The area of this rectangle is ____ circles'.
- Why are circles not a good shape to measure area with?
- Can you suggest a better shape to use?
- How many squares are there inside your rectangle?
- Copy and complete this sentence: 'The area of this rectangle is ____ squares'.

Counting squares

One way of working out area is by **counting squares**.

To measure area we use units like:

- square centimetres, written cm^2
- square metres, written m^2

This square, with sides of 1 cm, has an area of exactly 1 cm^2.

1 cm^2

Your exercise book is probably ruled up into smaller squares than this.
To make things easy, assume the squares in all the diagrams here are **unit squares**. In other words, assume they measure exactly 1 cm^2 even though they actually have other measurements.

Example By counting or estimating squares, work out the area in cm^2 of each of these shapes:

(a)

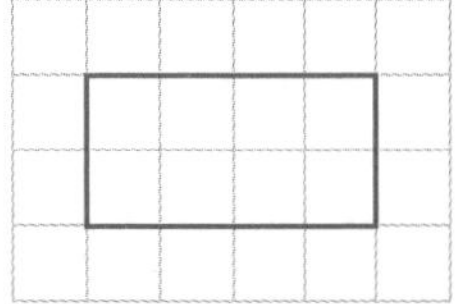

(b)

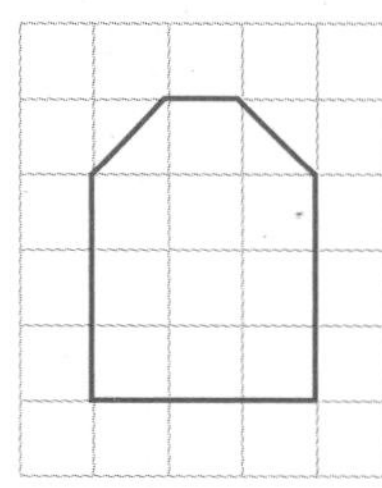

(c)

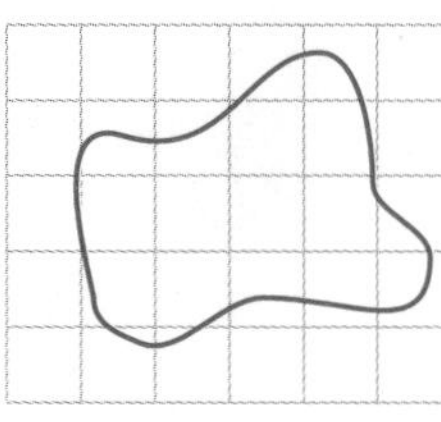

Answer (a) There are 8 squares, so the area is 8 cm^2.

(b) There is the equivalent of 11 squares—2 half-squares at the top make 1 square. So, the area is 11 cm^2.

(c) The area is about 12 cm^2.

With irregular shapes—like (c)—area is harder to work out. How do you know whether to count a part-square or not?
Here's a good way to estimate the area:

- if more than half of a square is inside the shape, count the square
- if less than half of a square is inside the shape, don't count it.

EXERCISE 11.1

1–4 *Work out the area of these shapes by counting squares. Each square represents 1 cm^2.*

1

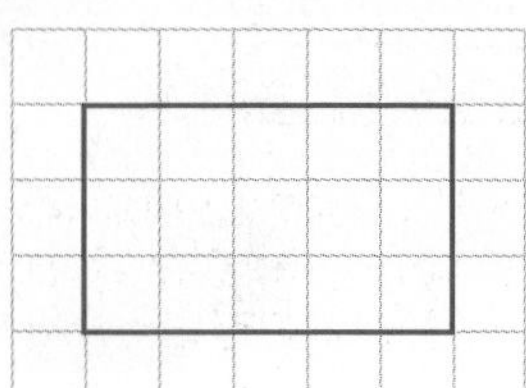

2

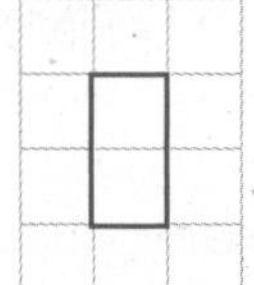

3

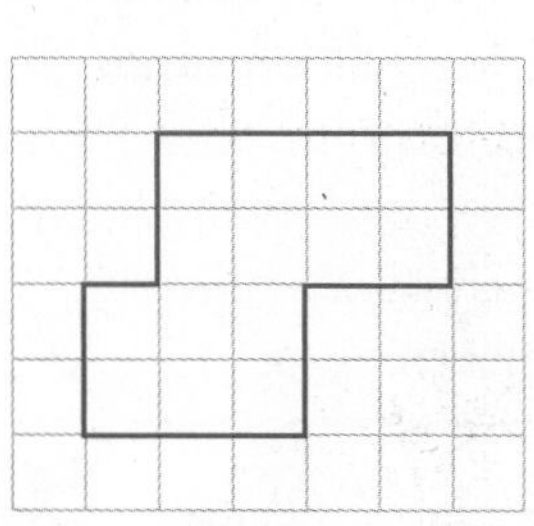

4

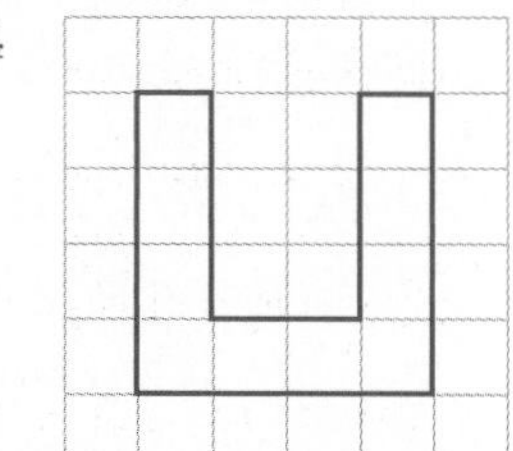

5 Often, shapes are not just made up of whole-unit squares. What fraction of a unit square are the shaded parts of these shapes?

(a)

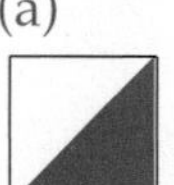

(b)

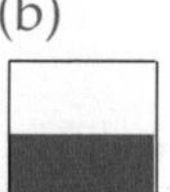

(c)

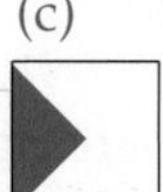

(d)

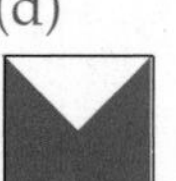

(e)

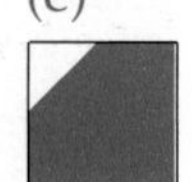

6–10 *Work out the area of these shapes, by counting squares and parts of squares. Each square represents 1 cm^2.*

6

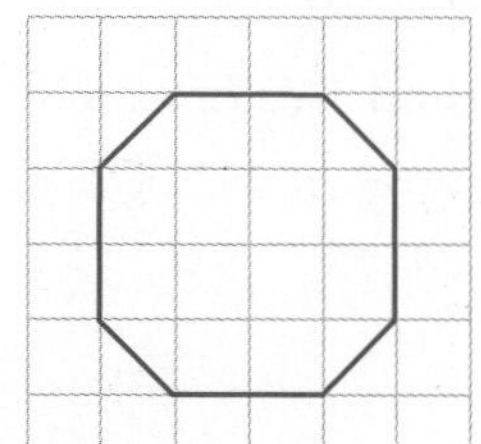

7

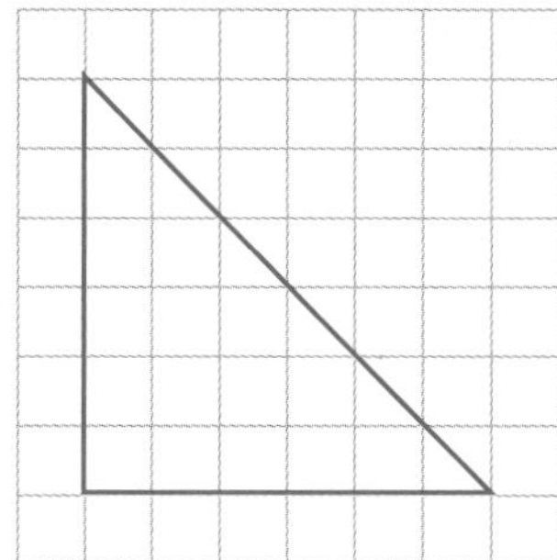

8

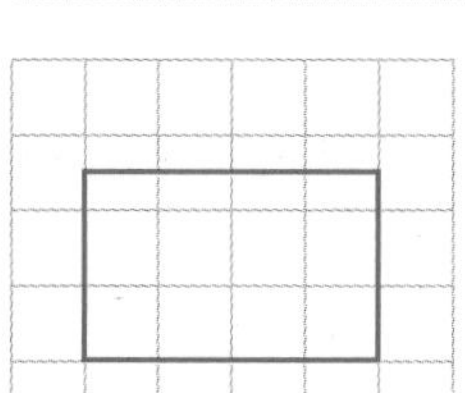

9

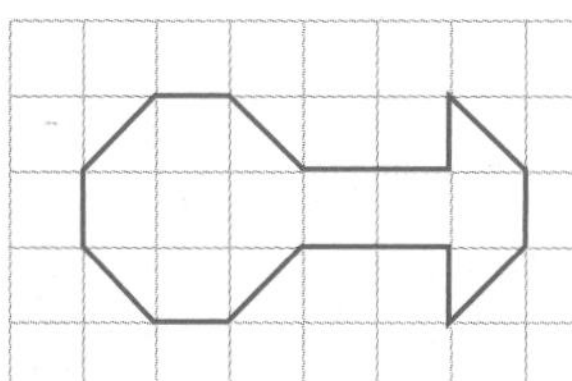

10

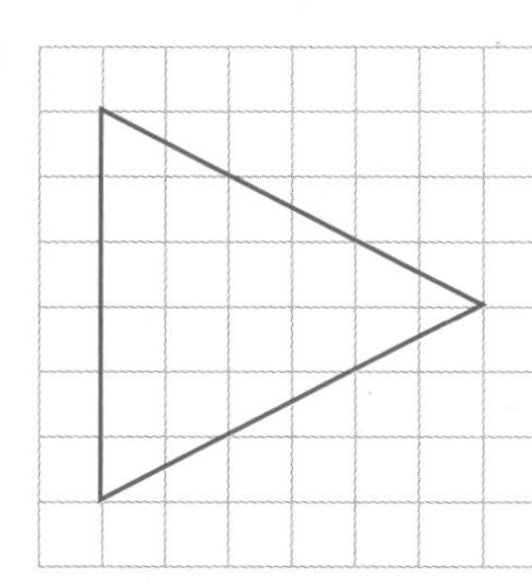

11–12 *Estimate the areas of these shapes, by counting or not counting part-squares.*

11

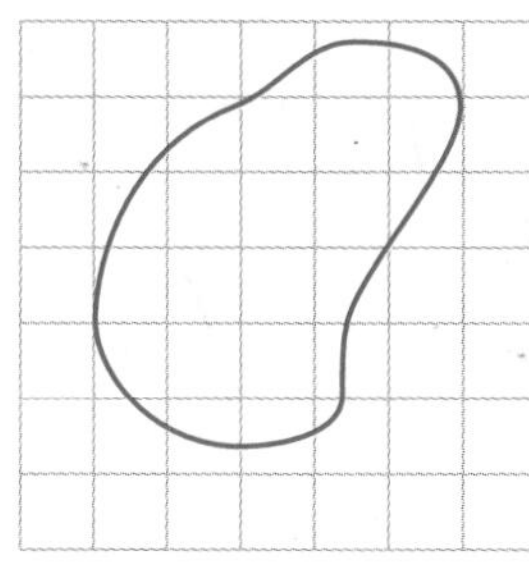

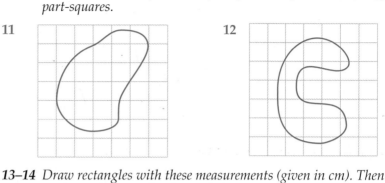

12

13–14 *Draw rectangles with these measurements (given in cm). Then work out the area of each one.*

13

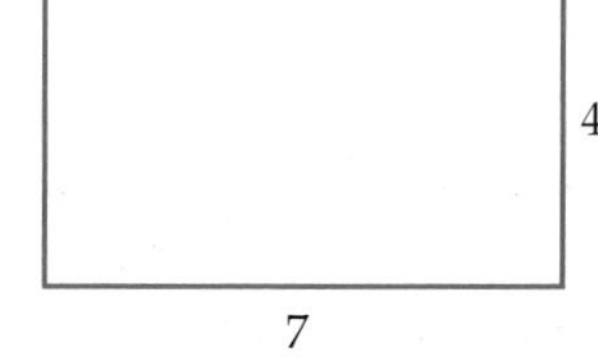

14

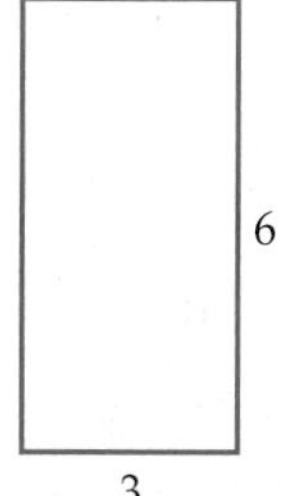

15–16 *Draw rectangles with these measurements. Assume a square in your book is 1 cm^2. Then work out the area of each rectangle.*

15 height 4 cm and width 5 cm

16 height 8 cm and width 3 cm

17 Another unit for area is the square millimetre (mm^2). This square has sides of 1 cm, which is 10 mm. How many mm^2 are there in 1 cm^2?

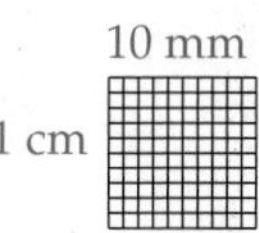

18 You could draw a rectangle that is 11 squares wide and 8 squares high. Counting squares, you would find that there are 88 of them. You could work out this answer directly from the numbers 8 and 11. Explain how.

Rectangles

To calculate the area of a rectangle, we multiply the length of the base by the height.

height

base

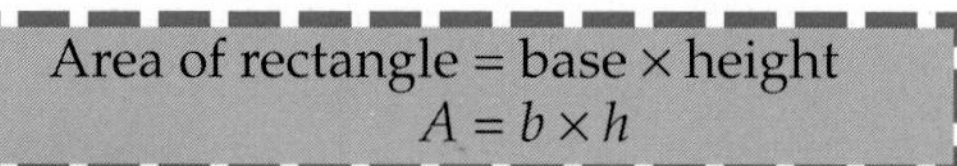

Area of rectangle = base × height
$A = b \times h$

Example What is the area of this rectangle?

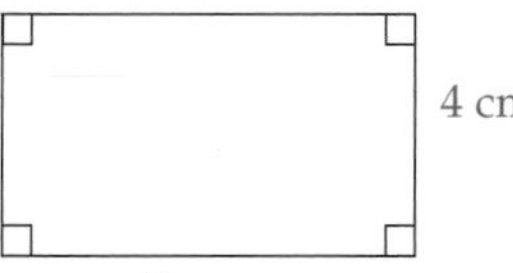

Answer Area $= b \times h$
$= 7 \text{ cm} \times 4 \text{ cm}$
$= 28 \text{ cm}^2$

Squares

Squares are special kinds of rectangles—all their sides are the same length. Therefore, we only need 1 measurement to calculate the area.

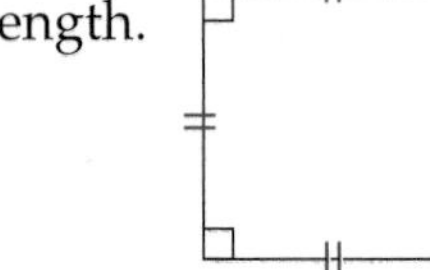

Area of square = side × side
$A = s \times s = s^2$

Example Calculate the area of this square.

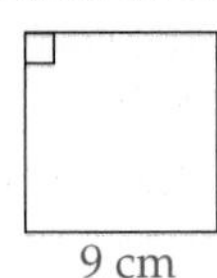

Answer Area = $s \times s$
= 9 cm × 9 cm
= 81 cm^2

EXERCISE 11.2

1–7 *Calculate the area of these rectangles.*

1

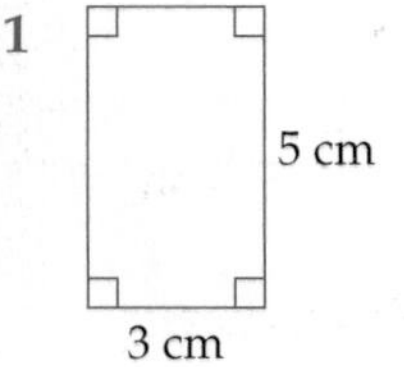

Choose your area units carefully. If the sides are in cm, the area will be in cm^2. If the sides are in m, the area will be in m^2.

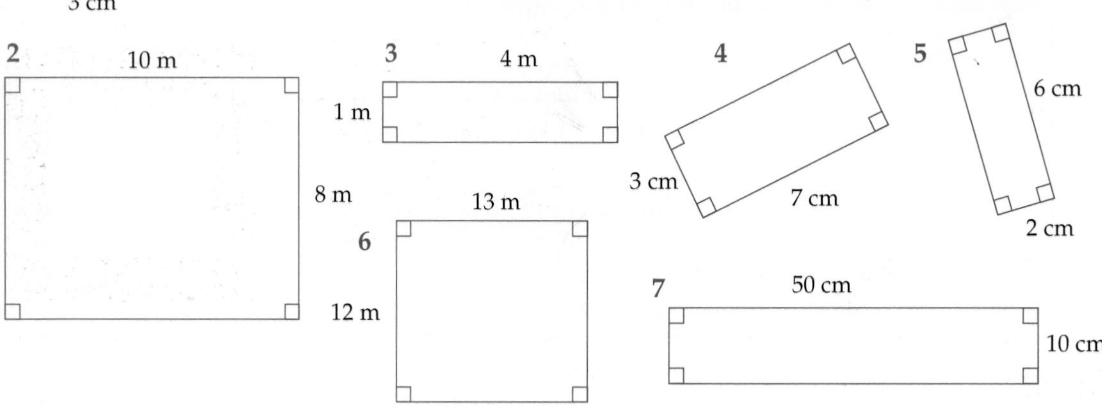

8 Measure the sides of each of these rectangles. Then calculate the area of each one in cm^2.

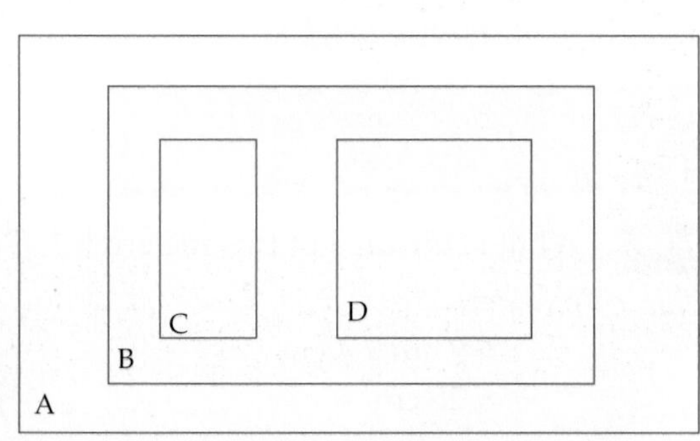

9–11 *Calculate the area of these squares.*

9

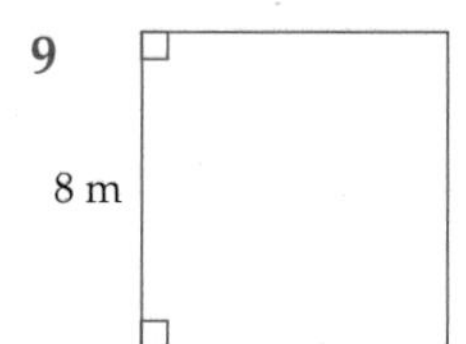

10

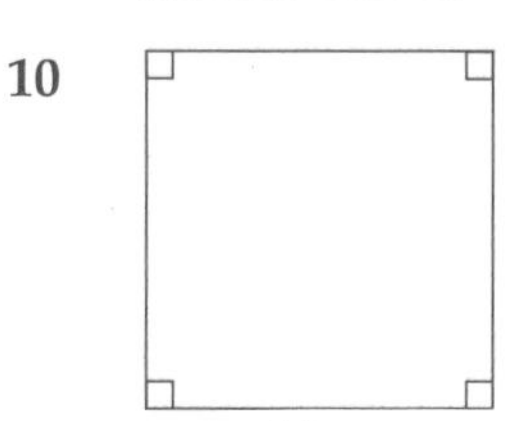

11

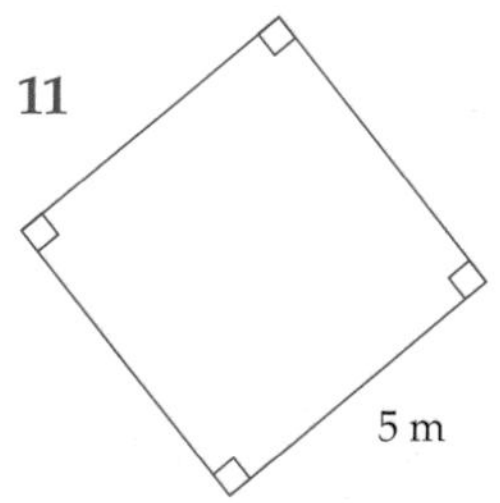

12 (a) Copy this diagram. Add a dashed line to divide it into two rectangles.

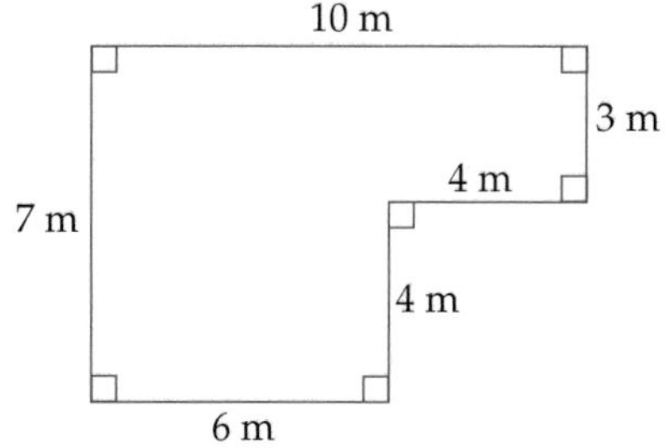

(b) Calculate the area of the whole shape.

13

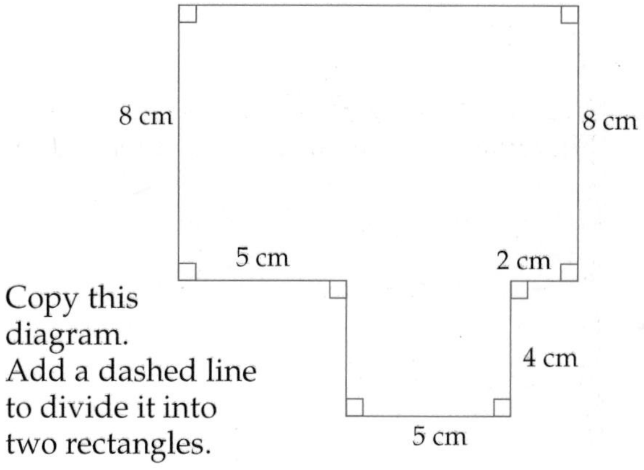

(a) Copy this diagram. Add a dashed line to divide it into two rectangles.

(b) Calculate the area of the whole shape.

14

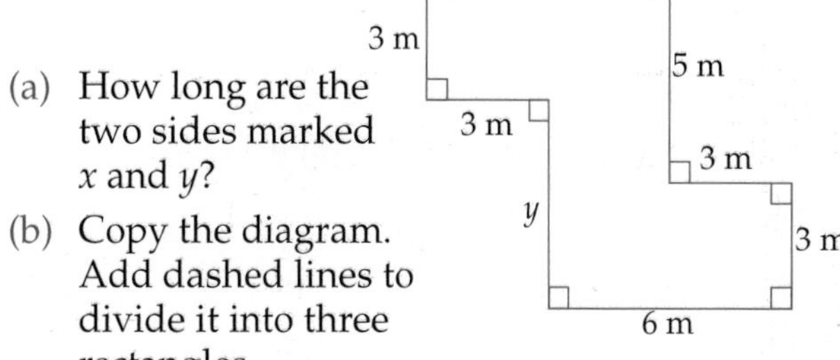

(a) How long are the two sides marked x and y?

(b) Copy the diagram. Add dashed lines to divide it into three rectangles.

(c) Calculate the area of the whole shape.

15 This diagram shows a black square with sides of 6 cm. A square with sides of 4 cm has been removed from it. Calculate the area of the part remaining.

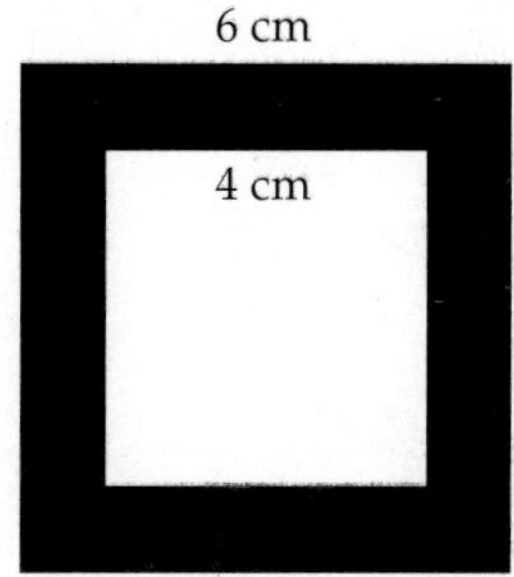

Triangles

- You could draw a line to split this rectangle into two equal triangles. Where would you draw the line?

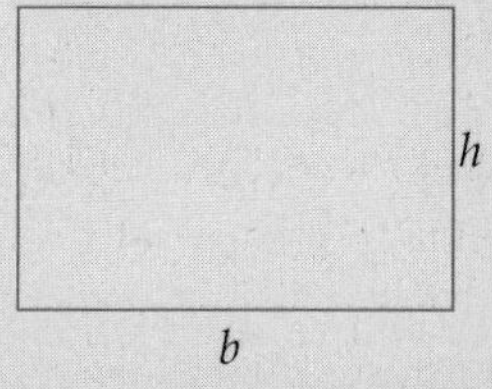

- Is the area of the rectangle twice the area of one of the triangles?
- Complete this sentence: 'The area of one of these triangles is _____ the area of the rectangle.'

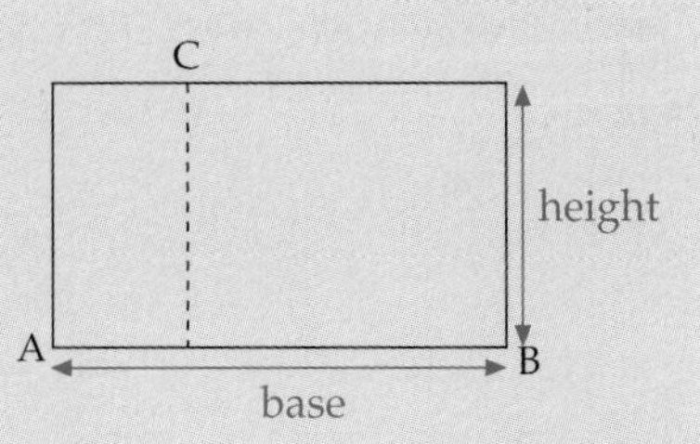

- Draw a rectangle. Add a vertical dashed line inside as shown on the right.
- Now draw a triangle ABC. One side (AB) is the base of the rectangle, and C is on the opposite side of the rectangle.
- The area of the triangle must be half the area of the rectangle. Can you explain why?

The area of this rectangle is twice the area of the triangle. So, the triangle area must be half the rectangle area $b \times h$.

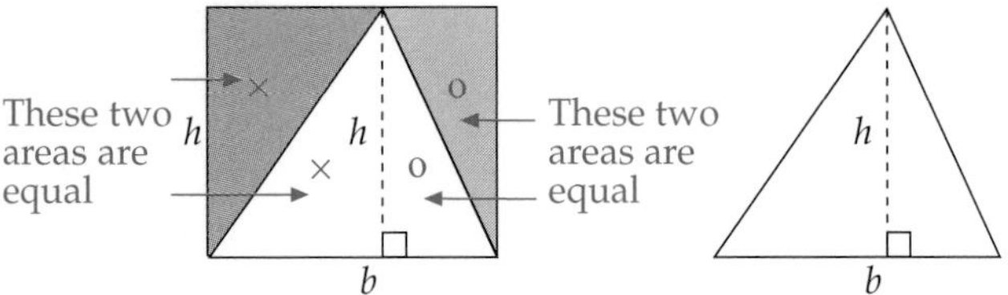

The area of a triangle is calculated from the rule 'half base times height'.

Area of △ = half base × height

$$A = \frac{1}{2}(b \times h)$$

Example Calculate the area of this triangle.

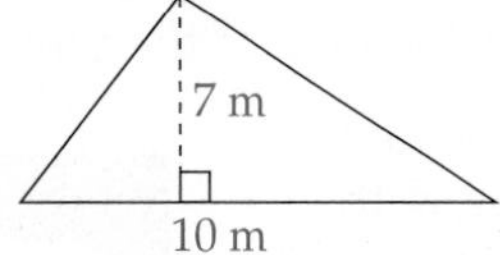

Answer

$$\text{Area} = \frac{1}{2}(b \times h)$$
$$= \frac{1}{2}(10 \times 7)$$
$$= \frac{1}{2} \times 70$$
$$= 35 \text{ m}^2$$

The height of a triangle is normally shown by a dashed line inside the triangle.
This height must be at right-angles to the base.
Sometimes, the height is shown by a line **outside** the triangle:

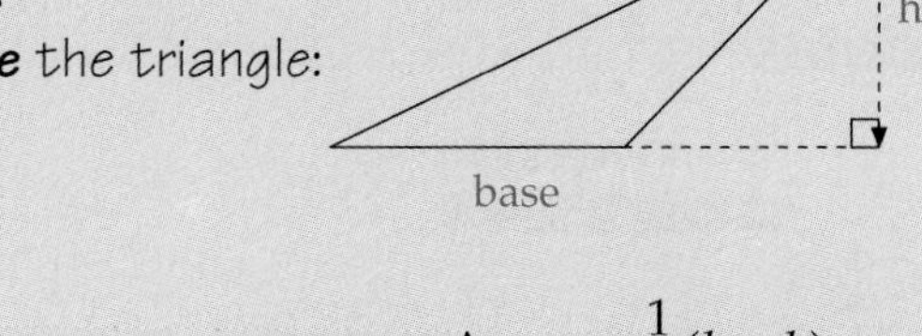

Any of the sides of the triangle can be the base.
If the triangle is right-angled, we can take one of the sides as the height.

4 cm, 3 cm, 5 cm

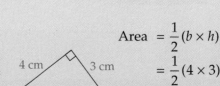

$$\text{Area} = \frac{1}{2}(b \times h)$$
$$= \frac{1}{2}(4 \times 3)$$
$$= \frac{1}{2} \times 12$$
$$= 6 \text{ cm}^2$$

EXERCISE **11.3**

1–12 *Calculate the area of these triangles. All the measurements are in cm.*

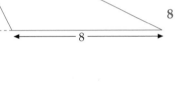

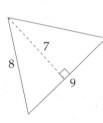

1

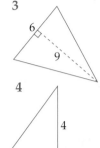

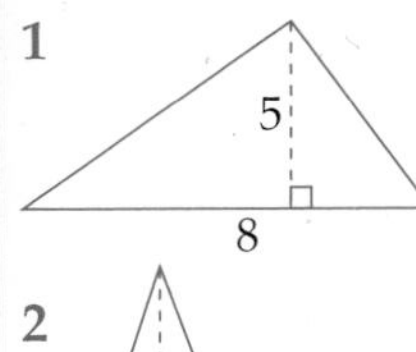

2

3

4

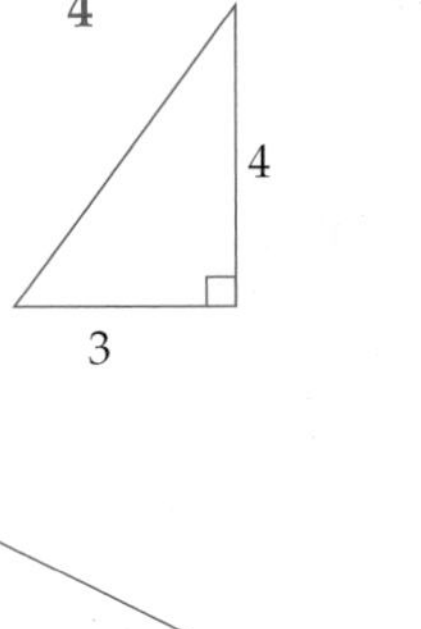

5

6

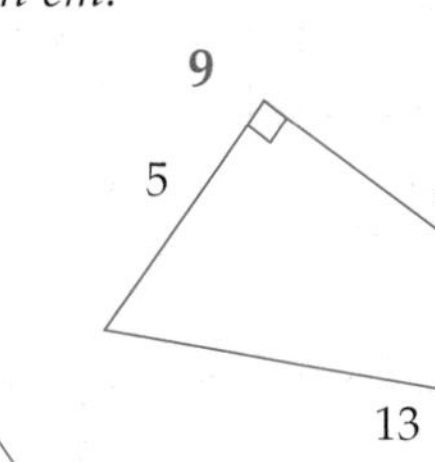

7

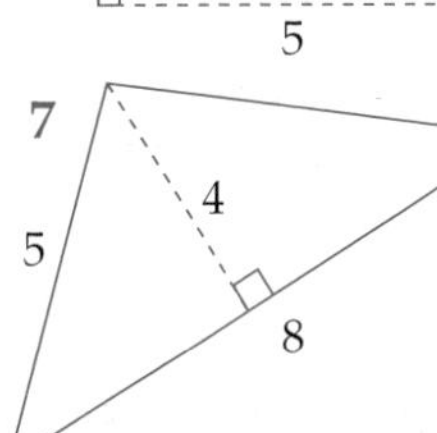

8

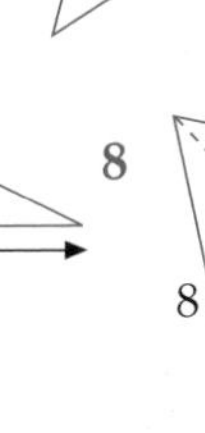

9

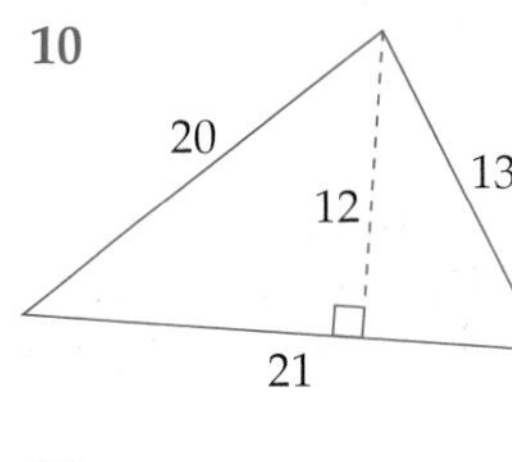

10

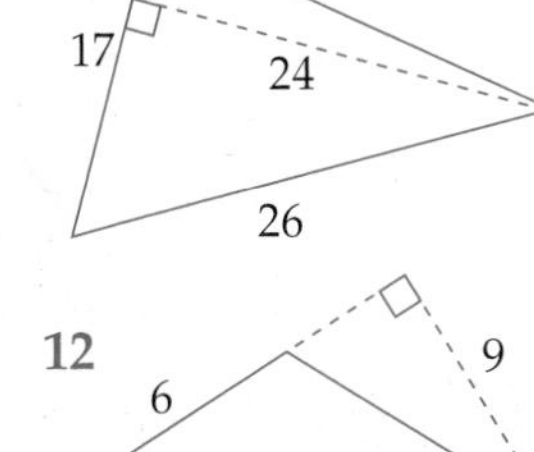

11

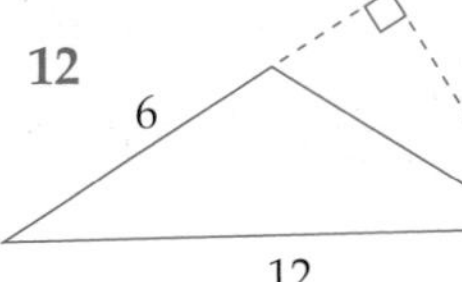

12

13 Calculate the area of this triangle. Assume each small square is 1 cm^2.

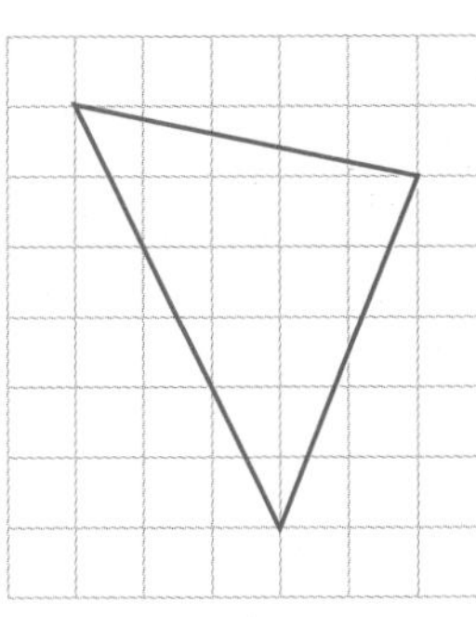

14 There are *two* ways of calculating the area of this shape. The measurements are in cm.

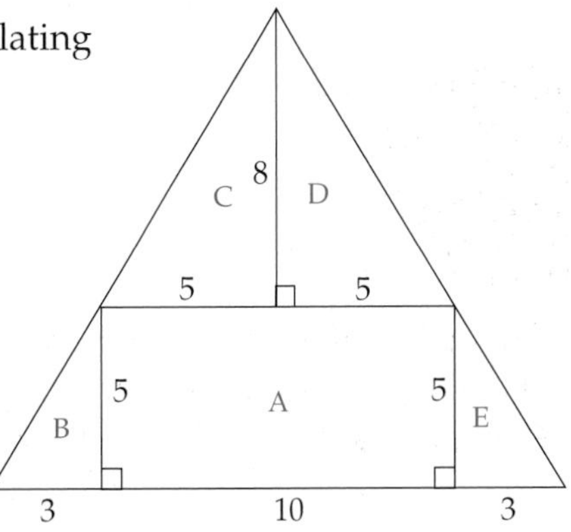

Method 1 (5 pieces)

(a) Calculate the size of triangles C and D.

(b) Calculate the size of triangles B and E.

(c) Calculate the size of rectangle A.

(d) Add together the areas of A, B, C, D and E.

Method 2 (1 shape)

(e) Use the formula $A = \frac{1}{2}(b \times h)$
Use a base of 16 cm and a height of 13 cm.

What has gone wrong?

(f) Explain why the two methods give different answers!

Parallelograms

A **parallelogram** is a quadrilateral (four-sided shape) with:

- both pairs of opposite sides parallel
- both pairs of opposite sides the same length.

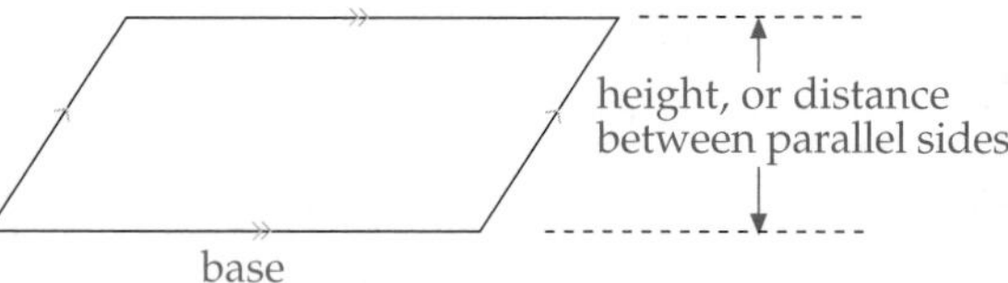

A parallelogram has the same area as a rectangle with the same base and height (distance between parallel sides). If a triangle is cut off one end of a parallelogram and moved to the other, you get a rectangle that must have the same area.

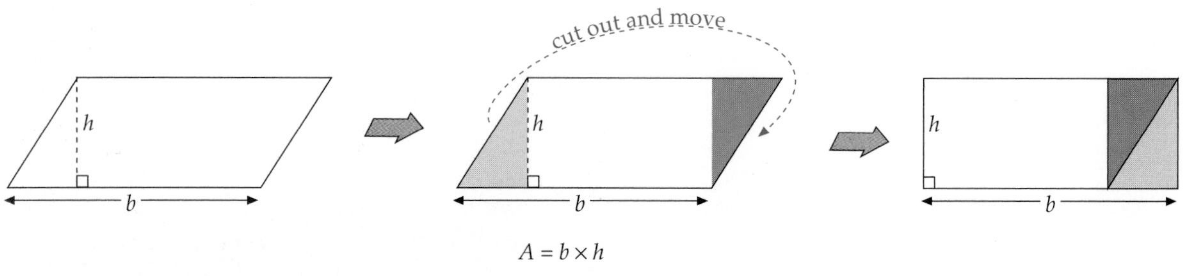

Area of parallelogram = length of base × distance between sides

$A = b \times h$

Example Calculate the area of each of these parallelograms:

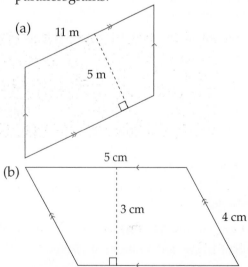

(a) 11 m, 5 m

(b) 5 cm, 3 cm, 4 cm

Answer

(a) The 'base' is the side marked 11 m. The distance between the sides is 5 m.

Area $= b \times h$

$= 11 \text{ m} \times 5 \text{ m}$

$= 55 \text{ m}^2$

(b) We don't use the length of 4 cm, because it is not at right-angles to the base.

Area $= b \times h$

$= 5 \text{ cm} \times 3 \text{ cm}$

$= 15 \text{ cm}^2$

EXERCISE 11.4

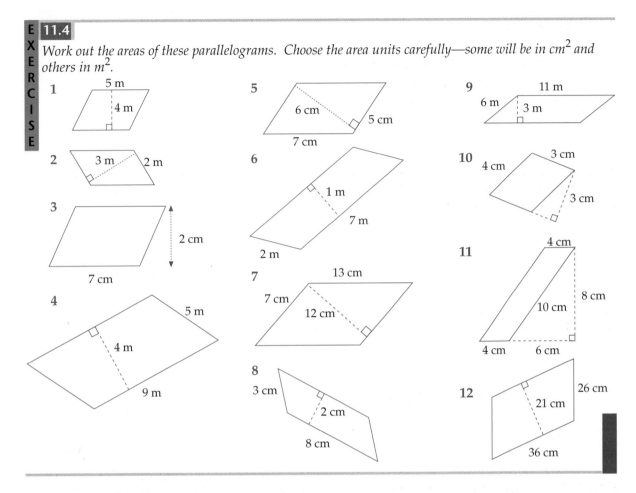

Work out the areas of these parallelograms. Choose the area units carefully—some will be in cm^2 and others in m^2.

1 (5 m, 4 m)

2 (3 m, 2 m)

3 (7 cm, 2 cm)

4 (5 m, 4 m, 9 m)

5 (6 cm, 5 cm, 7 cm)

6 (1 m, 7 m, 2 m)

7 (13 cm, 7 cm, 12 cm)

8 (3 cm, 2 cm, 8 cm)

9 (11 m, 6 m, 3 m)

10 (3 cm, 4 cm, 3 cm)

11 (4 cm, 8 cm, 10 cm, 4 cm, 6 cm)

12 (26 cm, 21 cm, 36 cm)

Compound areas

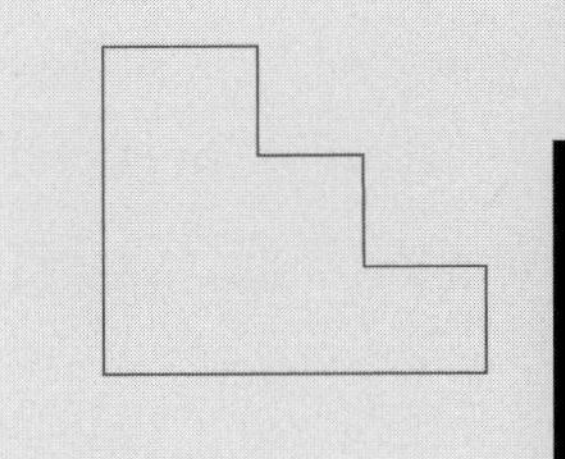

- You could add two dashed lines to this shape to split it up into 3 rectangles. Explain where.
- Are there any other ways of splitting this shape up into 3 rectangles?

Many shapes are made up of mixtures of rectangles, squares, triangles and parallelograms. We call these **compound** shapes.

To work out the area of a compound shape, split it up into other shapes first. Then add the areas of all the shapes. Sometimes you also use subtraction.

It helps to add dashed lines to the diagram to show how you are splitting it up.

Here is one example of each:

Adding areas

Example Work out the area of this shape.

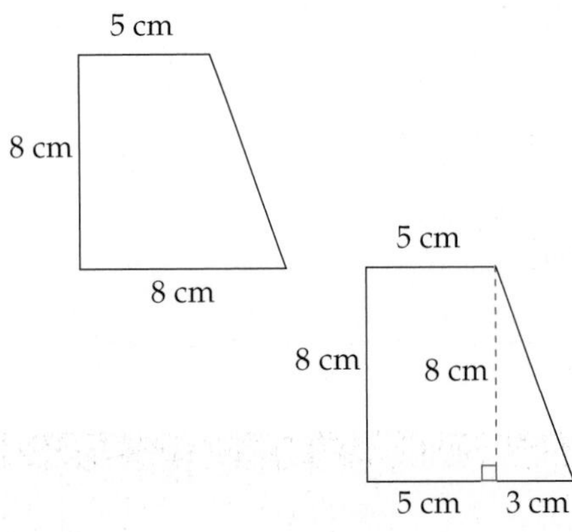

Answer Adding a dashed line shows the shape is made up of a rectangle and a triangle. Notice how the base of 8 cm can be separated into 5 cm and 3 cm.

$$
\begin{aligned}
\text{Area} &= \text{area of rectangle} + \text{area of triangle} \\
&= b \times h + \frac{1}{2}(b \times h) \\
&= 5 \times 8 + \frac{1}{2}(3 \times 8) \\
&= 40 + \frac{1}{2} \times 24 \\
&= 40 + 12 \\
&= 52 \text{ cm}^2
\end{aligned}
$$

Subtracting areas

Example Calculate the shaded area in this diagram.

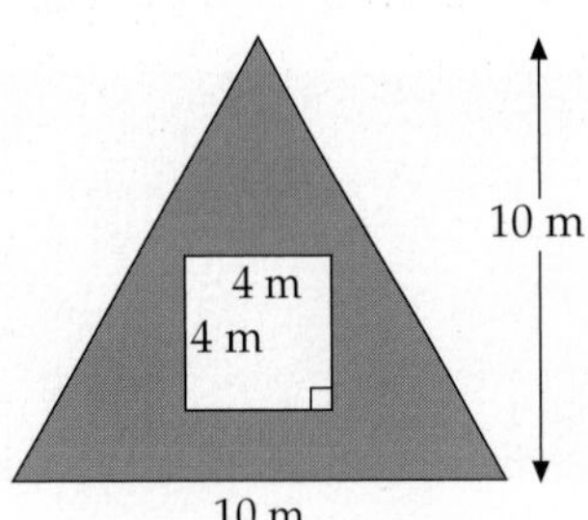

Answer This area is what is left over when the square is removed from the triangle.

$$
\begin{aligned}
\text{Area} &= \text{area of triangle} - \text{area of square} \\
&= \frac{1}{2}(b \times h) - s \times s \\
&= \frac{1}{2}(10 \times 10) - 4 \times 4 \\
&= \frac{1}{2} \times 100 - 16 \\
&= 50 - 16 \\
&= 34 \text{ m}^2
\end{aligned}
$$

EXERCISE 11.5

Work out the areas of these compound shapes. All the measurements are in cm.

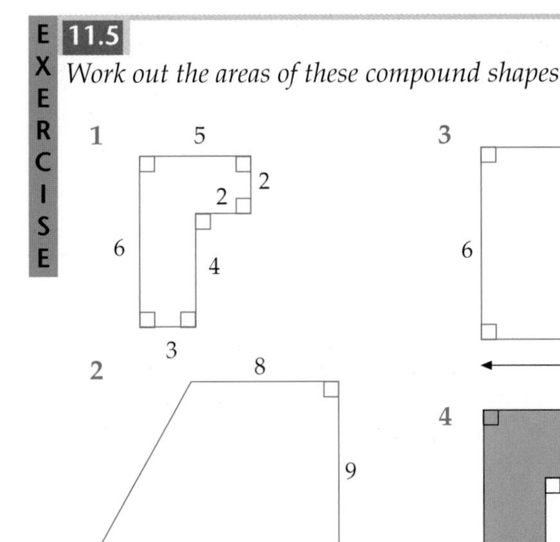

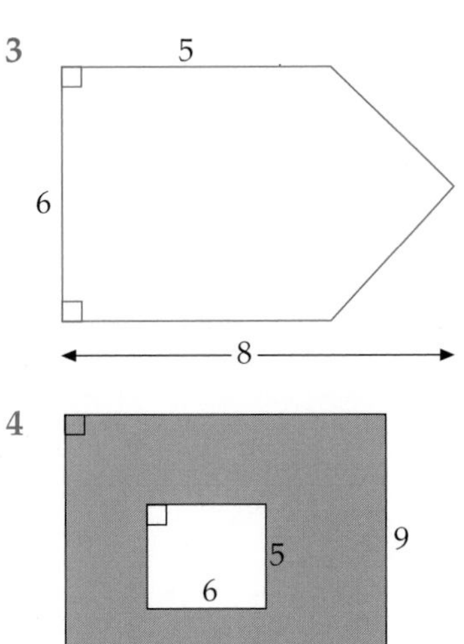

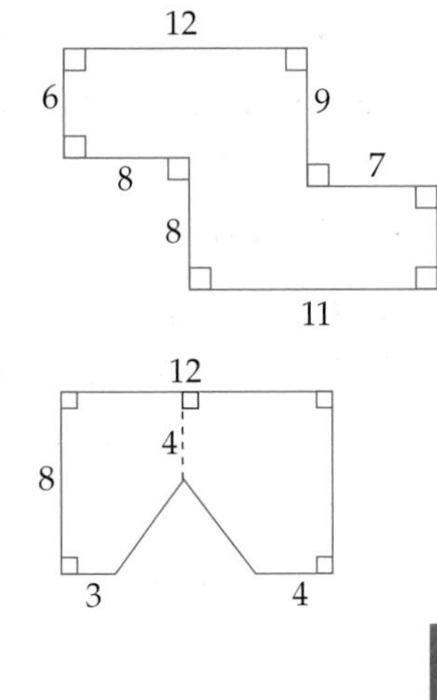

INVESTIGATION

PICK'S RULE

You can use the ideas from compound shapes to work out the area of any shapes with:

- straight sides
- all their corners on a square grid.

Sometimes, the shapes will be triangles and quadrilaterals— and the sides won't always be whole numbers or at right-angles.

Here's an example. It's a triangle drawn on a square grid of 1 cm squares. We want to work out the area.

The base and height aren't given, so we can't use the formula $\frac{1}{2}(b \times h)$.

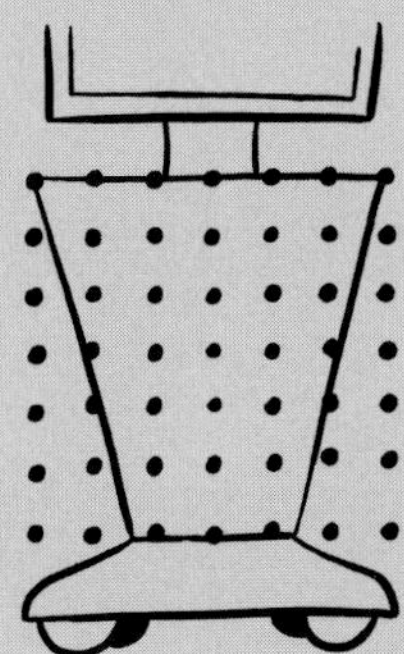

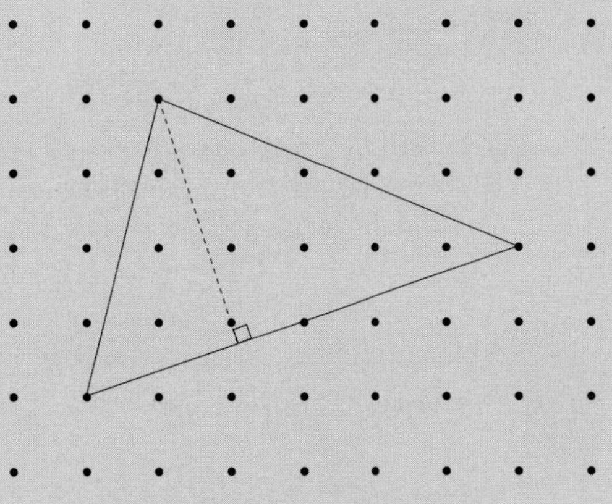

Instead, we could imagine the triangle was inside a rectangle:

The area we want is what is left over when areas A, B and C are subtracted from the area of the rectangle.

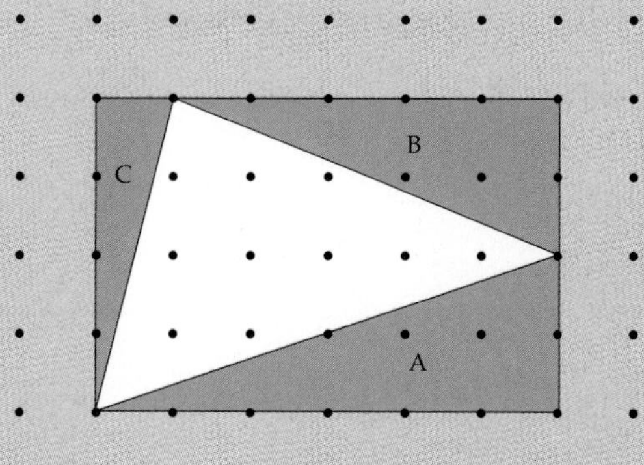

Area of rectangle $= 6 \times 4 = 24\ \text{cm}^2$

Area of triangle A $= \frac{1}{2}(b \times h) = \frac{1}{2} \times (6 \times 2) = \frac{1}{2} \times 12 = 6\ \text{cm}^2$

Area of triangle B $= \frac{1}{2}(b \times h) = \frac{1}{2} \times (5 \times 2) = \frac{1}{2} \times 10 = 5\ \text{cm}^2$

Area of triangle C $= \frac{1}{2}(b \times h) = \frac{1}{2} \times (1 \times 4) = \frac{1}{2} \times 4 = 2\ \text{cm}^2$

The area we want will be $24 - (6 + 5 + 2) = 24 - 13 = 11\ \text{cm}^2$

This is a complicated process. It was made much easier by a mathematician called Pick. He discovered a rule for the area of polygons with all their corners on dots on a square grid.

The rule just involves counting dots!

We use n for the number of dots inside the shape.
We use p for the number of dots on the perimeter.

The rule is:

Area of shape $= n - 1 + \frac{p}{2}$

or $A = n - 1 + \frac{1}{2}p$

Here is how the rule works for our triangle:

$n = 10$ (there are 10 dots inside the shape)
$p = 4$ (there are 4 dots on the perimeter. They are numbered ① to ④ to show you. The dots can be on sides as well as the corners!)

Area of shape $= n - 1 + \frac{p}{2}$

$= 10 - 1 + \frac{4}{2}$

$= 10 - 1 + 2$

$= 11\ \text{cm}^2$

EXERCISE 11.6

1–2 *These questions are about checking that Pick's Rule works. Each shape is drawn on a 1 cm square grid.*

1

(a) Write down the length of the base of this rectangle (in cm).

(b) Write down the height of this rectangle (in cm).

(c) Use the rule Area = $b \times h$ to calculate the area of the rectangle.

(d) Count the number of dots inside the rectangle.
Write your answer as $n =$ ___

(e) Count the number of dots on the perimeter of the rectangle. Write your answer as $p =$ ___

(f) Use Pick's rule $(A = n - 1 + \frac{1}{2}p)$ to work out the area of the rectangle.

(g) Are your answers to (c) and (f) the same?

2

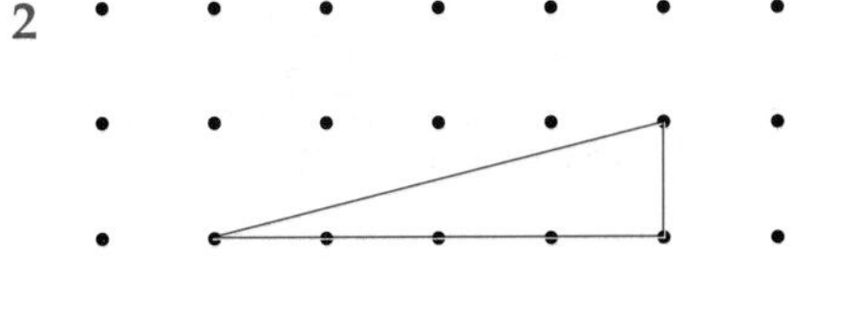

(a) Write down the length of the base of this triangle (in cm).

(b) Write down the height of this triangle (in cm).

(c) Use the rule Area = $\frac{1}{2}(b \times h)$ to calculate the area of the triangle.

(d) Count the number of dots inside the triangle. Write your answer as $n =$ ___

(e) Count the number of dots on the perimeter of the triangle. Write your answer as $p =$ ___

(f) Use Pick's rule $(A = n - 1 + \frac{1}{2}p)$ to work out the area of the triangle.

(g) Are your answers to (c) and (f) the same?

3–8 *Use Pick's rule to work out the area of these shapes.*

3

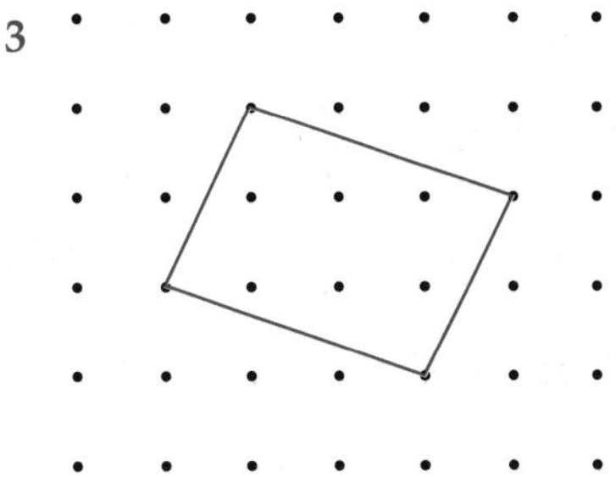

4

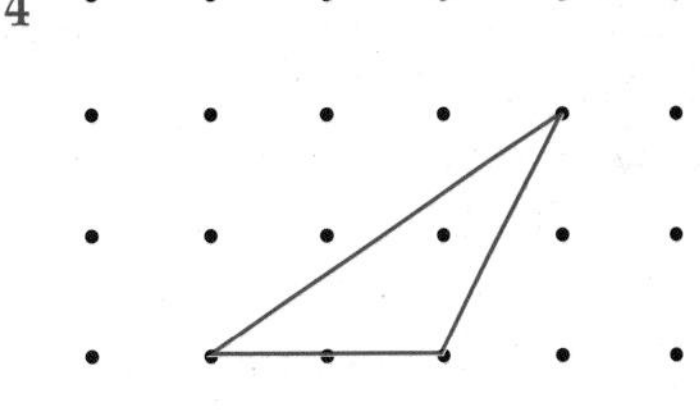

5

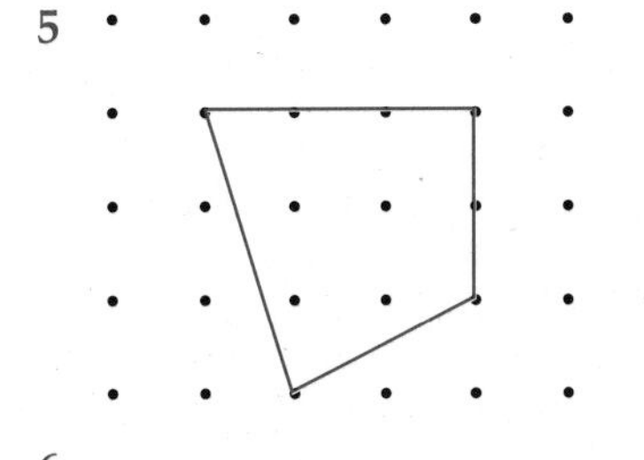

6

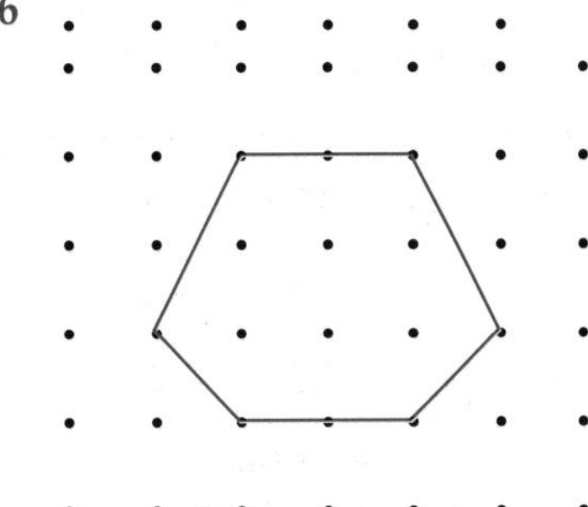

7

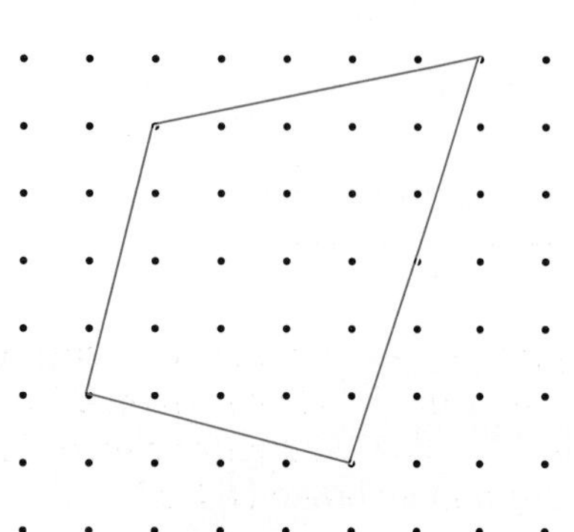

8

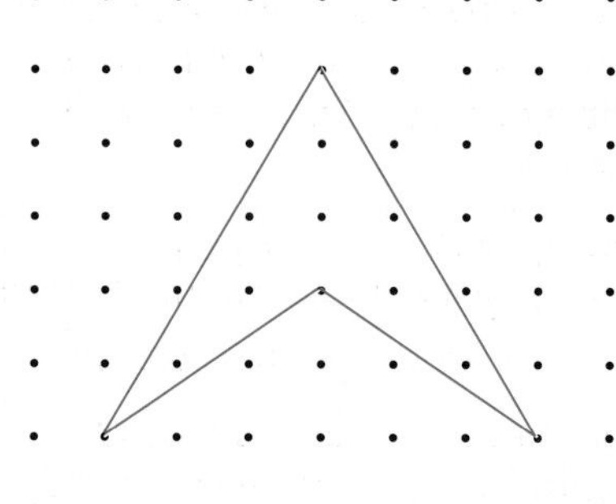

Using area ideas in real-life

Example A gardener has a rectangular garden measuring 10 m by 8 m. The gardener decides to lay a 1 m wide concrete path around the outside of the garden. What area of concrete will be needed?

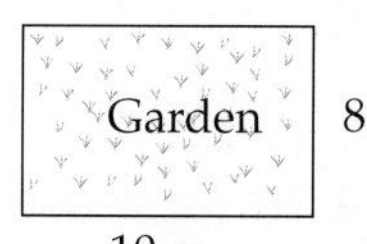

Answer When we add the path to the diagram, we get a larger rectangle measuring 12 m by 10 m.

The area of the path is the difference between the areas of the two rectangles.

Area of path = area of large rectangle – area of smaller rectangle

$= 12 \times 10 - 10 \times 8$

$= 120 - 80$

$= 40\text{ m}^2$

EXERCISE 11.7

1 Tui and Wiremu have to paint the front of a fence. The fence is rectangular, with a length of 24 m and a height of 2 m. 1 litre of fence paint covers about 6 m^2.

(a) Calculate the area to be painted.

(b) How many litres of paint will they need?

2 This wooden block has six identical square faces.

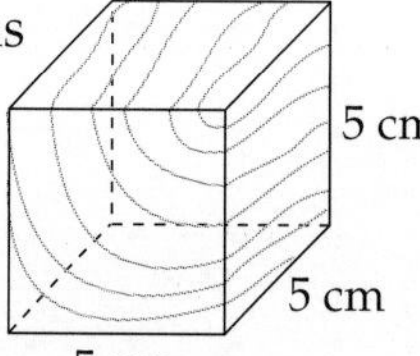

(a) What is the area of one face?

(b) What is the total area of all 6 faces?

3 Greenfingers Market Gardeners have a square field with sides of 40 m. They usually plant 2 pumpkins to every m^2 in this field.

(a) What is the area of the field?

(b) How many pumpkins can they plant?

4 A rectangular swimming pool is 50 m long by 16 m wide. Tiling is to be added, to a distance of 2 m from the edge of the pool on all sides.

(a) Draw a diagram and shade in the area to be tiled.

(b) Calculate the area of tiling needed.

5 Carpet tiles are square, and measure 0.5 m by 0.5 m. Jenny wants to tile the floor of a room measuring 6 m by 3 m. How many tiles does she need?

6 A school hockey field is rectangular. It measures 112 m by 49 m. Calculate its area:
(a) exactly (b) to the nearest 100 m^2.

7 In spring, the sheep on one farm need 40 m^2 of grazing each. How many sheep should be put in a paddock measuring 50 m by 100 m?

8

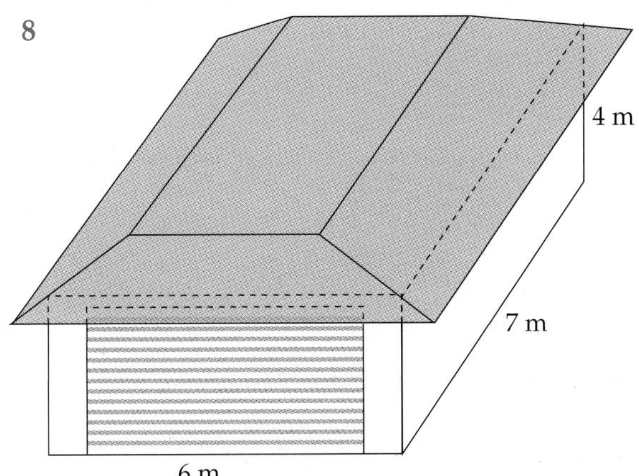

The four outside walls of this garage are to be painted. This includes the roller door at the front, but not the roof. Each litre of the paint chosen covers 5 m^2.

(a) What is the total area to be painted?
(b) How many litres of paint are needed?

9 

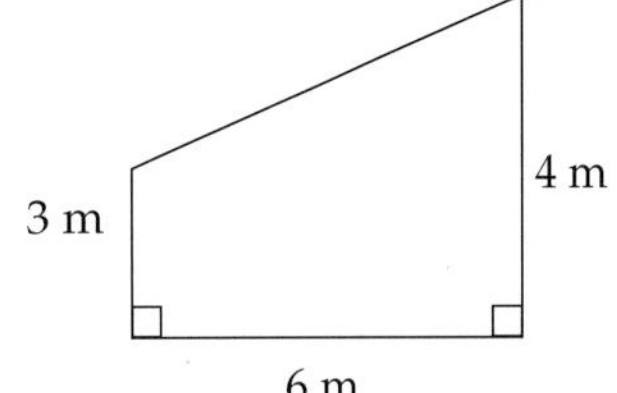

This diagram shows a wall at one end of a music classroom. It is to be covered in wallpaper. 1 roll of wallpaper covers 8 m^2. How many rolls will be needed?

10 A paper manufacturer sells boxes of 200 paper tissues. Each tissue is square, with sides of 21 cm. They also make rolls of paper towel. These have the same width (21 cm), and a length of 50 m.

(a) What is the area of a paper tissue?
(b) The area of the paper towel in m^2 is $0.21 \times 50 = 10.5$ m^2. Work out the area of the paper towel in cm^2.
(Note 1 m = 100 cm)
(c) Which contains more paper—a box of 200 tissues or a paper towel? Explain by writing down some calculations and saying what they refer to.

Hectares

Large areas of land are measured in **hectares**.

- 1 hectare is 10 000 m^2
- The short way of writing 1 hectare is 1 ha.

It helps to think of a hectare as a square measuring 100 m by 100 m. 100 m is the length of a running track. 1 ha is about two rugby/soccer/hockey fields in size.

Example A school occupies 4.67 ha of land. Write this area in m^2.

Answer $4.67 \text{ ha} = 4.67 \times 10\,000 \text{ m}^2 = 46\,700 \text{ m}^2$

Example The playground at the school has an area of 8700 m^2. Write this area in ha.

Answer $8700 \text{ m}^2 = \frac{8700}{10\,000} \text{ ha}$
$= 0.87 \text{ ha}$

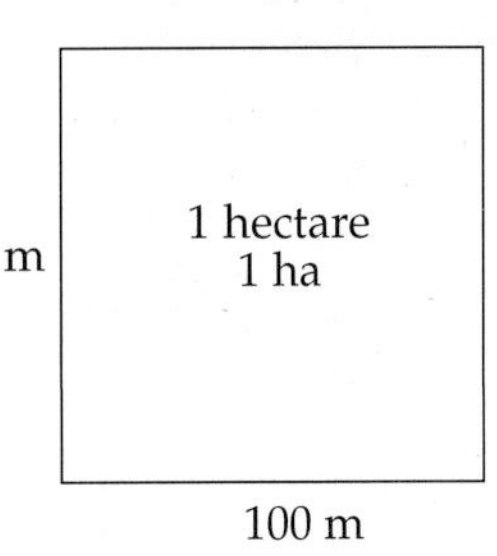

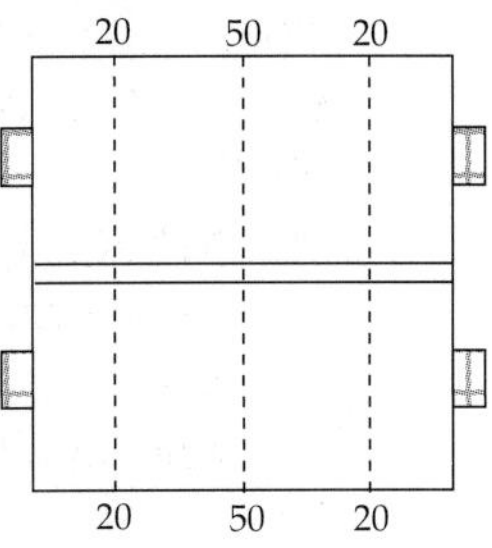

EXERCISE 11.8

1 Write these areas in m^2:
(a) 5 ha
(b) 3.2 ha
(c) 100 ha
(d) 0.55 ha
(e) 0.091 ha

2 Write these areas in ha:
(a) 40 000 m^2
(b) 68 000 m^2
(c) 1000 m^2
(d) 9500 m^2
(e) 39 500 m^2

3 This plan shows some land owned by a racing club.

How much land, in hectares, do the club own?

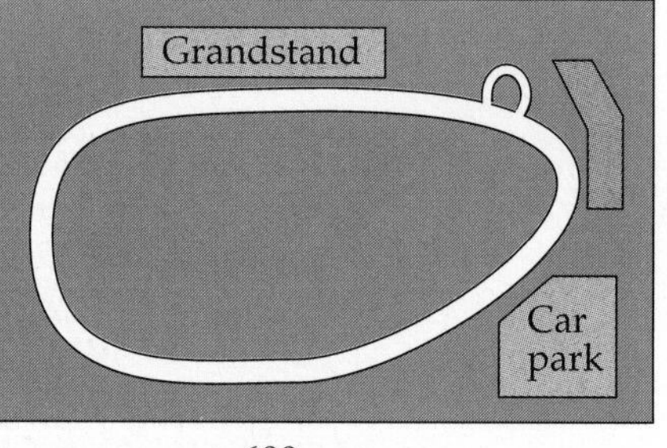

4 The giraffe enclosure at a safari park is 80 ha. The recommended space for 1 giraffe is 16 ha. How many giraffe should be kept in the enclosure?

5 A school has six playing fields. Each one measures about 50 m by 100 m. What area of land, in hectares, is playing fields?

6 A developer is selling sections in a new subdivision. The area of the subdivision is 4.6 ha. Each section is about 700 m^2. Estimate the number of sections for sale.

Perimeter

STARTER

Each of these sections of land has an area of 1 ha.

Each small square on the grid has a side length of 10 m.

The measurements of section A are 100 m by 100 m.

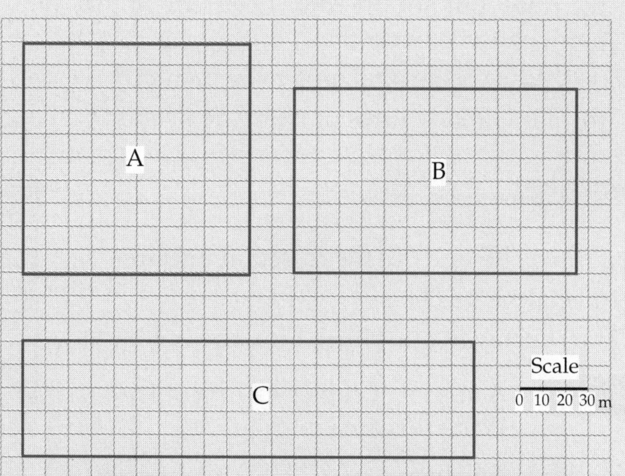

- What are the measurements of section B?
- What are the measurements of section C?
- Which section would take the longest to walk around the outside? Explain, by counting the edges of squares or otherwise.

The **perimeter** of a figure is the total length of its sides.

Example Work out the perimeter of this parallelogram.

Answer Perimeter = 10 + 8 + 10 + 8 = 36 cm.

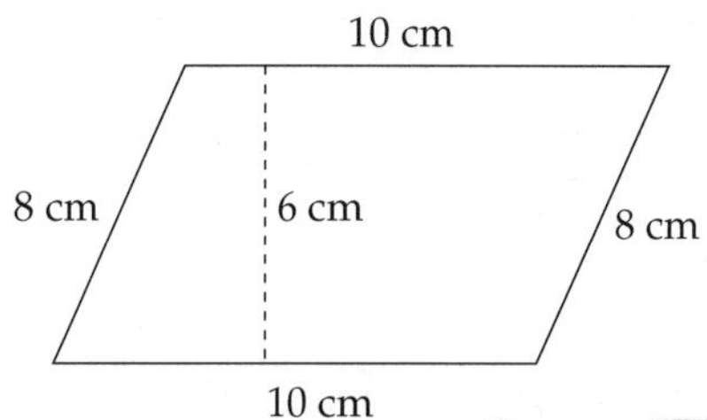

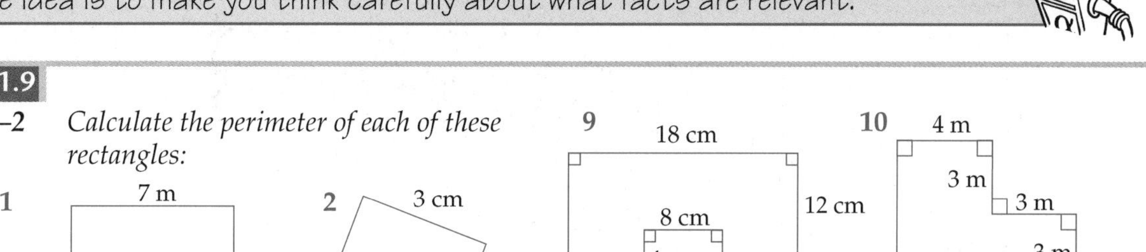

This is a good example of a maths problem where *unnecessary* information is given.
The idea is to make you think carefully about what facts are relevant.

EXERCISE 11.9

1–2 *Calculate the perimeter of each of these rectangles:*

1

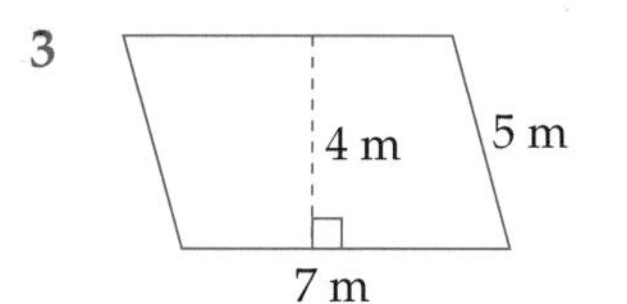

2

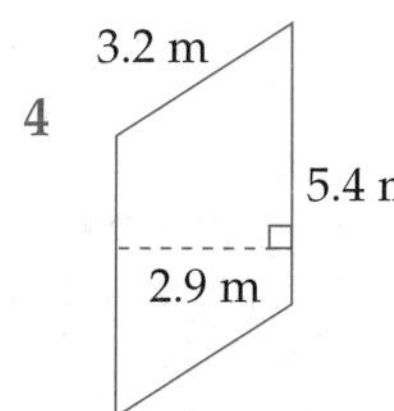

3–4 *Calculate the perimeter of each of these parallelograms:*

3

7 m, 4 m, 5 m

4

3.2 m, 5.4 m, 2.9 m

5–10 *Calculate the perimeter of each of these figures:*

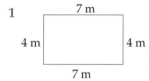

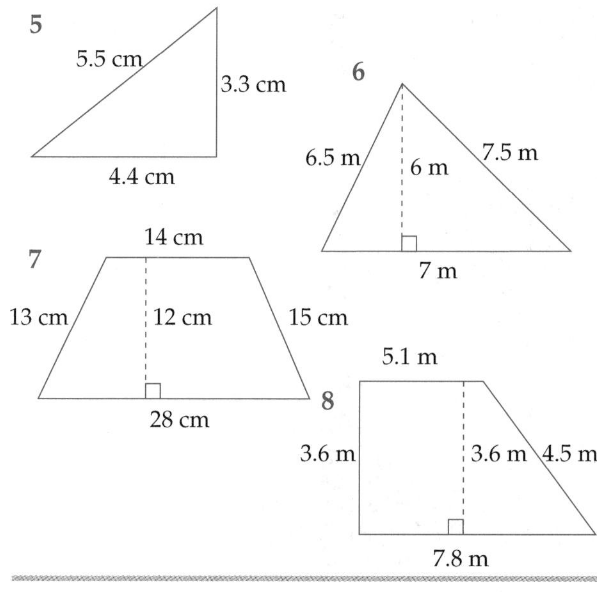

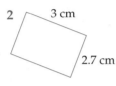

9

18 cm, 12 cm, 8 cm, 4 cm, 5 cm

10

4 m, 3 m, 3 m, 3 m, 3 m, 2 m

11 Estimate the perimeter of this Turkish rug. If you look carefully, you will see a 30 cm ruler on one edge.

12 This is a floor plan for a house. It is to be built on a concrete pad. Before pouring the concrete, a low wall needs to be built around the edge. How long will this wall be?

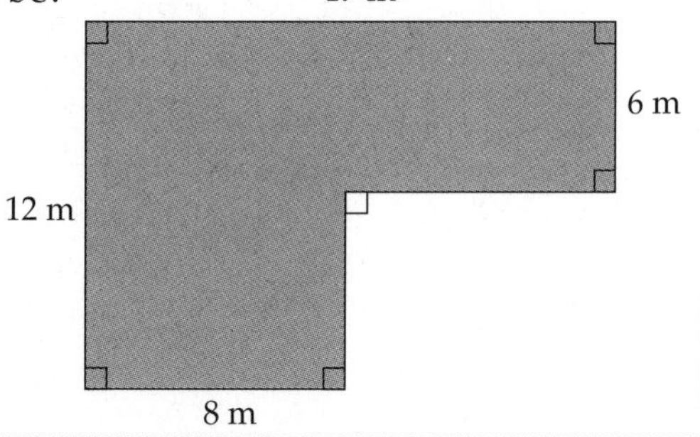

INVESTIGATION

THE SIX SHEET SHOW

- Take six sheets of A4 paper. A4 paper measures approximately 30 cm by 21 cm.
- Arrange the six pieces on a flat surface (a large table or the floor) so that
  —each sheet is right next to another sheet
  —the sheets do not overlap
  —the sides match (short next to short, long next to long)

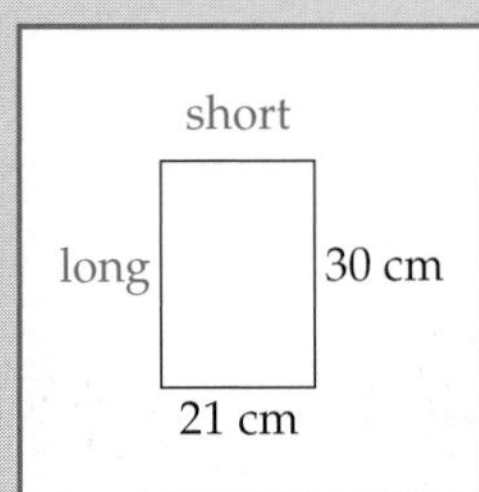

One way of doing this is shown here:

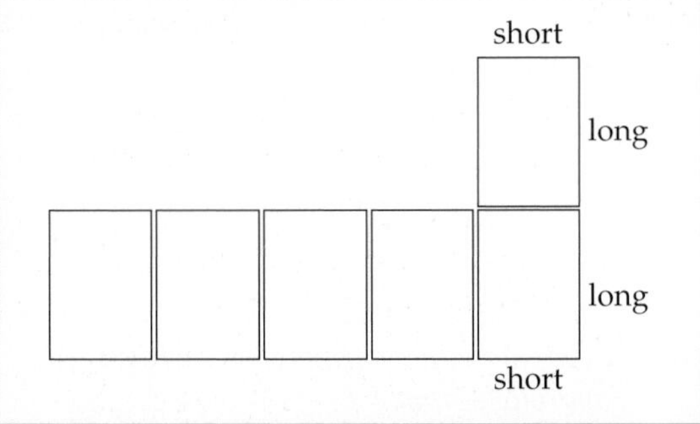

- Draw diagrams to show three other ways to arrange the six A4 sheets. Remember: next to each other, not overlapping, and with matching sides.

- Use a calculator to work out the perimeter for each of the four shapes. Use 21 cm for short sides and 30 cm for long sides. Write the perimeter of each shape on its diagram.
- Calculate the area of each shape. What do you notice?
- Which kind of shapes have the smallest perimeter? Which kind have the largest perimeter?

12 Area and circumference of circles

STARTER

Did you know it is impossible to calculate the area of a circle exactly? A circle can't be divided up exactly into squares.

Mathematicians thought about this problem (trying to work out the area of a circle) for many centuries.

They discovered they needed a special number. This was called 'pi', and is written with the symbol π. The value of π is quite close to 3. Let's use 3 as this special number.

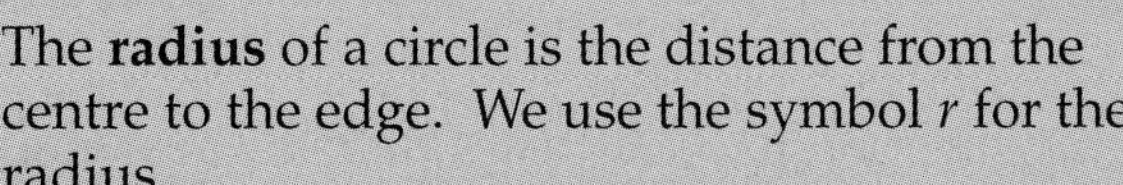

The **radius** of a circle is the distance from the centre to the edge. We use the symbol r for the radius.

The first mathematicians thought that the area of a circle, very roughly, could be worked out by multiplying $3 \times r \times r$.

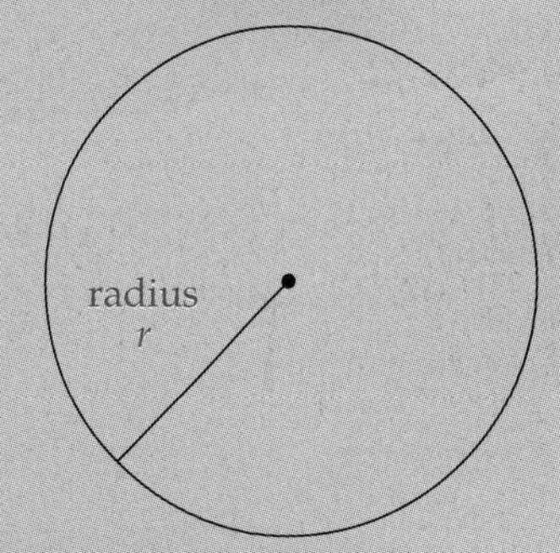

Let's see if this works in these examples:

A

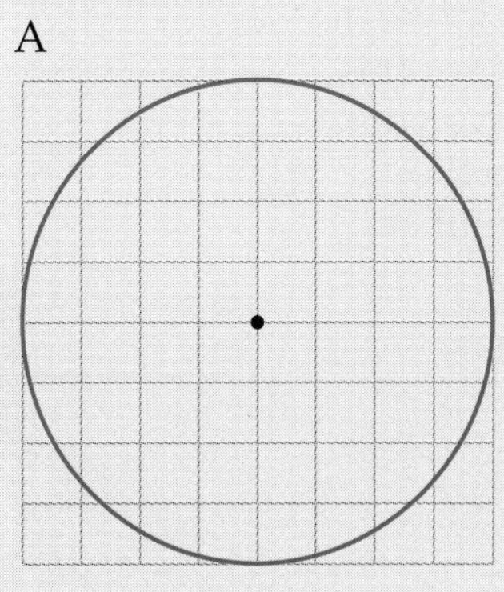

B

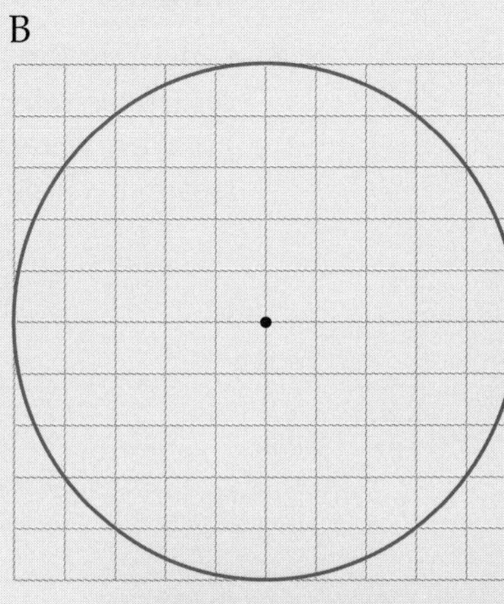

- Estimate the area of circle A by counting squares. Allow for part-squares.
- Now work out $3 \times 4 \times 4$. Is this close to your estimate?
- Estimate the area of circle B by counting squares. Allow for part-squares.
- Now work out $3 \times 5 \times 5$. Is this close to your estimate?

The **area of a circle** is calculated using a formula:

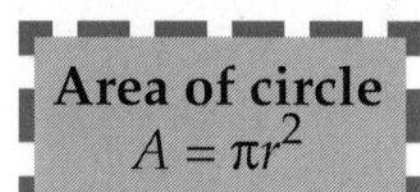

- This formula means $\pi \times r \times r$.
- π is the special number used in circle work.
- To 8 decimal places, π is 3.141 592 65.
- Press the special π key on a calculator to get its value.

Example Calculate the area of this circle. The radius is 6 cm.

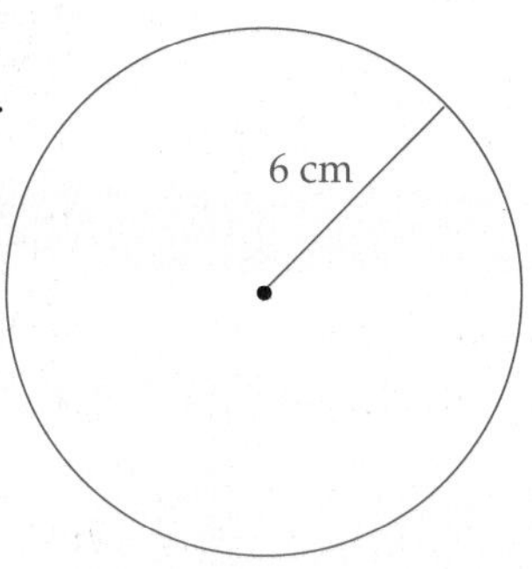

Answer

$$\begin{aligned} \text{Area} &= \pi r^2 \\ &= \pi \times 6^2 \\ &= \pi \times 6 \times 6 \\ &= \pi \times 36 \\ &= 113.1 \text{ cm}^2 \end{aligned}$$

Check you can get this answer on your calculator.

EXERCISE 12.1

1–4 *Calculate the area of each circle. Give your answers in the correct units, to the nearest whole number.*

1

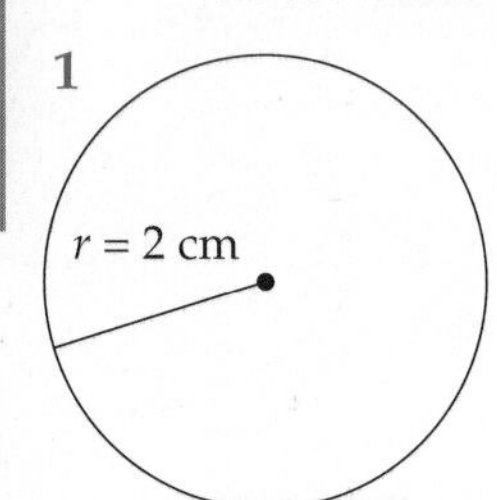

2

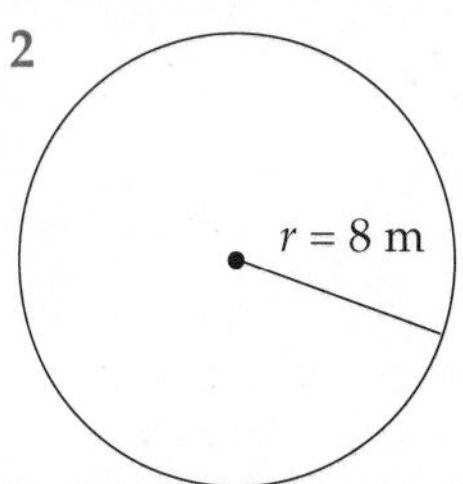

3

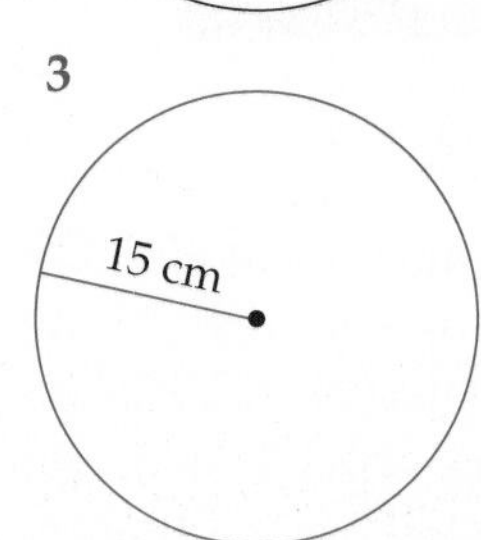

4

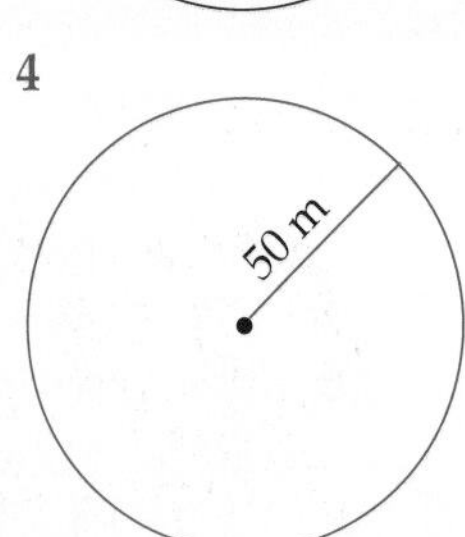

5 Calculate the area of a circle with a radius of 6.1 cm. Give your answer correct to 1 decimal place.

6 Calculate the area of a circle with a radius of 11.2 m. Give your answer correct to 1 decimal place.

7 Calculate the area of this semi-circle. Give your answer correct to the nearest whole number.

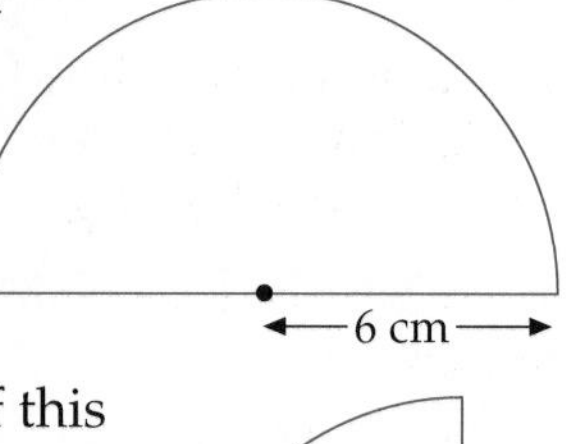

8 Calculate the area of this quarter-circle. Give your answer correct to the nearest whole number.

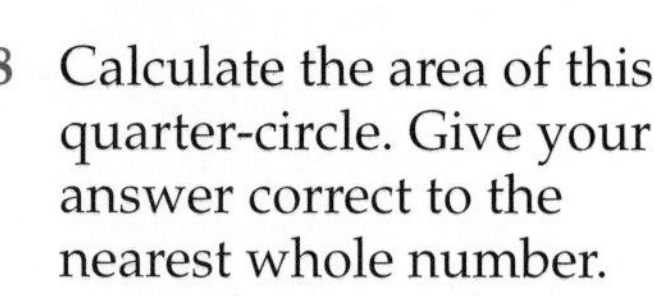

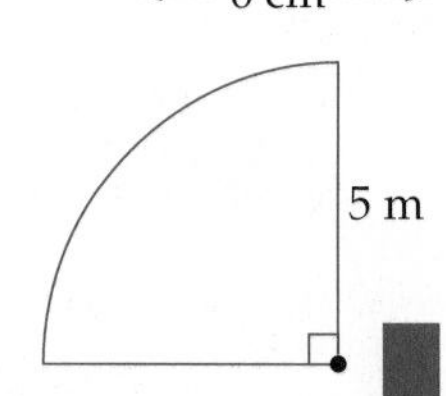

INVESTIGATION

PIZZA VALUE

- Find out whether a small, medium or large pizza is best value for money.
- Here is the information you will need from your local pizza place:
  —radius or diameter of the different sizes
  —price of the different sizes.
- Calculate the price per cm^2 (by dividing the price by the area) for each size.
- Explain what you are calculating. Write down your working at each step.

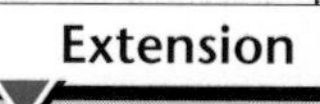

- Does the type of topping make a difference to your calculations? Explain.

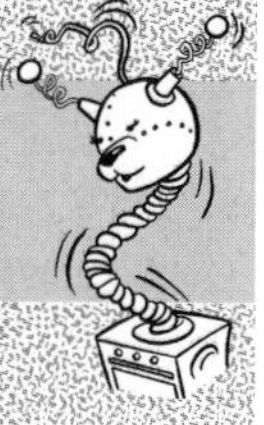

Circumference and diameter of a circle

The perimeter of a circle is called the **circumference.** It is the distance around the outside edge of the circle.

The **diameter** is a line that joins two points on opposite sides of the circle, through the centre. It is the longest distance across the circle, and is twice the length of the radius.

There is a formula that links the circumference (C) and diameter (d) of a circle:

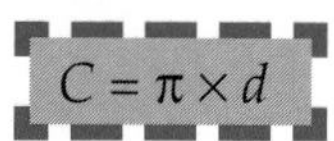

Example Calculate the circumference of this circle.
The diameter is 8.2 cm.

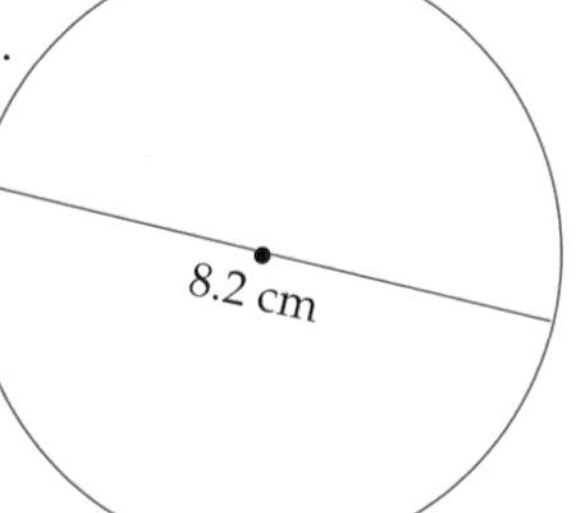

Answer
$C = \pi \times d$
$C = \pi \times 8.2$
$= 25.8$ cm (1 dp)

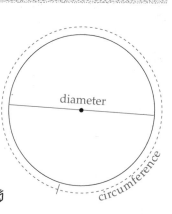

Sometimes we work with the radius (r) instead of the diameter.
The diameter is twice the radius ($d = 2r$). So, the formula becomes $C = \pi \times 2r$.
In algebra we would write this as $C = 2\pi r$.

EXERCISE 12.2

1–4 *Calculate the circumference of each circle. Give your answers in the correct units, to the nearest whole number.*

1 2

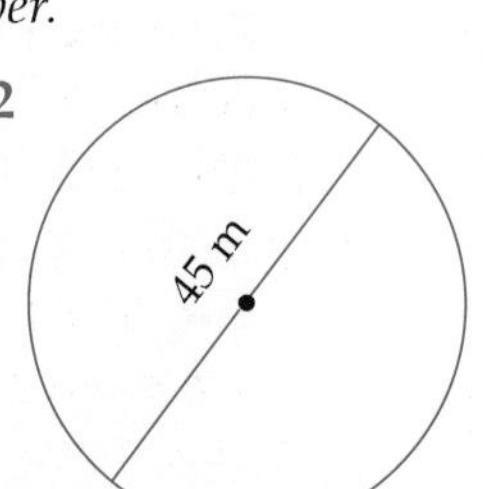

3 4

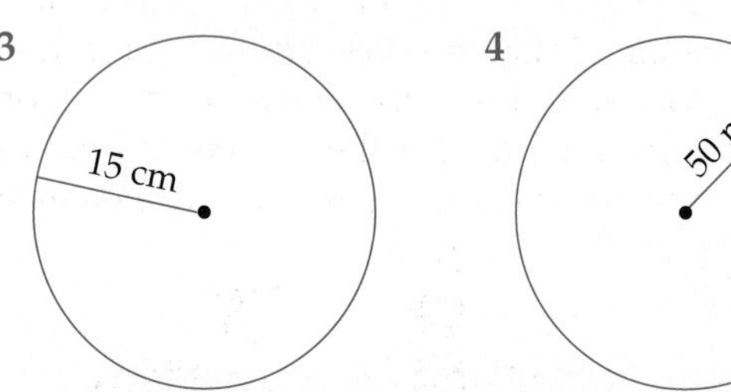

5 Calculate the circumference of a circle with a diameter of 61 cm.

6 Calculate the circumference of a circle with a radius of 19 m.

7 How many different diameters can be drawn in a circle?

8 This table shows measurements of the diameter and circumference of several round items. The measurements have been rounded to the nearest mm.

		Circumference (C)	Diameter (d)	$C \div d$
(i)	Top of coffee mug	267	85	3.1412
(ii)	Frisbee	785	250	
(iii)	Car tyre	1756	559	
(iv)	CD	374	119	

(a) Use a calculator to work out the values for the last column. (i) has been done for you.
(b) Explain what you are calculating when you divide C by d.
(c) Suggest a reason why the values in the last column are all slightly different.

9 Calculate the perimeter of this semi-circle. Give your answer correct to the nearest whole number.

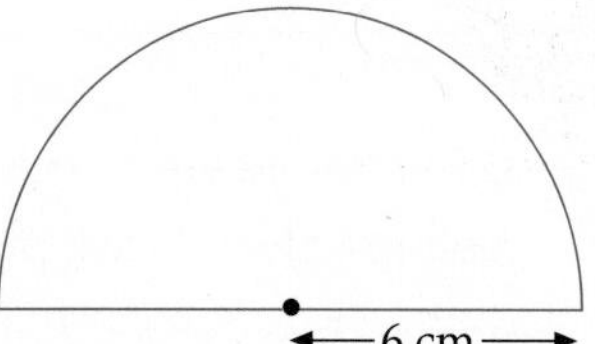

10 Calculate the perimeter of this quarter-circle. Give your answer correct to the nearest whole number.

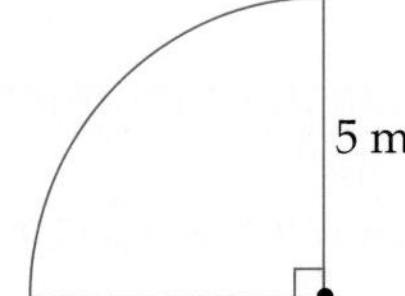

Here are some ways in which area of circles and circumference come into real life.

EXERCISE 12.3

1 A rotary sprinkler waters a lawn in a circular pattern. The water can reach up to 8 m from the sprinkler. What area of lawn can be watered from one position?

2 A tape measure is pulled tight around a circular tree trunk. The diameter of the trunk is 14 cm. What will be the reading on the tape measure (to the nearest cm)?

3 A cake is baked in a round tin, and is then iced on top. The diameter of the tin is 24 cm.

(a) What is the radius of the tin?

(b) Calculate the area of icing to the nearest cm^2.

4 A round rubber hose has a radius of 2.5 cm. To repair a leak, Chris has wound tape around the pipe exactly *three* times.
What length of tape is this? Give your answer to the nearest cm.

5 A goat is tied to a post by a rope. The rope measures 5 m. Estimate the area of grass the goat can reach, to the nearest $10\ m^2$.

6 A circular cricket ground has a diameter of 80 m. The boundary is marked by a length of rope. What will be the length of this rope, to the nearest m?

7 A round instant-coffee jar has a diameter of 8 cm. The top is sealed with foil to keep the contents fresh. What is the area of foil, to the nearest cm^2?

8 A bicycle has wheels with a radius of 61 cm. It is wheeled forward until the front wheel has gone around exactly once. Calculate how far the bicycle has moved. Give your answer correct to the nearest cm.

13 Volume

The **volume** of a solid object is the amount of space it occupies.

We measure volume using **cubic** units.

The two most common units for measuring volume are:

- the cubic centimetre cm^3
- the cubic metre m^3

We define 1 cm^3 as the volume of a cube with edges of 1 cm.

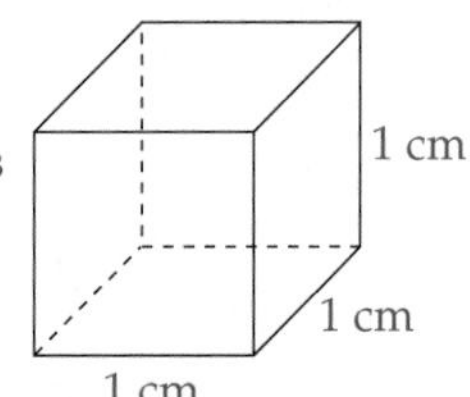

For example a new eraser (rubber) could have a volume of about 12 cm^3.

Here the eraser is photographed against a centimetre ruler. The length is about 6 cm, the width about 2 cm, and the height about 1 cm.

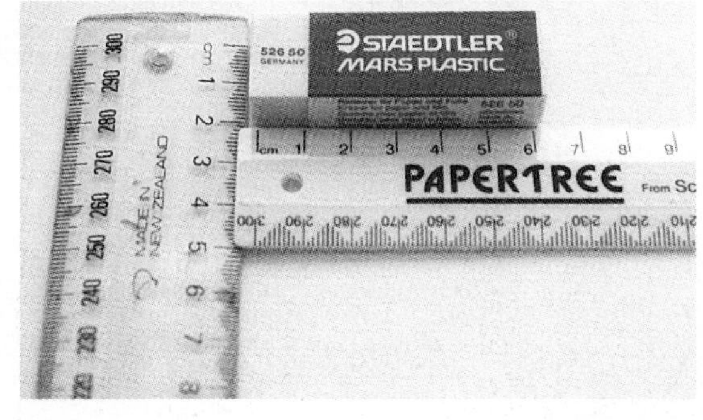

We can see the volume would be about 12 cm^3 by looking at a drawing of 1 cm^3 blocks representing the eraser.
If we count the 1 cm^3 blocks there are 12.

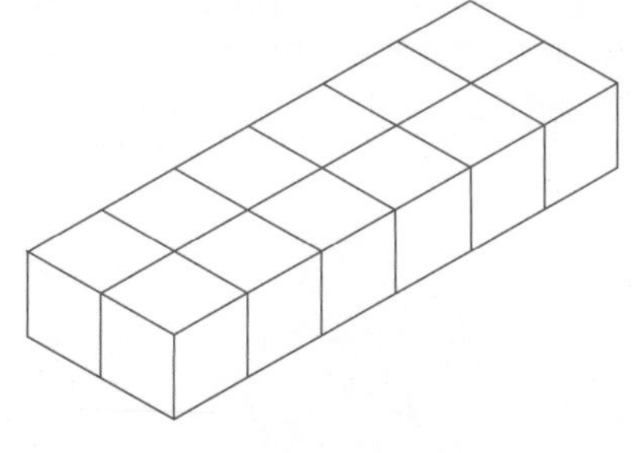

Larger objects, like shipping containers, buildings, etc. would usually have their volumes measured in m^3.

EXERCISE 13.1

Choose the most suitable unit to measure these volumes. Choose from the list { cm^3, m^3, km^3 }

1 the space inside your classroom

2 a pencil sharpener

3 a packet of tissues

4 the moon

5 a car battery

6 a packet of butter

7 a swimming pool

8 a truckload of gravel for road repairs

9 a calculator

10 a telephone handset

Counting blocks/adding layers

> Do you remember we used **squares** to estimate area? This applies to 2-dimensional shapes on a flat surface.
> Solid objects are different—they occupy space in 3 dimensions. So, their volumes can be estimated by counting **cubes**.

Here, we will assume each small cube measures 1 cm by 1 cm by 1 cm. So, each small cube has a volume of 1 cm^3.

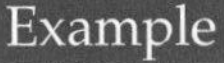

(a) Write down the volume of this shape.
(b) What would be the volume if another layer was added?

Answer

(a) Counting blocks, there are 15.
The volume is 15 cm^3.

(b) Another layer would also have 15 blocks.
This would give a total of 15 + 15 = 30 blocks. That is, the volume would be 30 cm^3.

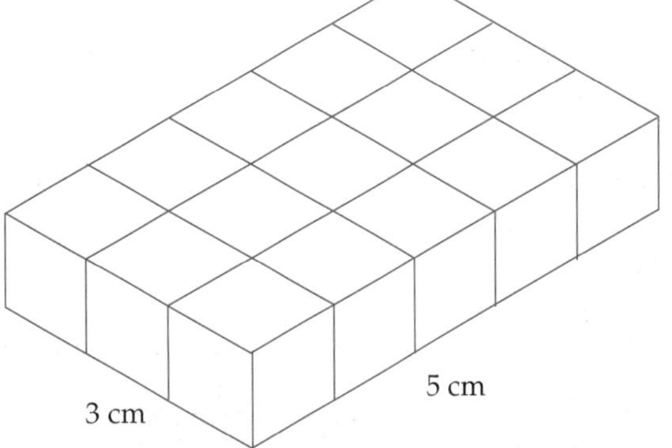

EXERCISE 13.2

1–7 *Work out the volumes of these shapes. They are made up of small cubes, each with a volume of* 1 cm^3.

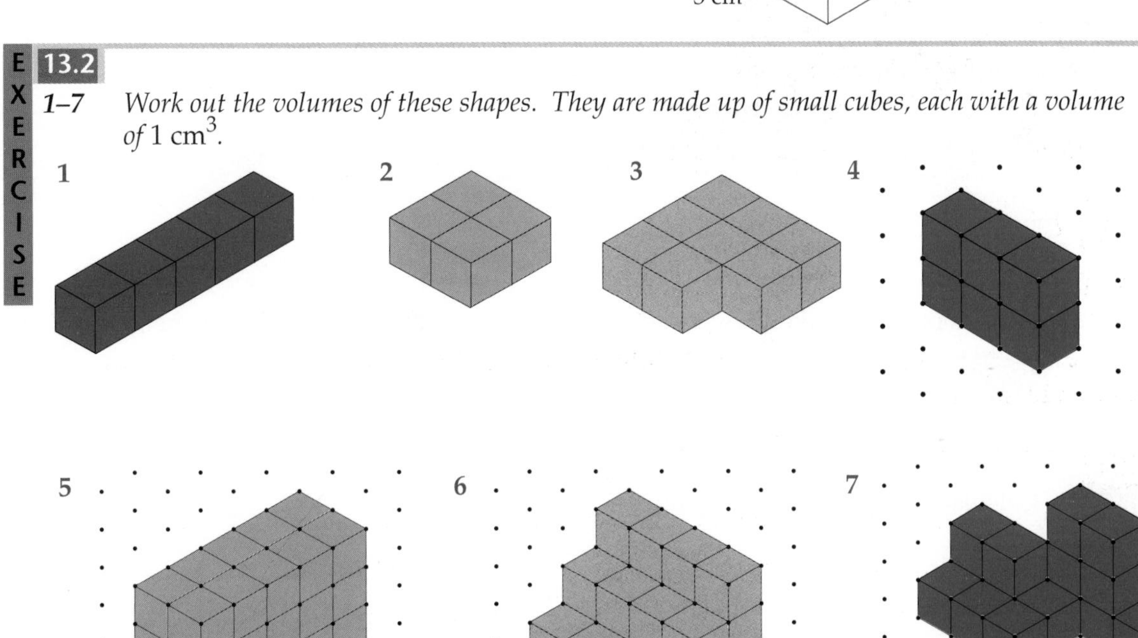

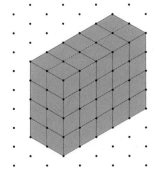

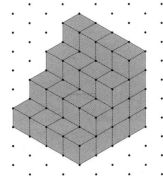

8

(a) What is the volume of this block?
(b) What would be the volume if:
  (i) 1 extra layer was added on top?
  (ii) 3 extra layers were added on top?

9

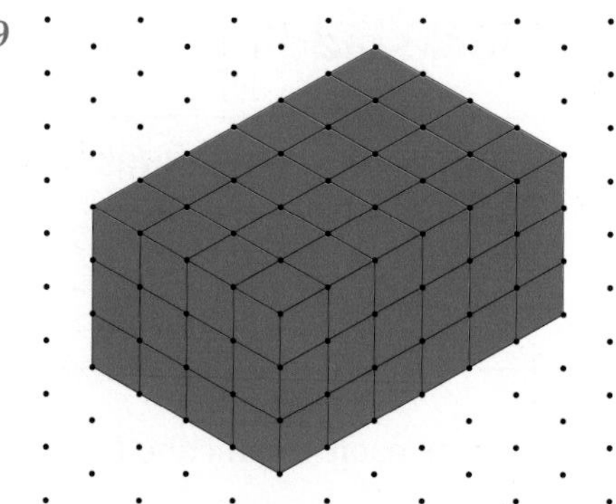

(a) What is the volume of this block?
(b) What would be the volume if the top layer was *removed*?

Volume of cuboids

STARTER

This shape has a volume of 60 cm^3.

- Explain how you can get the answer of 60 from the numbers 3, 4 and 5.

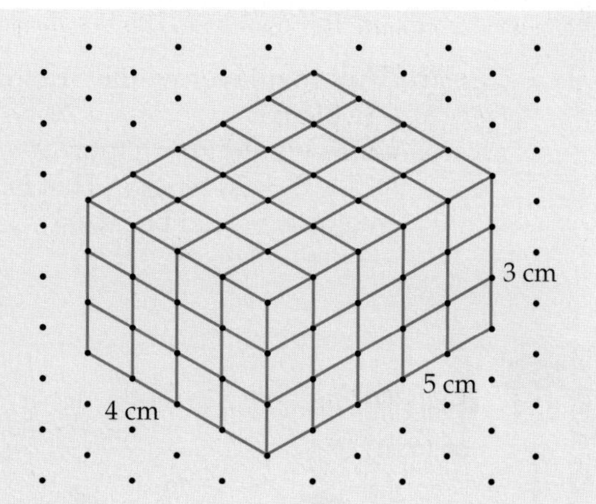

A **cuboid** is a solid shape where all six faces are rectangles.
The volume of a cuboid is calculated by multiplying the length by the width by the height.

Volume of cuboid = length × width × height

$$V = \ell \times w \times h$$

Example Calculate the volume of this cuboid.

Answer

$$V = \ell \times w \times h$$
$$= 6 \times 5 \times 3$$
$$= 90 \text{ m}^3$$

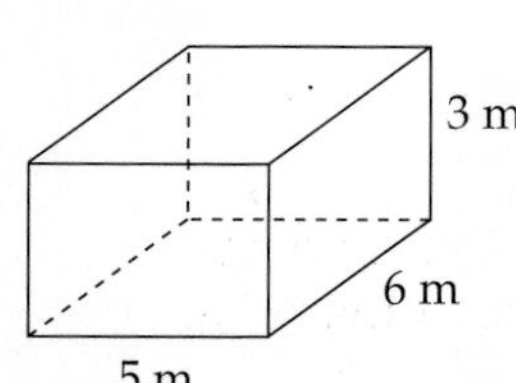

Cubes

A **cube** is a special kind of cuboid where all the edges are the same length.

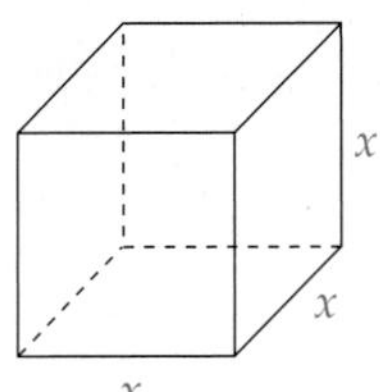

The volume of a cube is calculated by multiplying the edge length by itself three times. (In other words, raising the edge length to the power of 3.) This is why we often say 'x cubed' for 'x to the power of 3'.

$$V = x \times x \times x$$

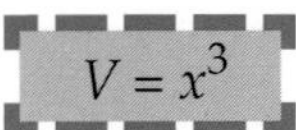

EXERCISE 13.3

1–4 *Calculate the volumes of these cuboids:*

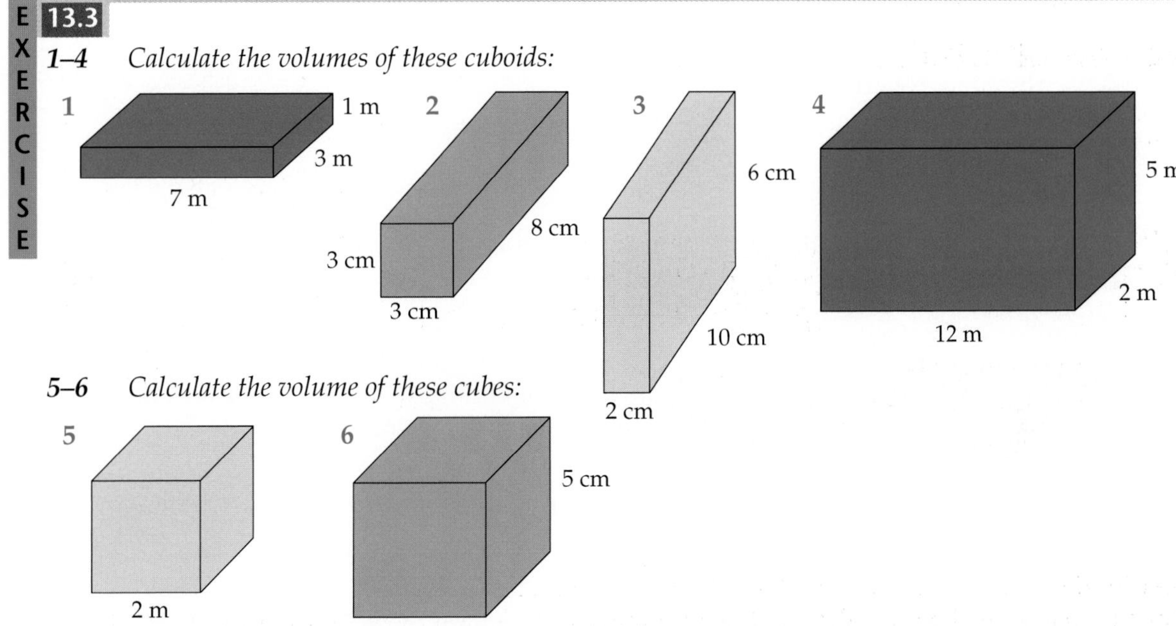

5–6 *Calculate the volume of these cubes:*

5 2 m

6 5 cm

7 This table gives the measurements, in cm, of some different cuboids. Calculate the values (a)–(h).

length	width	height	volume (cm^3)
2	5	4	(a)
10	1	2	(b)
3	12	4	(c)
6	6	5	(d)
8	2	4	(e)
(f)	3	5	15
2	(g)	5	20
6	3	(h)	72

8 Each edge of a cube is 3 cm long. Calculate the volume of the cube.

9 Each edge of a cube is 6 cm long. Calculate the volume of the cube.

INVESTIGATION

THE ORANGE-JUICE CARTON

Only Orange Ltd sell small cuboid cartons of orange juice. They contain 240 mL of orange juice. This means the volume of each carton is 240 cm^3.

Here's one possible design with dimensions giving a volume of 240 cm^3:

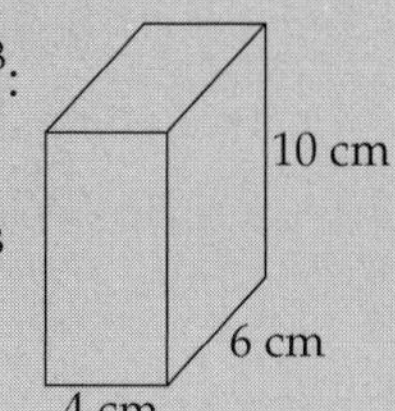

1 Draw designs for two other possible cuboids with a volume of 240 cm^3. Show the dimensions on each one. Make sure the designs are all different—for example $4 \times 6 \times 10$ is the same design as $6 \times 10 \times 4$.

Only Orange make their cartons by cutting out a net of special waxed cardboard foil, and sealing the edges together.

Here is the net for the 4 cm × 6 cm × 10 cm design. It shows the six faces of the carton before it is folded into position.

The total area of cardboard foil needed for this design is 248 cm^2.

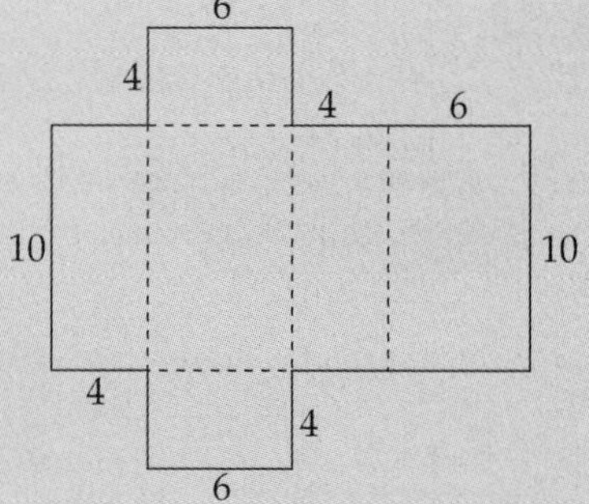

2 Explain why the area needed is 248 cm^2. Do this by working out the area of each face, and adding these together. Show your calculations.

3 Work out the total area of cardboard foil required for your two other designs (question 1).

4 What kind of design will need the smallest amount of cardboard foil? Explain.

Volume of prisms

STARTER

This is a drawing of a triangular wedge of cheese. It has been drawn on a 1 cm square grid.

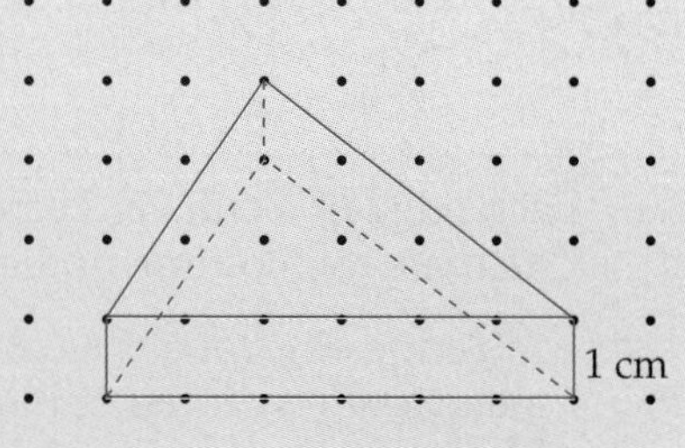

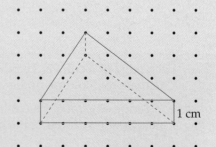

- Explain why the area of the triangle on top is 9 cm^2.

The **volume** of the wedge of cheese is 9 cm^3.

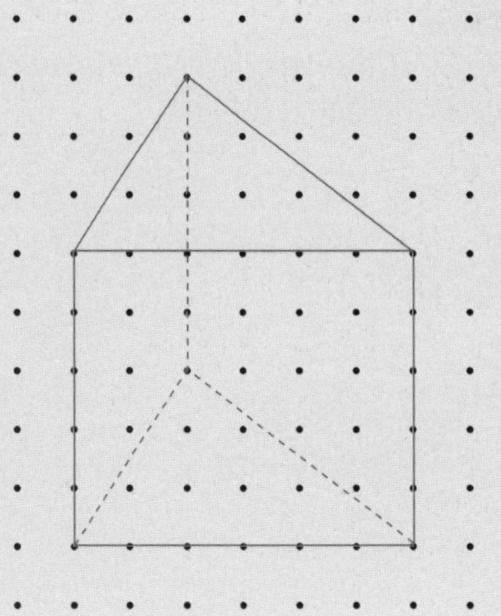

Four more identical wedges are now stacked on top of this one. This makes the height of the wedge 5 cm instead of 1 cm.

- What do you think the total volume is now?

Objects like this triangular wedge of cheese are called **prisms**.

A prism has the same cross-section all the way through its height (or length). It has two identical, parallel end faces.

All of these shapes are examples of prisms:

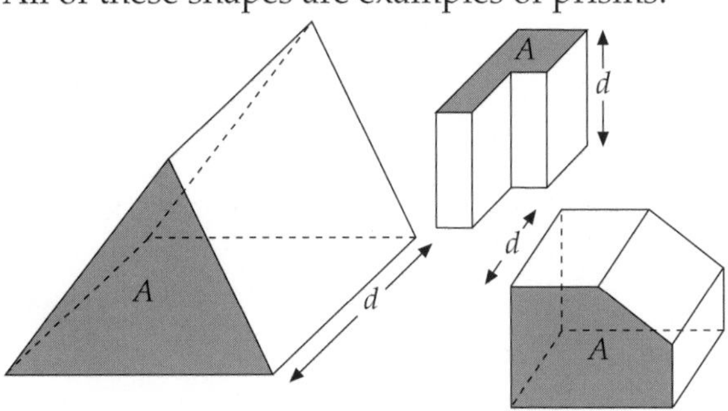

- In each case, one of the two end faces is shaded. This shows the cross-section.
- The end faces are the same distance (d) apart everywhere.

The volume of a prism is worked out by multiplying the area of the cross-section (A) by the distance between the two identical end faces (d).

Volume of prism = $A \times d$

- The distance (d) between the two end faces can either look like a *height* or a *length*. It depends on how the prism has been drawn.
- Sometimes, the area of the cross-section is given to you. If not, you work it out first. Then you multiply it by the distance (d) between the two end faces.

Examples Calculate the volume of each prism.

(a) 4 cm, $A = 7$ cm^2

(b) 5 cm, 3 cm, 4 cm

Answers

(a) Volume of prism = $A \times d$

$V = 7 \text{ cm}^2 \times 4 \text{ cm}$

$= 28 \text{ cm}^3$

(b) The cross-section is a triangle.

Triangle area $= \frac{1}{2}(b \times h) = \frac{1}{2}(3 \times 4) = \frac{1}{2} \times 12 = 6 \text{ cm}^2$

$V = 6 \text{ cm}^2 \times 5 \text{ cm}$

$= 30 \text{ cm}^3$

EXERCISE 13.4

1–12 *Calculate the volume of these prisms. The lengths are in cm. If the cross-section area is given, it is in* cm^2.

1

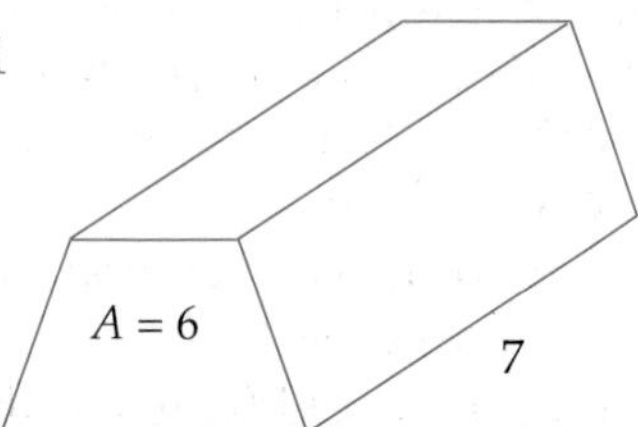

2

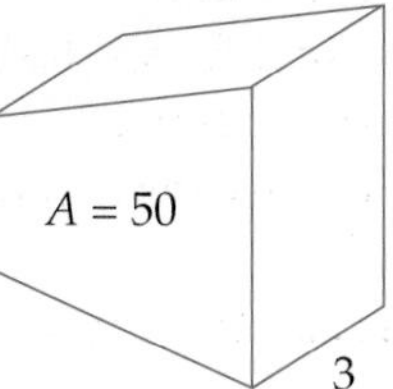

3

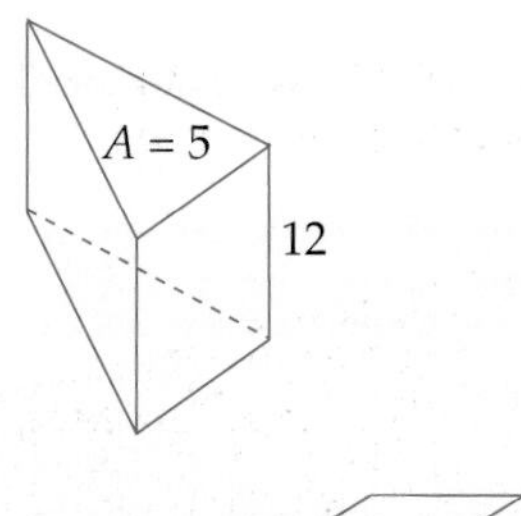

4

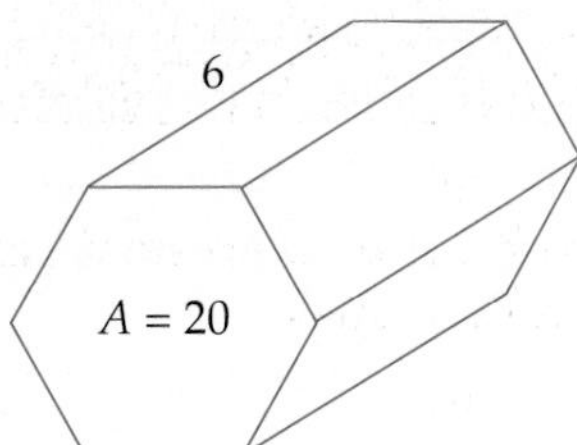

5

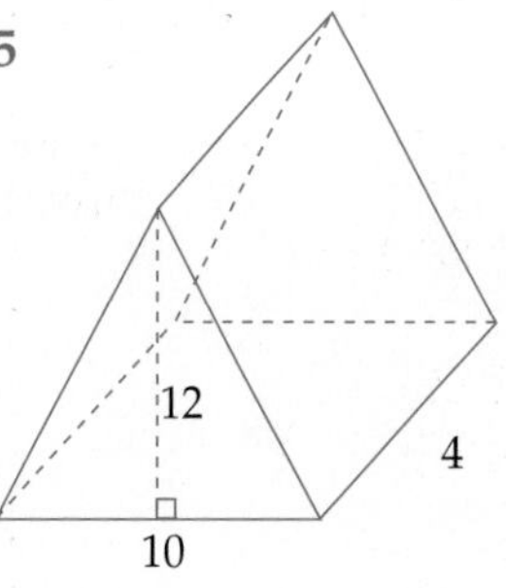

6

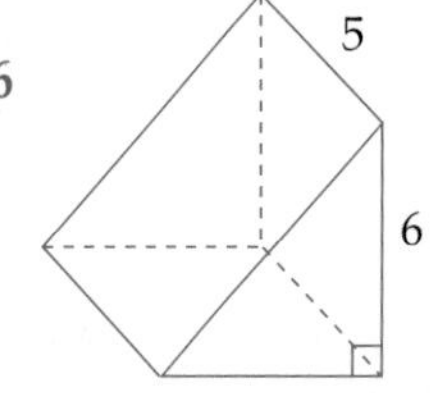

7

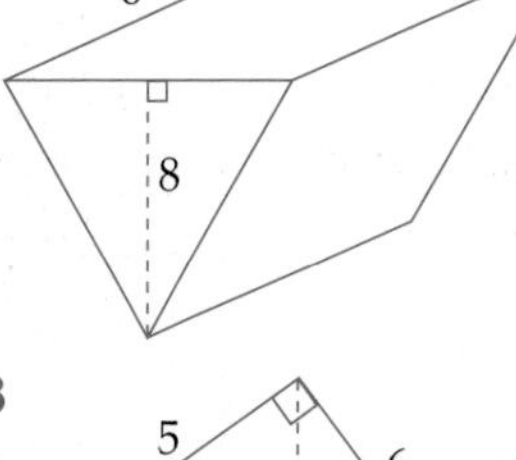

8

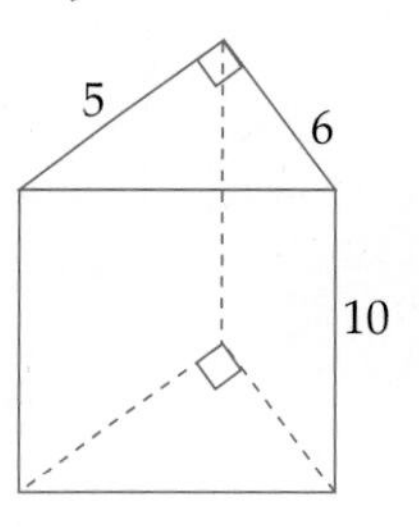

9 (note: area of circle is $A = \pi r^2$)

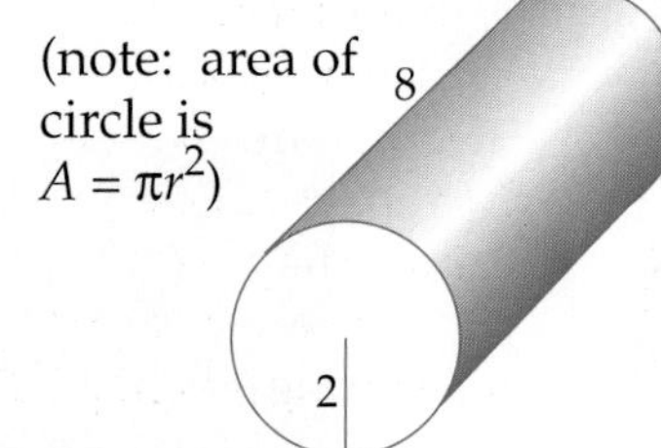

10

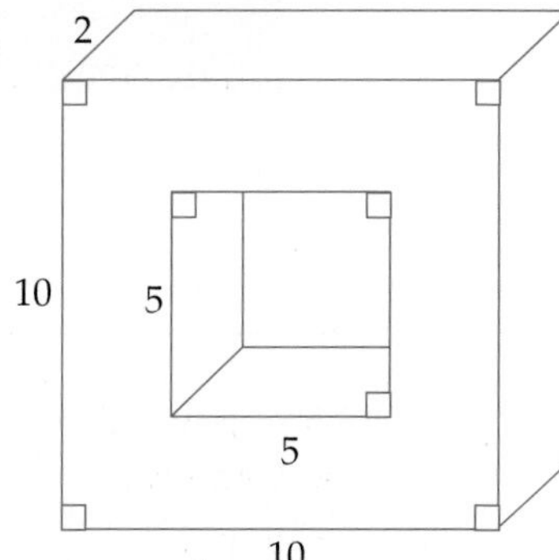

11

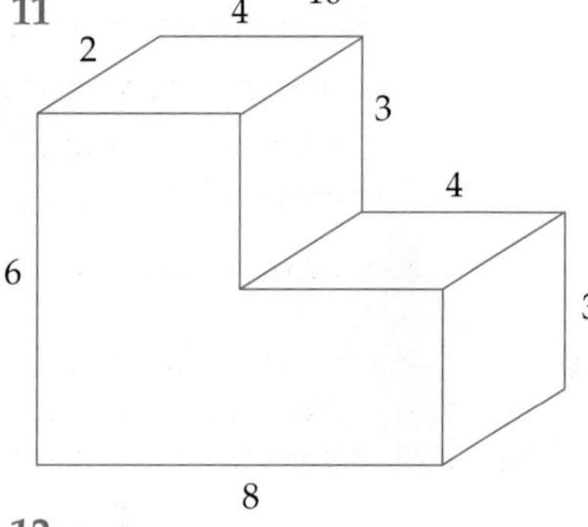

12

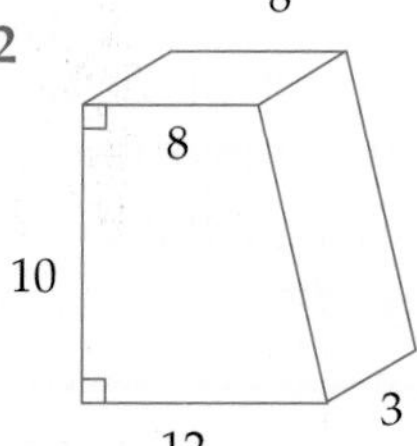

13 A prism has a triangular cross-section. The base is 6 cm and the height is 4 cm. The length of the prism from end to end is 8 cm.

(a) Copy this diagram. Add the three measurements in the correct positions.

(b) Calculate the volume of the prism.

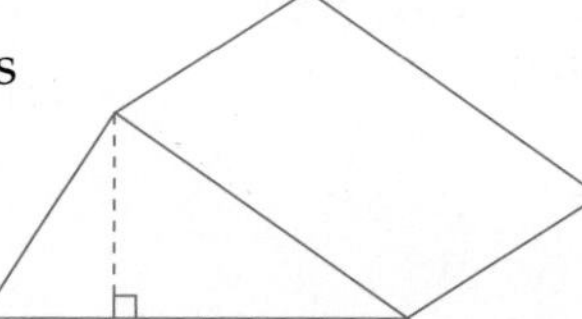

Using volume ideas

EXERCISE 13.5

1 A manufacturer of games makes dice. Each die measures 1 cm by 1 cm by 1 cm. They are packed into a carton measuring 12 cm by 10 cm by 8 cm.

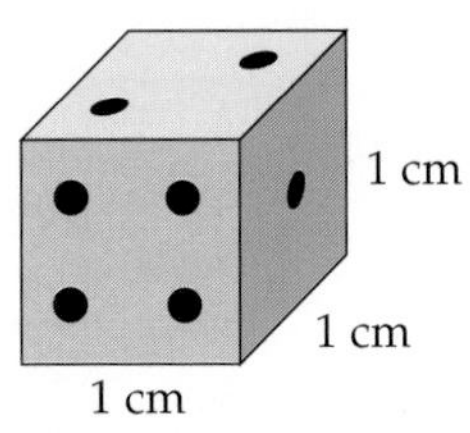

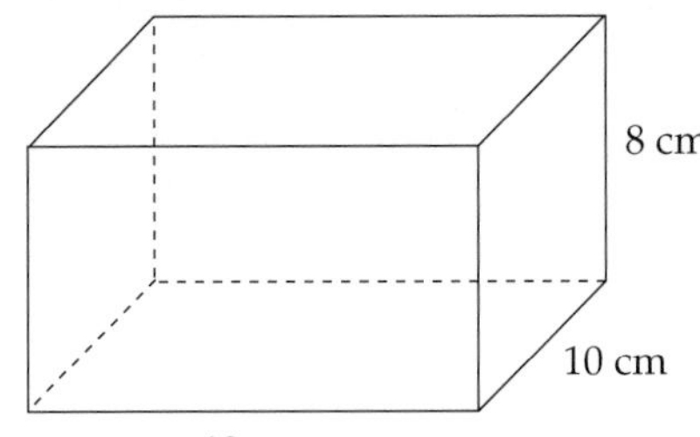

(a) How many dice can be placed in the bottom layer of the carton?

(b) How many layers of dice fit inside the carton altogether?

(c) Calculate the volume of the carton.

(d) Complete this label to go on the outside of the carton:

Contains exactly ____ dice

2 This diagram shows a two-tier wedding cake. All the measurements are in cm. Calculate the total volume of the cake.

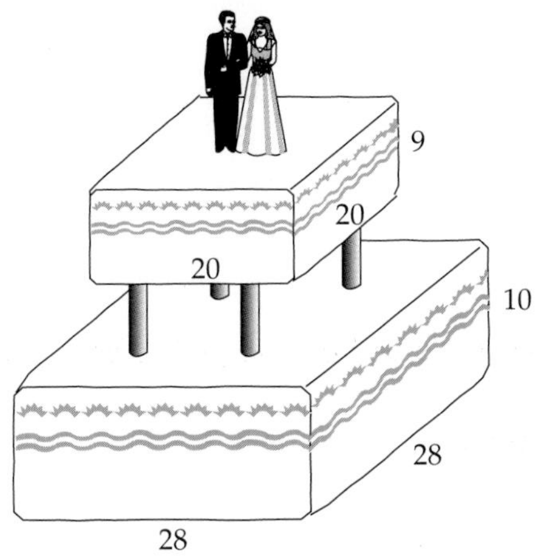

3 The storage space in a warehouse is 8 m long, 3 m wide and 4 m high. It will be filled with cubic cartons with each edge measuring 50 cm (or 0.5 m).

(a) How many cartons will fit along the length of the storage space?

(b) How many cartons will fit across the width of the storage space?

(c) How many cartons will fit on the floor of the storage space altogether?

(d) How many layers of cartons can be stored in the space?

(e) How many cartons can be stored altogether?

4 Here is a plan for a concrete ramp, for wheelchair access into a building.

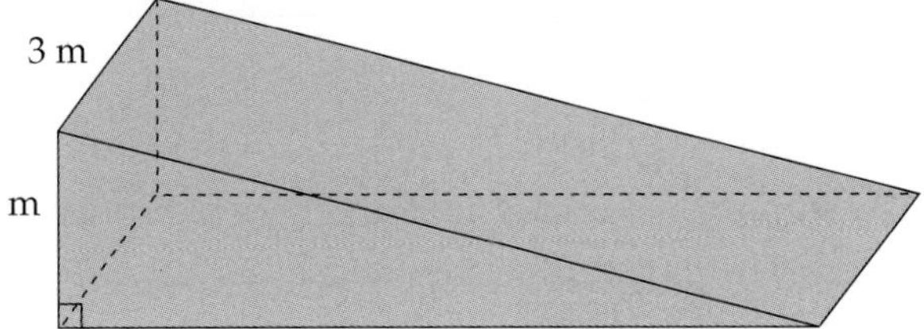

Calculate the volume of concrete (in m^3) needed to build this ramp.

5 A swimming pool is 50 m long, and 16 m wide. At the shallow end, the pool is 1 m deep. It slopes down steadily to the deep end, where the depth is 3 m.

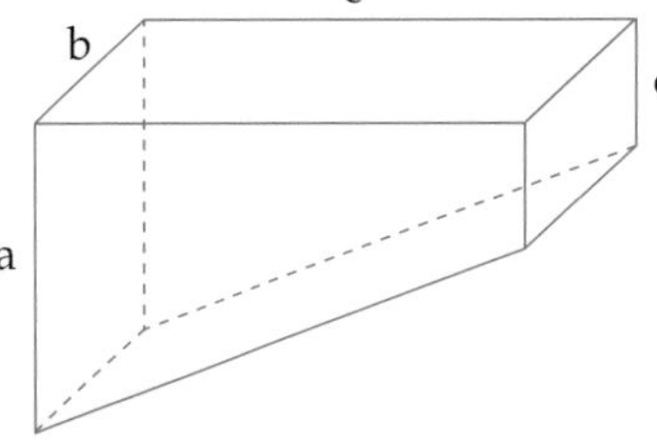

(a) What are the measurements marked a, b, c and d on this diagram?

(b) Calculate the area of the cross-section of the pool. *Hint*: you could draw the cross-section as (rectangle + triangle):

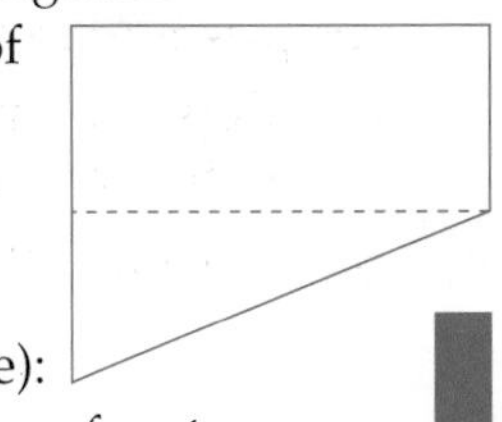

(c) Calculate the volume of water in the pool.

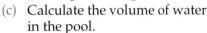

Liquid volume

STARTER

Here are advertisements for two cars:

TOYOTA Corolla, 98, red, auto, 1600, \$12999 o.n.o. Ph (9) 483 2153

TOYOTA Camry, 2.0, white, a/c, \$12500, Ph (9) 483 9449

- What do the numbers 1600 and 2.0 refer to?
- Which car is more powerful? Explain.

A space that can be filled with a liquid is often called a 'capacity' rather than a volume.

We use units like litres and millilitres (mL) for liquid volume.

- ordinary volume of 1 cm^3 = 1 mL liquid volume
- ordinary volume of 1000 cm^3 = 1 litre liquid volume

Centimetres (length), litres (liquid volume), and grams (mass) are all related. The common link is water!

- 1 mL of water weighs 1 g, and occupies (takes up) 1 cm^3.
- 1 litre of water weighs 1 kg, and occupies 1000 cm^3.

1 litre

1 kg

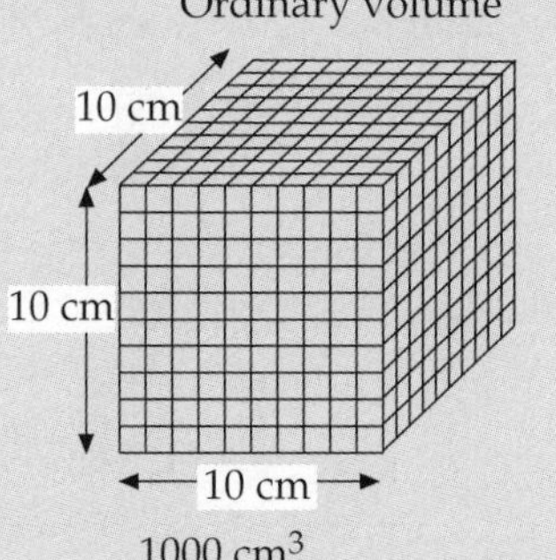

1000 cm^3

Example Change 600 cm^3 to mL.

Answer 600 cm^3 = 600 mL

Example What volume container would hold 2 litres of liquid?

Answer 2 litres = 2×1000 mL = 2000 cm^3

Example How many litres of water can this fish tank hold?

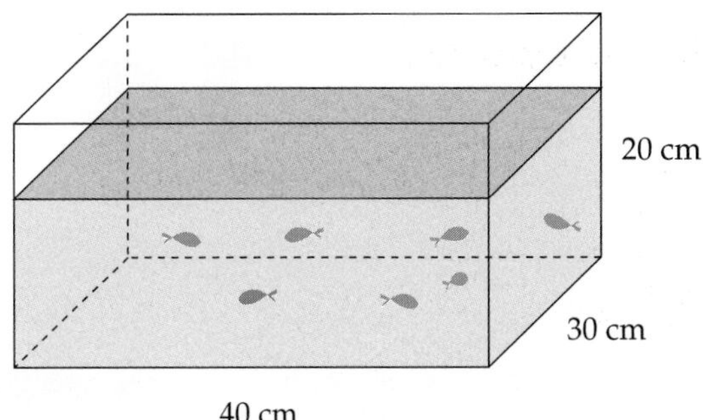

Answer The fish tank is a cuboid.

Volume = $40 \times 30 \times 20 = 24\ 000\ \text{cm}^3$

(Note $1000\ \text{cm}^3 = 1$ litre)

Volume = $\dfrac{24\ 000}{1000} = 24$ litres

EXERCISE 13.6

1 Change these car engine sizes (given in cm^3) to litres:
(a) 1300 (b) 4000 (c) 850

2 Change these car engine sizes to cm^3:
(a) 1 litre (c) 2.3 litres
(b) 2 litres (d) 4.2 litres

3 A powerful motorbike has an engine size of $500\ \text{cm}^3$. How many motorbikes would be equivalent in power to a 1 litre car engine?

4 Write down the weight (in g or kg) of these volumes of water:
(a) 400 mL (c) 1.2 litres
(b) 30 litres (d) 50 mL

5 This is a juice carton. Use its dimensions to complete the label correctly.

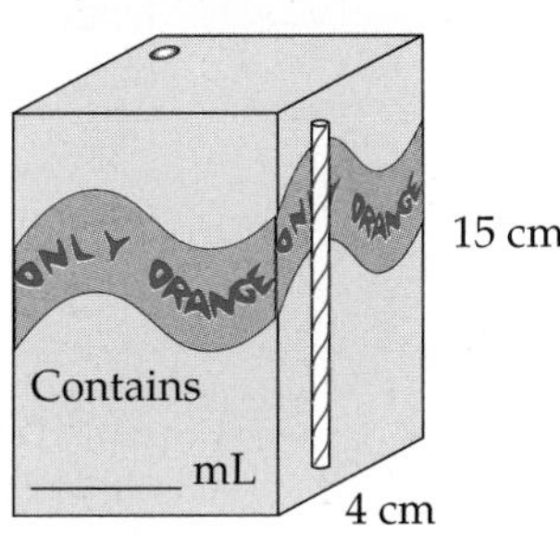

6 A laundry tub has a shape like a cuboid. It measures 40 cm by 25 cm, and is 20 cm deep. How many litres of water would it contain when full?

7 A cake tin has a square base. Its sides measure 18 cm, and it has a height of 10 cm. It is filled with water and left to soak before being cleaned. Calculate the volume of water in the tin in:
(a) cm^3 (b) mL (c) litres

8 We can cut this box to make a container holding exactly 1 litre. Calculate the height at which it should be cut.

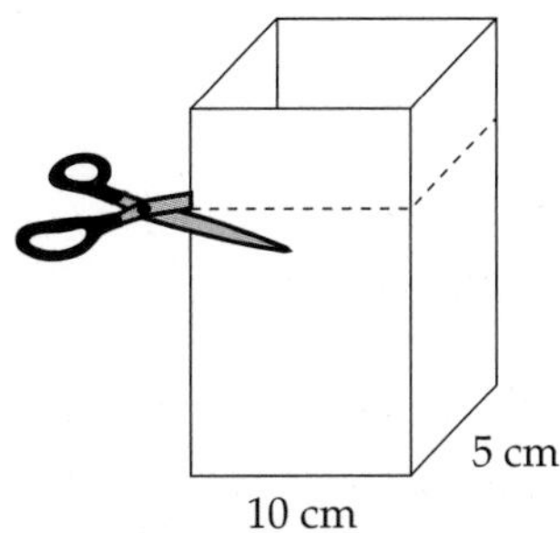

9 This glass has a radius of 3 cm and a height of 10 cm. Its cross-section area can be calculated from

$A = \pi r^2 = \pi \times 3 \times 3 = 28.3\ \text{cm}^2$.

(a) Calculate its volume in cm^3.
(b) Which of these is closest to the amount of water the glass will hold:

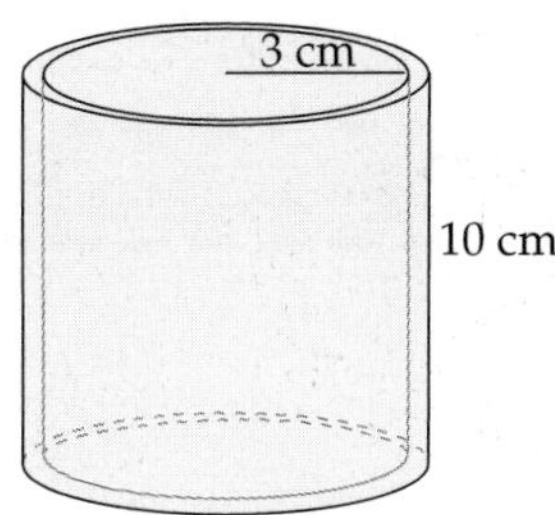

A 100 mL C 500 mL
B 250 mL D 1 litre

10 A cylindrical test-tube has a radius of 1 cm and a length of 12 cm. Calculate the volume of liquid it will hold. Give your answer to the nearest mL.

14 Angles

STARTER

- What do all of these diagrams have in common? Explain.

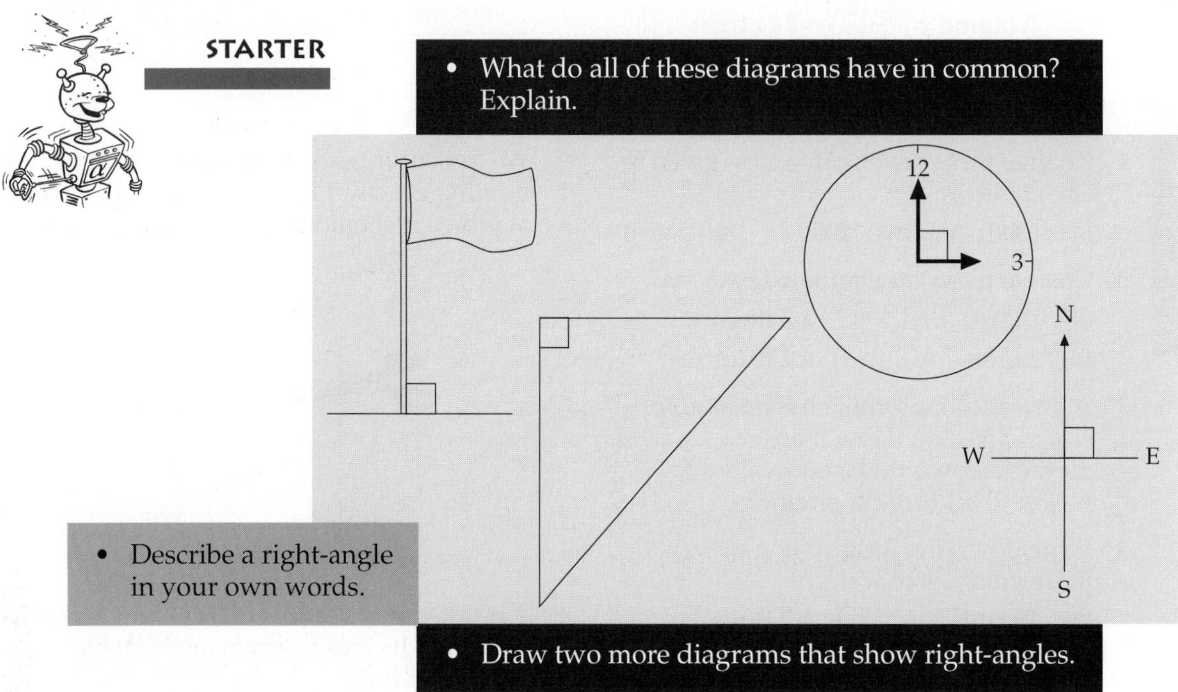

- Describe a right-angle in your own words.

- Draw two more diagrams that show right-angles.

Right-angles

A **right-angle** is a turn through a quarter of a circle.

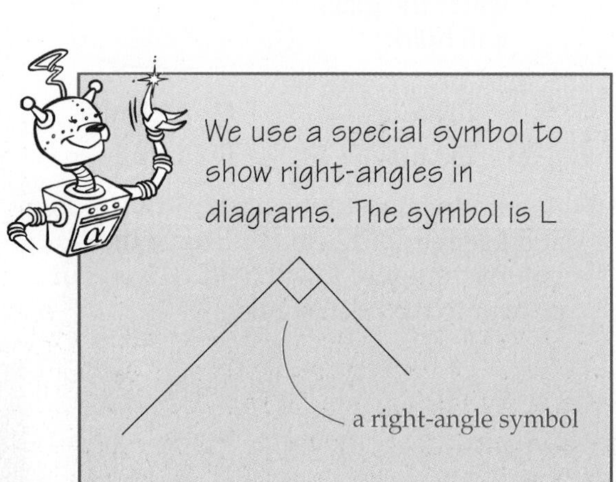

We use a special symbol to show right-angles in diagrams. The symbol is L
a right-angle symbol

Example This compass sign diagram shows a clockwise turn from the direction NE to NW. The turn is 3 right-angles.

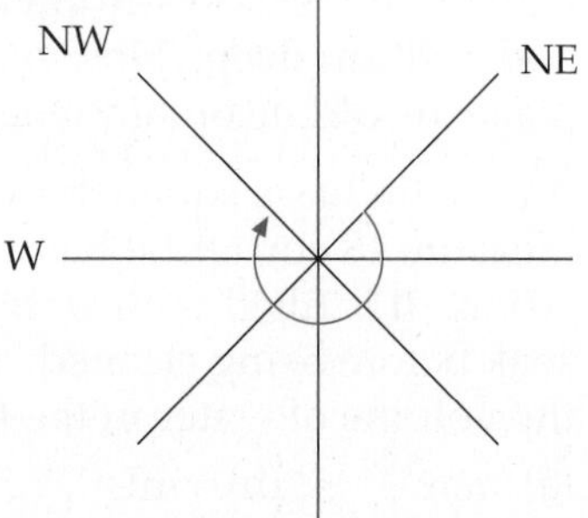

EXERCISE 14.1

1 Copy the compass sign diagram from the example into your book. Add the directions N, S, E, SE and SW to it.

2 How many right-angles are each of these turns? Choose from 1, 2, 3 or 4.
   (a) N to E clockwise
   (b) S to E clockwise
   (c) NW to NE clockwise
   (d) SW to NE clockwise
   (e) SE to SW clockwise
   (f) S to S clockwise
   (g) E to N clockwise
   (h) W to E clockwise

3 This is like the flag of Switzerland.
   (a) Copy the flag. Mark each right-angle with the right-angle symbol.
   (b) How many right-angles are there altogether?

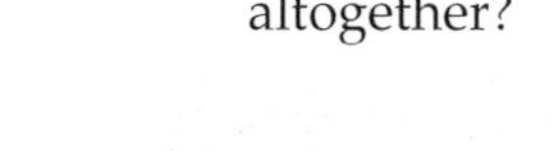

4 (a) How many right-angles does a clock's hour hand turn through when moving from:
      (i) 12 o'clock to 3 o'clock?
      (ii) 7 o'clock to 1 o'clock?
      (iii) 11 o'clock to 8 o'clock?
   (b) The hour hand of a clock starts at 5 o'clock. Where will it be when it has moved through:
      (i) 1 right-angle?
      (ii) 2 right-angles?
      (iii) 3 right-angles?

5 This line is the longest side of a right-angled triangle. It is about 6 cm long.
   (a) Copy the line. Draw the other two sides of the triangle.
   (b) Is it possible to draw a different answer to part (a)? Explain.

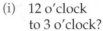

INVESTIGATION

PAPER-FOLDING

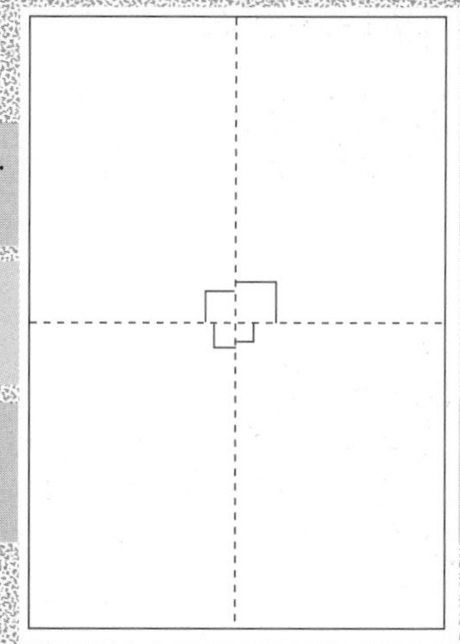

Take an A4 piece of paper. Fold it in half, then fold it in half again.

1 How many different right-angles are there in the centre?

Fold the piece of paper in half again.

2 Now how many right-angles are there?

3 Keep folding the paper a number of times. Copy this table and complete it as far as you can.

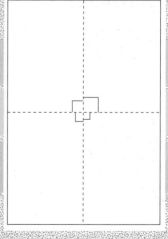

Number of folds	Number of right-angles
2	
3	
4	36
5	

4 How many right-angles would you get if you folded the piece of paper 6 times? Use the pattern shown in the table to predict this.

- Is it possible to keep folding the paper for ever?

Types of angle

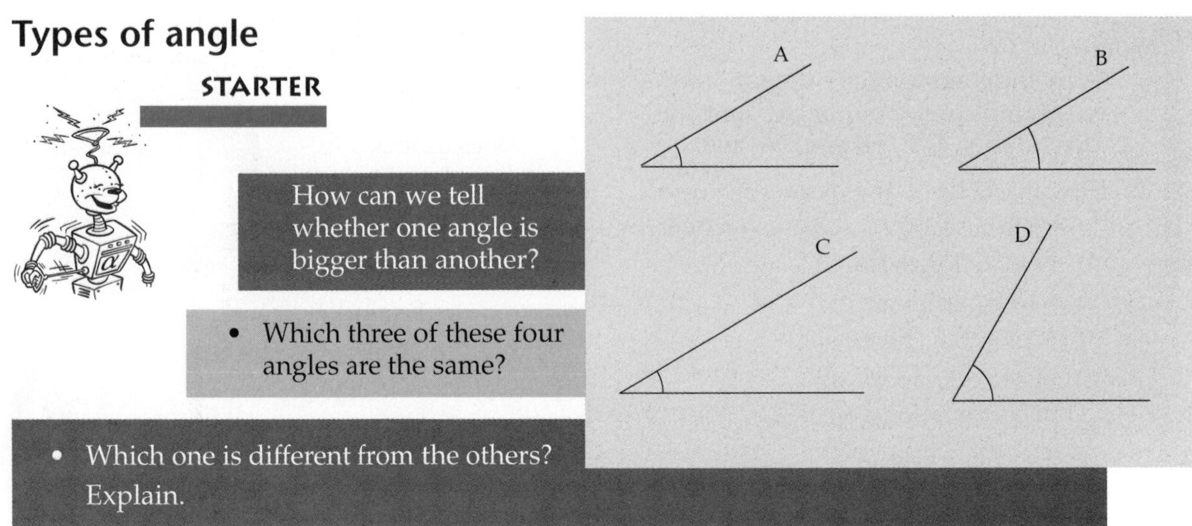

STARTER
How can we tell whether one angle is bigger than another?
• Which three of these four angles are the same?
• Which one is different from the others? Explain.
A
B
C
D

We can describe the size of an angle by saying whether it is **acute**, **obtuse** or **reflex**.

An **acute** angle is less than a right-angle	An **obtuse** angle is between 1 and 2 right-angles	A **reflex** angle is more than 2 right-angles

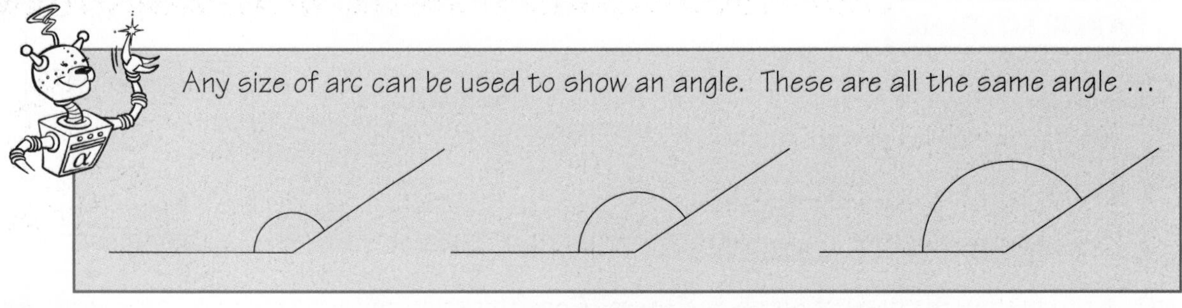

Any size of arc can be used to show an angle. These are all the same angle ...

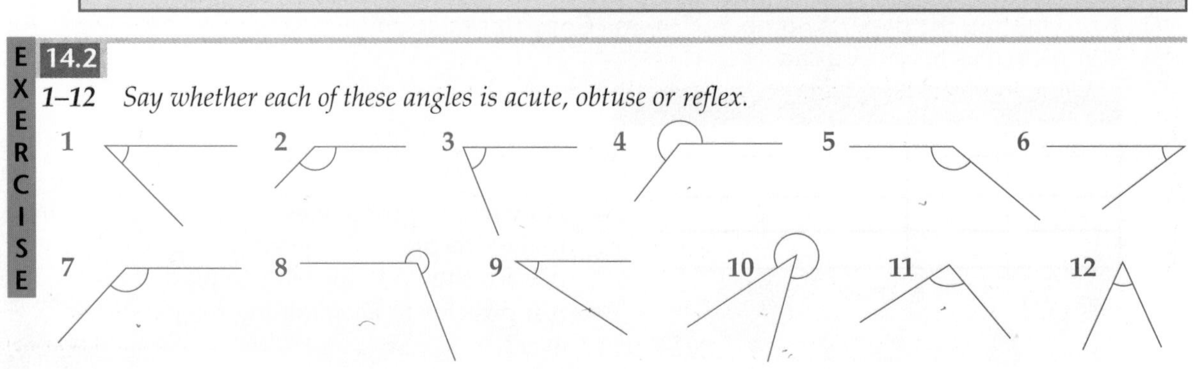

13 This is like the flag of Scotland. It is also known as the Cross of St. Andrew.

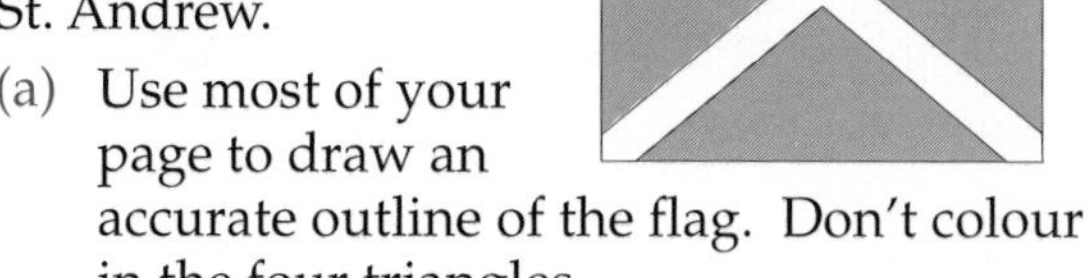

(a) Use most of your page to draw an accurate outline of the flag. Don't colour in the four triangles.

(b) Use a red pen to mark in the four reflex angles inside the flag.

(c) How many acute angles are there? Draw small blue arcs to show the acute angles.

(d) How many right-angles are there? Draw small right-angle symbols to show them.

(e) How many obtuse angles are there? Use another colour to show them.

14 The hour hand on my clock moved from 8 o'clock to 3 o'clock. Did it move through an acute, an obtuse or a reflex angle?

15

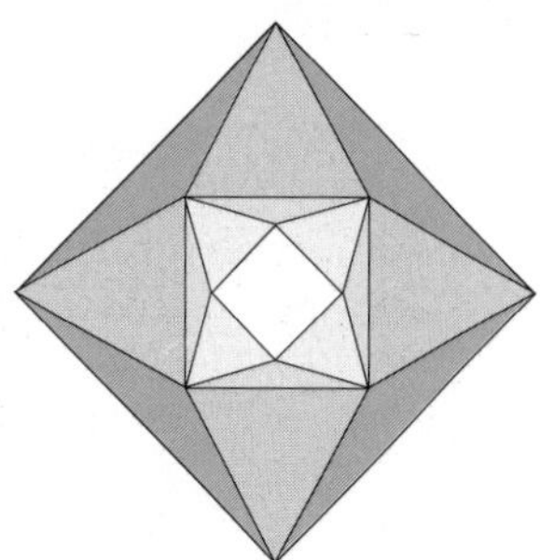

(a) How many right-angles are there in this shape? Don't count ones that have been split.

(b) How many obtuse angles are there? Again, don't count split ones.

Naming angles

STARTER

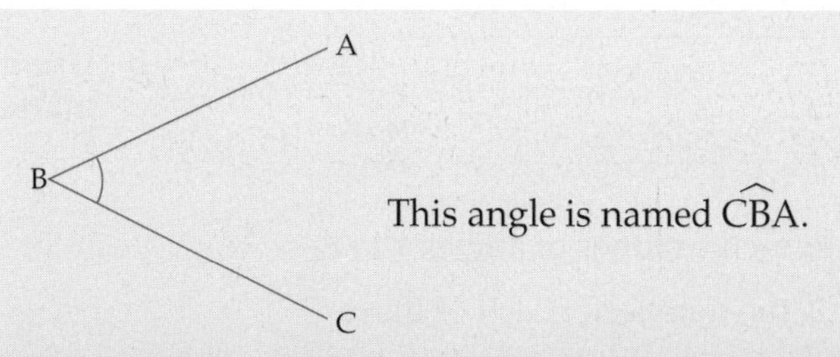

This angle is named $\widehat{CBA}$.

- What is the other way of naming this angle using three letters?
- Explain why $\widehat{BAC}$ is *not* the correct name for this angle.

Angles are formed when two lines meet at a point.
This point will be the *middle* letter of the angle name.
In the starter, B is where the lines meet—so B is the middle letter of the name.
The point where the lines meet is called the **vertex** of the angle.

EXERCISE 14.3

1 Name the marked angles. Use three letters for each one.

(a)

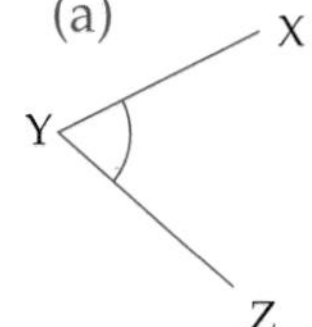

(b)

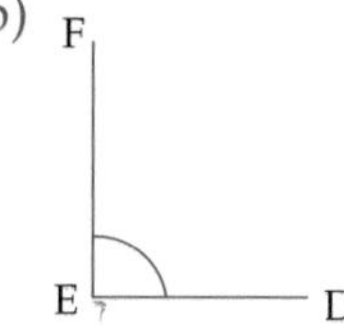

(c)

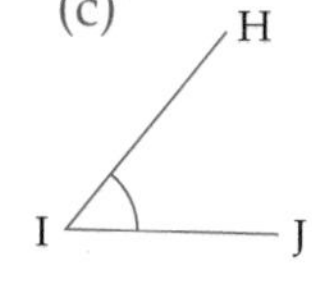

(d)

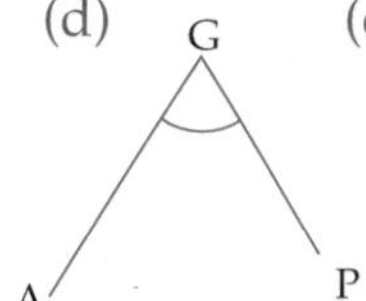

(e)

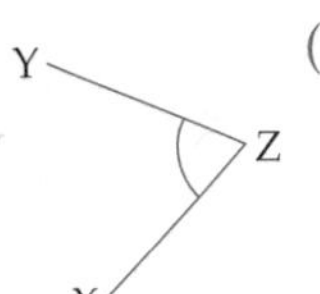

(f)

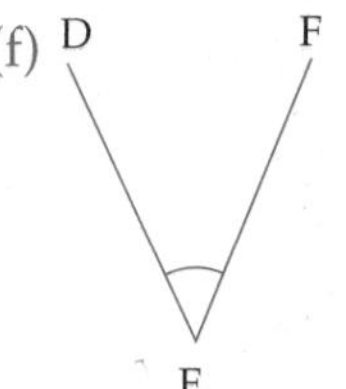

(continues)

(g)

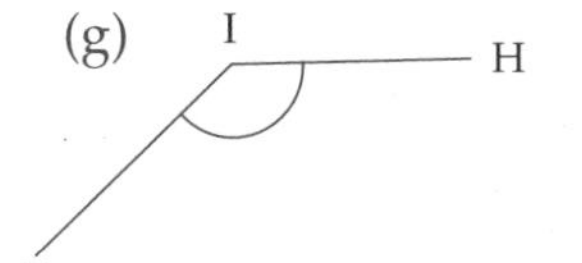

(h)

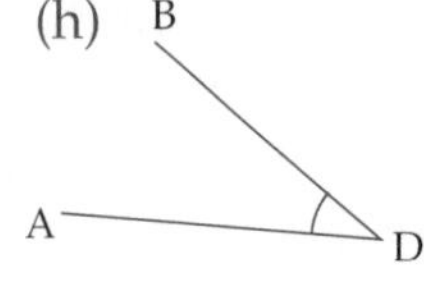

> There is more than one correct way to name an angle. In the answers, we will give both ways. You only have to give one!

2–3 *Use this diagram to answer the questions.*

2

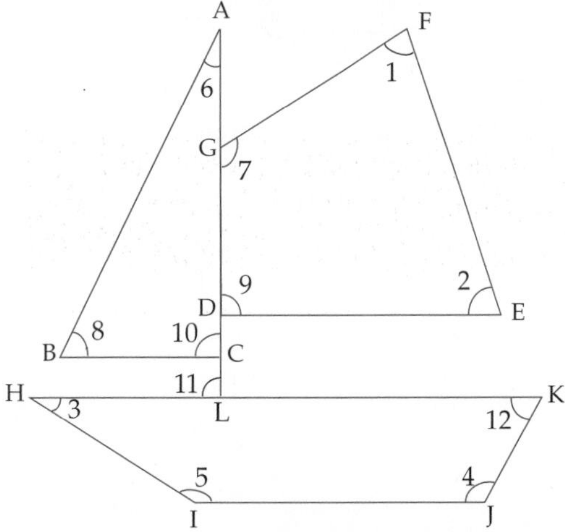

Write down the names of angles 1 to 8.

3 What is the number of each of these angles?

(a) $\widehat{ABC}$ (f) $\widehat{GCB}$

(b) $\widehat{BCD}$ (g) $\widehat{HIJ}$

(c) $\widehat{GDE}$ (h) $\widehat{HLA}$

(d) $\widehat{BAD}$ (i) $\widehat{BCA}$

(e) $\widehat{LGF}$ (j) $\widehat{HKJ}$

4 This diagram has three marked angles. All of them have Q as the vertex. Name the three angles.

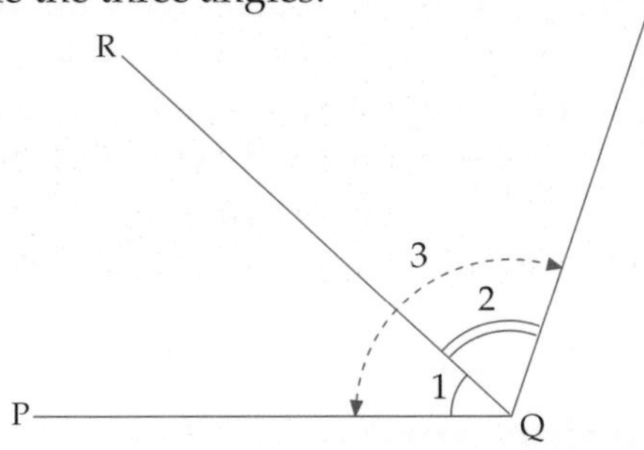

5 Use three letters to name the angles marked *a*, *b*, *c* and *d*.

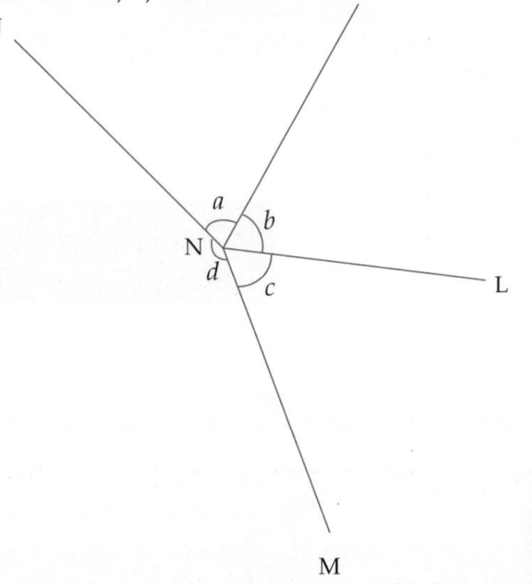

Measuring angles

> We use units called **degrees** to measure angles.

To work with angles more accurately, we take a right-angle as being 90°.

There are 4 right-angles in a full circle. So, there must be $4 \times 90° = 360°$ in a full circle.

> Degrees have been used for a long time. Many centuries ago, the Babylonians divided a full turn (or circle) into 360°. They believed (wrongly) that the Sun circled around the Earth. They also knew that a year was made up of about 360 days. This is where the measurement of degrees probably comes from.

STARTER

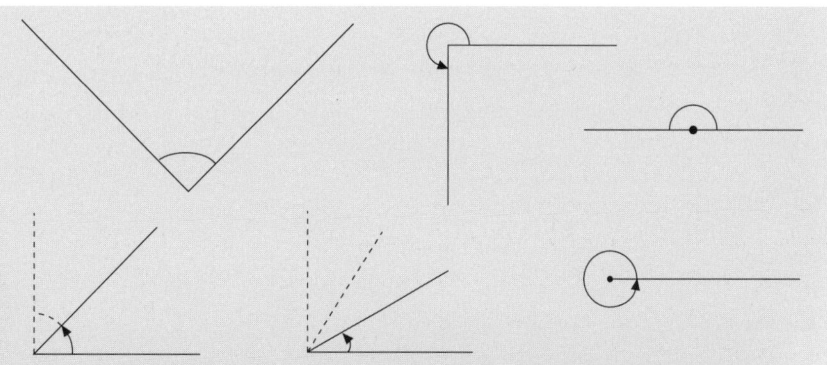

Six angles are shown here. They are all multiples or fractions of right-angles.

- Choose the size of each angle in degrees from the list { 30°, 180°, 360°, 270°, 45°, 90°}. In each case, explain your choice.

EXERCISE 14.4

1–6 *The diagram shows six angles. Match each angle with an angle size in degrees. Choose the angle size from this list:*

List of angle sizes
170°
100°
83°
67°
18°
215°

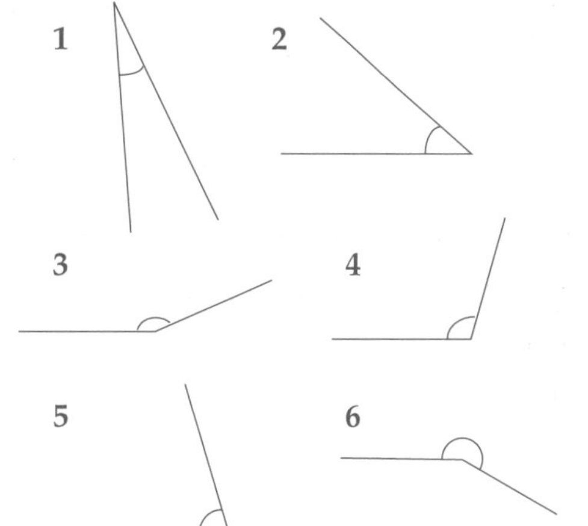

Using a protractor to measure angles

A **protractor** is a special instrument with an accurate scale in degrees around the outside.

On the next two pages we explain how to use a protractor.

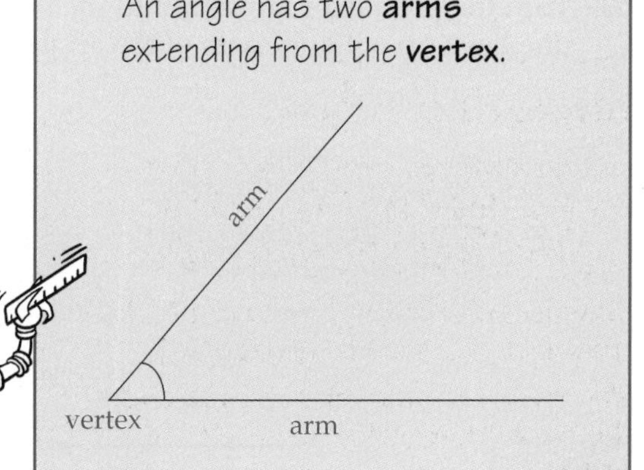

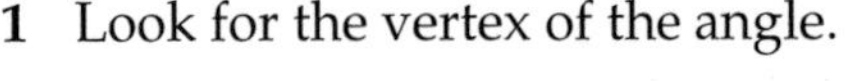

1 Look for the vertex of the angle.

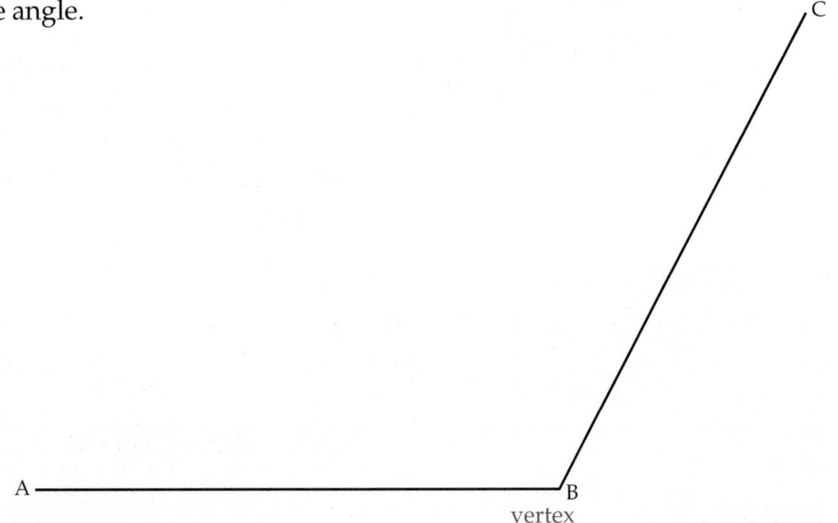

2 Place the protractor on the angle so that the centre of the protractor is exactly on the vertex.

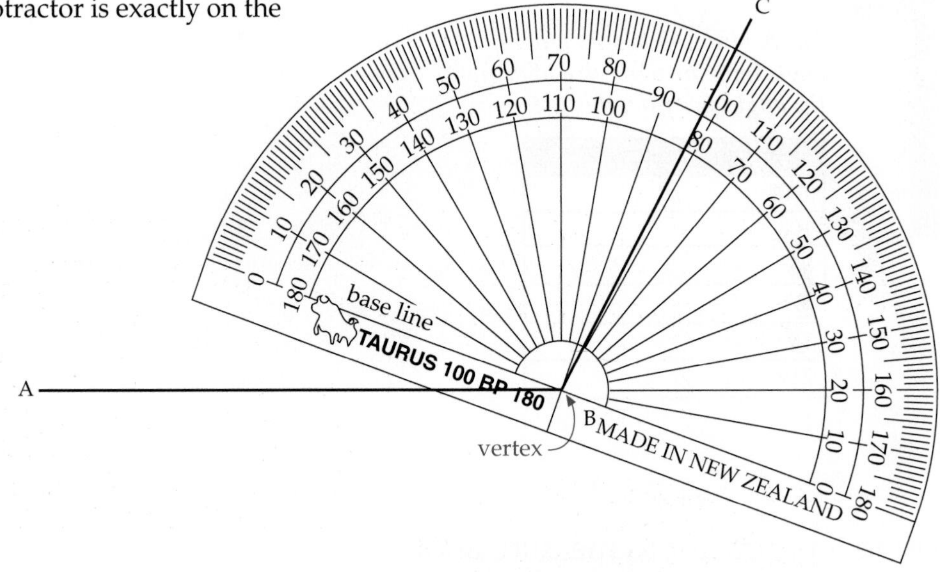

3 Turn the protractor around until the base line lines up with one arm of the angle.

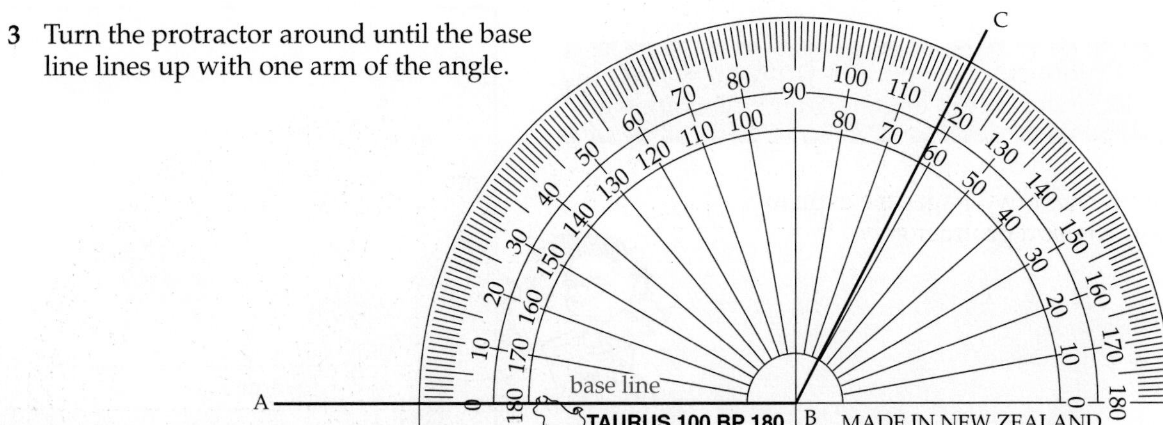

4 Look for the scale that starts with 0° on the base line.

5 On the other arm of the angle, read off the angle size on that scale.

Result:
$\widehat{ABC} = 118°$

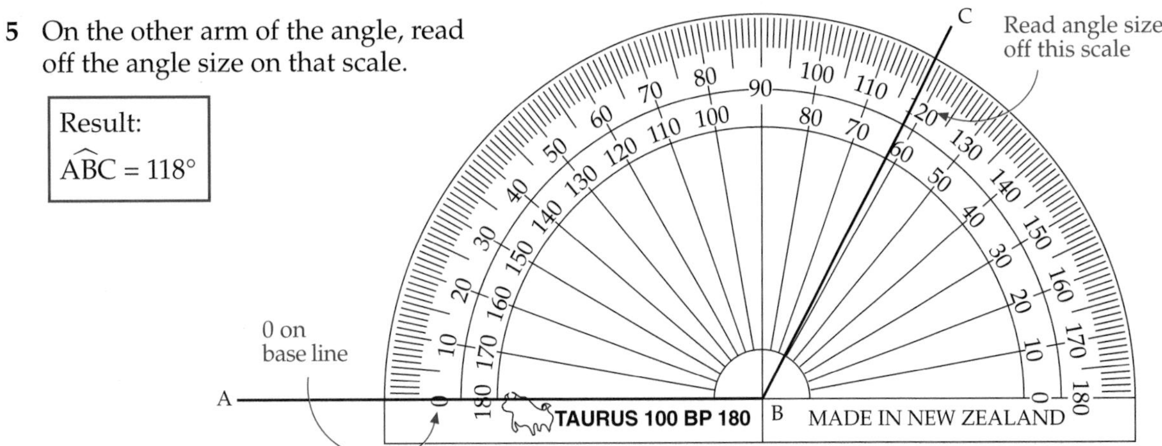

EXERCISE 14.5

1–4 *Write down the size of these angles.*

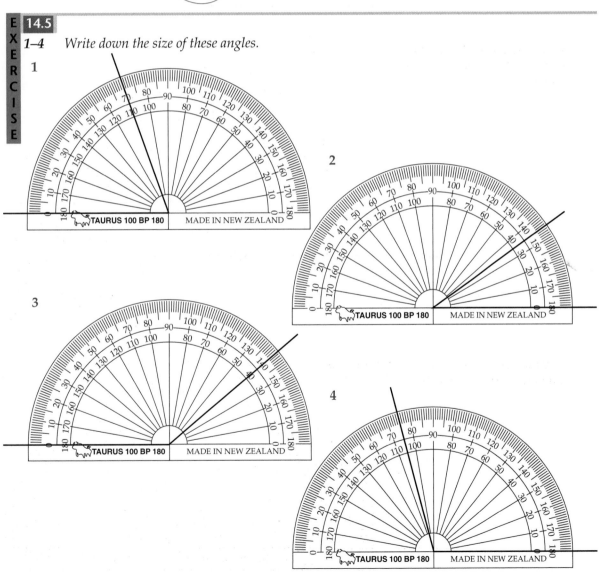

1

2

3

4

5–18 *Measure these angles with a protractor.*

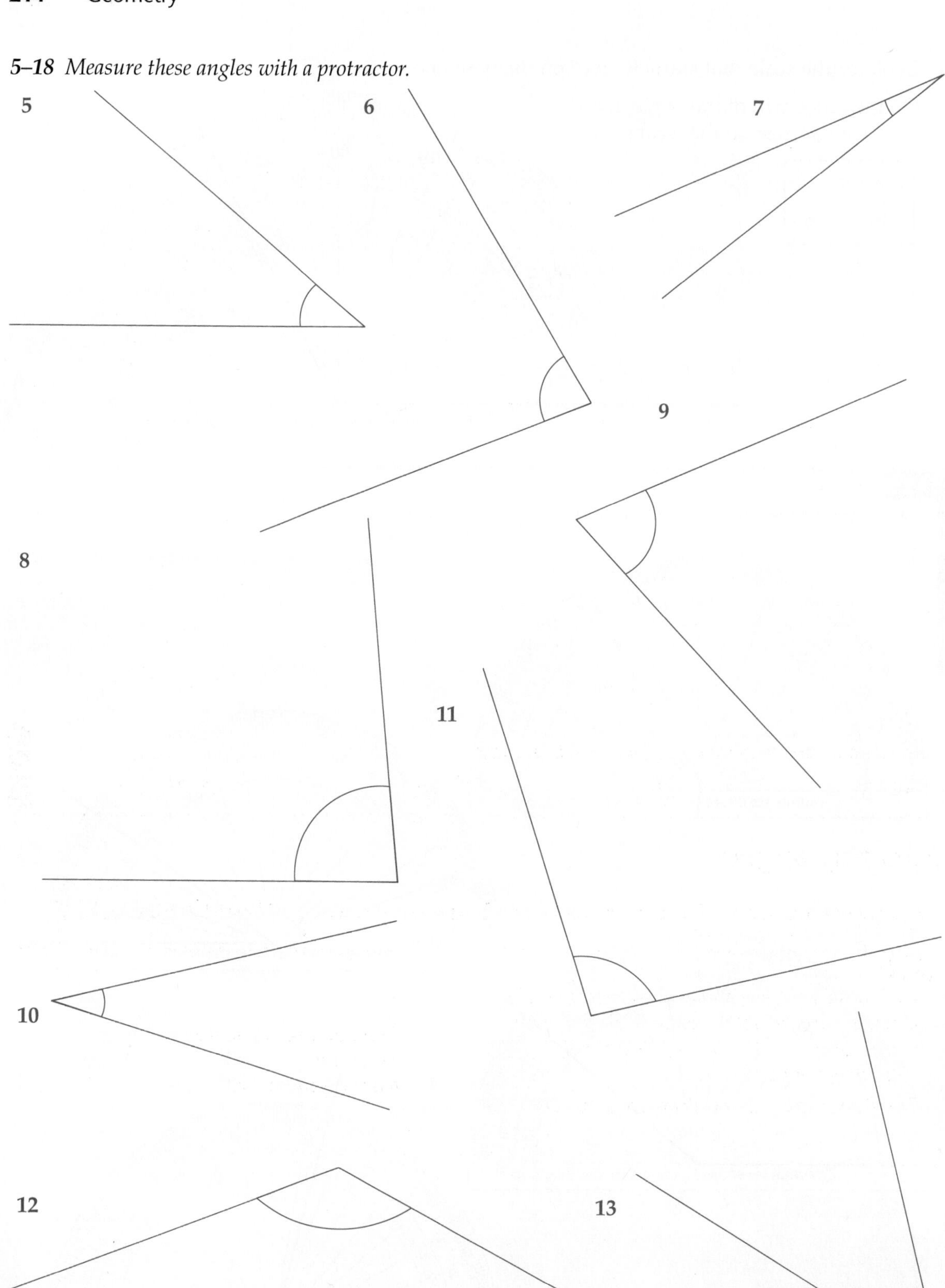

14

15

16

17

18

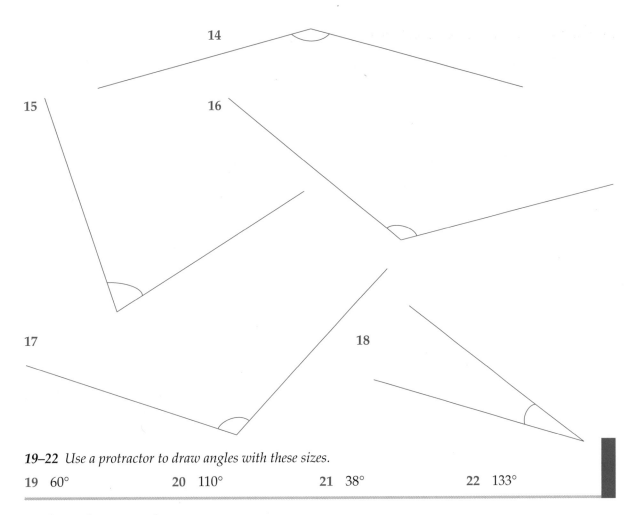

19–22 Use a protractor to draw angles with these sizes.

19 60° 20 110° 21 38° 22 133°

Estimating angles

Using a protractor should have given you a good idea about how big different angles look.

EXERCISE 14.6

Look at each of these angles. Decide whether it is acute, a right-angle or obtuse. Then estimate it to the nearest 10°. Finally, measure it accurately with a protractor.

The first one has been done for you:

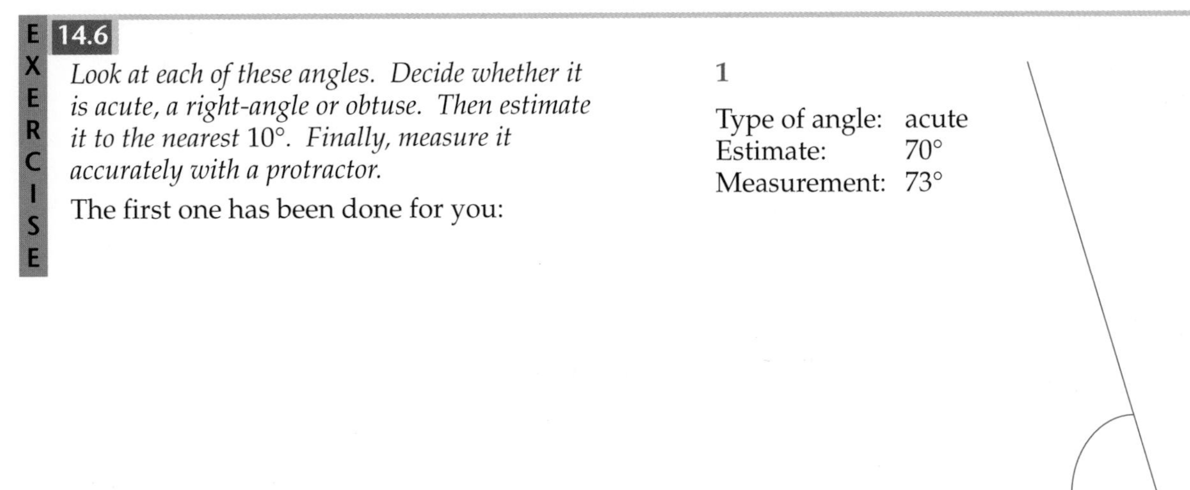

1

Type of angle: acute
Estimate: 70°
Measurement: 73°

2

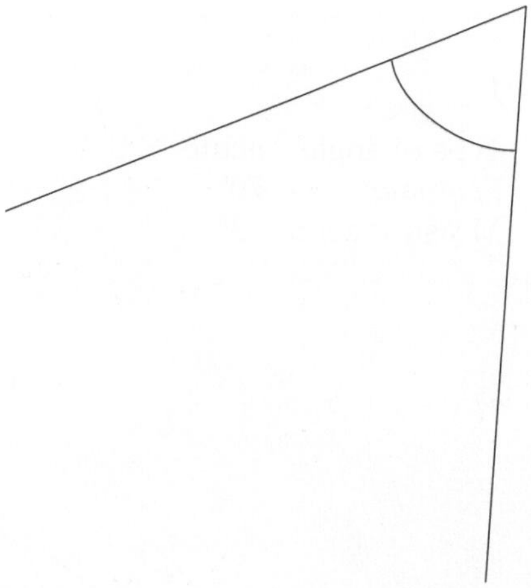

5

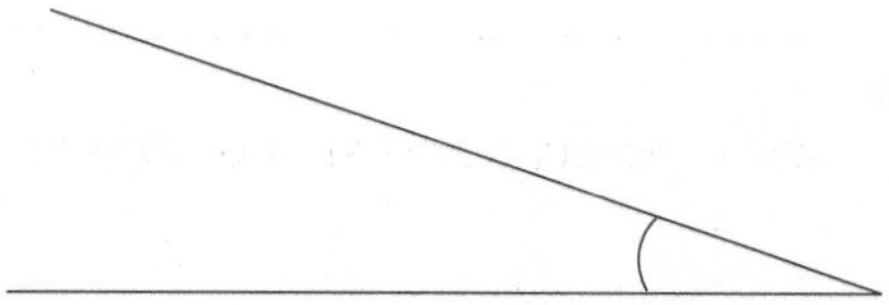

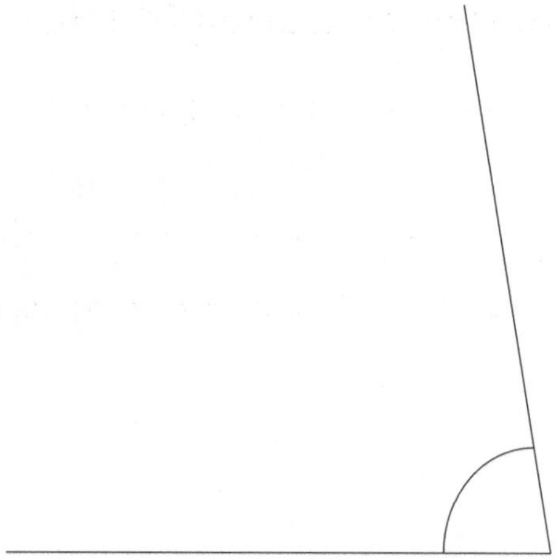

3

6

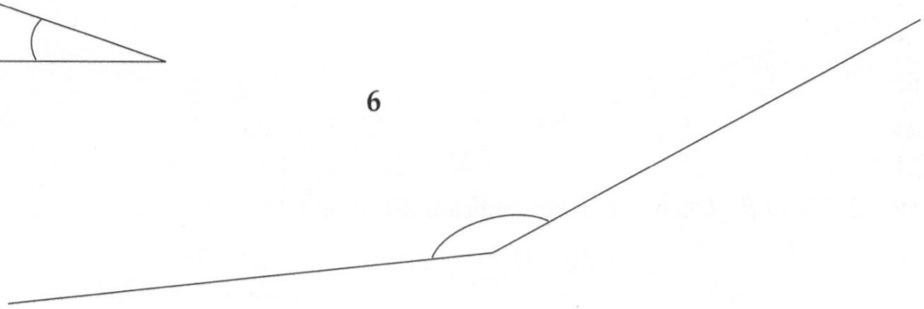

7

4

Angles on a straight line

A half-turn forms two right-angles.

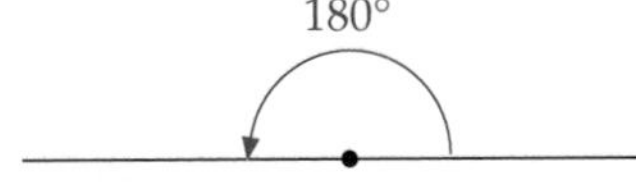

This means that:

> Angles which form a *straight line* add to 180°.

Example Work out the size of angle x.

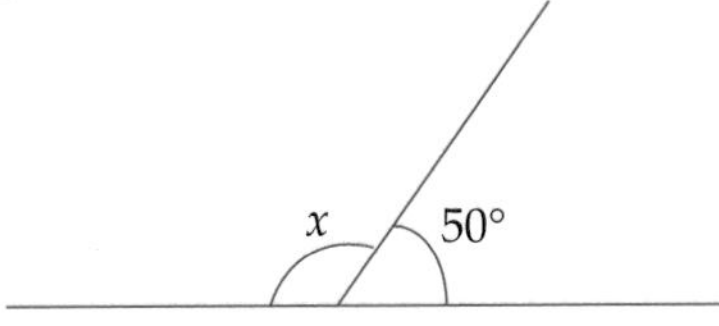

Answer

$$x + 50° = 180°$$
$$x = 180° - 50°$$
$$x = 130°$$

> This is an example of a **geometrical property**.
> We use it to work out angle sizes. The diagrams are not usually drawn to scale. This means you use the geometrical property, not a protractor, to work out the angle size!

EXERCISE 14.7

Work out the size of each marked angle. Don't use a protractor—the diagrams are not drawn to scale!

1

2

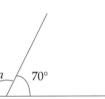

3

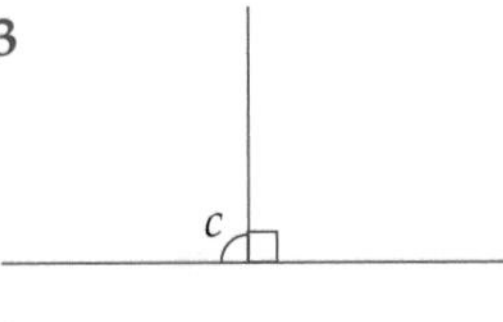

4

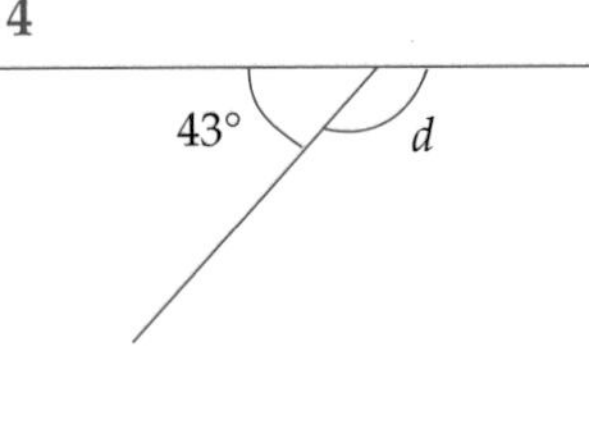

5

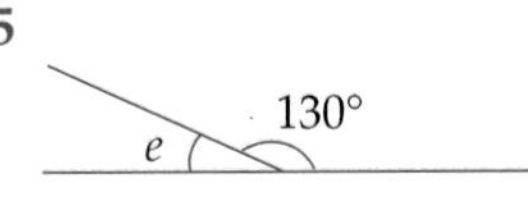

6

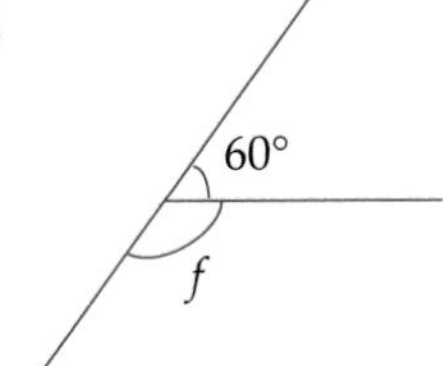

7

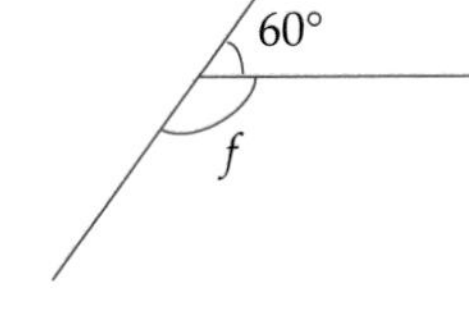

8

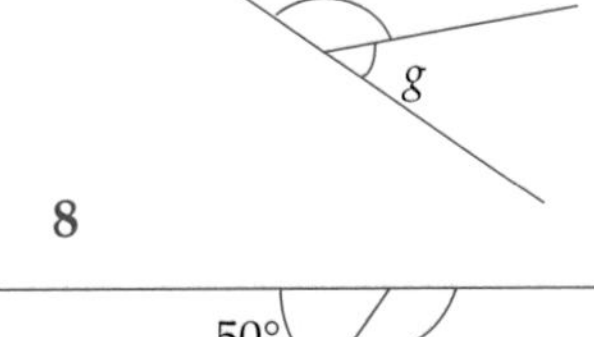

9

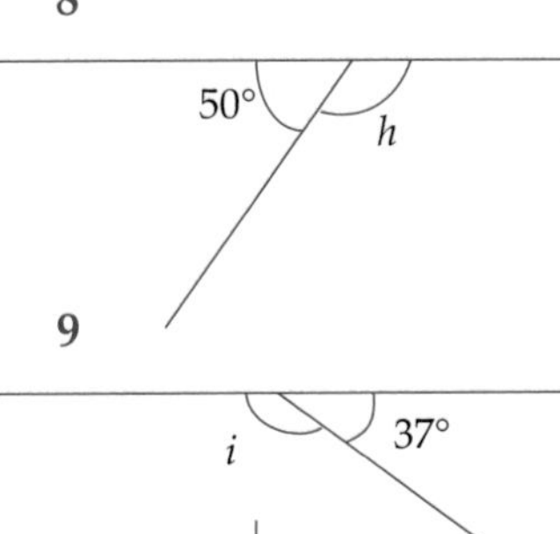

10

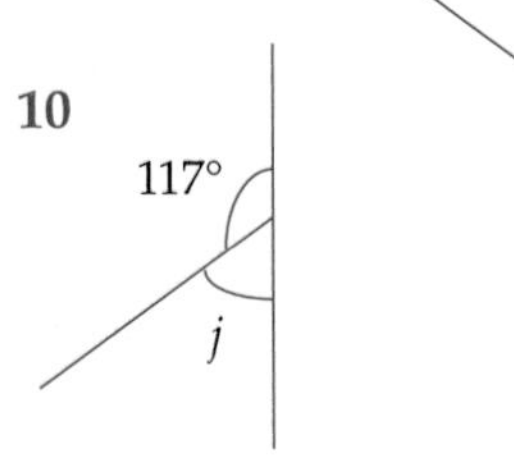

11

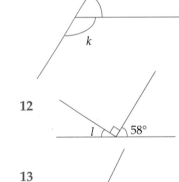

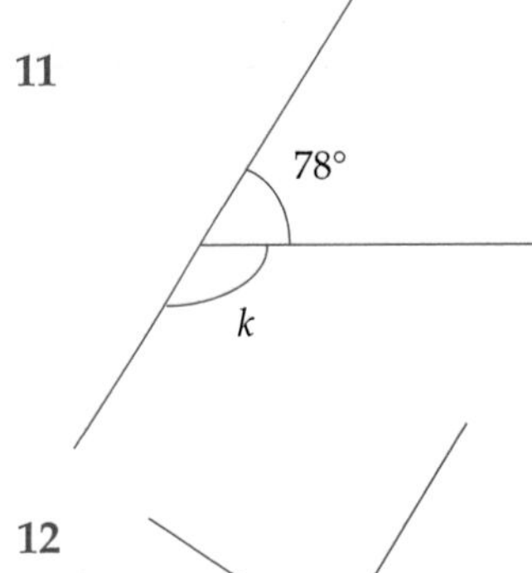

12

13

14

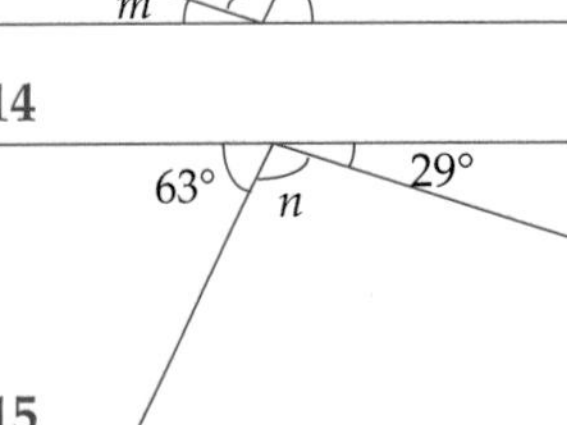

15

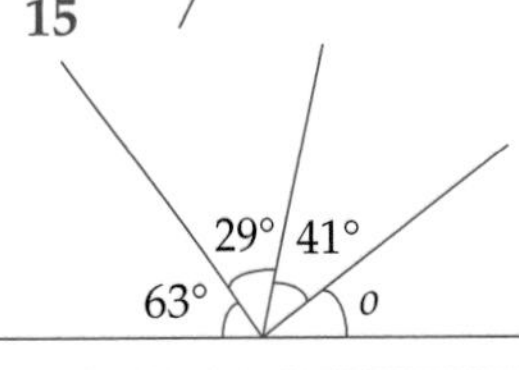

Complementary and supplementary angles

When two angles add to 90° they are called **complementary.**

Example 42° and 48° are complementary.

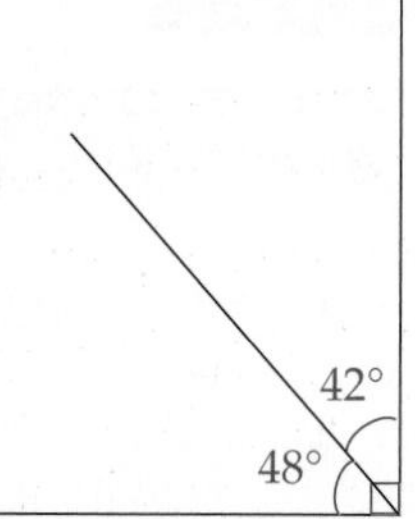

We say that one angle is the **complement** of the other.

Example The complement of 10° is 80°.

When two angles add to 180° they are called **supplementary.**

Example 55° and 125° are supplementary.

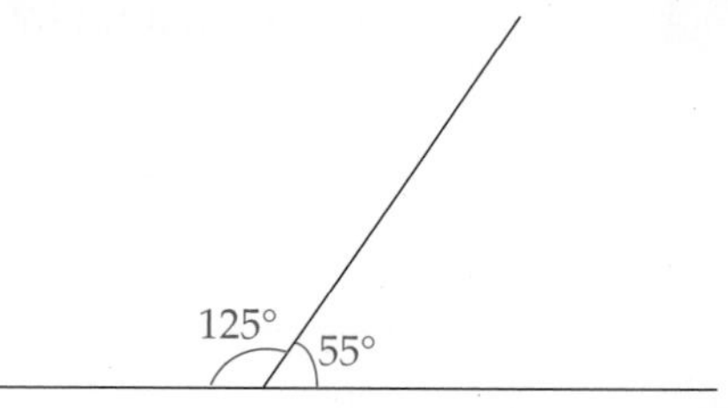

We say that one is the **supplement** of the other.

Example The supplement of 10° is 170°.

EXERCISE 14.8

1–3 Work out the size of the complementary angles a, b and c.

1

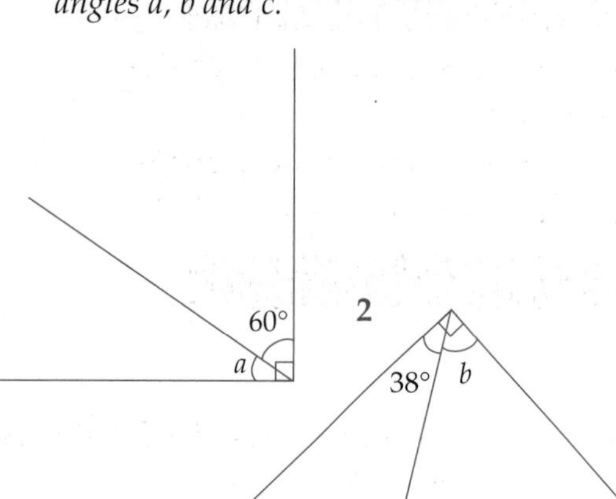

3

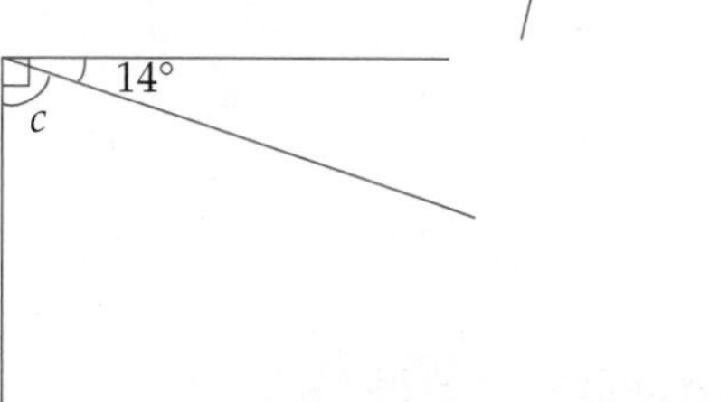

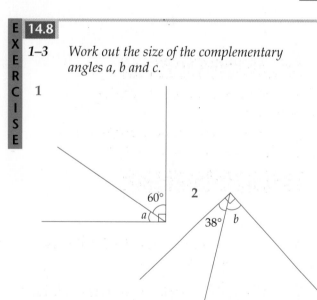

4 Write down the complement of each of these angles:

(a) 40° (d) 34°

(b) 9° (e) 90°

(c) 71°

5 A rectangle has four right-angles. Use this property to work out angles p and q.

(a)

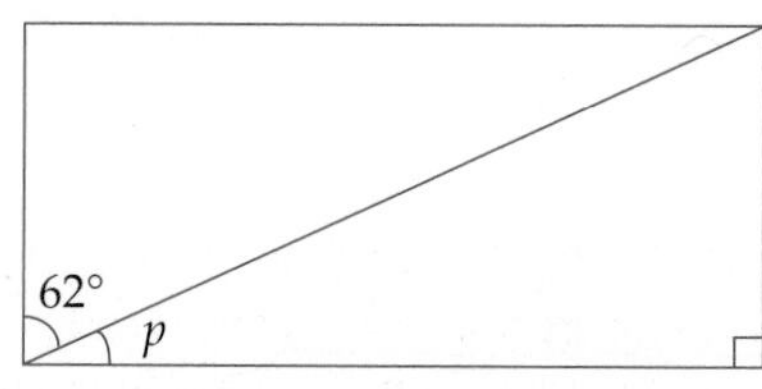

(b)

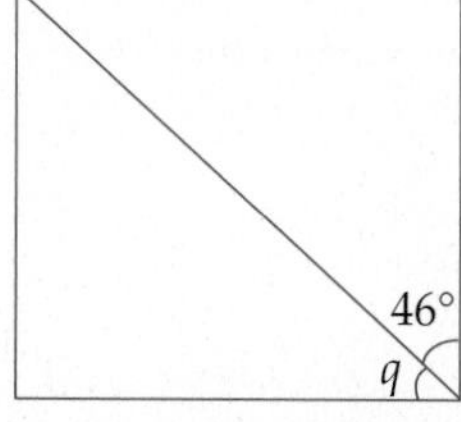

6–8 *Work out the size of these angles.*

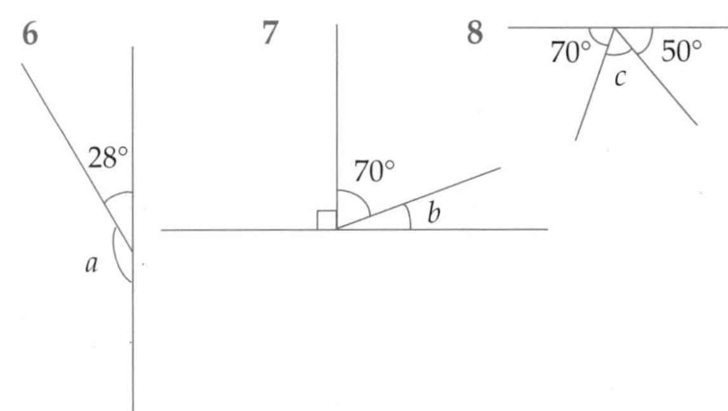

9 Write down the supplement of each of these angles:

(a) 80°
(b) 105°
(c) 74°
(d) 134°
(e) 90°

10 For each of these statements, write *true* or *false*.

(a) 60° and 30° are complementary
(b) 112° and 68° are supplementary
(c) 35° and 65° are complementary
(d) 42° and 48° are supplementary
(e) 90° and 90° are supplementary
(f) 102° and 88° are supplementary

Vertically opposite angles

STARTER

This diagram shows two straight lines.

- Are angle a and 130° a pair of supplementary angles?
- What is the value of angle a?
- Explain how you could work out the value of angle b.
- What can you say about the size of angles a and b?

Angles placed like p and q in this diagram are called **vertically opposite angles**.

Vertically opposite angles are always equal in size.

Example Work out the size of the angle marked x.

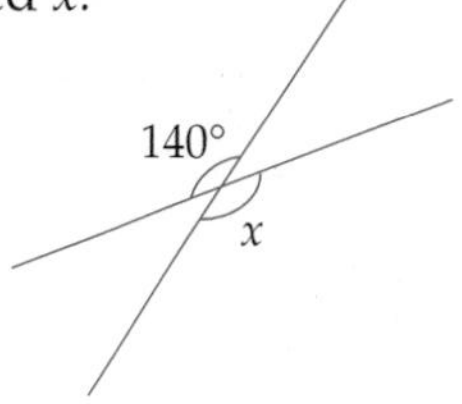

Answer $x = 140°$

EXERCISE 14.9

Work out the size of the marked angles. (All the lines that cross at a point are straight in this exercise.)

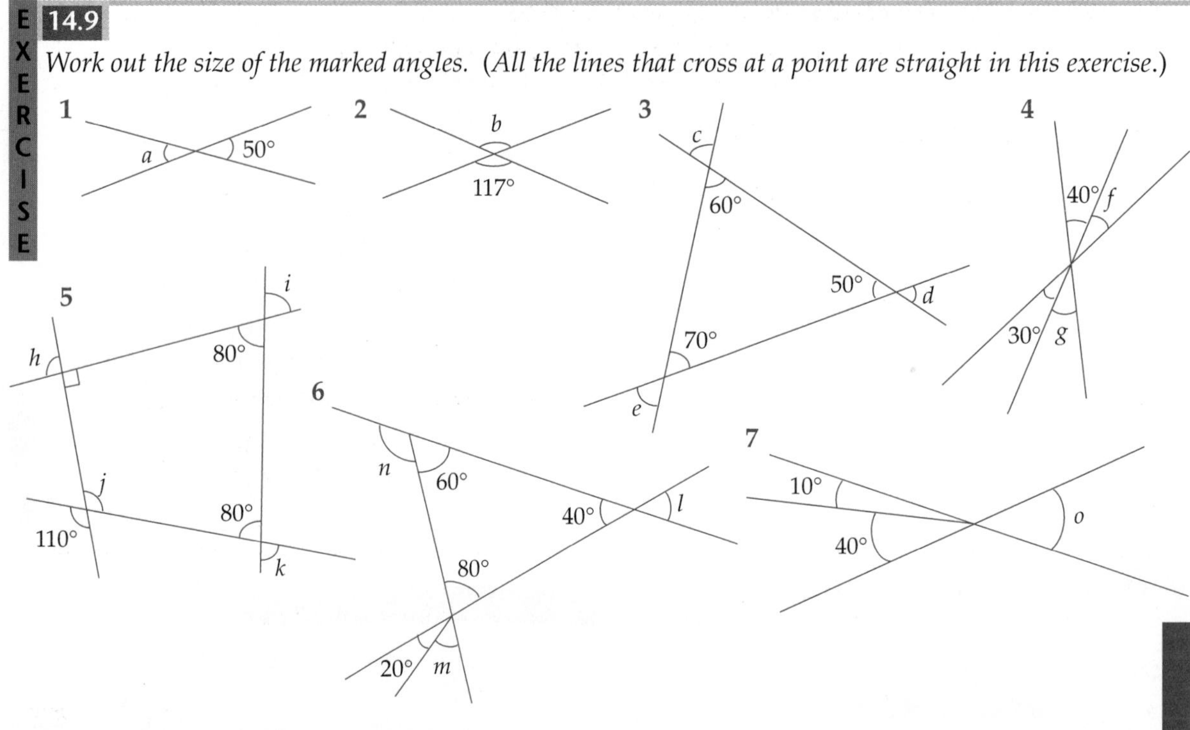

Angles at a point

STARTER

Work in pairs for this activity.

- Each person should take a sheet of paper, and draw four line segments all meeting at point P.

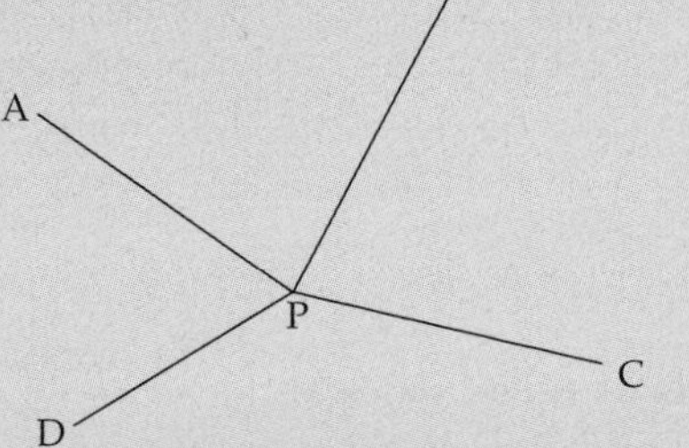

- Label your diagram and give it to the person you are working with.
- Take their diagram. Measure the four angles ($\widehat{APB}$, $\widehat{BPC}$, $\widehat{CPD}$ and $\widehat{DPA}$) with a protractor.
- Add up the sizes of your four angles.
- What total did you get?
- What total did the other person get for *your* diagram.?

- How could you decide who had measured the four angles most accurately? Discuss this as a class.

> When a group of angles meet at a single point, they add to 360°.

This is because a full turn is taken to be 360°.

Example Work out the size of angles p and q.

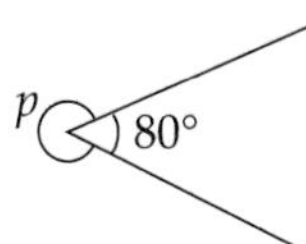

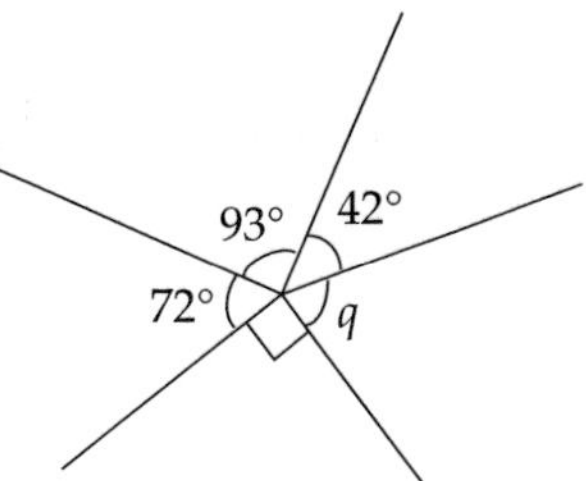

Answer

$$p + 80° = 360°$$
$$p = 360° - 80°$$
$$p = 280°$$

$$q + (90° + 72° + 93° + 42°) = 360°$$
$$q + 297° = 360°$$
$$q = 360° - 297°$$
$$q = 63°$$

EXERCISE 14.10

1–15 *Work out the size of the marked angles.*

1 a, 70°

2 b, 78°

3 c, 61°

4 d, 280°

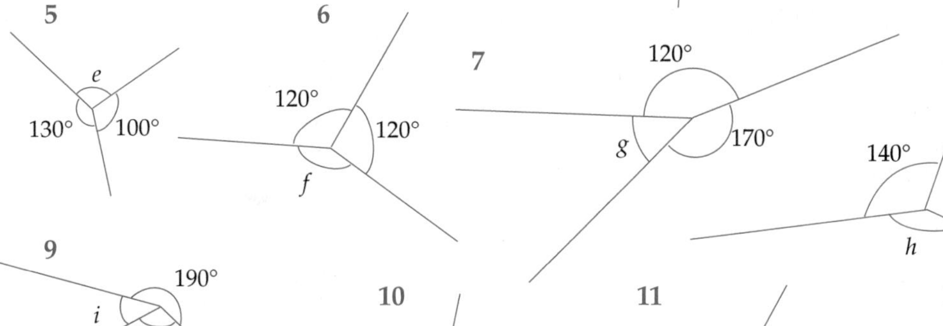

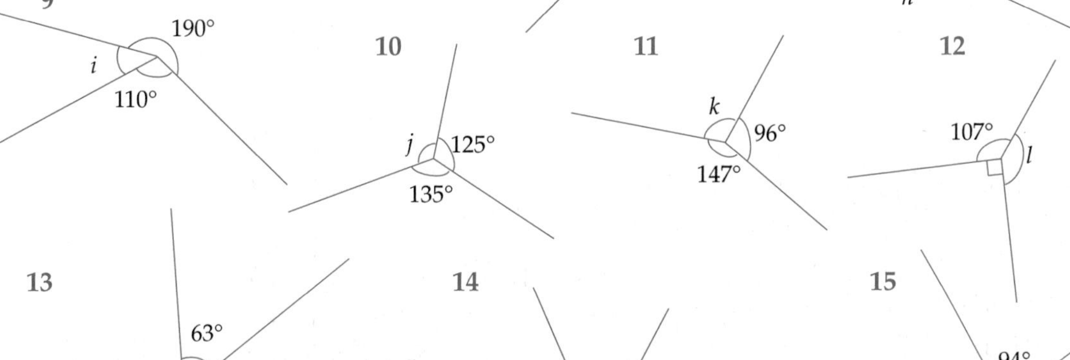

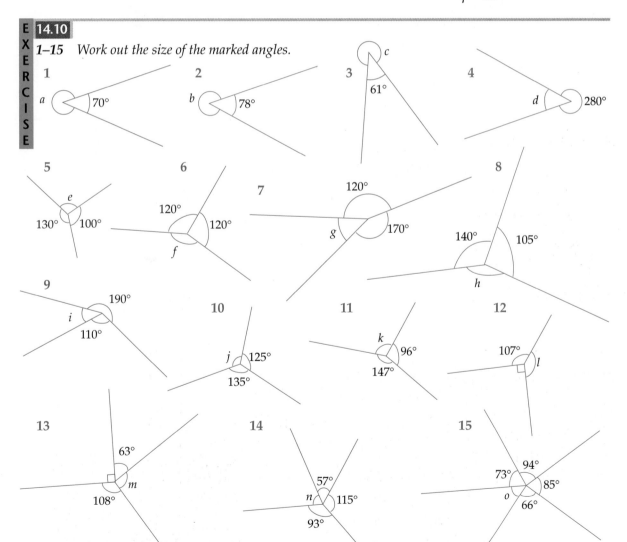

16 When an orange is sliced across it has nine identical sections.
Work out the angle at the centre of each section.

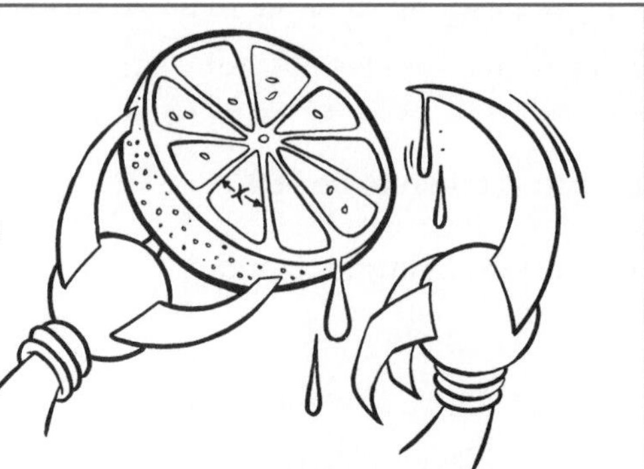

We can use the 'angles at a point' property to measure **reflex angles**. These are angles larger than 180°.

To measure angles larger than 180°, measure the smaller angle first.
Subtract this from 360°

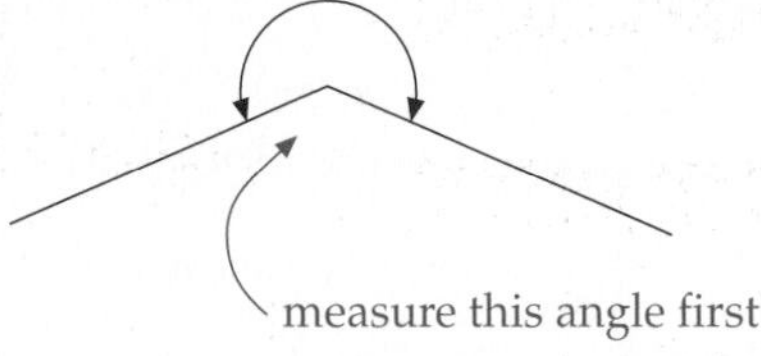

If the smaller angle measures, say, 148°, the larger angle must measure 212°.
This is because 360° − 148° = 212°.

14.11

Use a protractor to measure these reflex angles.

1

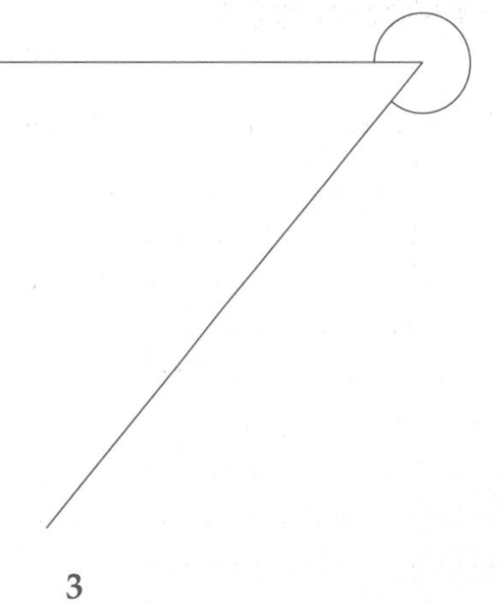

2

3

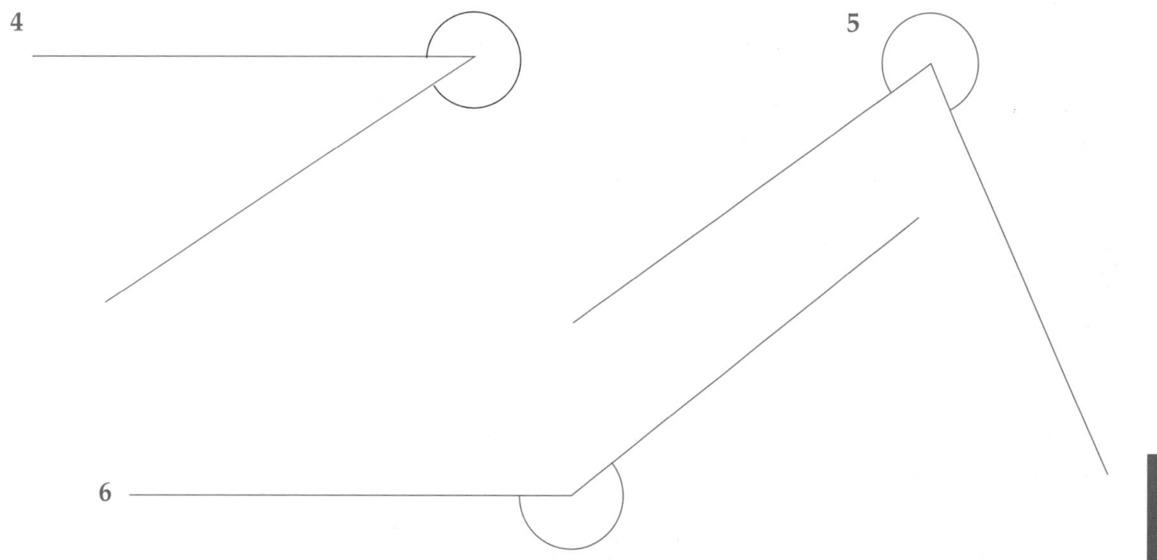

Angles in clocks

STARTER

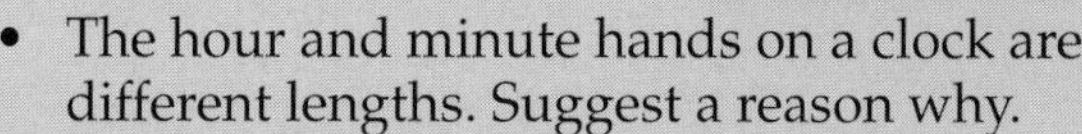

- What time does this clock show?

- The hour and minute hands on a clock are different lengths. Suggest a reason why.
- What is the angle between the hour hand and minute hand?
- What angle does the hour hand turn through in 1 hour?

EXERCISE 14.12

1 Make a copy of this table. Complete it to show the angle that the *hour* hand turns through.

Number of hours	Angle turned
1	
2	60°
3	
4	
5	
6	
7	
8	
9	
10	
11	
12	

2 What angle does the hour hand on a clock turn through:

(a) from 1 pm to 4 pm?

(b) from 2 pm to 9 pm?

(c) from 10 am to 3 pm?

3 Make a copy of this table. Complete it to show the angle that the *minute* hand turns through.

Number of minutes	Angle turned
5	
10	60°
15	
20	
25	150°
30	
35	
40	
45	
50	
55	
60	

4 What angle does the minute hand on a clock turn through:

(a) from 1.15 pm to 1.25 pm?

(b) from 3.35 pm to 3.50 pm?

(c) from 10.45 am to 11.30 am?

5 The minute hand of a clock turns through 60° in 10 minutes.

(a) Write down a calculation (using the numbers 60° and 10) to show that in 1 minute the minute hand turns though 6°.

(b) What angle does the minute hand turn through in 4 minutes?

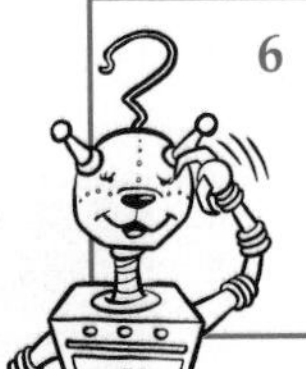

6 How many times in a twelve-hour period are the hour hand and minute hand of a clock at right-angles?

Angles in a triangle

STARTER

Work in pairs for this activity.

- Take a sheet of paper and draw two large triangles on it.
  - — The triangles should each have sides that are different lengths.
  - — One triangle should have all angles *acute* (less than 90°).
  - — The other triangle should have an *obtuse* angle (larger than 90°).

- Give your sheet with the two triangles to the other person.
- Take their diagram. Use a protractor to measure the three angles inside each triangle.
- Add up the sizes of the three angles inside each triangle.
- What total did you get?
- What total did the other person get?

INVESTIGATION

THE FOLDING TRIANGLE

Take a sheet of A4 paper and a ruler. Draw the outline of a triangle. Make the triangle as large as possible.

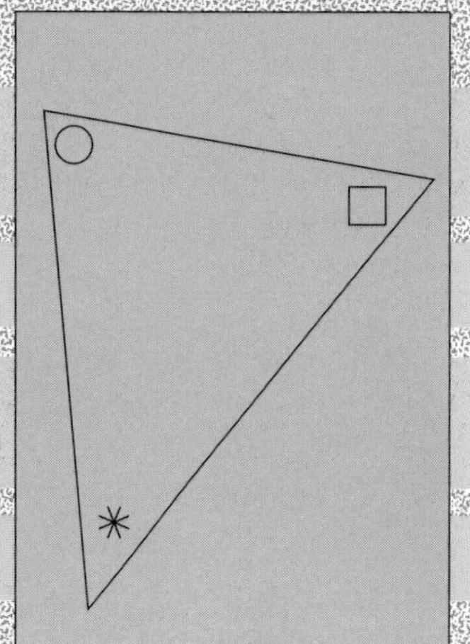

Use a pair of scissors to cut out the triangle.

Mark the three angles with different symbols— e.g. ✳, ○, □

Turn the triangle *upside down*.

Look for the longest side of your triangle. Fold the opposite corner so that it just touches the longest side

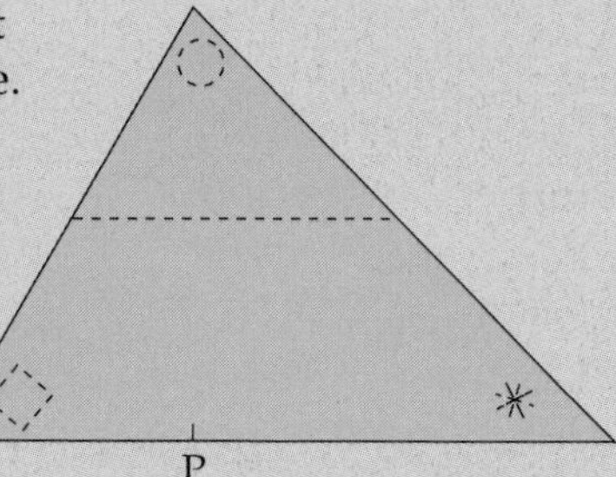

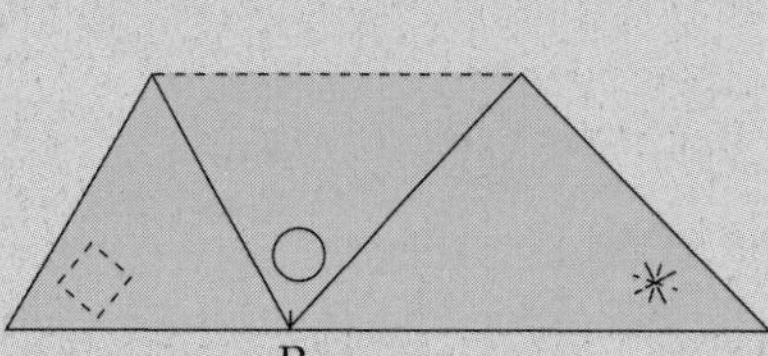

Now fold the other two corners of the triangle so that they all meet at P. You should have a rectangle shape.

1 Explain how the three different symbols ✳, ○, □ are now arranged.

2 What does this tell you about the sum of the three angles of a triangle?

The angles in a triangle add up to 180°.

$x + y + z = 180°$

Example Work out the size of the angle marked q.

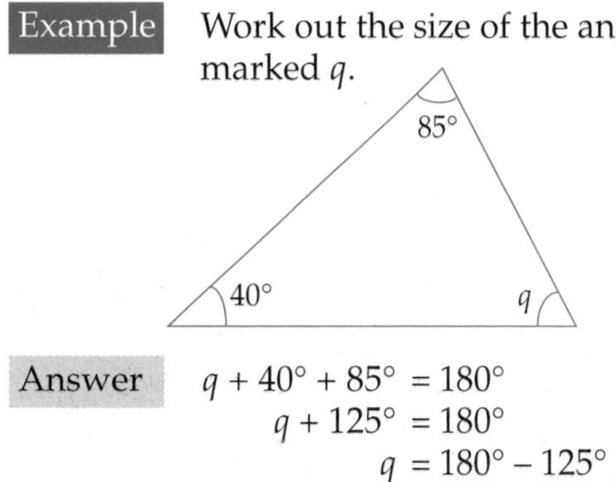

Answer

$$q + 40° + 85° = 180°$$
$$q + 125° = 180°$$
$$q = 180° - 125°$$
$$q = 55°$$

EXERCISE 14.13

1–12 *Work out the size of the marked angles.*

1

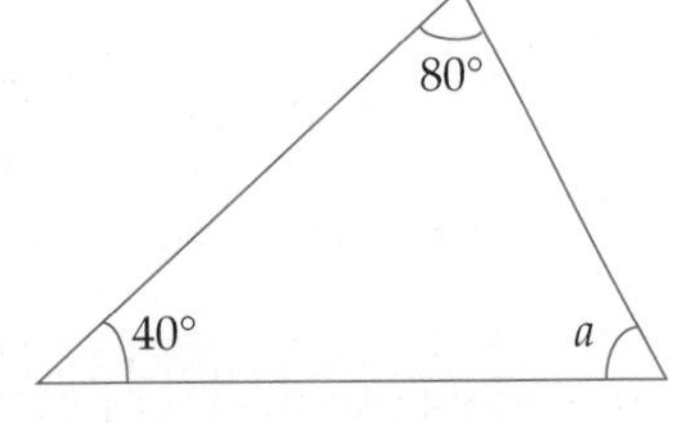

2

3

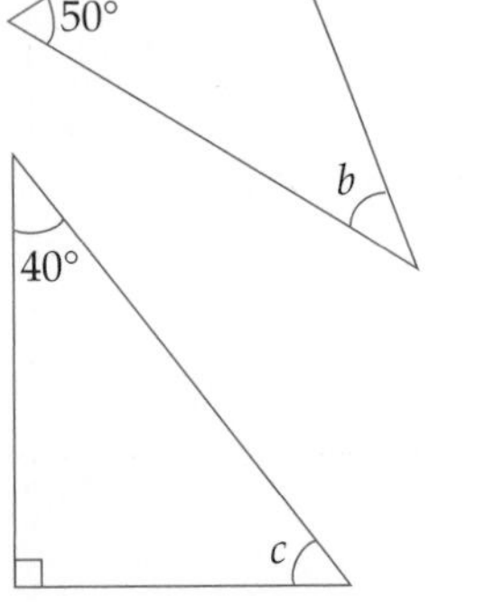

4

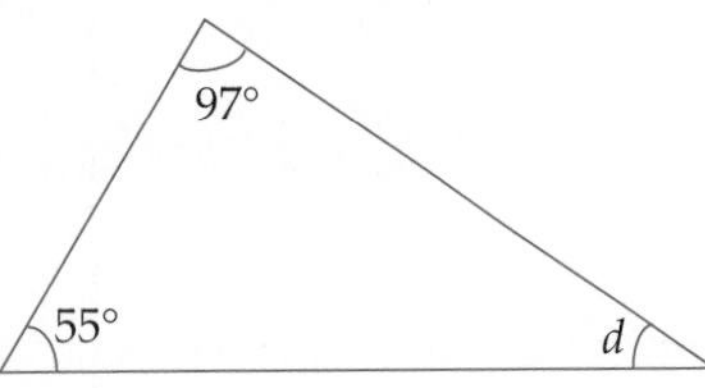

5

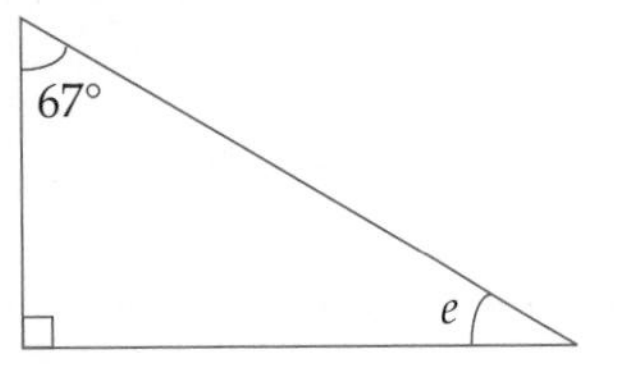

6

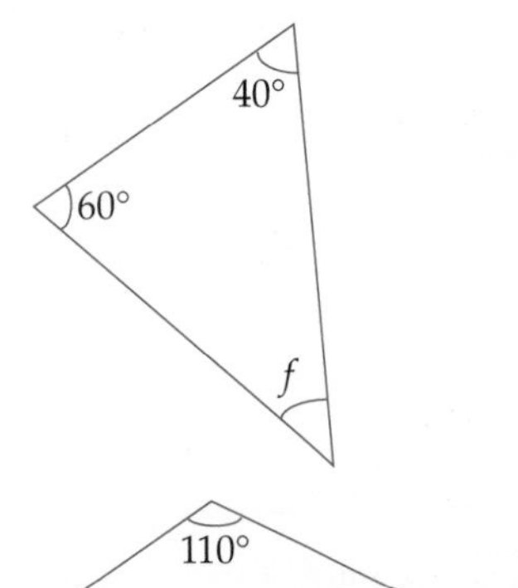

7

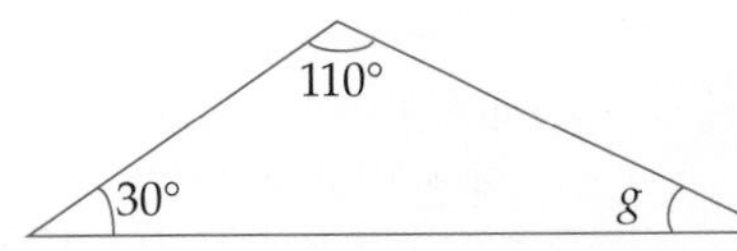

8

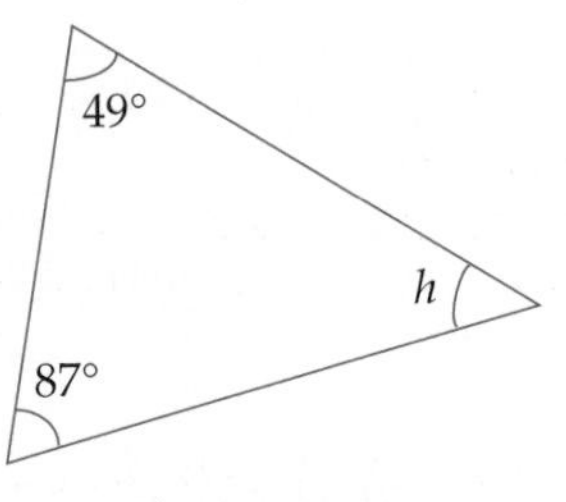

9

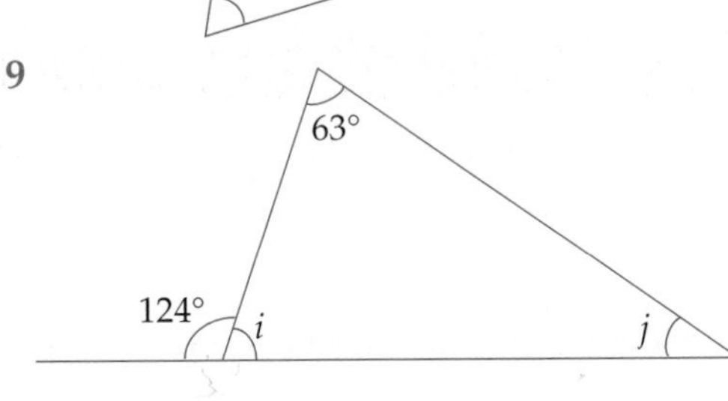

10

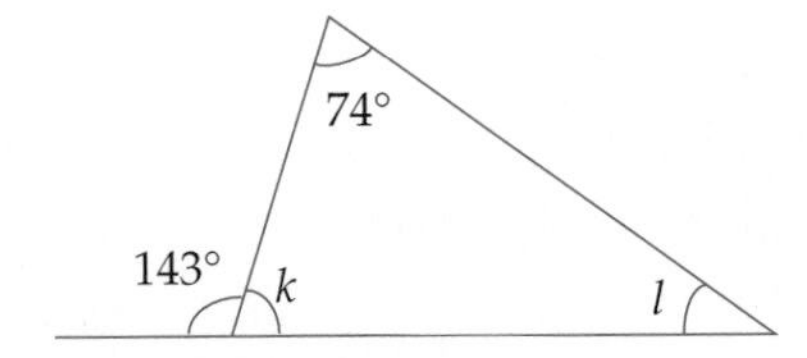

11

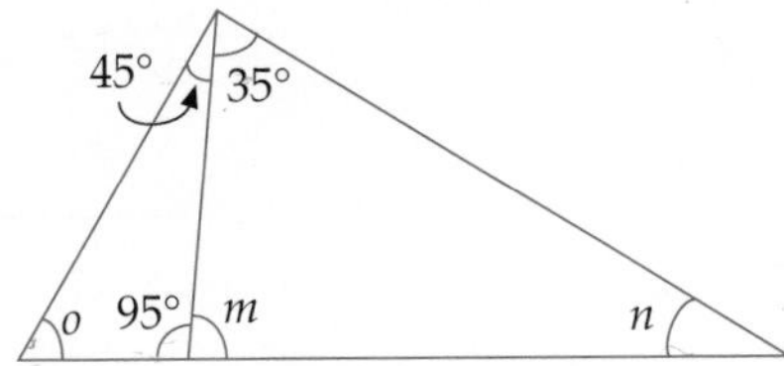

12

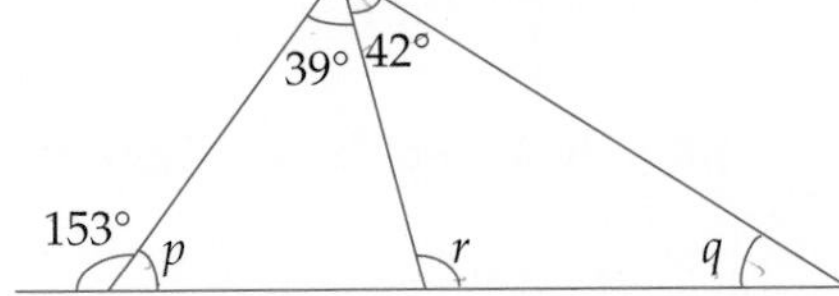

13 Here are two of the angles in some triangles. Write down the third angle each time.

(a) { 20°, 40°,   }   (d) { 83°, 90°,   }

(b) { 45°, 95°,   }   (e) { 1°, 178°,   }

(c) { 70°, 70°,   }   (f) { 60°, 60°,   }

14 Which of the triangles in Question 13 would look most like a straight line? Draw a diagram to explain.

15 (Multichoice) Which of these sets of angles could not form a triangle?

A { 40°, 60°, 80° }   C { 73°, 48°, 59° }

B { 105°, 15°, 60° }   D { 35°, 64°, 71° }

Some rules for finding angles

In geometry, you are sometimes asked to give a brief reason for an answer.
Here are four reasons we have covered in this chapter.
There is also a shortened way (*abbreviation*) of writing each reason.

Good maths students should be able to explain their results and give reasons for them.

	Reason	Abbreviation
$a + b = 180°$	adjacent angles on a straight line add to 180°	∠'s on line
$a = b$	vertically opposite angles are equal	vert. opp. ∠'s
$a + b + c = 360°$	angles at a point add to 360°	∠'s at pt
$a + b + c = 180°$	angles in a triangle add to 180°	∠ sum of △

EXERCISE 
14.14

1 In each diagram, the angle marked x is 70°. Give a reason why. Use one of the four reasons given above.

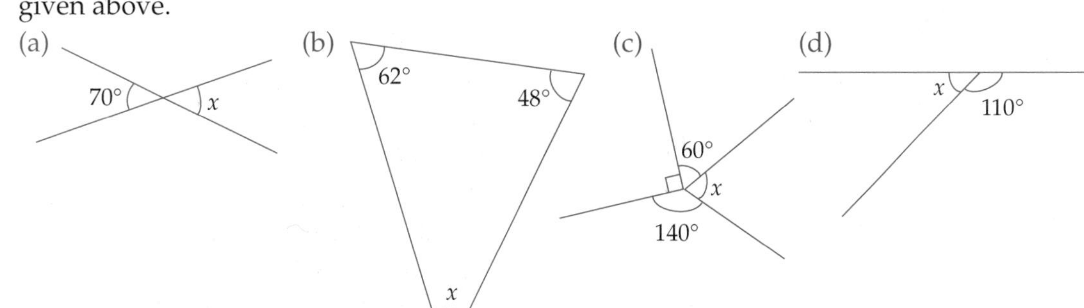

2 In a test on angles, Lee wrote down these answers. Draw a diagram that could have been in the question for each one.

(a) $a = 130°$ (∠'s at pt)
(b) $b = 40°$ (∠'s on line)
(c) $c = 80°$ (∠ sum of △)
(d) $d = 35°$ (vert. opp. ∠'s)

3–11 *In each diagram, work out the marked angles. Give a brief reason from the table for each one.*

∠'s on line
vert. opp. ∠'s
∠'s at pt
∠ sum of △

3
120°
a

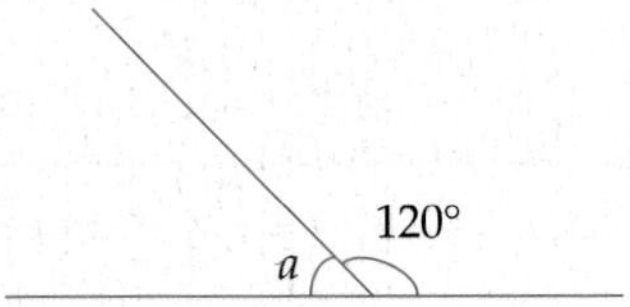

4
b
118°

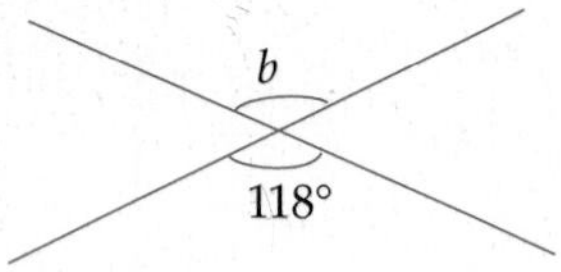

5
125°
c

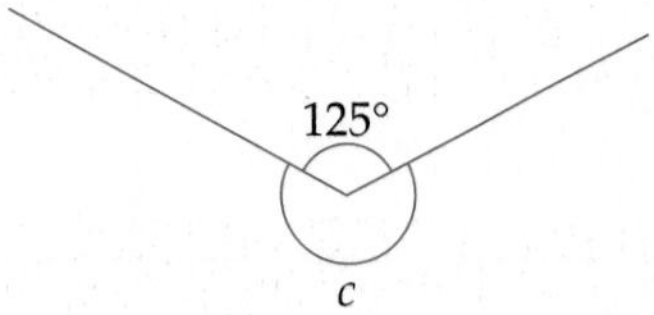

6
53°
d

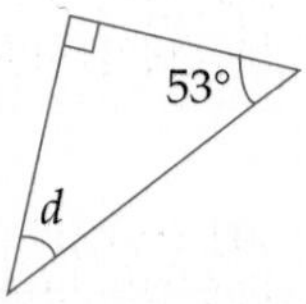

7
30°
e
40°

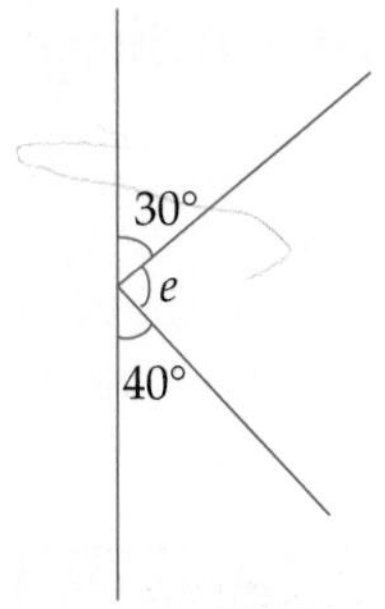

8
110°
f
130°

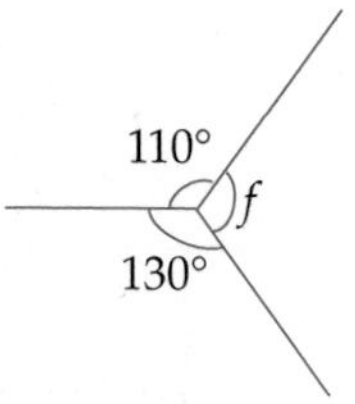

9
g
20°
55°

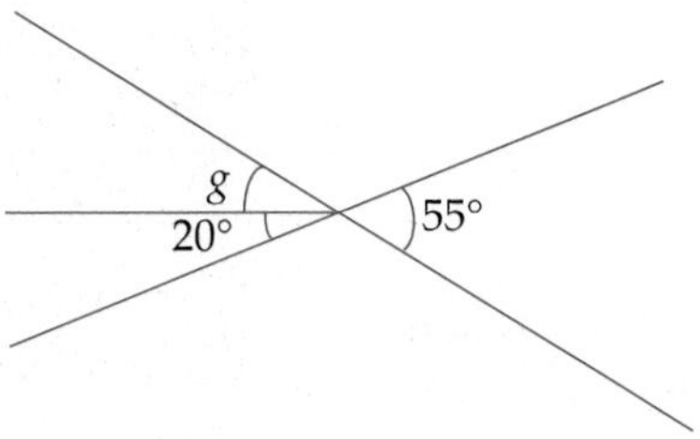

10
h
42°
29°

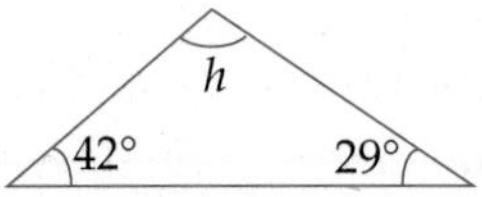

11
j
80°
k
50°
i

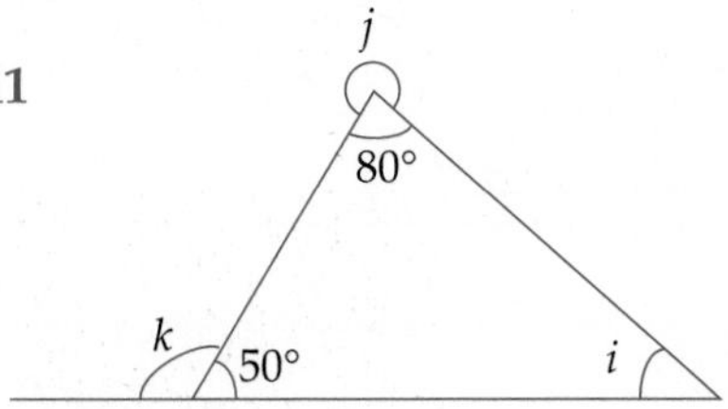

15 Reflection

STARTER

Both of these photos show reflection.

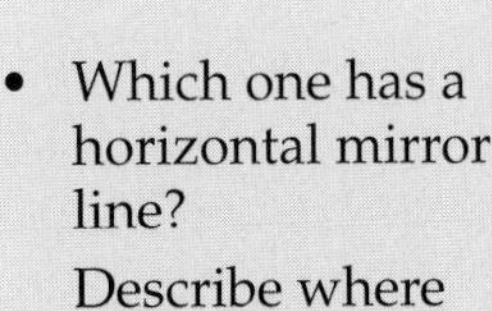

- Which one has a horizontal mirror line?

  Describe where this mirror line is.
- Which photo has a vertical line of symmetry?

  Describe where this line of symmetry is.

- Reflect this message in the dashed mirror line. What does it say?

HAVE YOU LIVED HERE ALL YOUR LIFE? NO, NOT YET!

In a **reflection**, an object and its image are on opposite sides of a line of symmetry.

This line of symmetry is often called a **mirror line**.

The object and its image are the **same distance** from the line of symmetry.

Example This diagram shows the number 4 and its image, reflected in a vertical mirror line.

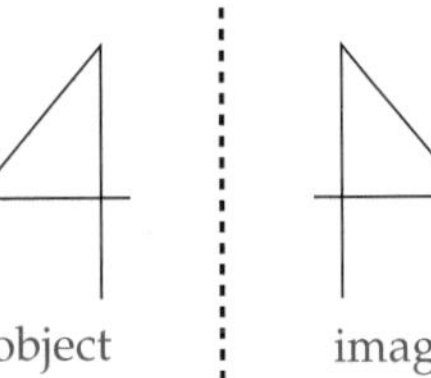

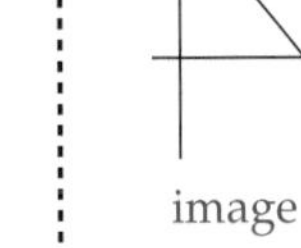

The mirror line is labelled m

Reflection can also be shown in paper-folding. When a shape is cut out from a folded piece of paper, it will look symmetric when unfolded.

The line of symmetry is the line of folding.

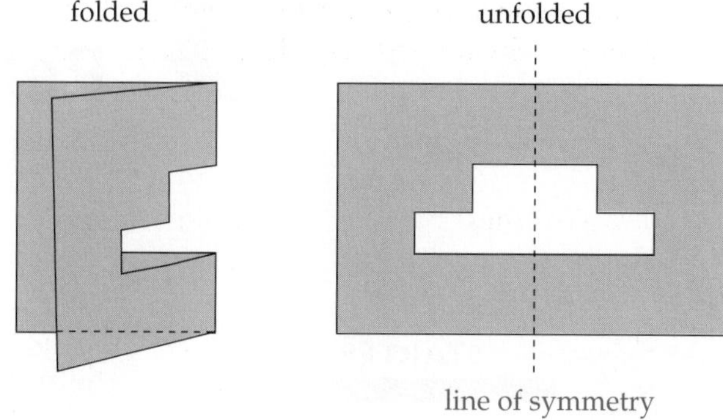

EXERCISE 15.1

1–10 *Copy these diagrams. Draw the image of each shape when it is reflected in the mirror line m.*

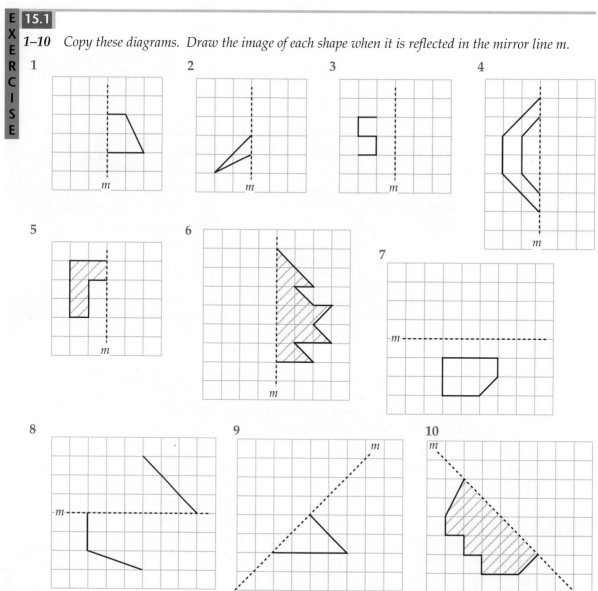

1 m

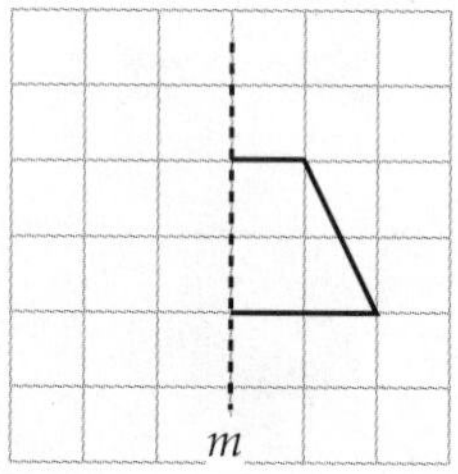

2 m

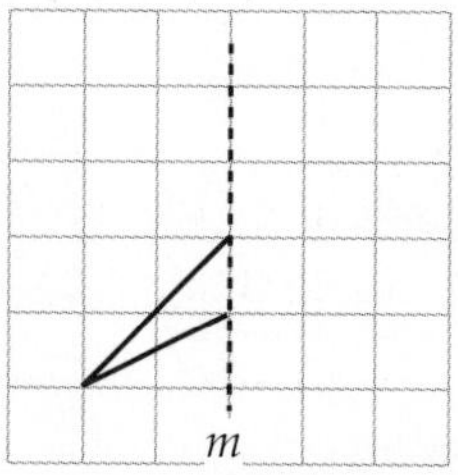

3 m

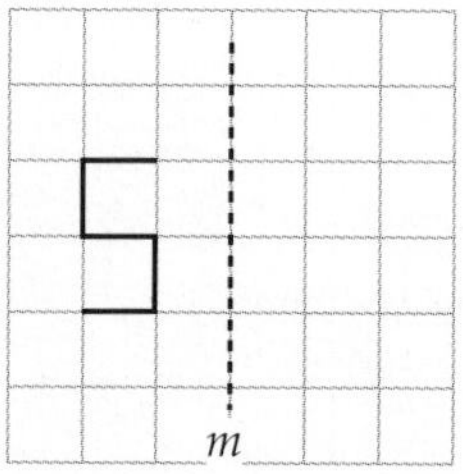

4 m

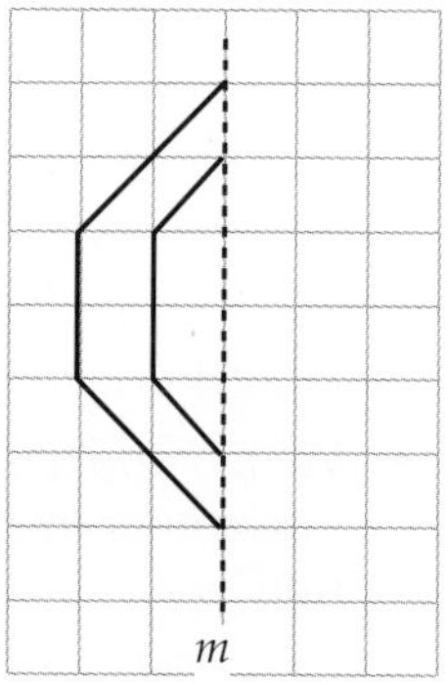

5 m

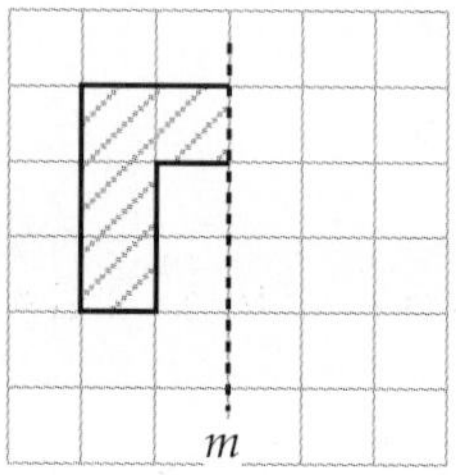

6 m

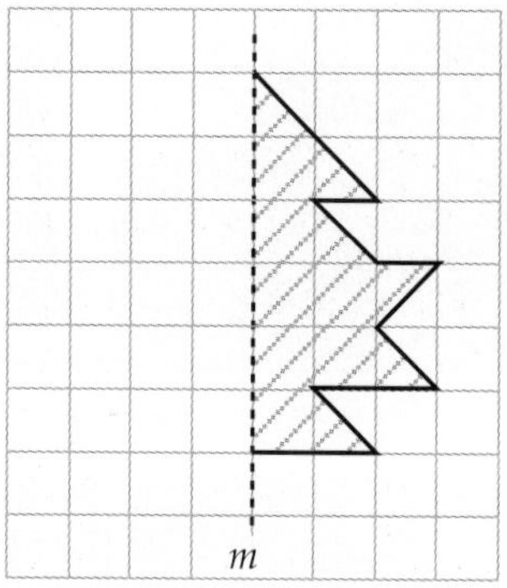

7 m

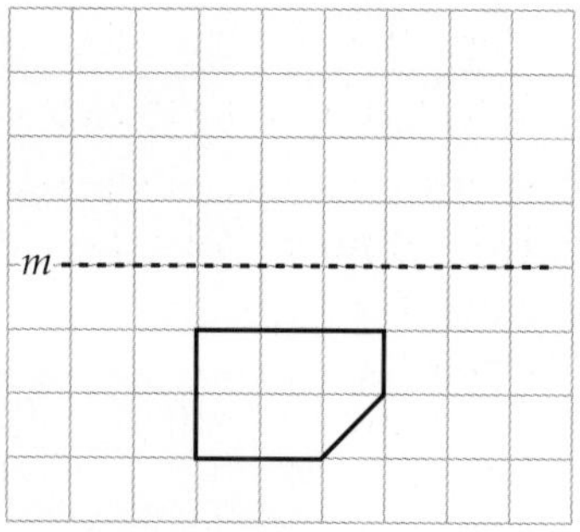

8 m

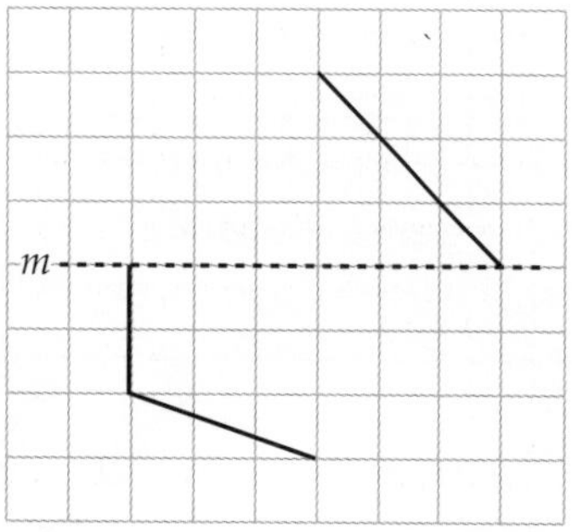

9 m

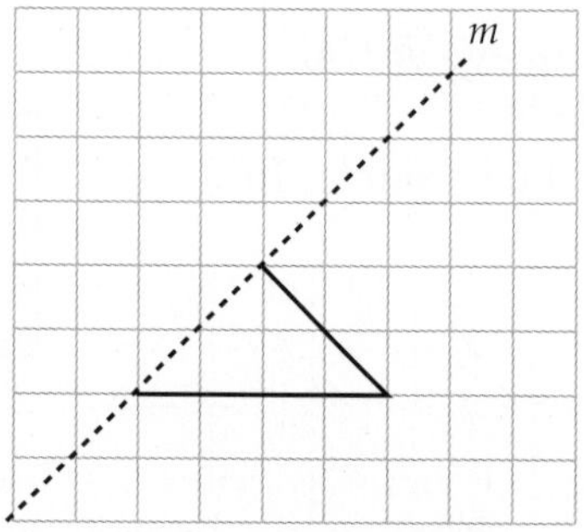

10 m

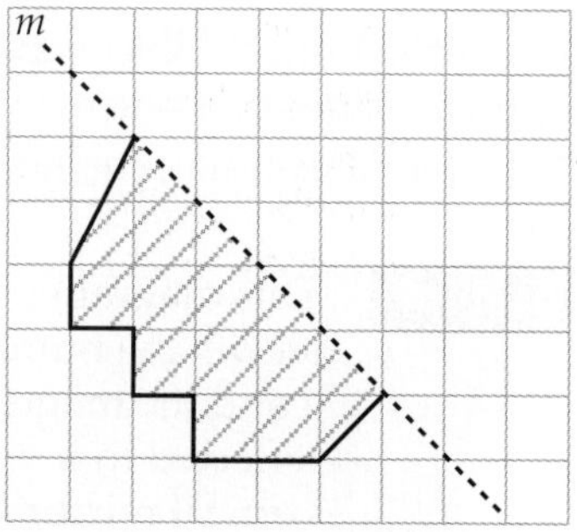

11 (Multichoice) This diagram shows part of a shape on the left side of a line of symmetry.

Which of these shows the complete shape?

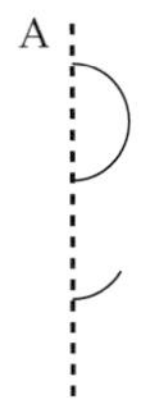

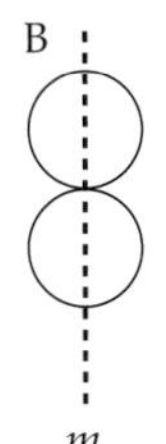

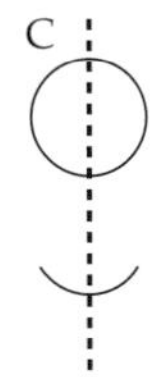

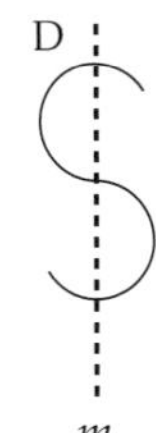

12 This diagram shows the 10 digits from 0 to 9, as they might look in a clock-radio display.

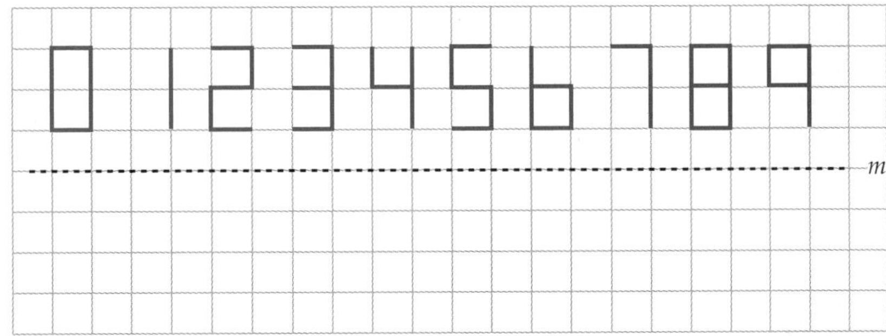

(a) Copy the diagram. Reflect each digit in the horizontal mirror line.

(b) Which four images look the same as the original digits?

13 When numbers on a calculator are reflected in a vertical line, they can look like letters. Here, a 5-digit number spells the word 'speed'.

(a) Copy the diagram. Draw the image of the 'word' on the other side of the mirror line.

(b) What is the 5-digit number on the calculator?

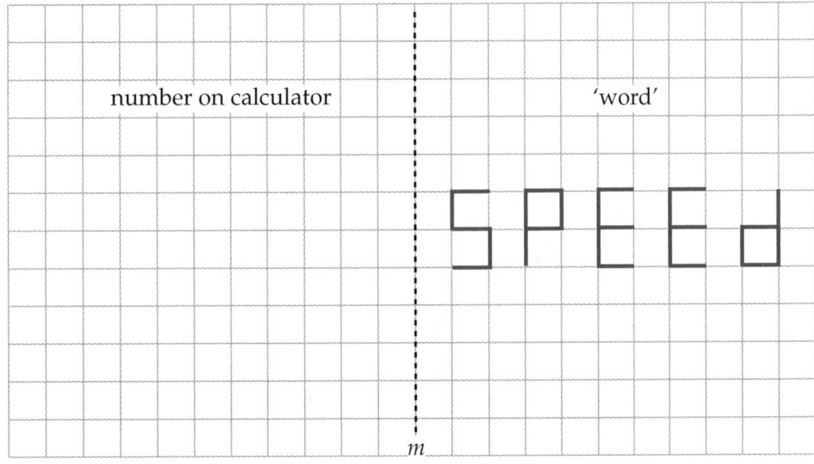

Where is the mirror line?

The mirror line is exactly half-way between each point and its image.

Example Draw in the lines of symmetry for each of these figures:

(a) object image

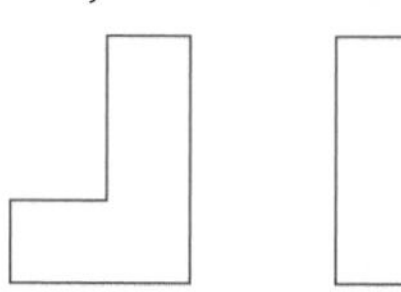

(b)

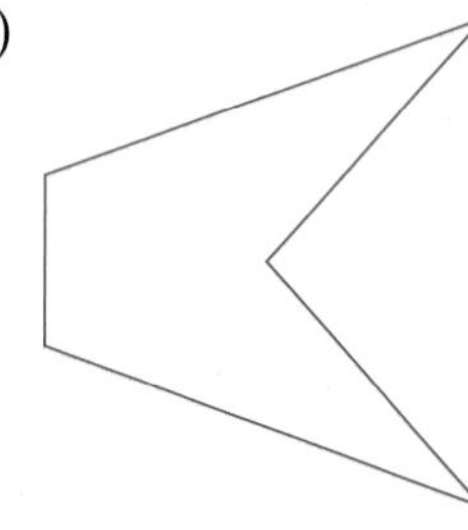

Answer

(a) object image

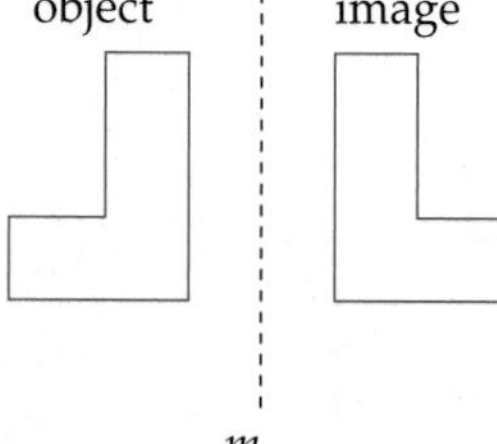

(b)

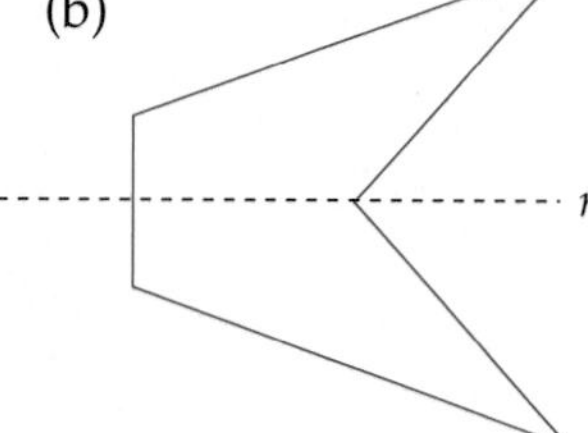

EXERCISE 15.2

1–4 *Copy these diagrams. Then draw in a dashed mirror line so that one figure is the reflection of the other.*

1

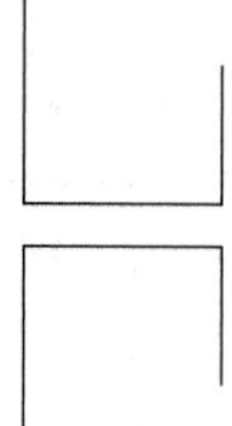

3

2

4

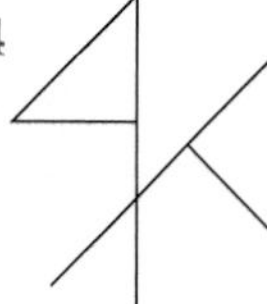

5 Which one of lines l and n is a line of symmetry for this rectangle?

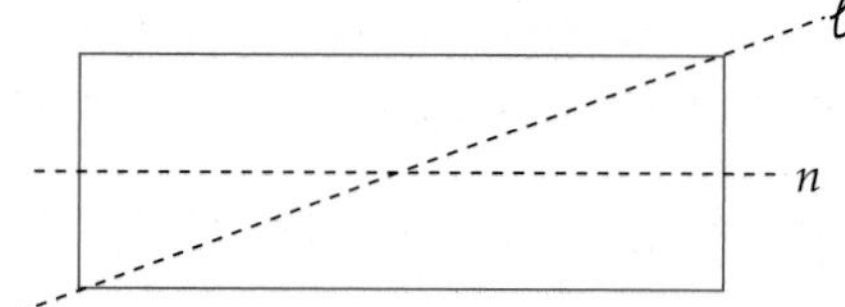

6 Which of these is a line of symmetry? Choose from the list { AC, AD, AF }.

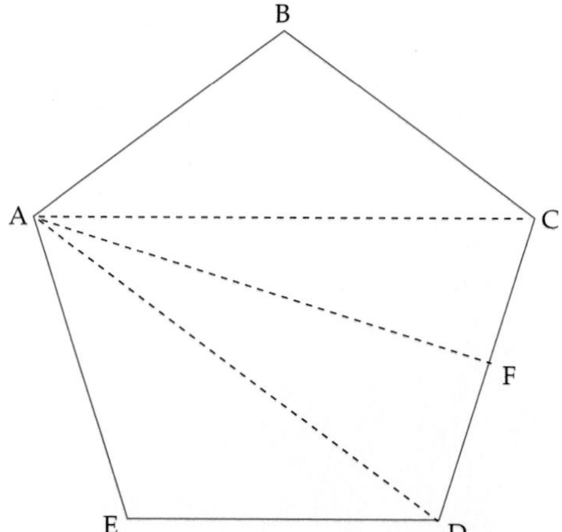

7 Write down the names (e.g. AB) of any lines of symmetry on each of these shapes.

(a)

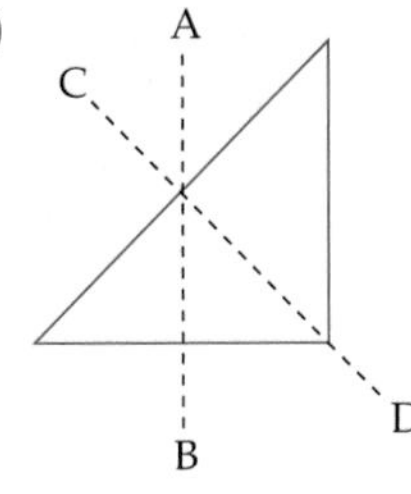

(b)

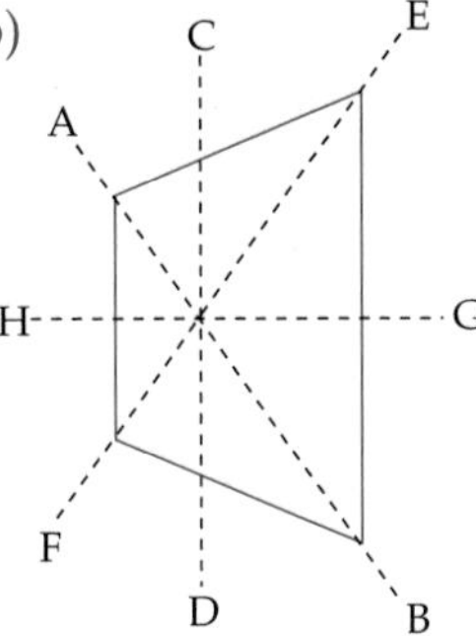

(c)

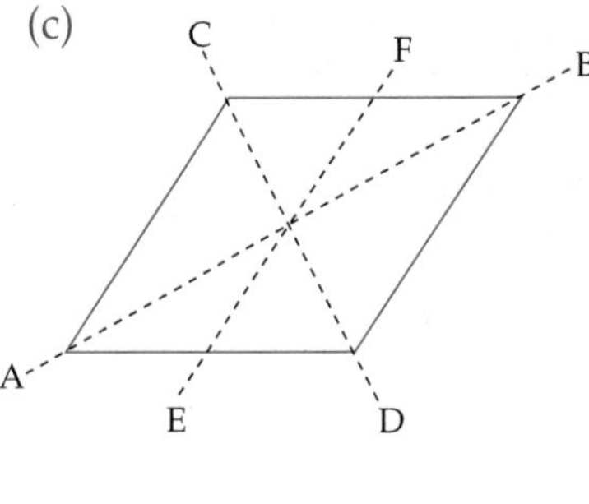

8 Write down the names (e.g. AB) of any lines of symmetry on these letters.

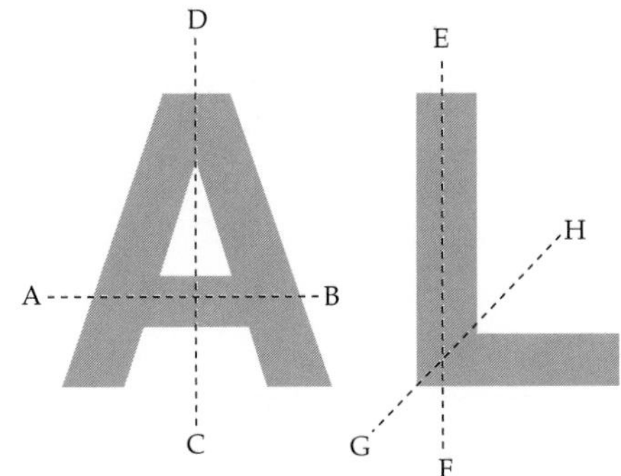

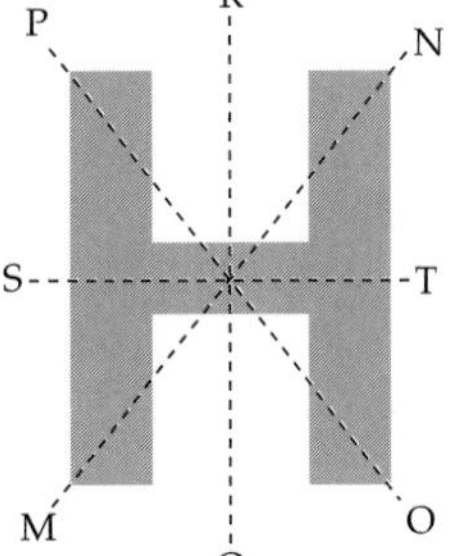

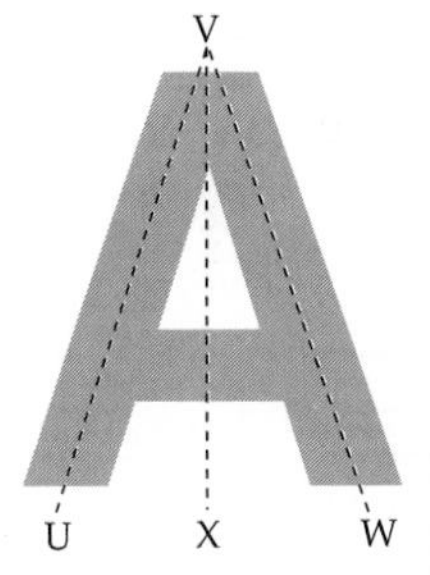

Points and images

Sometimes we refer to a point and its image using **labels**.

Example Reflect the rectangle ABCD in mirror line *m*.
Label the image.

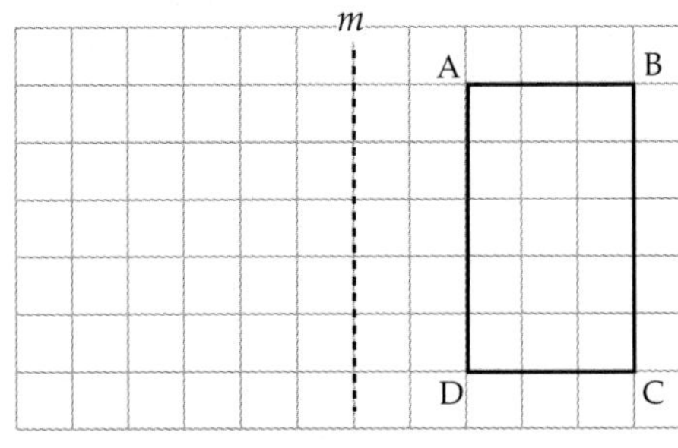

Answer

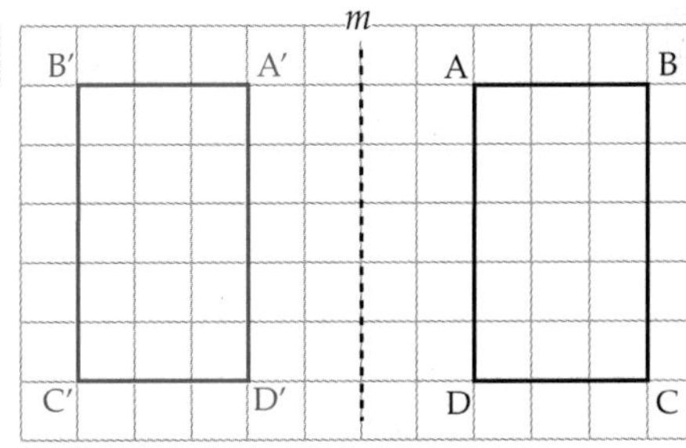

We use a 'dash' with a label to show which one is the image.
The image of A is A′.
B′ is the image of B.

Sometimes the figure is already drawn and labelled for us. We can then use those labels to identify points and their images.

Example This figure has m as a line of symmetry.

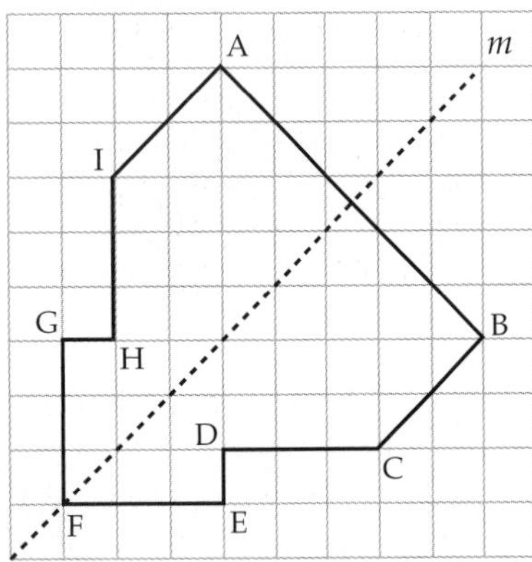

(a) Write down the images of these points when they are reflected in line m.
(i) A (ii) E (iii) F

(b) What is the image of the line AI?
(c) What is the image of angle $\widehat{BCD}$?

Answer

(a) (i) The image of A is B
(ii) The image of E is G
(iii) The image of F is F
(b) The image of AI is BC
(c) The image of is $\widehat{BCD}$ is $\widehat{AIH}$

Here's how to write down the image of a line or angle.
Just use the images of single points on the line or angle.
For example, if the image of P is R, and the image of Q is S, then the image of PQ will be RS.

EXERCISE 15.3

1–4 *Reflect the objects in the mirror lines given. Label each image A′B′C′ etc.*

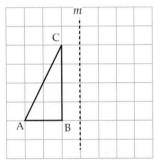

1

m
C
A
B

2

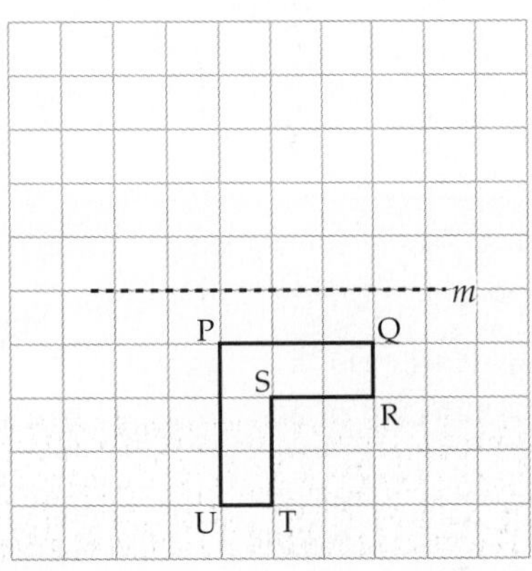

3

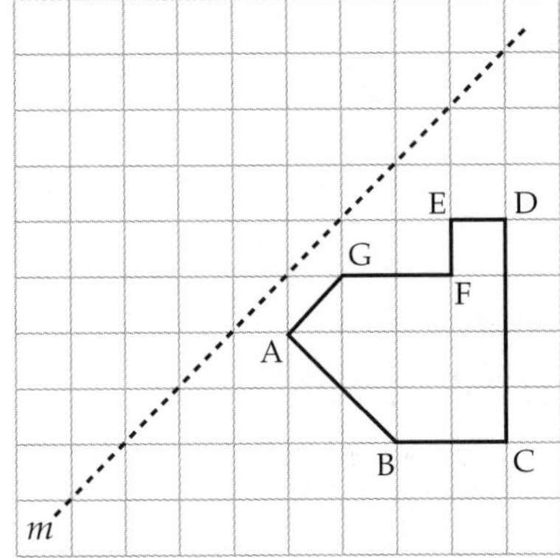

4

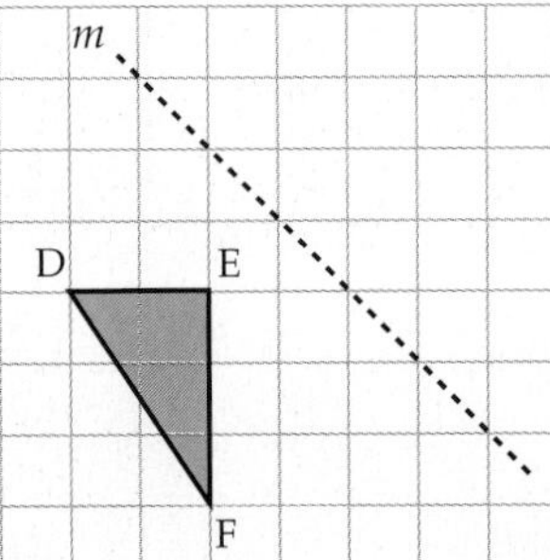

5 This diagram shows a reflection in the line of symmetry marked m.

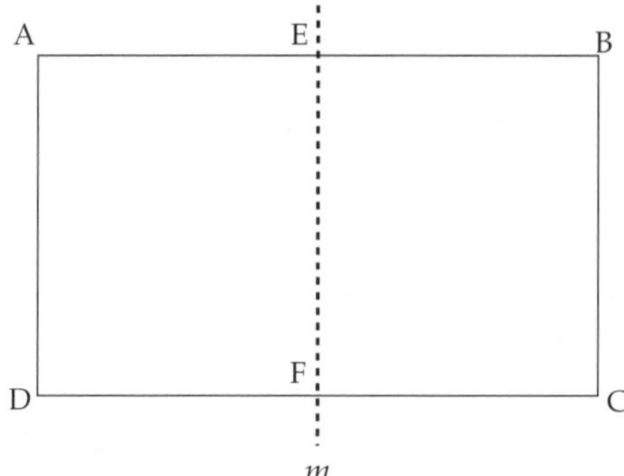

Write down the image of each of these:

(a) A
(b) C
(c) F
(d) AD
(e) CF
(f) $B\hat{C}F$

6 This diagram shows a reflection in the line of symmetry marked m.

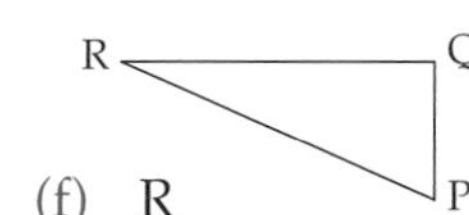

Write down the image of each of these:

(a) P
(b) RQ
(c) Q
(d) Y
(e) PQ
(f) R
(g) L
(h) WY
(i) $R\hat{Q}P$
(j) $Y\hat{W}X$

7

Use the diagram to decode what the ice-cream is thinking. Do this by copying the message, and writing the image of each letter beneath it. For example, the image of L is N.

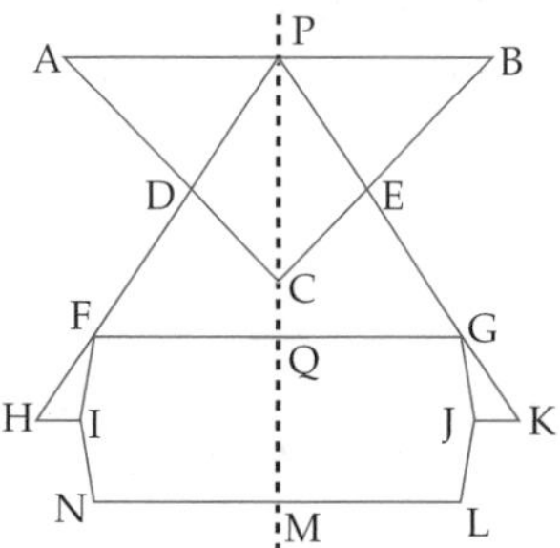

Properties of reflection

STARTER

Imagine a trail of ants crawling around the rectangle on the left. They go from A to B to C to D, and back to A.

- Is this direction clockwise or anti-clockwise?

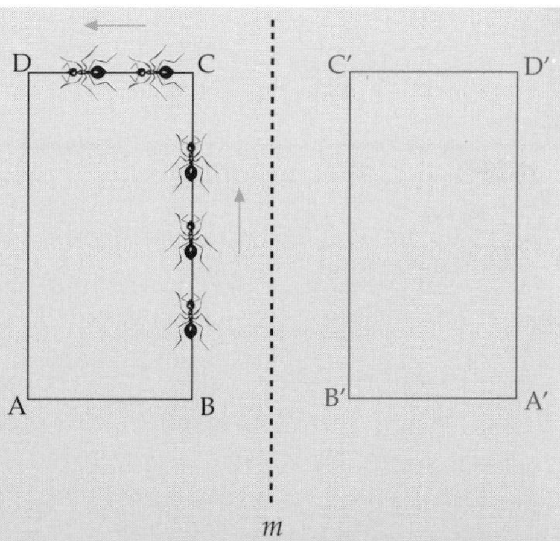

Now look at the reflection of the ant trail (the rectangle on the right). Follow the image of the ants moving from A′ to B′ to C′ to D′, and back to A′.

- Is this image direction clockwise or anti-clockwise?

- Has there been a change in the direction the ants appear to move in?

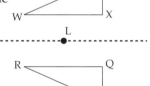

1 **Points on the mirror line stay where they are when reflected. These points are called invariant.**

Example The two invariant points are D and E.

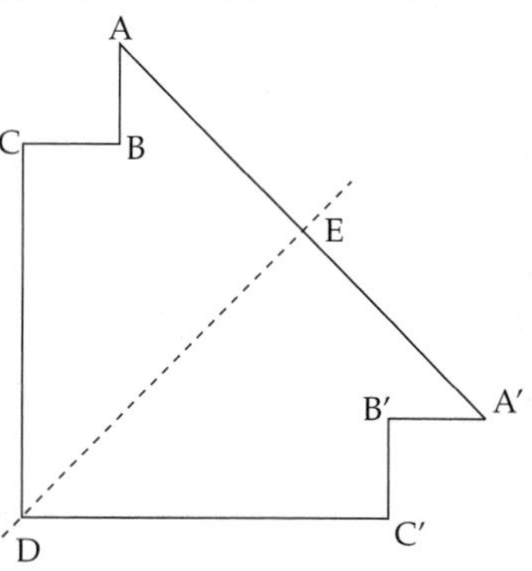

2 **When a line or angle is reflected, its image is the same size.**

Example What are the values of the lengths/angles marked x and y in this reflection?

Answer $x = 4$ cm $y = 60°$

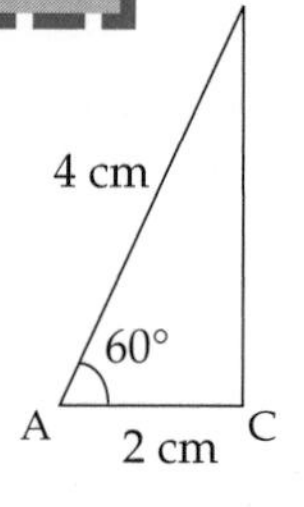

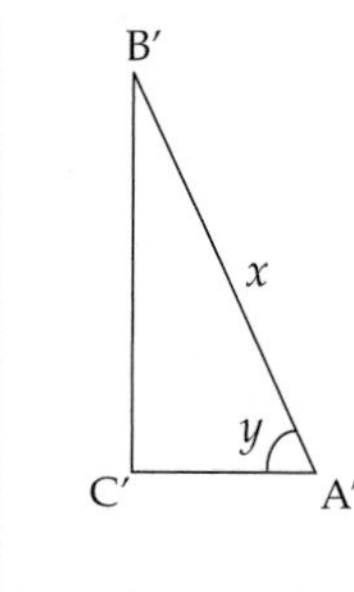

3 **When a shape is reflected, the 'sense' (direction around a figure) is reversed.**

Example B to C to D to B.... (object) is anti-clockwise

B′ to C′ to D′ to B′.... (image) is clockwise

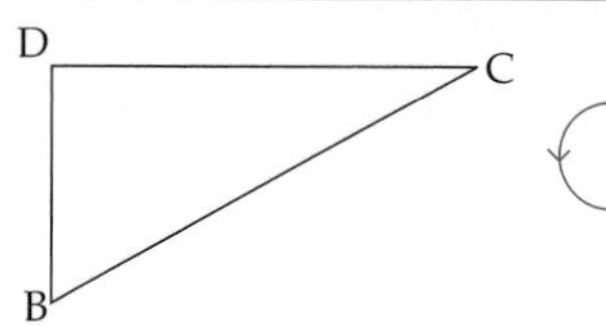

m

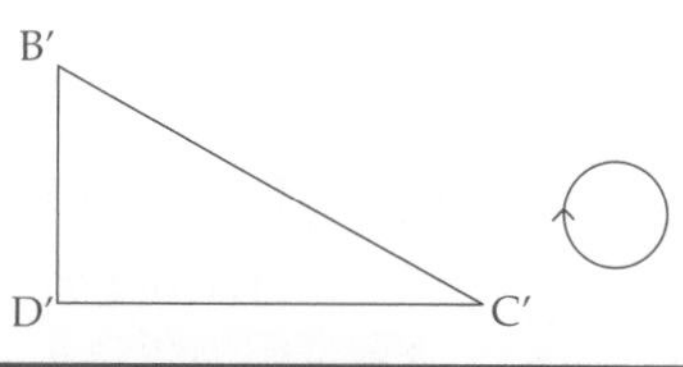

Did you know properties of reflection are very useful on ships and aircraft?

At sea, **sonar** can be used to estimate the depth of water below a ship. Sonar is a sound signal which bounces off the sea-bed. By measuring the time it takes for the signal to return, the sonar equipment can estimate the distance travelled by the signal.

- What is the name of the similar system used for locating aircraft?

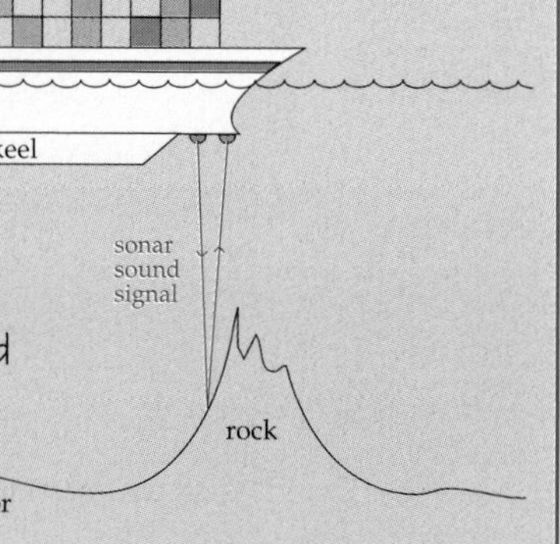

EXERCISE 15.4

1 The reflection in this diagram has three invariant points. Name them.

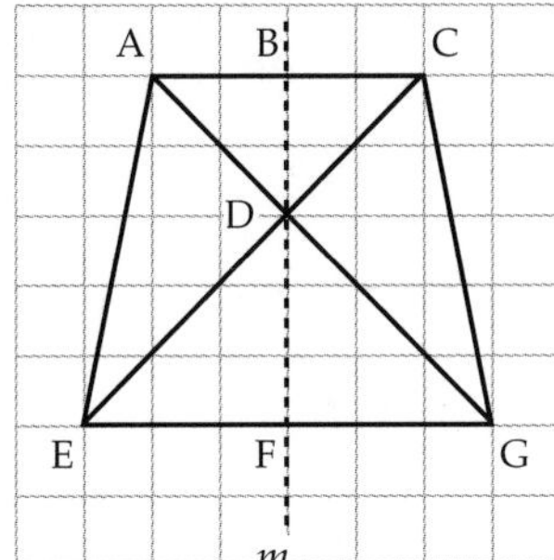

2 This diagram shows a reflection in the line marked *m*.

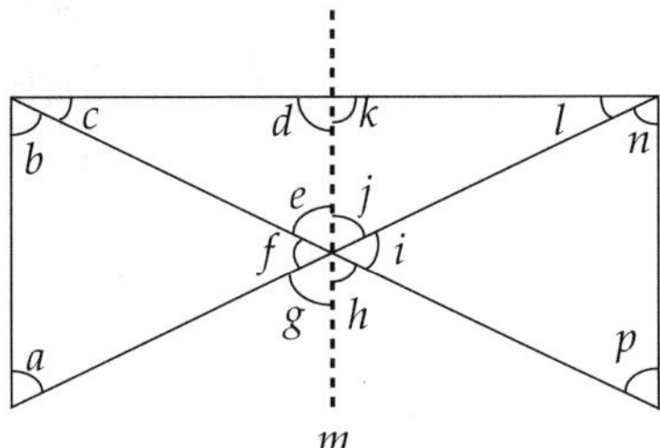

Look at each of these angles. Write down another angle that has the same size.

(a) *a*
(b) *e*
(c) *c*
(d) *n*
(e) *i*
(f) *d*

3

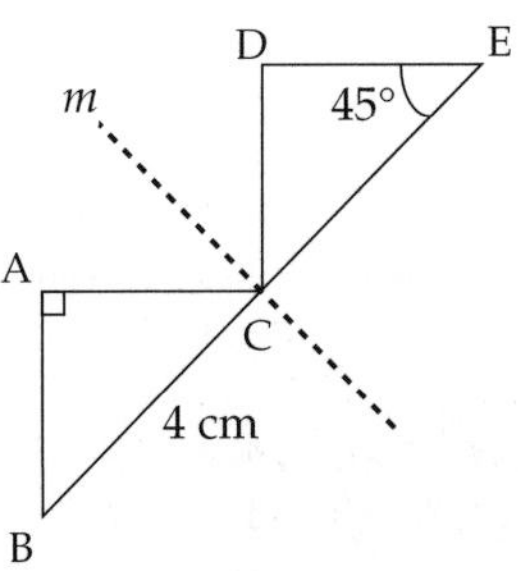

(a) Write down the invariant point(s).
(b) What line is the image of AC?
(c) What is the length of CE?
(d) What is the length of BE?
(e) What is the size of $\widehat{ABC}$?
(f) What is the size of $\widehat{CDE}$?

4

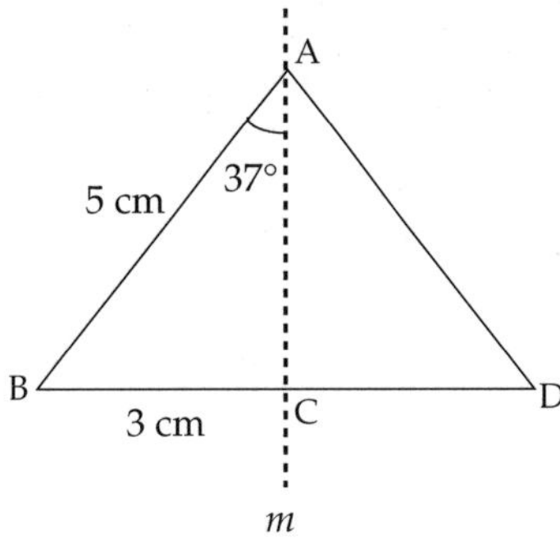

(a) Use the properties of reflection to write down the lengths of:
(i) AD (ii) CD (iii) BD

(b) If $\widehat{BAC} = 37°$, work out the size of $\widehat{BAD}$.

5

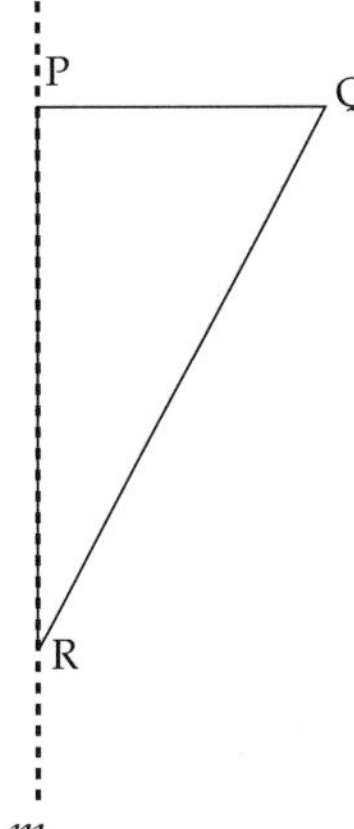

(a) Copy this diagram. Then draw the image of triangle PQR reflected in the line marked *m*. Label the image P′Q′R′.
(b) Is the direction of movement from P to Q to R to P (etc.) clockwise or anti-clockwise?
(c) Is the direction of movement from P′ to Q′ to R′ to P′ (etc.) clockwise or anti-clockwise?
(d) What do the answers to (b) and (c) show about 'sense' when an object is reflected?

6 This diagram shows a reflection in the line marked m.

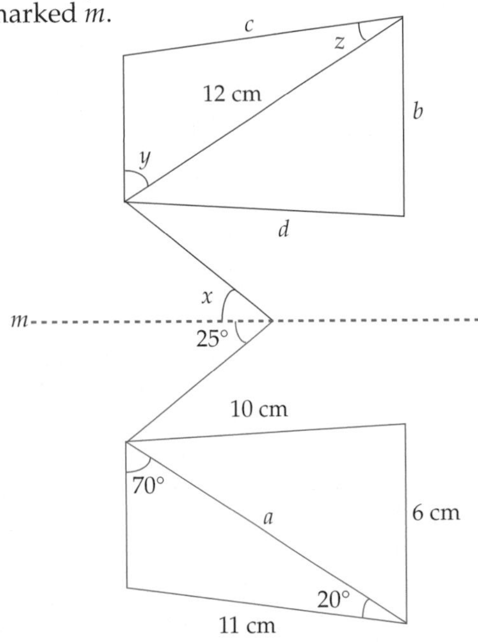

Use the properties of reflection to write down:

(a) the lengths of the lines marked a, b, c and d

(b) the sizes of the angles marked x, y and z.

7 Use the properties of reflection to write down the sizes of angles x, y and z.

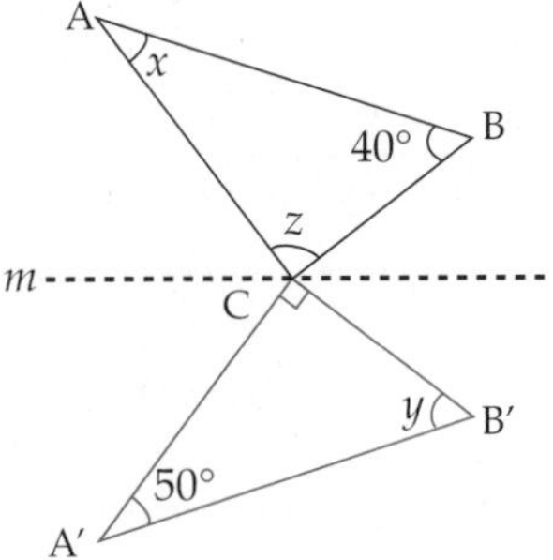

8 This diagram shows a shape called an arrowhead. The line of symmetry is m.

(a) Write down the images of:

(i) Q

(ii) P

(iii) PR

(iv) PQ

(v) $Q\hat{R}P$

(b) Name the invariant point(s).

(c) What is the size of $Q\hat{R}S$?

More than one mirror line

Both these photos show an indoor swimming pool at Hearst Castle. This property was built by William Randolph Hearst (a newspaper publisher) in California in the 1930s.

- How many lines of symmetry can you see in each photo?

INVESTIGATION

PREDICTING A REFLECTION

Take a piece of A4 paper.

Fold it in half twice:

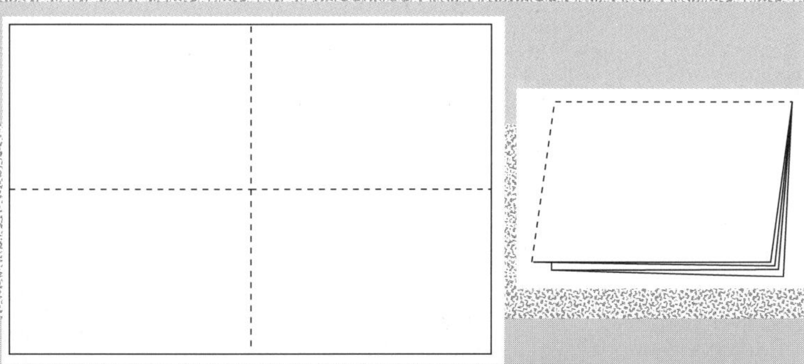

Try to predict the answers to these questions *before* you cut the paper.

- The paper will be cut along these green lines. The centre piece will be removed, and it will then be unfolded. What will it look like?

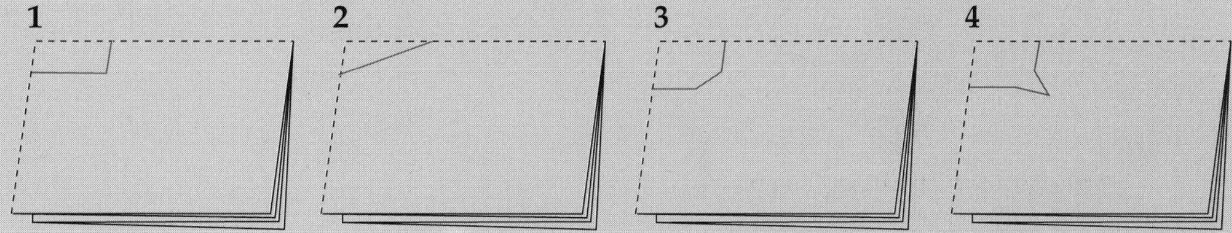

How could you predict what the unfolded piece of paper will look like when you know the shape of the centre piece?

Further investigation

If the paper is folded more than twice and cut, will the resulting shape have more than two lines of symmetry?

Shapes can have more than one line of symmetry.
There are several possible reflections.

Example This rectangle has two lines of symmetry, m and n.

- When reflected in m, the image of B is C.
- When reflected in n, the image of B is A.

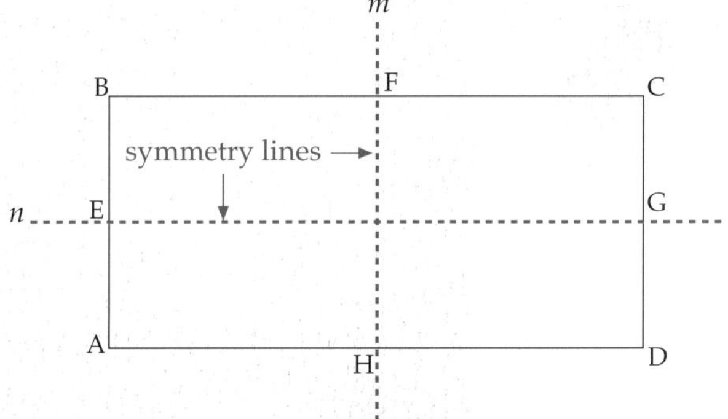

EXERCISE 15.5

1 Copy each diagram. Complete the figures so that both m and n are lines of symmetry.

(a)

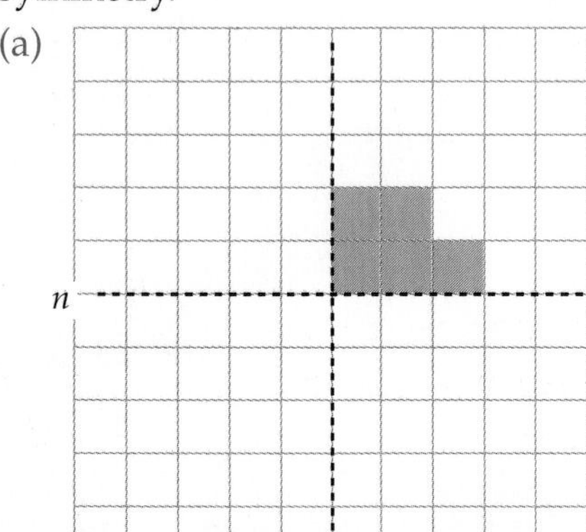

(b)

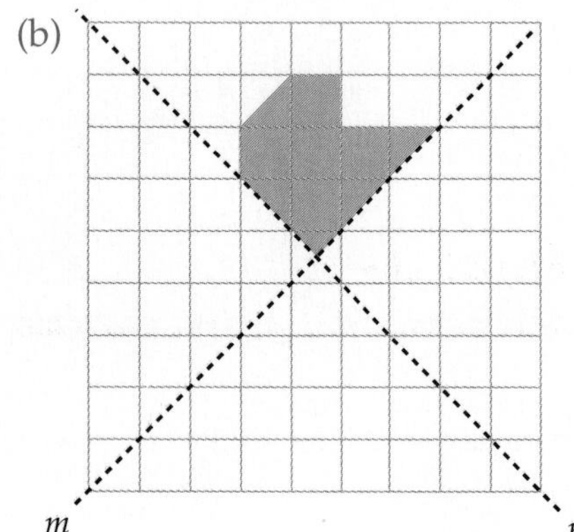

2

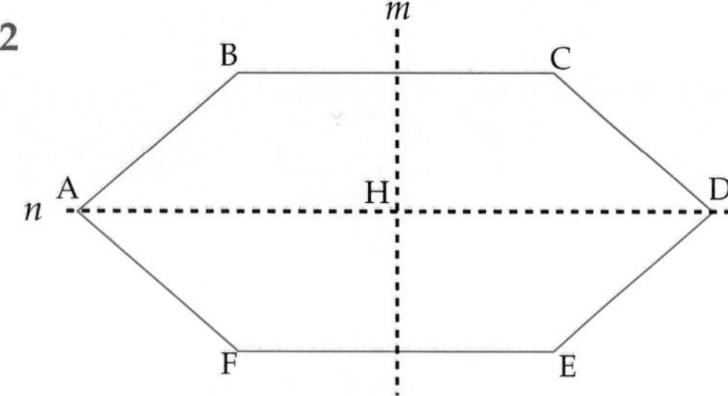

This shape has two lines of symmetry.

(a) What is the image of B when reflected in m?

(b) What is the image of B when reflected in n?

(c) Name three different line segments that must be the same length as AB.

(d) Which point is *invariant* when reflected in *both* lines m and n?

3 This rectangle ABCD has two lines of symmetry. ED = 5 cm and CD = 6 cm. Write down the length of these line segments:

(a) AE (c) AB

(b) BC (d) BF

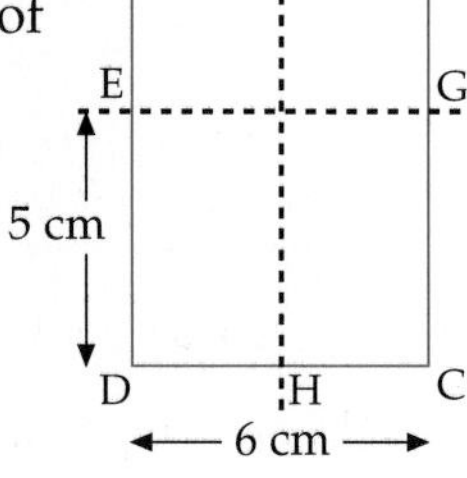

4 DEFG is a rhombus. It has two lines of symmetry.

(a) Use m as a line of symmetry. Write down the image of these lines and angles:

(i) DE

(ii) EF

(iii) $\widehat{DEF}$

(iv) $\widehat{EDF}$

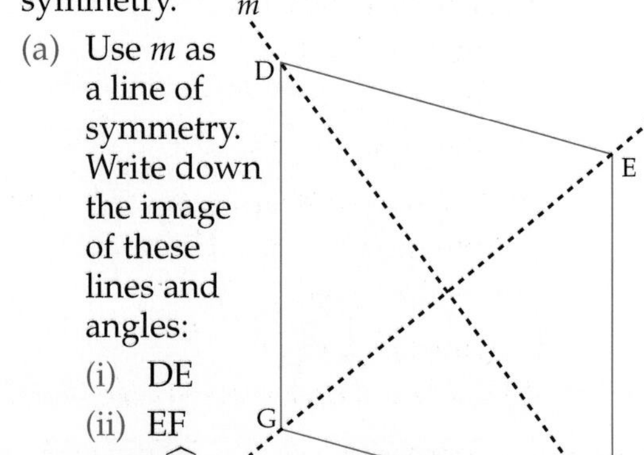

(b) Use n as a line of symmetry. Write down the image of these lines and angles:

(i) DE

(ii) DG

(iii) $\widehat{GDE}$

(c) Write down three different line segments that are the same length as DE.

5 This diagram has four different lines of symmetry: (p, q, r and s).

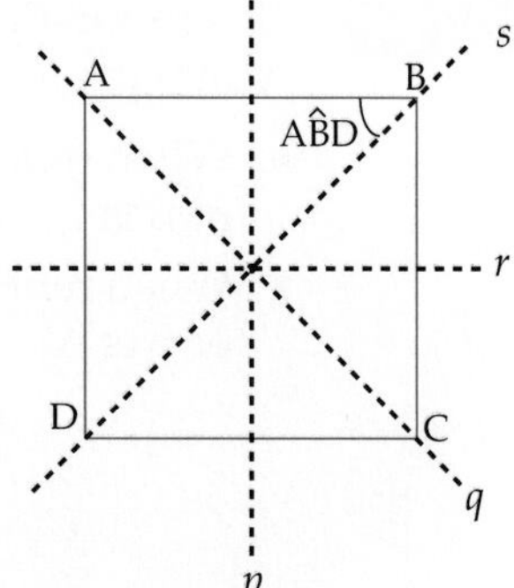

(a) Copy this table. Then complete it to give the images. One entry has been done in each column to show you how to answer.

Reflection in line	Image of C	Image of AB	Image of $\widehat{ABD}$
p	D		
q		AD	
r			
s			$\widehat{CBD}$

(b) What kind of figure is ABCD?

6 This is a regular hexagon. Two lines of symmetry are shown—m and n.

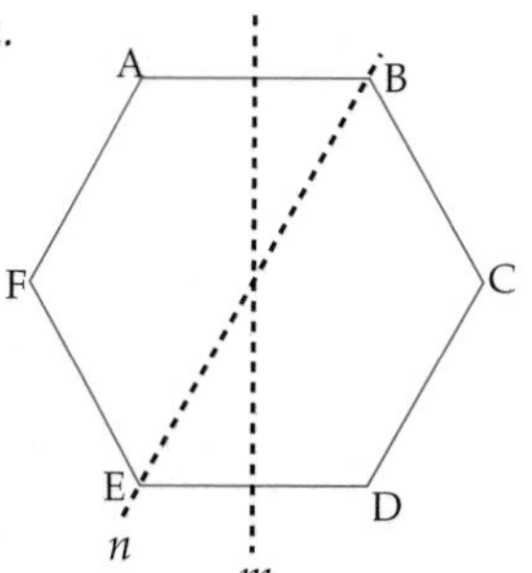

(a) How many more lines of symmetry could be added to this figure?

(b) Write down these images when reflecting in line m:

(i) the image of A

(ii) the image of C

(iii) the image of AF

(c) Write down these images when reflecting in line n:

(i) the image of B

(ii) the image of C

(iii) the image of DE

(d) Which two labelled points are *invariant* when reflecting in line n?

16 Rotation

STARTER

These pictures all show examples of rotation.

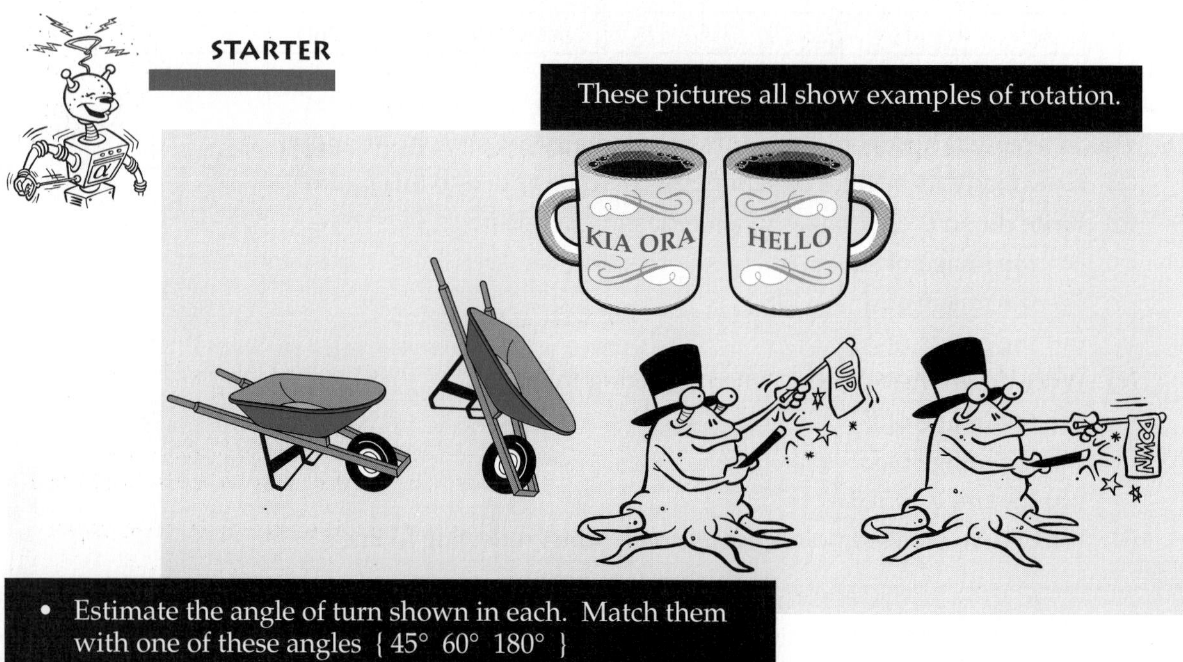

- Estimate the angle of turn shown in each. Match them with one of these angles { 45° 60° 180° }
- Describe where the centre of the rotation is for each one.

A **rotation** is a transformation where an object is *turned* around a fixed point to give its image. Each part of the object is turned through the same angle.

This example shows a rotation of 90° about the point marked ×.

The labels show what has happened as the object is transformed to the image.

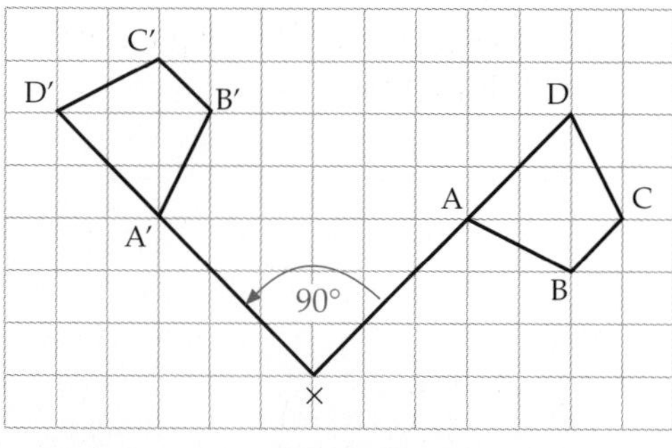

To do a rotation we need to know:

- the **centre** of rotation—all the points turn around this one fixed point
- the **angle of rotation**—this gives the amount of turning.

The angle of rotation can be given:

- in degrees (e.g. 90°, 180°, etc.)
- as a fraction of a turn (e.g. a quarter-turn or half-turn, etc.).

The direction can either be **clockwise** or **anti-clockwise**. If no direction is given, we take it as being anti-clockwise.

Take care over the direction of rotation. These two spirals, starting from the centre and moving outwards, show the two different directions:

anti-clockwise

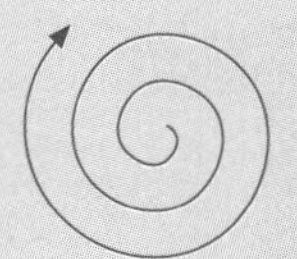
clockwise

Something to think about ... is a right-handed person more likely to draw a clockwise spiral? What about left-handers?

Activity—using tracing paper to do rotations

You will need:

- some tracing paper
- paper with a squared grid
- a sharp object to pin down the tracing paper as you turn it.

Example This example shows the method. A rectangle is going to be rotated 90° anti-clockwise about the point marked ×.

1 Copy this rectangle onto squared paper.

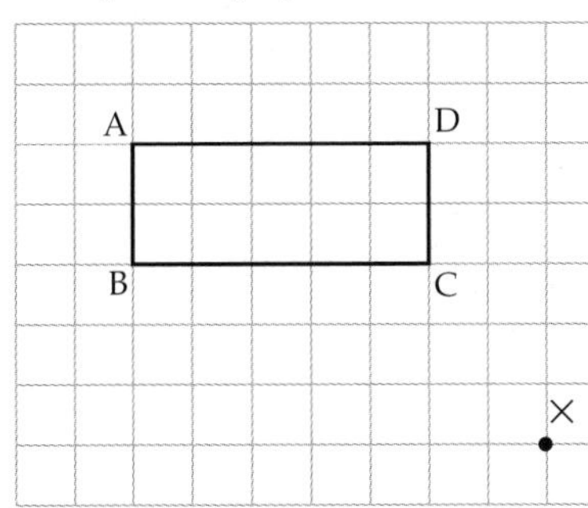

2 Place a piece of tracing paper on top, and draw the outline.

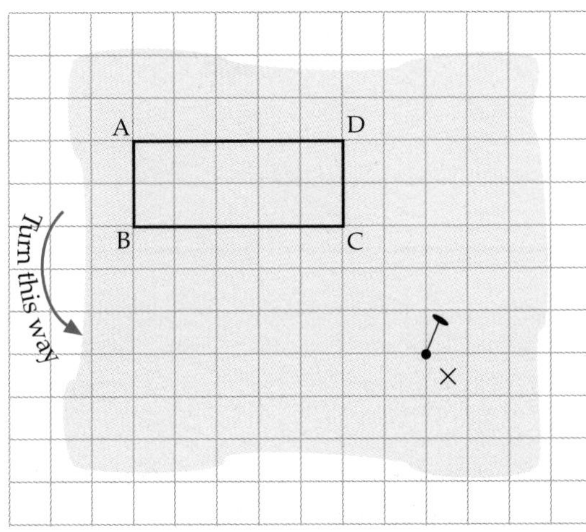

3 Pin down the piece of tracing paper. Now turn it through 90° anti-clockwise.

4 The final position of the tracing paper shows where the image will be.

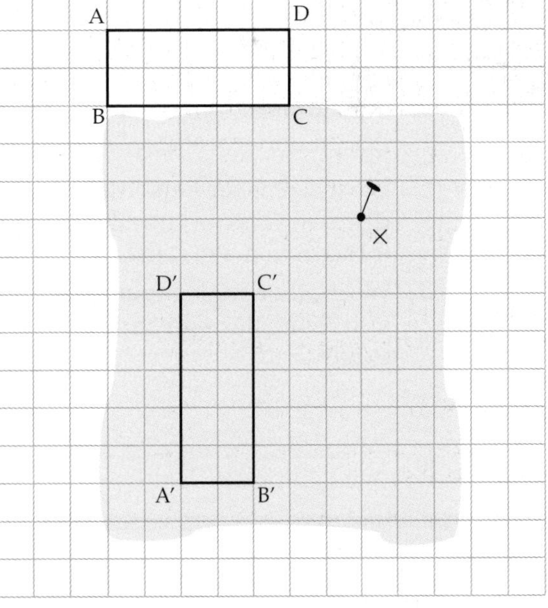

EXERCISE 16.1

1 (a) Make a tracing of this design.
(b) Can you turn it through 180° around the centre to match the design?

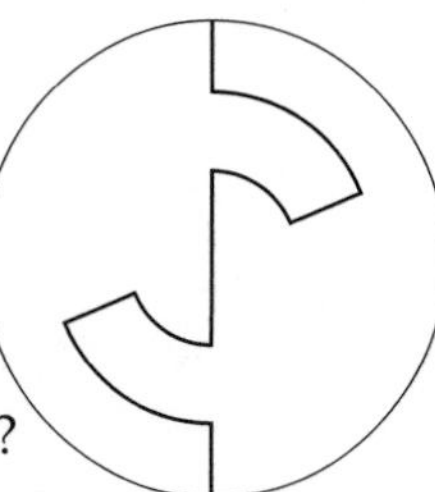

2 (a) Make a tracing of this letter.
(b) In how many different ways can the tracing fit on top of the letter?
(c) What size is the smallest angle (in degrees) you can turn the tracing through to make it fit?

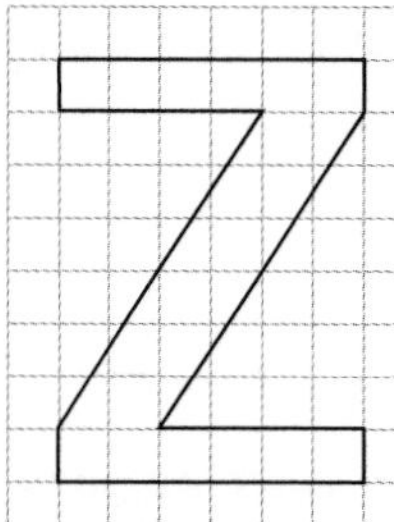

3 (a) Make a tracing of this design.
(b) Turn the tracing around the point marked O, until it matches the design underneath.
(c) What size is the smallest angle (in degrees) you can turn the tracing through to make it fit?
(d) What other angles could the tracing also rotate through and still fit exactly?

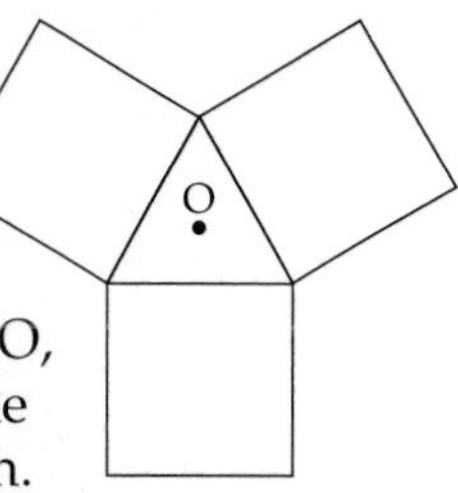

4 Make three copies of this diagram.

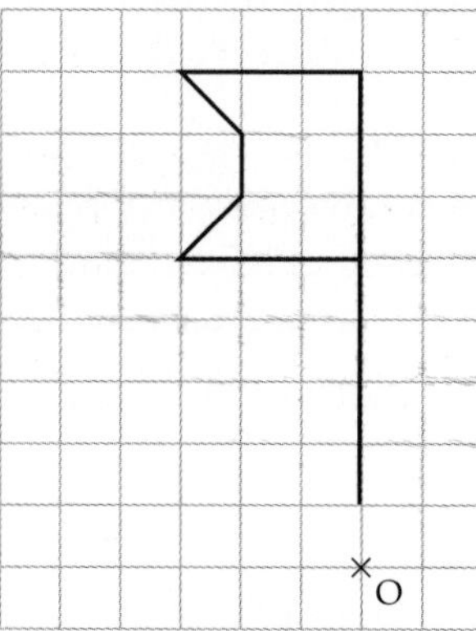

Draw the image when it is rotated:
(a) 90° anti-clockwise about O
(b) 180° anti-clockwise about O
(c) 90° *clockwise* about O.

5 Copy this figure. Draw its image when it is rotated 90° anti-clockwise about O.

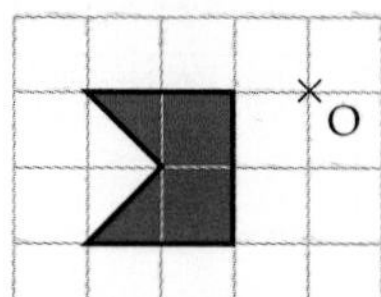

6 Copy this figure. Draw its image when it is rotated 180° anti-clockwise about O.

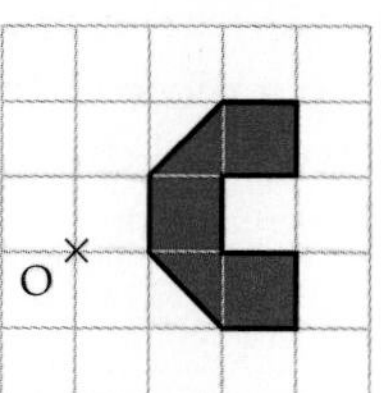

Drawing rotations accurately

Here are the steps to follow to draw a rotation accurately.

These instructions are for a 90° rotation.
The method is similar for other angles.

Example Rotate the triangle ABC through a quarter-turn (90° angle) anti-clockwise about O.

A
B
C
× O

1 Join the points O and A with a line.
Measure it. $\overline{OA}$ = 3.5 cm

A
3.5 cm
O
B
C

2 Draw a new line through O at right-angles to $\overline{OA}$. Mark A′ on this line. A′ will be the same distance from O as A was (here, $\overline{O'A'}$ = 3.5 cm)

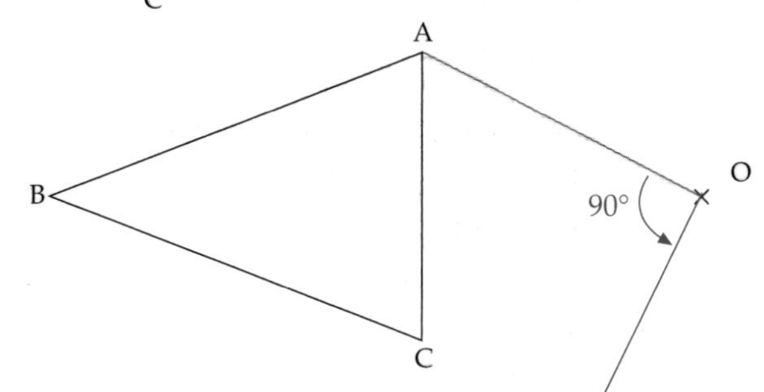

3 Locate B′ and C′ in a similar way.
Join the points A′, B′ and C′ to complete the image triangle.

A
O
B
C
A′
C′
B′

Usually, the shape to be rotated will be on a grid. This makes it easy to see where the image goes.

Sometimes, the centre of rotation is one of the points in the figure itself.

Example Rotate this rectangle through 180° about point C. Label the image of each point.

Answer The dashed arcs have been drawn in to show the half-turn. They are not part of the image.

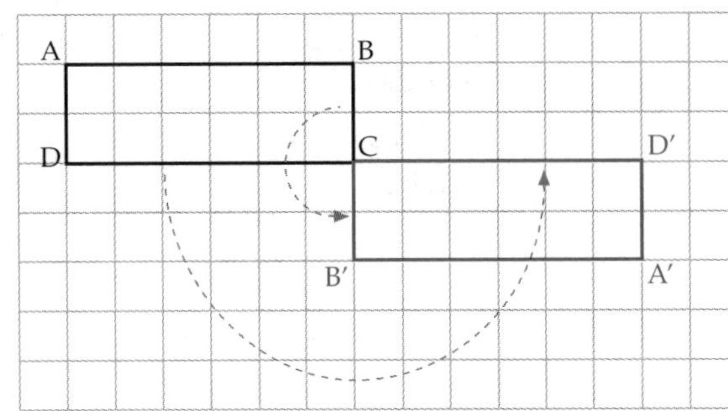

In this example, the angle of rotation was a half-turn (180°). So, we didn't have to say whether the direction was anti-clockwise or clockwise—for a 180° rotation, it makes no difference!

EXERCISE 16.2

Copy each figure. Rotate it through the angle given. Use the given point as the centre of rotation. Label the image A′, B′, etc.

1 through 90° about A

2 through 270° (i.e. 90° clockwise) about C

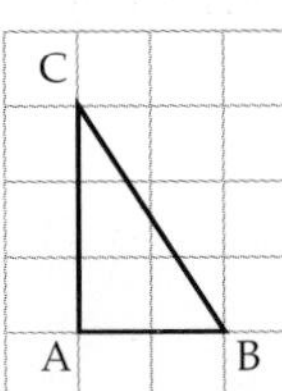

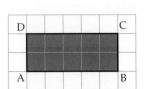

3 through 180° about A

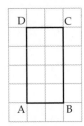

4 through 90° about O

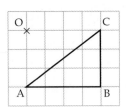

5 through 180° about O

6 through 270° about O

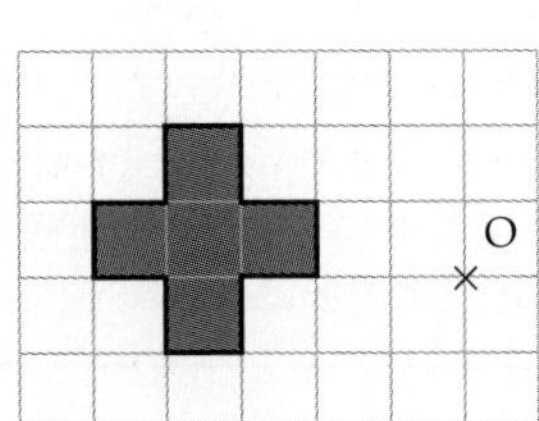

7 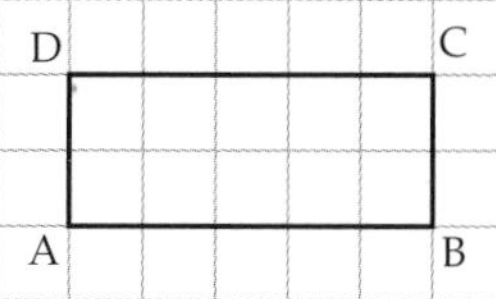

through 90° about B

8 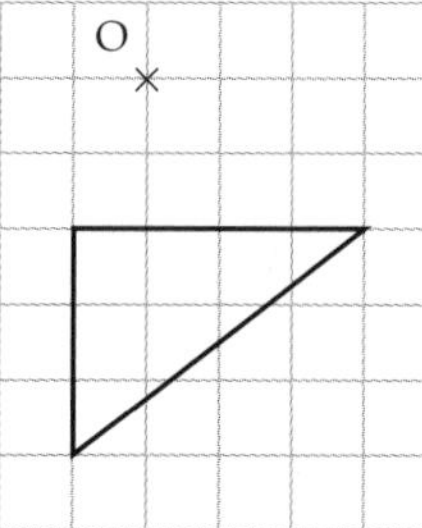

through 270° about O

9 through 180° about O

10 through 180° about C

Properties of rotation

Here are some properties of rotation:

- every point moves through the **same angle** around the centre of rotation
- each point and its image is the **same distance** from the centre of rotation
- there is only one **invariant point**. This is the centre of rotation.

Example This parallelogram has half-turn symmetry. It can be rotated through 180° onto itself about the point marked T.

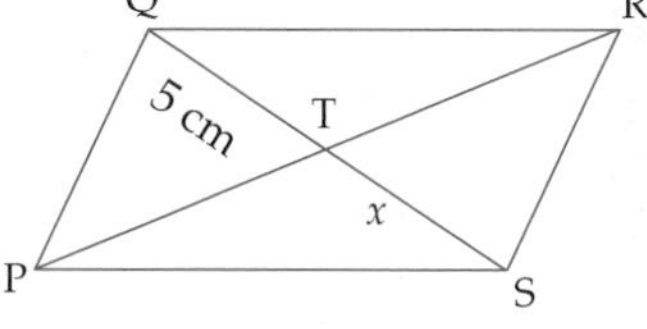

(a) Which point is the image of Q under this rotation?

(b) Explain why the length marked x is 5 cm.

(c) Which point is invariant in this rotation?

Answers (a) The image of Q is S.

(b) QT = ST because each point and its image is the same distance from the centre of rotation.

(c) T is invariant—it is the centre of rotation.

EXERCISE 16.3

1 This diagram shows a 90° rotation about O.

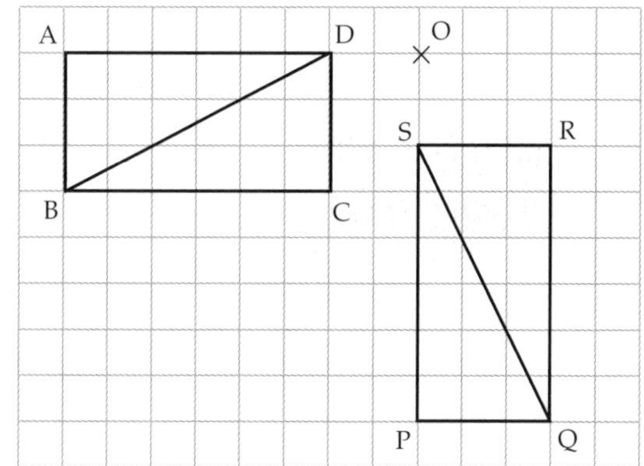

(a) Which point is the image of A?

(b) Which point is the image of C?

(c) Which line segment is the image of $\overline{BD}$?

2 This diagram shows a 180° rotation about O.

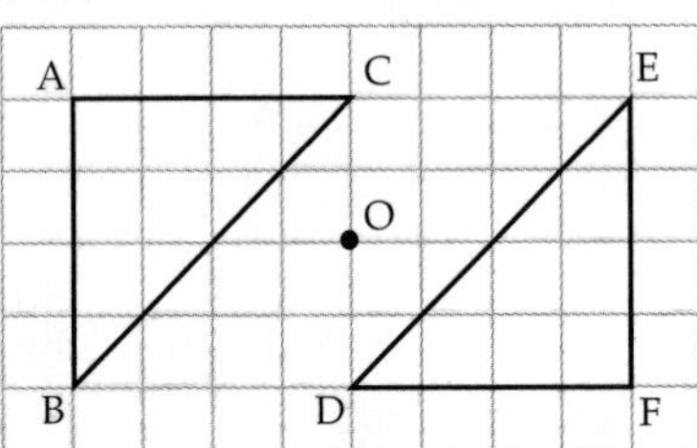

(a) Which point is the image of B?

(b) Which line segment is the image of $\overline{AC}$?

3 This regular pentagon maps onto itself when rotated through 72° about the centre O.

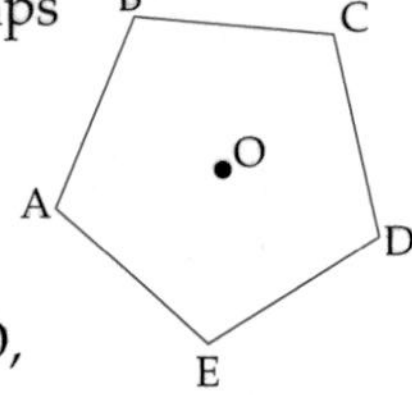

(a) When the pentagon is rotated 72° about O, what point is the image of D?

(b) What point is invariant in this rotation?

(c) There are five different angles through which the pentagon will rotate onto itself. Two of them are given. Copy and complete this list: { 72°, ….. , ……, ……. , 360° }

4 This octagon is regular. The centre is O.

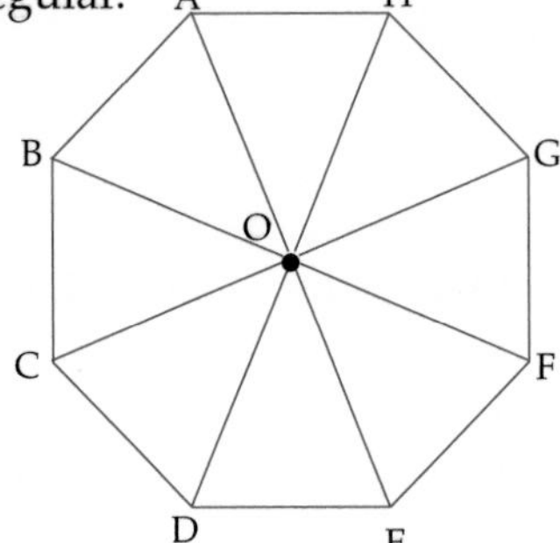

(a) Write down the images of:

(i) B after a rotation (anti-clockwise) of 90° about O

(ii) F after a rotation of 180° about O

(iii) C after a rotation (anti-clockwise) of 90° about O.

(b) The largest angle through which the octagon will rotate onto itself is 360°. What is the smallest? (Don't count 0° as an angle of rotation here!)

5 Look carefully at the labels of these objects and their images. Write down whether each is a *reflection* or a *rotation*.

(a)

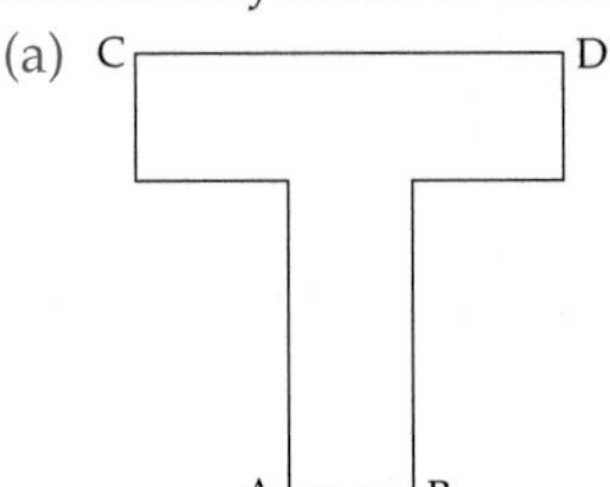

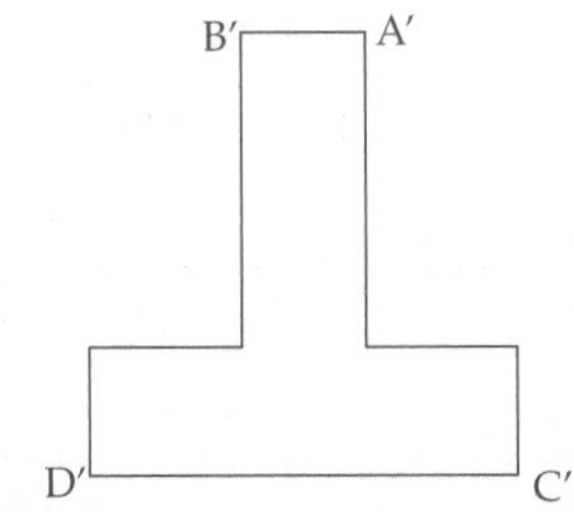

(b) (c)

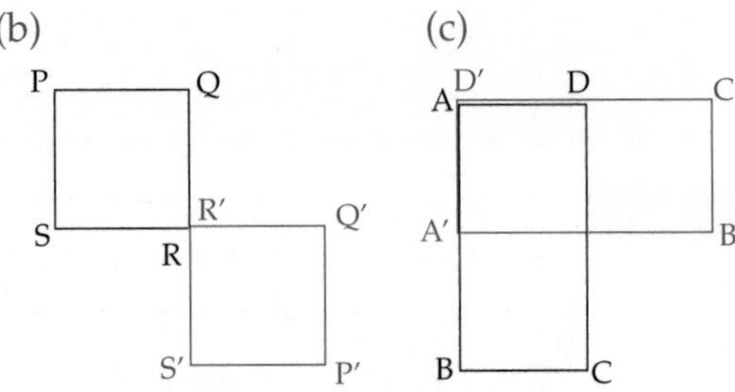

6 The diagram shows a rotation of the square ABCD to the square A′B′C′D′.

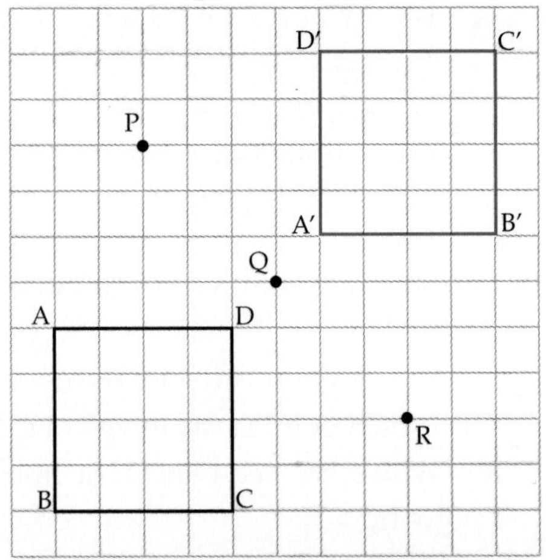

(a) What is the centre of rotation? Choose from the list { P, Q, R }

(b) What is the angle of rotation? Choose from the list { 90°, 180°, 270° }.

7 These diagrams all show rotations. For each one, write down the label of the centre of rotation.

(a)

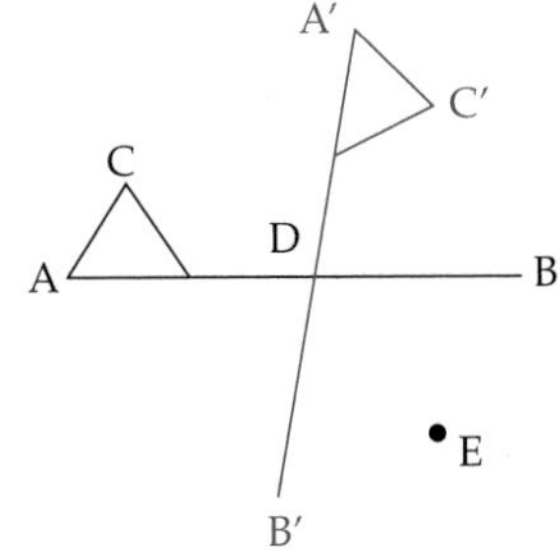

(b)

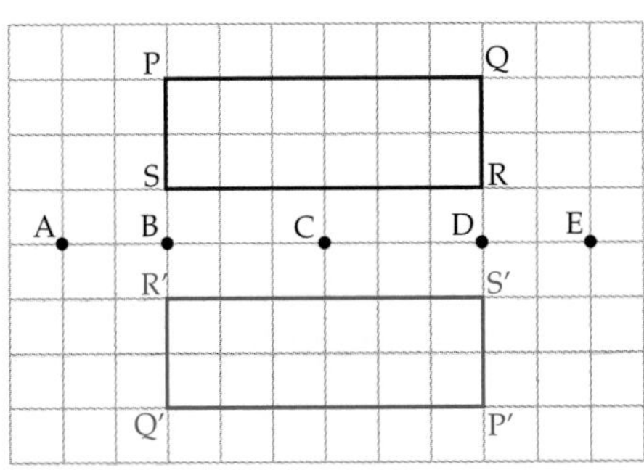

(c)

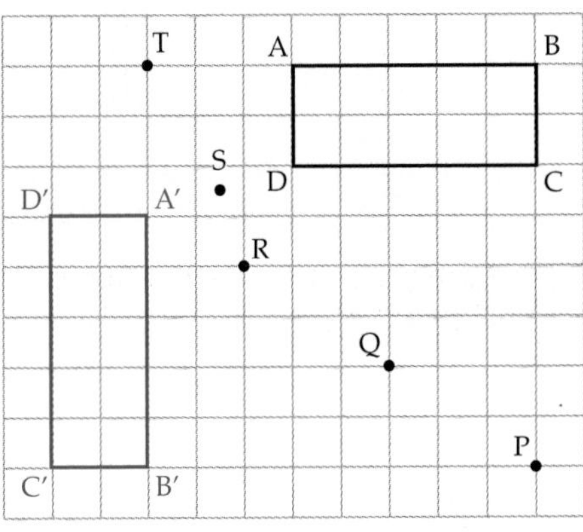

Extension

8 Copy this diagram and place a cross × on the centre of rotation.

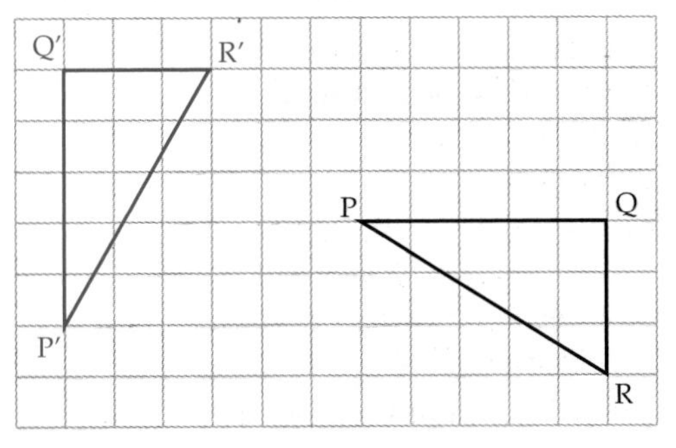

17 Translation

A **translation** is a movement where every point moves:

- the same distance
- in the same direction.

STARTER

This photograph was taken on an Italian motorway or *autostrada.* It shows several examples of translation.

- How many examples of translation can you see here? Write them down. You should be able to list at least five.

More translation!

- What do you think the Italian word 'sottopasso' means? Translate it!
- What country does Q8 petrol come from?

EXERCISE 17.1

1 This diagram shows a translation in which A moves to A′, B moves to B′, and so on.

(a) Measure these four lengths (in mm):

(i) AA′

(ii) BB′

(iii) CC′

(iv) DD′

(b) What do you notice about these four measurements?

2 This diagram shows a translation in which P moves to P′, Q to Q′, and so on.

(a) Measure these four lengths (in mm):

(i) PP′

(ii) QQ′

(iii) RR′

(iv) SS′

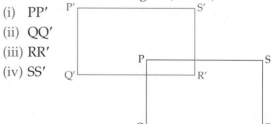

(b) What do you notice about these four measurements?

Drawing translations

To translate an object and draw its image, all we need to know is the image of *one point*. Then, every other point moves the *same distance* in the *same direction*.

All the points move along parallel lines!

Example Translate this flag.
The image of A is A′.

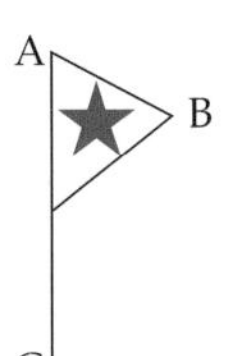

Answer

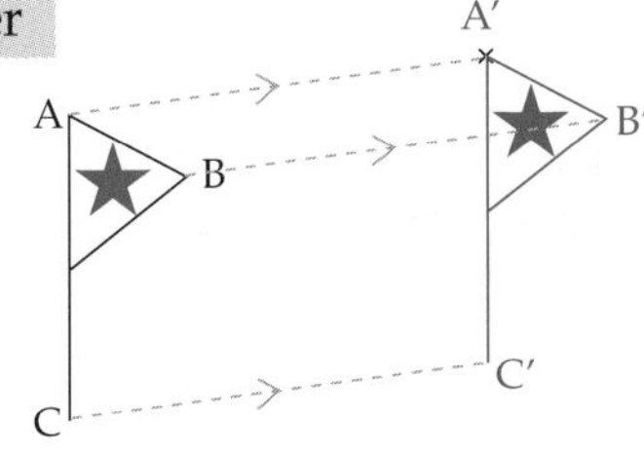

Notice how B and C have been 'translated' the same distance and in the same direction as A.

The arrow lines have been drawn to show you how far B and C move. These lines are not part of the answer.

Example This rectangle is to be translated so that A maps to C.
That is, the image of A is C.
Draw the image of the rectangle.

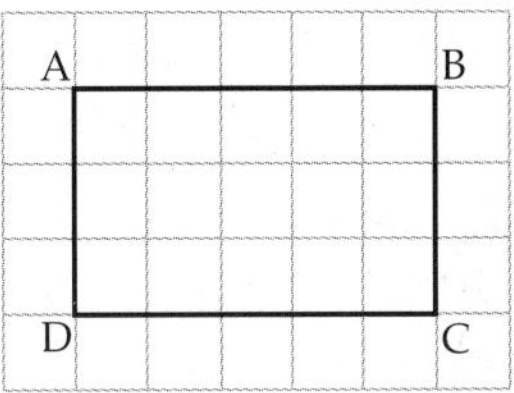

Answer

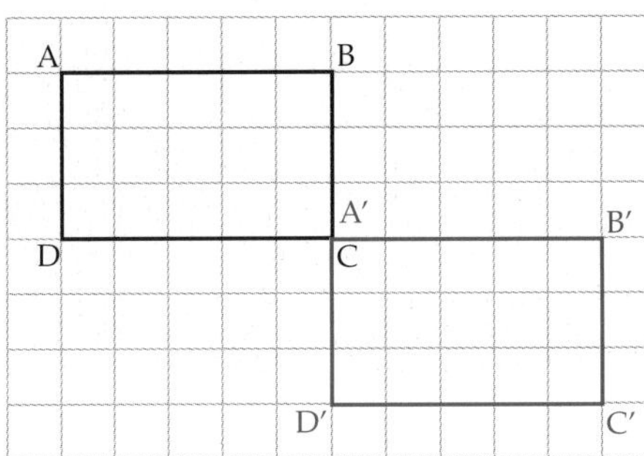

Notice how the grid of squares helps to draw the translation. In this example, each point moved across 5 squares and down 3 squares to give the image.

EXERCISE 17.2

1 This diagram shows a translation of a cross. Copy the diagram. Then add the labels B′, C′ and D′ in the correct positions.

A B C D A′

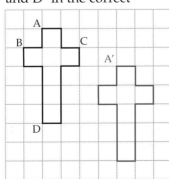

2–4 *Copy the diagram. Then draw the image of each shape. Each diagram shows a translation where A moves to A′.*

2

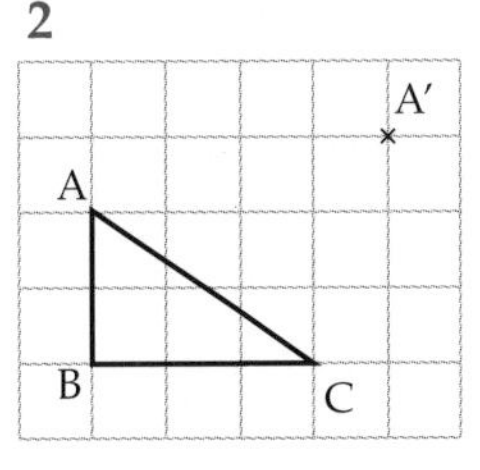

3

A D A′ B C

4

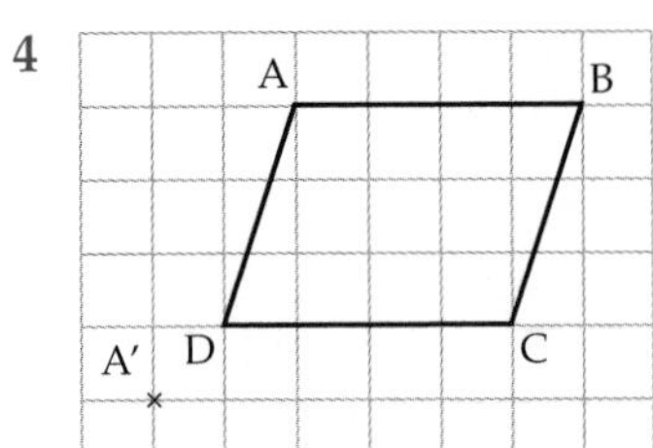

5–10 *Each of these diagrams has information about a translation. Copy the diagrams. Add the image of each shape when it is translated.*

5 The image of S is Q

Q R P S

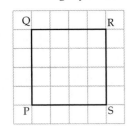

6 A → F

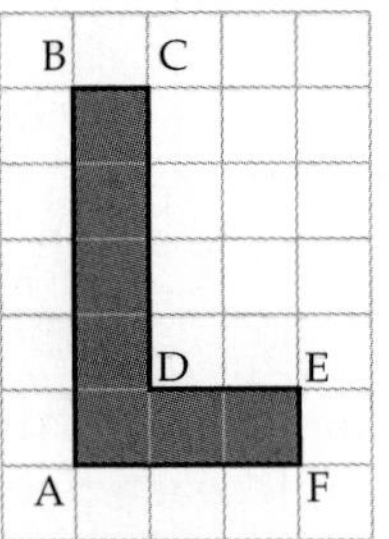

7 The image of A is E

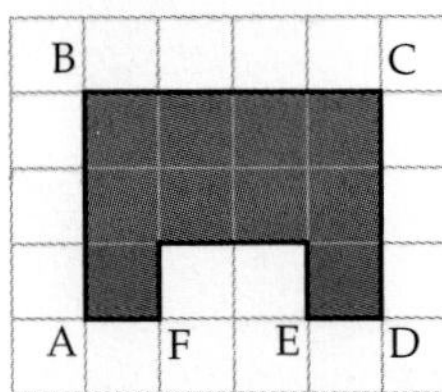

A short way of writing (for example) 'the image of A is B', is to write 'A → B'.

8 B → E

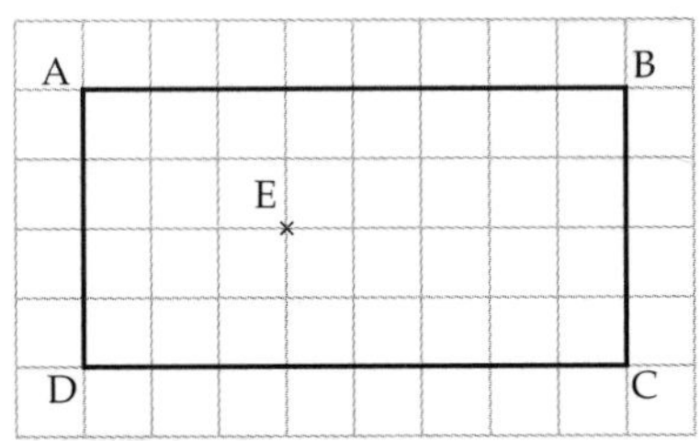

9 G → C

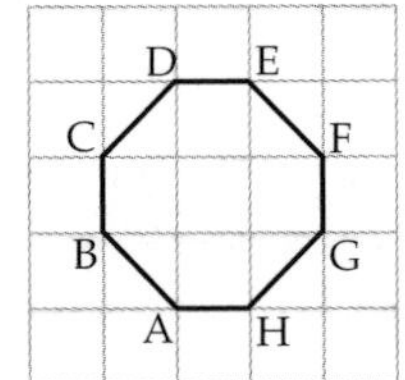

10 The image of R is R′

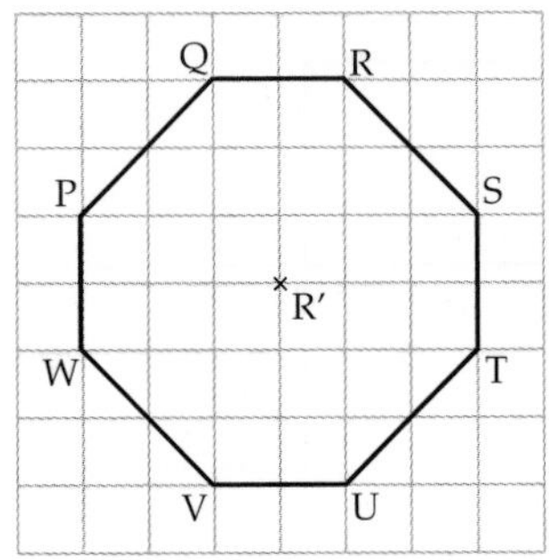

Using vectors to describe translations

When objects are translated on a grid of squares, we can use the squares to describe how far they move. We do this by saying how many squares a point moves up/down and sideways.

We have a special system for describing translations.
A translation can be written as a **vector**.
In two dimensions, a vector is a pair of numbers. The two numbers are written in large round brackets.

- The top number describes the sideways movement.
- The bottom number describes the up or down movement.

The next example shows a translation by the vector $\begin{pmatrix}5\\2\end{pmatrix}$.

Example In this translation A, B and C have each been moved 5 squares along to the right and 2 squares upwards.

We could represent this translation by an arrow:

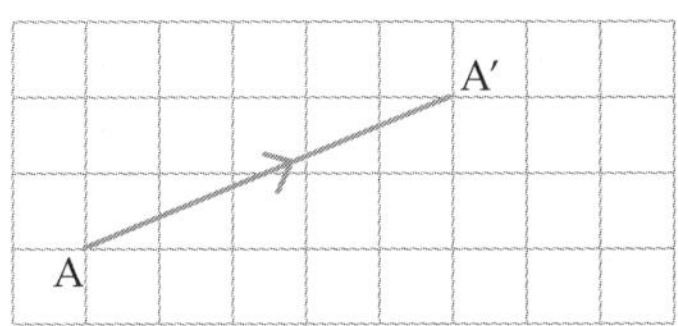

The translation that moves A to A′ can be written as $\begin{pmatrix}5\\2\end{pmatrix}$.

This arrow moves 5 squares to the right and 2 squares upwards from start to finish.

We write the two numbers in a vector in the same way each time. The rule is:

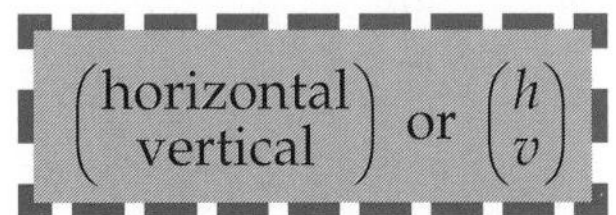

On top is the number of units of sideways movement:

- move **right** for *positive* numbers
- move **left** for *negative* numbers.

On the bottom is the number of units of movement up or down:

- move **up** for *positive* numbers
- move **down** for *negative* numbers.

This table makes it easy to see what happens.

$\begin{pmatrix}h\\v\end{pmatrix}$	**Negative**	**Positive**
Top number (h)	← move left	→ move right
Bottom number (v)	↓ move down	↑ move up

Examples

$\begin{pmatrix}{}^{-}1\\3\end{pmatrix}$

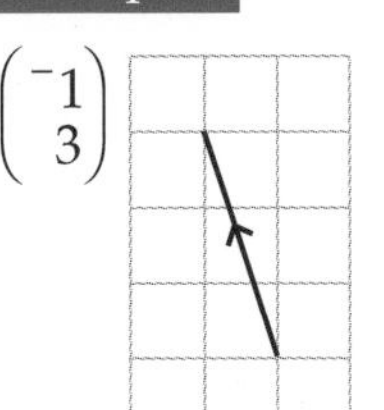

$\begin{pmatrix}4\\2\end{pmatrix}$

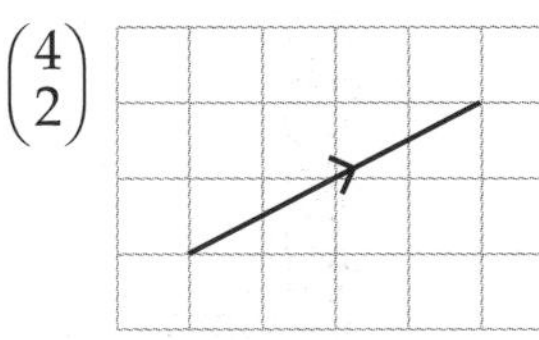

$\begin{pmatrix}{}^{-}2\\{}^{-}2\end{pmatrix}$

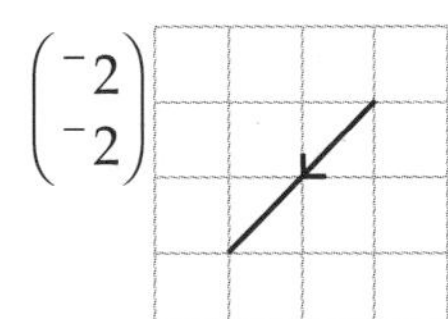

$\begin{pmatrix}2\\{}^{-}5\end{pmatrix}$

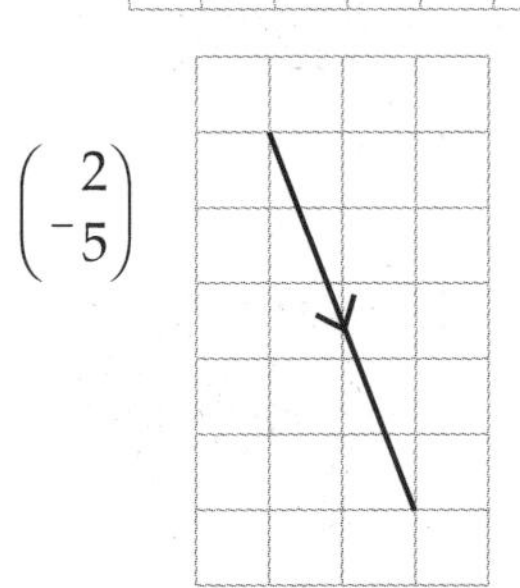

Sometimes the translation goes straight up or down only, or left or right only. Then, one of the numbers in the vector will be 0.

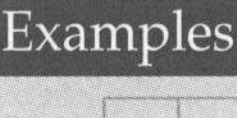

$\begin{pmatrix}0\\4\end{pmatrix}$

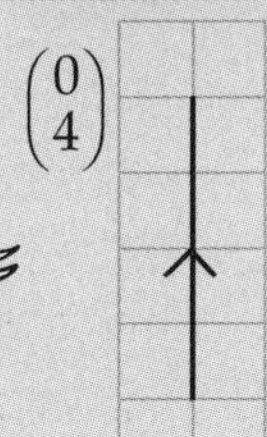

$\begin{pmatrix}{}^{-}3\\0\end{pmatrix}$

EXERCISE 17.3

1 Here are the vectors for eight different translations. In each vector, one number is missing. Copy the vectors and fill in the missing number.

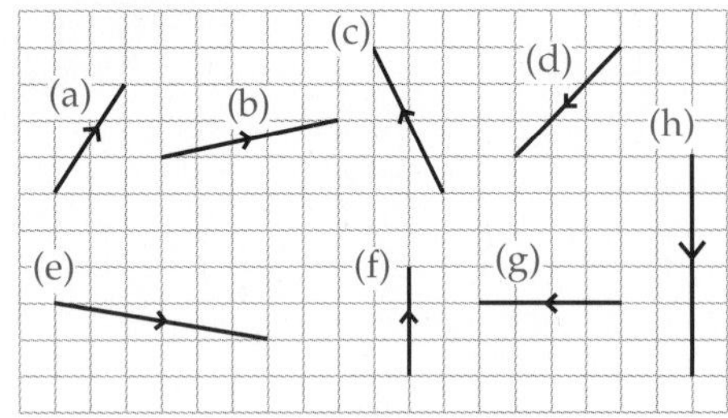

(a) $\begin{pmatrix} 2 \\ \dots \end{pmatrix}$ (e) $\begin{pmatrix} 6 \\ \dots \end{pmatrix}$

(b) $\begin{pmatrix} \dots \\ 1 \end{pmatrix}$ (f) $\begin{pmatrix} 0 \\ \dots \end{pmatrix}$

(c) $\begin{pmatrix} \dots \\ 4 \end{pmatrix}$ (g) $\begin{pmatrix} ^-4 \\ \dots \end{pmatrix}$

(d) $\begin{pmatrix} ^-3 \\ \dots \end{pmatrix}$ (h) $\begin{pmatrix} 0 \\ \dots \end{pmatrix}$

2–16 *Write down the vectors for each of these translations:*

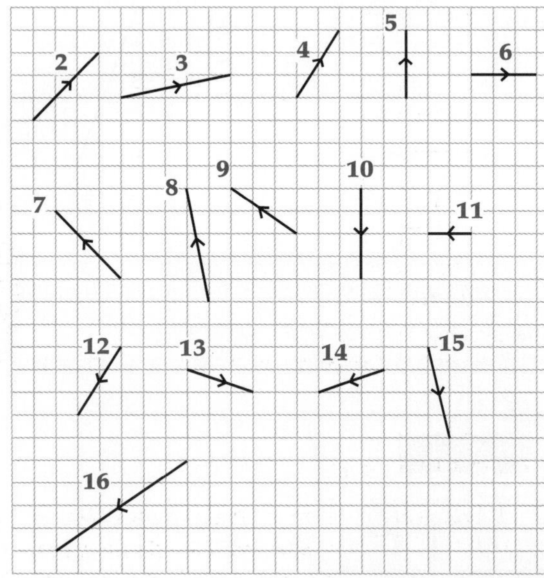

17–31 *Draw arrows to show translations by these vectors:*

17 $\begin{pmatrix} 5 \\ 4 \end{pmatrix}$

18 $\begin{pmatrix} 2 \\ 4 \end{pmatrix}$

19 $\begin{pmatrix} ^-1 \\ 3 \end{pmatrix}$

20 $\begin{pmatrix} 4 \\ ^-2 \end{pmatrix}$

21 $\begin{pmatrix} 3 \\ ^-1 \end{pmatrix}$

22 $\begin{pmatrix} 2 \\ 0 \end{pmatrix}$

23 $\begin{pmatrix} 0 \\ 5 \end{pmatrix}$

24 $\begin{pmatrix} ^-6 \\ 0 \end{pmatrix}$

25 $\begin{pmatrix} 0 \\ ^-3 \end{pmatrix}$

26 $\begin{pmatrix} 3 \\ ^-8 \end{pmatrix}$

27 $\begin{pmatrix} ^-5 \\ ^-1 \end{pmatrix}$

28 $\begin{pmatrix} ^-3 \\ ^-7 \end{pmatrix}$

29 $\begin{pmatrix} ^-1 \\ ^-1 \end{pmatrix}$

30 $\begin{pmatrix} 2 \\ ^-3 \end{pmatrix}$

31 $\begin{pmatrix} ^-2 \\ 3 \end{pmatrix}$

32 Each of these vectors is the same length. They all show different translations. Write down the vector for each one.

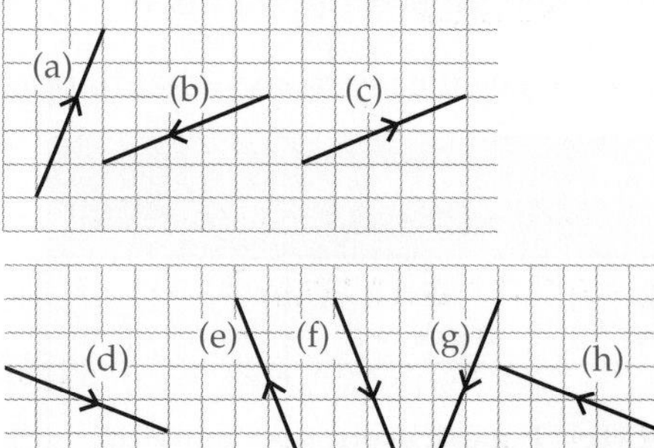

Using vectors to draw translations

Vectors give us an accurate way of describing how to do translations on squared paper.

Example Draw the image of this figure when it is translated by the vector $\begin{pmatrix} 2 \\ 5 \end{pmatrix}$.

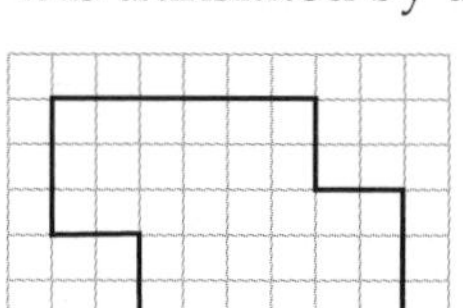

Answer

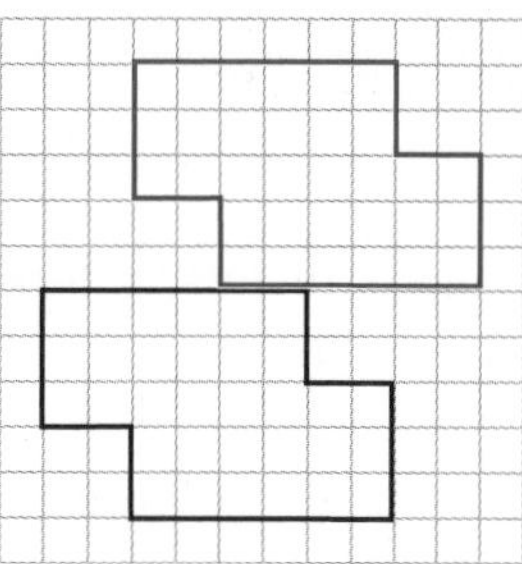

EXERCISE 17.4

Copy these figures. Then draw the image of each one when translated by the vector given.

1 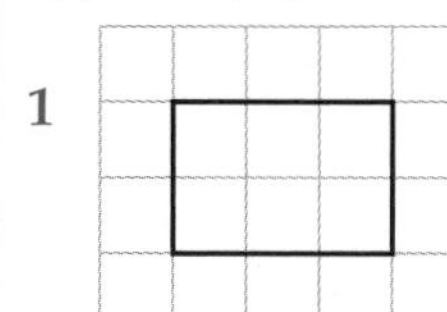 Vector: 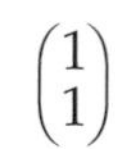 $\begin{pmatrix} 1 \\ 1 \end{pmatrix}$

2 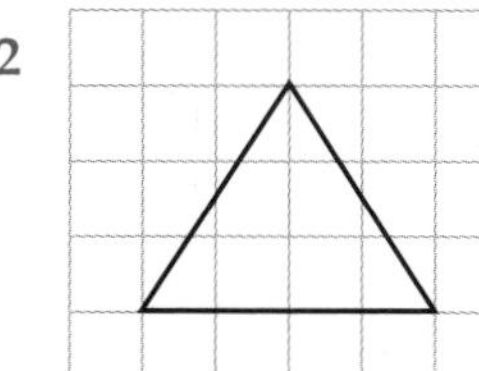 Vector: $\begin{pmatrix} 4 \\ 2 \end{pmatrix}$

3 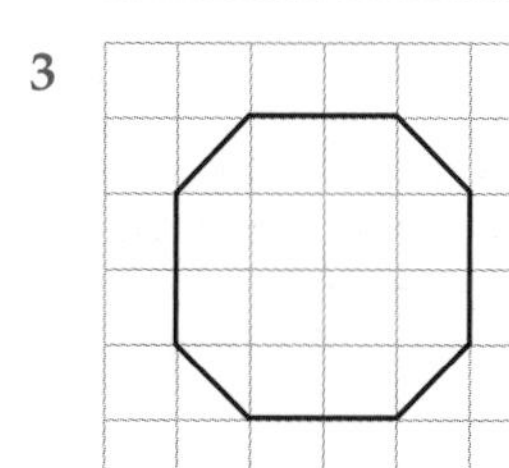 Vector: $\begin{pmatrix} 1 \\ -2 \end{pmatrix}$

4 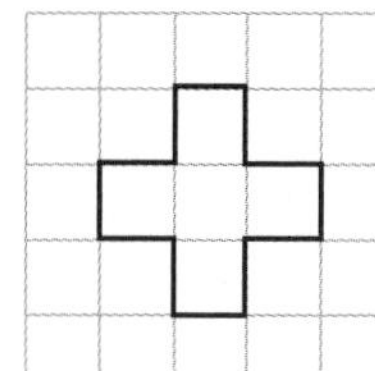 Vector: $\begin{pmatrix} 0 \\ 3 \end{pmatrix}$

5 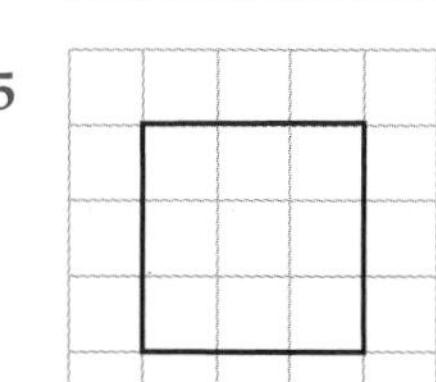 Vector: $\begin{pmatrix} -2 \\ -1 \end{pmatrix}$

6 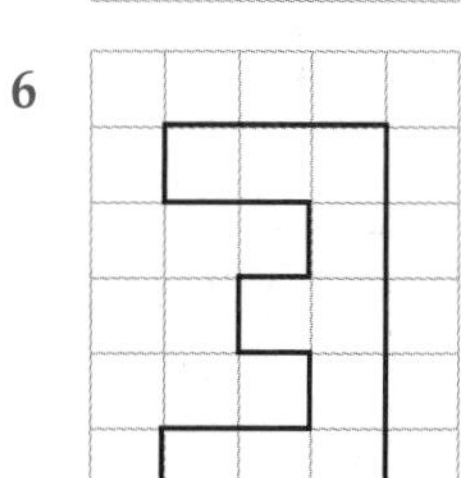 Vector: $\begin{pmatrix} -4 \\ 2 \end{pmatrix}$

What vector did that?

Sometimes we need to know which particular vector translates a shape to its image.

Example What translation moves triangle ABC to triangle A′B′C′?

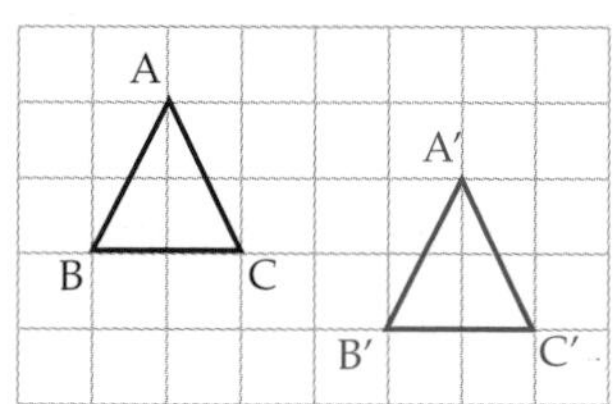

Answer Draw an arrow for the vector that starts at A and finishes at A′ (the image):

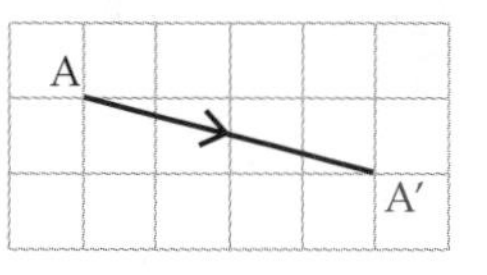

The vector for this translation is $\begin{pmatrix} 4 \\ -1 \end{pmatrix}$

Remember: every point shifts the same distance in the same direction. So, we can look for the vector linking one particular point to its image—e.g. A and A′.

EXERCISE 17.5

1–6 *Write down vectors for these translations.*

1

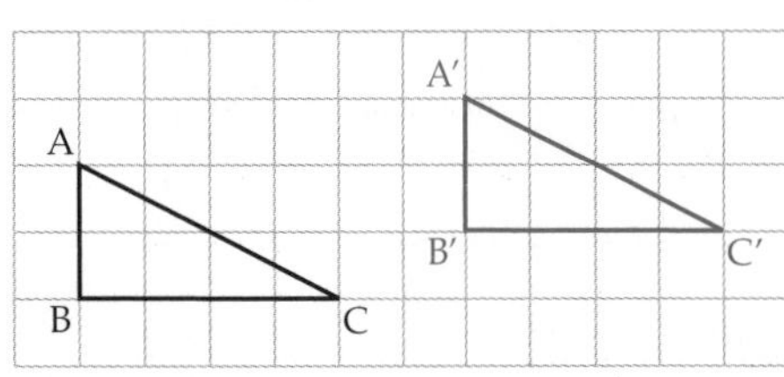

2

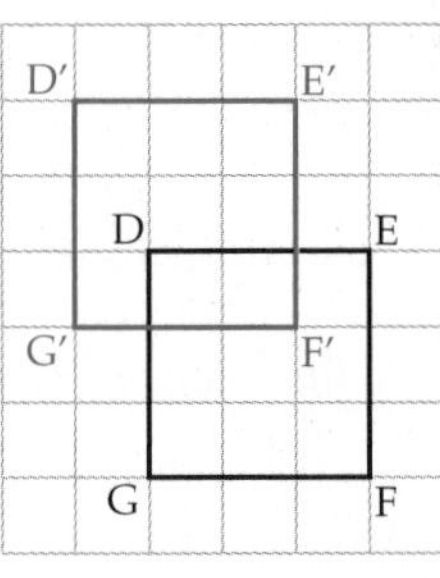

3

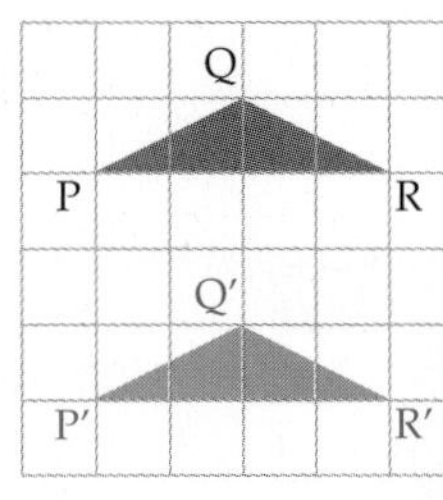

4

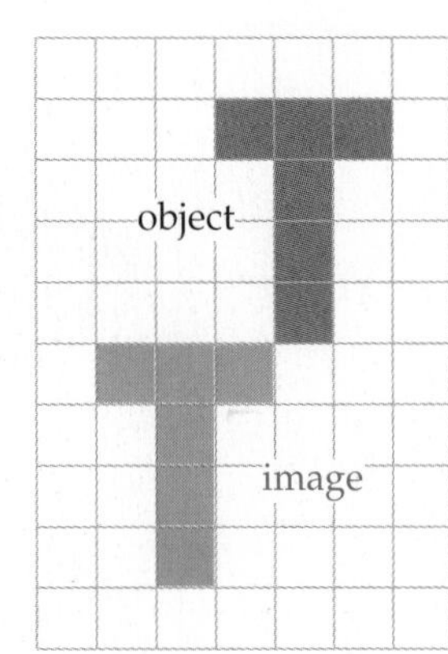

5

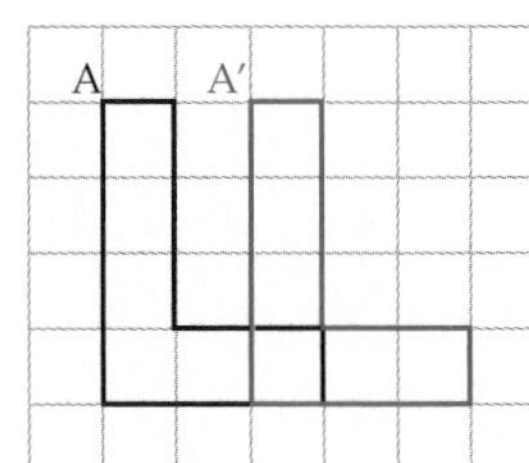

6

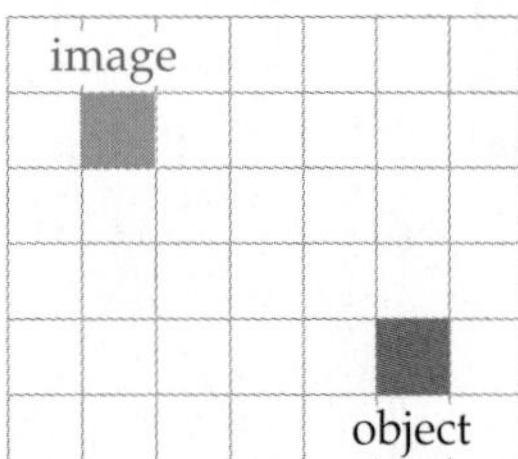

7 This is a rough plan of a cross-country course.

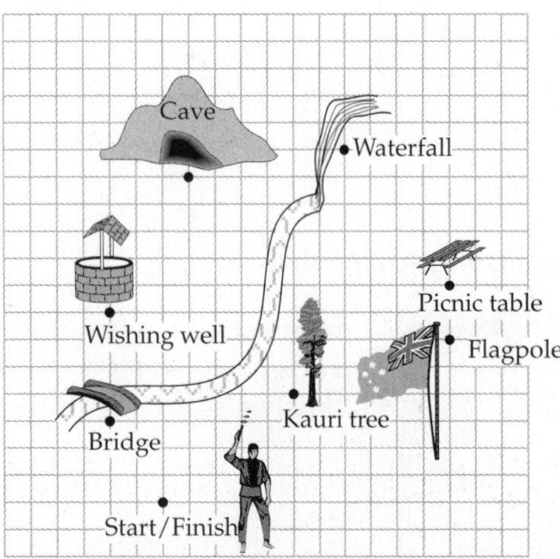

The race begins when the starter fires a pistol. The course goes from this point to a kauri tree, and then to a picnic table. From here the course goes to a flagpole nearby, and then to the base of a waterfall. From the waterfall the course continues to the entrance to a cave, and then via a wishing well to a bridge, before ending at the same place as it started.

Write down a list of 8 vectors that give the directions for the course.

INVESTIGATION

BACKTRACKING

What happens when we want to translate an image back to the object that it came from?
This is called an **inverse translation**.

1 Write down the vector that translates the object figure to the image figure.

2 Write down the vector that translates the image *back* to the object.

3 This arrow shows that A translates to B (i.e. A → B)

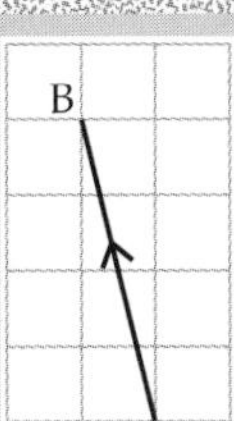

Draw an arrow for the translation where B → A

4 The vector for A → B in question 3 is $\begin{pmatrix} ^-1 \\ 4 \end{pmatrix}$

What is the vector for the translation B → A?

5 By drawing arrows (or otherwise), write down the *inverse* vectors for each of these.

(a) $\begin{pmatrix} 1 \\ 2 \end{pmatrix}$ (d) $\begin{pmatrix} ^-3 \\ 2 \end{pmatrix}$ (g) $\begin{pmatrix} 15 \\ ^-8 \end{pmatrix}$

(b) $\begin{pmatrix} ^-3 \\ ^-1 \end{pmatrix}$ (e) $\begin{pmatrix} 1 \\ 0 \end{pmatrix}$ (h) $\begin{pmatrix} ^-4 \\ 0 \end{pmatrix}$

(c) $\begin{pmatrix} 4 \\ ^-5 \end{pmatrix}$ (f) $\begin{pmatrix} 0 \\ 0 \end{pmatrix}$ (i) $\begin{pmatrix} 14 \\ ^-3 \end{pmatrix}$

6 How can you work out the *inverse* of a vector? Explain.

7 One translation is given by $\begin{pmatrix} a \\ b \end{pmatrix}$. Write down a vector for the *inverse* translation.

Properties of translation

Here are some properties of translation:

- there are no **invariant points**—all points move
- every point moves the **same distance** in the **same direction**
- when objects are translated, their **lengths and angle sizes stay the same**.

Example This diagram shows a translation. ABEF has moved to BCDE.

(a) What point is the image of E?

(b) What are the values of:

(i) the length marked x?

(ii) the angles marked y and z?

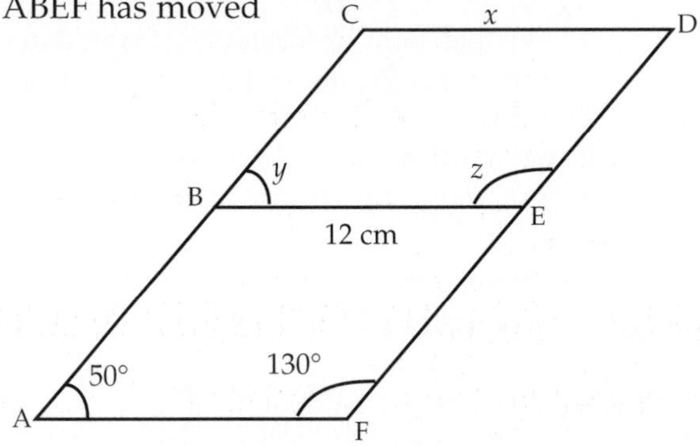

Answer (a) The image of E is D.

(b) (i) $x = 12$ cm

(ii) $y = 50°$, $z = 130°$

EXERCISE 17.6

1 The diagram shows a translation where A maps to B.

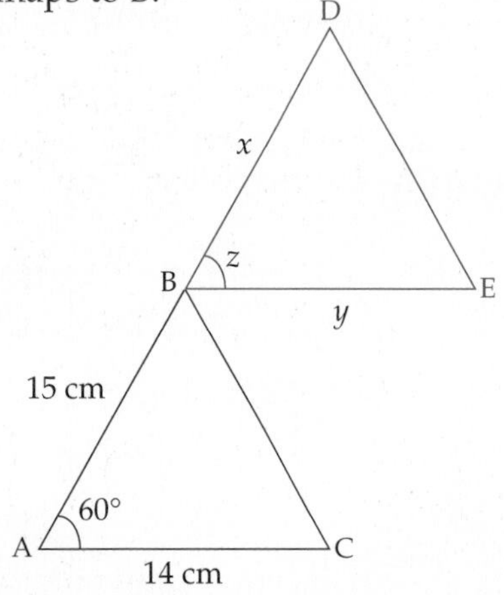

(a) What point is the image of C?

(b) What point is the image of B?

(c) Write down the values of x, y and z.

2 Several different translations are possible in this diagram.

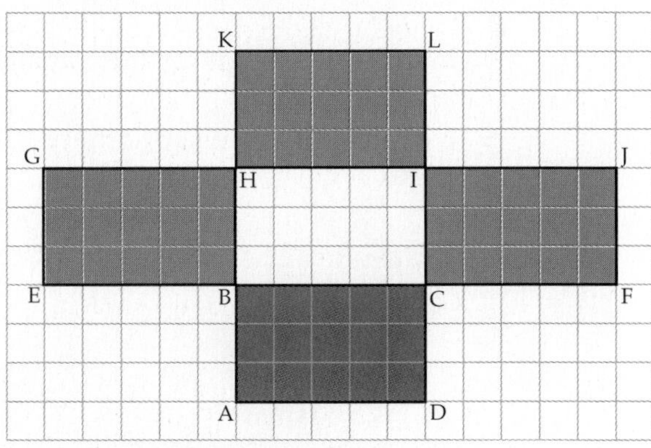

(a) If the image of A is C, which point is the image of E?

(b) If the image of D is I, which point is the image of C?

(c) Write down the vector for the translation ABCD → CIJF.

(d) Write down the vector for the translation CIJF → EGHB.

3 Here is a translation that moves A to B, and then another translation that moves B to C.

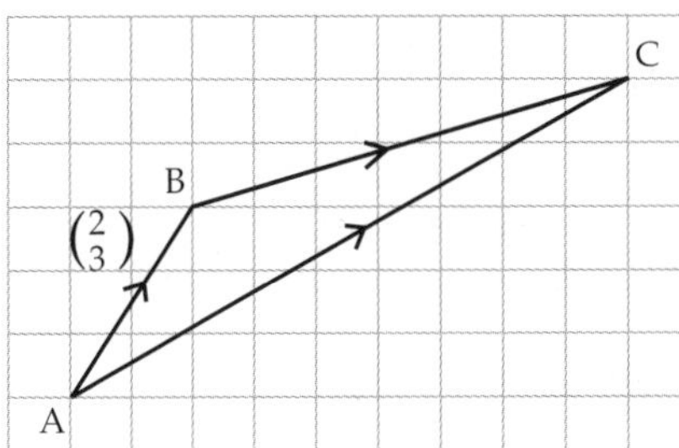

(a) Write down the vector for the translation B → C.

(b) What *single* vector would show how A translates to C?

4 A translation maps P to Q using the vector $\begin{pmatrix}5\\1\end{pmatrix}$. Then another translation maps Q to R using the vector $\begin{pmatrix}2\\3\end{pmatrix}$.
Draw a diagram, and use it to work out the *single* vector that would map P to R.

5 A translation maps D to E using the vector $\begin{pmatrix}3\\-4\end{pmatrix}$. Then another translation maps E to F using the vector $\begin{pmatrix}-2\\-5\end{pmatrix}$.
Draw a diagram, and use it to work out the *single* vector that would map D to F.

INVESTIGATION

SATURDAY KNIGHT FEVER

In chess, the piece called the 'knight' has a move that looks like the letter L.
For example: ⌈ or ⌊ or ⌊_
The knight moves to a square 2 rows away in any direction, and 1 row away at right-angles to that direction.

This diagram shows an example of *one* move the knight can make. (There are others.)

This particular move can be described by the vector $\begin{pmatrix}-1\\2\end{pmatrix}$.

1 Write down the eight vectors for all the possible moves for a knight. For example, the diagram shows the move using the vector $\begin{pmatrix}-1\\2\end{pmatrix}$.

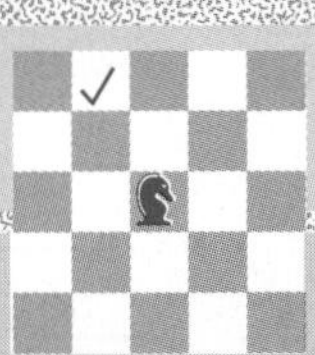

2 Copy this diagram. Tick all the squares that the knight can move to in one turn. One has been done for you.

3 Can a knight ever go from a black square to another black square in one move?

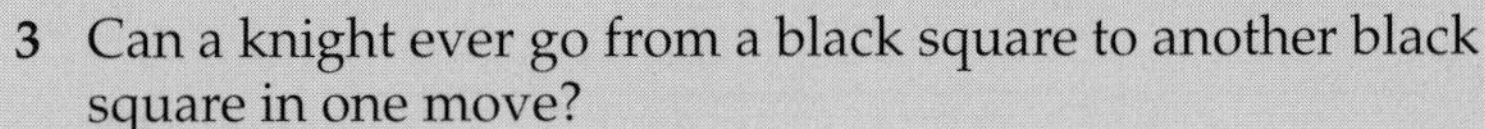

4 A chess-board has 64 squares altogether. Copy this grid. Then write numbers in each cell to show the number of moves a knight can make from each square.

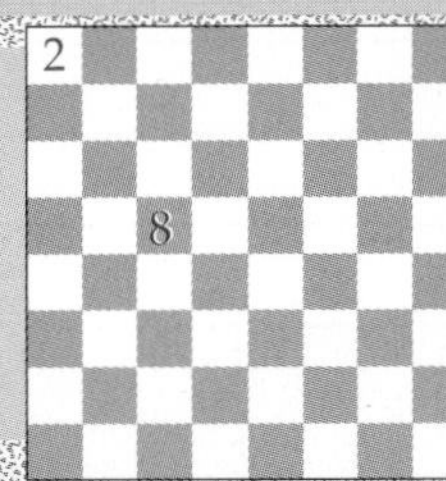

Further investigation

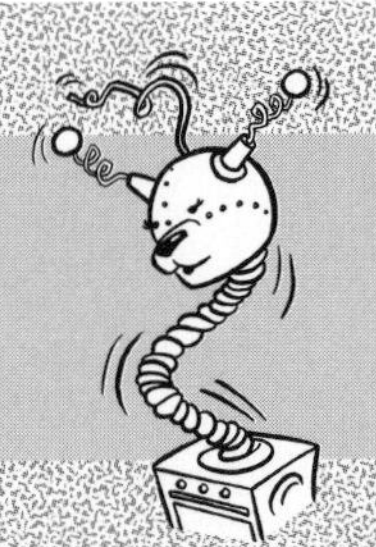

5 The Knight's Tour

- Is it possible for a knight to visit, once only, every square on a chess-board?

Draw an 8 by 8 square grid. Start at one corner and label each square 1, 2, 3, etc., (up to 64) as the knight visits it.

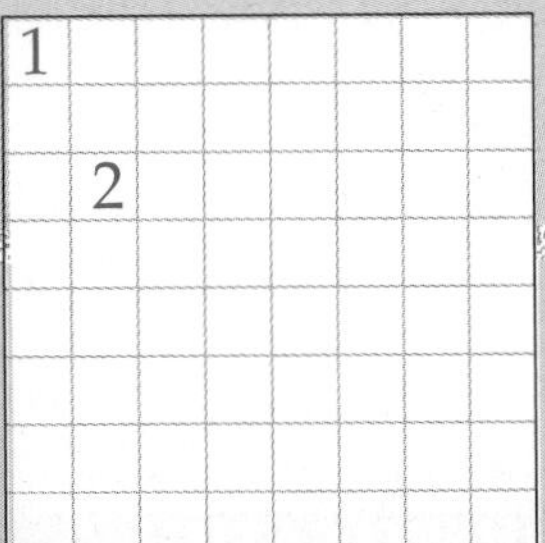

6 Other chess pieces

- The other pieces in chess are the pawn, bishop, rook (castle), Queen and King. Find out what kind of moves they can make.

pawn

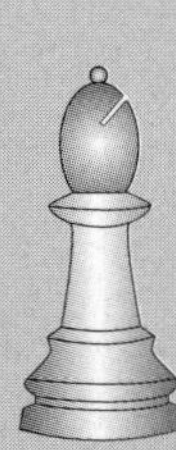

bishop

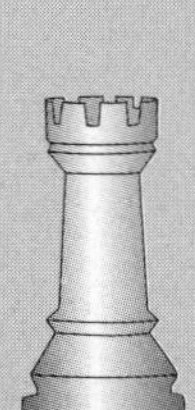

rook

Queen

King

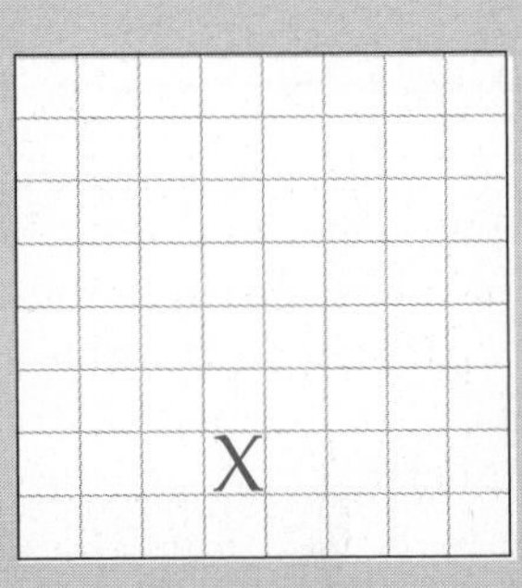

Make a list of all the possible moves for each chess piece. Start from the square marked X. Write the moves as column vectors.

Display your results in a table like this one:

Piece	Vector moves	Total number of possible moves
Pawn	$\begin{pmatrix}0\\1\end{pmatrix}, \begin{pmatrix} \\ \end{pmatrix}, \begin{pmatrix} \\ \end{pmatrix}, \begin{pmatrix} \\ \end{pmatrix}$	4
Knight		6
Bishop		9
Rook		14
Queen		23
King		8

18 Parallel lines

STARTER

What happens to lines when they are turned through an angle of 180° (a half-turn rotation)?

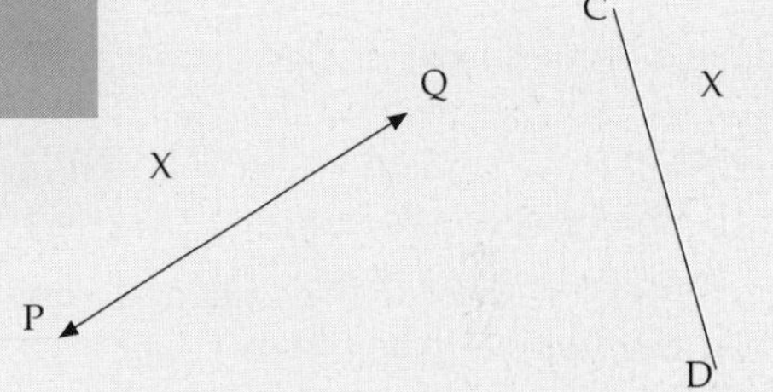

- Draw a line PQ anywhere. You could draw it on your page, or on the blackboard.
- Choose a point X not on the line.
- Rotate the line PQ through a half-turn (180°). Use X as the centre of rotation. You could use tracing paper to do this.
- Draw the image P′Q′.
- Repeat this with another line CD, that has a different slope. Turn it through 180°. Use any point as the centre of rotation. Draw the image C′D′.

- What can you say about any line and its image when it is rotated through a half-turn?

Parallel and perpendicular lines

Two lines are **parallel** if they map onto each other through a 180° rotation (or half-turn).

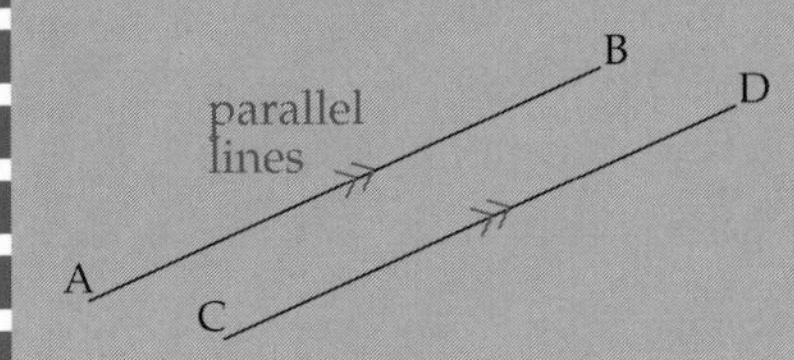

- Parallel lines never meet.
- Parallel lines are the same distance apart.

A line that crosses a pair of parallel lines is called a **transversal**.

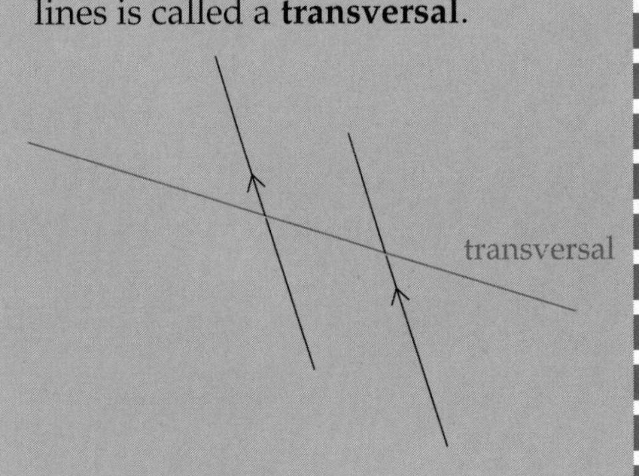

We show that two lines are parallel by placing small arrows on each one. We can also write AB II CD.

Two lines are **perpendicular** if they meet at right-angles (90°).

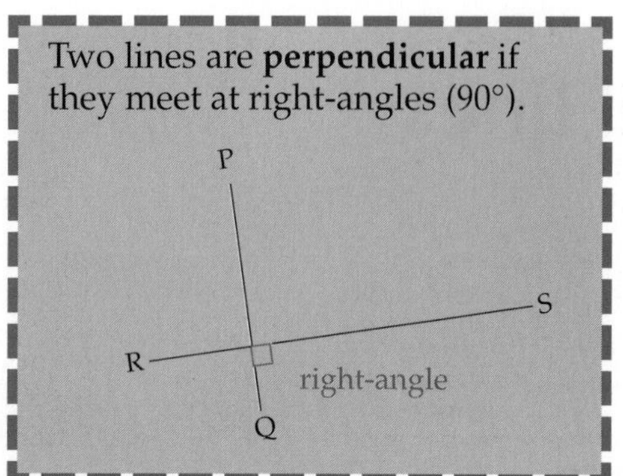

We show that two lines are perpendicular by placing a small right-angle symbol (∟) where they meet. We can also write PQ ⊥ RS.

Here's something for the technically-minded!

There is a difference between:

- a **line** (which extends forever in each direction)
- a **ray** (which extends in one direction) and
- a **line segment** (which has a fixed length).

Description	Name/Symbol	Diagram
line	$\overleftrightarrow{AB}$	A ⟷ B
ray	$\overrightarrow{CD}$	C ⟶ D
line segment	$\overline{EF}$	E —— F

In this chapter, what we say about parallel lines applies to the others too. Here, we'll only talk about parallel lines, not rays or line segments.

18.1

1

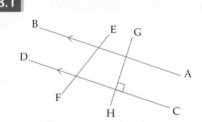

True or false?

(a) AB || CD
(b) EF || GH
(c) EF is a transversal
(d) GH ⊥ CD
(e) EF ⊥ AB
(f) AB ⊥ GH

2

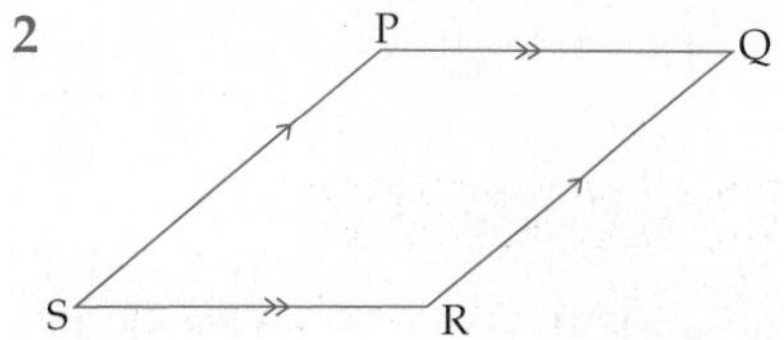

(a) Name a line parallel to PQ.
(b) Name a line parallel to QR.

3

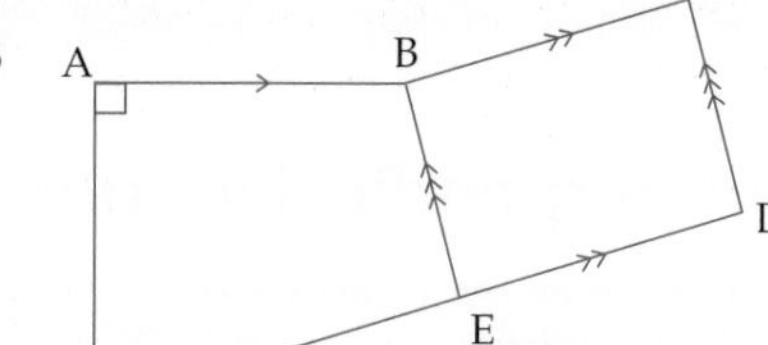

(a) Name a line parallel to AB.
(b) Name a line parallel to BC.
(c) Name a line parallel to CD.
(d) Name a line perpendicular to AB.

4 This is a drawing of a three-dimensional solid called a *cuboid*. The edges *behind* the solid that you can't see from the front have been drawn dashed.

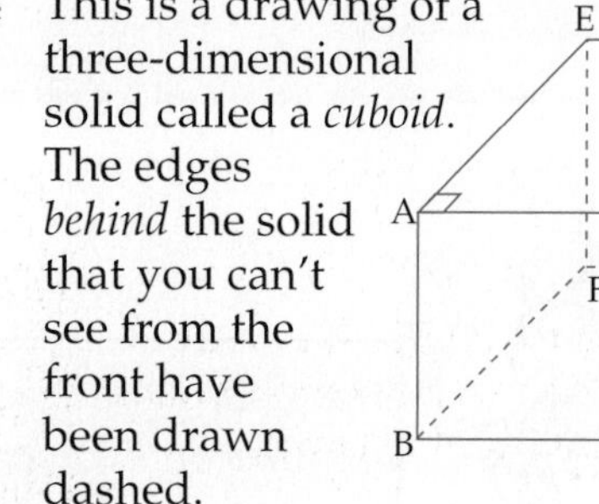
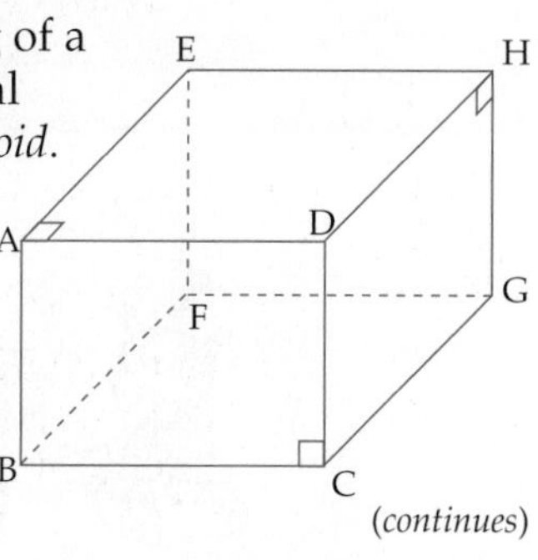

(*continues*)

(a) Name all three lines that are parallel to BC.

(b) Name a line that is perpendicular to BC.

True or false?

(c) AB || HG

(d) AE || CD

(e) DH ⊥ HG

(f) AE ⊥ AD

5 This diagram also shows a cuboid. This time it is drawn on *isometric* paper.

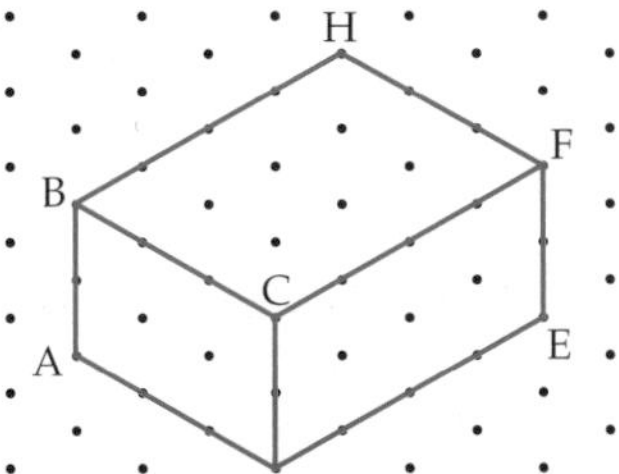

Copy these sentences. Complete them by placing either || or ⊥ in the box.

(a) DE ☐ HB (c) AB ☐ FE

(b) DE ☐ CD (d) FH ☐ FE

6 Write one or two sentences describing a set of *parallel* lines you have seen on a sports field.

7 Write one or two sentences describing a pair of *perpendicular* lines you have seen on a sports field.

8 Here are flags of six different countries. In each case, say what kind of stripes you can see. Choose from { parallel, perpendicular, both, neither }.

(a) United States

(d) France

(b) United Kingdom

(e) Denmark

(c) Greece

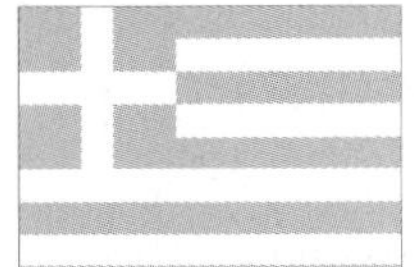

(f) Tonga

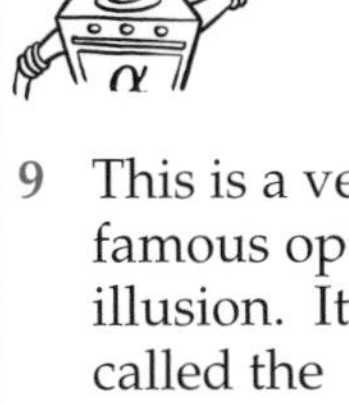

9 This is a very famous optical illusion. It is called the Hering illusion. Are the two bold lines parallel?

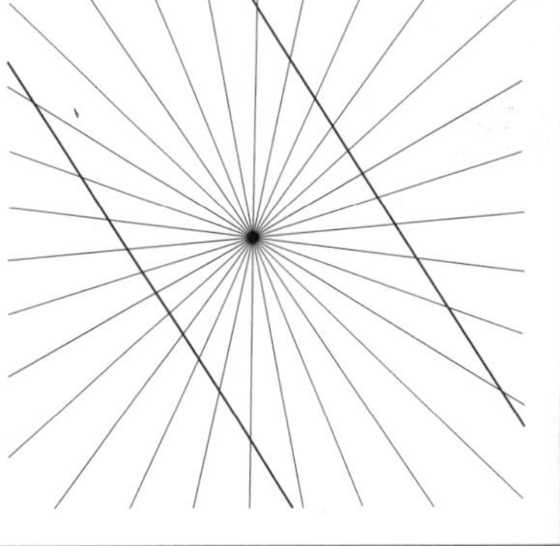

Alternate angles

STARTER

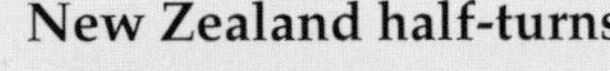

New Zealand half-turns

The pair of letters NZ are very similar.

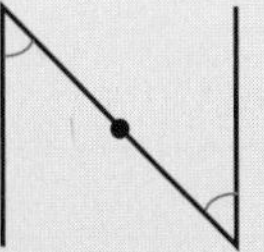

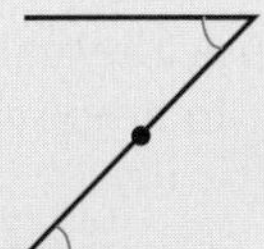

- What can you say about the two vertical lines of the letter N?
- Can you say the same about the two horizontal lines of the letter Z?

- Do the two letters each have half-turn symmetry?
- Are the marked angles equal? Explain.

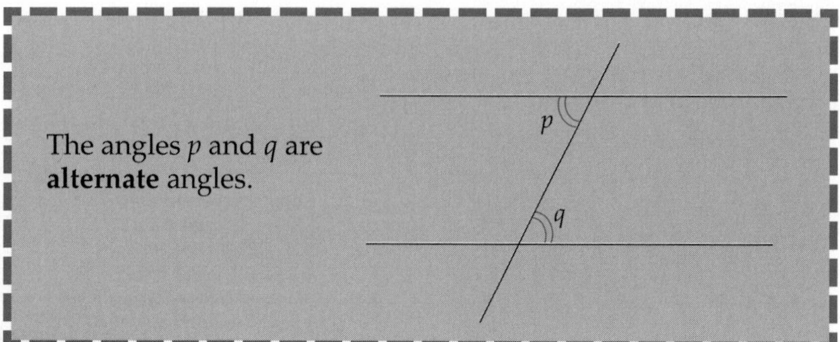

The angles p and q are **alternate** angles.

When a transversal crosses a pair of parallel lines, there are two pairs of alternate angles.
Alternate angles are:

- between the parallel lines
- on opposite sides of the transversal.

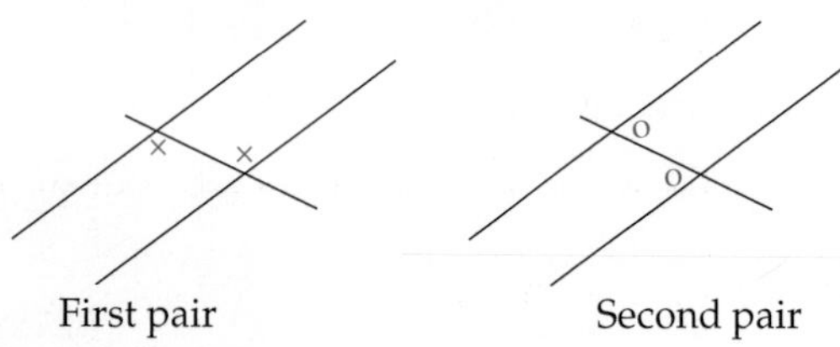

First pair Second pair

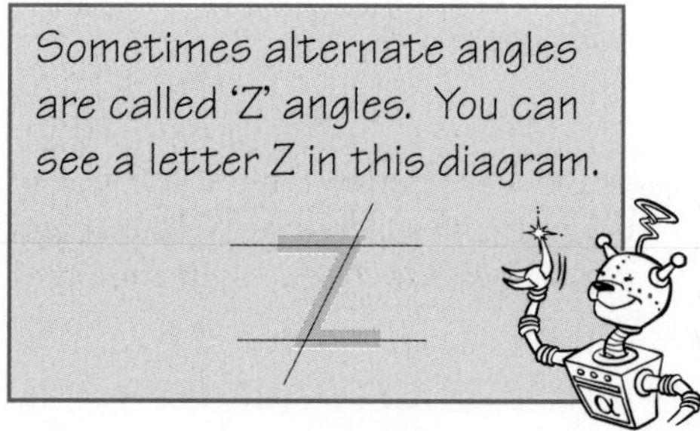

Sometimes alternate angles are called 'Z' angles. You can see a letter Z in this diagram.

- Each pair of angles is equal.
- One pair is acute.
- The other pair is obtuse.

EXERCISE 18.2

1 Copy these diagrams. Mark in the angle which is alternate to the angle × in each one.

(a) (b)

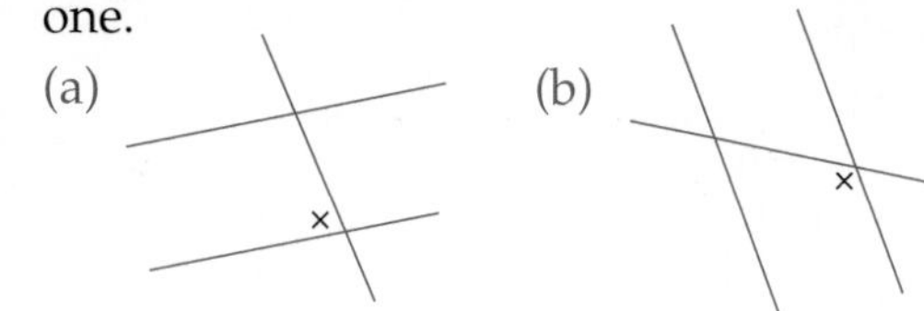

2 Which angle is alternate to angle a?

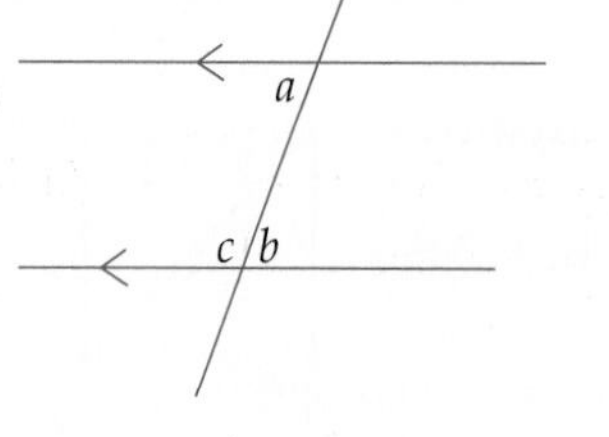

3 (a) Name the angle alternate to angle f.

(b) Name the angle alternate to angle g.

4 (a) Copy this table. Complete it to show pairs of alternate angles.

angle	angle
s	
u	
	t
m	
	n

(b) Are angles q and v alternate?

5–8 *Name two pairs of equal alternate angles in each figure.*

5

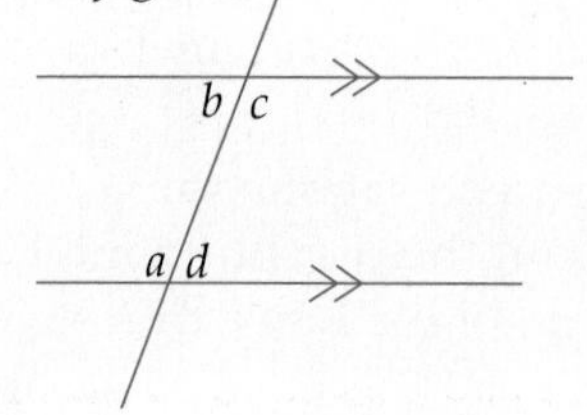

6

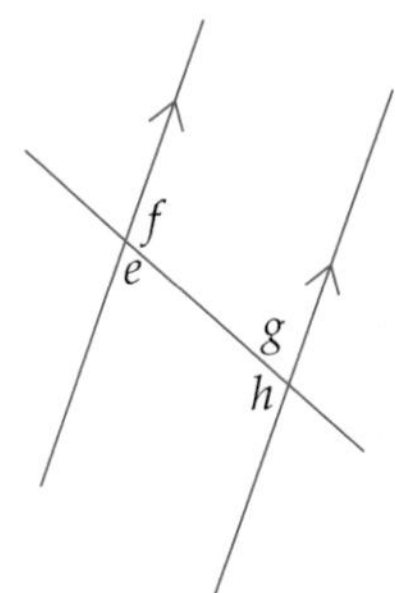

7

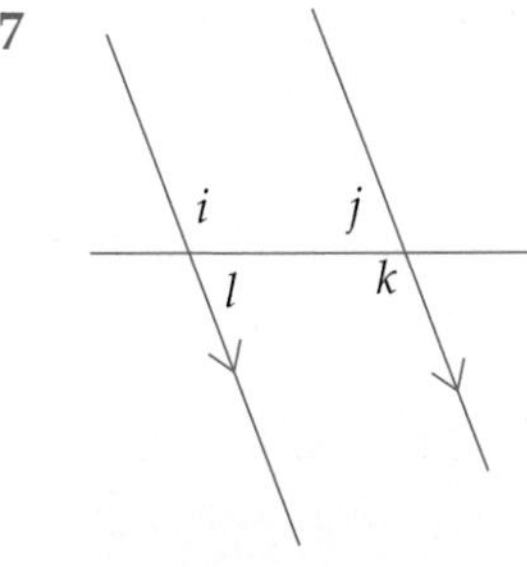

8

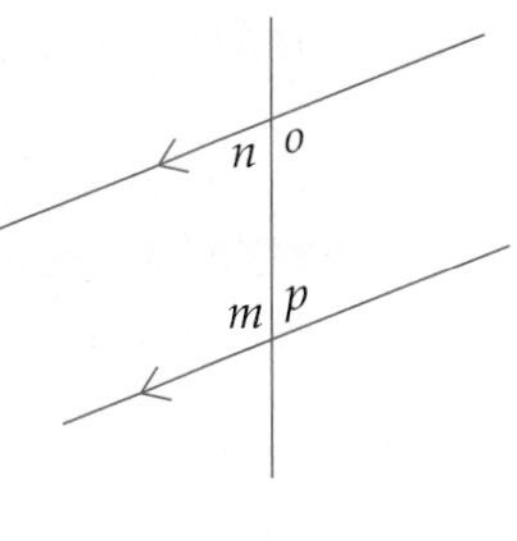

Using alternate angles to work out angle sizes

Example What is the size of the angles marked x and y?

Answer $x = 80°$
$y = 105°$

y 80° x 105°

EXERCISE 18.3

1–10 *In each diagram, work out the size of the unknown marked angles.*

1

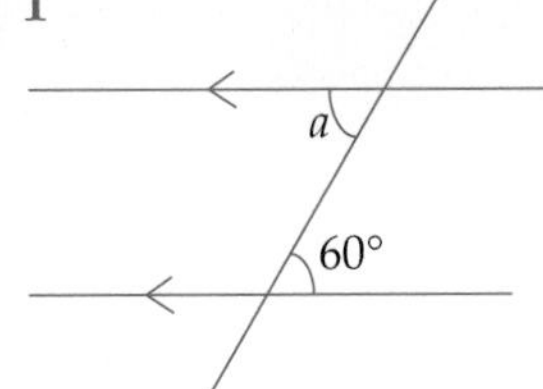

2

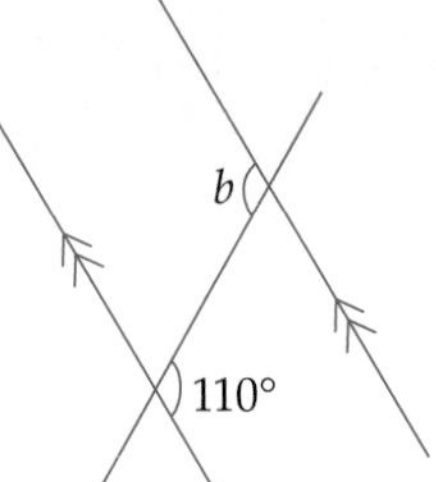

3

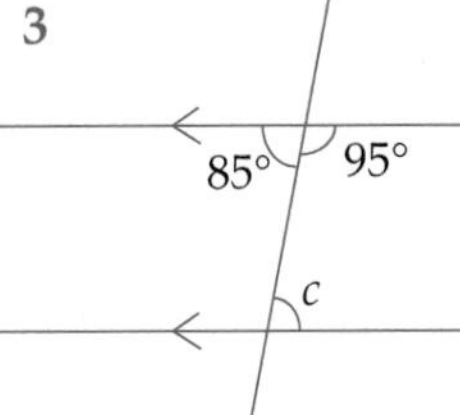

4

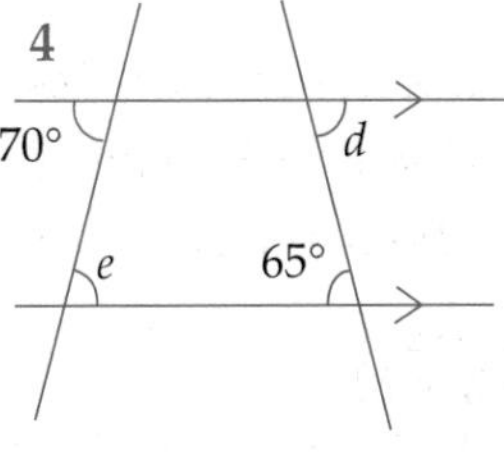

5

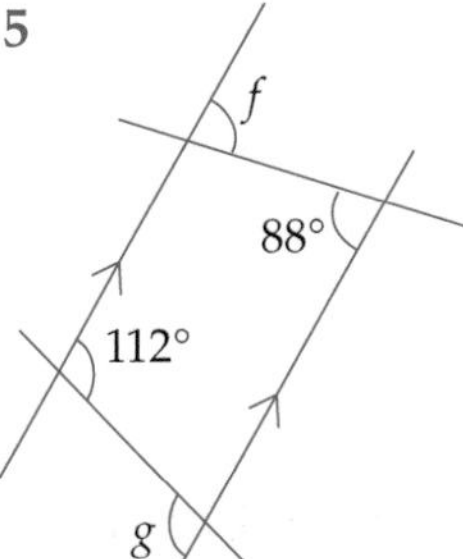

6

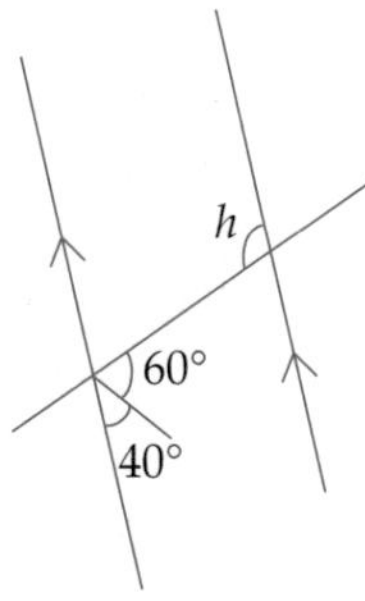

7

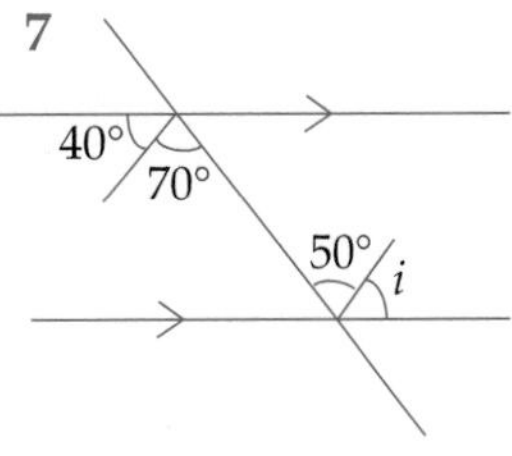

8

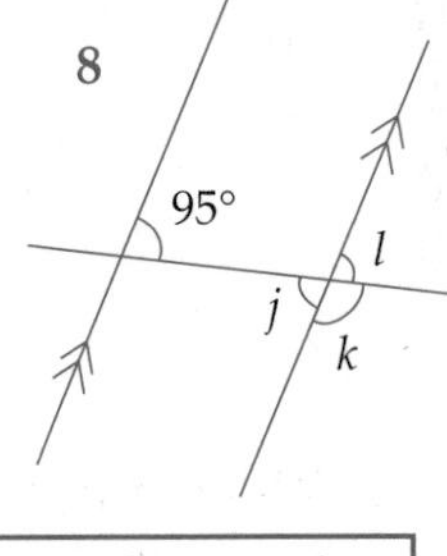

9

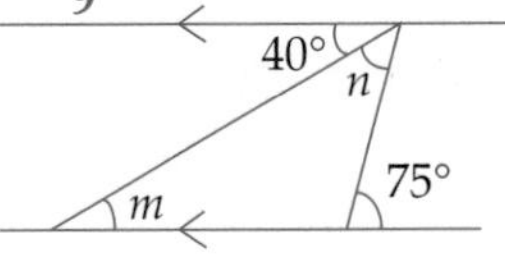

10

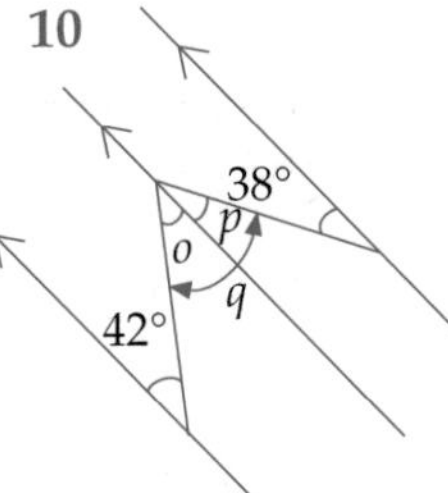

Copy the diagram. Calculate angles r and s.

11 12

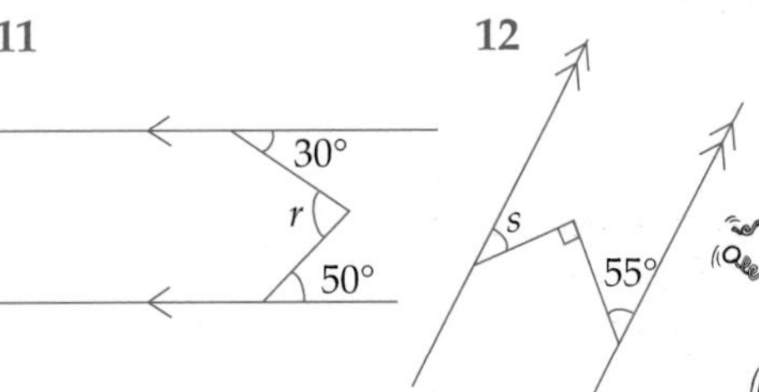

Hint: add an extra line.

Corresponding angles

STARTER

This photo shows several features of mathematical interest ....
.... a sphere,
.... curves called parabolas ....
(you'll work with these in Years 10 and 11 Mathematics!).

Look closely at the handrail leading up to the terrace. This diagram shows the support at the top, linked to two parallel rails.

- Are the two marked angles likely to be the same size?
- Are they on *opposite sides* or the *same side* of the transversal?
- Are they alternate angles?

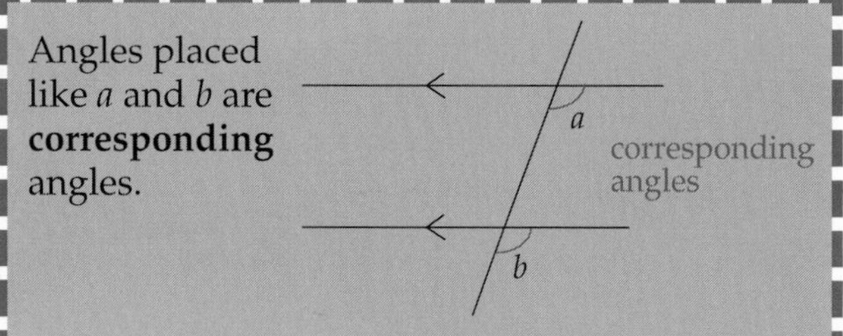

Angles placed like a and b are **corresponding** angles.

When a transversal crosses a pair of parallel lines, there are four pairs of corresponding angles. Corresponding angles are:

- *both above* or *both below* the parallel lines
- on the *same* side of the transversal.

This diagram shows the four pairs of corresponding angles:

- Each pair of angles is equal.
- Two pairs are acute.
- The other two pairs are obtuse.

Sometimes corresponding angles are called 'F' angles. You can see a letter F in this diagram.

EXERCISE 18.4

1 Copy these diagrams. Mark in the angle which is corresponding to angle × in each one.

(a)

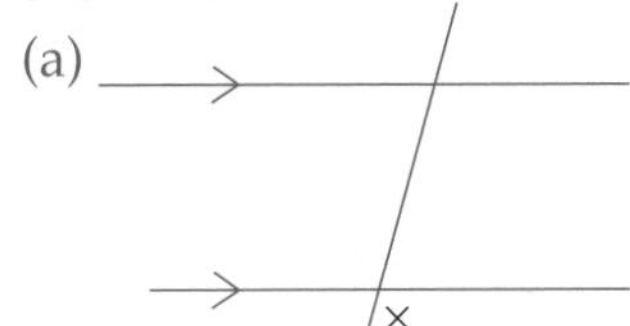

(b)

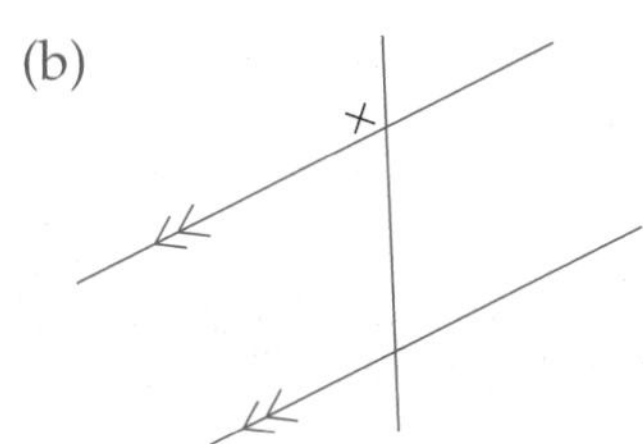

2

Which angle is corresponding to the angle marked *a*?

3

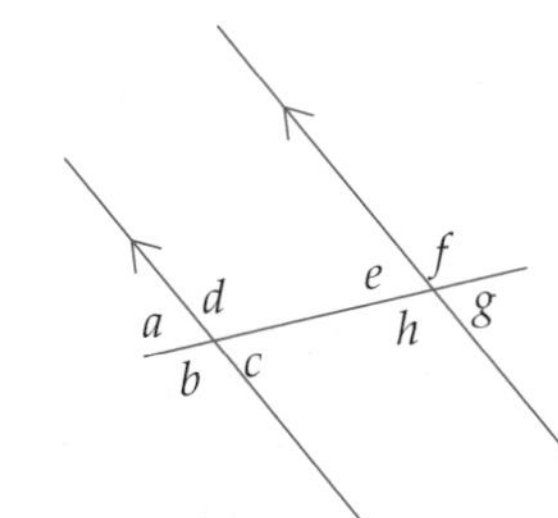

(a) Name the angle corresponding to angle *f*.

(b) Name the angle corresponding to angle *h*.

4

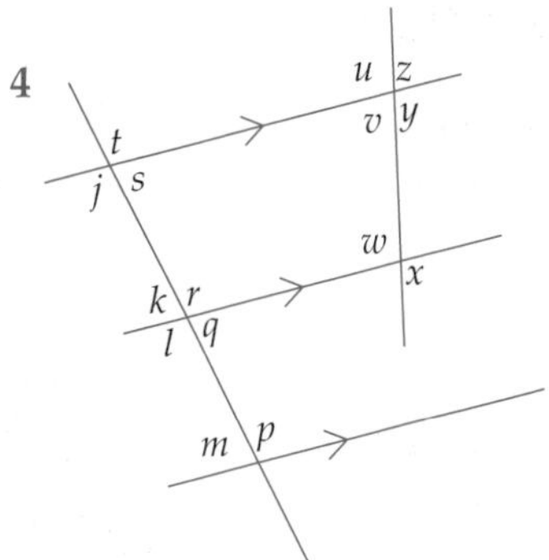

(a) Copy this table. Complete it to show pairs of corresponding angles.

angle	angle
j	
u	
	s
x	
	k

(b) Are angles *p* and *t* corresponding?

5–6 *Name four pairs of equal corresponding angles in each figure.*

5

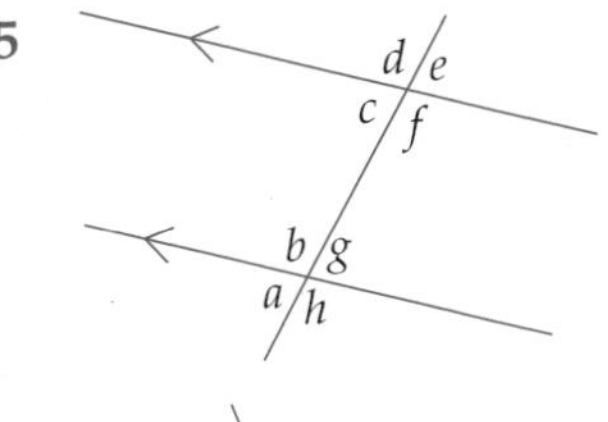

6

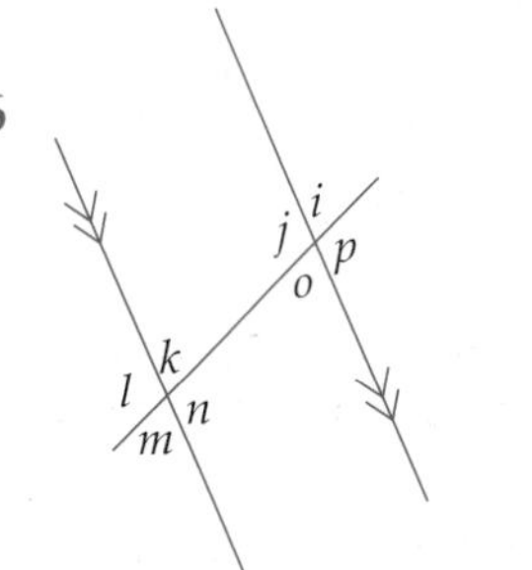

Using corresponding angles to work out angle sizes

Example What is the size of the angles marked x and y?

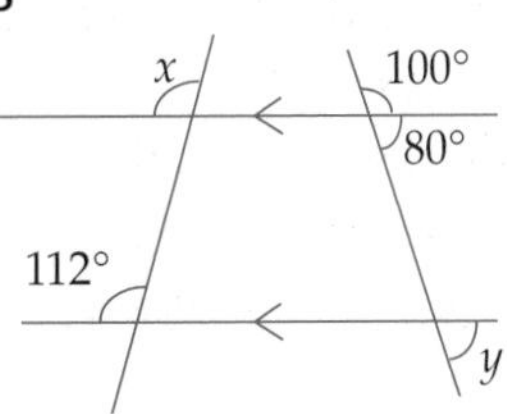

Answer $x = 112°$
$y = 80°$

EXERCISE 18.5

In each diagram work out the size of the unknown marked angles.

In some of these questions you may need to use other angle properties. For example, 'angles on a line add to 180°', etc.

1

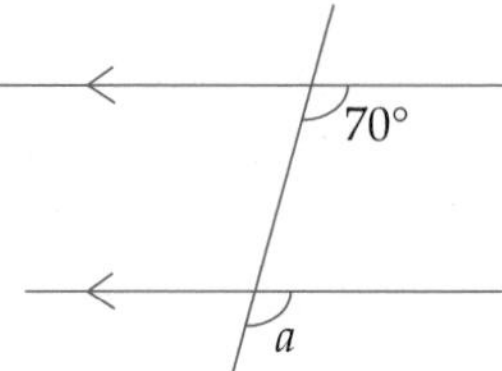

2

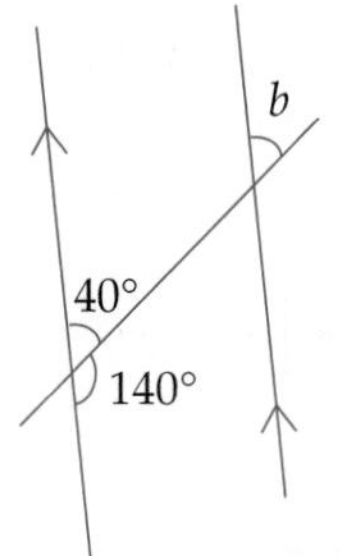

3

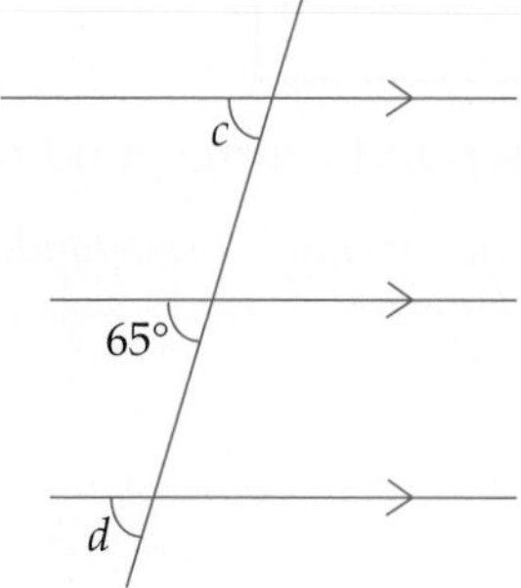

4

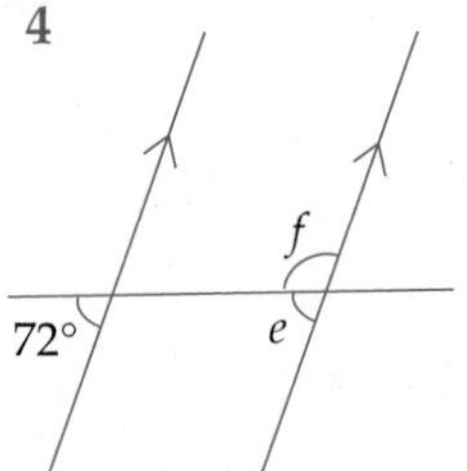

5

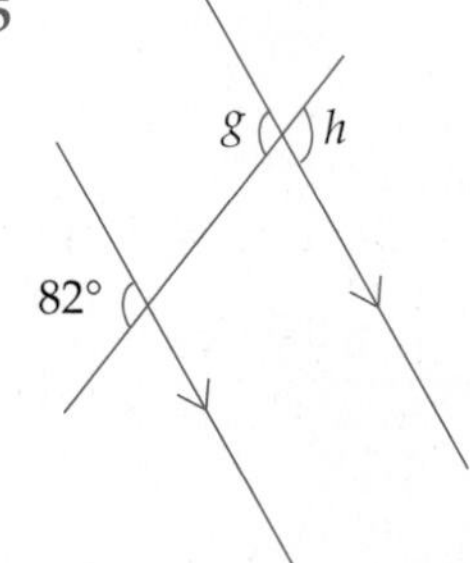

6

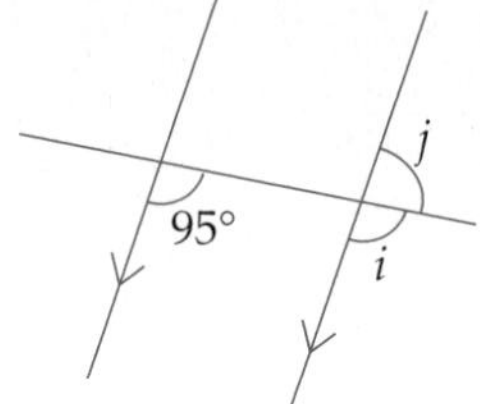

7

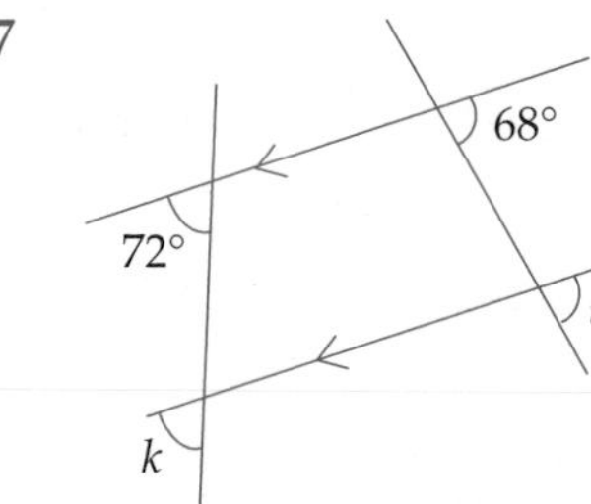

8

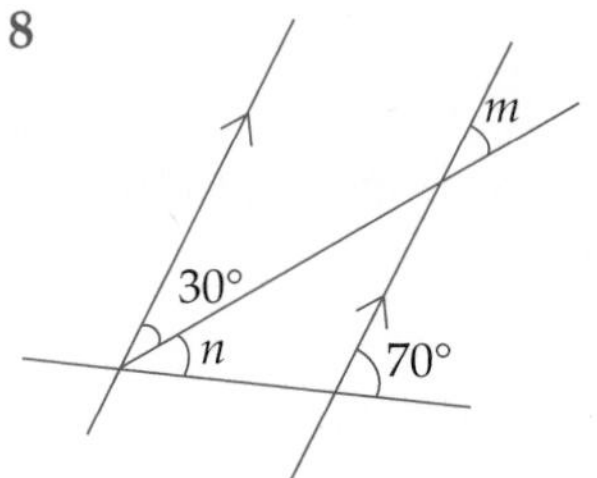

9

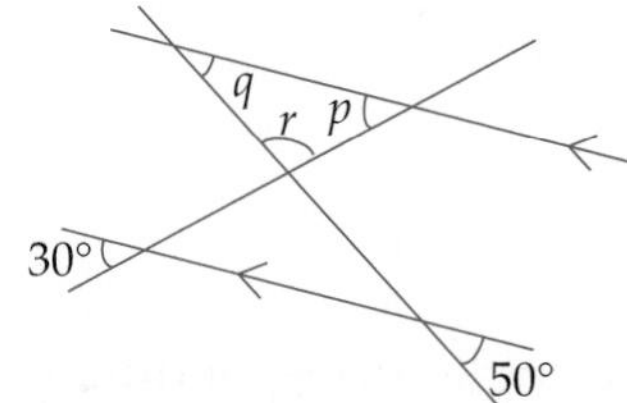

10

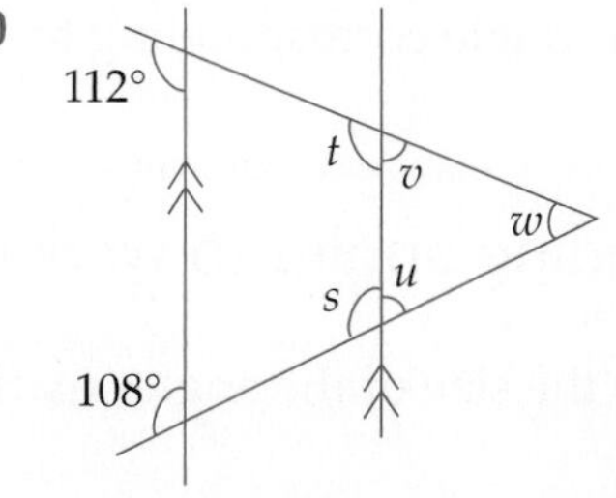

Co-interior angles

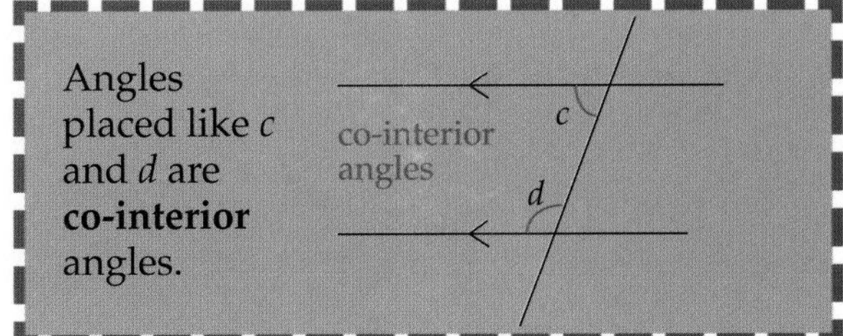

Angles placed like c and d are co-interior angles.
co-interior angles
c
d

Sometimes co-interior angles are called 'U' angles. You can see a letter U in this diagram.

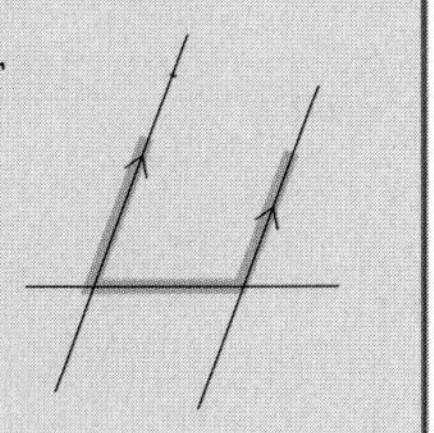

When a transversal crosses a pair of parallel lines, there are two pairs of co-interior angles.
Co-interior angles are:

- between the parallel lines
- on the *same* side of the transversal.

This diagram shows the two pairs of co-interior angles:

- Each pair of angles is *supplementary* (adds to 180°).

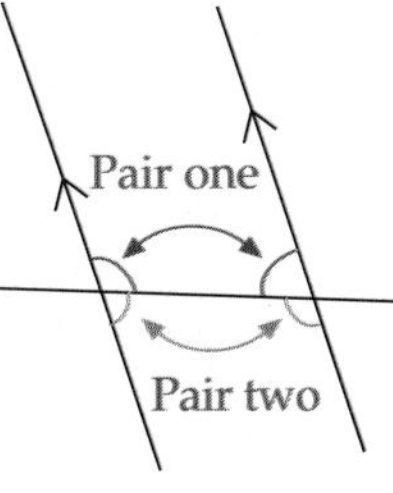

You can also use supplementary angles to work out angle sizes.

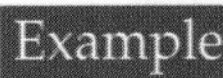

What is the size of the angle marked x?

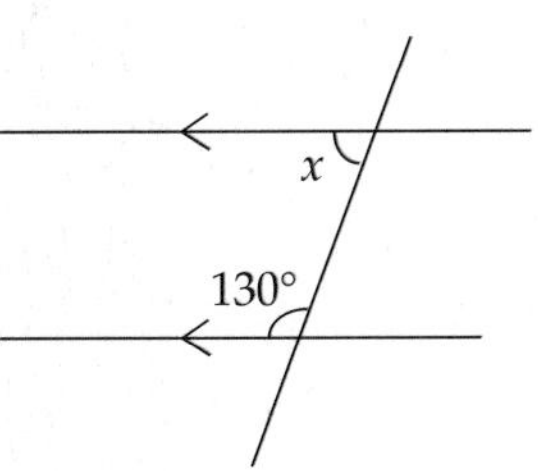

Answer $x = 180° - 130°$
$= 50°$

18.6

1 Copy these diagrams. Mark in the angle which is co-interior to angle × in each one.

(a)

(b)

2

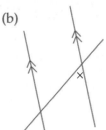

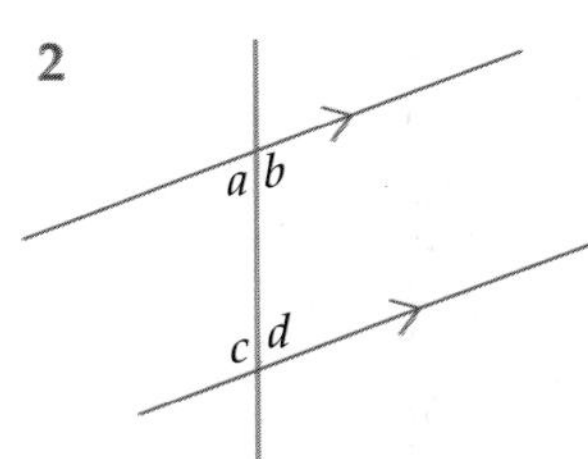

Which angle is co-interior to angle a?

3 (a) Name the angle co-interior to angle g.

(b) Name the angle co-interior to angle k.

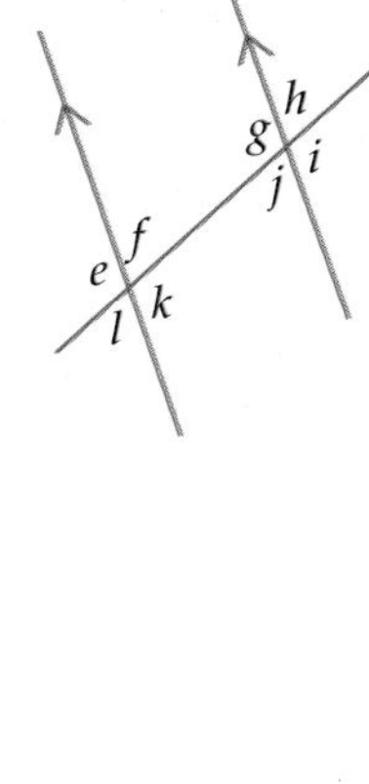

4

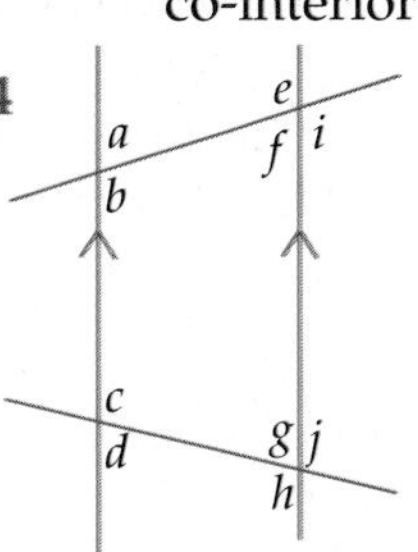

Copy this table. Complete it to show pairs of co-interior angles.

angle	angle
a	
f	
	c

5–10 *In each diagram, work out the size of the unknown marked angles.*

5

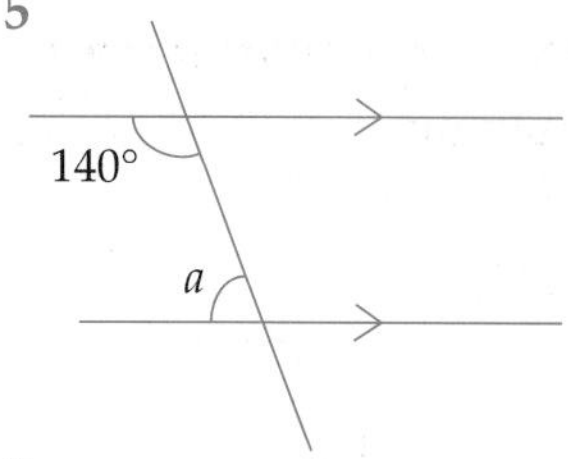

140°
a

6

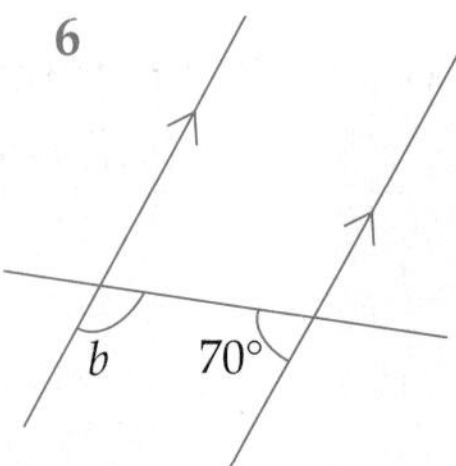

7

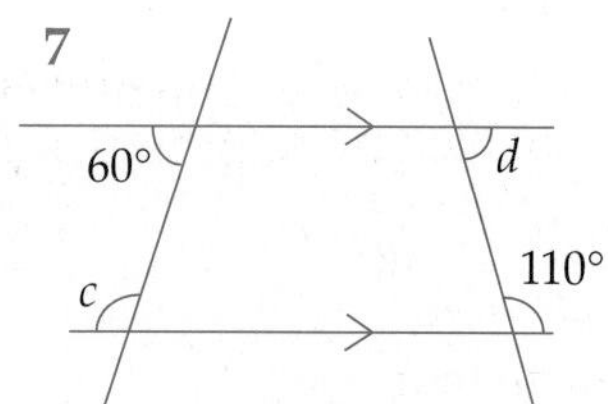

8

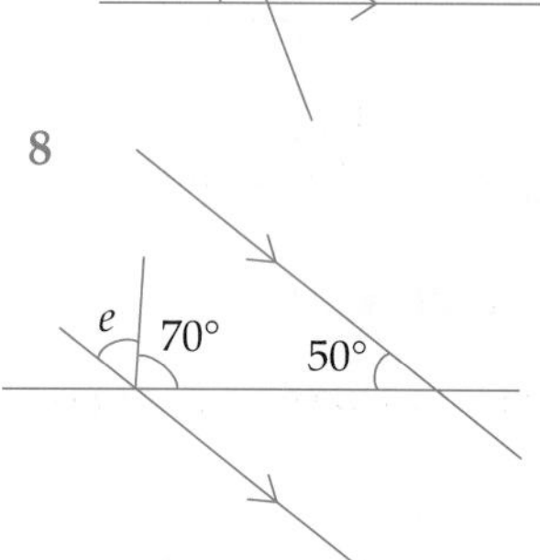

9

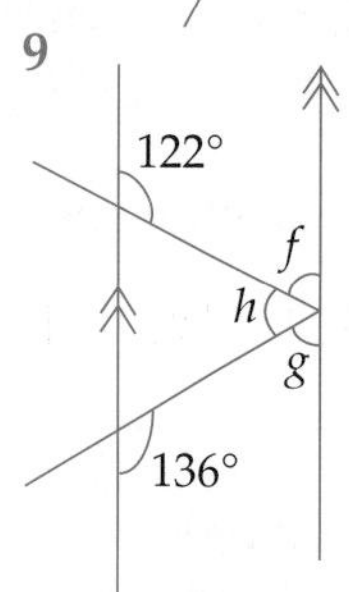

10

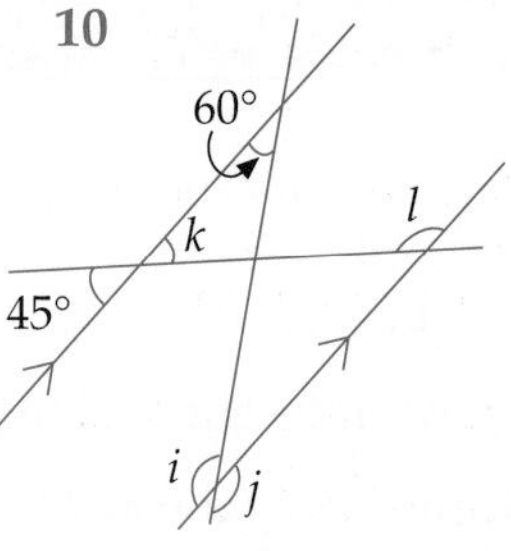

How many pairs of alternate, corresponding and co-interior angles can you see in this photograph?

The next exercise uses all three of the parallel-line angle relationships. This table shows the shortened ways (*abbreviations*) of writing these reasons:

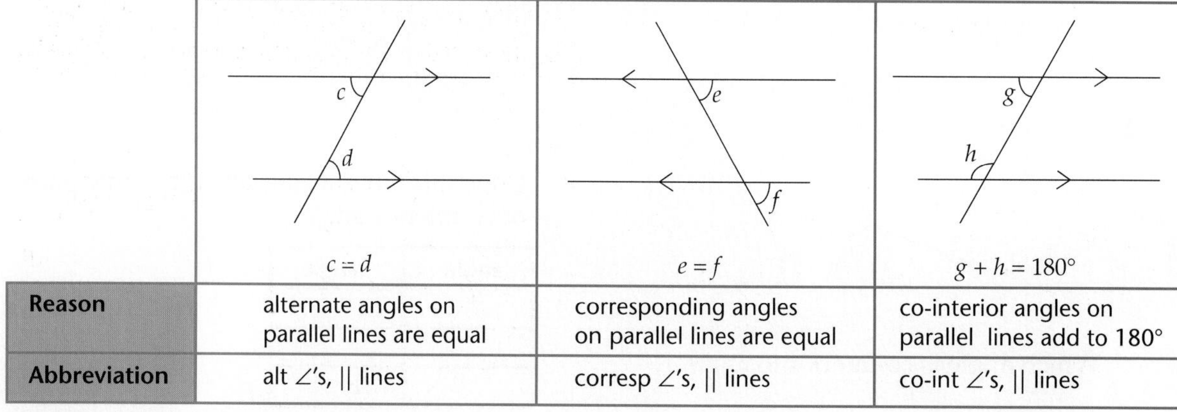

	$c = d$	$e = f$	$g + h = 180°$
Reason	alternate angles on parallel lines are equal	corresponding angles on parallel lines are equal	co-interior angles on parallel lines add to 180°
Abbreviation	alt ∠'s, || lines	corresp ∠'s, || lines	co-int ∠'s, || lines

EXERCISE 18.7

1 In each diagram, the angle marked x is 40°. Write down a reason why. Choose from the table on the previous page.

(a)

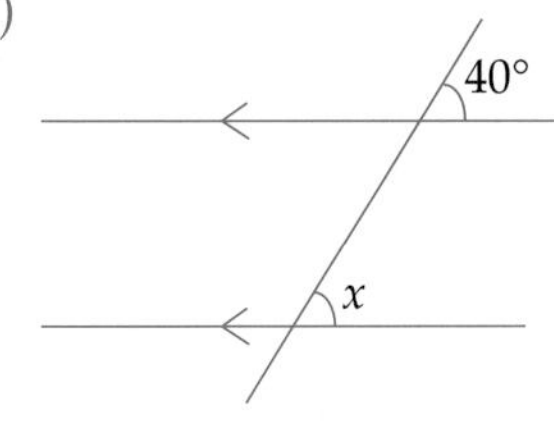

(b)

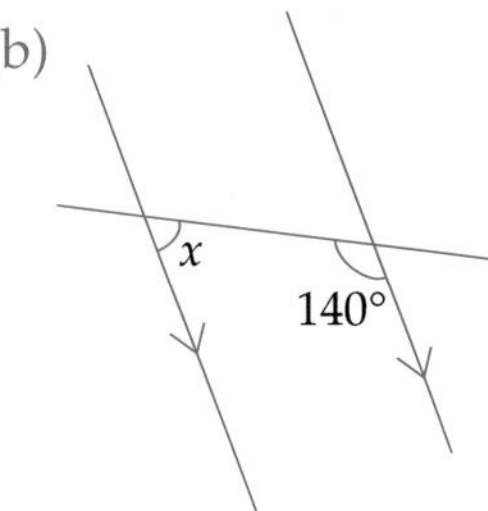

(c)

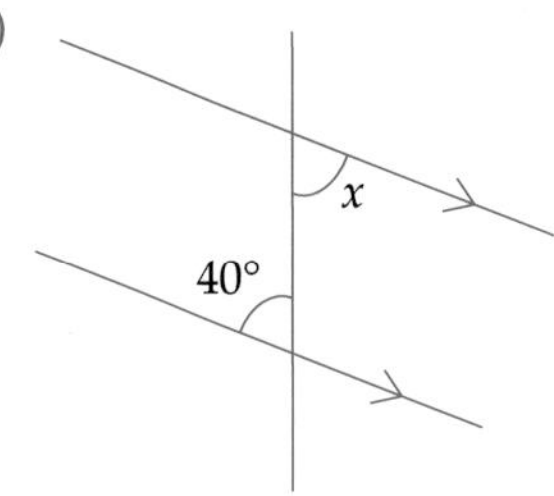

2 In each diagram the angle marked x is 112°. Write down a reason from this table to explain why:

∠'s on line
vert. opp. ∠'s
∠'s at pt
∠ sum of △
alt ∠'s, || lines
corresp ∠'s, || lines
co-int ∠'s, || lines

(a)

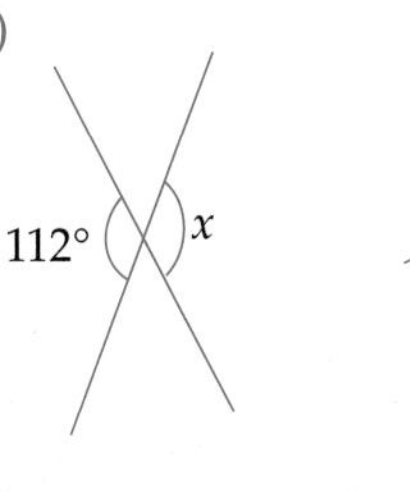

(b)

(c)

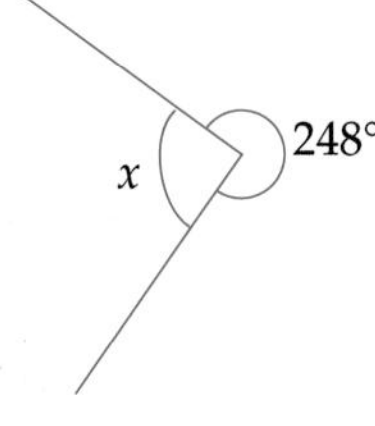

(d)

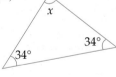

x
34°
34°

(e)

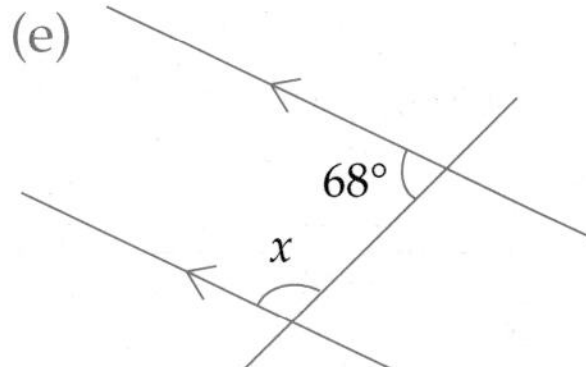

(f)

68°
x

(g)

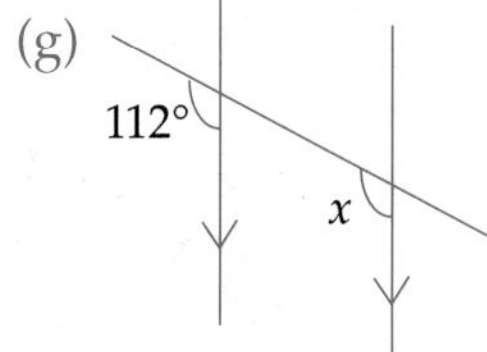

3–9 *Work out the sizes of the unknown marked angles in each diagram. Give a geometrical reason for each one.*

Sometimes you have to find the value of more than one angle. Often, they will be labelled alphabetically to show you the easiest order to work them out.

3

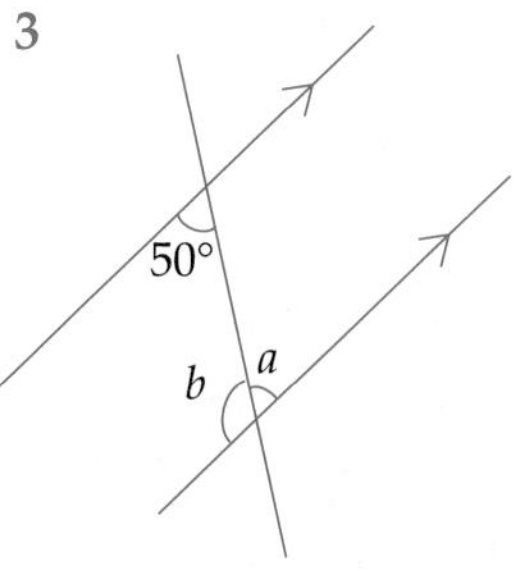

4

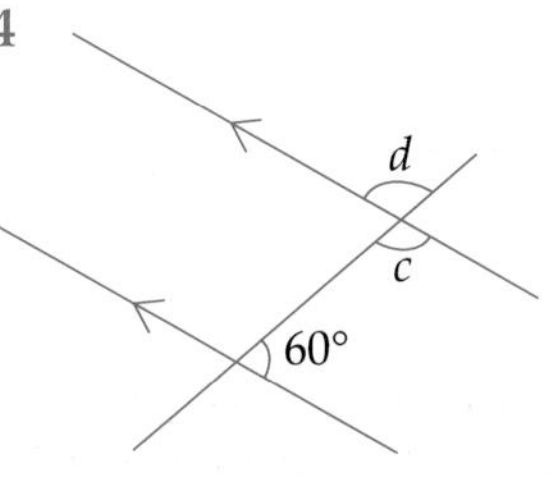

5

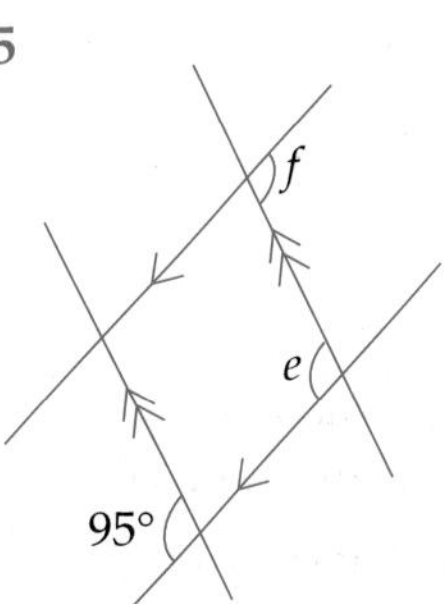

6

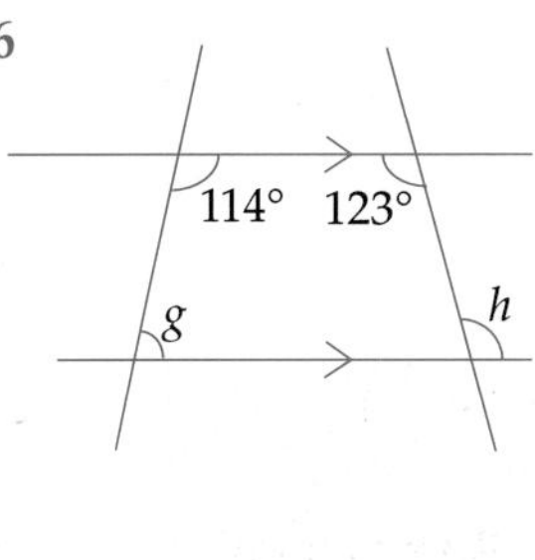

7

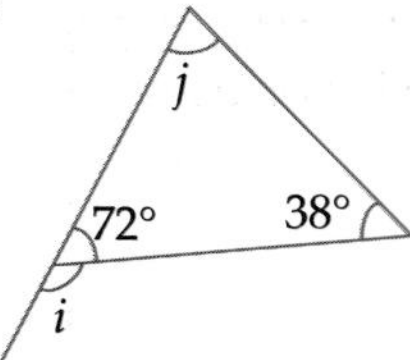

8

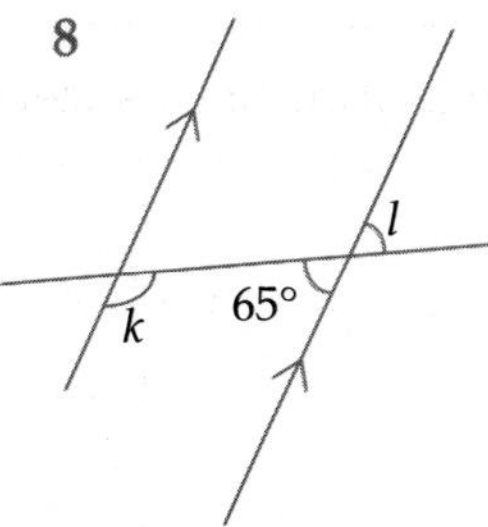

9

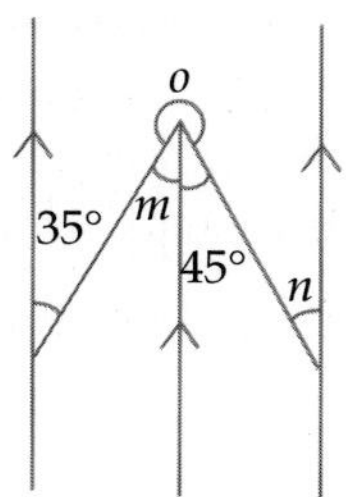

10–20 *Work out the sizes of the unknown marked angles in each diagram.*

10

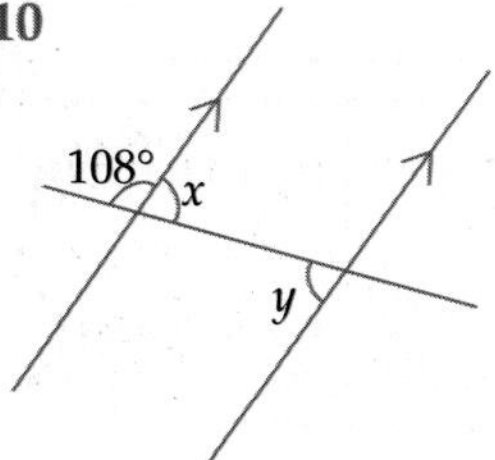

11

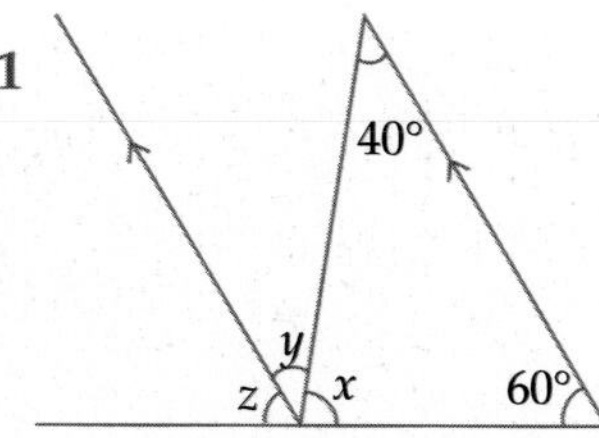

12

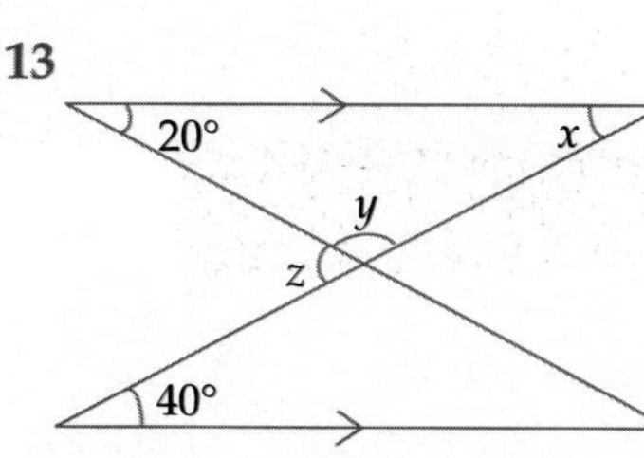

13

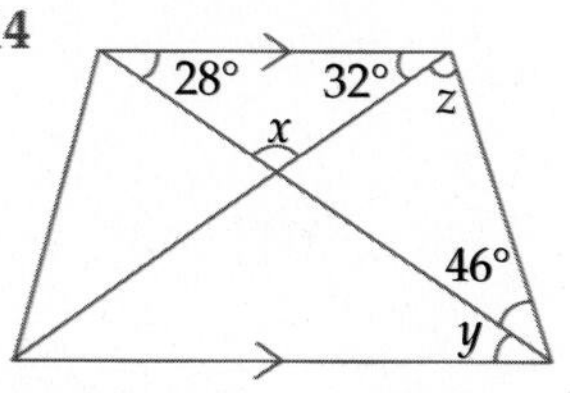

14

28°, 32°, z, x, 46°, y

15

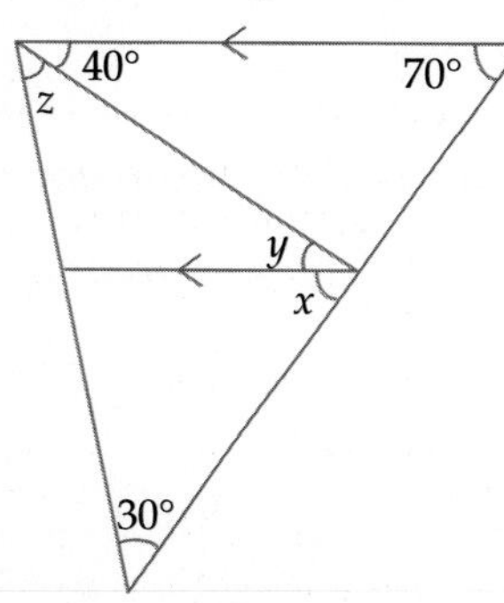

16

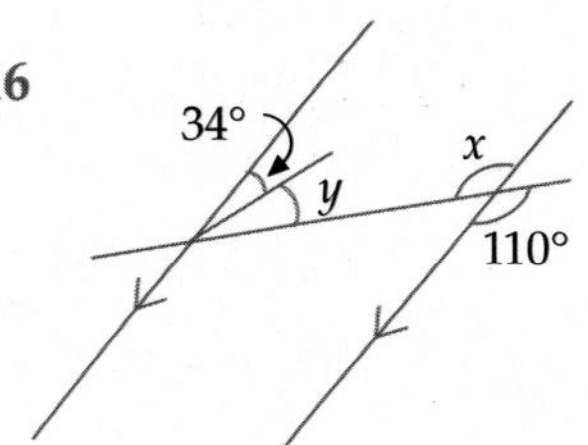

17

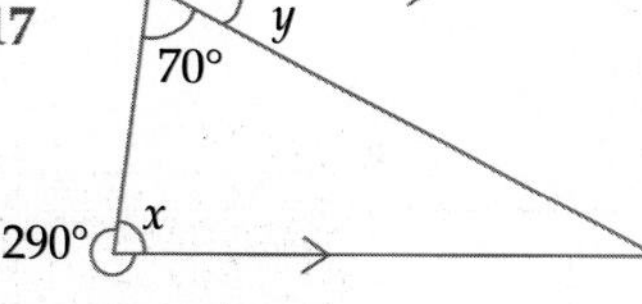

18

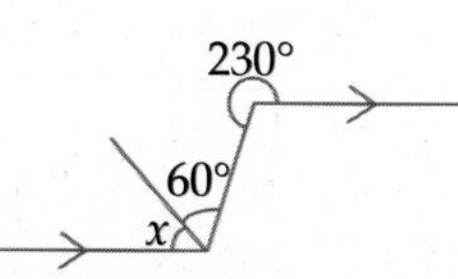

19

230°, 60°, x

20

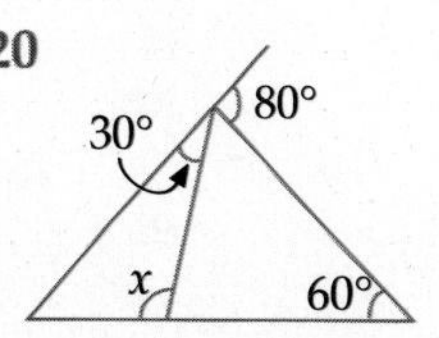

21 Copy and complete these sentences. Choose the missing words from this list: {alternate, corresponding, co-interior}.

Choose the missing letters from this list: $\{ a, b, d, e, f, g, h \}$.

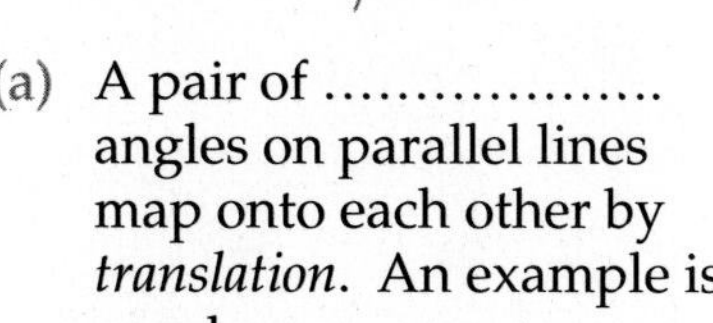

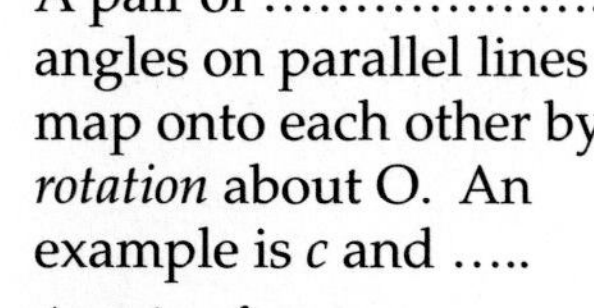

(a) A pair of .... angles on parallel lines map onto each other by *translation*. An example is c and .....

(b) A pair of .... angles on parallel lines map onto each other by *rotation* about O. An example is c and .....

(c) A pair of .... angles on parallel lines are supplementary. An example is c and .....

22 When a ray of light passes through a sheet of glass, it is *refracted* or bent.

Work out the sizes of the angles marked x and y.

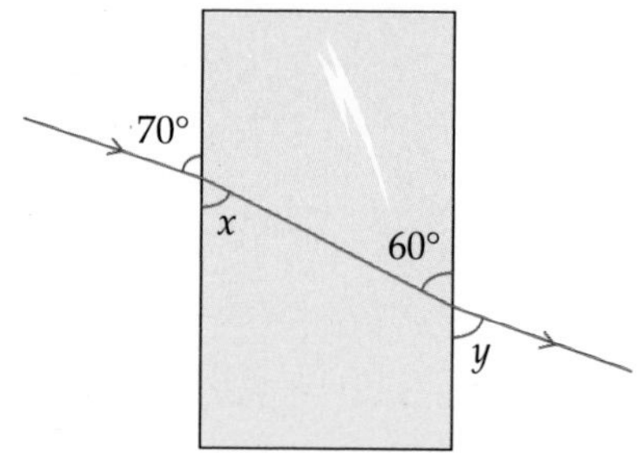

Bearings

STARTER

Cartography is a fascinating field. It combines parts of geography with some quite complicated mathematics.

It isn't easy to represent a *sphere* (round ball) like the Earth on a flat piece of paper.

- Some world maps distort land areas, like the Mercator projection.
- Other world maps break up land areas which are actually together, like Goode's projection.

Mercator projection distorts land areas

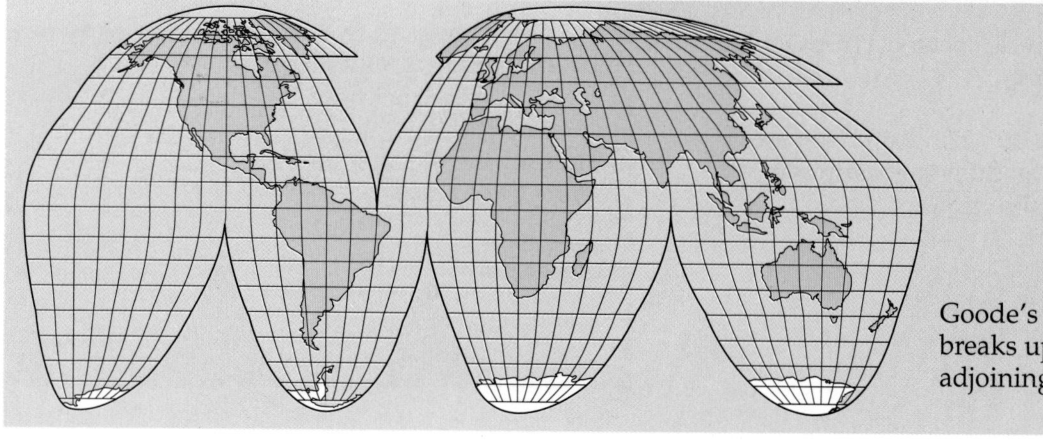

Goode's projection breaks up adjoining areas

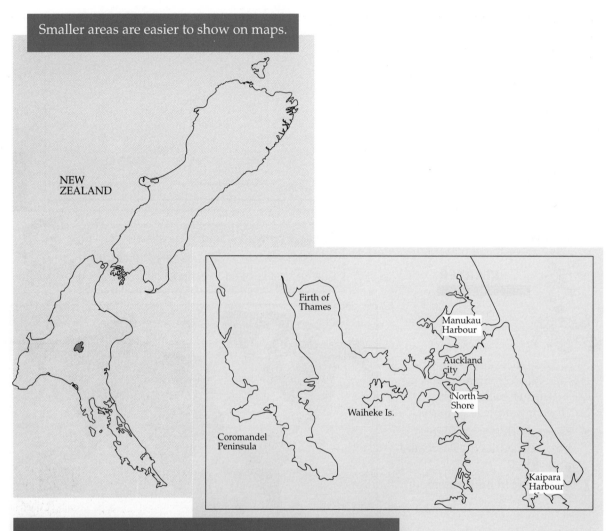

Smaller areas are easier to show on maps.

NEW ZEALAND

Firth of Thames
Manukau Harbour
Auckland city
North Shore
Waiheke Is.
Coromandel Peninsula
Kaipara Harbour

- What is unusual about these two smaller maps? Explain.
- How do we normally use maps of the Earth's surface?
- Give some reasons why maps are drawn this way.

A **bearing** gives a person a direction in which to steer.

Examples 060°, 220°, 005°, 340° are all different bearings or directions.

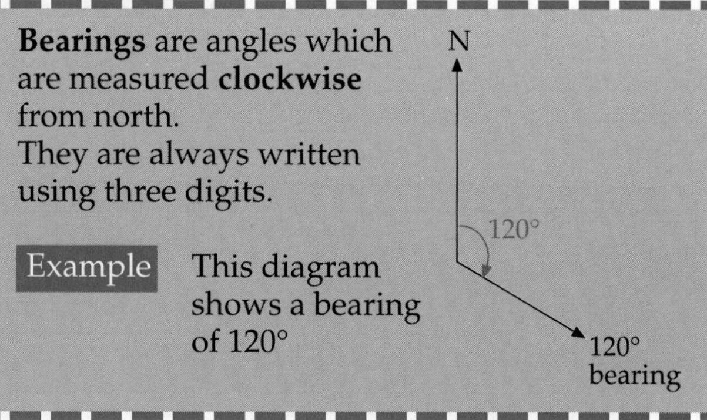

Bearings are angles which are measured **clockwise** from north.
They are always written using three digits.

Example This diagram shows a bearing of 120°

EXERCISE 18.8

1 Match each of these bearings with its most likely measurement from the box.

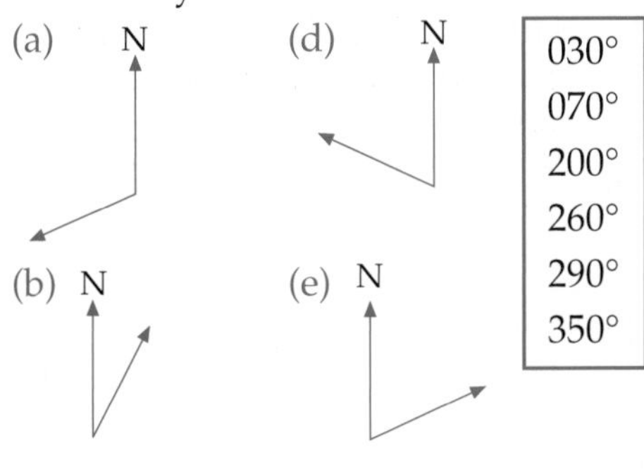

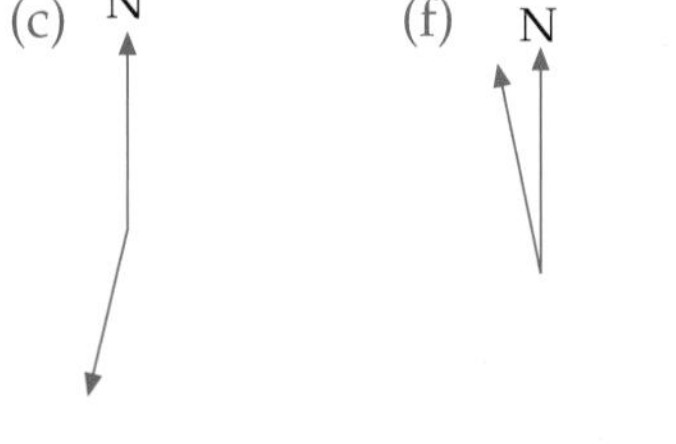

2 Copy this diagram. Complete the boxes so that they show *both* compass directions *and* bearings.

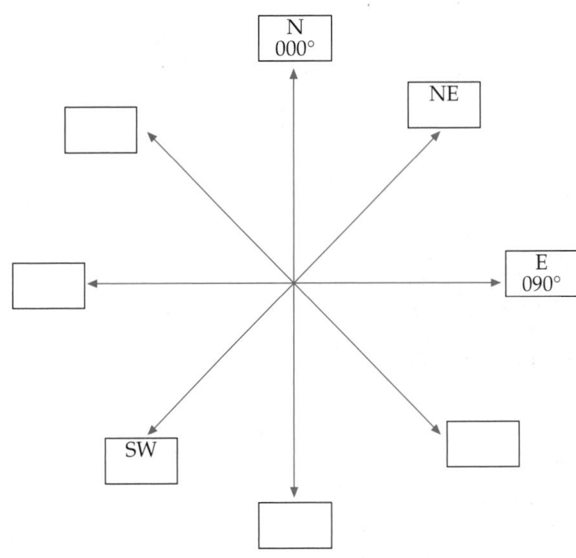

3 Use a protractor to measure these bearings:

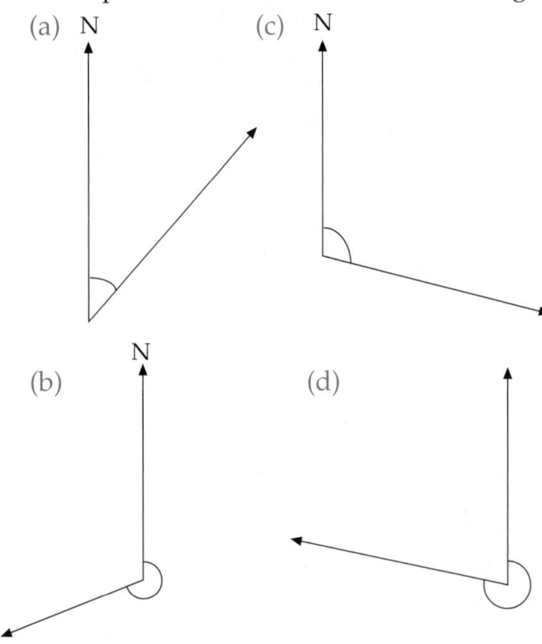

4 None of these are bearings. Explain why.

(a) 60° (b) 400° (c) NW

5 This is a map of Desolation Island.

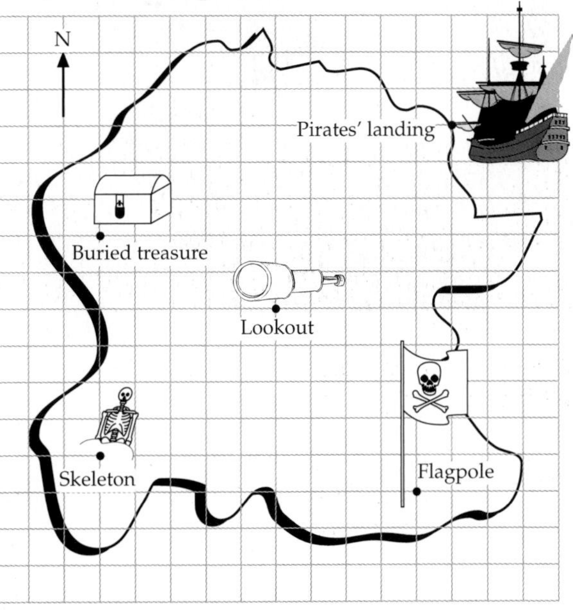

(a) Use a protractor to measure these bearings from the lookout:

(i) pirates' landing

(*continues*)

(ii) the skeleton
(iii) the flagpole
(iv) the buried treasure.

(b) What is the bearing of the buried treasure from the skeleton?

(c) What is the bearing of the skeleton from the buried treasure? You can work this out without having to use a protractor. Explain why.

(d) The bearing of the flagpole from the skeleton is 096°. You could work out the bearing of the skeleton from the flagpole without having to use a protractor. Explain how.

6 A search-and-rescue helicopter is based in Wellington. Use this map of central New Zealand to measure the bearings it would use to fly to:

(a) Cape Kidnappers
(b) Murchison
(c) Wanganui
(d) Mt Taranaki
(e) Farewell Spit

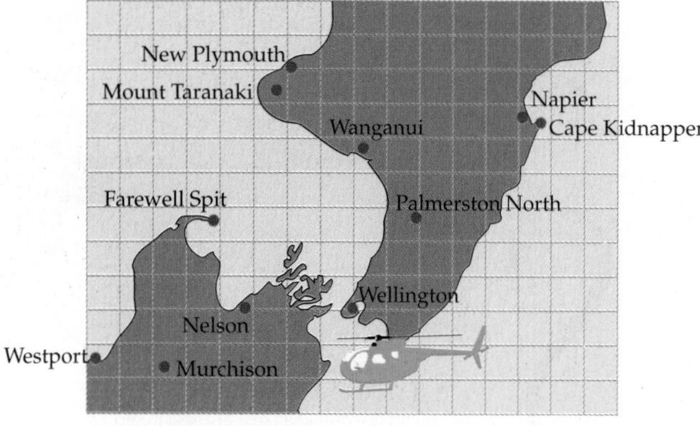

7 When a yacht sails a course it 'tacks', changing direction several times. This diagram shows the course of a yacht sailing from P to Q to R to S. The diagram isn't drawn to scale. However, you can work out the bearings by using angle properties of parallel lines.

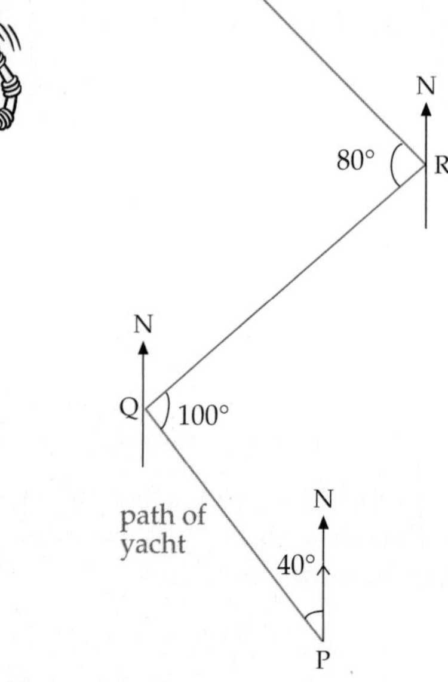

What is the bearing when the yacht is sailing:

(a) from P to Q?
(b) from Q to R?
(c) from R to S?

8 A small town has only three roads. The roads are all straight. There are seven houses. These have all been placed so that you have to cross a road to get from one house to another.

Copy the diagram. Draw in a possible position for the three roads.

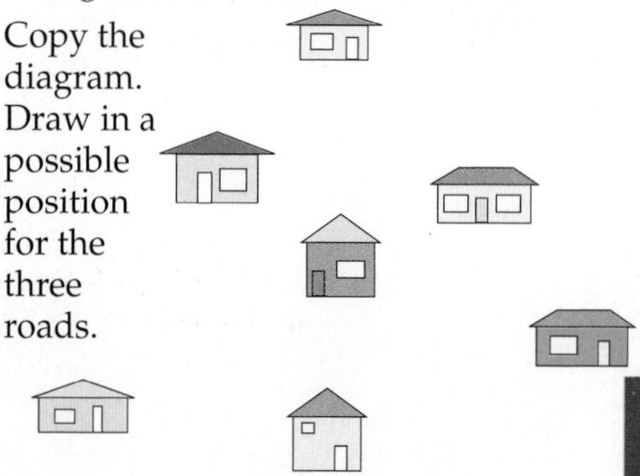

19 Symmetry

STARTER

Look at these photos and diagrams. They show parts of the airline industry, a business where symmetry is very important.

A Loading a Boeing 777 at Chicago's O'Hare Airport

B The intake of a rotary jet engine

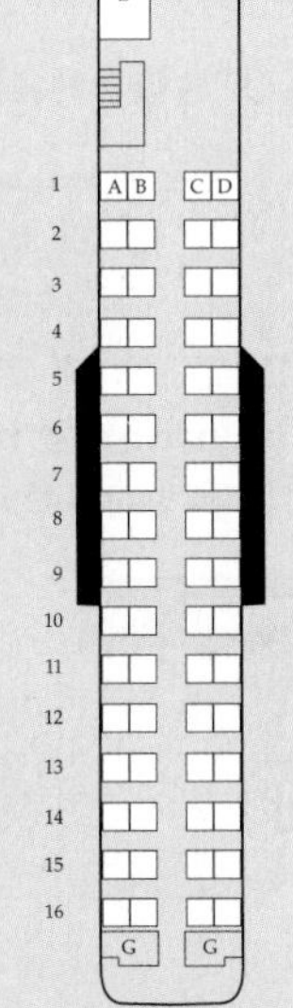

C A seating plan for the ATP aircraft

- Could the freight containers in photo A fit on either side of the aircraft?
- Explain how the freight containers are symmetric. Are they mirror images of each other?
- Explain how the blades in the engine (photo B) are symmetric.

- Suggest why an airline would refer to the seating plan in diagram C as 2-2.
- Suggest some advantages of having a symmetric seating plan on an aircraft.

- Which pictures(s) show(s) symmetry where reflection is involved?
- Which pictures(s) show(s) symmetry where rotation is involved?

STARTER

Each person should chose one kind of *transport* as a topic (not aircraft).

- Give this topic to the other person.
- Both of you now write down as many things to do with the topic that involve symmetry as you can.
- Write a short sentence about each one.

We see examples of symmetry all around us every day—in nature and in design. There are two different types of symmetry:

- symmetry when an object turns onto itself (rotation)
- symmetry when an object folds onto itself (reflection).

Rotational symmetry

A figure has **rotational symmetry** about a point if there is a rotation less than 360° through which the figure can turn and fit onto itself.

The **order of rotational symmetry** is the number of different rotations (including 360°) which map the figure onto itself.

Examples

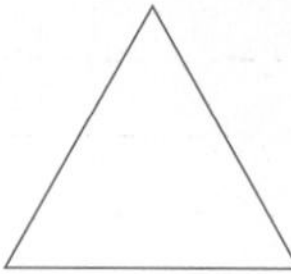

equilateral triangle
order of rotational symmetry = 3

Every shape has order of rotational symmetry of at least 1.

order of rotational symmetry = 4

Point symmetry is half-turn symmetry. That is, the figure can map onto itself by a half-turn (180°). Point symmetry has order 2, or 4, or 6, etc.

Example

A parallelogram has point symmetry.

EXERCISE 19.1

1 Which of these figures have rotational symmetry?

(a)

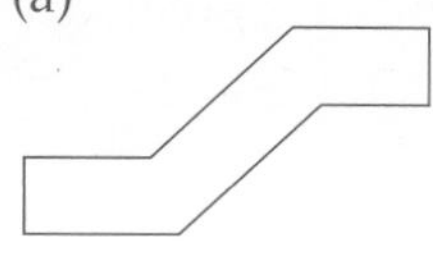

(b)

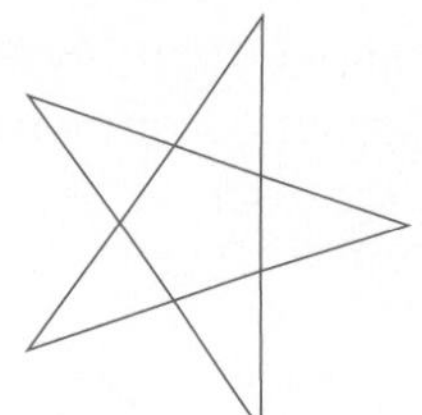

(c)

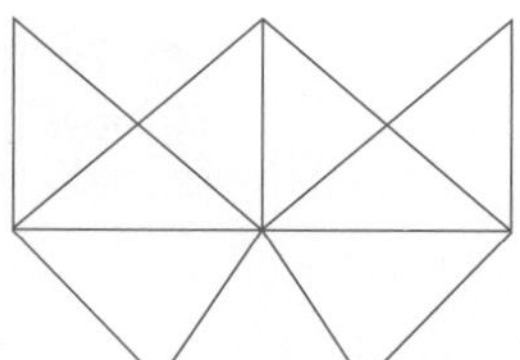

2 Write down the order of rotational symmetry for these crests:

(a)

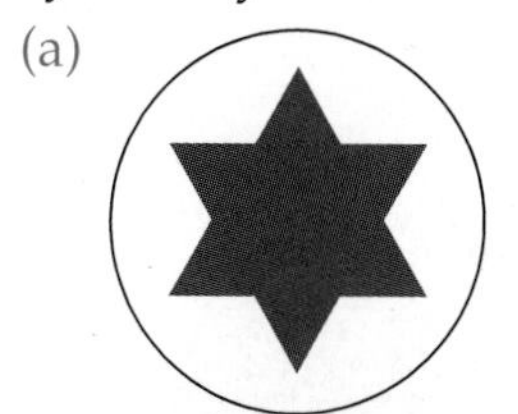

(c)

(b)

(d)

3 Write down the order of rotational symmetry for these designs:

(a)

(c)

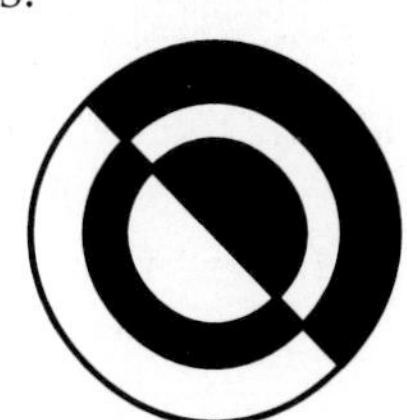

(b)

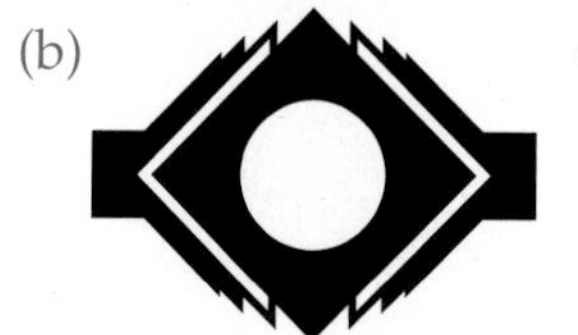

(d)

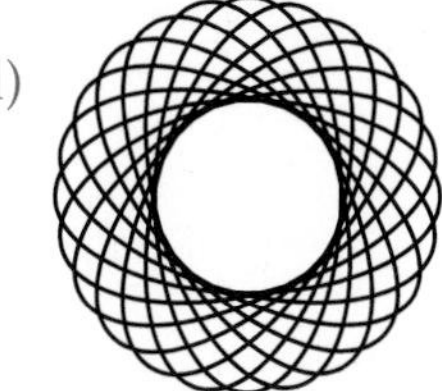

4 Look at the letters printed below. Write down the ones that have point (half-turn) symmetry.

ABCDEFGHIJKLMNOPQRSTUVWXYZ

5

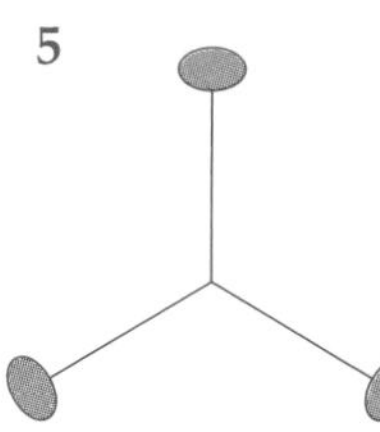

This shape has order of rotational symmetry of 3.

What is the size of the smallest turn, in degrees, that would make the shape fit onto itself again?

6 (a) How many ways are there in which this shape will turn onto itself?

(b) What is the size of the angle (in degrees) turned through each time?

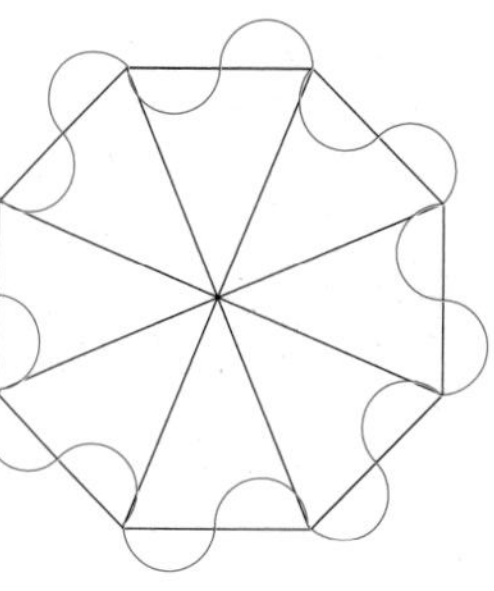

7 This table links the order of rotational symmetry of a shape with the smallest angle through which it can turn onto itself:

Order of rotational symmetry	Smallest angle through which the shape turns
1	360°
2	
3	120°
	90°
5	
6	
8	45°
	36°
12	

(a) Copy the table, and complete it.

(b) Explain in words what the link is.

8 Copy this diagram. Add to it so that your answer has rotational symmetry of order 2.

9 Copy this diagram. Add to it so that your answer has rotational symmetry of order 4.

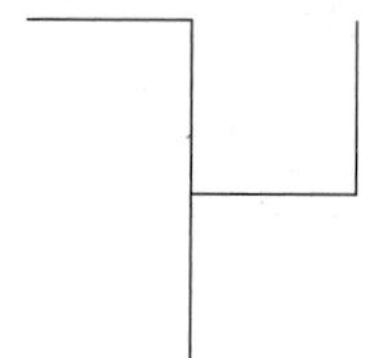

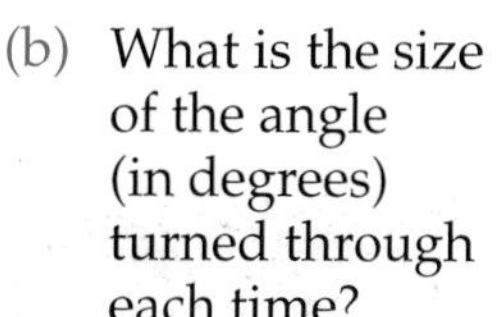

10 Most of the circular designs in this mosaic have the same order of rotational symmetry. What is it?

11 These crossword designs are on a 13 by 13 grid. They show rotational symmetry. Write down the order of rotational symmetry for each one.

(a)

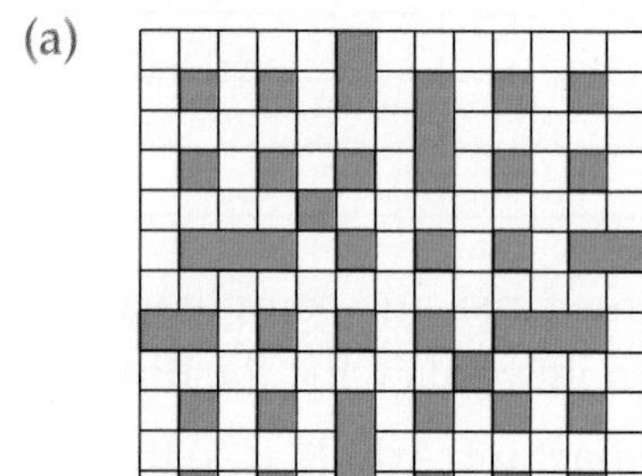

(b)

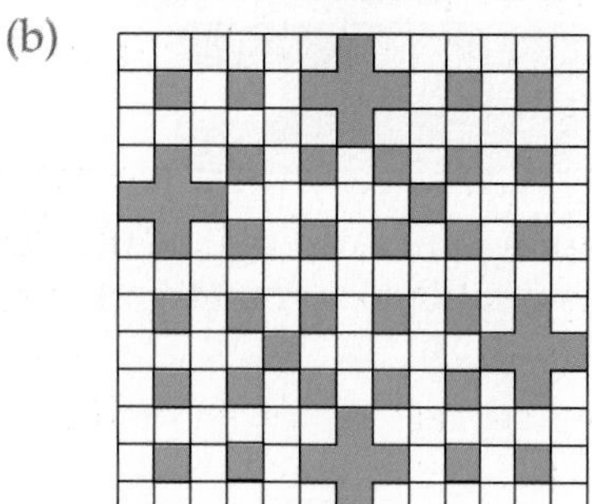

12 Make a crossword design on an 8 by 8 grid, with rotational symmetry of order 4.

13–15 You will need isometric paper for these questions.

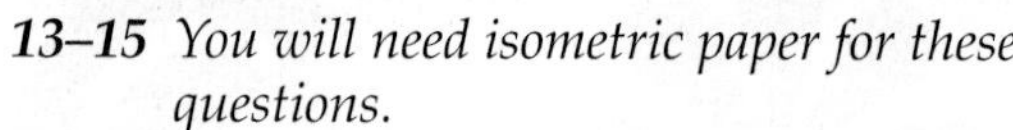

13

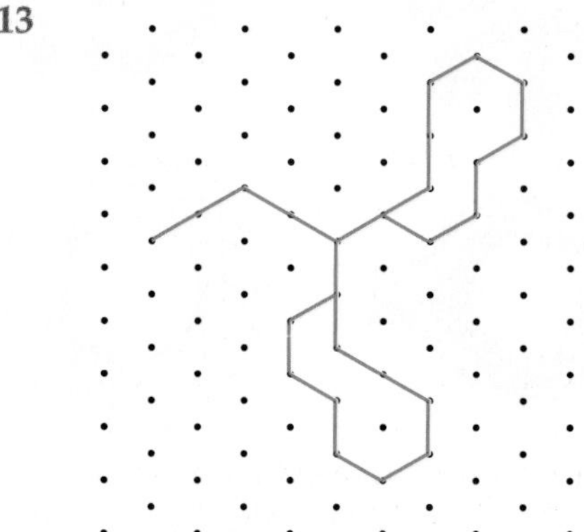

Copy this figure. Complete it so that it has rotational symmetry of order 3.

14 Use isometric paper to design a shape with rotational symmetry of order 6.

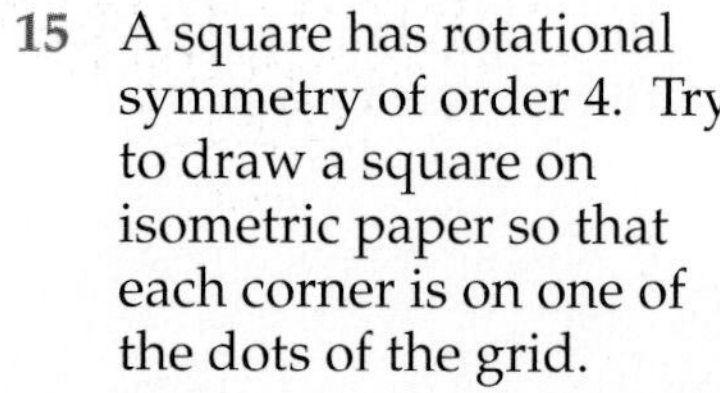

15 A square has rotational symmetry of order 4. Try to draw a square on isometric paper so that each corner is on one of the dots of the grid.

Line symmetry

STARTER

- Fold a sheet of paper in half.
- Cut out this pattern.
- What design will appear on the paper when it is unfolded?
- Does the design have symmetry?

A shape has **line symmetry** if it reflects or folds onto itself.
The line of folding, or mirror line, is called an **axis of symmetry**.

Example This rectangle has line symmetry. It has 2 axes of symmetry.

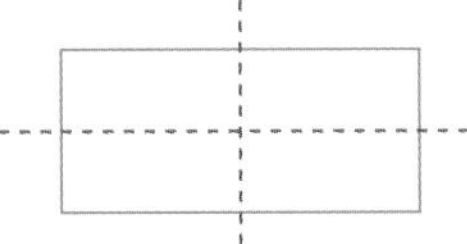

This diagram of a nut has 6 axes of symmetry.

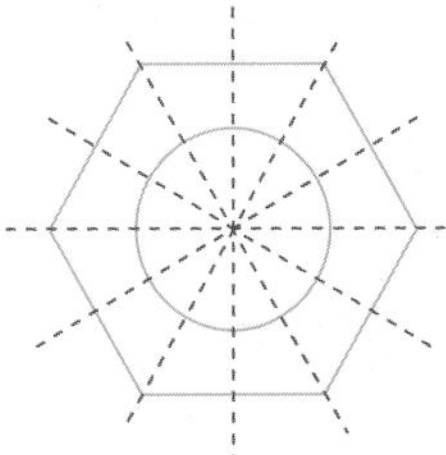

EXERCISE 19.2

1 Write down the number of axes of symmetry for each of these shapes.

(a) (b) (c) (d)

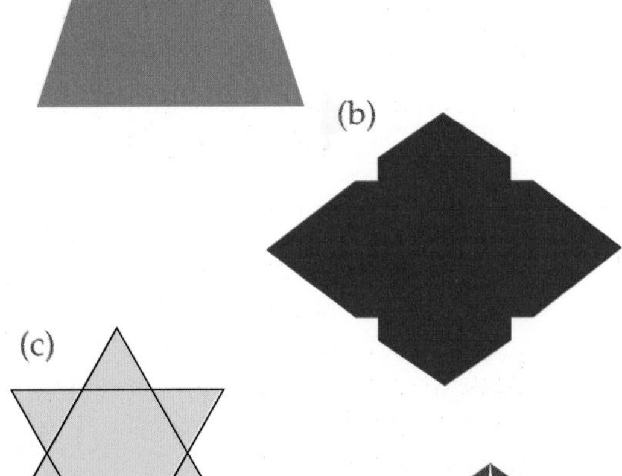

2 Here are five important mathematical symbols. Copy the table. Then write down the number of axes of symmetry each symbol has.

Symbol	+	−	×	÷	=
Number of axes of symmetry					

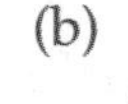

3 Copy these diagrams. Add dashed lines to show the axes of symmetry.

(a) (b) (c)

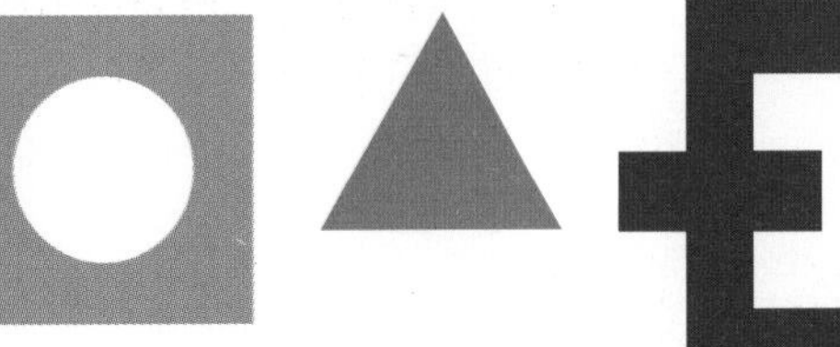

4 Copy this diagram. Then add to it so that it has two lines of symmetry. There is more than one way of doing this!

5 **ABCDEFGHIJKLMNOPQRSTUVWXYZ**

(a) Which of these letters printed have line symmetry?

(b) Which letters have a horizontal axis of symmetry?

(c) Which letters have a vertical axis of symmetry?

(d) Which letters have *two* axes of symmetry?

6 Which letter of the alphabet can be printed so that it has an *unlimited number* of axes of symmetry?

7 Copy this row of digits. Below each one, write down the number of axes of symmetry it has.

0 1 2 3 4 5 6 7 8 9

8 If these words are printed using CAPITAL letters, they can look symmetrical.

Mum, bike, boxed, wow

Write each one in capital letters. Then add a dashed line to show the symmetry.

9 Here are seating plans for several different types of aircraft:

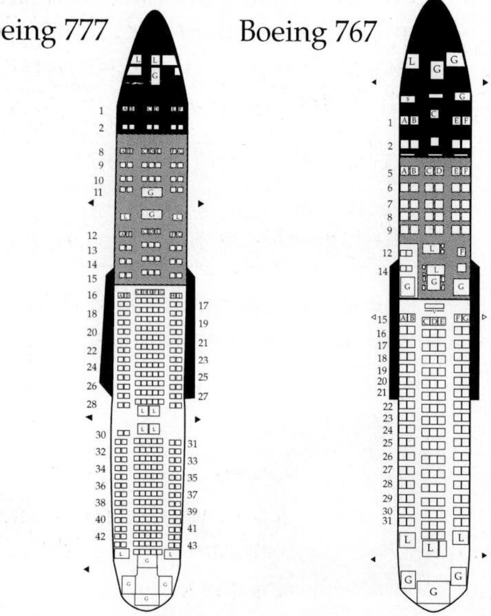

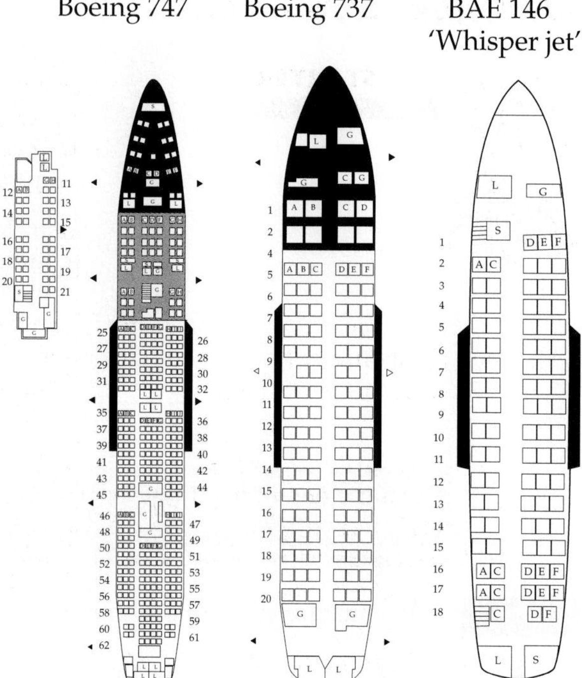

(a) Travel agents call the economy class seating plan in a Boeing 767 '2-3-2'. Explain why.

(b) Which aircraft has a 2-5-2 seating plan in economy class?

(c) Which aircraft does *not* have a symmetric seating plan?

(d) How many seats are there in most rows of a Boeing 747?

(e) Is it possible for an aircraft to have an odd number of seats in a row, and for them to be arranged symmetrically? Explain.

(f) Choose one kind of aircraft. Write a sentence or two to explain how airlines arrange seats in first/business class compared with economy.

Total order of symmetry

STARTER

A child's game involves placing these wooden shapes back into the holes in the board. The shapes are:
—an equilateral triangle
—an isosceles trapezium
—the letter L.

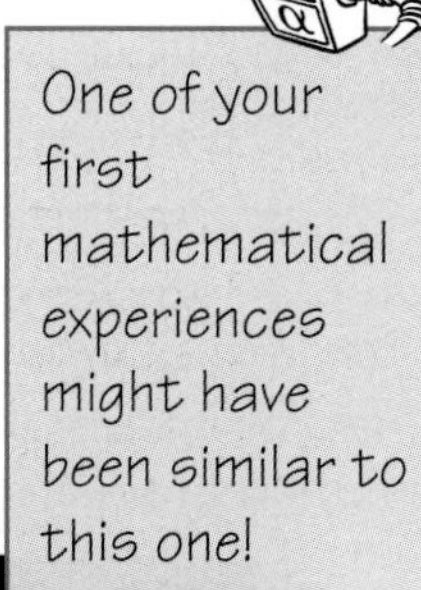

One of your first mathematical experiences might have been similar to this one!

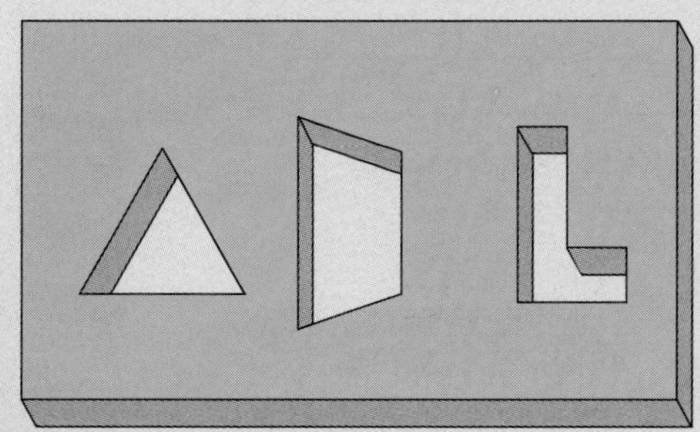

First, let's look at what happens with the equilateral triangle.

- How many different ways can the triangle be placed in its hole? Remember that the shapes can be turned upside down!
- What is the order of rotational symmetry of the triangle?
- How many axes of symmetry does the triangle have?

Now the others:

- How many ways can the isosceles trapezium be put back into its hole?
- How many ways can the letter L fit into its hole?
- Suggest a relationship between:
  —the number of ways a shape will fit in a hole
  —the number of axes of symmetry and
  —the order of rotational symmetry.

The **total order of symmetry** of a shape is:
- the number of axes of symmetry

  plus
- the order of rotational symmetry.

Figures always have a total order of symmetry of at least 1. This is because **any** figure can always turn through 360° onto itself again.

Example The total order of symmetry for a square is 8.

4 axes of symmetry

4 for order of rotational symmetry (90°, 180°, 270°, 360°)

$4 + 4 = 8$

EXERCISE 19.3

1 Copy this table.

	Order of rotational symmetry	Number of axes of symmetry	Total order of symmetry
(a)			
(b)			
(c)			
(d			
(e)			

Now complete it to show the *total* order of symmetry for each of these shapes:

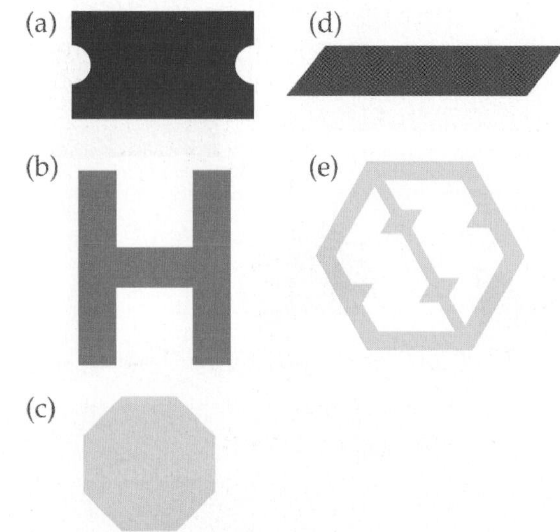

2 This is a photo of a Mexican rug.

Choose—and sketch—designs from the rug that have:

(a) rotational symmetry only
(b) line symmetry only
(c) both kinds of symmetry (total order 4)
(d) total order of symmetry of 1.

3 What is the total order of symmetry of the plate shown in this photo?

4 This sign advertises a brand of petrol called Esso.

(a) Which letter in the sign has rotational symmetry only?
(b) Which letter in the sign has line symmetry only?
(c) Which letter in the sign has both kinds of symmetry?
(d) What is the total order of symmetry of the sign?

5 Here are some flags from countries in the Commonwealth:

(a)  Nigeria

(b) Canada

(c)  Jamaica

(d)  United Kingdom

(e)  New Zealand

Copy this table, and complete it for each flag:

		Order of rotational symmetry	**Number of axes of symmetry**	**Total order of symmetry**
(a)	Nigeria			
(b)	Canada			
(c)	Jamaica			
(d)	United Kingdom			
(e)	New Zealand			

6 Each of these crossword designs is on a 13 by 13 grid. They all show symmetry.

(a)

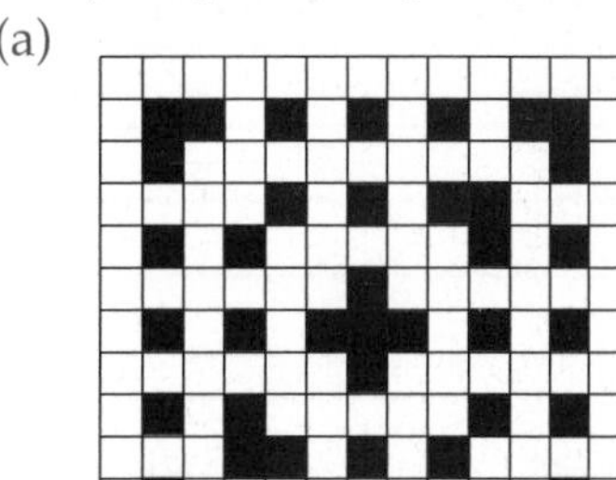

(b)

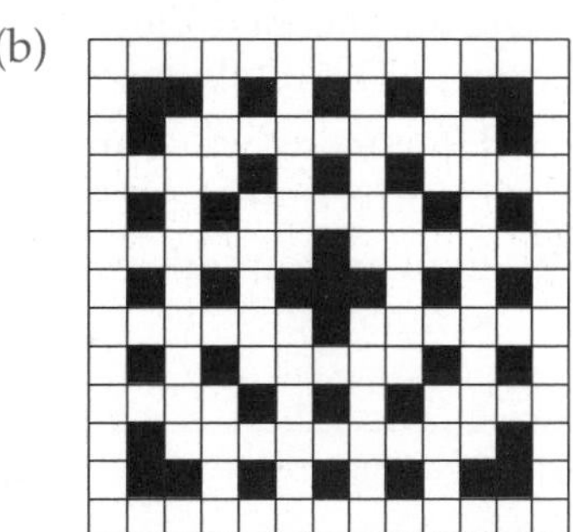

(c)

(d)

(continues)

Copy this table. Complete it to show the type of symmetry in each crossword design.

	Order of rotational symmetry	Number of axes of symmetry	Total order of symmetry
(a)			
(b)			
(c)			
(d)			

7 ATM means 'automatic teller machine'. This is the 'hole in the wall' where you insert a plastic card and money magically appears!

There are several different ways to insert your card into an ATM. Only one way is correct.

(a) How many ways are there *altogether* (correct and incorrect) to insert a card into an ATM?

(b) Explain your answer using the ideas of symmetry.

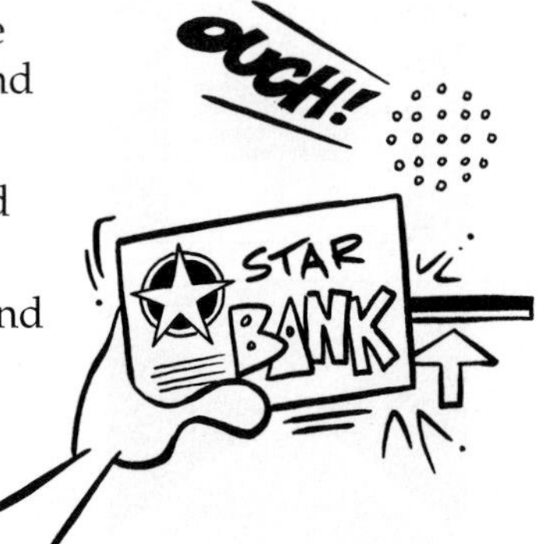

Triangles with symmetry

Triangles can be described by the *type of symmetry* they have.

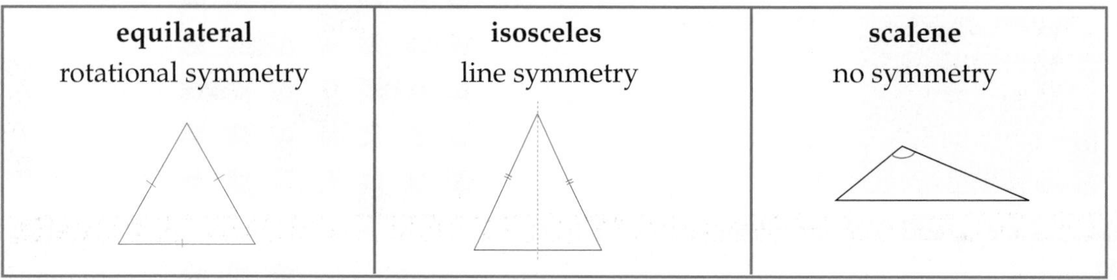

These symmetry properties mean that:

- an equilateral triangle has three sides the same length
- an isosceles triangle has two sides the same length.

Triangles can also be described by the *size of the largest angle* in them.

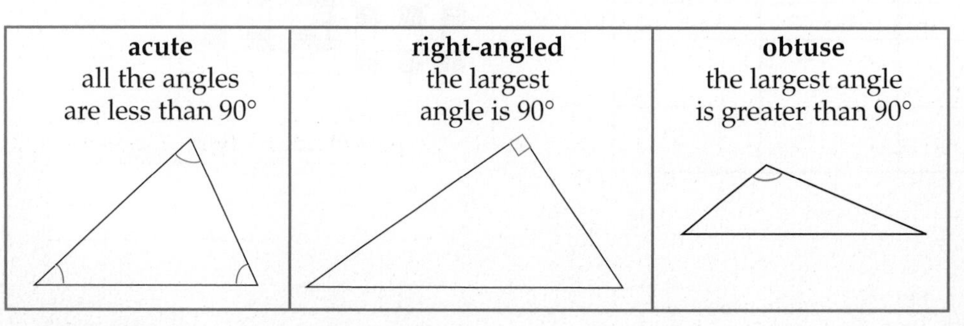

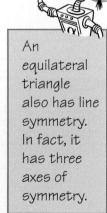

acute
all the angles are less than 90°
right-angled
the largest angle is 90°
obtuse
the largest angle is greater than 90°

An equilateral triangle also has line symmetry. In fact, it has three axes of symmetry.

EXERCISE 19.4

1 This diagram shows an isosceles triangle XYZ. Name the two equal sides.

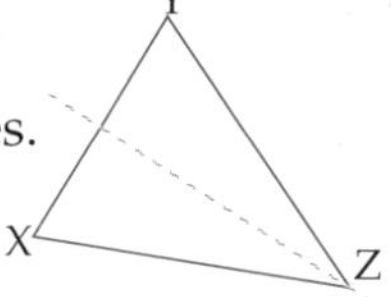

2 Triangle ABC is isosceles. The axis of symmetry is BD.
Write down the lengths of:
(a) AB
(b) CD
(c) AC

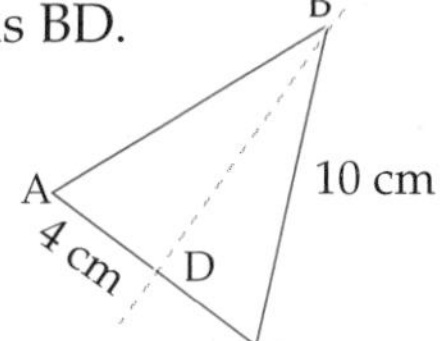

3

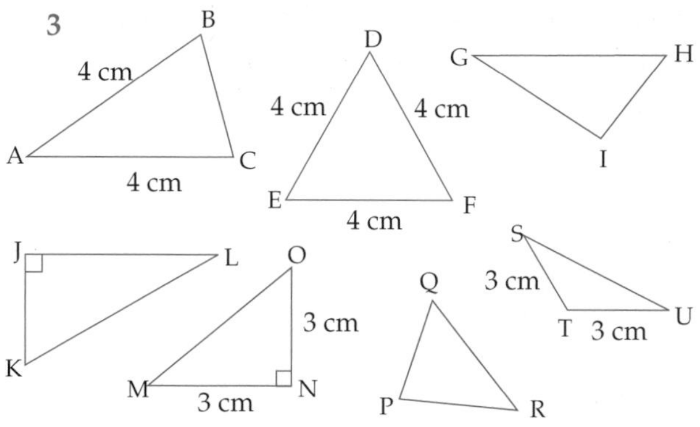

Write down the names (i.e. three letters) of the triangles here that are:
(a) equilateral
(b) isosceles *and* right-angled
(c) scalene *and* acute
(d) scalene *and* obtuse
(e) isosceles *and* acute
(f) isosceles *and* obtuse
(g) scalene *and* right-angled

4 Write down a sentence to describe the angles of each of these triangles:
(a) isosceles
(b) equilateral
(c) scalene

5 ABCDE is a regular pentagon. By drawing in two diagonals, it can be split into three isosceles triangles.
(a) Name the acute triangle(s).
(b) Name the obtuse triangle(s).

6 How many axes of symmetry does an isosceles triangle have?

7 Is it possible for a triangle to have two obtuse angles? Explain.

INVESTIGATION

WHOLE-NUMBER TRIANGLES

1 Is it possible to draw a triangle with sides 1 cm, 1 cm, and 3 cm? Explain.
2 What about drawing a triangle with sides 1 cm, 1 cm, and 2 cm?

3 How many different triangles can be drawn with:
- a perimeter of 12 cm, and
- sides that have whole-number lengths?

Draw up a table like this one to help.
Next to each set of side lengths, write whether the triangle is *equilateral*, *scalene* or *isosceles*.

Lengths of sides	Type of triangle
3 4 5	

4 There are seven different triangles you can draw with a perimeter of 18 cm and sides that have whole-number lengths. Copy this table.

Type of triangle	Lengths of sides
Scalene	
Isosceles	{ 2 8 8 }
Equilateral	

Complete it by writing in the other six sets of side lengths.

5 Complete these sentences:

- The longest side of a triangle must measure …………….. half the perimeter.
- The two shorter sides of a triangle must add to …………….. the longest side.

Choose from { less than, exactly, more than }

Angles in isosceles triangles

STARTER

Have you ever tried to cool down two pieces of toast without using a toast-rack?

Here's one way of doing this. Place the two pieces on a flat table. Balance the top edge of one piece against the top edge of the other.

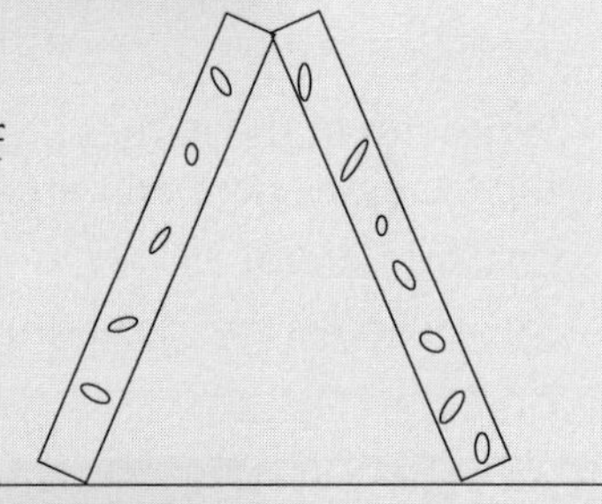

- Can you explain why the resulting triangle is isosceles?
- What can you say about the angles which the pieces of toast make with the table?

As well as having two sides that are the same length, isosceles triangles also have a pair of *equal-sized angles.*

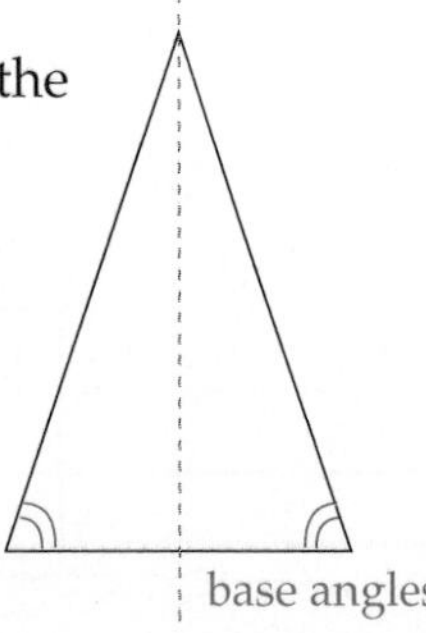

- We can show a triangle is **isosceles** by marking the two sides that are the same length with small // marks.
- We often call the two equal-sized angles the *base* angles.

We already know the sum of the angles in a triangle is 180°. So, this property of isosceles triangles means we can work out angles.

Example Work out the size of the angles marked x and y.

Answer $x = 75°$ (the line symmetry of the isosceles triangle means the base angles are the same)

$y = 30°$ (the two base angles add to 150°. This leaves $180° - 150° = 30°$ for the third angle of the triangle)

Example Work out the size of the angles marked p and q.

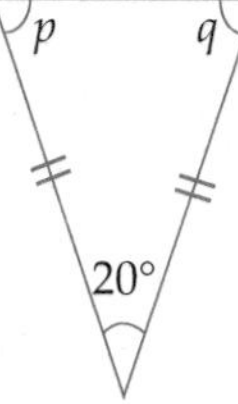

Answer The three angles in the triangle have to add to 180°.

One is 20°. This leaves $180° - 20° = 160°$ for the sum of the other two.

The angles p and q are equal, so each one must be $\frac{160°}{2} = 80°$

$p = 80°$ $q = 80°$

EXERCISE 19.5

1 Name the two equal angles in each of these isosceles triangles. Use three letters for each—e.g. $\widehat{ABC}$, $\widehat{CAB}$.

(a)

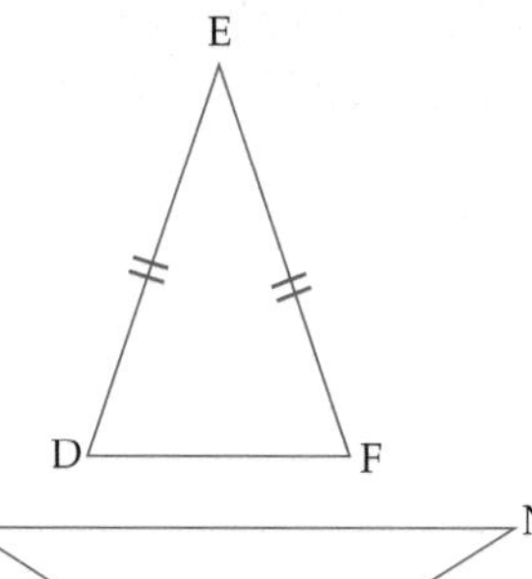

(b) L N M

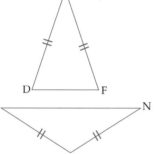

(c)

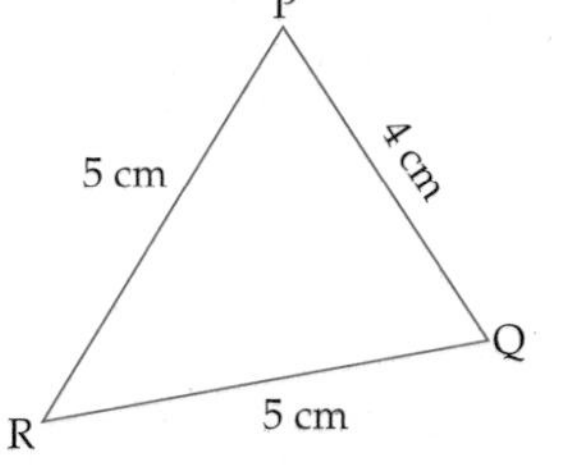

2–12 *Work out the size of the marked angles.*

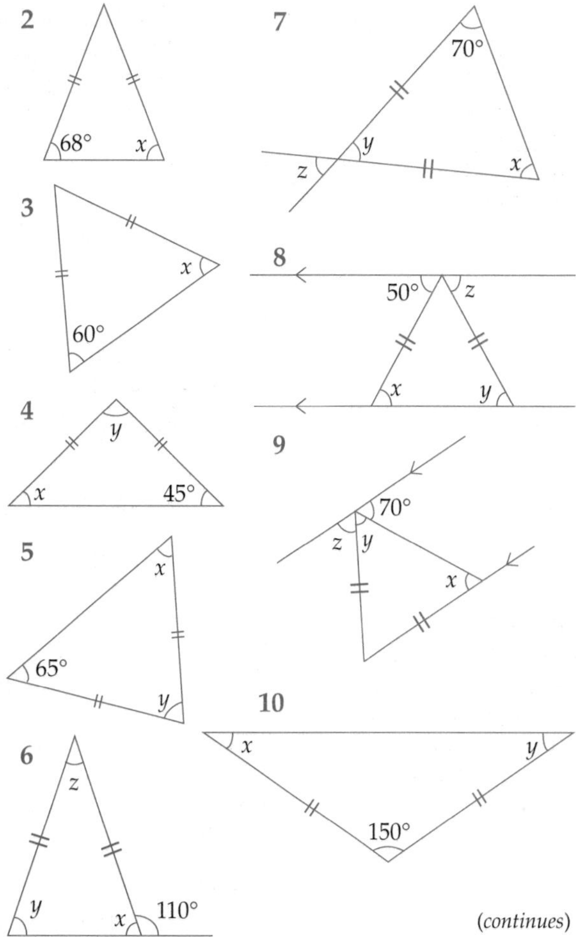

(continues)

11

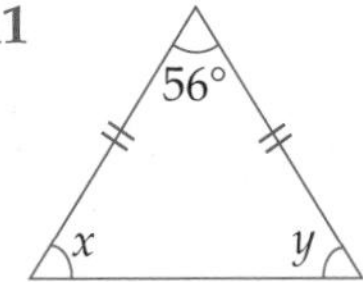

12

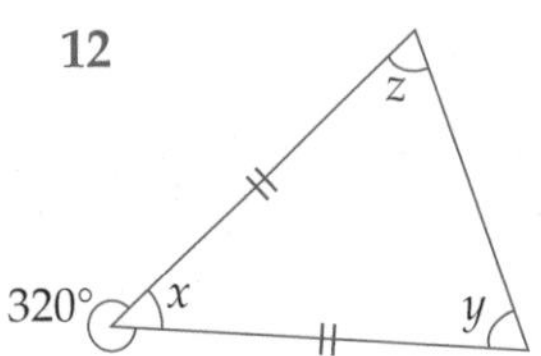

13 Write down the sizes of the three angles in a right-angled isosceles triangle.

14 On the right are two views of the same regular pentagon.

One view shows how the pentagon can be split up into 5 identical isosceles triangles joining up at the centre of the pentagon.

The other view shows an *interior* angle of the pentagon, labelled y.

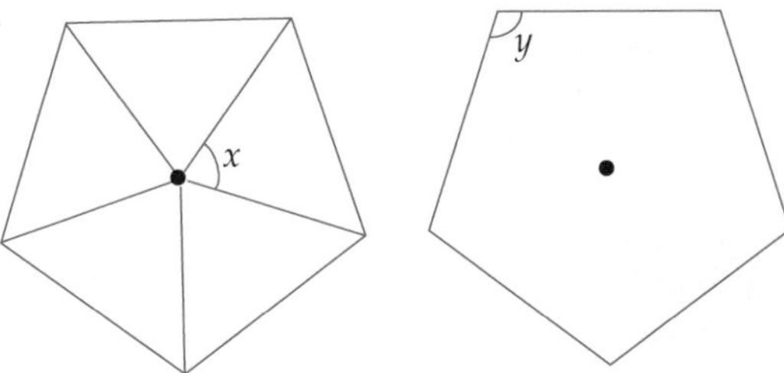

(a) Write down a mathematical calculation to show why angle x is 72°.

(b) Use the properties of isosceles triangles to help you work out the size of angle y.

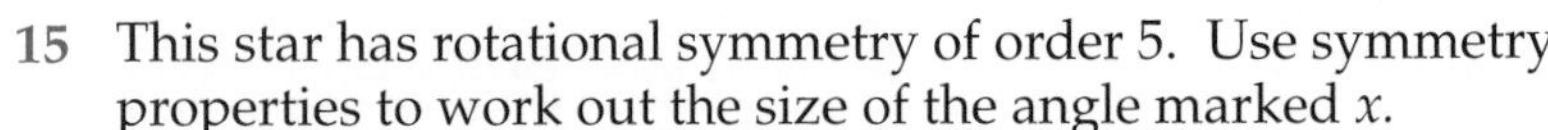

15 This star has rotational symmetry of order 5. Use symmetry properties to work out the size of the angle marked x.

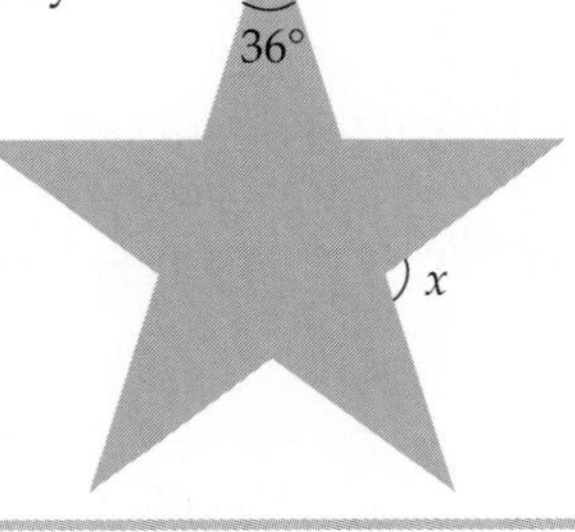

Quadrilaterals with symmetry

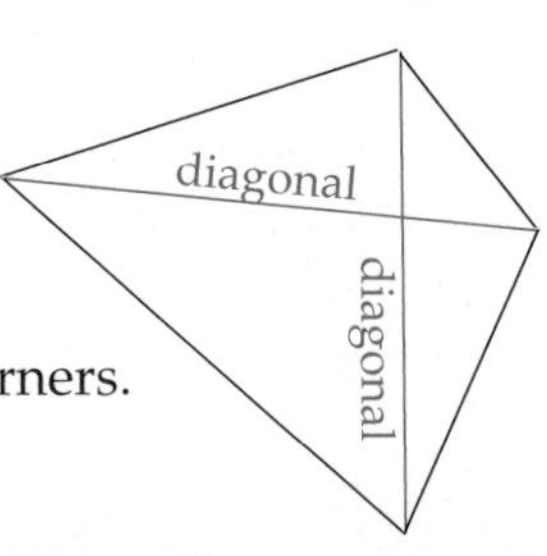

A quadrilateral is a four-sided figure.

Quadrilaterals have two **diagonals**. A diagonal in a quadrilateral is a line that joins a pair of opposite corners.

Some quadrilaterals have symmetry properties.

Rotational symmetry

A parallelogram has half-turn symmetry:

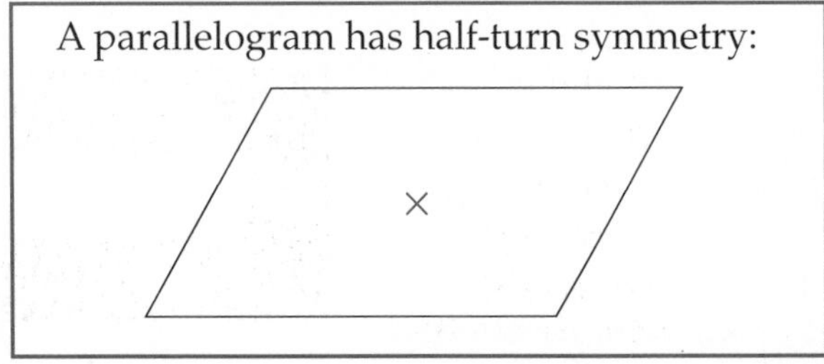

Chicago is famous for its skyscrapers. Look for the quadrilaterals!

Line symmetry

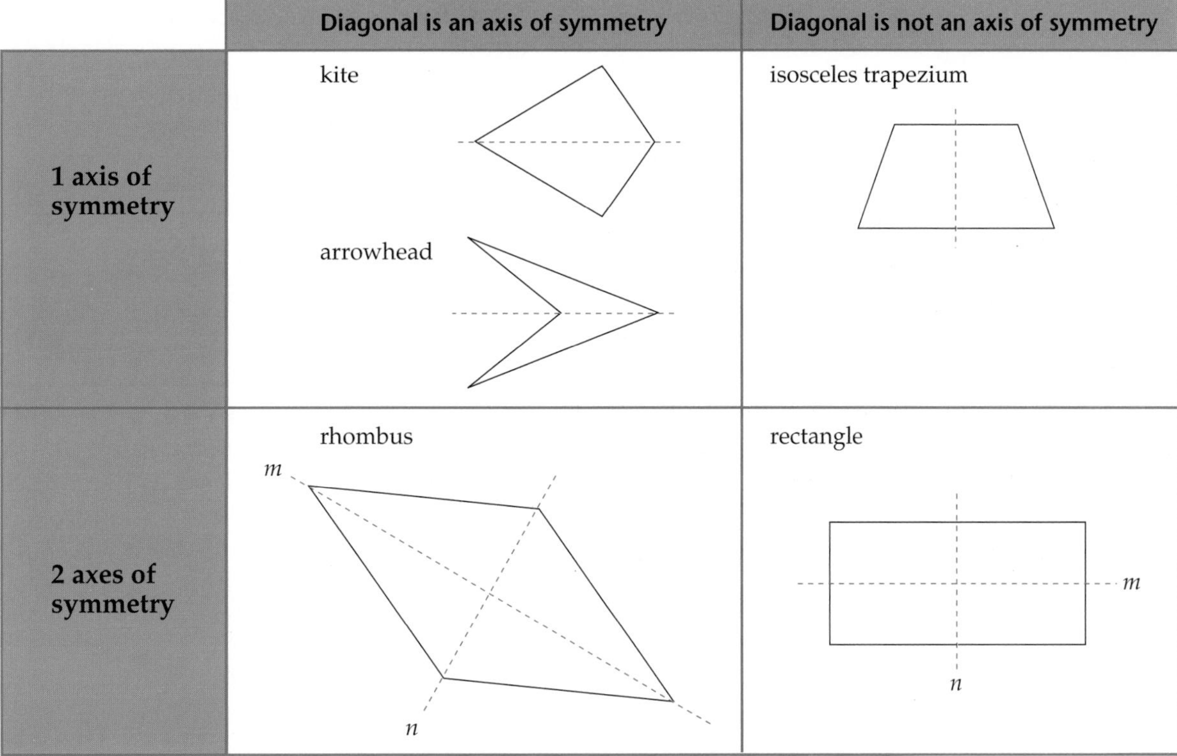

	Diagonal is an axis of symmetry	Diagonal is not an axis of symmetry
1 axis of symmetry	kite arrowhead	isosceles trapezium
2 axes of symmetry	rhombus	rectangle

A square has all of the symmetry properties.

A trapezium has a pair of parallel sides. Most trapeziums don't have any particular symmetry properties.

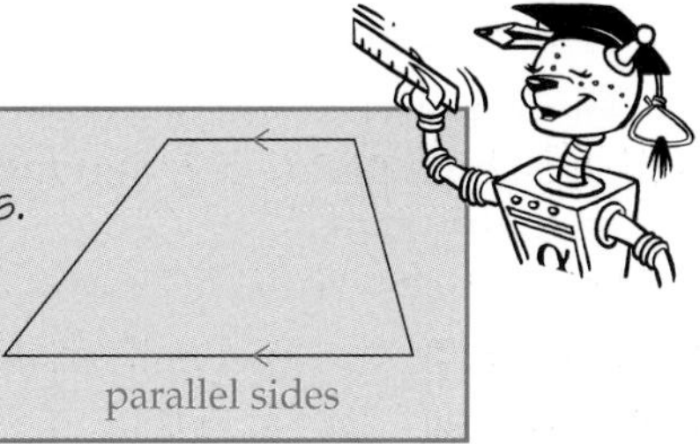

EXERCISE 19.6

1 Write down the names of these quadrilaterals.

(a)

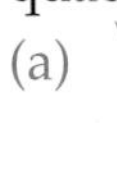

(b)

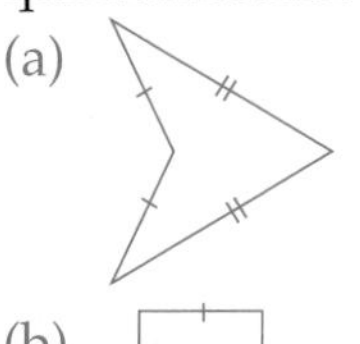

(c)

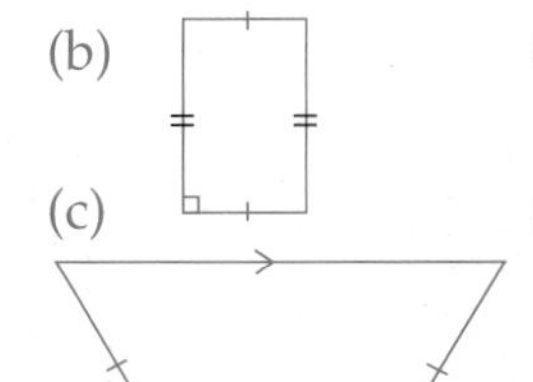

(d)

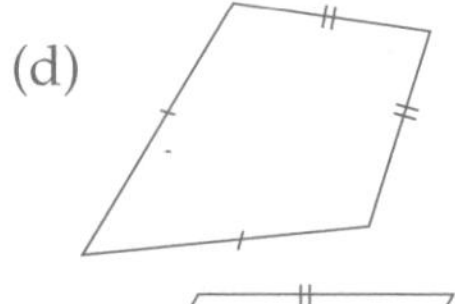

(e)

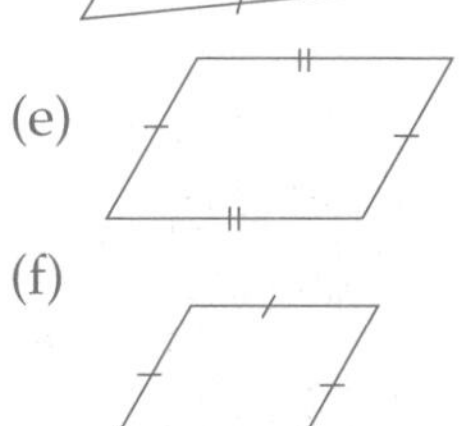

(f)

2 This is the flag of Kuwait. It is made up of four quadrilaterals (labelled A, B, C and D).

(a) Which is a rectangle?

(b) Which is an isosceles trapezium?

(c) Which is a trapezium with no symmetry properties?

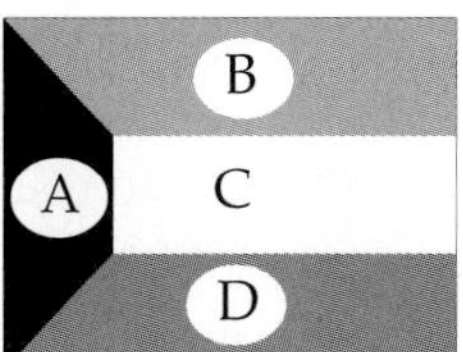

3 This diagram shows several different kinds of quadrilateral.

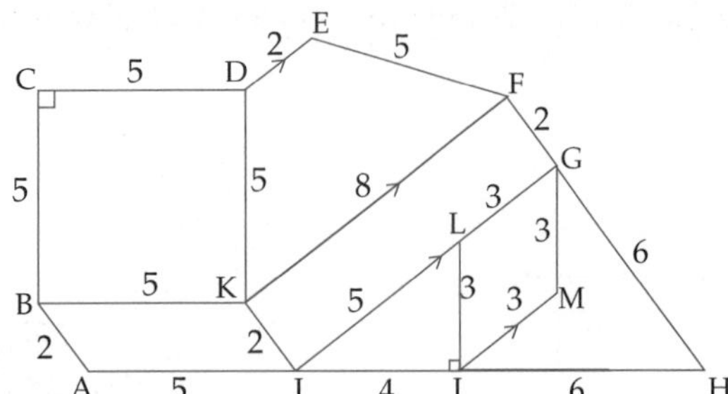

The numbers along the line segments show their lengths, in cm.

Write down the name of an example of each of these. (a) has been done for you.

(a) square BCDK
(b) rectangle
(c) rhombus
(d) parallelogram
(e) kite
(f) isosceles trapezium
(g) a trapezium with no symmetry properties
(h) arrowhead

4 Here are two views of a cube. A is drawn on a square grid. B is drawn on an isometric grid.

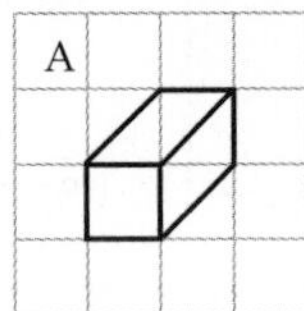

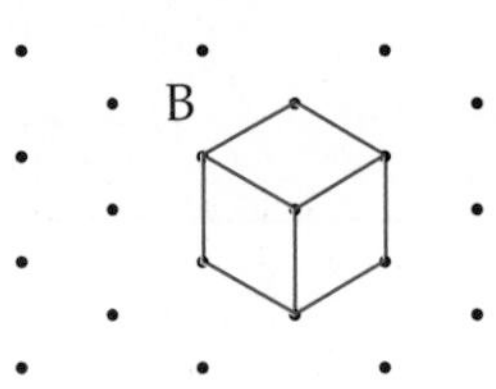

Copy and complete these two sentences:

(a) On a square grid, a cube can be represented by drawing one .... and two ....
(b) On an isometric grid, a cube can be represented by drawing three ....

5 A kite and an arrowhead both have a diagonal as one axis of symmetry. Explain the difference between a kite and an arrowhead.

6 Is it possible to draw a quadrilateral with one diagonal that is *outside* the quadrilateral? Explain.

7 Name the quadrilaterals with line symmetry that also have rotational symmetry.

8 This diagram shows that a regular hexagon can be split up into two equilateral triangles and two rhombuses:

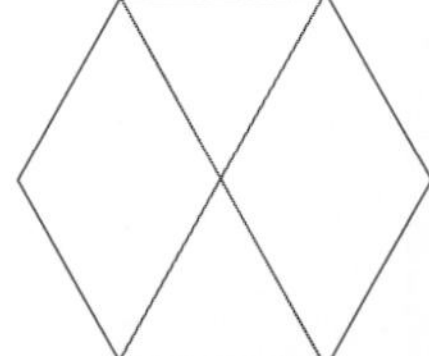

Draw diagrams to show how to split up a hexagon into:

(a) two isosceles trapeziums
(b) a rectangle and two isosceles triangles
(c) a kite and two isosceles triangles.

Properties of quadrilaterals

Quadrilaterals with symmetry may have special properties for their sides, angles and diagonals.

Here are special properties we can check for:

- sides (could be same length, or parallel)
- angles (could all be same size, or opposite pairs same size)
- diagonals (could be same length, could cut at right-angles, could bisect each other, could bisect the angles)

'Bisect' means cut in half.

Example Here is a list of the properties of a rhombus:

—all four sides are the same length
—each pair of opposite sides is parallel
—opposite angles are the same size
—the diagonals cut at right-angles
—the diagonals bisect each other
—the diagonals bisect the angles.

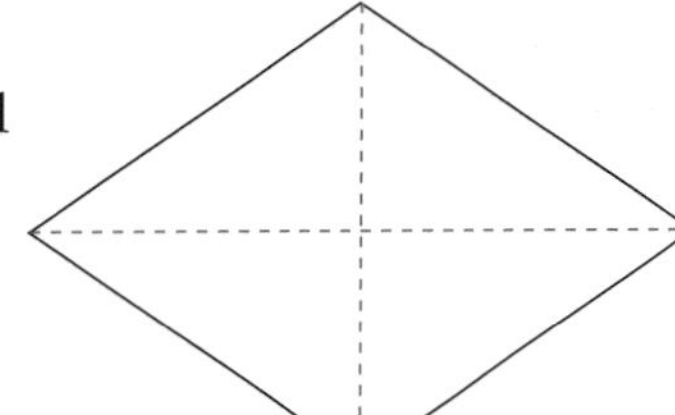

EXERCISE 19.7

1 Here is a parallelogram:

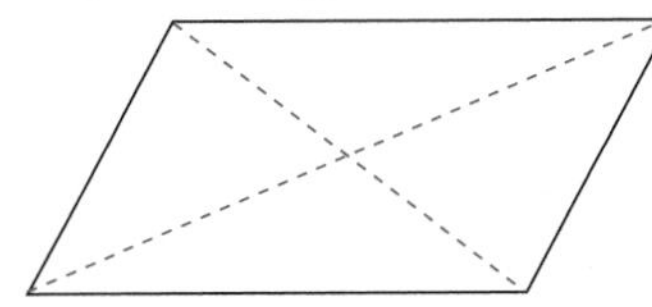

(a) Are all four sides the same length?
(b) Are opposite sides the same length?
(c) Are opposite angles the same size?
(d) Are the diagonals the same length?
(e) Do the diagonals cut at right-angles?
(f) Do the diagonals bisect each other?
(g) Do the diagonals bisect the angles?

2 Write down as many facts about the *sides*, *angles* and *diagonals* of a rectangle as you can.

3 Here is a list of quadrilaterals:

{ square, rectangle, rhombus, parallelogram, kite, isosceles trapezium }.

Write down all the quadrilaterals from this list that have these properties:

(a) two pairs of parallel sides
(b) all sides the same length
(c) each pair of opposite angles the same size
(d) both diagonals the same length.

4 ABCD is an isosceles trapezium.

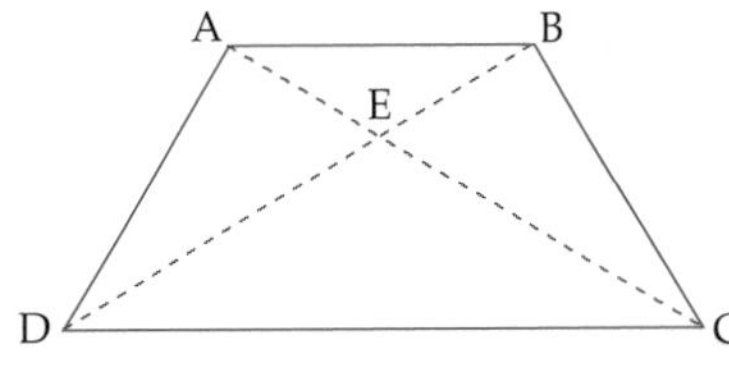

Use the diagram to complete statements (a) to (e).

(a) AD = ...
(b) AB || ....
(c) $\widehat{ADC}$ = ...
(d) $\widehat{ABC}$ = ...
(e) BD = ...
(f) Which point lies on the axis of symmetry? (The axis of symmetry hasn't been drawn in.)

5 A parallelogram has the property of rotational symmetry. Use this property to work out the marked unknown lengths and angles here:

(a)

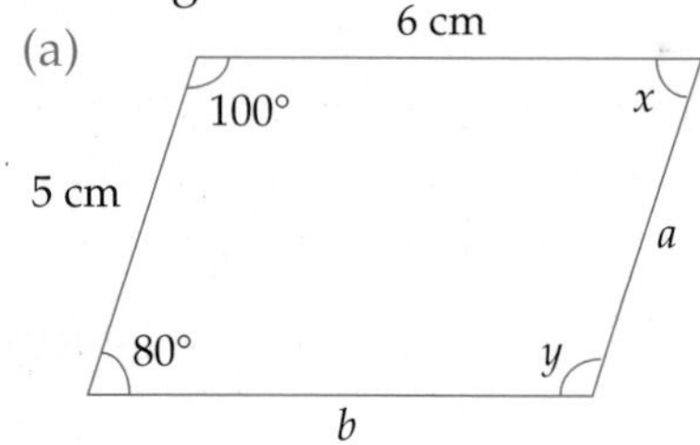

(b)

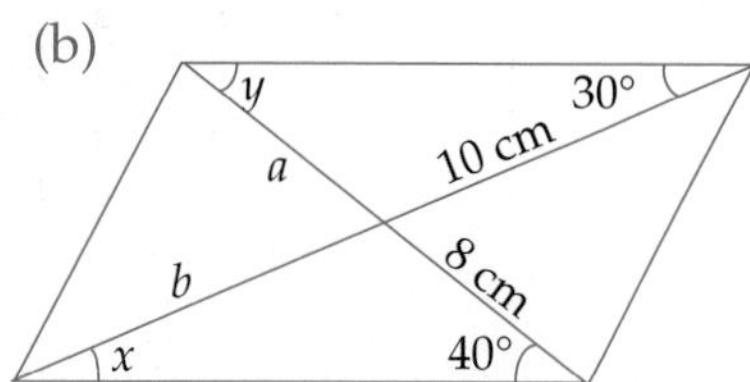

6 A kite has the property of line symmetry. Use this property to work out the marked unknown lengths and angles here:

(a)

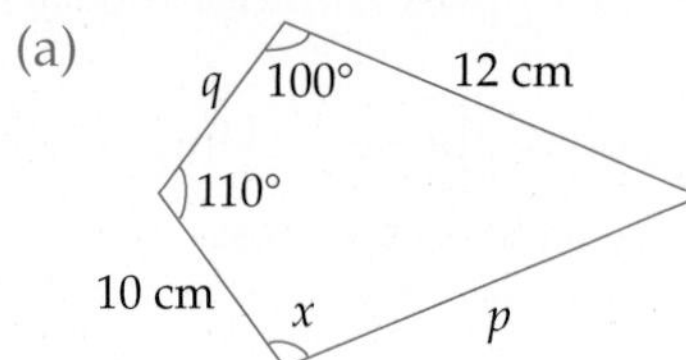

(b)

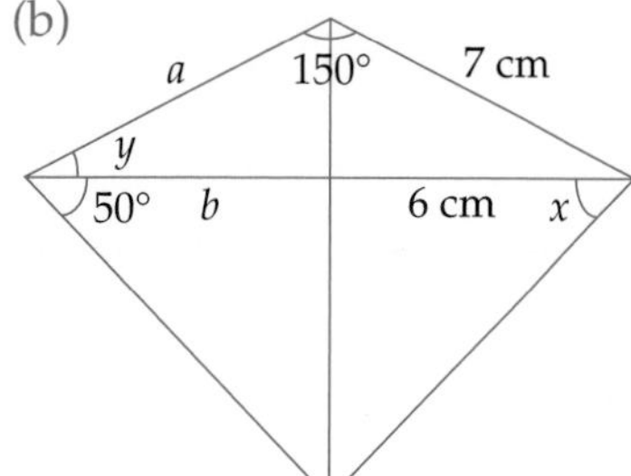

7 Are the diagonals of a rectangle perpendicular (cut at right-angles)?

8 Do the diagonals of an isosceles trapezium cut each other in half?

9 Quadrilaterals have two diagonals. What about pentagons (five sides)?

Draw a pentagon, and show all the diagonals. How many are there altogether?

10 Hone, Iaone and Joan each own a farm. Hone has five children, Iaone has four children, and Joan has four children. Each child will inherit an identical piece of land (i.e. same size and shape) as their brothers/sisters.

Hone's farm is square.

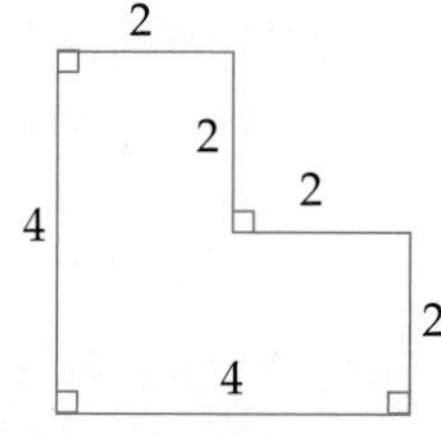

Iaone's farm is "L" shaped.

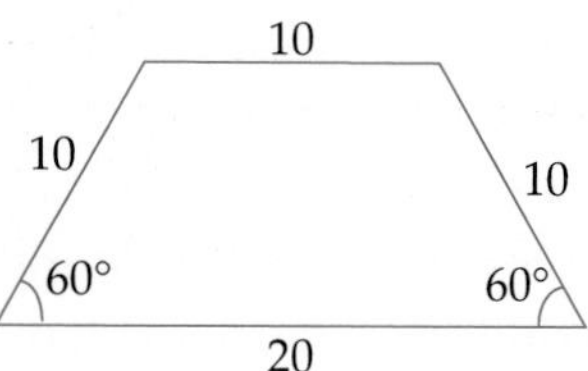

Joan's farm is an isosceles trapezium.

The measurements on the sides are in km.

(a) Show how Hone's farm can be divided into five identical pieces.

(b) Show how Iaone's farm can be divided into four identical pieces.

(c) Show how Joan's farm can be divided into four identical pieces.

INVESTIGATION

RUBBER QUADRILATERALS

This diagram shows a block of wood with 16 nails placed in a square grid. A rubber band has been put around four of the nails to form a square.

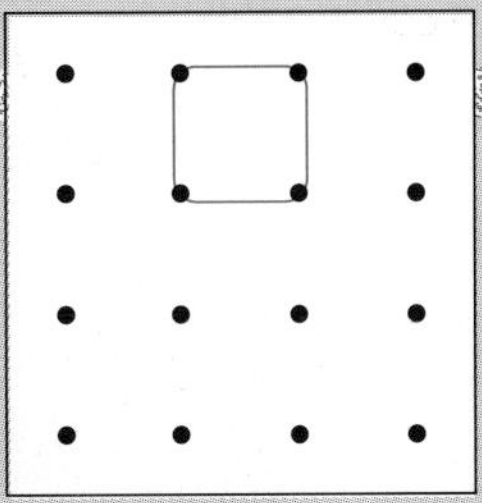

1 Draw diagrams to show how the rubber band could give each of these shapes:

(a) rectangle
(b) rhombus
(c) parallelogram
(d) kite
(e) isosceles trapezium
(f) a trapezium with no symmetry properties
(g) arrowhead
(h) a quadrilateral that is none of the above.

2 In how many different ways could you place the rubber band around the nails to form a square?

3 Is it possible to place a rubber band around *three* of the nails to form an equilateral triangle? Investigate.

20 3D shapes

STARTER

This wooden shape is called a Moebius (or Möbius) strip. It has been constructed by glueing many smaller pieces together.

- Would it be possible to make a Moebius strip out of one solid piece of wood?

- Imagine running your hand around an edge, starting at the top. How many edges does a Moebius strip have?
- How many *surfaces* does a Moebius strip have?

- Try making a Moebius strip of your own. Start by cutting out a band of paper. Explain what you do next.

- A Moebius strip looks 'impossible', but can be built. Would it be possible to build this shape?

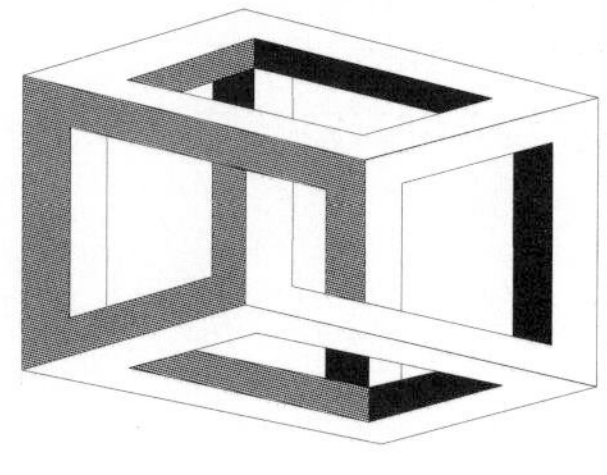

3-dimensional (3D) shapes

It has never been easy to show solid shapes on a flat surface. They appear to have no depth. The difficulty is that a flat surface has only 2 dimensions, while any solid shape has 3 dimensions.

The diagram on the right shows one way of representing 3 dimensions on a 2-dimensional surface.

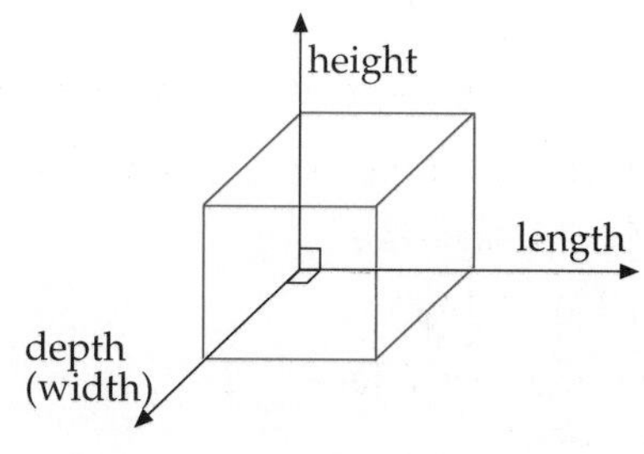

A shape like this is called a cuboid. All its faces are rectangles.

Sometimes it helps to show edges that are 'behind' the shape as seen from the front. We draw these 'hidden' edges with dashed lines.

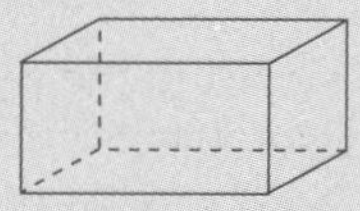

Here are some other important mathematical solids:

Cube all faces are square	**Sphere** a perfectly round solid
Prisms • triangular prism • hexagonal prism (the cross-section has 6 sides)	**Pyramids** • triangular base (often called a **tetrahedron**) • rectangular base
Cylinder a prism where the cross-section is a circle	**Cone** a pyramid with a circular base

Faces, edges and vertices

Most of the shapes above have *faces*, *edges* and *vertices*.

- CDHG is an example of a face
- AD is an edge
- D is a vertex.

A cuboid has 6 faces, 12 edges and 8 vertices.

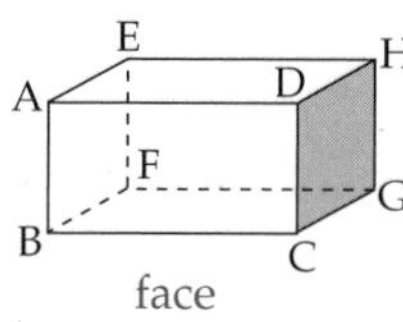

face

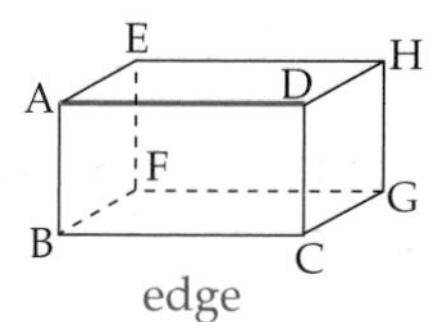

edge

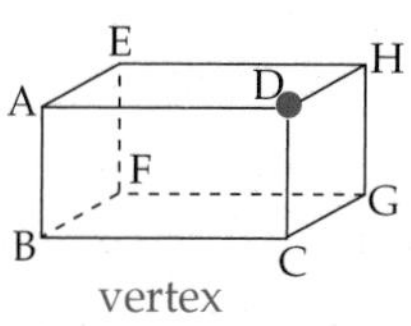

vertex

EXERCISE 20.1

1 What shape would make a good model for each of these objects? Choose from this list: { cuboid, triangular prism, pyramid, sphere, cylinder, cone }.

(a) a basketball

(b) a rectangular swimming pool with the same depth everywhere

(c) a tin of cat food

(d) a Jaffa

(e) a cobblestone

(f) a can of Coca Cola

(g) an ice-cream cone

(h) a wedge placed under a door to stop it moving

(i) the end of a pencil that has been in a sharpening machine

2 ABCDEFGH is a cuboid.

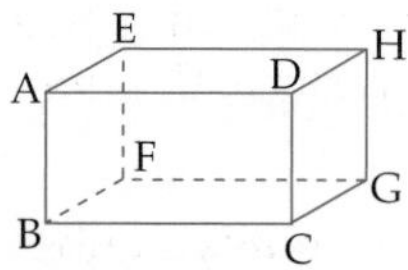

(a) Which vertex is the greatest distance from C?

(b) Name the three edges that are parallel to AE.

(c) Which face is opposite to CDHG?

3 ABCD is a tetrahedron.

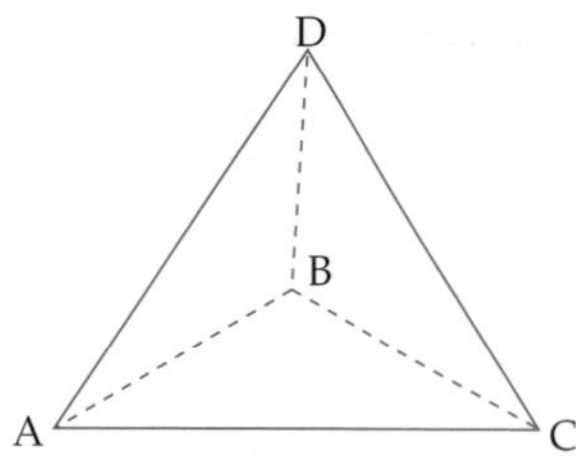

(a) How many faces does ABCD have?

(b) How many edges does ABCD have?

(c) How many vertices does ABCD have?

4 Rewi is planning to make a box kite in the shape of a cube. The frame will be made out of light wooden dowelling.

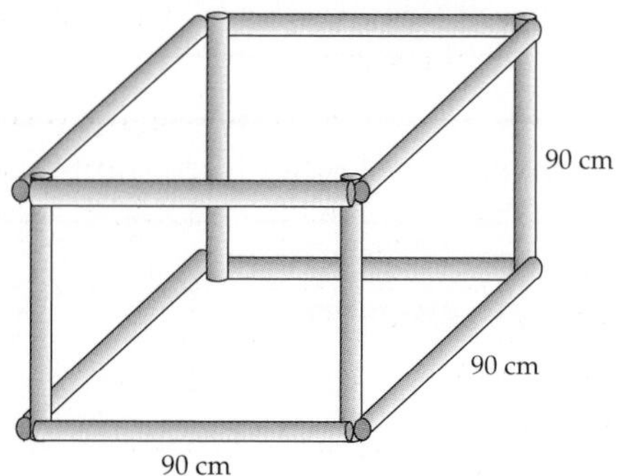

He buys 10 m (i.e. 1000 cm) of dowelling. Explain, showing some calculations, whether this amount will be enough.

5 Copy and complete these diagrams to show the *hidden* edges:

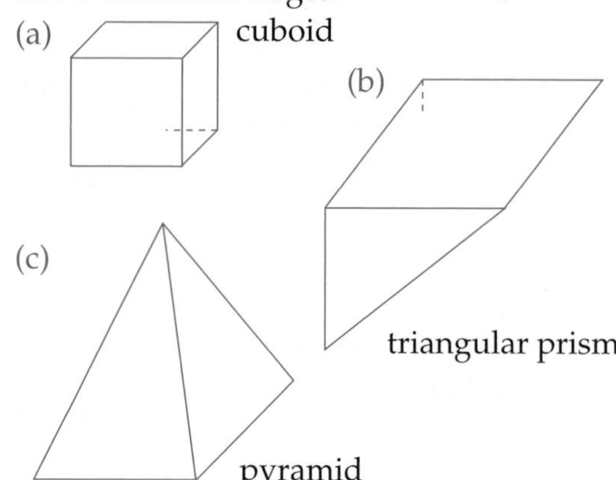

6 Quinta has started to draw a cuboid. She was interrupted after drawing three edges.

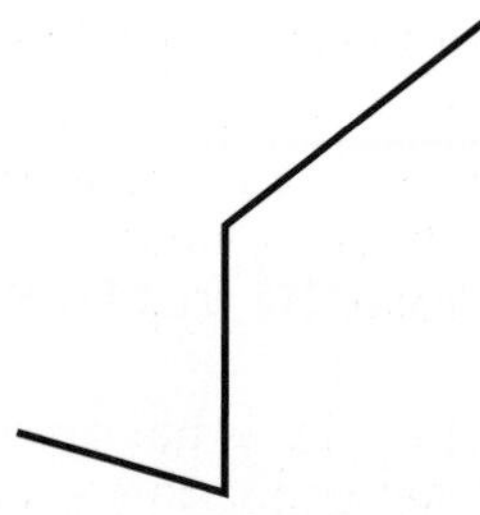

Copy the diagram. Then complete it to show where the other 9 edges would go, including the hidden ones.

7 (a) How many edges meet at each vertex of a cuboid?
(b) What shape is each face of a cube?

8 Copy this table. Complete it to show the number of faces, edges and vertices for each of these shapes.

		Number of faces	Number of edges	Number of vertices
(a)	cube			
(b)	triangular prism			
(c)	hexagonal prism			
(d)	pyramid			
(e)	cube where a triangular slice has been cut off			

(a)

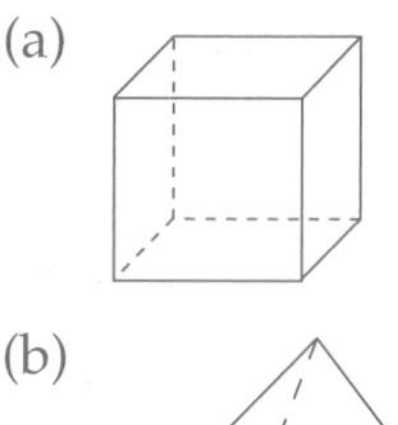

(d)

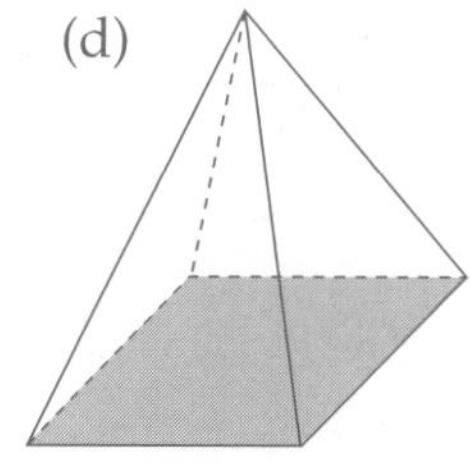

(b)

(e)

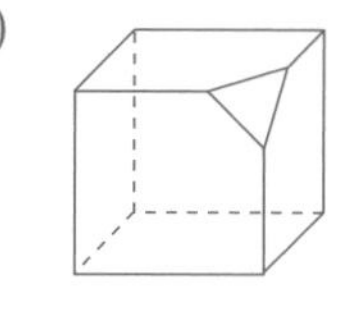

(c)

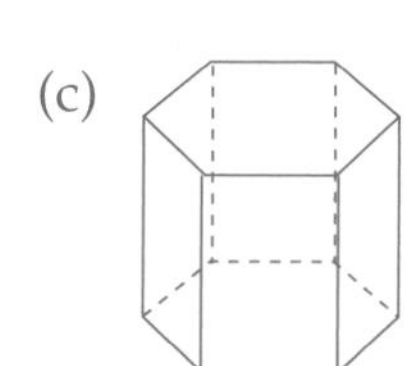

9 This hexagonal prism (cross-section has 6 edges) has 8 faces altogether.

Could you paint it with less than 8 colours so that any faces which meet have different colours? Explain.

10 Draw a pentagonal prism (cross-section has 5 sides).

11 Sheila is standing in front of a large cuboid. Bruce is standing behind the cuboid on the opposite side to Sheila.

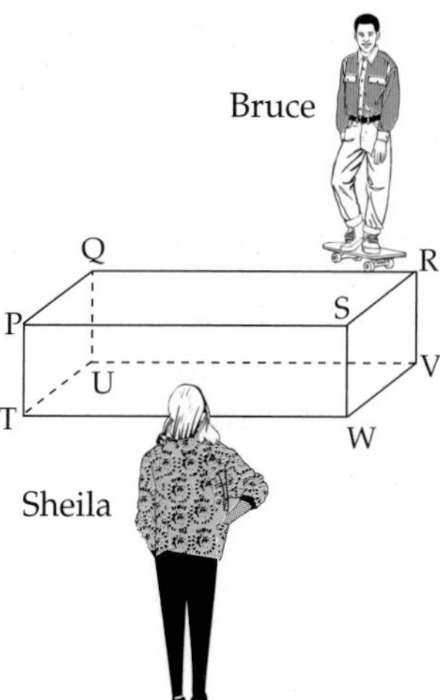

The diagram shows the view of the cuboid as Sheila sees it.

Make a copy of the diagram. Place the labels on it to show the view that Bruce would see.

12 This diagram shows a cube where a piece has been removed. This was done by slicing across the cube near a vertex. What is the name of the shape that has been *removed*?

13 The diagram shows a 'truncated' pyramid. The top has been removed by cutting a slice parallel to the base.

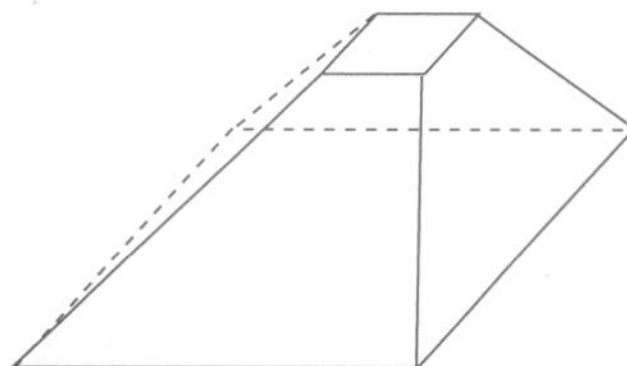

(a) Two of the faces are square. What shape are the other four faces?
(b) How many edges does the truncated pyramid have?
(c) What is the name of the shape that has been removed?

INVESTIGATION

COCKROACH IN THE CLASSROOM

A cockroach has a nest in one of the top corners (A) of a classroom. There is a tasty-looking rubbish bin at the opposite corner (G).

The cockroach reaches the rubbish bin by scuttling along the edges of the classroom. The cockroach never travels along the same edge more than once, and does not return to its nest until after it has reached the bin.

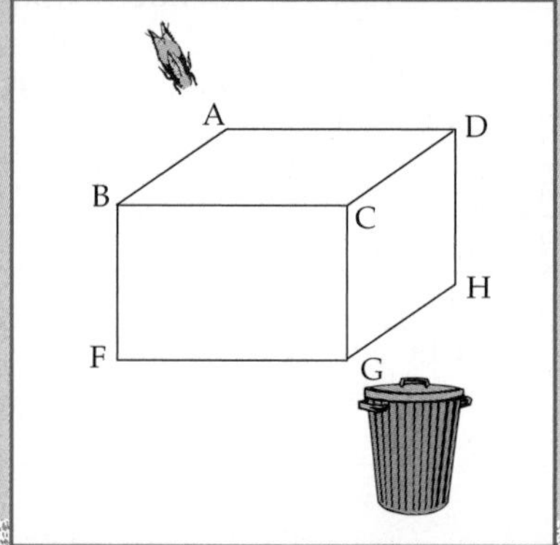

A cuboid makes a good model for the classroom.

- Draw a cuboid with all eight vertices (A to H) labelled. The cuboid should show all the hidden edges.
- Is it possible for the cockroach to reach the bin travelling along only 1 edge?
- Is it possible for the cockroach to reach the bin travelling along only 2 edges?
- Is it possible for the cockroach to reach the bin travelling along only 3 edges? If you think it is, write down a possible path from A to G.
- Is it possible for the cockroach to reach the bin travelling along only 4 edges? If you think it is, write down a possible path from A to G.
- Write down a path travelling along 5 different edges from A to G.

Investigate to work out the total number of different paths from the nest to the bin. Set out your working so that someone else can follow what you are doing.

Isometric drawings

The word **isometric** means *same distance*.

3D shapes are often drawn on an isometric grid. This is because all the measurements can be represented by an accurate scale.

An isometric grid has the same distance between each point on the grid.

Some advantages of using isometric grids

The cube on the right is drawn on an isometric grid. The height, length and width are each represented by lines that are the same length. Each face of the cube looks the same size.

If you use lines the same length to draw an **oblique** view of a cube, the cube looks distorted:

Example Show how to represent a cuboid with:

- a base measuring 2 m by 4 m
- a height of 3 m

on an isometric grid.

Answer

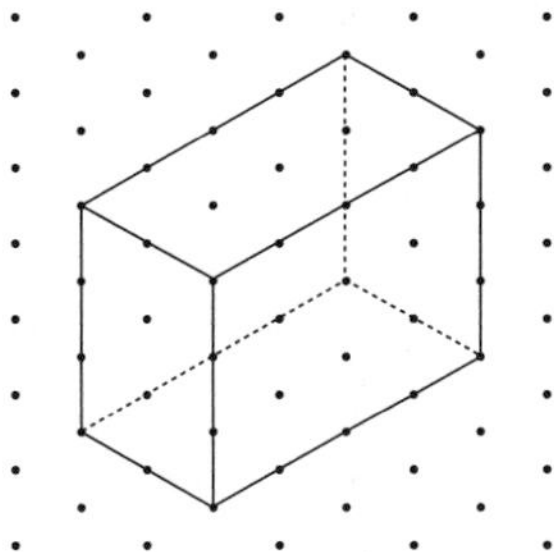

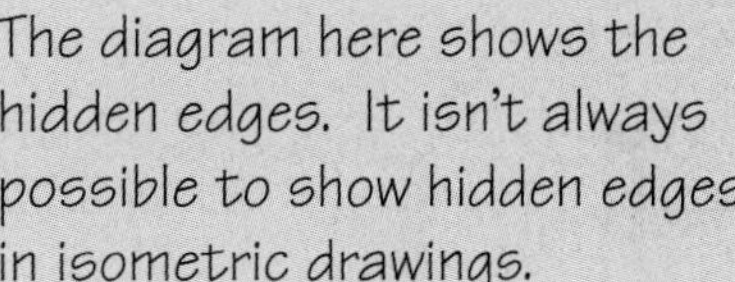

The diagram here shows the hidden edges. It isn't always possible to show hidden edges in isometric drawings.

Example This isometric drawing shows a shape made up by removing 8 small cubes from a large cube.

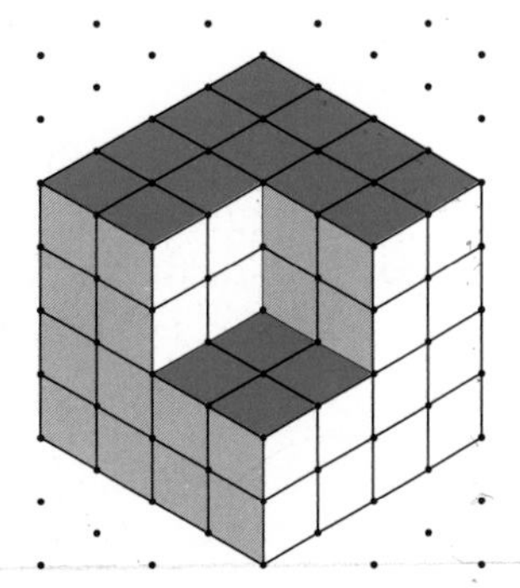

(a) How many small cubes make up the shape shown here?

(b) Draw the solid that has been removed.

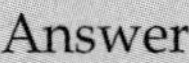

Answer (a) 56 (b)

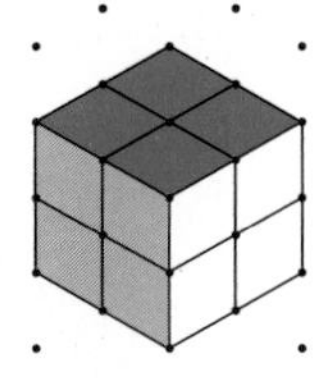

EXERCISE 20.2

*You will need several sheets of **isometric** paper for this exercise.*

1 Draw these shapes on isometric paper.

(a)

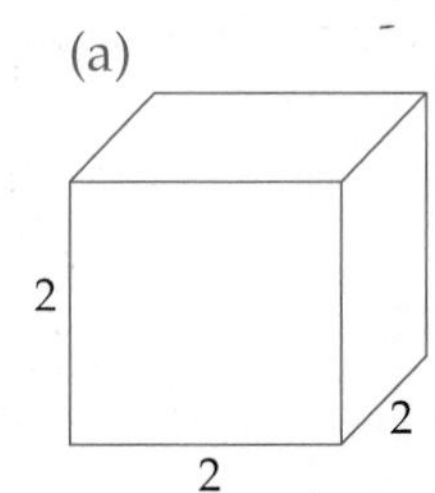

(b)

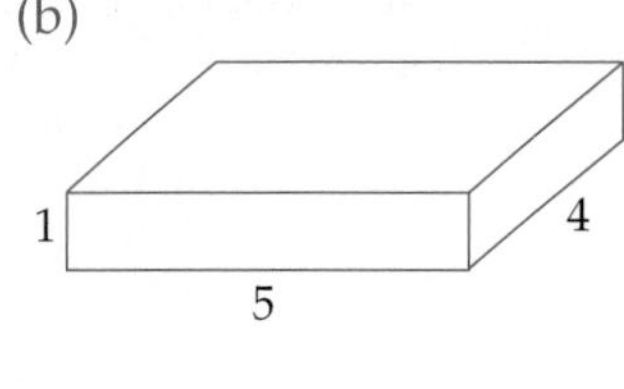

2 How many small cubes make up the shapes shown here?

(a)

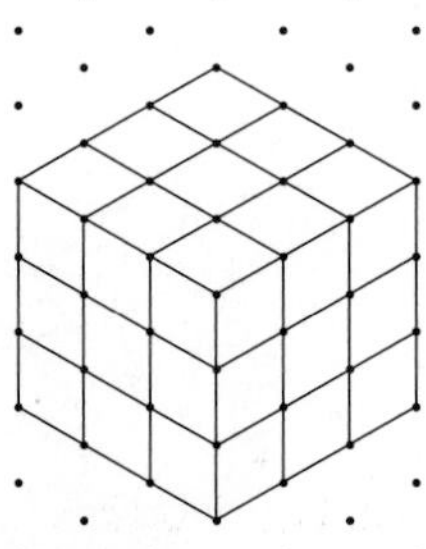

(c)

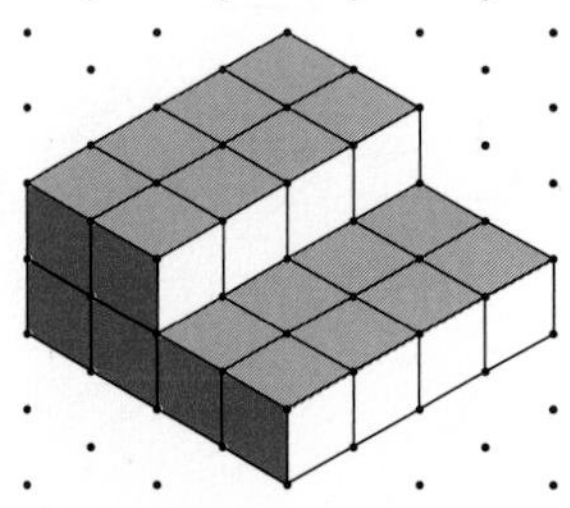

(b)

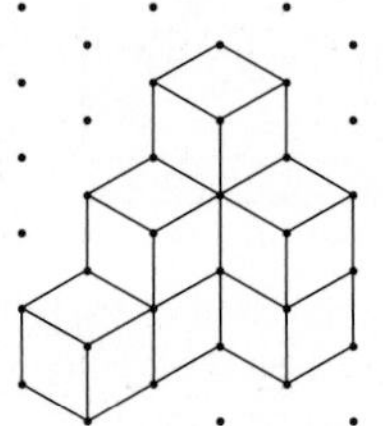

(d)

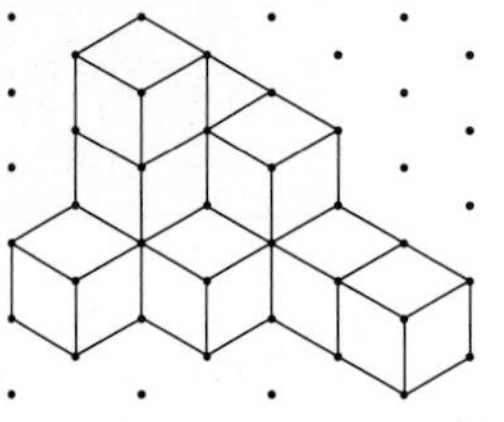

3 What would these shapes look like if the cubes marked with ∗ signs were removed? Use isometric paper to draw the new shapes.

(a)

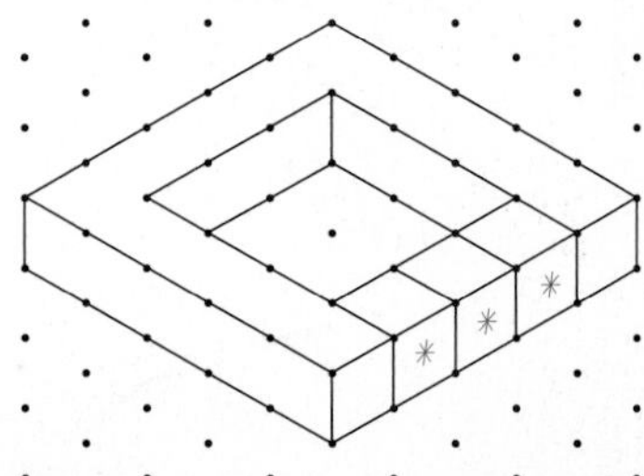

(b)

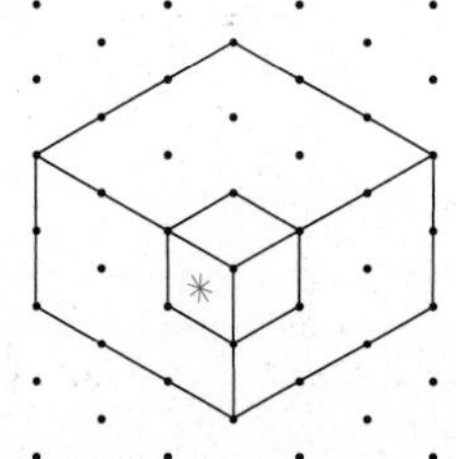

4 The cube marked A in this diagram will be moved and placed on top of the cube marked B. Make a drawing on an isometric grid to show the result.

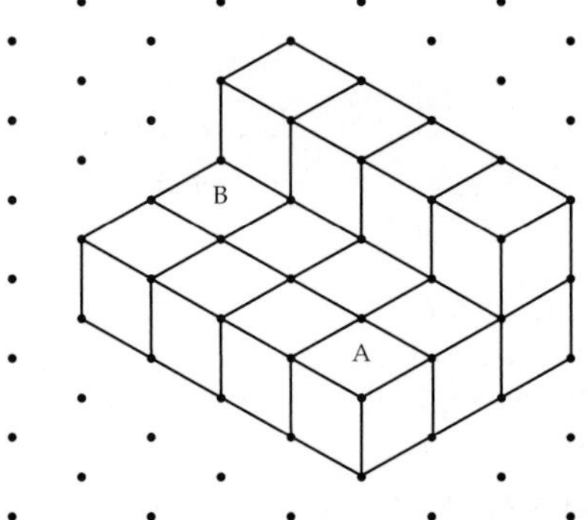

5 A furniture manufacturer makes up couches by working with foam-rubber cubes.

This diagram shows a '3-seater' couch.

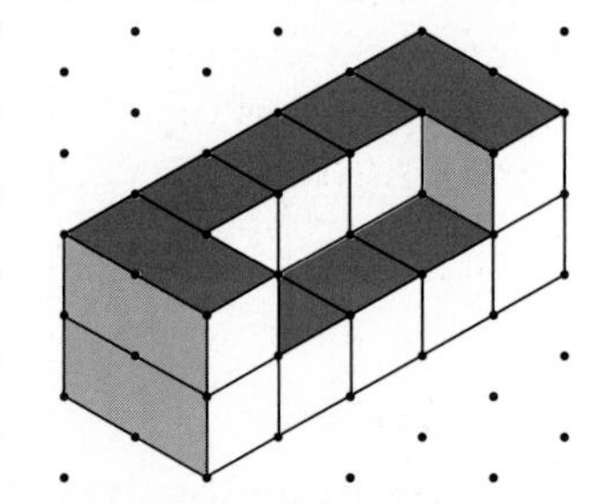

(a) How many cubes make up a '3-seater' couch?

(b) Draw a '4-seater' couch on an isometric grid.

(c) How many cubes would make up a '2-seater' couch?

6 Each of these solids is made up of 4 cubes.

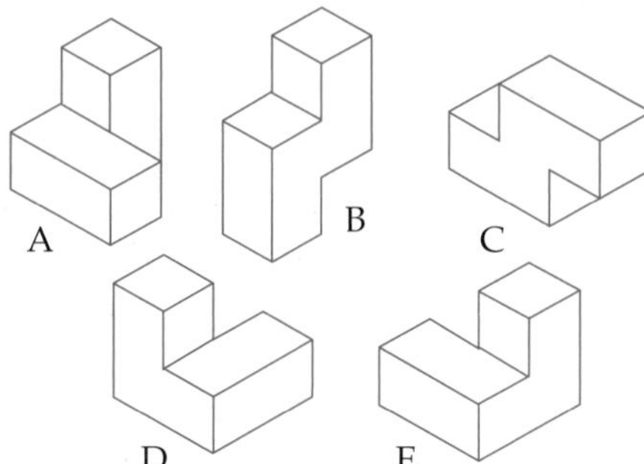

(a) Which solid is the same as B?

(b) Which solid is not the same as any others?

7 A designer is working with 3-dimensional models of letters of the alphabet. Here is the design of the letter 'L':

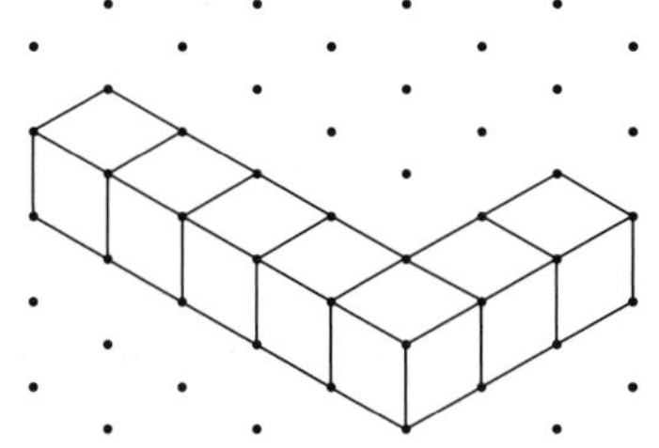

(a) Draw another design where the top of the L points to the right instead of the left. Part of the diagram has been drawn here to start you off.

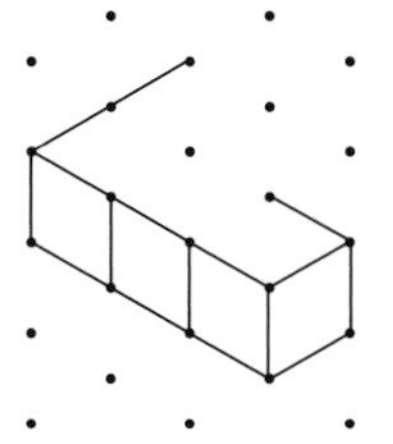

(b) Draw a design for the letter T.

(c) Draw a design for the letter E.

8 64 small cubes are glued together to form one large cube. How many of the 64 small cubes can still be seen?

9

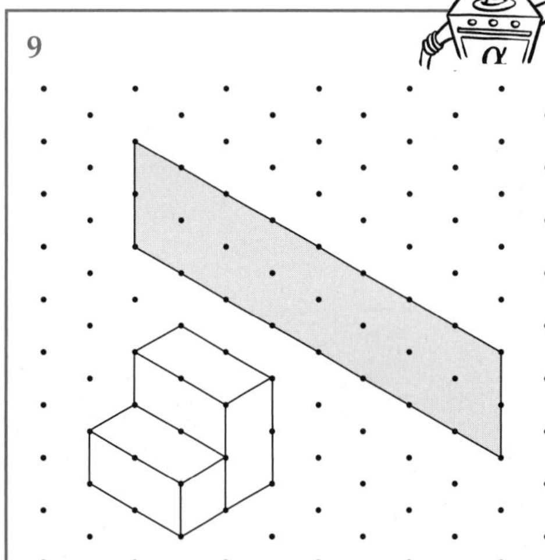

A mirror has been placed 3 units away from a shape. The mirror is parallel to one face of the shape. Copy the diagram. Add a drawing to show the reflection of the shape.

Nets

STARTER

Below is a plan for some vinyl liner to go inside a rectangular swimming pool. The pool measures 8 m by 6 m.

- Make a copy of this plan. Add four dashed lines to show where the vinyl would be folded.
- Mark two different points on this plan that will be in the same position after the vinyl has been folded and placed inside the pool.
- How deep is the pool?

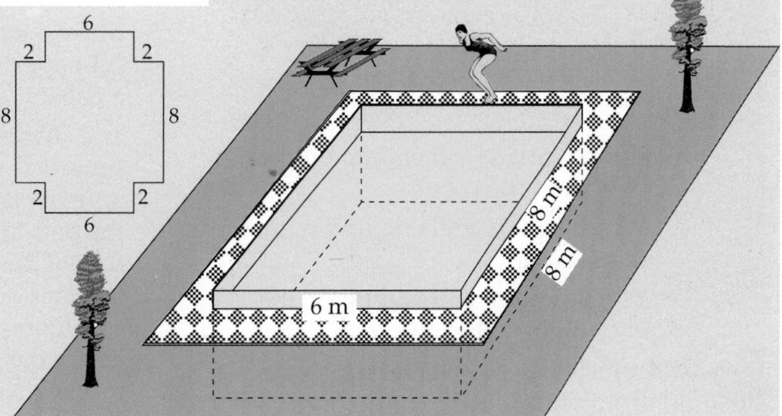

> A **net** of a solid is a plan that shows all the faces of the solid. It shows how the faces could be folded to make the shape.

Example This is the net of a cube.

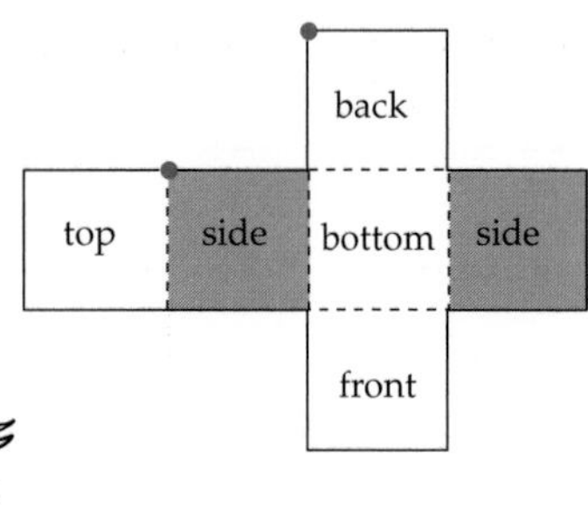

When the net is folded into position, it looks like this:

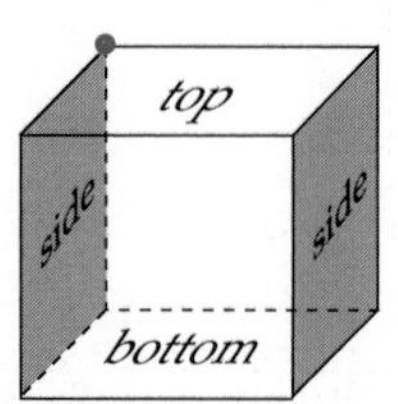

Notice how the two points marked with the large dot (•) end up in the same place on the completed cube.

A net shows the **minimum** amount of paper/canvas etc. needed to make up a solid shape. Often extra flaps of material (called **tabs**) would also be useful.

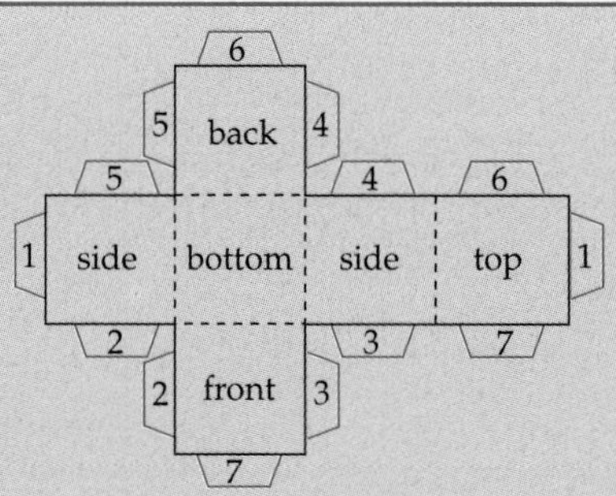

For example, the two tabs marked 3 join the cube together along the edge marked 3.

EXERCISE 20.3

1 Here is a drawing of a net, and the cube made when the net is folded. The six squares on the net have been numbered.

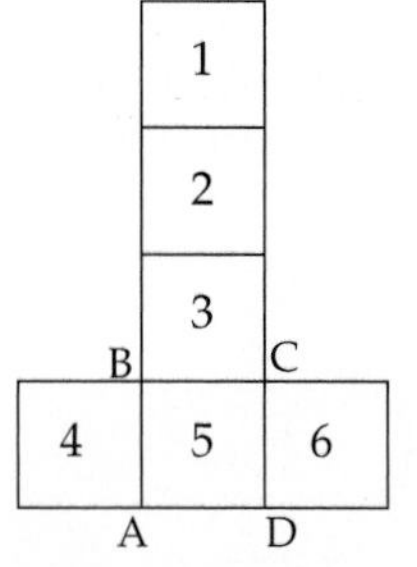

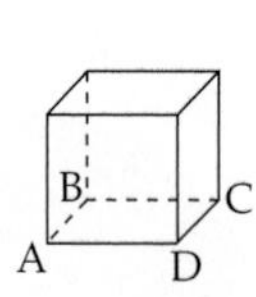

(a) Which square will end up on the bottom of the cube?

(b) Which square will end up on the top of the cube?

(c) Which square will end up on the back of the cube?

(d) Which square will end up on the front of the cube?

2 This is the net of a cube. Make a copy of it. Add the labels 'top', 'front' and 'side' (twice) to the diagram.

back
bottom

3 Make a large copy of this net on a piece of A4 paper. Cut your net out, and fold it into a cube.

The shaded square represents the bottom face of the cube. Which point will end up on the top face above the point marked X?

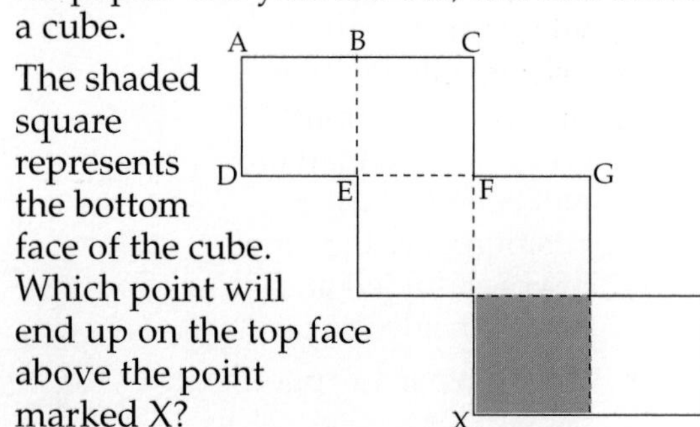

4 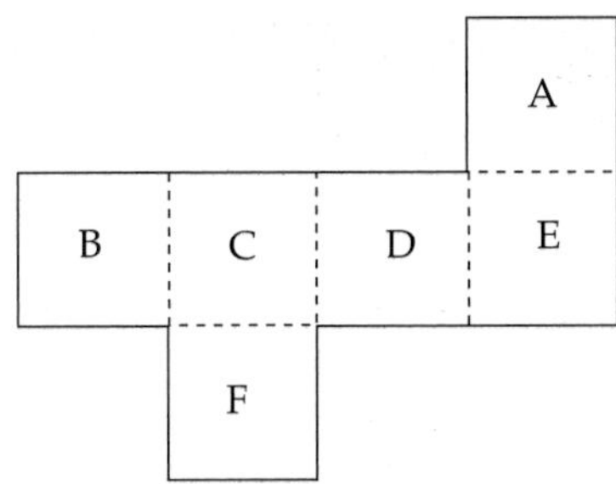

The six faces on this net have been labelled A, B, C, D, E and F. When the net is folded into a cube, there will be three pairs of opposite faces. Write down the labels for the face opposite:

(a) D

(b) E

(c) F

5 This cube has been labelled PQRSTUVW.

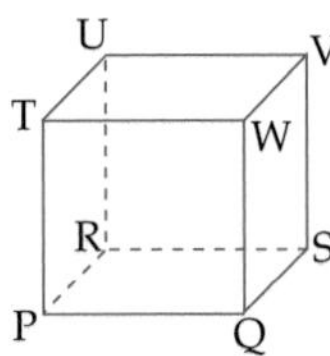

Here is the net for the cube. The square that will end up on the bottom is labelled PQRS.

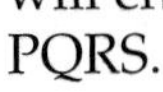

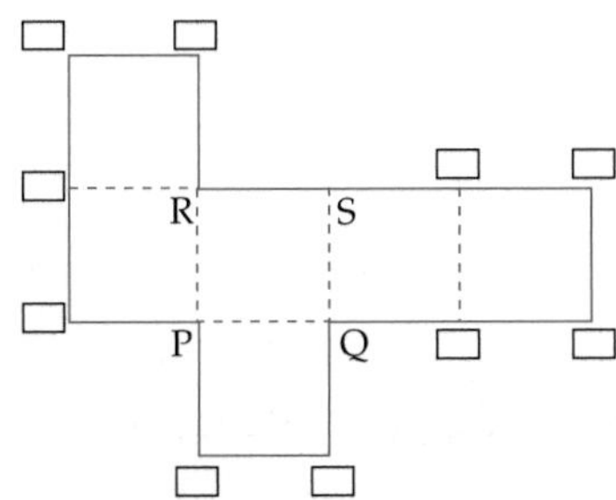

Copy the net. Add letters in each of the 10 boxes to show how the net will fold to make up the cube. Choose from { P, Q, R, S, T, U, V, W }.

6 Draw a net for this cuboid. The measurements are in cm.

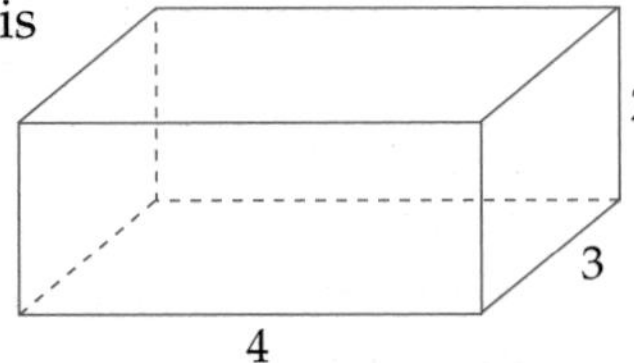

7 Draw a net for this tetrahedron. Each face is an equilateral triangle.

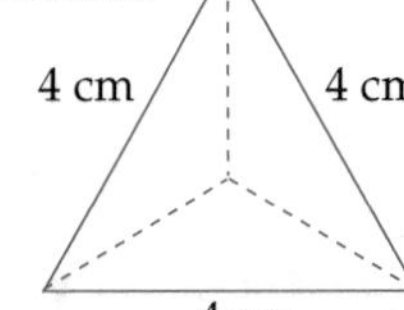

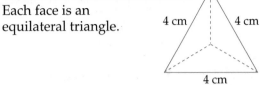

8 These nets fold into mathematical solids. Name the solids.

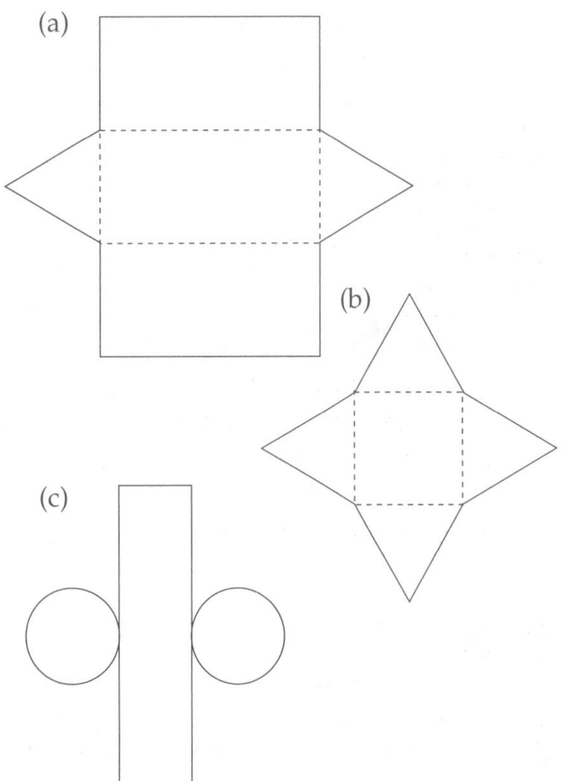

9 This is a net for a shape called a *dodecahedron*.

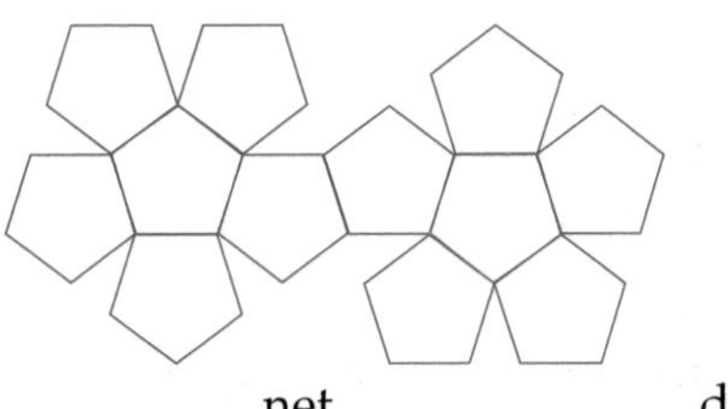

net

dodecahedron (front view)

(a) What shape is each face?

(b) How many faces does the dodecahedron have?

(c) How many faces meet at each vertex?

INVESTIGATION

THE ICOSAHEDRON

Take a large piece of paper or light cardboard. Draw this net on it.
Each triangle is equilateral.

Cut out the net and use it to construct a solid shape.

The solid is called an *icosahedron*.

- Write down as many facts about the faces, edges and vertices of an icosahedron as you can.

- Colour in the faces of your icosahedron.
- What is the smallest number of colours you will need if all faces that meet are different colours?

Views

STARTER

- How many $1 coins are shown here?

This plan shows how the coins in the photo are laid out.

This is an example of a **plan view.**
It shows the heights of different parts of a solid when viewed from above.

5	8
2	3

To calculate the total number of coins, we can *add* all the numbers in the plan view.

The same group of coins could also be viewed from in front, or from the side:

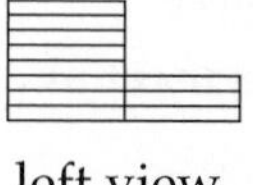

left view

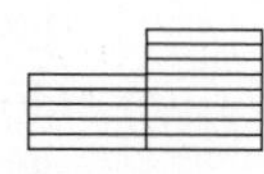

front view

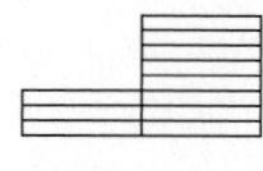

right view

Example Represent this solid by drawing:

(a) a plan view

(b) top, front and side views.

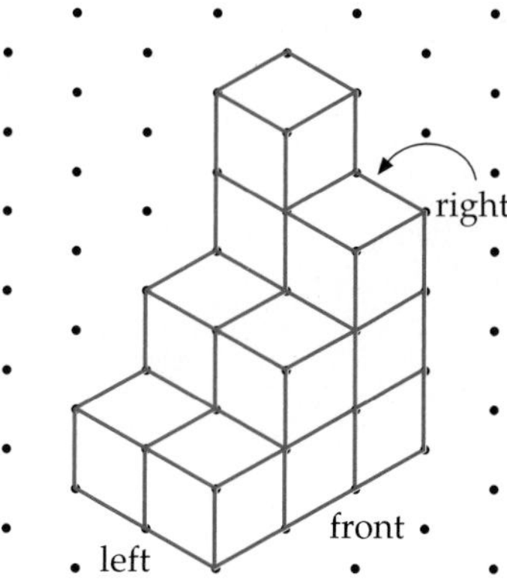

Answers (a)

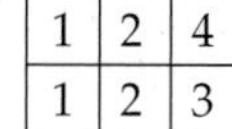

1	2	4
1	2	3

(b)

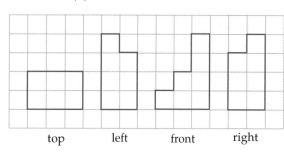

top left front right

EXERCISE 20.4

1 Examine this shape carefully.

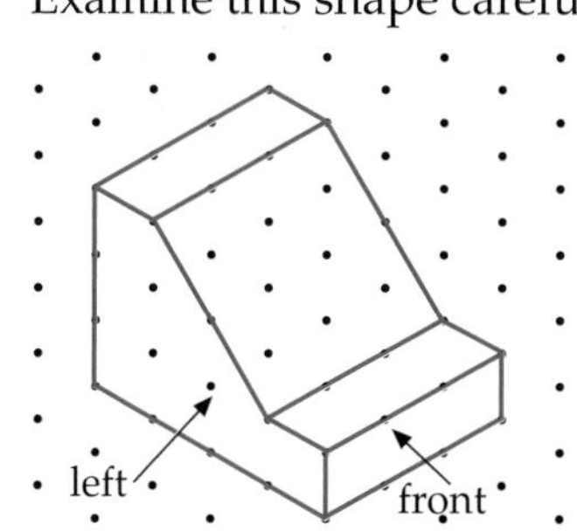

Here are three different views of it, labelled A, B and C.

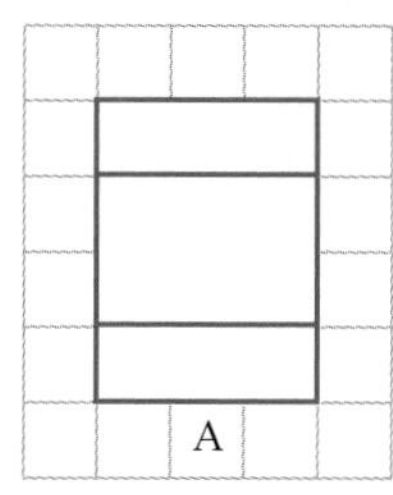

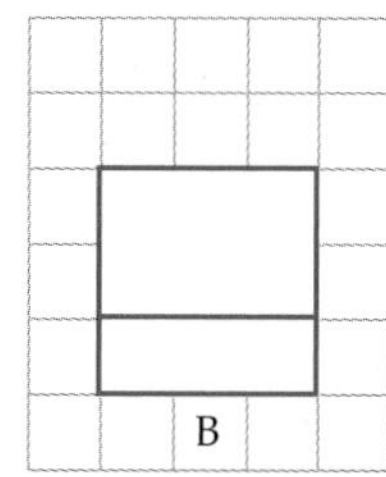

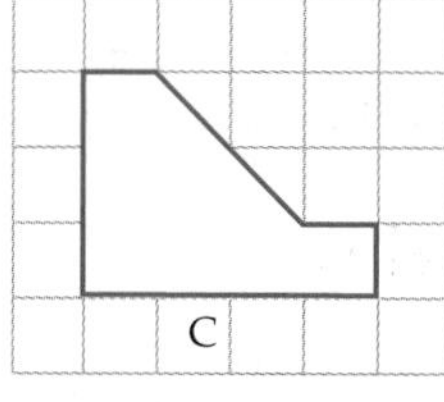

(a) Which view is the 'left' view?

(b) Which view is the 'top' view?

(c) Which view is the 'front' view?

(d) Draw a 'right' view for this shape.

2 Draw plan views of each of these solid shapes.

(a)

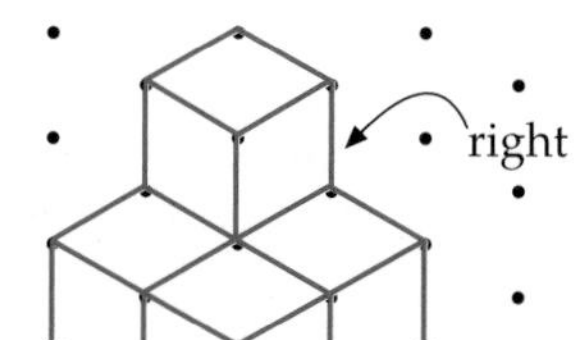

(b)

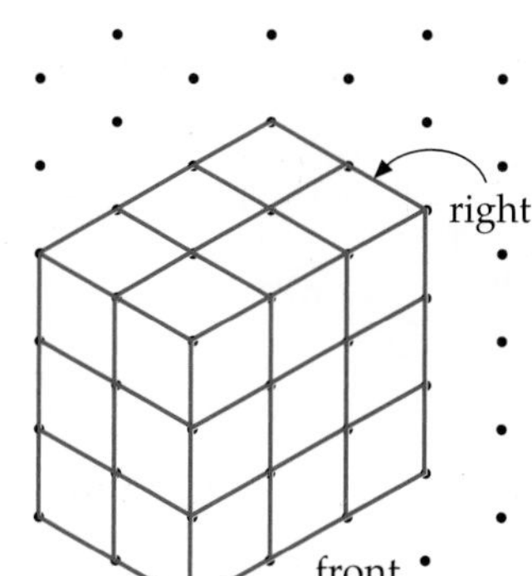

(c)

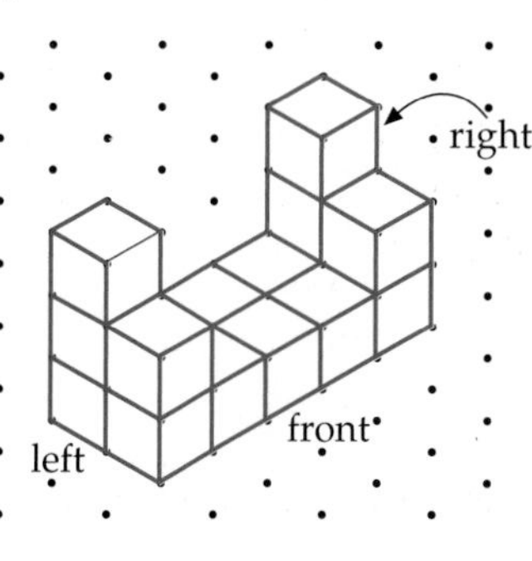

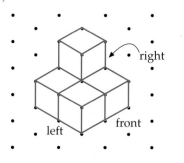

3 Draw top, front and side views for each of the shapes in Question 2.

4 Here are plan views of two shapes. Draw the front view and both side views for each one.

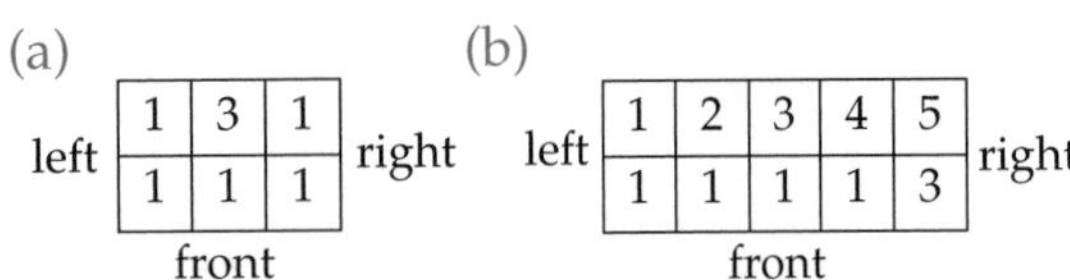

5 Use an isometric grid to draw the solids given by these plan views:

(a)

4	4
4	4

(b)

2	2
1	1

(c)

2	2
	1

6 Draw a plan view for the shapes given by these views:

(a)

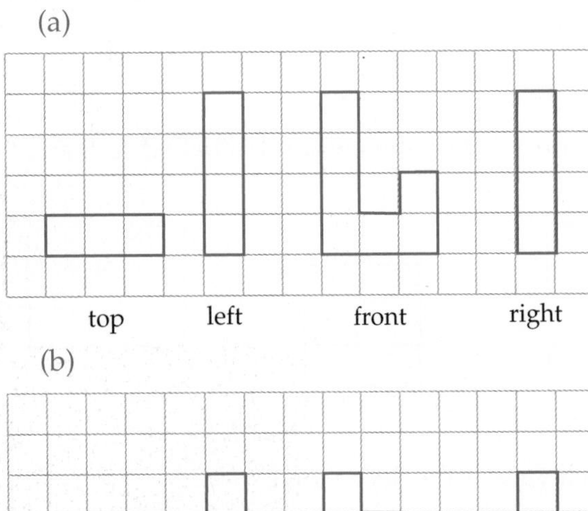

(b)

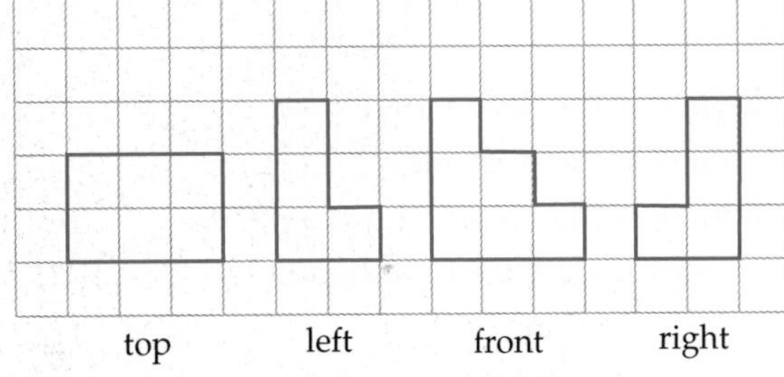

7 A furniture manufacturer makes up beds and couches from foam-rubber cubes.

This diagram shows a '3-seater' couch.

(a) Draw a plan view for this couch.

(b) A bed uses 8 foam-rubber cubes. Draw a plan view for a bed.

8 This is a part of a chart of Math Harbour, used by sailors. It shows the location of the wharf. The chart is a kind of plan view.

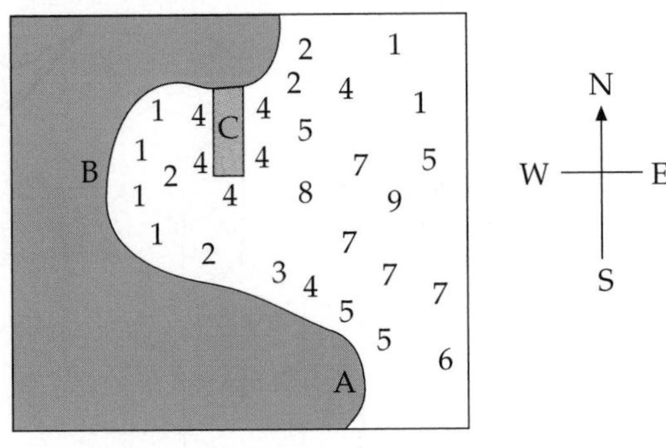

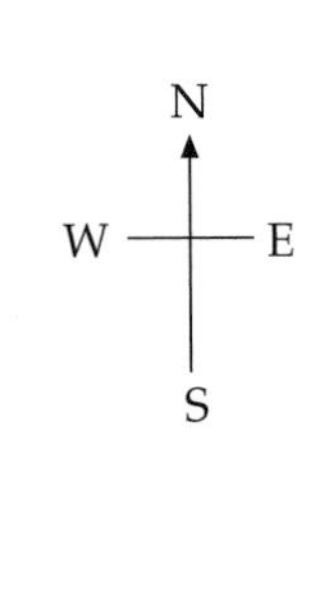

(a) Does the white part of the chart represent land or water?

(b) What do the numbers on the chart represent?

(c) Is the beach at Math Harbour most likely to be at A, B or C?

(d) What object is at the place marked C?

(e) The map shows the location of an underwater reef. Explain whether the reef is at the north or south entrance to Math Harbour.

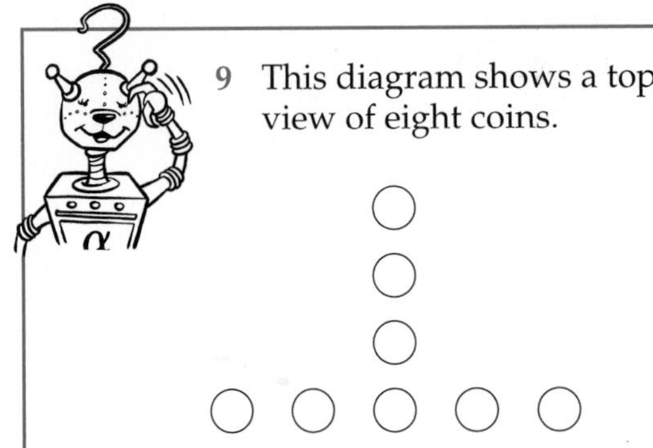

9 This diagram shows a top view of eight coins.

Show how to move one of these eight coins to make two lines of five coins.

21 Introducing expressions

STARTER

D, C, B, A; 2; x

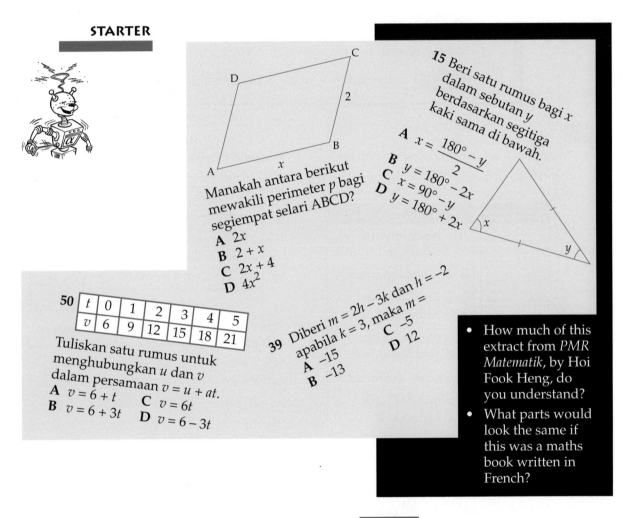

Manakah antara berikut mewakili perimeter p bagi segiempat selari ABCD?

A $2x$
B $2 + x$
C $2x + 4$
D $4x^2$

15 Beri satu rumus bagi x dalam sebutan y berdasarkan segitiga kaki sama di bawah.

A $x = \dfrac{180° - y}{2}$
B $y = 180° - 2x$
C $x = 90° - y$
D $y = 180° + 2x$

x, y

50

t	0	1	2	3	4	5
v	6	9	12	15	18	21

Tuliskan satu rumus untuk menghubungkan u dan v dalam persamaan $v = u + at$.

A $v = 6 + t$ **C** $v = 6t$
B $v = 6 + 3t$ **D** $v = 6 - 3t$

39 Diberi $m = 2h - 3k$ dan $h = -2$ apabila $k = 3$, maka $m =$

A −15 **C** −5
B −13 **D** 12

- How much of this extract from *PMR Matematik*, by Hoi Fook Heng, do you understand?
- What parts would look the same if this was a maths book written in French?

In Maths, we use **symbols** to represent *numbers*, *operations*, and *formulas*. It's important to understand how these are arranged.

It's useful to be able to explain mathematical ideas using words. However, it's equally important to be able to use symbols—such as numbers (e.g. 5), letters (e.g. x), and signs (e.g. +).

We often use x to represent some number in a mathematical calculation. Sometimes, we refer to the letter x as a **variable**.

Example $x + 4$ means 'a number with 4 added on'.
$x - 20$ means '20 less than x', or 'the result of taking away 20 from a number'.

Algebra is the language of mathematicians.

Multiplication and division

The two symbols × and ÷ are not used very often in algebra.

- We leave out a multiplication sign.

Example 5 lots of x, or $5 \times x$, is written as $5x$.

- Instead of writing a division sign, we use a fraction symbol.

Example x divided by 8, or $x \div 8$, is written as $\frac{x}{8}$

EXERCISE 21.1

1 Match each algebra expression with an English phrase from the box.

	Algebra
(a)	$x + 3$
(b)	$x - 2$
(c)	$5x$
(d)	$x + 5$
(e)	$2x$
(f)	$3x$
(g)	$x - 1$

English
A. a number with 2 subtracted from it
B. 2 times a number
C. a number with 5 added to it
D. a number with 1 subtracted from it
E. 5 times a number
F. a number with 3 added to it
G. 3 times a number

2 Write down algebra expressions for these English expressions.

(a) a number with 10 added to it

(b) a number with 15 subtracted from it

(c) a number multiplied by 4

(d) a number multiplied by 7

3 Write down the English expression for these algebra expressions.

(a) $6x$ (c) $x - 12$

(b) $x + 9$ (d) $5x$

4 For each English expression, write down an algebra expression chosen from the box.

(a) ten times a number

(b) a number divided by ten

(c) ten divided by a number

(d) ten more than a number

(e) ten less than a number

$x + 10$
$\frac{10}{x}$
$10x$
$x - 10$
$\frac{x}{10}$

5 Write down these expressions *without* using multiplication or division signs.

(a) $4 \times x$ (e) $p \times q$

(b) $x \div 6$ (f) $12 \times y$

(c) $20 \times x$ (g) $100 \div x$

(d) $x \div 30$ (h) $p \div q$

6 Write an equivalent algebraic expression for each of these:

(a) x take away 7

(b) 6 more than x

(c) 12 lots of x

(d) 10 less than x

(e) the number of cents in x dollars

(f) the number of days in x weeks

(g) the sum of p and q

7 Show the meaning of these expressions by including multiplication signs:

(a) $4p$ (c) pq

(b) $6p - 1$ (d) $2 + 3p$

Substitution

STARTER

One of the safety rules for a white-water rafting company is written this way:

> The number of life-jackets taken is always 3 more than the number of passengers

The rule can't be given more exactly than this, because the number of passengers on each trip varies.

The manager writes down this rule as:
Number of life-jackets = $x + 3$

- What does x stand for in this expression?
- If there are 11 passengers, what is the number of life-jackets that has to be taken?
- What is the value of $x + 3$ when $x = 16$?

In Maths, we often use a letter (such as x) to represent a number.

Example If $x = 7$, then $x + 3 = 10$
But if $x = 24$, then $x + 3 = 27$

The number represented by $x + 3$ depends on the value of x.

EXERCISE 21.2

1–15 *The value of x is 8. Calculate each of these expressions:*

1 $x + 2$
2 $x + 10$
3 $x + 27$
4 $x - 6$
5 $x - 8$
6 $x - 1$
7 $2 \times x$
8 $4 \times x$
9 $7 \times x$
10 $3x$
11 $10x$
12 $9x$
13 $x \div 4$
14 $\frac{x}{2}$
15 $\frac{x}{8}$

16 A car factory uses a rule to decide how many tyres it needs for its cars.

The rule is:

> Number of tyres = 5 × the number of cars

The manager writes down this rule as:
Number of tyres = $5x$

(a) What does x stand for in this expression?
(b) The factory is assembling 60 cars. How many tyres does it need?
(c) What is the value of $5x$ when $x = 40$?

17 The manager of a small office uses a rule to decide how many computers they need. The rule is:

> The number of computers we need is six less than the number of workers

This rule can also be written as:

Number of computers = $x - 6$

(a) What does x stand for in this expression?

(b) The office has 13 workers. How many computers should it have?

(c) What is the value of $x - 6$ when $x = 7$?

(d) Are there any values of x for which the rule does not work? Explain.

18 Wedding Breakfasts Ltd specialises in catering for receptions. First, they find out how many guests are invited. Then, they can decide how many tables to hire.

The rule is that each table seats four guests. For some values of x, this rule can be written as:

Number of tables = $\frac{x}{4}$

(a) What does x stand for in this rule?

(b) How many tables should be hired if there are 80 guests?

(c) What is the value of $\frac{x}{4}$ when $x = 100$?

(d) There are some values of x for which this rule does not work exactly. Describe these values. Explain what you would have to do to work out an answer.

Sometimes, an expression has more than one letter or *variable*.

Example The expression $x + y$ has two different variables. They can both be replaced by numbers.

Example $a = 7$ $b = 3$ $c = 5$
Calculate the value of $a + b + c + 17$.

Answer $a + b + c + 17 = 7 + 3 + 5 + 17 = 32$

EXERCISE 21.3

1–6 *Here, $a = 4$, $b = 5$, $c = 13$, $d = 28$. Calculate each of these expressions:*

1 $a + b$

2 $a + c + d$

3 $d + b$

4 $b - a$

5 $c - b$

6 $d - a$

7 An airline provides two types of dinner on a flight—chicken and fish.

The total number of meals served on the flight can be worked out using the rule $c + f$.

What is the value of $c + f$ when:

(a) $c = 41$ and $f = 35$?

(b) $c = 56$ and $f = 29$?

8 Sounds Unlimited use this rule to work out the number of CDs they sell each week:

> Number sold = Number in shop at start of week – Number in shop at end of week

They write down this rule as:

Number sold = $x - y$

(a) Explain what x stands for in this rule.

(b) Explain what y stands for in this rule.

(c) Calculate the value of $x - y$ when $x = 20$ and $y = 7$.

(d) Explain in words what you have worked out in part (c).

A rule can also show that two variables are multiplied.

Example $a \times b$ is written as ab

If $a = 4$ and $b = 7$, then $ab = a \times b = 4 \times 7 = 28$

EXERCISE 21.4

p = 3, *q* = 2 and *r* = 4. *Work out the following.*

1 $5p$	4 $5r$	7 pr	10 $6pq$
2 $2r$	5 $12p$	8 qr	11 $14r$
3 $6q$	6 pq	9 pqr	12 $15pq$

Simplifying algebraic expressions

Multiplying

There are two ways we can show multiplication:

- with a 'times' symbol (×)
- by placing the letters, or number and letter, next to each other.

In algebra we normally write a multiplication without the × symbol if we can. This is called **simplifying** the expression.

Example Each of these are equivalent:

Using the × symbol	Simplified
$2 \times x$	$2x$
$p \times q$	pq

Here are the rules for writing multiplication expressions as simply as possible:

Rule	Example
• Any numbers in the expression are multiplied	$4 \times 2x = 8x$
• If there is more than one letter, they are written in alphabetical order	$3d \times 5c = 15cd$
• Numbers are placed in front of letters when multiplying	$p \times 2q = 2pq$

The number 1 is not usually written in. For example, $1p$ is just written as p.

EXERCISE 

Simplify these expressions:

1 $4 \times 3x$	6 $7 \times 2x$	11 $2a \times 4b$	16 $3 \times 2a \times 5$
2 $2 \times 5x$	7 $b \times a$	12 $q \times 2p \times 3r$	17 $1 \times 10q \times 1$
3 $a \times c$	8 $4c \times 2d$	13 $f \times 2d \times 5e$	18 $2 \times 4p \times 2q \times r$
4 $3 \times p$	9 $2g \times 3f$	14 $3r \times q \times 2p$	19 $4a \times b \times 2c$
5 $1 \times d$	10 $p \times 2a$	15 $4d \times 2c \times e$	20 $q \times r \times p$

Adding or subtracting algebraic expressions

STARTER

- What is the value of $4 + 4 + 4 + 4 + 4 + 4 + 4$?
- Explain whether there is more than one way of working this out.

- What is the value of $x + x + x$ when $x = 20$?
- What is the value of $3x$ when $x = 20$?

- Will $x + x + x$ always have the same value as $3 \times x$?
- Which is simpler to write down: $x + x + x$ or $3x$?

Examples $x + x + x + x = 4x$ (because there are 4 lots of x)

$6x - x = 5x$

EXERCISE 21.6

1–6 *Write these expressions as simply as possible:*

1 $p + p$

2 $r + r + r + r$

3 $x + x + x + x$

4 $q + q + q + q + q + q$

5 $x + x + x$

6 $y + y + y + y + y$

7–12 *Write these expressions as simply as possible:*

7 $x + 2x$

8 $5x + x$

9 $6x + 2x$

10 $2y + 3y$

11 $5p + p$

12 $10x + 6x$

13–18 *Simplify these expressions by subtracting:*

13 $6x - 4x$

14 $10x - 7x$

15 $7p - 6p$

16 $11x - x$

17 $5x - 4x$

18 $20x - 19x$

19–24 *Simplify:*

19 $x + x + 2x$

20 $3x + x + 6x$

21 $2x + 3x + 4x$

22 $x + 8x + x$

23 $12p + p + 2p$

24 $8q + 3q + 9q$

25–30 *Simplify these expressions by adding and subtracting:*

25 $12x + 8x - 5x$

26 $x + 5x + 4x + 2x$

27 $6x + 3x - x$

28 $6p - 5p + p$

29 $3x + 2x - x + 8x$

30 $4x - 2x - x + 5x$

Like and unlike terms

Like terms are ones including exactly the same letter or combination of letters.

Examples Like terms: $2x, 3x, 31x$ Unlike terms: $2x, 3$

$4ab, 3ab$ $5p, 6q$

EXERCISE 21.7

1 Write down the like terms from each group:

(a) $\{6x, 9x, 8y\}$

(b) $\{5p, 4q, 3p, 5r\}$

(c) $\{x, 2y, 3x\}$

(d) $\{2p, 4q, q\}$

(e) $\{6a, b, 6c, 6d, 4b\}$

(f) $\{2x, 3y, y, 4y, 8z\}$

2 Write down the like terms in each expression:

(a) $2x + 3y + 6x$

(b) $4b + 6b + 2a$

(c) $2q - 4p + 8p$

(d) $x + 2y + 3x$

(e) $3x + 7y - z + 2x$

(f) $c + 3d + 5e - 2c$

Example $5p + 3q - 4p$ has like terms $5p$ and $4p$

3 For each of the following pairs of terms, say whether they are *like* or *unlike*.

(a) $2a, 5a$

(b) $3c, 2p$

(c) $14p, 23p$

(d) $4x, 4y$

(e) $r, 2r$

(f) $14r, 7$

(g) $15, ^{-}22$

(h) $3c, 6cd$

(i) $15pqr, pqr$

Simplifying expressions that have unlike terms

STARTER

Joanne and Leanne are planning a trip to the beach.

Joanne will take 8 cans of drink, and 3 towels.

Leanne will take 5 cans of drink, and 4 towels.

One of them writes this expression down on a piece of paper as a reminder to herself:

Mustn't forget! $5d + 4t$

- Which person does this expression (that is, $5d + 4t$) refer to?
- Write down a similar expression for the other person.
- How many cans of drink will they take altogether?
- How many towels will they take altogether?
- Suggest how you could write $5d + 4t + 8d + 3t$ more simply.
- Is it possible to add terms that have d and t, and get a sensible answer?

Some expressions have a mixture of terms that are **like** and **unlike**.

- Like terms can be collected or grouped together. They can then be added or subtracted to simplify them.
- When all the terms in a sum are unlike, no further simplification can be done.

Examples (a) $4r + 8r = 12r$

Both terms are like and can be added.

(b) $3p + 7q + 2p + 5q = (3p + 2p) + (7q + 5q)$

$= 5p + 12q$

The pairs of p and q terms can be simplified.
$5p + 12q$ can't be simplified further, because the p and q terms are unlike.

(c) $6x + 2 + 3x = (6x + 3x) + 2$

$= 9x + 2$

The x terms are like, and can be added.
$9x$ and 2 are unlike terms, so $9x + 2$ can't be simplified further.

EXERCISE 21.8

1–10 *Simplify these expressions, by collecting like terms together and adding them.*

1 $4x + 3y + 2x + 5y$

2 $6p + 2q + 2p + 3q$

3 $4x + 5x + 2y + 3y$

4 $10p + 7q + p + q$

5 $x + 2y + 3y + x$

6 $4x + y + 3x$

7 $12x + 3x + 7y$

8 $p + 2q + 3q$

9 $3a + 4b + b + 5b$

10 $x + 3x + 2y + 2x$

11 (a) Copy this table. Then complete it to show what happens when $x = 4$, $x = 6$ and $x = 11$.

	$2x + 3 + 5x + 7$	$7x + 10$
$x = 4$	$2 \times 4 + 3 + 5 \times 4 + 7$ $= 8 + 3 + 20 + 7$ $= ....$	$7 \times 4 + 10 = ...$
$x = 6$		
$x = 11$		

(b) What do you notice about the final results?

(c) Simplify $2x + 3 + 5x + 7$.

12–20 *Simplify:*

12 $2x + 5 + 2x + 1$

13 $6x + 2 + 2x + 3$

14 $5x + 3 + 10 + 2x$

15 $4x + 2x + 2$

16 $2x + 1 + 5x$

17 $x + 8 + 2x + 1$

18 $4x + 3x + 2 + 8$

19 $18 + x + 3x + 4$

20 $x + 1 + 9x + x$

21 One side of a triangle is 2 cm longer than the other two sides, which are each marked x.

(a) Write down, as simply as possible, an expression for the *perimeter* (total length of the sides).

(b) Calculate the perimeter if the value of x is 5 cm.

22 (a) Write down, as simply as possible, an expression for the *perimeter* of this quadrilateral. The lengths are in cm.
(b) If the value of p is 2 cm, calculate the perimeter.
(c) What is the length of the longest side of the quadrilateral?

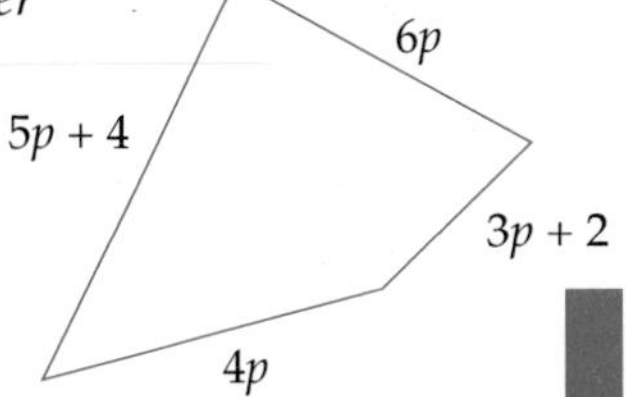

Simplifying expressions using addition *and* subtraction

Some expressions have a mixture of adding and subtracting. The '+' and '–' signs go with the terms on their right.

Example Simplify $6x + 2y - 4x + 5y$.

Answer Collect together the like x terms and the like y terms:

$6x + 2y - 4x + 5y = (6x - 4x) + (2y + 5y)$

The brackets show how the like terms are grouped.

$= 2x + 7y$

EXERCISE 21.9

Simplify these expressions, by collecting together like terms and adding or subtracting them.

1 $4x + 5y - 2x + 3y$

2 $6x + 8y - x - 5y$

3 $4x + 8 - x + 2$

4 $11x + 6 - 9x - 5$

5 $6x + 9y - 7y - 4x$

6 $10x + 3y - 6x$

7 $14c - 2c + 3d$

8 $5r + 4 - 2r + 11$

9 $4x - 3x + 8y - 7y$

10 $2x + 3x + 5x - 10$

11 $4c - c + 2$

12 $12x - 8x - x + 2$

13 $13x + 2y - 4x$

14 $8x + 2y + x - y$

15 $32 + 18p + 15 - 6p$

16 $6x + 14 - x - 5$

17 $15e + 3f - 2f - 14e$

18 $3c + 4c + 17 - 15 + c$

19 $y + 2y + 8 - 7 + y$

20 $6x - 5x - 1$

22 Formulas and patterns

Algebra gives us rules that explain relationships and show how to calculate quantities.

Formulas

A **formula** is a mathematical rule that explains how to calculate some quantity.

Let's look at two formulas used with squares.
Both formulas use the letter x for the side length.

	Formula 1	Formula 1
Here is the rule:	The **perimeter** of the square is four times the side length	The **area** of the square can be calculated by multiplying the side length by itself
We can write this using a formula:	$P = 4x$	$A = x \times x$
The formula shows how to calculate the result. We *substitute* the side length into the formula:	If $x = 6$ cm, then $P = 4 \times 6 = 24$ cm	If $x = 6$ cm, then $A = 6 \times 6 = 36\text{ cm}^2$

EXERCISE 22.1

1 My parents found the formula:

$f = a + 2$

gave them the right number of friends to invite to my birthday party each year. f is the number of friends, and a is my age.

(a) How many friends should have been invited to my 8th birthday party?

(b) How many friends should have been invited to my 5th birthday party?

2 The distance (in km) that a Boeing 747 can fly in h hours is given by this formula:

$d = 900h$

Use the formula to calculate the distance it can fly in:

(a) 2 hours
(b) 5 hours
(c) 6 hours
(d) $5\frac{1}{2}$ hours

3 $C = 2n + 3$

Calculate the value of C when:

(a) $n = 4$
(b) $n = 1$
(c) $n = 6$
(d) $n = 20$

4 This bag contains an unknown number of sweets. We will call this number x.

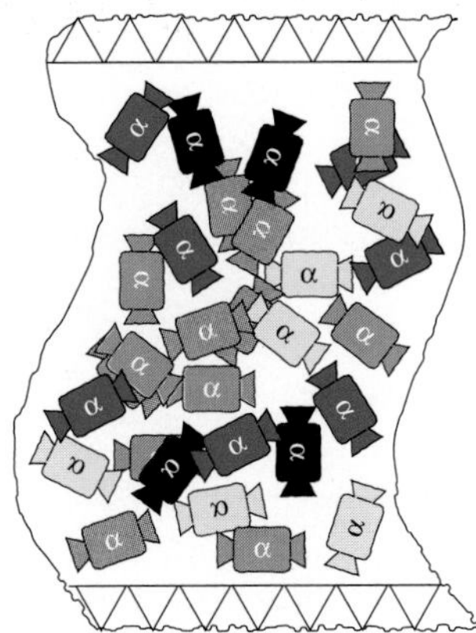

(a) 10 sweets are removed from the bag. How many sweets will still be in the bag?

(b) 6 sweets are added to a new bag. How many sweets will there be in the bag?

(c) You have bought 5 of these bags of sweets. How many sweets do you have altogether?

5 A lawnmowing contractor earns a basic wage of \$200 a week, and an extra \$6 for every lawn he mows.

His weekly wages (W) are given by the formula:

$$W = 6n + 200$$

n is the number of lawns he mows.

How much money does he earn in a week in which he mows:

(a) 10 lawns? (c) 25 lawns?

(b) 20 lawns? (d) no lawns?

6 A plumber uses the formula:

$$C = 40 + 50t$$

to calculate how much to charge for a job. In the formula, t stands for the number of hours worked on the job.

Calculate the charge for jobs with these hours worked:

(a) 2 hours (b) 1 hour (c) $\frac{1}{2}$ hour

7 A hotel pays a live-in porter \$10 an hour. Each week, the hotel deducts \$90 for living expenses. The porter's weekly earnings are given by the formula:

$$E = 10h - 90$$

(a) What does the h represent in this formula?

(b) Calculate the porter's earnings for a week in which 40 hours were worked.

8 This formula gives the number of strands of wire that are needed in a fence with n posts:

$$s = 5n - 5$$

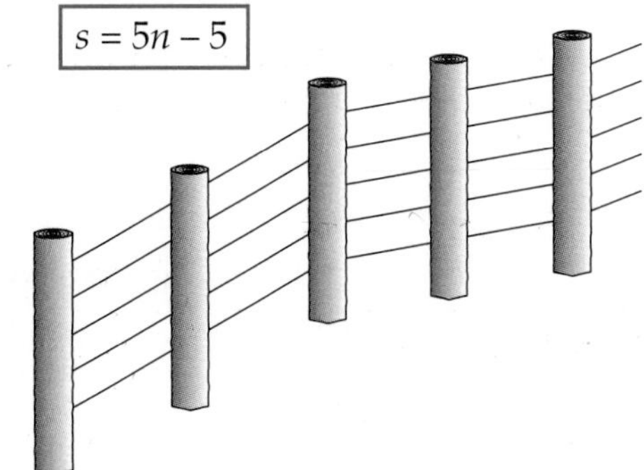

The formula says:
to work out the number of strands

- take the number of posts
- multiply by 5
- then subtract 5 from the result.

(a) Calculate s when $n = 3$.

(b) A fence has 10 posts. How many strands of wire will the fence have?

(c) Explain what happens if you substitute $n = 1$ into this formula.

(d) Howard substitutes $n = 4.2$, and gets a result of 16 for s. Is it sensible to substitute a number like 4.2 into this formula? Explain.

INVESTIGATION

THE RULE OF 72

The Rule of 72 has been used by banks and financial advisers for a long time. It gives a good indication of how long it will take to double money you have invested.

> **The Rule of 72**
>
> To work out the number of years it takes for money to double, divide 72 by the interest rate

If the interest rate is 6%, it will take you about 12 years to double your money.
If the interest rate is only 4%, it will take about 18 years.

- How long will it take you to double your money if the interest rate is 9%?
- How long if the interest rate is 12%?
- Write the Rule of 72 as a formula. Use y for the number of years, and r for the interest rate.

More than one variable

So far, we have only substituted one value into a formula to work out the result. Formulas where more than one value is substituted are handled in the same way.

STARTER

If you have done some work on area already, you probably know how to calculate the area of a triangle. *Two* measurements are needed—the length of the base, and the height.

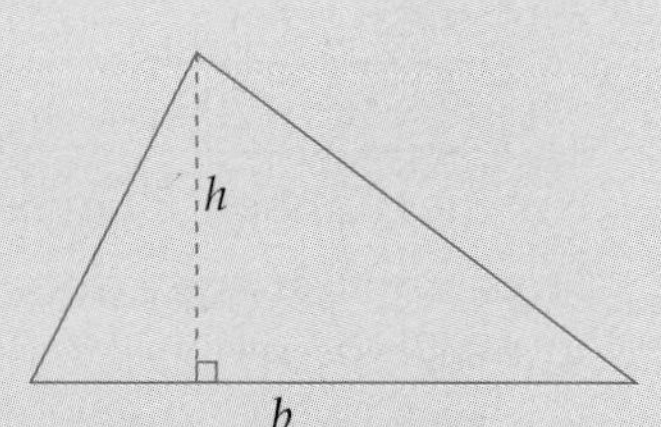

The rule is: to calculate the area, multiply the base length by the height, and divide by 2.

As a formula, we write this as $A = \frac{b \times h}{2}$ or just $A = \frac{bh}{2}$

- Why do you think we chose to use the letters b and h in this formula?
- How does the formula show we divide by 2?

Example Calculate the area of this triangle.

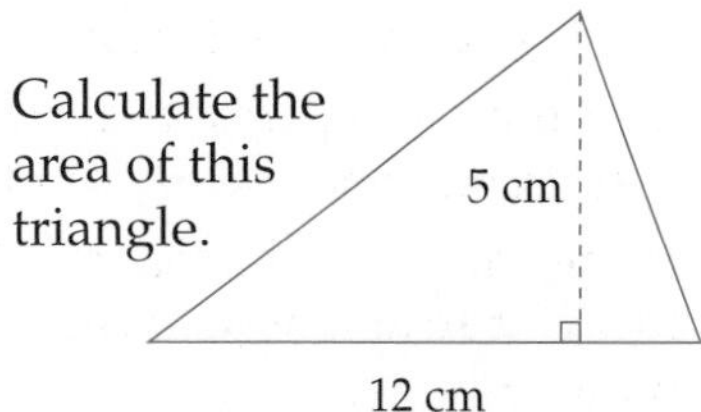

Answer The base length is 12 cm, so we take $b = 12$

The height is 5 cm, so we take $h = 5$

Then *substitute* into the formula $A = \frac{bh}{2}$

$$A = \frac{bh}{2} = \frac{12 \times 5}{2} = \frac{60}{2} = 30 \text{ cm}^2$$

EXERCISE 22.2

1 Here are some statements in words. They give rules for solving problems. Choose the matching formula from the box, and write it down for statements (a) to (f).

Choose a formula from this list
$A = bh$
$p = \ell + 2$
$n = 4t$
$C = 2a$
$s = \frac{d}{t}$
$C = b + g$

(a) The number of wheel nuts on a car is found by multiplying the number of tyres by 4.

(b) The average speed of a car is calculated by dividing the distance it has travelled by the time it has taken.

(c) The number of children in a family is the number of boys added to the number of girls.

(d) The area of a rectangle is calculated by multiplying the base by the height.

(e) A driver needs a parking space that measures 2 m more than the length of their car.

(f) Avocados sell for \$2 each. The total cost is \$2 times the number bought.

2 Here are some rules. Write them as formulas. Use the green letters in each one as your variables.

(a) The **n**umber of people on an aircraft = the number of **c**rew plus the number of **p**assengers.

(b) A **s**on's age = his **f**ather's age minus 24.

(c) The number of **w**heels in a bike rack = 2 times the number of **b**icycles.

(d) The **c**ost of petrol per litre = the **a**mount paid divided by the **n**umber of litres bought.

3 The formula for the time a cyclist takes for a journey is $t = \frac{d}{s}$.
d is the distance of the journey, and s is the average speed.

Use the formula to complete these sentences:

(a) When d = 60 km and s = 20 km/h, t = ... hours.

(b) When d = 50 km and s = 25 km/h, t = ... hours

4 A zoo uses this formula to calculate the cost of entrance (in dollars) for groups of adults and children. a stands for the number of adults in the group, and c stands for the number of children.

$$E = 12a + 4c$$

Calculate the cost of entrance for these groups:

(a) 2 adults and 1 child

(b) 3 adults and 7 children

(c) 6 adults

5

The PV2 rule helps town-planners decide if a pedestrian crossing is needed on a road.

This rule takes two factors into account:

- the number of pedestrians crossing the road in one hour. Use p for this number.
- the number of vehicles travelling along the road in one hour. Use v for this number.

Then multiply p by v by v. If the result is greater than 100 000 000, then a pedestrian crossing is needed.

(a) Copy and complete this table for each of these roads.

	Number of pedestrians p	**Number of vehicles v**	**Result of $p \times v \times v$**
Algebra Drive	350	500	
Bracket Road	200	600	
Calculator Street	60	1500	

(b) In which road is a pedestrian crossing justified?

6 Jupiter Cable Ltd supplies Internet services and pay-for-view movies to homes. They charge:

- 85 cents per day for *unlimited* Internet access
- \$4.50 per movie.

They use this formula to calculate the monthly charges (in dollars) to each home:

$C = 0.85d + 4.5m$

(a) Suggest what the letter d represents in this formula.

(b) Calculate the monthly charges to a family in June (30 days). The family watched four movies from Jupiter Cable in this month.

(c) Jupiter Cable decided to change their charges to 95 cents a day for Internet access and \$3 for each movie. Write down the new formula for their monthly charges.

INVESTIGATION

SILLY WALKS

This investigation is about using a formula to calculate the speed, or rate, at which people move.

The formula is $s = \frac{d}{t}$

- Explain in words what this formula tells you to do with a distance and a time.

- Mark out a distance of 40 metres (that's 4000 cm) in a straight line, as accurately as possible.
- Use a stop-watch to time how many seconds each of these takes:
  —speed at which a person walks normally
  —speed at which a person runs as fast as possible
  —speed at which a person moves when 'heeling and toeing'
- Use the formula to calculate the speed for each one.

Sequence patterns

STARTER

The motorway in this picture has five lanes.
The lanes are divided by white dashed lines. There are four of these divider lines on this motorway.

- Copy this table. Complete it to show how many divider lines are needed to mark the different numbers of lanes.

Number of lanes	1	2	3	4	5	6
Number of divider lines needed					4	

- Explain, in words, how you work out the number of divider lines when you know the number of lanes.

Suppose the number of lanes is n.

- Write down a formula for d, the number of divider lines. Write it as: $d = ...$
- Does it make sense to substitute the following numbers into the formula? Explain.

  (a) $2\frac{1}{2}$ (b) 3.7 (c) 0
- Describe the kinds of numbers that *can* be substituted into the formula.

Some formulas in Maths only work for counting numbers.
The counting numbers start at 1.

Counting numbers = { 1, 2, 3, 4, 5, 6, ... }

Many patterns in Maths can be described using formulas involving counting numbers.

A list like this is often called a **sequence.**
Here is another sequence:
1, 4, 9, 16, 25, 36, ...
These are the results of putting the counting numbers into the formula $n \times n$.

Example

This pattern can be described by writing down the numbers 1, 3, 5, 7, 9
It can also be described using algebra. The formula is $2n - 1$

The next (6th) shape in the pattern will have 11 dots.
This can be calculated by substituting $n = 6$ into the formula:
$2n - 1$ is $2 \times 6 - 1 = 12 - 1 = 11$

EXERCISE 22.3

1–6 *Write down the next two numbers in each of these patterns:*

1 1, 2, 3, 4, 5, 6, __ , __

2 4, 6, 8, 10, 12, 14, __ , __

3 1, 3, 5, 7, 9, 11, __ , __

4 2, 5, 8, 11, 14, 17, __ , __

5 1, 6, 11, 16, 21, 26, __ , __

6 25, 22, 19, 16, 13, 10, __ , __

7–12 *Draw the next shape in each of these patterns. Underneath the shape you have drawn, write in the number that goes with it.*

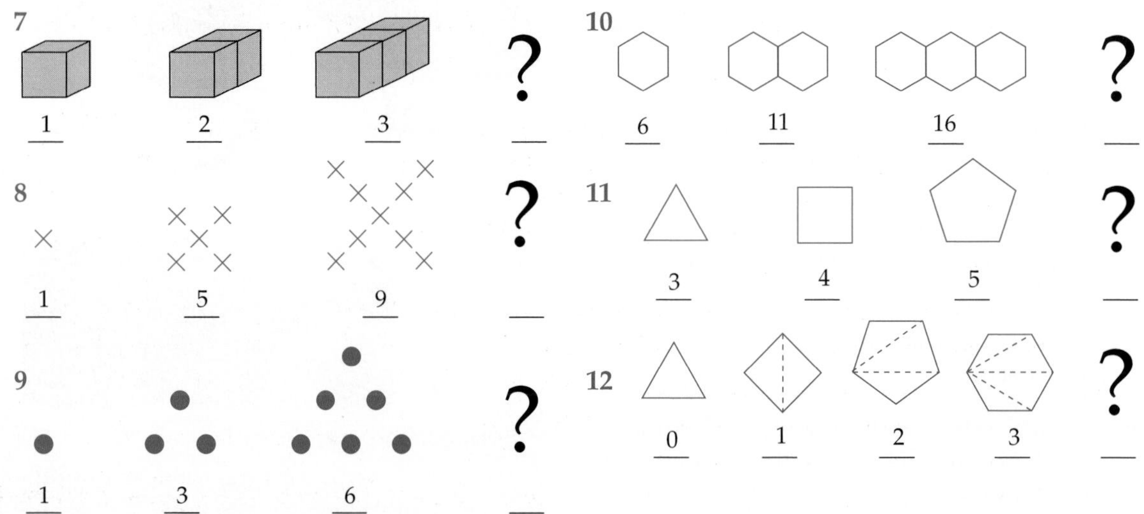

13–18 *Substitute the numbers 1, 2, 3 and 4 into each of these rules. Then write down the first four terms of the number sequences.*

Example $3n - 2$

$n = 1$	$n = 2$	$n = 3$	$n = 4$
$3 \times \mathbf{1} - 2 = 1$	$3 \times \mathbf{2} - 2 = 4$	$3 \times \mathbf{3} - 2 = 7$	$3 \times \mathbf{4} - 2 = 10$

Sequence is: 1, 4, 7, 10

13 $6 \times n$

14 $n + 8$

15 $4n$

16 $n - 1$

17 $2n - 1$

18 $4n + 1$

EXERCISE 22.4

1 These regular hexagons have side lengths of 1 cm, 2 cm and 3 cm.

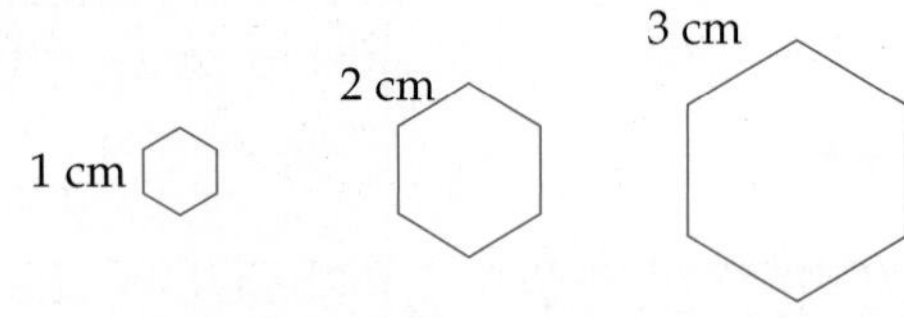

Perimeter: 6 cm __ __

The perimeter of each shape is the total length of the sides.

(a) What is the perimeter of the second hexagon?

(b) What is the perimeter of the third hexagon?

(c) What will be the perimeter of a regular hexagon with sides measuring 8 cm? Use the pattern to predict this.

(d) Explain, in words, what the rule is for calculating the perimeter of a regular hexagon when you know the length of one side.

(continues)

(e) P stands for the perimeter, and n stands for the length of a side. The rule can also be written as: $P = \square n$. What number goes in the space marked $\square$?

2 The diagram shows a pattern with 4, then 7, then 10, cubes.

				...
Shape number:	1	2	3	...

(a) How many cubes will the next shape in the pattern have?

(b) Write down a calculation for the number of cubes in shape number 5. Use this rule:

> Number of cubes $= 3n + 1$

3 A construction company builds office blocks that are several storeys high. A flight of stairs joins one storey to a landing, so that 2 flights of stairs link one storey to another.

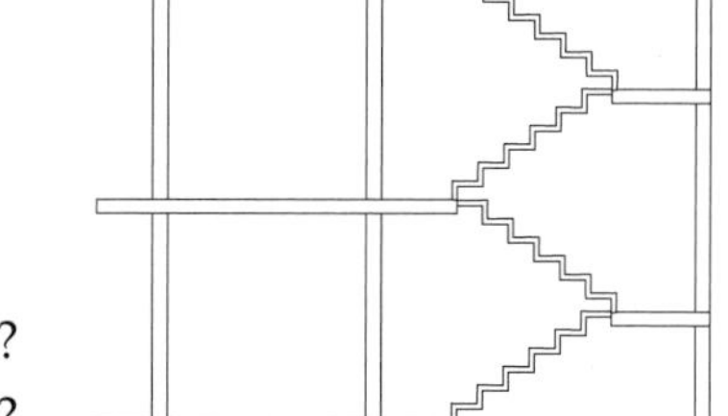

The diagram shows that a 3-storey building would have 4 flights of stairs.

(a) How many flights of stairs would a 2-storey building have?

(b) How many flights of stairs would a 4-storey building have?

(c) Let's take n as the number of storeys. Which of these is the correct formula for f, the number of flights of stairs?

(i) $f = n + 1$ (ii) $f = 2n - 2$

(d) The formula $f = 2n - 2$ gives a sensible answer when $n = 1$. Write down some working to show this. Explain.

4 Each shape in this pattern shows a row of white tiles surrounded on all sides by green tiles.

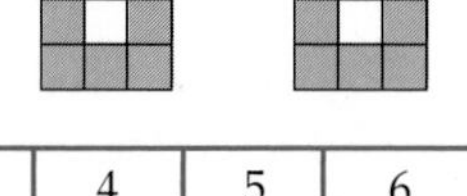

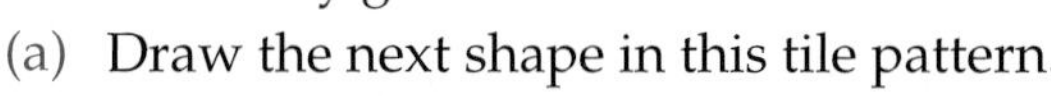

(a) Draw the next shape in this tile pattern.

(b) Copy this table. Complete it for the first six shapes in the pattern.

Number of white tiles (n)	1	2	3	4	5	6
Number of green tiles (g)	8	10				

(c) How many *green* tiles are added on at each step?

(d) n is the number of white tiles, and g is the number of green tiles. Which of the following is the correct rule for this pattern?

A $g = n + 7$ B $g = n + 8$ C $g = 4n$ D $g = 2n + 6$

(e) How many *green* tiles will there be when there are 20 white tiles?

5 This pattern is made up of matches and green dots:

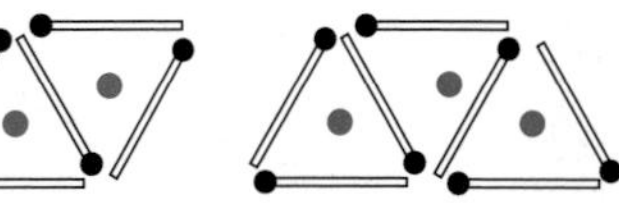

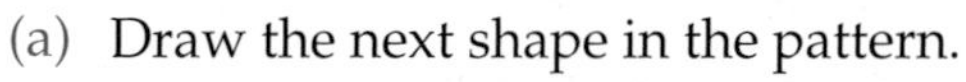

(a) Draw the next shape in the pattern.

(b) Copy this table. Complete it to show how the pattern continues.

Number of dots (d)	1	2	3	4	5	6
Number of matches (m)	3					

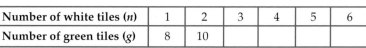

(c) How many matches would there be if there were:

(i) 8 dots (ii) 10 dots (iii) 100 dots?

(continues)

(d) Explain, in words, what you do to the number of dots to work out the number of matches.

(e) Write down a rule linking d and m: $m = ...$

6 This diagram shows a model for an office block. The top and all four sides of the model are to be covered with square mirror tiles. One tile will cover the top, and five tiles are needed for each face.

(a) How many tiles are needed altogether?

(b) How many tiles are needed for a model twice as high, but with the same-sized top?

(c) Investigate to suggest a rule for the number of tiles needed when there are n tiles on one face. Write the rule in two ways:

(i) in words (ii) using an algebraic formula.

7 A furniture store sells couches made out of foam-rubber cubes. The diagram shows their 3-seater design. This 3-seater couch takes 17 cubes to make.

(a) Copy this table. Complete it to show how many cubes are needed to make different-sized couches.

Number of seats (n)	1	2	3	4	5
Number of cubes			17		

(b) The rule for the number of cubes needed to make a couch with n seats looks like:

Number of cubes = $3n + \square$

What number should go in the box to make the rule correct?

INVESTIGATION

HYDROCARBONS

What do methane gas barbeques, butane cigarette lighters and the octane level of petrol all have in common?

They are all examples of products based on *hydrocarbons*. A hydrocarbon is a molecule that combines atoms of hydrogen with atoms of carbon.

The diagrams here show how the atoms are arranged:	**Methane**	**Ethane**	**Propane**	**Butane**
	H | H—C—H | H	H H | | H—C—C—H | | H H	H H H | | | H—C—C—C—H | | | H H H	
Number of carbon atoms (n)	1	2	3	4
Number of hydrogen atoms (h)	4			

1 Draw the next diagram in the sequence (for butane, which has four carbon atoms).

2 Copy the bottom two rows of the table. Now complete them.

3 Octane is a hydrocarbon with 8 carbon atoms. Use the pattern in the table to work out how many *hydrogen* atoms are present in a molecule of octane.

4 Write down the rule that links n with h. (*Hint*: it can be expressed as $h = \square n + \square$).

23 Working with expressions

Remember: it's simpler in algebra to leave out a multiplication sign (×) if you can!

Example Write $6 \times p + 2$ without the multiplication sign

Answer $6 \times p + 2 = 6p + 2$

EXERCISE 23.1

Write these expressions without multiplication signs.

1 $5 \times x + 1$
2 $4 \times y + 2$
3 $6 \times p - 8$
4 $8 \times y - 10$
5 $12 \times x - 3$
6 $4 + 3 \times p$
7 $5 - 2 \times y$
8 $x \times y + 5$
9 $p \times q + 3$
10 $a \times b + c$
11 $p \times q - r$
12 $x + y \times z$
13 $p - q \times r$
14 $6 \times x + 2 \times y$
15 $15 \times x - 4 \times y$

Mixing operations (+ – × ÷) in one problem

With numbers, we follow special rules that tell us what order to do operations in. The same rules work with algebraic expressions.

Always do multiplication and division before addition and subtraction.

Example $x = 3, y = 4$

(a) Calculate $xy - 2$

(b) Calculate $17 - 2x$

Answer

(a) $xy - 2 = 3 \times 4 - 2$
$= 12 - 2$
$= 10$

(b) $17 - 2x = 17 - 2 \times 3$
$= 17 - 6$
$= 11$

Example Calculate the value of $\frac{x}{2} + 7$ when $x = 6$

Answer $\frac{x}{2} + 7 = \frac{6}{2} + 7$
$= 3 + 7$
$= 10$

Note that $\frac{x}{2}$ is how we write $x \div 2$ in algebra

EXERCISE 23.2

1–8 *Calculate the value of each of these expressions when $x = 6$.*

1 $3x + 2$

2 $2x - 5$

3 $4x + 1$

4 $4x - 20$

5 $10x + 7$

6 $5 + 2x$

7 $15 - 2x$

8 $5x - 30$

9–14 *Calculate the value of each of these expressions when $x = 12$.*

9 $\frac{x}{2} + 4$

10 $\frac{x}{2} - 3$

11 $\frac{x}{3} + 5$

12 $20 + \frac{x}{6}$

13 $15 - \frac{x}{12}$

14 $2 - \frac{x}{6}$

15–28 *$e = 2, f = 3$ and $g = 7$. Evaluate these:*

15 $3e - 1$

16 $2f + 8$

17 $20 - 2g$

18 $ef + 1$

19 $4fg$

20 $2e + 4$

21 $eg - 13$

22 $29 - ef$

23 $efg + 2$

24 $4f + 2g$

25 $12e - 3g$

26 $3f - 1 + e$

27 $5f - 4e$

28 $8ef - 4g + 10$

A motorbike has a petrol tank with a capacity of 24 litres. The petrol tank is empty. The owner of the motorbike only has enough money to pay for 12 litres.

The owner decides to buy the petrol from a friend who has three full cans of petrol, holding 8 litres, 10 litres and 14 litres, respectively.

Explain how the owner can pour exactly 12 litres into the motorbike tank without wasting any.

Brackets

> When part of the expression is in brackets, that part is worked out first

Example Calculate the value of $2 \times (p + 6)$ if $p = 3$

Answer
$$\begin{aligned} 2 \times (p + 6) &= 2 \times (3 + 6) \\ &= 2 \times 9 \\ &= 18 \end{aligned}$$

Example Evaluate $4(x - 5)$ if $x = 8$

Answer
$$\begin{aligned} 4 \times (8 - 5) &= 4 \times 3 \\ &= 12 \end{aligned}$$

> A number in front of the first bracket multiplies it. The multiplication sign isn't always written in.

Example What is the value of $\dfrac{x+5}{2}$ when $x = 3$?

Answer The long fraction line here shows that *all* of the top line is divided by 2.
The expression is equivalent to writing $(x + 5) \div 2$

$$\frac{x+5}{2} = \frac{3+5}{2}$$
$$= \frac{8}{2}$$
$$= 4$$

The fraction line makes it obvious what has to be divided. So, brackets are not always necessary.

EXERCISE 23.3

1–12 *$x = 10$ and $y = 6$. Work out the following expressions:*

1 $3 \times (x + 2)$
2 $4 \times (y - 2)$
3 $5(x - 3)$
4 $2(y + 1)$
5 $3(x + y)$
6 $y(x - 2)$
7 $4(x - y)$
8 $x(y + 3)$
9 $5(2x - 1)$
10 $3(3y - 11)$
11 $2(2x - 3y)$
12 $x(x + y)$

13–24 *$x = 8$ and $y = 5$. Evaluate these expressions:*

13 $\dfrac{x+6}{7}$
14 $\dfrac{x-3}{5}$
15 $\dfrac{x+2}{y}$
16 $\dfrac{5x}{2}$
17 $\dfrac{3y}{5}$
18 $\dfrac{20-x}{4}$
19 $\dfrac{2x+9}{5}$
20 $\dfrac{3x-4}{2}$
21 $\dfrac{x-y}{3}$
22 $\dfrac{18}{x+1}$
23 $\dfrac{20}{x-7}$
24 $\dfrac{2x+10}{x+y}$

25–30 *Rewrite these expressions to show all the multiplication and division signs.*

25 $2p + 3$
26 $6(p + 4)$
27 $5p + 4q$
28 $\dfrac{p}{6}$
29 $\dfrac{p+1}{2}$
30 $\dfrac{10p-3}{4}$

Evaluate the expressions in the clues. The answer to each one will link a letter with a number. Swap the letters into the answer to decode it.
For example, the first answer is 2. So, replace 2 in the answer with the letter a.

What is the purpose of education?

Answer:

3 12 | 6 0 20 11 2 15 0 | 2 5 | 0 14 20 3 9
14 1 5 8 | 4 1 3 10 | 2 5 | 12 20 0 5 | 12 5 0

Clues: $x = 5, y = 3, z = 2$

a $x - y$
c xy
d $2(y + 1)$
e $x - (y + z)$
h $3y + 1$
i $2y - 5$
l $4z + 3$
m $2(x + z)$
n $x(y - z)$
o $z(x + 1)$
p $x(z + 2)$
r $\dfrac{4y}{z}$
t $\dfrac{x+1}{2}$
w $\dfrac{x+y}{z}$
y $\dfrac{xy+3}{z}$

Powers

When a variable (letter) is multiplied by itself several times, we use **powers**.
This is the same idea as in Chapter 5 in the Number strand—here we learned to write $3 \times 3 \times 3 \times 3$ as 3^4.
Instead of using *repeated multiplication,* we write expressions more simply in **index form.**

Examples $r \times r = r^2$ (which is said 'r to the power of 2' or 'r squared')
$p \times p \times p \times p \times p = p^5$

Sometimes there is more than one base number.

Example Simplify $x \times x \times y \times y \times y$

Answer $x \times x \times y \times y \times y = x^2y^3$

An expression like x^2y^3 can't be simplified further.

In **index form** (e.g. p^5) we give special names to the two terms:
base → p^5 ← index

EXERCISE 23.4

1–10 *Shorten these expressions by writing them in index form.*

1 $r \times r \times r$
2 $w \times w$
3 $x \times x \times x \times x \times x \times x \times x$
4 $d \times d \times d \times d$
5 $p \times p \times q \times q \times q \times q$
6 $c \times d \times d \times c \times c$
7 $x \times y \times y \times y \times x$
8 $u \times t \times u \times t$
9 $p \times q \times q$
10 $x \times x \times y \times y \times z \times z$

11–20 *Write these expressions in full, using multiplication symbols.*

11 x^5
12 r^3
13 w^2
14 xy^2
15 p^2q^2
16 x^4y^2
17 p^2q
18 t^3u^2
19 xy^2z
20 c^3d

21 The dots in these Maori place names stand for multiplication symbols. Write each word in index form:
(a) k.a.r.a.k.a
(b) p.a.p.a.k.u.r.a
(c) k.a.t.i.k.a.t.i
(d) k.a.i.w.a.k.a

22 Make up words from each of these index expressions. Arrange the letters in the correct order. Leave out the × symbols.
(a) hap^2y
(b) mo^2
(c) r^2a^2d
(d) p^2i^2

23 Write a^2b^2 in full, to form the name of a Swedish rock group famous in the 1970s.

Multiplying expressions with numbers and letters

Example Simplify $4x \times 6x$

Answer
$$4x \times 6x = 4 \times x \times 6 \times x$$
$$= 4 \times 6 \times x \times x$$
$$= 24x^2$$

Any numbers can be multiplied separately. Then, letters can be combined and written in index form. In the final, simplified answer, the number part is written first.

EXERCISE 23.5

1–4 Shorten these expressions by writing them in index form.

1 $6 \times p \times p$

2 $4 \times x \times 3 \times x$

3 $2 \times 5 \times x \times x$

4 $x \times 4 \times x$

5–22 Simplify these by multiplying and writing in index form where possible.

5 $5x \times 2x$

6 $2q \times 3q$

7 $3p \times p$

8 $4a \times 2a$

9 $q \times 6q$

10 $8p \times 8p$

11 $10x \times 10x$

12 $2x \times 10x \times 3$

13 $r \times 2r \times 4r$

14 $x \times 4x \times x$

15 $2x \times 2x \times 2x$

16 $5 \times 2x \times x$

17 $3c \times 2d \times d$

18 $4r \times 2q \times 2r$

19 $7x \times 4y$

20 $2p \times 3q \times p$

21 $x \times 4y \times 2y$

22 $4x \times 2x \times y \times 3y$

Substituting into expressions written in index form

Example If $x = 7$, work out the value of x^2.

Answer $x^2 = 7 \times 7 = 49$

Squaring a number means multiplying it by itself.

EXERCISE 23.6

$p = 1, q = 2, r = 4$. Work out the following.

1 q^2

2 r^2

3 p^2

4 $(q + 3)^2$

5 $(r - 1)^2$

6 $r^2 + 5$

7 $q^2 + 8$

8 $r^2 - 4$

9 $(r - 4)^2$

10 $p^2 + q^2$

11 $(p + q)^2$

12 $(2q + 3)^2$

SPREADSHEET INVESTIGATION

HOW DO SPREADSHEETS HANDLE POWERS?

Spreadsheets use the caret symbol (^) to represent powers. For example, the formula =A1^2 calculates the square of the number in cell A1.

Examples =A1^3 is the short way of writing =A1*A1*A1

=G10^4 means =G10*G10*G10*G10

1 Produce a spreadsheet that calculates these powers (x^2, x^3, x^4, x^5) for all the counting numbers from 1 to 12.

The extract here shows headings and the formulas you enter in some of the cells. You can complete the spreadsheet by entering the rest of the formulas and copying row 3 downwards.

What you enter:

	A	B	C	D	E
1	x	x^2	x^3	x^4	x^5
2					
3	1	=A3^2	=A3^3		
4	2	=A4^2	=A4^3		
5	3				
	4				
12					
13	11				
14	12				

What appears:

	A	B	C	D	E
1	x	x^2	x^3	x^4	x^5
2					
3	1	1	1		
4	2	4	8		
5	3				
	4				
12					
13	11				
14	12				

Now let's see how spreadsheet software handles a mixture of multiplications and powers. We will use it to see what happens when calculating $5x^2$ and $(5x)^2$.

2 Produce a spreadsheet which calculates the values of $5x^2$ and $(5x)^2$ for all the counting numbers from 1 to 10.

Use these headings and formulas. Complete the spreadsheet by copying row 3 downwards.

	A	B	C
1	x	5x^2	(5x)^2
2			
3	1	=5*A3^2	=(5*A3)^2
4	2		
5	3		
6	4		
7	5		
8	6		
9	7		
10	8		
11	9		
12	10		

3 Now produce a spreadsheet that calculates the values of $3x^2$ and $(3x)^2$ for all the counting numbers from 1 to 6.

4 Explain whether $5x^2$ and $(5x)^2$ always give the same result.

5 Which rule does squaring first, and then the multiplying?

6 Which rule does multiplying first, and then squares the result?

STARTER

Does squaring a number then multiplying by 3 give the same result as multiplying the number by 3, and then squaring it?

Copy these tables. Complete them to see what happens when the numbers we start with are 2, 5 and 1.

Number	Squaring	Then multiplying by 3
2	$2^2 = 2 \times 2 = 4$	$4 \times 3 = 12$
5		
1		

Number	Multiplying by 3	Then squaring
2		
5	$5 \times 3 = 15$	$15^2 = 15 \times 15 = 225$
1		

- What is your conclusion?

- How could you write 'squaring a number then multiplying by 3' using algebra, if the number was p?
- Is $p^2 \times 3$ the same as $3p^2$?

In algebra, we use brackets to show part of an expression has to be worked out first.

- In the expression $(4x)^2$, would you multiply x by 4 first, or square x first?
- In an expression like $4x^2$, would you square x first, or multiply x by 4 first?

- Explain whether $3p^2$ and $(3p)^2$ give the same result.
- Explain whether $4x^2$ and $(4x)^2$ are the same.

When there are no brackets, and you have a mixture of multiplication and squaring, always do the squaring first.

Example $p = 3$. Work out the value of $5p^2$.

Answer

$$5p^2 = 5 \times p \times p = 5 \times 3 \times 3 = 5 \times 9 = 45$$

EXERCISE 23.7

1–4 *$x = 1, y = 2, z = 3$. Evaluate these expressions:*

1 (a) $4x^2$ (b) $(4x)^2$

2 (a) $5y^2$ (b) $(5y)^2$

3 (a) $2z^2$ (b) $(2z)^2$

4 (a) $3y^2$ (b) $(3y)^2$

5–20 *$p = 1, q = 2, r = 4$. Work out the following:*

5 $3q^2$

6 $2p^2$

7 $3r^2$

8 $2q^2$

9 $5q^2$

10 $3 + p^2$

11 $r^2 - 7$

12 $2r^2 + 1$

13 $3p + r^2$

14 $5r - q^2$

15 rq^2

16 $3pr^2$

17 $2qp^2$

18 $6q^2 + p$

19 $2r^2 - q^2$

20 $5q^2 - 3p^2$

If Einstein were alive today, would he be a remarkable person?

Evaluate these expressions in the clues. Swap the letters you get into the answer to decode it.
For example, the first answer is 4. So, replace 4 in the answer with the letter a.

Answer:

12 20 64	23 20	1 24 8 16 3	10 20
24 13 20 36	24 9 20	23 8 9 3 36 20 3	
4 9 3	21 0 21 25 12	12 20 4 36 64	24 16 3

Clues: $x = 2$

a x^2	h $(2x)^2 + 7$	o $6x^2$	u x^3
b $x^2 + 6$	i $(x - 2)^2$	r $(3x)^2$	v $4x^2 - 3$
d $x^2 - 1$	l $2x^2 + 8$	s $(4x)^2$	w $(2x - 3)^2$
e $24 - x^2$	n $(x + 1)^2$	t $(2x + 1)^2$	y $16 - x^2$
f $5x^2 + 1$			

Multiplying using indices

STARTER

- Write x^3 in full using multiplication signs.
- Write x^5 in full using multiplication signs.

- What is the result of multiplying $(x \times x \times x)$ by $(x \times x \times x \times x \times x)$?
- Write the answer in index form.

- Suggest a method for multiplying x^3 by x^5 *without* writing out the working in full.

When multiplying index expressions with the **same base**, we can **add the powers** or indices.

Example Simplify $p^2 \times p^{10}$.

Answer $p^2 \times p^{10} = p^{12}$

Example Simplify $2x^3 \times 6x^4$.

Answer
$$2x^3 \times 6x^4 = 2 \times 6 \times x^3 \times x^4 = 12 \times x^{3+4} = 12x^7$$

Add the indices, but multiply the front numbers in an expression like this!

EXERCISE 23.8

1–15 *Simplify these expressions:*

1 $x^2 \times x^3$
2 $y^4 \times y^2$
3 $p^4 \times p^3$
4 $c^3 \times c^3$
5 $x^2 \times x^2$
6 $y^2 \times y$
7 $p^4 \times p$
8 $x \times x^6$
9 $t \times t^8$
10 $x^2 \times x^2 \times x^2$
11 $t^4 \times t^2 \times t^3$
12 $p^2 \times p^3 \times p^5$
13 $c \times c^2 \times c$
14 $x^2 \times x \times x^4$
15 $x^2 \times x^8 \times x \times x^4$

16–30 *Simplify these expressions:*

16 $2x^5 \times 4x^3$
17 $5y^2 \times 3y^4$
18 $8p^2 \times 2p^3$
19 $10t^2 \times 3t^5$
20 $x^4 \times 5x^3$
21 $4x^2 \times x^3$
22 $3t \times 4t^2$
23 $5p^2 \times 6p$
24 $2y \times 8y^3$
25 $c \times 2c^2$
26 $4x^2 \times x$
27 $2x \times 4x \times 3x$
28 $2x^4 \times 3x^3 \times 5x^2$
29 $6x \times 4x^3 \times 2x$
30 $x \times 5x^2 \times 3x$

Dividing using indices

When we **divide** expressions written in index form, we **subtract** the indices.
Here is how this works.

Example Show how to simplify $\frac{x^6}{x^2}$.

Answer

$$\frac{x^6}{x^2} = \frac{x \times x \times x \times x \times x \times x}{x \times x} \text{ (writing in full)}$$
$$= \frac{x}{x} \times \frac{x}{x} \times \frac{x \times x \times x \times x}{1}$$
$$= x \times x \times x \times x$$

(Notice that two of the x terms 'cancel' out, because $\frac{x}{x}$ is another name for 1 whole)

$$= x^4$$

Usually we just use the short-cut of *subtracting* the indices.

Example Simplify $\frac{p^5}{p}$

Answer $\frac{p^5}{p} = p^{5-1} = p^4$

Here, it is useful to think of p as being the same as p^1.

Example Simplify $12x^5 \div 6x^4$

Answer

$$12x^5 \div 6x^4 = \frac{12x^5}{6x^4}$$
$$= \frac{12\,x^{5-4}}{6}$$
$$= 2x^1 = 2x$$

Subtract the indices, but **divide the front numbers** in an expression like this!

EXERCISE 23.9

Simplify these expressions:

1 $\frac{x^5}{x^3}$
2 $\frac{p^7}{p^4}$
3 $\frac{x^8}{x^6}$
4 $\frac{x^3}{x}$
5 $\frac{p^3}{p^2}$
6 $\frac{y^2}{y}$
7 $x^4 \div x$
8 $y^5 \div y^4$
9 $p^8 \div p^7$
10 $y^{10} \div y^2$
11 $p^2 \div p$
12 $x^5 \div x^4$
13 $\frac{8x^5}{2x^3}$
14 $\frac{12y^7}{3y^2}$
15 $\frac{10x^2}{2x}$
16 $\frac{18y^3}{3y^2}$
17 $\frac{24n^4}{6n^2}$
18 $\frac{25x^8}{5x^2}$
19 $\frac{9p^2}{3p}$
20 $\frac{8x^6}{2x^2}$
21 $\frac{24x^5}{6x}$
22 $\frac{12x^4}{6}$
23 $\frac{14p^3}{2}$
24 $\frac{16y^4}{2y^3}$
25 $\frac{2x^5}{5x^2}$
26 $\frac{4x^2}{3x}$
27 $\frac{2x^4}{4x^3}$
28 $\frac{12x^6}{18x^2}$
29 $\frac{10n^3}{12n}$
30 $\frac{4p^{12}}{10p^4}$

24 Equations

STARTER

I am thinking of a number. If I multiply this number by 3, I get a result of 18. What is the number?"

- How could this question be written using algebra symbols?

Equations give information about the values of unknown numbers.

We use x to represent the unknown number.

The aim is to "solve" the equation to work out the value of x.

Examples $4x = 28$

$x + 5 = 13$

$\frac{x}{2} = 20$

EXERCISE 24.1

Write the following as mathematical equations. The first one has been done for you.

1 I think of a number and add 7 to it. The result is 20.

is the same as $x + 7 = 20$

2 I think of a number and add 2 to it. The result is 8.

3 I think of a number and add 5 to it. The result is 17.

4 I think of a number and multiply it by 4. The result is 12.

5 I think of a number and multiply it by 6. The result is 24.

6 I think of a number and subtract 8 from it. The result is 3.

7 I think of a number and subtract 17 from it. The result is 5.

8 I multiply 3 by a number, and get a result of 21.

9 I multiply 12 by a number, and get a result of 108.

10 I divide a number by 7, and get a result of 4.

11 Some number plus 8 is equal to 12.

12 Some number divided by 4 is equal to 7.

It is easy to guess the answer to simple equations. But they soon become harder! So, we look for rules to solve easy equations. Then we put these together to solve harder equations.

Equations involving multiplication

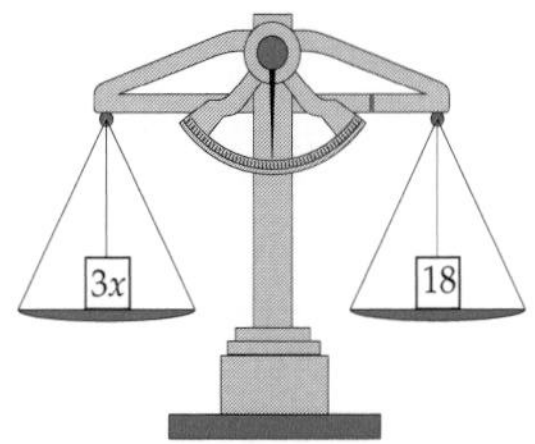

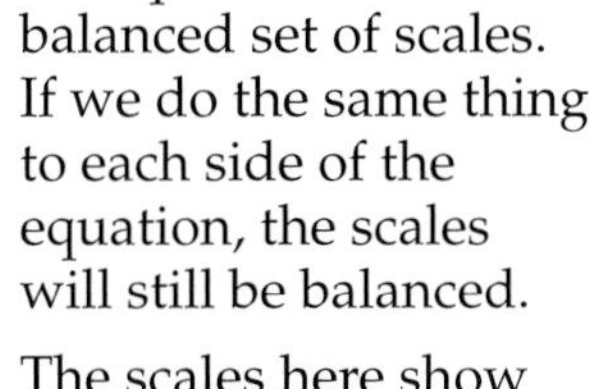

An equation is like a balanced set of scales. If we do the same thing to each side of the equation, the scales will still be balanced.

The scales here show how to solve the equation $3x = 18$.

Because x is multiplied by 3, we divide by 3 to work out x by itself.

This is how the working is set out:

$3x = 18$

$\frac{3x}{3} = \frac{18}{3}$ (divide both sides by 3)

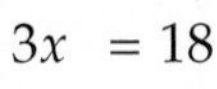

$x = 6$

EXERCISE 24.2

1 Copy and complete: To solve the equation $4x = 20$, divide 20 by .....

2 Copy and complete: To solve the equation $2x = 18$, divide 18 by .....

3 Copy and complete: To solve the equation $3x = 27$, divide .... by 3.

4 Copy and complete: To solve the equation $7x = 77$, divide .... by 7.

5–18 *Solve these equations. Show your working.*

5	$2x = 12$	12	$12x = 48$
6	$8x = 16$	13	$9x = 81$
7	$10x = 30$	14	$2x = 42$
8	$6x = 42$	15	$7x = 35$
9	$5x = 15$	16	$5x = 95$
10	$3x = 39$	17	$13x = 26$
11	$4x = 36$	18	$20x = 100$

Equations involving adding

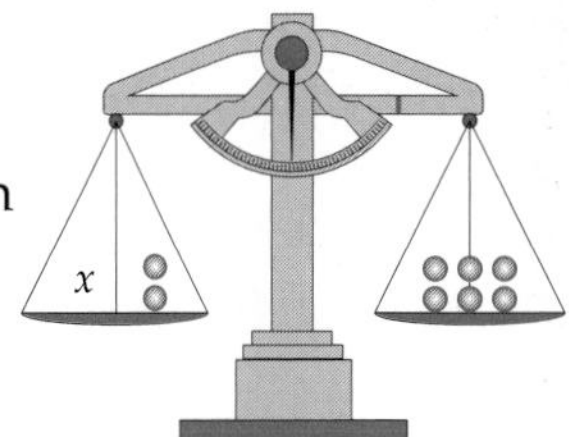

The scales show how to solve the equation $x + 2 = 6$.

Because x has 2 added to it, we subtract 2 to work out x by itself.

This is how the working is set out:

$x + 2 = 6$

$x + 2 - 2 = 6 - 2$ (subtract 2 from both sides)

$x = 4$

EXERCISE 24.3

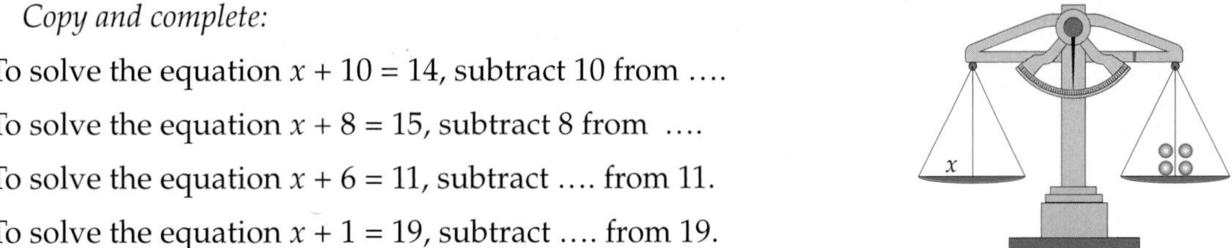

1–4 *Copy and complete:*

1 To solve the equation $x + 10 = 14$, subtract 10 from ....

2 To solve the equation $x + 8 = 15$, subtract 8 from ....

3 To solve the equation $x + 6 = 11$, subtract .... from 11.

4 To solve the equation $x + 1 = 19$, subtract .... from 19.

5–18 *Solve these equations. Show your working.*

5 $x + 2 = 3$
6 $x + 5 = 12$
7 $x + 4 = 30$
8 $x + 8 = 19$
9 $x + 12 = 15$
10 $x + 9 = 39$
11 $x + 10 = 53$
12 $x + 29 = 48$
13 $x + 7 = 81$
14 $x + 1 = 482$
15 $x + 65 = 90$
16 $x + 17 = 63$
17 $x + 2 = 2$
18 $x + 31 = 31$

Equations involving subtracting

We solve equations that involve adding by subtracting. In the same way, we solve equations that involve subtracting by adding.

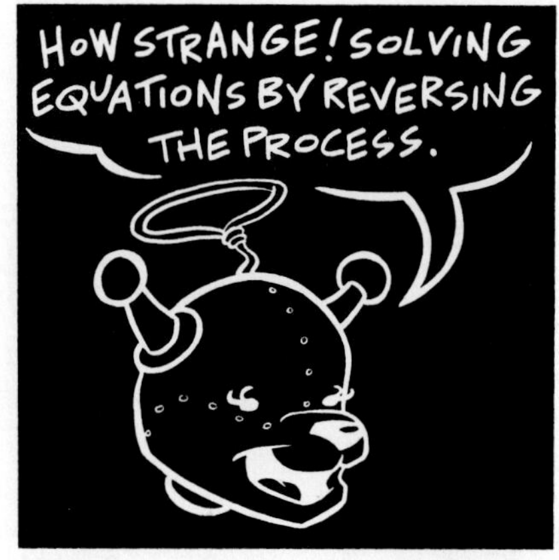

HOW STRANGE! SOLVING EQUATIONS BY REVERSING THE PROCESS.

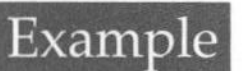
Example Solve the equation $x - 8 = 3$.

Answer This is how the working is set out:

$$x - 8 = 3$$
$$x - 8 + 8 = 3 + 8 \quad \text{(add 8 to both sides)}$$
$$x = 11$$

EXERCISE 24.4

1 Copy and complete: To solve the equation $x - 2 = 5$, add …. to 5.

2 Copy and complete: To solve the equation $x - 17 = 13$, add …. to 13.

3 Copy and complete: To solve the equation $x - 1 = 6$, …. 1 to 6.

4 Copy and complete: To solve the equation $x - 28 = 32$, …. 28 to 32.

5–18 *Solve these equations. Show your working.*

5 $x - 3 = 7$
6 $x - 2 = 4$
7 $x - 5 = 12$
8 $x - 8 = 20$
9 $x - 10 = 35$
10 $x - 7 = 36$
11 $x - 100 = 61$
12 $x - 23 = 23$
13 $x - 1 = 0$
14 $x - 8 = 0$
15 $x - 17 = 0$
16 $x - 34 = 34$
17 $x - 31 = 67$
18 $x - 49 = 38$

Equations involving division

The reverse of division is multiplication.

Example Solve the equation $\frac{x}{5} = 6$

Answer

$$\frac{x}{5} = 6$$
$$\frac{x}{5} \times 5 = 6 \times 5 \quad \text{(multiply both sides by 5)}$$
$$x = 30$$

EXERCISE 24.5

1 Copy and complete: To solve the equation $\frac{x}{6} = 2$, multiply 2 by ....

2 Copy and complete: To solve the equation $\frac{x}{3} = 12$, multiply 12 by ....

3 Copy and complete: To solve the equation $\frac{x}{4} = 9$, multiply .... by 4.

4 Copy and complete: To solve the equation $\frac{x}{2} = 1$, multiply .... by 2.

5–18 *Solve these equations. Show your working.*

5 $\frac{x}{2} = 5$

6 $\frac{x}{3} = 10$

7 $\frac{x}{8} = 9$

8 $\frac{x}{5} = 8$

9 $\frac{x}{4} = 3$

10 $\frac{x}{2} = 16$

11 $\frac{x}{6} = 12$

12 $\frac{x}{4} = 40$

13 $\frac{x}{13} = 4$

14 $\frac{x}{4} = 1$

15 $\frac{x}{3} = 0$

16 $\frac{x}{55} = 1$

17 $\frac{x}{16} = 0$

18 $\frac{x}{5} = 200$

Mixed examples

EXERCISE 24.6

Solve these equations. In each case, show your working.

1 $x + 2 = 8$

2 $2x = 8$

3 $\frac{x}{2} = 8$

4 $x - 2 = 8$

5 $3x = 18$

6 $x - 3 = 18$

7 $\frac{x}{3} = 18$

8 $x + 3 = 18$

9 $\frac{x}{6} = 10$

10 $6x = 24$

11 $x - 7 = 8$

12 $x + 3 = 15$

13 $3x = 27$

14 $x - 4 = 4$

15 $x + 5 = 5$

16 $\frac{x}{3} = 6$

Equations with *x* on both sides

Collect all the terms with x on the left side.

Example Solve the equation $5x = 3x + 8$.

Answer

$5x = 3x + 8$

$5x - 3x = 3x + 8 - 3x$ (take away $3x$ from both sides—equation is still balanced)

$2x = 8$ (simplify both sides)

$x = \frac{8}{2}$

$x = 4$

EXERCISE 24.7

Solve these equations. Show your working.

1 $7x = 2x + 20$
2 $9x = 5x + 24$
3 $6x = 3x + 6$
4 $3x = 2x + 1$
5 $5x = 3x + 18$
6 $13x = 9x + 28$
7 $8x = 7x + 9$
8 $4x = 5 + 3x$
9 $5x = 9 + 2x$
10 $4x = 3x + 7$
11 $7x = 6x + 18$
12 $13x = 3x + 40$
13 $14x = 36 + 11x$
14 $16x = x + 30$
15 $3x = 2x + 67$

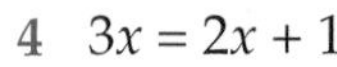

A small city has a business centre, a hospital and a high school.

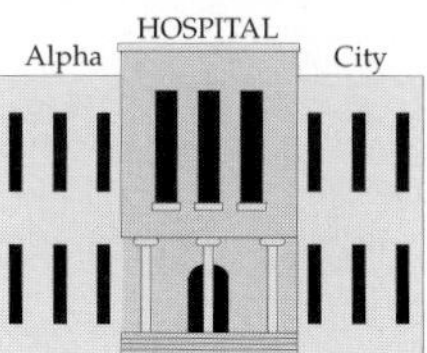

Each of these needs to be connected by underground cables to the local TV station, the phone company and the power station.

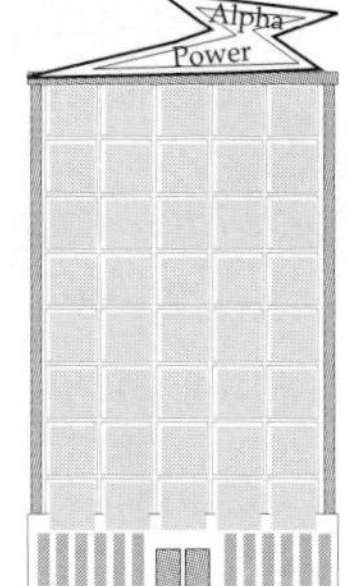

None of the cables are allowed to cross each other.

- Try to draw a diagram to show where the cables should be laid.

Equations with numbers on both sides

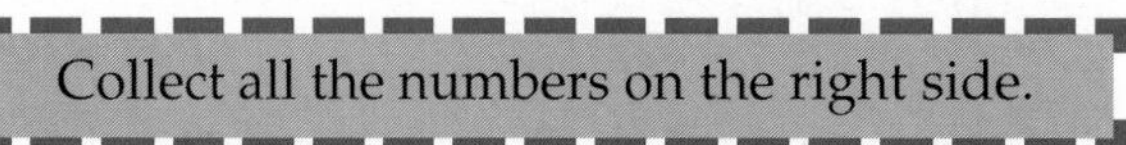

Collect all the numbers on the right side.

Example Solve the equation $6x - 5 = 13$.

Answer

$6x - 5 = 13$

$6x - 5 + 5 = 13 + 5$ (add 5 to both sides; equation is still balanced)

$6x = 18$ (simplify both sides)

$x = \frac{18}{6}$

$x = 3$

Example Solve the equation $8x + 12 = 20$.

Answer

$$8x + 12 = 20$$
$$8x + 12 - 12 = 20 - 12$$
$$8x = 8$$
$$x = \frac{8}{8} = 1$$

EXERCISE **24.8**

Solve these equations. Show your working.

1 $2x - 1 = 5$

2 $3x + 1 = 13$

3 $4x + 3 = 23$

4 $5x - 8 = 22$

5 $2x + 9 = 11$

6 $3x - 14 = 1$

7 $6x - 12 = 0$

8 $7x - 17 = 18$

9 $4x + 5 = 21$

10 $9x - 1 = 17$

11 $10x + 3 = 33$

12 $12x - 5 = 19$

13 $6x + 3 = 3$

14 $4x - 9 = 91$

15 $11x - 14 = 19$

Using equations to solve problems (1)

Solving equations is useful—we can use the process to solve *practical* problems.

Example Crazy Paving has a design for laying hexagonal paving stones to form a pathway.

The outside edges of the path are bordered with lengths of wood. These are shown as black lines on the diagram.

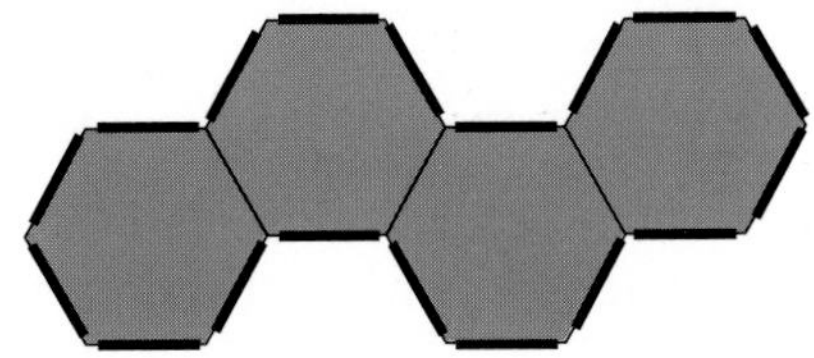

When there are 4 paving stones, 18 lengths of wood will be needed. The rule that gives the number of lengths of wood when there are x paving stones is: $\boxed{4x + 2}$

Write down an equation and then solve it to work out how many paving stones there are when 82 lengths of wood are used.

Answer

$$4x + 2 = 82$$
$$4x = 82 - 2$$
$$4x = 80$$
$$x = \frac{80}{4} = 20$$

24.9

1 Matthew and Cathy's ages add to 27. Cathy is 14. Let Matthew's age be x.

(a) Write down an equation that shows the two ages add to 27.

(b) Solve the equation to work out Matthew's age.

2 Freda is saving money for a school trip. So far she has saved x dollars. When she has saved another \$20 she will have reached \$100, which is what the trip costs.

(a) Use this information to write down an equation combining x, 20 and 100.

(b) Solve the equation to work out x.

3 The highest midday temperature in Auckland last year was 3 times the coldest midday temperature. The highest temperature was 27 °C. The lowest temperature was x °C.

(a) Use this information to write down an equation combining x, 27 and 3.

(b) Solve the equation to work out x.

4 Four identical calculators are placed on a set of scales. The total weight is 500 g.

(a) Use this information to write down an equation. Represent the weight of one calculator by x.

(b) Solve the equation.

5 Here is a pattern where matchsticks are placed to form a row of squares:

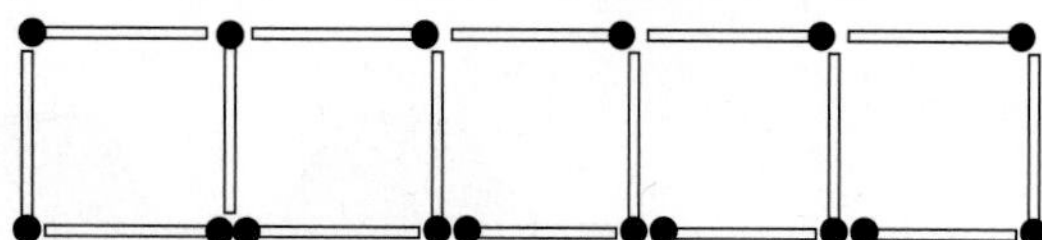

The rule for working out the number of matchsticks when there are x squares is $3x + 1$.

One of these patterns uses 19 matchsticks.

Solve the equation $3x + 1 = 19$ to work out how many squares there are in the pattern.

6 Another pattern has matchsticks arranged to make a row of triangles:

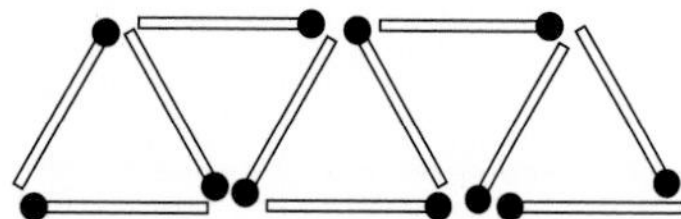

The rule for working out the number of matchsticks when there are x triangles is $2x + 1$.

(a) Use this information to write down an equation for working out the number of triangles when there are 17 matchsticks.

(b) Solve the equation.

7 A painter pours 4 litres of paint out of a bucket. This leaves 6 litres in the bucket. When full, the bucket holds x litres.

(a) Which of these equations could be used to work out the amount of paint in a full bucket?

A $4x = 6$ B $x + 4 = 6$

C $x - 4 = 6$ D $x + 6 = 4$

(b) Solve the equation to work out x.

8 Jill and Karen buy their father a gift that costs \$50. Karen pays \$6 more than Jill does.

This information can be represented by the equation:

$x + x + 6 = 50$

(a) What does x stand for in this equation?

The equation simplifies to:

$2x + 6 = 50$

(b) Solve the equation. Then write down how much each sister paid.

Boyd and Chris buy their mother a gift that costs \$75. Chris pays \$5 more than Boyd does.

(c) Use this information to write an equation.

(d) Solve the equation, and then write down how much each brother paid.

9 A large number (x) of boys register for school rugby. The sports co-ordinator divides them up into teams of 15, and gets exactly 5 teams.

(a) Which of these equations could be used to work out the number of boys who registered?

A $5x = 15$ B $x + 5 = 15$

C $x - 5 = 15$ D $\frac{x}{15} = 5$

(b) Work out the number of boys who registered.

10 Kevin shared a bag of 36 lollies with his friends. They each had 5, and there was 1 left over. There were x people in the group.
   (a) Use this information to write down an equation linking x, 36, 5 and 1.
   (b) Solve the equation to work out the number of people in the group.

11 Altogether, Carl took 39 eggs out of the fridge to make some Christmas cakes. He made four cakes. Each had the same number (x) of eggs. 3 of the eggs were not used in the cakes because they were rotten.
   (a) Which of these four equations is the correct one for working out the number of eggs in each cake?
   A $3x + 4 = 39$ B $4x + 3 = 39$
   C $4x - 3 = 39$ D $3x - 4 = 39$
   (b) Solve an equation to work out the number of eggs in each cake.

12 A taxi company charges $2 per km, plus a $3 'flagfall' fee. A passenger pays $19. x stands for the distance travelled.
   (a) Use this information to write down an equation linking x, 2, 3 and 19.
   (b) Solve the equation to work out the distance travelled.

13 The cost of a torch with batteries is $12. The torch costs $8 more than the batteries. How much do the batteries cost?

14 The school roll at Aotearoa High School is 757. There are 13 more boys than girls. Write an equation and solve it, to work out how many boys are on the roll.

Equations: combined types

Aim to end up with:
- letter terms on the left side of the = sign
- non-letter (number) terms on the right side of the = sign

Example Solve the equation $5x + 8 = 2x + 20$

Answer

$5x + 8 = 2x + 20$

$5x + 8 - 8 = 2x + 20 - 8$ (taking 8 from both sides, to end up with letter terms only on left)

$5x = 2x + 12$

$5x - 2x = 2x + 12 - 2x$ (taking $2x$ from both sides, to end up with non–letter terms only on right)

$3x = 12$

$x = \frac{12}{3} = 4$

EXERCISE 24.10

Solve these equations. Show your working.

1 $3x + 8 = 2x + 10$
2 $4x + 5 = 2x + 19$
3 $6x + 7 = x + 22$
4 $6x + 5 = 5x + 6$
5 $6x - 1 = 3x + 8$
6 $9x - 3 = 7x + 1$
7 $8x - 9 = 2x + 3$
8 $7x - 4 = 5x + 2$
9 $11x + 8 = x + 48$
10 $8x - 5 = 3x + 10$
11 $10x + 9 = 7x + 15$
12 $2x - 1 = 5 - x$
13 $5x + 2 = 18 - 3x$
14 $3x + 10 = 30 - 2x$
15 $8x - 23 = 7x + 17$

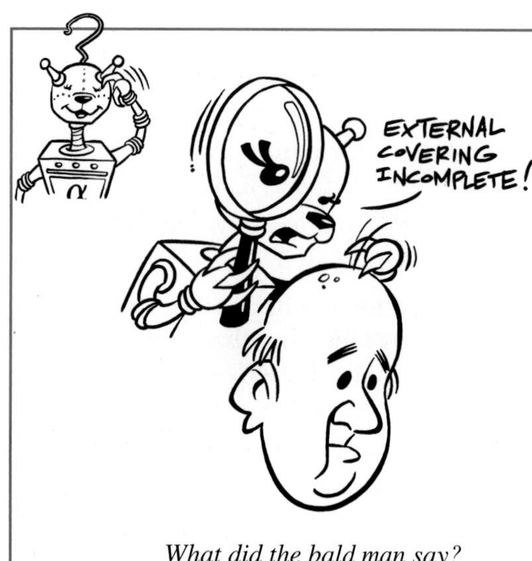

What did the bald man say?

Answer:

13 1 4 18	5 7 9 1 25	28 7 11 2
5 7 3 7 18 18 7 8		

Each equation is labelled A to W. Solve each equation, then swap the letters into the answer to decode it.

Clues

Y	$3x = 75$	I	$6x + 7 = 3x + 19$
E	$2x + 1 = 5$	D	$3x = x + 18$
G	$\frac{x}{2} = 14$	W	$4x - 3 = 29$
M	$9x = 4x + 15$	R	$\frac{x}{3} = 6$
A	$8x = 8$	O	$2x + 1 = x + 8$
N	$x - 3 = 8$	H	$x + 8 = 21$
T	$x + 4 = 9$		

Equations with integer answers

Equations don't always have whole numbers as answers. Sometimes, the answers can be negative integers. We still use the rules introduced earlier, and solve them the same way.

EXERCISE 24.11

Examples

$$x - 7 = {}^{-}8 \qquad x + 6 = 1$$
$$x - 7 + 7 = {}^{-}8 + 7 \qquad x + 6 - 6 = 1 - 6$$
$$x = {}^{-}1 \qquad x = {}^{-}5$$

Solve these equations.

1 $x - 3 = 12$
2 $x + 8 = 6$
3 $x - 8 = {}^{-}2$
4 $x - 4 = {}^{-}9$
5 $x + 7 = 0$
6 $x + 5 = {}^{-}2$
7 $x - 4 = {}^{-}11$
8 $x - 4 = {}^{-}1$
9 $x + 18 = 7$
10 $x + 20 = {}^{-}15$
11 $x - 10 = {}^{-}12$
12 $x - 18 = {}^{-}3$
13 $x + 14 = {}^{-}8$
14 $x - 17 = {}^{-}3$
15 $x + 12 = 0$
16 $x + 13 = 1$
17 $x - 9 = {}^{-}9$

EXERCISE 24.12

Examples

$$6x = {}^{-}24 \qquad \frac{x}{4} = {}^{-}3$$
$$x = \frac{{}^{-}24}{6} \qquad \frac{x}{4} \times 4 = {}^{-}3 \times 4$$
$$x = {}^{-}4 \qquad x = {}^{-}12$$

Solve these equations.

1 $4x = {}^{-}20$
2 ${}^{-}5x = 35$
3 $\frac{x}{2} = {}^{-}3$
4 ${}^{-}3x = 15$
5 ${}^{-}2x = {}^{-}18$
6 $\frac{x}{4} = {}^{-}7$
7 $10x = {}^{-}20$
8 ${}^{-}6x = {}^{-}48$
9 $3x = {}^{-}21$
10 $\frac{x}{6} = {}^{-}2$
11 $9x = {}^{-}9$
12 $\frac{x}{10} = {}^{-}4$
13 ${}^{-}x = 8$
14 ${}^{-}x = {}^{-}3$
15 $\frac{x}{5} = {}^{-}40$
16 ${}^{-}12x = {}^{-}24$

EXERCISE 24.13

Examples

$$2x + 15 = 1$$
$$2x + 15 - 15 = 1 - 15$$
$$2x = {}^{-}14$$
$$x = \frac{^{-}14}{2}$$
$$x = {}^{-}7$$

$$8x + 3 = 12x - 17$$
$$8x + 3 - 3 = 12x - 17 - 3$$
$$8x = 12x - 20$$
$$8x - 12x = 12x - 20 - 12x$$
$$^{-}4x = {}^{-}20$$
$$x = \frac{^{-}20}{^{-}4}$$
$$x = 5$$

Solve these equations.

1 $4x + 10 = 6$

2 $5x - 3 = {}^{-}13$

3 $2x + 11 = 5$

4 $4x - 11 = {}^{-}3$

5 $10x + 18 = {}^{-}12$

6 $^{-}4x + 3 = {}^{-}1$

7 $^{-}5x + 6 = 21$

8 $6x - 3 = {}^{-}39$

9 $4x + 3 = 2x - 7$

10 $7x - 13 = 4x + 5$

11 $8x + 3 = 7x - 1$

12 $9x - 15 = 2x - 1$

13 $2x + 3 = 5x + 6$

14 $x - 1 = 2x - 11$

SPREADSHEET INVESTIGATION

John decides to solve the equation $2x + 50 = 11 - x$.
He does this by calculating values of $(2x + 50)$ and $(11 - x)$ on a spreadsheet, and looking for when they are the *same*.

He has been told:

- the answer is an integer
- the answer is between $^{-}20$ and 20.

John sets up the spreadsheet so that values for x appear in column A. He puts formulas for $2x + 50$ and $11 - x$ in columns B and C.

Here is what he enters:

	A	B	C
1	x	2x+50	11-x
2			
3	-20	=2*A3+50	=11-A3
4	-19		
5	-18		
6	-17		

Here is what the first three rows look like:

	A	B	C
1	x	2x+50	11-x
2			
3	-20	10	31
4	-19		
5	-18		
6	-17		

1 Produce this spreadsheet yourself.

2 Copy the formulas in row 3 downwards about 40 times.

3 Compare the values in columns B and C.

4 What is the solution to the equation $2x + 50 = 11 - x$? Explain how the spreadsheet shows the answer.

Further investigation

Use the same method to solve these two equations.
The answer to each one is an integer between $^{-}25$ and 25.

5 $7x + 20 = 5x - 10$

6 $9x - 27 = 13x - 119$

Equations with fraction answers

Sometimes the answers are fractions. We still solve the equations in the same way.

EXERCISE 24.14

Examples

$$7x = 4$$
$$\frac{7x}{7} = \frac{4}{7}$$
$$x = \frac{4}{7}$$

$$6x + 1 = 9$$
$$6x + 1 - 1 = 9 - 1$$
$$6x = 8$$
$$x = \frac{8}{6} = \frac{4}{3}$$
$$x = 1\frac{1}{3}$$

$$5x + 2 = 3x + 1$$
$$5x + 2 - 2 = 3x + 1 - 2$$
$$5x = 3x - 1$$
$$5x - 3x = 3x - 1 - 3x$$
$$2x = {}^{-}1$$
$$\frac{2x}{2} = \frac{{}^{-}1}{2}$$
$$x = \frac{{}^{-}1}{2}$$

Solve these equations.

1 $3x = 2$
2 $5x = {}^{-}3$
3 $6x = 7$
4 $2x = 19$
5 $4x = 11$
6 ${}^{-}3x = 10$
7 $2x - 1 = 10$
8 $4x + 3 = 14$
9 $3x - 4 = 6$
10 $8x + 2 = {}^{-}5$
11 $5x + 2 = {}^{-}5$
12 ${}^{-}2x + 4 = 5$
13 $5x + 2 = 3x + 5$
14 $8x - 4 = 5x + 1$
15 $3x + 2 = x - 5$
16 $4x - 3 = 2x - 8$
17 $3x + 2 = 5x - 7$
18 $5x - 4 = x + 7$

Each of the pears here cost the same amount. How much does the banana cost?

Cost = \$1.05

Cost = \$1.25

Making up equations

Here, we take some information and turn it into an equation. We can then use these equations to solve problems (see next section).

Example Write an equation for this information:
I think of a number, multiply it by 3 and then add 5. This gives a result of 17.

Answer Suppose the number I think of is x.
Then the equation will be: $3x + 5 = 17$

EXERCISE 24.15

1–9 Write down equations for this information. You don't have to solve the equations.

1 I think of a number and subtract 5 from it. This gives a result of $^{-}2$.

2 I think of a number and multiply it by 6. This gives a result of 12.

3 I think of a number and add 8 to it. This gives a result of 17.

4 I think of a number and divide it by 4. This gives a result of 6.

5 I think of a number, multiply it by 2, then add 7 to it. This gives a result of 19.

6 I think of a number, multiply it by 4, then add 5 to it. This gives a result of 1.

7 I think of a number, and multiply it by 8. This gives the same result as if I had added 14 to the number.

8 A number is multiplied by 2, and then has 7 added to it. The result is the same as if 9 was added to the number.

9 A number is multiplied by 8, and then has 5 subtracted from it. The result is the same as if the number was multiplied by 6, and then had 3 added to it.

10 The rule for working out the number of biscuits needed for a meeting is this:

Multiply the number of people by 3 and add 2.

This gives a total of 23 biscuits. Suppose x is the number of people. Write down an equation for this information.

11 The rule for working out the number of pages in a newspaper is this:

Multiply the number of sections by 12, and add 6.

This gives a total of 42 pages. Suppose x is the number of sections. Write down an equation for this information.

12 The rule for working out the profit in dollars at a cinema is this:

Multiply the number of people by 7, and subtract 50.

x represents the number of people, and the profit is \$160. Write down an equation for this information.

Using equations to solve problems (2)

Example If I think of a number and multiply it by 7, I get the same result as if I had multiplied the number by 4 and then added 15.
Write down an equation for this information. Solve the equation to work out the number I am thinking of.

Answer The equation is

$$7x = 4x + 15$$
$$7x - 4x = 15$$
$$3x = 15$$
$$x = \frac{15}{3} = 5$$

Example A school has a drainage problem. They have to choose a drainlayer to employ:

- Advantage Drainlayers Ltd charge \$100 per hour plus a call-out fee of \$80
- Buildwell Drainlayers Ltd charge \$85 per hour plus a call-out fee of \$170.

(a) The Principal thinks the job will take 2 hours. Which firm should the school employ?

(b) The Deputy Principal thinks the job will take 7 hours. Which firm should the school employ?

(c) The rule for working out the total cost if Advantage Drainlayers Ltd are used is $100x + 80$. What does the letter x represent?

(d) Write down the rule for the total cost if Buildwell Drainlayers Ltd are used.

(e) There is one length of time for which the cost will be the same no matter which firm does the job. Make up and solve an equation to work out this time.

Answer (a) Cost of Advantage for 2 hours: $100 \times 2 + 80 = \$280$
Cost of Buildwell for 2 hours: $85 \times 2 + 170 = \$340$
Advantage is cheaper.

(b) Cost of Advantage for 7 hours: $100 \times 7 + 80 = \$780$
Cost of Buildwell for 7 hours: $85 \times 7 + 170 = \$765$
Buildwell is cheaper.

(c) x represents the number of hours for the job.

(d) $85x + 170$

(e) If the cost is the same, the two rules give the same result. That is:

$$100x + 80 = 85x + 170$$
$$100x - 85x = 170 - 80$$
$$15x = 90$$
$$x = \frac{90}{15} = 6$$

If the job takes 6 hours, the two firms both charge the same amount.

EXERCISE 24.16

1–6 *Write down an equation, and then solve it to work out the answer.*

1 What is my lucky number in Lotto? If you multiply it by 3, and then add 11, you get 38.

2 If I multiply the number on my letter-box by 5, I get the same result as if I added 60 to it. What is the number on my letter-box?

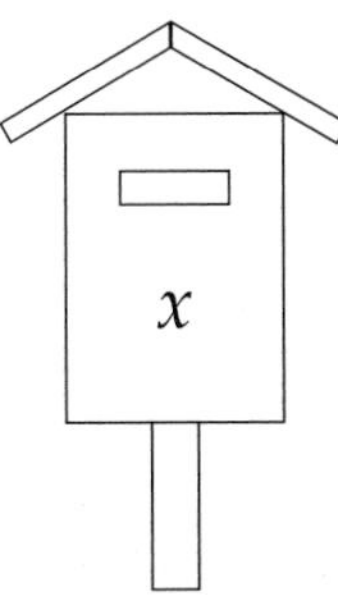

3 Gary works out that if he has saved 4 times as much money as he has now, and adds a $15 gift from his uncle, he will have the money he needs to buy a jacket that costs $95. How much money does he have now?

4 If you added 10 to the outside temperature, you would get the same result as if you subtracted the outside temperature from 8. What is the outside temperature?

5 To work out the number of sausage rolls she needs to make for a party, Hannah multiplies the number of guests by 3, and then subtracts 5. As a result, she makes 61 sausage rolls. How many guests is she expecting?

6 Debbie and Sandra are twins. If Debbie doubles her age and adds 1, and if Sandra takes her age away from 40, they both get the same answer. How old are they?

7 In a triathlon, the running leg is 8 times the length of the swimming leg. The total distance of both legs is 36 km. How long is the swimming leg?

8 The property manager at Aotearoa College is deciding which firm of painters to employ. The Board of Trustees wants the cheapest firm to be employed.

- Striped Painters charge $50 per hour plus an 'administration' fee of $80
- Landscape Painters charge $48 per hour plus a 'booking' fee of $100

(a) Which firm should the College employ if they think the job will take 20 hours?

(b) Which firm should the College employ if they think the job will take 5 hours?

(c) The rule for working out the total cost if Striped Painters are employed is $50x + 80$. What does the letter x represent?

(d) Write down the rule for the total cost if Landscape Painters are employed.

(e) There is one length of time for which the cost will be the same, no matter which firm is employed. Make up and solve an equation to work out this time.

9 The owners of a car-park are deciding on a rule to work out charges for each complete hour.

Here are two rules they could use. Each rule gives the charge in dollars for a car that parks for x hours:

Rule A: $2x - 1$	Rule B: $x + 3$

(a) Which rule would mean that cars parked for 1 hour would pay $1?

(b) There is one length of time for which both rules give the same result. Make up and solve an equation to work out this time.

10 Lee has a job filling bags of cement. He calculated that if he filled 4 bags, he would have 17 kg left over. However, if he tried to fill 5 bags, he would be 3 kg short. Write an equation and solve it to work out x, the amount of cement in a bag.

25 Expanding brackets and factorising

Expanding brackets

STARTER

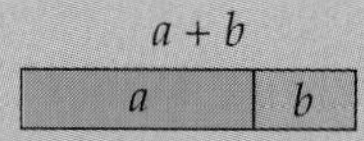

The diagram shows a block of wood, with lengths a and b marked in.

If we double the whole length we get:

$2 \times (a + b)$ | a | b | a | b |

If we double each length, and then add, we get:

$2a + 2b$

$2a$ $2b$

- **Is the total length of wood the same in each case? Explain.**

When an expression has brackets (or grouping symbols), the part **inside** the brackets is usually calculated first.

Example $4 \times (3 + 5) = 4 \times 8 = 32$

However, we would get the same result if we:

- first multiplied each number inside the brackets by 4
- then did the adding last.

$4 \times 3 \quad + \quad 4 \times 5 = 12 + 20 = 32$

This is called the **distributive rule.**
It also works in algebra.

Examples $6(x + y) = 6x + 6y$
$2(c - d) = 2c - 2d$

We call this process **expanding brackets**.
Each term inside the brackets is multiplied by the term that is outside.

EXERCISE 25.1

1–4 *Evaluate these:*

1 (a) two lots of $(3 + 5)$
  (b) two lots of 3 + two lots of 5

2 (a) $6 \times (10 + 1)$
  (b) $6 \times 10 + 6 \times 1$

3 (a) 4 lots of $(50 - 30)$
  (b) 4 lots of 50 – 4 lots of 30

4 (a) $7 \times (11 - 5)$
  (b) $7 \times 11 - 7 \times 5$

5–16 *Write down what needs to go in each box to expand the brackets correctly.*

5 $4 \times (10 + 3) = \square \times 10 + 4 \times 3$

6 $6 \times (8 - 2) = 6 \times \square - 6 \times 2$

7 $10 \times (6 + 7) = 10 \times 6 + \square \times 7$

8 $5 \times (14 - 3) = 5 \times 14 - 5 \times \square$

9 $8 \times (7 - 5) = \square \times 7 - \square \times 5$

10 $^{-}2 \times (3 + 4) = {}^{-}2 \times 3 + \square \times 4$

11 $5(x + y) = \square \times x + 5y$

12 $8(x - y) = 8 \times \square - 8y$

13 $6(p + q) = 6p + \square \times q$

14 $3(x - 12) = 3 \times \square - 3 \times 12$

15 $4(x + 8) = \square \times x + \square \times 8$

16 $3(x - 1) = 3x - 3 \times \square$

EXERCISE 25.2

Example Expand $6(x - y)$

Answer $6(x - y) = 6x - 6y$

Expand these brackets:

1 $3(x + y)$

2 $4(x + y)$

3 $5(p + q)$

4 $10(x + y)$

5 $7(c + d)$

6 $2(p - q)$

7 $3(x - y)$

8 $5(p + q + r)$

9 $4(p - q + r)$

10 $12(x - y + z)$

The number in front of the brackets can also be *negative*.

Example (a) Expand $^{-}3(x + y)$ (b) Expand $^{-}4(x - y)$

Answer

(a) $^{-}3(x + y) = {}^{-}3x + {}^{-}3y$
$= {}^{-}3x - 3y$

(b) $^{-}4(x - y) = {}^{-}4 \times x - {}^{-}4 \times y$
$= {}^{-}4x - {}^{-}4y$
$= {}^{-}4x + 4y$

EXERCISE 25.3

Expand these brackets:

1 $^{-}2(x + y)$

2 $^{-}4(p + q)$

3 $^{-}5(x + y)$

4 $^{-}6(u - v)$

5 $^{-}1(x - y)$

6 $^{-}4(p - q)$

7 $^{-}3(x + y - z)$

8 $^{-}1(x - y + z)$

Remember the rules for simplifying negative numbers here!

Sometimes, there are also numbers *inside* the brackets. These are multiplied by the number outside the brackets in the same way.

Example (a) Expand $2(x + 3)$ (b) Expand $^-4(x - 6)$

Answer (a) $2(x + 3) = 2 \times x + 2 \times 3$
$= 2x + 6$

(b) $^-4(x - 6) = {}^-4 \times x - {}^-4 \times 6$
$= {}^-4x - {}^-24$
$= {}^-4x + 24$

This diagram should help you to see how this expanding process works:

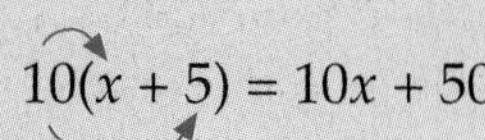

$10(x + 5) = 10x + 50$

EXERCISE 25.4

Expand these brackets:

1. $3(x + 6)$
2. $4(x + 5)$
3. $2(x - 4)$
4. $8(x - 2)$
5. $^-3(x + 3)$
6. $^-4(x + 6)$
7. $^-2(x - 4)$
8. $7(x - 11)$
9. $8(x + 4)$
10. $^-8(x - 2)$
11. $^-1(x - 2)$
12. $^-1(x + 3)$
13. $12(x - 2)$
14. $^-5(x - 10)$
15. $^-6(x + 4)$

EXERCISE 25.5

Example Expand $4(3x - 2)$

Answer $4(3x - 2) = 4 \times 3x - 4 \times 2$
$= 12x - 8$

Example Expand $^-5(2x - 1)$

Answer $^-5(2x - 1) = {}^-5 \times 2x - {}^-5 \times 1$
$= {}^-10x - {}^-5$
$= {}^-10x + 5$

Expand these brackets:

1. $5(2x + 3)$
2. $4(7x - 2)$
3. $10(4x - 2)$
4. $^-3(5x + 2)$
5. $^-2(4x - 3)$
6. $2(3x + 1)$
7. $6(3x - 4)$
8. $^-3(2x + 11)$
9. $^-1(5x + 4)$
10. $^-1(7x - 2)$
11. $10(2x + 1)$
12. $20(3x - 2)$
13. $^-8(7x - 6)$
14. $^-1(3x + 1)$
15. $^-6(4x - 1)$

The terms inside the brackets can also be multiplied by a letter outside.

Example (a) Expand $a(x + y)$ (b) Expand $x(2x + 3y)$

Answer (a) $a(x + y) = ax + ay$

(b) $x(2x + 3y) = x \times 2x + x \times 3y$
$= 2x^2 + 3xy$

EXERCISE 25.6 *Expand these brackets:*

1 $p(q + r)$
2 $a(b + c)$
3 $x(y - z)$
4 $p(q - r)$
5 $a(b + c - d)$
6 $x(a + b + c + d)$
7 $p(q + 3)$
8 $x(y - 4)$
9 $x(a + 1)$
10 $d(3 + c)$
11 $c(14 - d)$
12 $x(x + 2)$
13 $x(x - 3)$
14 $x(2x + 1)$
15 $x(3x - 2)$
16 $x(2x + 6)$
17 $x(7 - x)$
18 $x(x - 1)$

EXERCISE 25.7 *Expand these brackets:*

Example Expand $3p(x + y)$

Answer $3p(x + y) = 3px + 3py$

Example Expand $4x(2x - 5)$

Answer $4x(2x - 5) = 4x \times 2x - 4x \times 5$
$= 8x^2 - 20x$

1 $4a(c + d)$
2 $7x(p - q)$
3 $9p(q - r)$
4 $5y(x + z)$
5 $2x(x + 3)$
6 $4x(x - 2)$
7 $3x(2x + 1)$
8 $2x(x - y)$
9 $7x(x + 1)$
10 $3x(x - 6)$
11 $4x(x + 5)$
12 $6x(2x - 3)$
13 $5p(p + 2q)$
14 $5x(4x - 1)$
15 $^{-}3x(4x + 3)$
16 $^{-}2x(x - 1)$
17 $^{-}x(2x + 1)$
18 $^{-}4x(x - 2)$

INVESTIGATION

GIFT-GIVING

In many families, each person gives the other members of the family a gift for Christmas. The gifts are placed under a Christmas tree.

Let's investigate to see if there is a rule that gives the number of gifts under the tree.

If there are two people in a family (e.g. Mr and Mrs Smith), there will be two gifts under the tree. One will be from Mr Smith to Mrs Smith, and one will be from Mrs Smith to Mr Smith.

1 How many gifts will there be if there are three people in the family?
2 How many gifts will there be if there are four people in the family?

One way of checking the number of gifts would be to make a list of all the pairs of people. Do this for a family of five people—call the people A, B, C, D, and E. Some of the pairs are AB, AC, AD, AE, BA, etc.

3 Use this process to predict the number of gifts under the tree when there are five people.

Another way of working out the number of gifts is to count the number of people in the family. Each person has to give one gift less than there are people. So, if there are 11 people, each person will have to give 10 gifts. There will be 110 gifts altogether.

4 Investigate to find a formula for the number of gifts when there are n people in the family.

5 Express this rule in two ways: with brackets, and expanded.

Answer:

14 12 4	14 12 10 13 7	13 9 6 8
5 13 9 11	14 12 4	3 2 1

Here's how to decode the answer.
Each set of brackets is labelled with a letter.
The expansions are labelled with numbers.
Match each set of brackets with the correct expansion to find the answer.

Brackets

C $3a(b + c)$
D $^{-}3a(b + c)$
E $2(a - b - c)$
F $^{-}2(a + b)$
H $^{-}7(^{-}x - y - 4)$
I $5x(x + 1)$
K $^{-}3(a - b + c)$
M $^{-}7(x - y + 4)$
N $2(a + b)$
O $7(x - y + 4)$
R $5x(x + y)$
S $2(a + b - c)$
T $^{-}5x(x + y)$
U $2(a - b)$

Expansions

1 $2a + 2b$
2 $2a - 2b$
3 $2a + 2b - 2c$
4 $2a - 2b - 2c$
5 $^{-}2a - 2b$
6 $3ab + 3ac$
7 $^{-}3ab - 3ac$
8 $^{-}3a + 3b - 3c$
9 $7x - 7y + 28$
10 $5x^2 + 5x$
11 $^{-}7x + 7y - 28$
12 $7x + 7y + 28$
13 $5x^2 + 5xy$
14 $^{-}5x^2 - 5xy$

Expanding brackets and collecting like terms

Remember:
- like terms are ones like $5a$, $7a$, $36a$, etc. They can be added or subtracted.
- terms such as a, $2b$, $7c$ or x, 8, x^2, etc. are unlike terms. They can't be added or subtracted.

Example Expand and simplify $2(4x + y) + 8(3x - 2y)$

Answer

$$\begin{aligned} 2(4x + y) + 8(3x - 2y) &= 2 \times 4x + 2 \times y + 8 \times 3x - 8 \times 2y \quad \text{(expanding brackets)} \\ &= 8x + 2y + 24x - 16y \\ &= 8x + 24x + 2y - 16y \quad \text{(collecting like terms)} \\ &= 32x - 14y \end{aligned}$$

EXERCISE 25.8

Expand and simplify these expressions.

1. $2(x + y) + 3(x + y)$
2. $4(x + y) + 5(2x + 3y)$
3. $3(2x + y) + 2(x - y)$
4. $7(x + y) + 3(x + 4y)$
5. $5(x + 2y) + 4(3x + 7y)$
6. $3(x + 2y) - 2(x + y)$
7. $5(x - y) + 3(x + y)$
8. $7(x - y) + 2(x - y)$
9. $8(2x + y) - 3(x + 2y)$
10. $3(x + 2) + 4(x + 2)$
11. $4(x + 1) + 2(x + 8)$
12. $7(x - 1) + 3(x + 4)$
13. $5(x + 2) - 4(x + 3)$
14. $10(x + 4) - 2(x - 8)$
15. $6(3x + 2) + 4(x - 2)$
16. $2(4x - 1) + 5(x + 2)$

A farmer has to row a boat across a river to take a duck, a fox, and a bag of grain to the other side.

The boat only has enough room for the farmer and *one* of the other three things.

The duck can't be left alone with the fox or with the bag of grain.

- Explain how the farmer can take all three across the river.

Equations with brackets

Example Solve $2(3x - 1) = x + 8$

Answer

$$\begin{aligned} 2(3x - 1) &= x + 8 \\ 6x - 2 &= x + 8 \quad \text{(expanding brackets)} \\ 6x - 2 + 2 &= x + 8 + 2 \\ 6x &= x + 10 \\ 6x - x &= x + 10 - x \\ 5x &= 10 \\ x &= \frac{10}{5} \\ x &= 2 \end{aligned}$$

Expand the brackets first. Then solve like ordinary equations.

EXERCISE 25.9

Solve these equations:

1. $2(x + 1) = 6$
2. $4(x - 3) = 20$
3. $5(x + 3) = 10$
4. $3(x - 7) = {}^{-}6$
5. $5(x - 1) = 15$
6. $6(2x - 1) = 6$
7. $6(x + 5) = x$
8. $2(3x - 1) = 28$
9. $4(x + 2) = 2x$
10. $4x + 8 = 2(x - 3)$
11. $3x - 9 = 2(x + 8)$
12. $4(x - 3) = 2x + 8$
13. $5(x + 6) = 2x + 9$
14. $x - 4 = 2(x + 3)$
15. $3(x + 2) = 2(x - 1)$
16. $6(x + 3) = 7(x - 2)$
17. $2(2x - 3) = 3(x + 1)$
18. $5(x - 3) = 2(2x + 1)$
19. $3(2x - 5) = 5(x + 2)$
20. $12(x + 3) - 3(x - 7) = 3$

Factorising

STARTER

- How could an expression like $8x + 8y$ be written with brackets?
- If it *was* written using brackets, $8x + 8y = \square(x + y)$ what number would go in the box?
- If $4x - 4y$ was written as $4(\square - \square)$ what letters would go in the boxes?

Example Factorise $2x + 2y$.

Answer $2x$ and $2y$ each have a **common factor** of 2.

$2x + 2y = 2(x + y)$ (the common factor of 2 is written at the front of the brackets)

Factorising is the reverse process to expanding.

EXERCISE 25.10

Write down the number, letter or symbol that needs to go in the box to make the factorising work correctly.

1 $3x + 3y = \square(x + y)$
2 $7x - 7y = \square(x - y)$
3 $5x + 5y = \square(x + y)$
4 $10p - 10q = \square(p - q)$
5 $2p + 2q = 2(\square + q)$
6 $4x - 4y = 4(\square - y)$
7 $6p + 6q = 6(p + \square)$
8 $9x + 9y = \square(x + y)$
9 $12x + 12y = 12(x + \square)$
10 $7x - 7y = 7(x \square y)$
11 $2x + 2y = 2(x \square y)$
12 $15x + 15y = 15(\square + y)$

EXERCISE 25.11

Factorise these expressions:

1 $4p + 4q$
2 $10x + 10y$
3 $3x + 3y$
4 $8p - 8q$
5 $5c - 5d$
6 $30x - 30y$
7 $7p + 7q$
8 $3x + 3y + 3z$
9 $2a + 2b + 2c + 2d$
10 $5x + 5y - 5z$

Example Factorise $3x + 12$.

Answer $3x$ and 12 each have a common factor of 3

$3x + 12 = 3 \times x + 3 \times 4$

$= 3(x + 4)$ (the common factor of 3 goes to the front of the brackets)

EXERCISE 25.12

Copy each of these. Replace the box with a number, letter or symbol to make the factorising work correctly.

1 $3x + 15 = \square(x + 5)$
2 $7x - 28 = \square(x - 4)$
3 $5x + 30 = \square(x + 6)$
4 $10x - 20 = \square(x - 2)$
5 $2x + 12 = 2(\square + 6)$
6 $4x - 32 = 4(\square - 8)$
7 $6x + 42 = 6(x + \square)$
8 $9x + 108 = \square(x + 12)$
9 $12x + 60 = 12(x + \square)$
10 $7x - 28 = 7(x \square 4)$
11 $2x + 16 = 2(x \square 8)$
12 $15x + 45 = 15(\square + 3)$
13 $8x - 24 = 8(x - \square)$
14 $6x + 8 = 2(3x + \square)$
15 $12x - 16 = 4(\square - 4)$
16 $12x + 15 = \square(4x + 5)$

EXERCISE 25.13

Factorise these:

1 $2x + 6$
2 $10x + 20$
3 $4x + 12$
4 $3x + 21$
5 $6x + 24$
6 $5x - 10$
7 $12x - 24$
8 $3x - 36$
9 $7x - 21$
10 $8x + 24$
11 $7x - 63$
12 $5x + 55$

Taking out the highest common factor

Example Factorise $6x - 15$.

Answer The highest common factor of $6x$ and 15 is 3.
$6x - 15 = 3(2x - 5)$

EXERCISE 25.14

Factorise these expressions. The first four have been started for you.

1 $15x + 20 = 5(\quad)$
2 $32x + 24 = 8(\quad)$
3 $12x - 22 = 2(\quad)$
4 $15x - 24 = 3(\quad)$
5 $12x + 18$
6 $15x - 20$
7 $4x + 6$
8 $18x - 24$
9 $6x - 4$
10 $30x + 20$
11 $40x - 50$
12 $12x + 30$
13 $28x + 24$
14 $14x - 21$
15 $36x - 48$

Sometimes the number 1 is needed inside the brackets.

Example (a) Factorise $7x + 7$.
(b) Factorise $6x + 3$.

Answer (a) $7x + 7 = 7(x + 1)$
(b) $6x$ and 3 have a common factor of 3
$6x + 3 = 3(2x + 1)$

EXERCISE 25.15

Factorise these expressions:

1 $3x + 3$
2 $2x - 2$
3 $11x + 11$
4 $8x - 4$
5 $4x + 2$
6 $15x - 5$
7 $24x + 12$
8 $18x - 3$
9 $10x + 10$
10 $21x - 3$

INVESTIGATION

THE FARMER AND THE SQUARE PENS

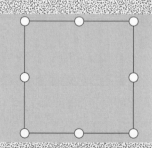

A farmer is investigating fencing patterns for square pens.
The first pen has 3 posts on each side.
Altogether, 8 posts are needed.

1 How many posts are needed for a pen with 4 posts on each side?
Draw a diagram to work this out.

2 Copy and complete this table:

Number of posts on each side	2	3	4	5	6
Total number of posts	4	8			

3 Predict how many posts will be needed altogether when there are 20 posts on each side.

4 Write down a formula that gives the number of posts, P, when there are n posts on each side. Write it as $P =$ ______

5 Show that the formula can be written in two ways—expanded and factorised.

Letters as common factors

To find common factors, write out the expression in full. Then look for letters that are the same.

Example Factorise $cd - ce$

Answer Common factor is c.

$cd - ce = c(d - e)$

Example Factorise $x^2 - xy$

Answer $x^2 - xy = x \times x - x \times y$ (writing in full)

The common factor is x.

$x^2 - xy = x(x - y)$

EXERCISE 25.16

Factorise these expressions:

1 $ax + ay$
2 $bp + bq$
3 $cd - bc$
4 $ax + bx$
5 $x^2 + xy$
6 $x^2 + 5x$
7 $x^2 - 3x$
8 $xy + 3x$
9 $xy - 5y$
10 $x^2 + 2xy$
11 $7x - xy$
12 $4x + 3xy$
13 $2x + x^2$
14 $3x - x^2$
15 $ax + 5a$

For always!

Can you explain why this number trick *always* gives the answer 4?

- Think of a number
- Multiply it by 6
- Add 8
- Divide by 2
- Subtract 3 times the number you started with

26 Co-ordinates

STARTER

- What information do co-ordinates give?

Co-ordinates on maps

Grid references follow a system where *two* items of information are needed. Each place on a map has:

- a reference that relates to a horizontal line, usually on the bottom of the map
- a reference that relates to a vertical line, usually on the left-hand side of the map.

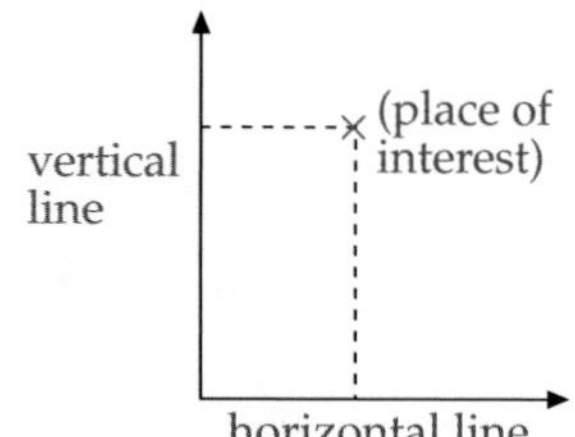

The two references, taken together, are called **co-ordinates**. They identify the place of interest.

To avoid confusion, we write down the horizontal reference **first**, and the vertical reference **second**.

You will find a map very useful if you have ever tried to find a street in an unfamiliar town or city.

When a map has a lot of points of interest, it will often have a *directory* or index. This tells you roughly where to look on the map.

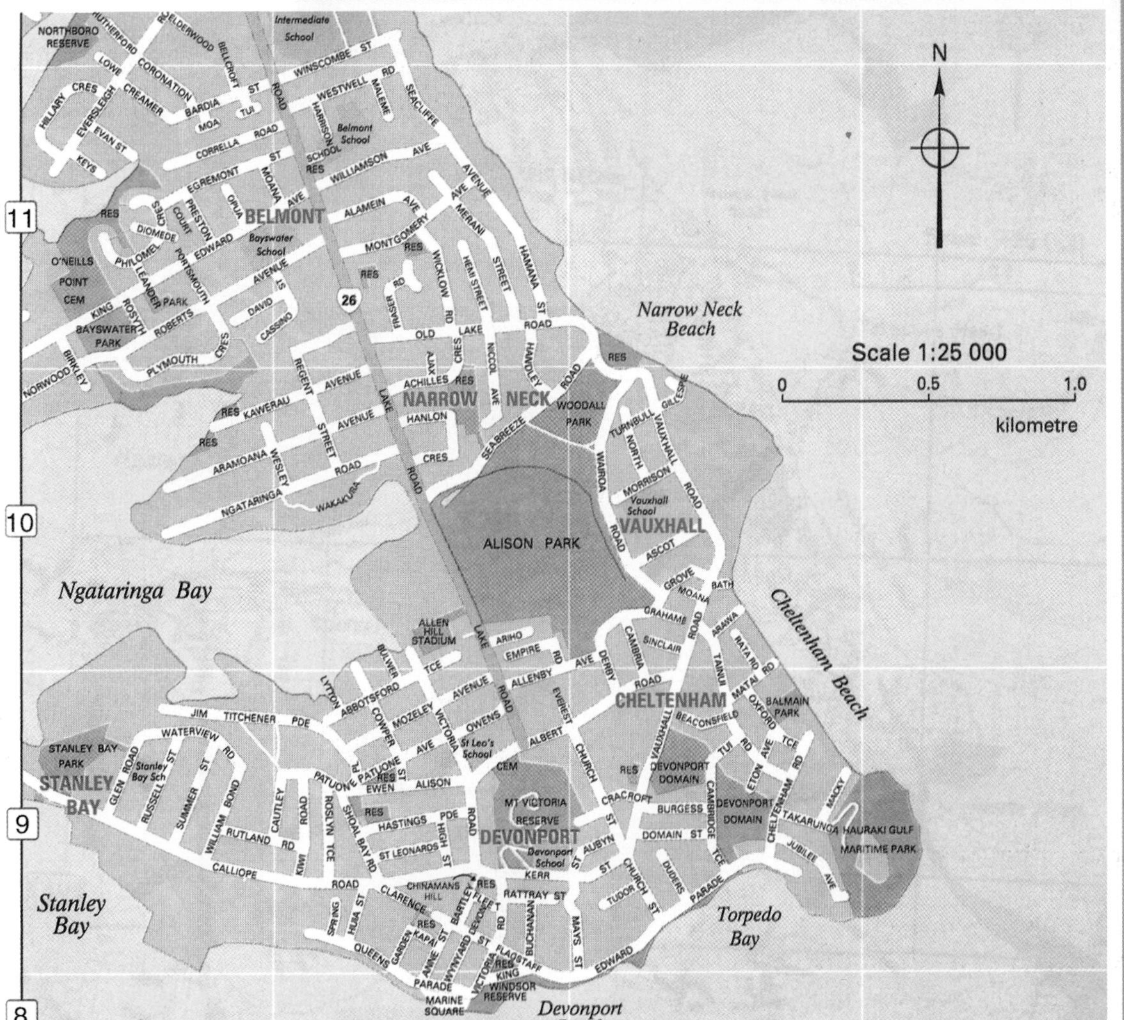

Directory	Grid reference
Glen Road	C9
Grove Road	E10
Jubilee Avenue	E9
Kiwi Road	D9
Moa Place	C11

- What school is in Glen Road?
- What is the nearest park to Grove Road?
- Which primary school has grid reference E10?
- What beach has grid reference E11?

EXERCISE 26.1

1 This map is a guide to Alphaworld Amusement Park.

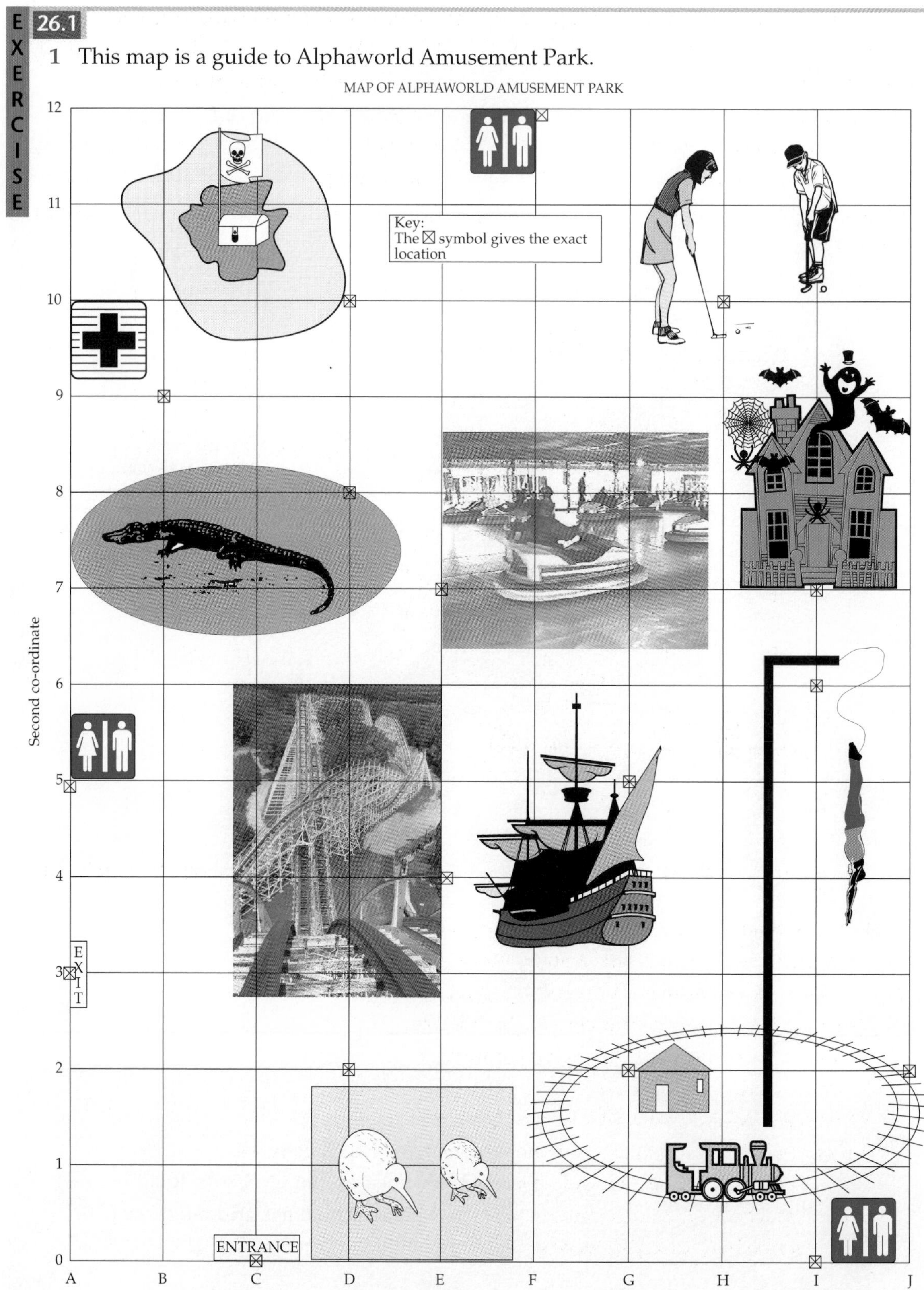

(a) Write down what you would find at or near the places with these co-ordinates:

(i) D2 (ii) I7 (iii) C0 (iv) A5 (v) B9 (vi) E7

(b) Write down the co-ordinates that give the location of each of these places:

(i) pirate ship
(ii) crocodile enclosure
(iii) treasure island
(iv) the exit
(v) minigolf
(vi) bungy-jump.

2 In Invercargill, the streets in the city centre are laid out exactly in North–South and East–West directions.

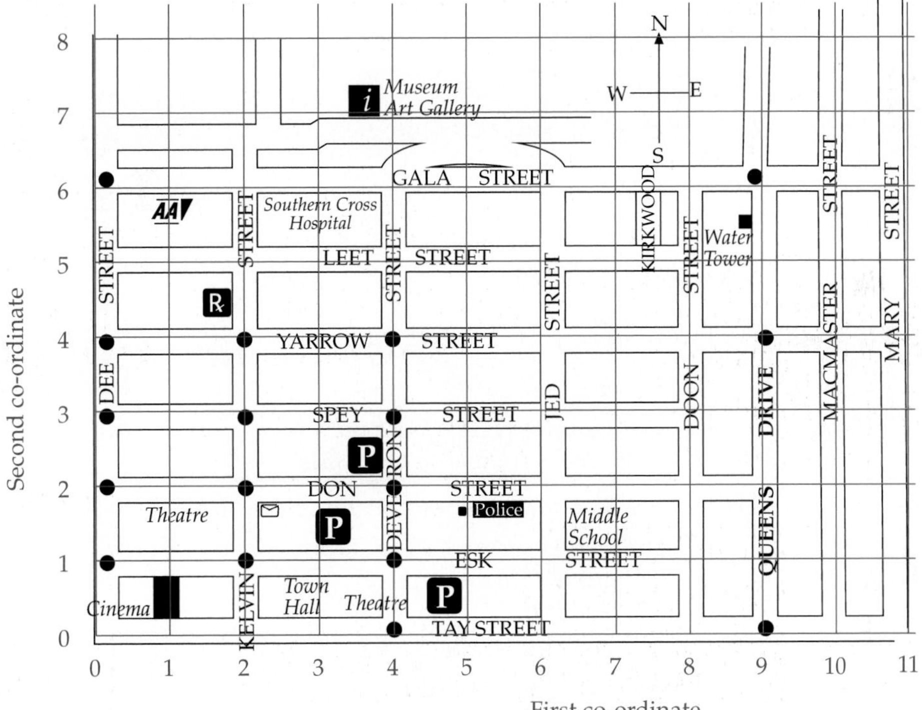

The grid shows that the Urgent Pharmacy is at (2, 4). This is represented on the map by the symbol ℞

(a) Which school is next to the intersection given by (6, 2)?

(b) What point of interest would you see from (9, 5)?

(c) What are the co-ordinates of the intersection of Leet and Jed Streets?

(d) What are the closest co-ordinates to the Post Shop (✉)?

(e) What are the co-ordinates of the police station?

(f) What street would you walk along to go from (0, 4) to (9, 4)?

(g) What street would you walk along to go from (6, 1) to (6, 5)?

(h) Simon cycled from (0, 0) to (0, 5), then to (4, 5) and finally to (4, 7).

(i) What street intersection did he start from?
(ii) What was his final destination?
(iii) Describe his journey in words.

Extension

Land Information New Zealand (*toitu te whenua*) publish specialist topographic maps of all parts of the North Island and South Island. They show enormous amounts of information.
These maps are printed using a scale of 1 : 50 000. The squares on the map are 2 cm wide.
This means 2 cm on the map represents $2 \times 50\,000 = 100\,000$ cm, or 1 km, on the ground. Each square represents an area of 1 km^2.

This map shows part of the Bay of Islands, in Northland. It uses a special six-figure system of co-ordinates. This gives locations accurately to within 100 metres.

Let's look at an example, for the Caravan Park at Orongo Bay. Its grid reference is 152569. How does this work?

Split the reference into two parts: 152 569

First three figures:	152	• the 15 appears along the horizontal scale at the bottom of the map • the 2 shows the caravan park is 200 metres further on— or 2 tenths further to the right
Last three figures:	569	• the 56 appears along the vertical scale at the side of the map • the 9 shows the caravan park is 900 metres further up— or 9 tenths further up

3 What features of interest will you find at these grid references?
(a) 128589 (b) 145565 (c) 110549 (d) 165562 (e) 178618

4 Give the grid references for these places as accurately as you can. (It doesn't matter if the 3rd and 6th digits are out by 1.)
(a) the cemetery at Paihia
(b) Oturori Rock
(c) the end of the railway line at Opua
(d) the Maori pa on Marriott Island
(e) Paroa Pa

5 Use the centimetre scale of your ruler to answer these questions. 2 cm on the map = 1 km on the ground OR 1 cm on the map = 500 m on the ground.
(a) What is the distance for the passenger ferry service from the jetty at Russell to the jetty at Paihia?
(b) How long is Toretore Island?
(c) What is the distance for the vehicular ferry route from Opua to Okiato?

6 Estimate the area of Motuarohia Island, to the nearest km^2.

7 What is the height (in metres) of the highest point on Motuarohia Island?

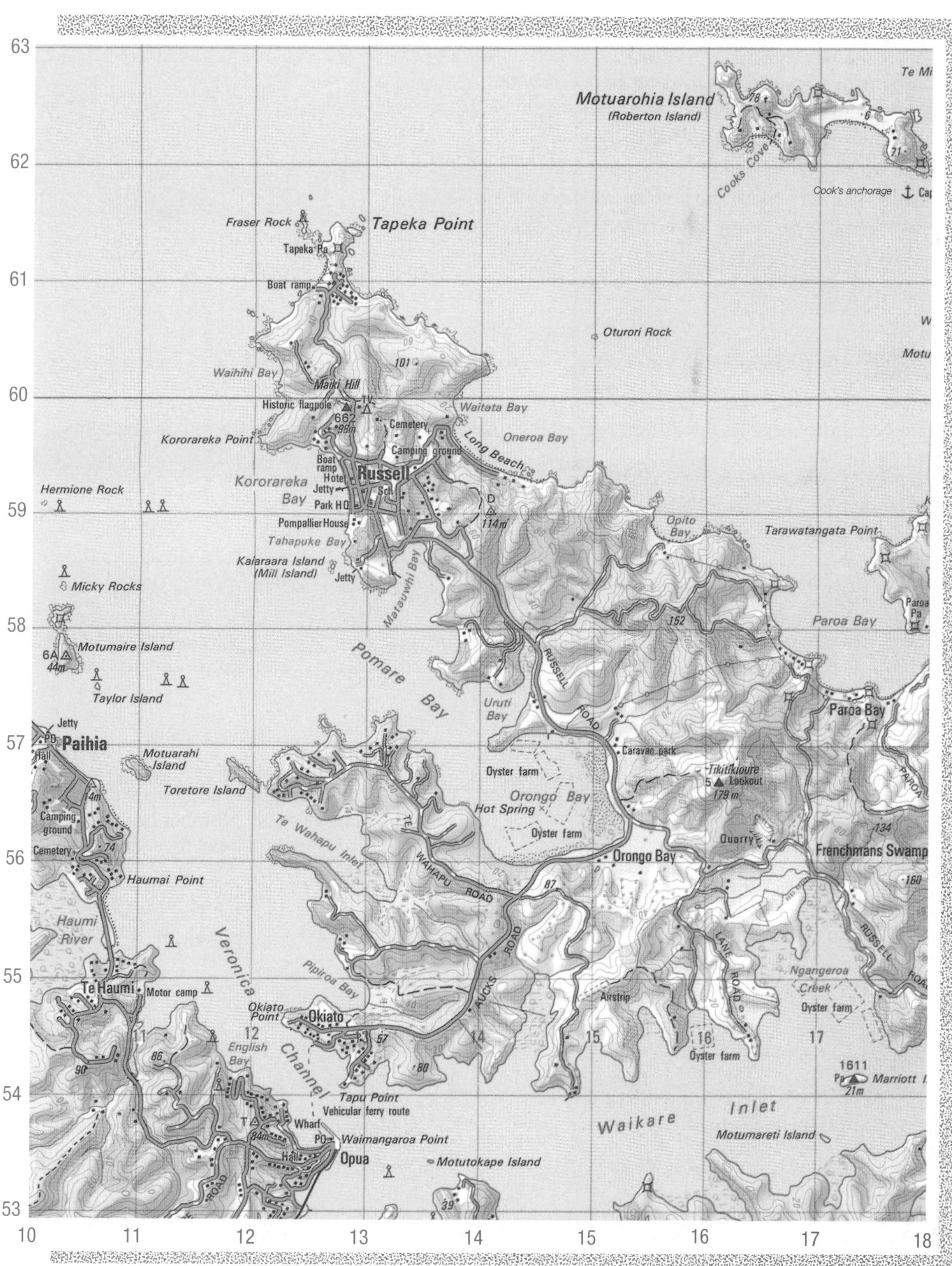

Motuarohia Island
(Roberton Island)
Cooks Cove
Cook's anchorage
Fraser Rock
Tapeka Point
Tapeka Pa
Boat ramp
Oturori Rock
Waihihi Bay
Maiki Hill
Historic flagpole
Waitata Bay
Cemetery
Oneroa Bay
Kororareka Point
Camping ground
Long Beach
Russell
Kororareka Bay
Hermione Rock
Pompallier House
Tahapuke Bay
Kaiaraara Island
(Mill Island)
Jetty
Opito Bay
Tarawatangata Point
Micky Rocks
Matauwhi Bay
Paroa Bay
Motumaire Island
Pomare Bay
Russell Road
Taylor Island
Uruti Bay
Paroa Bay
Paihia
Motuarahi Island
Caravan park
Tikitikioure
Lookout
Oyster farm
Toretore Island
Orongo Bay
Hot Spring
Te Wahapu Inlet
Quarry
Frenchmans Swamp
Camping ground
Cemetery
Orongo Bay
Haumai Point
Wahapu Road
Haumi River
Veronica Channel
Aucks Road
Lane Road
Ngangeroa Creek
Pipiroa Bay
Te Haumi
Motor camp
Okiato Point
Okiato
Airstrip
Oyster farm
English Bay
Oyster farm
Marriott
Tapu Point
Vehicular ferry route
Inlet
Waikare
Wharf
Waimangaroa Point
Motumareti Island
Opua
Mototukape Island

Mathematical co-ordinates

In Mathematics, we use co-ordinates to describe the position of points on a whole-number plane.

- The scales are at right-angles to each other.
- Both scales are number lines that start at 0.
- The horizontal scale at the bottom is called the ***x*-axis**.
- The vertical scale on the left is called the ***y*-axis**.

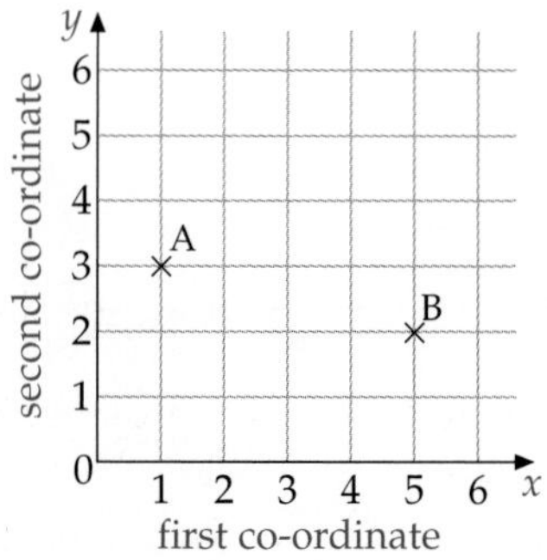

Examples The point marked A is (1, 3).
The point marked B is (5, 2).

The first co-ordinate gives the distance *across* the number plane. The scale on the *x*-axis gives this information—for A this is 1 unit.
The second co-ordinate gives the distance *up* the number plane. The scale on the *y*-axis gives this information—for A this is 3 units.

The **order** of the two co-ordinates is important. For example, (4, 1) is not the same point as (1, 4).
In a pair of co-ordinates, the x number comes first and the y number second.

EXERCISE 26.2

1 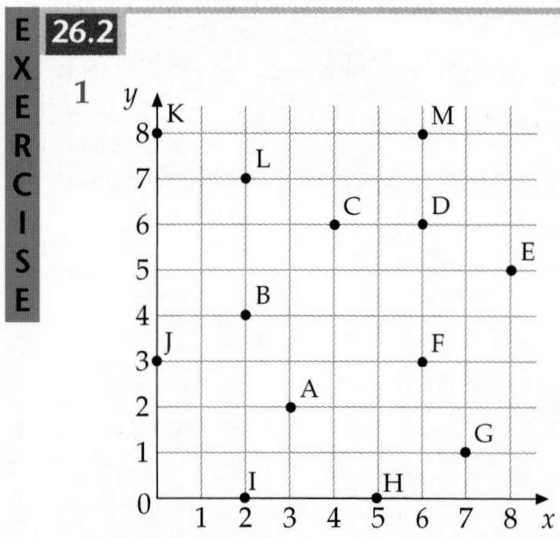

Write down the co-ordinates of the points labelled A to M.

2 Draw and label an *x*-axis and *y*-axis on a grid of squared paper. Number both axes from 0 to 10. Plot and label these points with a cross (×):

A = (2, 1)	F = (4, 9)
B = (3, 2)	G = (0, 4)
C = (5, 1)	H = (9, 0)
D = (1, 6)	I = (4, 0)
E = (8, 8)	J = (7, 5)

3 On a sheet of grid paper, draw an *x*-axis and a *y*-axis. Plot the four points E = (1, 3); F = (5, 4); G = (4, 8) and H = (0, 7). What kind of shape is EFGH?

4

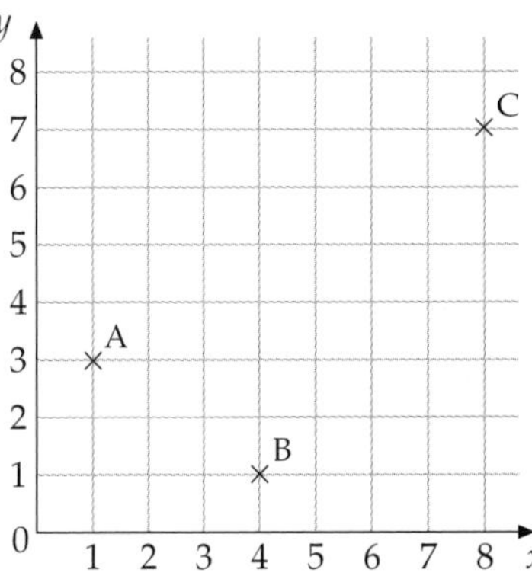

(a) Write down the co-ordinates of A, B and C.

(b) A, B and C are three of the four corners of a rectangle. What are the co-ordinates of D, the fourth corner?

5 A parallelogram is a four-sided shape with two pairs of parallel sides. It has half-turn symmetry.
An isosceles trapezium has one pair of parallel sides, and one pair of sides the same length. It has one axis of symmetry.

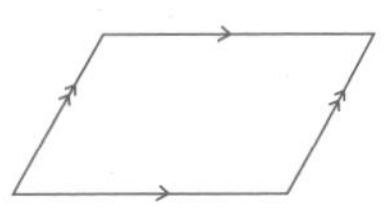
parallelogram

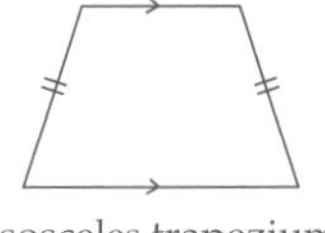
isosceles trapezium

(a) (2, 3), (4, 6) and (5, 3) are three of the four corners of a parallelogram. Plot these three points. Then write down the co-ordinates of the fourth corner. (There are three possible answers.)

(b) PQRS is an isosceles trapezium. P = (2, 5); Q = (4, 7); R = (8, 7). Draw a diagram and plot P, Q and R. What are the co-ordinates of S? (There is more than one possible answer.)

ACTIVITY

This is a game like Battleships™, and uses co-ordinates. The winner is the first person to find a hidden aircraft-carrier. The aircraft carrier has the outline of a parallelogram.

- Choose a partner. Each person then draws a grid, with both the x-axis and the y-axis numbered from 0 to 7.
- Draw a parallelogram on your grid. Place the four corners at points that have whole-number co-ordinates.

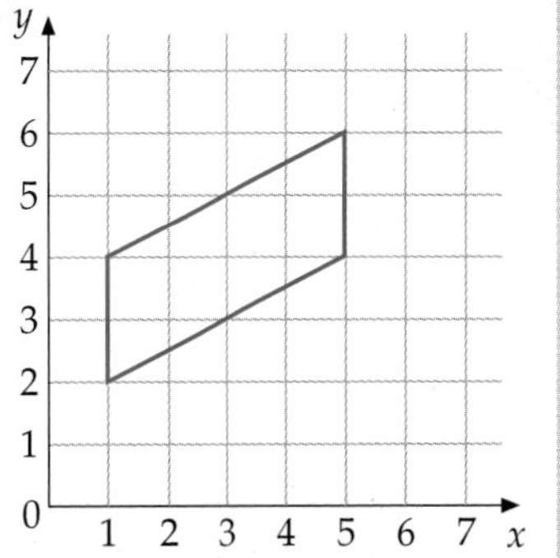

- Hide your grid from the other person.
- Now, take turns at guessing your partner's co-ordinates.

- If your partner guesses a point on the deck of the aircraft carrier (inside the parallelogram), tell him or her they have hit the deck.
- If they guess a point on the side of the parallelogram, they get an extra guess.
- If they guess one of the four corners, they get two extra turns.

The winner is the first person to locate the four corners of the parallelogram.

Using co-ordinates with integers

Remember how the whole-number line can be extended in reverse to show the integers?

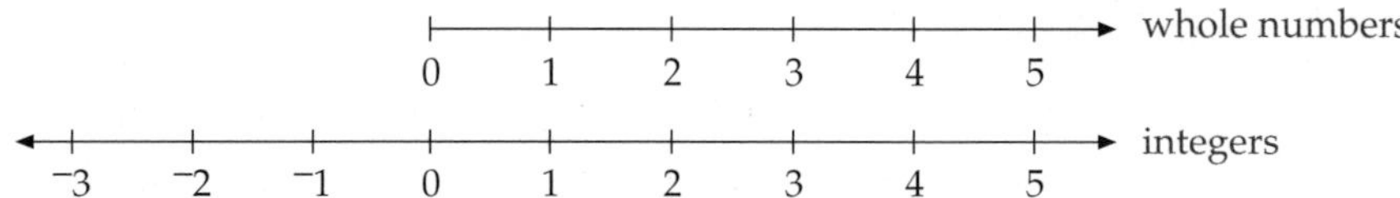

The same thing can be done to the *x*-axis and the *y*-axis.

We always write co-ordinates this way:
(*x* number first, *y* number second).

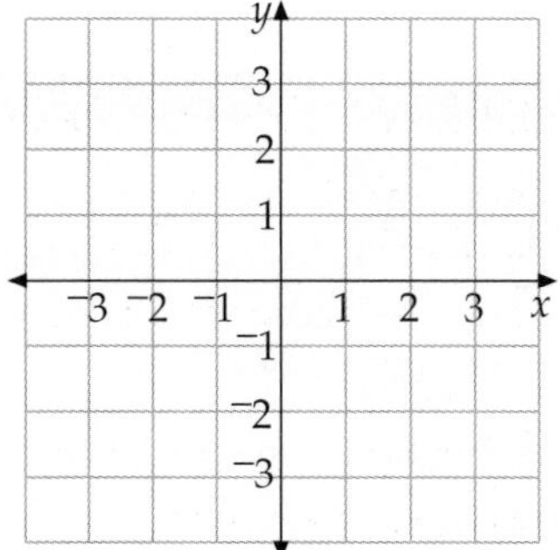

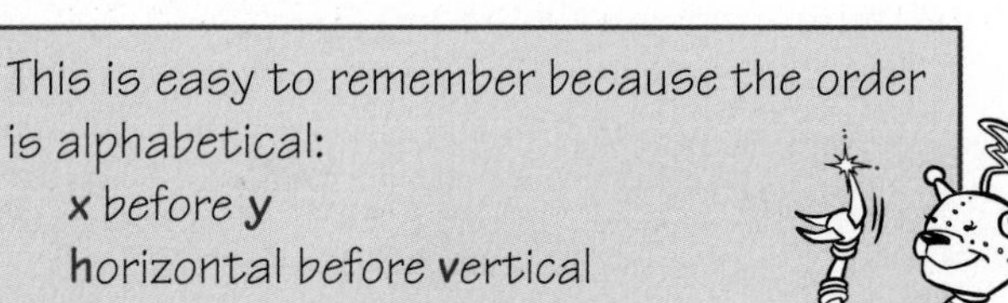

This is easy to remember because the order is alphabetical:
x before **y**
horizontal before **v**ertical
first before **s**econd

Example A is the point $(^-1, 3)$
B is the point $(^-2, ^-4)$
C is the point $(5, ^-2)$

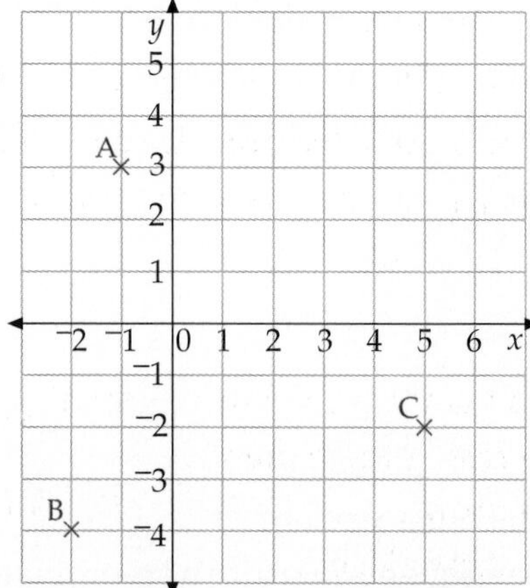

(0, 0) is the point where the x-axis and the y-axis intersect.
We often call this point the **origin**.

EXERCISE 26.3

1 Write down the co-ordinates of the points labelled A to T.

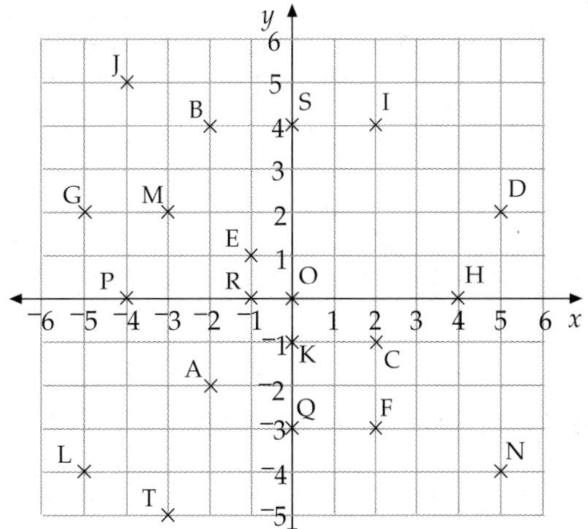

2 Draw and label an x-axis and a y-axis on a grid of squared paper. Number both axes from $^-6$ to 6. Plot and label these points with a cross (×).

A = (2, 3)	E = $(^-2, 0)$	I = $(^-5, 5)$	M = $(^-4, 2)$
B = $(^-2, ^-3)$	F = $(1, ^-2)$	J = $(0, ^-3)$	N = $(2, ^-4)$
C = $(5, ^-2)$	G = $(^-3, ^-3)$	K = $(^-2, 4)$	O = (0, 0)
D = $(^-1, 4)$	H = $(4, ^-4)$	L = $(^-3, ^-1)$	P = $(0, ^-1)$

3 Draw and label an x-axis and a y-axis on a grid of squared paper.

(a) Plot and label these points:
A = $(^-1, ^-2)$, B = $(2, ^-2)$, C = (2, 1).

(b) A, B, and C are three of the four corners of a square. What are the co-ordinates of the fourth corner, D?

4 Draw and label an x-axis and a y-axis on a grid of squared paper.

(a) Plot and label the points P = (1, 3), Q = $(^-4, 1)$, R = $(1, ^-1)$.

(b) P, Q and R are the three corners of a triangle. Explain why △PQR is isosceles.

(c) P, Q and R are also three corners of a rhombus. A rhombus has four equal sides. What are the co-ordinates of the fourth corner, S?

5 Draw a set of axes. Use your diagram to write down the co-ordinates of the points exactly half-way between these pairs of points:

(a) (2, 1) and (6, 3) (b) $(^-3, 5)$ and $(1, ^-3)$

6 Plot these points. Then join them up in the order given. Join the last point to the first.

$(2, ^-3)$ $(^-1, ^-3)$ $(^-4, ^-2)$ $(^-6, ^-2)$ $(^-8, ^-4)$ $(^-7, ^-1)$ $(^-7, 2)$ $(^-6, 0)$ $(^-1, 2)$ (0, 6) (1, 2)

(7, 2) (10, 1) $(9, ^-1)$ $(7, ^-1)$ (4, 0) $(5, ^-2)$

What creature is this?

7 This co-ordinate graph shows a cross-section of a swimming beach.

(a) Explain what you would find at these points:

(i) $(^-9, ^-2)$ (ii) (9, 6) (iii) (0, 0)

(b) Give the co-ordinates for these objects:

(i) the crab (ii) the seagull (iii) the top of the flag-pole.

(c) What is at each of these points? Choose from { air, water, ground }

(i) $(^{-}4, ^{-}3)$

(ii) $(^{-}4, 2)$

(iii) $(^{-}10, ^{-}2)$

(iv) $(7, ^{-}2)$

(v) $(2, 1)$

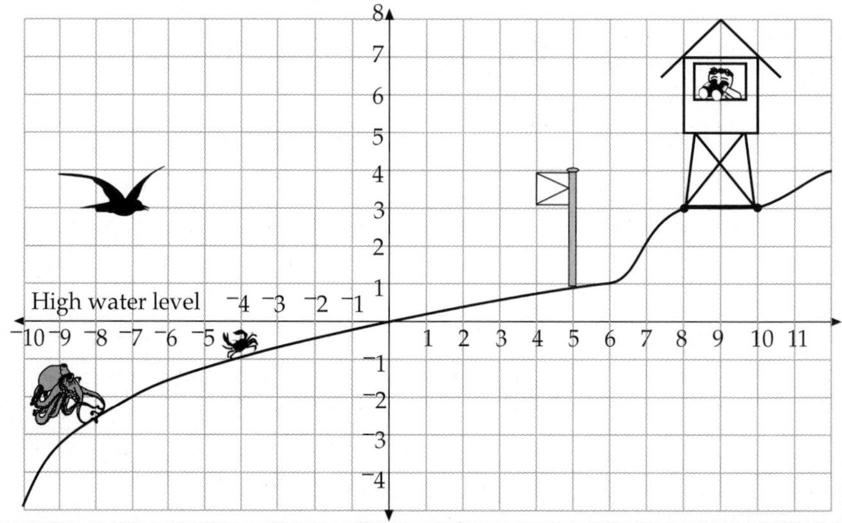

INVESTIGATION

THE QUEEN RULES

Chess co-ordinates are related to the ones we use in Maths.

The main similarity—the numbering of both axes starts from the bottom left.

The main differences—the labelling refers to the squares themselves, not the lines separating the squares.

—a letter and a number are used rather than a pair of numbers.

(iv) (iii) (ii) a3 a2 a1 c1 (i)

1 How many squares are there on a chess board?

2 Give the co-ordinates of the squares marked (i), (ii), (iii) and (iv).

Suppose the co-ordinates in chess were pairs of numbers, instead of a letter/number mix. For example: a1 = (1, 1); a2 = (1, 2); b1 = (2, 1), and so on.

3 Can you give a rule that links the numbers in a pair of co-ordinates for:

(a) the white squares? (b) the black squares?

4 The 8 Queens

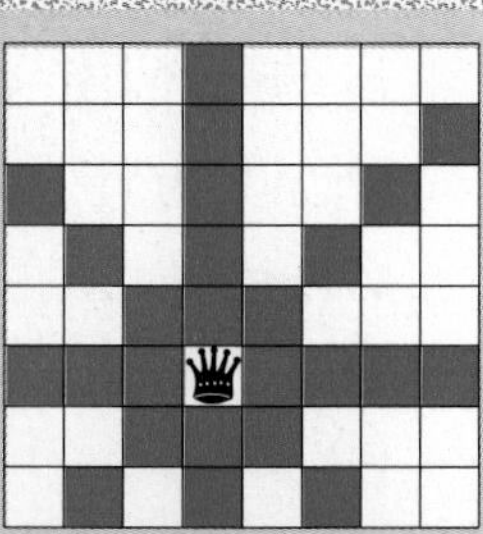

In chess, the most powerful piece is the queen. If the way is clear, a player's queen can take *any* piece belonging to the other player that is on the same row, column or diagonal.

Draw an 8 by 8 grid of 64 squares.

Try to place 8 queens on it so that no queen can take any other queen.

This is quite difficult. You'll probably need to use a pencil and rubber as you try to place the 8 queens in suitable positions!

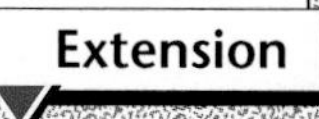

Latitude and longitude

The Earth is a round sphere (three-dimensional). It is not easy to show a large area of the world on a flat (two-dimensional) piece of paper. Cartographers (people who specialise in maps) have developed several ways of doing this.

Many world maps are based on a grid of horizontal and vertical lines.

- The horizontal lines are called lines of **latitude.** The lines run east to west. The best known of these lines is called the Equator.
- The vertical lines are called lines of **longitude.** One of these is called the meridian. This passes through Greenwich, in London, England.

These lines give us a grid, so we can use a form of co-ordinates. Just like in Maths, the horizontal scale is used before the vertical one.

Example The co-ordinates of Oamaru are approximately (171°E, 45°S). E stands for east (of the meridian). S stands for south (of the Equator).

This diagram shows why we use degrees in the co-ordinates. It also shows that any place with a second co-ordinate of 45°S is halfway between the Equator and the South Pole.

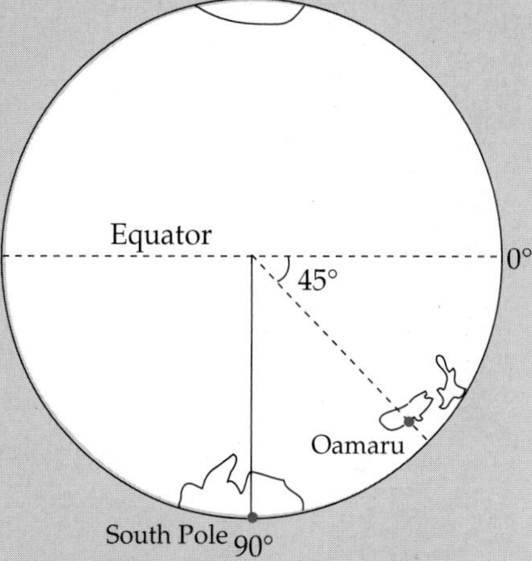

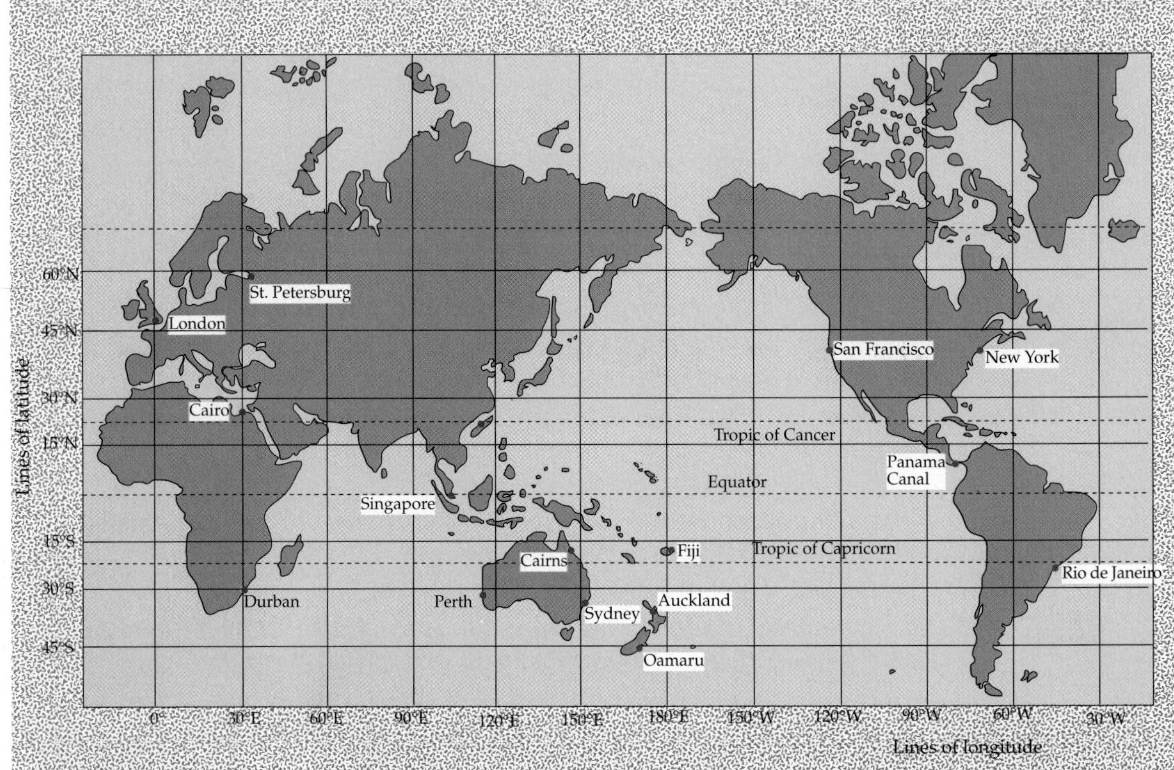

EXERCISE **26.4**

Match each of these places with one of the approximate co-ordinates. Use the map with the lines of latitude and longitude as a guide.

1 Auckland
2 Cairns
3 Cairo
4 Durban
5 Fiji
6 Hong Kong
7 London
8 New York
9 Panama Canal
10 Perth
11 Rio de Janeiro
12 St Petersburg
13 San Francisco
14 Singapore
15 Sydney

Co-ordinates

(116°E, 32°S)	(30°E, 28°N)
(180°, 20°S)	(175°E, 37°S)
(30°E, 60°N)	(0°, 51°N)
(105°E, 0°)	(145°E, 17° S)
(115°E, 23°N)	(74°W, 41°N)
(43°W, 23°S)	(80°W, 10°N)
(123°W, 37°N)	(30°E, 30°S)
(150°E, 34°S)	

27 2D graphs

Interpreting 2D graphs

STARTER

An adult usually has some control over their weight, but no way of changing their height! Good advice for any adult is to eat a healthy, well-balanced diet— and take enough exercise.

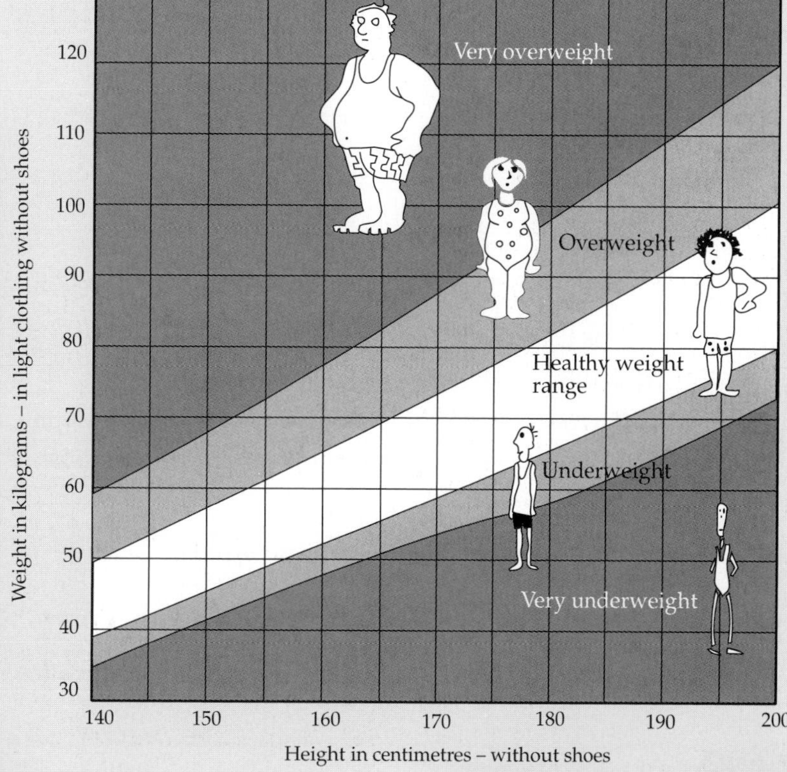

This graph shows the healthy weight ranges for people of various heights. It also shows weight ranges for over-weight and under-weight people.

- Estimate the healthy weight range for an adult who is 180 cm tall.
- Describe the weight range for each of these people:
  - — Mr Harris (170 cm tall, and weighs 85 kg)
  - — Dr Keppell (160 cm and weighs 61 kg)
  - — Mrs Jackson (175 cm tall, and weighs 59 kg)
  - — Ms Lloyd (165 cm tall, and weighs 90 kg)
  - — Mr Morris (185 cm tall, and weighs 60 kg).

- Where would you expect a point for a jockey to appear on this graph?

- Where would you expect a point for a sumo-wrestler to appear on this graph?

Scatter plots

We can draw graphs to show the relationship between two quantities. One way of doing this is to create a **scatter plot**.

- A scatter plot has two axes, drawn at right-angles to each other.
- Each axis shows a *different* quantity, and usually has a scale.

Example This scatter plot shows the heights and ages of 5 children in a family.

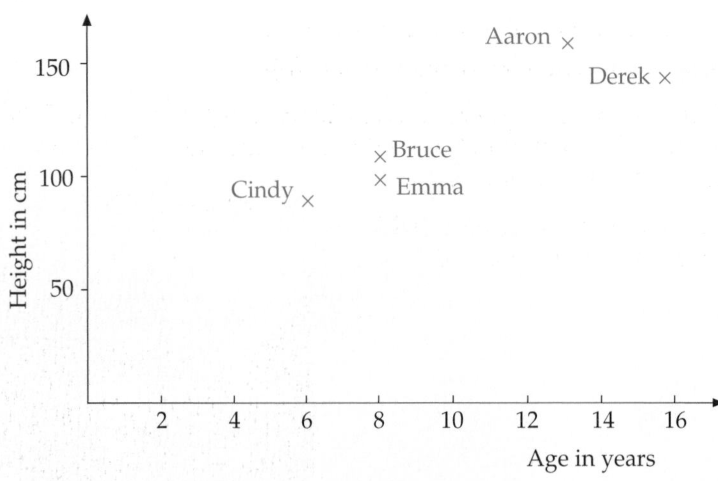

(a) Who is the youngest of the five children?
(b) Who is the tallest of the five children?
(c) How does the graph show that Bruce and Emma are twins?
(d) What does the graph show about the relationship between age and height for these children?

Answers (a) Cindy is the youngest (6 years old).
(b) Aaron is the tallest.
(c) Bruce and Emma both have the same age.
(d) In general, the older a child is, the taller they are.

EXERCISE 27.1

1 Which of these points represents a person who is:
(a) taller *and* younger than Lee?
(b) older *and* shorter than Lee?
(c) shorter *and* younger than Lee?
(d) older *and* taller than Lee?

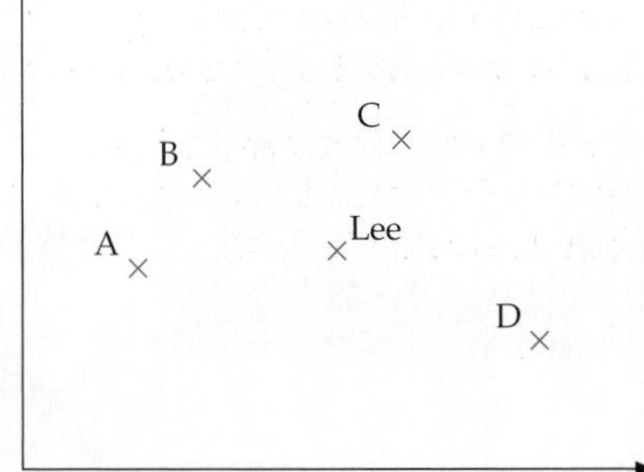

2 These two graphs show relationships between the climates of Auckland and Queenstown in June.

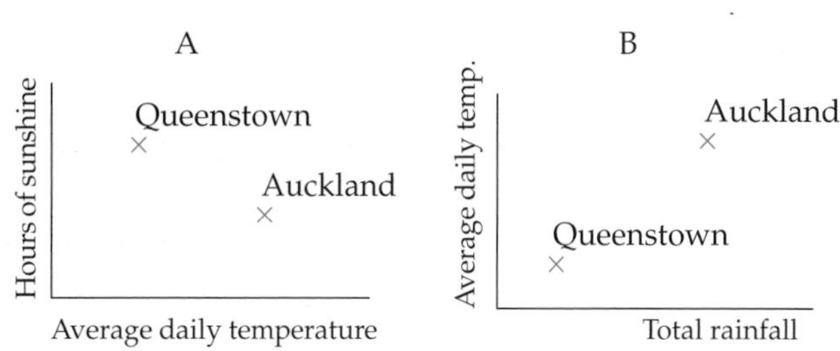

(a) Explain what graph A tells you about the climates of Auckland and Queenstown.

(b) Which place is wetter in June—Auckland or Queenstown?

(c) Which graph (A or B) did you use to answer part (b)?

The climate at Milford Sound in June is different to Auckland or Queenstown. It is wetter than both places. It is warmer than Queenstown, but colder than Auckland. It has fewer hours of sunshine than either Auckland or Queenstown.

(d) Make a copy of both graphs (A and B). Add an extra point on each to show the climate at Milford Sound.

Milford Sound

3 Make a copy of this graph. Add four points, labelled P, Q, R and S, to show possible positions for each of these people:

(a) Peter, who is heavier *and* younger than Chris

(b) Quinta, who is lighter *and* older than Chris

(c) Ricky, who is the same age *and* heavier than Chris

(d) Simone, who is the same weight *and* older than Chris.

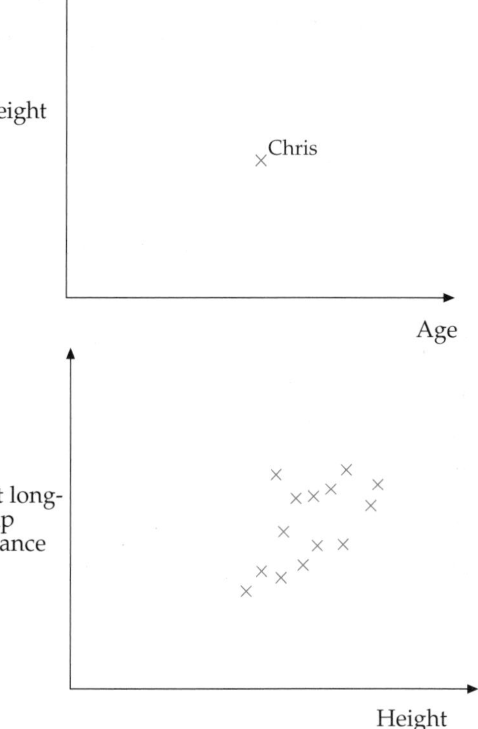

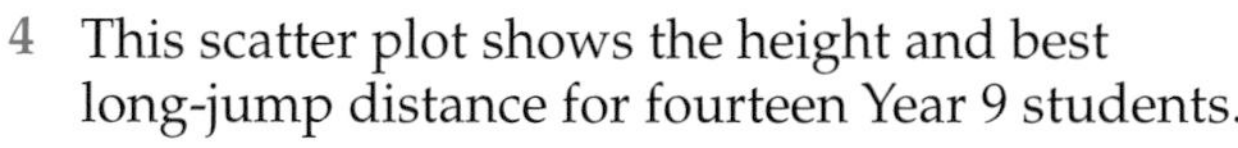

4 This scatter plot shows the height and best long-jump distance for fourteen Year 9 students.

What does the scatter plot tell you about the relationship between the distance a student can jump and their height?

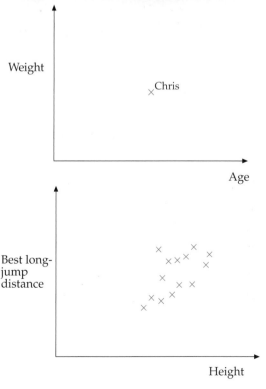

5 This table shows how different sporting activities affect different types of fitness.

Sport	Activity ratings					
	Aerobic fitness	Flexibility	Stamina	Body fat	Muscle tone	Total
Aerobics	8	8	7	8	8	**39**
Basketball	8	4	3	8	5	**28**
Cycling	8	1	4	6	5	**24**
Gymnastics	6	10	9	9	10	**44**
Hockey	7	4	3	8	5	**27**
Jogging	9	1	2	10	5	**27**
Martial arts	5	4	5	6	6	**26**
Netball	6	4	3	6	6	**25**
Rowing	7	3	5	5	6	**26**
Rugby	7	1	6	7	6	**27**
Soccer	7	4	2	8	5	**26**
Squash	6	1	4	6	5	**22**
Swimming	7	3	6	1	7	**24**
Table-tennis	5	5	1	3	3	**17**
Tai chi	3	6	1	3	2	**15**
Tennis	5	4	2	6	5	**22**
Walking	4	2	2	7	3	**18**

Data from *Health and Adolescence: Develop a Healthy You*, by Robert Burns.

Use the information in the table to answer these questions.

(a) This graph shows ratings of stamina and flexibility for four activities (gymnastics, squash, table-tennis and walking)

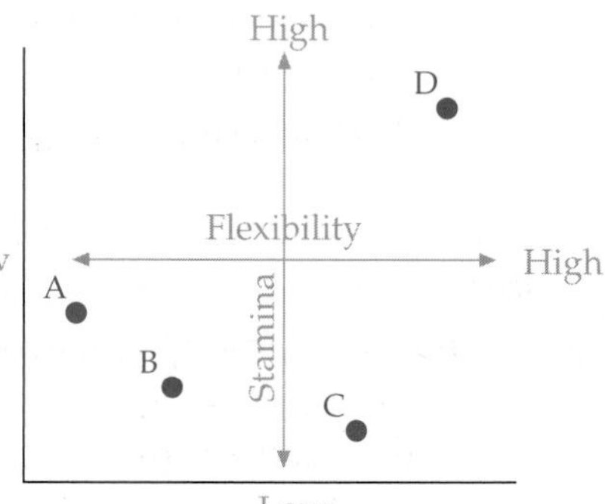

(i) Match each point (A–D) to one of these four activities.

(ii) Which other sport listed in the table would be plotted in the same place as squash?

(b) This graph shows ratings of muscle tone and body fat level for four activities (martial arts, swimming, table-tennis and walking).

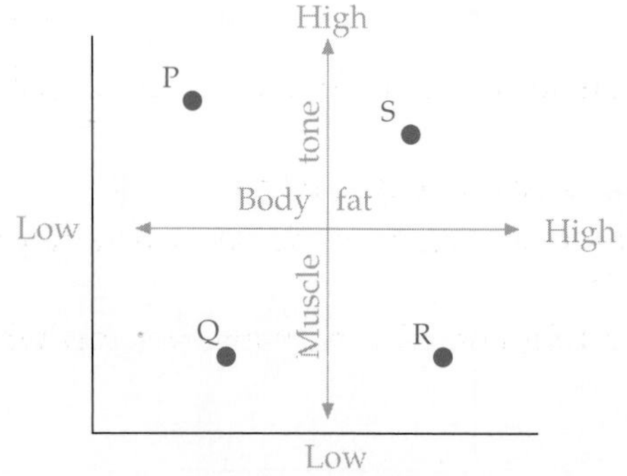

(i) Match each point (P–S) to one of these four activities.

(ii) Make a copy of the graph. Add a point to show where gymnastics would appear.

Line graphs

Graphs can also tell how one quantity changes as another one does. This is often done with a **line graph**.

Example This graph shows what happens to the temperature of an egg over a period of 100 minutes.

The egg is taken from the refrigerator and placed in a saucepan of boiling water. It is then left to cool down on a kitchen bench.

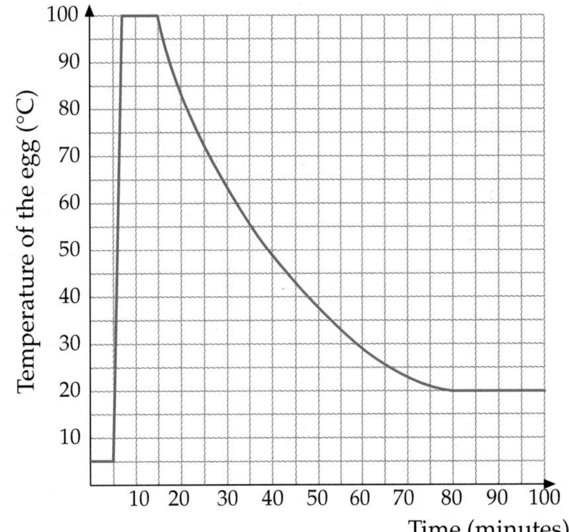

Use the graph to answer these questions:

(a) What was the temperature inside the refrigerator?

(b) For how long was the egg in the saucepan of water?

(c) What is the room temperature in the kitchen?

(d) How long did it take the egg to cool down to room temperature, after it was removed from the boiling water?

Answer

(a) 5 °C

(b) 10 minutes (read this off on the axis—from 5 minutes to 15 minutes)

(c) 20 °C

(d) 65 minutes (read this off on the axis—from 15 minutes to 80 minutes)

EXERCISE 27.2

1 Here are four graphs that tell a story.

(a) Match each one to one of these situations:

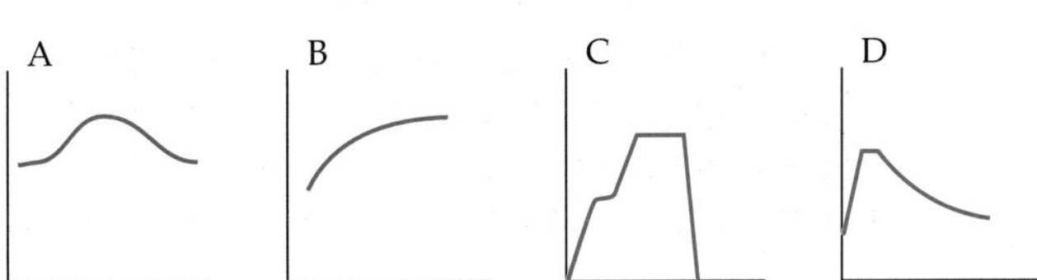

E Water is poured into a kettle, boiled, and then left to cool down.

F A weightlifter raises a bar over his head, holds it steady for a few seconds, and then drops it.

G The prices of groceries are not increasing as fast as they used to.

H People tend to earn more money in their 40s and 50s than they do when they are older or younger.

(b) Make a copy of each graph. Give the graph a title, and label each axis to show what it represents.

2 This graph shows the number of accidents at an intersection over a 12-month period.

(a) Which month had the fewest accidents?

(b) Which month had the most accidents?

(c) Which two consecutive months had the same number of accidents?

(d) How many accidents were there for the whole year?

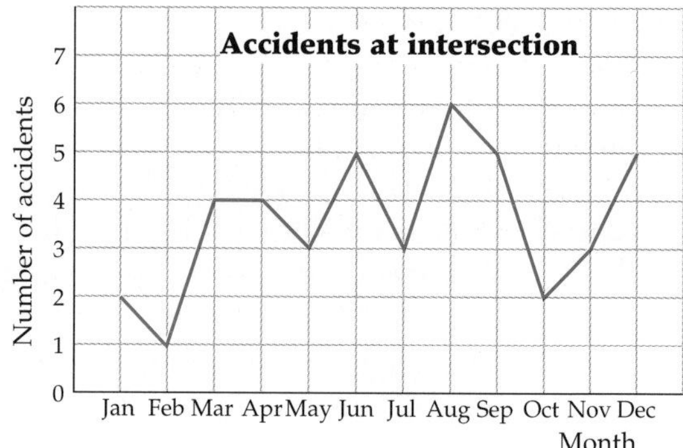

3 This graph shows the level of petrol in the tank of the school's tractor one day. The tractor was used to mow the school grounds.

(a) When did the mowing begin?

(b) Suggest what happened at 1 pm.

(c) If the tank hadn't been refilled at 10 am, when would the tractor have run out of petrol?

(d) How long did it take to mow the school grounds?

(e) How much petrol was used altogether?

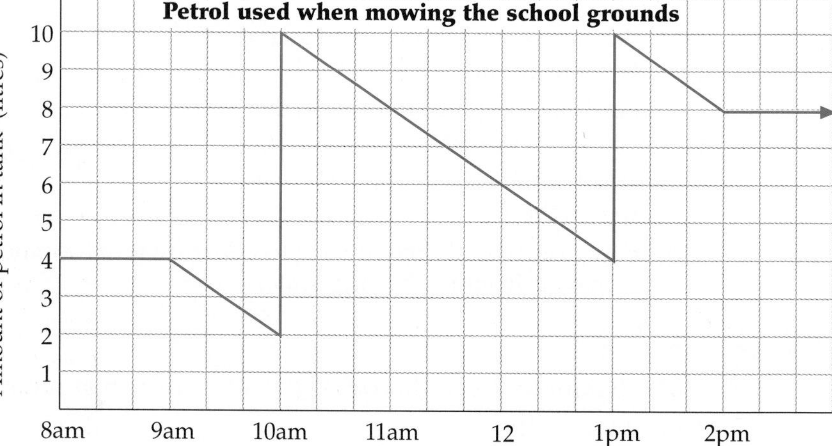

4 The graph shows what happens to the depth of water as a person takes a bath.

(a) Write a story describing what might have happened for each of these parts of the graph:

A–B, B–C, C–D, D–E, E–F, F–G, G–H and H–I.

(b) The part from H to I is steeper than the part from A to B. Does this mean the bath takes longer to fill, or longer to empty?

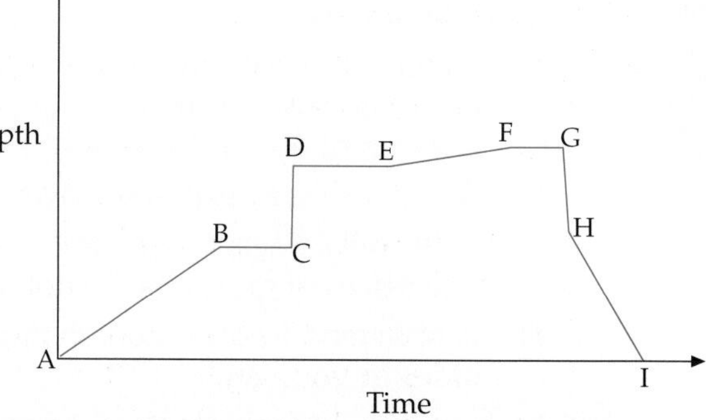

5 This graph shows the level of water in a kitchen sink over a period of 20 minutes. Write a story to describe what might have happened.

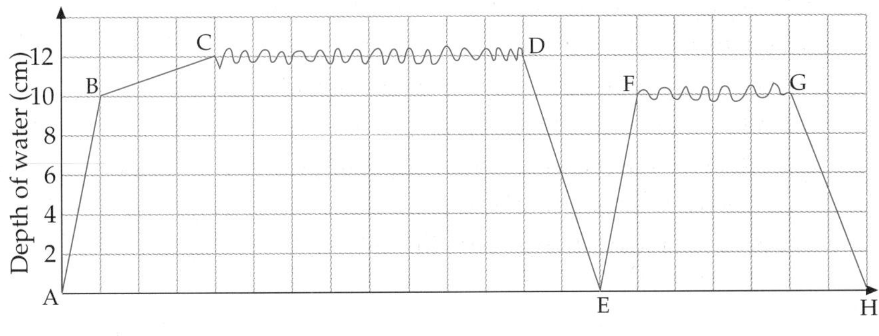

6 This graph shows what happened when Taine and Wiremu went bungy jumping.

Describe what happened in words.

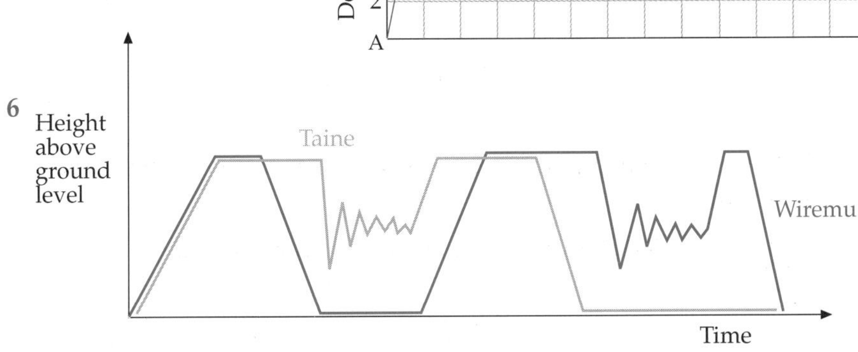

7

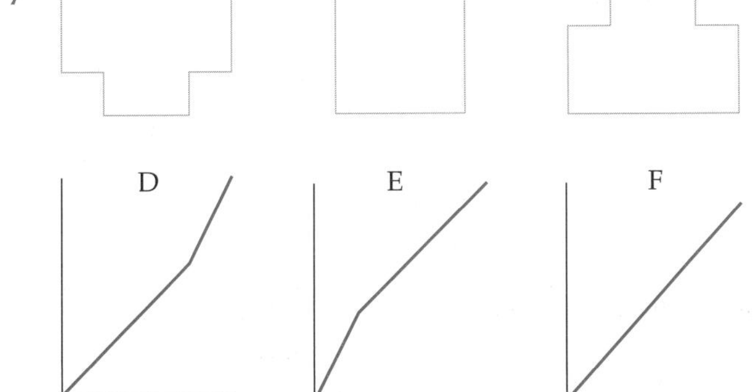

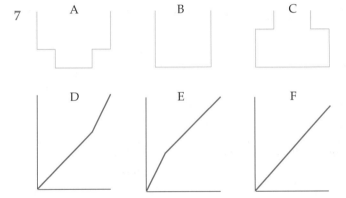

(a) Each of these containers (A–C) is filled with water at a steady rate. Match each one with a graph (D–F), showing the relationship between the height of water and the time taken to fill the container.

(b) Which container (A, B or C) contains the smallest amount of water?

8 These graphs show physical changes during adolescence for typical boys and girls. Individuals may develop at different times and rates from those shown here.

Both graphs show the 'growth spurt' which is typical of this age group.

(a) Which group has the earlier growth spurt: boys or girls?

(b) At what age does a typical girl stop growing in height?

(c) Explain how the graph shows that a typical boy stops gaining weight by about 18.

(d) At what age is the growth in height fastest for a typical boy?

(e) A typical girl gains weight fastest when she is 12. Explain how the graph shows this.

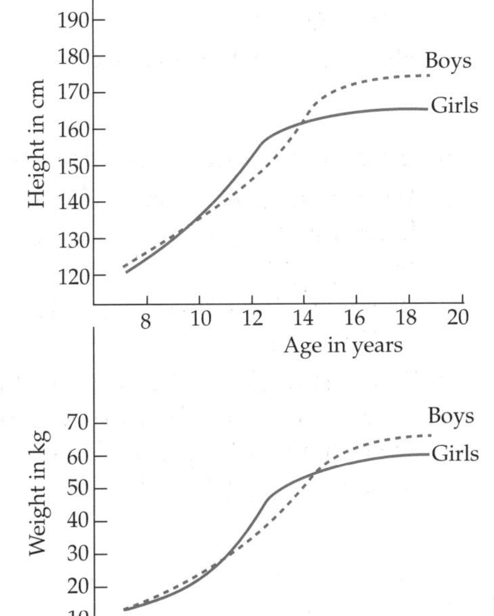

"Too many cooks spoil the broth."

A lunch bar produces the same number of sandwiches and bread rolls every day.

- There is a relationship between the time taken to produce the food and the number of cooks at the lunch bar. Which of these graphs (A–D) best shows this relationship?
- Explain your choice of answer.

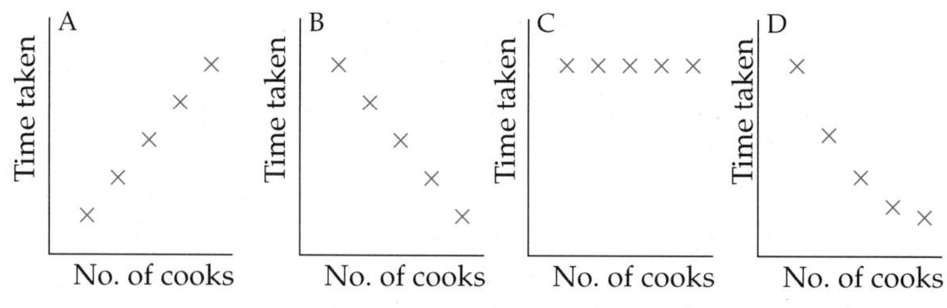

SPREADSHEET INVESTIGATION

This table shows the temperature in New Plymouth, measured every two hours for one day in January. The temperature has been measured to the nearest °C.

Time	Temperature	Time	Temperature	Time	Temperature
Midnight	14	10 am	19	8 pm	19
2 am	13	midday	21	10 pm	18
4 am	13	2 pm	23	midnight	16
6 am	13	4 pm	22		
8 am	16	6 pm	20		

1 Enter this data into two columns of a spreadsheet.
2 Produce a graph to show what happens to the temperature during the day.
3 At what time of the day does the temperature rise the fastest? Explain how the graph shows this.

INVESTIGATION

CAR PRICES

What would a graph showing the relationship between the price of a car and its mileage look like?

Here are some advertisements from a newspaper. Notice that the advertisers save money by using abbreviations—e.g. 57k means 57 000 km.

TOYOTA COROLLA WINDY 91 3dr, auto, p/s, a/c, red, 43 000 km, FSH, AA inspected; As new $10995.
TOYOTA COROLLA XL H/B 95 5 spd, 1 onr, 42 000 km, 12 mths warranty; $13995.
TOYOTA COROLLA, 1.6 GX sedan, auto, 95, private onr, Alpine stereo, unmarked; $14990.
TOYOTA COROLLA, 1995 XL Hatchback, 1300cc, 5 door, 80 000 km, forest green, as new cond; $13500 ono.
TOYOTA COROLLA 1.6 GL hatch, 95, 1 onr, 72 000 kms, 12 months Toyota wrty; $12495.
TOYOTA COROLLA 1.6 sedan 1998 brand new demo, air bag electrics three year factory warranty 5-speed; $20990.
TOYOTA COROLLA 1.6GS Liftback, 1992, NZ assemb, manual, 57km, 2 onrs, immaculate; $11350 ono.
TOYOTA COROLLA 1.8 GLX LB auto, 31 000 km, abs, a/c, now $19900.
TOYOTA COROLLA 1.8 GLX hatch 5 speed brand new 1998 demo, air cond, CD player, ABS brakes, alloys, dual air bags, electrics, 3 year factory warranty; $25990.
TOYOTA COROLLA 1987 5dr l/back, 2 onrs, 127 000 km, 5spd, new NZ; $3750
TOYOTA COROLLA 1997 1.6, 5dr hatch, 5 spd, 37 000 km, Signature Class vehicle, 8.49% interest rate; special price $15990.

1 Plot information for 20 of these cars on a graph like this one.
The point already plotted shows that one of the cars has done 37 000 km, and is selling for $15 990.

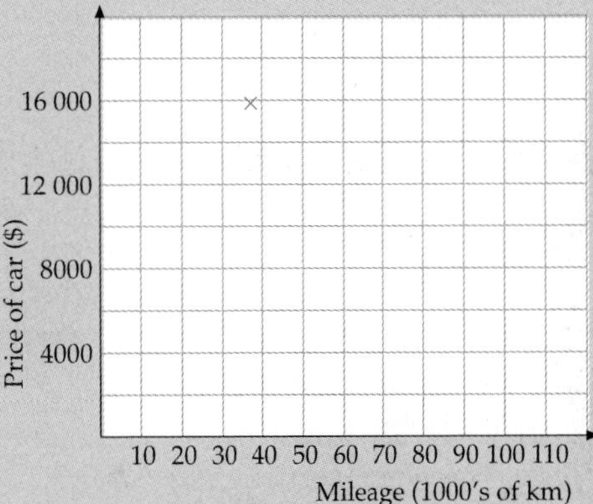

2 Describe the pattern shown in the graph. Explain what it shows about the relationship between the price and the mileage of Toyota Corollas.

3 Suggest some other factors that influence the price of a car. You should be able to name at least four.

4 Choose another model of car. Now investigate the relationship between the *age* of the car and its *mileage*.
You will need to research this using advertisements in a newspaper, or in a publication like *Trade and Exchange.*

Distance–time graphs

A special kind of 2D graph shows *travel*, or a journey of some kind.

- The time scale is on the horizontal axis
- The distance travelled is shown on the vertical axis.

Example This graph shows a student's journey one day. She went from home into town and back, via a bus stop.

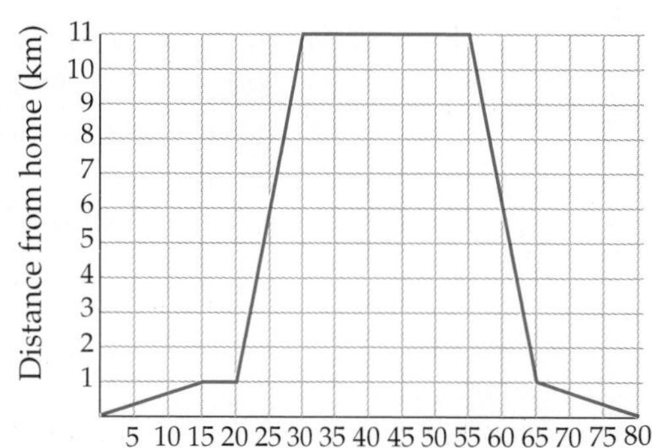

(a) How far is it from home to the bus stop?

(b) How far did the student travel by bus into town?

(c) How long did she have to wait at the bus stop?

(d) How many minutes did she spend in town?

(e) The bus travels 10 km in 10 minutes. How far would it travel in 60 minutes?

(f) What is the speed of the bus in km/h?

Answer

(a) 1 km

(b) 10 km (worked out from the difference of 11 km and 1 km on the vertical axis)

(c) 5 minutes (worked out from the difference of 20 minutes and 15 minutes on the horizontal axis)

(d) 25 minutes (worked out from the difference of 55 minutes and 30 minutes on the horizontal axis)

(e) 60 km

(f) 60 km in 60 minutes (one hour) is 60 km/h.

EXERCISE 27.3

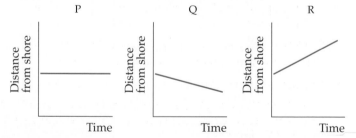

1 Michael is swimming at a lake. These graphs (P, Q and R) show his distance from the shore as time goes by.

P, Q, R: Distance from shore / Time

(a) Which graph shows he is moving closer to the shore as time goes by?

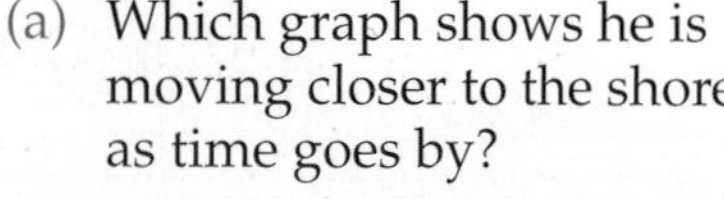

(b) Which graph shows he is moving away from the shore as time goes by?

(c) Which graph shows he is staying the same distance from the shore as time goes by?

2 Narelle goes to a lake to swim. She swims out from the shore, then swims parallel to the shore for a while, then swims back to the shore. Draw a graph to show what happens to her distance from the shore as time passes.

3 Draw a distance-time graph for each of the following. Graph time on the horizontal axis, and graph the distance from home on the vertical axis.

(a) Iona walks from home to the dairy. Here she buys some milk and heads back towards home. Halfway back, she remembers she forgot to buy some biscuits. So, she returns to the dairy, buys the biscuits and then walks home.

(continues)

(b) Ian walks to school. As soon as he arrives at school, he remembers he has forgotten his Maths homework. So, he returns home, collects the homework, and walks to school again.

(c) Ailsa walks to a friend's house. She waits there for a few minutes until her friend is ready, then they both walk to school. The friend lives halfway between school and Ailsa's house.

4 Chris cycled from a farm to town, and back. The graph shows this journey.

(a) How far is the farm from town?

(b) How long was Chris away from the farm altogether?

(c) How long did Chris stay in town?

(d) Chris had a puncture during the journey. Did this happen on the way to town, or on the way back to the farm? Explain how the graph shows this information.

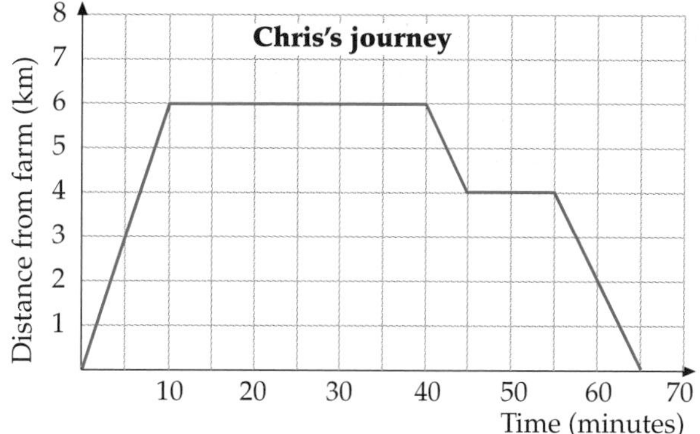

(e) Explain how the graph shows that Chris travelled faster going in to town than returning home to the farm.

5 Draw a distance–time graph for the Pearson family's motorway journey:

- for the first part of the journey they travelled 50 km in 30 minutes
- they then stopped at a rest area for 10 minutes
- they continued on, travelling 60 km in 40 minutes
- they spent one hour (60 minutes) in the city
- they returned home without stopping (110 km). The return journey took 80 minutes

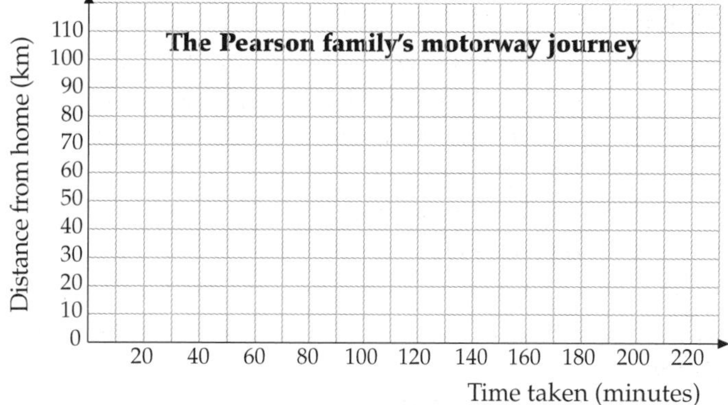

Use scales similar to the ones in this diagram.

6 The distance from Christchurch to Invercargill is about 600 km.

Kelly lives in Invercargill. She leaves home at 0800 hours, and drives towards Christchurch at a steady average speed of 75 km/h.

Kaye lives in Christchurch. She leaves home at 1000 hours on the same day, and drives towards Invercargill at a steady average speed of 100 km/h.

(a) This table shows the distance of each person from Invercargill at different times during the day. Copy it, and complete it.

Time	Distance from Invercargill	
	Kelly	Kaye
0800	0	600
0900	75	600
1000	150	600
1100		500
1200		
1300		
1400		
1500		
1600		

(continues)

(b) Use the information in the table to draw a distance–time graph for each person. Use the *same* set of axes.

(c) At about what time will Kelly and Kaye pass each other? Explain how you can work this out from the graph.

(d) When they pass each other, are they closer to Invercargill or to Christchurch?

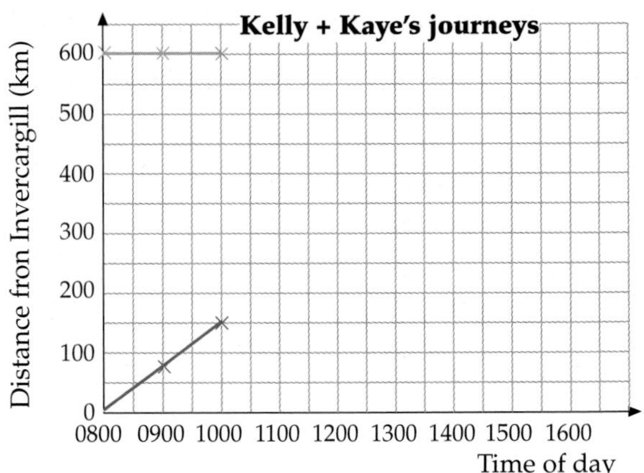

Co-ordinate patterns

STARTER

Sometimes there is a rule linking the x co-ordinate to the y co-ordinate. Let's investigate this.

We'll use $y = x + 2$.

This means that the second (y) co-ordinate is two more than the first (x) co-ordinate.

Some examples are: (1, 3), (2, 4), (3, 5)

- Complete these pairs of co-ordinates for the rule $y = x + 2$: (4, __), (5, __), (6, __)
- Plot the three example points and the other three you just worked out on a grid with an x-axis and a y-axis.
- Explain what you notice about the six points.

- Now complete these pairs of co-ordinates for the same rule, $y = x + 2$: ($^-1$, __), (0, __)
- Plot them on your graph. Do they fit the same pattern?

An algebra rule (linking x and y) can be used to plot co-ordinates and produce a pattern on a graph.

Example $y = 2x$

This means that the second number (y) in a pair of co-ordinates is 2 times the first number (x).

Some of the points that fit this rule are
($^-2$, $^-4$), ($^-1$, $^-2$), (0, 0), (1, 2), (2, 4), (3, 6)

When the points are plotted, the pattern is obvious:

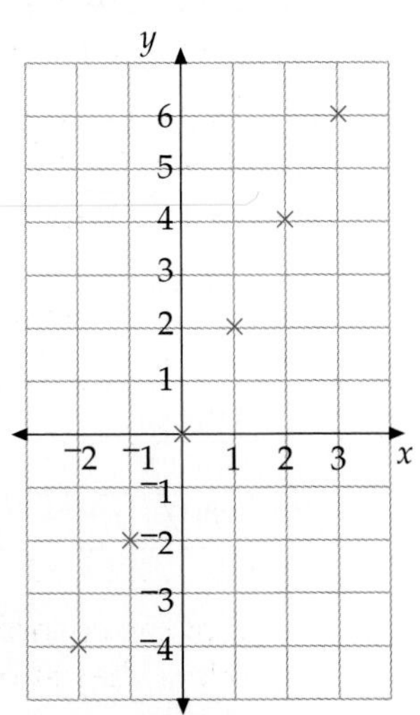

You can usually tell if the points have been worked out correctly: they should form a pattern when you plot them!

Example Plot some points that fit the rule $y = 3x - 1$.

Answer We can show what happens by using a table:

x	y (calculated from $y = 3x - 1$)	Co–ordinates (x, y)
$^{-}1$	$3 \times {}^{-}1 - 1 = {}^{-}3 - 1 = {}^{-}4$	$({}^{-}1, {}^{-}4)$
0	$3 \times 0 - 1 = 0 - 1 = {}^{-}1$	$(0, {}^{-}1)$
1	$3 \times 1 - 1 = 3 - 1 = 2$	$(1, 2)$
2	$3 \times 2 - 1 = 6 - 1 = 5$	$(2, 5)$
3	$3 \times 3 - 1 = 9 - 1 = 8$	$(3, 8)$

We start with x–values near 0. This is because we will be placing co–ordinates onto a graph, and we want points near the centre.

EXERCISE 27.4

1 (a) Copy and complete this table for the rule $y = 3x$.

x	y (calculated from $y = 3x$)	Co–ordinates (x, y)
$^{-}2$	$3 \times {}^{-}2 = {}^{-}6$	$({}^{-}2, {}^{-}6)$
$^{-}1$		
0		
1		
2		
3		

(b) Plot the co–ordinates from the table. (*Hint*: they should lie in a straight line!)

2 (a) Copy and complete this table for the rule $y = x + 4$.

x	y (calculated from $y = x + 4$)	Co–ordinates (x, y)
$^{-}2$	$^{-}2 + 4 = 2$	$({}^{-}2, 2)$
$^{-}1$		
0		
1		
2		
3	$3 + 4 = 7$	$(3, 7)$

(b) Plot the co–ordinates from the table. (*Hint*: they should lie in a straight line!)

3 (a) Copy and complete this table for the rule $y = {}^{-}2x$ (i.e. $y = {}^{-}2 \times x$)

x	y (calculated from $y = {}^{-}2x$)	Co–ordinates (x, y)
$^{-}2$		
$^{-}1$	$^{-}2 \times {}^{-}1 = 2$	$({}^{-}1, 2)$
0		
1		
2		
3		

(b) Plot the co–ordinates from the table.

4 (a) Copy and complete this table for the rule $y = 2x + 1$.

x	y (calculated from $y = 2x + 1$)	Co–ordinates (x, y)
$^{-}2$	$2 \times {}^{-}2 + 1 = {}^{-}4 + 1 = {}^{-}3$	$({}^{-}2, {}^{-}3)$
$^{-}1$		
0		
1		
2		
3		

(b) Plot the co–ordinates from the table.

5 (a) Copy and complete this table for the rule $y = x^2$.

x	y (calculated from $y = x^2$)	Co–ordinates (x, y)
$^{-}2$	$(^{-}2)^2 = {}^{-}2 \times {}^{-}2 = 4$	$(^{-}2, 4)$
$^{-}1$		
0		
1		
2		
3		

(b) Plot the co-ordinates from the table. (*Hint*: they will form a kind of curve.)

6–10 *Calculate co-ordinates for each of these rules. Then plot them on a set of x- and y-axes. Use a method similar to the one in questions 1–5.*

6 $y = x + 3$

7 $y = x - 1$

8 $y = 3x + 1$

9 $y = {}^{-}x$ (i.e. $y = {}^{-}1x$)

10 $y = 2x - 2$

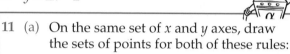

11 (a) On the same set of x and y axes, draw the sets of points for both of these rules:

$y = x + 2$ $\qquad$ $y = 2x + 1$

(b) What are the co-ordinates of the point that fits *both* rules?

SPREADSHEET INVESTIGATION

We can use spreadsheet software to plot points that fit rules connecting x and y.

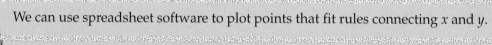

Let's investigate how we would do this for the rule $y = 4x - 5$.

- The x-values go in column A. These range from $^{-}3$ to 3.
- The y-values are calculated in column B. In cell B3, the formula that does this is entered as =4*A3–5
- When the formula is copied downwards, all the other y-values are automatically calculated.

	A	B
1	x	y
2		
3	-3	=4*A3-5
4	-2	
5	-1	
6	0	
7	1	
8	2	
9	3	

To draw the graph, follow these steps:

- Use the mouse to highlight the block A3:B9
- Click on the chart-wizard button on the toolbar

- Choose the XY(Scatter) chart type.
- Click on Finish.

You can improve the look of the graph by double-clicking on it, and then dragging the sides of the box up or down to make the scale look more realistic.

Here is the completed spreadsheet, together with the graph of the rule $y = 4x - 5$:

	A	B	C	D	E	F	G
1	x	y					
2							
3	-3	-17					
4	-2	-13					
5	-1	-9					
6	0	-5					
7	1	-1					
8	2	3					
9	3	7					
10							
11							
12							
13							
14							
15							
16							

y = 4x - 5

EXERCISE 27.5

Use spreadsheet software to create the graphs for these rules. In each case, draw up a table of values first. Print out your completed spreadsheets if possible.

1 $y = x + 1$

2 $y = {}^{-}4x$

3 $y = 5x + 3$

4 $y = 0.4x - 2$

5 $y = 6 - x$

Applications

Sometimes we can use a graph to explain a rule. The graph can be used to read off values. This is often faster than doing calculations.

STARTER

The rule for the amount of water in a leaking bucket is $W = 10 - 2n$. (This means $10 - 2 \times n$).

W stands for the amount of water (measured in litres)

n stands for the time or number of minutes since the bucket was full.

- What is the value of W when $n = 1$?
- How much water is left in the bucket after 2 minutes?

The answers to the first two questions help give some points on the graph:

- Copy the graph, and join the two points.
- This kind of graph is a straight line, so extend the line in both directions.
- How much water does the bucket hold when it is full?
- How long does it take for the bucket to be completely empty?

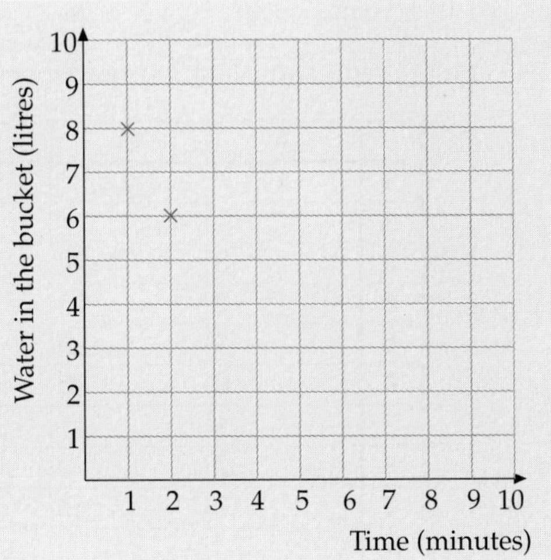

EXERCISE 27.6

1 A parking meter accepts any New Zealand coin. It gives 1 minute of parking for every 4 cents put in. For example, if coins worth 80 cents are put in, you will be allowed to park for 20 minutes.

This graph shows the relationship between the parking time and the value of coins put into the meter.

Use the graph to answer these questions:

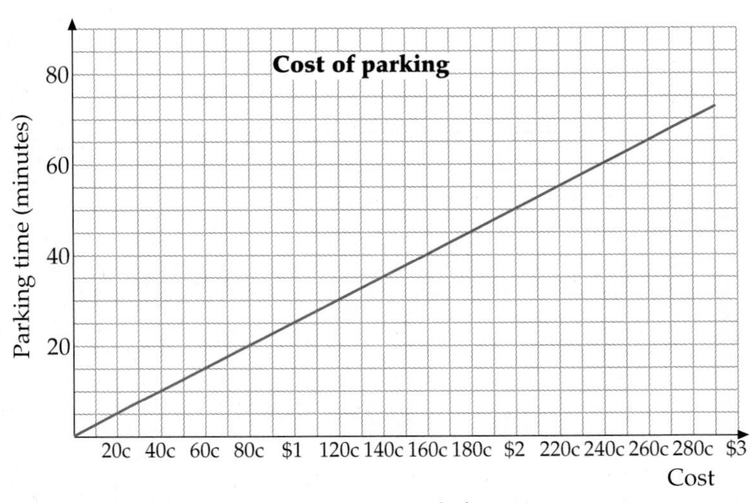

(a) How much parking time will you get if you put in coins worth \$1.60?
(b) How much parking time will you get if you put in *two* 50 c coins?
(c) How much will it cost you to park for 1 hour (60 minutes)?
(d) What will it cost to park for quarter of an hour?

2 Transit Taxi Ltd run a shuttle bus service. They charge as follows:

Call-out fee	\$3
Charge per km	\$2

For example, the charge for a 5 km journey would be \$13. This is calculated by working out $3 + 2 \times 5$.

(a) The charge for a 4 km journey is \$11. Write down the calculation that gives \$11.

(b) Copy and complete this table:

Length of journey (km)	Charge in \$
1	
2	
3	
4	11
5	13
6	
7	

(continues)

(c) Use the values in the table to draw a graph.

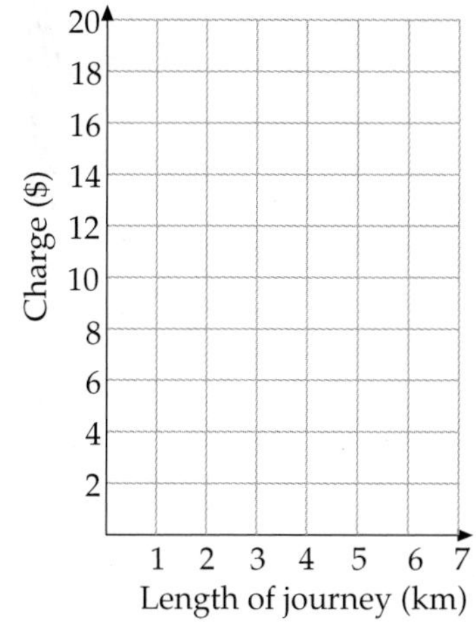

(d) Explain how you could use the graph to calculate the charge for a $2\frac{1}{2}$ km journey. What is this charge?

3 The battery in Mr Fairfax's car is fully charged. It delivers a current of 30 amps. Unfortunately he leaves the car lights on. The current in the battery drops by 5 amps every hour.

(a) Copy and complete this table:

Time (hours)	Battery current (amps)
0	30
1	25
2	
3	

(b) Draw a graph using the values from your table. The horizontal axis should show time. The vertical axis should show the battery current. Join up the points on the graph.

(c) Use the graph to estimate the current from the battery when the car lights have been left on for $1\frac{1}{2}$ hours.

(d) Assume the current from the battery continues to drop at the same rate. Extend your graph, and use it to predict when there will be no current.

(e) Mr Fairfax believes there is a rule that helps explain the relationship between the battery current (B) and the time (t) for which the lights are left on. Which of these is the most suitable rule?

A $B = 30 - t$

B $B = 30t$

C $B = 30 - 5t$

D $B = 5t + 25$

4 This graph shows the cost of train tickets.

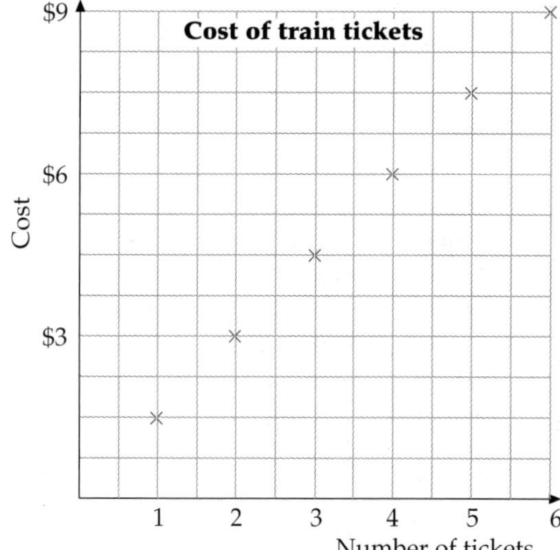

(a) What is the cost of 2 tickets?

(b) What is the cost of 6 tickets?

(c) What is the cost of 3 tickets?

(d) How many tickets can you buy for $9?

(e) One of the points on this graph has co-ordinates (4, 6). Explain what the values 4 and 6 tell you.

(f) If the graph was continued, which one of these three points would fit on it?

A (8, 10)

B (10, 15)

C (20, 24)

(g) Explain whether it is sensible to plot the point (2.5, 3.75) on this graph.

5 Cath and Derek both have jobs delivering newspapers. They each have a savings account at the same bank. At the beginning of every month, they each deposit a regular amount of money.

Here are the rules for the amount of money in each person's savings account. S stands for the money in the savings account. n stands for the number of deposits each person has made.

Cath: $S = 20n + 70$ Derek: $S = 30n + 30$

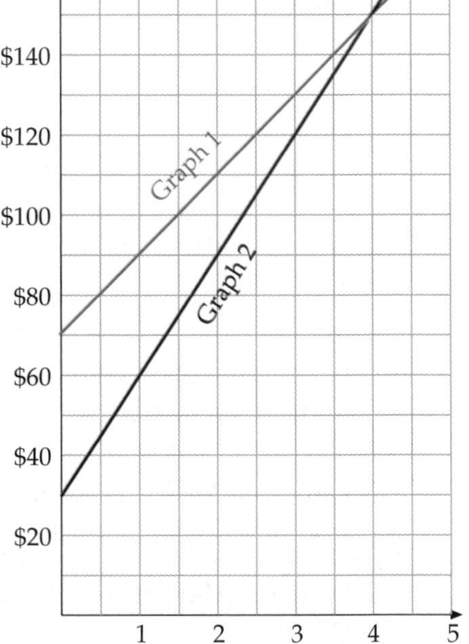

(a) How much money does Cath have after she has made 3 deposits?

(b) How much money does Cath have after she has made 4 deposits?

(c) Use your answers to (a) and (b) to work out how much money Cath deposits each month.

This diagram shows the graphs of the two rules. They are labelled Graph 1 and Graph 2.

(d) Which graph shows Cath's savings?

(e) Which graph shows Derek's savings?

(f) How much money did Derek have in his account to start with? Explain how the graph shows this.

(g) The two graphs cross when the value of n is 4. Explain what this means about the amount of money each person has.

6 An adult and *two* children pay $18 to play a round of mini-golf.

(a) If the charge for an adult is $14, how much is the charge for a child?

(b) If the charge for an adult is $12, how much is the charge for a child?

(c) Copy this table. Complete it to show some of the possibilities for the adult and child charges.

Adult charge	16	14	12	10	8	6
Child charge	1					

(d) Use the pairs of values from the table to draw a graph on axes like this. Join up the points. The graph will show the relationship between the adult charge and child charge. What kind of graph do you get?

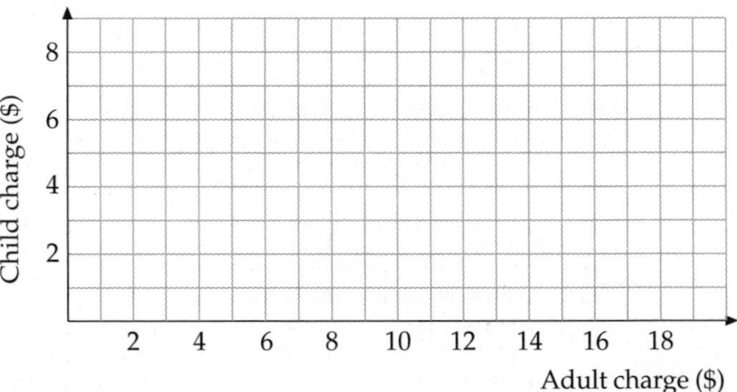

(e) It is unlikely the graph could be extended beyond the points given by the values in the table. Suggest a reason why, from your own experience of adult and child charges.

28 Interpreting data and statistical displays

Statistics is the collection and study of numerical facts or data.

Today, you live in a wired, digital world! A good understanding of statistical ideas will help you throughout your life. It is important to understand how to:

- collect data
- interpret data
- summarise them with calculations
- display the data suitably.

Interpreting data from articles, tables and graphs

STARTER This article extract was published in the *New Zealand Herald* in 1996. It is filled with statistics. Read the extract, and then answer the questions about it.

A nation running short of puff

The Ministry of Health's latest report on the smoking habits of New Zealanders, *Tobacco Statistics 1996*, says that 17 out of every 100 New Zealanders will die of a smoking-related illness, half of those having lost years from the end of their lives. Smoking is responsible for one in four cancer deaths, one in 10 deaths from heart attack or stroke, and two of every five deaths from respiratory illness, says the Ministry of Health.

Cost to the country is estimated at $250 million annually. On any given day, there is an average 828 people in hospital with smoking-related illness and their care costs $100 million. Another $150 million is spent on outpatient treatment; $30 million of that is paid by the government funding agency, Pharmac, to buy drugs to treat lung cancer or heart disease specifically caused by smoking.

But that $250 million cost provides little incentive for politicians to act to discourage smoking. For each of the past eight years, governments have taken around $600 million in tax on tobacco.

About 25 per cent of adult New Zealanders are smokers, the number having declined rapidly through the mid-to-late 80s but now seemingly levelling out. In 1984 they were smoking an average of 24 tailor-mades a day; now it's down to 15. In part that's because of the Smokefree Environments Act that came into force in late 1990, restricting smoking in the workplace, restaurants and other public places. Another factor is price increases.

Altogether, 3758 tonnes of tobacco were consumed in New Zealand in 1984, but the figure dropped to 2934 tonnes last year. But one in three women and one in four men aged 15 to 24 continues to smoke. Forty people take up the habit each day.

It's that uptake rate and the continued attraction of cigarettes, particularly to young women, that has health authorities worried. That's why they're taking action against retailers who sell to the underaged. A survey of fourth-form smokers found one third were supplied with cigarettes by a family member, but nearly half bought their own.

Take 1000 smokers now aged 20, and imagine they continue to smoke for the rest of their lives. One will die of Aids, two will be murdered, two will drown, 11 will commit suicide, 13 will die in road crashes. 500 of them will die early from smoking-related illness, 250 will die before the age of 70, (losing on average 21 years of life), 250 will die after age 70 (losing on average 8 years).

- Copy this table. Complete it using statistics from the extract.

	1984	1996
Tobacco consumed (tonnes)		
Average number of tailor-made cigarettes smoked per day		

- The extract implies that about a quarter of smokers now aged 20 will die of a smoking-related illness before they reach 70. Use numbers from the extract to write down a fraction that simplifies to $\frac{1}{4}$.
- Give two reasons from the extract why the percentage of adults who smoke has declined.
- It could be said that the government makes a 'profit' of $350 million from smokers each year. Write down a calculation, using two numbers from the extract, that results in this value.

Here are two pie-graphs that could be drawn to display information in this extract.

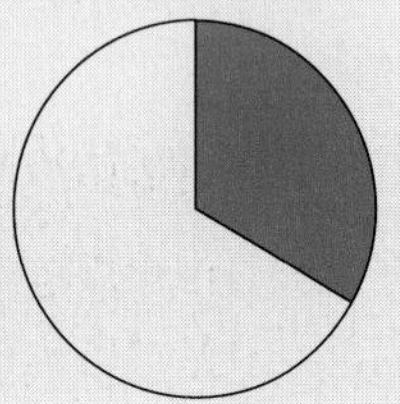

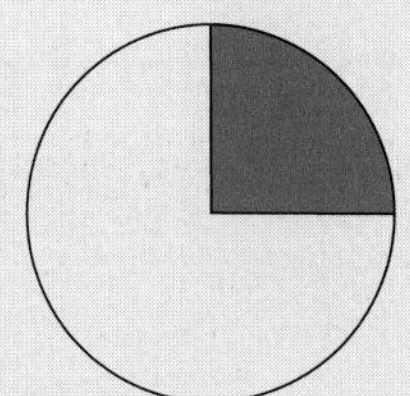

- Suggest a suitable heading. Describe how the graphs could be labelled.

EXERCISE 28.1

1 Here is some weather data for Hamilton:

Month	Average max. temperature (°C)	Average min. temperature (°C)	Raindays	Rainfall (mm)
January	25.7	16.3	5	54
February	23.8	16.0	6	67
March	22.1	14.9	4	102
April	19.4	10.9	11	83
May	17.5	6.8	13	110
June	15.8	3.4	12	118
July	15.0	3.1	18	132
August	16.1	5.8	15	143
September	17.2	7.9	11	83
October	18.0	10.4	8	23
November	20.4	12.6	8	74
December	22.5	14.9	6	68

(a) Which month was the warmest?

(b) Which month had the least amount of rain?

(c) Which month had the most rainy days?

(d) Which two months had the same average minimum temperature?

(e) How many months had an average minimum temperature of less than 10 °C?

(f) Calculate the total amount of rainfall during the year.

(g) Did the first or second half of the year have most rainy days?

2 This graph shows the leading causes of death in New Zealand.

(a) What are the two leading causes of death?

(b) What percentage of the deaths are due to some kind of accident?

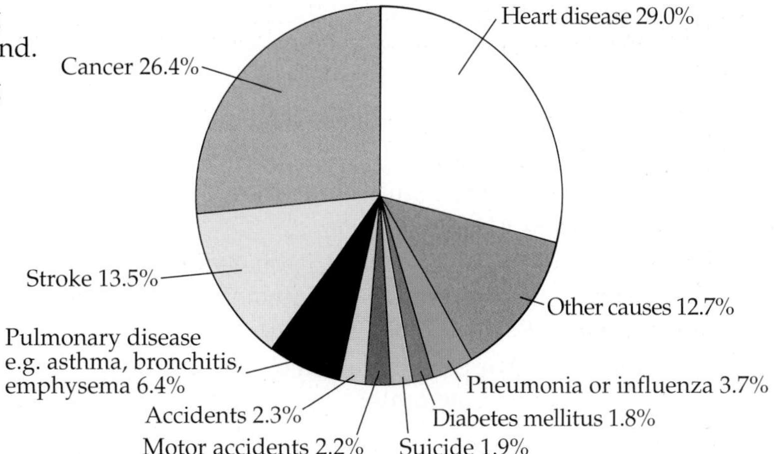

3 These two tables show a comparison of food prices in different countries. The prices have been converted to New Zealand dollars.

Rice 1 kg	
Germany	$4.15
Netherlands	$3.72
Sweden	$3.34
Ireland	$3.03
England	$2.23
Hong Kong	$2.17
South Africa	$2.03
Spain	$1.79
New Zealand	$1.50
Australia	$1.46
Singapore	$1.23
Fiji	$1.12
Indonesia	$0.66

Flour 1.5 kg	
England	$2.84
Sweden	$2.53
South Africa	$2.13
New Zealand	$1.91
Ireland	$1.91
Spain	$1.82
Hong Kong	$1.64
Australia	$1.61
Fiji	$1.40
Singapore	$1.34
Germany	$1.33
Netherlands	$1.26
Indonesia	$1.24

(a) In which two countries does flour cost the same?

(b) In which country does it cost the most to buy 1 kg of rice and 1.5 kg of flour?

(c) The amounts in the table show that the cost of rice in Sweden is about three times the cost in Fiji. Which of these calculations gives this result?

A $3.34 - 1.12 = 2.22$ B $3.34 \div 1.12 = 2.98$ C $3.34 \times 1.12 = 3.74$

(d) Calculate how many times more expensive it is to buy rice in Ireland than in New Zealand. Give your answer to the nearest whole number.

4 At most schools there is a choice of subjects in Year 12. This graph shows the proportions of male students and female students taking different subjects.

(a) Are there more male students or more female students taking Physics?

(b) Are there more male students or more female students taking Biology?

(c) Use the scale on a ruler to help you decide whether there are more male or female students taking Maths.

(d) Which subject appears to have equal numbers of male and female students?

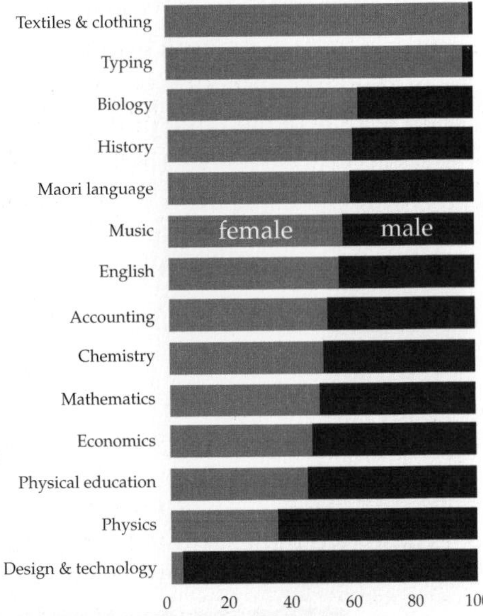

Calcium makes up a large part of your bone mass. It is important to maintain a calcium-rich diet, and get plenty of exercise, to maintain strong bones. There is a link between calcium loss and developing osteoporosis, a bone-thinning disease which makes fractures more likely.

5 This table shows the recommended amount of calcium needed per day for various age groups. It also shows some foods that are rich in calcium.

(a) Write down the amount of calcium each of these people need per day:
 (i) Matthew, aged 14
 (ii) Nga, aged 10
 (iii) Wiremu, aged 5
 (iv) Cathy, aged 17
 (v) Mr Tranh, aged 42
 (vi) Mrs Smith, aged 71

(b) Calculate the amount of calcium in each of these foods:
 (i) a litre of homogenised milk (1 litre = 1000 mL)
 (ii) six slices of cheddar cheese
 (iii) a bowl of muesli with half a glass of milk

(c) Write a sentence or two to explain whether eating a pottle of yoghurt and two glasses of calcium-fortified milk would be enough calcium for *your* daily needs.

Calcium: recommended daily intake

Foods rich in calcium		
Food		Calcium content
1 glass of homogenised milk (200 mL)		●
1 glass of calcium-fortified milk (200 mL)		● ◡
1 pottle of yoghurt (150 g)		●
3 slices of cheddar cheese (40 g)		● ◡
1 cup of ice cream (140 g)		●
Half a can of sardines (50 g)		● ◡
1 cup of salmon (240 g)		●
1 medium bowl of muesli (80 g)		●
1 cup of baked beans (270 g)		◡
Half a cup of dried figs (105 g)		●
Amount of calcium needed per day		
Young children (1 – 8 years)		● ● ● ●
Older children (8 – 11 years)		● ● ● ● ◡
Teenagers (12 – 18 years)	Girls	● ● ● ● ◡
	Boys	● ● ● ● ●
Adults		● ● ● ●
Older women (54+ years)		● ● ● ● ●
Pregnant women		● ● ● ● ● ◡
Breastfeeding women		● ● ● ● ● ●

● = approximately 200 mg of calcium

Calcium need per day based on recommended daily allowances which have been adopted for New Zealand.
Source: Dairy Advisory Bureau/Arthritis Foundation; *Consumer*.

Statistical displays

There are many ways of displaying statistical information.

A statistical graph should:
- have a title
- show the data as accurately as possible
- enable comparisons to be made.

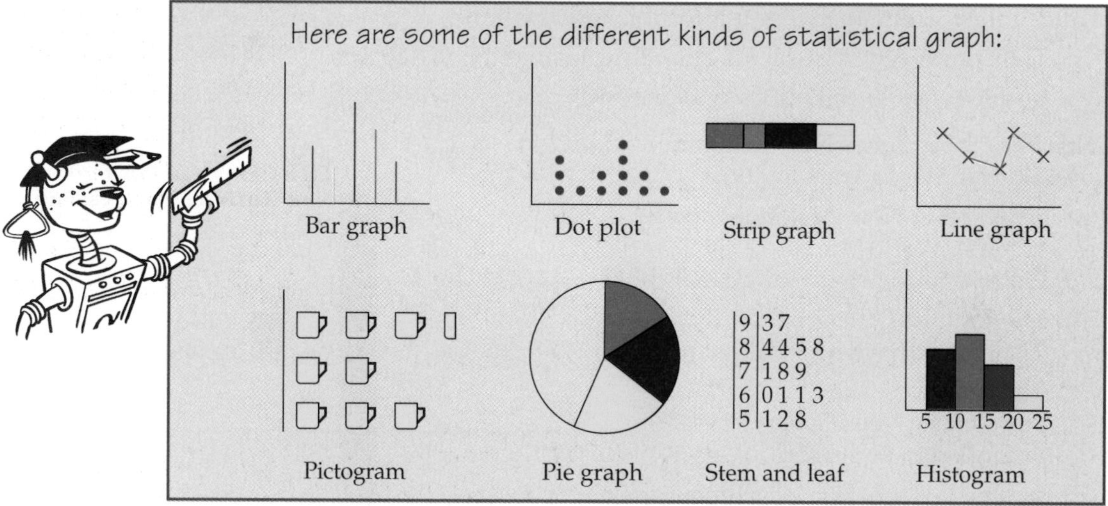

Bar graphs

- The height of the lines on a bar graph shows how many there are of each item.
- The vertical axis on the left should have an even scale.

Example This bar graph shows the number of television channels in four countries in 1995:

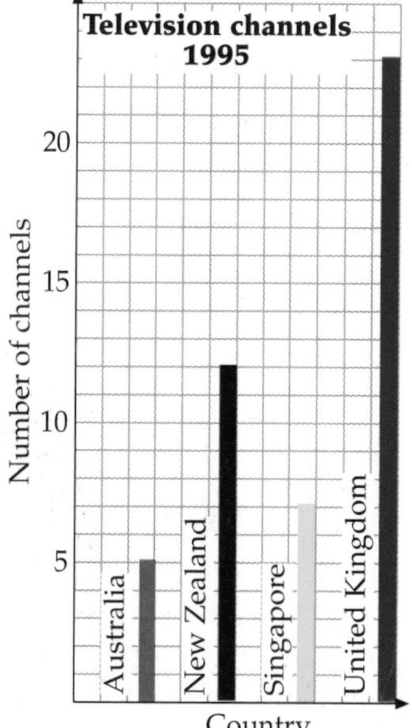

Sometimes a bar graph is called a **column graph**. The bars can be drawn as lines or as thin columns. They are not joined together.

EXERCISE 28.2

1 This table shows the different types of function that Gourmet & Gobble Ltd (a catering firm) provided food for in June last year. Represent the information in a bar graph.

Type of function	Number
Wedding	6
21st birthday	3
Corporate lunch	8
Midwinter Christmas	4
Others	5

2 Draw a neat, accurate, bar graph for this information:

Transport used by students attending Tasman High School:
bus 670, car 50, bike 230, walking 550.

3 This bar graph shows New Zealand casualties in World Wars I and II:

(a) How many New Zealanders were killed in World War I?
Give your answer to the nearest 1000.

(b) True or false? 'Fewer than 1000 New Zealanders have been killed in all other wars'.

(c) How many New Zealanders were wounded in both World Wars?

(d) In which World War was the number of New Zealanders killed more than half of the number wounded?

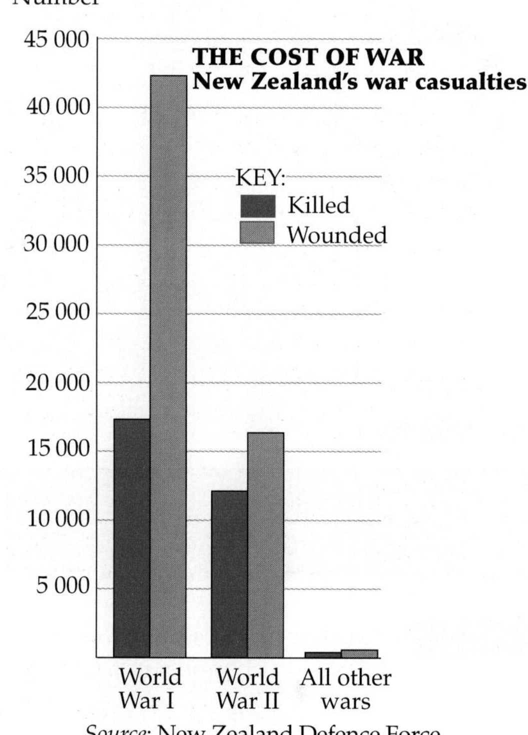

Source: New Zealand Defence Force, Statistics New Zealand

4 The annual average rainfall figures for nine North Island centres are shown on this map. Draw a bar graph to show this data.

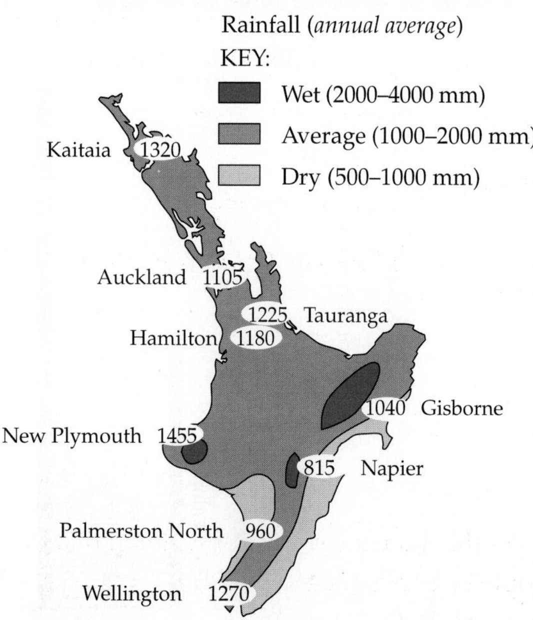

5 Explain what is misleading about this bar graph:

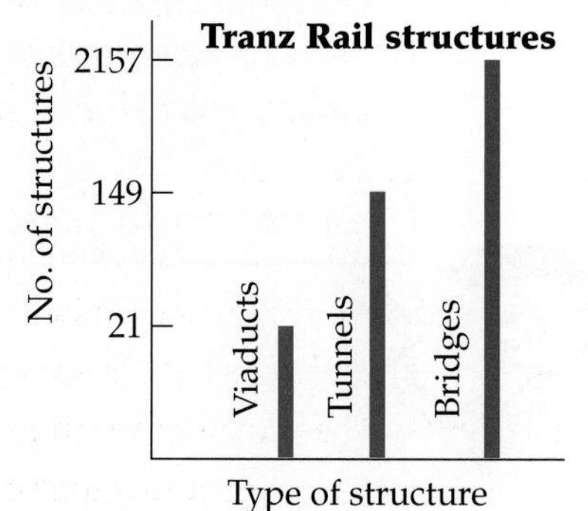

6 Spreadsheet software has been used to produce this bar graph. The data was collected by selecting a group of households and asking the occupants whether they have each of these appliances. The results show the percentage that have each appliance.

(a) Suggest a reason why the scale on the vertical axis does not start at 0.

(b) Explain how the heights of the columns give a misleading impression.

(c) Explain how you would read a value as accurately as possible from this graph.

	A	B
1	Appliance	Percentage of surveyed households
2		
3	Electric Range	95
4	Telephone	96
5	Washing machine	97.6
6	Colour TV	95.8
7		
8		
9		
10		
11		
12		
13		
14		
15		
16		
17		
18		
19		
20		
21		
22		
23		
24		

98
97
96
95
94
93
S1
Electric Range
Telephone
Washing machine
Colour TV

7 Use spreadsheet software to produce a bar graph to display this sunshine data. The data was collected over a thirty-year period starting in 1965. (Note: in the spreadsheet this might be called a column graph.)

City	Number of bright sunshine hours per year
Auckland	2071
Wellington	2024
Christchurch	2066
Dunedin	1595

Dot plots

- A dot plot uses a marked scale.
- Each time an item is counted, it is marked by a dot.

Example There are twenty houses in Division St. This dot plot gives information about the number of people living in the houses.

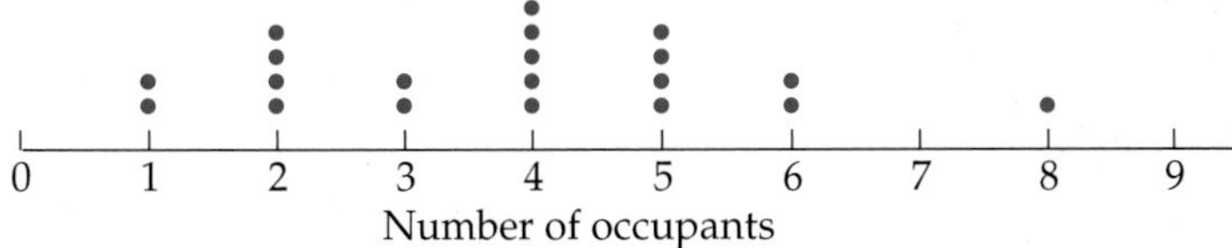

Some features of this dot plot are:

- it shows that there were two houses that had one person only living there
- the most common number of people in a house is 4
- the largest number of people in a house is 8.

EXERCISE 28.3

1 This is a list of temperatures taken at 3 pm in 25 locations throughout New Zealand one day last November. The temperatures are in °C.

22	17	20	25	19
19	14	18	24	17
19	20	17	24	22
24	17	19	15	17
22	14	23	20	18

Draw a line, and mark in a scale starting at 14 and ending at 25. Then use the data to produce a dot plot of these temperatures.

2 This dot plot shows the number of goals scored by sixteen teams at a one-day soccer tournament.

Soccer tournament

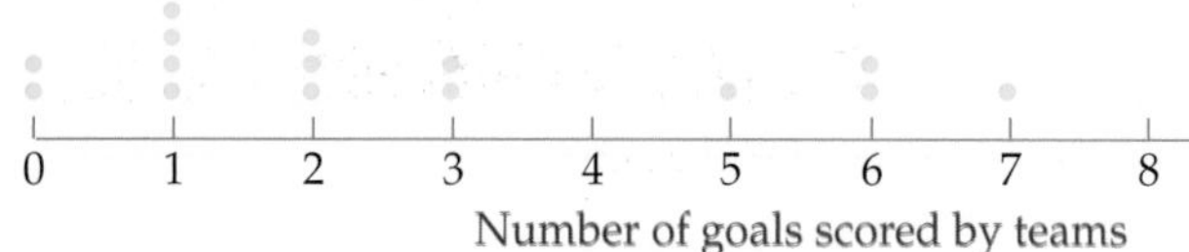

(a) What was the most number of goals scored by a team?

(b) How many teams scored one goal?

(c) What was the most common number of goals scored by these teams?

(d) How many goals were scored altogether?

3 Here is a list of the number of students in the ten classes in Year 9 at Aotearoa College.

Class	Number of students
9Ar	33
9Bh	30
9Ct	29
9Ew	30
9Lk	31
9Mn	32
9Re	28
9Sa	30
9St	31
9Wo	30

Display the information on a dot plot.

4 The Land Transport Safety Authority are considering whether the age at which people can first drive should be increased. This table shows the minimum age at which people can obtain a driver's licence in a number of different places.

Age	Place
14	South Dakota
15	New Zealand, Hawaii, Idaho, Montana, New Mexico, South Carolina
16	South Australia, Northern Territory, most Canadian provinces
17	New South Wales, Queensland, Western Australia, Tasmania, Canberra, Newfoundland, Ontario, Great Britain, Israel, New Jersey
18	Victoria, Nova Scotia, Denmark, Finland, France, Germany, the Netherlands, Norway, Sweden

(a) Use the data to construct a dot plot.

(b) Do you think a dot plot is an appropriate way to display this information? Explain.

Strip graphs

- A strip graph shows the proportion of each part to the whole very clearly.
- It should have a scale to make it easy to read off information.

Example Construct a strip graph to show the number of farmers in the four major types of agriculture in New Zealand. The numbers have been rounded to the nearest 100.

Farm type	Number of farmers
Dairy	21 300
Sheep	13 400
Beef	7200
Horticulture	9300

Answer A suitable scale to use would be 1 mm = 500 farmers.

To calculate the length of the 'dairy' strip, divide 21 300 by 500

Dairy: $\dfrac{21\,300}{500} = 42.6$ mm (approx. 43 mm)

Similar calculations for the other three types of farm give:

Sheep: 27 mm

Beef: 14 mm

Horticulture: 19 mm

Dairy Sheep Beef Hort.

Scale: 1 mm = 500 farmers

EXERCISE 28.4

1 This strip graph shows the proportions of different breeds of dairy cattle in New Zealand.

Breeds of NZ dairy cattle

Jersey	Friesian	Hereford	Others

Scale: 1 000 000 (1 million) cattle = 1 cm

(a) Measure the length of the Jersey part of the strip graph. Use your measurement to write down the number of Jersey cattle.

(b) How many Friesian cattle are there?

(c) How many Hereford cattle are there?

(d) How many dairy cattle are there altogether in New Zealand?

2 A survey of the eye colour of 30 students in a class gave the information in this table. Draw a strip graph 15 cm long. Divide it up to show the proportions of eye colours.

Eye colour	Number of students
Blue	8
Brown	17
Green	3
Hazel	2

3 This photo shows the result of fundraising by parents at St Mary's School in Northcote.
(a) How much money do the parents still have to raise?
(b) Describe how the graph is misleading.

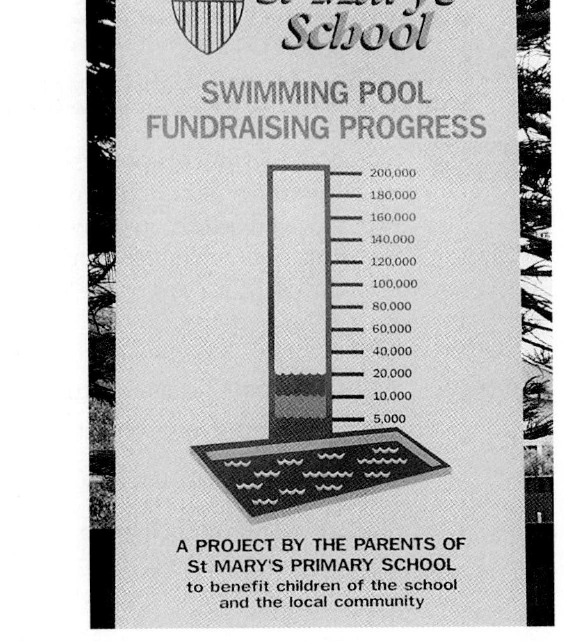

4 Here are figures from a recent survey of radio-listeners.
100 people who listen to the radio at breakfast time were asked to say what kind of programme they were listening to.

AM National Programme	15
AM News/Talkback	39
FM Music	46

(a) Which of these would be the most suitable scale on a strip bar?
A 1 cm = 1 listener
B 10 cm = 1 listener
C 1 cm = 10 listeners
(b) Show the information on a strip graph.

5 This table shows where overseas visitors to New Zealand have come from. The data was collected over a one-year period recently.

Country/continent	Number of visitors	Percentage (to nearest whole number)
Australia	409 326	28%
North America	180 741	
Europe	225 127	
Asia	397 462	
Other	229 182	
Total	1 441 838	

(a) The percentage of visitors from Australia was worked out on a calculator by evaluating $\frac{\square}{1\,441\,838} \times 100$. What number should replace the $\square$?
(b) Write down, in order from the table, the percentages for the other four places.
(c) Represent this information on a strip graph. Use a scale of 1 cm = 10%.

Pictograms

STARTER

This graph represents the number of medals won at the Kuala Lumpur Commonwealth Games by the leading four countries:

Australia

England 

Canada 

Malaysia 

Each symbol represents 10 medals
The graph shows that Malaysia won 36 medals.

- How many medals did England win?
- How many medals did Australia win?
- At the same Games, New Zealand won 35 medals. Describe how this would be shown on the graph.

- A pictogram (or pictograph) uses symbols to represent a fixed number of items.
- The key should show the value of each symbol.

EXERCISE 28.5

1 This graph shows the sizes for Mrs Johnson's six Mathematics classes. Each symbol represents 5 students.

(a) Which class has the most students? How many students are there in this class?

(b) Which class has the fewest students?

(c) Which classes are the same size?

(d) Estimate the total number of students in Mrs Johnson's classes.

Class	Number of students
9Br	α α α α α α (
10Jo	α α α α α α α'
10Hw	α α α α α α α
11 Maths	α α α α α α (
12 Maths	α α α α (
13 Calculus	α α α (

α = 5 students

2 This pictograph shows the number of spoons, forks and knives manufactured in a cutlery factory last month.

Key: 1 symbol = 500 pieces

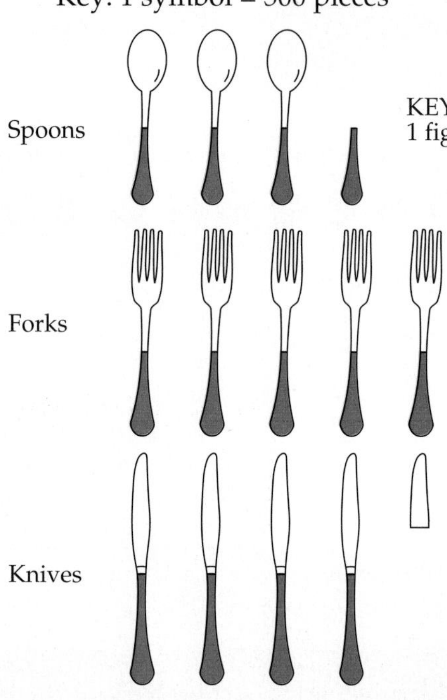

KEY:
1 figure = 500 pieces

(a) How many forks were made?
(b) How many spoons were made?
(c) How many knives were made?
(d) How many pieces of cutlery were made altogether?

3 This pictogram shows the number of tyres sold by four different tyre dealers one month. The information is correct to the nearest hundred. 1 symbol = 600 tyres.

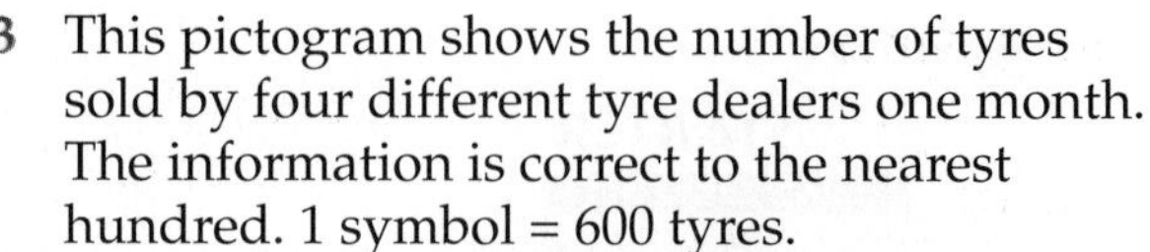

Rubber Runners

Gripwell

Brakefast

Tread-good

(a) How many tyres are represented by:
 (i) 2 symbols
 (ii) $\frac{1}{2}$ symbol
 (iii) $\frac{2}{3}$ symbol
(b) Which two dealers sold the same number of tyres?
(c) How many tyres were sold by all four dealers?
(d) A fifth dealer, Firmride, have been left off this graph. They sold 2700 tyres. Draw how their part of the pictograph should have looked.

4 This table gives the population of the six largest urban areas at the 1996 Census.

Urban area	Population
Auckland	997 940
Wellington	335 468
Christchurch	331 443
Hamilton	159 234
Dunedin	112 279
Tauranga	82 832

Represent this data in a pictogram. Choose a suitable symbol (e.g. a stick figure) to represent 100 000 people.

Pie graphs

What do you think the government spends most money on? The Police? Schools? Hospitals?

This pie graph shows how the government spends money on your behalf.

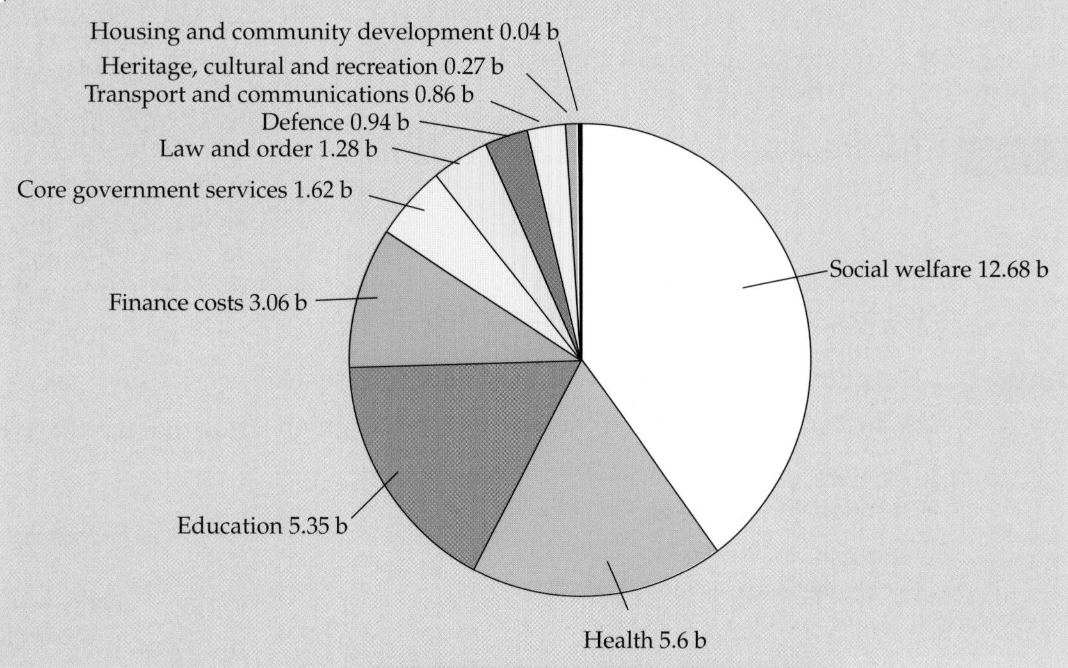

- What part of government spending takes more money than any other?
- There are 360° in a circle. Explain whether the angle at the centre of the Education sector is closest to 45°, 60° or 90°.
- The three largest parts of government spending (Social welfare, Health, and Education) make up about 75% of government spending. Explain how the graph shows this.

Here are two calculations that can be made from this data:

A $\frac{12.68}{31.70} \times 100 = 40\%$

- How has the number 31.70 been calculated. What does it represent?
- What does the answer of 40% represent?

B $40\% \times 360 = \frac{40}{100} \times 360 = 144°$

- Where in the graph is there an angle of 144°?

- Pie graphs are used to show comparisons.
- The 'slices of the pie' are called **sectors.** They show how the whole is divided up into different parts.

To work with pie graphs, we need to use some mathematics from elsewhere:

- percentages
- angles.

The angles at the centre of a pie graph are easy to calculate if the total divides into 360°.

You can use a protractor to draw in the angles at the centre of the pie graph. Usually you start the measuring from the top of the circle.

Example The 30 students in 9Bn come to school as follows:

Walk:	8
Bicycle:	5
Bus:	11
Car:	6

Represent this information on a pie graph.

Answer There are 30 students. So, each one will be represented by an angle of $\frac{360}{30} = 12°$ at the centre of the pie graph.

The angle for walk is $8 \times 12° = 96°$

The angle for bicycle is $5 \times 12° = 60°$

The angle for bus is $11 \times 12° = 132°$

The angle for car is $6 \times 12° = 72°$

How 9Bn travel to school

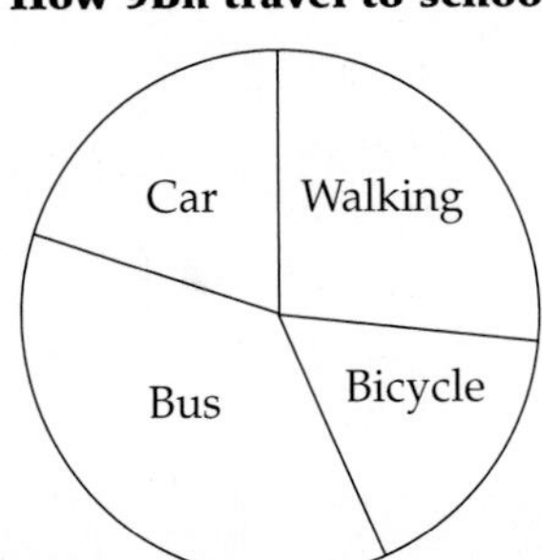

Often the data does not work out as conveniently as it does in the above example. So, we use percentages or fractions to calculate the angles at the centre of the pie graph.

Example A survey of 200 homes showed that 71 had at least one computer, and 129 did not. Show this information on a pie graph.

Answer Percentage with computer = $\frac{71}{200} \times 100 = 35.5\%$

Percentage with no computer = $\frac{129}{200} \times 100 = 64.5\%$

To calculate the angles at the centre of the pie graph, work out percentages of 360°:

$35.5\% \text{ of } 360 = \frac{35.5}{100} \times 360 = 127.8°$

$64.5\% \text{ of } 360 = \frac{64.5}{100} \times 360 = 232.2°$

Here, we round these angles to the nearest whole number: 128° and 232°

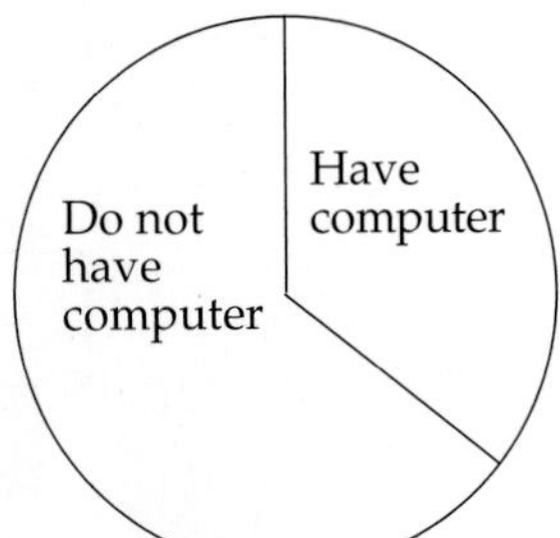

EXERCISE 28.6

1 A survey of 72 homes gives these results about the *main* method of home heating:

Heating method	Number of homes	Angle at centre
Electricity	29	
Gas	10	
Open fire	12	
Wood-burning stove	17	
Solar	1	5°
None	3	
Total	**72**	**360°**

A pie graph will be used to compare how popular each method is.

(a) Write down a calculation using the numbers 360 and 72, to show that the centre angle for *one* home in the pie graph will be 5°.

(b) Copy the table. Complete the third column.

(c) Draw a pie graph to display the results.

2 36 teams travel to a soccer tournament. They use these as their *main* method of transport:

Air 12
Bus 14
Train 9
Car 1

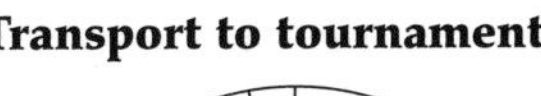

Transport to tournament

S
R
P
Q

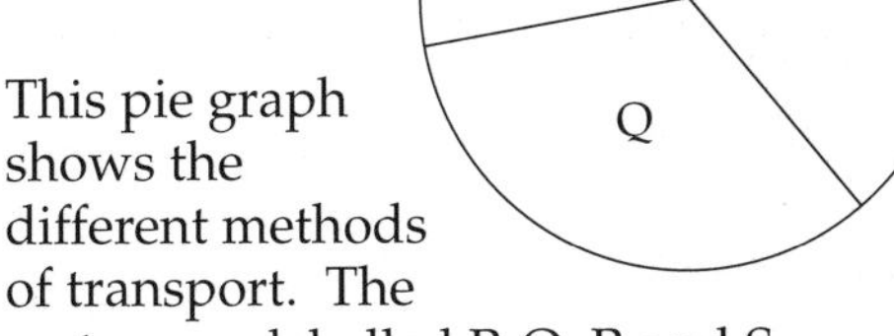

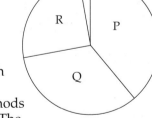

This pie graph shows the different methods of transport. The sectors are labelled P, Q, R and S.

(a) Match each sector (P, Q, R and S) with one of the methods of transport.

(b) What is the angle at the centre of sector Q?

(c) Which transport method do exactly one quarter of the teams use?

3 A football stadium has been designed with exactly 40 000 seats. This pie graph shows how the seats are split between covered and uncovered.

Stadium seating

Covered
Uncovered

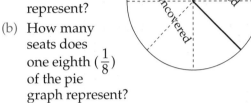

(a) How many seats does a right-angle (90°) at the centre represent?

(b) How many seats does one eighth ($\frac{1}{8}$) of the pie graph represent?

(c) How many seats are covered?

(d) How many seats are uncovered?

4 Tasman High School has 90 students in Year 9 classes. Each student was asked to find out what day of the week they were born.

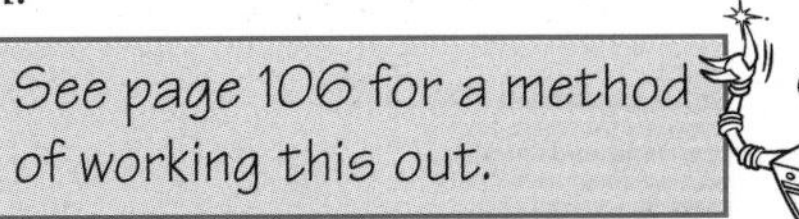

See page 106 for a method of working this out.

Here are the results:

Day of the week	Number of students	Angle at centre
Sunday	9	36°
Monday	12	
Tuesday	18	
Wednesday	15	
Thursday	15	
Friday	11	
Saturday	10	

(a) How many sectors will be needed to show this data on a pie graph?

(b) A single student would need an angle of 4° on this pie graph. Explain why.

(c) Copy the table. Complete it to show the angle needed for each day of the week.

(d) Draw the pie graph to display these results.

5 Anne asked her classmates this question:

'Are you the oldest child, one of the middle children or the youngest child in your family?'

The results were:

- exactly one-half said they were an oldest child
- one-sixth said they were a middle child
- one-third said they were a youngest child.

Display these results in a pie graph.

6 (a) Draw a pie graph to show the data in this bar graph.

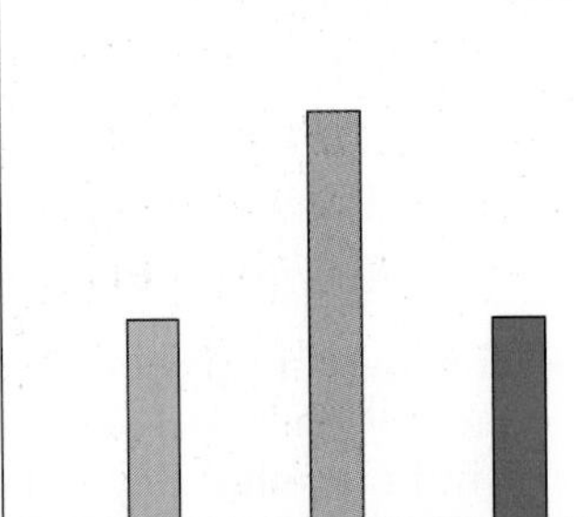

(b) Draw a bar graph to show the data in this pie graph.

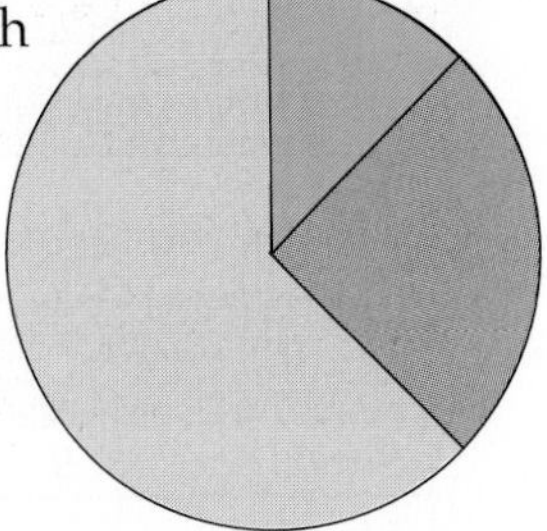

7 The most recent census gave these percentages to show how the population of greater Auckland is distributed:

City	Percentage
North Shore	18%
Waitakere	17%
Auckland	38%
Manukau	27%

The data can be displayed on a pie graph.

(a) The angle at the centre for the North Shore City sector is approximately 65°. Complete this calculation to work it out *exactly*:

$\frac{18}{100} \times 360 = ...$

(b) Calculate the angles at the centre for Waitakere City, Auckland City and Manukau City.

(c) Draw the pie graph.

8 Blood donor centres collect blood from volunteers and store it until it is needed (for operations and emergency transfusions after accidents, etc.). This table shows the percentages of the eight different types of human blood:

Blood type	Rhesus factor		Total
	positive	negative	
O	38	8	
A	32	7	
B	9	2	
AB	3	1	
Total			100

(a) Display these 8 blood percentages in a pie graph.

(b) Copy the table, and complete the totals.

(c) Construct a pie graph to display the proportions of the two different Rhesus factors.

(d) Construct a pie graph to display the four different blood types O, A, B and AB.

9 This table shows student roll numbers in New Zealand at 1 July one year recently.

Primary	459 221
Secondary	238 104
Polytechnic	95 346
University	105 690

Use spreadsheet software to produce a pie graph to show how the roll numbers compare with each other. You may find the instructions in Chapter 1 (on page 17) useful.

Stem and leaf diagrams

STARTER

Here are the daily absence data for a large secondary school over a six-week period. Each of the numbers has two digits.

38, 41, 34, 23, 55, 48, 37, 31, 30, 63, 17, 27, 35, 25, 43, 42, 66, 57, 54, 36, 32, 19, 25, 23, 41, 72, 49, 34, 24, 20.

The figures can also be shown in a **stem and leaf** graph.

stem	leaves
7	2
6	3 6
5	4 5 7
4	1 1 2 3 8 9
3	0 1 2 4 4 5 6 7 8
2	0 3 3 4 5 5 7
1	7 9

- Are the digits in the stem the first or second digits of the absence data?
- Explain what the leaves show.
- What was the most number of absences over this six-week period?
- What was the least number of absences over this six-week period?

- A stem and leaf diagram is a convenient way of writing down a group of numbers.
- The most significant digit(s) are placed in the vertical **stem**
- The last digits are placed in the horizontal **leaves**.
- Usually, the numbers in a leaf are in order from smallest to largest.

Advantages of using a stem and leaf display for data:

- it shows how the data are distributed
- it allows you to easily see the smallest and largest items of data
- it shows the data in order from smallest to largest.

EXERCISE 28.7

1 Here are scores for 25 players in a golf tournament:

84 78 75 94 101 77 88 87 91 72 100 94 82
81 73 68 76 83 77 104 83 71 82 85 74

(a) Construct a stem and leaf display for this data. Use numbers 6 to 10 in the stem. Make sure the digits in each leaf are in order from smallest to largest.

(b) What is the difference between the highest score and the lowest score?

2 Every Thursday, a newspaper allows people to advertise some items free of charge. They must be asking less than $100 for each item. Here is a stem and leaf display of the cost of items one Thursday.

Stem	Leaf
0	5 9
1	0 0 5
2	0 0 9 9
3	0 0 4 5 5 9 9
4	0 0 2 5 9 9
5	0 3 6 8
6	5 6 9
7	0 5
8	0 0 9
9	0 5 9 9 9 9

(a) How much is the cheapest item?

(b) How much is the most expensive item?

(c) What is the cheapest item that is over $60?

(d) How many items are advertised altogether?

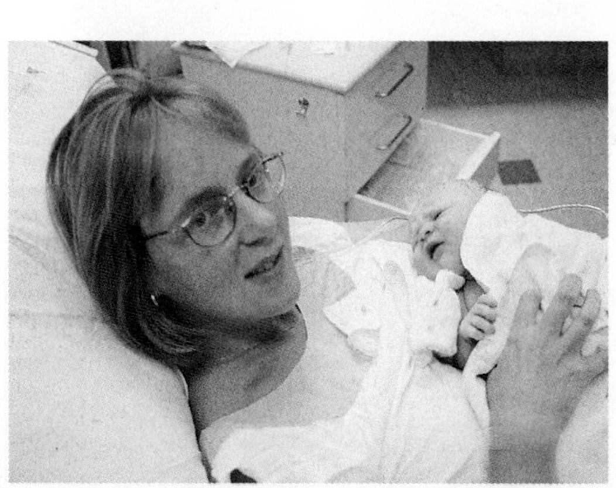

3 This stem and leaf diagram shows part of the Hutt Valley–Wellington train timetable for Mondays to Fridays. The times show when trains leave Taita to travel to Wellington.

Stem	Leaf
4	48
5	48
6	18 32 48 52
7	05 11 23 35 38 48 56
8	08 18 23 48
9	18 48
10	18 48
11	18 48
12	18 48
1	18 48
2	18 48
3	18 54
4	18 20 35 38 49
5	01 07 24 34 46 50
6	05 21 35 48
7	02 18 48
8	18 48
9	18 48
10	18 48
11	18

(a) The first train leaves Taita at 4.48 am. How much later does the second train leave?

(b) When does the last train leave Taita for Wellington?

(c) How frequently do the trains run during the middle of the day?

(d) What is the shortest time interval between trains in this timetable?

(e) Describe two significant features of this diagram. Suggest reasons for these features.

4 This stem and leaf diagram shows the ages of mothers in a maternity ward over a one-month period.

Stem	Leaf
1	6 7 9
2	0 0 1 2 2 4 4 4 5 5 6 8 8 9
3	1 2 4 4 5 6 7 7 8 9
4	0 0 1 2

(a) What age was the youngest mother?

(b) What age was the oldest mother?

(c) The most common age group for mothers is the twenties. How does the diagram show this?

5 Heights of students in 9Fr (in metres)

Girls	Alison 1.55 Denise 1.35 Lee 1.75 Wei-Li 1.58	Ann 1.40 Erin 1.46 Mary 1.68	Anna 1.60 Fleur 1.29 Nga 1.56	Becky 1.35 Hwan 1.51 Rachel 1.45	Cathy 1.27 Joanna 1.53 Teresa 1.62
Boys	Adam 1.57 Ioane 1.63 Stephen 1.81	Bryan 1.62 Kevin 1.52 Steven 1.72	Chris 1.74 Ki-Shu 1.46 Tim 1.79	David S 1.53 Martin 1.58 Xavier 1.54	David T 1.36 Roger 1.42 Wiremu 1.59

(a) Construct an ordered stem and leaf diagram to display the heights of all the students.

(b) How many students are there altogether?

(c) Give the names of the shortest and the tallest students in the class.

(d) Which one of 1.40–1.50 m or 1.50–1.60 m is the most common height interval?

(e) Construct a 'back-to-back' stem and leaf diagram to show the boys' and girls' heights separately.

6 This table gives the populations of New Zealand's medium-sized urban areas in 1961 and 1996.

Urban area	1961	1996
Blenheim	11 956	25 875
Dunedin	105 003	112 279
Gisborne	25 065	32 653
Hamilton	50 505	159 234
Hastings	32 490	58 675
Invercargill	41 088	49 306
Kapiti	12 305	30 004
Napier	32 716	55 044
Nelson	25 321	52 348
New Plymouth	32 387	49 079
Palmerston North	43 185	73 862
Rotorua	25 068	56 928
Tauranga	24 659	82 832
Timaru	26 424	27 521
Wanganui	35 694	41 320
Whangarei	21 790	45 785

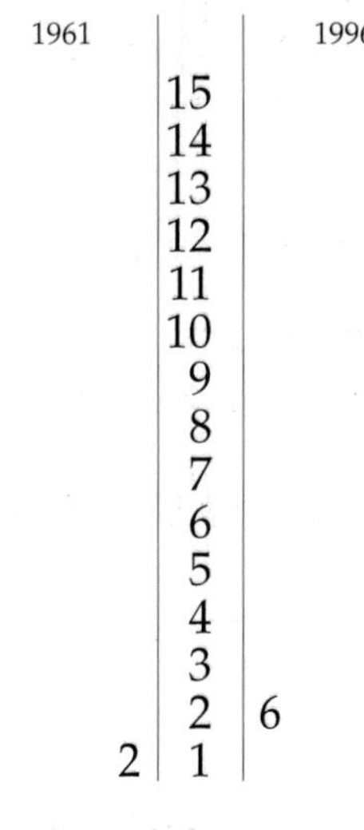

1961		1996
	15	
	14	
	13	
	12	
	11	
	10	
	9	
	8	
	7	
	6	
	5	
	4	
	3	
	2	6
2	1	

(a) Copy and complete the back-to-back stem and leaf graph to show the data. Round the figures to the nearest 1000. The figures for Blenheim have been included (notice that 11 956 rounds to 12 000, and 25 875 rounds to 26 000).

(b) Describe the most obvious difference between the 1961 figures and the 1996 figures.

Line graphs

STARTER

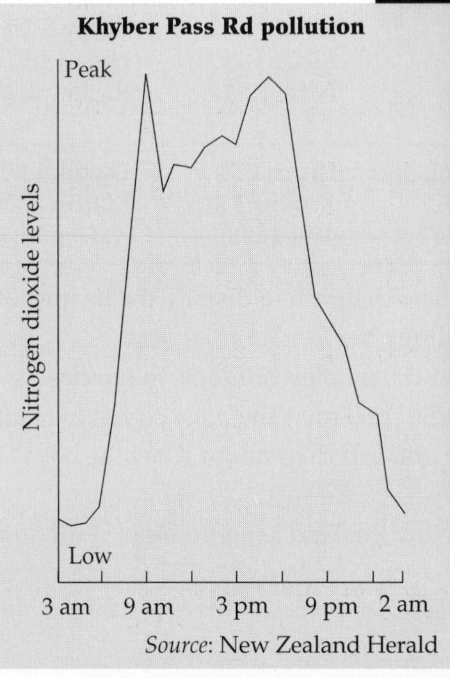

- Describe what this graph shows.
- Over what period of time have the measurements been taken?
- When are the two peaks? Suggest a reason why they occur at these times.
- Can you tell from the graph how often the measurements have been taken? Explain.
- The graph could be extended so that it covered a 48-hour period.
  What would you expect it to look like?
- Is there some information missing from this graph?

- A **line graph** shows what happens to data as time changes.
- Usually, the measurements are taken at regular time intervals.
- The time intervals are always shown on the horizontal scale.
- The data values can be read from the vertical scale.

Sometimes we call a line graph a **time series graph.**

The points on the graph are joined up, either with line segments or a smooth curve. This allows you to read off values in between.

EXERCISE 28.8

1

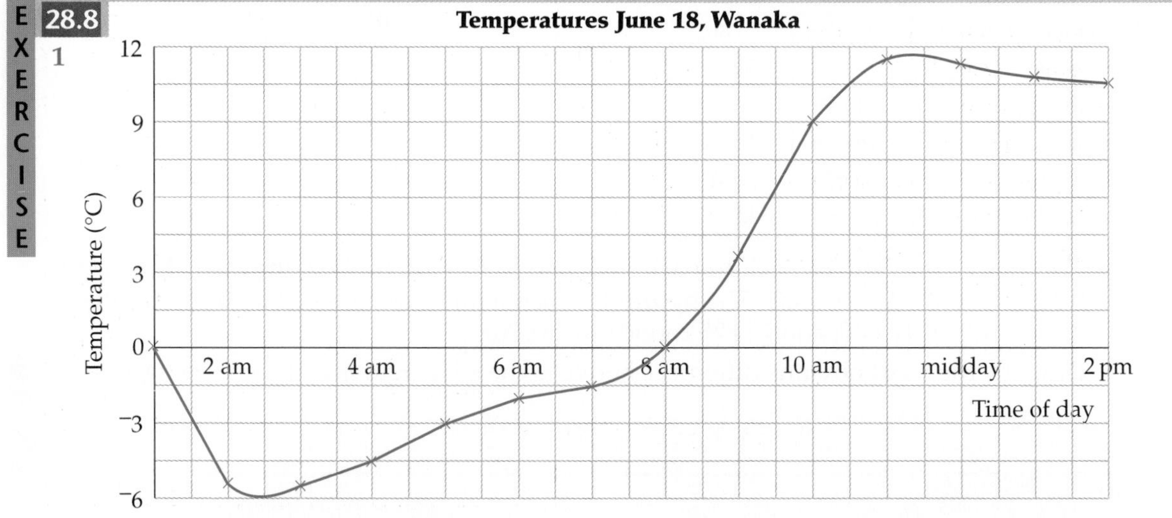

(a) What was the temperature at 10 am?

(b) What was the temperature at 3.30 am?

(continues)

(c) When was the temperature 0 °C?
(d) What was the coldest temperature shown? When was it recorded?
(e) Between which two times was the temperature *rising*?

2 This table gives the number of journeys made by taxi from a supermarket over a four- week period.

Week 1		Week 2		Week 3		Week 4	
Sun	12	Sun	14	Sun	15	Sun	16
Mon	10	Mon	8	Mon	11	Mon	9
Tue	14	Tue	16	Tue	13	Tue	12
Wed	15	Wed	16	Wed	15	Wed	17
Thu	28	Thu	23	Thu	29	Thu	31
Fri	27	Fri	29	Fri	26	Fri	30
Sat	18	Sat	21	Sat	22	Sat	19

(a) Display these 28 values on a line graph.
(b) Does the line graph show a repeating pattern? Explain.
(c) Which of these words best explains the long-term trend over the four- week period?
'Taxi hire from the supermarket is ....'
A increasing
B decreasing
C about the same each week

3 This line graph shows the number of calls through a telephone exchange from 6 am to 8 pm one day.

(a) How many calls were there at:
(i) 11 am?
(ii) 5 pm?
(b) Estimate the number of calls made at:
(i) 8.30 am
(ii) 6.45 pm
(c) At what *three* times were there 18 000 calls?
(d) When were there the *least* number of calls?

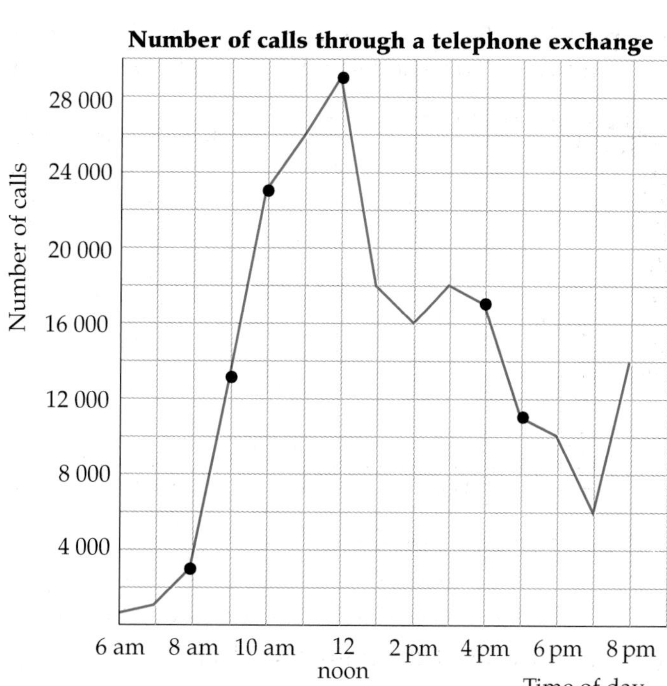

4 For a school project, Tanya measured the depth of water below the wharf at Westport one Sunday. As the tide comes in and out, the depth changes. Tanya rounded the depth to the nearest metre. Here are her results:

Time	Depth (m)	Time	Depth (m)
Sun 6 am	4	4 pm	5
7 am	3	5 pm	4
8 am	3	6 pm	3
9 am	4	7 pm	3
10 am	5	8 pm	4
11 am	7	9 pm	5
midday	8	10 pm	7
1 pm	8	11 pm	8
2 pm	7	midnight	8
3 pm	6	Mon 1 am	7

(a) Display this information on a line graph.
(b) What would you expect the depth to be at 2 am on Monday?
(c) Suggest what the depth might have been at 4 am on Sunday.
(d) Which of these is the best estimate of the time between high tide and low tide?

A 3 hours B $5\frac{1}{2}$ hours

C 7 hours D 11 hours

SPREADSHEET INVESTIGATION

This spreadsheet shows the number of farm sales in New Zealand over a six-year period.

	A	B	C	D	E	F	G	H
1	Half-year ended	Number of sales						
2								
3	Jun-91	1735						
4	Dec-91	1750						
5	Jun-92	2392						
6	Dec-92	1951						
7	Jun-93	2546						
8	Dec-93	1510						
9	Jun-94	2216						
10	Dec-94	1393						
11	Jun-95	2013						
12	Dec-95	1153						
13	Jun-96	2006						
14	Dec-96	1121						
15								
16	From NZ Yearbook, Statistics NZ							

Farm sales (six monthly)

Number sold: 0, 500, 1000, 1500, 2000, 2500, 3000

Time of Year: Dec-90, Dec-91, Dec-92, Dec-93, Dec-94, Dec-95, Dec-96, Dec-97

The graph shows two main features of interest:

- a **trend**—the total number of sales each year has been falling
- a **repeating pattern**—farm sales in the first half (ending in June) of the year are higher than the second half (ending in December).

1 Enter the data into a spreadsheet of your own, and produce the graph yourself.

You will need to use the graphing tools:

- Highlight the block of data (cell A2 at the top left down to cell B13 at the bottom right)
- Click on the Chart wizard.
- Choose the X-Y graph option
- Enter a suitable title, and axis labels.

2 This table shows the total population of New Zealand at ten-yearly intervals since 1886.

Census	Total population
1886	620 451
1896	743 214
1906	936 309
1916	1 149 225
1926	1 408 139
1936	1 573 812
1946	1 702 298
1956	2 174 062
1966	2 676 919
1976	3 129 383
1986	3 307 084
1996	3 681 546

(a) Enter the data into a spreadsheet.

(b) Produce a line graph to show how the population has increased over this period.

(c) Over which ten-year period was the population growing fastest? How does the graph show this?

Further investigation

3 Collect data from your own home for some kind of regular payments (e.g. the phone bill or the electricity bill).

(a) Enter the data into a spreadsheet.

(b) Produce a line graph that displays the data.

(c) Describe whether there is a long-term trend, and whether you notice any other features of interest.

(d) Comment on whether the graph shows obvious differences in the payments at certain times of the year.

Every five years, the government organisation Statistics New Zealand holds a census. This is a compulsory survey of every person in the country.

The information collected includes answers to questions about age, language, religion, employment and many other topics of interest.

The data is collected to identify changes, and help plan future development.

Census '96 – some facts

On Census night 5 March 1996 there were:
3 618 300 people in New Zealand; 1 777 461 males and 1 840 839 females. Males = 49%, Females = 51%.

Maori population
523 374 people identified with the Maori ethnic group, up 20.4% since 1991.

Age groups
Between the 1991 and 1996 Censuses, the number of people under 15 has risen by 48 435 to 832 080.
The retirement-aged group in 1996 made up 12% of the population and numbered 422 667 compared with 11% and numbering 379 767 in 1991. There is a slightly higher proportion of men in this age group than in 1991.

Median age
In 1996 the median age of the population was 32.95 years. In 1991 the median age was 31.32, up from 29.74 in 1986.

Language
2 892 681 or 84% of the population on Census night reported they speak only one language. 95% or 3 290 454 people who answered the language question said they speak English. There were 153 666 people who stated that they spoke Maori, and 111 777 who said they spoke other Polynesian languages, with Samoan being the most widely spoken of these with 70 875 speakers.

Census 96 religious affiliations
Over one half of New Zealanders (57.4%) specified a Christian denomination. The 1991 figure was 65.2%. Major denominations were Anglican 17.5% (22.1% in 1991), Presbyterian 12.7% (16.3%) and Catholic 13.1% (15%).

Smoking
21.9% of the population aged 15 and over (609 297 people) said they were regular smokers. Despite an increase in the size of the population, this is down from the 1981 total of 721 116 (the last time the census asked New Zealanders about their smoking habits).

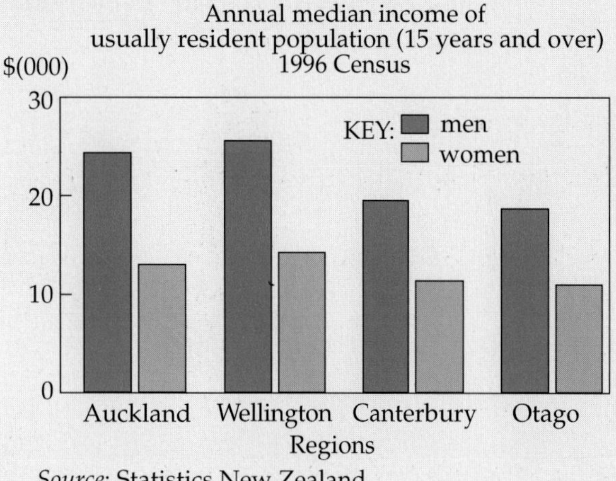

Source: Statistics New Zealand

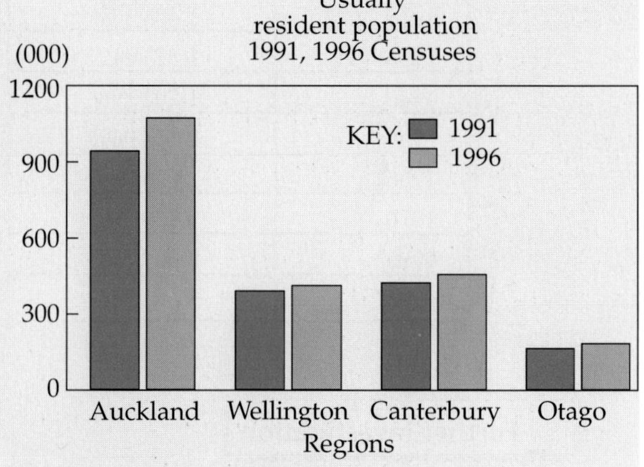

Source: Statistics New Zealand

Census information is available on the Internet.
The address is http://www.stats.govt.nz

EXERCISE 28.9

Twenty questions about the 1996 Census

1 What was the total population of New Zealand on Census night?

2 How many people reported that they speak the Maori language?

3 Which of the four regions given has the lowest annual median income for females?

4 What percentage of the population aged 15 and over said they were regular smokers?

5 Which of the four regions given has the highest annual median income for males?

6 What percentage of New Zealanders said they belonged to a Christian denomination?

7 The New Zealand census is conducted every five years. Write down the years in which the next three censuses will be held.

8 What Polynesian language (not including Maori) is the most widely spoken in New Zealand?

9 Which Christian denomination had the most people saying they belonged to it?

10 On what date was the 1996 Census conducted?

11 Did the median age of New Zealanders rise or fall between 1991 and 1996?

12 What percentage of New Zealanders speak only one language?

13 How many more females than males were there in New Zealand on census night?

14 Did the percentage of New Zealanders who smoke rise or fall from 1981 to 1996?

15 'On average, New Zealanders were about three years older in 1996 than in 1986'. Explain, using numbers from the article.

16 'The population of Auckland in 1996 was over one million'. *True* or *false*?

17 Did the percentage of New Zealanders of 'retirement age' rise or fall between 1991 and 1996?

18 A calculation that can be made using numbers given in this article is

$$\frac{523\ 374}{3\ 618\ 300} \times \frac{100}{1} = 14.5\% \text{ (approx.)}$$

What does this percentage tell us?

19 How many people were under 15 on Census night, 1991?

20 What does the graph show about the median income for males and females in New Zealand?

29 Working with data

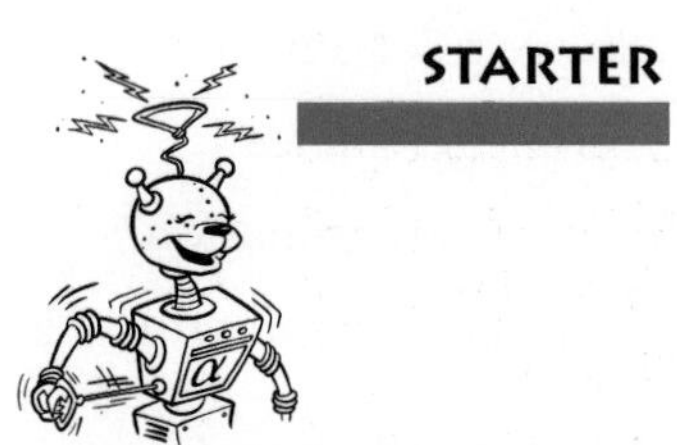

What is the 'average' age of the Maths family?

Mr Maths is 33 years old. Mrs Maths is 30. The oldest child, Gamma, is 10. The two twins, Alpha and Beta, are 6 years old.

Gamma says: 'the average age is 10. I have the middle age. Half the family are older than me, and half are younger.'

Alpha and Beta say: 'We think the average age is 6. We have the most common age!'

Mr and Mrs Maths add up the ages and make a calculation. They say: 'No, the average age is 17.'

The Maths family

- Who is correct?
- Explain what calculation Mr and Mrs Maths made to get an answer of 17.

Averages

The **average** of a set of numbers is a number which is typical of the set.
We use averages all the time:

- on average, I watch 4 videos each week
- my phone bill shows my average phone call lasts for 7.5 minutes
- on average, my electricity bill is $63.47
- the average age of people in my class is 13.

In Maths we use three different types of average—the **mean**, the **median** and the **mode**.

The mean

The **mean** of a set of numbers is calculated by dividing the total of the numbers by how many numbers there are.

$$\text{Mean} = \frac{\text{Sum of the values}}{\text{Number of values}}$$

Example Calculate the mean of the numbers 4, 7, 7, 10, 11, 9.

Answer There are six values altogether.

$$\text{Mean} = \frac{4+7+7+10+11+9}{6} = \frac{48}{6} = 8$$

- The mean doesn't have to be one of the original values.
- If one or more of the values is 0, include these when you count the number of values.

Example Calculate the mean of 5, 0, 8, 1, 0, 4, 3, 0, 2, 2.

Answer There are ten values altogether.

$$\text{Mean} = \frac{5+0+8+1+0+4+3+0+2+2}{10} = \frac{25}{10} = 2.5$$

EXERCISE 29.1

1–5 *Calculate the mean for each of these sets of numbers:*

1 { 1, 3, 1, 5, 7, 5, 6 }

2 { 6, 8, 5, 13, 12, 6, 7, 7 }

3 { 21, 27 }

4 { 3, 10, 12, 13 }

5 { 8, 0, 9, 2 }

6 Twenty numbers add up to 60. What is their mean?

7–9 *Calculate the mean for each of these sets of numbers. Give each answer correct to 2 decimal places, if they do not work out exactly.*

7 { 33, 76, 35, 34, 89, 0, 101 }

8 { 204, 1006, 0, 593, 87, 412 }

9 { 41.8, 32.8, 56.3, 38.0, 49.7, 51.8, 21.6 }

10 Dennis has these coins in his pocket. Calculate the mean value of the coins.

50c, 10c, \$2, 10c, 10c, 5c, \$1, \$2, 20c, 5c

11 Here are last week's takings at the school tuckshop:

Day	Amount taken
Monday	\$671
Tuesday	\$784.90
Wednesday	\$1041.25
Thursday	\$1188.60
Friday	949.20

Calculate the mean of these amounts.

12 A coxless four has a combined weight of 261 kg. Calculate the mean weight.

13 The mean weight of some apples is 151 g. Altogether they weigh 1208 g. How many apples are there?

14 Here are the times for ten swimmers to complete one length of a swimming pool:

Swimmer	Time	Swimmer	Time
Desley	1 min 12 sec	Anita	59 sec
Frank	49 sec	Julie	1 min 17 sec
Gary	50 sec	Ioane	1 min 5 sec
Hinemoa	49 sec	Colin	51 sec
Barry	1 min 17 sec	Eun-Wah	1 min 3 sec

(a) Calculate the mean time. (Remember to change minutes to seconds if necessary.)

(b) Which swimmer swam closest to the mean time?

Consecutive numbers follow each other in sequence—for example, 15, 16, 17, 18, 19.

15 Four consecutive numbers add up to 34.

(a) What is the mean of the numbers?

(b) What are the numbers?

16 Jelena and her brother have a mean height of 165 cm. Her brother is 172 cm tall. How tall is Jelena?

The median

The **median** is the *middle* value when all the values are placed in order.

Example The median of the set of numbers { 0, 0, 11, 14, 18, 21, 36 is 14 }

↑ median (under 14)

When there are an *even* number of values, the median is halfway between the two middle values. We find this by calculating the *mean* of the two middle values. We add them together, and divide by 2.

Example Calculate the median of these six birth-weights:
2.4 kg, 2.1 kg, 1.8 kg, 1.8 kg, 1.5 kg, 2.0 kg

Answer Write the weights in order: 1.5, 1.8, 1.8, 2.0, 2.1, 2.4
The two middle weights are 1.8 and 2.0

$$\text{Median} = \frac{1.8 + 2.0}{2} = \frac{3.8}{2} = 1.9 \text{ kg}$$

Sometimes you have to put the numbers in order first!

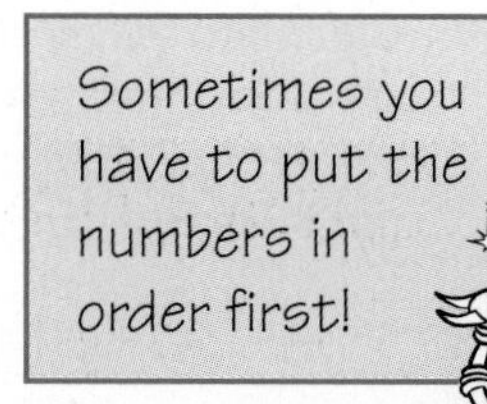

EXERCISE 29.2

1–5 *Write down the median of each of these sets of numbers:*

1 { 5, 9, 14, 15, 15 }

2 { 20, 21, 24, 26, 30, 31 }

3 { 6, 11, 17, 18, 18, 28, 35, 35, 35, 41, 42 }

4 { 93, 89, 58, 54, 48, 43, 43, 39, 33 }

5 { 9.3, 10.4, 10.8, 11.0, 11.3, 11.6, 12.2, 12.3, 13.8, 14.1, 14.1, 15.5, 18.6 }

6–10 *Put these sets of numbers in order. Then write down the median of each set.*

6 { 6, 2, 5, 4, 1 }

7 { 112, 98, 147 }

8 { 44, 66, 51, 49 }

9 { 46, 33, 49, 29, 51, 38, 52, 17 }

10 { 91, 105, 112, 89, 110, 89, 102, 114, 106, 99 }

11 This stem and leaf diagram shows the number of grapefruit collected one day from 20 trees.

Calculate the median number of fruit collected from each tree.

Stem	Leaf
12	7
11	1 1 8
10	0 5 7 9
9	2
8	3 9
7	6 7
6	0 3 3
5	
4	1 3
3	7
2	
1	
0	4

12 Colin has these stamps in his drawer:
$5 \times$ 40c stamps, $7 \times$ 80c stamps, $2 \times$ \$1 stamps, 1 \$1.50 stamp, and $2 \times$ \$1.80 stamps.
What is the median value of all the stamps?

13 Here is some weather data for Hamilton:

Month	Raindays	Rainfall (mm)
January	5	54
February	6	67
March	4	102
April	11	83
May	13	110
June	12	118
July	18	132
August	15	143
September	11	83
October	8	23
November	8	74
December	6	68

(a) Calculate the median number of raindays per month.

(b) Calculate the median amount of rainfall each month.

14

Age (years)	11	68	42	5	71	39	2
Height (cm)	212	198	192	118	95	61	38
Mass (kg)	63	98	75	102	63	41	14

(a) Are the aliens in order of age, height, or mass?

(b) Work out each of these:

(i) the median height

(ii) the median age

(iii) the median mass

15 A taxi driver writes down the odometer reading on the taxi at the end of each day. The distance travelled (in km) can be calculated from this. Some of the information is missing at the end of the week, but there is enough there to work out the missing entries.

(a) Copy and complete this table:

Day of week	Odometer at start of day	Odometer at end of day	Distance travelled (km)
Sunday	4018.6	4122.7	104.1
Monday	4122.7		223.6
Tuesday	4346.3		
Wednesday	4435.5		
Thursday	4548.2		156.0
Friday			193.1
Saturday	4897.3	5060.7	

(b) What is the median distance travelled this week? On what day did this occur?

16 Two children in a family with four children are twins. The other two children are 19 and 16. The median age of all four children is 14. How old are the twins?

There are spreadsheet formulas that calculate the **mean** and **median** of a *block* of cells.

Example Using the numbers in cells B3 down to B10, the formulas would be:

- mean: =AVERAGE(B3:B10)
- median =MEDIAN(B3:B10)

This extract from a spreadsheet shows what happens when the numbers 11.4, 19.4, 18, 31, 5.9, 9.6, 2.1 and 6.8 are entered.

What you enter:

	A	B
1		Number
2		
3		11.4
4		19.4
5		18
6		31
7		5.9
8		9.6
9		2.1
10		6.8
11		
12	Mean	=AVERAGE(B3:B10)
13		
14	Median	=MEDIAN(B3:B10)

What appears:

	A	B
1		Number
2		
3		11.4
4		19.4
5		18
6		31
7		5.9
8		9.6
9		2.1
10		6.8
11		
12	Mean	13.025
13		
14	Median	10.5

Check for yourself that the values 13.025 and 10.5 are correct!

EXERCISE 29.3

1 This table gives the populations of New Zealand's urban areas in 1996. The urban areas are in alphabetical order.

Urban area	1996
Auckland	997940
Blenheim	25875
Christchurch	331443
Dunedin	112279
Gisborne	32653
Hamilton	159234
Hastings	58675
Invercargill	49306
Kapiti	30004
Napier	55044
Nelson	52348
New Plymouth	49079
Palmerston North	73862
Rotorua	56928
Taupo	21044
Tauranga	82832
Timaru	27521
Wanganui	41320
Wellington	335468
Whangarei	45785

(a) Enter the information into columns A and B of a spreadsheet.

(b) Calculate the *median* population using a spreadsheet formula.

(c) Calculate the *mean* population using a spreadsheet formula.

(d) One of the two averages (median or mean) is influenced by the extremely large value of the Auckland population. Which one?

(e) Sort the data so that it is in order of population, with Auckland at the top. (Note: there are instructions given for spreadsheet sorting in Chapter 1, on page 15.)

2 Open a new worksheet in your spreadsheet program.

(a) Produce a spreadsheet of birthdates.

In column A, enter the names of the people whose birthdates you know.

Now highlight the cells in column B that you will be using for the birthdates. These need to be formatted as dates. Click on Format, Cell, Date to do this. Choose a date format that shows the day, month and year.

Then enter the birthdates.

> *Spreadsheets handle dates in a different way from other numbers. The program needs to know in advance that you have entered dates in this range of cells.*

(b) Calculate the mean and median birthdates for these people.

(c) Sort the list of people from oldest to youngest.

Print out your results if your computer is connected to a printer.

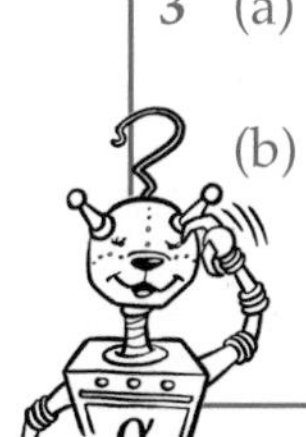

3 (a) Investigate how to show today's date in a spreadsheet.

(b) Use this to calculate the exact age in years, months and days for each of the people on your list in question 2.

The mode

STARTER

- Make a list of the ages of students in your class.
- Which age occurs most frequently (is the most common)? Is it 12, 13 or 14?

You have just found the *mode* age of students in your class.

The **mode** of a set of numbers is the one that occurs most often.

Example What is the mode of the numbers 3, 5, 5, 7, 8, 5, 9, 9, 10 ?

Answer The mode is 5, because 5 occurs more often than any of the other numbers.

- Sometimes there is no mode. For example, the set of numbers 0, 13, 41, 53, 6 has no mode.
- Sometimes there is more than one mode. For example, the set of coins { 20c, 50c, 10c, $1, 50c, $2, 10c } has two modes: 10c and 50c.

EXERCISE 29.4

1–7 *Write down the mode for each of these sets of numbers:*

1 { 3, 6, 7, 4, 6 }

2 { 5, 7, 8, 2, 0, 3, 7 }

3 { 10, 60, 20, 20, 70, 30, 40, 0, 40, 20, 50, 0 }

4 { 2, 0, 3, 0, 4, 5, 5, 8, 4, 0, 30, 44, 1, 7, 3, 3, 6, 5, 0, 4 }

5 { 13, 18, 14, 12, 11, 10 }

6 { 1, 8, 0, 5, 6, 4, 5, 1 }

7 { 70, 90, 40, 50, 70, 20, 90, 100, 20, 20, 50, 50, 20, 60, 40, 40 }

8 (Multichoice) Which one of these four sets of numbers has no mode?

A { 4, 4, 1, 3, 3 }

B { 6, 6, 6, 6 }

C { 18, 1, 12, 21 }

D { 5.1, 2.2, 3.2, 2.2 }

9 This dot plot shows the number of jeans in different sizes (8-22) sold one day by a clothing shop.

Jean sizes sold one day

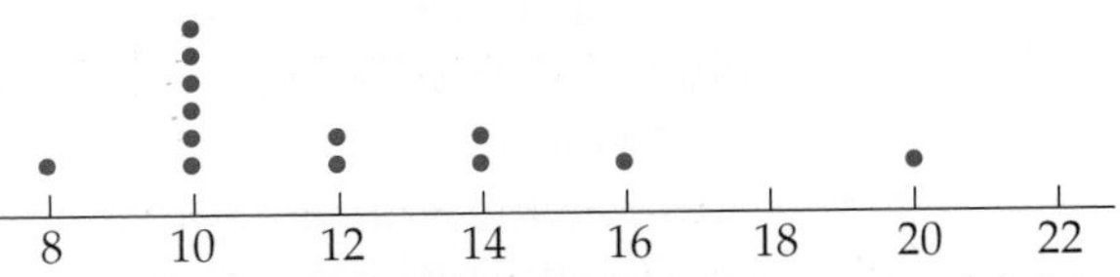

(a) What was the mode jeans size sold this day?

(b) Explain how the dot plot shows the value of the mode.

10

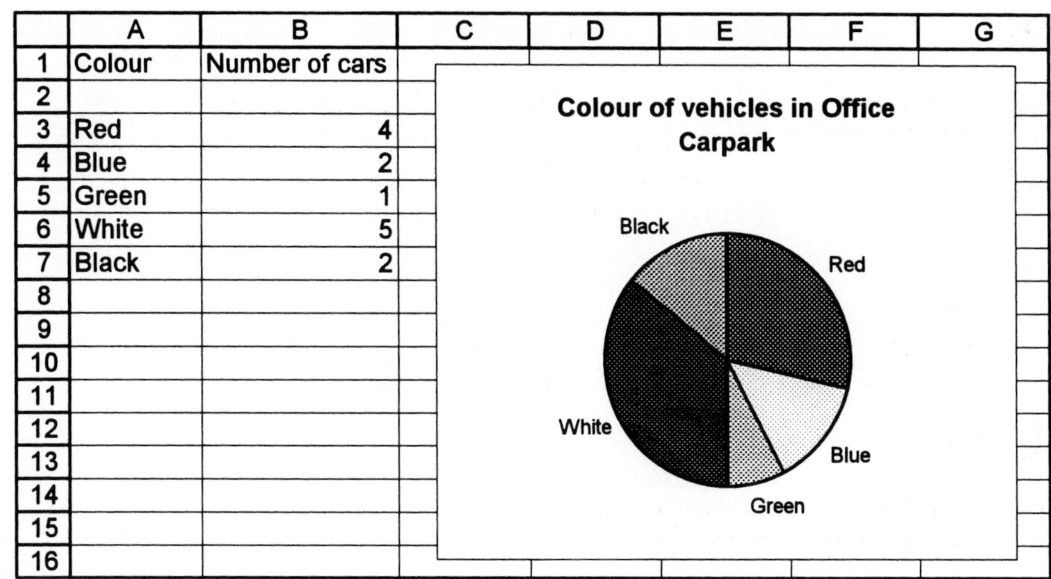

	A	B	C	D	E	F	G
1	Colour	Number of cars					
2							
3	Red	4					
4	Blue	2					
5	Green	1					
6	White	5					
7	Black	2					
8							
9							
10							
11							
12							
13							
14							
15							
16							

This spreadsheet shows the colours of all the vehicles in an office carpark.

(a) What is the mode colour?

(b) Explain how the pie graph shows which colour is the mode.

11 A class carried out an experiment to find out how many chocolate buttons there were in little 'fun' packets. This graph shows the results when they counted the number in each of 20 packets.

Number of chocolate buttons in packets

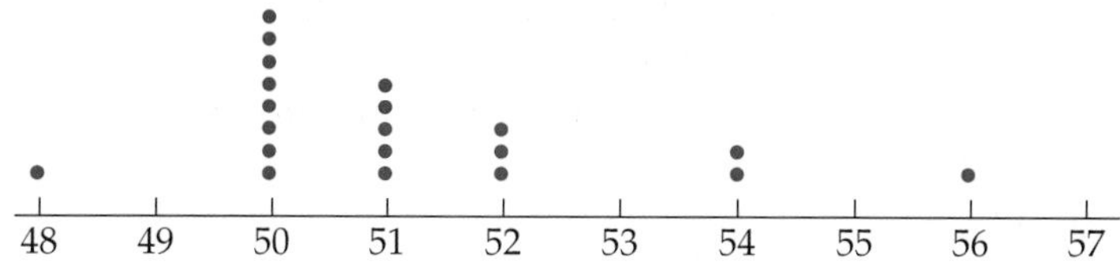

(a) What name do we give to this kind of graph?

(b) Make a prediction of how many chocolate buttons there might be in the next packet. Explain your reasoning.

12 A book has 105 pages altogether.

(a) How many pages will have a numeral 3 in their page number?

(b) What will be the mode of the numerals used in the page numbers?

INVESTIGATION

MEAN REACTION TIME

Do this in pairs.

In scientific investigations, an experiment is often repeated several times. This is because the measurements are slightly different every time. We can 'average out' the results by calculating the mean.

This experiment shows how you can calculate your reaction time!

Get a ruler with a scale in cm.

- The first person holds the top of the ruler in a vertical position, ready to drop it.
- The second person keeps their thumb and index finger wide apart, level with the bottom of the ruler.
- When the ruler is dropped, the second person should snap together their thumb and finger to stop it.
- Measure where the top of the thumb is on the ruler. This gives the distance the ruler has fallen.

Repeat this experiment ten times, writing down the distance each time.

Now calculate the *mean* distance.

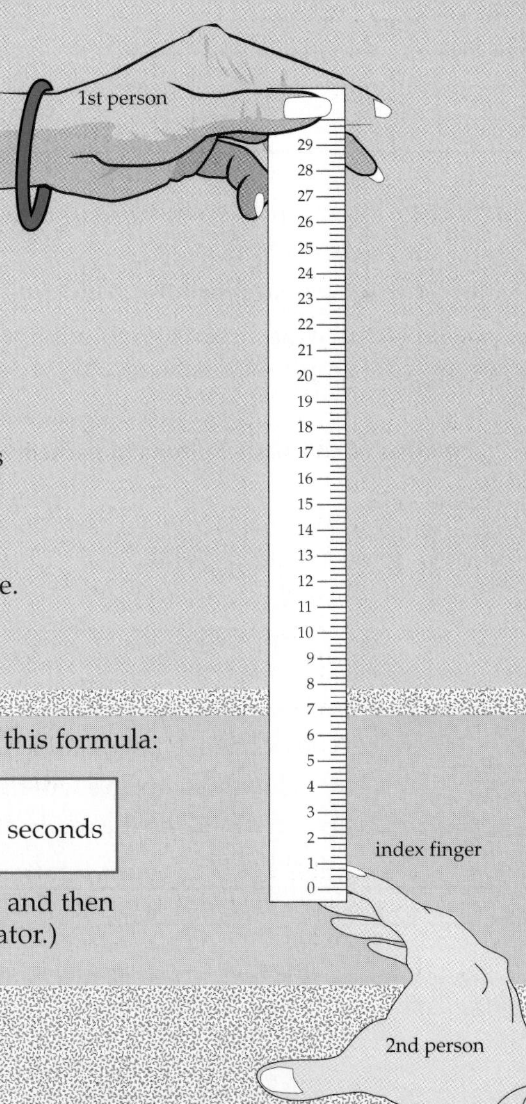

To calculate your reaction time, use this formula:

$$\text{Reaction time} = \sqrt{\frac{\text{mean distance}}{490.5}} \text{ seconds}$$

(Divide the mean distance by 490.5, and then use the 'square root' on your calculator.)

Frequency tables

STARTER

A class of Year 9 students was asked how many pets each one had at home. These were the results:

1, 1, 0, 2, 1, 3, 0, 4, 2, 1, 0, 0, 3, 2, 6, 2, 1, 0, 1, 1, 0, 3, 0, 1, 1, 2, 1, 2, 1, 4, 0, 1, 2

- How many students had 1 pet at home?
- How many had none?

- Suggest how this table should be completed:
- Explain how you could work out the number of students in the class from the table.
- If a student was chosen at random from the class, what number of pets would they be most likely to have? Explain how you can work this out from the table.

Number of pets	Frequency
0	
1	
2	7
3	
4	
5	
6	

- Do a survey like this in your class. The teacher can keep a tally on the board—e.g.

  0 ||||
  1 |||
  2 ~~||||~~ ||

- Make up a table like the one above for the number of pets owned by students in your class.

Sometimes lots of the numbers from a survey are the same. Then, it is easier to show how many of each one there is using a table rather than a list. This kind of table is called a **frequency table**.

The number of times a value occurs is called its **frequency**.

Example Here are the ages of the 40 students at a small primary school:

5, 5, 5, 5, 6, 6, 6, 6, 6, 6, 7, 7, 8, 8, 8, 8, 8, 8, 8, 9, 9, 9, 9, 9,
10, 10, 10, 10, 10, 11, 11, 11, 11, 11, 11, 11, 12, 12, 12, 12

This frequency table summarises the information in a compact, useful form:

Age of student	Frequency
5	4
6	6
7	2
8	7
9	5
10	5
11	7
12	4

← the frequency of age 9 is 5, because 9 occurred 5 times.

A frequency table helps show us how to draw a bar graph for the data:

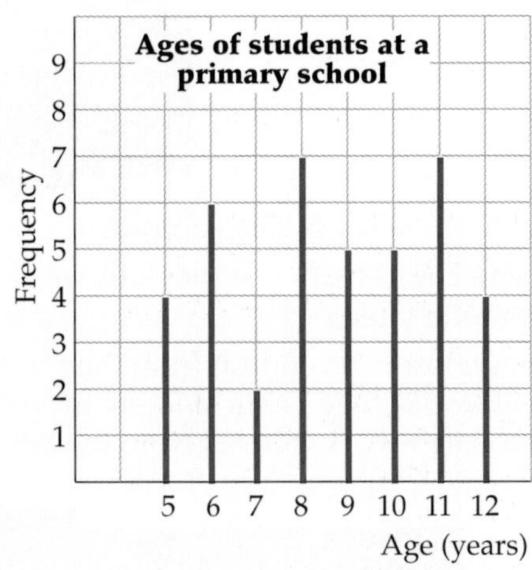

EXERCISE 29.5

1 This frequency table shows the marks out of 10 for a test taken by 30 students.

Mark	Frequency
0	0
1	1
2	1
3	0
4	4
5	7
6	7
7	6
8	3
9	1
10	0

(a) How many students got a mark of 8?
(b) What is the frequency of the mark 7?
(c) How often did the mark 6 occur?
(d) Which mark occurred 3 times?
(e) What was the lowest mark?
(f) What was the highest mark?
(g) Explain why the frequencies add up to 30.
(h) Draw a bar graph to show this data.

2 A motorcyclist bought petrol by the litre 45 times last year.

(a) Construct a frequency table for these purchases:

9, 8, 8, 5, 6, 8, 7, 4, 5, 6, 8, 8, 4, 9, 5
5, 6, 8, 3, 7, 7, 8, 5, 6, 5, 4, 8, 7, 7, 7
5, 8, 6, 7, 7, 6, 7, 5, 8, 4, 5, 6, 7, 8, 7

Give the table a suitable title.

The two columns for the table should be headed 'Number of litres bought' and 'Frequency'.

(b) Predict the amount of petrol the motorcyclist is most likely to buy next time. Explain how you worked this out from the table.

3 Jenny empties out her coin purse. These are the coins in there:

50c, 20c, 20c, \$1, \$1, 10c, 20c, 50c, 10c, 10c, \$2, 10c, 20c, 50c, 20c, \$1, 20c, 20c, 10c, 50c, \$1, 10c, 10c, 10c

(a) Copy and complete this frequency table:

Coin	Number of those coins	Value of those coins (\$)
10c	8	0.80
20c		
50c		
\$1		
\$2		
Totals		

(b) How many coins are in the purse?

(c) How much money did Jenny have in the purse?

4 This table shows the number of tickets sold to each person in a queue at a cinema.

Number of tickets sold	Frequency
1	7
2	50
3	31
4	22
5	8
6	3

(a) How many people in the queue bought 3 tickets?

(b) How many people do you think were going to watch a movie on their own? Explain.

(c) How many people were in the queue altogether?

(d) Another person joins the queue. What would be the most likely number of tickets they buy?

5 A restaurant takes bookings for tables on New Year's Eve. When people book, they give the number of guests per table.

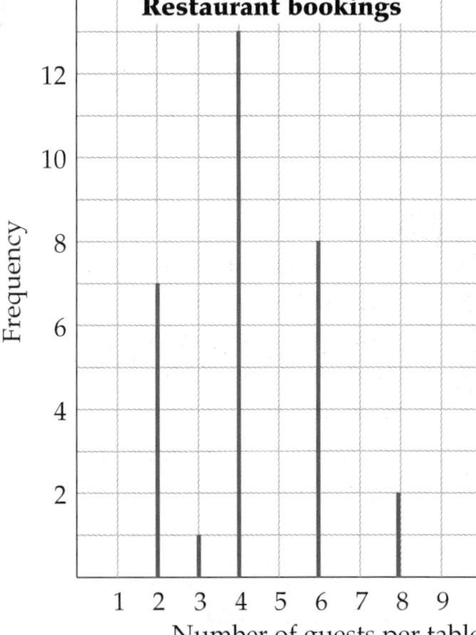

(a) Use the information in the bar graph to produce a frequency table.

(b) How many bookings were there altogether?

(c) Calculate the total number of guests.

INVESTIGATION

FIRST INITIALS

What is the most popular first letter of the first names of students in your class? For example, this would be the letter 'L' for Lee Smith.

1 Summarise this information in a frequency table. This is what the top of the table will look like:

First letter	Frequency
A	
B	

2 What is the most common first letter, and how often did it occur?

Grouping data and histograms

Sometimes, all—or nearly all—the items of data have different values. This often happens when we *measure* the data.

For example, you could measure the heights of students in your class accurately to the nearest mm. Most values will be different.

In this case, we place similar items together in groups.

STARTER

- Mark a scale in cm on one of the classroom walls.
- Use it to measure the height of everyone in the class as accurately as possible.

Each student should fit into one of the groups in this frequency table:

Height interval	Frequency (number of students)
130–140 cm	
140–150 cm	
150–160 cm	
160–170 cm	
170–180 cm	
180–190 cm	

- Complete the frequency table by counting the number of students who fit into each height interval.

When a frequency table has *grouped* data, we use a graph called a **histogram** to display it.

Example This table shows urban areas in New Zealand under 100 000 in population at the 1996 census. Summarise the information in a frequency table. Then display it in a histogram.

Urban area	1996
Blenheim	25 875
Gisborne	32 653
Hastings	58 675
Invercargill	49 306
Kapiti	30 004
Napier	55 044
Nelson	52 348
New Plymouth	49 079
Palmerston North	73 862
Rotorua	56 928
Tauranga	82 832
Timaru	27 521
Wanganui	41 320
Whangarei	45 785

Answer Frequency table:

Population	Frequency
20 000–30 000	2
30 000–40 000	2
40 000–50 000	4
50 000–60 000	4
60 000–70 000	0
70 000–80 000	1
80 000–90 000	1
90 000–100 000	0

Histogram:

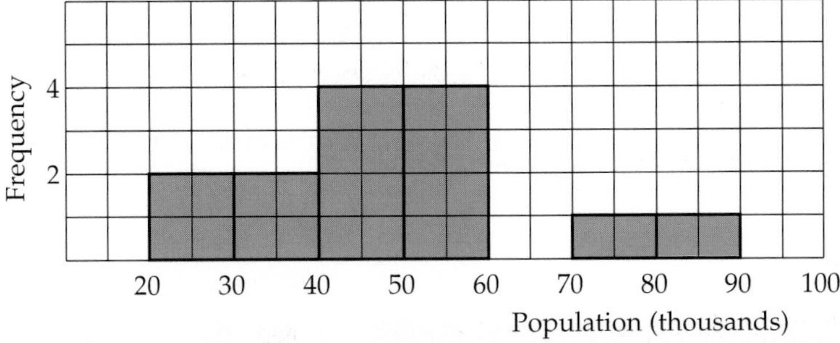

Features of a **histogram**:
- the intervals containing the measurements are shown on the horizontal axis
- the frequency scale appears on the vertical axis
- the columns are joined together.

EXERCISE 29.6

1 This frequency table gives information about birthweights in grams for children born at a hospital.

Birthweight (grams)	Frequency
0–500	0
500–1000	0
1000–1500	1
1500–2000	8
2000–2500	15
2500–3000	12
3000–3500	3
3500–4000	0

Display the information in a histogram.

2 The pumps at a petrol station are accurate to one-hundredth of a litre. Lee records data for 30 consecutive sales of petrol. Here are the results, in litres:

45.16, 29.02, 33.59, 58.30, 51.68, 51.68, 45.16, 48.93, 7.91, 23.21

38.04, 41.31, 25.29, 23.21, 5.31, 46.84, 51.39, 38.17, 23.21, 40.59

62.37, 32.15, 29.83, 51.68, 6.33, 27.29, 33.84, 28.54, 14.17, 38.04

(a) Summarise this information in a frequency table. Use intervals 0–10, 10–20, 20–30, etc.

(b) Display the information in a histogram.

3 This histogram shows the number of people in different salary brackets in an accountant's office.

(a) How many people earn a salary of between $30 000 and $40 000?

(b) How many people earn more than $50 000?

(c) How many people earn less than $50 000?

(d) How many people work at this office?

(e) If you chose a person at random from this office, what would be the most likely salary range?

(f) It isn't possible to work out the highest salary exactly. Explain why.

4 This table shows distances (in km) from Auckland Airport to some destinations. These can all be reached by direct flights.

Destination	Distance	Destination	Distance
Adelaide	3247	Perth	5400
Apia	2893	Port Moresby	4126
Bangkok	11 500	Rarotonga	3013
Brisbane	2293	San Francisco	10 503
Hong Kong	9145	Santiago	12 822
Honolulu	7086	Seoul	12 869
Los Angeles	10 480	Singapore	8410
Melbourne	2635	Suva	2141
Nadi	2156	Sydney	2158
Norfolk Island	1091	Taipei	10 654
Noumea	1859	Tokyo	8837
Pago Pago	2902	Tonga	2004
Papeete	4093	Townsville	3359

(a) Copy and complete this frequency table, to summarise these distances:

Distance (in km)	Frequency
0–2000	
2000–4000	
4000–6000	

(b) Draw a histogram to display the information.

30 Surveys and exploring probability

How do we go about finding out statistical information?
Surveys, and conclusions we draw from data, are only useful if:

- we have asked *suitable* questions
- we have measured items or asked people who are *representative* .

Sampling

Many surveys only involve asking a *few* people for information, or measuring a *limited number* of items. Often, it is inconvenient or time-consuming to ask everyone. Instead, we take a **sample.** A sample is only part of the whole group.

The **sample size** should be large enough to give fairly accurate results. However, it should also be small enough to be convenient and easy to collect information.

Usually a sample of, say, 4 or 5 items, is not enough.

Example We want to estimate the percentage of people who have read a certain magazine.
Only four people are asked.
The only possible results from the sample are 0%, 25%, 50%, 75% or 100%.

When organisations conduct opinion polls, they survey about a thousand people. This gives an accurate estimate most of the time.

A survey using a sample provides useful information if the people chosen are **representative** of others. If we choose some people at *random* from the whole group, this sample should be representative.

When items are chosen at **random**:

- there is no pattern to the choice
- each item is equally likely to be chosen.

Two ways of choosing items at random are:

- drawing names from a hat
- using a numbered list of items together with special random numbers to choose some of the items.

Example The results of spinning a roulette wheel give **random numbers**, from 1 to 36.
The wheel is equally likely to stop anywhere, and the results can't be predicted in advance.

Example The Board of Trustees at a school want to ask students what they think about changing the school uniform. There are a number of ways in which this could be done:

1 ask every student in the school
2 choose one Year 9 class at random, and ask every student
3 take a sample of 20 students at random from Year 13, and ask them
4 the Board could ask their own children for their views
5 invite interested students to a meeting after school, and ask them
6 take a sample of 100 students at random from the school roll, and ask them.

Comment on each one.

Answers

1 This would take a long time, and be inconvenient.
2 The class may not be typical of others; only one Year level is surveyed.
3 This would be a representative sample of Year 13, but not of other levels.
4 This would not be representative of all students; children of Board members may not tell their parents exactly what they think.
5 Students who have strong feelings about uniform would be most likely to attend. Some students might be excluded because they can't attend.
6 This would give the best results. It is fast, convenient, and sampling at *random* from all levels means any student *might* be chosen. This makes the survey representative of all students. The results should be similar to asking everyone, but obtained faster and with less effort.

EXERCISE 30.1

1 The managers of the school tuckshop are considering buying a deep-fryer and selling hot chips to students. They need to know how many students would buy hot chips, and how often.

Comment on each of these methods of choosing students. Explain whether the method is representative, and gives the needed information.

(a) The first 30 students who enter the tuckshop are surveyed one lunchtime.
(b) 100 students are chosen at random from the school roll.
(c) 4 students are chosen at random from the school roll.
(d) All the students in the Year 11 Food and Nutrition class are asked.

2 A market researcher is doing a phone survey for a company that sells home and contents insurance in the North Island. The researcher chooses people to survey by looking up phone numbers in the Auckland phone directory, and then calling that number between 5 pm and 8 pm.

A survey like this will not be representative. Write down at least three groups of people who will be excluded from the survey.

3 You have been asked to find out the percentage of customers who order a drink when they go to a fast food outlet.

(a) You could ask twenty friends whether they ordered a drink the last time they bought fast food. Give two reasons why you may not get a reliable answer.

(b) Describe a sampling method you could use to estimate this percentage.

4 A market researcher is running a survey by telephone. The first person to answer the phone is not automatically selected to answer the questions. Suggest a reason why.

5 A Member of Parliament decides to survey a sample of voters in her electorate, to help her decide how to vote on a proposal to ban casinos.

Match each of these possible sample sizes A, B and C with a description from the box.

Sample size	
A	12 000
B	10
C	1000

	Description
(i)	quick and easy to carry out the survey, but may not give an accurate estimate
(ii)	the best choice of sample size, because it will give a fairly accurate estimate
(iii)	will give an extremely accurate estimate, but will be expensive and time-consuming to carry out

6 You have been asked to select one of six people in a household to answer some questions. Which of these methods of choosing a person is *random*?

(a) Choosing the tallest person.

(b) Giving each person a number from 1 to 6, then tossing a fair six-sided die to see which number from 1 to 6 appears.

(c) Choosing the person with the most recent birthday.

(d) Phoning the household and speaking to whoever answers the phone.

(e) Visiting the household and speaking to the person who opens the door.

(f) Placing the people's names into a hat and choosing one without looking.

7 (Multichoice) The Land Transport Safety Authority are thinking about whether they should raise the minimum age for getting a driver's licence from 15 to 18. They want to find out whether adult New Zealanders agree with this. Which of the following sampling methods will be representative?

A Choosing a group of 30 students at random from your school.

B Choosing a group of 1000 people at random from the electoral roll (a list of New Zealanders who are entitled to vote).

C Asking members of the AA (Automobile Association) to post in a questionnaire.

D Interviewing twenty police officers and asking them for their opinion.

Questionnaires

Many surveys involve answering questions. To get reliable results, everyone should be asked exactly the same questions.

A good way of doing this is to design a **questionnaire.**

This is a set of carefully planned questions.

Features of questions in a good questionnaire:

- simple and easy to answer
- polite and don't invade people's privacy
- give results that are easy to process (yes/no results are ideal for this)
- cover all possible alternatives
- unambiguous, so that everyone understands them in the same way.

Examples

Questions	Why the question is unsuitable
Have you ever stolen anything from a shop?	Invades people's privacy, and is unlikely to get an honest answer in some cases
Have your results in Maths improved this year?	This is ambiguous. It's not clear whether it compares now to earlier in the year, or whether it compares this year to last year
Yesterday, did you arrive to work early or late?	This question doesn't cover all possible alternatives. Some people would want to answer 'on time'. Or, they may not have gone to work yesterday
How many times have you been to the beach in the last twelve months?	Not easy to answer, because those who go often may not remember

EXERCISE 30.2

1 Explain why these survey questions are not suitable.

(a) George is planning a survey on smoking habits. He asks: 'Do your parents smoke? Yes or No?'

(b) Marlene is finding out how her fellow students travel to school. She gives them this question to answer:

'How did you travel to school yesterday?' Tick one box:

Walk: ☐ Bus: ☐ Car: ☐

(c) George asks his teacher to hand out a questionnaire about smoking. One of the questions is:

'Do you ever smoke at school?'

(d) Marlene includes this question in her survey:

'If you travel to school by bus, do you find the bus clean and comfortable?'

(e) Marlene asks this question of those students who walk to school:

'How many times have you arrived to school late so far this year?'

(f) Marlene asks this question:

'Do you prefer travelling to school by bus?'

2 Terry is investigating whether people are satisfied with the service at their local bank. He only asks one question of each person.

Terry: Hello Mrs A! Did you have to wait too long in a queue the last time you visited the bank?

Mrs A: No—I was second in line.

Terry: Excuse me, Mr B, I'd like to ask you about your impressions of the service at the bank. How long did you have to wait in line last time you were there?

Mr B: Five minutes, and it seemed like ages!

Terry: Hi Glen! Whadd'ya reckon about the service at the bank here?

Glen: Gidday Terry! It's a cool bank—no worries!

(a) Give a reason why Terry's questions are unlikely to provide useful information.

(b) Design a questionnaire that would give more useful information about people's attitudes to the service at their bank.

3 Design a questionnaire that would accurately count the number of cats now owned by the students in your class.

4 Design a questionnaire that will collect this information from other students in your class:

- whether they play sport. If so—is it a team or individual sport?
- how much time they spend at this time of the year on sport—playing and practising.

5 You have been asked to investigate a claim that teenagers watch more videos than their parents.

(a) Design a questionnaire to collect some data that would help answer this claim.

(b) What kind of graph would be suitable to display the results of this kind of survey? Draw and label a graph using some values that you think you could possibly get. (Note—there is no need to actually carry out the survey).

Ideas for surveys:

1 Favourite news on television

Design a questionnaire to give to people to find out which channel of TV news they watch.

Here are some points you will need to consider when you make up your questions:

- How will you deal with people who don't watch TV news?
- Will you restrict your questions to the 6 pm news bulletin only?
- What about people who watch several channels of news? (Consider restricting your questions to last night's news bulletin.)
- Decide what to do if the person you ask has more than one TV set in their home.

Hand out the questionnaire to 30 people.

Summarise the results, and display them with a suitable graph.

2 Quick-stop petrol

One major New Zealand oil company advertises that its petrol stations are 'Quick Stop'. The advertisements claim that drivers will be able to fill their cars with petrol, pay quickly and then leave.

Select two petrol stations near your home or school.

Record the time spent by 20 different cars at each petrol station.

One way of doing this would be for one student to act as time-keeper. Another could record the registration numbers of the cars, writing down the arrival time and leaving time to the nearest second.

Example

Registration number	Arrival time	Leaving time	Time spent
UW9598	2.46.17	2.50.45	4.28 or 268 sec
PAWSHE	2.47.23	2.52.04	

Repeat the survey at another petrol station.

At home, make some calculations. Then produce a report in the form of a project.

- Work out the time spent by each car.
- Calculate the mean time spent.
- Draw a graph to show your results.
- Explain which petrol station provides the fastest service. Use your results to justify your answer.

Exploring probability

STARTER

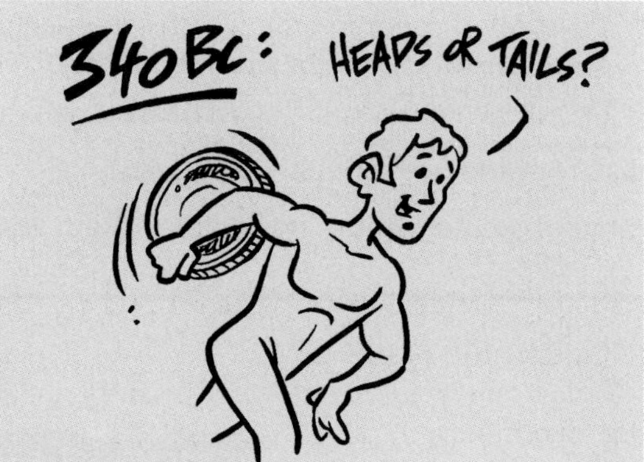

Explain why many games start with two players tossing a coin.

Probability is all about using mathematics to describe chance—how *likely* an event is to occur.

This scale shows how we can describe the probability of an event:

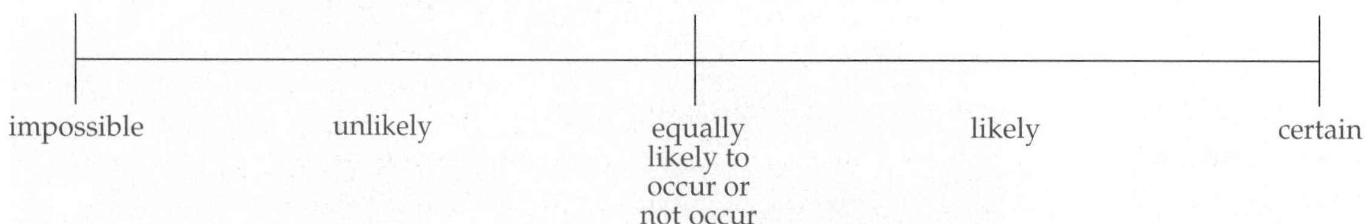

We can use a **frequency table** to predict how likely events are to occur. The **relative frequency** gives information about how often an event occurred, compared with other events.

Example 50 vehicles have passed Nga's house in the last half-hour. She has recorded the different types in this frequency table.

Type of vehicle	Frequency	Relative frequency
Bus	2	$\frac{2}{50}$ or 4%
Car	37	$\frac{37}{50}$ or 74%
Motorbike	1	$\frac{1}{50}$ or 2%
Truck	10	$\frac{10}{50}$ or 20%

Relative frequencies always add to exactly 1, or 100%.

She could use this information to *predict* how likely the next vehicle is to be:

- a car—*likely*
- a truck—*unlikely*
- a motorbike—*very unlikely*

INVESTIGATION

TOSSING A DIE

Six-sided dice are used in many games of chance. This is because, if they are fair, they are equally likely to land with any one of the numbers 1, 2, 3, 4, 5 or 6 facing upwards.

- Toss a tie 50 times. Make a note of the number that faces upwards. Copy and complete this table to summarise the results:

Number facing upwards	Frequency	Relative frequency
1		$\frac{}{50}$ or ____ %
2		
3		
4		
5		
6		

- Add the percentages in the relative frequency column. What is the sum?
- About how many times would you expect each number to appear?

EXERCISE 30.3

1 A survey of 100 vehicles in a carpark gave these relative frequencies:

Up-to-date registration	84%
Registration expired	14%
No registration sticker	2%

Another car was surveyed in the same carpark. Choose from these terms: {unlikely, very unlikely, likely} to describe the likelihood that this car:

(a) has an expired registration

(b) has an up-to-date registration

(c) has no registration sticker

2 Describe how likely these events are. Choose from { impossible, very unlikely, unlikely, equally likely to occur or not occur, likely, very likely, certain }

(a) You choose one card from a pack of 52, and get the Queen of Hearts.

(b) You will still be at your current school next term.

(c) You toss two six-sided dice (each numbered 1–6) and get a total of 13.

(d) You choose one card from a pack of 52, and get a diamond.

(e) The sun will rise in the East tomorrow.

(f) You toss a fair coin and it lands with heads facing upwards.

(g) You toss a six-sided die (with faces numbered 1–6) once, and get a number greater than 2.

3 The diagram shows two discs. Each has a spinner which can stop anywhere on the disc.

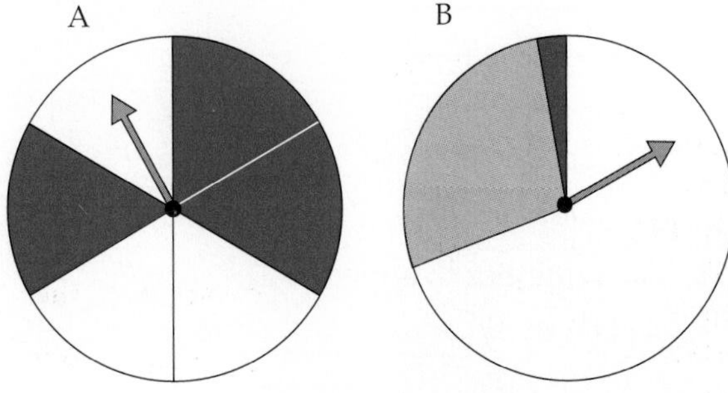

(a) Which spinner is equally likely to stop on a green or a white sector?

(b) Complete these sentences:

(i) It is likely that spinner __ will stop on a _________ sector.

(ii) It is very unlikely that spinner __ will stop on a _________ sector.

(c) Describe an event that is *unlikely* to happen with one of these spinners.

4 A telemarketer is a person who phones people at home, trying to sell them something. This table shows what happened with 100 calls made by a telemarketer one day:

Result of call	Frequency	Relative frequency
Answered	61	$\frac{61}{100} = 0.61$
Not answered	22	
Answer machine	11	
Out of order	1	
Engaged	5	

(a) Copy the table. Complete the relative frequency column.

(b) Match these results with one of these descriptions { unlikely, very unlikely, likely }

(i) the call will be answered

(ii) the phone being called will be out of order

(iii) the phone being called will reply with an answer machine

5 A large drama club has four different types of membership: adult, child, senior citizen and life member. Fifty membership records are chosen at random to take a survey. Here are the results:

Type of membership	Number in survey
Adult	25
Child	7
Senior citizen	17
Life member	1

(a) The relative frequency of child memberships in this survey is 14%. Write down a calculation to show how this is worked out.

(b) What is the relative frequency of senior citizen memberships:

(i) as a fraction?

(ii) as a percentage?

(c) Which type of membership is *equally likely to appear or not appear* in this survey?

(d) Which type of membership is *very unlikely* to appear in the survey?

6 The school librarian takes a survey of students who visit the school library one lunch hour. These are the results:

Year level	Frequency	Relative frequency	Relative frequency as a percentage (rounded)
Year 9	58	$\frac{58}{160}$	36%
Year 10	29		
Year 11	25		
Year 12	17		
Year 13	31		
Total	**160**		

(a) Copy the table. Complete the last two columns.

(b) A student was chosen at random from those in the library.

(i) What year level would they be *most likely* to be?

(ii) What year level would they be *least likely* to be?

7 A computer dealer keeps records of repairs needed on old and new models of computers.

Type of computer	Old model	New model
Needed repair	75	16
Did not need repair	425	24
Total	**500**	**40**

(a) Is it *likely* or *unlikely* that a computer sold by this dealer will need repair?

(b) Calculate the relative frequencies of computers that need repair for both the old and new models.

(c) Use your answers to (b) to explain which model seems the most reliable.

Tree diagrams

Sometimes, a process involving chance or making choices is repeated. If this happens, we can show the different outcomes by drawing a **tree diagram**.

Example Here are some alternative ways in which Wade could spend his Saturday. In the afternoon he has to do chores. He has a choice of tidying his room, painting a fence, doing the dishes, or washing the car. After dinner, he has a choice of watching a video or going to see friends.

Draw a tree diagram to show the different possibilities. How many are there altogether?

Answer

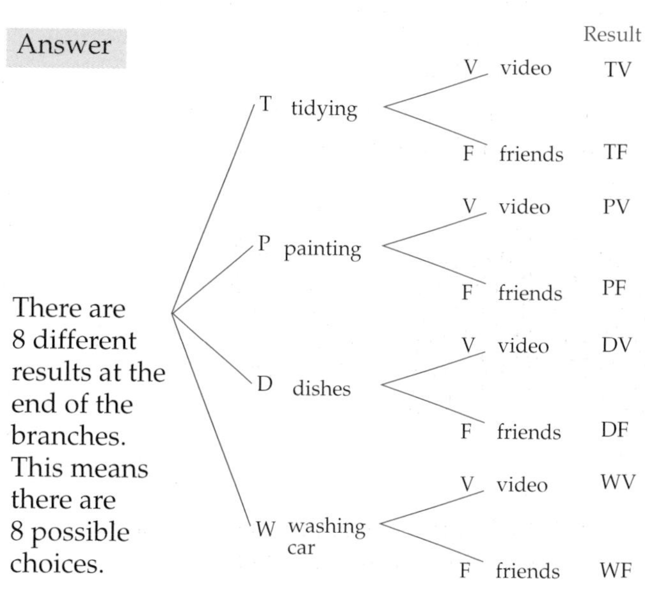

There are 8 different results at the end of the branches. This means there are 8 possible choices.

EXERCISE 30.4

1 Paula, Quinta and Rupert have booked three seats at a cinema.

This tree diagram shows the six different ways in which they can be seated:

1st seat | 2nd seat | 3rd seat | Result

P — Q — R — PQR
P — R — ☐ — ☐
Q — P — ☐ — ☐
Q — R — ☐ — ☐
R — ☐ — ☐ — ☐
R — ☐ — ☐ — ☐

(a) Copy and complete the diagram.

(b) Rupert will be in the middle in some of the six possible seating arrangements. How many?

(c) In some of the arrangements, Paula and Rupert will be sitting together. How many?

2 (a) Copy this tree diagram. Complete it to show the different possibilities for the sex of the first three children in a family:

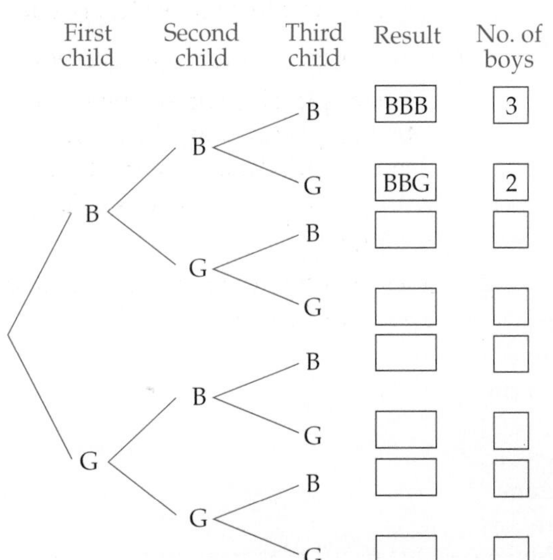

(b) How many possibilities are there altogether?

(c) How many of the possibilities will have exactly 1 boy?

3 In the game of basketball, a foul by one team is sometimes penalised by giving the other team *two* penalty shots at the hoop. These are either successful (S) or unsuccessful (U).

(a) Copy and complete the tree diagram to show the four possible results.

First shot | Second shot | Result

S — S — SS
S — U — __
U — ☐ — __
U — ☐ — __

(b) How many of the results will have exactly *one* of the shots at the hoop being successful?

4 A Year 9 class are voting for two representatives to go on the school council. Four students have been nominated: Aroha, Bryan, Cathy, and Derek.

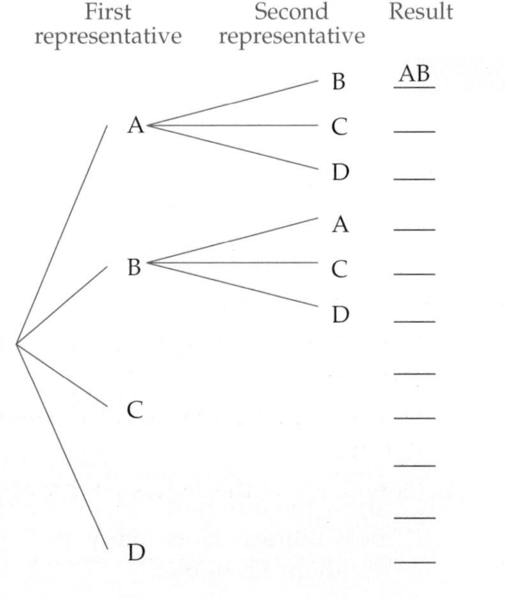

(a) Copy and complete the tree diagram to show the possibilities.

(b) How many possible results are there?

(c) How many of the results include Aroha?

(d) How many of the possible results include Cathy and/or Derek?

5 This diagram shows the different routes that a driver can use to travel from Napier to Mount Maunganui.

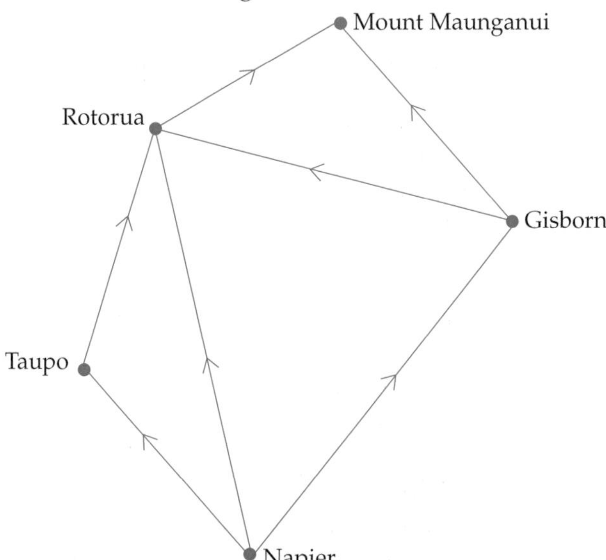

The choices can also be shown in a tree diagram:

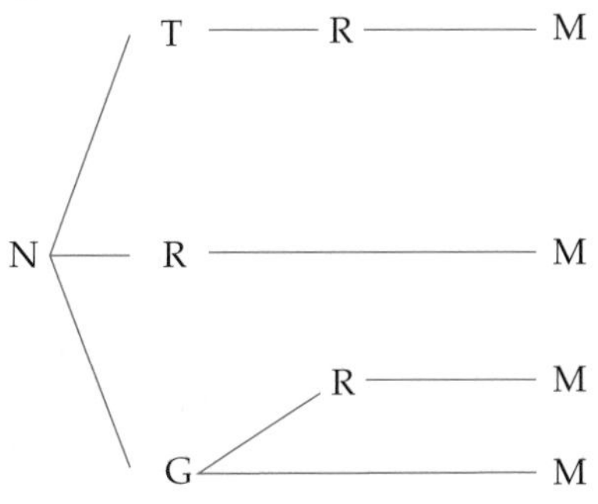

(a) How many different routes are possible?

(b) How many of the routes go through Rotorua?

(c) How many of the routes go through Gisborne?

6 A pizza delivery company offers these options:

Base:	*Pan or Crispy*
Topping:	*Vegetarian, Super Supreme, Hawaiian, Italian*

(a) Copy and complete this tree diagram to show the possible choices:

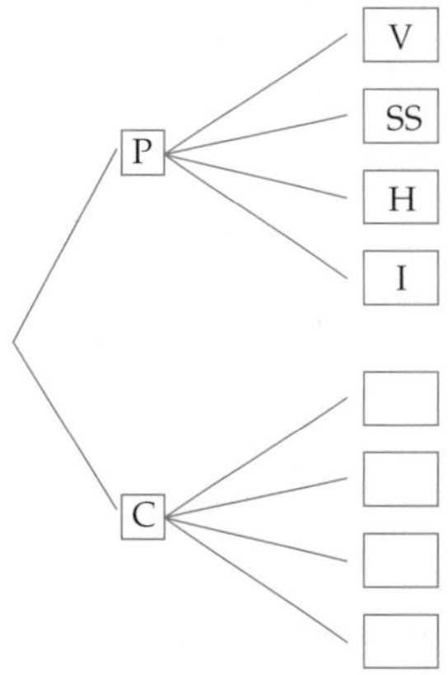

(b) How many of the possible choices come with:

(i) a Pan base?

(ii) an Italian or Hawaiian topping?

(c) Describe how the tree diagram would need to be changed if:

(i) the company introduced a new topping, called 'Meatlovers'

(ii) the company offered the choice of adding olives to each topping.

7 A family has four children altogether.

(a) Draw a tree diagram to show the different possibilities (boy/girl) for the first, second, third and fourth child.

(b) How many possibilities are there altogether?

(c) How many of the possibilities have 2 boys and 2 girls?

ANSWERS

Chapter 1—Spreadsheets

EXERCISE 1.1 (page 2)

1 (a) E7 (c) D8
(b) E9 (d) F8

2 (a) C11 (c) E11
(b) D12 (d) D10

3 Goes to A1. This works from anywhere in the spreadsheet.

4 (a) AA
(b) EA
(c) IV (in Excel – other programs may be different)

5 Moves to the last column at the right-hand end of the spreadsheet.

6 Moves to the last non-empty cell in the spreadsheet. All rows and columns after this are empty.

7 E11

8 (a) Moves to the bottom row of the spreadsheet (within the current column) if the rest of the column is empty. Otherwise, moves to the next non-empty cell.
(b) Moves to the top row of the spreadsheet (within the current column) if the rest of the column is empty. Otherwise, moves to the next non-empty cell.

9 16384 in Excel 7.0; 65536 in Excel 97.

10 IV 16384 in Excel 7.0; IV 65536 in Excel 97.

11 $256 \times 16384 = 4\ 194\ 304$ (in Excel 7); $256 \times 65536 = 16\ 777\ 216$ in Excel 97.

EXERCISE 1.2 (page 6)

2

	A	B
1	Month of Year	Number of Days
2		
3	Jan	31
4	Feb	28
5	Mar	31
6	Apr	30
7	May	31
8	Jun	30
9	Jul	31
10	Aug	31
11	Sep	30
12	Oct	31
13	Nov	30
14	Dec	31

3

	A	B	C	D
1	**New Zealand's Principal Lakes**			
2				
3	**Lake**	**Island**	**Maximum depth (m)**	**Area (sq. km)**
4				
5	Taupo	North	163	606
6	Rotorua	North	45	80
7	Wairarapa	North	3	80
8	Waikaremoana	North	248	54
9	Te Anau	South	417	344
10	Wakatipu	South	380	293
11	Wanaka	South	311	193
12	Ellesmere	South	2	181
13	Pukaki	South	70	169
14	Manapouri	South	444	142
15	Hawea	South	384	141
16	Tekapo	South	120	88
17	Benmore (artificial)	South	120	75
18	Hauroko	South	462	71

EXERCISE 1.3 (page 8)

1 160
2 80
3 4800
4 3
5 14.76
6 64
7 104
8 1
9 13
10 97
11 30
12 0
13 7
14 4662
15 141
16 0
17 9648
18 2
19 42.548
20 (a) E (or a similar error message)
(b) #DIV/0!

EXERCISE 1.4 (page 10)

1

	A	B	C
1	First number	Second number	Sum
2			
3	4	10	14
4	11	39	50
5	780	519	1299
6	8.9	17.1	26
7	19.83	0	19.83
8	0.4	0.7	1.1
9	519000	63700	582700
10	0.49	9.51	10

2

	A	B	C	D
1	First number	Second number	Multiplying	Dividing
2				
3	8	4	32	2
4	12	6	72	2
5	99	100	9900	0.99
6	6.45	3.18	20.511	2.0283
7	256	512	131072	0.5
8	6.0001	5.9999	36	1.00003
9	100	0.01	1	10000
10	0.003	0.0006	0.0000018	5

3 (a) \$15

(b) 150 (or 156 if infants are counted as children)

(c) the total amount received in entrance fees

	A	B	C	D	E
1	Type of visitor	Number	Entrance fee	Amount received	
2					
3	Adult	74	\$15	\$1,110.00	
4	Senior citizen	14	\$10	\$140.00	
5	Zoo member	63	\$9	\$567.00	
6	Child (2-14)	150	\$5	\$750.00	
7	Infant (0-2)	6	\$0	\$0.00	
8				\$2,567.00	
9					
10					
11					
12					

(d) \$2567 (e) \$1982

4

	A	B	C	D
1	Name	Hourly Rate	Hours worked	Amount paid
2				
3	Paolo Stella	\$19.20	45	\$864.00
4	Nga Taumanu	\$14.90	40	\$596.00
5	Darren Hinch	\$12.50	18	\$225.00
6	Vanessa Smith	\$12.50	23	\$287.50
7	Wiremu Ngatai	\$12.50	22	\$275.00
8	John Jones	\$9.50	16	\$152.00
9	Ki Lim Liu	\$9.50	19	\$180.50
10				
11			Total amount	\$2,580.00

5

	A	B	C	D	E
1	Country	Population	Number of doctors	Doctors per 1000 pop'n	
2					
3	New Zealand	3800000	8000	2.11	
4	Australia	18300000	40000	2.19	
5	Japan	125800000	214000	1.70	
6	Korea	45500000	45500	1.00	
7	Norway	4400000	12000	2.73	
8	UK	58800000	88000	1.50	
9	USA	266600000	586500	2.20	
10					
11					

EXERCISE 1.5 (page 14)

1 (a) 2, 4, 6, 8, 10, 12 , ...

(b) even numbers

(c) the sequence changes to { 1, 3, 5, 7, 9, 11, ... }, which is the odd numbers.

6 Day 21

Spreadsheet investigation—Magic square (page 12)

This spreadsheet shows the formulae and an arrangement of the numbers from 1 to 9. Other arrangements are possible.

	A	B	C	D	E
1					
2		6	7	2	=B2+C2+D2
3		1	5	9	=B3+C3+D3
4		8	3	4	=B4+C4+D4
5	=B4+C3+D2	=B2+B3+B4	=C2+C3+C4	=D2+D3+D4	=B2+C3+D4

EXERCISE 1.6 (page 16)

1 (b)

	A	B
1	**Lotto numbers**	
2		
3	1	
4	5	
5	11	
6	18	
7	29	
8	31	
9	34	

(c)

	A	B
1	**Lotto numbers**	
2		
3	34	
4	31	
5	29	
6	18	
7	11	
8	5	
9	1	

2

	A	B
1	Decimal numbers	
2		
3	0.7	
4	0.70001	
5	0.70017	
6	0.701	
7	0.71	
8	0.7107	
9	0.711	
10	0.71701	
11	0.77	

3 (b)

	A	B
1	City	Maximum Temperature (°C)
2		
3	Auckland	15
4	Christchurch	10
5	Dunedin	8
6	Hastings	10
7	Invercargill	9
8	Nelson	12
9	Palmerston North	10
10	Tauranga	17
11	Timaru	7
12	Wellington	10
13	Whangarei	15

(c)

	A	B
1	City	Maximum Temperature (°C)
2		
3	Tauranga	17
4	Auckland	15
5	Whangarei	15
6	Nelson	12
7	Christchurch	10
8	Hastings	10
9	Palmerston North	10
10	Wellington	10
11	Invercargill	9
12	Dunedin	8
13	Timaru	7

EXERCISE 1.7 (page 19)

1

	A	B	C	D
1	**River**	**Length in km**		
2				
3	Nile	6695		
4	Amazon	6570		
5	Mississippi	6020		
6	Waikato (NZ's longest)	425		

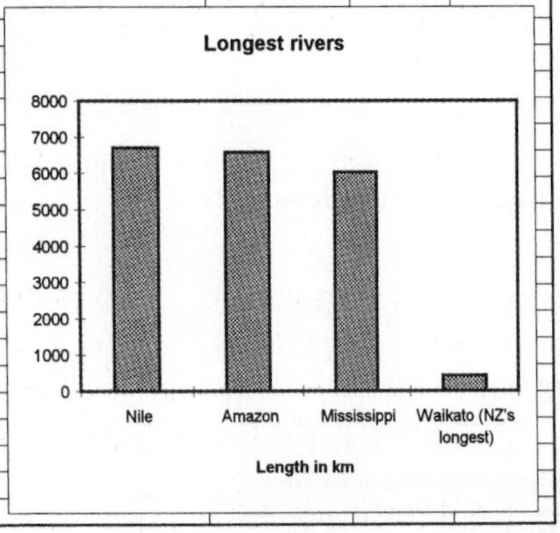

Longest rivers

8000 7000 6000 5000 4000 3000 2000 1000 0

Nile | Amazon | Mississippi | Waikato (NZ's longest)

Length in km

3 (b)

	A	B	C	D	E
1	**New Zealand's Principal Lakes**				
2					
3	**Lake**	**Maximum depth (m)**			
4					
5	Taupo	163			
6	Rotorua	45			
7	Wairarapa	3			
8	Waikaremoana	248			
9	Te Anau	417			
10	Wakatipu	380			
11	Wanaka	311			
12	Ellesmere	2			
13	Pukaki	70			
14	Manapouri	444			
15	Hawea	384			
16	Tekapo	120			
17	Benmore (artificial)	120			
18	Hauroko	462			

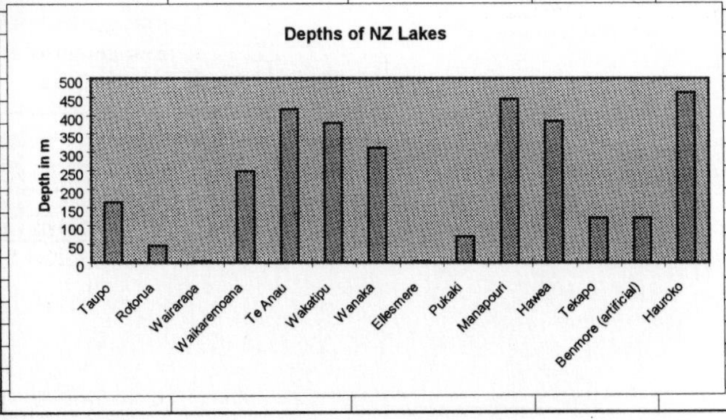

Depths of NZ Lakes

Depth in m

500 450 400 350 300 250 200 150 100 50 0

Taupo | Rotorua | Wairarapa | Waikaremoana | Te Anau | Wakatipu | Wanaka | Ellesmere | Pukaki | Manapouri | Hawea | Tekapo | Benmore (artificial) | Hauroko

4

	A	B	C	D	E	F	G	H
1	Month of Year	Number of Days						
2								
3	January	31						
4	February	28						
5	March	31						
6	April	30						
7	May	31						
8	June	30						
9	July	31						
10	August	31						
11	September	30						
12	October	31						
13	November	30						
14	December	31						
15								
16								
17								
18								
19								
20								

Spreadsheet investigation—Dominos (page 20)

	A	B
1	Highest number	Number of
2	on domino	dominos in set
3		
4	0	1
5	1	3
6	2	6
7	3	10
8	4	15
9	5	21
10	6	28
11	7	36
12	8	45
13	9	55
14	10	66
15	11	78
16	12	91
17	13	105
18	14	120
19	15	136
20	16	153
21	17	171
22	18	190
23	19	210
24	20	231
25	21	253
26	22	276
27	23	

Chapter 2—Decimals

Starter (page 21)

- 5009
- Using the end dial, with the digits on the white background.
- The tenths digit
- 0 0 0 0 0 0

EXERCISE 2.1 (page 22)

1 (b) $29.83 = 2 \times 10 + 9 \times 1 + 8 \times \frac{1}{10} + 3 \times \frac{1}{100}$

(c) $5.917 = 5 \times 1 + 9 \times \frac{1}{10} + 1 \times \frac{1}{100} + 7 \times \frac{1}{1000}$

(d) $30.05 = 3 \times 10 + 0 \times 1 + 0 \times \frac{1}{10} + 5 \times \frac{1}{100}$

(e) $0.028 = 2 \times \frac{1}{100} + 8 \times \frac{1}{1000}$

2 (a) 0.4 (b) 0.8 (c) 5.3 (d) 17.4 (e) 1.32 (f) 5.68 (g) 16.07 (h) 0.04

3 (a) 9 (b) 3 (c) 1 (d) 0

4 (a) 1 (b) 3 (c) 8 (d) 0

5 (a) 8 (b) 2 (c) 8 (d) 9

6 (a) 0.3 (b) 0.14 (c) 0.66 (d) 0.89

7 (b) eight tenths (c) four tens (d) six hundredths (e) five thousandths (f) one thousandth (g) one tenth (h) seven thousands

8 (a) 0.4 (b) 0.9 (c) 0.07 (d) 0.44 (e) 0.005 (f) 0.063 (g) 0.331 (h) 0.087

9 (a) 0.012 (b) 0.45 (c) 0.350

10 (a) false (b) true (c) true (d) false

11 (a) hundredths (b) 9.86 seconds

12 (a) tenths of a kilometre (b) 658.2 km (c) 999.9 km (d) 341.8 km

Puzzle—Place value cross-number (page 23)

4	7	5	3	6	■	4	7	■	8
9	■	2	6	■	3	7	■	■	4
8	4	■	8	■	■	9	■	8	2
3	■	4	■	4	9	3	3	6	■
3	■	9	■	7	■	5	■	9	8
6	9	8	3	3	6	■	2	3	■
■	■	3	■	5	■	■	■	3	0
5	9	3	5	■	7	0	3	6	■

EXERCISE 2.2 (page 26)

1 (a) 2 2.1 2.2 2.3 2.4 2.5 2.6 2.7 2.8 2.9 3 3.1 3.2 3.3 3.4 3.5 3.6 3.7 3.8 3.9 4

(b) 6.4 6.5 6.6 6.7 6.8 6.9 7 7.1 7.2 7.3 7.4

2 (a) 4.93 (b) 4.86 (c) 4.8 (d) 4.9 (e) 4.84

3 (a) 13 (b) 14.05 (c) 0.6 (d) 1.02

4 (a) true (b) false (c) false (d) true (e) false

5 (a) High jump (b) Shot-put (c) 100 m sprint

	(a) High jump	(b) Shot-put	(c) 100 m sprint
1st	Amanda	Wiremu	Ralph
2nd	Nga	Bruce	Derek
3rd	Sally	Temoana	Ioane
4th	Rachel	Ioane	Tuwhare
5th	Wei-Li	Mark	Bruce
6th	Christine	Steven	Wiremu

6 (a) B (Tiger) (b) C (Shell) (c) B (Tiger) (d) C (Shell) (e) A (Alpha) (f) C (Shell)

7 (a) { 11.993, 12.06, 12.5, 13.18, 14 }
(b) { 0.057, 0.072, 0.17, 0.705, 0.71 }

8 B

9 a = 8.5, b = 9.25, c = 10.5, d = 8.75

10 Many answers are possible. Here is one set of 12:

{ 6.12, 6.124, 6.125, 6.126, 6.127, 6.128, 6.129, 6.13, 6.14, 6.15, 6.16, 6.17 }

11 Two possible answers: 6298 or 8104

EXERCISE 2.3 (page 27)

1 536, 53.6
2 385, 3.85
3 4669, 4.669
4 1963, 1.963
5 115, 1.15
6 8.8
7 30.8
8 1.2
9 21.5
10 54.4
11 9.76
12 69.56
13 17.04
14 11.57
15 20.01

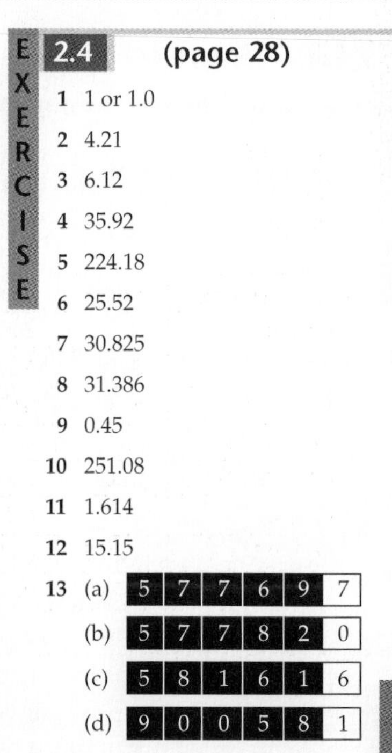

EXERCISE 2.4 (page 28)

1 1 or 1.0
2 4.21
3 6.12
4 35.92
5 224.18
6 25.52
7 30.825
8 31.386
9 0.45
10 251.08
11 1.614
12 15.15
13 (a) 5 7 7 6 9 7
(b) 5 7 7 8 2 0
(c) 5 8 1 6 1 6
(d) 9 0 0 5 8 1

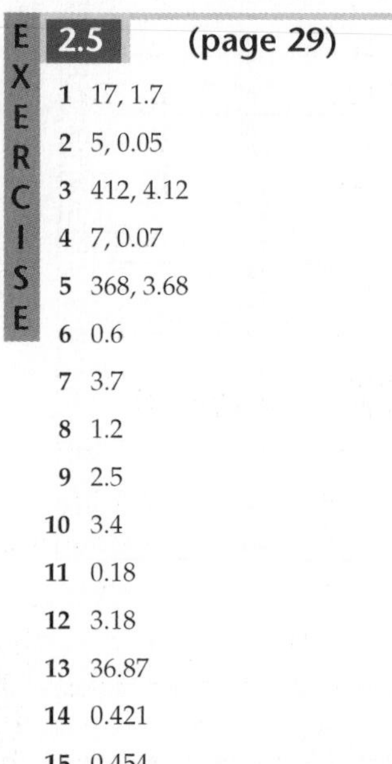

EXERCISE 2.5 (page 29)

1 17, 1.7
2 5, 0.05
3 412, 4.12
4 7, 0.07
5 368, 3.68
6 0.6
7 3.7
8 1.2
9 2.5
10 3.4
11 0.18
12 3.18
13 36.87
14 0.421
15 0.454

EXERCISE 2.6 (page 29)

1 2.6
2 0.1
3 2.69
4 4.68
5 1.14
6 13.84
7 17.98
8 524.14
9 0.25
10 0.025
11 6.982
12 29.813
13 (a) 1.33 seconds
(b) 64.24 seconds
14 (a) 4710.4 km
(b) 52193.8 km
15

+	1.14	0.02	2.15	0.2
0.7	1.84	0.72	2.85	0.9
2.18	3.32	2.2	4.33	2.38
3	4.14	3.02	5.15	3.2
4.35	5.49	4.37	6.5	4.55

16 Fill the large jug with water—this takes 1 litre exactly. Fill the small jug from the large jug twice. This leaves 0.4 litres in the large jug: 1 – 0.3 – 0.3 = 0.4

EXERCISE 2.7 (page 31)

1 2.73
2 1.408
3 1.89
4 21.6
5 36.04
6 12.093
7 16
8 0.9702
9 7.14
10 1.44
11 24.867
12 28.5

EXERCISE 2.10 (page 33)

1 0.15
2 0.06
3 0.56
4 0.036
5 0.45
6 3.2
7 0.3
8 4.9
9 0.09
10 0.016
11 0.0021
12 0.0008
13 0.0027
14 1.2
15 1
16 4.08
17 0.192
18 0.0018
19 2.4
20 0.1701

EXERCISE 2.8 (page 32)

1 1.08
2 9.6
3 1.68
4 1.21
5 0.6
6 14.8
7 31.5
8 3.22
9 13.12
10 22.91
11 13.04
12 1.33
13 19.65
14 561.4
15 270.04

EXERCISE 2.11 (page 33)

1 (a) 6
(b) 12
(c) 7.8
(d) 4
(e) 3124
(f) 311.8
(g) 0.04
(h) 0.507

2 (a) 55
(b) 60
(c) 134
(d) 1260
(e) 0.7
(f) 6518.2
(g) 0.031
(h) 73.12

3 (a) 625
(b) 900
(c) 0.4
(d) 1110
(e) 31 700
(f) 4500
(g) 11 125.5
(h) 8.066

4

	Number	× 10	× 100	× 1000	× 10 000
(a)	0.6	6	60	600	6000
(b)	53.1	531	5310	53 100	531 000
(c)	6.45	64.5	645	6450	64 500
(d)	0.026	0.26	2.6	26	260
(e)	0.0008	0.008	0.08	0.8	8
(f)	8.9	89	890	8900	89 000
(g)	0.161 25	1.6125	16.125	161.25	1612.5
(h)	93.182	931.82	9318.2	93 182	931 820

EXERCISE 2.9 (page 32)

1 0.56
2 0.008
3 0.0378
4 0.357
5 0.001 08
6 0.0003
7 0.1665
8 1.7667
9 0.000 001 4
10 8.74872
11 4
12 0.0545

EXERCISE 2.12 (page 34)

1 (a) $3.35
(b) $6.90
(c) $49.20
(d) $105.50
(e) $0.75

2 (a) 565 c
(b) 1490 c
(c) 10 050 c
(d) 60 c
(e) 5 c

3 (a) $1.78
(b) $6.87
(c) $23.28
(d) $5.87
(e) $10.57
(f) $20.48

4 $1.20

5 $15.65

6 Cost of 130 packets is 130 × $2.38 = $309.4
This costs more than $300, so $300 is not enough money.

7 a = $23.30, b = $233, c = $34.90, d = $349, e = $8.99, f = $89.90, g = $1.24, h = $124

8 (a) $3.14 US dollars
(b) $418.80 US dollars
(c) $44.74 Australian dollars
(d) $932.28 Australian dollars
(e) 20.78 pounds sterling
(f) 757.10 German marks
(g) 1 782 180 Japanese yen
(h) $726.96 US dollars

EXERCISE 2.13 (page 36)

1 (a) 7 (b) 0.7
2 (a) 42 (b) 0.42
3 (a) 125 (b) 1.25
4 (a) 116 (b) 1.16
5 (a) 26 (b) 0.26
6 (a) 196 (b) 1.96
7 0.52
8 7.75
9 0.0068
10 0.655
11 0.071
12 0.019 37

EXERCISE 2.14 (page 36)

1 0.56
2 0.105
3 7.5
4 0.125
5 0.005
6 0.0425
7 16.38
8 0.001 95

EXERCISE 2.15 (page 37)

1 (a) 2
(b) 5
(c) 600
(d) 2980
(e) 5
(f) 6
(g) 300
(h) 502

2 (a) 67 ÷ 5
(b) 800 ÷ 2
(c) 1573 ÷ 40
(d) 300 ÷ 5
(e) 60 200 ÷ 1
(f) 5931 ÷ 80
(g) 52 ÷ 20
(h) 1 ÷ 500

3 3
4 275
5 25
6 36.95
7 317.1
8 20
9 88.2
10 1.02
11 795
12 73

EXERCISE 2.16 (page 38)

1 (a) 9.06
(b) 0.12
(c) 0.078
(d) 0.4
(e) 31.24
(f) 3.118
(g) 0.0004
(h) 0.005 07

2 (a) 4.455
(b) 0.806
(c) 0.0134
(d) 0.126
(e) 0.000 07
(f) 0.6512
(g) 0.000 31
(h) 0.000 073 1

3 (a) 2.2025
(b) 6.0009
(c) 80
(d) 0.001 11
(e) 0.0317
(f) 0.0045
(g) 0.011 125 5
(h) 0.000 008 6

4

	Number	÷ 10	÷ 100	÷ 1000	÷ 10 000
(a)	33	3.3	0.33	0.033	0.0033
(b)	788	78.8	7.88	0.788	0.0788
(c)	6.45	0.645	0.0645	0.006 45	0.000 645
(d)	733.5	73.35	7.335	0.7335	0.073 35
(e)	0.8	0.08	0.008	0.0008	0.000 08
(f)	12.97	1.297	0.1297	0.012 97	0.001 297
(g)	556 67	5566.7	556.67	55.667	5.5667
(h)	1088.21	108.821	10.8821	1.088 21	0.108 821

EXERCISE 2.17 (page 39)

1 19.229
2 50.054
3 7.600 38
4 4230
5 24.57
6 0.0254
7 480.4
8 1.331
9 1.1745
10 1563.07

11

×	4	0.5	6.8	0.02
1.3	5.2	0.65	8.84	0.026
37.2	148.8	18.6	252.96	0.744
0.08	0.32	0.04	0.544	0.0016
0.75	3	0.375	5.1	0.015

EXERCISE 2.18 (page 39)

1 Calculation: 1.585 + 0.02
Answer: 1.605 m

2 Calculation: 0.65 + 1.125
Answer: 1.775 kg

3 Calculation: 94.08 – 1.27
Answer: 92.81 seconds

4 Calculation: 12.4 – 10.8
Answer: 1.6 cm

5 Calculation: 12 × 0.454 kg
Answer: 5.448 kg

6 Calculation: 0.268 + 0.957 + 0.037
Answer: 1.262 kg

7 Calculation: 3.48 ÷ 4
Answer: 0.87 m

8 Calculation: 1.8 – 1.32
Answer: 0.48 m

9 Calculation: 2.29 × 24
Answer: $54.96

10 Calculation: $30.60 ÷ 0.45
Answer: 68 stamps

11 Calculation: $9.20 ÷ 8
Answer: $1.15

12 Calculation: $17.48 ÷ 19
Answer: $0.92

13 (a) ←0.84→
×——×——×——×——×——×

(b) Calculation: 0.84 × 5
Answer: 4.2 m

14 50 lettuces

EXERCISE 2.19 (page 40)

1 (a) 0.6666….
(b) 15.2222….
(c) 18.272 727 27….
(d) 4.166 66….
(e) 0.003 333….
(f) 0.307 307 307 307….
(g) 23.181 281 281 281 2….
(h) 646.646 646 646 646….

2 (a) $0.\dot{8}$ (e) $0.5\dot{6}\dot{2}$
(b) $10.\dot{5}$ (f) $0.\dot{2}1\dot{8}$
(c) $1.6\dot{3}$ (g) $0.1\dot{1}\dot{3}$
(d) $0.\dot{1}\dot{8}$ (h) $6.8\dot{2}7\dot{7}$

3 The dot should be placed over the *first* 6, not the second. This is because that is where the repeating pattern starts.

4 (a) $1.3\dot{6}$ (e) $1.7\dot{5}$
(b) $0.81\dot{6}$ (f) $3227.\dot{2}\dot{7}$
(c) $7.\dot{2}\dot{7}$ (g) $44.78\dot{6}$
(d) $105.\dot{3}$ (h) $78.\dot{5}7142\dot{8}$

EXERCISE 2.20 (page 42)

1 (a) 3.1 (c) 0.4
(b) 4.9 (d) 0.1

2 (a) 1.39 (c) 0.06
(b) 0.44 (d) 10.02

3 (a) 0.447 (c) 12.063
(b) 2.695 (d) 0.005

4

		to 1 dp	to 2 dp	to 3 dp	to 4 dp
(a)	7.091 83	7.1	7.09	7.092	7.0918
(b)	0.117 78	0.1	0.12	0.118	0.1178
(c)	16.995 46	17.0	17.00	16.995	16.9955

5 (a) 2.14 (d) 1.21
(b) 4.03 (e) 0.69
(c) 1.80 (f) 5.05

6 (a) 0.4286 (d) 2.8462
(b) 0.3333 (e) 1358.6668
(c) 4.2678 (f) 13.2631

7 6.405, 6.408, 6.409, 6.411, 6.413, 6.4149

Any number between 6.405 and 6.415 (excluding 6.415 itself) will round to 6.41 (2 dp)

Using a spreadsheet to do rounding (page 42)

	A	B	C	D	E
1	Number	to 0 dp.	to 1 dp.	to 2 dp.	to 3 dp.
2					
3	7.09183	7	7.1	7.09	7.092
4	0.11778	0	0.1	0.12	0.118
5	16.99546	17	17.0	17.00	16.995
6	0.999888	1	1.0	1.00	1.000
7	0.004639	0	0.0	0.00	0.005

EXERCISE **2.21** **(page 43)**

1 7.9 cm

2 $11.63

3 $6.14

4 0.46 m or 46 cm

5 (a) $183.73
(b) Overpaid by 1 cent

6 (a) $164.10
(b) $675.23
(c) $6891.80
(d) $105.44
(e) $358.75
(f) $112 820.51

Chapter 3—Integers

Starter (page 45)

- sea-level
- 392 m below sea-level
- 397 m below sea-level

EXERCISE **3.1** **(page 46)**

1 (a) $^{-}40$ (b) below (c) $^{-}3$ (d) before (e) above (f) below

2 (a) $^{+}12, ^{-}100$ (b) $^{+}2, ^{-}8$ (c) $^{-}12, ^{+}19$ (d) $^{+}8, ^{-}2$ (e) $^{-}40, ^{+}65$ (f) $^{+}4, ^{-}15$ (g) $^{-}2, ^{+}5$

3 (a) $A = {}^{+}5, B = {}^{+}2, C = 0, D = {}^{-}4, E = {}^{-}7$
(b) (i) 3 °C (ii) $^{-}2$ °C
(c) (i) $^{-}9$ °C (ii) 3 °C (iii) $^{-}3$ °C (iv) 0 °C

4 (a) $600
(b) $^{-}$$700

5 (a) $^{-}16$ °C
(b) 2 °C
(c) Jan 10

EXERCISE **3.2** **(page 47)**

1 (a) { 0, 1, 3, 5, 6 }
(b) { 1, 2, 3, 4, 5, 7 }
(c) { 17, 29, 38, 49, 52 }
(d) { 27, 38, 42, 49, 93, 138, 192 }

2 (a) $3 > 1$ (b) $5 > 0$ (c) $1 < 3$ (d) $0 < 4$ (e) $1 > 0$

3 (a) 2 °C
(b) $^{-}7$ °C
(c) 0 °C
(d) $^{-}4$ °C
(e) $^{-}9$ °C, $^{-}8$ °C (other answers are possible)
(f) $^{-}12$ °C, $^{-}11$ °C (other answers are possible)

4 $^{+}7 > {}^{+}2$

5 $^{-}3 < {}^{+}4$

6 $^{-}2 > {}^{-}5$

7 $^{-}8 < {}^{-}3$

8 $^{+}5 > {}^{-}2$

9 $^{+}3 > {}^{-}8$

10 $^{-}10 < {}^{-}1$

11 $^{+}16 > {}^{-}11$

12 $^{+}57 < {}^{+}73$

13 $^{-}25 > {}^{-}84$

14 $^{-}93 < {}^{+}12$

15 $^{+}3 > {}^{-}467$

16 { $^{-}4, 0, ^{+}2$ }

17 { $^{-}5, ^{-}3, ^{+}2, ^{+}5, ^{+}7$ }

18 { $^{-}6, ^{-}5, ^{-}3, ^{-}2, ^{-}1$ }

19 { $^{-}7, ^{-}5, ^{-}3, ^{-}2, 0$ }

20 { $^{-}80, ^{-}78, ^{-}31, ^{+}98$ }

21 { $^{-}821, ^{-}392, ^{-}5, ^{-}3, ^{+}428$ }

22 (a) false (b) false (c) true (d) true (e) false (f) false (g) false (h) false

23 { Rex Hopkins, Tracey Meech, Jason Ng, Wiremu Rata, John Sutton, Alar Treial }

24 Lake Eyre, Caspian Sea, Valdes Peninsula, Death Valley, Lake Assai, Dead Sea

25

$^{-}8$
$^{-}6$ $^{-}10$
$^{-}9$ $^{-}7$

Exercise 3.3 (page 50)

1 $^{+}2$
2 -6
3 $^{+}4$
4 $^{+}1$
5 0
6 $^{-}2$
7 $^{-}8$
8 0
9 $^{+}2$
10 $^{+}4$
11 $^{-}9$
12 $^{-}4$
13 $^{-}1$
14 $^{+}2$
15 $^{+}10$
16 $^{-}9$
17 $^{+}12$
18 $^{-}13$
19 0
20 $^{-}13$
21 $^{-}6$
22 0
23 $^{-}3$
24 $^{-}13$
25 $^{+}8$
26 $^{-}10$
27 $^{-}5$
28 0
29 $^{-}9$
30 $^{+}7$
31 (a) $^{+}34$ (b) $^{+}90$ (c) $^{-}38$ (d) $^{-}38$ (e) $^{-}146$ (f) $^{+}247$ (g) $^{-}600$ (h) $^{+}211$

Exercise 3.4 (page 50)

1 $^{-}1 + {}^{-}7 = {}^{-}8$ (fell by 8 °C altogether)
2 $^{-}4 + {}^{+}9 = {}^{+}5$ (rose by 5 points)
3 $^{-}10 + {}^{+}7 = {}^{-}3$ (fell by 3 cm altogether)
4 $^{+}3 + {}^{-}5 = {}^{-}2$ (fell by 2 cents over the two day period)
5 $^{+}3 + {}^{-}5 + {}^{+}1 + {}^{-}2 = {}^{-}3$ (3 under)
6 Withdrawal of \$25

Exercise 3.7 (page 53)

1 $^{-}3$
2 $^{-}11$
3 $^{+}11$
4 $^{+}9$
5 $^{+}2$
6 $^{+}9$
7 $^{-}12$
8 $^{-}3$
9 $^{-}5$
10 $^{+}5$
11 $^{-}7$
12 $^{-}5$
13 $^{-}16$
14 $^{-}12$
15 $^{-}7$
16 $^{+}7$
17 $^{-}16$
18 $^{+}1$
19 $^{-}8$
20 0
21 $^{-}97$
22 $^{-}175$
23 $^{+}78$
24 $^{+}300$

Exercise 3.5 (page 52)

+	$^{-}11$	89	$^{-}32$	41
$^{-}8$	–	+	–	+
$^{-}35$	–	+	–	+
$^{-}66$	–	+	–	–
37	+	+	+	+

+	$^{-}11$	89	$^{-}32$	41
$^{-}8$	$^{-}19$	81	$^{-}40$	33
$^{-}35$	$^{-}46$	54	$^{-}67$	6
$^{-}66$	$^{-}77$	23	$^{-}98$	$^{-}25$
37	26	126	5	78

Exercise 3.6 (page 52)

1 $^{+}3$
2 $^{-}4$
3 $^{+}2$
4 $^{-}1$
5 0
6 $^{-}6$
7 $^{-}3$
8 $^{+}37$
9 $^{-}98$
10 $^{+}41$

Exercise 3.8 (page 53)

1 $^{-}5$ °C
2 $^{-}$\$200 (an overdraft of \$200)
3 (a) $^{-}1 - {}^{-}9 = 8$ °C
(b) $3 - {}^{-}5 = 8$ °C
(c) $^{-}5 - {}^{-}9 = 4$ °C
4 (a) $120 - 19 = 101$ °C
(b) $120 - {}^{-}6 = 126$ °C
(c) $4 - {}^{-}6 = 10$ °C
(d) $19 - {}^{-}6 = 25$ °C
5 7 metres ($2 - {}^{-}5 = 7$)

Exercise 3.9 (page 54)

1 9
2 $^{-}2$
3 3
4 $^{-}2$
5 3
6 3
7 1
8 3
9 $^{-}9$
10 $^{-}15$
11 5
12 $^{-}9$
13 3
14 $^{-}24$
15 $^{-}13$
16 15
17 $^{-}41$
18 $^{-}31$
19 $^{-}2$
20 $^{-}2$
21 $^{-}4$
22 $^{-}85$
23 40
24 $^{-}26$

Exercise 3.10 (page 54)

1 $^{-}5$
2 $^{-}5$
3 $^{-}14$
4 $^{-}7$
5 $^{-}2$
6 2
7 $^{-}8$
8 $^{-}16$
9 $^{-}3$
10 $^{-}8$

Exercise 3.11 (page 55)

1 4
2 11
3 $^{-}3$
4 10
5 7
6 $^{-}16$
7 $^{-}16$
8 13
9 $^{-}168$
10 55

Exercise 3.12 (page 55)

1 9
2 $^{-}1$
3 14
4 $^{-}13$
5 9
6 $^{-}2$
7 $^{-}9$
8 $^{-}32$
9 $^{-}12$
10 $^{-}25$
11 8
12 1

EXERCISE 3.13 (page 55)

1 27

2 A: 3 (3 over par)
B: 1 (1 over par)
C: 8 (8 over par)

3 (a) \$40
(b) \$35
(c) $^{-}$\$34

4 (a) 7
(b) level 3 of the parking garage

5

3	$^{-}2$	2	$^{-}9$
$^{-}7$	0	$^{-}4$	5
$^{-}8$	1	$^{-}3$	4
6	$^{-}5$	$^{-}1$	$^{-}6$

6

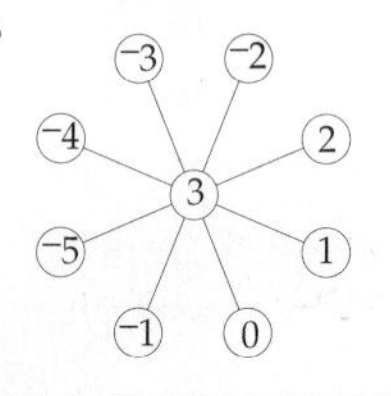

EXERCISE 3.14 (page 57)

1 15, 12, 9, 6, 3, 0, $^{-}3$, $^{-}6$, $^{-}9$, $^{-}12$, $^{-}15$, $^{-}18$

2 30, 24, 18, 12, 6, 0, $^{-}6$, $^{-}12$, $^{-}18$, $^{-}24$, $^{-}30$, $^{-}36$

3 $^{-}10$, $^{-}8$, $^{-}6$, $^{-}4$, $^{-}2$, 0, 2, 4, 6, 8, 10

4 $^{-}20$, $^{-}15$, $^{-}10$, $^{-}5$, 0, 5, 10, 15, 20, 25, 30

5 $^{-}28$, $^{-}21$, $^{-}14$, $^{-}7$, 0, 7, 14, 21, 28, 35, 42

EXERCISE 3.15 (page 58)

1 24
2 15
3 $^{-}12$
4 9
5 100
6 $^{-}16$
7 21
8 16
9 $^{-}24$
10 $^{-}40$
11 $^{-}8$
12 $^{-}4$
13 42
14 0
15 $^{-}20$
16 5
17 $^{-}18$
18 $^{-}120$
19 $^{-}72$
20 $^{-}70$

21

×	+	−
+	+	−
−	−	+

22 40
23 6
24 $^{-}32$
25 18
26 $^{-}8$
27 30
28 30
29 5
30 $^{-}24$
31 0
32 $^{-}100$
33 64
34 36
35 105
36 36
37 64
38 120
39 0
40 $^{-}200$

Puzzle (page 60)
See page 461 for answer

EXERCISE 3.16 (page 60)

1 $^{-}3$
2 $^{-}3$
3 $^{-}8$
4 $^{-}7$
5 6
6 2
7 $^{-}18$
8 $^{-}5$
9 $^{-}15$
10 2
11 1
12 $^{-}1$
13 $^{-}1$
14 $^{-}3$
15 $^{-}5$
16 0

17

÷	+	−
+	+	−
−	−	+

EXERCISE 3.17 (page 60)

1 11
2 4
3 $^{-}30$
4 $^{-}3$
5 $^{-}70$
6 2
7 24
8 $^{-}1$
9 $^{-}27$
10 13
11 $^{-}1$
12 $^{-}8$
13 5
14 $^{-}6$
15 $^{-}7$
16 14
17 80
18 4
19 $^{-}16$
20 $^{-}100$

Chapter 4—Multiples, factors and primes

EXERCISE 4.1 (page 62)

1 { 4, 8, 12, 16, 20, 24, ... }

2 { 7, 14, 21, 28, 35, 42, ... }

3 (10, 20, 30, 40, 50, 60, ... }

4 { 12, 24, 36, 48, 60, 72, ... }

5 { 200, 400, 600, 800, 1000, 1200, ... }

6 { 35, 40, 45, 50, 55 }

7 { 25, 50, 75, 100, 125 }

8 (a) { 24, 48, 72, 96, 120, 144, 168 }
(b) the number of hours in a week

9 (a) true
(b) true
(c) false
(d) false

10 (a) They are multiples of 6.
(b) They are multiples of 13.
(c) They are multiples of 4 that are between 43 and 61. (Other answers are possible.)

11 (a) even numbers (or multiples of 2)
(b) east
(c) 806
(d) 1214 and 1218
(e) the stairs
(f) 264

12 (a) An even number is a multiple of two.
(b) An odd number is an integer (or counting number) which is not a multiple of two.

13 (a)

+	Even	Odd
Even	Even	Odd
Odd	Odd	Even

(b)

–	Even	Odd
Even	Even	Odd
Odd	Odd	Even

(c)

×	Even	Odd
Even	Even	Even
Odd	Even	Odd

14 27

Investigation—Oddities (page 63)

- 1, 3, 5, 7, 9, 11, 13, 15, 17, 19, 21, 23, 25, 27, 29, 31
- 4
- 9
- 16
- 100
- $20 \times 20 = 400$
- To calculate the sum of some odd numbers (starting at 1), multiply the last one by itself. Another way of expressing this is: the sum of the first n odd numbers is $n \times n$ or n^2.

EXERCISE 4.2 (page 64)

1 { 6, 12, 18 }
2 { 15, 30, 45 }
3 { 24, 48, 72 }
4 { 30, 60, 90 }
5 18
6 42
7 18
8 90
9 12
10 $100
11 (a) Monday
(b) Tuesday 2 children; Friday 2 adults
(c) She either did haircuts for children only (5 altogether) or adults only (3 altogether).
12 42 seconds
13 12 days

EXERCISE 4.3 (page 65)

1 { 1, 2, 4 }
2 { 1, 7 }
3 { 1, 2, 3, 6, 9, 18 }
4 { 1, 13 }
5 { 1, 2, 4, 5, 8, 10, 20, 40 }
6 { 1, 2, 4, 5, 10, 20, 25, 50, 100 }
7 { 1, 2, 4, 5, 8, 10, 16, 20, 40, 80 }
8 (a) { 1, 3, 7, 9, 21, 63 }
(b) { 1, 2, 3, 6, 17, 34, 51, 102 }
(c) { 1, 3, 13, 39 }
(d) { 1, 7, 13, 91 }
9 (a) true (b) false (c) true (d) true (e) true (f) false (g) false (h) true
10 (a) $1 \times 96, 2 \times 48, 3 \times 32, 4 \times 24, 6 \times 16, 8 \times 12$
(b) $1 \times 144, 2 \times 72, 3 \times 48, 4 \times 36, 6 \times 24, 8 \times 18, 9 \times 16, 12 \times 12$

EXERCISE 4.4 (page 66)

1 yes
2 no
3 no
4 yes
5 no
6 no
7 yes
8 no
9 (a) leap year
(b) not a leap year
(c) not a leap year
(d) leap year

EXERCISE 4.5 (page 67)

1 { 1, 5 }
2 { 1, 2, 4, 8 }
3 { 1 }
4 { 1, 2, 3, 6 }
5

Number	Factors
4	1, 2, 4
6	1, 2, 3, 6

HCF = 2

6

Number	Factors
30	1, 2, 3, 5, 6, 10, 15, 30
75	1, 3, 5, 15, 25, 75

HCF = 15

7

Number	Factors
36	1, 2, 3, 4, 6, 9, 12, 18, 36
48	1, 2, 3, 4, 6, 8, 12, 16, 24, 48

HCF = 12

8 2
9 1
10 5
11 1
12 25
13 8
14 32 cm by 32 cm
15 60
16 (a) 11
(b) Q = 5, R = 8
17 121

Exercise 4.6 (page 69)

1 (a) prime
(b) composite
(c) prime
(d) composite
(e) prime
(f) composite
(g) composite
(h) prime

2 23, 29

3 53

4 neither

5 2

6 2, 3, 5, 7, 11, 13, 17, 19, 23, 29, 31, 37, 41, 43, 47, 53, 57, 59, 61, 67, 71, 73, 79, 83, 89, 97

Spreadsheet investigation—Terminating decimals (page 71)

Numbers that give terminating decimals when you divide by them are: "numbers that can be expressed as products of 2 and/or 5 only"

Exercise 4.7 (page 70)

1
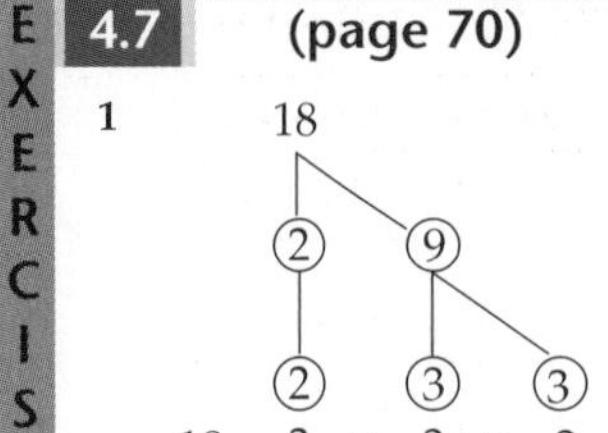

$18 = 2 \times 3 \times 3$

2
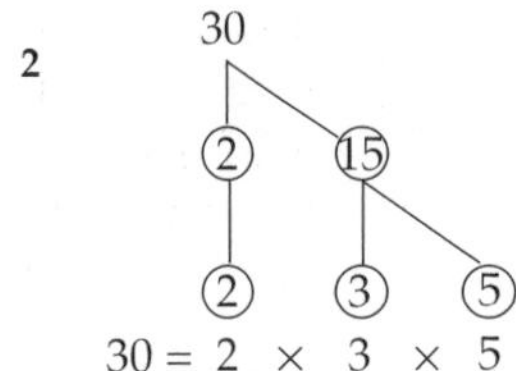

$30 = 2 \times 3 \times 5$

3
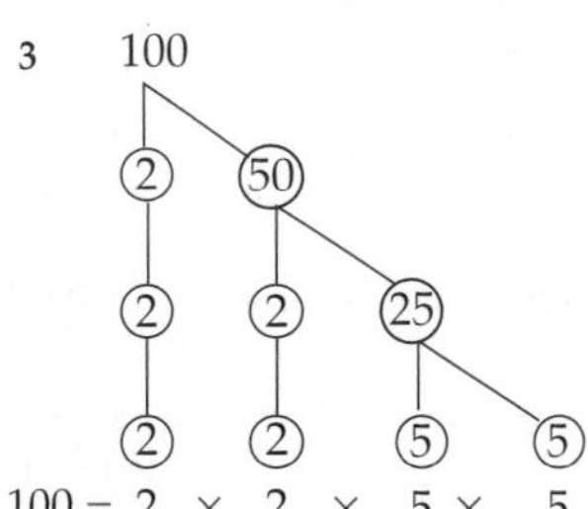

$100 = 2 \times 2 \times 5 \times 5$

4
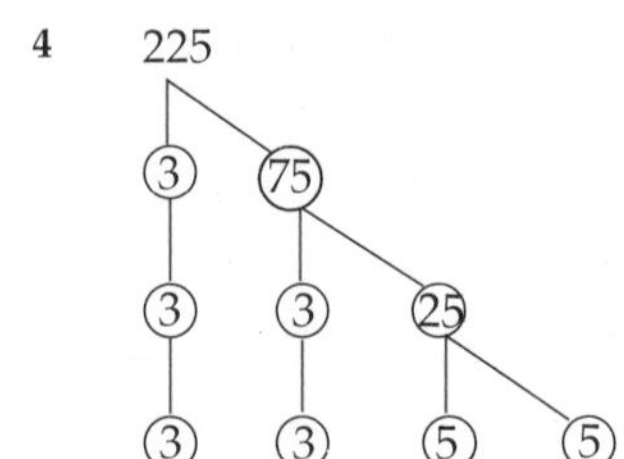

$225 = 3 \times 3 \times 5 \times 5$

5 $2 \times 2 \times 2 \times 7$

6 $2 \times 2 \times 2 \times 2 \times 3$

7 $2 \times 2 \times 2 \times 3 \times 3$

8 $2 \times 2 \times 2 \times 2 \times 5$

9 $2 \times 5 \times 5 \times 5$

10 3×5

11 7×13

12 $2 \times 2 \times 3 \times 3 \times 5 \times 5$

Chapter 5—Powers and roots

Exercise 5.1 (page 73)

1 4^3

2 8^6

3 2^5

4 3^3

5 6^2

6 7^8

7 20^3

8 15^4

9 $2 \times 2 \times 2$

10 $10 \times 10 \times 10 \times 10$

11 7×7

12 $3 \times 3 \times 3 \times 3 \times 3 \times 3$

13 6^4

14 4^6

15 5^2

16 8^3

17 10^2

18 2^3

19 (a) 3
(b) 8
(c) 5
(d) 7

20 (a) 2
(b) 1
(c) 5
(d) 1

Exercise 5.2 (page 73)

1 9

2 8

3 100

4 64

5 81

6 125

7 64

8 1024

9 1000

10 144

Exercise 5.3 (page 74)

1 16 384

2 243

3 1331

4 4913

5 20 736

6 4096

7 104 976

8 4096

9 531 441

10 2025

11 1 092 727

12 20 511 149

13 6889

14 74 618 461

15 3.375

16 1.4641

17 0.0081

18 571.787

19 304.5025

20 263.374 721

Exercise 5.4 (page 75)

1 1

2 64

3 –125

4 $^-128$

5 729

6 $^-1$

7

Column A	Column B
$(^-3)^7 = {}^-2187$	$(^-6)^4 = 1296$
$(^-18)^3 = {}^-5832$	$(^-1)^{10} = 1$
$(^-54)^3 = {}^-157\,464$	$(^-11)^4 = 14\,641$
$(^-8)^3 = {}^-512$	$(^-7)^6 = 117\,649$
$(^-29)^5 = {}^-20\,511\,149$	$(^-5)^8 = 390\,625$

8 (a) odd, negative
(b) even, positive

9 When a negative number is raised to an odd power the answer is negative. When a negative number is raised to an even power the answer is positive.

Exercise 5.5 (page 75)

1 9
2 225
3 36
4 5041
5 1.96
6 556.96
7 327.61
8 0.36
9 141.61
10 102 400
11 1849
12 1
13 0.7569
14 309.76

15

	A	B
1	Number	Square
2		
3	1	1
4	2	4
5	3	9
6	4	16
7	5	25
8	6	36
9	7	49
10	8	64
11	9	81
12	10	100
13	11	121
14	12	144
15	13	169
16	14	196
17	15	225
18	16	256
19	17	289
20	18	324
21	19	361
22	20	400

Exercise 5.6 (page 77)

1 25 m^2
2 36 cm^2
3 1.44 mm^2
4 1391.29 m^2
5 (a) 5329 m^2
(b) 20.25 m^2
(c) 973.44 cm^2
(d) 2401 mm^2
6 64 m^3
7 140.608 cm^3
8 4913 mm^3
9 8 120 601 m^3
10 (a) 125 m^3
(b) 512 cm^3
(c) 12 167 mm^3
(d) 4.913 m^3
11 26

Investigation—Larger and smaller squares (Page 76)

Number	Square	The square is ______ than the number
39	1521	bigger
2	4	bigger
0.3	0.09	smaller
0.767	0.588 289	smaller
15	225	bigger
1.2	1.44	bigger
0.98	0.9604	smaller
5.001	25.010 001	bigger

1 39, 2, 15, 1.2, 5.001
2 0.3, 0.767, 0.98
3 yes, the number is 1($1^2 = 1$)
4 (a) numbers greater than 1
(b) numbers less than 1 (except 0)

Investigation—Mersenne Primes (page 77)

1 15
2 Mersenne numbers are always odd, because powers of 2 are always even, and subtracting 1 gives an odd result.
3 3, 7, 31, 127

Exercise 5.7 (page 79)

1 6
2 3
3 10
4 9
5 5
6 8
7 2
8 4
9 1
10 0

Exercise 5.8 (page 80)

1 A: between 2 and 3
2 (a) (i) 16
(ii) 16.81
(iii) 17.64
(iv) 18.49
(b) 4.1
3 (a) (i) 56.25
(ii) 57.76
(iii) 59.29
(iv) 60.84
(b) 7.7
4 85 is between 81 (= 9^2) and 100 (=10^2)
5 1.73
6 22.58
7 71
8 13
9 7.02
10 14.14
11 0.94
12 6.2
13 0.07
14 0.61
15 5 m
16 6.87 m
17 32.06 cm
18 1.92 m
19 (a) 14 cm
(b) 56 cm
20 (a) 8 (b) 36 (c) 28
21 No, because the square root of 200 is not a whole number.
22 31.62 m
23 (a) By calculating the square root of 2.
(b)

Accuracy	Length
to nearest m	1 m
to 1 dp	1.4 m
to 2 dp	1.41 m
to 3 dp	1.414 m
to 4 dp	1.4142 m

(c) 1.414 m (or 1414 mm). It is not possible to measure much more accurately than this.

Chapter 6—Brackets and order of operations

EXERCISE 6.1 (page 81)

1	8	**11**	$2 \times (6 + 4)$
2	24	**12**	$(40 \div 8) \times 4$
3	4	**13**	$(10 - 7) + 17$
4	4	**14**	$24 - (2 + 2)$
5	15	**15**	$(3 + 7) \times (5 - 3)$
6	3	**16**	$(4 \times 2) + 3 = 11$
7	15	**17**	$(5 - 3) \times 8 = 16$
8	11	**18**	$(6 - 2) + 5 = 9$
9	2	**19**	$(10 + 3) \times 2 = 26$
10	18	**20**	$4 + (7 \times 2) = 18$

EXERCISE 6.2 (page 82)

1	15	**11**	$^{-}2$
2	5	**12**	10
3	$^{-}9$	**13**	2
4	$^{-}9$	**14**	8
5	14	**15**	1
6	2	**16**	$^{-}7$
7	13	**17**	24
8	28	**18**	60
9	$^{-}6$	**19**	$^{-}10$
10	14	**20**	$^{-}10$

EXERCISE 6.3 (page 84)

1	5	**15**	3	**29**	58
2	4	**16**	8	**30**	43
3	100	**17**	14	**31**	7
4	5	**18**	8	**32**	14
5	5	**19**	81	**33**	29
6	5	**20**	14	**34**	14
7	14	**21**	14	**35**	7
8	14	**22**	4	**36**	2
9	5	**23**	36	**37**	10
10	8	**24**	26	**38**	1
11	17	**25**	39	**39**	18
12	7	**26**	72	**40**	11
13	3	**27**	32		
14	4	**28**	102		

The NUT puzzle (page 84)

1 4 4 5 4—1—6
0
6 3 0 0 2 2
3
2 5 6—1—3 5

EXERCISE 6.4 (page 85)

1	40	**9**	38
2	8	**10**	9
3	39	**11**	14
4	29	**12**	12
5	15	**13**	5
6	22	**14**	60
7	34	**15**	2
8	2	**16**	$(7 - 2) \times (10 + 3) = 65$

The 3333 Puzzle (page 85)

(a) $2 = 3 \div 3 + 3 \div 3$
$3 = (3 + 3 + 3) \div 3$
$4 = (3 \times 3 + 3) \div 3$
$5 = 3 + (3 + 3) \div 3$
$6 = 3 + 3 + 3 - 3$
$7 = 3 + 3 + 3 \div 3$
$8 = 3 \times 3 - 3 \div 3$
$9 = 3 \times 3 + (3 - 3)$

(b) All the numbers appear.

Chapter 7—Fractions

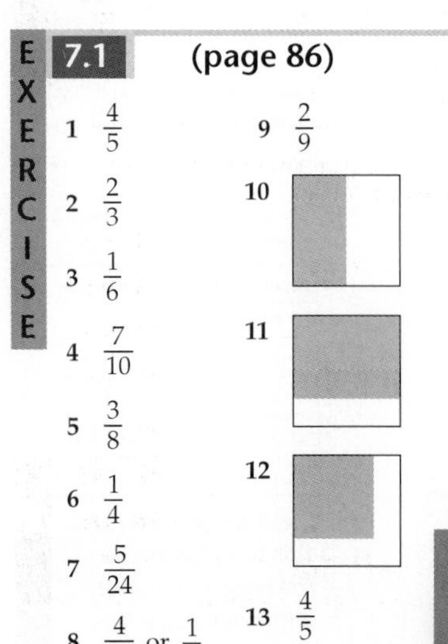

EXERCISE 7.1 (page 86)

1 $\frac{4}{5}$
2 $\frac{2}{3}$
3 $\frac{1}{6}$
4 $\frac{7}{10}$
5 $\frac{3}{8}$
6 $\frac{1}{4}$
7 $\frac{5}{24}$
8 $\frac{4}{16}$ or $\frac{1}{4}$
9 $\frac{2}{9}$
10
11
12
13 $\frac{4}{5}$

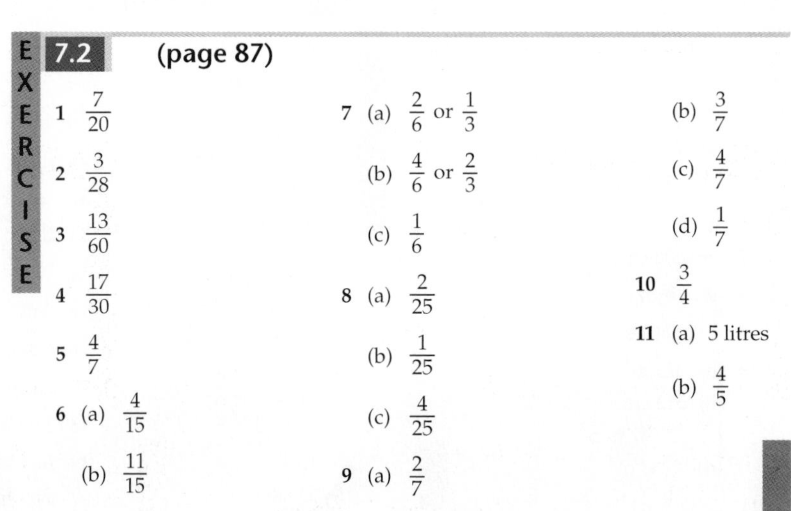

EXERCISE 7.2 (page 87)

1 $\frac{7}{20}$
2 $\frac{3}{28}$
3 $\frac{13}{60}$
4 $\frac{17}{30}$
5 $\frac{4}{7}$
6 (a) $\frac{4}{15}$ (b) $\frac{11}{15}$
7 (a) $\frac{2}{6}$ or $\frac{1}{3}$ (b) $\frac{4}{6}$ or $\frac{2}{3}$ (c) $\frac{1}{6}$
8 (a) $\frac{2}{25}$ (b) $\frac{1}{25}$ (c) $\frac{4}{25}$
9 (a) $\frac{2}{7}$ (b) $\frac{3}{7}$ (c) $\frac{4}{7}$ (d) $\frac{1}{7}$
10 $\frac{3}{4}$
11 (a) 5 litres (b) $\frac{4}{5}$

EXERCISE 7.3 (page 89)

1 (a) (i) $\frac{1}{10}$
(ii) $\frac{3}{10}$
(iii) $\frac{6}{10}$ $\left(\text{or } \frac{3}{5}\right)$
(iv) $\frac{10}{10}$ (or 1)

(b) (i) C
(ii) J
(iii) K
(iv) A

2 (a) (i) $\frac{3}{4}$
(ii) $\frac{4}{4}$ (or 1)
(iii) $\frac{9}{4}$
(iv) $\frac{0}{4}$ (or 0)

(b) (i) H
(ii) E
(iii) I
(iv) I

3
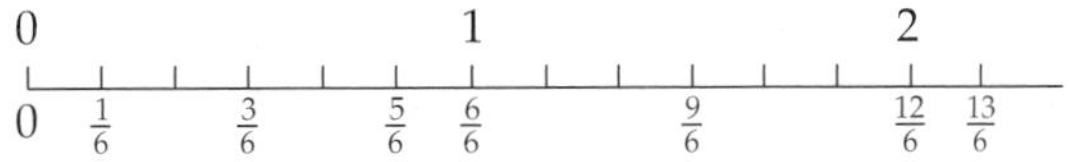

EXERCISE 7.4 (page 91)

1 $\frac{8}{10}$, $\frac{12}{15}$

2 $\frac{2}{6}$, $\frac{3}{9}$

3 $\frac{1}{2}$, $\frac{3}{6}$

4 $\frac{10}{12}$, $\frac{15}{18}$

5 $\frac{14}{20}$, $\frac{21}{30}$

6 $\frac{2}{3}$, $\frac{6}{9}$

7 A and E

8 (a) $\frac{5}{30}$ (b) $\frac{18}{32}$

9 (a) No, only $\frac{13}{30}$ has been completed.
(b) $\frac{17}{30}$

EXERCISE 7.5 (page 92)

1 (a) $\frac{1}{9}$ (d) $\frac{1}{2}$
(b) $\frac{1}{12}$ (e) $\frac{1}{4}$
(c) $\frac{1}{6}$ (f) $\frac{1}{8}$

2 (a) $\frac{1}{3}$
(b) $\frac{2}{3}$

3 (a) $\frac{2}{3}$, strips A and D
(b) $\frac{2}{3}$, strips B and D
(c) $\frac{1}{2}$, strips F and G
(d) $\frac{3}{4}$, strips G and H
(e) $\frac{3}{4}$, strips B and G

4 $\frac{4}{5}$

5 $\frac{1}{2}$

6 $\frac{2}{3}$

7 $\frac{3}{2}$

8 $\frac{3}{5}$

9 $\frac{1}{2}$

10 $\frac{1}{3}$

11 2

12 $\frac{3}{4}$

13 1

14 $\frac{1}{29}$

15 $\frac{2}{3}$

EXERCISE 7.6 (page 94)

1 $\frac{8}{15}$

2 $\frac{3}{20}$

3 $\frac{5}{24}$

4 $\frac{1}{6}$

5 $\frac{9}{20}$

6 $\frac{21}{100}$

7 $\frac{9}{16}$

8 $\frac{3}{50}$

9 $\frac{21}{40}$

10 $\frac{4}{15}$

11 $\frac{5}{8}$

12 2

13 $\frac{3}{16}$

14 4

15 8

16 6

17 $\frac{3}{2}$

18 4

19 $\frac{3}{4}$

20 0

21 10

22 1

23 $\frac{8}{45}$

24 $\frac{3}{20}$

EXERCISE 7.7 (page 94)

1 $\frac{1}{3}$

2 12

3 $\frac{1}{15}$

4 $\frac{1}{6}$

5 160 minutes

6 (a) \$24
(b) \$44

7 18 minutes

8 (a) 24
(b) 8

9 Each person could get three-quarters $\left(\frac{3}{4}\right)$ of a bar

10 $\frac{1}{5}$

11 (a) $\frac{1}{5}$
(b) $\frac{1}{5} \times 60 = 12$ minutes

EXERCISE 7.8 (page 95)

1 $\frac{3}{2}$

2 $\frac{3}{4}$

3 $\frac{2}{3}$

4 $\frac{6}{5}$

5 $\frac{10}{7}$

6 $\frac{2}{7}$

7 4

8 $\frac{1}{7}$

9 2

10 $\frac{1}{3}$

11 $\frac{1}{100}$

12 yes

13 no

14 yes

15 yes

16 no

17 yes

18 yes

EXERCISE 7.9 (page 96)

1 $\frac{2}{3} \div \frac{1}{4} = \frac{2}{3} \times \frac{4}{1}$
$= \frac{8}{3}$

2 $\frac{1}{5} \div \frac{2}{5} = \frac{1}{5} \times \frac{5}{2}$
$= \frac{1}{2}$

3 $\frac{3}{4} \div \frac{1}{3} = \frac{3}{4} \times \frac{3}{1}$
$= \frac{9}{4}$

4 $\frac{1}{2} \div \frac{7}{10} = \frac{1}{2} \times \frac{10}{7}$
$= \frac{10}{14}$
$= \frac{5}{7}$

5 $\frac{9}{10}$
6 $\frac{10}{21}$
7 $\frac{2}{3}$
8 $\frac{5}{8}$
9 $\frac{4}{15}$
10 $\frac{3}{4}$
11 $\frac{1}{4}$
12 3
13 $\frac{1}{2}$
14 $\frac{1}{2}$
15 $\frac{1}{2}$
16 32
17 20
18 $\frac{1}{6}$
19 $\frac{1}{10}$
20 $\frac{3}{2}$

EXERCISE 7.10 (page 98)

1 $\frac{4}{5}$
2 $\frac{5}{7}$
3 $\frac{3}{4}$
4 $\frac{2}{3}$
5 $\frac{5}{6}$
6 $\frac{4}{5}$
7 1
8 $\frac{2}{3}$
9 $\frac{4}{5}$
10 $\frac{3}{4}$
11 $\frac{1}{5}$
12 $\frac{2}{11}$
13 $\frac{2}{5}$
14 $\frac{1}{4}$
15 $\frac{1}{2}$
16 $\frac{3}{5}$
17 $\frac{2}{3}$
18 $\frac{1}{2}$
19 0
20 $\frac{7}{10}$

EXERCISE 7.11 (page 100)

1 $\frac{2}{3} + \frac{1}{5} = \frac{10}{15} + \frac{3}{15}$
$= \frac{13}{15}$

2 $\frac{3}{10} + \frac{2}{5} = \frac{3}{10} + \frac{4}{10}$
$= \frac{7}{10}$

3 $\frac{4}{5} + \frac{1}{7} = \frac{28}{35} + \frac{5}{35}$
$= \frac{33}{35}$

4 $\frac{1}{4} + \frac{5}{6} = \frac{3}{12} + \frac{10}{12}$
$= \frac{13}{12}$

5 $\frac{5}{6}$
6 $\frac{11}{15}$
7 $\frac{10}{9}$
8 $\frac{11}{12}$
9 $\frac{2}{3}$
10 $\frac{7}{10}$
11 $\frac{19}{12}$
12 $\frac{23}{30}$
13 $\frac{16}{63}$
14 $\frac{59}{60}$
15 $\frac{11}{20}$
16 $\frac{7}{8}$

EXERCISE 7.12 (page 100)

1 $\frac{2}{3} - \frac{1}{4} = \frac{8}{12} - \frac{3}{12}$
$= \frac{5}{12}$

2 $\frac{9}{10} - \frac{1}{5} = \frac{9}{10} - \frac{2}{10}$
$= \frac{7}{10}$

3 $\frac{2}{5} - \frac{1}{7} = \frac{14}{35} - \frac{5}{35}$
$= \frac{9}{35}$

4 $\frac{5}{6} - \frac{1}{9} = \frac{15}{18} - \frac{2}{18}$
$= \frac{13}{18}$

5 $\frac{1}{12}$
6 $\frac{3}{8}$
7 $\frac{17}{63}$
8 $\frac{1}{12}$
9 $\frac{1}{10}$
10 $\frac{1}{4}$

Puzzle—Hippie (page 96)
See page 461 for answer.

Puzzle—Prisoner (page 100)
See page 461 for answer.

EXERCISE 7.13 (page 101)

1 $\frac{9}{20}$
2 $\frac{1}{6}$
3 (a) $\frac{7}{12}$ (b) $\frac{5}{12}$
4 $\frac{5}{12}$
5 (a) $\frac{11}{12}$ (b) $\frac{1}{12}$
6 $\frac{1}{8}$

EXERCISE 7.14 (page 102)

1 $2\frac{1}{3}$
2 $1\frac{1}{2}$
3 $1\frac{5}{6}$
4 $2\frac{3}{4}$
5 $5\frac{4}{5}$
6 $10\frac{5}{6}$
7 $1\frac{7}{10}$
8 4
9 $1\frac{2}{17}$
10 $2\frac{5}{12}$
11 $3\frac{2}{3}$ cm
12 (a) $7\frac{1}{4}$ (b) 7 (c) 1
13 (a) $4\frac{4}{7}$
(b) No, 35 students would be needed.
(c) 4 teams, with each team having one reserve.
14 4

EXERCISE 7.15 (page 103)

1 $\frac{9}{4}$
2 $\frac{7}{2}$
3 $\frac{7}{5}$
4 $\frac{13}{10}$
5 $\frac{33}{5}$
6 $\frac{3}{2}$
7 $\frac{19}{8}$
8 $\frac{41}{2}$
9 $\frac{41}{20}$
10 $\frac{413}{100}$
11 (a) $\frac{9}{4}$ (b) 9

EXERCISE 7.16 (page 104)

1 $3\frac{1}{8}$

2 $1\frac{1}{4}$

3 2

4 $5\frac{2}{3}$

5 2

6 $2\frac{2}{5}$

EXERCISE 7.17 (page 104)

1 4

2 8

3 $6\frac{4}{5}$

4 1

5 $2\frac{2}{3}$

6 $1\frac{2}{3}$

7 $10\frac{1}{2}$

8 $7\frac{2}{5}$

9 $4\frac{1}{6}$

10 $5\frac{11}{20}$

11 $\frac{23}{24}$

12 $3\frac{9}{10}$

EXERCISE 7.18 (page 105)

1 $6\frac{1}{4}$ litres

2 $4\frac{3}{4}$ litres

3 (a)

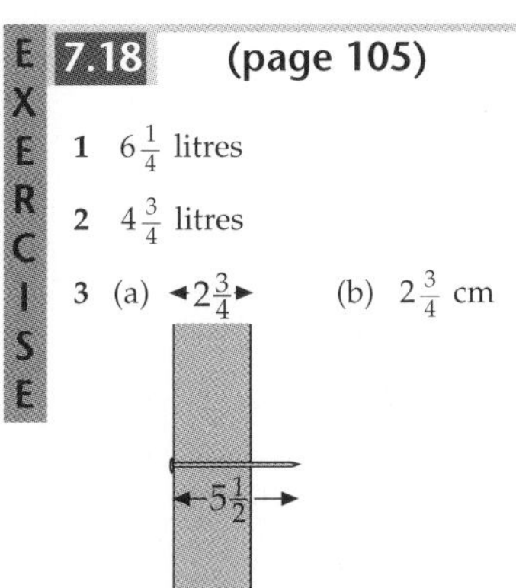

(b) $2\frac{3}{4}$ cm

4 $5\frac{1}{4}$ cups

5 $2\frac{1}{2}$ pies

6 (a) $10\frac{3}{10}$ lengths

(b) $\frac{7}{10}$ of a length

7 $1\frac{5}{6}$ glasses

8 $\frac{2}{15}$

9 $7\frac{1}{2}$ books per hour

10 $3\frac{3}{4} \div 5 = \frac{15}{4} \times \frac{1}{5}$

$= \frac{3}{4}$

Each person gets $\frac{3}{4}$ of an Easter egg

EXERCISE 7.19 (page 108)

1 (a) $\frac{7}{10}$

(b) 0.7

2 (a) $\frac{9}{100}$

(b) 0.09

3 (a) $\frac{41}{100}$

(b) 0.41

4 (a) $\frac{5}{1000}$

(b) 0.005

5 0.3

6 0.05

7 0.22

8 0.376

9 $\frac{9}{10}$

10 $\frac{7}{100}$

11 $\frac{61}{100}$

12 $\frac{3}{1000}$

13 3.5

14 6.75

15 22.03

16 1.041

17 $1\frac{9}{10}$

18 $5\frac{7}{100}$

19 $31\frac{3}{10}$

20 $7\frac{23}{1000}$

EXERCISE 7.20 (page 109)

1 $\frac{7}{10}$

2 $\frac{3}{10}$

3 $\frac{1}{10}$

4 $\frac{17}{100}$

5 $\frac{83}{100}$

6 $\frac{99}{100}$

7 $\frac{513}{1000}$

8 $\frac{1}{4}$

9 $\frac{3}{4}$

10 $\frac{2}{5}$

11 $\frac{1}{5}$

12 $\frac{9}{25}$

13 $\frac{1}{8}$

14 $\frac{21}{25}$

15 $\frac{3}{500}$

EXERCISE 7.21 (page 109)

1 0.4

2 0.5

3 0.55

4 0.875

5 0.075

6 0.4625

7 2.75

8 7.5

9 9.6

10 17.1875

11 0.3333

12 0.2857

13 0.8889

14 0.2308

15 0.4545

16 0.7364

EXERCISE 7.22 (page 110)

1 $\frac{1}{2}$

2 $\frac{4}{5}$

3 $\frac{4}{10}$

4 $\frac{4}{11}$

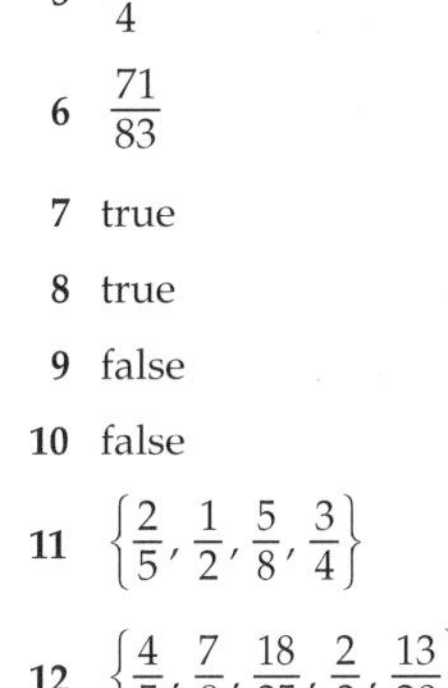

5 $\frac{3}{4}$

6 $\frac{71}{83}$

7 true

8 true

9 false

10 false

11 $\left\{\frac{2}{5}, \frac{1}{2}, \frac{5}{8}, \frac{3}{4}\right\}$

12 $\left\{\frac{4}{5}, \frac{7}{9}, \frac{18}{25}, \frac{2}{3}, \frac{13}{20}\right\}$

13 Peter

14 B

15 (a) $\frac{55}{106}$

(b) The best exchange rate was for Mr Bean.
Mr Atkinson: 0.5189,
Mr Bean: 0.5195,
Mr Rowan: 0.5111

16 Fraction infected at Daintree is

$\frac{17}{25} = 0.68$

Fraction infected at Trinity Bay is

$\frac{11}{16} = 0.6875$

The Trinity Bay farm has the higher rate of infection.

Investigation—Fraction approximations to π (page 111)

1

Fraction	Decimal
$\frac{22}{7}$	3.142 857 143
$\frac{103\,993}{33\,102}$	3.141 592 653
$\frac{355}{113}$	3.141 592 92
$\frac{223}{71}$	3.140 845 07
$\left(\frac{16}{9}\right)^2$	3.160 493 827
$\frac{25}{8}$	3.125

2

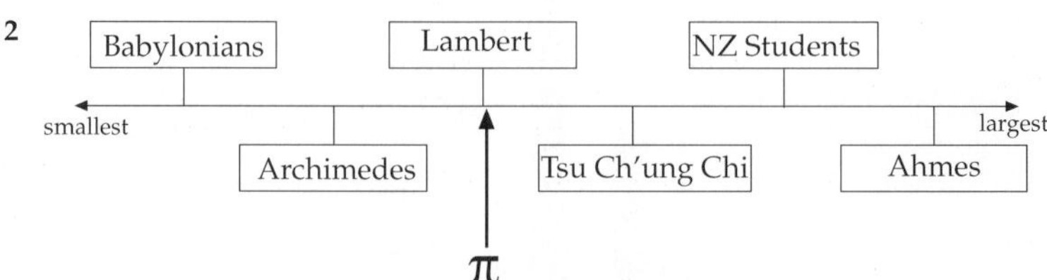

3 Lambert's approximation is the most accurate. The difference between it and the true value is only 0.000 000 000 5.

Chapter 8—Percentages

EXERCISE 8.1 (page 113)

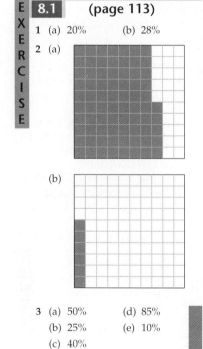

1 (a) 20% (b) 28%

2 (a)

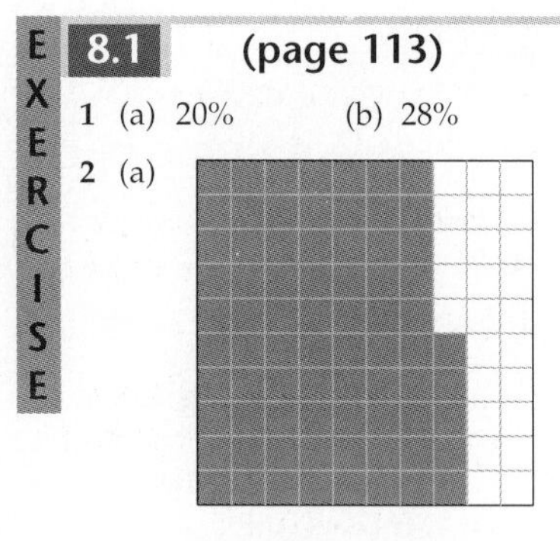

(b)

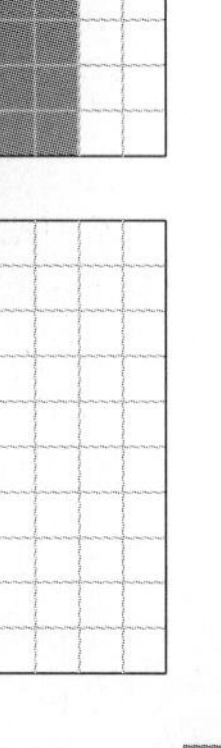

3 (a) 50% (b) 25% (c) 40% (d) 85% (e) 10%

EXERCISE 8.2 (page 113)

1 $\frac{17}{100}$
2 $\frac{3}{10}$
3 $\frac{99}{100}$
4 $\frac{49}{100}$
5 $\frac{3}{4}$
6 $\frac{1}{4}$
7 $\frac{1}{100}$
8 $\frac{1}{20}$
9 $\frac{3}{50}$
10 $\frac{3}{5}$
11 $\frac{1}{2}$
12 $\frac{2}{5}$
13 $\frac{7}{10}$
14 $\frac{11}{25}$
15 $\frac{24}{25}$

EXERCISE 8.3 (page 114)

1 40%
2 30%
3 49%
4 12%
5 50%
6 25%
7 35%
8 38%
9 33.33%
10 66.67%
11 44.44%
12 60.78%
13 42.86%
14 46.15%
15 83.33%

16 (a)

Topic	Mark out of total	Percentage
Integers	$\frac{11}{20}$	55%
Angles	$\frac{24}{30}$	80%
Area	$\frac{27}{50}$	54%
Fractions	$\frac{12}{25}$	48%

(b) Fractions

(c) Angles

(d) Assume that the tests were about the same difficulty; and that her mark reflects her understanding.

Exercise 8.4 (page 115)

1 53%
2 30%
3 1%
4 70%
5 64.9%
6 0.5
7 0.29
8 0.04
9 1.25
10 0.692

11

	Percentage (words)	Percentage (symbol)	Decimal (symbol)	Fraction	Fraction (words)
(a)	seventy-three per cent	73%	0.73	$\frac{73}{100}$	seventy-three hundredths
(b)	six per cent	6%	0.06	$\frac{3}{50}$	three fiftieths
(c)	thirty-five per cent	35%	0.35	$\frac{7}{20}$	seven twentieths
(d)	sixteen per cent	16%	0.16	$\frac{4}{25}$	four twenty-fifths

Exercise 8.5 (page 116)

1 35
2 192
3 72
4 10
5 $5.04
6 $10.80
7 2.31 m
8 12
9 $3500
10 4550 kg
11 45 kg
12 $72
13 $15 900
14 $180

Puzzle (page 60)
For fast acting relief try slowing down

Puzzle—Hippie (page 96)
Oh no, I've found one

Puzzle—Prisoner (page 100)
I shall dig ditches

Exercise 8.6 (page 118)

1 56%
2 90%
3 5%
4 68%
5 60%
6 (a) 40%
(b) 50%
7 8%
8 24%
9 42%
10 6%
11 (a) 932 km
(b) 47%
(c) 32 km
12 Yes—the mark has improved, going up from 60% to 68%.
13 (a) 75%
(b) 25%
(c) 70%
(d) 30%

Investigation—Compound interest (page 122)
1 $930.80

Exercise 8.7 (page 121)

1 (a) $3200 (b) $11 200
2 (a) 0.3 m (b) 20%
3 (a) $28 (b) 40%
4 25%
5 $3360
6 Discount on Eskifridge is 35% of $1300
$0.35 \times 1300 = 455$
New price = $1300 – $455 = $845
Discount on Chillway is 20% of $1150
$0.20 \times 1150 = 230$
New price = $1150 – $230 = $920
The Eskifridge is the cheaper refrigerator after the discount is taken off.
7 (a) 3.2 cents a litre
(b) 3.57%
8 75%
9 $6.59
10 18.68%

Chapter 9—Everyday measurements

Exercise 9.1 (page 125)

1 (a) 11.10 (b) 3.32 (c) 6.48 (d) 2.42
2 (a) half past ten in the morning
(b) quarter past nine in the morning
(c) quarter to nine in the morning
(d) half past seven in the evening
(e) ten past one in the afternoon
(f) quarter to one in the afternoon
(g) ten to midday
(h) twenty to three in the afternoon
3 (a) 4.30 pm (b) 3.00 am (c) 1.15 pm (d) 7.45 am (e) 3.05 pm (f) 10.50 am
4 (a) (b)

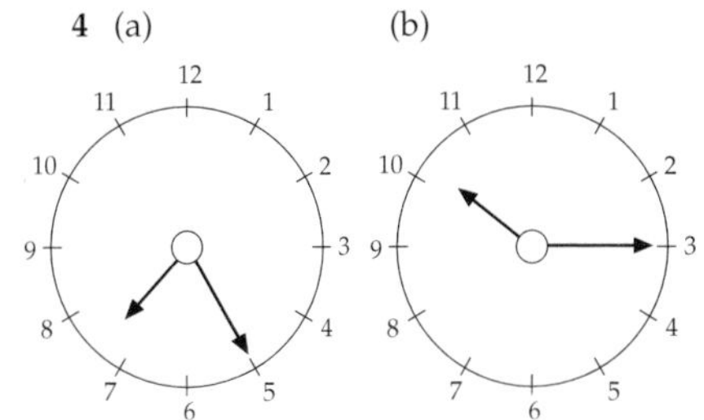

5 (a) 60 (d) 45
(b) 15 (e) 180
(c) 30

6 Records for 180 minutes, or 3 hours

7 Length of Dick Tracy is 1 hour 45 minutes, or 105 minutes.
Length of Star Trek is 2 hours 5 minutes, or 125 minutes.
The total time is 230 minutes, which is less than the 240-minute length of the video. However, she should not record the movie shown in between these two!

8 (a) 11 am (c) 5.55 pm
(b) 8.10 am (d) 1.15 pm

9 (a) 15 minutes
(b) 50 minutes
(c) 3 hours 45 minutes or 225 minutes

10 1 hour 25 minutes or 85 minutes

11 11.15 pm

12 (a) 31 minutes
(b) 19 minutes
(c) 2.37 pm
(d) 5.04 pm

13 (a) 7.15 pm
(b) 7.55 pm
(c)

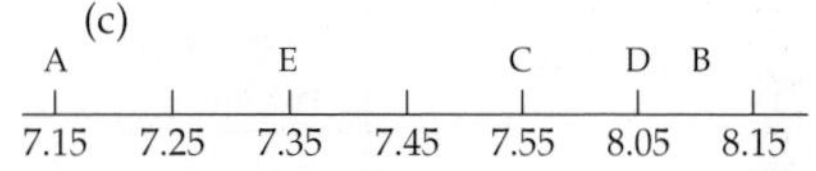

14 (a) entrance–lions–crocodiles–giraffes–kiwis–kiosk–snakes–exit (62 minutes).
Other answers are possible
(b) entrance–kiwis–kiosk–giraffes–crocodiles–snakes–lions–exit (58 minutes).
Other answers are possible.

Starter (page 129)

- 2010
- 10.35 pm
- 2 hours 25 minutes (or 145 minutes)
- hours
- minutes

EXERCISE 9.2 (page 130)

1

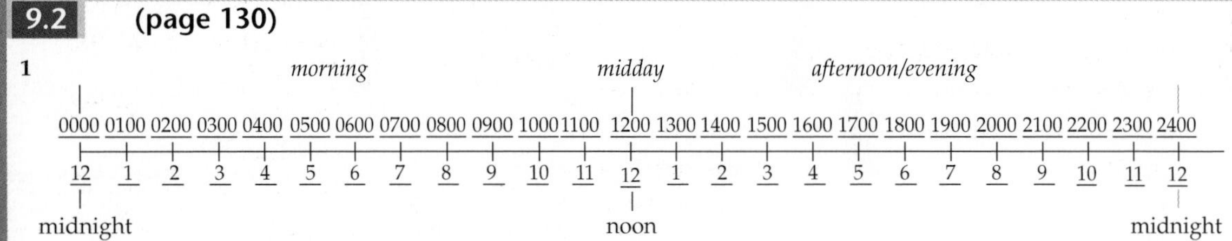

2 (a) 9.45 am (e) 8.20 pm
(b) 3 pm (f) 8.15 am
(c) 4.30 am (g) 11.30 pm
(d) 4.50 pm (h) 12.15 pm

3 (a) 1015 (f) 2310
(b) 1630 (g) 1728
(c) 2300 (h) 0840
(d) 0600 (i) 1200
(e) 0445 (j) 0000 or 2400

4 (a) 0730 (d) 2040
(b) 2015 (e) 1430
(c) 0345 (f) 1555

5 (a) midday (c) midday
(b) midnight (d) midnight

6 (a) 0000, 0125, 0300, 0445, 0615, 0645, 0830, 1100, 1315, 1445, 1630, 1815, 2030, 2205
(b) The Making of Daylight (30 minutes)
(c) Empire of the Sun (2 hours 30 minutes, or 150 minutes)

9 5 hours 45 minutes

10 (a) 8.45 am
(b)

Station	Southbound
Auckland	dep. 0830
Papakura	arr. 0914
Hamilton	arr. 1043
Taumarunui	arr. 1301
National Park	arr. 1353
Ohakune	arr. 1425
Marton	arr. 1627
Palmerston North	arr. 1712
Levin	arr. 1749
Porirua	arr. 1909
Wellington	arr. 1927

(c) Porirua and Levin
(d) Papakura and Auckland
(e) National Park and Ohakune
(f) The southbound train trip takes longer:
Southbound: 1927—0830 = 10 hours, 57 minutes
Northbound: 1935—0845 = 10 hours 50 minutes

EXERCISE 9.3 (page 133)

1 (a) 5 pm
(b) 1545
(c) quarter to eight at night
(d) 1 pm
2 (a) 10 am
(b) 0810
(c) half past six in the morning
(d) 11 pm
3 (a) 1 October (b) 19 March

EXERCISE 9.4 (page 135)

1 Fiji
2 2 hours
3 Adelaide
4 (a) 11 am (the previous day)
(b) 9 am
(c) midday (the previous day)
(d) 7.30 am
5 (a) midday
(b) 2 pm
(c) 10 am
(d) 11.30 am
6 (a) 6.30 pm, Thursday
(b) 10.30 pm, Wednesday
(c) 9.30 pm, Wednesday
7 (a) 5.15 am Tuesday
(b) 7.15 am Monday
(c) 1.15 am Tuesday
8 One of the first places in the world for the year to change from 1999 to 2000.
9 (a) 2 pm
(b) three
(c) Monday, Tuesday, Wednesday, Thursday, Friday, Sunday
(d) 1.30 am on Monday
(e) 2 pm
(f) 2 hours 55 minutes
(g) 3 hours 30 minutes

EXERCISE 9.5 (page 138)

1 (a) 180 (c) 30
(b) 48 (d) 48
2 hours, week
3 $\frac{365}{7} = 52\frac{1}{7}$
4 4
5 14
6 (a) Thursday
(b) Wednesday
(c) Saturday
7 (a) 31 (d) 30
(b) 30 (e) 28
(c) 31 (f) 29
8 (a) Tuesday
(b) Friday
(c) July 9
(d) six
9 (a) December, January, February
(b) March, April, May
(c) September, October, November
10 (a) a leap year
(b) not a leap year
(c) not a leap year
(d) not a leap year
(e) not a leap year
(f) not a leap year
(g) a leap year
(h) not a leap year
11 10
12 (a) 13th
(b) 6 837 480 minutes
(c) 28 900 days
13 (a) 12 October 2004
(b) 1 March 2000
(c) 29 February 2012
14 (a) 17th
(b) 19th
(c) 20th

EXERCISE 9.6 (page 140)

1 \$51
2 (a) \$7.40 (b) \$2.60
3 (a) \$3.05 (b) \$16.95
4 (a) \$17
(b) \$42.50
(c) \$29.75
5 \$20.55
6 \$2.10
7 6
8 (a) \$19.95 (b) \$30.05
9 two and a half hours
10 (a) 75 cents (c) \$10.85
(b) \$1.60 (d) \$15.40
11 (a) \$5.88 (c) \$15.11
(b) \$20.55 (d) \$20.48
12 (a) \$1.80 (c) \$15.75
(b) \$16.50 (d) \$43.45
13 (a) \$160 (b) \$3.85
14 \$42.90
15 (a) seven (b) \$32.55
16 1 hour

EXERCISE 9.7 (page 142)

1 (a) 35 cents (c) \$1
(b) 18 cents (d) 40 cents
2 (a) (i) \$7.70
(ii) \$10.00
(iii) \$11.35
(b) \$12.10
(c) (i) The cost of two large fries and a chicken sandwich.
(ii) The change they will get from a \$20 note if they buy a cheeseburger and large fries.
(d) A cheeseburger and a small fries.
3 (a) \$6.00
(b) ten times or more

(c) If they paid for ten months as ten lots of one month, this would cost $360. It would be cheaper to join for twelve months with a cost of $300.
If they paid for ten months as six months, three months and one month, this would cost $326. It would still be cheaper to join for twelve months.

(d) 6 months child/6 months student costs $215 altogether.
12 months student costs $220 altogether. Therefore, 6 months of each type is cheaper.

(e) $69

4 (a) $10.90 (b) $4.84 (c) $11.12 (d) $35.70

EXERCISE 9.8 (page 146)

1 26 °C, 25 °C, 21 °C, 18 °C, 16 °C, 11 °C, 9 °C

2 (a) 45 °C (b) $^{-}$120 °C (c) 12 °C (d) 800 °C (e) 85 °C (f) $^{-}$4 °C (g) 350 °C

3

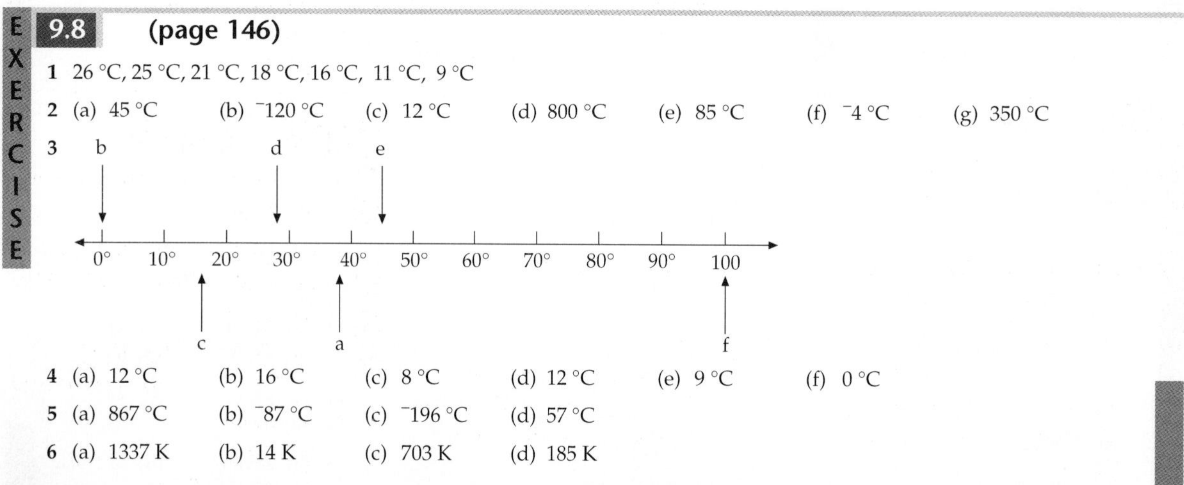

4 (a) 12 °C (b) 16 °C (c) 8 °C (d) 12 °C (e) 9 °C (f) 0 °C

5 (a) 867 °C (b) $^{-}$87 °C (c) $^{-}$196 °C (d) 57 °C

6 (a) 1337 K (b) 14 K (c) 703 K (d) 185 K

EXERCISE 9.9 (page 148)

1 a = 1.2, b = 5.8, c = 8.6

2 (a) 0.1
(b) a = 12.5, b = 14.9, c = 16.4, d = 19.3

3 (a) millimetres (mm)
(b) a = 3 cm, b = 6.5 cm, c = 7.7 cm, d = 8.9 cm, e = 9.6 cm

4 5.7 cm or 57 mm

5 (a) 10 km/h
(b) 105 km/h

6 37.6 °C

7 (a) 2.6 kg
(b) 3.4 kg
(c) 56 kg

8 (a) 350 mL
(b) 475 mL
(c) 190 mL

EXERCISE 9.10 (page 150)

1 A = National Radio Wellington 530 kHz
B = Sports Station 981 kHz
C = Newstalk ZB Auckland 1080 kHz
D = Radio Hauraki 1492 kHz

2 (a) 0.2 units
(b) a = 5.4, b = 6.6, c = 8.3, d = 4.5

3 (a) a = 100 Mhz, b = 104 MHz
(b) 88.8 MHz

4 (a) No. Between 30 and 50 the scale units are one decibel, and between 50 and 80 the scale units are two decibels.
(b) a = 35, b = 44, c = 56, d = 73

5 a = 8, b = 60, c = 1, d = 15, e = 1.8, f = 85

6 (a) a = 600 mL, b = 75 mL, c = 850 mL, d = 325 mL
(b) 1000
(c) the sides are sloping
(d) like a cylinder, with vertical sides

Chapter 10—More everyday measurements

EXERCISE 10.1 (page 154)

1 74 mm

2 4.5 cm

3 a = 50 mm, b = 10 mm, c = 20 mm, d = 30 mm, e = 60 mm, f = 55 mm, g = 75 mm

4 (Actual measured lengths) a = 8.7 cm, b = 1.6 cm, c = 2.3 cm, d = 5.9 cm, e = 7.5 cm, f = 6.1 cm

5 (a) 10 cm (b) 40 cm (c) 80 cm (d) 20 cm (e) 80 cm (f) 10 cm (g) 20 cm

EXERCISE 10.2 (page 155)

1 (a) cm (b) km (c) mm (d) m (e) m (f) mm

2 (a) A: 14 mm (b) A: 300 m (c) B: 15 cm (d) B: 7 m

3 (a) 1 mm (b) 2 m (c) 100 m (d) 9 mm (e) 35 m (f) 70 cm (g) 24 cm (h) 4 cm (i) 7 km (j) 14 cm

4 (a) km
(b) (i) 84 km (ii) 498 km
(c)

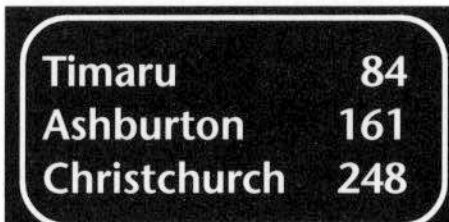

5 (a) 8 cm (b) 16 cm (c) 6 years

6 (a) 12 km (b) 36 km

7 2.7 km

8 (a) 548 km
(b) (i) 1380 km (or 1380.2 km or 1380.3 km, or 1380.25 km)
(ii) 380.2 km (or 380.3 km or 380.25 km)

9 (a) 12
(b) (i) 1.3 m (ii) 0.9 m (iii) 1.4 m
(c) size 8

EXERCISE 10.3 (page 159)

1 a = 26 mm, b = 45 mm, c = 61 mm, d = 80 mm

2 a = 2.6 cm, b = 4.5 cm, c = 6.1 cm, d = 8 cm

3 (a) 8 cm (b) 3.5 cm (c) 12 cm (d) 9.4 cm

4 (a) 60 mm (b) 42 mm (c) 130 mm (d) 83 mm

5 (a) 2 m (b) 1.3 m (c) 0.85 m (d) 1.479 m

6 (a) 3000 mm (b) 4600 mm (c) 130 mm (d) 18 mm

7 (a) 4 m (b) 5.3 m (c) 0.8 m (d) 0.73 m

8 (a) 200 cm (b) 170 cm (c) 58 cm (d) 8 cm

9 (a) 3000 m (b) 4200 m (c) 830 m (d) 75 m

10 (a) 5 km (b) 1.35 km (c) 14.8 km (d) 0.5 km

11 (a) 400 (b) 600 (c) 10 (d) 2000 (e) 800 (f) 4.4 (g) 0.83 (h) 9

12 (a) no (b) yes (c) no (d) yes

EXERCISE 10.4 (page 159)

1 4 km

2 7.3 km

3 900 mm

4 4 mm

5 (a) km (b) m (c) 1200 m, 4500 m (d) 472 cm (e) 3 km

EXERCISE 10.5 (page 161)

1 (a) width = 3 cm, height = 5 cm
(b) width = 9 cm, height = 15 cm

2 (a) length = 5 cm, width = 2.5 cm
(b) length = 100 m, width = 50 m
(c) 112 m

3 (a) 190 m (b) 920 m (c) 330 m (d) about 1450 m

4 (a) 8.4 m
(b) 100 cm
(c) length = 3.5 m width = 3.4 m

5 (a) 30 m (b) 40 m (c) 36.5 m

6 7.2 m

7 2 mm

8 (a) 18 m (b) B 4 m (c) 30 m

9 One of the students lying down at the edge might measure about 1.6 metres. Comparing a measurement of a student with the width of the heart, about 15 of them would fit. Therefore the width is about $15 \times 1.6 = 24$ metres.

EXERCISE 10.6 (page 166)

1 80 km/h
2 15 km/h
3 (a) 32 km
(b) 32 km/h
4 5100 km
5 (a) 300 km
(b) 150 km/h
6 72 km
7 4 hours
8 (a) 17 km/h
(b) 640 km/h
(c) 100 km/h
9 (a) 180 km
(b) 720 km
(c) 25 km
10 (a) 2 hours
(b) 45 hours
(c) half an hour (or 30 minutes)
11 18 km
12 2 minutes

EXERCISE 10.7 (page 167)

1 kg
2 mg
3 tonnes
4 g
5 kg
6 tonnes
7 kg
8 g
9 (a) A: 250 g
(b) B: 2 g
(c) B: 70 tonnes
10 (a) 2 t
(b) 1 kg
(c) 10 kg
(d) 380 t
(e) 30 g
(f) 3 kg
(g) 2 g
(h) 100 kg
(i) 500 g
(j) 45 kg

EXERCISE 10.8 (page 168)

1 (a) 8 g
(b) 3.59 g
(c) 0.18 g
2 (a) 6000 mg
(b) 12 900 mg
(c) 130 000 mg
3 (a) 2 kg
(b) 4.3 kg
(c) 0.85 kg
4 (a) 3000 g
(b) 8300 g
(c) 125 g
5 (a) 4 tonnes
(b) 6.53 tonnes
(c) 0.85 tonnes
6 (a) 3000 kg
(b) 5900 kg
(c) 580 kg
7 1.45 kg
8 4.25 kg
9 400 g
10 38.4 kg
11 750 g
12 (a) $19
(b) $34.20
(c) $4.75
13 (a) $66
(b) $2.20
(c) $5.50
14 (a) $1.20
(b) $480
(c) $81.60
15 (a) Cocoa
(b) Espresso
(c) 20 cups
(d) 80 mg
(e) Amount needed to poison is 5 g = 5000 mg. Each can of cola has 40 mg of caffeine. To calculate the number of cans, work out 5000 ÷ 40. This gives 125 cans. There are sixty minutes in an hour, so 125 ÷ 60 gives about 2 cans per minute!

EXERCISE 10.9 (page 170)

1 (a) 4 litres
(b) 2.25 litres
(c) 0.8 litres
2 (a) 5000 mL
(b) 1800 mL
(c) 500 mL
3 (a) 1800 mL
(b) 1.8 litres
4 950 mL
5 2400 mL or 2.4 litres
6 6 cans
7 5 litres
8 25 scoops
9 (a) 14 mugs
(b) 50 mL

EXERCISE 10.10 (page 171)

1 (a) litre
(b) metre
(c) litre
(d) gram
(e) kilometre
(f) millilitre or litre
(g) metre
(h) kilogram
2 (a) 1000
(b) 100
(c) 1000
(d) 10
(e) 1000
(f) 1000
(g) 1000
(h) 1000
3 (a) km
(b) cm
(c) g
(d) mL
(e) kg
4 (a) 3000 m
(b) 9.3 kg
(c) 6.3 m
(d) 400 cm
(e) 3200 g
(f) 5 tonnes
(g) 8 cm
(h) 2100 mL
(i) 13 km
(j) 0.5 litres
(k) 400 mm

Investigation—The Spectacular Sky Tower (page 172)

1	1 m, length
12	12 m, length
15	15 metres, length
30	30 minutes
40	40 seconds, time
60	60 minutes, time
170	170 tonnes, weight
200	200 km/h speed
328	328 m, length
360	360°, angle
660	660 tonnes, weight
1000	1000 years, time
2000	2000 tonnes, weight

Chapter 11—Area

EXERCISE 11.1 (page 174)

1 15 cm^2

2 2 cm^2

3 14 cm^2

4 10 cm^2

5 (a) $\frac{1}{2}$

(b) $\frac{1}{2}$

(c) $\frac{1}{4}$

(d) $\frac{3}{4}$

(e) $\frac{7}{8}$

6 14 cm^2

7 18 cm^2

8 10 cm^2

9 11 cm^2

10 18 cm^2

11 about 19 cm^2

12 about 12 cm^2

13 28 cm^2

14 18 cm^2

15 20 cm^2

16 24 cm^2

17 100

18 Calculate 8×11

EXERCISE 11.2 (page 176)

1 15 cm^2

2 80 m^2

3 4 m^2

4 21 cm^2

5 12 cm^2

6 156 m^2

7 500 cm^2

8 A = 28 cm^2
B = 15 cm^2
C = 2 cm^2
D = 4 cm^2

9 64 m^2

10 100 cm^2

11 25 m^2

12 54 m^2

13 116 cm^2

14 (a) $x = 6$ m
$y = 5$ m
(c) 42 m^2

15 20 cm^2

EXERCISE 11.3 (page 179)

1 20 cm^2

2 70 cm^2

3 27 cm^2

4 6 cm^2

5 12 cm^2

6 15 cm^2

7 16 cm^2

8 31.5 cm^2

9 30 cm^2

10 126 cm^2

11 204 cm^2

12 27 cm^2

13 13.5 cm^2

14 (a) Each triangle is 20 cm^2
(b) Each triangle is 7.5 cm^2
(c) 50 cm^2
(d) 105 cm^2
(e) 104 cm^2
(f) The answers are different because the entire shape (A+B+C+D+E) is *not* a triangle. If you draw the five small shapes carefully, you will notice the sloping sides of the large shape are not straight.

EXERCISE 11.4 (page 181)

1 20 m^2

2 6 m^2

3 14 cm^2

4 36 m^2

5 30 cm^2

6 7 m^2

7 84 cm^2

8 16 cm^2

9 33 m^2

10 9 cm^2

11 32 cm^2

12 756 cm^2

EXERCISE 11.5 (page 183)

1 22 cm^2

2 90 cm^2

3 39 cm^2

4 78 cm^2

5 139 cm^2

6 86 cm^2

EXERCISE 11.6 (page 185)

1 (a) 4 cm
(b) 3 cm
(c) 12 cm^2
(d) $n = 6$
(e) $p = 14$
(f) $A = n - 1 + \frac{1}{2}p$
$= 6 - 1 + \frac{1}{2} \times 14$
$= 5 + 7$
$= 12$ cm^2
(g) yes

2 (a) 4 cm
(b) 1 cm
(c) 2 cm^2
(d) $n = 0$
(e) $p = 6$
(f) $A = n - 1 + \frac{1}{2}p$
$= 0 - 1 + \frac{1}{2} \times 6$
$= {}^{-}1 + 3$
$= 2$ cm^2
(g) yes

3 $A = n - 1 + \frac{1}{2}p$
$= 6 - 1 + \frac{1}{2} \times 4 = 5 + 2 = 7$ cm^2

4 $A = n - 1 + \frac{1}{2}p$
$= 1 - 1 + \frac{1}{2} \times 4 = 0 + 2 = 2\text{ cm}^2$

5 $A = n - 1 + \frac{1}{2}p$
$= 4 - 1 + \frac{1}{2} \times 7 = 3 + 3\frac{1}{2} = 6\frac{1}{2}\text{ cm}^2$

6 $A = n - 1 + \frac{1}{2}p$
$= 6 - 1 + \frac{1}{2} \times 8 = 5 + 4 = 9\text{ cm}^2$

7 $A = n - 1 + \frac{1}{2}p$
$= 21 - 1 + \frac{1}{2} \times 5 = 20 + 2\frac{1}{2} = 22\frac{1}{2}\text{ cm}^2$

8 $A = n - 1 + \frac{1}{2}p$
$= 8 - 1 + \frac{1}{2} \times 4 = 7 + 2 = 9\text{ cm}^2$

EXERCISE 11.7 (page 186)

1 (a) 48 m^2 (b) 8 litres
2 (a) 25 cm^2 (b) 150 cm^2
3 (a) 1600 m^2 (b) 3200
4 (a)
54 m
16 m
50 m
20 m
(b) 280 m^2
5 72
6 (a) 5488 m^2 (b) 5500 m^2
7 125
8 (a) 104 m^2 (b) 21 litres
9 3 rolls
10 (a) 441 cm^2
(b) 105 000 cm^2
(c) Paper in a box of tissues is $200 \times 441\text{ cm}^2 = 88\,200\text{ cm}^2$
Paper in the towel is 105 000 cm^2
The paper towel has more paper.

EXERCISE 11.8 (page 188)

1 (a) 50 000 m^2
(b) 32 000 m^2
(c) 1 000 000 m^2
(d) 5500 m^2
(e) 910 m^2
2 (a) 4 ha
(b) 6.8 ha
(c) 0.1 ha
(d) 0.95 ha
(e) 3.95 ha
3 27 ha
4 5
5 3 ha
6 66 sections

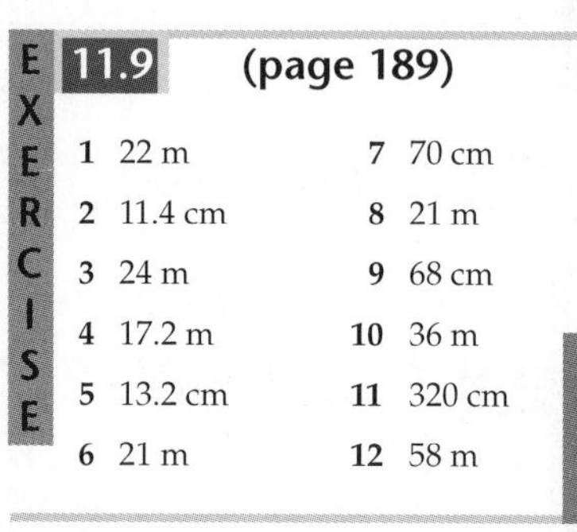

EXERCISE 11.9 (page 189)

1 22 m
2 11.4 cm
3 24 m
4 17.2 m
5 13.2 cm
6 21 m
7 70 cm
8 21 m
9 68 cm
10 36 m
11 320 cm
12 58 m

Chapter 12—Area and circumference of circles

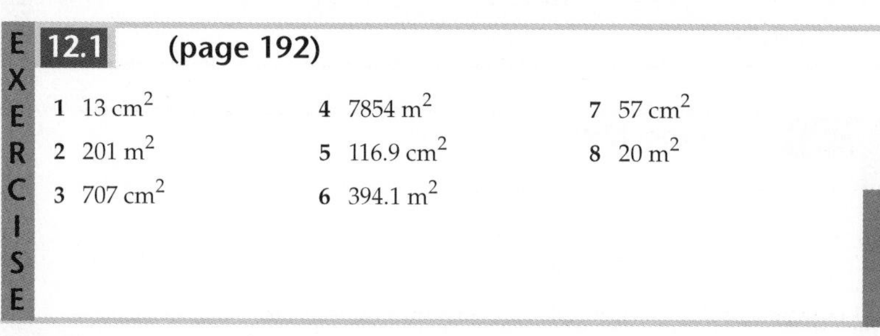

EXERCISE 12.1 (page 192)

1 13 cm^2
2 201 m^2
3 707 cm^2
4 7854 m^2
5 116.9 cm^2
6 394.1 m^2
7 57 cm^2
8 20 m^2

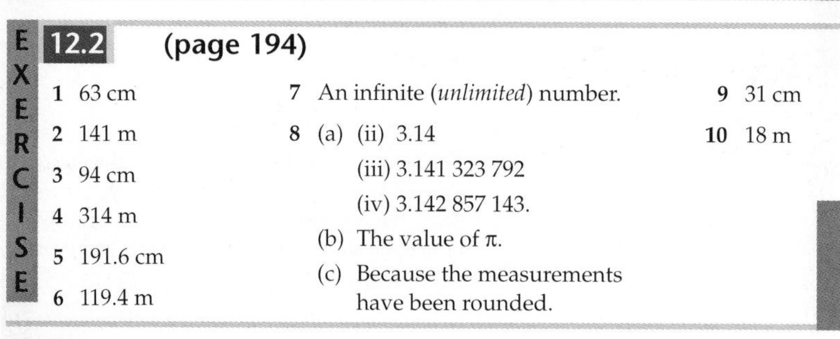

EXERCISE 12.2 (page 194)

1 63 cm
2 141 m
3 94 cm
4 314 m
5 191.6 cm
6 119.4 m
7 An infinite (*unlimited*) number.
8 (a) (ii) 3.14
(iii) 3.141 323 792
(iv) 3.142 857 143.
(b) The value of π.
(c) Because the measurements have been rounded.
9 31 cm
10 18 m

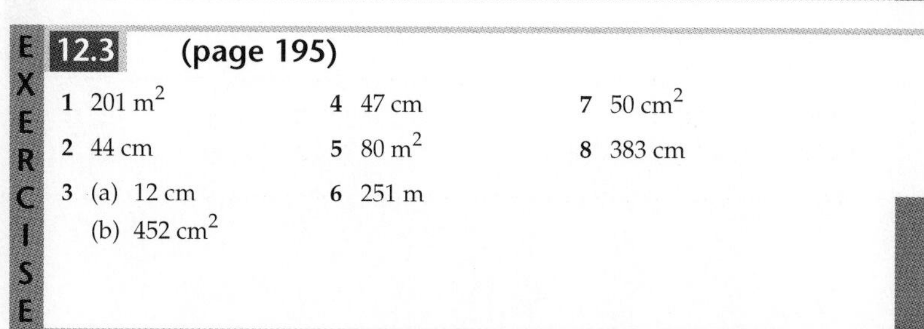

EXERCISE 12.3 (page 195)

1 201 m^2
2 44 cm
3 (a) 12 cm
(b) 452 cm^2
4 47 cm
5 80 m^2
6 251 m
7 50 cm^2
8 383 cm

Chapter 13—Volume

Exercise 13.1 (page 196)

1 m^3
2 cm^3
3 cm^3
4 km^3
5 cm^3
6 cm^3
7 m^3
8 m^3
9 cm^3
10 cm^3

Exercise 13.2 (page 197)

1 5 cm^3
2 4 cm^3
3 8 cm^3
4 6 cm^3
5 40 cm^3
6 40 cm^3
7 15 cm^3
8 (a) 20 cm^3
(b) (i) 40 cm^3
(ii) 80 cm^3
9 (a) 72 cm^3
(b) 48 cm^3

Exercise 13.3 (page 199)

1 21 m^3
2 72 cm^3
3 120 cm^3
4 120 cm^3
5 8 m^3
6 125 cm^3
7 (a) 40
(b) 20
(c) 144
(d) 180
(e) 64
(f) 1
(g) 2
(h) 4
8 27 cm^3
9 216 cm^3

Exercise 13.4 (page 202)

1 42 cm^3
2 150 cm^3
3 60 cm^3
4 120 cm^3
5 240 cm^3
6 120 cm^3
7 120 cm^3
8 150 cm^3
9 100.5 cm^3
10 150 cm^3
11 72 cm^3
12 300 cm^3
13 (a)

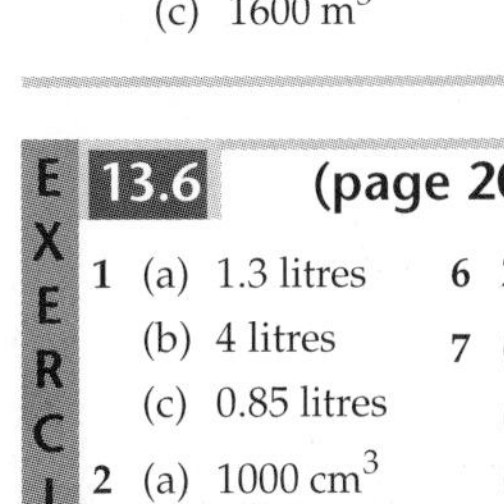

(b) 96 cm^3

Exercise 13.5 (page 203)

1 (a) 120
(b) 8
(c) 960 cm^3
(d) 960
2 11 440 cm^3
3 (a) 16
(b) 6
(c) 96
(d) 8
(e) 768
4 18 m^3
5 (a) a = 3, b = 16, c = 50, d = 1
(b) 100 m^2
(c) 1600 m^3

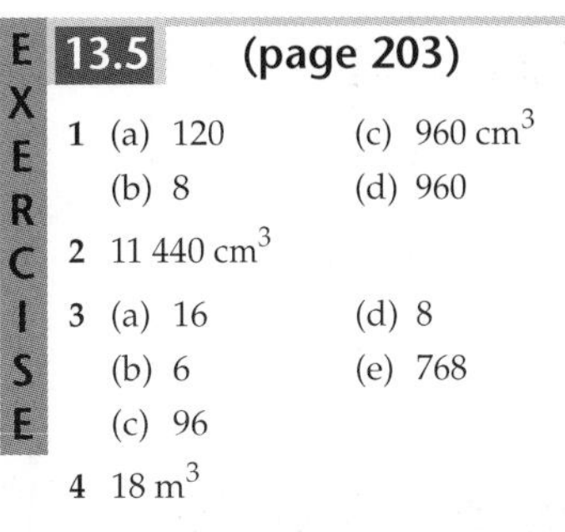

Exercise 13.6 (page 205)

1 (a) 1.3 litres
(b) 4 litres
(c) 0.85 litres
2 (a) 1000 cm^3
(b) 2000 cm^3
(c) 2300 cm^3
(d) 4200 cm^3
3 2
4 (a) 400 g
(b) 30 kg
(c) 1.2 kg
(d) 50 g
5 360 mL
6 20 litres
7 (a) 3240 cm^3
(b) 3240 mL
(c) 3.24 litres
8 20 cm
9 (a) 283 cm^3
(b) B: 250 mL
10 38 mL

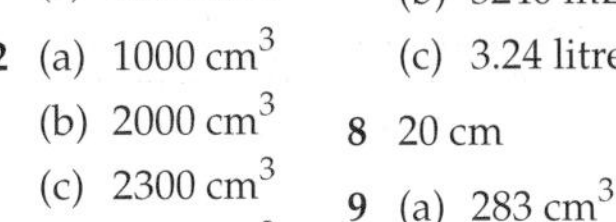

Chapter 14—Angles

Exercise 14.1 (page 207)

1

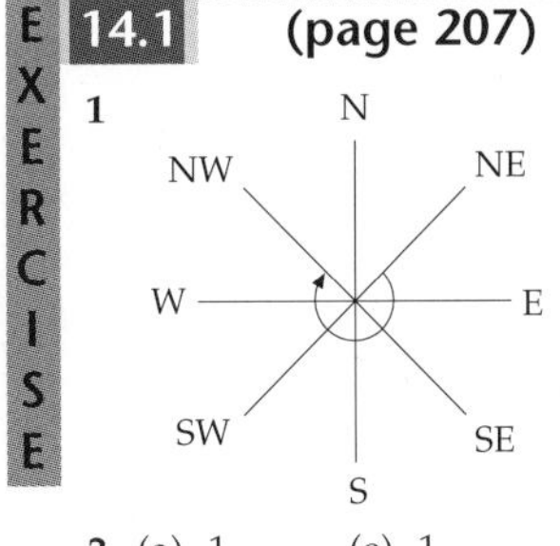

2 (a) 1
(b) 3
(c) 1
(d) 2
(e) 1
(f) 4
(g) 3
(h) 2

3 (a)

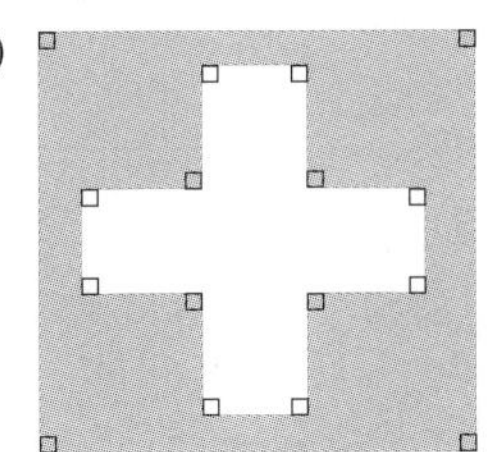

(b) 16

4 (a) (i) 1
(ii) 2
(iii) 3
(b) (i) 8 o'clock
(ii) 11 o'clock
(iii) 2 o'clock

5 (a)

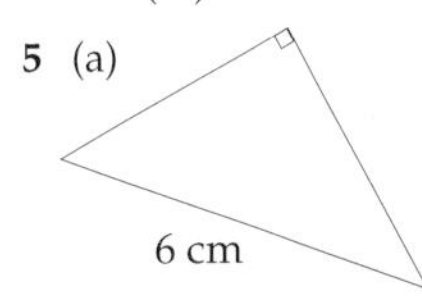

(one possible answer is shown)
(b) Yes, many answers are possible, both *below* and *above* the 6 cm line.

Exercise 14.2 (page 208)

1 acute
2 obtuse
3 acute
4 reflex
5 obtuse
6 acute
7 obtuse
8 reflex
9 acute
10 reflex
11 obtuse
12 acute
13 (c) 10
(d) 4
(e) 10
14 reflex
15 (a) 4
(b) 8

Exercise 14.3 (page 209)

1 (a) $\widehat{XYZ}$ or $\widehat{ZYX}$
(b) $\widehat{DEF}$ or $\widehat{FED}$
(c) $\widehat{HIJ}$ or $\widehat{JIH}$
(d) $\widehat{AGP}$ or $\widehat{PGA}$
(e) $\widehat{XZY}$ or $\widehat{YZX}$
(f) $\widehat{DEF}$ or $\widehat{FED}$
(g) $\widehat{GIH}$ or $\widehat{HIG}$
(h) $\widehat{ADB}$ or $\widehat{BDA}$

2 1 = $\widehat{EFG}$ or $\widehat{GFE}$
2 = $\widehat{DEF}$ or $\widehat{FED}$
3 = $\widehat{IHL}$ or $\widehat{IHK}$ or $\widehat{KHI}$ or $\widehat{LHI}$
4 = $\widehat{IJK}$ or $\widehat{KJI}$
5 = $\widehat{HIJ}$ or $\widehat{JIH}$
6 = $\widehat{BAG}$ or $\widehat{GAB}$ (other answers are also possible)
7 = $\widehat{DGF}$ or $\widehat{FGD}$ (other answers are also possible)
8 = $\widehat{ABC}$ or $\widehat{CBA}$

3 (a) 8
(b) 10
(c) 9
(d) 6
(e) 7
(f) 10
(g) 5
(h) 11
(i) 10
(j) 12

4 1 = $\widehat{PQR}$ or $\widehat{RQP}$
2 = $\widehat{RQS}$ or $\widehat{SQR}$
3 = $\widehat{PQS}$ or $\widehat{SQP}$

5 a = $\widehat{JNK}$ or $\widehat{KNJ}$
b = $\widehat{KNL}$ or $\widehat{LNK}$
c = $\widehat{LNM}$ or $\widehat{MNL}$
d = $\widehat{JNM}$ or $\widehat{MNJ}$

Exercise 14.4 (page 211)

1 18°
2 67°
3 170°
4 100°
5 83°
6 215°

Exercise 14.5 (page 213)

1 70°
2 35°
3 140°
4 105°
5 40°
6 80°
7 15°
8 85°
9 70°
10 30°
11 95°
12 132°
13 45°
14 150°
15 77°
16 127°
17 115°
18 21°

19

60°

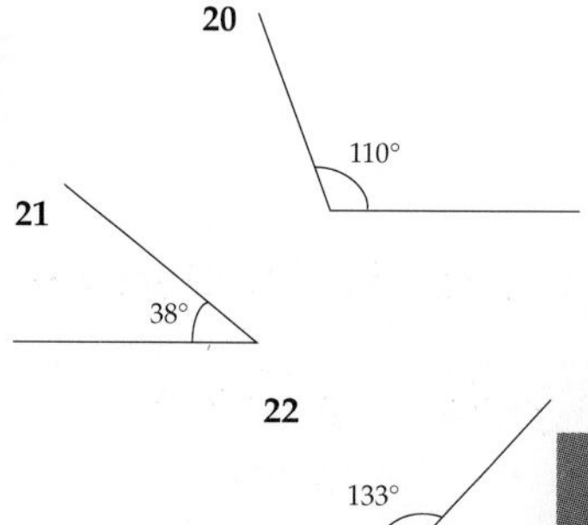

22

133°

Exercise 14.6 (page 215)

2 obtuse, 110°, 111°
3 acute, 20°, 18°
4 acute, 60° or 70°, 65°
5 acute, 80°, 81°
6 obtuse, 160°, 158°
7 right, 90°, 90°

Exercise 14.7 (page 217)

1 a = 110°
2 b = 150°
3 c = 90°
4 d = 137°
5 e = 50°
6 f = 120°
7 g = 70°
8 h = 130°
9 i = 143°
10 j = 63°
11 k = 102°
12 l = 32°
13 m = 3°
14 n = 88°
15 o = 47°

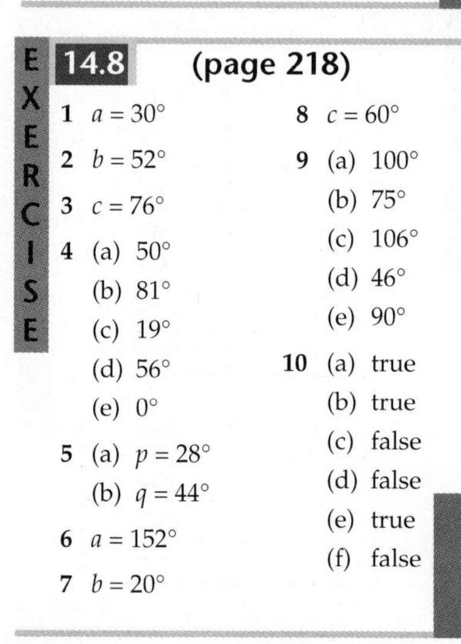

Exercise 14.8 (page 218)

1 a = 30°
2 b = 52°
3 c = 76°
4 (a) 50°
(b) 81°
(c) 19°
(d) 56°
(e) 0°
5 (a) p = 28°
(b) q = 44°
6 a = 152°
7 b = 20°
8 c = 60°
9 (a) 100°
(b) 75°
(c) 106°
(d) 46°
(e) 90°
10 (a) true
(b) true
(c) false
(d) false
(e) true
(f) false

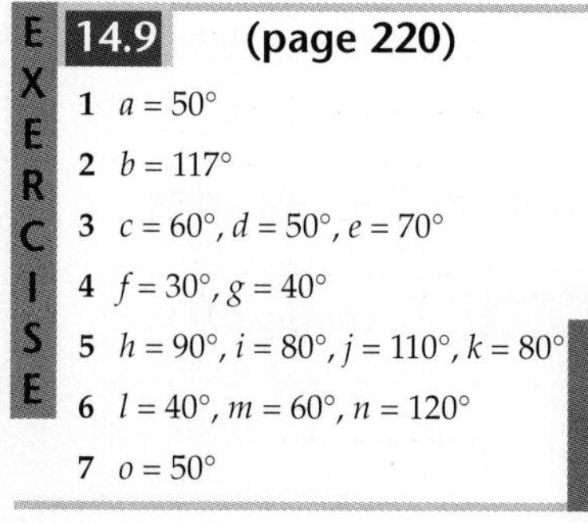

Exercise 14.9 (page 220)

1 a = 50°
2 b = 117°
3 c = 60°, d = 50°, e = 70°
4 f = 30°, g = 40°
5 h = 90°, i = 80°, j = 110°, k = 80°
6 l = 40°, m = 60°, n = 120°
7 o = 50°

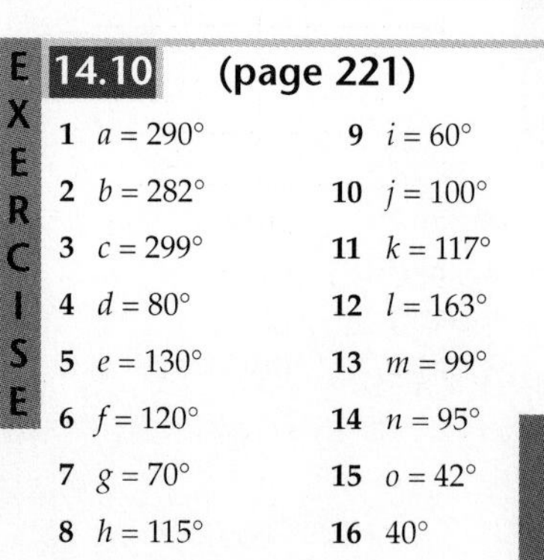

Exercise 14.10 (page 221)

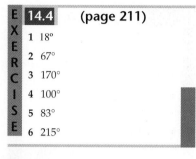

1 a = 290°
2 b = 282°
3 c = 299°
4 d = 80°
5 e = 130°
6 f = 120°
7 g = 70°
8 h = 115°
9 i = 60°
10 j = 100°
11 k = 117°
12 l = 163°
13 m = 99°
14 n = 95°
15 o = 42°
16 40°

EXERCISE 14.11 (page 222)

1 310°
2 265°
3 200°
4 327°
5 281°
6 219°

EXERCISE 14.12 (page 223)

1

Number of hours	Angle turned
1	30°
2	60°
3	90°
4	120°
5	150°
6	180°
7	210°
8	240°
9	270°
10	300°
11	330°
12	360°

2 (a) 90° (b) 210° (c) 150°

3

Number of minutes	Angle turned
5	30°
10	60°
15	90°
20	120°
25	150°
30	180°
35	210°
40	240°
45	270°
50	300°
55	330°
60	360°

4 (a) 60° (b) 90° (c) 270°
5 (a) 60° ÷ 10 = 6°
(b) 24°
6 24 times

EXERCISE 14.13 (page 226)

1 $a = 60°$
2 $b = 60°$
3 $c = 50°$
4 $d = 28°$
5 $e = 23°$
6 $f = 80°$
7 $g = 40°$
8 $h = 44°$
9 $i = 56°, j = 61°$
10 $k = 37°, l = 69°$
11 $m = 85°, n = 60°, o = 40°$
12 $p = 27°, q = 72°, r = 66°$
13 (a) 120° (d) 7°
(b) 40° (e) 1°
(c) 40° (f) 60°
14 The triangle in (e) { 1°, 178°, 1° }

15 D: (the three angles add to only 170°)

EXERCISE 14.14 (page 227)

1 (a) vertically opposite angles are equal
(b) angles in a triangle add to 180°
(c) angles at a point add to 360°
(d) adjacent angles on a straight line add to 180°

2

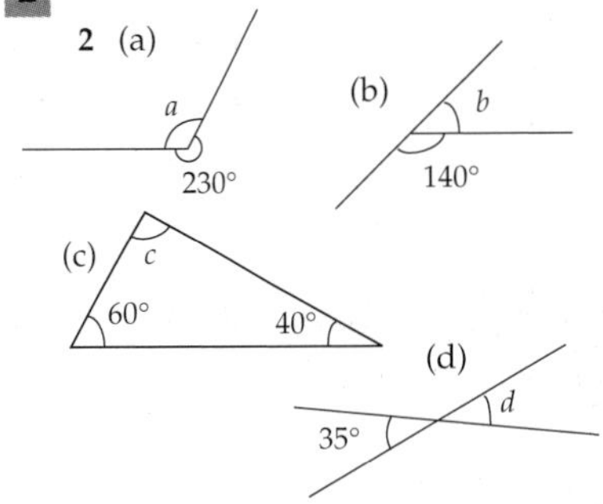

3 $a = 60°$ (∠'s on line)
4 $b = 118°$ (vert. opp. ∠'s)
5 $c = 235°$ (∠'s at pt)
6 $d = 37°$ (∠ sum of △)
7 $e = 110°$ (∠'s on line)
8 $f = 120°$ (∠'s at pt)
9 $g = 35°$ (vert. opp. ∠'s)
10 $h = 109°$ (∠ sum of △)
11 $i = 50°$ (∠ sum of △)
$j = 280°$ (∠'s at pt)
$k = 130°$ (∠'s on line)

Chapter 15—Reflection

EXERCISE 15.1 (page 230)

1
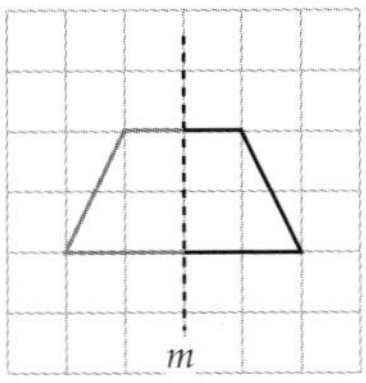

2
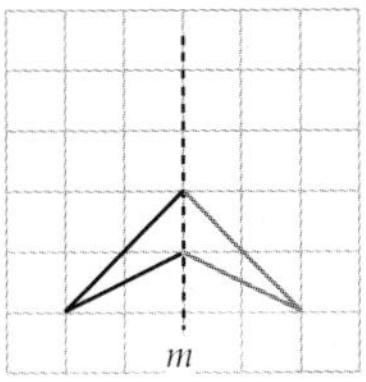

3
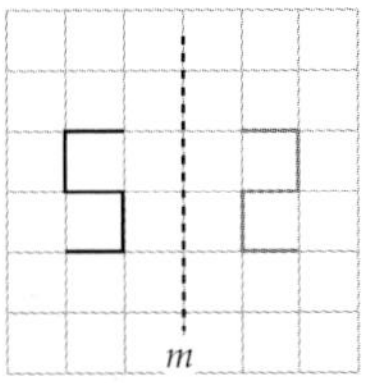

4
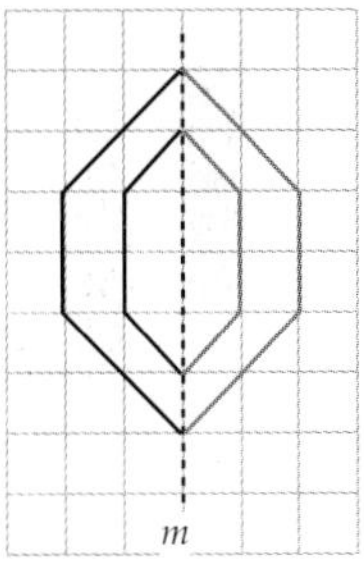

5
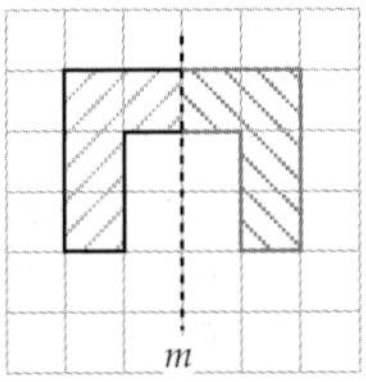

6
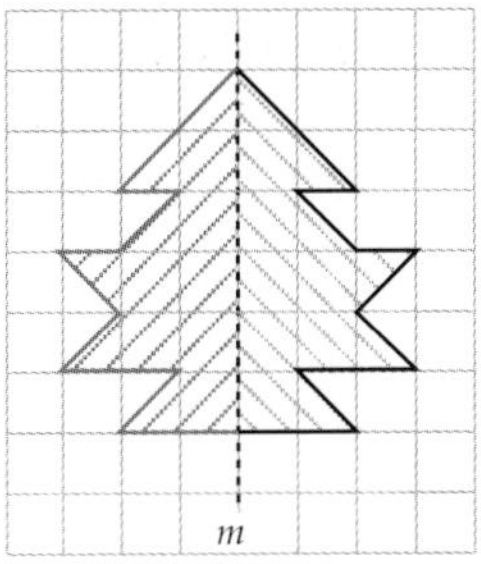

7

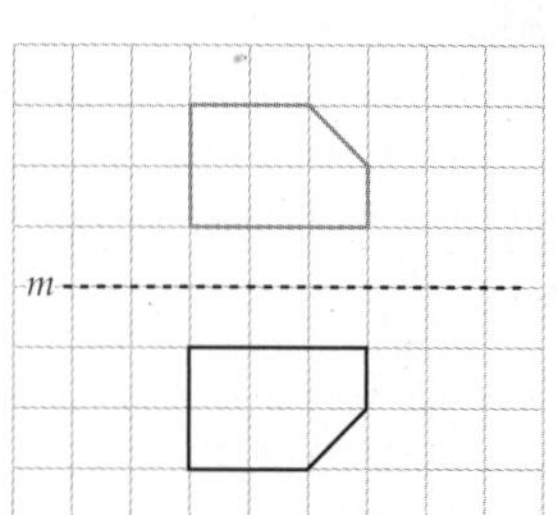

8

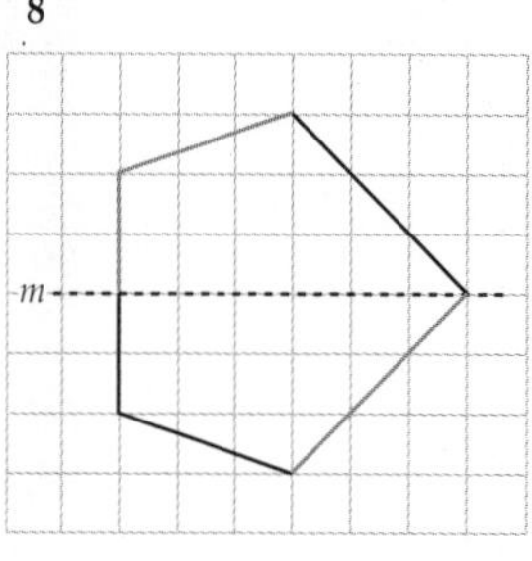

9

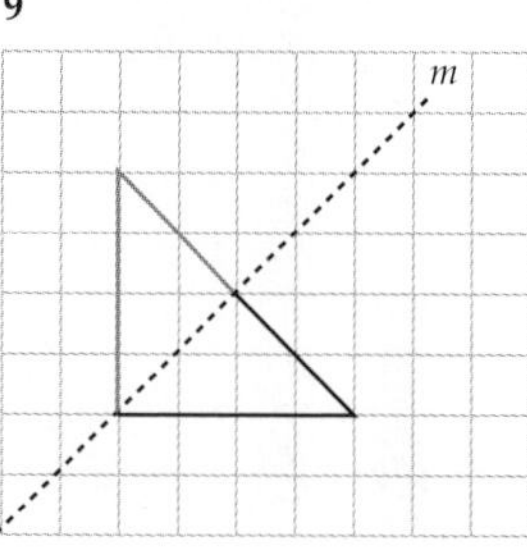

10

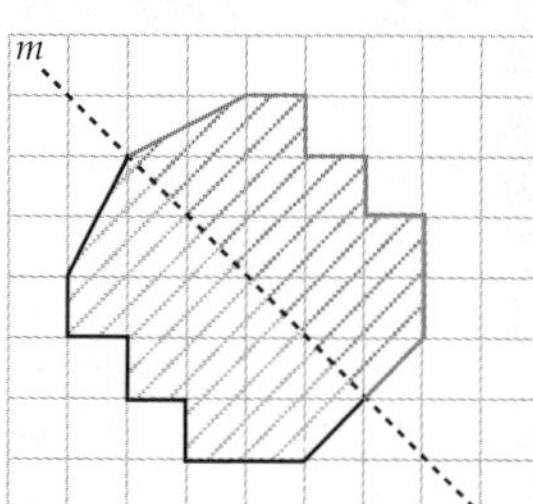

11 C

12 (a)

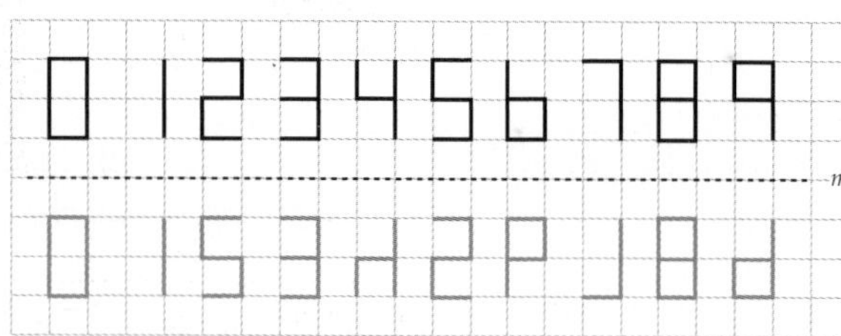

(b) 0, 1, 3, 8

13 (a)

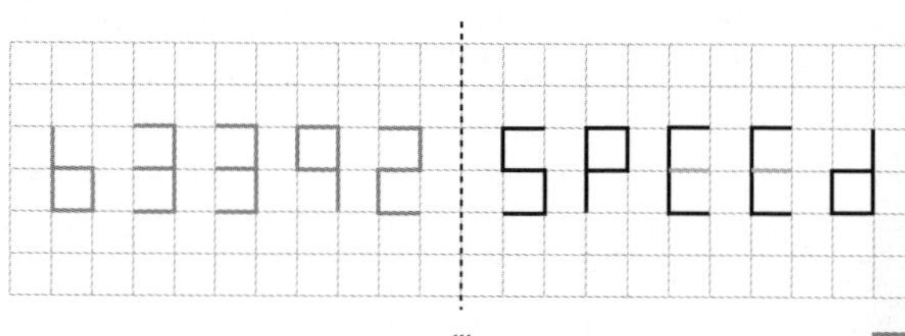

(b) 63 392

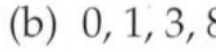

EXERCISE 15.2 (page 232)

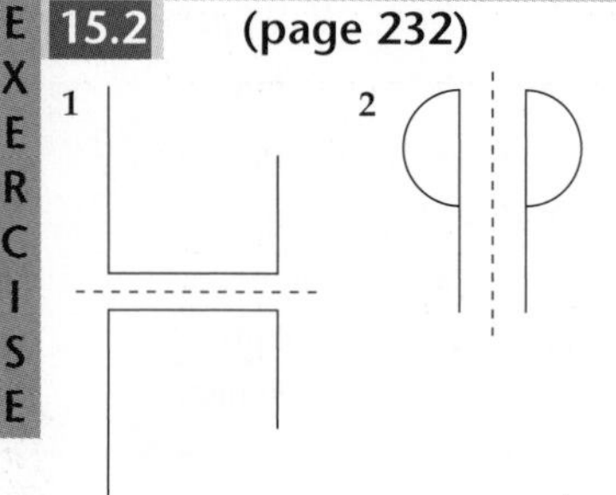

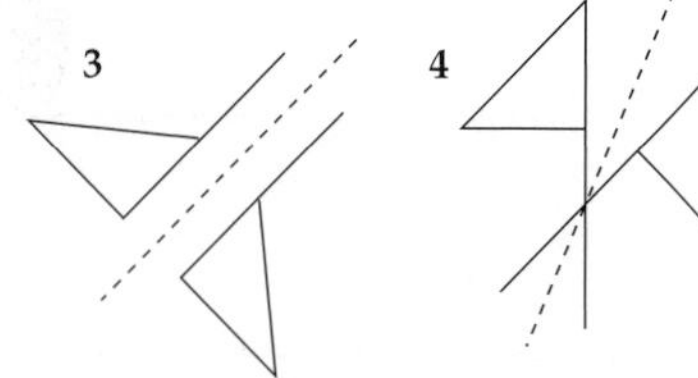

5 *n*

6 AF

7 (a) CD
(b) GH
(c) AB and CD

8 CD, QR, ST, VX

EXERCISE 15.3 (page 234)

1

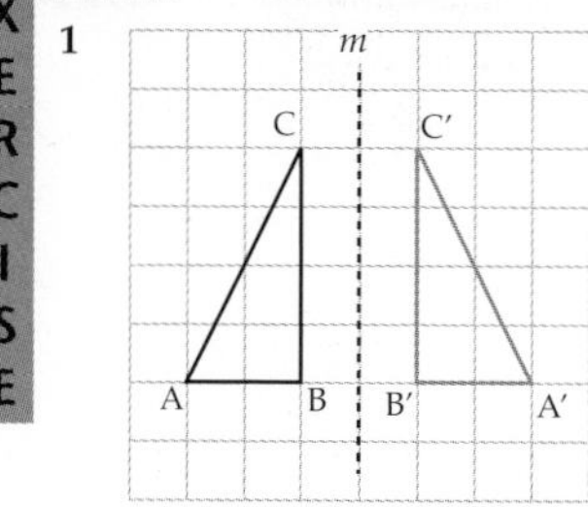

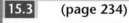

2

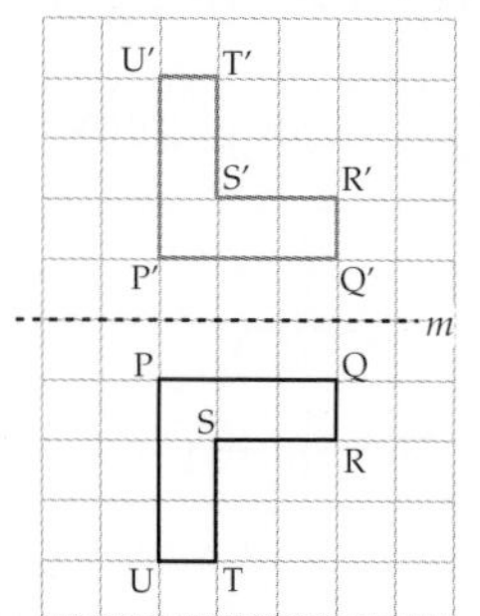

3

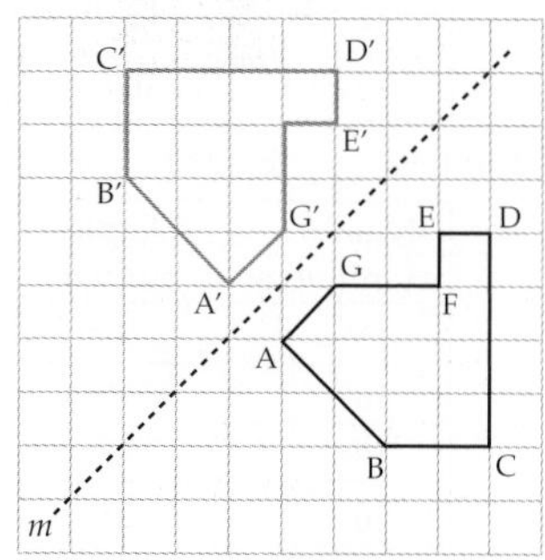

4

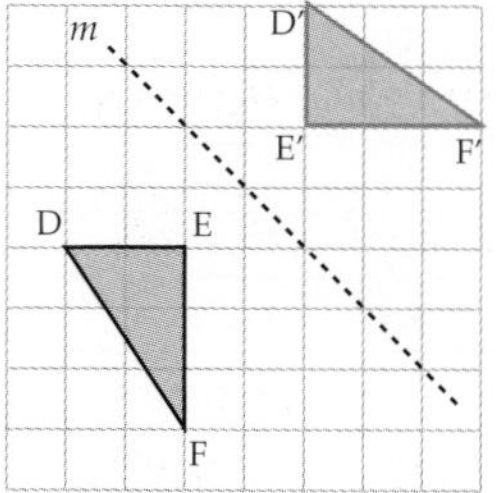

5 (a) B	(b) D	(c) F	(d) BC	(e) DF	(f) $A\widehat{D}F$
6 (a) Y	(b) WX	(c) X	(d) P	(e) YX	
(f) W	(g) L	(h) RP	(i) $W\widehat{X}Y$	(j) $P\widehat{R}Q$	

7 See page 483 for answer.

EXERCISE 15.4 (page 237)

1 B, D, F

2 (a) p (b) j (c) l (d) b (e) f (f) k

3 (a) C (b) DC (c) 4 cm (d) 8 cm (e) 45° (f) 90°

4 (a) (i) 5 cm (ii) 3 cm (iii) 6 cm
(b) 74°

5 (a)

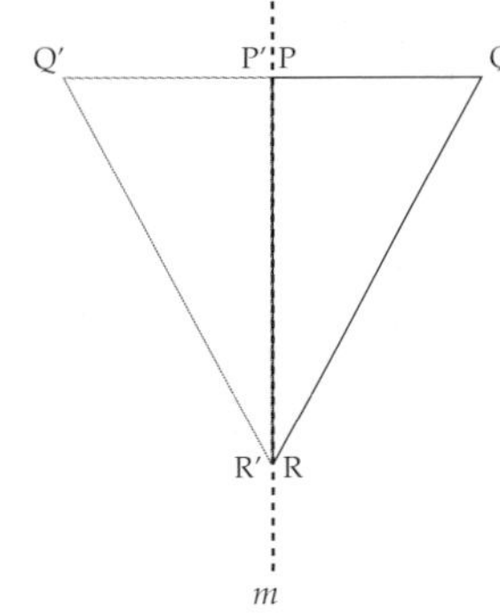

(b) clockwise
(c) anti-clockwise
(d) sense changes when an object is reflected

6 (a) $a = 12$ cm, $b = 6$ cm, $c = 11$ cm, $d = 10$ cm
(b) $x = 25°$, $y = 70°$, $z = 20°$

7 $x = 50°$, $y = 40°$, $z = 90°$

8 (a) (i) S (ii) P (iii) PR (iv) PS (v) $\widehat{SRP}$
(b) P and R
(c) 90°

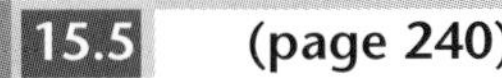
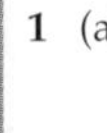

EXERCISE 15.5 (page 240)

1 (a)

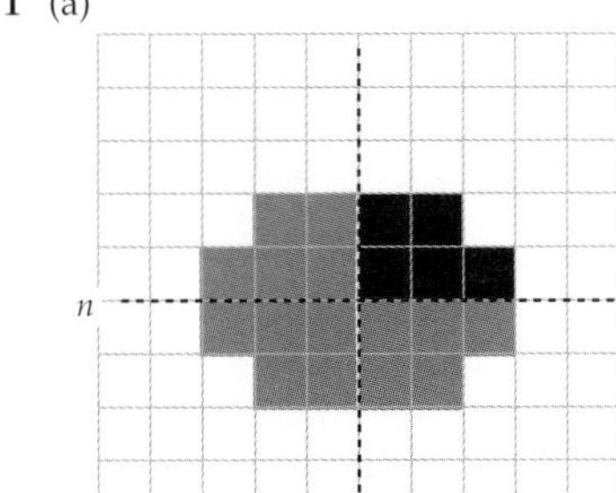

(b)

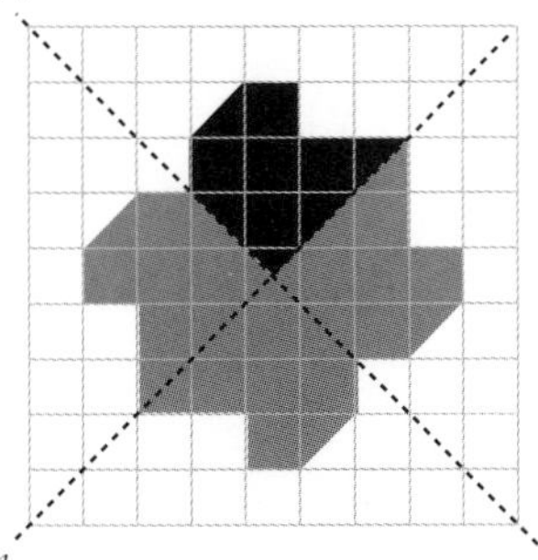

2 (a) C (b) F (c) AF, CD, DE (d) H

3 (a) 5 cm (b) 10 cm (c) 6 cm (d) 3 cm

4 (a) (i) DG (ii) GF (iii) $\widehat{DGF}$ (iv) $\widehat{GDF}$
(b) (i) FE (ii) FG (iii) $\widehat{GFE}$
(c) DG, EF, FG

5 (a)

Reflection in line	Image of C	Image of AB	Image of $\widehat{ABD}$
p	D	BA	$\widehat{BAC}$
q	C	AD	$\widehat{BDA}$
r	B	DC	$\widehat{DCA}$
s	A	CB	$\widehat{CBD}$

(b) square

6 (a) 4
(b) (i) B (ii) F (iii) BC
(c) (i) B (ii) A (iii) FE
(d) B and E

Chapter 16—Rotation

EXERCISE 16.1 (page 244)

1 (b) yes

2 (b) 2 (c) 180°

3 (c) 120° (d) 240°, 360°

4 (a)

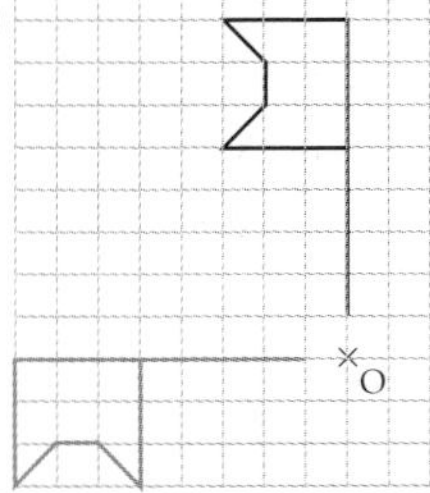

(b)

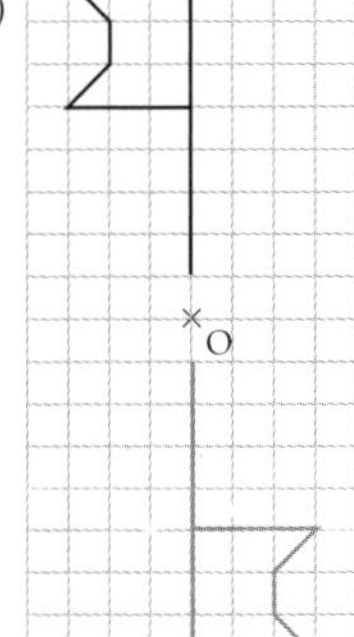

(c)

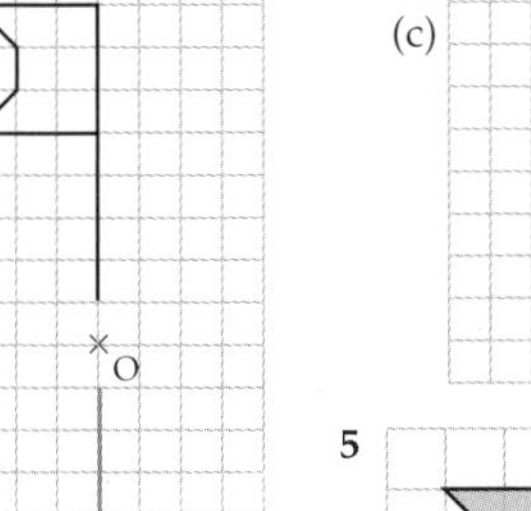
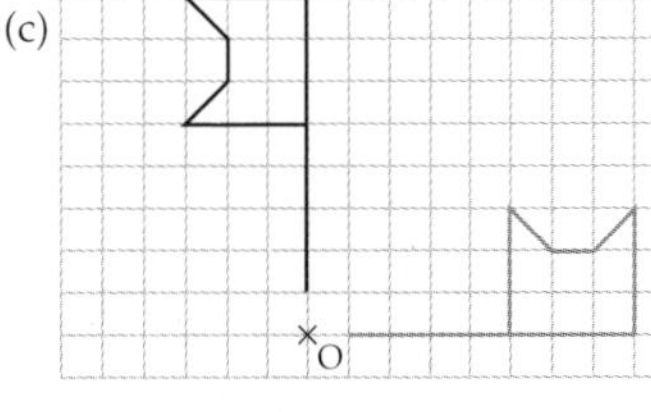

5

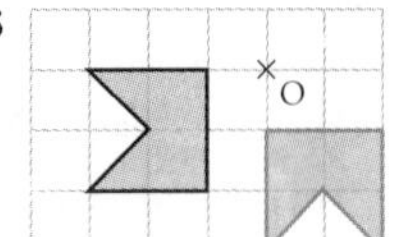

6

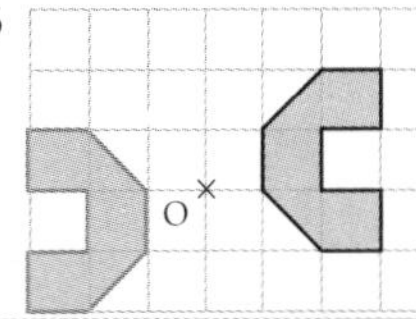

EXERCISE 16.2 (page 246)

1

2

3

4

5

6

7

8

9

10

EXERCISE 16.3 (page 247)

1 (a) P
(b) R
(c) QS

2 (a) E
(b) FD

3 (a) C
(b) O
(c) 144°, 216°, 288°

4 (a) (i) D
(ii) B
(iii) E
(b) 45°

5 (a) rotation
(b) reflection
(c) rotation

6 (a) P (b) 90°

7 (a) D
(b) C
(c) T

8

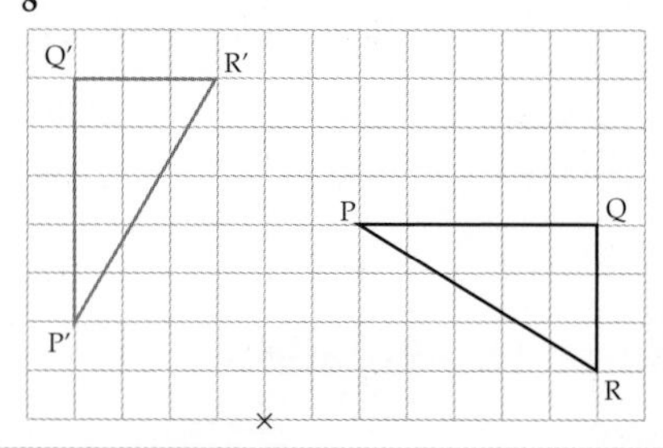

Chapter 17—Translation

Starter (page 250)

- *sottopasso* means 'underpass'
- Q8 petrol comes from Kuwait

EXERCISE 17.1 (page 250)

1 (a) (i) 24 mm (iii) 24 mm
(ii) 24 mm (iv) 24 mm
(b) All four measurements are the same.

2 (a) (i) 23 mm (iii) 23 mm
(ii) 23 mm (iv) 23 mm
(b) All four measurements are the same.

EXERCISE 17.2 (page 251)

1

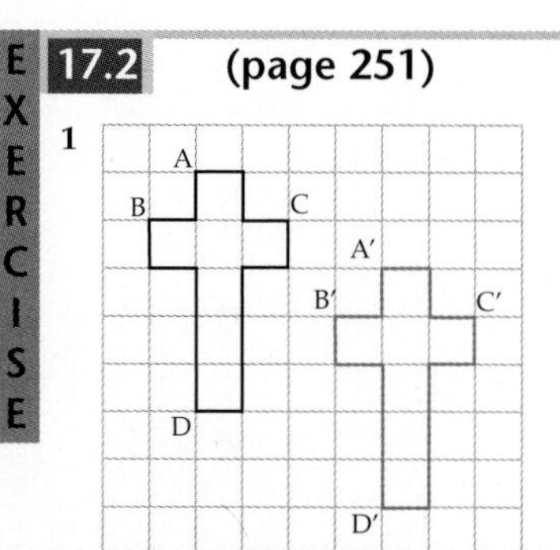

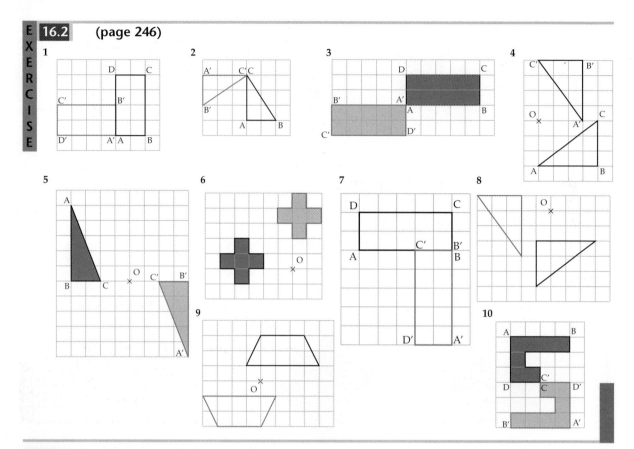

2

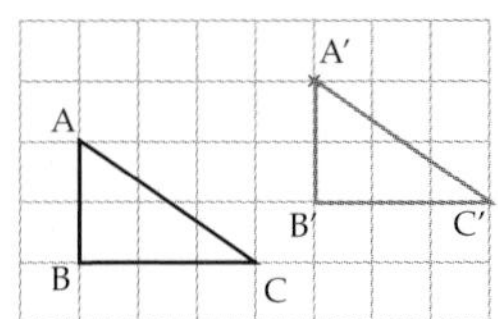

3

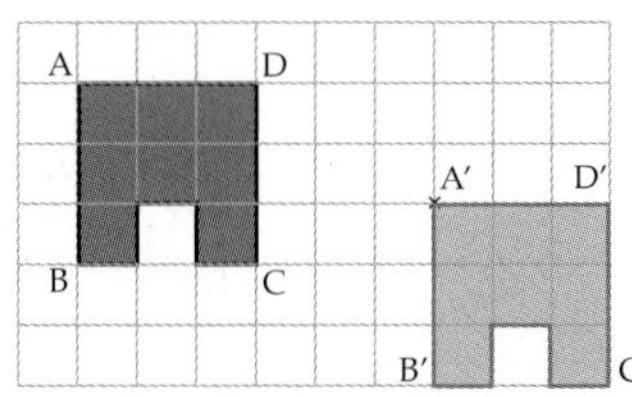

4

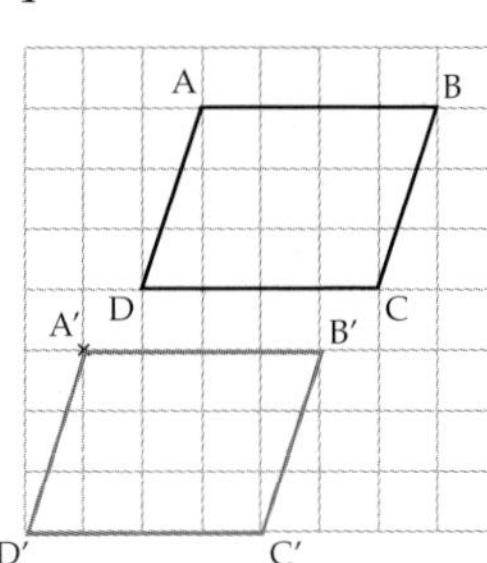

5

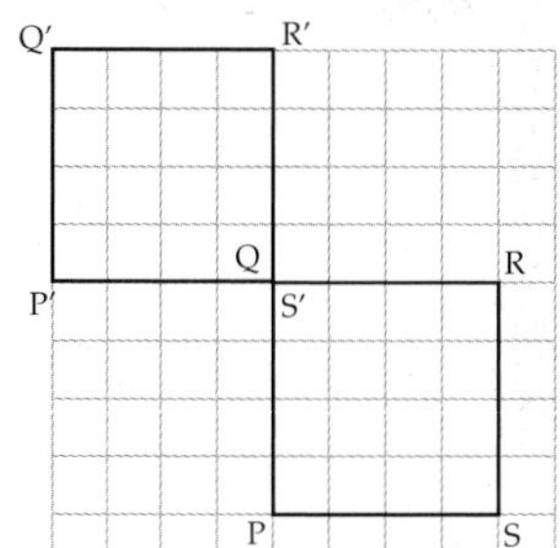

6

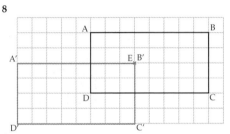

7

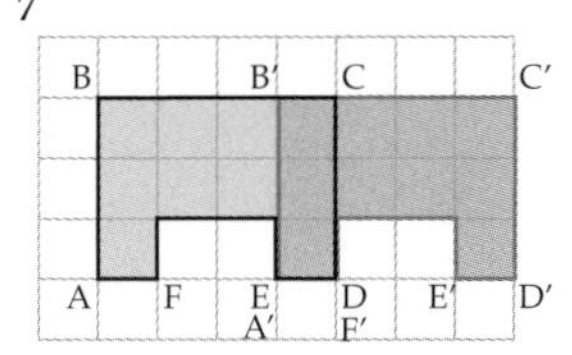

8

9

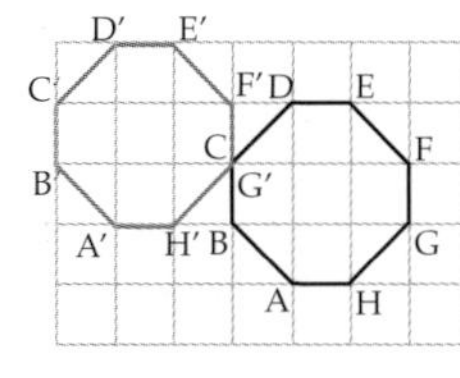

10

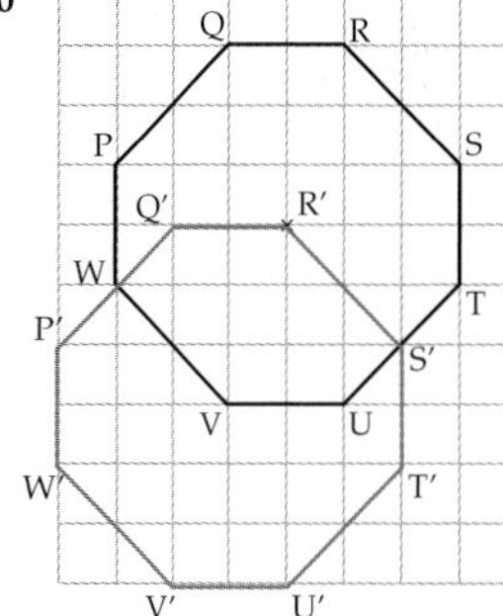

EXERCISE 17.3 (page 254)

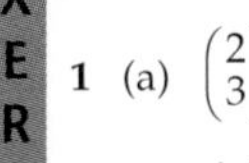

1 (a) $\begin{pmatrix}2\\3\end{pmatrix}$ (b) $\begin{pmatrix}5\\1\end{pmatrix}$ (c) $\begin{pmatrix}-2\\4\end{pmatrix}$ (d) $\begin{pmatrix}-3\\-3\end{pmatrix}$ (e) $\begin{pmatrix}6\\-1\end{pmatrix}$ (f) $\begin{pmatrix}0\\3\end{pmatrix}$ (g) $\begin{pmatrix}-4\\0\end{pmatrix}$ (h) $\begin{pmatrix}0\\-6\end{pmatrix}$

2 $\begin{pmatrix}3\\3\end{pmatrix}$

3 $\begin{pmatrix}5\\1\end{pmatrix}$

4 $\begin{pmatrix}2\\3\end{pmatrix}$

5 $\begin{pmatrix}0\\3\end{pmatrix}$

6 $\begin{pmatrix}3\\0\end{pmatrix}$

7 $\begin{pmatrix}-3\\3\end{pmatrix}$

8 $\begin{pmatrix}-1\\5\end{pmatrix}$

9 $\begin{pmatrix}-3\\2\end{pmatrix}$

10 $\begin{pmatrix}0\\-4\end{pmatrix}$

11 $\begin{pmatrix}-2\\0\end{pmatrix}$

12 $\begin{pmatrix}-2\\-3\end{pmatrix}$

13 $\begin{pmatrix}3\\-1\end{pmatrix}$

14 $\begin{pmatrix}-3\\-1\end{pmatrix}$

15 $\begin{pmatrix}1\\-4\end{pmatrix}$

16 $\begin{pmatrix}-6\\-4\end{pmatrix}$

17–31

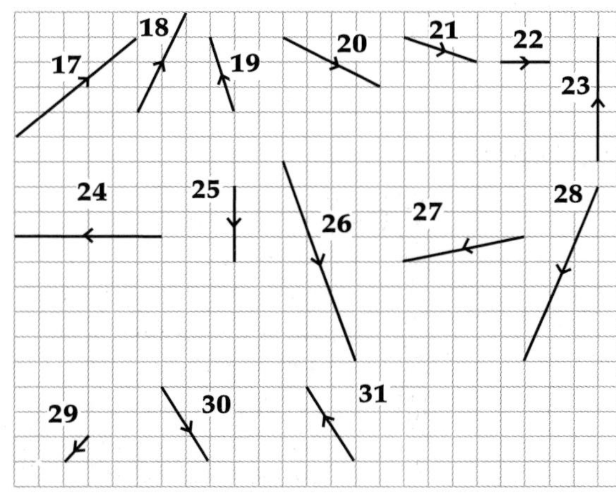

32 (a) $\begin{pmatrix}2\\5\end{pmatrix}$ (b) $\begin{pmatrix}-5\\-2\end{pmatrix}$ (c) $\begin{pmatrix}5\\2\end{pmatrix}$ (d) $\begin{pmatrix}5\\-2\end{pmatrix}$ (e) $\begin{pmatrix}-2\\5\end{pmatrix}$ (f) $\begin{pmatrix}2\\-5\end{pmatrix}$ (g) $\begin{pmatrix}-2\\-5\end{pmatrix}$ (h) $\begin{pmatrix}-5\\2\end{pmatrix}$

17.4 (page 255)

1

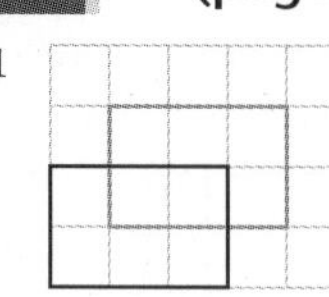

2

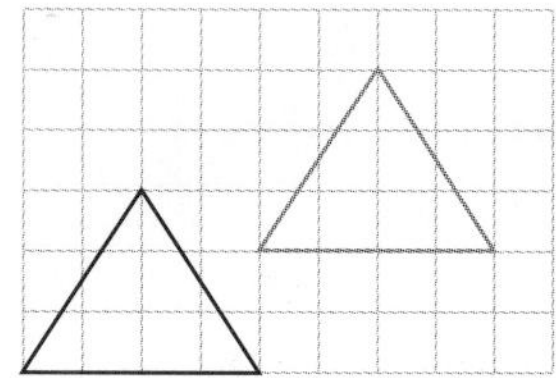

3

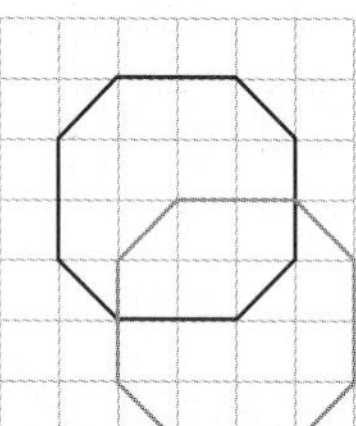

4

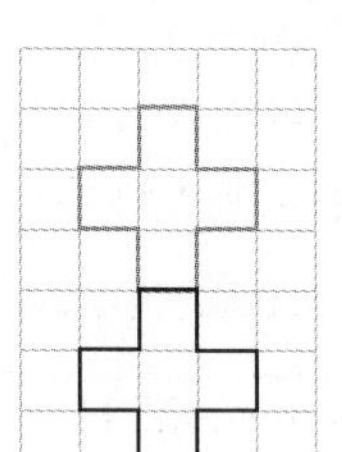

5

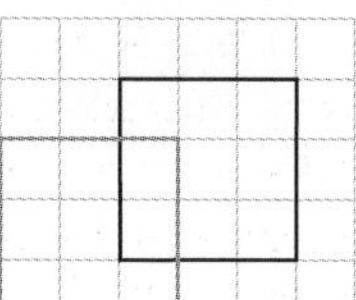

6

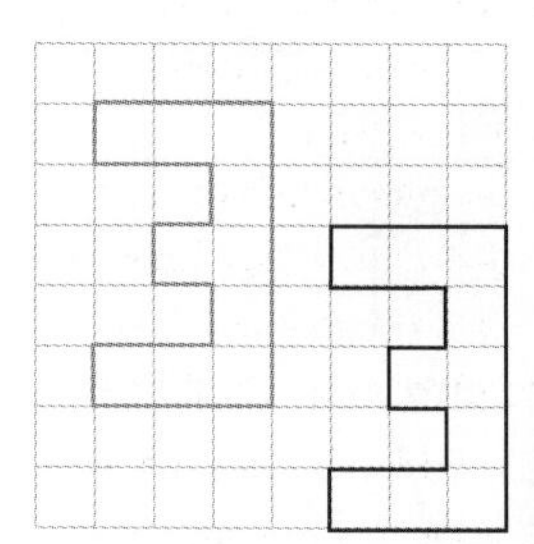

EXERCISE 17.5 (page 256)

1 $\begin{pmatrix} 6 \\ 1 \end{pmatrix}$

2 $\begin{pmatrix} -1 \\ 2 \end{pmatrix}$

3 $\begin{pmatrix} 0 \\ -3 \end{pmatrix}$

4 $\begin{pmatrix} -2 \\ -4 \end{pmatrix}$

5 $\begin{pmatrix} 2 \\ 0 \end{pmatrix}$

6 $\begin{pmatrix} -4 \\ 3 \end{pmatrix}$

7 $\begin{pmatrix} 5 \\ 4 \end{pmatrix}$, $\begin{pmatrix} 6 \\ 4 \end{pmatrix}$, $\begin{pmatrix} 0 \\ -2 \end{pmatrix}$, $\begin{pmatrix} -4 \\ 7 \end{pmatrix}$, $\begin{pmatrix} -6 \\ -1 \end{pmatrix}$, $\begin{pmatrix} -3 \\ -5 \end{pmatrix}$, $\begin{pmatrix} 0 \\ -4 \end{pmatrix}$, $\begin{pmatrix} 2 \\ -3 \end{pmatrix}$

Investigation—Back-tracking (page 257)

1 $\begin{pmatrix} 8 \\ 4 \end{pmatrix}$

2 $\begin{pmatrix} -8 \\ -4 \end{pmatrix}$

3 B

A

4 $\begin{pmatrix} 1 \\ -4 \end{pmatrix}$

5 (a) $\begin{pmatrix} -1 \\ -2 \end{pmatrix}$ (b) $\begin{pmatrix} 3 \\ 1 \end{pmatrix}$ (c) $\begin{pmatrix} -4 \\ 5 \end{pmatrix}$ (d) $\begin{pmatrix} 3 \\ -2 \end{pmatrix}$

(e) $\begin{pmatrix} -1 \\ 0 \end{pmatrix}$ (f) $\begin{pmatrix} 0 \\ 0 \end{pmatrix}$ (g) $\begin{pmatrix} -15 \\ 8 \end{pmatrix}$ (h) $\begin{pmatrix} 4 \\ 0 \end{pmatrix}$

(i) $\begin{pmatrix} -14 \\ 3 \end{pmatrix}$

6 Change the sign (positive to negative, or negative to positive) of *both* the numbers in the vector.

7 $\begin{pmatrix} -a \\ -b \end{pmatrix}$

EXERCISE 17.6 (page 258)

1 (a) E

(b) D

(c) $x = 15$ cm, $y = 14$ cm, $z = 60°$

2 (a) H (c) $\begin{pmatrix} 5 \\ 3 \end{pmatrix}$

(b) L (d) $\begin{pmatrix} -10 \\ 0 \end{pmatrix}$

3 (a) $\begin{pmatrix} 7 \\ 2 \end{pmatrix}$ (b) $\begin{pmatrix} 9 \\ 5 \end{pmatrix}$

4 $\begin{pmatrix} 7 \\ 4 \end{pmatrix}$

5 $\begin{pmatrix} 1 \\ -9 \end{pmatrix}$

Investigation—Saturday Knight Fever (page 259)

1 $\begin{pmatrix} 1 \\ 2 \end{pmatrix}$, $\begin{pmatrix} 1 \\ -2 \end{pmatrix}$, $\begin{pmatrix} -1 \\ 2 \end{pmatrix}$, $\begin{pmatrix} -1 \\ -2 \end{pmatrix}$, $\begin{pmatrix} 2 \\ 1 \end{pmatrix}$, $\begin{pmatrix} 2 \\ -1 \end{pmatrix}$, $\begin{pmatrix} -2 \\ 1 \end{pmatrix}$, $\begin{pmatrix} -2 \\ -1 \end{pmatrix}$

2

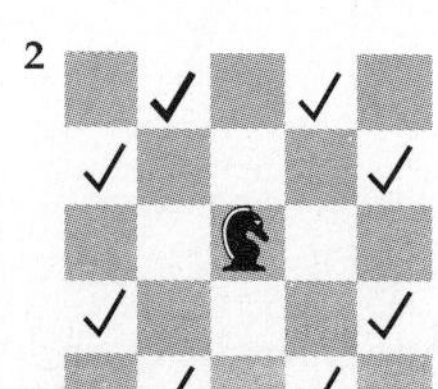

3 no

4

2	3	4	4	4	4	3	2
3	4	6	6	6	6	4	3
4	6	8	8	8	8	6	4
4	6	8	8	8	8	6	4
4	6	8	8	8	8	6	4
4	6	8	8	8	8	6	4
3	4	6	6	6	6	4	3
2	3	4	4	4	4	3	2

5 One possible answer is shown.

1	24	55	36	11	22	57	34
54	37	12	23	56	35	10	21
13	2	25	48	43	46	33	58
26	53	38	45	40	49	20	9
3	14	51	42	47	44	59	32
52	27	64	39	50	41	8	19
15	4	29	62	17	6	31	60
28	63	16	5	30	61	18	7

Chapter 18—Parallel lines

Exercise 18.1 (page 262)

1. (a) true (b) false (c) true (d) true (e) false (f) true
2. (a) SR (b) PS
3. (a) GF (b) ED or FD (c) BE (d) AG
4. (a) AD, EH, FG
   (b) AB or DC or BF or CG
   (c) true
   (d) false
   (e) true
   (f) true
5. (a) DE || HB (b) DE ⊥ CD (c) AB || FE (d) FH ⊥ FE
8. (a) parallel (b) both (c) both (d) parallel (e) perpendicular (f) perpendicular
9. yes

Exercise 18.2 (page 264)

1. (a)

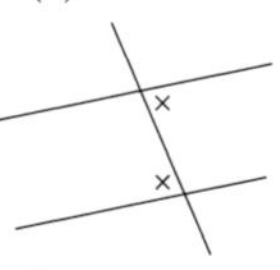

(b)

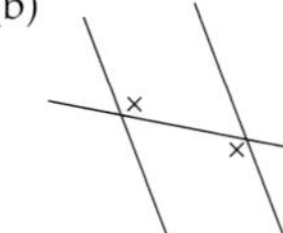

2. b
3. (a) d (b) e
4. (a) Alternate angles:

angle	angle
s	p
u	v
w	t
m	o
l	n

   (b) yes
5. a and c, b and d
6. e and g, f and h
7. i and k, j and l
8. m and o, n and p

Exercise 18.3 (page 265)

1. $a = 60°$
2. $b = 110°$
3. $c = 85°$
4. $d = 65°, e = 70°$
5. $f = 88°, g = 112°$
6. $h = 100°$
7. $i = 60°$
8. $j = 95°, k = 85°, l = 95°$
9. $m = 40°, n = 35°$
10. $o = 42°, p = 38°, q = 80°$
11. $r = 80°$
12. $s = 35°$

Exercise 18.4 (page 267)

1. (a) (b)

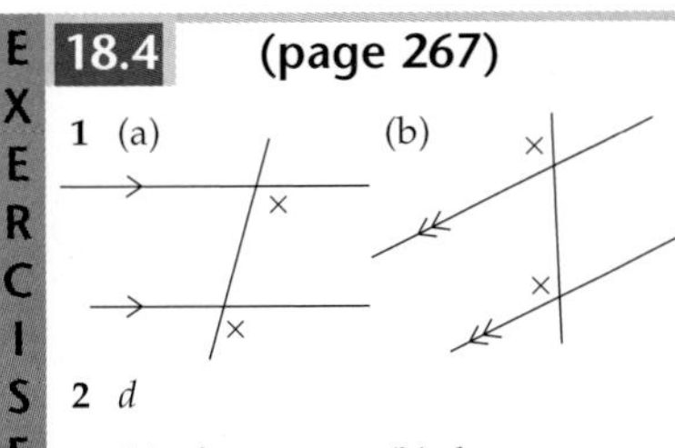

2. d
3. (a) d (b) b
4. (a) Corresponding angles:

angle	angle
j	l
u	w
q	s
x	y
m	k

   (b) yes
5. a and c, b and d, e and g, f and h
6. i and k, j and l, m and o, n and p

Exercise 18.5 (page 268)

1. $a = 70°$
2. $b = 40°$
3. $c = 65°$, $d = 65°$
4. $e = 72°$, $f = 108°$
5. $g = 82°$, $h = 82°$
6. $i = 95°$, $j = 85°$
7. $k = 72°, l = 68°$
8. $m = 30°, n = 40°$
9. $p = 30°, q = 50°$, $r = 100°$
10. $s = 108°$, $t = 112°$, $u = 72°$, $v = 68°$, $w = 40°$

Exercise 18.6 (page 269)

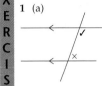

1. (a) (b)
2. c
3. (a) f (b) j
4. Co-interior angles:

angle	angle
a	e
f	b
g	c

5. $a = 40°$
6. $b = 110°$
7. $c = 120°, d = 70°$
8. $e = 60°$
9. $f = 58°, g = 44°, h = 78°$
10. $i = 120°, j = 120°, k = 45°$, $l = 135°$

Exercise 18.7 (page 271)

1. (a) Corresponding angles on parallel lines are equal.
   (b) Co-interior angles on parallel lines add to 180°.
   (c) Alternate angles on parallel lines are equal.
2. (a) vert. opp. ∠'s
   (b) alt ∠'s, || lines
   (c) ∠'s at pt
   (d) ∠ sum of △
   (e) co-int ∠'s, || lines
   (f) ∠'s on line
   (g) corresp ∠'s, || lines
3. $a = 50°$ (alt ∠'s, || lines)
   $b = 130°$ (corresp ∠'s, || lines or ∠'s on line)
4. $c = 120°$ (co-int ∠'s, || lines)
   $d = 120°$ (vert. opp. ∠'s)
5. $e = 95°$ (corresp ∠'s, || lines)
   $f = 95°$ (alt ∠'s, || lines)

6 $g = 66°$ (co-int ∠'s, || lines)
$h = 123°$ (alt ∠'s, || lines)
7 $i = 108°$ (∠'s on line)
$j = 70°$ (∠ sum of △)
8 $k = 115°$ (co-int ∠'s, || lines)
$l = 65°$ (vert. opp. ∠'s)
9 $m = 35°$ (alt ∠'s, || lines)
$n = 45°$, (alt ∠'s, || lines)
$o = 280°$ (∠'s at pt)
10 $x = 72°, y = 72°$
11 $x = 80°, y = 40°, z = 60°$
12 $x = 62°, y = 58°, z = 60°$
13 $x = 40°, y = 120°, z = 60°$
14 $x = 120°, y = 28°, z = 74°$
15 $x = 70°, y = 40°, z = 40°$
16 $x = 110°, y = 36°$
17 $x = 70°, y = 40°$
18 $x = 70°$
19 $x = 70°$
20 $x = 130°$
21 (a) corresponding, *a*
(b) alternate, *g*
(c) co-interior, *b*
22 $x = 60°, y = 70°$

EXERCISE 18.8 (page 275)

1 (a) 260° (d) 290°
(b) 030° (e) 070°
(c) 200° (f) 350°

2

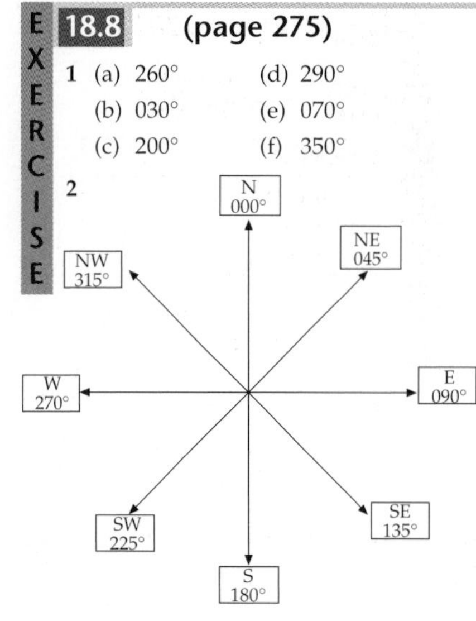

3 (a) 041° (c) 104°
(b) 249° (d) 281°

4 (a) 60° does not have three digits; should be written as 060°.
(b) 400° is outside the range 000° to 359°.
(c) NW is a compass direction, not a bearing.

5 (a) (i) 045°
(ii) 231°
(iii) 141°
(iv) 292°
(b) 000°
(c) 180°; Protractor not needed because the direction is exactly south
(d) 276° - can add 180° - use alternate angles

6 (a) 046°
(b) 252°
(c) 002°
(d) 340°
(e) 301°

7 (a) 320°
(b) 040°
(c) 300°

8

Chapter 19—Symmetry

EXERCISE 19.1 (page 278)

1 (a) Has rotational symmetry.
(b) Has rotational symmetry.
(c) Does not have rotational symmetry.

2 (a) 6 (c) 4
(b) 12 (d) 5

3 (a) 8 (c) 1
(b) 2 (d) 24

4 HINOSXZ

5 120°

6 (a) 8 (b) 45°

7 (a)

Order of rotational symmetry	Smallest angle through which the shape turns
1	360°
2	180°
3	120°
4	90°
5	72°
6	60°
8	45°
10	36°
12	30°

(b) The order of rotational symmetry × smallest angle = 360° OR to calculate the smallest angle through which the shape turns, divide 360° by the order of rotational symmetry.

8

9

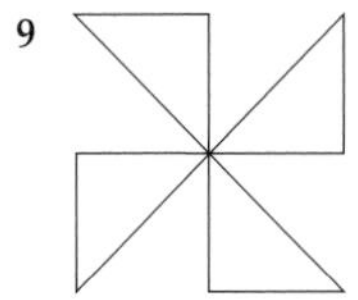

10 8

11 (a) 4 (b) 2

13

15 not possible!

Starter (page 283)

- 6
- 3
- 3
- 2
- 1
- The number of ways a shape will fit in its hole is the sum of the number of axes of symmetry and the order of rotational symmetry.

EXERCISE 19.2 (page 281)

1 (a) 1 (c) 6
(b) 2 (d) 5

2

Symbol	+	−	×	÷	=
Number of axes of symmetry	4	2	4	2	2

3 (a) (b) (c)

4

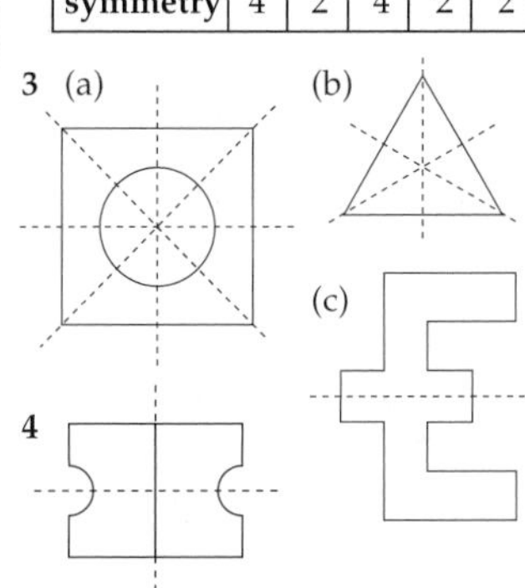

5 (a) ABCDEHIKMOTUVWXY
(b) BCDEHIKOX
(c) AHIMOTUVWXY
(d) HIOX

6 o

7

0	1	2	3	4	5	6	7	8	9
2	0	0	1	0	0	0	0	2	0

8 MUM
BIKE
BOXED
WOW

9 (a) 2 seats on left side, 3 in the middle, 2 seats on right side.
(b) Boeing 777
(c) BAE146 'Whisper jet'
(d) 10
(e) Yes, but only if there are two aisles
(f) Seating plan is still symmetrical, but with fewer seats

EXERCISE 19.3 (page 284)

1

	Order of rotational symmetry	Number of axes of symmetry	Total order of symmetry
(a)	2	2	4
(b)	2	2	4
(c)	8	8	16
(d)	2	0	2
(e)	2	2	4

3 8

4 (a) S (c) O
(b) E (d) 1

5

		Order of rotational symmetry	Number of axes of symmetry	Total order of symmetry
(a)	Nigeria	2	2	4
(b)	Canada	1	1	2
(c)	Jamaica	2	2	4
(d)	United Kingdom	2	0	2
(e)	New Zealand	1	0	1

6

	Order of rotational symmetry	Number of axes of symmetry	Total order of symmetry
(a)	2	2	4
(b)	4	4	8
(c)	2	0	2
(d)	2	0	2

7 (a) 4
(b) A plastic credit card is a rectangular shape. Rectangles have two axes of symmetry, and order of rotational symmetry of 2. This gives 4 as the total order of symmetry.

EXERCISE 19.4 (page 287)

1 XZ and YZ are equal

2 (a) 10 cm
(b) 4 cm
(c) 8 cm

3 (a) DEF (e) ABC
(b) MNO (f) STU
(c) PQR (g) JKL
(d) GHI

4 (a) Two angles are the same size.
(b) All three angles are the same size.
(c) None of the angles are the same size.

5 (a) BCE
(b) ABE, CDE

6 1

7 No, because then the two obtuse angles (each greater than 90°) would add to more than 180°. 180° is the sum of all *three* angles of a triangle.

EXERCISE 19.5 (page 289)

1 (a) $\widehat{DFE}$, $\widehat{EDF}$
(b) $\widehat{LNM}$, $\widehat{MLN}$
(c) $\widehat{PQR}$, $\widehat{QPR}$

2 $x = 68°$

3 $x = 60°$

4 $x = 45°, y = 90°$

5 $x = 65°, y = 50°$

6 $x = 70°, y = 70°, z = 40°$

7 $x = 70°, y = 40°, z = 40°$

8 $x = 50°, y = 50°, z = 50°$

9 $x = 70°, y = 70°, z = 40°$

10 $x = 15°, y = 15°$

11 $x = 62°, y = 62°$

12 $x = 40°, y = 70°, z = 70°$

13 45°, 45°, 90°

14 (a) $360° \div 5 = 72°$
(b) $y = 108°$

15 108°

Investigation—Whole-number triangles (page 287)

1 No. The 1 cm sides linked to each end of the 3 cm side cannot possibly join to form a triangle.

2 Not possible.

3 3 different triangles:

Lengths of sides	Type of triangle
3 4 5	Scalene
4 4 4	Equilateral
5 5 2	Isosceles

4

Type of triangle	Lengths of sides
Scalene	{5 6 7} {3 7 8} {4 6 8}
Isosceles	{2 8 8} {4 7 7} {8 5 5}
Equilateral	{6 6 6}

5 • less than
• more than

EXERCISE 19.6 (page 291)

1 (a) arrowhead
(b) rectangle
(c) isosceles trapezium
(d) kite
(e) parallelogram
(f) rhombus

2 (a) C
(b) A
(c) B or D

3 (a) BCDK (e) GHIL
(b) FGJK (f) DEFK
(c) GMIL (g) GMIJ
(d) ABKJ (h) GHIM

4 (a) one *square* and two *parallelograms*
(b) three *rhombuses*

5 An arrowhead has a reflex angle, whereas each angle in a kite is less than 180°.

6 Yes, an arrowhead.

7 Rectangle, rhombus and square.

8 (a) (b) (c)

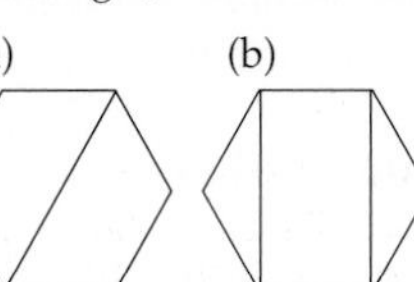

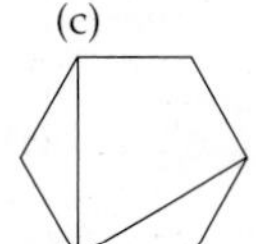

EXERCISE 19.7 (page 293)

1 (a) no (e) no
(b) yes (f) yes
(c) yes (g) no
(d) no

2 Opposite pairs of sides are the same length, and parallel. All angles are the same size (90°). The diagonals are the same length, and bisect each other.

3 (a) square, rectangle, rhombus, parallelogram
(b) square, rhombus
(c) square, rectangle, rhombus, parallelogram
(d) square, rectangle, isosceles trapezium

4 (a) BC (d) $\widehat{BAD}$
(b) DC (e) AC
(c) $\widehat{BCD}$ (f) E

5 (a) $a = 5$ cm, $b = 6$ cm, $x = 80°$, $y = 100°$
(b) $a = 8$ cm, $b = 10$ cm, $x = 30°$, $y = 40°$

6 (a) $p = 12$ cm, $q = 10$ cm, $x = 100°$
(b) $a = 7$ cm, $b = 6$ cm, $x = 50°$, $y = 15°$

7 no

8 no

9 5

10 (a)

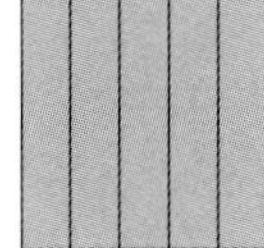

(b) 2 2 2 4 2 4

(c) 10 10 10 60° 60° 20

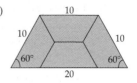

Chapter 20—3D shapes

Starter (Page 296)

- yes
- 1
- 1
- Twist it, then join the ends.
- no

EXERCISE 20.1 (page 298)

1 (a) sphere
(b) cuboid
(c) cylinder
(d) sphere
(e) cuboid
(f) cylinder
(g) cone
(h) triangular prism
(i) cone

2 (a) E
(b) BF, CG, DH
(c) BAEF

3 (a) 4 (b) 6 (c) 4

4 Altogether the cube shape has 12 edges. This will take a total of $12 \times 90 = 1080$ cm (or 10.8 m). 10 m of dowelling will not be enough.

5 (a)

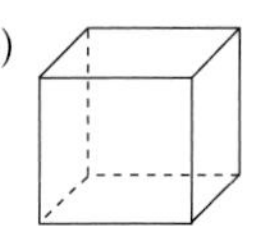

(b)

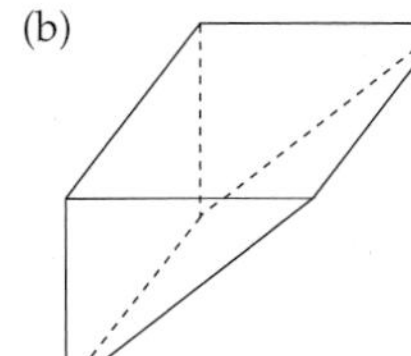

(c)

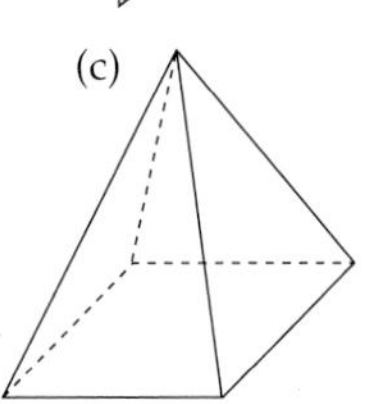

6

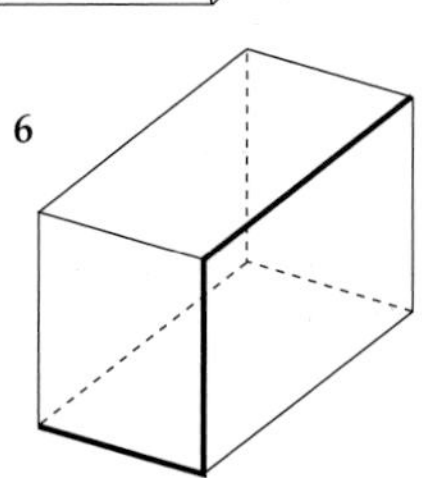

7 (a) 3 (b) square

8

	Number of faces	Number of edges	Number of vertices
cube	6	12	8
triangular prism	5	9	6
hexagonal prism	8	18	12
pyramid	5	8	5
cube where a triangular slice has been cut off	7	15	10

9 Yes, three colours would be enough—e.g. red for each end, and blue/green on alternate side faces.

10

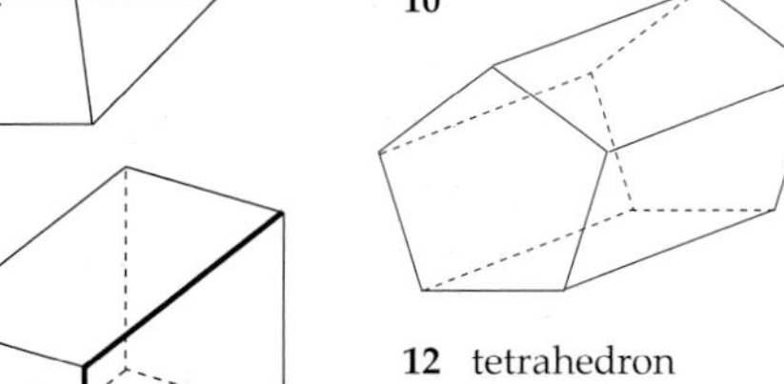

11

S P R Q W T V U

12 tetrahedron

13 (a) isosceles trapeziums
(b) 12
(c) pyramid

EXERCISE 20.2 (page 302)

1 (a)

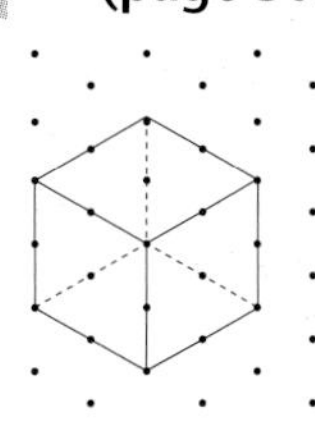

(b)

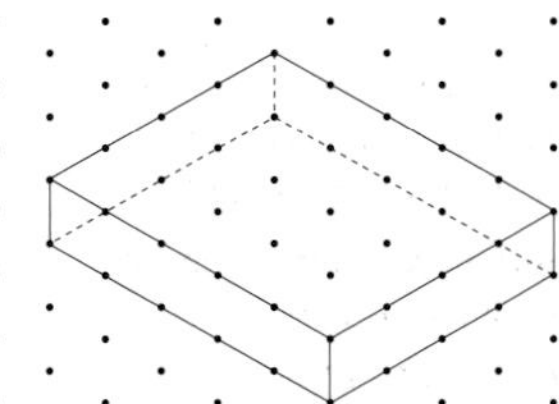

2 (a) 27 (b) 8 (c) 24 (d) 11

3 (a)

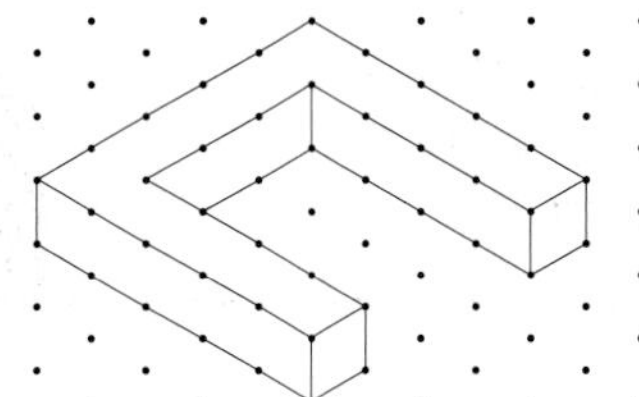

3 (b)

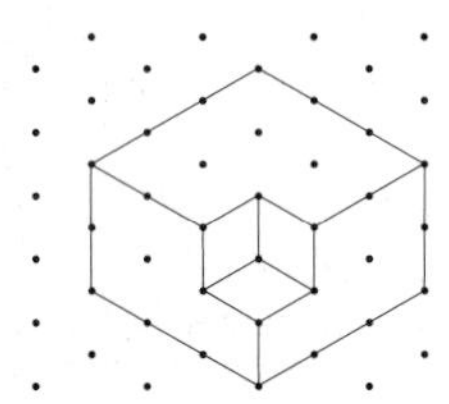

4

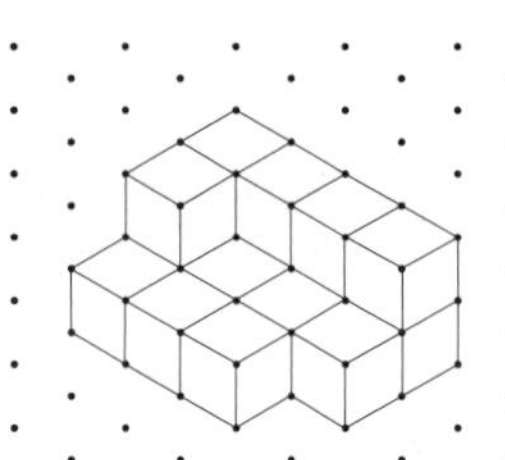

5 (a) 17 (b)

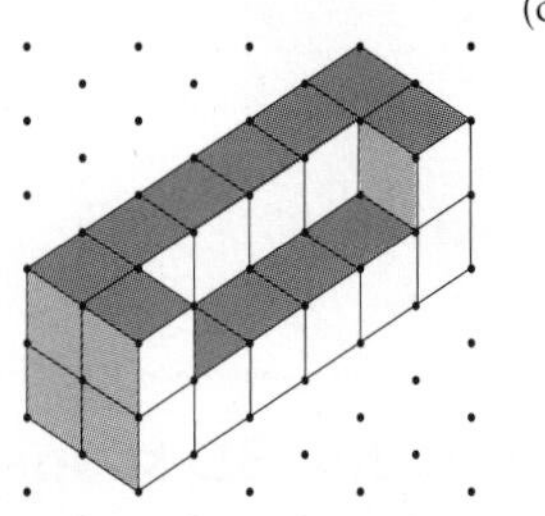

(c) 14

6 (a) C (b) E

7 (a)

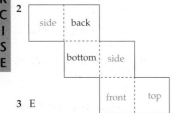

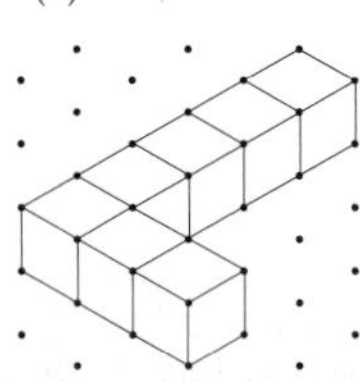

(b)

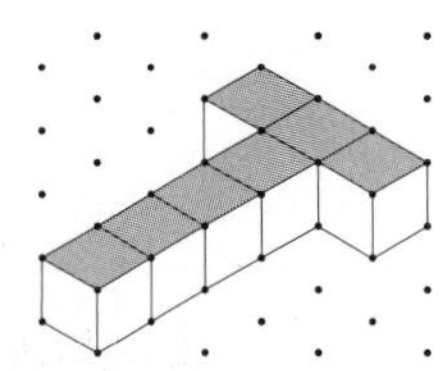

(c)

8 56

9

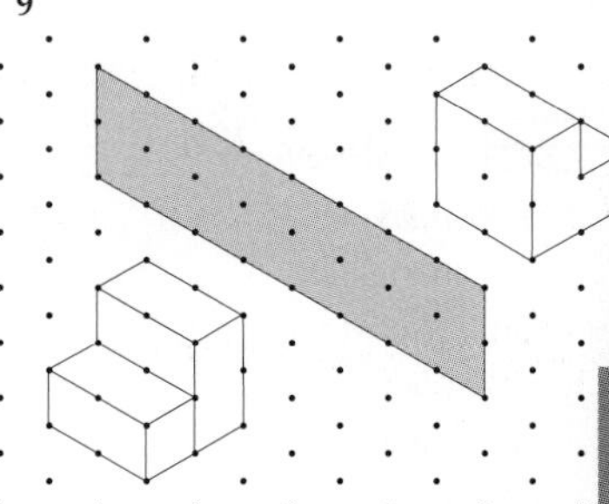

EXERCISE 20.3 (page 304)

1 (a) 5 (b) 2 (c) 3 (d) 1

2

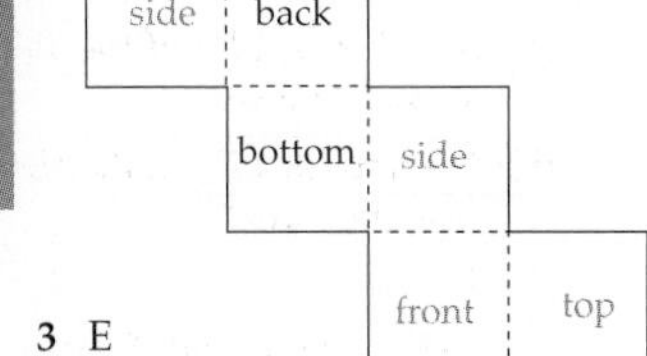

3 E

4 (a) B (b) C (c) A

5

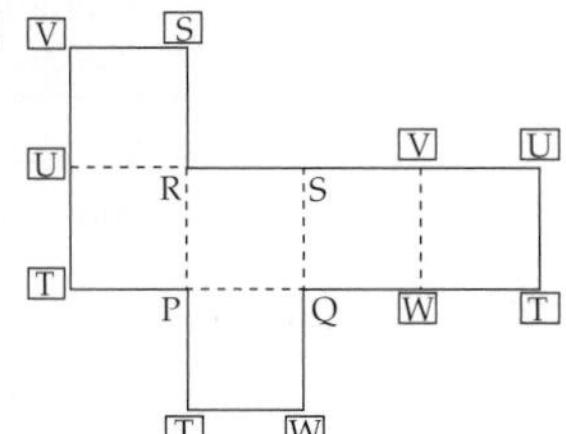

6

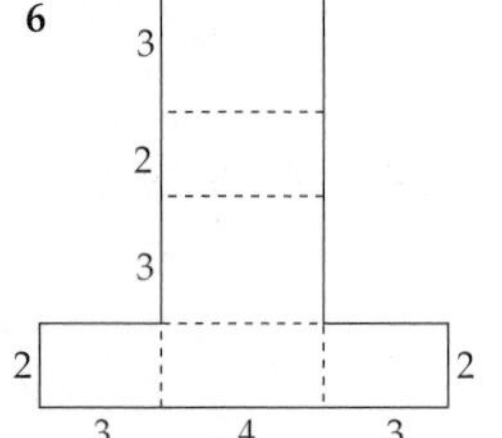

7

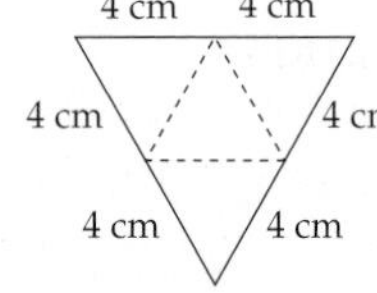

8 (a) triangular prism
(b) pyramid
(c) cylinder

9 (a) pentagon
(b) 12
(c) 3

EXERCISE 20.4 (page 307)

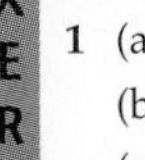

1 (a) C
(b) A
(c) B
(d)

2 (a) left

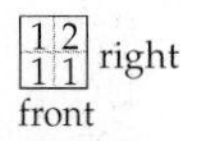

1	2
1	1

right
front

(b) left

3	3	3
3	3	3

right
front

(c) left

3	1	1	1	3
2	1	1	1	2

right
front

3 (a) (b) (c)

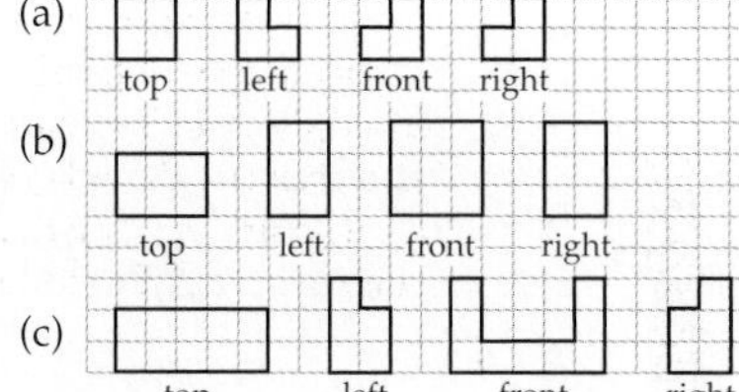

4 (a) (b)

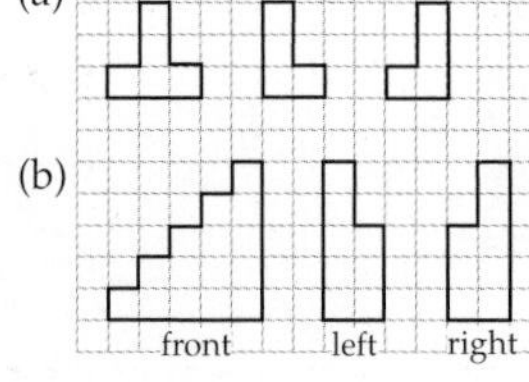

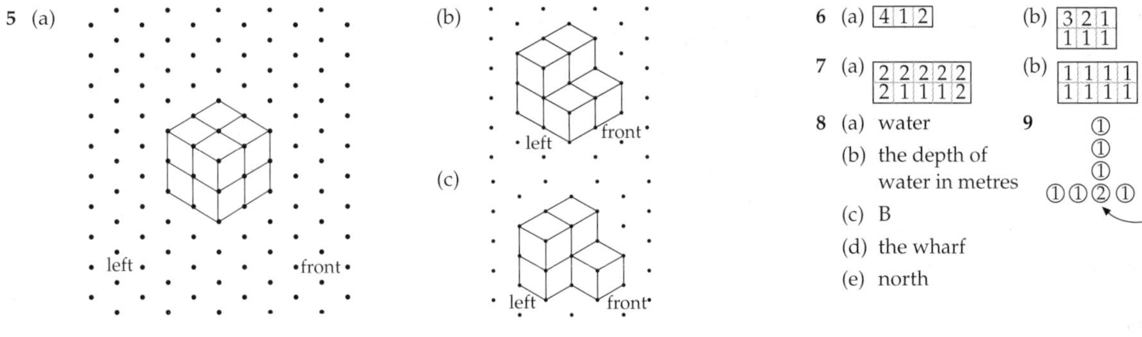

Exercise 15.3 7 "HELP, I'M BEING LICKED"

Chapter 21—Introducing expressions

EXERCISE 21.1 (page 310)

1 (a) F (b) A (c) E (d) C (e) B (f) G (g) D

2 (a) $x + 10$ (b) $x - 15$ (c) $4x$ (d) $7x$

3 (a) 6 times a number, or a number multiplied by 6
(b) a number with 9 added to it
(c) a number with 12 subtracted from it
(d) 5 times a number, or a number multiplied by 5

4 (a) $10x$ (b) $\frac{x}{10}$ (c) $\frac{10}{x}$ (d) $x + 10$ (e) $x - 10$

5 (a) $4x$ (b) $\frac{x}{6}$ (c) $20x$ (d) $\frac{x}{30}$ (e) pq (f) $12y$ (g) $\frac{100}{x}$ (h) $\frac{p}{q}$

6 (a) $x - 7$ (b) $x + 6$ (c) $12x$ (d) $x - 10$ (e) $100x$ (f) $7x$ (g) $p + q$

7 (a) $4 \times p$ (b) $6 \times p - 1$ (c) $p \times q$ (d) $2 + 3 \times p$

EXERCISE 21.2 (page 311)

1 10
2 18
3 35
4 2
5 0
6 7
7 16
8 32
9 56
10 24
11 80
12 72
13 2
14 4
15 1

16 (a) The number of cars.
(b) 300
(c) 200

17 (a) The number of workers.
(b) 7
(c) 1
(d) Numbers less than 6; the rule would not give a sensible answer.

18 (a) The number of guests.
(b) 20
(c) 25
(d) Numbers that are not multiples of 4. We need to round up so that there will be enough tables available (some will have empty seats). Take the nearest multiple of 4 *above* the number, and then use the rule. OR: use a calculator to work out the rule, then round *upwards*.

EXERCISE 21.3 (page 312)

1 9
2 45
3 33
4 1
5 8
6 24

7 (a) 76
(b) 85

8 (a) Number of CDs in the shop at start of week.
(b) Number of CDs in the shop at end of week.
(c) 13
(d) 13 CDs were sold if there were 20 CDs in the shop at the beginning of the week, and 7 in the shop at the end of the week.

EXERCISE 21.4 (page 313)

1 15
2 8
3 12
4 20
5 36
6 6
7 12
8 8
9 24
10 36
11 56
12 90

EXERCISE 21.5 (page 313)

1 $12x$
2 $10x$
3 ac
4 $3p$
5 d
6 $14x$
7 ab
8 $8cd$
9 $6fg$
10 $2ap$
11 $8ab$
12 $6pqr$
13 $10def$
14 $6pqr$
15 $8cde$
16 $30a$
17 $10q$
18 $16pqr$
19 $8abc$
20 pqr

EXERCISE 21.6 (page 314)

1 $2p$
2 $4r$
3 $4x$
4 $6q$
5 $3x$
6 $5y$
7 $3x$
8 $6x$
9 $8x$
10 $5y$
11 $6p$
12 $16x$
13 $2x$
14 $3x$
15 p
16 $10x$
17 x
18 x
19 $4x$
20 $10x$
21 $9x$
22 $10x$
23 $15p$
24 $20q$
25 $15x$
26 $12x$
27 $8x$
28 $2p$
29 $12x$
30 $6x$

Starter (Page 315)

- Leanne
- $8d + 3t$
- 13
- 7
- $13d + 7t$
- no

EXERCISE 21.7 (page 315)

1 (a) $6x$ and $9x$
(b) $5p$ and $3p$
(c) x and $3x$
(d) $4q$ and q
(e) b and $4b$
(f) $3y$, y and $4y$

2 (a) $2x$ and $6x$
(b) $4b$ and $6b$
(c) $4p$ and $8p$
(d) x and $3x$
(e) $3x$ and $2x$
(f) c and $2c$

3 (a) like
(b) unlike
(c) like
(d) unlike
(e) like
(f) unlike
(g) like
(h) unlike
(i) like

EXERCISE 21.8 (page 316)

1 $6x + 8y$
2 $8p + 5q$
3 $9x + 5y$
4 $11p + 8q$
5 $2x + 5y$
6 $7x + y$
7 $15x + 7y$
8 $p + 5q$
9 $3a + 10b$
10 $6x + 2y$

11 (a)

	$2x + 3 + 5x + 7$	$7x + 10$
$x = 4$	38	38
$x = 6$	52	52
$x = 11$	87	87

(b) They are the same.
(c) $7x + 10$

12 $4x + 6$
13 $8x + 5$
14 $7x + 13$
15 $6x + 2$
16 $7x + 1$
17 $3x + 9$
18 $7x + 10$
19 $4x + 22$
20 $11x + 1$
21 (a) $3x + 2$
(b) 17 cm
22 (a) $18p + 6$
(b) 42 cm
(c) 14 cm

EXERCISE 21.9 (page 317)

1 $2x + 8y$
2 $5x + 3y$
3 $3x + 10$
4 $2x + 1$
5 $2x + 2y$
6 $4x + 3y$
7 $12c + 3d$
8 $3r + 15$
9 $x + y$
10 $10x - 10$
11 $3c + 2$
12 $3x + 2$
13 $9x + 2y$
14 $9x + y$
15 $12p + 47$ (or $47 + 12p$)
16 $5x + 9$
17 $e + f$
18 $8c + 2$
19 $4y + 1$
20 $x - 1$

Chapter 22—Formulas and patterns

EXERCISE 22.1 (page 318)

1 (a) 10 friends (b) 7 friends

2 (a) 1800 km (b) 4500 km (c) 5400 km (d) 4950 km

3 (a) 11 (b) 5 (c) 15 (d) 43

4 (a) $x - 10$ (b) $x + 6$ (c) $5x$

5 (a) \$260 (b) \$320 (c) \$350 (d) \$200

6 (a) \$140 (b) \$90 (c) \$65

7 (a) The number of hours worked.
(b) \$310

8 (a) 10
(b) 45 strands
(c) You get 0 strands. A fence with only 1 post can't have any strands!
(d) No. The number of posts must be a whole number.

EXERCISE 22.2 (page 321)

1 (a) $n = 4t$ (b) $s = \frac{d}{t}$ (c) $C = b + g$
(d) $A = bh$ (e) $p = l + 2$ (f) $C = 2a$

2 (a) $n = c + p$ (b) $s = f - 24$ (c) $w = 2b$
(d) $c = \frac{a}{n}$

3 (a) 3 hours (b) 2 hours

4 (a) \$28 (b) \$64 (c) \$72

5 (a)

	Number of pedestrians p	Number of vehicles v	Result of $p \times v \times v$
Algebra Drive	350	500	87 500 000
Bracket Road	200	600	72 000 000
Calculator Street	60	1500	135 000 000

(b) Calculator Street

6 (a) The number of days in the month.
(b) \$43.50
(c) $C = 0.95d + 3m$

Investigation—The Rule of 72 (page 320)

- 8 years
- 6 years
- $y = \frac{72}{r}$

Starter (page 323)

Number of lanes	1	2	3	4	5	6
Number of divider lines needed	0	1	2	3	4	5

- The number of divider lines is one less than the number of lanes
- $d = n - 1$
- not sensible to substitute any of these numbers
- counting numbers only

EXERCISE 22.3 (page 324)

1 7, 8
2 16, 18
3 13, 15
4 20, 23
5 31, 36
6 7, 4

7
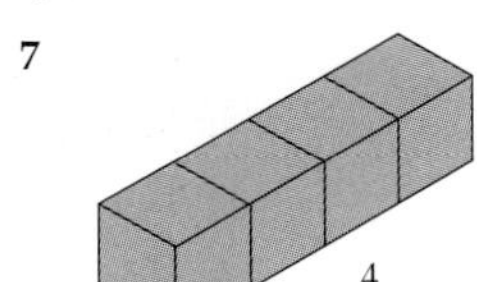
4

8
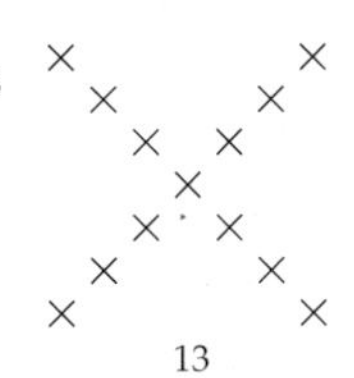
13

9
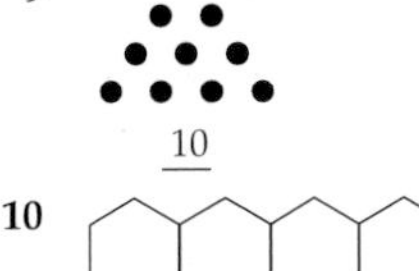
10

10
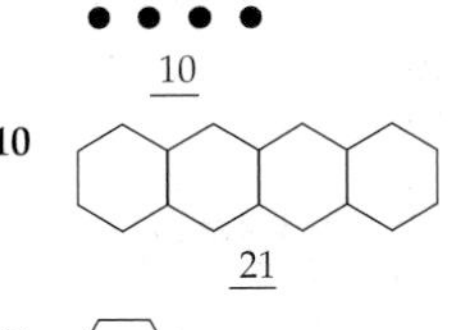
21

11
6

12
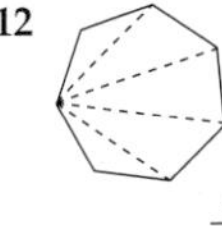
4

13 6, 12, 18, 24, 30
14 9, 10, 11, 12, 13
15 4, 8, 12, 16, 20
16 0, 1, 2, 3, 4
17 1, 3, 5, 7, 9
18 5, 9, 13, 17, 21

EXERCISE 22.4 (page 324)

1 (a) 12 cm
(b) 18 cm
(c) 48 cm
(d) Multiply the length of one side by 6.
(e) 6

2 (a) 13
(b) Number of cubes $= 3 \times 5 + 1 = 16$

3 (a) 2
(b) 6
(c) (ii) $f = 2n - 2$
(d) $f = 2 \times 1 - 2 = 0$. This is a sensible answer—a 1-storey building has no stairs!

4 (a)
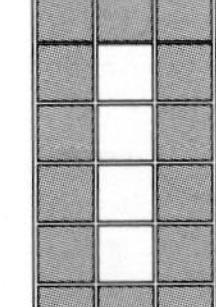

(b)

Number of white tiles (n)	1	2	3	4	5	6
Number of green tiles (g)	8	10	12	14	16	18

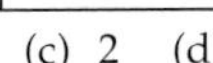
(c) 2 (d) D: $g = 2n + 6$ (e) 46

5 (a)
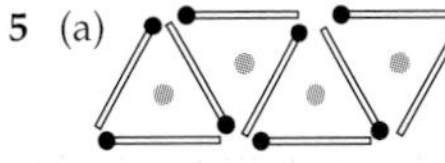

(b)

Number of dots (d)	1	2	3	4	5	6
Number of matches (m)	3	5	7	9	11	13

(c) (i) 17 (ii) 21 (iii) 201
(d) Multiply the number of dots by 2, and then add 1.
(e) $m = 2d + 1$

6 (a) 21
(b) 41
(c) (i) Multiply n by 4, and then add 1.
(ii) $4n + 1$

7 (a)

Number of seats (n)	1	2	3	4	5
Number of cubes	11	14	17	20	23

(b) 8

Investigation—Hydrocarbons (page 326)

(a)

```
    H   H   H   H
    |   |   |   |
H — C — C — C — C — H
    |   |   |   |
    H   H   H   H
```

(b)

	Methane	Ethane	Propane	Butane
Number of carbon atoms (n)	1	2	3	4
Number of hydrogen atoms (h)	4	6	8	10

(c) 18
(d) $h = 2n + 2$

Chapter 23—Working with expressions

Exercise 23.1 (page 327)

1 $5x + 1$
2 $4y + 2$
3 $6p - 8$
4 $8y - 10$
5 $12x - 3$
6 $4 + 3p$
7 $5 - 2y$
8 $xy + 5$
9 $pq + 3$
10 $ab + c$
11 $pq - r$
12 $x + yz$
13 $p - qr$
14 $6x + 2y$
15 $15x - 4y$

Puzzle (page 328)
Pour 10 litres into the motorbike tank from the 10-litre can. Refill the 10-litre can from the 14-litre can. Pour all of the 8-litre can into the 14-litre can. Now fill the 8-litre can from the 10-litre can. This will leave 2 litres in the 10-litre can, which can be added to the petrol already in the motorbike tank, making 12 litres altogether.

Puzzle (page 329)
See page 496 for answer.

Exercise 23.2 (page 328)

1 20
2 7
3 25
4 4
5 67
6 17
7 3
8 0
9 10
10 3
11 9
12 22
13 14
14 0
15 5
16 14
17 6
18 7
19 84
20 8
21 1
22 23
23 44
24 26
25 3
26 10
27 7
28 30

Exercise 23.3 (page 329)

1 36
2 16
3 35
4 14
5 48
6 48
7 16
8 90
9 95
10 21
11 4
12 160
13 2
14 1
15 2
16 20
17 3
18 3
19 5
20 10
21 1
22 2
23 20
24 2
25 $2 \times p + 3$
26 $6 \times (p + 4)$
27 $5 \times p + 4 \times q$
28 $p \div 6$
29 $(p + 1) \div 2$
30 $(10 \times p - 3) \div 4$

Exercise 23.4 (page 330)

1 r^3
2 w^2
3 x^7
4 d^4
5 p^2q^4
6 c^3d^2
7 x^2y^3
8 t^2u^2
9 pq^2
10 $x^2y^2z^2$
11 $x \times x \times x \times x \times x$
12 $r \times r \times r$
13 $w \times w$
14 $x \times y \times y$
15 $p \times p \times q \times q$
16 $x \times x \times x \times x \times y \times y$
17 $p \times p \times q$
18 $t \times t \times t \times u \times u$
19 $x \times y \times y \times z$
20 $c \times c \times c \times d$
21 (a) a^3k^2r (b) a^3kp^2ru (c) $a^2i^2k^2t^2$ (d) a^3ik^2w
22 (a) happy (b) moo (c) radar (d) pipi
23 ABBA

EXERCISE 23.5 (page 331)

1	$6p^2$	12	$60x^2$
2	$12x^2$	13	$8r^3$
3	$10x^2$	14	$4x^3$
4	$4x^2$	15	$8x^3$
5	$10x^2$	16	$10x^2$
6	$6q^2$	17	$6cd^2$
7	$3p^2$	18	$16qr^2$
8	$8a^2$	19	$28xy$
9	$6q^2$	20	$6p^2q$
10	$64p^2$	21	$8xy^2$
11	$100x^2$	22	$24x^2y^2$

EXERCISE 23.6 (page 331)

1	4	7	12
2	16	8	12
3	1	9	0
4	25	10	5
5	9	11	9
6	21	12	49

EXERCISE 23.7 (page 333)

1	(a) 4 (b) 16	9	20
		10	4
2	(a) 20 (b) 100	11	9
		12	33
3	(a) 18 (b) 36	13	19
		14	16
4	(a) 12 (b) 36	15	16
		16	48
5	12	17	4
6	2	18	25
7	48	19	28
8	8	20	17

Puzzle—Einstein (page 334)
See page 496 for answer.

EXERCISE 23.8 (page 334)

1	x^5	16	$8x^8$
2	y^6	17	$15y^6$
3	p^7	18	$16p^5$
4	c^6	19	$30t^7$
5	x^4	20	$5x^7$
6	y^3	21	$4x^5$
7	p^5	22	$12t^3$
8	x^7	23	$30p^3$
9	t^9	24	$16y^4$
10	x^6	25	$2c^3$
11	t^9	26	$4x^3$
12	p^{10}	27	$24x^3$
13	c^4	28	$30x^9$
14	x^7	29	$48x^5$
15	x^{15}	30	$15x^4$

EXERCISE 23.9 (page 335)

1	x^2	17	$4n^2$
2	p^3	18	$5x^6$
3	x^2	19	$3p$
4	x^2	20	$4x^4$
5	p	21	$4x^4$
6	y	22	$2x^4$
7	x^3	23	$7p^3$
8	y	24	$8y$
9	p	25	$\frac{2x^3}{5}$
10	y^8	26	$\frac{4x}{3}$
11	p	27	$\frac{x}{2}$
12	x	28	$\frac{2x^4}{3}$
13	$4x^2$	29	$\frac{5n^2}{6}$
14	$4y^5$	30	$\frac{2p^8}{5}$
15	$5x$		
16	$6y$		

Chapter 24—Equations

EXERCISE 24.1 (page 336)

2	$x + 2 = 8$	8	$3x = 21$
3	$x + 5 = 17$	9	$12x = 108$
4	$4x = 12$	10	$\frac{x}{7} = 4$
5	$6x = 24$	11	$x + 8 = 12$
6	$x - 8 = 3$	12	$\frac{x}{4} = 7$
7	$x - 17 = 5$		

EXERCISE 24.2 (page 337)

1	4	10	$x = 13$
2	2	11	$x = 9$
3	27	12	$x = 4$
4	77	13	$x = 9$
5	$x = 6$	14	$x = 21$
6	$x = 2$	15	$x = 5$
7	$x = 3$	16	$x = 19$
8	$x = 7$	17	$x = 2$
9	$x = 3$	18	$x = 5$

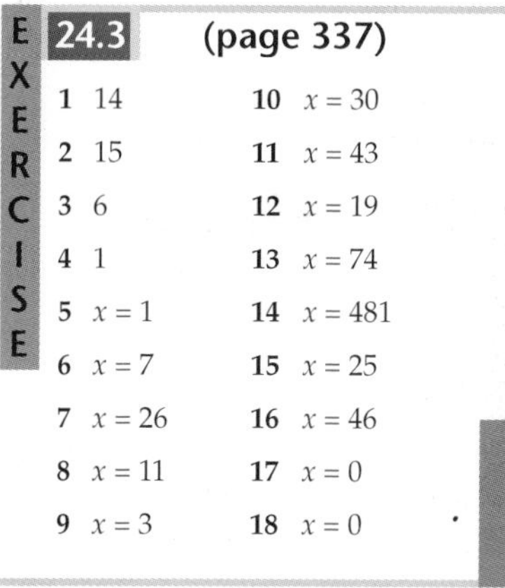

EXERCISE 24.3 (page 337)

1	14	10	$x = 30$
2	15	11	$x = 43$
3	6	12	$x = 19$
4	1	13	$x = 74$
5	$x = 1$	14	$x = 481$
6	$x = 7$	15	$x = 25$
7	$x = 26$	16	$x = 46$
8	$x = 11$	17	$x = 0$
9	$x = 3$	18	$x = 0$

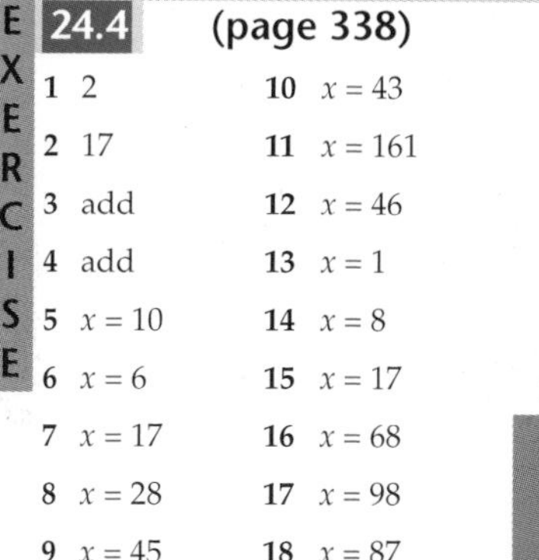

EXERCISE 24.4 (page 338)

1	2	10	$x = 43$
2	17	11	$x = 161$
3	add	12	$x = 46$
4	add	13	$x = 1$
5	$x = 10$	14	$x = 8$
6	$x = 6$	15	$x = 17$
7	$x = 17$	16	$x = 68$
8	$x = 28$	17	$x = 98$
9	$x = 45$	18	$x = 87$

Exercise 24.5 (page 339)

1 6
2 3
3 9
4 1
5 $x = 10$
6 $x = 30$
7 $x = 72$
8 $x = 40$
9 $x = 12$
10 $x = 32$
11 $x = 72$
12 $x = 160$
13 $x = 52$
14 $x = 4$
15 $x = 0$
16 $x = 55$
17 $x = 0$
18 $x = 1000$

Exercise 24.6 (page 339)

1 $x = 6$
2 $x = 4$
3 $x = 16$
4 $x = 10$
5 $x = 6$
6 $x = 21$
7 $x = 54$
8 $x = 15$
9 $x = 60$
10 $x = 4$
11 $x = 15$
12 $x = 12$
13 $x = 9$
14 $x = 8$
15 $x = 0$
16 $x = 18$

Exercise 24.7 (page 340)

1 $x = 4$
2 $x = 6$
3 $x = 2$
4 $x = 1$
5 $x = 9$
6 $x = 7$
7 $x = 9$
8 $x = 5$
9 $x = 3$
10 $x = 7$
11 $x = 18$
12 $x = 4$
13 $x = 12$
14 $x = 2$
15 $x = 67$

Exercise 24.8 (page 341)

1 $x = 3$
2 $x = 4$
3 $x = 5$
4 $x = 6$
5 $x = 1$
6 $x = 5$
7 $x = 2$
8 $x = 5$
9 $x = 4$
10 $x = 2$
11 $x = 3$
12 $x = 2$
13 $x = 0$
14 $x = 25$
15 $x = 3$

Exercise 24.9 (page 341)

1 (a) $x + 14 = 27$
(b) $x = 13$
2 (a) $x + 20 = 100$
(b) $x = 80$
3 (a) $3x = 27$
(b) $x = 9$
4 (a) $4x = 500$
(b) $x = 125$
5 6 squares
6 (a) $2x + 1 = 17$
(b) $x = 8$
7 (a) C: $x - 4 = 6$
(b) $x = 10$
8 (a) The amount that Jill pays.
(b) $x = 22$: Jill pays \$22, Karen pays \$28
(c) $x + x + 5 = 75$ OR $2x + 5 = 75$
(d) Boyd pays \$35 and Chris pays \$40
9 (a) D: $\frac{x}{15} = 5$
(b) $x = 75$
10 (a) $5x + 1 = 36$
(b) $x = 7$
11 (a) B: $4x + 3 = 39$
(b) $x = 9$
12 (a) $2x + 3 = 19$
(b) $x = 8$ km
13 \$2
14 $x + x + 13 = 757$ OR $2x + 13 = 757$
$x = 372$
372 girls on the roll, and 385 boys.

Exercise 24.10 (page 343)

1 $x = 2$
2 $x = 7$
3 $x = 3$
4 $x = 1$
5 $x = 3$
6 $x = 2$
7 $x = 2$
8 $x = 3$
9 $x = 4$
10 $x = 3$
11 $x = 2$
12 $x = 2$
13 $x = 2$
14 $x = 4$
15 $x = 40$

Exercise 24.11 (page 344)

1 $x = 15$
2 $x = {}^{-}2$
3 $x = 6$
4 $x = {}^{-}5$
5 $x = {}^{-}7$
6 $x = {}^{-}7$
7 $x = {}^{-}7$
8 $x = 3$
9 $x = {}^{-}11$
10 $x = {}^{-}35$
11 $x = {}^{-}2$
12 $x = 15$
13 $x = {}^{-}22$
14 $x = 14$
15 $x = {}^{-}12$
16 $x = {}^{-}12$
17 $x = 0$

Exercise 24.12 (page 344)

1 $x = {}^{-}5$
2 $x = {}^{-}7$
3 $x = {}^{-}6$
4 $x = {}^{-}5$
5 $x = 9$
6 $x = {}^{-}28$
7 $x = {}^{-}2$
8 $x = 8$
9 $x = {}^{-}7$
10 $x = {}^{-}12$
11 $x = {}^{-}1$
12 $x = {}^{-}40$
13 $x = {}^{-}8$
14 $x = 3$
15 $x = {}^{-}200$
16 $x = 2$

Exercise 24.13 (page 345)

1 $x = {}^{-}1$
2 $x = {}^{-}2$
3 $x = {}^{-}3$
4 $x = 2$
5 $x = {}^{-}3$
6 $x = 1$
7 $x = {}^{-}3$
8 $x = {}^{-}6$
9 $x = {}^{-}5$
10 $x = 6$
11 $x = {}^{-}4$
12 $x = 2$
13 $x = {}^{-}1$
14 $x = 10$

Puzzle—Bald man (page 344)
See page 496 for answer.

Spreadsheet investigation
(page 345)

5 $x = {}^{-}15$
6 $x = 23$

Exercise 24.14 (page 346)

1 $x = \frac{2}{3}$

2 $x = \frac{^-3}{5}$

3 $x = \frac{7}{6}$ or $1\frac{1}{6}$

4 $x = \frac{19}{2}$ or $9\frac{1}{2}$

5 $x = \frac{11}{4}$ or $2\frac{3}{4}$

6 $x = \frac{^-10}{3}$ or $^-3\frac{1}{3}$

7 $x = \frac{11}{2}$ or $5\frac{1}{2}$

8 $x = \frac{11}{4}$ or $2\frac{3}{4}$

9 $x = \frac{10}{3}$ or $3\frac{1}{3}$

10 $x = \frac{^-7}{8}$

11 $x = \frac{^-7}{5}$ or $^-1\frac{2}{5}$

12 $x = \frac{^-1}{2}$

13 $x = \frac{3}{2}$ or $1\frac{1}{2}$

14 $x = \frac{5}{3}$ or $1\frac{2}{3}$

15 $x = \frac{^-7}{2}$ or $^-3\frac{1}{2}$

16 $x = \frac{^-5}{2}$ or $^-2\frac{1}{2}$

17 $x = \frac{9}{2}$ or $4\frac{1}{2}$

18 $x = \frac{11}{4}$ or $2\frac{3}{4}$

Banana puzzle (page 346)

30 cents

Exercise 24.15 (page 347)

1 $x - 5 = {}^-2$

2 $6x = 12$

3 $x + 8 = 17$

4 $\frac{x}{4} = 6$

5 $2x + 7 = 19$

6 $4x + 5 = 1$

7 $8x = x + 14$

8 $2x + 7 = x + 9$

9 $8x - 5 = 6x + 3$

10 $3x + 2 = 23$

11 $12x + 6 = 42$

12 $7x - 50 = 160$

Exercise 24.16 (page 349)

1 $3x + 11 = 38$; $x = 9$

2 $5x = x + 60$; $x = 15$

3 $4x + 15 = 95$; $x = \$20$

4 $x + 10 = 8 - x$; $x = {}^-1$ °C

5 $3x - 5 = 61$; $x = 22$

6 $2x + 1 = 40 - x$; $x = 13$

7 $8x + x = 36$; $x = 4$ km

8 (a) Landscape Painters
(b) Striped Painters
(c) The number of hours worked.
(d) $48x + 100$
(e) $50x + 80 = 48x + 100$; $x = 10$ hours

9 (a) Rule A
(b) $2x - 1 = x + 3$; $x = 4$ hours

10 $4x + 17 = 5x - 3$; $x = 20$ kg

Chapter 25—Expanding brackets and factorising

Exercise 25.1 (page 351)

1 (a) 16 (b) 16

2 (a) 66 (b) 66

3 (a) 80 (b) 80

4 (a) 42 (b) 42

5 4

6 8

7 10

8 3

9 8, 8

10 $^-2$

11 5

12 x

13 6

14 x

15 4, 4

16 1

Exercise 25.2 (page 351)

1 $3x + 3y$

2 $4x + 4y$

3 $5p + 5q$

4 $10x + 10y$

5 $7c + 7d$

6 $2p - 2q$

7 $3x - 3y$

8 $5p + 5q + 5r$

9 $4p - 4q + 4r$

10 $12x - 12y + 12z$

Exercise 25.3 (page 351)

1 $^-2x - 2y$

2 $^-4p - 4q$

3 $^-5x - 5y$

4 $^-6u + 6v$

5 $^-x + y$

6 $^-4p + 4q$

7 $^-3x - 3y + 3z$

8 $^-x + y - z$

Exercise 25.4 (page 352)

1 $3x + 18$

2 $4x + 20$

3 $2x - 8$

4 $8x - 16$

5 $^-3x - 9$

6 $^-4x - 24$

7 $^-2x + 8$

8 $7x - 77$

9 $8x + 32$

10 $^-8x + 16$

11 $^-x + 2$

12 $^-x - 3$

13 $12x - 24$

14 $^-5x + 50$

15 $^-6x - 24$

Exercise 25.5 (page 352)

1 $10x + 15$

2 $28x - 8$

3 $40x - 20$

4 $^-15x - 6$

5 $^-8x + 6$

6 $6x + 2$

7 $18x - 24$

8 $^-6x - 33$

9 $^-5x - 4$

10 $^-7x + 2$

11 $20x + 10$

12 $60x - 40$

13 $^-56x + 48$

14 $^-3x - 1$

15 $^-24x + 6$

Exercise 25.6 (page 353)

1 $pq + pr$

2 $ab + ac$

3 $xy - xz$

4 $pq - pr$

5 $ab + ac - ad$

6 $ax + bx + cx + dx$

7 $pq + 3p$

8 $xy - 4x$

9 $ax + x$

10 $3d + cd$

11 $14c - cd$

12 $x^2 + 2x$

13 $x^2 - 3x$

14 $2x^2 + x$

15 $3x^2 - 2x$

16 $2x^2 + 6x$

17 $7x - x^2$

18 $x^2 - x$

EXERCISE 25.7 (page 353)

1 $4ac + 4ad$
2 $7px - 7qx$
3 $9pq - 9pr$
4 $5xy + 5yz$
5 $2x^2 + 6x$
6 $4x^2 - 8x$
7 $6x^2 + 3x$
8 $2x^2 - 2xy$
9 $7x^2 + 7x$
10 $3x^2 - 18x$
11 $4x^2 + 20x$
12 $12x^2 - 18x$
13 $5p^2 + 10pq$
14 $20x^2 - 5x$
15 ${}^{-}12x^2 - 9x$
16 ${}^{-}2x^2 + 2x$
17 ${}^{-}2x^2 - x$
18 ${}^{-}4x^2 + 8x$

Investigation—Gift-giving (page 353)

1 6
2 12
3 20
5 $n(n-1)$ OR $n^2 - n$

Puzzle—What is this place? (page 354)

See page 496 for answer.

EXERCISE 25.8 (page 355)

1 $5x + 5y$
2 $14x + 19y$
3 $8x + y$
4 $10x + 19y$
5 $17x + 38y$
6 $x + 4y$
7 $8x - 2y$
8 $9x - 9y$
9 $13 + 2y$
10 $7x + 14$
11 $6x + 20$
12 $10x + 5$
13 $x - 2$
14 $8x + 56$
15 $22x + 4$
16 $13x + 8$

Puzzle—The farmer, fox, duck and grain (page 355)

Take the duck over. Come back alone. Take the grain over. Come back with the duck. Take the fox over. Come back alone. Take the duck over.

EXERCISE 25.9 (page 356)

1 $x = 2$
2 $x = 8$
3 $x = {}^{-}1$
4 $x = 5$
5 $x = 4$
6 $x = 1$
7 $x = {}^{-}6$
8 $x = 5$
9 $x = {}^{-}4$
10 $x = {}^{-}7$
11 $x = 25$
12 $x = 10$
13 $x = {}^{-}7$
14 $x = {}^{-}10$
15 $x = {}^{-}8$
16 $x = 32$
17 $x = 9$
18 $x = 17$
19 $x = 25$
20 $x = {}^{-}6$

EXERCISE 25.10 (page 357)

1 3
2 7
3 5
4 10
5 p
6 x
7 q
8 9
9 y
10 –
11 +
12 x

EXERCISE 25.11 (page 357)

1 $4(p + q)$
2 $10(x + y)$
3 $3(x + y)$
4 $8(p - q)$
5 $5(c - d)$
6 $30(x - y)$
7 $7(p + q)$
8 $3(x + y + z)$
9 $2(a + b + c + d)$
10 $5(x + y - z)$

EXERCISE 25.12 (page 357)

1 3
2 7
3 5
4 10
5 x
6 x
7 7
8 9
9 5
10 –
11 +
12 x
13 3
14 4
15 $3x$
16 3

EXERCISE 25.13 (page 357)

1 $2(x + 3)$
2 $10(x + 2)$
3 $4(x + 3)$
4 $3(x + 7)$
5 $6(x + 4)$
6 $5(x - 2)$
7 $12(x - 2)$
8 $3(x - 12)$
9 $7(x - 3)$
10 $8(x + 3)$
11 $7(x - 9)$
12 $5(x + 11)$

EXERCISE 25.14 (page 358)

1 $5(3x + 4)$
2 $8(4x + 3)$
3 $2(6x - 11)$
4 $3(5x - 8)$
5 $6(2x + 3)$
6 $5(3x - 4)$
7 $2(2x + 3)$
8 $6(3x - 4)$
9 $2(3x - 2)$
10 $10(3x + 2)$
11 $10(4x - 5)$
12 $6(2x + 5)$
13 $4(7x + 6)$
14 $7(2x - 3)$
15 $12(3x - 4)$

EXERCISE 25.15 (page 358)

1 $3(x + 1)$
2 $2(x - 1)$
3 $11(x + 1)$
4 $4(2x - 1)$
5 $2(2x + 1)$
6 $5(3x - 1)$
7 $12(2x + 1)$
8 $3(6x - 1)$
9 $10(x + 1)$
10 $3(7x - 1)$

Investigation—The farmer and the square pens (page 359)

1

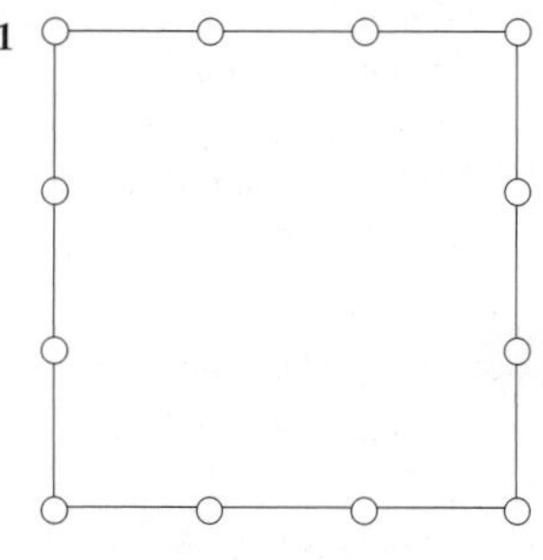

2

Number of posts on each side	2	3	4	5	6
Total number of posts	4	8	12	16	20

3 76

4 $P = 4(n - 1) = 4n - 4$

EXERCISE 25.16 (page 359)

1 $a(x + y)$
2 $b(p + q)$
3 $c(d - b)$
4 $x(a + b)$
5 $x(x + y)$
6 $x(x + 5)$
7 $x(x - 3)$
8 $x(y + 3)$
9 $y(x - 5)$
10 $x(x + 2y)$
11 $x(7 - y)$
12 $x(4 + 3y)$
13 $x(2 + x)$
14 $x(3 - x)$
15 $a(x + 5)$

Puzzle—For always! (page 359)

$$\frac{6x+8}{2} - 3x = \frac{1}{2}(6x+8) - 3x$$
$$= 3x + 4 - 3x$$
$$= 4$$

Chapter 26—Co-ordinates

Starter (page 361)

- Stanley Bay School
- Alison Park
- Vauxhall School
- Narrow Neck Beach

EXERCISE 26.1 (page 362)

1 (a) (i) Kiwi House
(ii) Haunted house
(iii) The entrance to Alphaworld Amusement Park
(iv) Toilets
(v) First Aid point
(vi) Dodgems

(b) (i) G5 (ii) D8 (iii) D10 (iv) A3 (v) H10 (vi) I6

2 (a) Middle School
(b) Water Tower
(c) (6, 5)
(d) (2, 2)
(e) (5, 2)
(f) Yarrow Street
(g) Jed Street
(h) (i) Intersection of Tay St and Dee St.
(ii) Museum Art Gallery
(iii) He cycled along Dee St, then along Leet St, then along Deveron St.

3 (a) Pompallier House
(b) Hot Spring at Orongo Bay
(c) Motor camp near Te Haumi
(d) Quarry
(e) Captain Cook's Anchorage

4 (a) 105561 (b) 150605 (c) 127536 (d) 173542 (e) 178581

5 (a) 3.5 km (b) 400 m (c) 900 m

6 1 km^2

7 78 m

EXERCISE 26.2 (page 366)

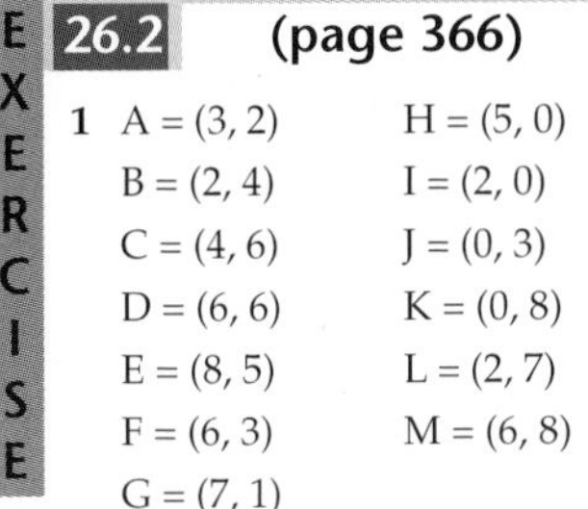

1 A = (3, 2)
B = (2, 4)
C = (4, 6)
D = (6, 6)
E = (8, 5)
F = (6, 3)
G = (7, 1)
H = (5, 0)
I = (2, 0)
J = (0, 3)
K = (0, 8)
L = (2, 7)
M = (6, 8)

2

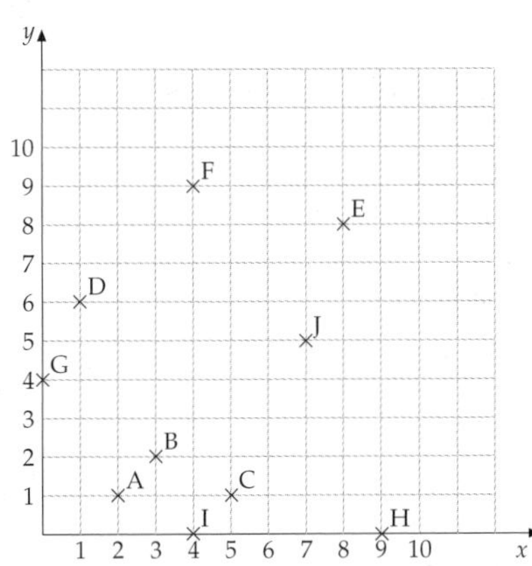

3 square

4 (a) A = (1, 3); B = (4, 1); C = (8, 7)
(b) D = (5, 9)

5 (a) (3, 0) or (7, 6) or (1, 6)
(b) (10, 5) or (2, 1)

EXERCISE 26.3 (page 369)

1 $A = (^-2, ^-2)$
$B = (^-2, 4)$
$C = (2, ^-1)$
$D = (5, 2)$
$E = (^-1, 1)$
$F = (2, ^-3)$
$G = (^-5, 2)$
$H = (4, 0)$
$I = (2, 4)$
$J = (^-4, 5)$
$K = (0, ^-1)$
$L = (^-5, ^-4)$
$M = (^-3, 2)$
$N = (5, ^-4)$
$O = (0, 0)$
$P = (^-4, 0)$
$Q = (0, ^-3)$
$R = (^-1, 0)$
$S = (0, 4)$
$T = (^-3, ^-5)$

2

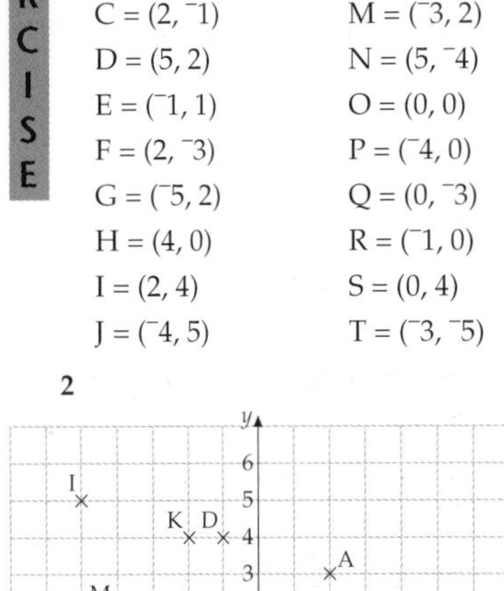

3 (a)

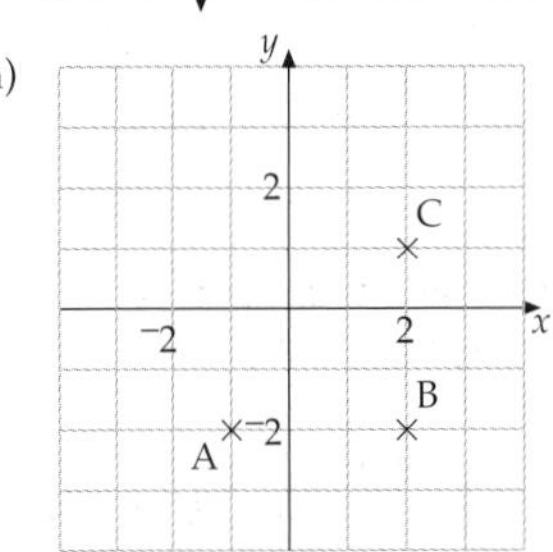

(b) $D = (^-1, 1)$

4 (a)

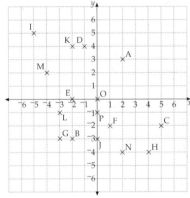

(b) The two sides PQ and QR are the same length.

(c) S = (6, 1)

5 (a) (4, 2)

(b) (⁻1, 1)

6 See page 496 for answer.

7 (a) (i) octopus

(ii) lifeguard

(iii) the edge of the water

(b) (i) (⁻4, ⁻1)(ii) (⁻7, 3)

(iii) (5, 4)

(c) (i) ground

(ii) air

(iii) water

(iv) ground

(v) air

Investigation—the Queen rules (page 370)

1 64

2 (i) d1 (ii) e4 (iii) b7 (iv) g8

3 (a) In the white squares the sum of the numbers is odd.

(b) In the black squares the sum of the numbers is even.

4 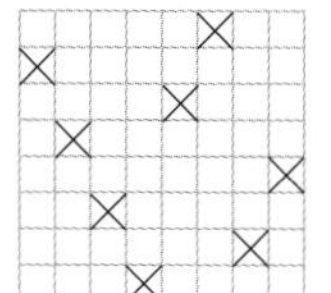

Other answers are possible.

EXERCISE 26.4 (page 372)

1 (175°E, 37°S)

2 (145°E, 17°S)

3 (30°E, 28°N)

4 (30°E, 30°S)

5 (180°, 20°S)

6 (115°E, 23°N)

7 (0°, 51°N)

8 (74°W, 41°N)

9 (80°W, 10°N)

10 (116°E, 32°S)

11 (43°W, 23°S)

12 (30°E, 60°N)

13 (123°W, 37°N)

14 (105°E, 0°)

15 (150°E, 34°S)

Chapter 27—2D graphs

Starter (page 373)

- 65-82 kg.
- Mr Harris is overweight.
- Dr Keppell has a healthy weight.
- Mrs Jackson is underweight.
- Ms Lloyd is very overweight.
- Mr Morris is very underweight.
- Bottom left.
- In the very over-weight section.

EXERCISE 27.1 (page 374)

1 (a) B (c) A

(b) D (d) C

2 (a) In June, Queenstown is sunnier and colder than Auckland.

(b) Auckland

(c) B

(d)

3

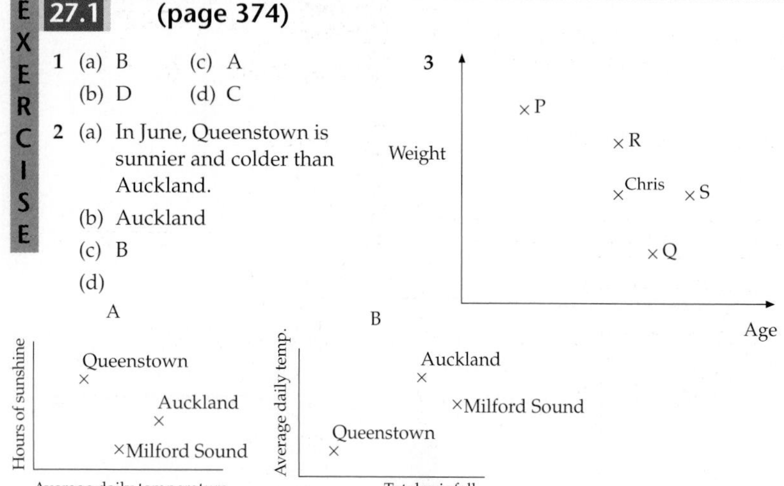

4 In general, the taller a person is, the further they can long-jump.

5 (a) (i) A = squash

B = walking

C = table-tennis

D = gymnastics

(ii) cycling

(b) (i) P = swimming

Q = table-tennis

R = walking

S = martial arts

(ii)

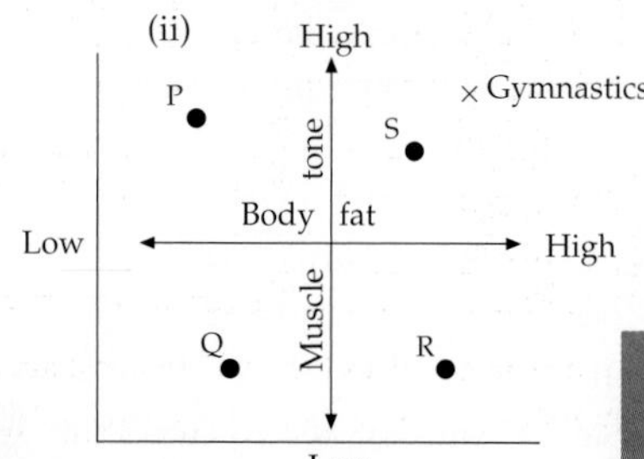

EXERCISE 27.2 (page 377)

1 (a) Graph A: H
Graph B: G
Graph C: F
Graph D: E

(b) Graph A: horizontal axis is age, vertical axis is earnings.
Graph B: horizontal axis is time, vertical axis is prices.
Graph C: horizontal axis is time, vertical axis is height above the ground.
Graph D: horizontal axis is time, vertical axis is temperature.

2 (a) February
(b) August
(c) March and April
(d) 43

3 (a) 9 am
(b) Tank was refilled with petrol.
(c) 11 am
(d) 5 hours
(e) 10 litres

4 (a) A–B bath was being filled
B–C tap(s) turned off for a while
C–D person gets into the bath
D–E person lies in the bath
E–F more water added to the bath
F–G person lies in the bath
G–H person gets out of the bath
H–I bath is emptied
(b) longer to fill

5 A–B shows the kitchen sink is filled with water. B–C shows dishes etc. are placed in the sink, raising the water level. C–D shows the level varies slightly as items are put in the sink and taken out again.
D–E–F shows the sink is emptied and refilled to change the water.
F–G shows more dishes are washed.
G–H shows the sink is emptied.

6 Wiremu climbed up to the bungy jump first, followed closely by Taine. Wiremu changed his mind, and climbed down to watch Taine jump. As Taine was pulled up to the jump again, Wiremu climbed up, and then waited while Taine climbed down. Then Taine watched as Wiremu jumped. Taine stayed on the ground while Wiremu was pulled back up. Finally, Wiremu climbed down.

7 (a) Container A matches graph E
Container B matches graph F
Container C matches graph D
(b) Container B holds the least amount of water.

8 (a) Girls
(b) 16
(c) At 18 the graph becomes level.
(d) 14
(e) The graph for girls' weights is steepest at 12 years of age.

Puzzle (page 380)

D. As more cooks are employed the food will be able to be prepared faster, but the time will never reach zero (as implied in graph B) because they will get in each other's way to some extent.

Spreadsheet investigation —Temperatures in New Plymouth (page 380)

	A	B	C	D	E	F	G	H
1	Time	Temperature						
2								
3	12:00 AM	14						
4	2:00 AM	13						
5	4:00 AM	13						
6	6:00 AM	13						
7	8:00 AM	16						
8	10:00 AM	19						
9	12:00 PM	21						
10	2:00 PM	23						
11	4:00 PM	22						
12	6:00 PM	20						
13	8:00 PM	19						
14	10:00 PM	18						
15	12:00 AM	16						

New Plymouth Temperatures
Temperature: 0, 5, 10, 15, 20, 25
Time: 12:00 AM, 12:00 PM, 12:00 AM, 12:00 PM

The temperature rises fastest between 8 am and 10 am. This is the steepest part of the graph.

EXERCISE 27.3 (page 382)

1 (a) Q (b) R (c) P

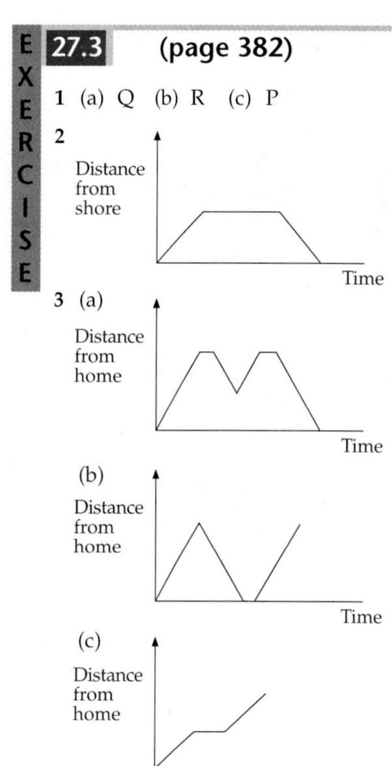

4 (a) 6 km
(b) 65 minutes
(c) 30 minutes
(d) The graph shows Chris stopped for 10 minutes on the way home, so this must be where the puncture took place.
(e) The graph is steeper for the part that shows Chris cycling to town.

5

The Pearson family's motorway journey

Distance from home (km): 0, 10, 20, 30, 40, 50, 60, 70, 80, 90, 100, 110

Time taken (minutes): 20, 40, 60, 80, 100, 120, 140, 160, 180, 200, 220

6 (a)

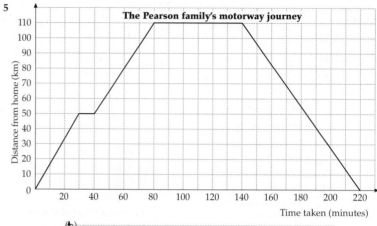

Time	Distance from Invercargill	
	Kelly	Kaye
0800	0	600
0900	75	600
1000	150	600
1100	225	500
1200	300	400
1300	375	300
1400	450	200
1500	525	100
1600	600	0

(b)

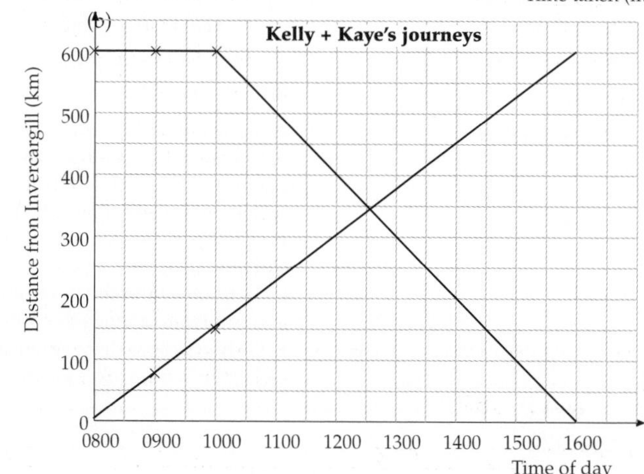

(c) 12.30 pm. This is the time where the lines cross on the graph.
(d) Christchurch

EXERCISE 27.4 (page 385)

1 (a)

x	y	Co-ordinates (x, y)
$^{-}2$	$^{-}6$	$(^{-}2, ^{-}6)$
$^{-}1$	$^{-}3$	$(^{-}1, ^{-}3)$
0	0	(0, 0)
1	3	(1, 3)
2	6	(2, 6)
3	9	(3, 9)

(b)

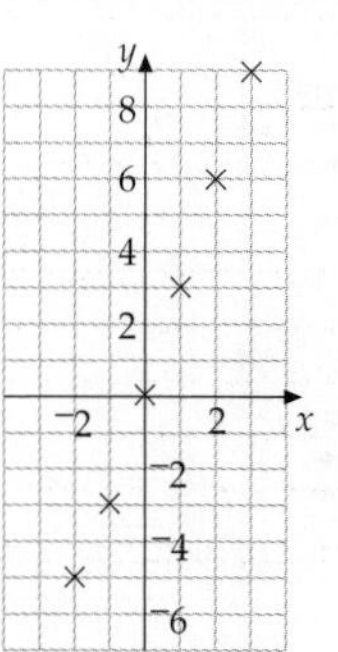

2 (a)

x	y	Co-ordinates (x, y)
$^{-}2$	2	$(^{-}2, 2)$
$^{-}1$	3	$(^{-}1, 3)$
0	4	(0, 4)
1	5	(1, 5)
2	6	(2, 6)
3	7	(3, 7)

(b)

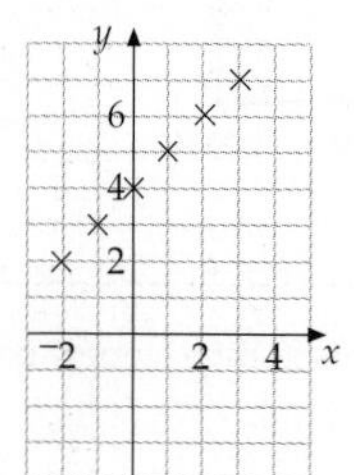

3 (a)

x	y	Co-ordinates (x, y)
$^{-}2$	4	$(^{-}2, 4)$
$^{-}1$	2	$(^{-}1, 2)$
0	0	(0, 0)
1	$^{-}2$	$(1, ^{-}2)$
2	$^{-}4$	$(2, ^{-}4)$
3	$^{-}6$	$(3, ^{-}6)$

(b)

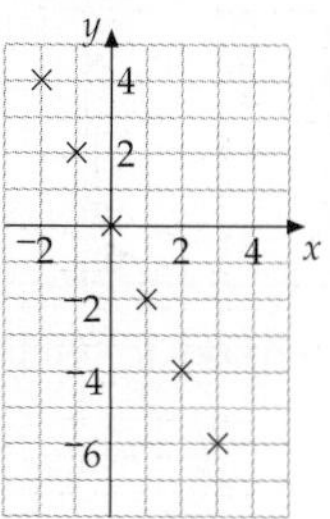

4 (a)

x	y	Co-ordinates (x, y)
$^-2$	$^-3$	$(^-2, ^-3)$
$^-1$	$^-1$	$(^-1, ^-1)$
0	1	(0, 1)
1	3	(1, 3)
2	5	(2, 5)
3	7	(3, 7)

(b)

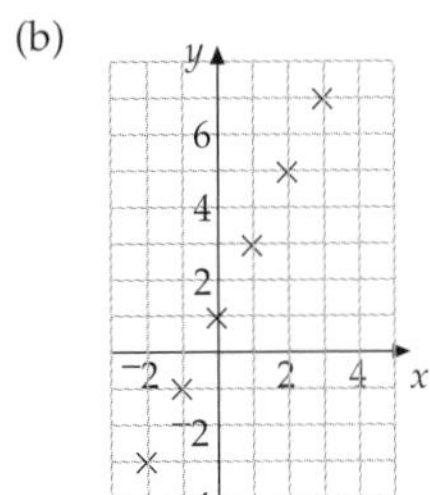

5 (a)

x	y	Co-ordinates (x, y)
$^-2$	4	$(^-2, 4)$
$^-1$	1	$(^-1, 1)$
0	0	(0, 0)
1	1	(1, 1)
2	4	(2, 4)
3	9	(3, 9)

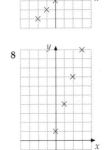

(b)

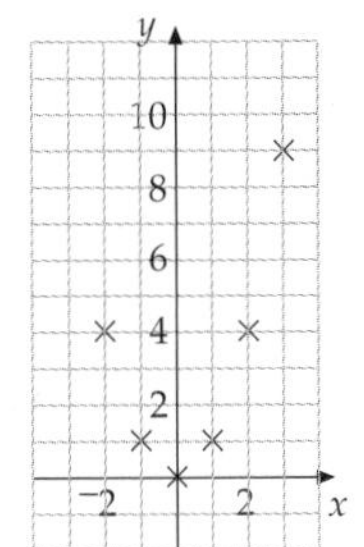

6

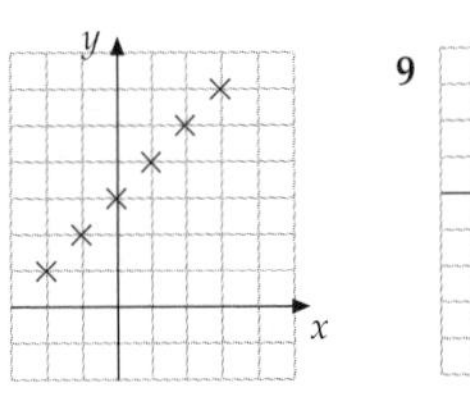

7

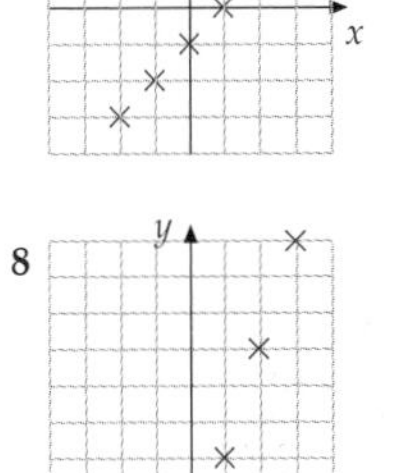

8

9

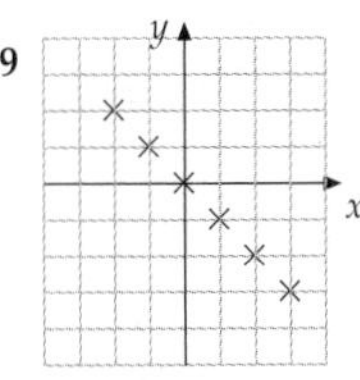

10

11 (a)

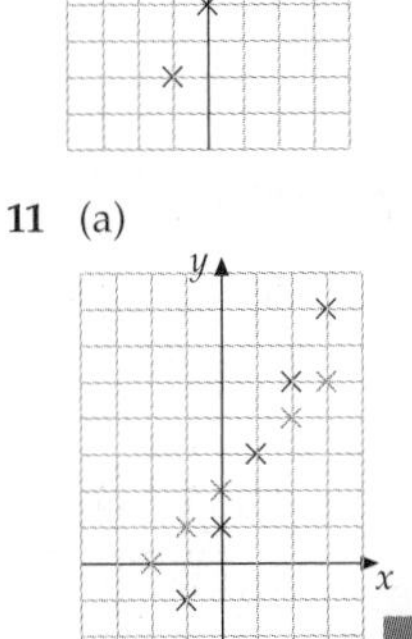

(b) (1, 3)

EXERCISE 27.5 (page 387)

1

	A	B	C	D	E	F	G
1	x	y					
2							
3	-3	-2					
4	-2	-1					
5	-1	0					
6	0	1					
7	1	2					
8	2	3					
9	3	4					
10							
11							
12							
13							
14							
15							
16							

y = x + 1

3

	A	B	C	D	E	F	G
1	x	y					
2							
3	-3	-12					
4	-2	-7					
5	-1	-2					
6	0	3					
7	1	8					
8	2	13					
9	3	18					
10							
11							
12							
13							
14							
15							
16							

y = 5x + 3

2

	A	B	C	D	E	F	G
1	x	y					
2							
3	-3	12					
4	-2	8					
5	-1	4					
6	0	0					
7	1	-4					
8	2	-8					
9	3	-12					
10							
11							
12							
13							
14							
15							
16							

y = -4x

4

	A	B	C	D	E	F	G
1	x	y					
2							
3	-3	-3.2					
4	-2	-2.8					
5	-1	-2.4					
6	0	-2					
7	1	-1.6					
8	2	-1.2					
9	3	-0.8					
10							
11							
12							
13							
14							
15							
16							

y = 0.4x - 2

5

	A	B	C	D	E	F	G
1	x	y					
2							
3	-3	9					
4	-2	8					
5	-1	7					
6	0	6					
7	1	5					
8	2	4					
9	3	3					
10							
11							
12							
13							
14							
15							
16							

y = 6 - x

Puzzle (page 329)
To replace an empty mind with an open one

Puzzle—Einstein (page 334)
Yes, he would be over one hundred and fifty years old

Puzzle—Bald man (page 344)
Hair today, gone tomorrow

Puzzle— What is this place? (page 354)
The third rock from the sun

Exercise 26.3

6 a shark

EXERCISE 27.6 (page 388)

1 (a) 40 minutes (b) 25 minutes (c) \$2.40 (d) 60 cents

2 (a) $3 + 2 \times 4 = 11$

(b)

Length of journey (km)	Charge in \$
1	5
2	7
3	9
4	11
5	13
6	15
7	17

(c)

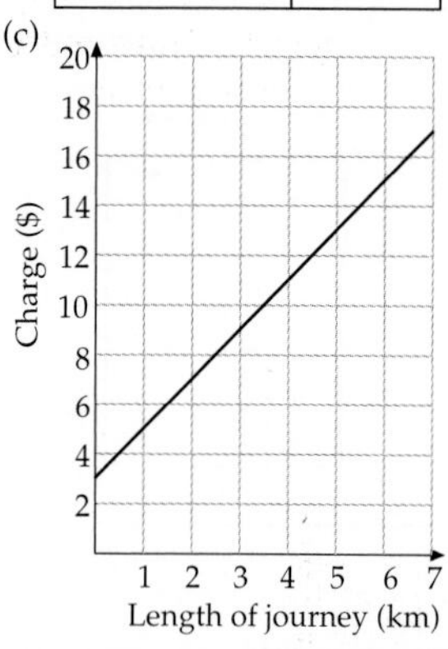

(d) Go up from 2.5 on the x-axis to the graph, then read across to the y-axis. The charge is \$8.

3 (a)

Time (hours)	Battery current (amps)
0	30
1	25
2	20
3	15

(b & d)

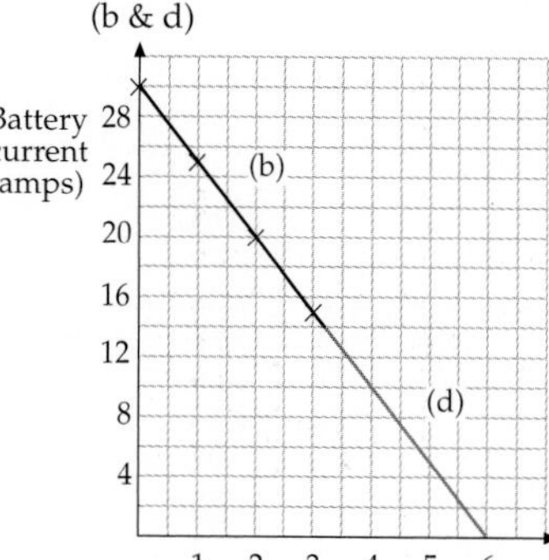

(c) 22.5 amps

(d) 6 hours

(e) C: $B = 30 - 5t$

4 (a) \$3

(b) \$9

(c) \$4.50

(d) 6 tickets

(e) You can buy 4 tickets for \$6.

(f) B: (10, 15)

(g) No, because the number of tickets must be a whole number —you can't have two and a half tickets.

5 (a) \$130

(b) \$150

(c) \$20

(d) Graph 1

(e) Graph 2

(f) \$30. This is the value when n is 0, and is where the graph starts on the y-axis.

(g) When n is 4, both Cath and Derek have the *same* amount of money—that is, \$150.

6 (a) \$2

(b) \$3

(c)

Adult charge	16	14	12	10	8	6
Child charge	1	2	3	4	5	6

(d) A straight line.

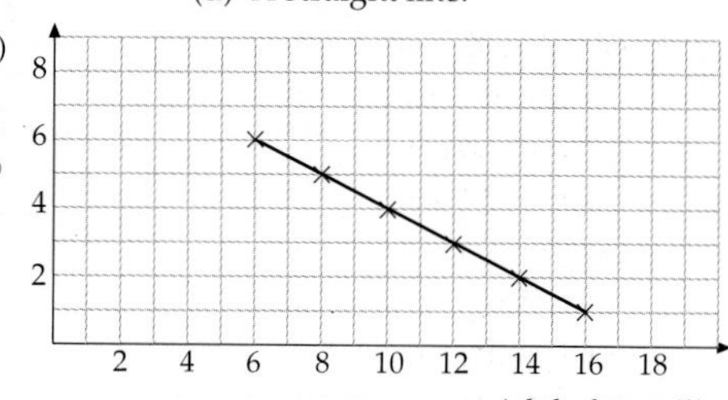

(e) It is unlikely the charge for children would be more than the adult charge (so cannot extend beyond (6, 6) to the left), and if the graph was extended as far as the x-axis it would mean children would be getting in free.

Chapter 28—Interpreting data and statistical displays

Starter (page 391)

	1984	1996
Tobacco consumed (tonnes)	3758	2934
Average number of tailor-made cigarettes smoked per day	24	15

- $\frac{250}{1000}$
- The Smokefree Environments Act, price increases
- \$600 million – \$250 million = \$350 million
- Proportion of young adults who smoke; women, men

EXERCISE 28.1 (page 392)

1 (a) January
(b) October
(c) July
(d) March and December
(e) 5
(f) 1057 mm
(g) second half

2 (a) Heart disease and cancer
(b) 4.5%

3 (a) New Zealand and Ireland
(b) Sweden
(c) B: 3.34 ÷ 1.12 = 2.98
(d) 2

4 (a) males
(b) females
(c) males
(d) Chemistry

5 (a) (i) 1000 mg
(ii) 900 mg
(iii) 800 mg
(iv) 900 mg
(v) 800 mg
(vi) 1000 mg
(b) (i) 1000 mg
(ii) 600 mg
(iii) 300 mg
(c) A pottle of yoghurt gives 200 mg of calcium, and two glasses of calcium fortified milk give 600 mg, making 800 mg altogether. Teenagers (12–18 years) need at least 900 mg daily, so this would not be enough.

EXERCISE 28.2 (page 396)

1

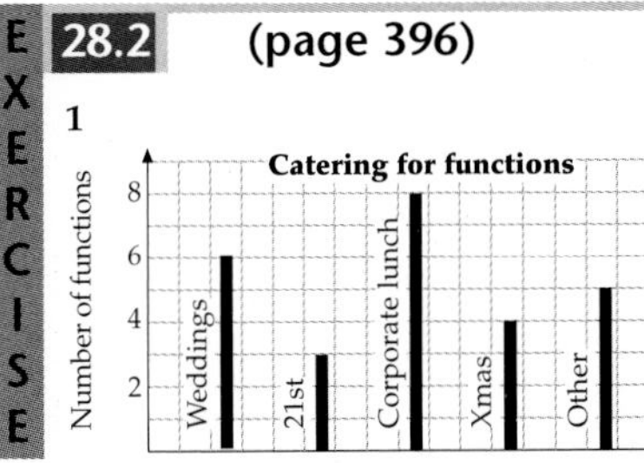

2

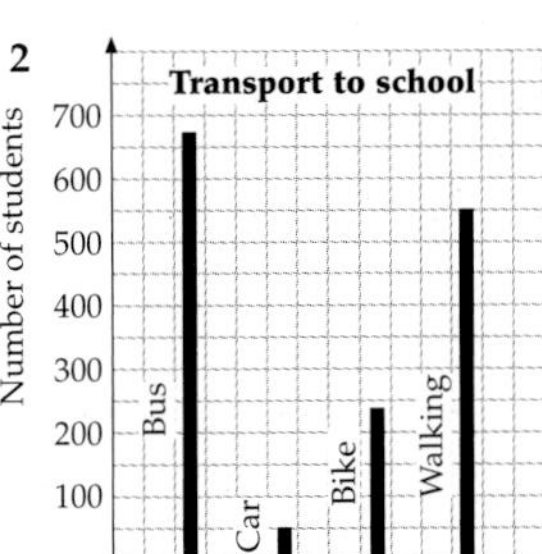

3 (a) 17 000
(b) true
(c) 58 000
(d) World War II

4

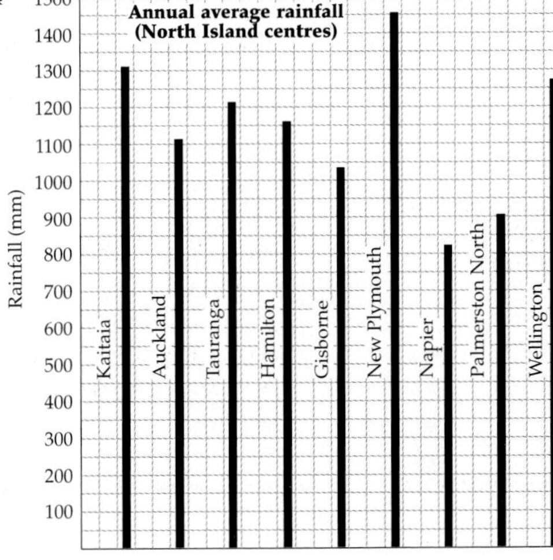

5 The scale on the vertical axis is not *uniform* (going up in equal steps).

6 (a) The columns would all look about the same height, and it would be harder to see the detail for the exact heights of the columns.
(b) It is hard to tell what part (front or back) of the top of the columns represents the height, and the graph has been drawn on a slope.
(c) Use a ruler and hold it horizontally.

7

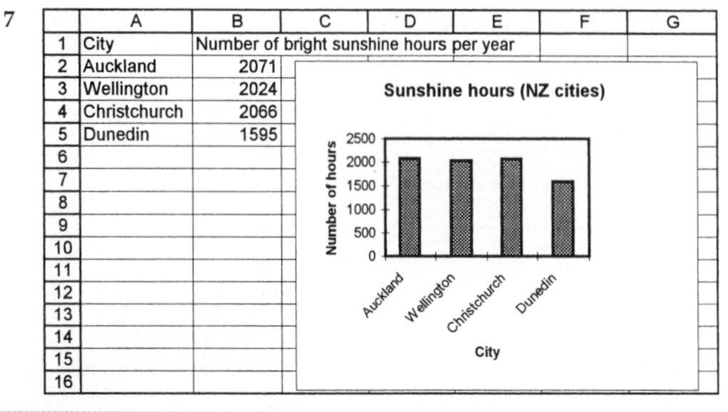

	A	B	C	D	E	F	G
1	City	Number of bright sunshine hours per year					
2	Auckland	2071					
3	Wellington	2024					
4	Christchurch	2066					
5	Dunedin	1595					
6							
7							
8							
9							
10							
11							
12							
13							
14							
15							
16							

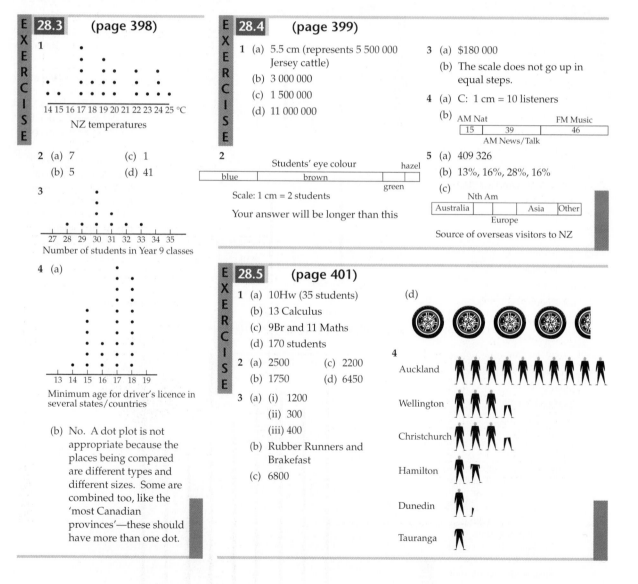

EXERCISE 28.3 (page 398)

1

14 15 16 17 18 19 20 21 22 23 24 25 °C

NZ temperatures

2 (a) 7 (b) 5 (c) 1 (d) 41

3

27 28 29 30 31 32 33 34 35

Number of students in Year 9 classes

4 (a)

13 14 15 16 17 18 19

Minimum age for driver's licence in several states/countries

(b) No. A dot plot is not appropriate because the places being compared are different types and different sizes. Some are combined too, like the 'most Canadian provinces'—these should have more than one dot.

EXERCISE 28.4 (page 399)

1 (a) 5.5 cm (represents 5 500 000 Jersey cattle)

(b) 3 000 000

(c) 1 500 000

(d) 11 000 000

2

Students' eye colour

blue	brown	green	hazel

Scale: 1 cm = 2 students

Your answer will be longer than this

3 (a) $180 000

(b) The scale does not go up in equal steps.

4 (a) C: 1 cm = 10 listeners

(b)

AM Nat	AM News/Talk	FM Music
15	39	46

5 (a) 409 326

(b) 13%, 16%, 28%, 16%

(c)

Australia	Nth Am	Europe	Asia	Other

Source of overseas visitors to NZ

EXERCISE 28.5 (page 401)

1 (a) 10Hw (35 students)

(b) 13 Calculus

(c) 9Br and 11 Maths

(d) 170 students

2 (a) 2500 (b) 1750 (c) 2200 (d) 6450

3 (a) (i) 1200

(ii) 300

(iii) 400

(b) Rubber Runners and Brakefast

(c) 6800

(d)

4

Auckland

Wellington

Christchurch

Hamilton

Dunedin

Tauranga

EXERCISE 28.6 (page 405)

1 (a) 360° ÷ 72 = 5°

(b)

Heating method	Number of homes	Angle at centre
Electricity	29	145°
Gas	10	50°
Open fire	12	60°
Wood-burning stove	17	85°
Solar	1	5°
None	3	15°
Total	72	360°

(c) Home heating methods

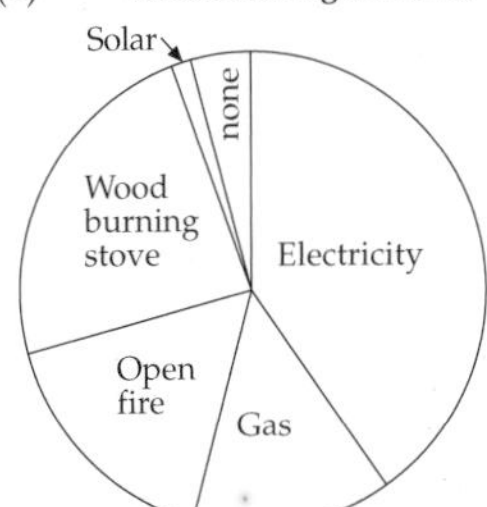

2 (a) P = Bus, Q = Air, R = Train, S = Car

(b) 120°

(c) Train

3 (a) 10 000 (c) 15 000

(b) 5000 (d) 25 000

4 (a) 7

(b) There are 90 students. 360° ÷ 90 = 4°

(c)

Day the week	Number of students	Angle at centre
Sunday	9	36°
Monday	12	48°
Tuesday	18	72°
Wednesday	15	60°
Thursday	15	60°
Friday	11	44°
Saturday	10	40°

(d) Day of birth

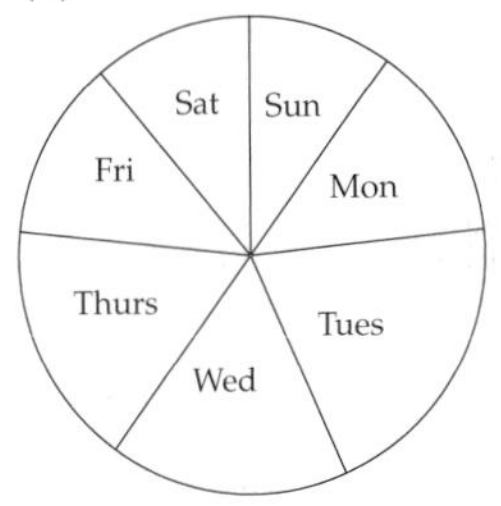

5 Status in family

6 (a)

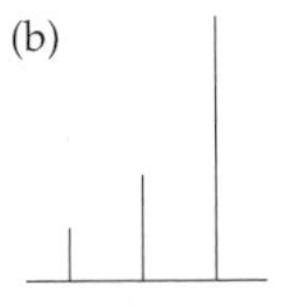

(b)

7 (a) 64.8°

(b) 61.2° or 61°, 136.8° or 137°, 97.2° or 97°

(c) Population of greater Auckland

8 (a) Blood types

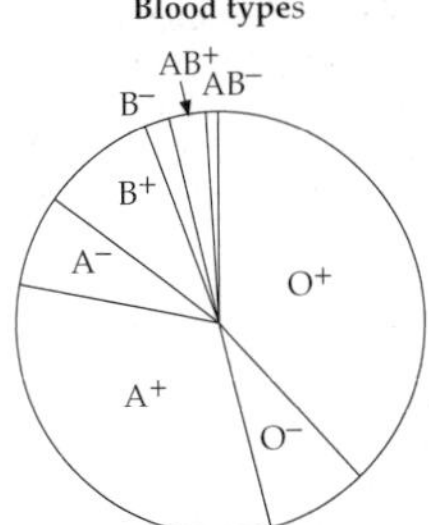

(b)

Blood type	Rhesus factor positive	Rhesus factor negative	total
O	38	8	46
A	32	7	39
B	9	2	11
AB	3	1	4
Total	**82**	**18**	**100**

(c) Rhesus factor

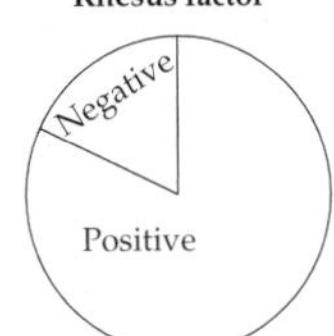

(d) Blood type

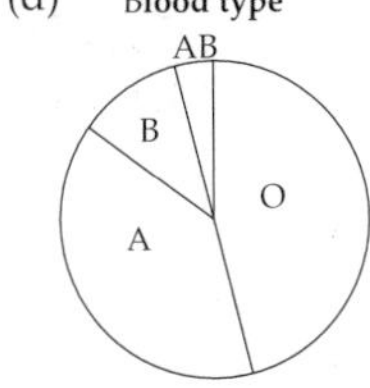

9

	A	B	C	D	E	F	G
1	NZ student roll numbers						
2							
3	Primary	459221					
4	High School	238104					
5	Polytechnic	95346					
6	University	105690					

NZ Student Roll Numbers

University 12%

Polytechnic 11%

Primary 50%

High School 27%

EXERCISE 28.7 (page 408)

1 Scores in golf tournament

Stem	Leaf
6	8
7	1 2 3 4 5 6 7 7 8
8	1 2 2 3 3 4 5 7 8
9	1 4 4
10	0 1 4

(b) 36

2 (a) $5 (c) $65
(b) $99 (d) 40

3 (a) 1 hour later
(b) 11.18 pm
(c) Every 30 minutes (half hour).
(d) 2 minutes
(e) There are two peak times, showing more trains are timetabled for going in to work in the morning and returning in the late afternoon. Other times show a regular pattern of two trains per hour.

4 (a) 16
(b) 42
(c) The 'twenties' leaf is the longest.

5 (a)

Heights of students in 9Fr (in m)

Stem	Leaf
1.8	1
1.7	2 4 5 9
1.6	0 2 2 3 8
1.5	1 2 3 3 4 5 6 7 8 8 9
1.4	0 2 5 6 6
1.3	5 5 6
1.2	7 9

(b) 31
(c) Cathy is the shortest, and Stephen is the tallest
(d) 1.50-1.60 m
(e)

Heights of students in 9Fr (in m)

Boys		Girls
1	1.8	
9 4 2	1.7	5
3 2	1.6	0 2 8
9 8 7 4 3 2	1.5	1 3 5 6 8
6 2	1.4	0 5 6
6	1.3	5 5
	1.2	7 9

6 (a)

1961		1996
	15	9
	14	
	13	
	12	
	11	2
5	10	
	9	
	8	3
	7	4
	6	
1	5	2 5 7 9
3 1	4	1 6 9 9
6 3 2 2	3	0 3
6 5 5 5 5 1	2	6 8
2 2	1	

(b) The numbers have increased (and spread out).

Starter (page 410)

- The graph shows high levels of nitrogen dioxide during the daytime.
- One day.
- 8 am and 5 pm (rush hour).
- Once every hour (each line segment represents a one-hour change).
- The pattern would be repeated.
- Yes—the scale on the vertical axis is missing.

EXERCISE 28.8 (page 410)

1 (a) 9 °C
(b) ⁻5 °C
(c) 1 am and 8 am
(d) ⁻6 °C at 2.30 am
(e) 2.30 am and 11.30 am

2 (a)

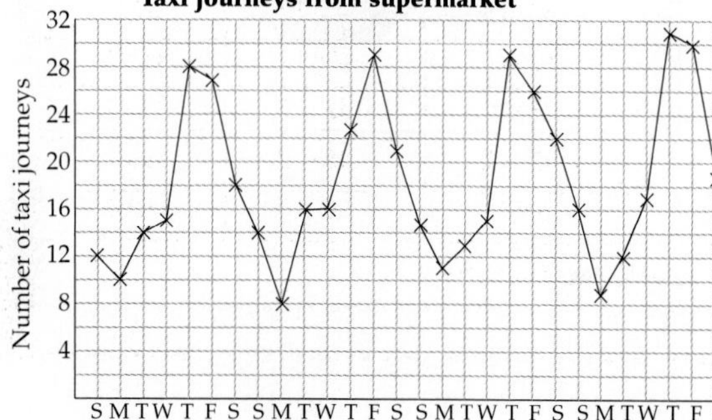

(b) Yes, the pattern repeats with high use on Thursdays and Fridays and low use on Mondays and Tuesdays.
(c) C: about the same each week.

3 (a) (i) 26 000 (ii) 11 000
(b) (i) 8000 (ii) 7000
(c) 9.30 am, 1 pm, 3 pm
(d) 6 am

4 (a)

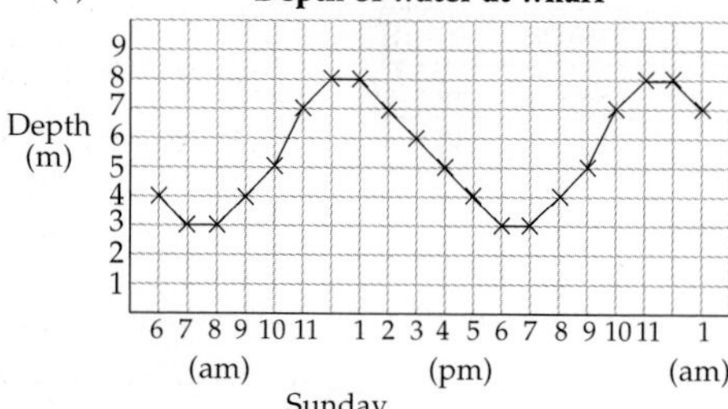

(b) 6 metres
(c) 6 metres
(d) B: $5\frac{1}{2}$ hours

Spreadsheet investigation (page 412)

2

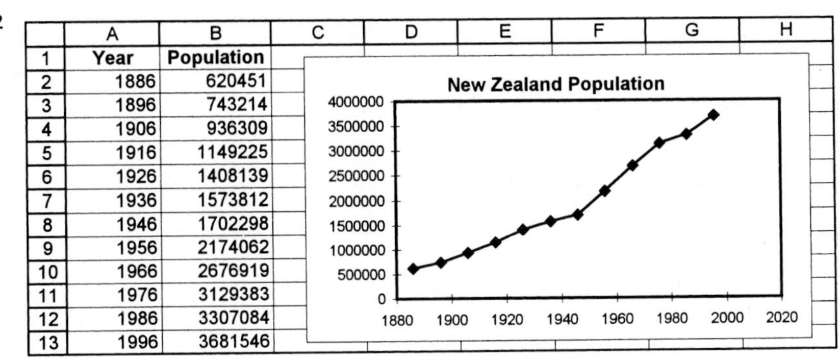

	A	B
1	Year	Population
2	1886	620451
3	1896	743214
4	1906	936309
5	1916	1149225
6	1926	1408139
7	1936	1573812
8	1946	1702298
9	1956	2174062
10	1966	2676919
11	1976	3129383
12	1986	3307084
13	1996	3681546

Population is growing fastest between 1956–1966—this is where the graph is steepest.

Exercise 28.9 (page 415)

1 3 618 300

2 153 666

3 Otago

4 21.9%

5 Wellington

6 57.4%

7 2001, 2006, 2011 (then 2016, 2021, etc.)

8 Samoan

9 Anglican

10 5 March 1996

11 It rose

12 84%

13 63 378

14 It fell

15 The median age increased from 29.74 to 32.95. This is a difference of 3.21, or about 3 years.

16 true

17 It rose

18 The percentage of Maori is about 14.5%.

19 783 645

20 NZ men have a higher median income than NZ women.

Chapter 29—Working with data

Exercise 29.1 (page 417)

1 4

2 8

3 24

4 9.5

5 4.75 or $\frac{19}{4}$ or $4\frac{3}{4}$

6 3

7 52.57

8 383.67

9 41.71

10 61 cents

11 $926.99

12 65.25 kg

13 8

14 (a) 61.2 seconds, or 1 minute, 1.2 seconds
(b) Eun-Wah

15 (a) 8.5
(b) 7, 8, 9, 10

16 158 cm

Exercise 29.2 (page 419)

1 14

2 25

3 28

4 48

5 12.2

6 4

7 112

8 50

9 42

10 103.5

11 86

12 80 cents

13 (a) 9.5 (b) 83 mm

14 (a) height
(b) (i) 118 cm (ii) 39 years (iii) 63 kg

15 (a)

Day of week	Odometer at start of day	Odometer at end of day	Distance travelled (km)
Sunday	4018.6	4122.7	104.1
Monday	4122.7	4346.3	223.6
Tuesday	4346.3	4435.5	89.2
Wednesday	4435.5	4548.2	112.7
Thursday	4548.2	4704.2	156.0
Friday	4704.2	4897.3	193.1
Saturday	4897.3	5060.7	163.4

(b) 156.0 km on Thursday

16 12

EXERCISE 29.3 (page 421)

1 The mean is a lot higher than the median because of the extremely large value of Auckland's population.

	A	B	C	D	E
1	**Urban area**	**1996**			
2	Auckland	997940		Median =	53696
3	Wellington	335468			
4	Christchurch	331443		Mean =	131932
5	Hamilton	159234			
6	Dunedin	112279			
7	Tauranga	82832			
8	Palmerston North	73862			
9	Hastings	58675			
10	Rotorua	56928			
11	Napier	55044			
12	Nelson	52348			
13	Invercargill	49306			
14	New Plymouth	49079			
15	Whangarei	45785			
16	Wanganui	41320			
17	Gisborne	32653			
18	Kapiti	30004			
19	Timaru	27521			
20	Blenheim	25875			
21	Taupo	21044			

EXERCISE 29.4 (page 422)

1 6

2 7

3 20

4 0

5 No mode.

6 Two modes: 1 and 5.

7 20

8 C

9 (a) 10
(b) In a dot plot, the mode is the number with the most dots above it.

10 (a) white
(b) In a pie graph, the mode is represented by the largest sector (largest angle at centre) .

11 (a) dot plot
(b) 50 would be a good prediction—being the mode, it is the most likely result.

12 (a) 20 (b) 1

EXERCISE 29.5 (page 426)

1 (a) 3
(b) 6
(c) 7 times
(d) 8
(e) 1
(f) 9
(g) Because there are 30 students.
(h)

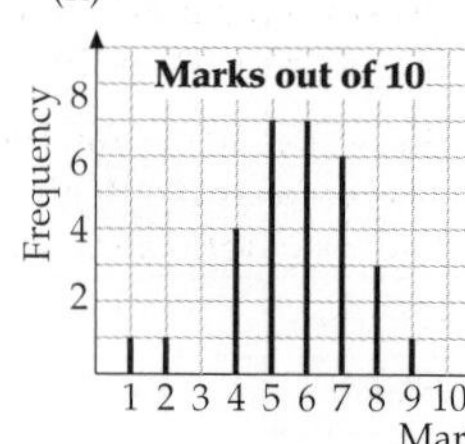

2 (a)

Number of litres bought	Frequency
0	0
1	0
2	0
3	1
4	4
5	9
6	7
7	11
8	11
9	2

(b) 7 or 8 litres. These were the two amounts with the highest frequency

3 (a)

Coin	Number of those coins	Value of those coins ($)
10c	8	0.80
20c	7	1.40
50c	4	2.00
$1	4	4.00
$2	1	2.00
Totals	24	10.20

(b) 24 (c) $10.20

4 (a) 31
(b) 7; there were 7 people who bought only one ticket.
(c) 121
(d) 2

5 (a)

Number of guests per table	Frequency
1	0
2	7
3	1
4	13
5	0
6	8
7	0
8	2

(b) 31 (c) 133

EXERCISE 29.6 (page 429)

1

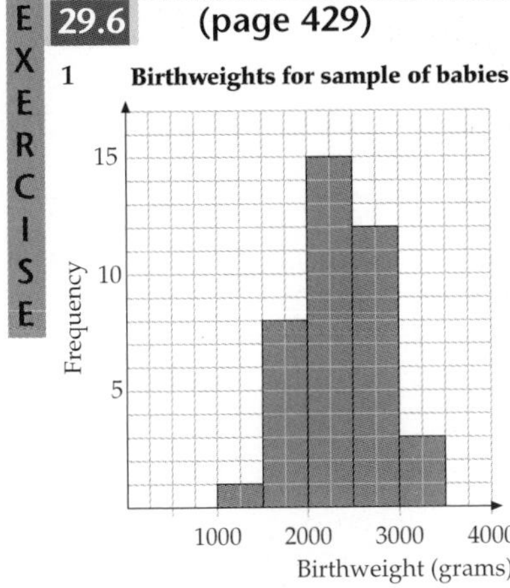

2 (a)

Amount of petrol sold (litres)	Frequency
0–10	3
10–20	1
20–30	8
30–40	6
40–50	6
50–60	5
60–70	1

(b)

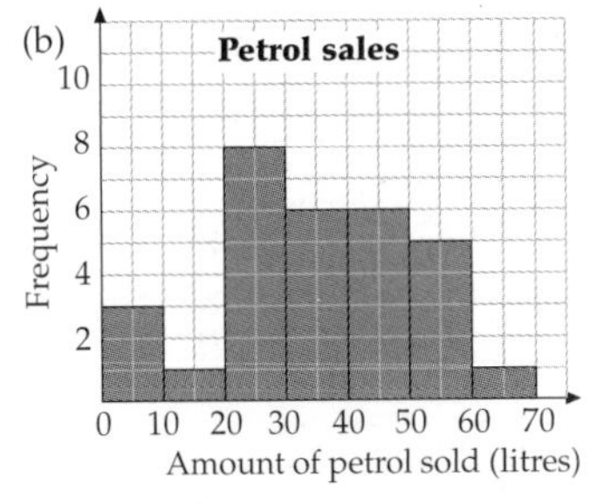

3 (a) 8 (b) 10 (c) 18 (d) 28
(e) \$40 000–\$50 000
(f) The top salary could be anywhere in the range \$80 000–\$90 000; no more information is available than that.

4 (a)

Distance (in km)	Frequency
0–2000	2
2000–4000	11
4000–6000	3
6000–8000	1
8000–10 000	3
10 000–12 000	4
12 000–14 000	2

(b)

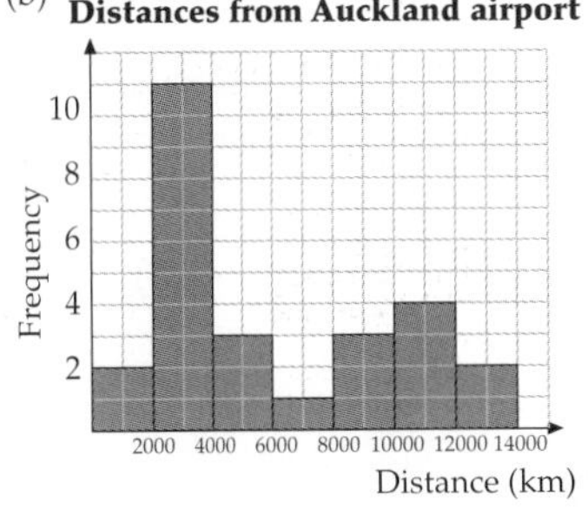

Chapter 30—Surveys and exploring probability

EXERCISE 30.1 (page 432)

1 A: not representative; first 30 students would be hungry and *more likely* to buy hot chips. Doesn't survey views of students who don't go to the tuckshop.

B: representative, gives the required information.

C: representative, but not enough students chosen to give accurate information.

D: not representative, views of other students not collected and students may be *less likely* to buy hot chips because in that class they would be taught that junk food is unhealthy!

2 People who do not live in Auckland.

People who do not have a telephone.

People who are not at home between 5 pm and 8 pm.

People whose phone line is engaged.

People who have unlisted phone numbers.

3 (a) They may not remember; your friends may not be typical of all customers.

(b) You could watch some consecutive customers, say 50 or 100, and observe whether they purchase a drink.

4 Some people in a house may be more likely to be the first person to answer the phone, and this could exclude others.

5 A (iii) will give an extremely accurate estimate, but will be expensive and time-consuming to carry out.

B (i) quick and easy to carry out the survey, but may not give an accurate estimate.

C (ii) the best choice of sample size, because it will give a fairly accurate estimate.

6 (a) not random
(b) random
(c) random
(d) not random
(e) not random
(f) random

7 B

EXERCISE 30.2 (page 434)

1 (a) Does not cover all possible alternatives—one parent may smoke, while the other one doesn't. The person's parents may not be alive.
(b) Does not cover all possible alternatives—for example, some students may cycle to school.
(c) Invades privacy and may not get an honest answer.
(d) Does not cover all possible alternatives—the person might think the bus is clean and uncomfortable, perhaps
(e) Students may not remember, and 'late' needs to be clearly defined.
(f) Question is unclear—what is travelling by bus being compared to?

2 (a) Terry should be asking the *same* questions each time.
(b) Please show your satisfaction with the service at your bank by circling a number below:

0	1	2	3	4	5	6	7	8	9	10
very unsatisfied			unsatisfied			satisfied				very satisfied

EXERCISE 30.3 (page 438)

1 (a) unlikely
(b) likely
(c) very unlikely

2 (a) very unlikely
(b) very likely
(c) impossible
(d) unlikely
(e) certain
(f) equally likely to occur or not occur
(g) likely

3 (a) Spinner A
(b) (i) It is likely that spinner B will stop on a white sector.
(ii) It is very unlikely that spinner B will stop on a green sector.
(c) Spinner B is unlikely to stop on the grey sector.

4 (a)

Result of call	Frequency	Relative frequency
Answered	61	$\frac{61}{100} = 0.61$
Not answered	22	$\frac{22}{100} = 0.22$
Answer-machine	11	$\frac{11}{100} = 0.11$
Out of order	1	$\frac{1}{100} = 0.01$
Engaged	5	$\frac{5}{100} = 0.05$

(b) (i) likely
(ii) very unlikely
(iii) unlikely

5 (a) $\frac{7}{50} \times 100 = 14\%$
(b) (i) $\frac{17}{50}$ (ii) 34%
(c) adult membership
(d) life membership

6 (a)

Year level	Frequency	Relative frequency	Relative frequency as a percentage (rounded)
Year 9	58	$\frac{58}{160}$	36%
Year 10	29	$\frac{29}{160}$	18%
Year 11	25	$\frac{25}{160}$ or $\frac{5}{32}$	16%
Year 12	17	$\frac{17}{160}$	11%
Year 13	31	$\frac{31}{160}$	19%
Total	**160**	**1**	**100%**

(b) (i) Year 9 (ii) Year 12

7 (a) unlikely
(b) Old: $\frac{75}{500}$ or 15%
New: $\frac{16}{40}$ or 40%
(c) The old model is more reliable, because only 15% need repair compared with 40% for the new model.

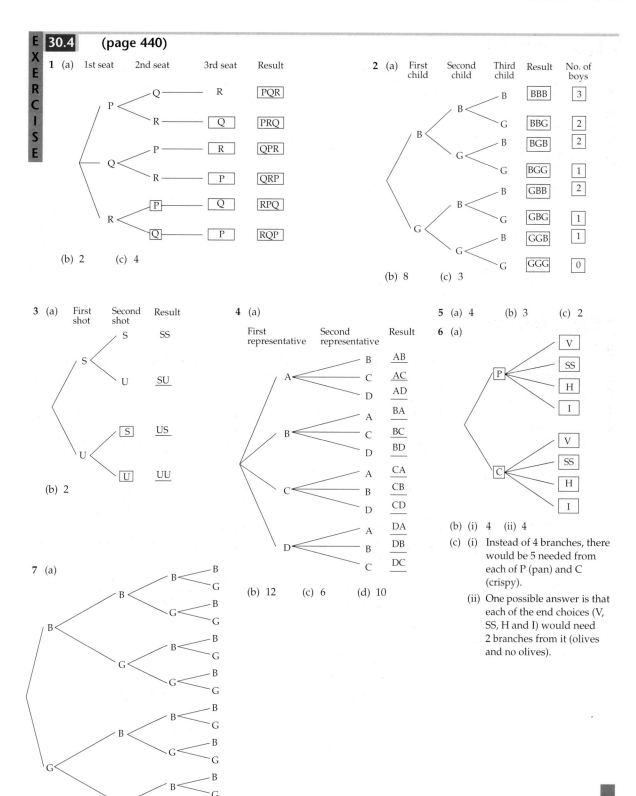

EXERCISE 30.4 (page 440)

1 (a)

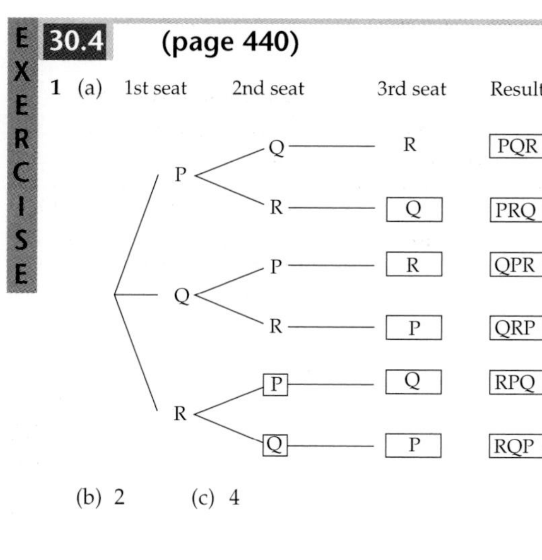

(b) 2 (c) 4

2 (a)

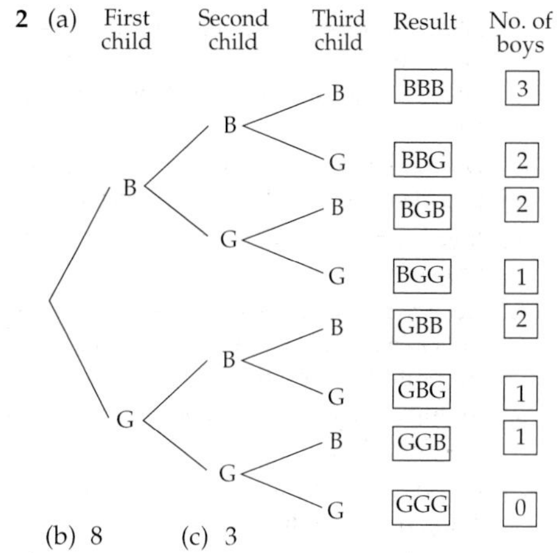

(b) 8 (c) 3

3 (a)

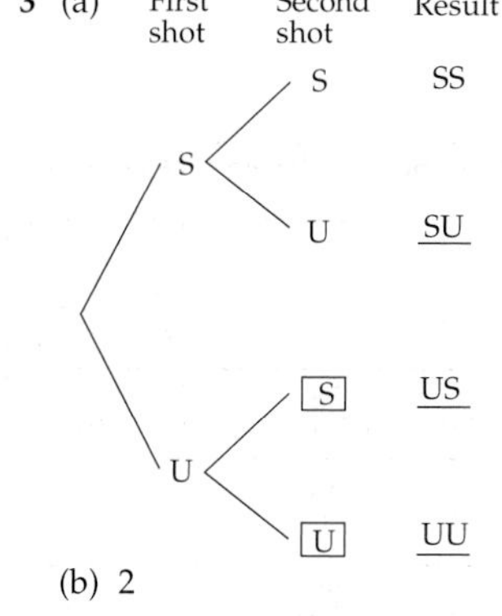

(b) 2

4 (a)

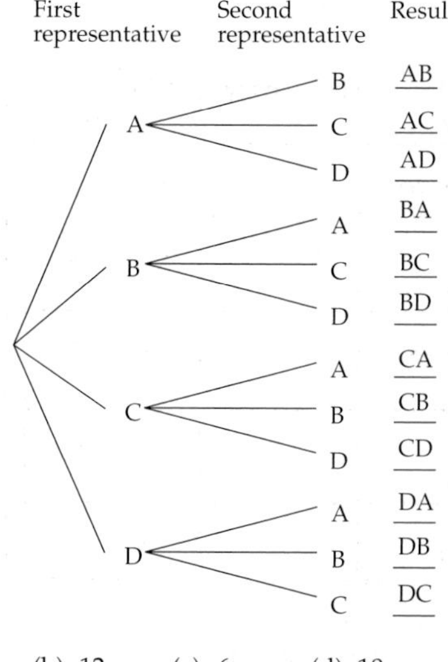

(b) 12 (c) 6 (d) 10

5 (a) 4 (b) 3 (c) 2

6 (a)

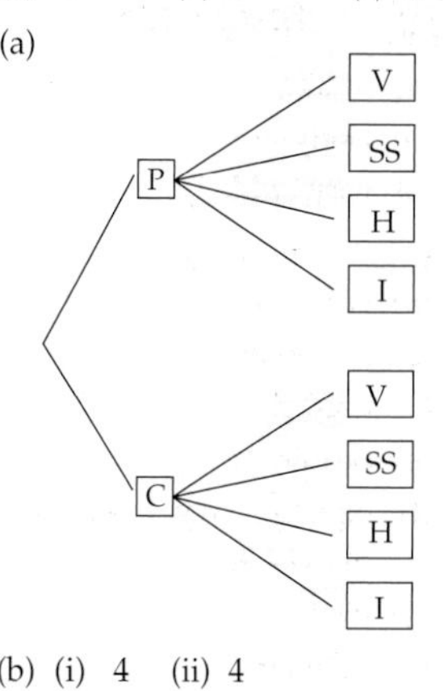

(b) (i) 4 (ii) 4

(c) (i) Instead of 4 branches, there would be 5 needed from each of P (pan) and C (crispy).

(ii) One possible answer is that each of the end choices (V, SS, H and I) would need 2 branches from it (olives and no olives).

7 (a)

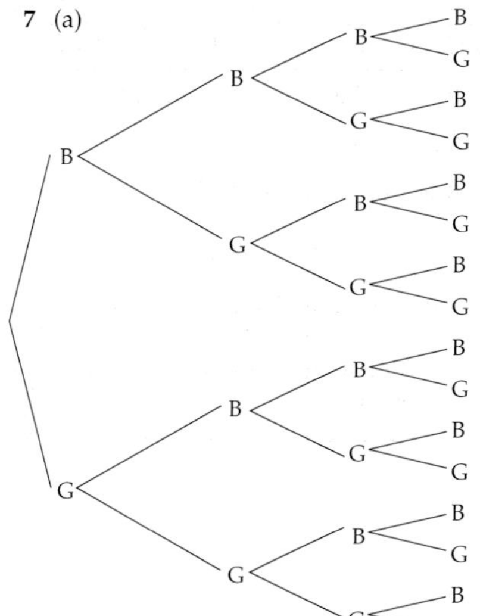

(b) 16 (c) 6

Index

To teachers

Alpha Mathematics has been written for the new Mathematics curriculum introduced recently into New Zealand schools. This curriculum encourages students to be able to explain their mathematical understanding, developed in a context of meaningful problems. The learning experiences in *Alpha Mathematics* are aimed largely at levels 4 and 5.

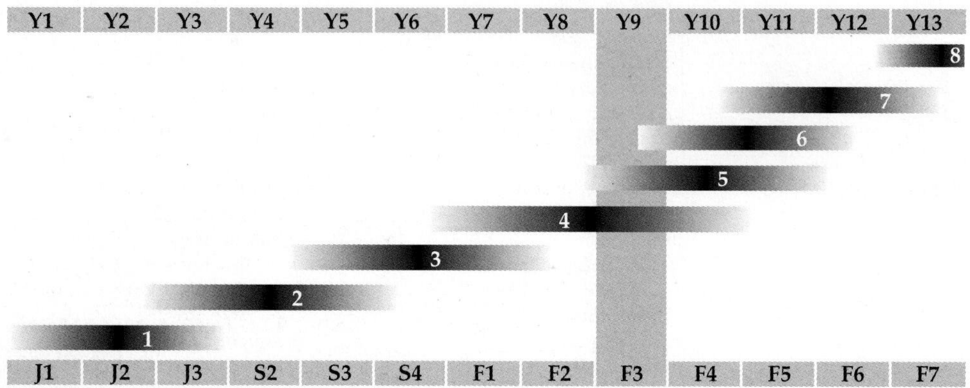

The content of *Alpha Mathematics* has been arranged into the five main strands of the New Zealand Mathematics curriculum – these are Number, Measurement, Geometry, Algebra and Statistics. The chapters are not necessarily a teaching order, and it would be best for teachers to develop their own programmes by selecting material from this textbook to meet the needs of students in their class.

Alpha Mathematics includes a substantial core of exercises which are designed to help students build good foundations for future learning in Mathematics. The questions are graded in difficulty and the exercises should be suitable for students of most abilities. A special feature is the inclusion of many puzzles to extend the faster-working students.

Many topics are introduced with special 'starters' – these are often open-ended and can be used in a variety of ways. The material in *Alpha Mathematics* has been designed to work with a variety of teaching styles, with plenty of 'interest' activities that you can use as required. The designers have paid particular attention to the layout – this is logical and mathematically correct, but the pages have deliberately been broken up into manageable chunks, laid out in a magazine-type style with plenty of fun illustrations to hold the students' interest.

A special feature of *Alpha Mathematics* is the inclusion of a full chapter to introduce students to using spreadsheets on computers. A well-resourced Mathematics Department should have access to computers, and I hope you get regular opportunities to use them with your students. By carrying out these activities you will be meeting the aim of using technology in the Mathematics programme.

Year 9 is your opportunity to introduce Mathematics for the first time to new students at secondary level, and lay solid foundations for the work you do at higher levels in the subject. I hope *Alpha Mathematics* proves to be a useful and helpful resource in assisting you to have an enjoyable and worthwhile year with your students as they learn Mathematics.

David Barton
September 1999